Understanding Health Insurance

A Guide to Billing and Reimbursement

Twelfth Edition

Understanding Health Insurance

A Guide to Billing and Reimbursement

Twelfth Edition

Michelle A. Green, MPS, RHIA, FAHIMA, CPC
SUNY Distinguished Teaching Professor
Alfred State College, Alfred, NY

JoAnn C. Rowell
Founder and Former Chairperson
Medical Assisting Department
Anne Arundel Community College, Arnold, MD

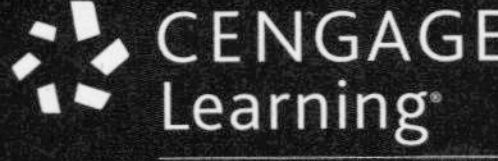

Australia • Brazil • Mexico • Singapore • United Kingdom • United States

**Understanding Health Insurance:
A Guide to Billing and Reimbursement,
Twelfth Edition**
Michelle Green

Vice President, GM Skills & Product Planning: Dawn Gerrain

Product Manager: Jadin B. Kavanaugh

Director, Development-Career and Computing: Marah Bellegarde

Product Development Manager: Juliet Steiner

Content Developer: Amy Wetsel

Product Assistant: Courtney Cozzy

Market Development Manager: Jonathan Sheehan

Marketing Manager, Special Markets: Erica Glisson

Senior Production Director: Wendy A. Troeger

Production Manager: Andrew Crouth

Senior Content Project Manager: Kara A. DiCaterino

Senior Art Director: Jack Pendleton

Media Editor: Deborah Bordeaux

For product information and technology assistance, contact us at
Cengage Learning Customer & Sales Support, 1-800-354-9706.

For permission to use material from this text or product,
submit all requests online at **www.cengage.com/permissions.**
Further permissions questions can be e-mailed to
permissionrequest@cengage.com.

Library of Congress Control Number: 2013947428

Book Only ISBN-13: 978-1-285-73759-1

Package ISBN-13: 978-1-285-73752-2

Cengage Learning
200 First Stamford Place, 4th Floor
Stamford, CT 06902
USA

Cengage Learning is a leading provider of customized learning solutions with office locations around the globe, including Singapore, the United Kingdom, Australia, Mexico, Brazil, and Japan. Locate your local office at **www.cengage.com/global**

Cengage Learning products are represented in Canada by Nelson Education, Ltd.

To learn more about Cengage Learning Solutions, visit **www.cengage.com**

Purchase any of our products at your local college store or at our preferred online store **www.cengagebrain.com**

Printed in the United States of America
1 2 3 4 5 6 7 18 17 16 15 14

Contents

List of Tables

Some chapter material is located in tables so that content is easy to read (and learn). Tables allow additional material (e.g., history of health care reimbursement in Chapter 2, history of managed care in Chapter 3) to be included in the textbook. The instructor has the option of assigning the review of such content as homework instead of covering that material in class.

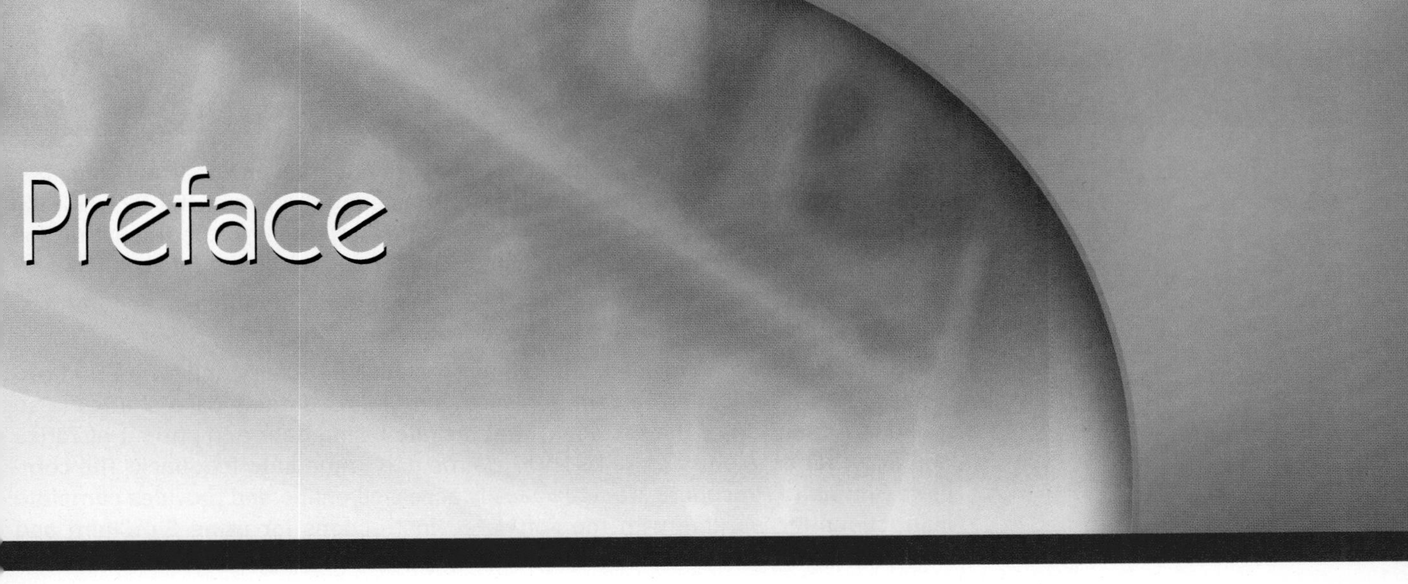

Preface

INTRODUCTION

Accurate processing of health insurance claims has become more exacting and rigorous as health insurance plan options have rapidly expanded. These changes, combined with modifications in state and federal regulations affecting the health insurance industry, are a constant challenge to health care personnel. Those responsible for processing health insurance claims require thorough instruction in all aspects of medical insurance, including plan options, payer requirements, state and federal regulations, abstracting of source documents, accurate completion of claims, and coding of diagnoses and procedures/services. *Understanding Health Insurance* provides the required information in a clear and comprehensive manner.

OBJECTIVES

The objectives of this text are to:

1. Introduce information about major insurance programs and federal health care legislation.
2. Provide a basic knowledge of national diagnosis and procedure coding systems.
3. Simplify the process of completing claims.

This text is designed to be used by college and vocational school programs to train medical assistants, medical insurance specialists, coding and reimbursement specialists, and health information technicians. It can also be used as an in-service training tool for new medical office personnel and independent billing services, or individually by claims processors in the health care field who want to develop or enhance their skills.

FEATURES OF THE TEXT

Major features of this text have been updated and expanded:

- Key terms, section headings, and learning objectives at the beginning of each chapter help to organize the material. They can be used as a self-test for checking comprehension and mastery of chapter content. Boldfaced key terms appear throughout each chapter to help learners master the technical vocabulary associated with claims processing.
- Coding exercises are located in textbook Chapters 6 through 8 and 10, and claims completion exercises are located in Chapters 11 through 17. Answers to exercises are available from your instructor.
- Numerous examples are provided in each chapter to illustrate the correct application of rules and guidelines.

- Notes clarify chapter content, focusing the student's attention on important concepts. Coding tips provide practical suggestions for mastering the use of the CPT, HCPCS, and ICD-10-CM coding manuals. HIPAA alerts draw attention to the impact of this legislation on privacy and security requirements for patient health information.
- End-of-chapter reviews reinforce learning and are in multiple-choice format. Answers to chapter reviews are available from your instructor.
- The practice software provided with the text includes SimClaim and a free trial version of Optum's *EncoderPro.com* software. SimClaim contains case studies (also found in Appendix I of the textbook) that include billing data and patient histories and allow for data entry on CMS-1500 claims and immediate feedback. The complete SimClaim *Procedure Manual* is easily accessed online and provides complete instructions for working with the software. (Instructions for using SimClaim and *EncoderPro.com* are located at the end of this preface.)

NEW TO THIS EDITION

- Chapter 1: New content about an employee's professional appearance, with an image, was added to the *Professionalism* section of the chapter. New content about the information to record about phone calls was added to the *Telephone Skills for the Health Care Setting* section. ICD-10-CM content replaced ICD-9-CM content.
- Chapter 2: Table 2-1 (the significant events in health care reimbursement) was updated to add content about *Accountable Care Organizations (ACOs)*. Content about meaningful use measures was added, and a new table contains the stages of meaningful use objectives and measures.
- Chapter 3: Content about ICD-10-CM was included to replace ICD-9-CM.
- Chapter 4: Content about secondary insurance was added, the sample encounter form was edited to replace ICD-9-CM codes with ICD-10-CM codes, and examples about calculating copayments and coinsurance were added.
- Chapter 5: Content about medical identity theft, the Medicare Drug Integrity Contractors (MEDIC) Program, the HITECH Act, the Health Care Fraud Prevention and Enforcement Action Team (HEAT), and the Health Plan Identifier (HPID) was added.
- Chapter 6: ICD-10-CM and ICD-10-PCS guidelines and codes were updated.
- Chapter 7: CPT coding guidelines and codes were updated.
- Chapter 8: HCPCS level II guidelines and codes were updated.
- Chapter 9: Content about reimbursement systems and the revenue cycle was updated. Content about chargemaster maintenance, revenue cycle monitoring, revenue cycle auditing, and resource allocation and data analytics was added. Instructions for completing the UB-04 were updated, and ICD-10-CM codes replaced ICD-9-CM codes in the outpatient case and completed UB-04 claim.
- Chapter 10: ICD-10-CM codes replaced ICD-9-CM codes throughout, and new images of revised CMS-1500 blocks were included.
- Chapters 11 to 17: ICD-10-CM codes replaced ICD-9-CM codes throughout. Insurance claims completion instructions and the CMS-1500 claim were revised according to the latest industry guidelines and standards.
- SimClaim practice software (located online) was revised to replace ICD-9-CM codes with ICD-10-CM codes. The option to print completed claims to PDF for easy e-mailing and printing remains.
- Scenario-based coding cases were updated and include multimedia to enhance coding practice.

ORGANIZATION OF THIS TEXTBOOK

- Chapter outlines, key terms, objectives, chapter exercises, end-of-chapter summaries, and reviews facilitate student learning.
- A Study Checklist at the end of each chapter directs learners to various methods of review, reinforcement, and testing.
- Chapter 1, Health Insurance Specialist Career, contains an easy-to-read table that delineates training requirements for health insurance specialists.
- Chapter 2, Introduction to Health Insurance, contains content about health care insurance developments.
- Chapter 3, Managed Health Care, contains content about managed care plans, consumer-directed health plans, health savings accounts, and flexible spending accounts.
- Chapter 4, Processing an Insurance Claim, contains content about managing an office visit for a new or established patient, claims processing steps, and the denials/appeals process.
- Chapter 5, Legal and Regulatory Issues, emphasizes confidentiality of patient information, retention of patient information and health insurance records, the Federal False Claims Act, the Health Insurance Portability and Accountability Act of 1996, and federal laws and events that affect health care.
- Chapter 6, ICD-10-CM Coding, contains coding conventions and coding guidelines with examples. An overview about ICD-10-PCS is also provided, and additional content can be found at the www.cengagebrain.com Student Resources online companion. The coding conventions for the ICD-10-CM Index to Disease and Injuries and ICD-10-CM Tabular List of Diseases and Injuries are clearly explained and include examples. In addition, examples of coding manual entries are included. The chapter review includes coding statements, which are organized according to the ICD-10-CM chapters.

> **NOTE:** The ICD-10-CM chapter is sequenced before the CPT and HCPCS level II chapters in this textbook because diagnosis codes are reported for medical necessity (to justify procedures and/or services provided).

- Chapter 7, CPT Coding, follows the organization of CPT sections. The chapter review includes coding statements organized by CPT section.

> **NOTE:** CPT codes were updated using the AMA's downloadable CPT data files.

- Chapter 8, HCPCS Level II Coding, has been updated to reflect revised codes and descriptions.
- Chapter 9, CMS Reimbursement Methodologies, contains information about reimbursement systems implemented since 1983 (including the Medicare physician fee schedule), hospital revenue cycle management, the chargemaster, and the UB-04 (CMS-1450) claim. (A separate chapter about the UB-04 claim is not included in this textbook. The UB-04 claim is automatically generated upon entry of chargemaster data in the facility's patient accounting system.)
- Chapter 10, Coding for Medical Necessity, contains tables that allow learners to organize answers to exercises. A chapter review contains evaluation and management coding practice exercises.
- Chapter 11, Essential CMS-1500 Claim Instructions, contains universal instructions that are followed when entering data on the CMS-1500 claim, a discussion of common errors made on claims, guidelines for maintaining the practice's insurance claim files, and the processing of assigned claims.
- Claims completion instructions in Chapters 12 to 17 are revised according to changes implemented by third-party and government payers. Claims completion instructions are located in an easy-to-read table format.

SUPPLEMENTS

The following supplements accompany the text:

Instructor's Manual (available on the Instructor Companion Website)

The Instructor's Manual contains the following sections:

- **Section I – Preparing Your Course**
- **Section II – Answer Keys to Textbook Chapter Exercises and Reviews**
- **Section III – Answer Keys to Textbook Appendix Case Studies**
- **Section IV – Instructor's Materials**
- **Section V – Answer Keys to Workbook Chapter Assignments**
- **Section VI – Answer Key to Mock CMRS Exam**
- **Section VII – Answer Key to Mock CPC-P Exam**

Student Workbook (ISBN 978-1-285-76767-6)

The Workbook follows the text's chapter organization and contains application-based assignments. Each chapter assignment includes a list of objectives, an overview of content relating to the assignment, and instructions for completing the assignment. Other components may be present depending on the assignment. Each chapter contains review questions, in multiple-choice format, to emulate credentialing exam questions. In Chapters 11 through 17, additional case studies allow more practice in completing the CMS-1500 claim. Appendix A contains a mock CMRS exam; Appendix B contains a mock CPC-P exam.

Instructor Resources (available on the Instructor Companion Website)

Spend less time planning and more time teaching with Cengage Learning's Instructor Resources to Accompany the Twelfth Edition of *Understanding Health Insurance*. As an instructor, you will find these resources offer invaluable assistance anywhere, at any time.

All instructor resources can be accessed by going to www.cengagebrain.com to create a unique user login. Contact your sales representative for more information. Online instructor resources at the Instructor Companion Website are password-protected and include the following:

- **The Instructor's Manual in Adobe's PDF format, which contains class preparation information, sample syllabi, and complete answer keys for each chapter of the book.**
- **The computerized test bank in Cognero® makes generating tests and quizzes a snap. With approximately 1,500 questions, including ICD-10-CM/PCS questions, you can create customized assessments for your students with the click of a button. New to the Twelfth Edition are practice test banks to provide to students with additional exam prep.**
- **Customizable instructor support slide presentations in PowerPoint® format focus on key points for each chapter.**
- **Insurance Billing & Coding Curriculum Guide helps you plan your course using *Understanding Health Insurance* and other Cengage resources.**

Companion Websites

Additional Instructor Resources at the Instructor Companion Site

- **Curriculum Guide**
- **Conversion grid mapping the Eleventh Edition to the Twelfth Edition, as well as to competing texts, to make transitioning a snap**
- **Revisions to the Instructor's Manual and computerized test bank (CTB) due to coding updates**
- **Grids comparing the Twelfth Edition of *Understanding Health Insurance* with competitive titles**
- **Access to all student supplements and additional textbook content**

Student Resources at the Student Companion Site

Additional textbook resources for both students and instructors can be found online. Some resources located at the Student Companion site to accompany *Understanding Health Insurance* are free, whereas others will require passcode entry. To access passcode-protected content, follow the instructions on the printed access card bound into the front of this textbook.

Student resources include:

- **CMS-1500 and UB-04 claims (blank)**
- **1995 and 1997 documentation guidelines for evaluation and management services**
- **Revisions to the textbook and workbook due to coding updates**
- **E/M CodeBuilder (that can be printed to use as a worksheet)**
- **Final test for AAPC CEU approval**

Premium Website

Additional textbook resources for students and instructors can be found online by following these instructions:

Some resources located on the Premium Website to accompany *Understanding Health Insurance, 12e*, are free, whereas others (such as SimClaim) will require passcode entry. To access passcode-protected content, follow the instructions on the printed access card bound into this textbook. Student resources include:

- **SimClaim, interactive CMS-1500 claims completion software—brand new software with updated cases!**
- **25 fully revised coding case studies**
- **Revisions to textbook due to coding changes as they become available**

CourseMate (Printed Access Card ISBN with access code: 978-1-285-73770-6)

Go beyond the textbook and complement your text and course content with study and practice materials through CourseMate. CourseMate includes:

- **Interactive eBook with highlighting, note taking, and interactive glossary**
- **Additional assignable chapter quizzes, flashcards, and games**
- **Engagement Tracker tool that monitors student engagement in the course**

Want to give CourseMate a try? Go to **www.cengagebrain.com**, enter the ISBN of this textbook (978-1-285-73752-2), and you can access a free sample of the CourseMate to accompany *Understanding Health Insurance, 12e*.

ABOUT THE AUTHOR

Michelle A. Green, MPS, RHIA, FAHIMA, CPC, SUNY Distinguished Teaching Professor, Alfred State College, Alfred, New York, has been a full-time college professor since 1984. She taught traditional classroom-based courses until 2000, when she transitioned all of the health information technology and coding/reimbursement specialist courses to an Internet-based format. Michelle A. Green's teaching responsibilities include health information management, insurance and reimbursement, and ICD-9-CM, ICD-10-CM, ICD-10-PCS, CPT, and HCPCS level II coding courses. Prior to 1984, she worked as a director of health information management at two acute care hospitals in the Tampa Bay, Florida, area. Both positions required her to assign ICD-9-CM codes to inpatient cases. Upon becoming employed as a college professor, she routinely spent semester breaks coding for a number of health care facilities so that she could further develop her inpatient and outpatient coding skills.

REVIEWERS

Special thanks are extended to the reviewers, technical reviewers, and supplement authors who provided recommendations and suggestions for improvement throughout the development of the Twelfth Edition. Their experience and knowledge has been a valuable resource for the authors.

Deborah Bennett, BS, AA, CCS-P
Instructor
Remington
North Olmsted, OH

Sue Butler, CPC, CIMC
Adjunct Faculty
Lansing Community College
Lansing, MI

Dianne M. Carrington, CCA
Instructor
Southern Hills Joint Voc Career Center
Georgetown, OH

Rhoda Cooper, CPC, RMC, NCICS
Director of HIM
Piedmont Virginia Community College
Charlottesville, VA

Donna Firn, CMA(AAMA), CPC-A
Medical Coding and Advisory Board Member
Delaware County Community College
Media, PA

Terri Gist-Grace, BA, CPC, PAHM
Program Director/Instructor
Medtech College-Indianapolis
Indianapolis, IN

Judy Hurtt, MEd
Instructor
East Central Community College
Decatur, MS

Cheryl D. Jerzak, BSHA, CMA (AAMA)
Director of Health Care Administration and Medical Assistant Programs
Four-D College
Colton, CA

Pat King, MA, BS, RHIA
Adjunct Faculty
Baker College
Auburn Hills, MI

Cheryl E. Riffe
Coding QM Specialist
Adjunct Faculty
National College
Princeton, WV
Calarion Health Care
Roanoke, VA

TECHNICAL REVIEWERS AND SUPPLEMENT AUTHORS

Crystal A. Clack, MS, RHIT, CCS
Adjust Faculty
DeVry University
Ilwaco, WA

Linda Hernandez, CPC-P
Billing Specialist
MedAmerica, Ontario, CA

Jessica Villar Rosati, RN
Comfort Keepers #157
Cape Girardeau, MO

ACKNOWLEDGMENTS

To my son, Eric, who understands and supports my passion for teaching and writing. Thank you for always checking in with me to find out if I've finished the next chapter!

To my students, throughout the world, who motivate me to want to learn everything so I can teach them everything. You are my inspiration.

Special appreciation is expressed to OptumInsight Publishing Group for granting permission to reprint selected tables and pages from:

- ***EncoderPro.com***
- ***HCPCS Level II Professional***
- ***ICD-10-CM Professional***
- ***ICD-10-PCS Professional***

FEEDBACK

Contact the author at **delmarauthor@yahoo.com** with questions, suggestions, or comments about the text or supplements.

How to Use This Text

Health Insurance Specialist Career

CHAPTER OUTLINE

Health Insurance Overview
Health Insurance Career Opportunities
Education and Training
Job Responsibilities
Professionalism

OBJECTIVES

Upon successful completion of this chapter, you should be able to:

1. Define key terms.
2. Discuss introductory health insurance concepts.
3. Identify career opportunities available in health insurance.
4. List the education and training requirements of a health insurance specialist.
5. Describe the job responsibilities of a health insurance specialist.
6. Explain the role of workplace professionalism in career success.

KEY TERMS

American Academy of Professional Coders (AAPC)
American Association of Medical Assistants (AAMA)
American Health Information Management Association (AHIMA)
American Medical Billing Association (AMBA)
bonding insurance
business liability insurance
Centers for Medicare and Medicaid Services (CMS)
claims examiner
coding
Current Procedural Terminology (CPT)
embezzle
errors and omissions insurance
ethics
explanation of benefits (EOB)
HCPCS level II codes
Healthcare Common Procedure Coding System (HCPCS)
hold harmless clause
independent contractor
International Classification of Diseases, 10th Revision, Clinical Modification (ICD-10-CM)
International Classification of Diseases, 10th Revision, Procedural Coding System (ICD-10-PCS)
internship

Objectives and Key Terms

The **Objectives** section lists the outcomes expected of the learner after a careful study of the chapter. Review the Objectives before reading the chapter content. When you complete the chapter, read the Objectives again to see if you can say for each one, "Yes, I can do that." If you cannot, go back to the appropriate content and reread it.

Key Terms represent new vocabulary in each chapter. Each term is highlighted in color in the chapter, is used in context, and is defined on first usage. A complete definition of each term appears in the Glossary at the end of the text.

STUDY CHECKLIST

- ☐ Read this textbook chapter and highlight key concepts. (Use colored highlighter sparingly throughout the chapter.)
- ☐ Create an index card for each k… concept on the other. Learn the…
- ☐ Access chapter Internet links to…
- ☐ Answer the chapter review ques…
- ☐ Complete the Workbook chapte…
- ☐ Form a study group with classm…

Study Checklist

The **Study Checklist** appears at the end of each chapter. This list directs you to other learning and application aids. Completing each of the items in the checklist helps you to gain confidence in your understanding of the key concepts and in your ability to apply them correctly.

Introduction

The **Introduction** provides a brief overview of the major topics covered in the chapter.

The Introduction and the Objectives provide a framework for your study of the content.

INTRODUCTION

Managed health care (managed care) combines health care delivery with the financing of services provided. The intent was to replace conventional fee-for-service plans with more affordable quality care to health care consumers and providers who agreed to certain restrictions (e.g., patients would receive care only from providers who are members of a managed care organization). Managed care is currently being challenged by the growth of consumer-directed health plans (CDHPs), which define employer contributions and ask employees to be more responsible for health care decisions and cost-sharing. You might think of a CDHP as a sort of "401(k) plan for health care" (recalling the shift from employer defined-benefit pension plans to employer defined-contribution 401(k) plans).

NOTE: Health insurance specialists and medical assist… obtain employment in clini… health care clearinghouses… health care facility billing departments, insurance co… nies, and physicians' office… well as with third-party adr… istrators (TPAs). When emp… by clearinghouses, insuran… companies, or TPAs, they o… have the opportunity to wo… home, where they process… verify health care claims u… an Internet-based applicat… server provider (ASP).

Notes

Notes appear throughout the text and serve to bring important points to your attention. The Notes may clarify content, refer you to reference material, provide more background for selected topics, or emphasize exceptions to rules.

HIPAA ALERT!

Traditionally, claims attachments containing medical documentation that supported procedures and services reported on claims were copied from patient records and mailed to payers. Effective 2006, providers submit electronic attachments with electronic claims or send ... in response to requests for medical documentation to su... (e.g., scanned images of paper records).

CODING TIP

Make sure that diagnoses, procedures, and services selected on the encounter form are documented in the patient's medical record before reporting codes on the insurance claim.

Icons

Icons draw attention to critical areas of content or provide experience-based recommendations. For example, the **HIPAA ALERT!** identifies issues related to the security of personal health information in the medical office. The **CODING TIP** provides recommendations and hints for selecting codes and for the correct use of the coding manuals. Other icons include **MANAGED CARE ALERT, HINT, REMEMBER!**, and **CAUTION**.

INTERNET LINKS

- Great Plains Regional Medical Center
  Go to **www.gprmc-ok.com** and select the About GPRMC link to learn more about Dr. Shadid and the history of the Great Plains Regional Medical Center, a managed care system started in 1929.
- HealthEast
  Go to **www.healtheast.org** to view informat... grated care delivery system that provides ac... services, ambulatory/outpatient services, ph...
- The Joint Commission
  Go to **www.jointcommission.org** to learn ab...
- The Joint Commission Quality Check
  Go to **www.qualitycheck.org** and conduct a... The Joint Commission's patient safety and ...
- Kaiser Permanente
  Go to **www.kaiserpermanente.org** to learn abo...
- National Committee for Quality Assurance ...
  Go to **www.ncqa.org** to learn about the NCQ...
- NCQA's Health Plan Report Card
  Go to **reportcard.ncqa.org** and click the Hea... create a customized report card of managed...

Internet Links

Internet Links are provided to encourage you to expand your knowledge at various state and federal government agency sites, commercial sites, and organization sites. Some exercises require you to obtain information from the Internet to complete the exercise.

EXERCISE 10-1

Choosing the First-Listed Diagnosis

Review the list of symptoms, complaints, and disorders in each case and underline the first-listed diagnosis, which is reported in Block 21 of the CMS-1500 claim.

1. Occasional bouts of urinary frequency, but symptom-free today
   Sore throat with swollen glands and enlarged tonsils
   Acute pharyngitis with negative rapid strep test
   Urinalysis test negative
2. Edema, left lateral malleolus
   Limited range of motion due to pain
   Musculoligamentous sprain, left ankle
   X-ray negative for fracture
3. Distended urinary bladder
   Benign prostatic hypertrophy (BPH) with urinary retention
   Enlarged prostate

SUMMARY

The financing of America's health care system has changed the way health care services are organized and delivered, as evidenced by a movement from traditional fee-for-service systems to managed care networks. These range from structured staff model HMOs to less structured preferred provider organizations (PPOs).

Currently, more than 60 million Americans are enrolled in some type of managed care program in response to regulatory initiatives affecting health care cost and quality.

A managed care organization (MCO) is responsible for the health of its enr... istered by the MCO that serves as a health plan or contracts with a hos... health system.

Most managed care financing is achieved through a method called capitati... assigned to or select a primary care provider who serves as the patient'...

Federal legislation mandated that MCOs participate in quality assuran... activities, including utilization management, case management, req... surgical opinions, non-use of gag clauses in MCO contracts, and di... incentives.

Managed care is categorized according to six models: exclusive provider o... ery systems, health maintenance organizations, point-of-service plans, ... tions, and triple option plans.

Consumer-directed health plans (CDHPs) provide incentives for controllin... give individuals an alternative to traditional health insurance and man...

Accreditation organizations, such as the NCQA, evaluate MCOs according...

Summary

The **Summary** at the end of each chapter recaps the key points of the chapter. It also serves as a review aid when preparing for tests.

REVIEW

MULTIPLE CHOICE Select the most appropriate response.

1. **Which means that the patient and/or insured has authorized the payer to reimburse the provider directly?**
   a. accept assignment
   b. assignment of benefits
   c. coordination of benefits
   d. medical necessity
2. **Providers who do not accept assignment of Medicare benefits do not receive information included on the _____, which is sent to the patient.**
   a. electronic flat file
   b. encounter form
   c. ledger
   d. Medicare Summary Notice
3. **The transmission of claims data to payers or clearinghouses is called claims**
   a. adjudication.
   b. assignment.
   c. processing.
   d. submission.
4. **A patient received services on April 5, totaling $1,000. He paid a $90 coinsurance at the time services were rendered. (The payer required the patient to pay a 20 percent coinsurance at the time services were provided.) The physician accepted assignment, and the insurance company established the reasonable charge as $450. On July 1, the provider received $360 from the insurance company. On August 1, the patient received a check from the insurance company in the amount of $450. The overpayment was _____, and the _____ must reimburse the insurance company. (Remember! Coinsurance is the percentage of costs a patient shares with the health plan.)**
   a. $450, patient
   b. $450, physician
   c. $550, patient
   d. $640, physician
5. **A series of fixed-length records submitted to payers to bill for health care services is an electronic**
   a. flat file format.

Reviews and Exercises

The **Reviews** test student understanding about chapter content and critical thinking ability. Reviews in coding chapters require students to assign correct codes and modifiers using coding manuals. Answers are available from your instructor.

Exercises provide practice applying critical thinking skills. Answers to exercises are available from your instructor.

BLUECROSS BLUESHIELD 469

TABLE 13-1 CMS-1500 claims completion instructions for BCBS fee-for-service plans

NOTE: Refer to Chapter 11 for clarification of claims completion (e.g., entering names, mailing addresses, ICD-10-CM codes, diagnosis pointer letters, NPI, and so on).

BLOCK	INSTRUCTIONS
1	Enter an X in the *Other* box if the patient is covered by an individual or family health plan. Or, enter an X in the *Group Health Plan* box if the patient is covered by a group health plan. **NOTE:** The patient is covered by a group health plan if a group number is printed on the patient's insurance identification card (or a group number is included on case studies located in this textbook, workbook, and SimClaim software).
1a	Enter the BCBS plan identification number as it appears on the patient's insurance card. *Do not enter hyphens or spaces in the number.*
2	Enter the patient's last name, first name, and middle initial (separated by commas) (e.g., DOE, JANE, M).
3	Enter the patient's birth date as MM DD YYYY (with spaces). Enter an X in the appropriate box to indicate the patient's gender. If the patient's gender is unknown, leave blank.
4	Enter the policyholder's last name, first name, and middle initial (separated by commas).
5	Enter the patient's mailing address and telephone number. Enter the street address on line 1, enter the city and state on line 2, and enter the five- or nine-digit zip code and phone number on line 3.
6	Enter an X in the appropriate box to ... ried domestic partner, enter an X in ...
7	Enter the policyholder's mailing add... state on line 2, and enter the five- ...
8	Leave blank.
9, 9a, 9d	Leave blank. *Blocks 9, 9a, and 9d ... in this chapter).*
9b–9c	Leave blank.
10a–c	Enter an X in the appropriate boxes ... accident, and/or another accident. ... abbreviation of the patient's residen...
10d	Leave blank.
11	Enter the policyholder's BCBS group ... *spaces in the policy or group num...*
11a	Enter the policyholder's birth date a... cyholder's gender. If the policyholde...
11b	Leave blank. This is reserved for pro...
11c	Enter the name of the policyholder's...
11d	Enter an X in the NO box. *Block 11c ... insurance coverage (discussed late...*
12	Enter SIGNATURE ON FILE. Leave the...
13	Leave blank. *Assignment of benefit... BCBS to reimburse providers direc...*

Claims Instructions

Claims instructions simplify the process of completing the CMS-1500 for various types of payers. These instructions are provided in tables in Chapters 12 to 17. Each table consists of step-by-step instructions for completing each block of the CMS-1500 for commercial, BlueCross BlueShield, Medicare, Medicaid, TRICARE, and Workers' Compensation payers.

How to Use SimClaim CMS-1500 Software

SimClaim software is an online educational tool designed to familiarize you with the basics of the CMS-1500 claims completion. Because in the real world there are many rules that can vary by payer, facility, and state, the version of SimClaim that accompanies the Twelfth Edition of this textbook maps to the specific instructions found in your *Understanding Health Insurance* textbook.

How to Access SimClaim

To access the SimClaim student practice software program online, please refer to the information on the printed access card found in the front of this textbook. The SimClaim case studies are also available for reference in Appendix I of this textbook.

Main Menu

From the Main Menu, you can access the SimClaim program three different ways: Study Mode, Test Mode, and Blank Form Mode. You can now save your work in all three modes and return to it later.

- Click on **Study Mode** to get feedback as you fill out claim forms for the case studies. If you need help entering information in a block of the form, you may click on Block Help for block-specific instructions while in Study Mode.
- Click on **Test Mode** to fill out claim forms for the case studies to test yourself. The completed claim is graded and can be printed and e-mailed to your instructor.
- Use **Blank Form Mode** if you wish to utilize the SimClaim program to fill out a blank CMS-1500 form with another case study in the textbook or student workbook.

You can access SimClaim support documentation from the Main Menu as well, including Block Help, a glossary, and a list of abbreviations.

General Instructions and Hints for Completing CMS-1500 Claims in SimClaim

Please read through the following general instructions before beginning work in the SimClaim program:

- **Certain abbreviations are allowed in the program**—for example, 'St' for Street, 'Dr' for Drive, 'Rd' for Road, 'Ct' for Court. No other abbreviations will be accepted as correct by the program.
- **Only one Diagnosis Pointer in Block 24E per line**—though SimClaim allows for more than one Diagnosis Pointer to be entered, only one diagnosis pointer is allowed in Block 24E for each line item as per textbook instructions.
- **No Amount Paid Indicated**—If there is no amount paid indicated on the case study, *leave the field blank.*
- **Secondary Insurance Claims**—If a Case Study indicates that a patient's Primary Insurance carrier has paid an amount, fill out a second claim for the Secondary Insurance that reflects the amount reimbursed by primary insurance when indicated.
- **Fill out Block 32** only when the facility is other than the office setting, as indicated on the Case Study.
- **Enter all dates** as listed on the Case Study.
- **For additional help using SimClaim, refer to the Block Help within SimClaim or to the specific carrier guidelines found in your textbook.**

How to Use *EncoderPro.com Expert* Online Software

Optum's *EncoderPro.com Expert* is a powerful medical coding software solution that allows you to locate CPT, HCPCS, ICD-10-CM, and ICD-10-PCS codes. The software provides users with fast searching capabilities across all code sets, it greatly reduces the time needed to build or review an insurance claim, and it helps improve overall coding accuracy. The software includes additional features such as ICD-10-CM and ICD-10-PCS crosswalks for ICD-9-CM codes and coding guidance (e.g., 1995 E/M guidelines). This software can be used to assign codes to any of the exercises in the *Understanding Health Insurance* textbook and workbook.

NOTE: Appendix III of this textbook contains a *Coding Practice Using EncoderPro.com* assignment, which allows students to become familiar with the use of an encoder (after having learned how to code using paper-based coding manuals).

HOW TO ACCESS THE FREE TRIAL OF *ENCODERPRO.COM EXPERT*

Information about how to access your 59-day trial of *EncoderPro.com Expert* is included on the printed tear-out card located in the front cover of this textbook. The card contains a unique user access code and password. Once you log in, scroll down to the bottom of the *License Agreement* page and click the *I Accept* link. Then, click the *I Accept* link on the *Terms of Use* page.

Permission to reprint granted by Optum

NOTE: Be sure to check with your instructor before beginning your free trial because it will expire 59 days after your initial login.

MENUS AND TOOLBARS

Optum's *EncoderPro.com Expert* contains a black toolbar with an *All Code Sets* drop-down menu that allows you to select the CPT, HCPCS (level II), ICD-10-CM, or ICD-10-PCS coding system.

- Use the *All Code Sets* drop-down menu on the far left to select a coding system. Then, enter a condition (e.g., diabetes) or procedure/service in the Search box. Click the Search button to view tabular list results, which can be expanded.
- Use the *Coding* drop-down menu (located below the *All Code Sets* drop-down menu) to view features of each coding system (e.g., new codes, reinstated codes, neoplasm table, and so on).

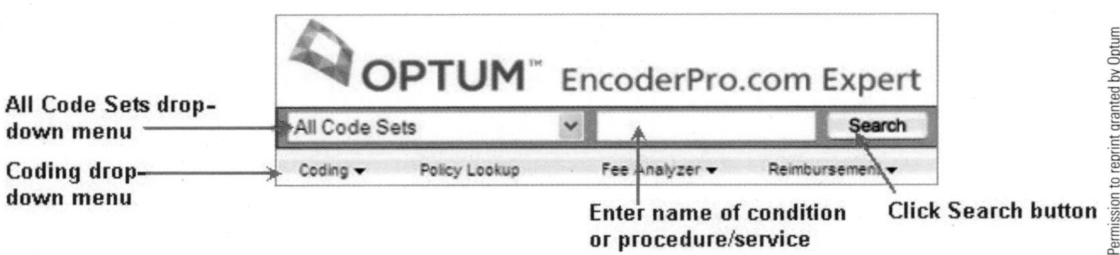

Permission to reprint granted by Optum

SOFTWARE FEATURES

The Expert version of *EncoderPro.com* contains the following features:

- *CodeLogic™ Search Technology*, which allows simultaneous code search across the CPT, HCPCS (level II), ICD-10-CM, and ICD-10-PCS code sets. Search results can display all four code sets or can be limited to one code set.
- *Search Terms*, which allow entry of up to four search terms, acronyms, and/or abbreviations that result in the ability to narrow down results when initiating a search. An automatic spell check feature ensures that valid terms are entered.
- *Code Detail*, which is a comprehensive reference page for *each* CPT and HCPCS level II code with access to modifiers, CCI edits, and cross-coding data. CPT and HCPCS level II codes are organized by section and subsection. For ICD-10-CM codes, excludes and includes notes as well as "code first" and "code also" references are displayed.
- *Code-Specific Edits and Information for ICD-10-CM*, which allows you to view instructional notes, AHA coding clinic references, and annotations for the selected ICD-10-CM code.
- *Code-Specific Edits and Information for CPT*, which allows you to view lay descriptions, *CPT® Assistant* references, AMA guidelines, and modifiers for the selected CPT code. You can also view primary CPT procedure codes (for add-on codes), surgical and anesthesia cross-codes, Medicare physician fee schedule information, and the unbundle edits from Medicare's Correct Coding Initiative.
- *Code-Specific Edits and Information for HCPCS (level II)*, which allows you to view annotations, section notes, modifiers, and coverage instruction references from the Pub-100 References for the selected HCPCS code.
- *Color Codes*, which allows you to look up all codes with their color codes in sorted lists.
- *User Notes*, which allows organizations to establish *global notes* based on company-wide rules. Individuals can also add and edit comments to codes, and each code with a User Note attached is flagged for quick reference.
- *Claim Compliance*, which allows you to check claim charge detail for coding compliancy so any billing errors can be edited as needed.

FEATURES OF *ENCODERPRO.COM EXPERT*

Optum's *EncoderPro.com Expert* includes the following software features:

- **CPT color codes that identify add-on codes, modifier -51 exempt status, age- and gender-specific codes, and so on**

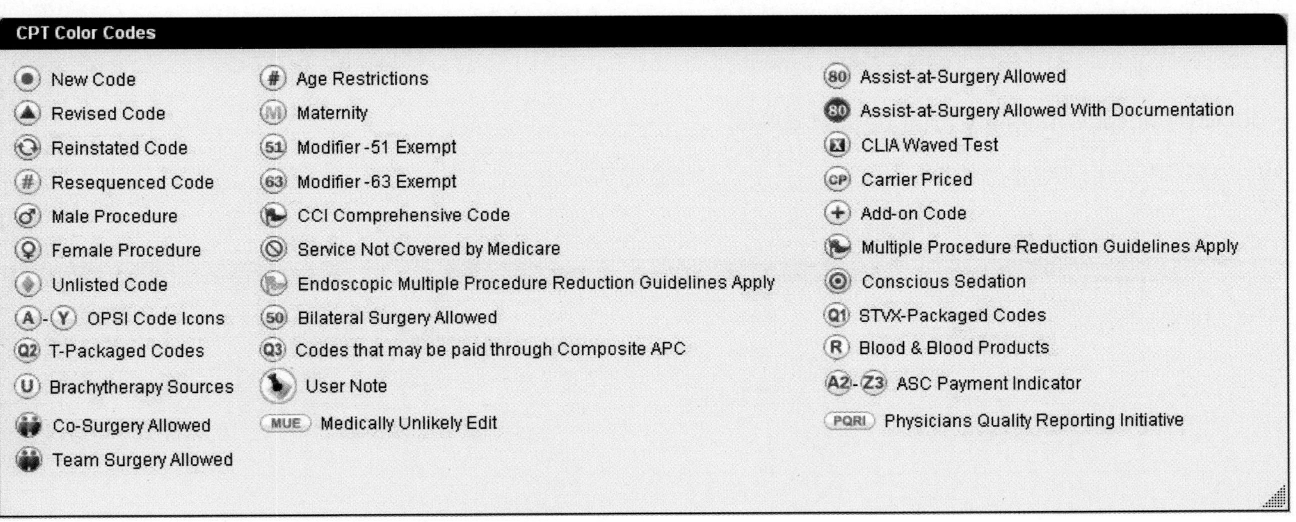

Permission to reprint granted by Optum

- **HCPCS level II color codes that identify new or revised codes or those that contain special coverage instructions, policy flags, and so on**

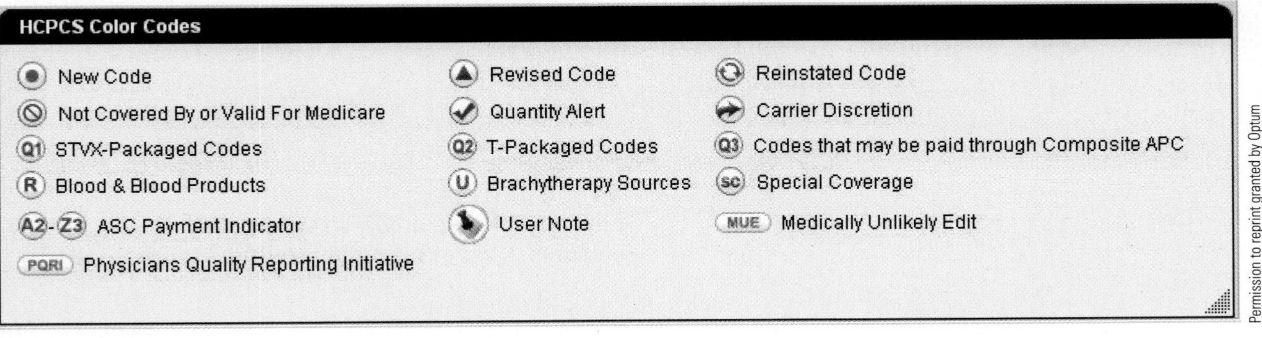

Permission to reprint granted by Optum

- **ICD-10-CM color codes that identify codes that require fourth and fifth digits, are age- and gender-specific, and so on**

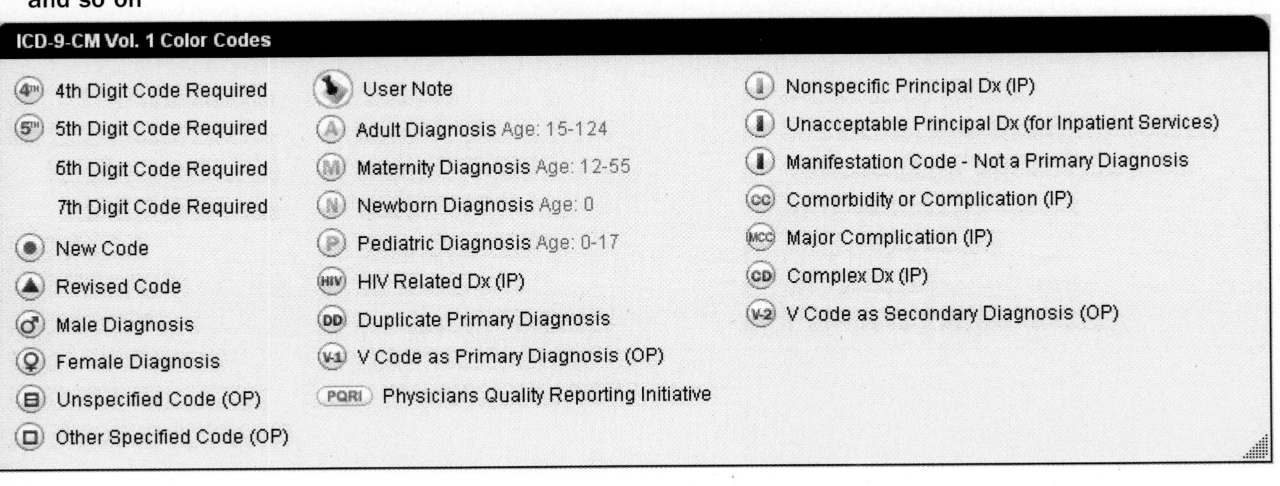

Permission to reprint granted by Optum

- User notes, notepad, HCPCS level II notes, and lay descriptions

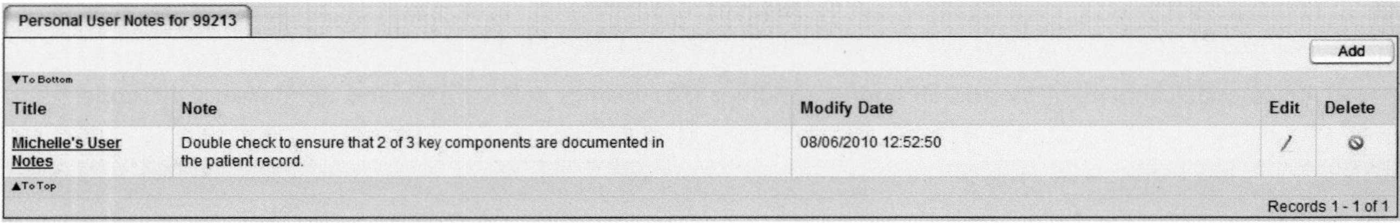

Permission to reprint granted by Optum

- ICD-10-CM code mapping (to ICD-9-CM codes)

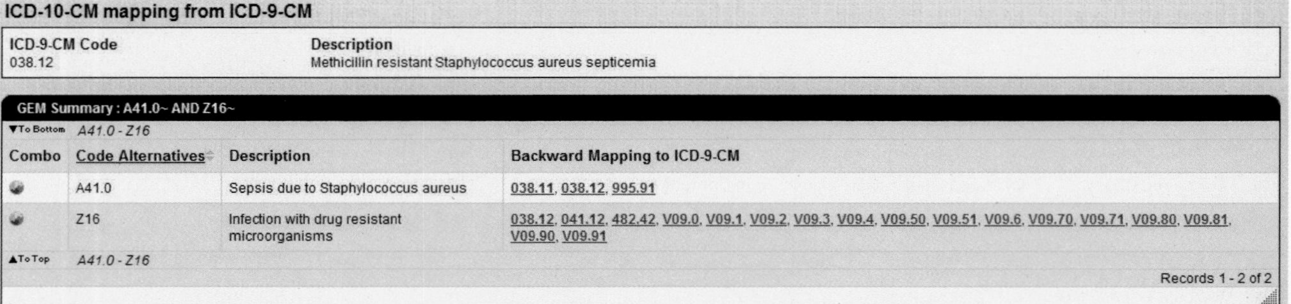

Permission to reprint granted by Optum

- CPT and HCPCS level II modifiers

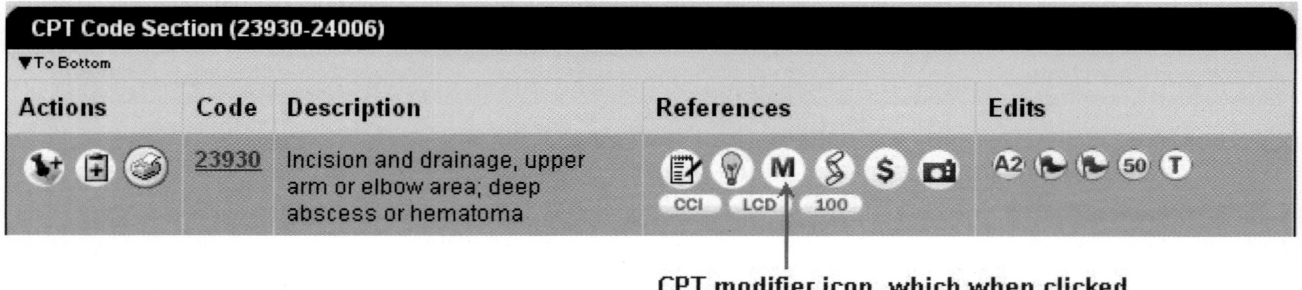

Permission to reprint granted by Optum

- LCD and NCD coverage determinations and medical necessity edits, CCI unbundle edits, and Medicare Pub-100 references

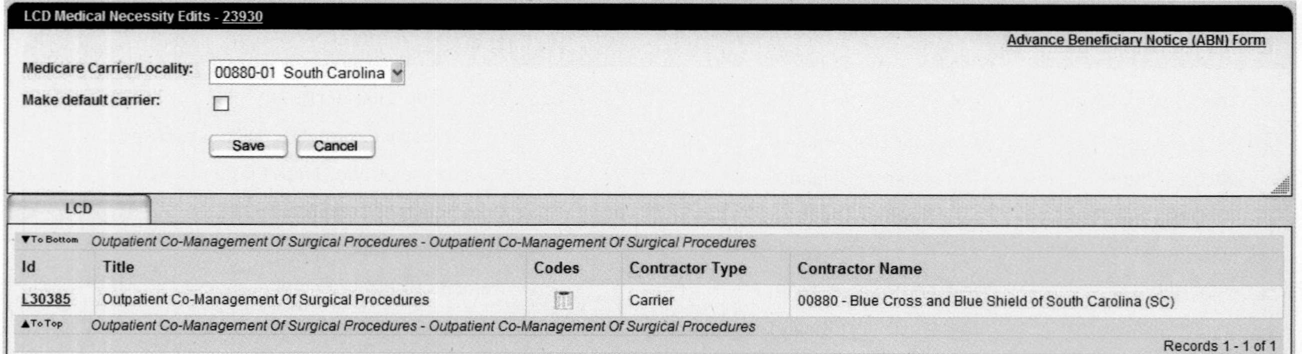

Permission to reprint granted by Optum

- **Modifier crosswalk**

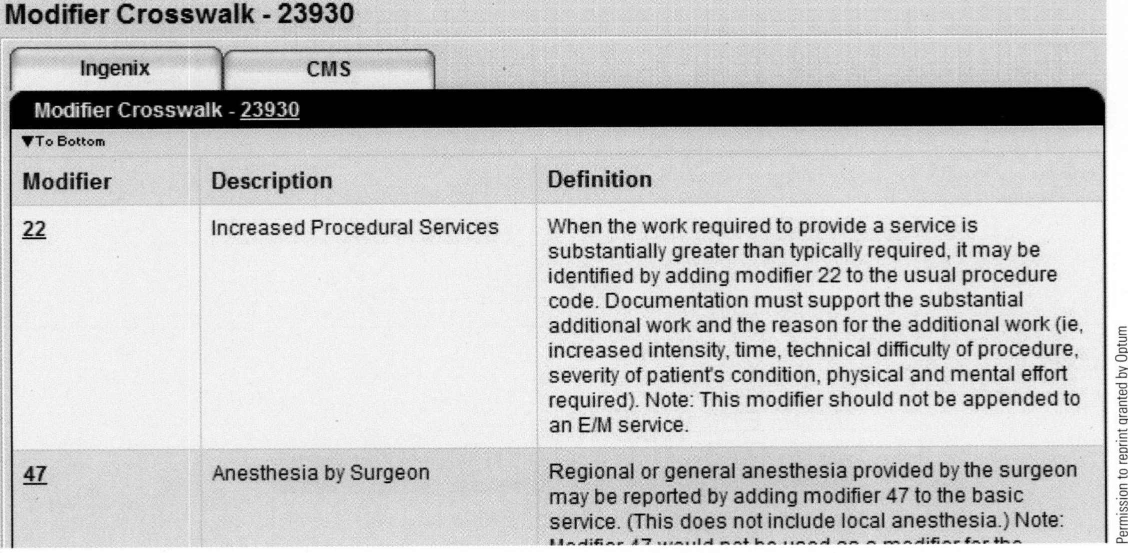

Modifier Crosswalk - 23930

Ingenix | CMS

Modifier Crosswalk - 23930

▼To Bottom

Modifier	Description	Definition
22	Increased Procedural Services	When the work required to provide a service is substantially greater than typically required, it may be identified by adding modifier 22 to the usual procedure code. Documentation must support the substantial additional work and the reason for the additional work (ie, increased intensity, time, technical difficulty of procedure, severity of patient's condition, physical and mental effort required). Note: This modifier should not be appended to an E/M service.
47	Anesthesia by Surgeon	Regional or general anesthesia provided by the surgeon may be reported by adding modifier 47 to the basic service. (This does not include local anesthesia.) Note:

- **Medicare physician fee schedule dialog box and fee calculation by locality**

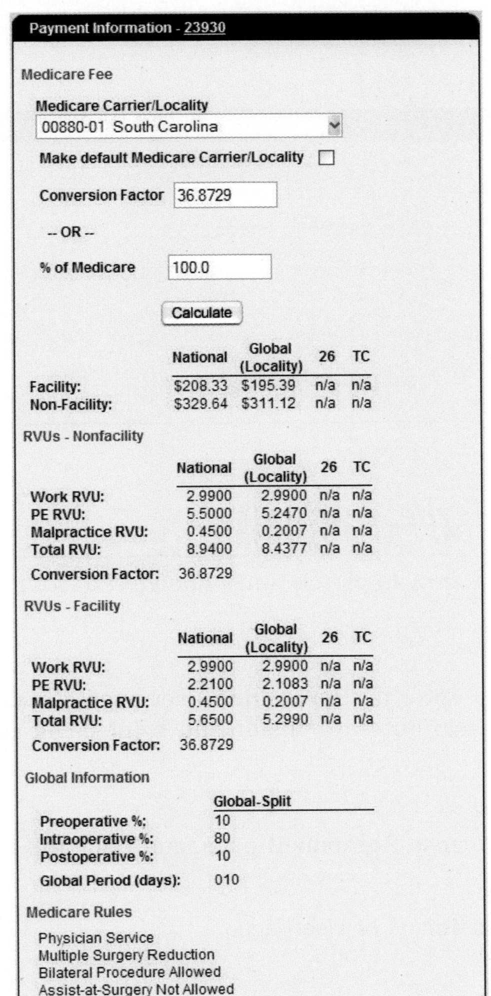

Payment Information - 23930

Medicare Fee

Medicare Carrier/Locality

00880-01 South Carolina

Make default Medicare Carrier/Locality

Conversion Factor 36.8729

-- OR --

% of Medicare 100.0

Calculate

	National	Global (Locality)	26	TC
Facility:	$208.33	$195.39	n/a	n/a
Non-Facility:	$329.64	$311.12	n/a	n/a

RVUs - Nonfacility

	National	Global (Locality)	26	TC
Work RVU:	2.9900	2.9900	n/a	n/a
PE RVU:	5.5000	5.2470	n/a	n/a
Malpractice RVU:	0.4500	0.2007	n/a	n/a
Total RVU:	8.9400	8.4377	n/a	n/a

Conversion Factor: 36.8729

RVUs - Facility

	National	Global (Locality)	26	TC
Work RVU:	2.9900	2.9900	n/a	n/a
PE RVU:	2.2100	2.1083	n/a	n/a
Malpractice RVU:	0.4500	0.2007	n/a	n/a
Total RVU:	5.6500	5.2990	n/a	n/a

Conversion Factor: 36.8729

Global Information

	Global-Split
Preoperative %:	10
Intraoperative %:	80
Postoperative %:	10
Global Period (days):	010

Medicare Rules

Physician Service
Multiple Surgery Reduction
Bilateral Procedure Allowed
Assist-at-Surgery Not Allowed

- **Compliance edit**

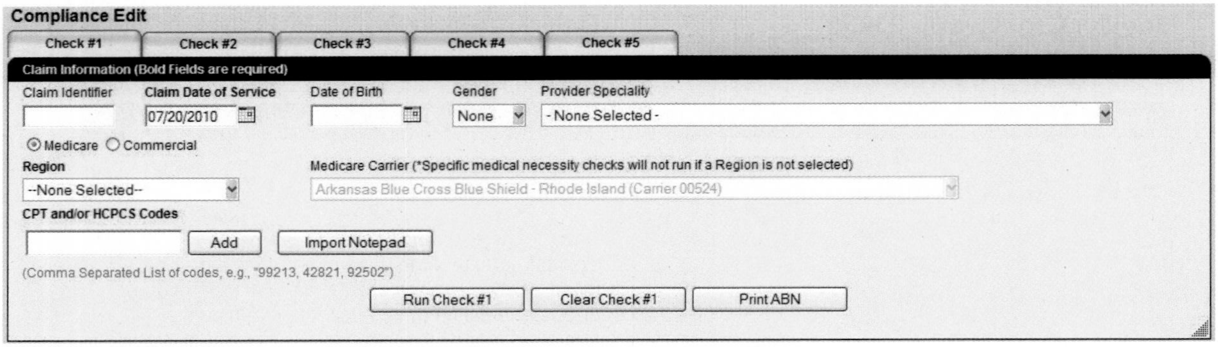

Compliance Edit

Check #1 | Check #2 | Check #3 | Check #4 | Check #5

Claim Information (Bold Fields are required)

Claim Identifier | Claim Date of Service 07/20/2010 | Date of Birth | Gender None | Provider Speciality - None Selected -

Medicare / Commercial

Region --None Selected--

Medicare Carrier (*Specific medical necessity checks will not run if a Region is not selected) Arkansas Blue Cross Blue Shield - Rhode Island (Carrier 00524)

CPT and/or HCPCS Codes

Add | Import Notepad

(Comma Separated List of codes, e.g., "99213, 42821, 92502")

Run Check #1 | Clear Check #1 | Print ABN

Permission to reprint granted by Optum

- **Edit reports**

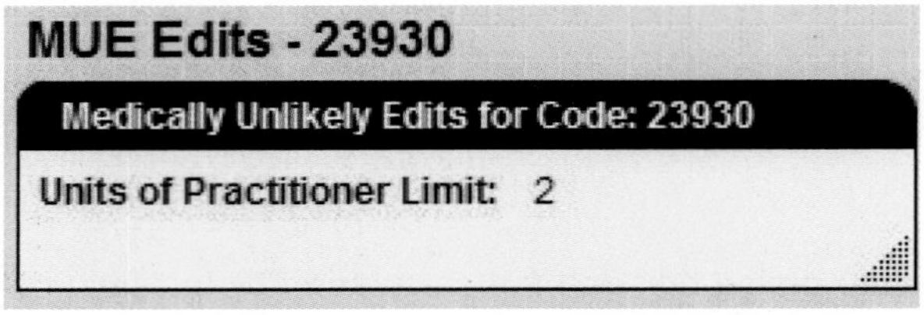

MUE Edits - 23930

Medically Unlikely Edits for Code: 23930

Units of Practitioner Limit: 2

Permission to reprint granted by Optum

- **Claims batch editor**

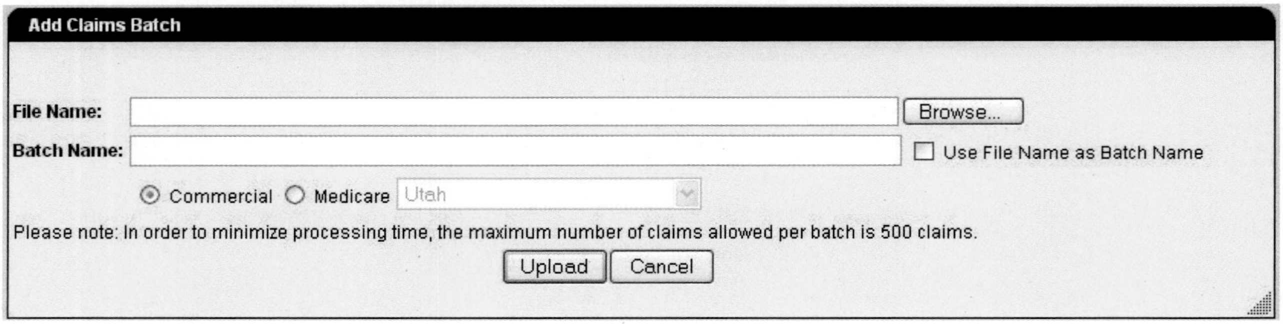

Add Claims Batch

File Name: Browse...

Batch Name: Use File Name as Batch Name

Commercial / Medicare Utah

Please note: In order to minimize processing time, the maximum number of claims allowed per batch is 500 claims.

Upload | Cancel

Permission to reprint granted by Optum

OPTUM'S *ENCODERPRO.COM EXPERT* TUTORIAL

Instructions: Use this tutorial to learn how to use Optum's *EncoderPro.com Expert* software.

NOTE: Be sure to check with your instructor before beginning your free trial because it will expire 59 days after your initial login.

Step 1

Log in to *www.EncoderPro.com* by entering the unique user access code and password (located on the printed tear-out card inside the front cover of this textbook).

Step 2

Scroll down to the bottom of the **License Agreement** page, and click the **I Accept** link.

Step 3

Then, click the **I Accept** link on the **Terms of Use** page.

Step 4

Locate the black toolbar that contains the **All Code Sets** drop-down list, which allows you to select a coding system. Refer to the following image, which identifies the location of the black toolbar on the software page.

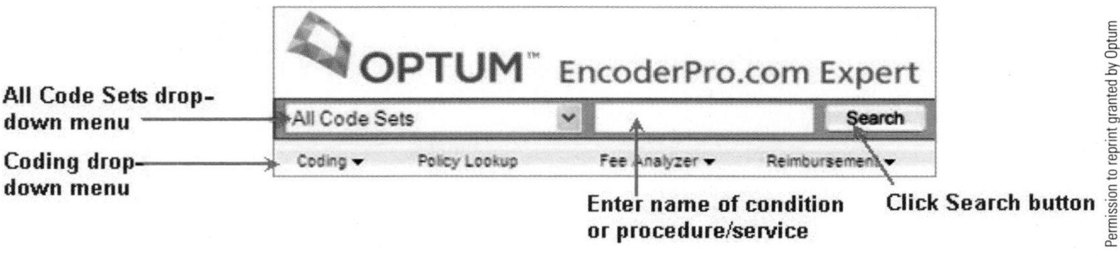

Permission to reprint granted by Optum

Step 5

- You will use *EncoderPro.com Expert* to automate the process of locating ICD-10-CM codes for:
  - Hypertension
  - Myocardial Infarction
- Select ICD-10-CM from the **All Code Sets** drop-down menu.
- Click in the empty Search box, located to the right of the **ICD-10-CM** menu item.
- Enter HYPERTENSION as the condition search term. (You can enter hypertension or Hypertension, if you prefer.)
- Click the **Search** button.

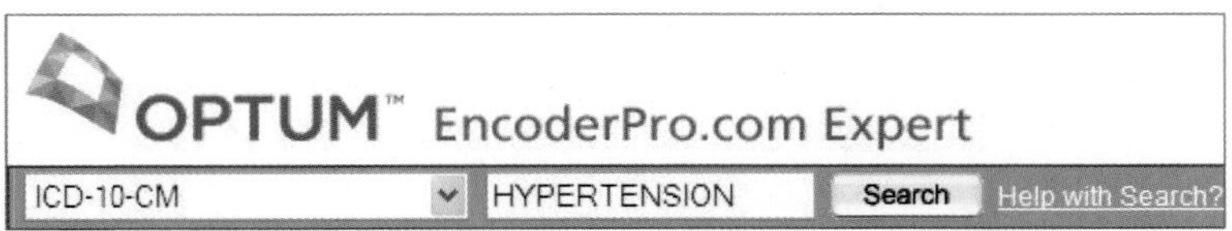

Permission to reprint granted by Optum

Step 6

- Search results for HYPERTENSION include category code I10.

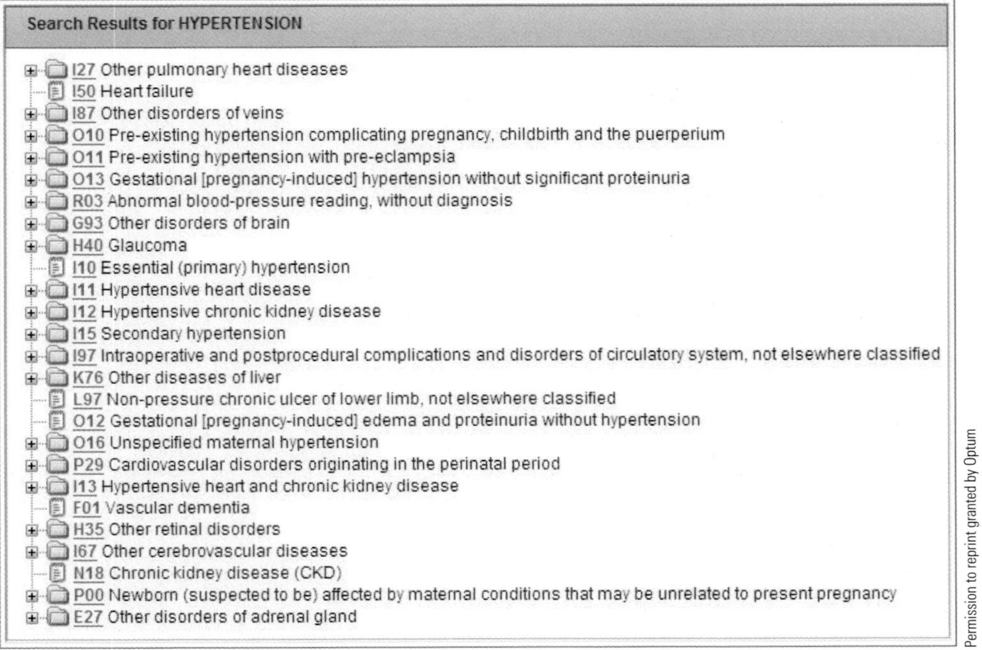

Permission to reprint granted by Optum

- Click on code I10 to view the tabular listing entry for the code.

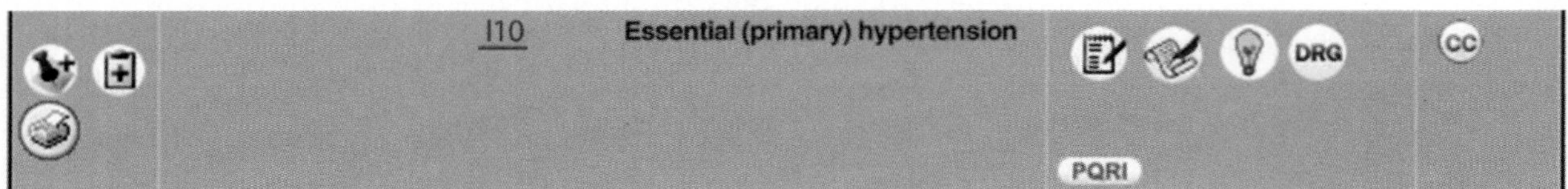

Permission to reprint granted by Optum

Step 7

- Now you try it! The physician documents "angina pectoris" as the patient's diagnosis.
- Enter ANGINA in the search box. Notice that many Search Results display. This condition requires more advanced coding skills than "hypertension," which means the *EncoderPro.com* index feature should be used to locate the code(s).

Step 8

- Scroll your mouse over the Coding drop-down menu, then scroll your mouse over the ICD-10-CM index menu item, and select Index to Diseases.
- Enter ANGINA to the right of the Term starts with: empty box.
- Click Find.
- Click on the Angina Pectoris I20.9 link.
- Notice that Myocardial Infarction displays on the right side of the page.
- Click on code I20.9 to display the tabular list entry.
- When you click on code I20.9 again, code information displays.

Health Insurance Specialist Career

CHAPTER 1

CHAPTER OUTLINE

Health Insurance Overview
Health Insurance Career Opportunities
Education and Training
Job Responsibilities
Professionalism

OBJECTIVES

Upon successful completion of this chapter, you should be able to:

1. Define key terms.
2. Discuss introductory health insurance concepts.
3. Identify career opportunities available in health insurance.
4. List the education and training requirements of a health insurance specialist.
5. Describe the job responsibilities of a health insurance specialist.
6. Explain the role of workplace professionalism in career success.

KEY TERMS

American Academy of Professional Coders (AAPC)
American Association of Medical Assistants (AAMA)
American Health Information Management Association (AHIMA)
American Medical Billing Association (AMBA)
bonding insurance
business liability insurance
Centers for Medicare and Medicaid Services (CMS)
claims examiner
coding
Current Procedural Terminology (CPT)
embezzle
errors and omissions insurance
ethics
explanation of benefits (EOB)
HCPCS level II codes
Healthcare Common Procedure Coding System (HCPCS)
health care provider
health information technician
health insurance claim
health insurance specialist
hold harmless clause
independent contractor
International Classification of Diseases, 10th Revision, Clinical Modification (ICD-10-CM)
International Classification of Diseases, 10th Revision, Procedural Coding System (ICD-10-PCS)
internship
medical assistant
Medical Association of Billers (MAB)
medical malpractice insurance

medical necessity
national codes
preauthorization
professional liability insurance
professionalism
property insurance
reimbursement specialist
remittance advice (remit)
respondeat superior
scope of practice
workers' compensation insurance

INTRODUCTION

The career of a health insurance specialist is a challenging one, with opportunities for professional advancement. Individuals who understand claims processing and billing regulations, possess accurate coding skills, have the ability to successfully appeal underpaid or denied insurance claims, and demonstrate workplace professionalism are in demand. A review of medical office personnel help-wanted advertisements indicates the need for individuals with all of these skills.

NOTE: Reimbursement specialist is another title for health insurance specialist.

HEALTH INSURANCE OVERVIEW

Most health care practices in the United States accept responsibility for filing health insurance claims, and some third-party payers (e.g., BlueCross BlueShield) and government programs (e.g., Medicare) require providers to file claims. A **health insurance claim** is the documentation submitted to a third-party payer or government program requesting reimbursement for health care services provided. In the past few years, many practices have increased the number of employees assigned to some aspect of claims processing. This increase is a result of more patients having some form of health insurance, many of whom require **preauthorization** (prior approval) for treatment by specialists and documentation of post-treatment reports. If preauthorization requirements are not met, payment of the claim is denied. According to BlueCross BlueShield, an insurance plan that has a **hold harmless clause** (patient is not responsible for paying what the insurance plan denies) in the contract, the health care provider cannot collect the fees from the patient. It is important to realize that not all insurance policies contain *hold harmless* clauses. However, many policies contain a *no balance billing* clause that protects patients from being billed for amounts not reimbursed by payers (except for copayments, coinsurance amounts, and deductibles). (Chapter 2 contains more information about these concepts.) In addition, patients referred to nonparticipating providers (e.g., a physician who does not participate in a particular health care plan) incur significantly higher out-of-pocket costs than they may have anticipated. Competitive insurance companies are fine-tuning procedures to reduce administrative costs and overall expenditures. This cost-reduction campaign forces closer scrutiny of the entire claims process, which in turn increases the time and effort medical practices must devote to billing and filing claims according to the insurance policy filing requirements. Poor attention to claims requirements will result in lower reimbursement rates to the practices and increased expenses.

A number of health care providers sign managed care contracts as a way to combine health care delivery and financing of services to provide more affordable quality care. A **health care provider** (Figure 1-1) is a physician or other health care practitioner (e.g., physician's assistant). Each new provider-managed care contract increases the practice's patient base, the number of claims requirements and reimbursement regulations, the time the office staff must devote to fulfilling contract requirements, and the complexity of referring patients for specialty care. Each insurance plan has its own authorization requirements, billing deadlines, claims requirements, and list of participating providers or networks. If a health care provider has signed 10 participating contracts, there are 10 different

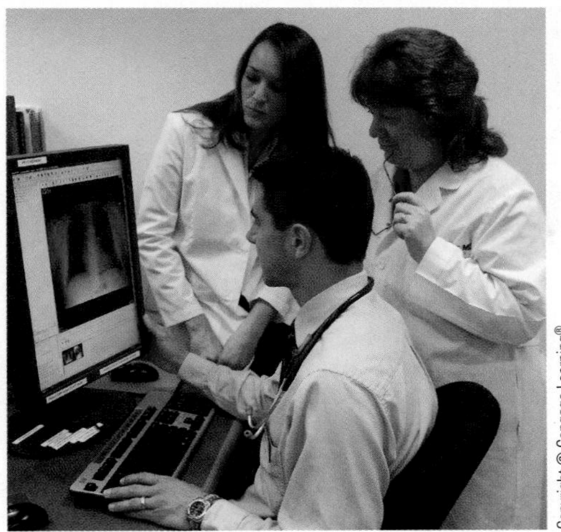

FIGURE 1-1 Health care providers viewing an electronic image of a patient's chest x-ray.

sets of requirements to follow and 10 different panels of participating health care providers from which referrals can be made.

Rules associated with health insurance processing (especially government programs) change frequently; to remain up-to-date, insurance specialists should be sure they are on mailing lists to receive newsletters from third-party payers. It is also important to remain current regarding news released from the **Centers for Medicare and Medicaid Services (CMS)**, which is the administrative agency within the federal Department of Health and Human Services (DHHS). The Secretary of the DHHS, as often reported on by the news media, announces the implementation of new regulations about government programs (e.g., Medicare, Medicaid).

The increased hiring of insurance specialists is a direct result of employers' attempts to reduce the cost of providing employee health insurance coverage. Employers renegotiate benefits with existing plans or change third-party payers altogether. The employees often receive retroactive notice of these contract changes; in some cases, they must then wait several weeks before receiving new health benefit booklets and new insurance identification cards. These changes in employer-sponsored plans have made it necessary for the health care provider's staff to check on patients' current eligibility and benefit status at each office visit.

HEALTH INSURANCE CAREER OPPORTUNITIES

According to the *Occupational Outlook Handbook* published by the U.S. Department of Labor—Bureau of Labor Statistics, the employment growth of claims adjusters and examiners will result from more claims being submitted on behalf of a growing elderly population. Rising premiums and attempts by third-party payers to minimize costs will also result in an increased need for examiners to scrupulously review claims. Although technology reduces the amount of time it takes an adjuster to process a claim, demand for these jobs will increase anyway because many tasks cannot be easily automated (e.g., review of patient records to determine medical necessity of procedures or services rendered).

NOTE: Information about salaries can be located at the www.bls.gov, www.aapc.com, and www.ahima.org websites.

Health insurance specialists (or **reimbursement specialists**) review health-related claims to determine the medical necessity for procedures or services performed before payment (reimbursement) is made to the provider. A **claims examiner** employed by a third-party payer reviews health-related claims to determine whether the

FIGURE 1-2 Health insurance specialist locating code number for entry in CMS-1500 claims software.

FIGURE 1-3 Medical assistant performing the administrative task of reviewing a record for documentation completeness.

> **NOTE:** Health insurance specialists and medical assistants obtain employment in clinics, health care clearinghouses, health care facility billing departments, insurance companies, and physicians' offices, as well as with third-party administrators (TPAs). When employed by clearinghouses, insurance companies, or TPAs, they often have the opportunity to work at home, where they process and verify health care claims using an Internet-based application server provider (ASP).

charges are reasonable and for medical necessity. **Medical necessity** involves *linking every procedure or service code reported on the claim to a condition code (e.g., disease, injury, sign, symptom, other reason for encounter) that justifies the need to perform that procedure or service* (Figure 1-2).

The claims review process requires verification of the claim for completeness and accuracy, as well as comparison with third-party payer guidelines (e.g., expected treatment practices) to (1) authorize appropriate payment or (2) refer the claim to an investigator for a more thorough review. A **medical assistant** (Figure 1-3) is employed by a provider to perform administrative and clinical tasks that keep the office or clinic running smoothly. Medical assistants who specialize in administrative aspects of the profession answer telephones, greet patients, update and file patient medical records, complete insurance claims, process correspondence, schedule appointments, arrange for hospital admission and laboratory services, and manage billing and bookkeeping.

> **EXAMPLE 1:** Procedure: Knee x-ray
>
> Diagnosis: Shoulder pain
>
> In this example, the provider is not reimbursed because the reason for the x-ray (shoulder pain) does not match the type of x-ray performed (knee). For medical necessity, the provider would need to document a diagnosis such as "fractured patella (knee bone)."

> **EXAMPLE 2:** Procedure: Chest x-ray
>
> Diagnosis: Severe shortness of breath
>
> In this example, the provider is reimbursed because medical necessity for performing the procedure is demonstrated.

Coding is the process of assigning ICD-10-CM, ICD-10-PCS CPT, and HCPCS level II codes to diagnoses, procedures, and services. Coding systems include:

> **NOTE:** ICD-10-PCS codes are assigned to inpatient hospital procedures only.

- ***International Classification of Diseases, 10th Revision, Clinical Modification* (ICD-10-CM)** **(coding system used to report diseases, injuries, and other reasons for inpatient** and outpatient encounters, such as an annual physical examination performed at a physician's office)

- *International Classification of Diseases, 10th Revision, Procedural Coding System* (ICD-10-PCS) (coding system used to report procedures and services on inpatient hospital claims)
- Healthcare Common Procedure Coding System (HCPCS, pronounced "hick picks"), which currently consists of two levels:
  - *Current Procedural Terminology* (CPT) (coding system published by the American Medical Association that is used to report procedures and services performed during outpatient and physician office encounters, and professional services provided to inpatients)
  - HCPCS level II codes (or national codes) (coding system published by CMS that is used to report procedures, services, and supplies not classified in CPT)

NOTE: On December 31, 2003, CMS phased out the use of local codes, previously known as HCPCS level III codes. However, some third-party payers continue to use HPCS level III codes.

In addition to an increase in insurance specialist positions available in health care practices, opportunities are also increasing in other settings. These opportunities include:

- Claims benefit advisors in health, malpractice, and liability insurance companies.
- Coding or insurance specialists in state, local, and federal government agencies, legal offices, private insurance billing offices, and medical societies.
- Medical billing and insurance verification specialists in health care organizations.
- Educators in schools and companies specializing in medical office staff training.
- Writers and editors of health insurance textbooks, newsletters, and other publications.
- Self-employed consultants who provide assistance to medical practices with billing practices and claims appeal procedures.
- Consumer claims assistance professionals who file claims and appeal low reimbursement for private individuals. In the latter case, individuals may be dissatisfied with the handling of their claims by the health care provider's insurance staff.
- Practices with poorly trained health insurance staff who are unwilling or unable to file a proper claims appeal.
- Private billing practices dedicated to claims filing for elderly or disabled patients.

NOTE: In addition to many other functions, health information technicians perform insurance specialist functions by assigning codes to diagnoses and procedures and, when employed in a provider's office, by processing claims for reimbursement. (Health information technicians manage patient health information and medical records, administer computer information systems, and code diagnoses and procedures for health care services provided to patients.) The *Occupational Outlook Handbook* states that physician offices offer the fastest employment growth and majority of new jobs for health information technicians because of an increasing demand for detailed records, especially in large group practices.

EDUCATION AND TRAINING

Training and entry requirements vary widely for health insurance specialists, and the Bureau of Labor Statistics' *Occupational Outlook Handbook* states that opportunities will be best for those with a college degree. Academic programs should include coursework (Table 1-1) in general education (e.g., anatomy and physiology, English composition, oral communications, human relations, computer applications, and so on) and health insurance specialist education (e.g., health information management, medical terminology, pharmacology, coding and reimbursement, insurance processing, and so on). The characteristics of a successful health insurance specialist include an ability to work independently, a strong sense of ethics, attention to detail, and the ability to think critically. The *American Heritage Concise Dictionary* defines ethics as the principles of right or good conduct, and rules that govern the conduct of members of a profession.

TABLE 1-1 Training requirements for health insurance specialists

COURSEWORK	DESCRIPTION
Anatomy and Physiology, Medical Terminology, Pharmacology, and Pathophysiology	Knowledge of anatomic structures and physiological functioning of the body, medical terminology, and essentials of pharmacology are necessary to recognize abnormal conditions (pathophysiology). Fluency in the language of medicine and the ability to use a medical dictionary as a reference are crucial skills.
Diagnosis and Procedure/ Service Coding	Understanding the rules, conventions, and applications of coding systems ensures proper selection of diagnosis and procedure/service codes, which are reported on insurance claims for reimbursement purposes. **EXAMPLE:** Patient undergoes a simple suture treatment of a 3-cm facial laceration. When referring to the CPT index, there is no listing for "Suture, facial laceration." There is, however, an instructional notation below the entry for "Suture" that refers the coder to "Repair." When "Repair" is referenced in the index, the coder must then locate the subterms "Skin," "Wound," and "Simple." The code range in the index is reviewed, and the coder must refer to the tabular section of the coding manual to select the correct code.
Verbal and Written Communication	Health insurance specialists explain complex insurance concepts and regulations to patients and must effectively communicate with providers regarding documentation of procedures and services (to reduce coding and billing errors). Written communication skills are necessary when preparing effective appeals for unpaid claims.
Critical Thinking	Differentiating among technical descriptions of similar procedures requires critical thinking skills. **EXAMPLE:** Patient is diagnosed with spondy*losis,* which is defined as any condition of the spine. A code from category M47 of ICD-10-CM would be assigned. If the diagnosis was mistakenly coded as spondy*lolysis,* which is a defect of the articulating portion of the vertebra, ICD-10-CM category Q76 (if congenital) or M43 (if acquired) codes would be reported in error.
Data Entry	Federal regulations require electronic submission of most government claims, which means that health insurance specialists need excellent keyboarding skills and basic finance and math skills. Because insurance information screens with different titles often contain identical information, the health insurance specialist must carefully and accurately enter data about patient care. **EXAMPLE:** Primary and secondary insurance computer screens require entry of similar information. Claims are rejected by insurance companies if data are missing or erroneous.
Internet Access	Online information sources provide access to medical references, insurance company manuals, and procedure guidelines. The federal government posts changes to reimbursement methodologies and other policies on websites. Internet forums allow health insurance specialists to network with other professionals.

Student Internship

> **NOTE:** Chapter 1 of the *Workbook to Accompany Understanding Health Insurance* contains an assignment entitled "Ready, Set, Get a Job" that teaches students how to create a résumé and cover letter, and helps them prepare for a job interview.

An **internship** benefits students and facilities that accept students for placement. Students receive on-the-job experience prior to graduation, and the internship assists them in obtaining permanent employment. Facilities benefit from the opportunity to participate in and improve the formal education process. Quite often, students who complete internships obtain employment at the internship facility. The students report to the internship supervisor at the site. Students are often required to submit a professional résumé to the internship supervisor and schedule an interview prior to acceptance for placement. While this

FIGURE 1-4 Medical assistant and internship student prepare for their next patient.

NOTE: Breach of patient confidentiality can result in termination of the internship, which means failing the internship course. Suspension or expulsion from your academic program are other possible consequences. Be sure to ask about your academic program's requirements regarding this issue.

process can be intimidating, students gain experience with the interview process, which is part of obtaining permanent employment. Students should research résumé writing and utilize interview technique services available from their school's career services office. This office typically reviews résumés and provides interview tips. (Some offices even videotape mock interviews for students.)

The internship is on-the-job training even though it is unpaid, and students should expect to provide proof of immunizations (available from a physician) and possibly undergo a pre-employment physical examination and participate in an orientation. In addition, because of the focus on privacy and security of patient information, the facility will likely require students to sign a nondisclosure agreement (to protect patient confidentiality), which is kept on file at the college and by the internship site.

During the internship, students are expected to report to work on time. Students who cannot participate in the internship on a particular day (or who arrive late) should contact their internship supervisor or program faculty, whoever is designated for that purpose. Students are also required to make up any lost time. Because the internship is a simulated job experience, students are to be well groomed and should dress professionally (Figure 1-4). Students should show interest in all aspects of the experience, develop good working relationships with coworkers, and react appropriately to criticism and direction. If any concerns arise during the internship, students should discuss them with their internship supervisor or program faculty.

JOB RESPONSIBILITIES

This section provides an overview of the major responsibilities delegated to health insurance specialists. In practices where just one or two persons work with insurance billing, each individual must be capable of performing all the listed responsibilities. In multispecialty practices that employ many health insurance specialists, each usually processes claims for a limited number of insurance companies (e.g., an insurance specialist may be assigned to processing only Medicare claims). Some practices have a clear division of labor, with specific individuals accepting responsibility for only a few assigned tasks. Typical tasks are listed in the following job description.

Health Insurance Specialist Job Description

1. Review patient record documentation to accurately code all diagnoses, procedures, and services using ICD-10-CM for diagnoses and CPT and HCPCS level II for procedures and services. (ICD-10-PCS codes are reported for inpatient hospital procedures only.)

   The accurate coding of diagnoses, procedures, and services rendered to the patient allows a medical practice to

   - **Communicate diagnostic and treatment data to a patient's insurance plan to assist the patient in obtaining maximum benefits.**
   - **Facilitate analysis of the practice's patient base to improve patient care delivery and efficiency of practice operations to contain costs.**
2. Research and apply knowledge of all insurance rules and regulations for major insurance programs in the local or regional area.
3. Accurately post charges, payments, and adjustments to patient accounts and office accounts receivable records.
4. Prepare or review claims generated by the practice to ensure that all required data are accurately reported and to ensure prompt reimbursement for services provided (contributing to the practice's cash flow).
5. Review all insurance payments and remittance advice documents to ensure proper processing and payment of each claim. The patient receives an **explanation of benefits (EOB)**, which is a report detailing the results of processing a claim (e.g., payer reimburses provider $80 on a submitted charge of $100). The provider receives a **remittance advice** (or **remit**), which is a notice sent by the insurance company that contains payment information about a claim.

NOTE: Chapter 4 contains additional information about EOBs and remits, including samples of each.

6. Correct all data errors and resubmit all unprocessed or returned claims.
7. Research and prepare appeals for all underpaid, unjustly recoded, or denied claims.
8. Rebill all claims not paid within 30 to 45 days, depending on individual practice policy and the payers' policies.
9. Inform health care providers and staff of changes in fraud and abuse laws, coding changes, documentation guidelines, and third-party payer requirements that may affect the billing and claims submission procedures.
10. Assist with timely updating of the practice's internal documents, patient registration forms, and billing forms as required by changes in coding or insurance billing requirements.
11. Maintain an internal audit system to ensure that required pretreatment authorizations have been received and entered into the billing and treatment records. Audits comparing provider documentation with codes assigned should also be performed.
12. Explain insurance benefits, policy requirements, and filing rules to patients.
13. Maintain confidentiality of patient information.

Scope of Practice and Employer Liability

Regardless of the employment setting, health insurance specialists are guided by a **scope of practice** that defines the profession, delineates qualifications and responsibilities, and clarifies supervision requirements (Table 1-2). Health insurance

TABLE 1-2 Scope of practice for health insurance specialists

Definition of Profession	One who interacts with patients to clarify health insurance coverage and financial responsibility, completes and processes insurance claims, and appeals denied claims.
Qualifications	Graduate of health insurance specialist certificate or degree program or equivalent. One year of experience in health insurance or related field. Detailed working knowledge and demonstrated proficiency in at least one insurance company's billing and/or collection process. Excellent organizational skills. Ability to manage multiple tasks in a timely manner. Proficient use of computerized registration and billing systems and personal computers, including spreadsheet and word processing software applications. Certification through AAPC, AHIMA, or AMBA.
Responsibilities	Use medical management computer software to process health insurance claims, assign codes to diagnoses and procedures/services, and manage patient records. Communicate with patients, providers, and insurance companies about coverage and reimbursement issues. Remain up-to-date regarding changes in health care industry laws and regulations.
Supervision Requirements	Active and continuous supervision of a health insurance specialist is required. However, the physical presence of the supervisor at the time and place responsibilities are performed is not required.

FIGURE 1-5 Self-employed health insurance specialist.

specialists who are self-employed are considered independent contractors (Figure 1-5). The *'Lectric Law Library's Lexicon* defines an **independent contractor** as "a person who performs services for another under an express or implied agreement and who is not subject to the other's control, or right to control, of the manner and means of performing the services. The organization that hires an independent contractor is not liable for the acts or omissions of the independent contractor."

Independent contractors should purchase **professional liability insurance** (or **errors and omissions insurance**), which provides protection from claims that contain errors and omissions resulting from professional services provided to clients as expected of a person in the contractor's profession. Professional associations often include a membership benefit that allows purchase of liability insurance coverage at reduced rates.

DETERMINING INDEPENDENT CONTRACTOR STATUS

One way to determine independent contractor status is to apply the common law "right to control" test, which includes five factors:

- Amount of control the hiring organization exerted over the worker's activities
- Responsibility for costs of operation (e.g., equipment and supplies)
- Method and form of payment and benefits
- Length of job commitment made to the worker
- Nature of occupation and skills required

The Internal Revenue Service applies a 20-factor independent contractor test to decide whether an organization has correctly classified a worker as an independent contractor for purposes of wage withholdings. The Department of Labor uses the "economic reality" test to determine worker status for purposes of compliance with the minimum wage and overtime requirements of the Fair Labor Standards Act.

EXAMPLE: The American Health Information Management Association makes information about the purchase of a professional liability plan available to its membership. If a member is sued for malpractice, the plan covers legal fees, court costs, court judgments, and out-of-court settlements. The coverage includes up to $2 million per incident and up to $4 million in any one policy year.

A health care facility (or physician) that employs health insurance specialists is legally responsible for employees' actions performed within the context of their employment. This is called ***respondeat superior,*** Latin for "let the master answer," which means that the employer is liable for the actions and omissions of employees as performed and committed within the scope of their employment. Employers purchase many types of insurance to protect their business assets and property (Table 1-3).

EXAMPLE: Linda Starling is employed by Dr. Pederson's office as a health insurance specialist. As part of her job, Linda has access to confidential patient information. While processing claims, she notices that her mother-in-law has been a patient, and she later tells her husband about the diagnosis and treatment. Her mother-in-law finds out about the breach of confidentiality and contacts her lawyer. Legally, Dr. Pederson can be sued by the mother-in-law. Although Linda could also be named in the lawsuit, it is more likely that she will be terminated.

TABLE 1-3 Types of professional insurance purchased by employers

INSURANCE	DESCRIPTION
Bonding Insurance	An insurance agreement that guarantees repayment for financial losses resulting from an employee's act or failure to act. It protects the financial operations of the employer. **NOTE:** Physician offices should bond employees who have financial responsibilities. The U.S. Department of Commerce estimates $500 billion in annual losses to all types of employers due to employees who **embezzle** (steal).
Business Liability Insurance	An insurance agreement that protects business assets and covers the cost of lawsuits resulting from bodily injury (e.g., customer slips on wet floor), personal injury (e.g., slander or libel), and false advertising. **Medical malpractice insurance**, a type of liability insurance, covers physicians and other health care professionals for liability relating to claims arising from patient treatment. **NOTE:** Liability insurance does *not* protect an employer from nonperformance of a contract, sexual harassment, race and gender discrimination lawsuits, or wrongful termination of employees. **NOTE:** An alternative to purchasing liability insurance from an insurance company is to *self-fund,* which involves setting aside money to pay damages or paying damages with current operating revenue should the employer ever be found liable. Another option is to join a *risk retention* or *risk purchasing group,* which provides lower-cost commercial liability insurance to its members. A third option is to obtain coverage in a *surplus lines market* that has been established to insure unique risks.
Property Insurance	An insurance agreement that protects business contents (e.g., buildings and equipment) against fire, theft, and other risks.
Workers' Compensation Insurance	Protection mandated by state law that covers employees and their dependents against injury and death occurring during the course of employment. Workers' compensation is not health insurance, and it is not intended to compensate for disability other than that caused by injury arising from employment. The purpose of workers' compensation is to provide financial and medical benefits to those with work-related injuries, and their families, regardless of fault.

PROFESSIONALISM

The *Merriam-Webster Dictionary* defines **professionalism** as the conduct, aims, or qualities that characterize a professional person. Health care facility managers establish rules of professional behavior (e.g., codes of conduct, policies, and procedures) so employees know how to behave professionally. Employees are expected to develop the following skills to demonstrate workplace professionalism, which results in personal growth and success:

Attitude and Self-Esteem

"For success, attitude is equally as important as ability."

Harry F. Banks

Attitude impacts an individual's capacity to effectively perform job functions, and an employee's attitude is perceived as positive, negative, or neutral. This subconscious transfer of feelings results in colleagues determining whether someone has a positive attitude about his or her work. Self-esteem impacts attitude: low self-esteem causes lack of confidence, and higher self-esteem leads to self-confidence, improved relationships, self-respect, and a successful career.

Communication

"And he goes through life, his mouth open, and his mind closed."

William Shakespeare

Successful interpersonal communication includes self-expression and active listening to develop understanding about what others are saying. To listen effectively, be sure to understand the message instead of just hearing words. This active involvement in the communication process helps avoid miscommunication.

Conflict Management

"When angry, count to ten before you speak; if very angry, a hundred."

Thomas Jefferson

Conflict occurs as a part of the decision-making process, and the way it is handled makes it positive or negative. People often have different perspectives about the same situation, and actively listening to the other's viewpoint helps neutralize what could become negative conflict.

Customer Service

"If we don't take care of our customers, someone else will."

Unknown

Health insurance specialists serve as a direct point of contact for a provider's patients, and they are responsible for ensuring that patients receive an excellent level of service or assistance with questions and concerns. It is equally important to remember that colleagues deserve the same respect and attention as patients.

Diversity Awareness

"The real death of America will come when everyone is alike."

James T. Ellison

Diversity is defined as differences among people and includes demographics of age, education, ethnicity, gender, geographic location, income, language, marital status, occupation, parental status, physical and mental ability, race, religious beliefs, sexual orientation, and veteran status. Developing tolerance, which is the opposite of bigotry and prejudice, means dealing with personal attitudes, beliefs, and experiences. Embracing the differences that represent the demographics of our society is crucial to becoming a successful health professional.

Leadership

"The difference between a boss and a leader: a boss says, 'Go!' A leader says, 'Let's go!'"

E. M. Kelly

Leadership is the ability to motivate team members to complete a common organizational goal display. Leaders have earned the trust of their team, which is the reason the entire team is able to achieve its objective and set the standard for productivity, as well as revenue goals. Interestingly, the leader identified by the team might not be the organization's manager or supervisor. Leaders emerge from within the organization because they have demonstrated beliefs, ethics, and values with which team members identify. Managers who are not threatened by the natural emergence of leaders benefit from team harmony and increased productivity. They receive credit for excellent management skills, and they begin the process to leadership when they begin to acknowledge the work ethic of the team and its leader.

Managing Change

"If we don't change, we don't grow. If we don't grow, we aren't really living."
Gail Sheehy

Change is crucial to the survival of an organization because it is a necessary response to implementation of new and revised federal and state programs, regulations, and so on. While the organization that does not embrace change becomes extinct, such change disrupts the organization's workflow (and productivity) and is perceived as a threat to employees. Therefore, it is the role of the organization's leadership team to provide details about the impending change, including periodic updates as work processes undergo gradual revision. Employees also need to understand what is being changed and why, and the leadership team needs to understand employees' reluctance to change.

Productivity

"Even if you are on the right track, you'll get run over if you just sit there."
Will Rogers

Health care providers expect health insurance and medical coding/billing specialists to be productive regarding completion of duties and responsibilities. Pursuing professional certification and participating in continuing education helps ensure individual compliance with the latest coding rules and other updates. Increased knowledge leads to increased productivity and performance improvement on the job.

Professional Ethics

"Always do right—this will gratify some and astonish the rest."
Mark Twain

The characteristics of a successful health insurance specialist include an ability to work independently, attention to detail, ability to think critically, and a strong sense of ethics. The *American Heritage Concise Dictionary* defines ethics as the principles of right or good conduct, and rules that govern the conduct of members of a profession.

Team-Building

"Michael, if you can't pass, you can't play."
Coach Dean Smith to Michael Jordan in his freshman year

Colleagues who share a sense of community and purpose work well together and can accomplish organizational goals more quickly and easily because they rely on one another. This means colleagues provide help to, and receive help from, other members of the team. Sharing the leadership role and working together to complete difficult tasks facilitates team-building.

Telephone Skills for the Health Care Setting

The telephone can be an effective means of patient access to the health care system because a health care team member serves as an immediate contact for the patient. Participating in telephone skills training and following established protocols (policies) allow health care team members to respond appropriately to patients.

When processes for handling all calls are developed *and* followed by health care team members, the result is greater office efficiency and less frustration for health care team members and patients. Avoid problems with telephone communication in your health care setting by implementing the following protocols:

NOTE: Although a receptionist is the initial point of contact for the office, all health care team members must effectively handle or transfer telephone calls. This requires sensitivity to patient concerns about health care problems, and the health care professional must communicate a caring environment that leads to patient satisfaction.

Establish a telephone-availability policy that works for patients and office staff. Telephone calls that are unanswered, result in a busy signal, and/or force patients to be placed on hold for long periods frustrate callers (Figure 1-6). The outcome can be a receptionist who sounds impatient and too busy to properly resolve callers' questions and concerns. Avoid such problems by increasing telephone availability so that the calls are answered outside of the typical 9 to 5 workday (which often includes not answering the telephone during lunch). Consider having employees (who have undergone telephone skills training) answer calls on a rotating basis one hour before the office opens, during the noon hour, and one hour after the office closes. This telephone protocol will result in satisfied patients (and other callers) and office employees (who do not have to return calls to individuals who otherwise leave messages on the answering machine).

Set up an appropriate number of dedicated telephone lines (e.g., appointment scheduling, insurance and billing) based on the function and size of the health care setting. Publish the telephone numbers on the office's website and in an office brochure or local telephone directory, and instruct employees to avoid using the lines when making outgoing calls. Another option is to install an interactive telephone response system that connects callers with appropriate staff (e.g., appointment scheduling, insurance and billing, and so on) based on the caller's keypad or voice responses to instructions provided.

Inform callers who ask to speak with the physician (or another health care provider) that the physician (or provider) is with a patient. Do *not* state, "The physician is busy," which implies that the physician is too busy for the patient and could offend the caller. Ask for the caller's name, telephone number, and reason for the call, and explain that the call will be returned.

NOTE: Assigning the 15-minute time periods must be approved by physicians because they may prefer to return telephone calls prior to the first appointment of the day or after the last appointment of the day.

Assign 15-minute time periods every 2 to 3 hours when creating the schedule, to allow time for physicians (and other health care providers) to return telephone calls. This allows the receptionist to tell callers an approximate time when calls will be returned (and patient records can be retrieved).

Physically separate front desk check-in/check-out and receptionist/patient appointment scheduling offices. It is unlikely that an employee who manages the registration of patients as they arrive at the office (and the check-out of patients at the conclusion of an appointment) has time to answer telephone calls. Office receptionists and appointment schedulers who work in private offices will

Copyright © Cengage Learning®.

FIGURE 1-6 Unanswered telephone calls frustrate callers.

comply with federal and state patient privacy laws when talking with patients. In addition, appointment scheduling, telephone management, and patient check-in (registration) and check-out procedures will be performed with greater efficiency.

Require office employees to learn professional telephone skills. Schedule professional telephone skills training as part of new employee orientation, and arrange for all employees to attend an annual workshop to improve skills. Training allows everyone to learn key aspects of successful telephone communication, which include developing an effective telephone voice that focuses on tone. During a telephone conversation, each person forms an opinion based on *how* something is said (rather than *what* is said). Therefore, speak clearly and distinctly, do not speak too fast or too slow, and vary your tone by letting your voice rise and fall naturally. The following rules apply to each telephone conversation:

- When answering the telephone, state the name of the office and your name (e.g., "Hornell Medical Center, Shelly Dunham speaking").
- Do not use slang (e.g., nope, yep, uh-huh) or health care jargon (e.g., ICU—the patient hears "eye see you").
- Use the caller's name (e.g., Betty Smith calls the office, stating her name as soon as her call is answered, and the receptionist asks, "How may I help you today, Mrs. Smith?").
- Provide clear explanations (e.g., "The doctor will return your call between 3 and 4 p.m. today.").
- Be pleasant, friendly, sincere, and helpful (e.g., smile as you talk with the caller and your tone will be friendly) (Figure 1-7).
- Give the caller your undivided attention to show personal interest, and do not interrupt.
- Before placing the caller on hold or transferring a call, ask him or her for permission to do so (e.g., "May I place you on hold?," "May I transfer you to the appropriate office?").
- When the individual with whom the caller wants to talk is unavailable, ask if you can take a message (e.g., "Dr. Smith is with a patient right now. May I take a message and have him return your call after 3 p.m.?").
- Use a preprinted message form (or commercial message pad) when taking a message (Figure 1-8). Document the following about each call, and file it in the patient's

FIGURE 1-7 Smile as you talk with a caller so your tone is pleasant.

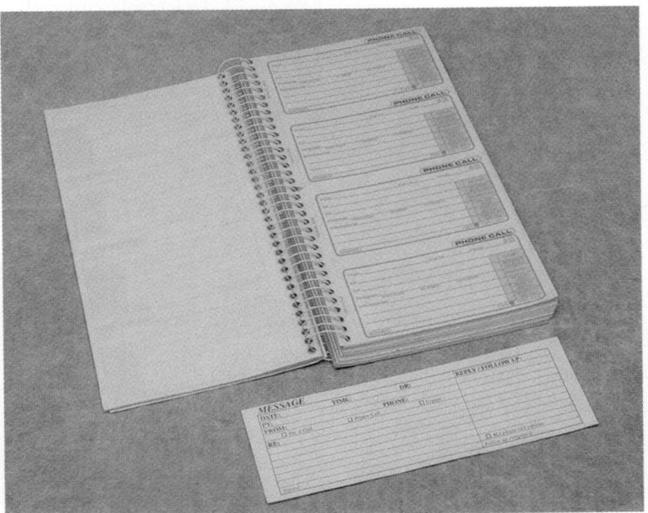

FIGURE 1-8 Message pads with carbonless copy.

record: date of call, name of patient, name and credentials of individual talking with patient, and a brief note about the contents of the telephone conversation.

Professional Appearance

Appropriate professional attire and personal presentation (Figure 1-9) provide an employee's first impression to colleagues, managers, physicians, patients or clients, and others. Well-groomed employees convey professional images about themselves and the quality of services provided by the organization. Employers establish the dress code policy, which is usually conservative and stylish but not trendy, and some require a uniform.

An employee's appearance provides that important first impression, and well-groomed professionals look self-confident, display pride in themselves, and appear capable of performing whatever duties need to be done. We have all experienced days when we didn't feel good about the way we looked, which, in turn, affected our performance. In order to present yourself in the best possible light, be sure to adhere to the following general guidelines for a professional appearance:

- ***Cleanliness*** **is the first essential for good grooming. Take a daily bath or shower. Use a deodorant or antiperspirant. Shampoo your hair often. Brush and floss your teeth daily.**
- ***Hand care*** **is critical. Take special care of your hands. Keep hand cream or lotion in convenient places to use after washing your hands. Because this is done frequently, hands tend to chap and crack, which can allow organisms entry into your body—a risk you cannot afford. Also, keep your fingernails manicured at a moderate length (and those who provide health care services to patients should not use false nails because bacteria and fungi can grow beneath such nails). If you work in a uniform and your organization's policy allows you to use nail polish, choose clear or light shades. Even when wearing street clothes, bright or trendy colors are not appropriate for the office.**
- ***Hair*** **must be clean and away from your face. Long hair should be worn up or at least fastened back. It is not appropriate to keep pushing your hair out of the way while working (because you can add organisms to your environment and perhaps**

Copyright © Cengage Learning®.

FIGURE 1-9 Present a professional appearance.

take them home with you). Patients who receive health care services from employees may also be susceptible to "receiving" something from your hair if you touch them after arranging your hair.

- *Proper attire* may vary with medical specialty. When a uniform is not required, it may be appropriate to wear a white laboratory coat over a dress shirt and slacks or a skirt. Depending on the organization (e.g., pediatric office), it might also be acceptable for the laboratory coat to be a color other than white. For instance, many pediatric practices prefer that medical assistants wear colorful prints with patterns of cartoon characters that children will recognize to help them feel more at ease. Psychiatry and psychology medical office assistants may not be required to wear uniforms, as their clinical duties would be limited. Looking like a professional will not only encourage the respect of others for your profession, but will also help you to feel like an integral part of the health care team. When uniforms are required, they must be clean, fit well, and be free from wrinkles. Uniform shoes should be kept clean and have clean shoestrings; hose must not have runs. Pay attention to the undergarments that you wear beneath the uniform so that they do not show through the fabric of your uniform.
- *Jewelry*, except for a watch or wedding ring, is not appropriate with a uniform. Small earrings may be worn but still may get in the way when you use the telephone. Not only does jewelry look out of place, but it is a great collector of microorganisms. Novelty piercings, such as nose rings and tongue studs, are not appropriate for professional grooming. Save the wearing of these for after work hours.
- *Fragrances*, such as perfumes, colognes, and aftershave lotions, may be offensive to some patients, especially if they are suffering from nausea. Thus, it is recommended that you not use fragrances.
- *Cosmetics* should be tasteful and skillfully applied. All major department stores have salespeople who can help you select and learn to apply products that will enhance your appearance.
- *Gum chewing* is very unprofessional. A large piece of gum interferes with speech, and cracking gum is totally unacceptable. If you feel you need gum for a breath concern, use a breath mint or mouthwash instead.
- *Posture* affects not only your appearance but also the amount of fatigue you experience. The ease at which you move around reflects your poise and confidence. To check your posture, back up to a wall, place your feet apart (straight down from your hips), and try to insert your hand through the space between your lower back and the wall. If you can, you need to improve your posture. Pull your stomach in, tuck under your buttocks, and try to place your spine against the wall. Your shoulders should be relaxed with your head held erect. This will probably feel very unnatural, but practice keeping your body straight and head erect when you walk and you will see how much better you look and feel.

Remember! Your personal hygiene must be impeccable because setting a good example for others is a part of your responsibility in the care of others. Daily showering, clean attractive hair, and neatly manicured nails show others that you take pride in yourself and provide a model that others can imitate. A lot of different elements compose our personal characteristics, and each has an impact about how we feel about ourselves and how others perceive us. It is important to evaluate yourself and help identify what you can do to improve your effectiveness when interacting with people. Your course instructor is an excellent resource with whom you could have a private conversation, asking whether there is anything you should be doing differently to improve your professional appearance (and communication skills). For example, during one of her classes, your author noticed that a student who was otherwise impeccably dressed and groomed frequently flipped her long hair from one side to the other. She met with the student to recommend that her hair be pulled back for interviews, internships, and employment. Prior to an on-campus interview for employment, the student stopped into the office to ask the instructor whether her hairstyle was appropriate; this was something the instructor did not ask the student to do, and she was very pleased at how well the student incorporated constructive criticism about her grooming. And, most importantly, the student got the job!

Professional Credentials

The health insurance specialist who joins one or more professional associations (Table 1-4) receives useful information available in several formats, including professional journals and newsletters, access to members-only websites, notification of professional development, and so on. A key feature of membership is an awareness of the importance of professional certification. Once certified, the professional is responsible for maintaining that credential by fulfilling continuing education requirements established by the sponsoring association. Join professional associations by going to their websites to locate membership links. Membership fees (and testing fees) vary, and some associations allow students to join for a reduced fee. Professional certification examination fees also vary according

TABLE 1-4 Professional associations that offer coding and reimbursement credentials

American Academy of Professional Coders (AAPC)	• Founded to elevate the standards of medical coding by providing certification, ongoing education, networking, and recognition for coders. • Publishes the *Coding Edge* monthly newsmagazine and hosts continuing education. • *Credentials:* Certified Professional Biller (CPB), Certified Professional Coder (CPC), Certified Professional Coder-Hospital (CPC-H), Certified Professional Coder-Payer (CPC-P), and specialty credentials in many different fields of expertise.
American Association of Medical Assistants (AAMA)	• Enables medical assisting professionals to enhance and demonstrate knowledge, skills, and professionalism required by employers and patients, and protects medical assistants' right to practice. • Publishes monthly *Certified Medical Assistant* journal. • *Credential:* Certified Medical Assistant, abbreviated as CMA (AAMA).
American Health Information Management Association (AHIMA)	• Founded in 1928 to improve the quality of medical records, and currently advances the health information management (HIM) profession toward an electronic and global environment, including implementation of ICD-10-CM and ICD-10-PCS. • Publishes monthly *Journal of AHIMA*. • *Credentials:* Certified Coding Assistant (CCA), Certified Coding Specialist (CCS), and Certified Coding Specialist-Physician-office (CCS-P). (Additional HIM credentials are offered by AHIMA.)
American Medical Billing Association (AMBA)	• Provides industry and regulatory education and networking opportunities for members. • *Credential:* Certified Medical Reimbursement Specialist (CMRS).
Medical Association of Billers (MAB)	• Created in 1995 to provide medical billing and coding specialists with a reliable source for diagnosis and procedure coding education and training. • Publishes the *CodeTrends* bimonthly newsletter and hosts continuing education programs. • *Credentials:* Certified Medical Billing Specialist (CMBS), Certified Medical Billing Specialist for Chiropractic Assistants (CMBS-CA), Certified Medical Billing Specialist for Hospitals (CMBS-H), and Certified Medical Billing Specialist for Instructors (CMBS-I).

to association. Once students decide where they want to seek employment (e.g., physician's office, hospital), they can research each professional association's website (located in Internet links in this chapter) to research certification examinations offered. For example, a physician's office will require different certifications as compared with hospitals. It is important for students to have an excellent understanding about the career path they want to pursue so as to obtain the appropriate certification credentials. For example, hospitals may prefer the AHIMA credentials, while physician's offices may prefer the AAPC credentials.

SUMMARY

A health insurance specialist's career is challenging and requires professional training to understand claims processing and billing regulations, possess accurate coding skills, and develop the ability to successfully appeal underpaid or denied insurance claims. A health insurance claim is submitted to a third-party payer or government program to request reimbursement for health care services provided. Many health insurance plans require preauthorization for treatment provided by specialists.

While the requirements of health insurance specialist programs vary, successful specialists will develop skills that allow them to work independently and ethically, focus on attention to detail, and think critically. Medical practices and health care facilities employing health insurance specialists require them to perform various functions. Smaller practices and facilities require specialists to process claims for all types of payers, while larger practices and facilities expect specialists to process claims for a limited number of payers.

Health insurance specialists are guided by a scope of practice, which defines the profession, delineates qualifications and responsibilities, and clarifies supervision requirements. Self-employed health insurance specialists are independent contractors who should purchase professional liability insurance. Health care providers and facilities typically purchase bonding, liability, property, and workers' compensation insurance to cover their employees. Employees who demonstrate professional behavior are proud of their work, and they are recognized as having integrity and discipline. They earn the respect of their colleagues, develop a reputation for being loyal and trustworthy, and are considered team players. The AAMA, AAPC, AHIMA, AMBA, and MAB offer exams leading to professional credentials. Becoming credentialed demonstrates competence and knowledge in the field of health insurance processing as well as coding and reimbursement.

INTERNET LINKS

- American Academy of Professional Coders (AAPC)
  www.aapc.com
- American Association of Medical Assistants (AAMA)
  www.aama-ntl.org
- American Health Information Management Association (AHIMA)
  www.ahima.org
- American Medical Billing Association (AMBA)
  www.ambanet.net
- Centers for Medicare and Medicaid Services (CMS)
  www.cms.gov
- Medical Association of Billers (MAB)
  www.physicianwebsites.com
- U.S. Department of Labor, Bureau of Labor Statistics (BLS)
  www.bls.gov

STUDY CHECKLIST

- ☐ Read this textbook chapter and highlight key concepts. (Use colored highlighter sparingly throughout the chapter.)
- ☐ Create an index card for each key term. (Write the key term on one side of the index card and the concept on the other. Learn the definition of each key term, and match the term to the concept.)
- ☐ Access chapter Internet links to learn more about concepts.
- ☐ Answer the chapter review questions, verifying answers with your instructor.
- ☐ Complete the Workbook chapter, verifying answers with your instructor.
- ☐ Form a study group with classmates to discuss chapter concepts in preparation for an exam.

REVIEW

MULTIPLE CHOICE Select the most appropriate response.

1. The document submitted to the payer requesting reimbursement is called a(n)

a. explanation of benefits.
b. health insurance claim.
c. remittance advice.
d. preauthorization form.

2. The Centers for Medicare and Medicaid Services (CMS) is an administration within the

a. Administration for Children and Families.
b. Department of Health and Human Services.
c. Food and Drug Administration.
d. Office of the Inspector General.

3. A health care practitioner is also called a health care

a. dealer.
b. provider.
c. purveyor.
d. supplier.

4. Which is the most appropriate response to a patient who calls the office and asks to speak with the physician?

a. Politely state that the physician is busy and cannot be disturbed.
b. Explain that the physician is unavailable, and ask if the patient would like to leave a message.
c. Transfer the call to the exam room where the physician is located.
d. Offer to schedule an appointment for the patient to be seen by the physician.

5. The process of assigning diagnoses, procedures, and services using numeric and alphanumeric characters is called

a. coding.
b. data processing.
c. programming.
d. reimbursement.

6. **If a health insurance plan's preauthorization requirements are not met by providers,**
   a. administrative costs are reduced.
   b. patients' coverage is cancelled.
   c. payment of the claim is denied.
   d. they pay a fine to the health plan.
7. **Which coding system is used to report diagnoses and conditions on claims?**
   a. CPT
   b. HCPCS level II
   c. ICD-10-CM
   d. ICD-10-PCS
8. **The CPT coding system is published by the**
   a. ADA.
   b. AHIMA.
   c. AMA.
   d. CMS.
9. **National codes are associated with**
   a. CDT.
   b. CPT.
   c. HCPCS level II.
   d. ICD.
10. **Which report is sent to the patient by the payer to clarify the results of claims processing?**
    a. explanation of benefits
    b. health insurance claim
    c. preauthorization form
    d. remittance advice
11. **A remittance advice contains**
    a. payment information about a claim.
    b. provider qualifications and responsibilities.
    c. detected errors and omissions from claims.
    d. documentation of medical necessity.
12. **Which type of insurance guarantees repayment for financial losses resulting from an employee's act or failure to act?**
    a. bonding
    b. liability
    c. property
    d. workers' compensation
13. **Physicians and other health care professionals purchase __________ insurance to protect them from liability relating to claims arising from patient treatment.**
    a. bonding
    b. medical malpractice
    c. third-party payer
    d. workers' compensation

14. Which mandates workers' compensation insurance to cover employees and their dependents against injury and death occurring during the course of employment?

a. state law

b. county law

c. local law

d. municipal law

15. The American Medical Billing Association offers which certification exam?

a. CCS

b. CMRS

c. CPC

d. RHIT

CHAPTER 2

Introduction to Health Insurance

CHAPTER OUTLINE

What Is Health Insurance?

Health Insurance Coverage Statistics

Major Developments in Health Insurance

Health Care Documentation

Electronic Health Record (EHR)

OBJECTIVES

Upon successful completion of this chapter, you should be able to:

1. Define key terms.
2. State the difference between medical care and health care, as well as the difference between insurance and health insurance.
3. Discuss the significant events in health care reimbursement from 1850 to the present.
4. Interpret health insurance coverage statistics.
5. List and describe medical documentation concepts.
6. Discuss the advantages to implementing the electronic health record.

KEY TERMS

ambulatory payment classifications (APCs)

American Recovery and Reinvestment Act of 2009 (ARRA)

Balanced Budget Act of 1997 (BBA)

CHAMPUS Reform Initiative (CRI)

Civilian Health and Medical Program of the Department of Veterans Affairs (CHAMPVA)

Civilian Health and Medical Program–Uniformed Services (CHAMPUS)

Clinical Laboratory Improvement Act (CLIA)

CMS-1500

coinsurance

Consolidated Omnibus Budget Reconciliation Act of 1985 (COBRA)

consumer-driven health plans (CDHPs)

continuity of care

copayment (copay)

deductible

diagnosis-related group (DRG)

electronic health record (EHR)

electronic medical record (EMR)

Employee Retirement Income Security Act of 1974 (ERISA)

Evaluation and Management (E/M)

Federal Employees' Compensation Act (FECA)

Federal Employers' Liability Act (FELA)

fee schedule

Financial Services Modernization Act (FSMA)

Gramm-Leach-Bliley Act

group health insurance

health care

Health Care and Education Reconciliation Act (HCERA)

- Health Information Technology for Economic and Clinical Health Act (HITECH Act)
- health insurance
- health insurance exchange
- health insurance marketplace
- Health Insurance Portability and Accountability Act of 1996 (HIPAA)
- Hill-Burton Act
- Home Health Prospective Payment System (HH PPS)
- individual health insurance
- Inpatient Psychiatric Facility Prospective Payment System (IPF PPS)
- Inpatient Rehabilitation Facility Prospective Payment System (IRF PPS)
- International Classification of Diseases (ICD)
- Investing in Innovations (i2) Initiative
- lifetime maximum amount
- major medical insurance
- meaningful EHR user
- meaningful use
- Medicaid
- medical care
- medical record
- Medicare
- Medicare Catastrophic Coverage Act
- Medicare contracting reform (MCR) initiative
- Medicare, Medicaid, and SCHIP Benefits Improvement and Protection Act of 2000 (BIPA)
- Medicare Prescription Drug, Improvement, and Modernization Act (MMA)
- Minimum Data Set (MDS)
- National Correct Coding Initiative (NCCI)
- Omnibus Budget Reconciliation Act of 1981 (OBRA)
- Outcomes and Assessment Information Set (OASIS)
- Outpatient Prospective Payment System (OPPS)
- Patient Protection and Affordable Care Act (PPACA)
- patient record
- *per diem*
- personal health record (PHR)
- policyholder
- preventive services
- problem-oriented record (POR)
- prospective payment system (PPS)
- public health insurance
- quality improvement organization (QIO)
- record linkage
- Resource Utilization Groups (RUGs)
- Resource-Based Relative Value Scale (RBRVS) system
- self-insured (or self-funded) employer-sponsored group health plans
- single-payer system
- Skilled Nursing Facility Prospective Payment System (SNF PPS)
- socialized medicine
- State Children's Health Insurance Program (SCHIP)
- Tax Equity and Fiscal Responsibility Act of 1982 (TEFRA)
- third-party administrators (TPAs)
- third-party payer
- total practice management software (TPMS)
- universal health insurance
- usual and reasonable payments
- World Health Organization (WHO)

INTRODUCTION

According to the *American Heritage Concise Dictionary*, insurance is a contract that protects the insured from loss. An insurance company guarantees payment to the insured for an unforeseen event (e.g., death, accident, and illness) in return for the payment of premiums. In addition to health insurance, types of insurance include automobile, disability, liability, malpractice, property, and life (discussed in Chapter 12). (This textbook covers health insurance in detail.) This chapter includes information about terms and concepts as an introduction to health insurance processing. These terms and concepts are explained in greater detail in later chapters of this text.

WHAT IS HEALTH INSURANCE?

To understand the meaning of the term *health insurance* as used in this text, differentiation must be made between medical care and health care. **Medical care** includes the identification of disease and the provision of care and treatment to persons who are sick, injured, or concerned about their health status. **Health care** expands the definition of medical care to include **preventive services**, which are designed to help individuals avoid health and injury problems. Preventive examinations may result in the early detection of health problems, allowing less drastic and less expensive treatment options. Health care insurance or **health insurance** is a contract between a policyholder and a third-party payer or government health program to reimburse the policyholder for all or a portion of the cost of medically necessary treatment or preventive care provided by health care professionals. A **policyholder** is a person who signs a contract with a health insurance company and who, thus, owns the health insurance policy. The policyholder is the insured (or enrollee). In some cases, the policy might include coverage for dependents. A **third-party payer** is a health insurance company that provides coverage, such as BlueCross BlueShield. Because both the government and the general public speak of "health insurance," this text uses that term exclusively. Health insurance is available to individuals who participate in group (e.g., employer sponsored), individual (or personal insurance), or prepaid health plans (e.g., managed care). Chapters 12 to 17 of this textbook contain content about the following types of health insurance, including definitions, claims completion instructions, sample completed CMS-1500 claims, and so on:

- Commercial
- BlueCross BlueShield
- Medicare
- Medicaid
- TRICARE
- Workers' Compensation

Employees who process patient registrations and insurance claims may be required to assist patients with information about copayments, coinsurance, and so on. For detailed information about the patient's insurance coverage, it would be appropriate to refer the patient to their health insurance representative.

HEALTH INSURANCE COVERAGE STATISTICS

U.S. Census Bureau data from 2011 estimate that most people in the United States are covered by some form of health insurance:

- Approximately 64 percent are covered by private health insurance
- Approximately 55 percent are covered by employment-based plans

GLOSSARY OF HEALTH INSURANCE TERMS	
Group health insurance	Health insurance coverage subsidized by employers and other organizations (e.g., labor unions, rural and consumer health cooperatives). These plans distribute the cost of health insurance among group members so that the cost is typically less per person and broader coverage is provided than that offered through individual health insurance plans. The Patient Protection and Affordable Care Act of 2010 includes a small business health care tax credit to help small businesses and small tax-exempt organizations afford the cost of covering their employees.
Individual health insurance	Private health insurance policy purchased by individuals or families who do not have access to group health insurance coverage. Applicants can be denied coverage, and they can also be required to pay higher premiums due to age, gender, and/or pre-existing medical conditions.
Public health insurance	Federal and state government health programs (e.g., Medicare, Medicaid, SCHIP, TRICARE) available to eligible individuals.
Single-payer system	Centralized health care system adopted by some Western nations (e.g., Canada, Great Britain) and funded by taxes. The government pays for each resident's health care, which is considered a basic social service.
Socialized medicine	A type of single-payer system in which the government owns and operates health care facilities and providers (e.g., physicians) receive salaries. The VA health care program is a form of socialized medicine.
Universal health insurance	The goal of providing every individual with access to health coverage, regardless of the system implemented to achieve that goal.

- **Approximately 32 percent are covered by government plans (e.g., Medicare, TRICARE)**
- **Approximately 16.5 percent are covered by Medicaid**

The reason the insurance coverage breakdown of covered persons is greater than 100 percent is because some people are covered by more than one insurance plan (e.g., employment-based plan plus Medicare). Thus, they are counted more than once when percentages are calculated.

CENGAGE brain.com

Go to www.cengagebrain.com and log in to UHI's Student Resources to view Table 2-A, which contains more about the significant events in health care reimbursement.

MAJOR DEVELOPMENTS IN HEALTH INSURANCE

Since the early 1900s, when solo practices prevailed, managed care and group practices have increased in number, and health care services (like other aspects of society in this country) have undergone tremendous changes (Table 2-1 and Figure 2-1).

TABLE 2-1 Significant events in health care reimbursement

YEAR	EVENT	DESCRIPTION
1850	First health insurance policy	The Franklin Health Assurance Company of Massachusetts was the first commercial insurance company in the United States to provide private health care coverage for injuries not resulting in death.
1908	FELA	President Theodore Roosevelt signed **Federal Employers' Liability Act (FELA)** legislation that protects and compensates railroad workers who are injured on the job.
1916	FECA	The **Federal Employees' Compensation Act (FECA)** provides civilian employees of the federal government with medical care, survivors' benefits, and compensation for lost wages. The Office of Workers' Compensation Programs (OWCP) administers FECA as well as the Longshore and Harbor Workers' Compensation Act of 1927 and the Black Lung Benefits Reform Act of 1977.
1929	Blue Cross	Justin Ford Kimball, an official at Baylor University in Dallas, introduced a plan to guarantee school teachers 21 days of hospital care for $6 a year. Other groups of employees in Dallas joined, and the idea attracted nationwide attention. This is generally considered the first Blue Cross plan.
1939	Blue Shield	The first Blue Shield plan was founded in California. The Blue Shield concept grew out of the lumber and mining camps of the Pacific Northwest at the turn of the century. Employers wanted to provide medical care for their workers, so they paid monthly fees to *medical service bureaus*, which were composed of groups of physicians.
1940	Group health insurance	To attract wartime labor during World War II, group health insurance was offered for the first time to full-time employees. The insurance was not subject to income or Social Security taxes, making it an attractive part of an employee benefit package. *Group health insurance* is health care coverage available through employers and other organizations (e.g., labor unions, rural and consumer health cooperatives); employers usually pay part or all of the premium costs.
1946	Hill-Burton Act	The **Hill-Burton Act** provided federal grants for modernizing hospitals that had become obsolete because of a lack of capital investment during the Great Depression and WWII (1929 to 1945). In return for federal funds, facilities were required to provide services free or at reduced rates to patients unable to pay for care.
1947	Taft-Hartley Act	The Taft-Hartley Act of 1947 amended the National Labor Relations Act of 1932, restoring a more balanced relationship between labor and management. An indirect result of Taft-Hartley was the creation of **third-party administrators (TPAs)**, which administer health care plans and process claims, thus serving as a system of checks and balances for labor and management.

(continues)

TABLE 2-1 (continued)

YEAR	EVENT	DESCRIPTION
1948	ICD	The **World Health Organization (WHO)** developed the **International Classification of Diseases (ICD)**, a classification system used to collect data for statistical purposes.
1950	Major medical insurance	Insurance companies began offering **major medical insurance**, which provided coverage for catastrophic or prolonged illnesses and injuries. Most of these programs incorporate large deductibles and lifetime maximum amounts. A **deductible** is the amount for which the patient is financially responsible before an insurance policy provides payment. A **lifetime maximum amount** is the maximum benefits payable to a health plan participant.
1966	Medicare and Medicaid	**Medicare** (Title XVIII of the Social Security Amendments of 1965) provides health care services to Americans over the age of 65. (It was originally administered by the Social Security Administration.)
		Medicaid (Title XIX of the Social Security Amendments of 1965) is a cost-sharing program between the federal and state governments to provide health care services to low-income Americans. (It was originally administered by the Social and Rehabilitation Service [SRS].)
	CHAMPUS	Amendments to the Dependents' Medical Care Act of 1956 created the **Civilian Health and Medical Program—Uniformed Services (CHAMPUS)**, which was designed as a benefit for dependents of personnel serving in the armed forces as well as uniformed branches of the Public Health Service and the National Oceanic and Atmospheric Administration. The program is now called TRICARE.
	CPT	*Current Procedural Terminology* (CPT) was developed by the American Medical Association in 1966. Each year an annual publication is prepared, which includes changes that correspond to significant updates in medical technology and practice.
1970	Self-insured group health plans	**Self-insured (or self-funded) employer-sponsored group health plans** allow large employers to assume the financial risk for providing health care benefits to employees. The employer does not pay a fixed premium to a health insurance payer, but establishes a trust fund (of employer and employee contributions) out of which claims are paid.
	OSHA	The *Occupational Safety and Health Administration Act of 1970 (OSHA)* was designed to protect all employees against injuries from occupational hazards in the workplace.
1973	CHAMPVA	The Veterans Healthcare Expansion Act of 1973 authorized Veterans Affairs (VA) to establish the **Civilian Health and Medical Program of the Department of Veterans Affairs (CHAMPVA)** to provide health care benefits for dependents of veterans rated as 100 percent permanently and totally disabled as a result of service-connected conditions, veterans who died as a result of service-connected conditions, and veterans who died on duty with less than 30 days of active service.
	HMOs	The *Health Maintenance Organization Assistance Act of 1973* authorized federal grants and loans to private organizations that wished to develop *health maintenance organizations (HMOs)*, which are responsible for providing health care services to subscribers in a given geographic area for a fixed fee.
1974	ERISA	The **Employee Retirement Income Security Act of 1974 (ERISA)** mandated reporting and disclosure requirements for group life and health plans (including managed care plans), permitted large employers to self-insure employee health care benefits, and exempted large employers from taxes on health insurance premiums. A **copayment (copay)** is a provision in an insurance policy that requires the policyholder or patient to pay a specified dollar amount to a health care provider for each visit or medical service received. **Coinsurance** is the percentage of costs a patient shares with the health plan. For example, the plan pays 80 percent of costs and the patient pays 20 percent.

(continues)

TABLE 2-1 (continued)

YEAR	EVENT	DESCRIPTION
1977	HCFA	To combine health care financing and quality assurance programs into a single agency, the Health Care Financing Administration (HCFA) was formed within the Department of Health and Human Services (DHHS). The Medicare and Medicaid programs were also transferred to the newly created agency. (HCFA is now called the Centers for Medicare and Medicaid Services, or CMS.)
1980	DHHS	With the departure of the Office of Education, the Department of Health, Education and Welfare (HEW) became the Department of Health and Human Services (DHHS).
1981	OBRA	The **Omnibus Budget Reconciliation Act of 1981 (OBRA)** was federal legislation that expanded the Medicare and Medicaid programs.
1983	DRG	The **Tax Equity and Fiscal Responsibility Act of 1982 (TEFRA)** created Medicare risk programs, which allowed federally qualified HMOs and competitive medical plans that met specified Medicare requirements to provide Medicare-covered services under a risk contract. TEFRA also enacted a **prospective payment system (PPS)**, which issues a predetermined payment for inpatient services. Previously, reimbursement was generated on a ***per diem*** basis, which issued payment based on daily rates. The PPS implemented in 1983, called **diagnosis-related groups (DRG)**, reimburses hospitals for inpatient stays.
1984	HCFA-1500	HCFA (now called CMS) required providers to use the *HCFA-1500* (now called the **CMS-1500**) to submit Medicare claims. The HCFA Common Procedure Coding System (HCPCS) (now called Healthcare Common Procedure Coding System) was created, which included CPT, level II (national), and level III (local) codes. Commercial payers also adopted HCPCS coding and use of the HCFA-1500 claim.
1985	COBRA	The **Consolidated Omnibus Budget Reconciliation Act of 1985 (COBRA)** allows employees to continue health care coverage beyond the benefit termination date.
1988	TRICARE	The **CHAMPUS Reform Initiative (CRI)** of 1988 resulted in a new program, TRICARE, which includes options such as TRICARE Prime, TRICARE Extra, and TRICARE Standard. (Chapter 16 covers TRICARE claims processing.)
	CLIA	**Clinical Laboratory Improvement Act (CLIA)** legislation established quality standards for all laboratory testing to ensure the accuracy, reliability, and timeliness of patient test results regardless of where the test was performed. The **Medicare Catastrophic Coverage Act** mandated the reporting of ICD-9-CM (now ICD-10-CM) diagnosis codes on Medicare claims; in subsequent years, private third-party payers adopted similar requirements for claims submission.
1991	CPT E/M codes	The American Medical Association (AMA) and HCFA (now called CMS) implemented major revisions of CPT, creating a new section called **Evaluation and Management (E/M)**, which describes patient encounters with providers for the purpose of evaluation and management of general health status.
1992	RBRVS	A new fee schedule for Medicare services was implemented as part of the Omnibus Reconciliation Acts (OBRA) of 1989 and 1990, which replaced the regional "usual and reasonable" payment basis with a fixed fee schedule calculated according to the **Resource-Based Relative Value Scale (RBRVS) system**. The RBRVS payment system reimburses physicians' practice expenses based on relative values for three components of each physician's service: physician work, practice expense, and malpractice insurance expense. **Usual and reasonable payments** were based on fees typically charged by providers according to specialty within a particular region of the country. A **fee schedule** is a list of predetermined payments for health care services provided to patients (e.g., a fee is assigned to each CPT code). The patient pays a copayment or coinsurance amount for services rendered, the payer reimburses the provider according to its fee schedule, and the remainder is a "write off" (or loss).

(continues)

TABLE 2-1 (continued)

YEAR	EVENT	DESCRIPTION
1992	RBRVS (continued)	**EXAMPLE:** A patient received preventive care evaluation and management services from his family practitioner. The total charges were $125, and the patient paid a $20 copayment during the office visit. The third-party payer reimbursed the physician the fee schedule amount of $75. The remaining $30 owed is recorded as a loss (write off) for the business.
1996	NCCI	The **National Correct Coding Initiative (NCCI)** was created to promote national correct coding methodologies and to eliminate improper coding. NCCI edits are developed based on coding conventions defined in the American Medical Association's *Current Procedural Terminology* (CPT) *manual*, current standards of medical and surgical coding practice, input from specialty societies, and analysis of current coding practice.
	HIPAA	The **Health Insurance Portability and Accountability Act of 1996 (HIPAA)** mandates regulations that govern privacy, security, and electronic transactions standards for health care information. The primary intent of HIPAA is to provide better access to health insurance, limit fraud and abuse, and reduce administrative costs.
1997	SCHIP	The **Balanced Budget Act of 1997 (BBA)** addresses health care fraud and abuse issues. The DHHS Office of the Inspector General (OIG) provides investigative and audit services in health care fraud cases. The **State Children's Health Insurance Program (SCHIP)** was also established to provide health assistance to uninsured, low-income children, either through separate programs or through expanded eligibility under state Medicaid programs.
1998	SNF PPS	The **Skilled Nursing Facility Prospective Payment System (SNF PPS)** is implemented (as a result of the BBA of 1997) to cover all costs (routine, ancillary, and capital) related to services furnished to Medicare Part A beneficiaries. The SNF PPS generates *per diem* payments for each admission; these payments are case-mix adjusted using a resident classification system called **Resource Utilization Groups (RUGs)**, which is based on data collected from resident assessments (using data elements called the **Minimum Data Set (MDS)**) and relative weights developed from staff time data.
1999	HH PPS	The Omnibus Consolidated and Emergency Supplemental Appropriations Act (OCE-SAA) of 1999 amended the BBA of 1997 to require the development and implementation of a **Home Health Prospective Payment System (HH PPS)**, which reimburses home health agencies at a predetermined rate for health care services provided to patients. The HH PPS was implemented October 1, 2000, and uses the **Outcomes and Assessment Information Set (OASIS)**, a group of data elements that represent core items of a comprehensive assessment for an adult home care patient and form the basis for measuring patient outcomes for purposes of outcome-based quality improvement.
	FSMA	The **Financial Services Modernization Act (FSMA)** (or **Gramm–Leach–Bliley Act**) prohibits sharing of medical information among health insurers and other financial institutions for use in making credit decisions.

(continues)

TABLE 2-1 (continued)

YEAR	EVENT	DESCRIPTION
2000	OPPS	The **Outpatient Prospective Payment System (OPPS)**, which uses **Ambulatory Payment Classifications (APCs)** to calculate reimbursement, is implemented for billing of hospital-based Medicare outpatient claims.
	BIPA	The **Medicare, Medicaid, and SCHIP Benefits Improvement and Protection Act of 2000 (BIPA)** required implementation of a $400 billion prescription drug benefit, improved Medicare Advantage (formerly called Medicare+Choice) benefits, required faster Medicare appeals decisions, and more.
	CDHPs	**Consumer-driven health plans (CDHPs)** are introduced as a way to encourage individuals to locate the best health care at the lowest possible price with the goal of holding down health care costs. These plans are organized into three categories: 1. *Employer-paid high-deductible insurance plans* with special health spending accounts to be used by employees to cover deductibles and other medical costs when covered amounts are exceeded. 2. *Defined contribution plans,* which provide a selection of insurance options; employees pay the difference between what the employer pays and the actual cost of the plan they select. 3. *After-tax savings accounts,* which combine a traditional health insurance plan for major medical expenses with a savings account that the employee uses to pay for routine care.
2001	CMS	On June 14, 2001, the Centers for Medicare and Medicaid Services (CMS) became the new name for the Health Care Financing Administration (HCFA).
2002	IRF PPS	The **Inpatient Rehabilitation Facility Prospective Payment System (IRF PPS)** is implemented (as a result of the BBA of 1997), which utilizes information from a patient assessment instrument to classify patients into distinct groups based on clinical characteristics and expected resource needs. Separate payments are calculated for each group, including the application of case- and facility-level adjustments.
	QIOs	CMS announced that **quality improvement organizations (QIOs)** will perform utilization and quality control review of health care furnished, or to be furnished, to Medicare beneficiaries. QIOs replaced peer review organizations (PROs), which previously performed this function.
	EIN	The employer identification number (EIN), assigned by the Internal Revenue Service (IRS), is adopted by DHHS as the National Employer Identification Standard for use in health care transactions.
2003	MMA	The **Medicare Prescription Drug, Improvement, and Modernization Act (MMA)** adds new prescription drug and preventive benefits, provides extra assistance to people with low incomes, and calls for implementation of a Medicare contracting reform (MCR) initiative to improve and modernize the Medicare fee-for-service system and to establish a competitive bidding process to appoint MACs. The *Recovery Audit Contractor (RAC) program* was also created to identify and recover improper Medicare payments paid to health care providers under fee-for-service Medicare plans. (RAC program details are in Chapter 5 of this textbook.)
	MCR	The **Medicare contracting reform (MCR) initiative** was established to integrate the administration of Medicare Parts A and B fee-for-service benefits with new entities called Medicare administrative contractors (MACs). MACs replaced Medicare carriers, DMERCs, and fiscal intermediaries to improve and modernize the Medicare fee-for-service system and establish a competitive bidding process for contracts.

(continues)

TABLE 2-1 (continued)

YEAR	EVENT	DESCRIPTION
2005	IPF PPS	The **Inpatient Psychiatric Facility Prospective Payment System (IPF PPS)** is implemented as a requirement of the Medicare, Medicaid, and SCHIP Balanced Budget Refinement Act of 1999 (BBRA). The IPF PPS includes a patient classification system that reflects differences in patient resource use and costs; the new system replaces the cost-based payment system with a per diem IPF PPS. About 1,800 inpatient psychiatric facilities, including freestanding psychiatric hospitals and certified psychiatric units in general acute care hospitals, are impacted.
	NPI	The Standard Unique Health Identifier for Health Care Providers, or National Provider Identifier (NPI), is implemented.
2009	ARRA	The **American Recovery and Reinvestment Act of 2009 (ARRA)** authorized an expenditure of $1.5 billion for grants for construction, renovation, and equipment, and for the acquisition of health information technology systems. DHHS established electronic health record (EHR) meaningful use objectives and measures during three stages to achieve the goal of improved patient care outcomes and delivery as well as data capture and sharing (2011–2012), advance clinical processes (2014), and improved outcomes (2016). Effective 2011, Medicare provided annual incentives to physicians and group practices for being a "meaningful EHR user"; Medicare will ultimately decrease Medicare Part B payments to physicians who are eligible to be, but fail to become, "meaningful EHR users."
	HITECH Act	The **Health Information Technology for Economic and Clinical Health Act (HITECH Act)** (included in American Recovery and Reinvestment Act of 2009) amended the Public Health Service Act to establish an Office of National Coordinator for Health Information Technology (ONC) within HHS to improve health care quality, safety, and efficiency. HealthIT rules and regulations include the *CLIA Program and HIPAA Privacy/Patients' Access to Test Reports* (amending CLIA of 1988 to specify that a laboratory may provide patient access to completed test reports that, using the laboratory's authentication process, can be identified as belonging to that patient); *HIPAA Privacy, Security, and Enforcement Rules* modifications; *HITECH Breach Notification; Standards and Certification Criteria for Electronic Health Records;* and *Meaningful Use of Electronic Health Records.*
2010	PPACA	The **Patient Protection and Affordable Care Act (PPACA)** focuses on private health insurance reform to provide better coverage for individuals with pre-existing conditions, improve prescription drug coverage under Medicare, and extend the life of the Medicare Trust fund by at least 12 years. Its goal is to provide quality affordable health care for Americans, improve the role of public programs, improve the quality and efficiency of health care, and improve public health. Americans will purchase health coverage that fits their budget and meets their needs by accessing the **health insurance marketplace** (or **health insurance exchange**) in their state. Individuals complete one application that allows them to view all options and enroll. Individuals will be able to determine if they can lower the costs of curruent monthly premiums for private insurance plans and qualify for lower out-of-pocket costs. The marketplace also indicates if individuals qualify for free or low-cost coverage available through Medicaid or the Children's Health Insurance Program (CHIP). Open enrollment began October 1, 2013, for coverage effective January 1, 2014. *PPACA also amended the time period for filing Medicare fee-for-service (FFS) claims to one calendar year after the date of service.* PPACA resulted in creation of risk adjustment, reinsurance, and risk corridors programs to help ensure that insurance plans compete on the basis of quality and service (and not on the basis of attracting the healthiest individuals). The result is improved coverage so that consumers—whether they are healthy or sick—can select the best plan for their needs.

(continues)

TABLE 2-1 (continued)

YEAR	EVENT	DESCRIPTION
2010	HCERA	The **Health Care and Education Reconciliation Act (HCERA)** amended the PPACA to implement health care reform initiatives, such as increasing tax credits to buy health care insurance, eliminating special deals provided to senators, closing the Medicare "donut hole," delaying taxes on "Cadillac health care plans" until 2018, implementing revenue changes (e.g., 10 percent tax on indoor tanning services effective 2010), and so on. HCERA also modified higher education assistance provisions, such as implementing student loan reform.
2011	i2 Initiative	The **Investing in Innovations (i2) Initiative** is designed to spur innovations in health information technology (health IT) by promoting research and development to enhance competitiveness in the United States. Examples of health IT competition topics include applications that: • Allow an individual to securely and effectively share health information with members of his or her social network • Generate results for patients, caregivers, and/or clinicians by providing them with access to rigorous and relevant information that can support real needs and immediate decisions • Allow individuals to connect during natural disasters and other periods of emergency • Facilitate the exchange of health information while allowing individuals to customize the privacy allowances for their personal health records
2012	ACOs	Accountable care organizations (ACOs) help physicians, hospitals, and other health care providers work together to improve care for people with Medicare. Under the new Medicare Shared Savings Program (Shared Savings Program), 27 ACOs entered into agreements with CMS, taking responsibility for the quality of care furnished to Medicare beneficiaries in return for the opportunity to share in savings realized through improved care. The Shared Savings Program and other initiatives related to ACOs were made possible by the PPACA (Affordable Care Act) of 2010. Participation in an ACO is purely voluntary for providers and beneficiaries, and Medicare beneficiaries retain their current ability to seek treatment from any provider they wish.

NOTE: Health care documentation must be dated and authenticated (with a legible signature or electronic authentication), and it may be:

- Dictated and transcribed
- Typed
- Handwritten
- Computer-generated

HEALTH CARE DOCUMENTATION

Health care providers are responsible for documenting and authenticating legible, complete, and timely patient records in accordance with federal regulations (e.g., Medicare *Conditions of Participation*) and accrediting agency standards (e.g., The Joint Commission). The provider is also responsible for correcting or altering errors in patient record documentation. A **patient record** (or **medical record**) documents health care services provided to a patient and includes patient demographic (or identification) data, documentation to support diagnoses and justify treatment provided, and the results of treatment provided. The primary purpose of the record is to provide for **continuity of care**, which involves documenting patient care services so that others who treat the patient have a source of information to assist with additional care and treatment. The record also serves as a communication tool for physicians and other patient care professionals, and assists in planning individual patient care and documenting a patient's illness and treatment.

Secondary purposes of the record do not relate directly to patient care and include:

- **Evaluating the quality of patient care**
- **Providing data for use in clinical research, epidemiology studies, education, public policy making, facilities planning, and health care statistics**

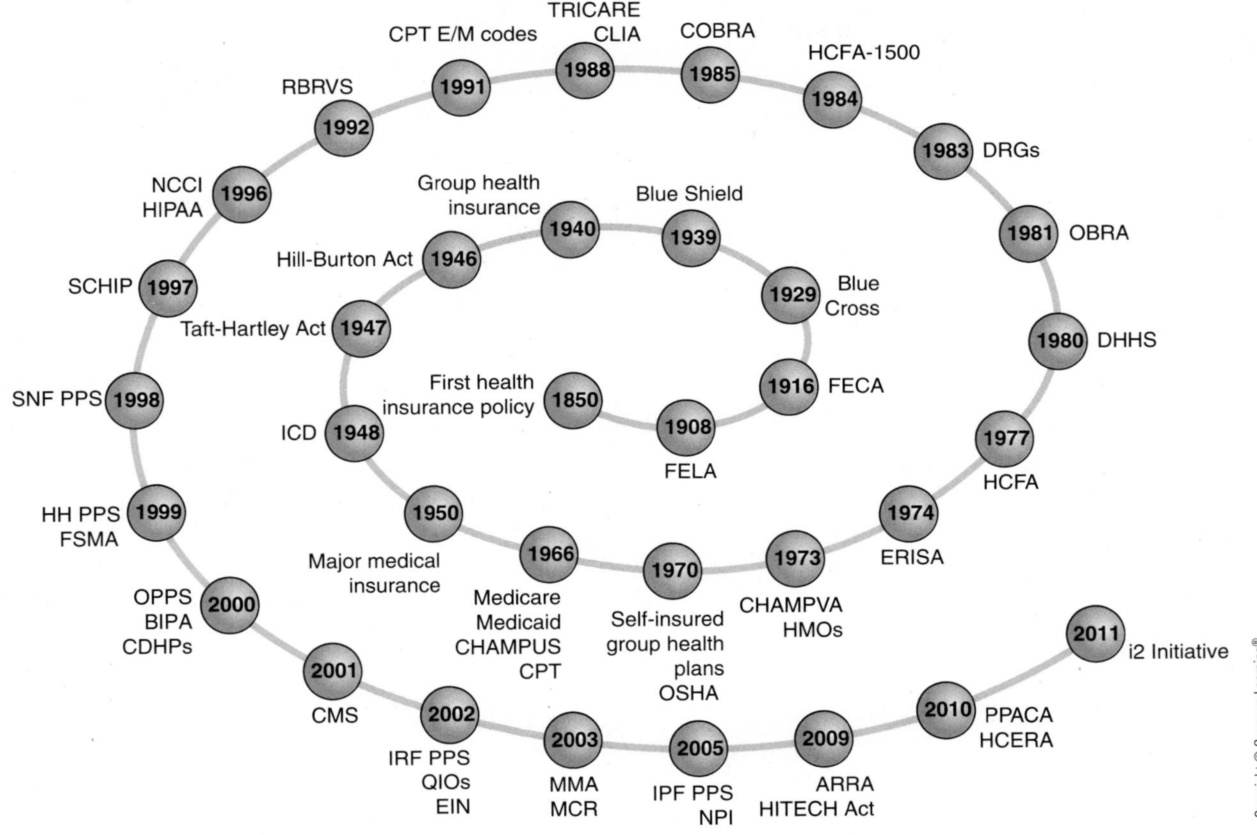

FIGURE 2-1 Timeline of dates and significant events in health care reimbursement.

- **Providing information to third-party payers for reimbursement**
- **Serving the medico-legal interests of the patient, facility, and providers of care**

CENGAGE**brain**.com

Go to www.cengagebrain.com and log in to UHI 12th edition's Student Resources to view CMS *Guidelines for Teaching Physicians, Interns, and Residents*, which cover documentation guidelines for Medicare reimbursement.

In a teaching hospital, general documentation guidelines allow both residents and teaching physicians to document physician services in the patient's medical record.

- **A *teaching hospital* participates in an approved Graduate Medical Education Residency Program in medicine, osteopathy, dentistry, or podiatry.**
- **A *teaching physician* is a physician, other than an intern or resident, who involves residents in patient's care. Generally, the teaching physician must be present during all critical or key portions of the procedure and immediately available to furnish services during the entire service (for services to be payable under the Medical Physician Fee Schedule).**

Documentation in the patient record serves as the basis for coding. The information in the record must support codes submitted on claims for third-party payer reimbursement processing. The patient's diagnosis must also justify diagnostic and/or therapeutic procedures or services provided. This is called *medical necessity* and requires providers to document services or supplies that are:

- **Proper and needed for the diagnosis or treatment of a medical condition**
- **Provided for the diagnosis, direct care, and treatment of a medical condition**

- **Consistent with standards of good medical practice in the local area**
- **Not mainly for the convenience of the physician, patient, or health care facility**

It is important to remember the familiar phrase "If it wasn't documented, it wasn't done." The patient record serves as a medico-legal document and a business record. If a provider performs a service but does not document it, the patient (or third-party payer) can refuse to pay for that service, resulting in lost revenue for the provider. In addition, because the patient record serves as an excellent defense of the quality of care administered to a patient, missing documentation can result in problems if the record has to be admitted as evidence in a court of law.

EXAMPLE:

Missing Documentation: A representative from XYZ Insurance Company reviewed 100 outpatient claims submitted by the Medical Center to ensure that all services billed were documented in the patient records. Upon reconciliation of claims with patient record documentation, the representative denied payment for 13 services (totaling $14,000) because reports of the services billed were not found in the patient records. The facility must pay back the $14,000 it received from the payer as reimbursement for the claims submitted.

Lack of Medical Necessity: The patient underwent an x-ray of his right knee, and the provider documented "severe right shoulder pain" in the record. The coder assigned a CPT code to the "right knee x-ray" and an ICD-10-CM code to the "right shoulder pain." In this example, the third-party payer will deny reimbursement for the submitted claim because the *reason* for the x-ray (shoulder pain) does not match the *type* of x-ray performed. For medical necessity, the provider should have documented a diagnosis such as "right knee pain."

Support of Medical Necessity: The patient underwent a chest x-ray, and the provider documented "severe shortness of breath" in the record. The coder assigned a CPT code to "chest x-ray" and an ICD-10-CM code to "severe shortness of breath." In this example, the third-party payer will reimburse the provider for services rendered because medical necessity for performing the procedure has been shown.

Problem-Oriented Record (POR)

The **problem-oriented record (POR)** is a systematic method of documentation that consists of four components:

- **Database**
- **Problem list**
- **Initial plan**
- **Progress notes**

The POR database contains the following information collected on each patient:

- **Chief complaint**
- **Present conditions and diagnoses**
- **Social data**
- **Past, personal, medical, and social history**

- **Review of systems**
- **Physical examination**
- **Baseline laboratory data**

The POR problem list serves as a table of contents for the patient record because it is filed at the beginning of the record and contains a numbered list of the patient's problems, which helps to index documentation throughout the record.

The POR initial plan contains the strategy for managing patient care, as well as any actions taken to investigate the patient's condition and to treat and educate him or her. The initial plan consists of three categories:

- **Diagnostic/management plans (plans to learn more about the patient's condition and the management of the conditions)**
- **Therapeutic plans (specific medications, goals, procedures, therapies, and treatments used to treat the patient)**
- **Patient education plans (plans to educate the patient about conditions for which he or she is being treated)**

The POR progress notes are documented for each problem assigned to the patient, using the SOAP format:

- **Subjective (S) (patient's statement about how he or she feels, including symptomatic information [e.g., "I have a headache"])**
- **Objective (O) (observations about the patient, such as physical findings, or lab or x-ray results [e.g., chest x-ray negative])**
- **Assessment (A) (judgment, opinion, or evaluation made by the health care provider [e.g., acute headache])**
- **Plan (P) (diagnostic, therapeutic, and education plans to resolve the problems [e.g., patient to take Tylenol as needed for pain])**

ELECTRONIC HEALTH RECORD (EHR)

Although the terms *electronic health record (EHR)* and *electronic medical record (EMR)* are often used interchangeably, the **electronic health record (EHR)** is a more global concept that includes the collection of patient information documented by a number of providers at different facilities regarding one patient. The EHR uses multidisciplinary (many specialties) and multi-enterprise (many facilities) recordkeeping approaches to facilitate **record linkage**, which allows patient information to be created at different locations according to a unique patient identifier or identification number. The electronic health record:

- **Provides access to complete and accurate patient health problems, status, and treatment data**
- **Allows access to evidence-based decision support tools (e.g., drug interaction alerts) that assist providers with decision making**
- **Automates and streamlines a provider's workflow, ensuring that all clinical information is communicated**
- **Prevents delays in health care response that result in gaps in care (e.g., automated prescription renewal notices)**
- **Supports the collection of data for uses other than clinical care (e.g., billing, outcome reporting, public health disease surveillance/reporting, and quality management)**

NOTE: Some disadvantages of the EHR include concerns about initial purchase costs, direct and indirect training costs, and ongoing maintenance costs; issues of privacy and security expressed by patients and providers; and the possibility that evaluation and management elements not actually performed during an encounter will be automatically documented (populated) by the software.

NOTE: The personal health record (PHR) is a web-based application that allows individuals to maintain and manage their health information (and that of others for whom they are authorized, such as family members) in a private, secure, and confidential environment.

The electronic medical record (EMR) has a more narrow focus because it is the patient record created for a single medical practice using a computer, keyboard, mouse, optical pen device, voice recognition system, scanner, and/or touch screen. The electronic medical record:

- Includes a patient's medication lists, problem lists, clinical notes, and other documentation
- Allows providers to prescribe medications, as well as order and view results of ancillary tests (e.g., laboratory, radiology)
- Alerts the provider about drug interactions, abnormal ancillary testing results, and when ancillary tests are needed

Total practice management software (TPMS) (Figure 2-2) is used to generate the EMR, automating the following medical practice functions:

- Registering patients
- Scheduling appointments
- Generating insurance claims and patient statements
- Processing payments from patient and third-party payers
- Producing administrative and clinical reports

Physician Incentive Payments for "Meaningful EHR Users"

Effective 2011, Medicare provides annual incentives to physicians and group practices for being a meaningful EHR user, which is defined by Medicare as:

- Physicians who demonstrate that *certified EHR technology* is used for the purposes of electronic prescribing, electronic exchange of health information in accordance with law and health information technology (HIT) standards, and submission of information on clinical quality measures (Table 2-2)
- Hospitals that demonstrate that *certified EHR technology* is connected in a manner that provides for the electronic exchange of health information to improve the quality of health care (e.g., promoting care coordination) and that *certified EHR technology* is used to submit information on clinical quality measures according to stages of meaningful use (objectives and measures that achieve goals of improved patient care outcomes and delivery through data capture and sharing, advance clinical processes, and improved patient outcomes) (Table 2-3)

The secretary of the Department of Health and Human Services determines whether physicians and hospitals have satisfactorily demonstrated "meaningful EHR use," and the secretary also selects criteria upon which clinical quality measures are based.

Meaningful Use Measures

The *American Recovery and Reinvestment Act (ARRA)*, enacted in 2009, implemented measures to modernize the nation's infrastructure, including the *Health Information Technology for Economic and Clinical Health (HITECH) Act*, which supports the concept of EHRs/meaningful use. *Meaningful use* requires the use of certified EHR technology in a meaningful manner (e.g., electronic prescribing) to ensure that certified EHR technology is connected so as to provide for the electronic exchange of health information to improve the quality of care.

FIGURE 2-2 Total practice management software (TPMS) data flow.

TABLE 2-2 Maximum Medicare incentive payments to physicians who are "meaningful EHR users"

	FIRST CALENDAR YEAR IN WHICH ELIGIBLE PROFESSIONAL (EP) RECEIVES AN INCENTIVE PAYMENT				
	2011	**2012**	**2013**	**2014**	**2015 and Beyond**
2011	$18,000	$0	$0	$0	$0
2012	$12,000	$18,000	$0	$0	$0
2013	$8,000	$12,000	$15,000	$0	$0
2014	$4,000	$8,000	$12,000	$12,000	$0
2015	$2,000	$4,000	$8,000	$8,000	$0
2016	$0	$2,000	$4,000	$4,000	$0
Total	**$44,000**	**$44,000**	**$39,000**	**$24,000**	**$0**

TABLE 2-3 Stages of meaningful use objectives and measures

STAGE 1 (2011–2012) DATA CAPTURE AND SHARING	STAGE 2 (2014) ADVANCE CLINICAL PROCESSES	STAGE 3 (2016) IMPROVED OUTCOMES
• Capture electronic health information in a standardized format • Communicate captured information for patient care coordination processes • Initiate the reporting of clinical quality measures and public health information • Use captured information to track key clinical conditions and engage patients (and their families) in the delivery of care	• Electronically transmit patient care summaries across multiple settings • Establish more patient-controlled data • Increase requirements for e-prescribing and incorporating lab results • Provide more rigorous health information exchange (HIE) among multiple settings	• Facilitate patient access to self-management tools • Implement decision support for national high-priority conditions • Improve population health • Improve quality, safety, and efficiency, leading to improved health care outcomes • Provide access to comprehensive patient data through patient-centered HIEs

Health care providers that use certified EHR technology must submit information about quality of care and other measures to the Secretary of Health and Human Services (HHS). The concept of meaningful use includes the following health outcomes policy priorities:

- **Engaging patients and families in their health**
- **Ensuring adequate privacy and security protection for personal health information**
- **Improving care coordination**
- **Improving population and public health**
- **Improving quality, safety, and efficiency and reducing health disparities**

CMS implemented an incentive payment to eligible professionals (EPs) and eligible hospitals (EHs) that demonstrate they have engaged in efforts to adopt, implement, or upgrade certified EHR technology. To encourage widespread EHR

TABLE 2-4 Reduction in Medicare Part B payments to providers who do not implement an EHR

REDUCTION IN MEDICARE PART B PAYMENTS	
2015	1% if physician is an e-prescriber
	2% if physician is not an e-prescriber
2016	2%
2017 and later	3%

adoption, promote innovation, and avoid imposing excessive burden on health care providers, *meaningful use* was implemented using a phased-in approach, subdivided into three stages from 2011 and 2012 (data capture and sharing) through 2014 (advance clinical processes) and 2016 (improved outcomes).

Physician Payment Reductions for Non-EHR Use

Physicians will receive decreased Medicare Part B payments beginning in 2015 if they were eligible to be "meaningful EHR users" by 2015 but did not implement an electronic health record (EHR) (Table 2-4). After 2017, Medicare Part B payments may be reduced an additional 1 percent for each year in which less than 75 percent of physicians eligible to be "meaningful EHR users" are using electronic health records. The maximum Medicare Part B payment decrease is 5 percent, and the DHHS may exempt physicians for whom becoming a "meaningful EHR user" would be a "significant hardship." Such an exemption will end after five years.

SUMMARY

Health insurance is a contract between a policyholder and a third-party payer or government program for the purpose of providing reimbursement of all or a portion of medical and health care costs.

The history of health care reimbursement can be traced back to 1850, when the Franklin Health Assurance Company of Massachusetts wrote the first health insurance policy.

Subsequent years, through the present, have seen significant changes and advances in health care insurance and reimbursement, from the development of the first BlueCross and BlueShield plans to legislation that resulted in government health care programs (e.g., to cover individuals age 65 and older), payment systems to control health care costs (e.g., diagnosis-related groups), and regulations to govern privacy, security, and electronic transaction standards for health care information.

A *patient record* (or *medical record*) documents health care services provided to a patient, and health care providers are responsible for documenting and authenticating legible, complete, and timely entries according to federal regulations and accreditation standards. The records include patient demographic (or identification) data, documentation to support diagnoses and justify treatment provided, and the results of treatment provided. The primary purpose of the record is to provide for continuity of care, which involves documenting patient care services so that others who treat the patient have a source of information to assist with additional care and treatment. The *problem-oriented record (POR)* is a systematic method of documentation that consists of four components: database, problem list, initial plan, and progress notes (documented using the SOAP format).

The *electronic health record (EHR)* is a global concept (as compared with the EMR) that includes the collection of patient information documented by a number of providers at different facilities regarding one patient. The EHR uses multidisciplinary (many specialties) and multi-enterprise (many facilities) recordkeeping approaches to facilitate *record linkage*, which allows patient information to be created at different locations according to a unique patient identifier or identification number. The *personal health record* (PHR) is a web-based application that allows individuals to maintain and manage their health information (and that of others for whom they are authorized, such as family members) in a private, secure, and confidential environment. The electronic medical record (EMR) has a more narrow focus (as compared with the EHR) because it is the patient record created for a single medical practice and uses total practice management software (TPMS) to generate the EMR and automate medical practice functions.

INTERNET LINKS

- Consolidated Omnibus Budget Reconciliation Act (COBRA)
  Go to **www.cobrainsurance.com** to learn more about COBRA.
- Healthcare Insurance Marketplace—Taking health care into your own hands
  Go to **www.healthcare.gov** to shop for health insurance that meets your needs.
- InteliHealth—In partnership with the Harvard Medical School to provide clinically accurate and relevant medical content
  Go to **www.intelihealth.com**, and click on *Look It Up* to explore the website's health care resources.
- THOMAS (Library of Congress)
  Go to **http://thomas.loc.gov** and browse House of Representatives and Senate bills to determine their current status. (The name THOMAS was selected "in the spirit of Thomas Jefferson" to provide legislative information available from the Library of Congress.)

STUDY CHECKLIST

- ☐ Read this textbook chapter and highlight key concepts.
- ☐ Create an index card for each key term.
- ☐ Access the chapter Internet links to learn more about concepts.
- ☐ Answer the chapter review questions, verifying answers with your instructor.
- ☐ Complete the Workbook chapter, verifying answers with your instructor.
- ☐ Form a study group with classmates to discuss chapter concepts in preparation for an exam.

REVIEW

MULTIPLE CHOICE **Select the most appropriate response.**

1. **Which was the first commercial insurance company in the United States to provide private health care coverage for injuries not resulting in death?**
   a. Baylor University Health Plan
   b. BlueCross and BlueShield Association
   c. Franklin Health Assurance Company
   d. Office of Workers' Compensation Program

2. Which replaced the 1908 workers' compensation legislation and provided civilian employees of the federal government with medical care, survivors' benefits, and compensation for lost wages?

a. Black Lung Benefits Reform Act
b. Federal Employees' Compensation Act
c. Longshore and Harbor Workers' Compensation Act
d. Office of Workers' Compensation Programs

3. The first Blue Cross policy was introduced by

a. Baylor University in Dallas, Texas.
b. Harvard University in Cambridge, Massachusetts.
c. Kaiser Permanente in Los Angeles, California.
d. American Medical Association representatives.

4. The Blue Shield concept grew out of the lumber and mining camps of the _____ region at the turn of the century.

a. Great Plains
b. New England
c. Pacific Northwest
d. Southwest

5. Health care coverage offered by _____ is called group health insurance.

a. a state
b. CMS
c. employees
d. employers

6. The Hill-Burton Act provided federal grants for modernizing hospitals that had become obsolete because of a lack of capital investment during the Great Depression and WWII (1929 to 1945). In return for federal funds,

a. facilities were required to provide services free or at reduced rates to patients unable to pay for care.
b. medical group practices were formed to allow providers to share equipment, supplies, and personnel.
c. national coordinating agencies for physician-sponsored health insurance plans were created.
d. universal health insurance was provided to those who could not afford private insurance.

7. Third-party administrators (TPAs) administer health care plans and process claims, serving as a

a. clearinghouse for data submitted by government agencies.
b. Medicare administrative contractor (MAC) for business owners.
c. system of checks and balances for labor and management.
d. third-party payer (insurance company) for employers.

8. Major medical insurance provides coverage for _____ illnesses and injuries, incorporating large deductibles and lifetime maximum amounts.

a. acute care (short-term)
b. catastrophic or prolonged
c. recently diagnosed
d. work-related

9. The government health plan that provides health care services to Americans over the age of 65 is called

a. Medicare.
b. Medicaid.
c. CHAMPUS.
d. TRICARE.

10. The percentage of costs a patient shares with the health plan (e.g., plan pays 80 percent of costs and patient pays 20 percent) is called

a. coinsurance.

b. copayment.

c. deductible.

d. maximum.

11. The Tax Equity and Fiscal Responsibility Act of 1982 (TEFRA) enacted the _____ prospective payment system (PPS).

a. ambulatory payment classifications

b. diagnosis-related groups

c. fee-for-service reimbursement

d. resource-based relative value scale system

12. The Clinical Laboratory Improvement Act (CLIA) established quality standards for all laboratory testing to ensure the accuracy, reliability, and timeliness of patient test results

a. only at hospitals and other large institutions.

b. regardless of where the test was performed.

13. The National Correct Coding Initiative (NCCI) promotes national correct coding methodologies and eliminates improper coding. NCCI edits are developed based on coding conventions defined in _____, current standards of medical and surgical coding practice, input from specialty societies, and analysis of current coding practice.

a. CPT

b. ICD-10-CM

c. HCPCS level II

d. NDC

14. The primary intent of HIPAA legislation is to

a. combine health care financing and quality assurance programs into a single agency.

b. create better access to health insurance, limit fraud and abuse, and reduce administrative costs.

c. provide health assistance to uninsured, low-income children by expanding the Medicaid program.

d. protect all employees against injuries from occupational hazards in the workplace.

15. Effective 2002, the utilization and quality control review of health care furnished, or to be furnished, to Medicare beneficiaries is performed by

a. consumer-driven health plans.

b. peer review organizations.

c. professional standards review organizations.

d. quality improvement organizations.

16. Which is a primary purpose of the patient record?

a. ensure continuity of care

b. evaluate quality of care

c. provide data for use in research

d. submit data to third-party payers

17. The problem-oriented record (POR) includes the following four components:

a. chief complaint, review of systems, physical examination, laboratory data

b. database, problem list, initial plan, progress notes

c. diagnostic plans, management plans, therapeutic plans, patient education plans

d. subjective, objective, assessment, plan

18. The electronic health record (EHR) allows patient information to be created at different locations according to a unique patient identifier or identification number, which is called

a. evidence-based decision support.

b. health data management.

c. record linkage.

d. surveillance and reporting.

19. When a patient states, "I haven't been able to sleep for weeks," the provider who uses the SOAP format documents that statement in the _____ portion of the clinic note.

a. assessment

b. objective

c. plan

d. subjective

20. The provider who uses the SOAP format documents the physical examination in the _____ portion of the clinic note.

a. assessment

b. objective

c. plan

d. subjective

CHAPTER 3

Managed Health Care

CHAPTER OUTLINE

History of Managed Health Care

Managed Care Organizations

Managed Care Models

Consumer-Directed Health Plans

Accreditation of Managed Care Organizations

Effects of Managed Care on a Physician's Practice

OBJECTIVES

Upon successful completion of this chapter, you should be able to:

1. Define key terms.
2. Discuss the history of managed care in the United States.
3. Explain the role of a managed care organization.
4. Describe six managed care models, and provide details about each.
5. List and define consumer-directed health plans.
6. Identify the organization that accredits managed care organizations.
7. Describe the effects of managed care on a physician's practice.

KEY TERMS

accreditation
adverse selection
Amendment to the HMO Act of 1973
cafeteria plan
capitation
case management
case manager
closed-panel HMO
competitive medical plan (CMP)
concurrent review
consumer-directed health plan (CDHP)
customized sub-capitation plan (CSCP)
direct contract model HMO
discharge planning
enrollees
exclusive provider organization (EPO)
external quality review organization (EQRO)
federally qualified HMO
fee-for-service
flexible benefit plan
flexible spending account (FSA)
gag clause
gatekeeper
group model HMO
group practice without walls (GPWW)
Healthcare Effectiveness Data and Information Set (HEDIS)
health care reimbursement account (HCRA)

health maintenance organization (HMO)
Health Maintenance Organization (HMO) Assistance Act of 1973
health reimbursement arrangement (HRA)
health savings account (HSA)
health savings security account (HSSA)
independent practice association (IPA) HMO
individual practice association (IPA) HMO
integrated delivery system (IDS)
integrated provider organization (IPO)
legislation
managed care organization (MCO)
managed health care (managed care)
management service organization (MSO)
mandates
medical foundation
Medicare risk program
National Committee for Quality Assurance (NCQA)
network model HMO
network provider
Office of Managed Care
open-panel HMO
physician incentive plan
physician incentives
physician-hospital organization (PHO)
point-of-service plan (POS)
preadmission certification (PAC)
preadmission review
Preferred Provider Health Care Act of 1985
preferred provider organization (PPO)
primary care provider (PCP)
prospective review
quality assessment and performance improvement (QAPI)
quality assurance program
Quality Improvement System for Managed Care (QISMC)
report card
retrospective review
risk contract
risk pool
second surgical opinion (SSO)
self-referral
staff model HMO
standards
sub-capitation payment
subscribers (policyholders)
survey
triple option plan
utilization management (utilization review)
utilization review organization (URO)

INTRODUCTION

Managed health care (managed care) combines health care delivery with the financing of services provided. The intent was to replace conventional fee-for-service plans with more affordable quality care to health care consumers and providers who agreed to certain restrictions (e.g., patients would receive care only from providers who are members of a managed care organization). Managed care is currently being challenged by the growth of consumer-directed health plans (CDHPs), which define employer contributions and ask employees to be more responsible for health care decisions and cost-sharing. You might think of a CDHP as a sort of "401(k) plan for health care" (recalling the shift from employer defined-benefit pension plans to employer defined-contribution 401(k) plans).

CENGAGEbrain.com

Go to www.cengagebrain.com and log in to UHI 12th edition's Student Resources to view Table 3-A, which contains the history of managed care.

HISTORY OF MANAGED HEALTH CARE

Managed health care (or managed care) (Table 3-1 and Figure 3-1) was developed as a way to provide affordable, comprehensive, prepaid health care services to **enrollees**, also called **subscribers (policyholders)**, who are employees and dependents who join a managed care plan and are also known as *beneficiaries* in private insurance plans.

MANAGED CARE ORGANIZATIONS

NOTE: Some managed care organizations have discontinued capitation and have adopted fee-for-service payment plans.

A **managed care organization (MCO)** is responsible for the health of a group of enrollees and can be a health plan, hospital, physician group, or health system. Unlike traditional **fee-for-service** plans, which reimburse providers for individual health care services rendered, managed care is financed according to a method called **capitation**, where providers accept pre-established payments for providing health care services to enrollees over a period of time (usually one year). If the physician provides services that cost less than the capitation

TABLE 3-1 Significant managed care federal legislation

YEAR	LEGISLATIVE TITLE	LEGISLATIVE SUMMARY
1973	HMO Assistance Act	The **Health Maintenance Organization (HMO) Assistance Act of 1973**: ● Authorized grants and loans to develop HMOs under private sponsorship ● Defined a **federally qualified HMO** (certified to provide health care services to Medicare and Medicaid enrollees) as one that has applied for and met federal standards established in the HMO Act of 1973 ● Required most employers with more than 25 employees to offer HMO coverage if local plans were available
1974	ERISA	The Employee Retirement Income Security Act of 1974 (ERISA): ● Mandated reporting and disclosure requirements for group life and health plans (including managed care plans) ● Permitted large employers to self-insure employee health care benefits ● Exempted large employers from taxes on health insurance premiums
1981	OBRA	The Omnibus Budget Reconciliation Act of 1981 (OBRA): ● Provided states with flexibility to establish HMOs for Medicare and Medicaid programs ● Increased managed care enrollment resulted
1982	TEFRA	The Tax Equity and Fiscal Responsibility Act of 1982 (TEFRA): ● Modified the HMO Act of 1973 ● Created **Medicare risk programs**, which allowed federally qualified HMOs and competitive medical plans that met specified Medicare requirements to provide Medicare-covered services under a risk contract ● Defined **risk contract** as an arrangement among providers to provide capitated (fixed, prepaid basis) health care services to Medicare beneficiaries ● Defined **competitive medical plan (CMP)** as an HMO that meets federal eligibility requirements for a Medicare risk contract but is not licensed as a federally qualified plan
1985	**Preferred Provider Health Care Act of 1985**	● Eased restrictions on preferred provider organizations (PPOs) ● Allowed subscribers to seek health care from providers outside of the PPO
	COBRA	The Consolidated Omnibus Budget Reconciliation Act of 1985 (COBRA) established an employee's right to continue health care coverage beyond the scheduled benefit termination date (including HMO coverage)
1988	**Amendment to the HMO Act of 1973**	● Allowed federally qualified HMOs to permit members to occasionally use non-HMO physicians and be partially reimbursed
1989	HEDIS	The **Healthcare Effectiveness Data and Information Set (HEDIS)**: ● Is developed by the National Committee for Quality Assurance (NCQA) ● Created standards to assess managed care systems in terms of membership, utilization of services, quality, access, health plan management and activities, and financial indicators
1994	**Office of Managed Care**	● Established as an office of HCFA (now called CMS) to facilitate innovation and competition among Medicare HMOs
1996	HIPAA	The Health Insurance Portability and Accountability Act of 1996 (HIPAA) created federal standards for insurers, HMOs, and employer plans, including those who self-insure

(continues)

TABLE 3-1 (continued)

YEAR	LEGISLATIVE TITLE	LEGISLATIVE SUMMARY
1997	Medical Savings Accounts	A *medical savings account (MSA)* allows individuals to withdraw tax-free funds for health care expenses that are not covered by a qualifying high-deductible health plan. Health care expenses that may be reimbursed from the MSA include the following: ● Dental expenses, including uncovered orthodontia ● Eye exams, contact lenses, and eyeglasses ● Hearing care expenses ● Health plan deductibles and copayments ● Prescription drugs **NOTE:** Legislation passed in 2003 replaced MSAs with health savings accounts (HSAs) (defined in Table 3-3). Existing MSAs are "grandfathered," or they can be moved to an HSA.
	BBA	The Balanced Budget Act of 1997 (BBA): ● Encouraged formation of provider service networks (PSNs) and provider service organizations (PSOs) ● Mandated risk-based managed care organizations to submit encounter data related to inpatient hospital stays of members ● Established the *Medicare+Choice* program, which expanded Medicare coverage options by creating managed care plans to include HMOs, PPOs, and MSAs (now called Medicare Advantage or Medicare Part C) ● Required organizations to implement a **quality assessment and performance improvement (QAPI)** program so that quality assurance activities are performed to improve the functioning of M+C organizations
	State managed care legislation	● In 1997, Texas was the first state to enact legislation allowing consumers to sue an HMO for medical malpractice. (Other states have since passed similar legislation.) ● Other state-enacted legislation since 1997 includes that relating to mandated benefits, high-risk pools, method and philosophy of treatment for Alzheimer's disease, Medicaid eligibility, banning financial incentives, independent appeals measures, insuring liability, and prompt payment.
2003	MMA	The Medicare Prescription Drug, Improvement, and Modernization Act (MMA) (or Medicare Modernization Act): ● Amended the Internal Revenue Code of 1986 to allow a deduction to individuals for amounts contributed to health savings security accounts and health savings accounts, and to provide for the disposition of unused health benefits in cafeteria plans and flexible spending arrangements ● Title I of the Act established a voluntary program for prescription drug coverage under Medicare

EXAMPLE: In June, Hillcrest Medical Group received a capitated payment of $15,000 for the 150 members (enrollees) of the ABC Managed Care Health Plan. The Group spent $12,500 of the capitated payment on preventive, chronic, and acute health care services provided to member patients. The services were provided at the Group's office and local hospital, which included inpatient, outpatient, and emergency department care. (The Group is responsible for paying the enrollees' hospital bills.) In this scenario, health care services provided to enrollees cost less than the capitated payment received. The Hillcrest Medical Group, therefore, made a profit of $2,500. If health care services had cost more than the capitated amount of $15,000, the Group would have experienced a loss.

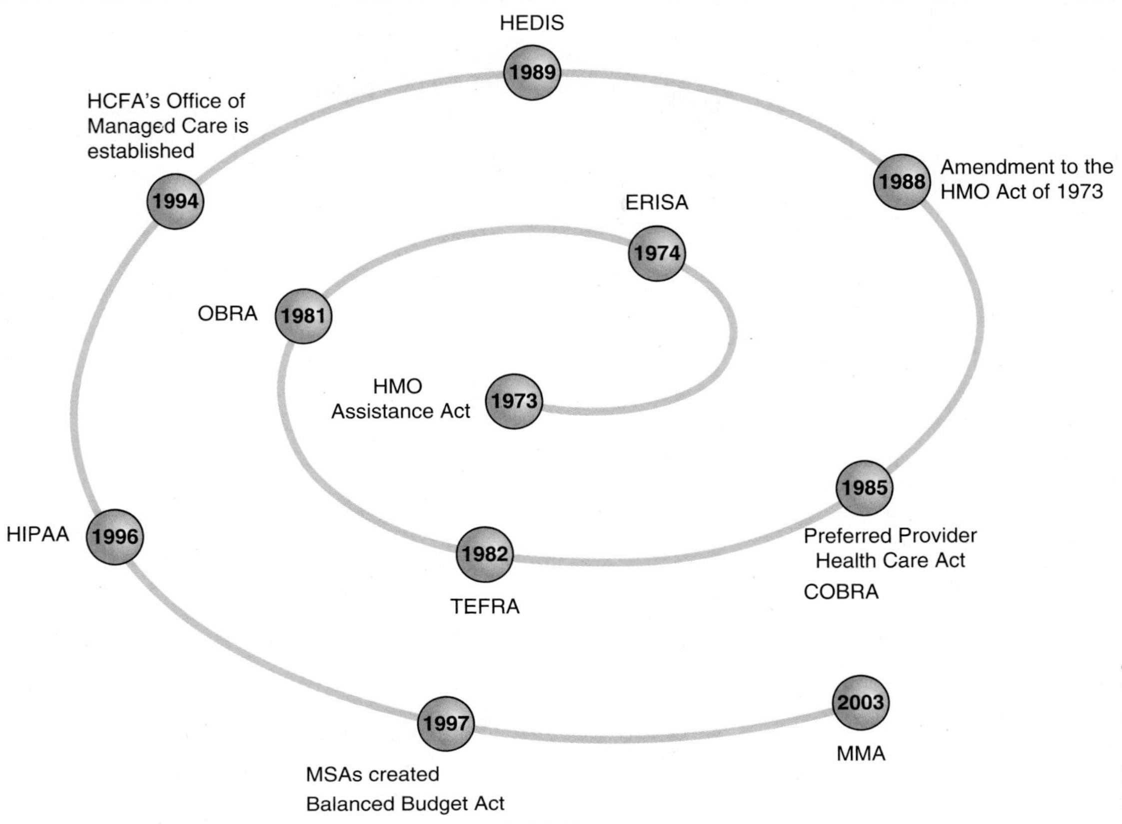

FIGURE 3-1 Timeline of dates and significant events in health care reimbursement.

amount, there is a profit (which the physician keeps). If services provided to subscribers cost more than the capitation amount, the physician loses money.

Primary Care Providers

Managed care plan enrollees receive care from a primary care provider selected from a list of participating providers. The **primary care provider (PCP)** is responsible for supervising and coordinating health care services for enrollees and approves referrals to specialists (Figure 3-2) and inpatient hospital admissions (except in emergencies). The PCP serves as a **gatekeeper** by providing essential health care services at the lowest possible cost, avoiding nonessential care, and referring patients to specialists.

Quality Assurance

Managed care plans that are "federally qualified" and those that must comply with state quality review **mandates** (laws) are required to establish quality assurance programs. A **quality assurance program** includes activities that assess the quality of care provided in a health care setting. Many states have enacted **legislation** (laws) requiring an **external quality review organization (EQRO)** (e.g., QIO) to review health care provided by managed care organizations. The types of quality reviews performed include government oversight, patient satisfaction surveys, data collected from grievance procedures, and reviews conducted by independent organizations. Independent organizations that perform reviews include

Guardian Managed Care Plan

101 Main St. ■ Anywhere, US 12345 ■ (101) 555-1234

PRIMARY CARE PROVIDER PREAUTHORIZATION REFERRAL FORM FOR CONSULTATION

Patient Name	Preauthorization Number	Name of Consulting Physician
Member Identification Number	Member Name (Last, First, MI)	Member Birthdate
Primary Care Physician Identification Number	Name of Primary Care Physician (PCP)	PCP Phone Number

This referral authorizes the services listed below. All services must be rendered by provider stated below.

Diagnosis: ICD-10-CM code(s):

Medical History:

Reason for Referral:

Consultant may provide services listed below. All authorized visits must occur within 90 days of date authorized by PCP. If surgical procedure is listed below, Consultant Treatment Plan is not required. For initial consultation, specialist must submit Consultant Treatment Report of findings and treatment recommendations.

Diagnostic tests indicated: CPT / HCPCS level II code(s):

Procedure(s) to be performed: CPT / HCPCS level II code(s):

Primary Care Physician Signature	Date

Consultant billing procedures for services authorized by Primary Care Physician:

1. Enter Preauthorization Number listed above in Block 23 of the CMS-1500 claim.
2. For first submission, submit CMS-1500 claim with original PCP Preauthorization Referral Form for Consultation.
3. For subsequent submissions, no attachments are required.
4. Consultant must complete Consultant Treatment Plan to obtain authorization for any surgical procedure not specified on this form.

Improperly completed forms will be returned.

Care Management Use Only
Expiration date: _______________
Referral number: _______________

FIGURE 3-2 Sample primary care provider preauthorization referral for consultation with a specialist.

accreditation agencies such as the National Committee for Quality Assurance and The Joint Commission.

Medicare established the **Quality Improvement System for Managed Care (QISMC)** to ensure the accountability of managed care plans in terms of objective, measurable **standards** (requirements). Plans are required to meet minimum performance levels and to show demonstrable and measurable improvement in specified broad clinical areas (e.g., preventive services, acute ambulatory care, chronic care, and hospital care) based on performance improvement projects that each plan identifies. Beginning in 2006, the *Physician Quality Reporting System* (formerly called Physician Quality Reporting Initiative or PQRI system) established a financial incentive for eligible professionals who participate in a *voluntary* quality reporting program. The Healthcare Effectiveness Data and Information Set (HEDIS), sponsored by the National Committee for Quality Assurance, consists of performance measures used to evaluate managed care plans (e.g., rate of Pap smears performed among women of a certain age). The National Committee for Quality Assurance (NCQA) reviews managed care plans and develops report cards to allow health care consumers to make informed decisions when selecting a plan. The **report card** contains data regarding a managed care plan's quality, utilization, customer satisfaction, administrative effectiveness, financial stability, and cost control.

Utilization Management

Utilization management (or utilization review) is a method of controlling health care costs and quality of care by reviewing the appropriateness and necessity of care provided to patients prior to the administration of care (**prospective review**) or after care has been provided (**retrospective review**). Utilization management activities performed by managed care plans include:

- **Preadmission certification (PAC)** or **preadmission review**, which is a review for medical necessity of inpatient care prior to the patient's admission
- *Preauthorization*, which is a review that grants prior approval for reimbursement of a health care service (e.g., elective surgery)
- **Concurrent review**, which is a review for medical necessity of tests and procedures ordered during an inpatient hospitalization
- **Discharge planning**, which involves arranging appropriate health care services for the discharged patient (e.g., home health care)

Some managed care plans contract out utilization management services to a **utilization review organization (URO)**, an entity that establishes a utilization management program and performs external utilization review services. Other plans contract with a *third-party administrator (TPA)*, an organization that provides health benefits claims administration and other outsourced services for self-insured companies.

Case Management

Case management involves the development of patient care plans for the coordination and provision of care for complicated cases in a cost-effective manner. For example, instead of admitting a patient to the hospital, a managed care plan might authorize 24-hour home health care services when appropriate. The **case manager** (e.g., physician, physician's assistant, nurse practitioner, nurse, or social worker) submits written confirmation, authorizing treatment, to the provider (Figure 3-3).

NOTE: Managed care programs have been successful in containing costs and limiting unnecessary services, resulting in the current trend for health care plans to offer the SSO as a benefit, not a requirement.

Second Surgical Opinions

Prior to scheduling elective surgery, managed care plans often require a **second surgical opinion (SSO)**; that is, a second physician is asked to evaluate the necessity of surgery and recommend the most economical, appropriate facility in which to perform the surgery (e.g., outpatient clinic or doctor's office versus inpatient hospitalization).

Guardian Managed Care Plan

101 Main St. ■ Anywhere, US 12345 ■ (101) 555-1234

DATE:

RE: ______________________________
DATE OF BIRTH: ______________________
IDENTIFICATION NUMBER: _______________
START TREATMENT DATE: ________________

NAME OF CONSULTANT: ________________
MAILING ADDRESS: ___________________

Dear Dr. ________________

________________ was referred to you by the Guardian Managed Care Plan on ____________. I am authorizing the following medically necessary treatment. This is subject to patient eligibility and contract limitations at the time treatment is performed.

Procedure	Units	From	To	Preauthorization Number
________	________	________	________	________

When filing for reimbursement, please send the CMS-1500 claim to the Guardian Managed Care Plan at the above address. In order to expedite payment, please be certain to include in Block 23 the preauthorization number indicated above.

Please note that any services provided beyond those listed in this letter require additional preauthorization. If you anticipate that the patient will require additional services, you must complete an outpatient treatment report two weeks prior to rendering any additional treatment. If the patient fails to keep appointments, please inform us by telephone. If treatment is discontinued, submit a written discharge summary within two weeks of termination.

Although eligibility and benefit information has been corroborated to the best of our ability, certification for medically necessary care does not guarantee financial reimbursement related to these matters. If you need further information, or if there are any significant changes in the patient's medical status, please contact me at the Guardian Managed Care Plan at (800) 555-1212, extension 1234.
Thank you for your cooperation.

Sincerely,

Case Manager
Original:
cc:

FIGURE 3-3 Sample case manager written confirmation order.

Gag Clauses

Medicare and many states prohibit managed care contracts from containing **gag clauses**, which prevent providers from discussing all treatment options with patients, whether or not the plan would provide reimbursement for services. Medicare beneficiaries are entitled to advice from their physicians on medically necessary treatment options that may be appropriate for their condition or disease. Because a gag clause would have the practical effect of prohibiting a physician from giving a patient the full range of advice and counsel that is clinically appropriate, it would result in the managed care plan not providing all covered Medicare services to its enrollees, in violation of the managed care plan's responsibilities.

Physician Incentives

Physician incentives include payments made directly or indirectly to health care providers to encourage them to reduce or limit services (e.g., discharge an inpatient from the hospital more quickly) so as to save money for the managed care plan. The federal **physician incentive plan** requires managed care plans that contract with Medicare or Medicaid to disclose information about physician incentive plans to CMS or state Medicaid agencies before a new or renewed contract receives final approval.

NOTE: Government and private payers have implemented managed care programs to control health care costs. Chapters 12 to 17 of this textbook include details about such managed care programs (e.g., Medicare managed care plans are discussed in Chapter 14).

MANAGED CARE MODELS

Managed care originally focused on cost reductions by restricting health care access through utilization management and availability of limited benefits. Managed care organizations (MCOs) were created to manage benefits and to develop participating provider networks. Managed care can now be categorized according to six models:

1. Exclusive provider organization (EPO)
2. Integrated delivery system (IDS)
3. Health maintenance organization (HMO)
    a. Direct contract model
    b. Group model
    c. Individual practice association (IPA)
    d. Network model
    e. Staff model
4. Point-of-service plan (POS)
5. Preferred provider organization (PPO)
6. Triple option plan

NOTE: *Exclusive provider organization (EPO)* patients must receive care from participating providers, which can include emergency departments at participating hospitals, or they pay for all costs incurred.

Exclusive Provider Organization (EPO)

An **exclusive provider organization (EPO)** is a managed care plan that provides benefits to subscribers who are required to receive services from network providers. A **network provider** is a physician or health care facility under contract to the managed care plan. Usually, network providers sign exclusive contracts with the EPO, which means they cannot contract with other managed care plans. (Network providers are usually reimbursed on a fee-for-service basis.) Subscribers are generally required to coordinate health care services through their primary care physician (PCP). EPOs are regulated by state insurance departments (unlike HMOs, which are regulated by either the state commerce or department of corporations, depending on state requirements).

NOTE: An *integrated delivery system (IDS)* is the result of a joint venture between hospitals and members of their medical staff.

Integrated Delivery System (IDS)

An **integrated delivery system (IDS)** is an organization of affiliated providers' sites (e.g., hospitals, ambulatory surgical centers, or physician groups) that offer joint health care services to subscribers. Models include physician-hospital organizations, management service organizations, group practices without walls, integrated provider organizations, and medical foundations. A **physician-hospital organization (PHO)** is owned by hospital(s) and physician groups that obtain managed care plan contracts; physicians maintain their own practices and provide health care services to plan members. A **management service organization (MSO)** is usually owned by physicians or a hospital and provides practice management (administrative and support) services to individual physician practices. A **group practice without walls (GPWW)** establishes a contract that allows physicians to maintain their own offices and share services (e.g., appointment scheduling and billing). An **integrated provider organization (IPO)** manages the delivery of health care services offered by hospitals, physicians (who are employees of the IPO), and other health care organizations (e.g., an ambulatory surgery clinic and a nursing facility). A **medical foundation** is a nonprofit organization that contracts with and acquires the clinical and business assets of physician practices; the foundation is assigned a provider number and manages the practice's business. An *integrated delivery system* may also be referred to by any of the following names: integrated service network (ISN), delivery system, vertically integrated plan (VIP), vertically integrated system, horizontally integrated system, health delivery network, or accountable health plan.

NOTE: *Health maintenance organizations (HMOs)* manage patient health care services by expending a monthly capitation amount paid by a third-party payer.

Health Maintenance Organization (HMO)

A **health maintenance organization (HMO)** is an alternative to traditional group health insurance coverage and provides comprehensive health care services to voluntarily enrolled members on a prepaid basis. In contrast, traditional health insurance coverage is usually provided on a fee-for-service basis in which reimbursement increases if the health care service fees increase, if multiple units of service are provided, or if more expensive services are provided instead of less expensive ones (e.g., brand-name versus generic prescription medication).

HMOs provide preventive care services to promote "wellness" or good health, thus reducing the overall cost of medical care. Annual physical examinations are encouraged for the early detection of health problems. Health risk assessment instruments (surveys) and resources are also available to subscribers. A primary care provider (PCP) assigned to each subscriber is responsible for coordinating health care services and referring subscribers to other health care providers.

NOTE: Coinsurance may also be required of managed care plans when out-of-network (nonparticipating) providers render health care services to plan subscribers.

HMOs often require a *copayment* (or *copay*), which is a fee paid by the patient to the provider at the time health care services are rendered. Copayments range from $1 to $35 per visit, and some services are exempt because coinsurance payments are required instead.

HMOs must meet the requirements of the HMO Act of 1973 as well as the rules and regulations of individual states. There are five HMO models (Table 3-2): direct contract model, group model, individual practice association, network model, and staff model.

EXAMPLE: Dr. Sanders provided Nancy Jones with evaluation and management (E/M) services at the Center City HMO during an office visit. The contracted E/M service rate is $64, and Nancy is required to pay a $10 copayment. She has a $100 annual deductible, which was met earlier this year. She is not required to pay a coinsurance amount.

Provider fee (contracted E/M service rate)	$64
Patient copayment	- $10
Insurance payment	$54

TABLE 3-2 Closed-panel and open-panel health maintenance organization models

CLOSED-PANEL HMO	Health care is provided in an HMO-owned center or satellite clinic or by physicians who belong to a specially formed medical group that serves the HMO.
CLOSED-PANEL MODELS	**DESCRIPTION**
Group Model HMO	Contracted health care services are delivered to subscribers by *participating physicians who are members of an independent multispecialty group practice.* The HMO reimburses the physician group, which is then responsible for reimbursing physician members and contracted health care facilities (e.g., hospitals). The physician group can be owned or managed by the HMO, or it can simply contract with the HMO.
Staff Model HMO	Health care services are provided to subscribers by *physicians employed by the HMO.* Premiums and other revenue are paid to the HMO. Usually, all ambulatory services are provided within HMO corporate buildings.
OPEN-PANEL HMO	Health care is provided by individuals who are *not* employees of the HMO or who do not belong to a specially formed medical group that serves the HMO.
OPEN-PANEL MODELS	**DESCRIPTION**
Direct Contract Model HMO	Contracted health care services are delivered to subscribers by *individual physicians in the community.*
Individual Practice Association (IPA) HMO	Also called **independent practice association (IPA) HMO**, contracted health services are delivered to subscribers by *physicians who remain in their independent office settings.* The IPA is an intermediary (e.g., physician association) that negotiates the HMO contract and receives and manages the capitation payment from the HMO, so that physicians are paid on either a fee-for-service or capitation basis.
Network Model HMO	Contracted health care services are provided to subscribers by *two or more physician multispecialty group practices.*

NOTE: A POS plan is not an HMO, but it is a managed care plan that combines the characteristics of an HMO and a preferred provider organization (PPO) (discussed below). POS enrollees pay less if they use the plan's in-network providers. POS enrollees who receive care from out-of-network providers pay higher deductible and coinsurance amounts.

NOTE: A PPO is not an HMO, but it is similar to an HMO because it is a managed care plan that provides enrollees with discounted health care through a network of providers. PPO enrollees can also receive health care outside of the network if they are willing to pay higher costs.

Point-of-Service Plan (POS)

To create flexibility in managed care plans, some HMOs and preferred provider organizations have implemented a **point-of-service plan (POS)**, under which patients have freedom to use the managed care panel of providers or to self-refer to out-of-network providers. If enrollees choose to receive all medical care from the managed network of health care providers, or obtain an authorization from their POS primary care provider for specialty care with an out-of-network provider, they pay only the regular copayment or a small charge for the visit and they pay no deductible or coinsurance costs. If the enrollee sees a non-managed care panel specialist without a referral from the primary care physician, this is known as a **self-referral**. The enrollee will have greater out-of-pocket expenses, as he must pay both a large deductible (usually $200 to $250) and 20 to 25 percent coinsurance charges, similar to those paid by persons with fee-for-service plans.

Preferred Provider Organization (PPO)

A **preferred provider organization (PPO)** (sometimes called a *participating provider organization*) is a managed care network of physicians and hospitals that have joined together to contract with insurance companies, employers, or other organizations to provide health care to subscribers for a discounted fee. PPOs do not routinely establish contracts for laboratory or pharmacy services, but they do offer reduced-rate contracts with specific hospitals. Most PPOs are open-ended plans allowing patients to use non-PPO providers in exchange for larger out-of-pocket expenses. Premiums, deductibles, and copayments are usually higher than those paid for HMOs, but lower than those paid for regular fee-for-service plans.

Triple Option Plan

NOTE: A *triple option plan* provides patients with more choices than a traditional managed care plan.

A **triple option plan**, which is usually offered either by a single insurance plan or as a joint venture among two or more insurance payers, provides subscribers or employees with a choice of HMO, PPO, or traditional health insurance plans. It is also called a **cafeteria plan** (or **flexible benefit plan**) because of the different benefit plans and extra coverage options provided through the insurer or third-party administrator. Triple option plans are intended to prevent the problem of covering members who are sicker than the general population (called **adverse selection**). A **risk pool** is created when a number of people are grouped for insurance purposes (e.g., employees of an organization); the cost of health care coverage is determined by employees' health status, age, sex, and occupation.

CONSUMER-DIRECTED HEALTH PLANS

Consumer-directed health plans (CDHPs) include many choices that provide individuals with an incentive to control the costs of health benefits and health care. Individuals have greater freedom in spending health care dollars, up to a designated amount, and receive full coverage for in-network preventive care. In return, individuals assume significantly higher cost-sharing expenses after the designated amount has been expended. (The catastrophic limit is usually higher than those common in other plans.) CDHPs have become a popular alternative to the increased costs of traditional health insurance premiums and the limitations associated with managed care plans. They include the following tiers:

- **Tax-exempt account, which is used to pay for health care expenses and provides more flexibility than traditional managed care plans in terms of access to providers and services**
- **Out-of-pocket payments for health care expenses, which are made after the tax-exempt account is expended and before the deductible for high-deductible insurance has been met; this tier actually represents a gap in coverage**
- **High-deductible insurance policy, which reimburses allowable health care expenses after the high deductible has been paid**

CDHPs usually provide Internet-based support so individuals can track health care expenses, improve their health by viewing useful information and learning about preventive services, obtain information about provider quality, and receive notification about provider group-rate pricing. Various CDHPs are available to individuals (Table 3-3), all of which are subject to modification as legislation is passed and payers alter program requirements.

NOTE: Effective January 1, 2006, The Joint Commission (formerly called the Joint Commission on Accreditation of Healthcare Organizations, or JCAHO, pronounced jāy cō) discontinued its Network Accreditation Program for Managed Care Organizations. In July 2002, The Joint Commission approved its first National Patient Safety Goals, and annual national patient safety goals were published. The Joint Commission International Collaborating Center on Patient Safety was then established in 2005 to provide patient safety solutions to health care organizations.

ACCREDITATION OF MANAGED CARE ORGANIZATIONS

The National Committee for Quality Assurance (NCQA) evaluates managed care organizations. **Accreditation** is a voluntary process that a health care facility or organization (e.g., hospital or managed care plan) undergoes to demonstrate that

TABLE 3-3 Types of consumer-directed health plans (CDHPs)

TYPE OF CDHP	DESCRIPTION
Customized Sub-Capitation Plan (CSCP)	• Health care expenses are funded by insurance coverage; the individual selects one of each type of provider to create a customized network and pays the resulting customized insurance premium. • Each provider is paid a fixed amount per month to provide only the care that an individual needs from that provider (**sub-capitation payment**). **NOTE:** In managed care, the primary care provider usually receives a *capitation payment* and is responsible for managing *all* of an individual's health care, which includes reimbursing other caregivers (e.g., specialists).
Flexible Spending Account (FSA)	• Tax-exempt accounts offered by employers to any number of employees, which individuals use to pay health care bills. • Employees contribute funds to the FSA through a salary reduction agreement and withdraw funds to pay medical bills. • Funds in an FSA are exempt from both income tax and Social Security tax (employers may also contribute to FSAs). • By law, employees forfeit unspent funds remaining in the FSA at the end of the year.
Health Savings Account (HSA); Health Savings Security Account (HSSA)	• Participants enroll in a relatively inexpensive high-deductible insurance plan, and a tax-deductible savings account is opened to cover current and future medical expenses. • Money deposited (and earnings) is tax-deferred, and money withdrawn to cover qualified medical expenses is tax-free. • Money can be withdrawn for purposes other than health care expenses after payment of income tax plus a 15 percent penalty. • Unused balances "roll over" from year to year; if an employee changes jobs, he or she can continue to use the HSA to pay for qualified health care expenses.
Health Care Reimbursement Account (HCRA)	• Tax-exempt account used to pay for health care expenses. • Individual decides, in advance, how much money to deposit in the HCRA (unused funds are forfeited).
Health Reimbursement Arrangement (HRA)	• Tax-exempt accounts offered by employers with more than 50 employees, which individuals use to pay health care bills. • U.S. Treasury Department and Internal Revenue Service issued tax guidance information for HRAs in 2002. • Must be used for qualified health care expenses and allows individuals to accumulate unspent money for future years. • If an employee changes jobs, he or she can continue to use the HRA to pay for qualified health care expenses.

it has met standards beyond those required by law. Accreditation organizations develop standards (requirements) that are reviewed during a **survey** (evaluation) process that is conducted both offsite (e.g., managed care plan submits an initial document for review) and onsite (at the managed care plan's facilities).

National Committee for Quality Assurance (NCQA)

The **National Committee for Quality Assurance (NCQA)** of Washington, DC, is a private, not-for-profit organization that assesses the quality of managed care plans in the United States and releases the data to the public for consideration when selecting a managed care plan. The NCQA began accrediting managed care programs in 1991 when a need for consistent, independent information about the quality of care provided to patients was originally identified.

EFFECTS OF MANAGED CARE ON A PHYSICIAN'S PRACTICE

Managed care organizations (MCOs) impact a practice's administrative procedures by requiring:

- **Separate bookkeeping systems for each capitated plan to ensure financial viability of the contract**
- **A tracking system for preauthorization of specialty care and documented requests for receipt of the specialist's treatment plan or consultation report**
- **Preauthorization and/or precertification for all hospitalizations and continued certification if the patient's condition requires extension of the number of authorized days**
- **Up-to-date lists for referrals to participating health care providers, hospitals, and diagnostic test facilities used by the practice**
- **Up-to-date lists of special administrative procedures required by each managed care plan contract**
- **Up-to-date lists of patient copayments and fees for each managed care plan contract**
- **Special patient interviews to ensure preauthorization and to explain out-of-network requirements if the patient is self-referring**
- **Additional paperwork for specialists to complete and the filing of treatment and discharge plans**
- **Some case managers employed by the MCO to monitor services provided to enrollees and to be notified if a patient fails to keep a preauthorized appointment**
- **The attachment of preauthorization documentation to health insurance claims submitted to some MCOs**

NOTE: It is important to realize that managed care is an option many payers use to reimburse health care, as covered in Chapters 12 to 17.

SUMMARY

The financing of America's health care system has changed the way health care services are organized and delivered, as evidenced by a movement from traditional fee-for-service systems to managed care networks. These range from structured staff model HMOs to less structured preferred provider organizations (PPOs).

Currently, more than 60 million Americans are enrolled in some type of managed care program in response to regulatory initiatives affecting health care cost and quality.

A managed care organization (MCO) is responsible for the health of its enrollees, which can be administered by the MCO that serves as a health plan or contracts with a hospital, physician group, or health system.

Most managed care financing is achieved through a method called capitation, and enrollees are assigned to or select a primary care provider who serves as the patient's gatekeeper.

Federal legislation mandated that MCOs participate in quality assurance programs and other activities, including utilization management, case management, requirements for second surgical opinions, non-use of gag clauses in MCO contracts, and disclosure of any physician incentives.

Managed care is categorized according to six models: exclusive provider organizations, integrated delivery systems, health maintenance organizations, point-of-service plans, preferred provider organizations, and triple option plans.

Consumer-directed health plans (CDHPs) provide incentives for controlling health care expenses and give individuals an alternative to traditional health insurance and managed care coverage.

Accreditation organizations, such as the NCQA, evaluate MCOs according to pre-established standards.

INTERNET LINKS

- Great Plains Regional Medical Center
  Go to **www.gprmc-ok.com** and select the About GPRMC link to learn more about Dr. Shadid and the history of the Great Plains Regional Medical Center, a managed care system started in 1929.
- HealthEast
  Go to **www.healtheast.org** to view information about the HealthEast Care System, which is an integrated care delivery system that provides acute care, chronic care, senior services, community-based services, ambulatory/outpatient services, physician clinics, and preventive services.
- The Joint Commission
  Go to **www.jointcommission.org** to learn about The Joint Commission.
- The Joint Commission Quality Check
  Go to **www.qualitycheck.org** and conduct a search to identify health care organizations that meet The Joint Commission's patient safety and quality standards.
- Kaiser Permanente
  Go to **www.kaiserpermanente.org** to learn about the history of the country's first HMO, Kaiser Permanente.
- National Committee for Quality Assurance (NCQA)
  Go to **www.ncqa.org** to learn about the NCQA.
- NCQA's Health Plan Report Card
  Go to **http://reportcard.ncqa.org** and click the Health Insurance Plans link to use an interactive tool to create a customized report card of managed care plans.

STUDY CHECKLIST

- ☐ Read this textbook chapter and highlight key concepts.
- ☐ Create an index card for each key term.
- ☐ Access the chapter Internet links to learn more about concepts.
- ☐ Answer the chapter review questions, verifying answers with your instructor.
- ☐ Complete the Workbook chapter, verifying answers with your instructor.
- ☐ Form a study group with classmates to discuss chapter concepts in preparation for an exam.

REVIEW

MULTIPLE CHOICE Select the most appropriate response.

1. **The intent of managed health care was to**
   a. dramatically improve the health care delivery system in the United States.
   b. have employees of a managed care organization provide patient care.
   c. replace fee-for-service plans with affordable, quality care to health care consumers.
   d. retrospectively reimburse patients for health care services provided.
2. **Which term best describes those who receive managed health care plan services?**
   a. employees
   b. enrollees
   c. payers
   d. providers

3. The Medical Center received a $100,000 capitation payment in January to cover the health care costs of 150 managed care enrollees. By the following January, $80,000 had been expended to cover services provided. The remaining $20,000 is

a. distributed equally among the 150 enrollees.
b. retained by the Medical Center as profit.
c. submitted to the managed care organization.
d. turned over to the federal government.

4. A nonprofit organization that contracts with and acquires the clinical and business assets of physician practices is called a

a. medical foundation.
b. Medicare risk program.
c. physician-hospital organization.
d. triple option plan.

5. A _____ is responsible for supervising and coordinating health care services for enrollees.

a. case manager
b. primary care provider
c. third-party administrator
d. utilization review manager

6. The term that describes requirements created by accreditation organizations is

a. laws.
b. mandates.
c. regulations.
d. standards.

MATCHING: Match the term with its definition.

a. preadmission review
b. preauthorization
c. concurrent review
d. discharge planning

_____ **7. Arranging appropriate health care services for discharged patients.**
_____ **8. Review for medical necessity of inpatient care prior to admission.**
_____ **9. Review for medical necessity of tests/procedures ordered during inpatient hospitalization.**
_____ **10. Grants prior approval for reimbursement of a health care service.**

MATCHING: Match the type of managed care model with its definition.

a. EPO
b. IDS
c. HMO
d. POS
e. PPO

_____ **11. Contracted network of health care providers that provide care to subscribers for a discounted fee.**
_____ **12. Organization of affiliated providers' sites that offer joint health care services to subscribers.**
_____ **13. Provides benefits to subscribers who are required to receive services from network providers.**
_____ **14. Provides comprehensive health care services to voluntarily enrolled members on a prepaid basis.**
_____ **15. Patients can use the managed care panel of providers (paying discounted health care costs) or self-refer to out-of-network providers (and pay higher health care costs).**

CHAPTER 4

Processing an Insurance Claim

CHAPTER OUTLINE

Processing an Insurance Claim
Managing New Patients
Managing Established Patients
Managing Office Insurance Finances
Insurance Claim Life Cycle
Maintaining Insurance Claim Files
Credit and Collections

OBJECTIVES

Upon successful completion of this chapter, you should be able to:

1. Define key terms.
2. Describe the processing of an insurance claim.
3. Explain how claims processing for new and established patients differs.
4. Manage the office's insurance finances.
5. Discuss the life cycle of an insurance claim, including electronic data interchange (EDI).
6. Maintain a medical practice's insurance claim files.
7. Explain the role of credit and collections in processing claims.

KEY TERMS

accept assignment
accounts receivable
accounts receivable aging report
accounts receivable management
allowed charges
ANSI ASC X12
appeal
assignment of benefits
bad debt
beneficiary
birthday rule
chargemaster
claims adjudication
claims attachment
claims processing
claims submission
clean claim
clearinghouse
closed claim
coinsurance
common data file
Consumer Credit Protection Act of 1968
coordination of benefits (COB)
covered entity
day sheet
deductible

delinquent account
delinquent claim
delinquent claim cycle
downcoding
electronic data interchange (EDI)
electronic flat file format
electronic funds transfer (EFT)
Electronic Funds Transfer Act
Electronic Healthcare Network Accreditation Commission (EHNAC)
electronic media claim
electronic remittance advice (ERA)
encounter form
Equal Credit Opportunity Act
Fair Credit and Charge Card Disclosure Act
Fair Credit Billing Act
Fair Credit Reporting Act
Fair Debt Collection Practices Act (FDCPA)
guarantor
litigation
manual daily accounts receivable journal
noncovered benefit
nonparticipating provider (nonPAR)
open claim
out-of-pocket payment
outsource
participating provider (PAR)
past-due account
patient account record
patient ledger
pre-existing condition
primary insurance
Provider Remittance Notice (PRN)
secondary insurance
source document
superbill
suspense
Truth in Lending Act
two-party check
unassigned claim
unauthorized service
unbundling
value-added network (VAN)

INTRODUCTION

This chapter provides an overview of the processing of a health insurance claim in the health care provider's office and the major steps taken to process that claim by the insurance company. *Electronic Data Interchange (EDI)* content is also located in this chapter.

PROCESSING AN INSURANCE CLAIM

The processing of an insurance claim is initiated when the patient contacts a health care provider's office and schedules an appointment. (Procedures for obtaining information on new and established patients are discussed next in this chapter.) The insurance claim used to report professional and technical services is known as the *CMS-1500 claim* (Figure 4-1). The provider's claim for payment is generated from information located on the patient's encounter form (or superbill), ledger/account record, and source document (e.g., patient record or chart). Information from these documents is transferred to the CMS-1500 claim. Such information includes patient and insurance policy identification, CPT and HCPCS level II codes and charges for procedures and/or services, and ICD-10-CM codes for diagnoses treated and/or managed during the encounter. (The selection of CPT and HCPCS level II codes for procedures, services, and diagnoses is discussed in later chapters.) The CMS-1500 claim requires responses to standard questions pertaining to whether the patient's condition is related to employment, an auto accident, or any other accident; additional insurance coverage; use of an outside laboratory; and whether the provider accepts assignment. To **accept assignment** means the provider agrees to accept what the insurance company allows or approves as payment in full for the claim. The patient is responsible for paying any copayment and/or coinsurance amounts.

> **NOTE:** To *accept assignment* is sometimes confused with **assignment of benefits**, which means the patient and/or insured authorizes the payer to reimburse the provider directly.

Health insurance plans may include an **out-of-pocket payment** provision, which usually has limits of $1,000 or $2,000. The physician's office manager must be familiar with the out-of-pocket payments provision of a patient's health insurance plan so that when the patient has reached the limit of an out-of-pocket payment for the year, appropriate patient reimbursement to the provider is determined. The patient may still be responsible for another out-of-pocket

HEALTH INSURANCE CLAIM FORM

APPROVED BY NATIONAL UNIFORM CLAIM COMMITTEE (NUCC) 02/12

PICA | PICA

CARRIER

1. MEDICARE (Medicare#) | MEDICAID (Medicaid#) | TRICARE (ID#/DoD#) | CHAMPVA (Member ID#) | GROUP HEALTH PLAN (ID#) | FECA BLK LUNG (ID#) | OTHER (ID#)

1a. INSURED'S I.D. NUMBER (For Program in Item 1)

2. PATIENT'S NAME (Last Name, First Name, Middle Initial)

3. PATIENT'S BIRTH DATE MM DD YY SEX M F

4. INSURED'S NAME (Last Name, First Name, Middle Initial)

5. PATIENT'S ADDRESS (No., Street)

6. PATIENT RELATIONSHIP TO INSURED Self Spouse Child Other

7. INSURED'S ADDRESS (No., Street)

CITY STATE

8. RESERVED FOR NUCC USE

CITY STATE

ZIP CODE TELEPHONE (Include Area Code) ( )

ZIP CODE TELEPHONE (Include Area Code) ( )

9. OTHER INSURED'S NAME (Last Name, First Name, Middle Initial)

10. IS PATIENT'S CONDITION RELATED TO:

11. INSURED'S POLICY GROUP OR FECA NUMBER

a. OTHER INSURED'S POLICY OR GROUP NUMBER

a. EMPLOYMENT? (Current or Previous) YES NO

a. INSURED'S DATE OF BIRTH MM DD YY SEX M F

b. RESERVED FOR NUCC USE

b. AUTO ACCIDENT? YES NO PLACE (State)

b. OTHER CLAIM ID (Designated by NUCC)

c. RESERVED FOR NUCC USE

c. OTHER ACCIDENT? YES NO

c. INSURANCE PLAN NAME OR PROGRAM NAME

d. INSURANCE PLAN NAME OR PROGRAM NAME

10d. CLAIM CODES (Designated by NUCC)

d. IS THERE ANOTHER HEALTH BENEFIT PLAN? YES NO *If yes*, complete items 9, 9a, and 9d.

READ BACK OF FORM BEFORE COMPLETING & SIGNING THIS FORM.

12. PATIENT'S OR AUTHORIZED PERSON'S SIGNATURE I authorize the release of any medical or other information necessary to process this claim. I also request payment of government benefits either to myself or to the party who accepts assignment below.

SIGNED ______ DATE ______

13. INSURED'S OR AUTHORIZED PERSON'S SIGNATURE I authorize payment of medical benefits to the undersigned physician or supplier for services described below.

SIGNED ______

PATIENT AND INSURED INFORMATION

14. DATE OF CURRENT ILLNESS, INJURY, or PREGNANCY (LMP) MM DD YY QUAL.

15. OTHER DATE QUAL. MM DD YY

16. DATES PATIENT UNABLE TO WORK IN CURRENT OCCUPATION MM DD YY FROM MM DD YY TO

17. NAME OF REFERRING PROVIDER OR OTHER SOURCE

17a.

17b. NPI

18. HOSPITALIZATION DATES RELATED TO CURRENT SERVICES MM DD YY FROM MM DD YY TO

19. ADDITIONAL CLAIM INFORMATION (Designated by NUCC)

20. OUTSIDE LAB? YES NO $ CHARGES

21. DIAGNOSIS OR NATURE OF ILLNESS OR INJURY Relate A-L to service line below (24E) ICD Ind.

A. B. C. D.

E. F. G. H.

I. J. K. L.

22. RESUBMISSION CODE ORIGINAL REF. NO.

23. PRIOR AUTHORIZATION NUMBER

24. A. DATE(S) OF SERVICE From MM DD YY To MM DD YY	B. PLACE OF SERVICE	C. EMG	D. PROCEDURES, SERVICES, OR SUPPLIES (Explain Unusual Circumstances) CPT/HCPCS MODIFIER	E. DIAGNOSIS POINTER	F. $ CHARGES	G. DAYS OR UNITS	H. EPSDT Family Plan	I. ID. QUAL.	J. RENDERING PROVIDER ID. #
1								NPI	
2								NPI	
3								NPI	
4								NPI	
5								NPI	
6								NPI	

25. FEDERAL TAX I.D. NUMBER SSN EIN

26. PATIENT'S ACCOUNT NO.

27. ACCEPT ASSIGNMENT? (For govt. claims, see back) YES NO

28. TOTAL CHARGE $

29. AMOUNT PAID $

30. Rsvd for NUCC Use

31. SIGNATURE OF PHYSICIAN OR SUPPLIER INCLUDING DEGREES OR CREDENTIALS (I certify that the statements on the reverse apply to this bill and are made a part thereof.)

SIGNED DATE

32. SERVICE FACILITY LOCATION INFORMATION

a. NPI b.

33. BILLING PROVIDER INFO & PH # ( )

a. NPI b.

PHYSICIAN OR SUPPLIER INFORMATION

NUCC Instruction Manual available at: www.nucc.org *PLEASE PRINT OR TYPE*

Courtesy of the Centers for Medicare & Medicaid Services, www.cms.gov

FIGURE 4-1 Blank CMS-1500 claim (For instructional use only).

provision, such as 20 percent of the cost for services or procedures performed. (Not all health insurance plans include an out-of-pocket payments provision.)

EXAMPLE: Mary Smith's annual deductible has been met for her health insurance plan, but she is still required to pay a $20 copayment per encounter. Thus, the office staff no longer collects an annual deductible out-of-pocket payment from Mary; however, they do continue to collect a $20 copayment for each encounter (e.g., office visit).

Health insurance plans may also include a *pre-existing conditions clause*, which is used to determine patient eligibility for coverage. If the patient was treated for a medical condition prior to the effective date of health insurance coverage, the health insurance plan will not pay benefits for that particular illness. Usually, the clause expires one year after the health insurance plan's effective date. This means that the health care provided to the patient for a pre-existing condition is then covered by the health insurance plan.

NOTE: During the insurance verification and eligibility process, patient payments are determined. During the check-out process, all copayments, coinsurance, and deductibles are collected.

Management of Accounts Receivable

Accounts receivable management assists providers in the overall collection of appropriate reimbursement for services rendered, and includes the following functions:

- **Insurance verification and eligibility (confirming the patient's insurance plan and eligibility information with the third-party payer to determine the patient's financial responsibility for services rendered)**

INSURANCE VERIFICATION FORM

Patient's Last Name, First Name, Middle Initial	Patient's DOB	Patient's Mailing Address
Insurance Specialist or Office Manager's Name	Date of Call	Physician's Name
Health Insurance Plan Name	Group No.	Health Insurance Policy Number
Health Insurance Plan Effective Date	PlanID	Health Insurance Plan Termination Date

Plan Type (circle one): PPO HMO Regular Group MC Capitated WC

$ ________ Deductible Amount $ ________ Amount Not Satisfied $ ________ Copayment Amount

Percentage of Reimbursement: ________ % Coinsurance ☐ Yes ☐ No Pre-existing Clause

List plan exclusions: ________

Name of plan representative: ________

- **Patient and family counseling about insurance and payment issues (assessing patient financial requirements; advising patients and families about insurance benefits, copayments, and other financial obligations; resolving patient billing questions and complaints; adjusting accounts as necessary; and establishing financial arrangements for patients as necessary)**
- **Patient and family assistance with obtaining community resources (assisting patients in researching financial resources, housing, transportation, and medications and pharmaceutical supplies)**
- **Preauthorization of services (contacting third-party payers to obtain approval before services are provided, ensuring appropriate reimbursement)**

- **Capturing charges and posting payments (entering charges for services and procedures in the billing system, entering adjustments to patient accounts for payments received, generating balance receipts, reconciling daily work batches, preparing an audit trail, and preparing bank deposits)**
- **Billing and claims submission (completing, submitting, and processing CMS-1500 claims for payment; and researching and resolving claims payment delay issues)**
- **Account follow-up and payment resolution (reviewing explanation of benefits and remittance advice documents, contacting payers to resolve claims denials, resubmitting CMS-1500 claims, responding to payer and patient correspondence, following up on assigned accounts, and using collection techniques to maintain current accounts, including monitoring for delinquent payments)**

EXAMPLE: The patient's insurance plan has a $200 deductible, and just $100.00 has been met so far this year. The insurance specialist will inform the patient that the remaining deductible amount must be met (in addition to any copayments, coinsurance, and other out-of-pocket payments).

The patient's health insurance information is verified by the insurance specialist (or office manager) by calling the health insurance company and completing an "insurance verification form."

Completing the CMS-1500 Claim

The health insurance specialist completes the claim (e.g., identify the type of insurance, patient's sex, patient's relationship to insured, provider's federal tax identification number, and so on). The CMS-1500 claim includes several areas that require the signature of the patient and the provider. When submitting claims, "SIGNATURE ON FILE" can be substituted for the patient's signature (as long as the patient's signature is actually on file in the office). The completed claim is proofread and double-checked for accuracy (e.g., verification that a signature statement is on file, and so on). Any supporting documentation that has to be attached to the claim is copied from the patient's chart (e.g., operative report) or developed (e.g., letter delineating unlisted service provided, referred to in the CPT coding manual as a "special report").

The Privacy Act of 1974 prohibits payers from notifying providers about payment or rejection information on claims for which the provider did not accept assignment. Therefore, *providers who do not accept assignment of Medicare benefits do not receive a copy of the Medicare Summary Notice (MSN) information (called a provider remittance notice, or PRN)* that is sent to the Medicare beneficiary (patient). Information released to providers is limited to whether the claim was received, processed, and approved or denied. To assist in an appeal of a denied claim, the patient must furnish the nonparticipating provider with a copy of the MSN. In addition, a letter signed by the patient must accompany the request for review. If the beneficiary writes the appeal, the provider must supply supporting documentation (e.g., copy of patient record).

MANAGING NEW PATIENTS

The interview and check-in procedure for a patient who is new to the provider's practice is more extensive than for a returning (or established) patient. The purpose of the new patient interview and check-in procedure is to obtain information, schedule the patient for an appointment, and generate a patient record.

Basic office policies and procedures (e.g., copayments must be paid at the time of visit) should also be explained to each new patient.

NOTE: To increase office efficiency, mail new patients an information form to be completed and brought to the office 15 minutes prior to the scheduled appointment.

NOTE: For a minor child, obtain the name, address, and signature of the parent or guardian.

NOTE: Instruct the patient to bring his or her health insurance card (Figure 4-2) to the appointment because the office will need to make a copy of its front and back. The card contains the subscriber's insurance and group number, as well as payer telephone numbers and provider network information.

NOTE: The patient is responsible for copayments and/or deductibles, but does not pay more than the allowed negotiated charge.

STEP 1 Preregister the new patient who calls to schedule an appointment. After determining that the patient has contacted the appropriate office, obtain the following information:

- **Patient's name (last, first, and middle initial)**
- **Home address and telephone number**
- **Name of employer, as well as employer's address and telephone number**
- **Date of birth**
- **Guarantor (person responsible for paying the charges)**
- **Social security number**
- **Spouse's name, occupation, and place of employment**
- **Referring provider's name**
- **Emergency contact (e.g., relative), including address and telephone number**
- **Health insurance information (so the claim can be processed)**
    - **Name and phone number of health insurance company**
    - **Name of policyholder (which is the person in whose name the insurance policy is issued)**
    - **Health insurance identification number, which is sometimes the policyholder's social security number (SSN)**
    - **Health insurance group number**
    - **Whether health care treatment must be preauthorized**

Be sure to explain office policies regarding appointment cancellations, billing and collections (e.g., copayments are to be paid at the time of the office visit), and health insurance filing. Patients may ask whether the provider participates in their health insurance plan. A **participating provider (PAR)** contracts with a health insurance plan and accepts whatever the plan pays for procedures or services performed. PARs are not allowed to bill patients for the difference between the contracted rate and their normal fee.

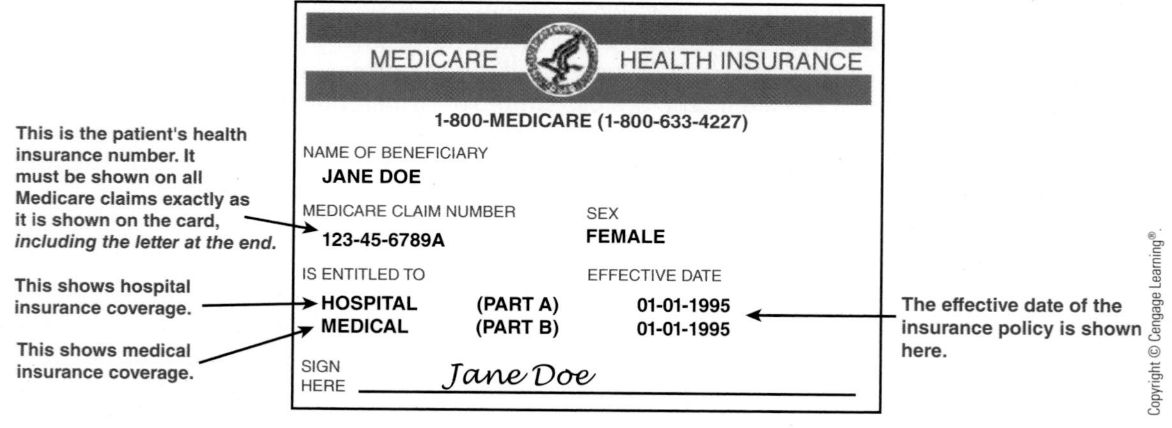
MEDICARE
HEALTH INSURANCE
1-800-MEDICARE (1-800-633-4227)
NAME OF BENEFICIARY
JANE DOE
MEDICARE CLAIM NUMBER
123-45-6789A
SEX
FEMALE
IS ENTITLED TO
EFFECTIVE DATE
HOSPITAL (PART A) 01-01-1995
MEDICAL (PART B) 01-01-1995
SIGN HERE
Jane Doe
This is the patient's health insurance number. It must be shown on all Medicare claims exactly as it is shown on the card, including the letter at the end.
This shows hospital insurance coverage.
This shows medical insurance coverage.
The effective date of the insurance policy is shown here.
Copyright © Cengage Learning®.

FIGURE 4-2 Medicare insurance card.

A **nonparticipating provider (nonPAR)** (or out-of-network provider) does not contract with the insurance plan, and patients who elect to receive care from nonPARs will incur higher out-of-pocket expenses. The patient is usually expected to pay the difference between the insurance payment and the provider's fee.

EXAMPLE 1:

Dr. Smith is a *participating provider (PAR)* for the ABC Health Insurance Plan. Kathe Bartron is treated by Dr. Smith in the office, for which a $50 fee is charged. Dr. Smith collects $10 from the patient and is reimbursed a total of $40.

PAR provider fee	$50
PAR provider contracted rate (or allowable charge)	$40
Patient copayment	- $10
Insurance payment	$30
PAR provider write-off amount	$10

EXAMPLE 2:

Dr. Jones is a *nonparticipating provider (nonPAR).* Lee Noffsker is treated by Dr. Jones in the office, for which a $50 fee is charged. Dr. Jones collects $13 ($8 + $5) from the patient and is reimbursed a total of $50 (because he does not participate in the insurance plan and can collect the difference between his fee and the patient's coinsurance plus the insurance payment).

nonPAR provider fee	$50
nonPAR allowable charge	$45
Patient copayment	- $8
Insurance payment	$37
nonPAR provider may bill patient	$5

MANAGED CARE ALERT!

Prior to scheduling an appointment with a specialist, a managed care patient must obtain a referral from the primary care provider (Figure 4-3) or case manager (i.e., preauthorization number is required). In addition, depending on the managed care plan, certain procedures and services must be preauthorized before the patient undergoes treatment.

STEP 2 **Upon arrival for the office appointment, have the patient complete a patient registration form (Figure 4-4).**

NOTE: It is fraudulent for patients to withhold information about secondary health insurance coverage, and penalties may apply.

The patient registration form is used to create the patient's financial and medical records. Be sure to carefully review the completed form for identification, financial, and medical history information. Sometimes patients do not know how to answer a question or they feel that the requested information does not apply to their situation. If information is missing, be sure to interview the patient appropriately to complete the form.

Consultation Referral Form

Date of Referral:	Payer Information:
Patient Information:	Name:
Name (Last, First, MI)	Address:
Date of Birth (MM/DD/YYYY) / Phone: ( )	
Member #:	Phone Number: ( )
Site #:	Facsimile / Data #: ( )

Primary or Requesting Provider:

Name: (Last, First, MI)		Specialty:
Institution / Group Name:	Provider ID #: 1	Provider ID #: 2 (If Required)
Address: (Street #, City, State, Zip)		
Phone Number: ( )	Facsimile / Data Number: ( )	

Consultant / Facility / Provider:

Name: (Last, First, MI)		Specialty:
Institution / Group Name:	Provider ID #: 1	Provider ID #: 2 (if Required)
Address: (Street #, City, State, Zip)		
Phone Number: ( )	Facsimile / Data Number: ( )	

Referral Information:

Reason for Referral:

Brief History, Diagnosis and Test Results: ______

______

Services Desired: Provide Care as indicated:	**Place of Service:**
☐ Initial Consultation Only	☐ Office
☐ Diagnostic Test: (specify) ______	☐ Outpatient Medical/Surgical Center*
☐ Consultation with Specific Procedures: (specify) ______	☐ Radiology ☐ Laboratory
______	☐ Inpatient Hospital*
☐ Specific Treatment: ______	☐ Extended Care Facility*
☐ Global OB Care & Delivery	☐ Other: (explain)
☐ Other: (explain) ______	*(Specific Facility Must Be Named)

Number of visits: (If blank, 1 visit is assumed)	Authorization #: (If Required)	Referral Is Valid Until: (Date) (See Payer Instructions)
Signature: (Individual Completing This Form)		Authorizing Signature (If Required)

Referral certification is not a guarantee of payment. Payment of benefits is subject to a member's eligibility on the date that the service is rendered and to any other contractual provisions of the plan.

White: Payer • Yellow: Primary or Requesting Provider • Pink: Consultant / Facility / Provider • Goldenrod: Patient

See Health Care Plan Manual For Specific Instructions.

FIGURE 4-3 Sample consultation referral form.

> **NOTE:** Generate a separate financial record and medical record for each patient.

STEP 3 Photocopy the front and back of the patient's insurance identification card(s), and file the copy in the patient's financial record.

STEP 4 Confirm the patient's insurance information and eligibility status by contacting the payer via telephone, Internet, or fax. (Payer contact information can be found on the insurance card.) Collect copayment from the patient.

> **NOTE:** Steps in this chapter apply to both computerized and noncomputerized practices. The ✓ icon identifies steps completed for computerized practices only.

STEP 5 ✓ Enter all information using computer data entry software. Verify information with the patient or subscriber, and make appropriate changes.

When the patient has more than one policy, perform a coordination of benefits (COB) to be sure the patient has correctly determined which policy is primary,

DOCTORS GROUP • MAIN STREET • ALFRED, NY 12345 **PATIENT REGISTRATION FORM**

PATIENT INFORMATION

Last Name	First Name	Middle Name
Street	City	State/Zip Code
Patient's Date of Birth	Social Security Number	Home Phone Number
Student Status ☐ Full-time ☐ Part-time	Employment Status ☐ Full-time ☐ Part-time ☐ Unemployed	Marital Status ☐ Single ☐ Married ☐ Separated ☐ Divorced ☐ Widowed
Sex ☐ Male ☐ Female	Name/Address of Employer	Occupation
Employer Phone Number	Referred by	
Emergency Contact	Address	Telephone Number
Visit is related to on-the-job injury ☐ No ☐ Yes Date: ____	Prior treatment received for injury ☐ No ☐ Yes Doctor: ____	WC Number: ____

Visit is related to automobile accident ☐ No ☐ Yes Date: ____ Name & Address of Insurance Company/Policy Number

GUARANTOR'S BILLING INFORMATION

Last Name	First Name	Middle Name
Street	City	State/Zip Code
Relationship to Patient	Social Security Number	Home Phone Number
Employer	Employer Address	Employer Phone Number

INSURANCE INFORMATION

PRIMARY INSURED INFORMATION			SECONDARY INSURED INFORMATION		
Last Name	First Name/Middle Initial		Last Name	First Name/Middle Initial	
Address	City/State/Zip Code		Address	City/State/Zip Code	
Relationship to Insured ☐ Self ☐ Spouse ☐ Child ☐ Other			Relationship to Insured ☐ Self ☐ Spouse ☐ Child ☐ Other		
Sex ☐ Male ☐ Female			Sex ☐ Male ☐ Female		
Insured's Date of Birth	Home Phone Number		Insured's Date of Birth	Home Phone Number	
Name and Address of Insurance Company			Name and Address of Insurance Company		
Insured Identification Number	Group Number	Effective Date	Insured Identification Number	Group Number	Effective Date
Name of Employer Sponsoring Plan			Name of Employer Sponsoring Plan		

CONSENT TO PAYMENT

I have listed all health insurance plans from which I may receive benefits. I hereby authorize payment of medical benefits bill ed to my insurance to the Doctors Group. I hereby accept responsibility for payment for any service(s) provided to me that is not covered by my insurance. I also accept responsibility for fees that exceed the payment made by my insurance, if the Doctors Group does not participate with my insurance. I agree to pay all copayments, coinsurance, and deductibles at the time services are rendered. I, (Patient's Name), hereby authorize the Doctors Group to use and/or disclose my health information which specifically identifies me or which can reasonably be used to identify me to carry out my treatment, payment, and health care operations.

I understand that while this consent is voluntary, if I refuse to sign this consent, the Doctors Group can refuse to treat me.

I have been informed that the Doctors Group has prepared a notice ("Notice") that more fully describes the uses and disclosures that can be made of my individually identifiable health information for treatment, payment and health care operations. I understand that I have the right to review such Notice prior to signing this consent. I understand that I may revoke this consent at any time by notifying the Doctors Group, in writing, but if I revoke my consent, such revocation will not affect any actions that the Doctors Group took before receiving my revocation.

I understand that the Doctors Group has reserved the right to change his/her privacy practices and that I can obtain such changed notice upon request. I understand that I have the right to request that the Doctors Group restrict how my individually identifiable health information is used and/or disclosed to carry out treatment, payment or health operations. I understand that the Doctors Group does not have to agree to such restrictions, but that once such restrictions are agreed to, the Doctors Group must adhere to such restrictions.

Signature of Patient or Patient's Representative ____ Date ____

Printed Name of Patient: ____ Relationship of representative to patient: ____

FIGURE 4-4 Sample patient registration form.

secondary, and so on. The determination of primary or secondary status for patients with two or more commercial policies is different for adults than for children.

- ***Adult patient named as policyholder:*** **The patient is the policyholder.**
- ***Adult patient named as dependent on policy:*** **The patient is a dependent on the insurance policy.**

NOTE: Per HIPAA privacy standards, when contacting the payer to verify insurance eligibility and benefit status, be prepared to provide the following information:

- Beneficiary's last name and first initial
- Beneficiary's date of birth
- Beneficiary's health insurance claim number (HICN)
- Beneficiary's gender

EXAMPLE: Mary Jones works for Alfred State College and is enrolled in the group health insurance's family plan. She is named as the primary policyholder on this plan. Her husband, Bill, is a full-time college student and is named as a dependent on Mary's health insurance plan. (Bill does not have other health insurance coverage.)

NOTE: Certain insurance plans are always considered primary to other plans (e.g., workers' compensation insurance is primary to an employee's group health care plan if the employee is injured on the job). These situations are discussed in Chapters 12 to 17.

- ***Primary versus secondary insurance:*** **Primary insurance is the insurance plan responsible for paying health care insurance claims first. Secondary insurance is the insurance plan that is billed after the primary insurance plan has paid its contracted amount (e.g., 80 percent of billed charges) and the provider's office has received a remittance advice from the primary payer. (Depending on office policy, providers may be required to submit secondary claims to Medicare.)**
- **Provider offices should share with patients their policy about submitting claims to a secondary payer, which is often courtesy service because providers are often not required to submit claims to secondary payers. Larger provider group practices might employ insurance specialists who process secondary payer claims, but smaller group practices often require patients to submit secondary claims because projected reimbursement may not justify employing dedicated staff for such processing (even though such processing results in faster reimbursement by secondary payers).**
- **When the patient is responsible for submitting claims to secondary payers, they are responsible for submitting an explanation of benefits (EOB) received from the primary payer. The EOB communicates to the secondary payer the reimbursement amount the provider received from the primary payer; then, the secondary payer calculates any additional reimbursement to be paid to the provider (or to the patient).**
- **Both primary insurance and secondary insurance plans provide reimbursement for qualified procedures or services only, which are those that meet medical necessity. If the patient's primary payer denies coverage due to a determination that procedures and services were not covered (because they did not meet medical necessity provisions), the secondary payer is likely to do the same. When patients are covered by group health insurance plans (e.g., employer plans), reimbursement cannot exceed the total cost of procedures and services rendered.**

EXAMPLE: Cindy Thomas has two health insurance policies, a group insurance plan through her full-time employer and another group insurance plan through her husband's employer. Cindy's plan through her own employer is primary, and the plan through her husband's employer is secondary. When Cindy receives health care services at her doctor's office, the office first submits the insurance claim to Cindy's employer's health plan; once that health plan has paid, the insurance claim can be submitted to Cindy's secondary insurance (her husband's group insurance plan).

NOTE: Total reimbursement cannot exceed the total charges for health care services rendered by Cindy's doctor.

- ***Child of divorced parents:*** **The custodial parent's plan is primary. If the parents are remarried, the custodial parent's plan is primary, the custodial stepparent's plan**

is secondary, and the noncustodial parent's plan is tertiary (third). An exception is made if a court order specifies that a particular parent must cover the child's medical expenses.

- ***Child living with both parents:*** **If each parent subscribes to a different health insurance plan, the primary and secondary policies are determined by applying the birthday rule. Physician office staff must obtain the birth date of each policyholder because the** **birthday rule** **states that the policyholder whose birth month and day occurs earlier in the calendar year holds the primary policy for dependent children. The year of birth is not considered when applying the birthday rule determination. If the policyholders have identical birthdays, the policy in effect the longest is considered primary.**

> **EXAMPLE 1:** A child is listed as a dependent on both his father's and his mother's group policy. Which policy is primary?
>
> Mother—birthdate 03/06/89—works for IBM
>
> Father—birthdate 03/20/87—works for General Motors
>
> **Answer:** The mother's policy is primary; her birthday is earlier in the calendar year.

> **EXAMPLE 2:** A child is listed as a dependent on his father's group health insurance policy and his mother's group health insurance policy. The father was born on 01/01/86, and the mother was born on 03/04/85. Which policy is considered primary?
>
> **Answer:** The father's policy is primary because his birthday is earlier in the calendar year.

> **EXAMPLE 3:** A dependent child is covered by both parents' group policies. The parents were born on the same month, day, and year. Which policy is primary?
>
> The father's policy took effect 03/06/86.
>
> The mother's policy took effect 09/06/92.
>
> **Answer:** The father's policy is primary because it has been in effect six years longer.

> **NOTE:** Determination of primary and secondary coverage for one or more government-sponsored programs is discussed in detail in the respective Medicare, Medicaid, and TRICARE chapters.

- ***Gender rule:*** **Some self-funded health care plans use the *gender rule*, which states that the father's plan is always primary when a child is covered by both parents. This provision can cause problems if one parent's coverage uses the *birthday rule* and the other uses the *gender rule*. Be sure to contact the health plan administrators to determine which rule to follow.**

> **NOTE:** At this point, clinical assessment and/or treatment of the patient is performed, after which the provider documents all current and pertinent diagnoses, services rendered, and special follow-up instructions on the encounter form. The medical record and encounter form are then returned to the employee responsible for checking out patients.

STEP 6 Create a new patient's medical record.

STEP 7 Generate the patient's encounter form.

The **encounter form** (Figure 4-5) is the financial record source document used by health care providers and other personnel to record treated diagnoses and services rendered to the patient during the current encounter. In the physician's office, it is also called a **superbill**; in the hospital it is called a **chargemaster**.

ENCOUNTER FORM

Tel: (101) 555-1111	Kim Donaldson, M.D.	EIN: 11-9876543
Fax: (101) 555-2222	INTERNAL MEDICINE	NPI: 1234567890
	101 Main Street, Suite A	
	Alfred, NY 14802	

OFFICE VISITS	NEW	EST	OFFICE PROCEDURES		INJECTIONS	
❑ Level I	99201	99211	❑ EKG with interpretation	93000	❑ Influenza virus vaccine	____
❑ Level II	99202	99212	❑ Oximetry with interpretation	94760	❑ Admin of Influenza vaccine	G0008
❑ Level III	99203	99213	**LABORATORY TESTS**		❑ Pneumococcal vaccine	90732
❑ Level IV	99204	99214	❑ Blood, occult (feces)	82270	❑ Admin of pneumococcal vaccine	G0009
❑ Level V	99205	99215	❑ Skin test, Tb, intradermal (PPD)	86580	❑ Hepatitis B vaccine	90746
					❑ Admin of Hepatitis B vaccine	G0010
					❑ Tetanus toxoid vaccine	90703
					❑ Immunization administration	90471

DIAGNOSIS

❑ Abnormal heart sounds	R00.9	❑ Chronic ischemic heart disease	I25.9	❑ Hypertension	I10
❑ Abdominal pain	R10.8__	❑ Chronic obstructive lung disease	J44.9	❑ Hormone replacement	Z79.890
❑ Abnormal feces	R19.5	❑ Congestive heart failure	I50.9	❑ Hyperlipidemia	E78.5
❑ Allergic rhinitis	J30.9	❑ Cough	R05	❑ Hyperthyroidism	E05.9__
❑ Anemia, pernicious	D51.0	❑ Depressive disorder	F32.9	❑ Influenza	J11.1
❑ Anxiety	F41.9	❑ Diabetes mellitus, type 2	E11.___	❑ Loss of weight	R63.4
❑ Asthma	J45.909	❑ Diarrhea	R19.7	❑ Nausea	R11.0
❑ Atrophy, cerebral	G31.9	❑ Dizziness	R42	❑ Nausea with vomiting	R11.2
❑ B-12 deficiency	D51.9	❑ Emphysema	J43.__	❑ Pneumonia	J18.__
❑ Back pain	M54.9	❑ Fatigue	R53.83	❑ Sore throat	J02.9
❑ Bronchitis	J40	❑ Fever	R50.9	❑ Vaccine, hepatitis B	Z23
❑ Cardiovascular disease	I25.1__	❑ Gastritis	K29.50	❑ Vaccine, influenza	Z23
❑ Cervicalgia	M54.2	❑ Heartburn	R12	❑ Vaccine, pneumococcus	Z23
❑ Chest pain	R07.9	❑ Hematuria	R31.9	❑ Vaccine, tetanus toxoid	Z23
❑	____	❑	____	❑	____

PATIENT IDENTIFICATION		FINANCIAL TRANSACTION DATA	
PATIENT NAME:		INVOICE NO.	
PATIENT NUMBER:		ACCOUNT NO.	
DATE OF BIRTH:		TOTAL FOR SERVICE:	$
ENCOUNTER DATE		AMOUNT RECEIVED:	$
DATE OF SERVICE:	/ /	PAID BY:	❑ Cash ❑ Check ❑ Credit Card
RETURN VISIT DATE			
DATE OF RETURN VISIT:	/ /	CASHIER'S INITIALS:	

FIGURE 4-5 Sample encounter form.

CODING TIP:

A short blank line is located after some of the codes in the encounter form (Figure 4-5) to allow entry of additional character(s) to report the specific ICD-10-CM diagnosis code. Medicare administrative contractors reject claims with missing, invalid, or incomplete diagnosis codes.

The minimum information entered on the form at this time is the date of service, patient's name, and balance due on the account.

Attach the encounter form to the front of the patient's medical record so that it is available for clinical staff when the patient is escorted to the treatment area.

If patient scheduling is performed on the computer, generate encounter forms for all patients scheduled on a given day by selecting the "print encounter forms" function from the computer program.

MANAGING ESTABLISHED PATIENTS

STEP 1 **Depending on the provider's plan of treatment, either schedule a return appointment when checking out the patient or when the patient contacts the office.**

> **EXAMPLE:** The highlighted phrase in this example indicates that a follow-up visit is scheduled only if the patient contacts the office.
>
> S: Patient states that her stomach hurts and she has been vomiting.
>
> O: Abdominal exam reveals mild tenderness. Her throat is red.
>
> A: Flu.
>
> P: Bed rest. Return to office if symptoms worsen.
>
> (SOAP notes are typically used in a provider's office to document patient visits. S = subjective, O = objective, A = assessment, and P = plan. SOAP notes are discussed in Chapter 10.)

MANAGED CARE ALERT!

Approximately one week prior to an appointment with a specialist for nonemergency services, the status of preauthorization for care must be verified. If the preauthorization has expired, the patient's nonemergency appointment may have to be postponed until the required treatment reports have been filed with the primary care provider or case manager and a new preauthorization for additional treatment has been obtained.

NOTE: Once clinical assessment and/or treatment has been completed, the patient enters the postclinical phase of the visit. Services and diagnosis(es) are selected on the encounter form, and the patient's medical record and encounter form are given to the employee responsible for checking out patients.

STEP 2 **Verify the patient's registration information when the patient registers at the front desk.**

As the cost of health care increases and competition for subscribers escalates among insurers, many employers who pay a portion of health care costs for their employees purchase health insurance contracts that cover only a three- or six-month period. Therefore, it is important to ask all returning (or established) patients if there have been any changes in their name, address, phone number, employer, or insurance plan. If the answer is yes, a new registration form should be completed and the computerized patient database should be updated.

STEP 3 **Collect copayment from the patient.**

STEP 4 **Generate an encounter form for the patient's current visit.**

Attach the encounter form to the front of the patient's medical record so it is available for clinical staff when the patient is escorted to the treatment area.

MANAGING OFFICE INSURANCE FINANCES

The following procedures are the same for new and established patients.

STEP 1 **Assign CPT and HCPCS level II (national) codes to procedures and services, and assign ICD-10-CM codes to diagnoses documented on the encounter form. (Coding is discussed in Chapters 6 to 8.)**

CODING TIP:

Make sure that diagnoses, procedures, and services selected on the encounter form are documented in the patient's medical record before reporting codes on the insurance claim.

NOTE: Practice management software makes use of the patient ledger and manual daily accounts receivable journal (or day sheet) obsolete. However, discussion about these items, with figures, is included to familiarize students with them in the event that they are required to use them on the job.

STEP 2 **Use the completed encounter form to determine the charges for procedures performed and/or services provided, and total all charges.**

STEP 3 **Post all charges to the patient's ledger/account record and the daily accounts receivable journal, either manually or using practice management software.**

The **patient ledger** (Figure 4-6), known as the **patient account record** (Figure 4-7) in a computerized system, is a permanent record of all financial transactions

BC/BS R2345678 STATEMENT PATIENT, IMA

IMA PATIENT
900 RANDELL RD
ANYWHERE, MD 20000

DATE	CODE	DESCRIPTION	CHARGE	CREDITS PAYMENTS	CREDITS ADJ	CURRENT BALANCE
		BALANCE FOR WARD →				30 -
5/23/YYYY		ROA per ck		30 -		0
6/25/YYYY	99213	OV copayment per check	38 -	15 -		0
6/25/YYYY		BCBS billed	23 -			23 -
8/1/YYYY		BCBS check		23 -		0 -

PLEASE PAY LAST AMOUNT IN THIS COLUMN

OV — Office Visit
OS — Office Surgery
TC — Telephone Consultation
FA — Failed Appointment
RP — Report

HOSP — Hospital Visit
HS — Hospital Surgery
SA — Surgical Assistant
SC — Surgical Consultation
ER — Emergency Room

ROA — Received on Account
NC — No Charge
INS — Insurance

THIS IS A COPY OF YOUR ACCOUNT AS IT APPEARS ON YOUR LEDGER CARD.

FIGURE 4-6 Sample patient ledger card.

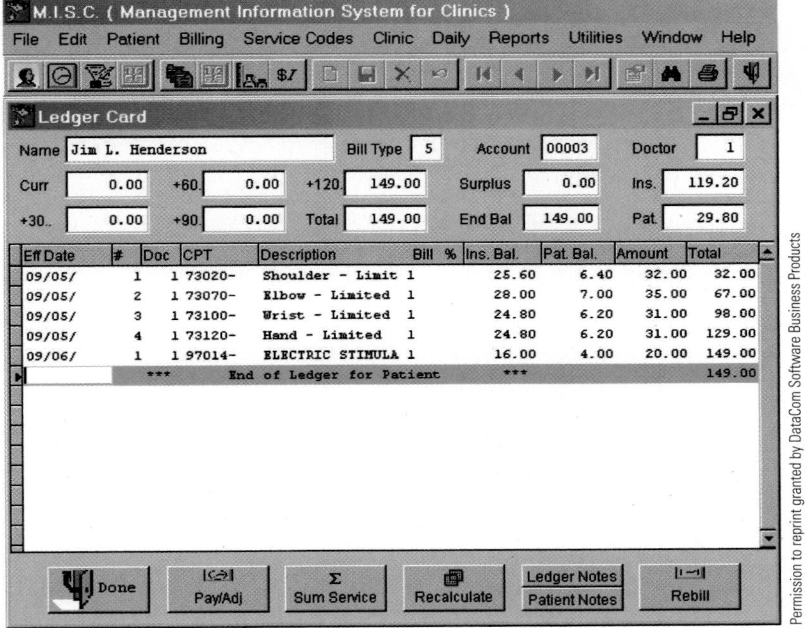

FIGURE 4-7 Sample patient account record generated from practice management software.

between the patient and the practice. The charges, along with personal or third-party payments, are all posted on the patient's account.

Each procedure performed must be individually described and priced on the patient's ledger/account record.

The **manual daily accounts receivable journal**, also known as the **day sheet**, is a chronologic summary of all transactions posted to individual patient ledgers/accounts on a specific day (Figure 4-8).

STEP 4 Complete the insurance claim.

Review completed claims prior to submission to ensure accuracy.

> **EXAMPLE:** Barbara was reviewing a recently completed claim for newborn care when she noticed that the patient (policyholder) was 58 years old. Upon further review, Barbara discovered that during her pregnancy the policyholder's daughter was providing her mother's insurance information. The result was the denial of all previous claims paid to the provider, and the provider was required to pay back all reimbursement paid by the payer. Although the provider was allowed to bill the patient for unpaid claims, the patient was unable to pay and the account was submitted to collections for processing.

STEP 5 Attach supporting documentation to the claim (e.g., copies of operative reports, pathology reports, and written authorization). ✓ For electronic claims, check with the payer to determine how to submit attachments (e.g., fax, postal mail, scanned image).

DATE 6/25/YYYY

DAY SHEET

	PT. NAME	DESCRIPTION	OLD BAL.	CHARGE	PAYMENT	NEW BAL.
1.	Patient, Ima	OV-99213 per ck	0	38 —	38 —	0
2.						
3.						
4.						
5.						
6.						
7.						
8.						
9.						
10.						
11.						
20.						
21.						
22.						
		TOTALS				

PROOF
Old Bal. ______
+ Charges ______
- Payments ______
= New Bal. ______

FIGURE 4-8 Sample day sheet with one patient entry.

NOTE: In July 2000, federal electronic signature legislation was enacted. Physicians who contract with government and/or managed care plans are considered to have valid signatures on file.

STEP 6 Obtain the provider's signature on the claim, if manually processed. Special arrangements may be made with some payers to allow the provider's name to be keyboarded or a signature stamp to be used. No signature is possible on electronic claims.

STEP 7 File a copy of the claim and copies of the attachment(s) in the practice's insurance files. ✓ Electronic claims are stored in the computer.

STEP 8 Log completed claims in an insurance registry (Figure 4-9). Be sure to include the date the claim was filed with the insurance payer. ✓ For computerized

INSURANCE CLAIMS REGISTRY

Date Filed	Patient Name	Insurance Company	Unusual Procedure Reported	Amount Due	Amount Paid
6/13/YYYY	Patient, Ima	BC/BS FEP	n/a	$ 38.00	

FIGURE 4-9 Insurance claim registry.

claims processing, medical practice management software should generate a claims log.

STEP 9 **Mail or electronically send the claims to the third-party payer.**

STEP 10 **Post payment(s) to the patient's account.**

The source of each payment should be identified, either as third-party payment (e.g., name of payer and payment type) or patient's payment (e.g., cash, check, credit card, money order, personal check). (Refer to the 5/23/YYYY entry in Figure 4-6.)

NOTE: *Copayments* (fixed payment amounts for an office visit, outpatient encounter, or outpatient surgery) are obtained from the patient at the beginning or end of the encounter, depending on office policy. *Coinsurance* amounts may be billed to patients after services are provided.

STEP 11 **Bill the patient for the coinsurance or copayment amounts not paid at the start or end of the encounter.**

The patient's health insurance policy may stipulate a coinsurance payment (e.g., 20 percent of charges) or a copayment (e.g., $20). Health care providers bill patients for coinsurance amounts after reimbursement from the third-party payer has been received and posted.

HINT:

To save the expense of mailing invoices, ask patients to pay their portion of the bill as they depart the office.

NOTE: Electronic data interchange (EDI) content is located on page 78 of this chapter.

INSURANCE CLAIM LIFE CYCLE

The life cycle of a claim consists of four stages (Figure 4-10):

- **Claims submission and electronic data interchange (EDI)**
- **Claims processing**
- **Claims adjudication**
- **Payment**

For claims assigned a "pending status" by the payer, the provider can respond by correcting errors and omissions on the claim and resubmitting for reconsideration.

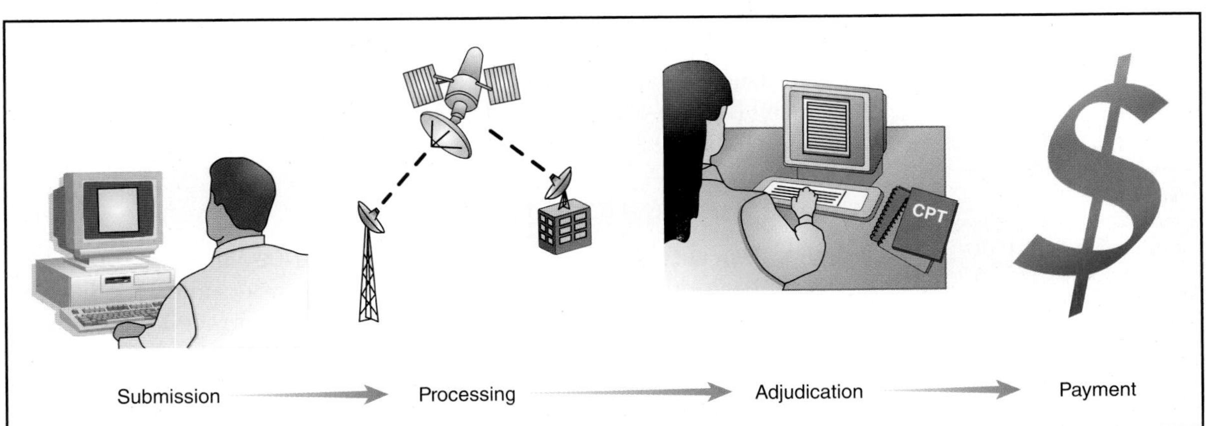

FIGURE 4-10 Life cycle of an insurance claim.

When the claim is denied (or rejected), the provider can appeal the payer's decision and resubmit the claim for reconsideration, attaching supporting documentation to justify procedures or services provided.

NOTE: Providers can purchase software from a vendor, contract with a billing service or clearinghouse that will provide software or programming support, or use HIPAA-compliant free billing software that is supplied by Medicare administrative contractors.

Claims Submission and Electronic Data Interchange (EDI)

The American Medical Billing Association (AMBA) estimates that more than six billion insurance claims are filed each year (around 500 million claims each month) and just 40 percent are filed electronically. About 60 percent are filed manually (on a paper-based CMS-1500 claim). Medicare alone receives more than 500 million claims per year.

Courtesy of the American

NOTE: Health care clearinghouses perform centralized claims processing for providers and health care plans. They receive claims from providers, transmit claims to payers, receive remittance advice and payment instructions from payers, and transmit that information to providers (all in a HIPAA-compliant format). A health care clearinghouse also conducts eligibility and claim status queries in the format prescribed by HIPAA.

The life cycle of an insurance claim begins in the provider's office when the health insurance specialist completes CMS-1500 claims using medical management software. **Claims submission** is the electronic or manual transmission of claims data to payers or clearinghouses for processing. A **clearinghouse** is a public or private entity that processes or facilitates the processing of nonstandard data elements (e.g., paper claim) into standard data elements (e.g., electronic claim). Clearinghouses also convert standard transactions (e.g., electronic remittance advice) received from payers to nonstandard formats (e.g., remittance advice that looks like an explanation of benefits) so providers can read them. Clearinghouses use secure networks to receive and remit electronic transactions that flow among payers, providers, and employees. A **value-added network (VAN)** is a clearinghouse that involves value-added vendors, such as banks, in the processing of claims. Using a VAN is more efficient and less expensive for providers than managing their own systems to send and receive transactions directly from numerous entities.

When selecting a clearinghouse, it is important to determine which one processes a majority of claims for health plans billed by the provider. Although a provider might be able to contract with just one clearinghouse *if a health plan does not require submission of claims to a specific clearinghouse*, some plans have established their own clearinghouses, and providers must submit claims to them. Clearinghouses typically charge providers a start-up fee, a monthly flat fee, and/or a per-claim transaction fee based on volume. They also offer additional services, such as claims status tracking, insurance eligibility determination, and secondary billing services. (Providers may also want to determine whether a clearinghouse is accredited by the **Electronic Healthcare Network Accreditation Commission [EHNAC]**.)

Clearinghouses process claims in an electronic flat file format, which requires conversion of CMS-1500 claims data to a standard format. Providers can also use software to convert claims to an **electronic flat file format** (or **electronic media claim**) (Figure 4-11), which is a series of fixed-length records (e.g., 25 spaces for patient's name) submitted to payers as a bill for health care services.

NOTE: **ANSI ASC X12** is an electronic format standard that uses a variable length file format to process transactions for institutional, professional, dental, and drug claims. The ANSI organization facilitates the development of standards for health informatics and other industries (e.g., international exchange of goods and services).

Electronic Data Interchange (EDI)

Electronic data interchange (EDI) is the computer-to-computer transfer of data between providers and third-party payers (or providers and health care clearinghouses) in a data format agreed upon by sending and receiving parties. HIPAA's administrative simplification provisions directed the federal government to adopt national electronic standards for the automated transfer of certain health care data among health care payers (e.g., Medicare administrative contractors), payers (e.g., BCBS), and providers (e.g., hospitals, physicians). These provisions enable the entire health care industry to communicate electronic data using a

```
MSG_HDR|BCBS|ECM_Y06|SndApp|SndFac|RcApp|RcFac|YYYY01052369|56941
INS_CLM||||562697|YYYY0105|YYYY0110|ADLO5691|125.00
PRV_DT1|M_P|Smith|DKSL23659
PRV_DT1|M_H|Jones|DLEP65915
PAT_IDF|DCB5432|Green|19941205
CRD_STS|Y|Y|N
SRV_CMN|GM|YYYY0105|50.00
SRV_FEE|CP|45.00
SRV_FEE|CK|12.00
SRV_CMN|GM|YYYY0106|55.00
SRV_FEE|CO|10.00
SRV_FEE|RK|
```


FIGURE 4-11 Sample electronic flat file format.

single set of standards. Health care providers submit standard transactions for eligibility, authorization, referrals, claims, or attachments to any payer. This "simplifies" clinical, billing, and other financial applications and reduces costs. Three electronic formats are supported for health care claims transactions:

- **UB-04 flat file format**
- **National Standard Format (NSF)**
- **ANSI ASC X12 837 format (American National Standards Institute, Accredited Standards Committee, Insurance Subcommittee X12, claims validation table 837)**

NOTE: Electronic claims data submission has almost entirely replaced the paper-based claims processing.

The Health Insurance Portability and Accountability Act of 1996 (HIPAA) mandated national standards for the electronic exchange of administrative and financial health care transactions (e.g., CMS-1500 claim) to improve the efficiency and effectiveness of the health care system. Standards were adopted for the following transactions:

- **Eligibility for a health plan**
- **Enrollment and disenrollment in a health plan**
- **First report of injury**
- **Health care payment and remittance advice**
- **Health claim status**
- **Health claims and equivalent encounter information**
- **Health claims attachments**
- **Health plan premium payments**
- **Referral certification and authorization**
- **Coordination of benefits (COB)**

NOTE: *Computer-generated paper claims are not considered electronic data interchange (EDI).* Providers that generate paper-based claims submit them to health care clearinghouses, which convert them to a standardized electronic format for submission to payers.

Covered entities (Figure 4-12) are required to use mandated national standards when conducting any of the defined transactions covered under HIPAA. **Covered entities** include all private-sector health plans (excluding certain small self-administered health plans); managed care organizations; ERISA-covered health benefit plans (those covered by the Employee Retirement Income Security Act of 1974); government health plans (including Medicare, Medicaid, Military Health System for active duty and civilian personnel, Veterans Health Administration, and Indian Health Service programs); all health care

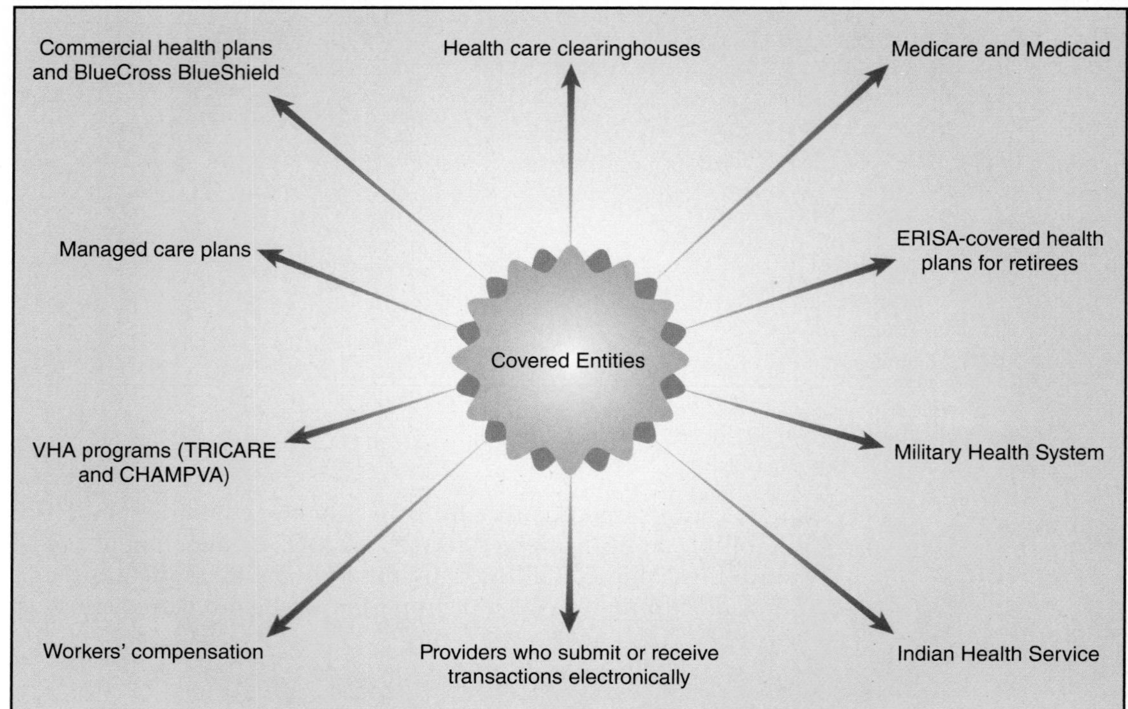

FIGURE 4-12 Covered entities.

clearinghouses; and all health care providers that choose to submit or receive these transactions electronically.

> **NOTE:** HIPAA's health care transaction standards require covered entities to submit electronic transactions using the same format. HIPAA *does not require* providers to submit transactions electronically, but DHHS suggests that providers may want to adopt the electronic transaction standards so that they can benefit from reductions in the costs and administrative burdens of health care.

Implementation of the HIPAA health care transaction standards has caused concern among providers, especially small physician practices that are not computerized or do not currently submit electronic claims. It is important to understand that only those providers that submit electronic claims are required to comply with the transaction standards. If the provider's office uses paper CMS-1500 claims, that office usually contracts with a health care clearinghouse to conduct standard electronic transactions. The administrative simplification provisions of HIPAA were passed with the support of the health care industry, which believed that standards would lower the cost and administrative burdens of health care. Industry members needed the federal government's help to establish a uniform way of processing transactions. In the past, providers had to submit transactions in whatever format the particular health plan required. Health plans could not agree on a standard without giving their competitors a (short-term) market advantage.

The American Medical Billing Association delineates the following advantages of electronic claims processing:

- **Reduction in payment turnaround time by shortening payment cycle**
- **Reduction in claims submission error rates to 1 to 2 percent**

Paper claims that can contain errors result in payment delays, and approximately 30 to 35 percent of all paper claims are rejected due to errors and omissions. Electronic claims are submitted directly to the payer after being checked for accuracy by billing software or a health care clearinghouse, and this audit/edit process reduces the normal rejection rate to 1 to 2 percent. The audit/edit process results in a **clean claim**, which contains all required data elements needed to process and pay the claim (e.g., valid diagnosis and procedure/service codes, modifiers, and so on). In addition, if an electronic claim is rejected due to an error or omission, the provider is notified more quickly than with paper claims, and the claim can be edited and resubmitted for processing.

Electronic claims are submitted using the following transmission media:

- ***Dial-up*** **(telephone line or digital subscriber line [DSL] is used for claims submission, and providers install software on office computers)**
- ***Extranet*** **(direct submission of claims to payers using Internet technology that emulates a system connection; provider can access information about collaborating parties only, such as payer and patient data elements)**
- ***Internet*** **(secure transmission of claims over the Internet, eliminating the need for additional software)**
- ***Magnetic tape, disc, or compact disc media*** **(physical movement of transmissions from one location to another using media)**

NOTE: Claims submitted via facsimile (fax) are not electronic transmissions because the information exchanged did not exist in electronic form before the transmission.

ELECTRONIC SUBMISSION OF MEDICARE CLAIMS BY PROVIDERS

The insurance claim is electronically transmitted in data "packets" (called batches) from the provider's computer modem to the Medicare administrative contractor's modem over a telephone line. Medicare administrative contractors perform a series of initial edits (called front-end edits or pre-edits), which determine whether the claims in a batch meet basic requirements of the HIPAA standard. If errors are detected at this level, the entire batch of claims is rejected and returned to the provider for correction and resubmission. Claims that pass initial edits are re-edited to compare data with implementation guide requirements in those HIPAA claim standards. If errors are detected at this level, individual claims containing errors are rejected and returned to the payer for correction and resubmission. Once the claim has passed the first two levels of edits, each claim undergoes a third editing process for compliance with Medicare coverage and payment policy requirements. Edits at this level could result in rejection of individual claims and be returned to the provider for correction. If individual claims are denied, the reason for the denial is communicated to the provider. Upon successful transmission of claims, an acknowledgement report is generated and either transmitted to the provider or placed in an electronic mailbox for downloading by the provider.

Claims Attachments

A **claims attachment** is a set of supporting documentation or information associated with a health care claim or patient encounter. Claims attachment information can be found in the remarks or notes fields of an electronic claim or paper-based claim forms. Claims attachments are used for:

- **Medical evaluation for payment**
- **Past payment audit or review**
- **Quality control to ensure access to care and quality of care**

NOTE: Claims are sometimes delayed or rejected because the payer needs to obtain a copy of patient records for review prior to making a determination. In this situation, the provider is notified of the request for information and has an opportunity to submit supporting documentation from the record to justify the medical necessity of procedures or services performed. This delay in claims processing can sometimes be avoided if the practice contacts payers to request a list of CPT and HCPCS level II codes that require supporting documentation.

EXAMPLE: CPT modifiers are reported on claims to provide clarification about procedures and services performed, and they are entered as two-digit numbers. Providers that submit supporting documentation when reporting the following modifiers on claims assist the payer in making payment determinations:

- –22 (Increased Procedural Services)
- –53 (Discontinued Procedure)
- –59 (Distinct Procedural Service)

EXAMPLE: When a provider performs a procedure for which there is no CPT or HCPCS level II code and an unlisted code is reported on the claim, supporting documentation must be submitted (e.g., copy of operative report).

HIPAA ALERT!

Traditionally, claims attachments containing medical documentation that supported procedures and services reported on claims were copied from patient records and mailed to payers. Effective 2006, providers submit electronic attachments with electronic claims or send electronic attachments in response to requests for medical documentation to support claims submitted (e.g., scanned images of paper records).

How to Avoid Resubmitting Claims

In April 2002, the American Association of Health Plans (AAHP) and the National Specialty Society Insurance Coalition met with health plans and medical specialty societies to discuss claims submission concerns. A work group, which included representatives from health plans, the Healthcare Financial Management Association (HFMA), hospitals, and physician specialty organizations, was created to improve administrative processes and claims processing; among other things, the group identified ways that health plans and providers could improve claims submission processes. The result was the development of "tools & tips" documents that can assist health plans and providers to improve claims processing efficiency by decreasing duplicate, ineligible, and delayed claims.

Delayed claims contain incomplete and inaccurate information. Although hospitals and large group practices collect data about these problems and address them, smaller provider practices often do not have the tools to evaluate their claims submission processes. A major reason for delays in claims processing is incompleteness or inaccuracy of the information necessary to coordinate benefits among multiple payers. If the remittance advice from the primary payer is not attached to the claim submitted to the secondary payer, delays will also result. **Coordination of benefits (COB)** is a provision in group health insurance policies intended to keep multiple insurers from paying benefits covered by other policies; it also specifies that coverage will be provided in a specific sequence when more than one policy covers the claim. Some payers electronically transfer data to facilitate the coordination of benefits on a submitted claim. (Medicare calls this concept "crossover.") Becoming educated about how to correctly process claims for crossover patients will reduce payment delays and improve accounts receivable.

NOTE: Edits and validation at the claims processing stage are limited to verification of insured status, patient identification number and demographic information, provider identification number, and the like. If analysis of the claim reveals incorrect or missing information that cannot be edited by the claims examination, the claim is rejected and returned to the provider. The provider can correct the errors and omissions and resubmit the claim for processing.

Claims Processing

Claims processing involves sorting claims upon submission to collect and verify information about the patient and provider (Figure 4-13). Clearinghouses and payers use software to automate the scanning and imaging functions associated with claims processing. Scanning technology "reads" the information reported on the claim and converts it to an image so that claims examiners can analyze, edit, and validate the data. The claims examiner views the image (or electronic data if submitted in that format) on a split computer screen (Figure 4-14) that contains the claim on the top half and information verification software on the bottom half.

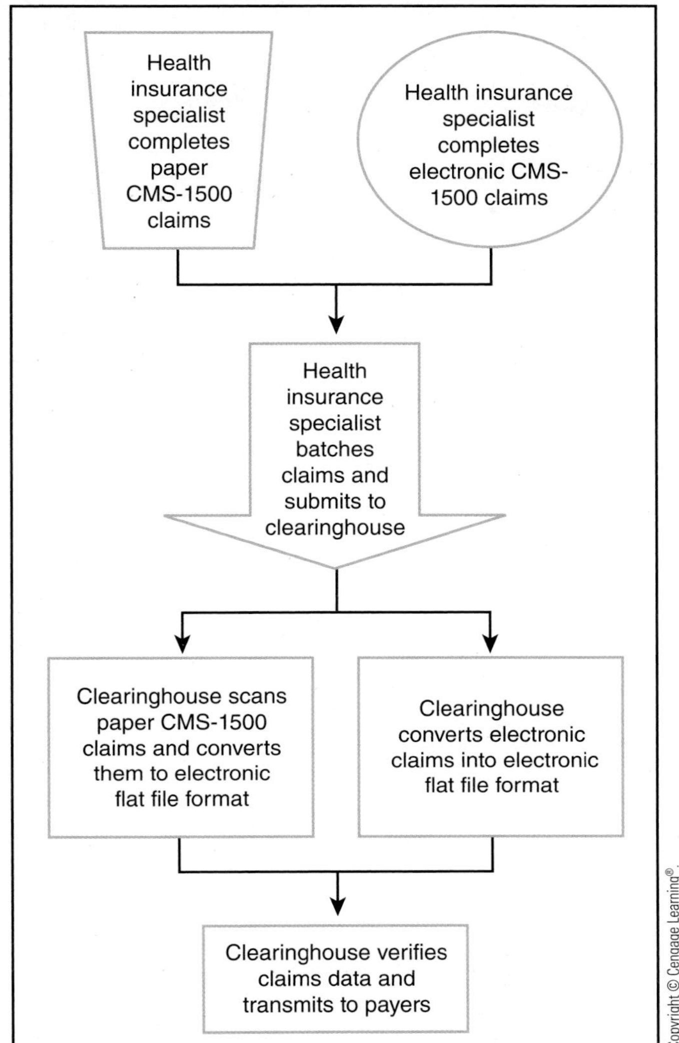

FIGURE 4-13 Claims submission and processing.

Claims Adjudication

After the claim has been validated by the payer's claims examiner, it undergoes the **claims adjudication** process (Figure 4-15), in which the claim is compared to payer edits and the patient's health plan benefits to verify that the:

- **Required information is available to process the claim**
- **Claim is not a duplicate**
- **Payer rules and procedures have been followed**
- **Procedures performed or services provided are covered benefits**

NOTE: Patients can be billed for noncovered procedures but not for unauthorized services. Providers process denials of unauthorized services as a business loss.

The payer analyzes each claim for patient and policy identification and compares data with its computerized database. Claims are automatically rejected if the patient and subscriber names do not match exactly with names in the computerized database. Use of nicknames or typographical errors on claims will cause rejection and return, or delay in reimbursement

Insurance Identification Number		Payer	Payer PlanID Number
123456789		BCBS	987654321
First Name	Middle Name	Last Name	Home Phone
Mary	Sue	Patient	(101) 111-1234

Address	City	State	ZIP Code	Work Phone
2 Tiger Street	Anywhere	NY	12345-1234	(101) 111-9876

1. MEDICARE [ ] (Medicare#) MEDICAID [ ] (Medicaid#) TRICARE [ ] (ID#/DoD#) CHAMPVA [ ] (Member ID#) GROUP HEALTH PLAN [ ] (ID#) FECA BLK LUNG [ ] (ID#) OTHER [X] (ID#)

1a. INSURED'S I.D. NUMBER (For Program in Item 1): 123456789

2. PATIENT'S NAME (Last Name, First Name, Middle Initial)	3. PATIENT'S BIRTH DATE / SEX	4. INSURED'S NAME (Last Name, First Name, Middle Initial)
PATIENT, MARY, S	MM 10 DD 05 YY 1935 M [ ] F [X]	PATIENT, MARY, S
5. PATIENT'S ADDRESS (No., Street)	6. PATIENT RELATIONSHIP TO INSURED	7. INSURED'S ADDRESS (No., Street)
2 TIGER STREET	Self [X] Spouse [ ] Child [ ] Other [ ]	2 TIGER STREET
CITY: ANYWHERE STATE: NY	8. RESERVED FOR NUCC USE	CITY: ANYWHERE STATE: NY
ZIP CODE: 12345-1234 TELEPHONE (Include Area Code): (101) 1111234		ZIP CODE: 1234-1234 TELEPHONE (Include Area Code): (101) 1111234

FIGURE 4-14 Sample split screen viewed by claims examiner.

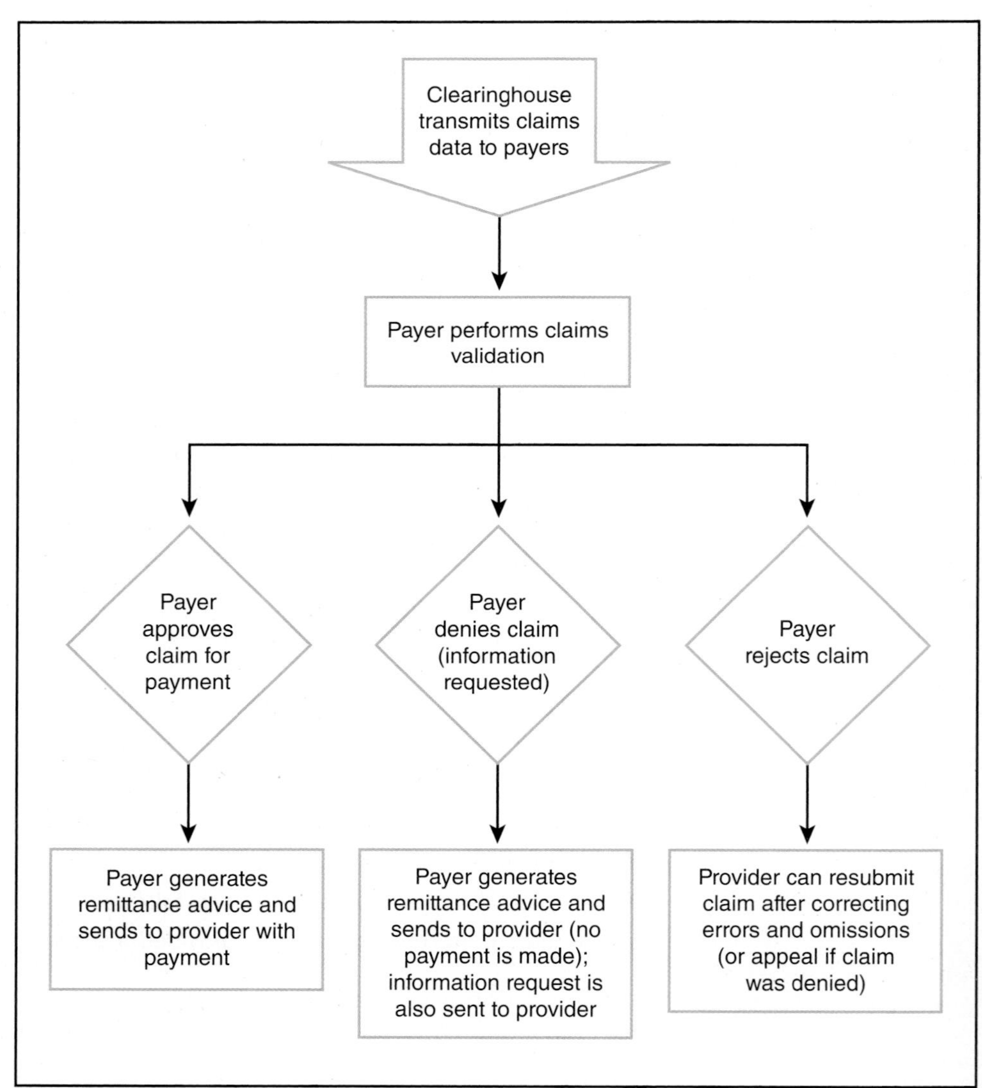

FIGURE 4-15 Claims adjudication and payment.

to the provider, because the claim cannot be matched. Procedure and service codes reported on the claim are compared with the policy's master benefit list to determine if they are covered. Any procedure or service reported on the claim that is not included on the master benefit list is a **noncovered benefit**, and will result in denial (rejection) of the claim. This means that the patient's insurance plan will not reimburse the provider for having performed those procedures or services. Procedures and services provided to a patient without proper authorization from the payer, or that were not covered by a current authorization, are **unauthorized services**. This means that the payer requires the provider to obtain preauthorization before performing certain procedures and services; and because it was not obtained, the claim is denied (rejected).

MANAGED CARE ALERT!

For managed care claims, both procedures and dates of service are verified to ensure that the services performed were both preauthorized and performed within the preauthorized time frame.

NOTE: Payers will identify a claim as a third-party liability responsibility based on review of codes. For example, submitting a claim on a patient who was injured in an automobile accident will trigger the payer to identify the automobile insurance as the primary payer on the claim.

The payer matches procedure and service codes (e.g., CPT) with diagnosis codes reported on the CMS-1500 claim to ensure the medical necessity of all procedures and services provided. Any procedure or service that is not medically necessary is denied. The claim is also checked against the **common data file**, which is an abstract of all recent claims filed on each patient. This process determines whether the patient is receiving concurrent care for the same condition by more than one provider, and it identifies services that are related to recent surgeries, hospitalizations, or liability coverage.

A determination is made as to **allowed charges**, which is the maximum amount the payer will allow for each procedure or service, according to the patient's policy. If no irregularity or inconsistency is found on the claim, the allowed charge for each covered procedure is determined. Allowed charges vary from policy to policy, and they are less than or equal to the fee charged by the provider. This means that payment is never greater than the fee submitted by the provider. A determination of the patient's annual deductible, copayment, and/or coinsurance amounts is also made. The **deductible** is the total amount of covered medical expenses a policyholder must pay each year out-of-pocket before the insurance company is obligated to pay any benefits. A policyholder (or subscriber or **beneficiary**) is the person in whose name the insurance policy is issued. **Coinsurance** is the percentage the patient pays for covered services after the deductible has been met and the copayment has been paid. For example, with an 80/20 plan, the insurance company pays 80 percent and the patient pays 20 percent. A *copayment* (or *copay*) is the fixed amount the patient pays each time he or she receives health care services.

EXAMPLE 1: Adam Appel is a patient of Dr. Phillips. He received preventive services for his annual physical examination on April 7. The third-party payer determined the allowed charge for preventive services to be $112, for which the payer reimbursed the physician 80 percent of that amount. Adam is responsible for paying the remaining 20 percent directly to the physician. Thus, the physician will receive a check in the amount of $89.60 from the payer, and the patient will pay $22.40 to the physician.

EXAMPLE 2: The patient underwent office surgery on September 8, and the third-party payer determined the allowed charge to be $680. The patient paid the 20 percent coinsurance at the time of the office surgery. The physician and patient each received a check for $544, and the patient signed the check over to the physician. The overpayment was $544, and the physician must reimburse the third-party payer.

Once the claims adjudication process has been completed, the payer generates a remittance advice that contains information about payment, denials, and pending status of claims. If a claim is denied, the provider can appeal the decision by resubmitting the claim and attaching supporting documentation. Claims that are assigned pending status contain errors and omissions, and providers can correct those problems and resubmit the claim for processing.

EXAMPLE: CPT contains laboratory panel codes (e.g., electrolyte panel), which bundle several laboratory tests into one code number. Some payers prefer to receive claims that contain individual code numbers for each laboratory test performed as part of the panel (e.g., carbon dioxide, chloride, potassium, and sodium). The payer's rationale is that a provider could order a series of tests and call it a panel, which is reimbursed at a higher rate than individual tests, even if not all of the panel tests were actually performed.

NOTE: Physician claims are adjudicated by line item (not for total charges), which means that payers bundle and edit code numbers for individual procedures and services. Because rules and procedures vary among payers, what one payer bundles, another may not. In addition, payers routinely change the rules and procedures that affect coverage policies and reimbursement to the provider. Another concern is that payers often do not apply official coding guidelines for diagnosis and procedure/service coding. Thus, CPT and HCPCS level II codes reported on a claim are sometimes changed by the payer, affecting payment to the provider.

During the adjudication process, the status location of a claim can be monitored and providers can track claims within a health plan's internal claims processing, adjudication, and payment systems. (HIPAA standardized the status locations for all health care claims transactions.) Providers can even verify, through a batch transmission, the status of multiple claims. Providers can also verify patients' insurance coverage and eligibility for services, and they can find out when to expect reimbursement for claims processed.

EXAMPLE: As part of Heather's job as a health insurance specialist for Dr. Miller's office, she queries the status of any claim that is 60 days old or older. A typical onscreen display appears as follows:

```
ABC1234 MEDICARE B ONLINE SYSTEM
SC CLAIM SUMMARY INQUIRY

HIC PROVIDER 123456 S/LOC TOB
OPERATOR ID ABCDE FROM DATE TO DATE DDE SORT
MEDICAL REVIEW SELECT

HIC PROV/MRN S/LOC TOB ADM DT FRM DT THRU DT
REC DT
SEL LAST NAME FIRST INIT TOT CHG PROV REIMB PD DT
CAN DT REAS NPC #DAYS
449999999A 179999 T B9997 131 0726YY 0726YY
SMITH M R 250.00 F1
```

Heather verifies that she is viewing the Medicare Part B claim status for M. R. Smith, a patient who was seen in the office on July 26, YY, for a service that was billed for $250. She notes that the claim has been paid, which is the interpretation of the F1 code on the last line. Because Heather queried the status of the claim, thinking that it was 60 days old or older, she will need to investigate whether the provider actually received the payment.

From:	To:
Medicare Administrative Contract # 09999	Medicare Provider # 987ABC654
	Medical Associates
EDI Exchange # 000000999	100 Main Street
Jun 16, YYYY @ 9:00 AM	Suite B
EDI Receiver ID: PAYER	Alfred, NY 14802

Adjustment applied: $0.00
Payment of $200.00 by CHECK #999999 dated Jun 16, YYYY

Patient Ref #	12345SANDERS	Internal Control #	99S7654321
Patient Name:	Jane Sanders	Paid as:	PRIMARY
Patient HIC #	98765432	Claim Total:	$ 500.00
Date of Claim:	May 08, YYYY	Amount Paid:	$ 200.00
Service # 1			
Date of Service:	May 08, YYYY	Allowable:	$ 200.00
Place of Service:	11	Deductible:	$ 0.00
Procedure Code:	10040	Coinsurance:	$ 0.00
Units:	1	Copayment:	$ 0.00
Charge:	$ 300.00	Paid:	$ 200.00
Provider ID:	987ABC654	Reasons:	Amount above fee schedule
Service # 2			
Date of Service:	May 15, YYYY	Allowable:	$ 100.00
Place of Service:	11	Deductible:	$ 100.00
Procedure Code:	99213	Coinsurance:	$ 0.00
Units:	1	Copayment:	$ 0.00
Charge:	$ 200.00	Paid:	$ 0.00
Provider ID:	987ABC654	Reasons:	Deductible applies

FIGURE 4-16 Sample remittance advice for one patient (two office visits).

NOTE: Chapter 4 of the *Workbook to Accompany Understanding Health Insurance* contains assignments to help students interpret data located on EOB and RA or ERA documents.

Payment of Claims

Once the adjudication process has been finalized, the claim is either denied or approved for payment. A remittance advice (Figure 4-16) is sent to the provider, and an explanation of benefits (EOB) (Figure 4-17) is mailed to the policyholder and/or patient. A remittance advice submitted to the provider electronically is called an **electronic remittance advice (ERA)**. It contains the same information as a paper-based remittance advice, but the provider receives ERAs more quickly. Providers use remittance advice information to process payments and adjustments to patient accounts. The remittance advice should be reviewed to make sure there are no processing errors (e.g., code changes, denial of benefits, and so on). (Patients should review EOBs to find out whether claims were paid; if denied, the patient should contact the provider's office to determine whether the claim was resubmitted, requested information was sent to the payer, and so on.) After reviewing the remittance advice and posting payments and adjustments, any code changes, denials, and partial payments should be followed up on. The payer may need additional information to make a determination about a claim, and prompt compliance with such requests will expedite payment.

NOTE: Medicare calls the remittance advice a **Provider Remittance Notice (PRN)** and the explanation of benefits a Medicare Summary Notice (MSN).

It is common for payers to include multiple patients on one remittance advice and to send the provider one check for multiple claims. Providers also have the option of arranging for **electronic funds transfer (EFT)**, which means that payers deposit funds to the provider's account electronically.

THE KEYSTONE PLAN

P.O. BOX 900
ALFRED, NY 14802-0900
(800) 555-9000

DATE: 04/05/YY
ID #: BLS123456789
ENROLLEE: MARY SUE PATIENT
CONTRACT: 300500
BENEFIT PLAN: STATE OF NEW YORK

MARY SUE PATIENT
100 MAIN ST
ALFRED, NY 14802

EXPLANATION OF BENEFITS

SERVICE DETAIL

PATIENT/RELAT CLAIM NUMBER	PROVIDER/ SERVICE	DATE OF SERVICE	AMOUNT CHARGED	AMOUNT NOT COVERED	AMOUNT ALLOWED	COPAY/ DEDUCTIBLE	%	PLAN BENEFITS	REMARK CODE
ENROLLEE 5629587	D MILLER OFFICE VISITS	04/05/YYYY	40.25		40.25	8.00	100	32.25*	D1
						PLAN PAYS		32.25	

*THIS IS A COPY OF INFORMATION SENT TO THE PROVIDER. THANK YOU FOR USING THE PARTICIPATING PROVIDER PROGRAM.

REMARK CODE(S) LISTED BELOW ARE REFERENCED IN THE *SERVICE DETAIL* SECTION UNDER THE HEADING *REMARK CODE*

(D1) THANK YOU FOR USING A NETWORK PROVIDER. WE HAVE APPLIED THE NETWORK CONTRACTED FEE. THE MEMBER IS NOT RESPONSIBLE FOR THE DIFFERENCE BETWEEN THE AMOUNT CHARGED AND THE AMOUNT ALLOWED BY THE CONTRACT.

BENEFIT PLAN PAYMENT SUMMARY INFORMATION	
D MILLER	$32.25

PATIENT NAME	MEDICAL/SURGICAL DEDUCTIBLE		MEDICAL/SURGICAL OUT OF POCKET		PHYSICAL MEDICINE DEDUCTIBLE	
	ANNUAL DEDUCT	YYYY YEAR TO-DATE	ANNUAL MAXIMUM	YYYY YEAR TO-DATE	ANNUAL DEDUCT	YYYY YEAR TO-DATE
ENROLLEE	$249.00	$249.00	$1804.00	$121.64	$250.00	$0.00

THIS CLAIM WAS PROCESSED IN ACCORDANCE WITH THE TERMS OF YOUR EMPLOYEE BENEFITS PLAN. IN THE EVENT THIS CLAIM HAS BEEN DENIED, IN WHOLE OR IN PART, A REQUEST FOR REVIEW MAY BE DIRECTED TO THE KEYSTONE PLAN AT THE ALFRED ADDRESS OR PHONE NUMBER SHOWN ABOVE. THE REQUEST FOR REVIEW MUST BE SUBMITTED WITHIN 60 DAYS AFTER THE CLAIM PAYMENT DATE, OR THE DATE OF THE NOTIFICATION OF DENIAL OF BENEFITS. WHEN REQUESTING A REVIEW, PLEASE STATE WHY YOU BELIEVE THE CLAIM DETERMINATION OR PRE-CERTIFICATION IMPROPERLY REDUCED OR DENIED YOUR BENEFITS. ALSO, SUBMIT ANY DATA OR COMMENTS TO SUPPORT THE APPEAL.

THIS IS NOT A BILL.

FIGURE 4-17 Sample explanation of benefits (EOB).

State Prompt Payment Laws and Regulations

The Prompt Payment Act of 1982 requires federal agencies to pay their bills on time or risk paying penalty fees if payments are late. Many states have also enacted prompt pay laws that apply to health insurance plans, requiring them to either pay or deny claims within a specified time frame (e.g., electronic claims must typically be paid within 30 days). In addition, many states apply penalty fees for late payments.

A federal regulation requires that Medicare Advantage organizations (previously called Medicare Choice, M+C, or Medicare Part C) make prompt payments for services provided by nonparticipating providers. Such organizations must pay 95 percent of clean claims within 30 days of submission, and the organization must pay interest on clean claims not paid within 30 days. (All other claims must be paid or denied within 60 days from the date of the receipt.)

Medicare claims must also be paid promptly by Medicare administrative contractors. Clean claims must be paid or denied within 30 days from receipt, and interest must be paid on claims that are paid after 30 days.

INTERPRETING A REMITTANCE ADVICE (REMIT) AND AN EXPLANATION OF BENEFITS (EOB)

Third-party payers review submitted claims to determine whether services are covered by the patient's insurance plan (e.g., cosmetic surgery is usually not covered) and for coordination of benefits to determine which payer is responsible for reimbursement (e.g., services provided to a patient treated for a work-related injury are reimbursed by the employer's workers' compensation payer). Once a payer has completed the claims adjudication (decision-making) process, the claim is denied or approved for payment. The provider receives a remittance advice (remit), and the patient receives an explanation of benefits (EOB). (Some payers send providers an EOB instead of a remittance advice.) The remit and EOB each contains information about denied services, reimbursed services, and the patient's responsibility for payment (e.g., copayment). The remittance advice typically includes the following items:

- Third-party payer's name and contract number
- Electronic data interchange (EDI) information, including EDI exchange number, date and time remittance advice was generated, and EDI receipt identifier
- Provider's name and mailing address
- Adjustments applied to the submitted claim (e.g., reduced payment, partial payment, zero payment, and so on)
- Amount and date of payment
- Patient's reference number, name and health insurance contract number, claim date, internal control number, paid status (e.g., primary, secondary, supplemental), claim total, and amount paid
- Date and place of service, procedure/service code, units, charge(s), provider identification number, allowable charges, deductible and coinsurance amounts, amount paid, and reasons (to explain payment amount)

The explanation of benefits typically includes the following items:

- Third-party payer's name, mailing address, and telephone number
- Date the EOB was generated, payer's identification number, contract number, and benefit plan
- Patient's name and mailing address
- Details of services reported on claim, including claim number, name of provider, date of service, amount charged, amount not covered by plan, amount allowed by plan, copayment and/or deductible amounts (that are the responsibility of the patient), amount paid under plan's benefits, and any remark codes (e.g., reason for denied claim)
- Benefit plan payment summary information, including provider's name and amount paid under plan's benefits
- Summary information about plan deductible and out-of-pocket amounts (paid by patient)
- Statement (at the bottom or top) that says THIS IS NOT A BILL

The count starts on the day after the receipt date and ends on the date payment is made.

EXAMPLE: If a clean claim received October 1 of this year is paid within 30 days, the Medicare requirement is met.

OUT WITH THE OLD AND IN WITH THE NEW

The Old Days: Traditional Claims Processing

Payers receive health claim forms by mail, and they are opened, date-stamped, sorted, and grouped according to physician specialty. Data from the claim forms are keyed into a claims database, and the validity of the claim is determined. If valid, payment is mailed to the physician. If not valid, an exception report is printed, the claim is manually retrieved from the file system, and it is faxed to a review panel of physicians. The physician may receive a request for information from the payer so that further review can occur prior to approval for payment.

The New Way: Electronic Claims Processing

Paper claims are scanned for image archiving and sent to a database for electronic routing and processing. Tracking of claims is automated; when a claim has to be retrieved for review, instead of searching through paper files, the image is quickly located and viewed onscreen or routed to a printer. Medicare is now enforcing mandatory submission of electronic claims, which means paper claims will be denied (except for those submitted by physician offices with fewer than 10 full-time equivalents, or FTEs). (The FTE abbreviation also refers to full-time employees.)

NOTE: Medicare *Conditions of Participation* require providers to maintain medical records for at least five years, and state retention laws are sometimes stricter (e.g., New York State requires medical records to be maintained for at least six years).

MAINTAINING INSURANCE CLAIM FILES

CMS requires providers to retain copies of any government insurance claims and copies of all attachments filed by the provider for a period of six years (unless state law stipulates a longer period). (The provider could be audited during that period.)

CMS stipulated in March 1992 that providers and billing services filing claims electronically can comply with this federal regulation by retaining the financial **source document** (routing slip, charge slip, encounter form, or superbill) from which the insurance claim was generated. In addition, the provider should keep the e-mailed report of the summary of electronic claims received from the insurance company.

It is recommended that the following types of claims and files be securely stored as electronic claims files (e.g., folders created using a computer) or manual claims files (e.g., labeled folders):

1. **Open claims** are organized by month and insurance company and have been submitted to the payer, but processing is not complete. Open claims include those that were rejected due to an error or omission (because they must be reprocessed).
2. **Closed claims** are filed according to year and insurance company and include those for which all processing, including appeals, has been completed.
3. *Remittance advice documents* are organized according to date of service because payers often report the results of insurance claims processed on different patients for the same date of service and provider. This mass report is called a *batched remittance advice.*

NOTE: If a patient requests a copy of the remittance advice received by the provider, all patient identification except that of the requesting patient must be removed.

EXAMPLE: Samantha Bartlett contacts the office to request a copy of the transmittal notice for her last date of service, explaining that she did not receive her copy. Because the information is on a batched remittance advice, the insurance specialist makes a copy of the page on which Samantha's information is found. Using the copy, the insurance specialist removes patients' information other than Samantha's, and mails the redacted (edited) copy to Samantha. The rest of the copy, which contains other patients' information, is shredded.

4. **Unassigned claims** are organized by year and are generated for providers who do not accept assignment; the file includes all unassigned claims for which the provider is not obligated to perform any follow-up work.

Tracking Unpaid Claims

The insurance specialist is responsible for tracking insurance claims submitted to third-party payers and clearinghouses, and tracking unpaid claims is especially important. To ensure that claims are processed in a timely manner (and payment is received), effective claims tracking requires the following activities:

- **Maintaining a paper or electronic copy of each submitted claim**
- **Logging information about claims submitted in a paper-based insurance claims registry or by using medical practice management software**
- **Reviewing the remittance advice (remit) to ensure that accurate reimbursement was received**

The remittance advice contains reason codes for "denied claims" (e.g., incorrect policy number, invalid CPT code), which are interpreted by the insurance specialist. If the claim was denied because the service is not covered by the payer, the claim is not resubmitted. (A bill is mailed to the patient, who receives an explanation of benefits from the payer that indicates the reason for the denial.) If the claim was denied due to errors, a corrected claim is submitted to the payer. The insurance specialist should carefully review the entire claim prior to resubmission, because processing of the original claim was halted by the payer (or clearinghouse) upon activation of a reason for denial. Other errors may exist in that claim, which need to be corrected prior to resubmission.

Remittance Advice Reconciliation

When the remittance advice and payment are received, retrieve the claim(s) and review and post payments to the patient accounts. Be sure to post the date payment was received, amount of payment, processing date, and any applicable transmittal notice number. Claims containing no errors are moved to the *closed claims* file. (Single-payment notices are attached to paper claims before filing in the *closed claims* file. Batched remittance advices are placed in the *batched remittance advice* file.)

Appeals Process

NOTE: Medicare appeals are now called redeterminations or reconsiderations, per BIPA-mandated changes.

An **appeal** is documented as a letter (Figure 4-18) signed by the provider explaining why a claim should be reconsidered for payment. If appropriate, include copies of medical record documentation. Be sure the patient has signed a release-of-information authorization.

Doctors Group
Main Street
Anywhere, NY 12345
March 15, YYYY

Medicare B Review Department
P.O. Box 1001
Anywhere, US 12345

NAME OF PATIENT: ______________________________
MEDICARE HICN*: ______________________________
I do not agree with the determination you made on HICN* ___________.

The reason I disagree with this determination is/are: (Check all that apply.)

☐ Service/Claim underpaid/reduced ☐ Service/Claim overpaid ☐ Service(s) overutilized
☐ Services not medically necessary ☐ Duplicate claim submitted ☐ Other: ___________

Services in question are delineated as follows:

Date(s) of Service:	Quantity Billed:	Modifier:	Procedure Code(s):

Additional information to consider, including specific diagnosis, illness and/or condition:
____
____

Attachments to consider: (Check all that apply)

☐ Medical Records ☐ Ambulance Run Sheet ☐ Copy of Claim ☐ Certificate of Medical Necessity
☐ Other: ______________________________

______________________________ ______________
Signature of Claimant or Representative Telephone Number

* HICN = Health Insurance Claim Number

FIGURE 4-18 Sample Medicare appeal letter.

NOTE: When questioning the payer about a remittance advice that includes multiple patients, circle the pertinent patient information. Do not use a highlighter, because payer scanning equipment does not recognize highlighted information.

NOTE: If the medical record does not support medical necessity, discuss the case with the office manager and provider.

Appealing Denied Claims

A remittance advice may indicate that payment was denied for a reason other than a processing error. The reasons for denials may include (1) procedure or service not medically necessary, (2) pre-existing condition not covered, (3) noncovered benefit, (4) termination of coverage, (5) failure to obtain preauthorization, (6) out-of-network provider used, (7) lower level of care could have been provided, (8) incorrect codes or incorrectly linked codes reported on claim, (9) bundled service or global period service is not eligible for separate payment, or (10) claim contained incomplete information or another insurance plan is primary.The following steps should be taken to appeal each type of denial.

1. *Procedure or service not medically necessary:* The payer has determined that the procedure performed or service rendered was not

medically necessary based on information submitted on the claim. To respond, first review the original source document (e.g., patient record) for the claim to determine whether significant diagnosis codes or other important information have been clearly documented or may have been overlooked. Next, write an appeal letter to the payer providing the reasons the treatment is medically necessary.

> **NOTE:** Beginning 2014, health insurance plans cannot refuse to cover individuals or charge more because of a pre-existing condition. An exception includes grandfathered *individual* health insurance plans, which individuals purchase privately (*not* through an employer).

2. *Pre-existing condition:* The payer has denied this claim based on the wording of the pre-existing condition clause in the patient's insurance policy. A **pre-existing condition** is any medical condition that was diagnosed and/or treated within a specified period of time immediately preceding the enrollee's effective date of coverage. The wording associated with these clauses varies from policy to policy (e.g., length of time pre-existing condition clause applies). It is possible for an insurance company to cancel a policy (or at least deny payment on a claim) if the patient failed to disclose pre-existing conditions. Respond to this type of denial by determining whether the condition associated with treatment for which the claim was submitted was indeed pre-existing. If it is determined that an incorrect diagnosis code was submitted on the original claim, for example, correct the claim and resubmit it for reconsideration of payment.

> **NOTE:** Office staff must be familiar with federal regulations regarding insurance coverage of pre-existing conditions when a patient changes jobs and/or an employer switches insurance plans.

3. *Noncovered benefit:* The claim was denied based on a list developed by the insurance company that includes a description of items covered by the policy as well as those excluded. Excluded items may include procedures such as cosmetic surgery. Respond to this type of denial by determining whether the treatment submitted on the claim for payment is indeed excluded from coverage. If it is determined that an incorrect procedure code was submitted, for example, correct the claim and resubmit it for reconsideration of payment along with a copy of medical record documentation to support the code change.
4. *Termination of coverage:* The payer has denied this claim because the patient is no longer covered by the insurance policy. Respond to this type of denial by contacting the patient to determine appropriate coverage, and submit the claim accordingly. For example, a patient may have changed jobs and may no longer be covered by his former employer's health insurance plan. The office needs to obtain correct insurance payer information and submit a claim accordingly. This type of denial reinforces the need to interview patients about current address, telephone number, employment, and insurance coverage each time they come to the office for treatment.

> **NOTE:** Denial types 5 and 6 are *not* restricted to managed care plans.

5. *Failure to obtain preauthorization:* Many health plans require patients to call a toll-free number located on the insurance card to obtain prior authorization for particular treatments. Problems can arise during an emergency situation when there is a lack of communication between provider and health plan (payer), because treatment cannot be delayed while awaiting preauthorization. Although such a claim is usually paid, payment might be less and/or penalties may apply because preauthorization was not obtained. If failure to obtain preauthorization was due to a medical emergency, it is possible to have penalties waived. Respond to this situation by requesting a retrospective review of a claim, and be sure to submit information explaining special circumstances that might not be evident from review of the patient's chart.

> **EXAMPLE:** The patient was admitted to the labor and delivery unit for an emergency cesarean section. The patient's EOB contained a $250 penalty notice (patient's responsibility) and a reduced payment to the provider (surgeon). The remittance advice stated that preauthorization for the surgical procedure (cesarean section) was not obtained. The provider appealed the claim, explaining the circumstances of the emergency surgery, and the payer waived the $250 penalty and reimbursed the provider at the regular rate.

6. *Out-of-network provider used:* The payer has denied payment because treatment was provided outside the provider network. This means that the provider is not eligible to receive payment for the services/procedures performed. Respond to this denial by writing a letter of appeal explaining why the patient sought treatment from outside the provider network (e.g., medical emergency when patient was out of town). Payment received could be reduced and penalties could also apply.
7. *Lower level of care could have been provided:* This type of denial applies when (a) care rendered on an inpatient basis is normally provided on an outpatient basis, (b) outpatient surgery could have been performed in a provider's office, or (c) skilled nursing care could have been performed by a home health agency. Respond to this type of denial by writing a letter of appeal explaining why the higher level of care was required. Be prepared to forward copies of the patient's chart for review by the insurance payer.
8. *Incorrect codes or incorrectly linked codes reported on claim.* When the payer denies payment because an incorrect code (e.g., CPT code reported on Medicare claim instead of HCPCS level II G code) was reported or the diagnosis and procedure/service codes are incorrectly linked on a claim, resubmit the claim with correct codes and/or correct linkage of diagnosis to procedure/service codes.
9. *Bundled service or global period service is not eligible for separate payment.* The payer will deny reimbursement when it is determined that multiple CPT and/or HCPCS level II codes were reported when just one code should have been reported for a bundled service. Likewise, the payer will deny payment for claims that contain codes for services that are not eligible for separate payment because they were performed during a global period. (Bundled services and global periods are discussed further in Chapter 7 of this textbook.)
10. *Claim contained incomplete information or another insurance plan is primary.* When the payer denies payment because the claim was incomplete, resubmit the claim with complete information. When another insurance plan is primary, submit the claim to that third-party payer; when a remittance advice (RA) is received from the primary payer, submit a claim with a copy of the RA to the secondary payer.

> **NOTE:** When a patient presents a new insurance card during his or her visit, edit third-party payer information in the patient's file so that claims are submitted to the appropriate payer.

CREDIT AND COLLECTIONS

Health care providers establish patient billing policies to routinely collect payments from patients that are due at the time services are delivered (e.g., copayments). Because most of a provider's fees are reimbursed by insurance plans, implementing consistent credit and collection practices is crucial to the operation of the organization.

Credit

Ideally, all payments are collected at the time the patient receives health care services. The reality is that alternate payment options are offered to patients (e.g., credit card billing, payment plans, and so on) to improve the organization's accounts receivable and reduce the need for collection practices. (**Accounts receivable** are the amounts owed to a business for services or goods provided.) If credit arrangements are available for patients, they must be consistently offered to all patients in accordance with the following federal laws:

- **Consumer Credit Protection Act of 1968** (or **Truth in Lending Act**), which requires providers to make certain written disclosures concerning all finance charges and related aspects of credit transactions (including disclosing finance charges expressed as an annual percentage rate).
- **Electronic Funds Transfer Act**, which establishes the rights, liabilities, and responsibilities of participants in electronic fund transfer systems. Financial institutions are required to adopt certain practices respecting such matters as transaction accounting, preauthorized transfers, and error resolution. The act also sets liability limits for losses caused by unauthorized transfers. (This law applies to financial institutions that partner with providers to process electronic funds transfers.)
- **Equal Credit Opportunity Act**, which prohibits discrimination on the basis of race, color, religion, national origin, sex, marital status, age, receipt of public assistance, or good-faith exercise of any rights under the Consumer Credit Protection Act.
- **Fair Credit and Charge Card Disclosure Act**, which amended the Truth in Lending Act and requires credit and charge card issuers to provide certain disclosures in direct mail, telephone, and other applications and solicitations for open-ended credit and charge accounts and under other circumstances (Figure 4-19). (This law applies to providers that accept credit cards.)
- **Fair Credit Billing Act**, which amended the Truth in Lending Act and requires prompt written acknowledgment of consumer billing complaints and investigation of billing errors by creditors.
- **Fair Credit Reporting Act**, which protects information collected by consumer reporting agencies such as credit bureaus, medical information companies, and tenant screening services. Organizations that provide information to consumer reporting agencies also have specific legal obligations, including the duty to investigate disputed information.
- **Fair Debt Collection Practices Act (FDCPA)**, which states that third-party debt collectors are prohibited from employing deceptive or abusive conduct in the collection of consumer debts incurred for personal, family, or household purposes. Such collectors may not, for example, contact debtors at odd hours, subject them to repeated telephone calls, threaten legal action that is not actually contemplated, or reveal to other persons the existence of debts.

NOTE: The provider is also responsible for adhering to any state laws that affect credit and collection policies.

Collections

As important as it is for a provider's employees to adhere to billing policies (e.g., verify current insurance information for each patient at the time of visit), following up on past-due accounts is crucial to the success of the business. A **past-due account** (or **delinquent account**) is one that has not been paid within a certain time frame (e.g., 120 days). Providers also track the status of **delinquent claims**, which have not been paid within a certain time frame (also about

NOTE: Delinquent claims awaiting payer reimbursement are never outsourced. They are resolved with the payer.

Forest Hills Medical Center
Forest Hills, NY 10001

TRUTH-IN-LENDING STATEMENT

Account Number ______________________________ Date ______________________________

Name of Patient (or Responsible Party) ______________________________

Address ______________________________

ANNUAL PERCENTAGE RATE (cost of your credit as a yearly rate)	**FINANCE CHARGE** (dollar amount credit will cost you)	**AMOUNT FINANCED** (amount of credit provided to you or on your behalf)	**TOTAL OF PAYMENTS** (amount you will have paid if you make all of the payments as scheduled)
_____ %	$ __________	$ __________	$ __________

Your payment schedule is as follows:

NUMBER OF PAYMENTS	AMOUNT OF PAYMENTS	WHEN PAYMENTS ARE DUE

Late Charge: If a payment is late, you may be charged $ __________

Repayment: If you pay off early, there will be no penalty.

Itemization of the amount financed of $ __________

$ __________ Amount given to you directly.

$ __________ Amount paid to the institution on your behalf.

I have received a copy of this statement.

____
Signature of Patient (or Responsible Party)

FIGURE 4-19 Sample Truth-in-Lending statement.

120 days) (Table 4-1). The **delinquent claim cycle** advances through aging periods (e.g., 30 days, 60 days, 90 days, and so on), and providers typically focus internal recovery efforts on older delinquent claims (e.g., 120 days or more). As a result, many accounts in the earlier stages of the delinquency cycle are overlooked as they begin to age.

NOTE: Payers establish time frames after which they will not process a claim, such as 180 days from the date of service. Once the claims submission date has passed, it is extremely difficult to obtain reimbursement from the payer, and *the provider is prohibited from billing the patient for payment.*

The best way to deal with delinquent claims is to prevent them by:

- **Verifying health plan identification cards on all patients**
- **Determining each patient's health care coverage (e.g., to ensure that a pre-existing condition is not submitted for reimbursement on the claim)**
- **Electronically submitting a *clean claim* that contains no errors**
- **Contacting the payer to determine that the claim was received**
- **Reviewing records to determine whether the claim was paid, denied, or is in suspense (pending) (e.g., subject to recovery of benefits paid in error on another patient's claim)**
- **Submitting supporting documentation requested by the payer to support the claim**

To determine whether a claim is delinquent, generate an **accounts receivable aging report** (Figure 4-20), which shows the status (by date) of outstanding claims from each payer, as well as payments due from patients. At this point

TABLE 4-1 Reasons to track claims

PROBLEM	DESCRIPTION
Coding errors	• **Downcoding** (assigning lower-level codes than documented in the record)
	• Incorrect code reported (e.g., incomplete code)
	• Incorrect coding system used (e.g., CPT code reported when HCPCS level II national code should have been reported)
	• Medical necessity does not correspond with procedure and service codes
	• **Unbundling** (submitting multiple CPT codes when just one code should have been submitted) **NOTE:** Unbundling is associated with the National Correct Coding Initiative (NCCI), which is further explained in Chapter 7 of this textbook.
	• Unspecified diagnosis codes are reported
Delinquent payment	• Payment is overdue, based on practice policy
Denied claim	• Medical coverage cancelled
	• Medical coverage lapsed beyond renewal date
	• Medical coverage policy issues prevent payment (e.g., pre-existing condition, noncovered benefit)
	• No-fault, personal injury protection (PIP), automobile insurance applies
	• Payer determines that services were not medically necessary
	• Procedure performed was experimental and therefore not reimbursable
	• Services should have been submitted to workers' compensation payer
	• Services were not preauthorized, as required under the health plan
	• Services were provided before medical coverage was in effect
Lost claim	• Claim was not received by payer
Overpayment	• Payer may apply offsets to future provider payments to recoup funds
	• Payer overpays provider's fee or managed care contract rate
	• Provider receives payment intended for patient
	• Provider receives duplicate payments from multiple payers
	• Payment is received on a claim not submitted by the provider
Payment errors	• Patient is paid directly by the payer when the provider should have been paid
	• Patient cashes a **two-party check** in error (check made out to both patient and provider)
Pending claim (suspense)	• Claim contains an error
	• Need for additional information
	• Review required by payer (e.g., high reimbursement, utilization management, complex procedures)
Rejected claim	• Also called *soft denials*
	• Claim contains a technical error (e.g., transposition of numbers, missing or incorrect data, duplicate charges or dates of service)
	• Payer instructions when submitting the claim were not followed
	• Resubmitted claim is returned (consider submitting a review request to payer)

1500 A/R Aging All
SOFTAID DEMO DATA
03/19/YYYY 16:11:34

Options
Entry Date 03/01/YYYY to 03/10/YYYY

Status Payer Code	Claim ID	Last Bill	Current	31 to 60	61 to 90	91 to 120	>120
CLAIM STATUS: PRIMARY							
AETNA OF CALIFORNIA – AETNA5						**510 382-8563**	
PETERS, GEORGE 58698775501	135741	03/05/YYYY	160.00	0.00	0.00	0.00	0.00
AETNA OF CALIFORNIA			160.00	0.00	0.00	0.00	0.00
HOME HEALTH AGENCY - AG						**958 855-4454**	
REYNOLDS, SAMUEL 56969885625	135740	03/04/YYYY	60.00	0.00	0.00	0.00	0.00
HOME HEALTH AGENCY			60.00	0.00	0.00	0.00	0.00
BLUE CROSS BLUE SHIELD OF FLOR - BCBS						**305 336-3727**	
LANGE, MATTHEW 12536521588	135735	03/01/YYYY	160.00	0.00	0.00	0.00	0.00
MAJORS, MARTIN 56236598541	135736	03/01/YYYY	240.00	0.00	0.00	0.00	0.00
NEVERETT, WILLIAM 56213598471	135738	03/10/YYYY	80.00	0.00	0.00	0.00	0.00
SANDERS, JOHN 56236985214	135739	03/04/YYYY	113.00	0.00	0.00	0.00	0.00
BLUE CROSS BLUE SHIELD OF FLOR			593.00	0.00	0.00	0.00	0.00
TOTAL: PRIMARY			813.00	0.00	0.00	0.00	0.00
CLAIM STATUS: SECONDARY							
MEDICAID - MCD							
TINDER, VERONICA 52623659814	135737	03/03/YYYY	1,580.00	0.00	0.00	0.00	0.00
MEDICAID			1,580.00	0.00	0.00	0.00	0.00
TOTAL: SECONDARY			1,580.00	0.00	0.00	0.00	0.00

Current	31 to 60	61 to 90	91 to 120	>120	Grand Total
2,393.000	0.00	0.00	0.00	0.00	2,393.00
100.00%	0.00%	0.00%	0.00%	0.00%	

FIGURE 4-20 Sample accounts receivable aging report.

> **NOTE:** **Litigation** (legal action) to recover a debt is usually a last resort for a medical practice. If legal action is taken, it usually occurs in small claims court where individuals can sue for money only without a lawyer. (Each state establishes limits for small claims, ranging from $2,000 to $25,000.)

many practices **outsource** (contract out) delinquent accounts to a full-service collections agency that utilizes collection tactics, including written contacts and multiple calls from professional collectors. (Collection agencies are regulated by federal laws, such as the FDCPA, which specifies what a collection source may or may not do when pursuing payment of past-due accounts.) Agencies that collect past-due charges directly from patients can add a fee to the delinquent account balance *if the practice originally notified the patient that a fee would be added if the account was sent to an outside collection source for resolution.*

An account receivable that cannot be collected by the provider or a collection agency is called a bad debt. To deduct a **bad debt**, the amount must have been previously included in the provider's income. Providers cannot deduct bad debts for money they expected to receive but did not (e.g., for money owed for services performed) because that amount was never included in their income.

NOTE: The *largest* past-due charges from the aging report are sent to collections first, followed by past-due charges in descending order. In Figure 4-20, the collections order would be MCD, BCBS, AG, and AETNA.

EXAMPLE: An insurance company mails a check in the amount of $350 to the patient because the physician who treated the patient is a nonparticipating provider (nonPAR) for that health plan. The check is reimbursement for CRNA anesthesia services provided to the patient during outpatient surgery. The patient cashes the check and spends it on a weekend vacation. When he receives the bill for CRNA anesthesia services, he no longer has the money to pay it. That account becomes delinquent and is outsourced to a collection agency, which attempts to collect the payment. The collection agency is unable to obtain payment from the patient, and the amount is considered a "bad debt" for the provider's practice.

TEN STEPS TO AN EFFECTIVE COLLECTION PROCESS	
Step 1	Call the patient within one week after providing services to determine patient satisfaction, and mention that an invoice for the outstanding balance is payable upon receipt.
Step 2	Mail a duplicate invoice ten days after the due date with "past due" stamped on it to alert the patient that the due date has passed.
Step 3	Mail a reminder letter with a duplicate invoice as the second overdue notice to remind the patient that the account needs attention.
Step 4	Make the first collection call, determine the reason for nonpayment, and obtain a promise to pay.
Step 5	Mail the first collection letter to the patient.
Step 6	Make the second collection call to the patient to request full payment, and obtain a promise to pay.
Step 7	Mail the second collection letter.
Step 8	Make the third collection phone call, and explain that the account will be submitted to a collection agency if payment is not made.
Step 9	Mail the final collection letter, and state that the account is being turned over to a collection agency.
Step 10	Submit the account to a collection agency.

State Insurance Regulators

Insurance is regulated by the individual states, not the federal government. State regulatory functions include registering insurance companies, overseeing compliance and penalty provisions of the state insurance code, supervising insurance company formation within the state, and monitoring the reinsurance market. State regulators ascertain that all authorized insurance companies meet and maintain financial, legal, and other requirements for doing business in the state. Regulators also license a number of insurance-related professionals, including agents, brokers, and adjusters.

If the practice has a complaint about an insurance claim, contact the state insurance regulatory agency (e.g., state insurance commission) for resolution. Although the commissioner will usually review a health care policy to determine whether the claims denial was based on legal provisions, the commissioner does not have legal authority to require a payer to reimburse a specific claim.

Improper Payments Information Act (IPIA) of 2002

IPIA legislated the Comprehensive Error Rate Testing (CERT) program, which was implemented in 2003 to assess and measure improper payments in the Medicare fee-for-service program. CERT produces a national *paid claims error rate*, which is used to target improvement efforts.

SUMMARY

The insurance claim used to report professional and technical services is called the CMS-1500 claim. The processing of an insurance claim begins when the new or established patient contacts the medical practice to schedule an appointment for health care. New patients should be pre-registered so that identification and health insurance information can be obtained prior to the scheduled office visit. Established patients are usually rescheduled at checkout of a current appointment.

The life cycle of a claim includes four stages: claims submission and electronic data interchange (EDI), claims processing, claims adjudication, and payment. Remittance advice reconciliation is an essential medical practice function that allows providers to determine the status of outstanding claims. Insurance claims processing problems arise as the result of a variety of issues, including coding errors, delinquent claims, denied claims, lost claims, overpayment, payment errors, pending (suspense) claims, and rejected claims.

INTERNET LINKS

- A.M. Best Company
  Go to **www.ambest.com**, and click on the Support & Resources link. Then, scroll down and click on the State Insurance Regulators link to view a list of government regulators organized by state.
- HIPAA-Related Code Lists
  Go to **www.wpc-edi.com**, and click on the Code Lists link to view health care EDI code lists (e.g., claim adjustment reason codes). The code lists contain narrative descriptions that assist in the interpretation of claims status data and information included on a remittance advice.
- Medicare Remit Easy Print (MREP) software
  Go to **www.cms.gov**; click on the Research, Statistics, Data and Systems link; click on the Access to CMS Data & Application link; and click on the Medicare Remit Easy Print (MREP) link to learn how to download the free (to Medicare providers and suppliers) software that is used to access and print remittance advice information, including special reports.

STUDY CHECKLIST

- ☐ Read this textbook chapter and highlight key concepts.
- ☐ Create an index card for each key term.
- ☐ Access the chapter Internet links to learn more about concepts.
- ☐ Answer the chapter review questions, verifying answers with your instructor.
- ☐ Complete the Workbook chapter, verifying answers with your instructor.
- ☐ Form a study group with classmates to discuss chapter concepts in preparation for an exam.

REVIEW

MULTIPLE CHOICE Select the most appropriate response.

1. **Which means that the patient and/or insured has authorized the payer to reimburse the provider directly?**
   a. accept assignment
   b. assignment of benefits
   c. coordination of benefits
   d. medical necessity

2. **Providers who do not accept assignment of Medicare benefits do not receive information included on the _____, which is sent to the patient.**
   a. electronic flat file
   b. encounter form
   c. ledger
   d. Medicare Summary Notice

3. **The transmission of claims data to payers or clearinghouses is called claims**
   a. adjudication.
   b. assignment.
   c. processing.
   d. submission.

4. **A patient received services on April 5, totaling $1,000. He paid a $90 coinsurance at the time services were rendered. (The payer required the patient to pay a 20 percent coinsurance of the reasonable charge at the time services were provided.) The physician accepted assignment, and the insurance company established the reasonable charge as $450. On July 1, the provider received $360 from the insurance company. On August 1, the patient received a check from the insurance company in the amount of $450. The overpayment was _____, and the _____ must reimburse the insurance company. (Remember! Coinsurance is the percentage of costs a patient shares with the health plan.)**
   a. $450, patient
   b. $450, physician
   c. $550, patient
   d. $640, physician

5. **A series of fixed-length records submitted to payers to bill for health care services is an electronic**
   a. flat file format.
   b. funds transfer.
   c. remittance advice.
   d. source document.

6. **Which is considered a covered entity?**
   a. EHNAC, which accredits clearinghouses
   b. private-sector payers that process electronic claims
   c. provider that submits paper-based CMS-1500 claims
   d. small self-administered health plan that processes manual claims

7. **A claim that is rejected because of an error or omission is considered a(n)**
   a. clean claim.
   b. closed claim.
   c. delinquent claim.
   d. open claim.

8. An electronic claim is submitted using _____ as its transmission media.

a. a facsimile machine
b. magnetic tape
c. a scanning device
d. software that prints claims

9. Which supporting documentation is associated with submission of an insurance claim?

a. accounts receivable aging report
b. claims attachment
c. common data file
d. electronic remittance advice

10. Which is a group health insurance policy provision that prevents multiple payers from reimbursing benefits covered by other policies?

a. accept assignment
b. assignment of benefits
c. coordination of benefits
d. pre-existing condition

11. The sorting of claims upon submission to collect and verify information about the patient and provider is called claims

a. adjudication.
b. authorization.
c. processing.
d. submission.

12. Which of the following steps would occur first?

a. Clearinghouse converts electronic claims into electronic flat file format.
b. Clearinghouse verifies claims data and transmits to payers.
c. Health insurance specialist batches and submits claims to clearinghouse.
d. Health insurance specialist completes electronic or paper-based claim.

13. Comparing the claim to payer edits and the patient's health plan benefits is part of claims

a. adjudication.
b. processing.
c. submission.
d. transmission.

14. Which describes any procedure or service reported on a claim that is not included on the payer's master benefit list?

a. medically unnecessary
b. noncovered benefit
c. pre-existing condition
d. unauthorized service

15. Which is an abstract of all recent claims filed on each patient, used by the payer to determine whether the patient is receiving concurrent care for the same condition by more than one provider?

a. common data file
b. encounter form
c. patient ledger
d. remittance advice

16. Which is the fixed amount patients pay each time they receive health care services?

a. coinsurance
b. copayment
c. deductible
d. insurance

17. Which of the following steps would occur first?

a. Clearinghouse transmits claims data to payers.
b. Payer approves claim for payment.
c. Payer generates remittance advice.
d. Payer performs claims validation.

18. Which must accept whatever a payer reimburses for procedures or services performed?

a. nonparticipating provider
b. out-of-network provider
c. participating provider
d. value-added provider

19. Which is an interpretation of the birthday rule regarding two group health insurance policies when the parents of a child covered on both policies are married to each other and live in the same household?

a. The parent whose birth month and day occurs earlier in the calendar year is the primary policyholder.
b. The parent who was born first is the primary policyholder.
c. Both parents are primary policyholders.
d. The parent whose income is higher is the primary policyholder.

20. Which is the financial record source document usually generated by a hospital?

a. chargemaster
b. day sheet
c. encounter form
d. superbill

21. Refer to Figure 4-20 in this chapter. Which payer's claim should be followed up first to obtain reimbursement?

a. Aetna of California
b. BlueCross BlueShield of Florida
c. Home Health Agency
d. Medicaid

22. Which requires providers to make certain written disclosures concerning all finance charges and related aspects of credit transactions?

a. Equal Credit Opportunity Act
b. Fair Credit Reporting Act
c. Fair Debt Collection Practices Act
d. Truth in Lending Act

23. Which protects information collected by consumer reporting agencies?

a. Equal Credit Opportunity Act
b. Fair Credit Reporting Act
c. Fair Debt Collection Practices Act
d. Truth in Lending Act

24. Which is the best way to prevent delinquent claims?

a. Attach supporting medical documentation on all claims.
b. Enter all claims data in the practice's suspense file.
c. Submit closed claims to all third-party payers.
d. Verify health plan identification information on all patients.

25. Which is a characteristic of delinquent commercial claims awaiting payer reimbursement?

a. Delinquent claims are outsourced to a collection agency.
b. The delinquent claims are resolved directly with the payer.
c. The accounts receivable aging report was not submitted.
d. The provided remittance notice was delayed by the payer.

CHAPTER 5

Legal and Regulatory Issues

CHAPTER OUTLINE

Introduction to Legal and Regulatory Considerations

Federal Laws and Events That Affect Health Care

Retention of Records

Health Insurance Portability and Accountability Act (HIPAA)

OBJECTIVES

Upon successful completion of this chapter, you should be able to:

1. Define key terms.
2. Provide examples of a statute, regulation, and case law, and explain the use of the *Federal Register*.
3. Summarize federal legislation and regulations affecting health care.
4. Explain retention of records laws.
5. List and explain HIPAA's provisions.

KEY TERMS

abuse
ANSI ASC X12N 837
authorization
black box edit
breach of confidentiality
case law
check digit
civil law
Clinical Data Abstracting Center (CDAC)
common law
Comprehensive Error Rate Testing (CERT) program
confidentiality
criminal law
Current Dental Terminology (CDT)
decrypt
Deficit Reduction Act of 2005
deposition
digital
electronic transaction standards
encrypt
False Claims Act (FCA)
Federal Claims Collection Act (FCCA)
Federal Register
First-look Analysis for Hospital Outlier Monitoring (FATHOM)
fraud
Health Plan Identifier (HPID)
Hospital Inpatient Quality Reporting (Hospital IQR) program
Hospital Payment Monitoring Program (HPMP)
hospital value-based purchasing (VBP) program
Improper Payments Information Act of 2002 (IPIA)
interrogatory

listserv
Medicaid Integrity Program (MIP)
medical identity theft
medical review (MR)
Medicare administrative contractor (MAC)
Medicare Drug Integrity Contractors (MEDIC) Program
Medicare Integrity Program (MIP)
Medicare Shared Savings Program
message digest
National Drug Code (NDC)
National Individual Identifier
National Plan and Provider Enumeration System (NPPES)
National Practitioner Data Bank (NPDB)
National Provider Identifier (NPI)
National Standard Employer Identification Number (EIN)
National Standard Format (NSF)
overpayment
Part A/B Medicare administrative contractor (A/B MAC)
Patient Safety and Quality Improvement Act
Payment Error Prevention Program (PEPP)
payment error rate
Payment Error Rate Measurement (PERM) program
Physician Quality Reporting System
physician self-referral law
Physicians at Teaching Hospitals (PATH)
precedent
privacy
Privacy Act of 1974
privacy rule
privileged communication
Program for Evaluating Payment Patterns Electronic Report (PEPPER)
program transmittal
protected health information (PHI)
qui tam
record retention
Recovery Audit Contractor (RAC) program
regulations
release of information (ROI)
release of information log
security
security rule
Stark I
statutes
statutory law
subpoena
subpoena *duces tecum*
Tax Relief and Health Care Act of 2006 (TRHCA)
UB-04
unique bit string
upcoding
whistleblower
Zone Program Integrity Contractor (ZPIC)

INTRODUCTION

The health insurance specialist must be knowledgeable about laws and regulations for maintaining patient records and processing health insurance claims. This chapter defines legal and regulatory terminology and summarizes laws and regulations that affect health insurance processing. Internet links are also included as a resource for remaining up to date and obtaining clarification of legal and regulatory issues.

INTRODUCTION TO LEGAL AND REGULATORY CONSIDERATIONS

Federal and state **statutes** (or **statutory law**) are laws passed by legislative bodies (e.g., federal Congress and state legislatures). These laws are then implemented as **regulations**, which are guidelines written by administrative agencies (e.g., CMS). **Case law** (or **common law**) is based on court decisions that establish a **precedent** (or standard).

Federal laws and regulations affect health care in that they govern programs such as Medicare, Medicaid, TRICARE, and the Federal Employees Health Benefit Plans (FEHBP). State laws regulate insurance companies, recordkeeping practices, and provider licensing. State insurance departments determine coverage issues for insurance policies (contracts) and state workers' compensation plans.

Civil law deals with all areas of the law that are not classified as criminal. **Criminal law** is public law (statute or ordinance) that defines crimes and their prosecution. A **subpoena** is an order of the court that requires a witness to appear at a particular time and place to testify. A **subpoena *duces tecum*** requires documents (e.g., patient record) to be produced. A subpoena is used to obtain witness testimony at trial and at **deposition**, which is testimony under oath taken outside of court (e.g., at the provider's office). In civil cases (e.g., malpractice), the provider might be required to complete an **interrogatory**, which is a document containing a list of questions that must be answered in writing.

Qui tam is an abbreviation for the Latin phrase *qui tam pro domino rege quam pro sic ipso in hoc parte sequitur*, meaning "who as well for the king as for himself sues in this matter." It is a provision of the Federal False Claims Act, which allows a private citizen to file a lawsuit in the name of the U.S. government, charge government contractors and other entities that receive or use government funds with fraud, and share in any money recovered. Common defendants in *qui tam* actions involving Medicare/Medicaid fraud include physicians, hospitals, HMOs, and clinics.

To accurately process health insurance claims, especially for government programs like Medicare and Medicaid, you should become familiar with the *Code of Federal Regulations* (Figure 5-1). Providers and health insurance specialists can locate legal and regulatory issues found in such publications as the *Federal Register* and *Medicare Bulletin*. The **Federal Register** (Figure 5-2) is a legal newspaper published every business day by the National Archives and Records Administration (NARA). It is available in paper form, on microfiche, and online.

EXAMPLE 1: FEDERAL STATUTE, IMPLEMENTED AS STATE PROGRAM

Congress passed Title XXI of the Social Security Act as part of the Balanced Budget Act of 1997, which called for implementation of the State Children's Health Insurance Program. In response, New York implemented Child Health Plus, which expanded insurance eligibility to children under age 19 who are not eligible for Medicaid and have limited or no health insurance. Even if family income is high, children can be eligible to enroll in Child Health Plus; an insurance premium in the form of a monthly family contribution may be required (e.g., a family of two with an income ranging from $24,977 to $25,920 pays $15 per month per child).

Title 42--Public Health

CHAPTER IV--CENTERS FOR MEDICARE & MEDICAID SERVICES, DEPARTMENT OF HEALTH AND HUMAN SERVICES

PART 405--FEDERAL HEALTH INSURANCE FOR THE AGED AND DISABLED

405.201	Scope of subpart and definitions.
405.203	FDA categorization of investigational devices.
405.205	Coverage of a non-experimental/investigational (Category B) device.
405.207	Services related to a noncovered device.
405.209	Payment for a non-experimental/investigational (Category B) device.
405.211	Procedures for Medicare contractors in making coverage decisions for a non-experimental/investigational (Category B) device.
405.213	Re-evaluation of a device categorization.
405.215	Confidential commercial and trade secret information.
405.301	Scope of subpart.
405.350	Individual's liability for payments made to providers and other persons for items and services furnished the individual.
405.351	Incorrect payments for which the individual is not liable.

Reprinted according to National Archives and Records Administration permissions notice

FIGURE 5-1 Portion of table of contents from *Code of Federal Regulations*, Title 42, Public Health, Chapter IV, Centers for Medicare & Medicaid Services.

69840 **Federal Register**/Vol. 68, No. 240/Monday, December 15, 2003/Rules and Regulations

DEPARTMENT OF HEALTH AND HUMAN SERVICES

Centers for Medicare & Medicaid Services

42 CFR Parts 402 and 408
[CMS–0463–IFC]
RIN 0938–AM71

Medicare Program; Medicare Prescription Drug Discount Card

Agency: Centers for Medicare & Medicaid Services (CMS), HHS.
ACTION: Interim final rule with comment period.

SUMMARY: Section 101, subpart 4 of the Medicare Prescription Drug, Improvement, and Modernization Act of 2003, codified in section 1860D—31 of the Social Security Act, provides for a voluntary prescription drug discount card program for Medicare beneficiaries entitled to benefits, or enrolled, under Part A or enrolled under Part B, excluding beneficiaries entitled to medical assistance for outpatient prescription drugs under Medicaid, including section 1115 waiver demonstrations. Eligible beneficiaries may access negotiated prices on prescription drugs by enrolling in drug discount card programs offered by Medicare-endorsed sponsors.

Eligible beneficiaries may enroll in the Medicare drug discount card program beginning no later than 6 months after the date of enactment of the Medicare Prescription Drug, Improvement, and Modernization Act of 2003 and ending December 31, 2005. After December 31, 2005, beneficiaries enrolled in the program may continue to use their drug discount card during a short transition period beginning January 1, 2006 and ending upon the effective date of a beneficiary's outpatient drug coverage under Medicare Part D, but no later than the last day of the initial open enrollment period under Part D.

Beneficiaries with incomes no more than 135 percent of the poverty line applicable to their family size who do not have outpatient prescription drug coverage under certain programs—Medicaid, certain health insurance coverage or group health insurance (such as retiree coverage), TRICARE, and Federal Employees Health Benefits Program (FEHBP)—also are eligible for transitional assistance, or payment of $600 in 2004 and up to $600 in 2005 of the cost of covered discount card drugs obtained under the program. In most case, any transitional assistance remaining available to a beneficiary on December 31, 2004 may be rolled over to 2005 and applied toward the cost of covered discount card drugs obtained under the program during 2005. Similarly, in most cases, any transitional assistance remaining available to a beneficiary on December 31, 2005 may be applied toward the cost of covered discount card drugs obtained under the program during the transition period.

The Centers for Medicare & Medicaid Services will solicit applications from entities seeking to offer beneficiaries negotiated prices on covered discount card drugs. Those meeting the requirements described in the authorizing statute and this rule, including administration of transitional assistance, will be permitted to offer a Medicare-endorsed drug discount card program to eligible beneficiaries. Endorsed sponsors may charge beneficiaries enrolling in their endorsed programs an annual enrollment fee for 2004 and 2005 of nor more than $30; CMS will pay this fee on behalf of enrollees entitled to transitional assistance.

To ensure that eligible Medicare beneficiaries take full advantage of the Medicare drug discount card program and make informed choices, CMS will educate beneficiaries about the existence and features of the program and the availability of transitional assistance for certain low-income beneficiaries; and publicize information that will allow Medicare beneficiaries to compare the various Medicare-endorsed drug discount card programs.

DATES: Effective Date: The provisions of this interim final rule with comment period are effective December 15, 2003.

Comment date: Comments will be considered if we receive them no later than 5 p.m. on January 14, 2004, at the appropriate address, as provided below.

ADDRESSES: In commenting, please refer to file code CMS–4063–IFC. Because of staff and resource limitations, we cannot accept comments by facsimile (FAX) transmission.

Mail written comments (1 original and 3 copies) to the following address ONLY: Centers for Medicare & Medicaid Services, Department of Health and Human Services, Attention: CMS–4063–FC, P.O. Box 8013, Baltimore, MD 21244–8012.

Please allow sufficient time for mailed comments to be timely received in the event of delivery delays.

If you prefer, you may deliver (by hand or courier) your written comments (1 original and 3 copies) to one of the following addresses: Room 445–G, Hubert H. Humphrey Building, 200 Independence Avenue, SW., Washington, DC 20201, or Room C5–14–03, 7500 Security Boulevard, Baltimore, MD 21244–1850.

(Because access to the interior of the Hubert H. Humphrey Building is not readily available to persons without Federal Government identification, commenters are encouraged to leave their comments in the CMS drop slots located in the main lobby of the building. A stamp-in clock is available for commenters wishing to retain a proof of filing by stamping in and retaining an extra copy of the comments being filed.)

Comments mailed to the addresses indicated as appropriate for hand or courier delivery may be delayed and could be considered late.

For information on viewing public comments, see the beginning of the **SUPPLEMENTARY INFORMATION** section.

FOR FURTHER INFORMATION CONTACT: Teresa DeCaro, (410) 786-6604.

SUPPLEMENTARY INFORMATION: Copies: To order copies of the **Federal Register** containing this document, send your request to: New Orders, Superintendent of Documents, P.O. Box 371954, Pittsburgh, PA 15250–7954. Specify the date of the issue requested an enclose a check or money order payable to the Superintendent of Documents, or enclose your Visa or Master Card number and expiration date. Credit card orders can also be placed by calling the order desk at (202) 512–1800 (or toll free at 1–888–293–6498) or by faxing to (202) 512–2250. The cost for each copy is $10. As an alternative, you can view and photocopy the **Federal Register** document at most libraries designated as Federal Depository Libraries and at many other public and academic libraries throughout the country that receive the **Federal Register**. This **Federal Register** document is also available from the **Federal Register** online database through GPO Access, a service of the U.S. Government Printing Office. The Web site address is: http://www.access.gpo.gov/nara/index.html.

Inspection of Public Comments: Comments received timely will be available for public inspection as they are received, generally beginning approximately 3 weeks after publication of a document, at the headquarters of the Centers for Medicare & Medicaid Services, 7500 Security Boulevard, Baltimore, Maryland 21244, Monday through Friday of each week from 8:30 a.m. to 4 p.m. To schedule an appointment to view public comments, please call: (410) 786-7197.

FIGURE 5-2 Sample page from the *Federal Register*.

EXAMPLE 2: FEDERAL STATUTE, IMPLEMENTED AS A FEDERAL REGULATION, AND PUBLISHED IN THE *FEDERAL REGISTER*

Congress passed the Balanced Budget Refinement Act of 1999 (Public Law No. 106-113), which called for a number of revisions to Medicare, Medicaid, and the State Children's Health Insurance Program. On May 5, 2000, the Department of Health and Human Services published a proposed rule in the *Federal Register* to revise the Medicare hospital inpatient prospective payment system for operating costs. This proposed rule was entitled "Medicare Program; Changes to the Hospital Inpatient Prospective Payment Systems and Fiscal Year 2001 Rates; Proposed Rule." The purpose of publishing the proposed rule is to allow for comments from health care providers. Once the comment period has ended, the final rule is published in the *Federal Register.*

EXAMPLE 3: CASE LAW

When originally passed, New York State Public Health Law (PHL) sections 17 and 18 allowed a *reasonable charge* to be imposed for copies of patient records. Health care facilities, therefore, charged fees for locating the patient's record and making copies. These fees were later challenged in court, and reasonable charge language in the PHL was interpreted in *Hernandez v. Lutheran Medical Center* (1984), *Ventura v. Long Island Jewish Hillside Medical Center* (1985), and *Cohen v. South Nassau Communities Hospital* (1987). The original interpretation permitted charges of $1.00 to $1.50 per page, plus a search and retrieval fee of $15. However, sections 17 and 18 of the PHL were amended in 1991 when the phrase, "the reasonable fee for paper copies shall not exceed seventy-five cents per page" was added to the law.

NOTE: All 17 *carriers* (processed Medicare Part B claims) and all 23 *fiscal intermediaries (FI)* (processed Medicare Part A claims) were eliminated in 2010 to create 23 Medicare administrative contractors (MACs). *Durable Medical Equipment Carriers [DMERCs]* that process durable medical equipment, prosthetics, orthotics, and supplies [DMEPOS] have been replaced with DME MACs. Home health and hospice claims are processed by HH&H MACs. New jurisdictions were created for administration by MACs, which consolidate the administration of Medicare Parts A and B benefits so that Medicare beneficiaries have claims processed by one contractor.

Program transmittals (Figure 5-3) contain new and changed Medicare policies and/or procedures that are to be incorporated into a specific CMS program manual (e.g., *Medicare Claims Processing Manual*). The cover page (or transmittal page) summarizes new and changed material, and subsequent pages provide details. The transmittals are sent to each **Medicare administrative contractor (MAC)** (or **Part A/B Medicare administrative contractor**, abbreviated as **A/B MAC**), which is an organization (e.g., insurance company) that contracts with CMS to process fee-for-service health care claims and perform program integrity tasks for both Medicare Part A and Part B. Each contractor makes program coverage decisions and publishes a newsletter, which is sent to providers who receive Medicare reimbursement.

Membership in professional associations can also prove helpful in accessing up-to-date information about the health insurance industry (refer to Chapter 1 for information on joining professional associations). Newsletters and journals published by professional associations routinely include articles that clarify implementation of new legal and regulatory mandates. They also provide resources for obtaining the most up-to-date information about such issues. Another way to remain current is to subscribe to a **listserv**, a subscriber-based question-and-answer forum available through e-mail.

FEDERAL LAWS AND EVENTS THAT AFFECT HEALTH CARE

The health care industry is heavily regulated by federal and state legislation (Figure 5-4). Table 5-1 summarizes major federal laws and events that affect health care. (Because state laws vary, it is recommended that they be researched individually.)

CMS Manual System

Pub. 100-08 Program Integrity Manual

Department of Health & Human Services (DHHS)
Centers for Medicare & Medicaid Services (CMS)

Transmittal 91 | **Date: DECEMBER 10, YYYY**

CHANGE REQUEST 3560

SUBJECT: Revision of Program Integrity Manual (PIM), Section 3.11.1.4

I. SUMMARY OF CHANGES: Revising the PIM to correct inconsistencies with section 3.4.1.2.

NEW/REVISED MATERIAL – EFFECTIVE DATE*: January 1, YYYY
IMPLEMENTATION DATE: January 3, YYYY

MANUALIZATION/CLARIFICATION – EFFECTIVE/IMPLEMENTATION DATES: Not Applicable.

Disclaimer for manual changes only: The revision date and transmittal number apply to the red italicized material only. Any other material was previously published and remains unchanged. However, if this revision contains a table of contents, you will receive the new/revised information only, and not the entire table of contents.

II. CHANGES IN MANUAL INSTRUCTIONS: (R = REVISED, N = NEW, D = DELETED)

R/N/D	CHAPTER/SECTION/SUBSECTION/TITLE
R	3/11.1.4/Requesting Additional Documentation

III. FUNDING: Medicare contractors shall implement these instructions within their current operating budgets.

IV. ATTACHMENTS:

X	**Business Requirements**
X	**Manual Instruction**
	Confidential Requirements
	One-Time Notification
	Recurring Update Notification

***Unless otherwise specified, the effective date is the date of service.**

FIGURE 5-3 Sample Medicare program transmittal.

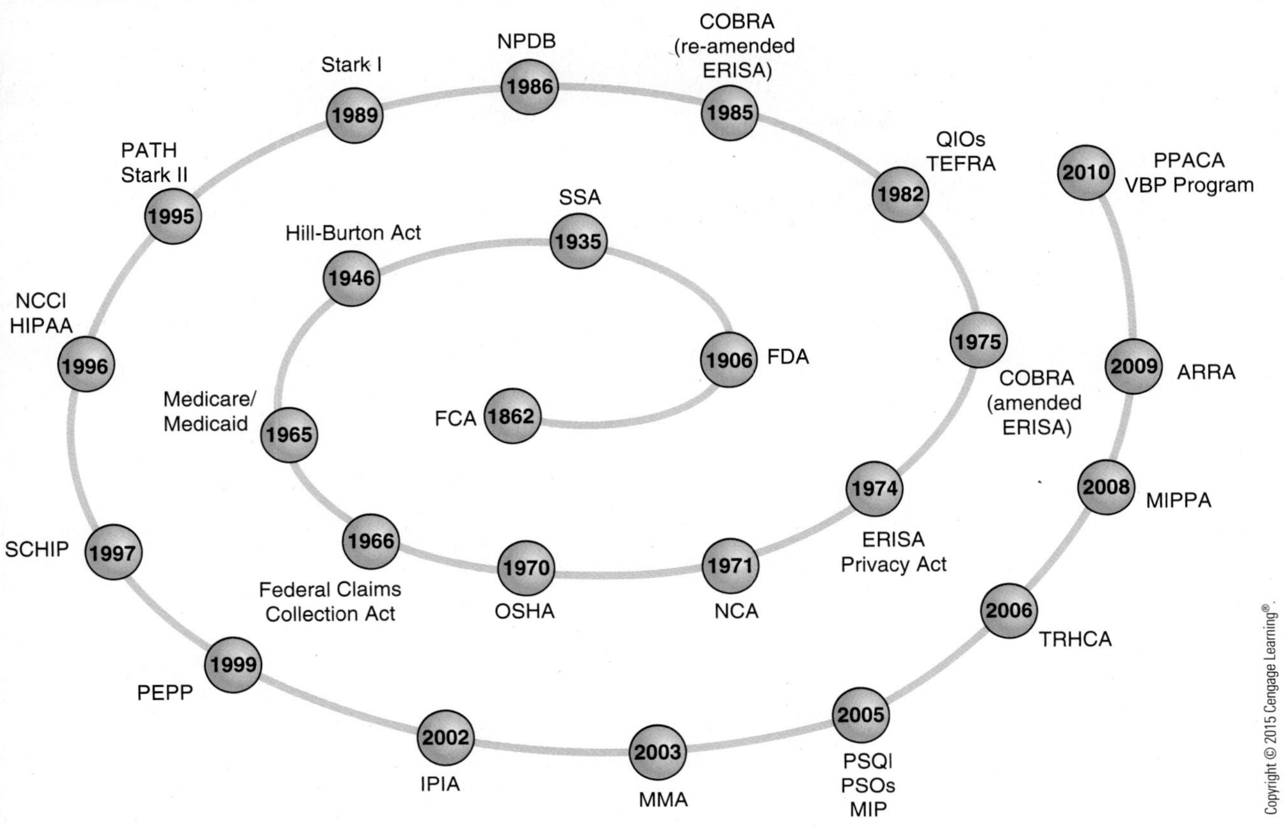

FIGURE 5-4 Timeline of dates and significant health care laws and events.

TABLE 5-1 Federal laws that affect health care

YEAR	FEDERAL LAW	DESCRIPTION
1863	False Claims Act (FCA)	• Regulated fraud associated with military contractors selling supplies and equipment to the Union Army • Used by federal agencies to regulate the conduct of any contractor that submits claims for payment to the federal government for any program (e.g., Medicare) • Amended in 2011 to increase civil monetary penalties (CMPs) to impose a maximum of $20,000 per false claim, plus three times the amount of damages that the government sustains; civil liability on those who submit false or fraudulent claims to the government for payment; and exclusion of violators from participation in Medicare and Medicaid **NOTE:** Control of fraud and abuse has been of great interest since the implementation of DRGs. Prior to DRGs, the cost-based reimbursement system for Medicare claims made fraud almost unnecessary, because the system rewarded high utilization of services. The implementation of DRGs resulted in the first serious "gaming" of the system to find ways to maximize revenues for hospitals. Because the diagnosis and procedure codes reported affect the DRG selected (and resultant payment), some hospitals engaged in a practice called **upcoding**, which is the assignment of an ICD-10-CM diagnosis code that does not match patient record documentation for the purpose of illegally increasing reimbursement (e.g., assigning the ICD-10-CM code for heart attack when angina was actually documented in the record). As a result, upcoding became a serious fraud concern under DRGs.

(continues)

TABLE 5-1 (continued)

YEAR	FEDERAL LAW	DESCRIPTION
1906	Food and Drug Act	• Authorized federal government to monitor the purity of foods and the safety of medicines • Now a responsibility of the Food and Drug Administration (FDA)
1935	Social Security Act (SSA)	• Included unemployment insurance, old-age assistance, aid to dependent children, and grants to states to provide various forms of medical care • Amended in 1965 to add disability coverage and medical benefits
1946	*Hill-Burton Act* (or Hospital Survey and Construction Act)	• Provided federal grants to modernize hospitals that had become obsolete due to lack of capital investment throughout the period of the Great Depression and World War II (1929 to 1945) • Required facilities to provide free or reduced-charge medical services to persons who were unable to pay, in return for federal funds • Program now addresses other types of infrastructure needs, and it is managed by the Health Resources and Services Administration (HRSA), within the Department of Health and Human Services (DHHS)
1962	Migrant Health Act	• Provided medical and support services to migrant and seasonal farm workers and their families
1965	Social Security Act Amendments	• Created Medicare and Medicaid programs, making comprehensive health care available to millions of Americans • Established *Conditions of Participation (CoP)* and *Conditions for Coverage (CfC)*, which are federal regulations that health care facilities must comply with to participate in (receive reimbursement from) the Medicare and Medicaid programs; physicians must comply with billing and payment regulations published by CMS
1966	**Federal Claims Collection Act (FCCA)**	• Required carriers (processed Medicare Part B claims) and fiscal intermediaries (processed Medicare Part A claims), both of which were replaced by Medicare administrative contractors (that administer the Medicare fee-for-program), to attempt the collection of **overpayments** (funds a provider or beneficiary receives in excess of amounts due and payable under Medicare and Medicaid)
1970	Occupational Safety and Health Act	• Created the Occupational Safety and Health Administration (OSHA), whose mission is to ensure safe and healthful workplaces in America • Since the agency was created in 1971, workplace fatalities have been cut in half and occupational injury and illness rates have declined 40 percent; at the same time, U.S. employment has doubled from 56 million workers at 3.5 million work sites to 111 million workers at 7 million sites
1971	National Cancer Act (NCA)	• Amended the Public Health Service Act of 1798 to more effectively carry out the national effort against cancer • Part of President Nixon's "War on Cancer," which centralized research at the National Institutes of Health (NIH)
1972	Federal Anti-Kickback Law	• Protected patients and federal health care programs from fraud and abuse by curtailing the corrupting influence of money on health care decisions • Violations of the law (as amended in 2011) are punishable by up to 10 years in prison, criminal fines up to $100,000, administrative civil money penalties up to $100,000, and exclusion from participation in federal health care programs • In 1987, DHHS published regulations designating specific "safe harbors" for various payment and business practices that, while potentially prohibited by the law, would not be prosecuted (e.g., investments in group practices)

(continues)

TABLE 5-1 (continued)

YEAR	FEDERAL LAW	DESCRIPTION
1972	Drug Abuse and Treatment Act	• Required that drug and alcohol abuse patient records be kept confidential and not subject to disclosure except as provided by law • Applied to federally assisted alcohol or drug abuse programs, which are those that provide diagnosis, treatment, and referral for treatment of drug and/or alcohol abuse **NOTE:** General medical care facilities are required to comply with this legislation *only* if they have an identified drug/alcohol abuse treatment unit or their personnel provide drug/alcohol diagnosis, treatment, or referral.
	Social Security Amendments	• Strengthened the utilization review process by creating professional standard review organizations (PSROs), which were independent peer review organizations that monitored the appropriateness, quality, and outcome of the services provided to beneficiaries of the Medicare, Medicaid, and Maternal and Child Health Programs • PSROs are now called quality improvement organizations (QIOs)
1974	Employment Retirement Income Security Act (ERISA)	• Ensured that pension and other benefits were provided to employees as promised by employers
	Privacy Act of 1974	• Implemented to protect the privacy of individuals identified in information systems maintained by federal government hospitals (e.g., military hospitals) and to give individuals access to records concerning themselves • Does not preempt state laws that are more restrictive **NOTE:** Although this law has no effect on records maintained by nonfederal hospitals, effective April 14, 2003, the Health Insurance Portability and Accountability Act of 1996 (HIPAA) requires *all* health plans, health care clearinghouses, and health care providers that conduct electronic financial or administrative transactions (e.g., electronic billing) to comply with national patient privacy standards, which contain safeguards to protect the security and confidentiality of patient information.
1975	Consolidated Omnibus Budget Reconciliation Act (COBRA)	• Amended ERISA to include provisions for continuation of health care coverage, which apply to group health plans of employers with two or more employees • Participants maintain, at their own expense, health care plan coverage that would have been lost due to a triggering event (e.g., termination of employment); cost is comparable to what it would be if they were still members of the employer's group
1977	Utilization Review Act	• Facilitated ongoing assessment and management of health care services • Required hospitals to conduct continued-stay reviews to determine the medical necessity and appropriateness of Medicare and Medicaid inpatient hospitalizations
1979	Department of Education Organization Act	• Established a separate Department of Education • Health, Education and Welfare (HEW) became known as the Department of Health and Human Services (DHHS) on May 4, 1980
1982	Peer Review Improvement Act	• Replaced PSROs with peer review organizations (PROs) (now called QIOs), which were statewide utilization and quality control peer review organizations • In 1985, PROs incorporated a focused second-opinion program, which referred certain cases for diagnostic and treatment verification

(continues)

TABLE 5-1 (continued)

YEAR	FEDERAL LAW	DESCRIPTION
1982	Tax Equity and Fiscal Responsibility Act (TEFRA)	• Established the first Medicare prospective payment system, which was implemented in 1983 • Diagnosis-related groups (DRGs) required acute care hospitals to be reimbursed a predetermined rate according to discharge diagnosis (instead of a *per diem* rate, which compensated hospitals retrospectively based on charges incurred for the total inpatient length of stay, usually 80 percent of charges) **NOTE:** Additional prospective payment systems were implemented in subsequent years for other health care settings, as discussed in Chapter 9.
1985	Consolidated Omnibus Budget Reconciliation Act (COBRA)	• Allowed former employees, retirees, spouses, domestic partners, and eligible dependent children who lose coverage due to certain qualifying events the right to temporary continuation of health coverage at group rates; benefits can continue for 18 or 36 months, depending on the qualifying event.
1986	Health Care Quality Improvement Act (HCQIA)	• Established the **National Practitioner Data Bank (NPDB)**, which improves the quality of health care by encouraging state licensing boards, hospitals and other health care entities, and professional societies to identify and discipline those who engage in unprofessional behavior; restricts the ability of incompetent physicians, dentists, and other health care practitioners to move from state to state without disclosure or discovery of previous medical malpractice payment and adverse action history; and impacts licensure, clinical privileges, and professional society memberships as a result of adverse actions • The *Health Integrity and Protection Data Base (HIPDB)*, established in 1996 as a result of HIPAA, was merged into the NPDB on May 6, 2013; the HIPDB combats fraud and abuse in health insurance and health care delivery by serving as a national data collection program for reporting and disclosing certain final adverse actions taken against health care practitioners, providers, and suppliers • Authorized entities use an *Integrated Querying and Reporting Service (IQRS)* to report adverse actions and submit a single query to obtain information from the NPDB (www.npdb-hipdb.hrsa.gov)
1987	Nursing Home Reform Act (part of the Omnibus Budget Reconciliation Act of 1987)	• Ensured that residents of nursing homes receive quality care, required the provision of certain services to each resident, and established a Resident's Bill of Rights • Allowed nursing homes to receive Medicaid and Medicare payments for long-term care of residents if the homes were certified by the state in which they were located and were in substantial compliance with the requirements of the Nursing Home Reform Act
1988	McKinney Act	• Provided health care to the homeless
1989	Omnibus Budget Reconciliation Act (OBRA 1989)	• Enacted a **physician self-referral law** (or **Stark I**) that prohibits physicians from referring Medicare patients to *clinical laboratory services* in which the physicians or their family members had a financial ownership/investment interest and/or compensation arrangement • In 1994, because some providers routinely waived coinsurance and copayments, the DHHS Office of Inspector General (OIG) issued the following fraud alert: "Routine waiver of deductibles and copayments by charge-based providers, practitioners or suppliers is unlawful because it results in (1) false claims, (2) violations of the anti-kickback statute, and (3) excessive utilization of items and services paid for by Medicare"

(continues)

TABLE 5-1 (continued)

YEAR	FEDERAL LAW	DESCRIPTION
1995	Physicians at Teaching Hospitals (PATH)	• Audits implemented by DHHS that examine the billing practices of physicians at teaching hospitals • Focus was on two issues: (1) compliance with the Medicare rule affecting payment for physician services provided by residents (e.g., whether a teaching physician was present for Part B services billed to Medicare between 1990 and 1996), and (2) whether the level of the physician service was coded and billed properly
	Stark II Physician Self-Referral Law	• Stark II (physician self-referral laws) expanded Stark I by including referrals of Medicare and Medicaid patients for the following designated health care services (DHCS): clinical laboratory services, durable medical equipment and supplies, home health services, inpatient and outpatient hospitalization services, occupational therapy services, outpatient prescription drugs, parenteral and enteral nutrients, equipment and supplies, physical therapy services, prosthetics, orthotics and prosthetic devices and supplies, radiation therapy services and supplies, and radiology services, including MRIs, CAT scans, and ultrasound services • Hospitals must also comply with Stark II regulations because of relationships they establish with physicians • In 2001, new regulations clarified what a *designated health service* was and under what circumstances physicians can have a financial relationship with an organization and still make referrals of Medicare patients for services or products provided by that organization **EXAMPLE:** Home care physicians who served as home health agency medical directors were prohibited from making in excess of $25,000/year if they wanted to make referrals to that agency. That cap was removed in the revised Stark II regulations.
1996	National Correct Coding Initiative (NCCI)	• Developed by CMS to reduce Medicare program expenditures by detecting inappropriate codes on claims and denying payment for them
	Health Insurance Portability and Accountability Act (HIPAA)	• Mandated administrative simplification regulations that govern privacy, security, and electronic transaction standards for health care information • Amended ERISA and COBRA to improve portability and continuity of health insurance coverage in connection with employment; protects health insurance coverage for workers and their families when they change or lose their jobs • Created the Healthcare Integrity and Protection Data Bank (HIPDB), which was merged with the National Practitioner Data Bank (NPDB) on May 6, 2013 • Established the Medicare Integrity Program (MIP), which authorizes CMS to enter into contracts with entities to perform cost report auditing, medical review, anti-fraud activities, and the Medicare Secondary Payer (MSP) program
1997	State Children's Health Insurance Program (SCHIP)	• Established a health insurance program for infants, children, and teens that covers health care services such as doctor visits, prescription medicines, and hospitalizations

(continues)

TABLE 5-1 (continued)

YEAR	FEDERAL LAW	DESCRIPTION
1999	Payment Error Prevention Program (PEPP)	• Initiated by DHHS to require facilities to identify and reduce improper Medicare payments and, specifically, the Medicare payment error rate (number of dollars paid in error out of the total dollars paid for inpatient prospective payment system services) • Established Clinical Data Abstracting Centers (CDACs), which became responsible for initially requesting and screening medical records for PEPP surveillance sampling for medical review, DRG validation, and medical necessity; medical review criteria were developed by peer review organizations (now called quality improvement organizations or QIOs)
	Ticket to Work and Work Incentives Improvement Act	• Made it possible for millions of Americans with disabilities to join the workforce without fear of losing their Medicaid and Medicare coverage • Modernized employment services system for people with disabilities • Launched initiative on combating bioterrorism
	Program Safeguard Contractors (PSCs)	CMS transferred responsibility for fraud and abuse detection from carriers and fiscal intermediaries (FIs) to Program Safeguard Contractors (PSCs) (PSCs were replaced by the Zone Program Integrity Contractor, or ZPIC, program in 2009.)

2002	Improper Payments Information Act of 2002 (IPIA)	• Established the Payment Error Rate Measurement (PERM) program to measure improper payments in the Medicaid program and the State Children's Health Insurance Program (SCHIP)
		• Established the Comprehensive Error Rate Testing (CERT) program to assess and measure improper Medicare fee-for-service payments (based on reviewing selected claims and associated medical record documentation)
		• Established the Hospital Payment Monitoring Program (HPMP) to measure, monitor, and reduce the incidence of Medicare fee-for-service payment errors for short-term, acute care, inpatient PPS hospitals, which included development of the:
		  • First-look Analysis for Hospital Outlier Monitoring (FATHOM) data analysis tool, which provides administrative hospital and state-specific data for specific CMS target areas
		  • Program for Evaluating Payment Patterns Electronic Report (PEPPER), which contains hospital-specific administrative claims data for a number of CMS-identified problem areas (e.g., specific DRGs, types of discharges) (A hospital uses PEPPER data to compare their performance with that of other hospitals.)

2003	Medicare Prescription Drug, Improvement, and Modernization Act (MMA)	• Mandated implementation of the Recovery Audit Contractor (RAC) program to find and correct improper Medicare payments paid to health care providers participating in fee-for-service Medicare • CMS created the Zone Program Integrity Contractor (ZPIC) program to review billing trends and patterns, focusing on providers whose billings for Medicare services are higher than the majority of providers in the community. CMS programs for detecting fraud and abuse were originally assigned to carriers' fiscal intermediaries (FIs), all of which were replaced by Medicare administrative contractors (MACs) by 2009. ZPICs are assigned to the MAC jurisdictions, replacing Program Safeguard Contractors (PSCs). (RAC and ZPIC programs were implemented in 2009.) • Developed the Hospital Inpatient Quality Reporting (Hospital IQR) program to equip consumers with quality of care information so they can make more informed decisions about health care options. The Hospital IQR program requires hospitals to submit specific quality measures data about health conditions common among Medicare beneficiaries and that typically result in hospitalization. Eligible hospitals that do not participate in the Hospital IQR program will receive an annual market basket update with a 2.0 percentage point reduction. (The Hospital IQR program was previously called the *Reporting Hospital Quality Data for Annual Payment Update program.*)

(continues)

TABLE 5-1 (continued)

YEAR	FEDERAL LAW	DESCRIPTION
2003	FACT Act	The *Fair and Accurate Credit Transaction Act of 2003 (FACT Act)* includes the Federal Trade Commission's *Identity Theft Red Flags Rule* (or *Red Flags Rule*), which requires businesses and organizations to implement a written *Identity Theft Prevention Program* designed to detect the warning signs (or red flags) of identity theft in their day-to-day operations. Health care organizations are required to comply with the Red Flags Rule because they extend credit to patients. Their *Identity Theft Prevention Program* will help prevent **medical identity theft**, which occurs when someone uses another person's name and/or insurance information to obtain medical and/or surgical treatment, prescription drugs, and medical durable equipment; it can also occur when dishonest people who work in a medical setting use another person's information to submit false bills to health care plans. The program must include the following four criteria: (1) what patterns, practices, or specific activities the business or organization will identify as red flags indicating potential identity theft; (2) how the business or organization intends to detect the red flags it has identified; (3) how the business or organization will respond to the detection of a red flag it has identified; and (4) how the business or organization intends to evaluate the success of its program and maintain it in the future.
2005	**Patient Safety and Quality Improvement Act**	• Amends Title IX of the Public Health Service Act to provide for improved patient safety by encouraging voluntary and confidential reporting of events that adversely affect patients (e.g., preventable medical errors known as *never events* or *adverse events*, which include surgery performed on the wrong site, medications administered in error, and so on) • Creates Patient Safety Organizations (PSOs) to collect, aggregate, and analyze confidential information reported by health care providers • Designates information reported to PSOs as privileged and not subject to disclosure (except when a court determines that the information contains evidence of a criminal act or each provider identified in the information authorizes disclosure)
	Deficit Reduction Act of 2005	• Created **Medicaid Integrity Program (MIP)**, which increased resources available to CMS to combat abuse, fraud, and waste in the Medicaid program. Congress requires annual reporting by CMS about the use and effectiveness of funds appropriated for the MIP.
2006	**Tax Relief and Health Care Act of 2006 (TRHCA)**	• Created **Physician Quality Reporting System** (previously called the Physician Quality Initiative or PQRI system) that establishes a financial incentive for eligible professionals who participate in a *voluntary* quality reporting program
2008	MIPPA	The *Medicare Improvements for Patients and Providers Act (MIPPA)* amended Titles XVIII (Medicare) and XIX (Medicaid) of the Social Security Act to extend expiring provisions under the Medicare Program, improve beneficiary access to preventive and mental health services, enhance low-income benefit programs, and maintain access to care in rural areas including pharmacy access.

(continues)

TABLE 5-1 (continued)

YEAR	FEDERAL LAW	DESCRIPTION
2009	ARRA	The *American Recovery and Reinvestment Act (ARRA)* protects **whistleblowers**, who are individuals that make specified disclosures relating to funds covered by the act (e.g., Medicare payments). ARRA prohibits retaliation (e.g., termination) against such employees who disclose information that they believe is: ● Evidence of gross mismanagement of an agency contract or grant relating to covered funds ● A gross waste of covered funds ● A substantial and specific danger to public health or safety related to the implementation or use of covered funds ● An abuse of authority related to the implementation or use of covered funds ● A violation of law, rule, or regulation related to an agency contract or grant awarded or issued relating to covered funds
	HITECH Act	The *Health Information Technology for Economic and Clinical Health Act (HITECH Act) of 2009* published final rules in the January 2013 *Federal Register*, which impact the HIPAA privacy and security rules. (Content about specific provisions is included in the HITECH Act section of this chapter.)
2010	PPACA	The *Patient Protection and Affordable Care Act (PPACA)* includes a health care reform measure that requires implementation of the **hospital value-based purchasing (VBP) program** to promote better clinical outcomes and patient experiences of care. Beginning October 2012, value-based incentive payments will be made to hospitals that meet performance standards with respect to a performance period for the fiscal year involved. This means that reimbursement for inpatient acute care services will be based on care *quality* (instead of the *quantity* of the services provided). The program's measures are a subset of those already adopted for the existing *Hospital Inpatient Quality Reporting Program* (Hospital IQR program).
2011	MEDIC	The **Medicare Drug Integrity Contractors (MEDIC) Program** was implemented to assist with CMS audit, oversight, anti-fraud, and anti-abuse efforts related to the Medicare Part D benefit. The goal is to identify cases of suspected fraud, investigate them thoroughly and in a timely manner, and take immediate action to ensure that the Medicare Trust Fund does not inappropriately pay claims and that inappropriate payments are recommended for recoupment.

RETENTION OF RECORDS

Record retention is the storage of documentation for an established period of time, usually mandated by federal and/or state law. (The state in which the health care provider practices determines whether federal or state law mandates the retention period.) Its purpose is to ensure the availability of records for use by government agencies and other third parties (e.g., insurance audit, quality of care review). It is acceptable to store medical records and insurance claims (including attachments submitted to third-party payers) in a format other than original hard copy if the storage medium (e.g., microfilm, scanned images) accurately reproduces all original documents.

- **Medicare *Conditions of Participation* mandate the retention of patient records in their original or legally reproduced form (e.g., microfilm) for a period of at least 5 years. (Individual state laws may require retention of patient records for a longer period, such as 6 years in New York State.)**

- **The Health Insurance Portability and Accountability Act (HIPAA) mandates the retention of health insurance claims and accounting records for a minimum of 6 years, unless state law specifies a longer period.**
- **HIPAA also mandates that health insurance claims be retained for a minimum of 2 years after a patient's death.**

EXAMPLE 1: Community Hospital is located in North Carolina (NC), which mandates that hospital medical records be retained for a minimum of 11 years following the discharge of an adult, and for a minor the record must be retained until the patient's 30th birthday. Because NC law is stricter than the HIPAA mandate regarding retention of records, Community Hospital must retain adult patient records for a period of 11 years and minor patient records until the patient's 30th birthday.

EXAMPLE 2: Dr. Smith practices in Delaware (DE), which mandates that medical records be retained for 5 years. Because the HIPAA mandate is stricter than DE state law, Dr. Smith must retain patient records for a period of 6 years. For any patient who has died, Dr. Smith must retain the record for a period of 2 years after the date of death.

HEALTH INSURANCE PORTABILITY AND ACCOUNTABILITY ACT (HIPAA)

In 1996, Congress passed the Health Insurance Portability and Accountability Act (HIPAA) because of concerns about fraud (e.g., coding irregularities, medical necessity issues, and waiving of copays and deductibles). While the Federal False Claims Act provides CMS with regulatory authority to enforce fraud and abuse statutes for the Medicare program, HIPAA extends that authority to all federal and state health care programs.

The Health Insurance Portability and Accountability Act of 1996 (HIPAA), Public Law No. 104-191, amended the Internal Revenue Code of 1986 to:

- **Improve the portability and continuity of health insurance coverage in the group and individual markets**
- **Combat waste, fraud, and abuse in health insurance and health care delivery**
- **Promote the use of medical savings accounts**
- **Improve access to long-term care services and coverage**
- **Simplify the administration of health insurance by creating unique identifiers for providers, health plans, employers, and individuals**
- **Create standards for electronic health information transactions**
- **Create privacy standards for health information**

A discussion on each HIPAA component follows. Although HIPAA standards are still being finalized, health care organizations should develop and implement a response to each component.

HIPAA legislation is organized according to five titles (Figure 5-5):

- ***Title I—Health Care Access, Portability, and Renewability***
- ***Title II—Preventing Health Care Fraud and Abuse, Administrative Simplification, and Medical Liability Reform***

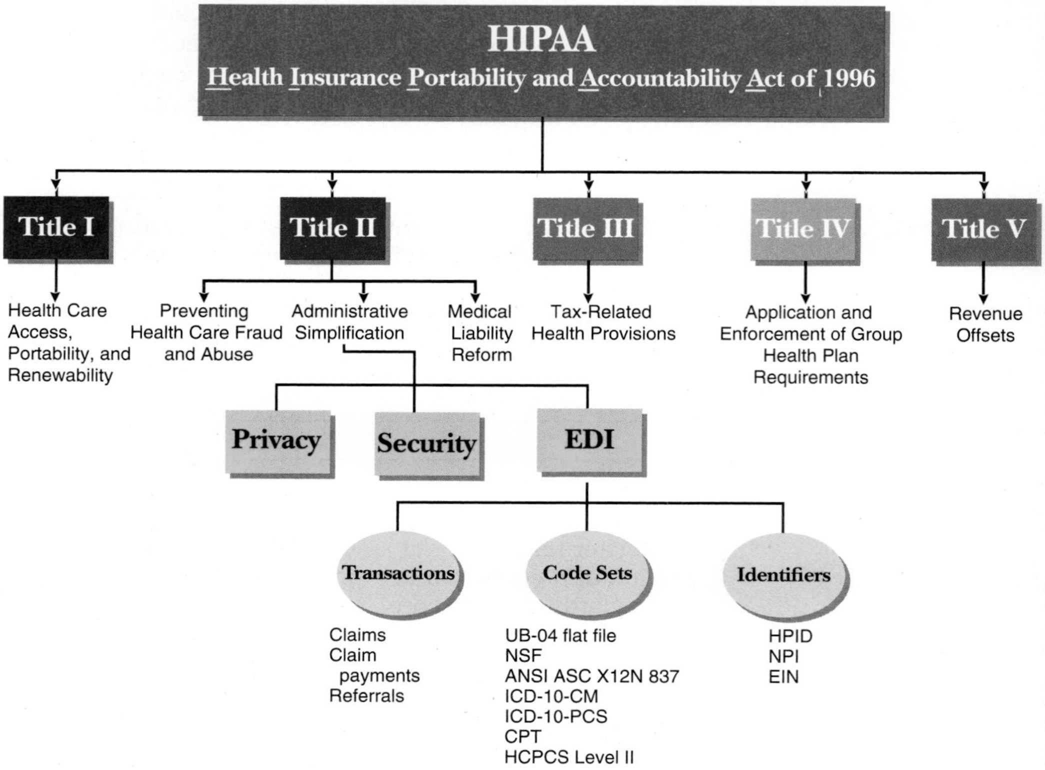

FIGURE 5-5 HIPAA provisions.

- ***Title III—Tax-Related Health Provisions***
- ***Title IV—Application and Enforcement of Group Health Plan Requirements***
- ***Title V—Revenue Offsets***

HIPAA Title I—Health Care Access, Portability, and Renewability

HIPAA provisions were designed to improve the portability and continuity of health coverage by:

- **Limiting exclusions for pre-existing medical conditions**
- **Providing credit for prior health coverage and a process for transmitting certificates and other information concerning prior coverage to a new group health plan or issuer**
- **Providing new rights that allow individuals to enroll for health coverage when they lose other health coverage, change from group to individual coverage, or gain a new dependent**
- **Prohibiting discrimination in enrollment and premiums against employees and their dependents based on health status**
- **Guaranteeing availability of health insurance coverage for small employers and renewability of health insurance coverage in both the small and large group markets**
- **Preserving, through narrow preemption provisions, the states' traditional role in regulating health insurance, including state flexibility to provide greater protections**

HIPAA Title II—Preventing Health Care Fraud and Abuse

HIPAA defines **fraud** as "an intentional deception or misrepresentation that someone makes, knowing it is false, that could result in an unauthorized payment." The attempt itself is considered fraud, regardless of whether it is successful. **Abuse** "involves actions that are inconsistent with accepted, sound medical, business, or fiscal practices. Abuse directly or indirectly results in unnecessary costs to the program through improper payments." The difference between fraud and abuse (Table 5-2) is the individual's intent; however, both have the same impact in that they steal valuable resources from the health care industry.

When a Medicare provider commits fraud, an investigation is conducted by the Department of Health and Human Services (DHHS) Office of the Inspector General (OIG). The OIG Office of Investigations prepares the case for referral to the Department of Justice for criminal and/or civil prosecution. A person found guilty of Medicare fraud faces criminal, civil, and/or administrative sanction penalties, including:

- **Civil penalties of $20,000 per false claim plus triple damages under the False Claims Act. (The provider pays an amount equal to three times the claim submitted, in addition to the civil penalties fine.)**
- **Criminal fines and/or imprisonment of up to 10 years if convicted of the crime of health care fraud as outlined in HIPAA or, for violations of the Medicare/Medicaid Anti-Kickback Statute, imprisonment of up to 10 years and/or a criminal penalty fine of up to $100,000.**
- **Administrative sanctions, including up to a $20,000 civil monetary penalty per line item on a false claim, assessments of up to triple the amount falsely claimed, and/or exclusion from participation in Medicare and state health care programs.**

TABLE 5-2 Fraud and abuse examples and possible outcomes

EXAMPLES OF FRAUD	POSSIBLE OUTCOMES OF FRAUD

• Accepting or soliciting bribes, kickbacks, and/or rebates
• Altering claims to increase reimbursement
• Billing for services or supplies not provided
• Misrepresenting codes to justify payment (e.g., upcoding)
• Entering a health insurance identification number other than the patient's to ensure reimbursement
• Falsifying certificates of medical necessity, plans of treatment, and/or patient records to justify payment
	• Administrative sanctions
	• Civil monetary penalties
	• Exclusion from the health program (e.g., Medicare)
	• Referral to the Office of Inspector General:
	  • Exclusion from Medicare program
	  • Sanctions and civil monetary penalties
	  • Criminal penalties (e.g., fines, incarceration, loss of license to practice, restitution, seizure of assets)

EXAMPLES OF ABUSE	**POSSIBLE OUTCOMES OF ABUSE**

• Billing noncovered services as covered services
• Billing or claim processing errors
• Reporting duplicative charges on a claim
• Charging excessively for services, equipment, and/or supplies
• Improper billing that results in payment by a government program when another payer is responsible
• Submitting claims for services not medically necessary
• Violating participating provider agreements with third-party payers
	• Education
	• Referral for Medical Review:
	  • Prepayment review of submitted claims
	  • Postpayment review (audit) of submitted claims
	• Recoup overpaid funds:
	  • Provider refunds payer
	  • Payment is withheld from future processed claims
	  • Suspension of payer payments (e.g., MAC holds checks)
	• Warnings

In addition to these penalties, those who commit health care fraud can also be tried for mail and wire fraud.

EXAMPLE: Medical review of claims submitted to Medicare by a physician group practice that contains mental health providers identified a pattern of psychiatric services billed on behalf of nursing facility patients with a medical history of dementia. Review of patient records revealed no mental health care physician orders or plans of treatment. This is an example of billing for services not furnished.

The DHHS Office of Inspector General (OIG) published the final *Compliance Program Guidance for Individual and Small Group Physician Practices* in the October 5, 2000, *Federal Register*. The intent of the guidance document is to help physicians in individual and small group practices design voluntary compliance programs that best fit the needs of their individual practices. By law, physicians are not subject to civil, administrative, or criminal penalties for innocent errors, or even negligence. The civil False Claims Act covers only offenses that are committed with *actual knowledge* of the falsity of the claim, or *reckless disregard* or *deliberate ignorance* of the truth or falsity of a claim. (The False Claims Act does not cover mistakes, errors, or negligence.) The OIG has stated that it is mindful of the difference between innocent errors (e.g., erroneous claims) and reckless or intentional conduct (e.g., fraudulent claims).

A voluntary compliance program can help physicians avoid generating erroneous and fraudulent claims by ensuring that submitted claims are true and accurate, expediting and optimizing proper payment of claims, minimizing billing mistakes, and avoiding conflicts with self-referral and antikickback statutes. Unlike other guidance previously issued by the OIG (e.g., *Third-Party Medical Billing Company Compliance Program Guidance*), the final physician guidance does not require that physician practices implement all seven standard components of a full-scale compliance program. (Although the seven components provide a solid basis upon which a physician practice can create a compliance program, the OIG acknowledges that full implementation of all components may not be feasible for smaller physician practices.) Instead, the guidance emphasizes a step-by-step approach for those practices to follow in developing and implementing a voluntary compliance program.

As a first step, physician practices can begin by identifying risk areas which, based on a practice's specific history with billing problems and other compliance issues, might benefit from closer scrutiny and corrective/educational measures. The step-by-step approach is as follows:

1. Perform periodic audits to internally monitor billing practices.
2. Develop written practice standards and procedures.
3. Designate a compliance officer to monitor compliance efforts and enforce practice standards.
4. Conduct appropriate training and education about practice standards and procedures.
5. Respond appropriately to detected violations by investigating allegations and disclosing incidents to appropriate government entities.
6. Develop open lines of communication (e.g., discussions at staff meetings regarding erroneous or fraudulent conduct issues) to keep practice employees updated regarding compliance activities.
7. Enforce disciplinary standards through well-publicized guidelines.

The final guidance further identifies four specific compliance risk areas for physicians: (1) proper coding and billing; (2) ensuring that services are reasonable and necessary; (3) proper documentation; and (4) avoiding improper inducements, kickbacks, and self-referrals. These risk areas reflect areas in which the OIG has focused its investigations and audits related to physician practices. The final guidance also provides direction to larger practices in developing compliance programs by recommending that they use both the physician guidance and previously issued guidance, such as the *Third-Party Medical Billing Company Compliance Program Guidance* or the *Clinical Laboratory Compliance Program Guidance*, to create a compliance program that meets the needs of the larger practice.

Medicare Integrity Program (MIP)

HIPAA includes a provision that established the *Medicare Integrity Program (MIP)*, which gives CMS specific contracting authority to enter into contracts with entities to promote the integrity of the Medicare program, such as medical review (MR), which requires Medicare administrative contractors (MACs) to verify inappropriate billing and to develop interventions to correct the problem. **Medical review (MR)** is defined by CMS as a review of claims to determine whether services provided are medically reasonable and necessary, as well as to follow up on the effectiveness of previous corrective actions. The national objectives and goals of medical review (MR) are to:

- Increase the effectiveness of medical review payment safeguard activities
- Exercise accurate and defensible decision making on medical review of claims
- Place emphasis on reducing the paid claims error rate by notifying individual billing entities (e.g., providers, DME suppliers) of medical review findings and making appropriate referrals to provider outreach and education
- Collaborate with other internal components and external entities to ensure correct claims payment and to address situations of potential fraud, waste, and abuse

If a MAC reviews a small sample of claims and verifies that an error exists, the MAC classifies the severity of the problem as minor, moderate, or significant. Then, the MAC imposes corrective actions that are appropriate for the severity of the infraction. The following types of corrective actions can result from medical review:

- *Provider Notification/Feedback*. Problems detected at minor, moderate, or significant levels require the MAC to inform the provider of appropriate billing procedures.
- *Prepayment Review*. When medical review of a claim prior to payment results in identified problems, the provider may be placed on prepayment review, which means a percentage of claims are subjected to medical review before payment is authorized. Once providers have re-established the practice of submitting claims correctly, they are removed from prepayment review.
- *Postpayment Review*. Medical review of claims after payment has been made is commonly performed by using statistically valid sampling, which allows underpayments or overpayments (if they exist) to be estimated without requesting the provider to submit copies of patient records for all claims submitted. This reduces the administrative burden for Medicare and costs for both Medicare and providers.

New signature guidelines for MR purposes require all health care services provided and/or ordered to be authenticated by the author (e.g., provider). Reviewers will disregard an entry that has a missing or illegible signature, and they will make claims review determinations based on authenticated documentation only.

This means that providers can no longer use signature stamps, and their signatures must be handwritten or generated electronically, except for:

- **Facsimiles of original written or electronic signatures for terminal illness for hospice care**
- **Clinical diagnostic test orders, which do not require a signature (but do require authenticated documentation)**
- **In cases where the relevant regulation, National Coverage Determination (NCD), Local Coverage Determination (LCD), and *Medicare Claims Processing Manual* have specific signature requirements, those take precedence.**

Medicaid Integrity Program (MIP)

NOTE: The Medicaid Integrity Program (MIP) was mandated by the Deficit Reduction Act of 2005. MIP content is included in this section of the chapter because of preceding HIPAA content about fraud and abuse.

The *Medicaid Integrity Program (MIP)* was mandated by the Deficit Reduction Act of 2005, which provides funds ($5 million in 2007 to $75 million by 2009 and each year thereafter) to combat fraud, waste, and abuse. Contractors will review the actions of those seeking payment from Medicaid (e.g., providers), perform audits, identify overpayments, and educate providers and others about program integrity and quality of care. Congress mandated that CMS devote at least 100 full-time staff members to the project, who will collaborate with state Medicaid officials. The MIP is based on four key principles:

- **Accountability for the MIP's activities and those of its contractors and the states**
- **Collaboration with internal and external partners and stakeholders**
- **Flexibility to address the ever-changing nature of Medicaid fraud**
- **National leadership in Medicaid program integrity**

The major strategies will include:

- **Balancing the role of the MIP between providing training and technical assistance to states while conducting oversight of their activities; and between supporting criminal investigations of suspect providers while concurrently seeking administrative sanctions**
- **Collaborating and coordinating with internal and external partners**
- **Consulting with interested parties in the development of the comprehensive Medicaid integrity plan**
- **Developing effective return on investment strategies**
- **Employing lessons learned in developing guidance and directives aimed at fraud prevention**
- **Targeting vulnerabilities in the Medicaid program**

Recovery Audit Contractor (RAC) Program

NOTE: The Patient Protection and Affordable Care Act of 2009 requires state Medicaid programs to contract with RACs to identify and recoup overpayment and underpayment of fees to providers. The Medicaid RAC program was implemented in January 2012.

The *Recovery Audit Contractor (RAC) program* is mandated by the Medicare Prescription Drug, Improvement, and Modernization Act of 2003 (MMA) to find and correct improper Medicare payments paid to health care providers participating in fee-for-service Medicare.

Medicare processes more than 1.2 billion Medicare claims annually, submitted by more than one million health care providers, including hospitals, skilled nursing facilities, physicians, and medical equipment suppliers. (*The federal surety bond*, a contract established between DME suppliers and Medicare, is now $500,000. In previous years, it was just $25,000.) Errors in claims submitted by these health care providers for services provided to Medicare beneficiaries can account for billions of dollars in improper payments each year.

The goal of the RAC program is to identify improper payments made on claims of health care services provided to Medicare beneficiaries. *Improper payments* include:

- ***Overpayments*** **(e.g., submitted claims do not meet Medicare's National Correct Coding Initiative or medical necessity policies, documentation in the patient record does not support codes reported on the claim, or Medicare administrative contractors reimburse providers more than once for the same patient encounter or calculate reimbursement using an incorrect fee schedule)**
- ***Underpayments*** **(e.g., submitted claims report codes simple procedures, when review of the record indicates a more complicated procedure was performed)**

Health care providers subject to review include hospitals, physician practices, nursing homes, home health agencies, durable medical equipment suppliers, and any other provider or supplier that bills Medicare Parts A and B.

The national RAC program is an outgrowth of a successful demonstration program that used RACs to identify Medicare overpayments and underpayments to health care providers and suppliers in California, Florida, New York, Massachusetts, South Carolina, and Arizona. The demonstration project resulted in over $900 million in overpayments that were returned to the Medicare Trust Fund between 2005 and 2008 as well as nearly $38 million in underpayments that were returned to health care providers. The RAC program uses *program integrity contractors (RAC auditors)* who review billing trends and patterns across Medicare programs. RAC auditors will focus on facilities and organizations (e.g., home health agency, hospitals) and individuals (e.g., providers) where billings for Medicare services are higher than the majority of providers and suppliers in the community. The recovery auditor (or RAC auditor) in each jurisdiction includes:

- **Region A: Performant Recovery, Livermore, California (www.dcsrac.com)**
- **Region B: CGI Federal, Fairfax, Virginia (http://racb.cgi.com)**
- **Region C: Connolly Consulting Associates, Inc., Wilton, Connecticut (www.connollyhealthcare.com/rac)**
- **Region D: Health Data Insights, Inc., Las Vegas, Nevada (https://racinfo.healthdatainsights.com)**

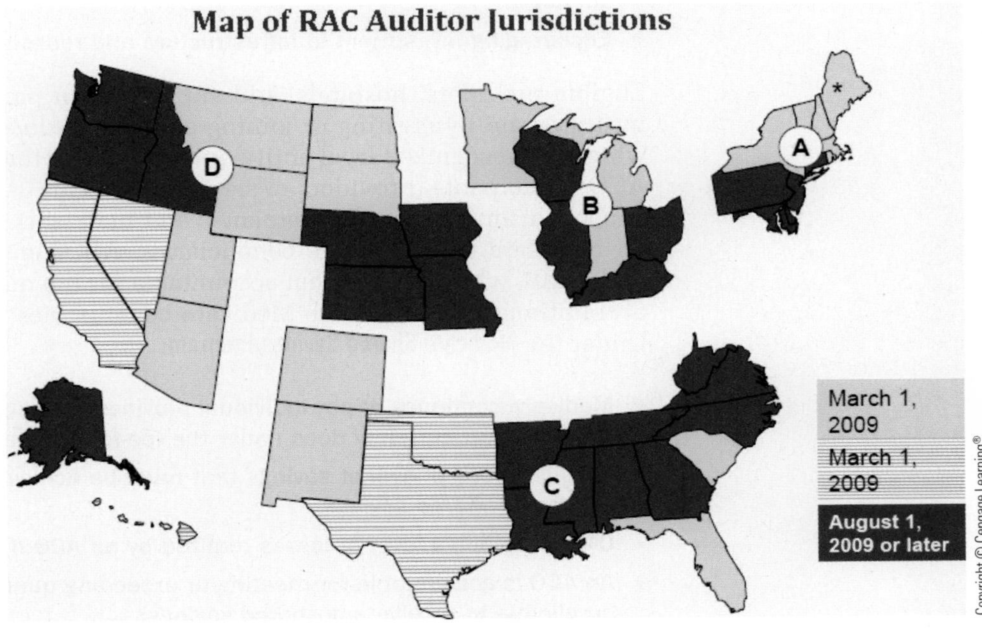

Health Care Fraud Prevention and Enforcement Action Team (HEAT)

The PPACA created the Health Care Fraud Prevention and Enforcement Action Team (HEAT) in 2009, which is a joint effort between the DHHS and Department of Justice (DOJ) to fight health care fraud by increasing coordination, intelligence sharing and training among investigators, agents, prosecutors, analysts, and policymakers. A key component of HEAT includes Medicare Strike Force teams, which are comprised of interagency teams of analysts, investigators, and prosecutors who can target emerging or migrating fraud schemes, including fraud by criminals masquerading as health care providers or suppliers. This effort received a boost in 2012 with the formation of a ground-breaking new Healthcare Fraud Prevention Partnership among DHHS, DOJ, and private organizations designed to find and stop scams that cut across public and private payers. This partnership facilitates industry anti-fraud efforts through shared insights among investigators, prosecutors, policymakers, and others.

EXAMPLE: The Medicare Strike Force coordinated three major actions in 2012, with the largest in May 2012 when 107 individuals, including doctors, nurses, and other licensed medical professionals, were charged in seven cities for their alleged participation in Medicare fraud schemes involving more than $452 million in alleged false billing.

Medicare Shared Savings Program

The *Patient Protection and Affordable Care Act (PPACA)* requires CMS to establish a Medicare shared savings program to facilitate coordination and cooperation among providers so as to improve the quality of care for Medicare fee-for-service beneficiaries and to reduce unnecessary costs. The Medicare shared savings program is designed to improve beneficiary outcomes and increase value of care by:

- **Promoting accountability for the care of Medicare fee-for-service beneficiaries**
- **Requiring coordinated care for all services provided under Medicare fee-for-service**
- **Encouraging investment in infrastructure and redesigned care processes**

Eligible providers, hospitals, and suppliers can participate in the shared savings program by creating or joining an *Accountable Care Organization (ACO)*, which is a recognized legal entity under state law that is comprised of a group of ACO participants (providers of services and suppliers). ACOs have established a mechanism for shared governance, and they work together to coordinate care for Medicare fee-for-service beneficiaries. ACOs enter into a 3-year agreement with CMS, which holds them accountable for the quality, cost, and overall care of traditional fee-for-service Medicare beneficiaries who may be assigned to it. Under the **Medicare Shared Savings Program**:

- **Medicare continues to pay individual providers and suppliers for specific items and services as it currently does under the fee-for-service payment systems.**
- **CMS develops a level of savings that must be achieved by each ACO *if the ACO is to receive shared savings.***
- **CMS develops a level of losses realized by an ACO *if it is held liable for losses.***
- **An ACO is accountable for meeting or exceeding quality performance standards to be eligible to receive any shared savings.**

Overpayments

Overpayments are funds a provider or beneficiary receives in excess of amounts due and payable under Medicare and Medicaid statutes and regulations. Once a determination of overpayment has been made, the amount so determined is a debt owed to the U.S. government. The Federal Claims Collection Act of 1966 requires Medicare administrative contractors (MACs) (as agents of the federal government) to attempt the collection of overpayments. Examples of overpayments include:

- Payment based on a charge that exceeds the reasonable charge
- Duplicate processing of charges/claims
- Payment to a physician on a nonassigned claim or to a beneficiary on an assigned claim (payment made to wrong payee)
- Payment for noncovered items and services, including medically unnecessary services
- Incorrect application of the deductible or coinsurance
- Payment for items or services rendered during a period of nonentitlement
- Primary payment for items or services for which another entity is the primary payer
- Payment for items or services rendered after the beneficiary's date of death (post-payment reviews are conducted to identify and recover payments with a billed date of service that is after the beneficiary's date of death)

When a Medicare administrative contractor determines that an overpayment was made, it proceeds with recovery by issuing an overpayment demand letter (Figure 5-6) to the provider. The letter contains information about the review and statistical sampling methodology used as well as corrective actions to be taken. (An explanation of the sampling methodology that was followed is included.) Corrective actions include payment suspension, imposition of civil money penalties, institution of pre- or post-payment review, additional edits, and so on.

Providers and beneficiaries can receive a *waiver of overpayment recovery* if one or more of the following provisions apply:

- Overpayment was discovered subsequent to the third calendar year after the year of payment.
- If an overpaid physician is found to be without fault or is deemed without fault, overpayment shifts to the beneficiary (e.g., medically unnecessary services).
- When both provider and beneficiary are without fault with respect to an overpayment on an assigned claim for medically unnecessary services, liability is waived for the overpayment (e.g., no action is taken to recover the overpayment).
- If a beneficiary is liable for an incorrect payment, CMS or SSA may waive recovery if the beneficiary was without fault with respect to the overpayment and recovery would cause financial hardship or would be against equity and good conscience.

Medicare administrative contractors are prohibited from seeking overpayment recovery when the following two time limitations apply:

- Overpayment is not reopened within 4 years (48 months) after the date of payment, unless the case involves fraud or similar fault.

[Insert Medicare administrative contractor letterhead here]

May 15, YYYY

Doug M. Smith, M.D.
393 Main St
Anywhere, US 12345

RE: SSN: **123-45-6789**
PATIENT: **Nathan A. Sanders**
CLAIM #: **939395SLD0005**

Dear Provider:

Please be advised that an overpayment of benefits has been made for the above named patient. In order to resolve this matter we are asking you to make reimbursement. Please make your check payable to:

EMPIRE STATE HEALTH PLAN

in the amount of

$675.00

and forward it to:

EMPIRE STATE HEALTH PLAN
P.O. BOX 93902
ANYWHERE, US 12345

We are requesting this refund due to the following reason:

CLAIM WAS PROCESSED UNDER THE WRONG PATIENT FOR DATES OF SERVICE 4/15 & 4/20/YYYY.

If you have any questions, please feel free to contact us.

Sincerely,

Mary Louise Smith
Claims Analyst (39-392)

FIGURE 5-6 Sample overpayment recovery letter.

- **Overpayment is discovered later than three full calendar years after the year of payment, unless there is evidence that the provider or beneficiary was at fault with respect to the overpayment.**

Provider Liability for Overpayments Providers are liable for refunding an overpayment in the following situations:

- **Overpayment resulted from incorrect reasonable charge determination (because providers are responsible for knowing Medicare reasonable charges for services).**

  Exception: **If the provider's reasonable charge screen was increased and the physician had no reason to question the amount of the increase, the physician is not liable and the case is referred to CMS for review.**
- **Provider received duplicate payments from the Medicare administrative contractor (because the claim was processed more than once, or the provider submitted duplicate claims).**
- **Provider received payment after agreeing to accept assignment (the provider agreed to accept as payment whatever the payer deemed a reasonable charge),**

and a beneficiary received payment on an itemized bill and submitted that payment to the provider.

EXAMPLE: Mary Sue Patient underwent office surgery on May 15, performed by Dr. Smith. Medicare determined the reasonable charge for the office surgery to be $360. In July, Dr. Smith and Mary Sue Patient each received a check from Medicare in the amount of $300. Mary Sue Patient then signed her $300 over to Dr. Smith. Thus, Dr. Smith received a total of $600 for services provided on May 15, an overpayment of $240 (the amount received in excess of the reasonable charge). Mary Sue Patient is liable for the remaining $60 of the duplicate payment. (If Mary Sue Patient had also previously paid Dr. Smith the $60 as coinsurance, Dr. Smith would be liable for the entire $300 overpayment. Remember! *Coinsurance* is the percentage of costs a patient shares with the health plan.) *Dr. Smith is responsible for contacting the Medicare administrative contractor (MAC) to report the overpayment and make arrangements to provide a refund.*

- **Provider received duplicate payments from Medicare and another payer directly or through the beneficiary, which happens to be the primary payer (e.g., automobile medical or no-fault insurer, liability insurer, or workers' compensation).**
- **Provider was paid but does not accept assignment.**
- **Provider furnished erroneous information, or provider failed to disclose facts known or that should have been known and that were material to the payment of benefits.**

EXAMPLE 1: A beneficiary is referred to a provider by an employer for a fracture that occurred during a fall at work. The physician billed Medicare and neglected to indicate on the claim that the injury was work related (although that information had been provided by the patient). If Medicare benefits are paid to the provider for services and the injury would have been covered by workers' compensation, the provider is liable for an overpayment because of failure to disclose that the injury was work related. Thus, the provider is liable whether or not the beneficiary was also paid.

EXAMPLE 2: A provider submitted an assigned claim showing total charges of $1,000. The provider did not indicate on the claim that any portion of the bill had been paid by the patient. The MAC determined the reasonable charge to be $600 and paid the physician $480 (80 percent of $600) on the assumption that no other payment had been received. The MAC later learned that the beneficiary had paid the physician $200 (which included the $120 coinsurance amount) before the provider submitted his claim. Thus, the payment should have been split between provider and beneficiary, with $400 paid to the provider and an $80 overpayment refund to the beneficiary. The provider is liable for causing the $80 overpayment, as the amount received from the beneficiary was not reported on the claim. (Remember! *Coinsurance* is the percentage of costs a patient shares with the health plan.)

- **Provider submitted a claim for services other than medically necessary services, but should have known they would not be covered (e.g., conversation with a relative of a beneficiary).**

- **Provider submitted a claim for medically unnecessary services.**
- **Items or services were furnished by a provider or supplier not qualified for Medicare reimbursement.**

> **EXAMPLE 1:** A lab test is performed by a nonqualified independent laboratory.

> **EXAMPLE 2:** Services are rendered by a naturopath (practitioner who uses natural remedies instead of drugs and surgery).

- **Overpayment was due to a mathematical or clerical error. (Failing to properly collect coinsurance, copayment, or deductible amounts is not a mathematical or clerical error.)**
- **Provider does not submit documentation to substantiate services billed, or there is a question as to whether services were actually performed (e.g., fraud is suspected).**
- **Overpayment was for rental of durable medical equipment, and supplier billed under the one-time authorization procedure. Suppliers of durable medical equipment that have accepted assignment can be reimbursed for rental items on the basis of a one-time authorization by the beneficiary (without the need to obtain the beneficiary's signature each month).**

Absence of Provider Liability for Overpayments A provider is liable for overpayments received unless found to be *without fault* as determined by the Medicare administrative contractor (MAC). A provider can be considered without fault if reasonable care was exercised in billing for and accepting payment, and the provider had a reasonable basis for assuming that payment was correct. In addition, if the provider had reason to question the payment and promptly brought the question to the attention of the MAC, she may be found without liability.

These criteria are always met in the case of overpayments due to an error with respect to the beneficiary's entitlement to Medicare benefits and the MAC's failure to properly apply the deductible. Normally, it is clear from the circumstances of the overpayment whether the provider was without fault in causing the overpayment. When this is not clear from the record, the MAC must review the issue (as long as the review occurs within three calendar years after the year in which the overpayment was made).

> **NOTE:** The National Correct Coding Initiative (NCCI) was started by CMS in 1996 (and it was *not* mandated by HIPAA). NCCI content is included in this section of the chapter because of preceding HIPAA content about fraud and abuse.

National Correct Coding Initiative (NCCI)

The Centers for Medicare and Medicaid Services (CMS) developed the *National Correct Coding Initiative (NCCI)* in 1996 to reduce Medicare program expenditures by detecting inappropriate codes submitted on claims and denying payment for them, promote national correct coding methodologies, and eliminate improper coding practices. (The National Correct Coding Initiative is covered in more detail in Chapter 7 of this textbook.)

NCCI code edits (Table 5-3) are used to process Medicare Part B claims, and NCCI coding policies are based on the:

- **Analysis of standard medical and surgical practice**
- **Coding conventions included in CPT**

> **NOTE:** Under a previous CMS contract, a private company refused to publish NCCI code edits it developed because it considered them proprietary; these nonpublished code edits were called **black box edits**. Use of these edits was discontinued when CMS did not renew its contract with the company, and future CMS contracts do not allow for such restrictions.

TABLE 5-3 Partial listing of National Correct Coding Initiative (NCCI) edits

NCCI EDIT	DESCRIPTION	DISPOSITION OF CLAIM
1	Invalid diagnosis code	Return to provider
2	Diagnosis and age conflict	Return to provider
3	Diagnosis and sex conflict	Return to provider
4	Medicare secondary payer alert	Suspend

- **Coding guidelines developed by national medical specialty societies (e.g., CPT advisory committee, which contains representatives of major medical societies)**
- **Local and national coverage determinations**
- **Review of current coding practices**

HIPAA Title II (continued)—Administrative Simplification

HIPAA was part of a congressional attempt at incremental health care reform, with the *administrative simplification* aspect requiring DHHS to develop standards for maintenance and transmission of health information required to identify individual patients. These standards are designed to:

NOTE: California implemented a regulation that prohibits the use of Social Security numbers on health plan ID cards and health-related correspondence.

- **Improve efficiency and effectiveness of the health care system by standardizing the interchange of electronic data for specified administrative and financial transactions**
- **Protect the security and confidentiality of electronic health information**

The requirements outlined by law and the regulations implemented by DHHS require compliance by *all* health care organizations that maintain or transmit electronic health information (e.g., health plans; health care clearinghouses; and health care providers, from large integrated delivery networks to individual physician offices).

The law also establishes significant financial penalties for violations.

General penalty for failure to comply:

- **Each violation: $100**
- **Maximum penalty for all violations of an identical requirement may not exceed $100,000**

Wrongful disclosure of individually identifiable health information:

- **Wrongful disclosure offense: $50,000; imprisonment of not more than 1 year; or both**
- **Offense under false pretenses: $100,000; imprisonment of not more than 10 years; or both**
- **Offense with intent to sell information: $250,000; imprisonment of not more than 10 years; or both**

Unique Identifiers

The administrative simplification (AS) provision of HIPAA requires establishment of standard identifiers for third-party payers (e.g., insurance companies, Medicare, and Medicaid), providers, and employers, as follows:

- **Health Plan Identifier (HPID) (formerly called PAYERID and PlanID) is assigned to third-party payers; it has 10 numeric positions, including a check digit as the tenth position. (A check digit is a one-digit character, alphabetic or numeric, used to verify the validity of a unique identifier.)**
- **National Individual Identifier (patient identifier) has been put on hold. Several bills in Congress would eliminate the requirement to establish a National Individual Identifier.**
- **National Provider Identifier (NPI) is assigned to health care providers as a 10-digit numeric identifier, including a check digit in the last position.**
- **National Standard Employer Identification Number (EIN) is assigned to employers who, as sponsors of health insurance for their employees, must be identified in health care transactions. It is the federal employer identification number (EIN) assigned by the Internal Revenue Service (IRS) and has nine digits with a hyphen (00-0000000). EIN assignment by the IRS began in January 1998.**

The Centers for Medicare and Medicaid Services (CMS) developed the **National Plan and Provider Enumeration System (NPPES)** to assign unique identifiers to health care providers and health plans. (Health plans also use NPPES to apply for their HPID.) Providers can apply for the national provider identifier (NPI) online, on paper, or through an organization (e.g., professional association). When applying for the NPI, it is important to remember that providers must:

- **Apply just once because every health plan, including Medicare and Medicaid, will use the same NPI for the provider**
- **Obtain an NPI even if they use a billing agency to prepare standard insurance transactions**
- **Continue to participate in health plan enrollment and/or credentialing processes**
- **Safeguard the NPI because it is a private identification number**

Electronic Health Care Transactions

HIPAA requires payers to implement **electronic transaction standards** (or transaction rules), which result in a uniform language for electronic data interchange. *Electronic data interchange (EDI)* is the process of sending data from one party to another using computer linkages. The CMS Standard EDI Enrollment Form must be completed prior to submitting electronic media claims (EMC) to Medicare. The agreement must be executed by each provider of health care services, physician, or supplier that intends to submit EMC.

> **EXAMPLE:** Health care providers submit electronic claims data to payers on computer tape or disk, or by computer modem or fax. The payer receives the claim, processes the data, and sends the provider the results of processing electronic claims (an electronic remittance advice).

The proposed standard for electronic signature is **digital**, which applies a mathematical function to the electronic document, resulting in a **unique bit string** (computer code) called a **message digest** that is encrypted and appended to the electronic document. (**Encrypt** means to encode a computer file, making it safe for electronic transmission so that unauthorized parties cannot read it.) The recipient of the transmitted electronic document **decrypts** (decodes) the message digest and compares the decoded digest with the transmitted version. If they are identical, the message is unaltered and the identity of the signer is proven.

The final rule on transactions and code sets was effective October 16, 2002, for large plans and October 16, 2003, for small plans. It requires the following to be used by health plans, health care clearinghouses (which perform centralized claims processing for providers and health plans), and health care providers who participate in electronic data interchanges:

NOTE: Computer-generated paper claims are not categorized as EDI.

- Three electronic formats are supported for health care claim transactions: the UB-04 flat file format, the National Standard Format (NSF), and the ANSI ASC X12N 837 (American National Standards Institute [ANSI], Accredited Standards Committee [ASC], Insurance Subcommittee [X12N], Claims validation tables [837]).
  - The **UB-04** flat file is a series of fixed-length records that is used to bill institutional services, such as services performed in hospitals. (The UB-04 is discussed in Chapter 9.)
  - The **National Standard Format (NSF)** flat file format is used to bill physician and noninstitutional services, such as services reported by a general practitioner on a CMS-1500 claim.
  - The **ANSI ASC X12N 837** variable-length file format is used to bill institutional, professional, dental, and drug claims.
- Dental services use *Current Dental Terminology (CDT)* codes. ***Current Dental Terminology (CDT)*** is a medical code set maintained and copyrighted by the American Dental Association.
- Diagnoses and inpatient hospital services are reported using *ICD-10-CM*.
- Physician services are reported using *Current Procedural Terminology (CPT)* codes.
- Procedures are reported using ICD-10-PCS (hospital inpatient) and CPT and HCPCS level II (outpatient and physician office).
- Institutional and professional pharmacy transactions are reported using *HCPCS level II (national)* codes.
- Retail pharmacy transactions are reported using the *National Drug Code* manual. No standard code set was adopted for nonretail pharmacy drug claims.

The ***National Drug Code (NDC)***, maintained by the Food and Drug Administration (FDA), identifies prescription drugs and some over-the-counter products. Each drug product is assigned a unique 11-digit, three-segment number, which identifies the vendor, product, and trade package size. The Deficit Reduction Act (DRA) of 2005 requires states to collect Medicaid rebates for physician-administered medications. Effective 2007, National Drug Codes (NDC) are reported on Medicaid CMS-1500 claims (in addition to the HCPCS level II codes) when physicians administer medication(s) to a patient during an encounter.

EXAMPLE: During an office encounter, a physician administered 4 milligrams of Zofran intravenously (IV) to a Medicaid patient. Enter the following codes on the CMS-1500 claim:

- J2405 as the HCPCS level II code for "ondansetron hydrochloride, per 1 mg," which is the generic form of Zofran. (Also enter the number 4 in the Units field of the CMS-1500 claim.)
- 00173044202 as the National Drug Code for "Zofran 2 mg/mL in solution form." (The NDC is located on the medication container.)

Privacy and Security Standards

NOTE: Providers should develop a policy that prohibits taking cell phone pictures of patients unless taken with the patient's own phone at the patient's request. Cell phone pictures of patients have appeared on the Internet, and employees have been terminated as a result because that is a breach of patient privacy.

Any information communicated by a patient to a health care provider is considered **privileged communication**, and HIPAA provisions address the privacy and security of protected health information. **Protected health information (PHI)** is information that is identifiable to an individual (individual identifiers) such as name, address, telephone numbers, date of birth, Medicaid ID number and other medical record numbers, Social Security number (SSN), and name of employer. In most instances, covered entities (providers, payers, and clearinghouses) are required to obtain an individual's **authorization** prior to disclosing the individual's health information, and HIPAA has established specific requirements for an authorization form. **Privacy** is the right of individuals to keep their information from being disclosed to others. Once information is disclosed (e.g., for the purpose of obtaining health care), it is essential that confidentiality of the information be maintained. **Confidentiality** involves restricting patient information access to those with proper authorization and maintaining the security of patient information. **Security** involves the safekeeping of patient information by:

- **Controlling access to hard copy and computerized records (e.g., implementing password protection for computer-based patient records)**
- **Protecting patient information from alteration, destruction, tampering, or loss (e.g., establishing office policies)**
- **Providing employee training in confidentiality of patient information (e.g., conducting annual in-service education programs)**
- **Requiring employees to sign a confidentiality statement that details the consequences of not maintaining patient confidentiality (e.g., employee termination)**

NOTE: Computerized practices must obtain the patient's signature on the special release form and provide a copy to the patient's insurance company upon request. With this method, the CMS-1500 claim generated will contain "SIGNATURE ON FILE" in Block 12 (Figure 5-8).

Because patient information is readily available through computerized databases and other means, it is essential to take steps to maintain confidentiality. **Breach of confidentiality**, often unintentional, involves the unauthorized release of patient information to a third party, as in the following examples:

- **Discussing patient information in public places (e.g., elevators)**
- **Leaving patient information unattended (e.g., computer screen display)**
- **Communicating patient information to family members without the patient's consent**
- **Publicly announcing patient information in a waiting room or registration area**
- **Accessing patient information without a job-related reason**

Although HIPAA privacy regulations do not require providers to obtain patient authorization for the release of health care information to payers for

NOTE: A dated, signed special release form is generally considered valid for 1 year. Be sure to obtain the patient's signature on the special release form each year. Undated signed forms are assumed to be valid until revoked by the patient or guardian. CMS regulations permit government programs to accept both dated and undated authorizations. Established medical practices must update patient information and obtain the necessary authorization forms. Patients who regularly seek care must sign a new authorization each year.

processing insurance claims, many providers continue to obtain patient authorization. The best practice is to advise patients that they have the right to restrict the release of their health care information (e.g., patient writes a letter informing the provider that medical records are not to be released to insurance companies). When a patient restricts the release of health care information, the provider should obtain the patient's signature on a consent form accepting financial responsibility for the cost of treatment. An insurance company that is prohibited from reviewing patient records will probably refuse to reimburse the provider for a submitted claim. The signed consent form accepting financial responsibility allows the provider to collect payment from the patient.

If patient authorization is obtained, be sure the patient has signed an "authorization for release of medical information" statement before completing the claim. The release can be obtained in one of two ways:

- **Ask the patient to sign a special release form that is customized by each practice and specifically names the patient's insurance company (Figure 5-7) or**
- **Ask the patient to sign Block 12, "Patient's or Authorized Person's Signature," on the CMS-1500 claim (Figure 5-8).**

When third parties (e.g., attorneys, family members, and others) request copies of patient information, be sure to obtain the patient's signature on an authorization to release medical information (Figure 5-9). Exceptions to the expectation of privacy include information released via subpoena duces tecum and according to statutory reporting requirements (e.g., communicable disease reporting).

Release of PHI for Legal Proceedings

It is usually acceptable to submit a copy of the medical record for legal proceedings. If the original record is required, obtain a receipt from the court clerk and retain a copy of the record in the storage area. Be sure to properly protect the original record when transporting it to court by placing the record in a locked storage container. Make sure that the original record remains in the custody of the health care personnel transporting the record until the record is entered into evidence.

Release of PHI for HIV Patients

Patients who undergo screening for the human immunodeficiency virus (HIV) or AIDS infection should sign an additional authorization statement for release of information regarding their HIV/AIDS status (Figure 5-10). Several states require very specific wording on this form. Be sure to determine if your state requires a special form.

Release of PHI for Drug and Alcohol Abuse Patients

The Drug Abuse and Treatment Act of 1972 is a federal law that requires drug and alcohol abuse patient records be kept confidential and not subject to disclosure except as provided by law. This law applies to federally assisted alcohol or drug abuse programs, which are those that provide diagnosis, treatment, or referral for treatment of drug and/or alcohol abuse. General medical care facilities are required to comply with the legislation only if they have an identified drug/alcohol abuse treatment unit or their personnel provide drug/alcohol diagnosis, treatment, or referral.

[Insert letterhead]

Authorization for Release of Medical Information to the Payer and Assignment of Benefits to Physician

COMMERCIAL INSURANCE

I hereby authorize release of medical information necessary to file a claim with my insurance company and ASSIGN BENEFITS OTHERWISE PAYABLE TO ME TO ____*(fill in provider's name)*____

I understand that I am financially responsible for any balance not covered by my insurance carrier. A copy of this signature is as valid as the original.

Signature of patient or guardian________________ Date ________

MEDICARE

BENEFICIARY ________________ Medicare Number ________

I request that payment of authorized Medicare benefits be made on my behalf to ____*(fill in provider's name)*____ for any service furnished to me by that provider. I authorize any custodian of medical information about me to release to the Centers for Medicare & Medicaid Services and its agents any information needed to determine these benefits or the benefits payable for related services.

Beneficiary Signature ________________ Date ________

MEDICARE SUPPLEMENTAL INSURANCE

BENEFICIARY ________________ Medicare Number ________

Medigap ID Number ________

I hereby give ____*(Name of Physician or Practice)*____ permission to bill for Medicare Supplemental Insurance payments for my medical care.

I understand that ____*(Name of Medicare Supplemental Insurance Carrier)*____ needs information about me and my medical condition to make a decision about these payments. I give permission for that information to go to ____*(Name of Medicare Supplemental Insurance Company)*____.

I request that payment of authorized Medicare Supplemental benefits be made either to me or on my behalf to ____*(Name of Physician or Practice)*____ for any services furnished me by that physician. I authorize any holder of medical information about me to release to ____*(Name of Medicare Supplemental Insurance Company)*____ any information required to determine and pay these benefits.

Beneficiary Signature ________________ Date ________

FIGURE 5-7 Sample authorization form for release of medical information and assignment of benefits.

READ BACK OF FORM BEFORE COMPLETING & SIGNING THIS FORM.

12. PATIENT'S OR AUTHORIZED PERSON'S SIGNATURE I authorize the release of any medical or other information necessary to process this claim. I also request payment of government benefits either to myself or to the party who accepts assignment below.

SIGNED SIGNATURE ON FILE DATE ________

FIGURE 5-8 Release of medical information (Block 12 on a CMS-1500 claim).

[Insert letterhead]

AUTHORIZATION FOR DISCLOSURE OF PROTECTED HEALTH INFORMATION (PHI)

(1) I hereby authorize Alfred Medical Center to disclose/obtain information from the health records of:

Patient Name	Date of Birth (mmddyyyy)	Telephone (w/ area code)
Patient Address		Medical Record Number

(2) Covering the period(s) of health care:

From (mmddyyyy)	To (mmddyyyy)	From (mmddyyyy)	To (mmddyyyy)

(3) I authorize the following information to be released by (Name of Provider) (check applicable reports):

☐ Face Sheet	☐ Doctors Orders	☐ Scan Results	☐ Mental Health Care	☐ Other:
☐ Discharge Summary	☐ Progress Notes	☐ Operative Report	☐ Alcohol Abuse Care	
☐ History & Physical Exam	☐ Lab Results	☐ Pathology Report	☐ Drug Abuse Care	
☐ Consultation	☐ X-ray Reports	☐ HIV Testing Results	☐ Nurses Notes	

This information is to be disclosed to or obtained from:

Name of Organization	Address of Organization	Telephone Number

for the purpose of: ____________________

Statement that information used or disclosed may be subject to redisclosure by the recipient and may no longer be protected by this rule. I understand that I have a right to revoke this authorization at any time. I understand that if I revoke this authorization I must do so in writing and present my written revocation to the Health Information Management Department. I understand that the revocation will not apply to information that has already been released in response to this authorization. I understand that the revocation will not apply to my insurance company when the law provides my insurer with the right to contest a claim under my policy. Unless otherwise revoked, this authorization will expire on the following date, event, or condition:

Expiration Date	Expiration Event	Expiration Condition

If I fail to specify an expiration date, event or, condition, this authorization will expire within six (6) months.

Signature of individual and date. I understand that authorizing the disclosure of this health information is voluntary. I can refuse to sign this authorization. I need not sign this form in order to ensure treatment. I understand that I may inspect or copy the information to be used or disclosed, provided in CFR 164.534. I understand that any disclosure of information carries with it the potential for an unauthorized redisclosure and may not be protected by federal confidentiality rules. If I have questions about disclosure of my health information, I can contact the Privacy Officer at Alfred Medical Center.

Signed:

Signature of Patient or Legal Representative	Date

If signed by legal representative:

Relationship to Patient	Signature of Witness

FIGURE 5-9 Sample authorization to release medical information.

[Insert letterhead]

Name and address of facility/provider obtaining release:

Name of person whose HIV related information will be released:

Name(s) and address(es) of person(s) signing this form (if other than above):

Relationship to person whose HIV information will be released:

Name(s) and address(es) of person(s) who will be given HIV related information:

Reason for release of HIV related information:

Time during which release is authorized:
From: To:

The Facility/Provider obtaining this release must complete the following:

Exceptions, if any, to the right to revoke consent for disclosure: (for example, cannot revoke if disclosure has already been made)

Description of the consequences, if any, of failing to consent to disclosure upon treatment, payment, enrollment, or eligibility for benefits:

(Note: Federal privacy regulations may restrict some consequences.)

My questions about this form have been answered. I know that I do not have to allow release of HIV related information, and that I can change my mind at any time and revoke my authorization by writing the facility/provider obtaining this release.

Date Signature

Figure 5-10 Sample authorization for release of confidential HIV-related information.

HIPAA Privacy Rule

The HIPAA **privacy rule** creates national standards to protect individuals' medical records and other personal health information. This rule also gives patients greater access to their own medical records and more control over how their personal health information is used. The rule addresses the obligations of health care providers and health plans to protect health information, requiring doctors, hospitals, and other health care providers to obtain a patient's written consent and an authorization before using or disclosing the patient's protected health information to carry out *treatment, payment, or health care operations (TPO).*

Privacy violations are subject to a penalty of no more than $100 per person per violation, not to exceed $25,000 per person per year per violation of a single standard. More serious violations are subject to more severe penalties, including the following:

- **$50,000 and/or up to 1 year in prison for persons who knowingly obtain and disclose protected health information**
- **$100,000 and/or up to 5 years in prison for persons who under "false pretense" obtain and disclose protected health information**
- **$250,000 and/or up to 10 years in prison for persons with intent to sell, transfer, or use PHI for malicious reasons or personal gain**

EXAMPLE: The DHHS Office for Civil Rights announced in 2011 that it has imposed a $4.3 million civil monetary penalty for violations of the HIPAA privacy rule on Cignet Health of Prince George's County, Maryland, as follows:

- $1.3 million for failing to grant 41 individuals access to their health records within 30 days.
- $3 million for "willful negligence" when the organization failed to cooperate with the investigation.

HIPAA ALERT!

Patient Access to Records. The HIPAA privacy rule states that "an individual has the right to inspect and obtain a copy of the individual's protected health information (PHI) in a designated record set," except for the following:

- Psychotherapy notes
- Information compiled in anticipation of use in a civil, criminal, or administration action or proceeding
- PHI subject to the Clinical Laboratory Improvements Amendments (CLIA) of 1988, which is the federal law that delineates requirements for certification of clinical laboratories
- PHI exempt from CLIA (e.g., information generated by facilities that perform forensic testing procedures)

HIPAA Security Rule

The HIPAA **security rule** adopts standards and safeguards to protect health information that is collected, maintained, used, or transmitted *electronically*. Covered entities affected by this rule include health plans, health care clearinghouses, and certain health care providers. Effective with implementation of the HITECH Act of 2009, health care business associates and their subcontractors must also follow the HIPAA security rule for electronic protected health information (PHI). Business associates must obtain HIPAA-compliant agreements with their subcontractors (instead of the business associate's covered entity doing so).

In general, security provisions should include the following policies and procedures:

NOTE: Individual states (e.g., New York) may have passed laws or established regulations for patient access to records; providers must follow these laws or regulations if they are stricter than HIPAA provisions.

- **Define authorized users of patient information to control access**
- **Implement a tracking procedure to sign out records to authorized personnel**
- **Limit record storage access to authorized users**
- **Lock record storage areas at all times**
- **Require the original medical record to remain in the facility at all times**

HITECH Act

The *Health Information Technology for Economic and Clinical Health Act (HITECH Act) of 2009* published final rules in the January 2013 *Federal Register*, which impacts HIPAA as follows:

- **Health care business associates and their subcontractors must comply with the HIPAA security rule for electronic protected health information (PHI). This means** that business associates must obtain HIPAA-compliant agreements with their subcontractors (instead of the business associate's covered entity doing so).

- Patients must authorize any health marketing they receive, except for notices such as prescription refill reminders, and business associates must obtain patient authorization prior to marketing.
- The sale of PHI by a covered entity or business associate (and their subcontractors) is prohibited.
- Compound authorizations for research are permitted, with adherence to applicable rules.
- Individually identifiable health information of a person deceased for more than 50 years is no longer considered PHI under the HIPAA privacy rule.
- Covered entities are permitted to disclose a decedent's PHI to family members and others who were involved in the care or payment for care of a decedent prior to death, unless doing so is inconsistent with any known prior expressed preference of the individual.
- Covered entities can disclose proof of immunization to a school where state or other law requires it prior to admitting a student. Written authorization is no longer required, but an agreement must still be obtained, and it can be oral.
- Covered entities must provide recipients of fundraising communication with a clear and conspicuous opportunity to opt out of receiving further such communications.
- Patients can restrict health plan (third-party payer) access to medical records that pertain to treatment paid for by the patient out of pocket.
- Patient access to electronic PHI is required, which means covered entities must provide a copy of protected health information that is maintained electronically and located in one or more designated record sets.
  - Covered entities must produce a copy of the electronic record in the format requested by the patient (or authorized individual).
  - Fees for paper and electronic copies are defined, which means providers can charge for costs of labor and materials required to copy PHI (whether in paper or electronic form). A reasonable cost-based fee for skilled technical staff time spent creating and copying the electronic file can be included in labor costs.
  - A covered entity cannot withhold copies of records due to the failure to pay for services above and beyond copying costs.
  - Timeliness for the provision of paper and electronic records was defined.
  - The breach notification rule's "harm threshold" was replaced with the new "low probability standard" with respect to breach of patient information notifications. This standard, which is used to determine whether a disclosure constitutes a breach, requires covered entities and business associates (and their subcontractors) to send breach notification letters to all individuals whose information has been compromised and report the incident (including detailed, publicly reported information about the breach based on the risk assessment system) to the Office of Civil Rights (OCR).
  - DHHS adopted a new risk assessment system that must be used to assess a possible breach, and it is mandatory that the following four factors are addressed during risk assessment analysis:
    1. What are the nature and extent of the PHI involved in the breach (e.g., types of identifiers, likelihood of re-identification of PHI involved in the breach)?

2. Who is the unauthorized person who used the PHI or to whom was the disclosure made?
3. Was PHI actually acquired or viewed by an inappropriate recipient?
4. To what extent has risk to the PHI been mitigated (e.g., disclosing entity received receipt of assurances from recipient that PHI was not used inappropriately)?

- Changes were made to the Genetic Information Nondiscrimination Act (GINA). Title I of GINA required a revision of the HIPAA Privacy Rule. Genetic information is defined as health information, and it may not be used or disclosed for underwriting purposes.
- Revised notice of privacy practices (NPP) requirements require providers to revise the document patients read and sign before their first visit. Providers are *not* required to print and distribute a revised NPP to all individuals seeking treatment. However, providers are required to provide a copy of the NPP to and obtain a good faith acknowledgement of receipt from *new patients*. The revised NPP must be posted in a clear and prominent location with copies available for individuals to easily take one. (Individuals should not have to ask the receptionist for a copy of the revised NPP.) The NPP contains the following new requirements:
  - Statement indicating that most uses and disclosures of psychotherapy notes (where appropriate) require patient (or authorized individual) authorization
  - Statement indicating that uses and disclosures of PHI for marketing purposes require patient (or authorized individual) authorization
  - Statement that disclosures constituting a sale of PHI require patient (or authorized individual) authorization
  - Statement that other uses and disclosures *not* described in the NPP will be made only upon authorization from the patient (or authorized individual)
  - Statement about fundraising communications and an individual's right to opt out
  - Statement informing individuals about their new right to restrict certain disclosures of PHI to a health plan if they pay for a service in full and out of pocket
  - Statement about an individual's right to be notified of a breach of unsecured PHI in the event the individual is affected

Protecting Patients from Identify Theft

According to the Federal Trade Commission (FTC), medical identity theft is a concern for patients, health care providers, and health care plans, and the victims of medical identity theft are typically identified when they are contacted by a debt collector about medical debt they do not owe, find erroneous listings of office visits or treatments on an explanation of benefits (EOB), have been denied insurance because their patient records document a condition they do not have, receive a bill for medical services that they did not receive, see medical collection notices on their credit report that they do not recognize, and/or were informed by their health care plan that they have reached their limit on benefits. Health care providers and insurers can help minimize the risk to patients who report one or more of the above occurrences by:

- *Conducting an investigation*. If patients report they were billed for services not received, review financial and medical records relating to services performed to verify identities of persons receiving services. If medical identity theft is identified, notify everyone who accessed the patient's records to let them know what information is inaccurate and ask them to correct the records.

- *Understanding provider obligations under the Fair Credit Reporting Act (FCRA).* If patients report that debts have been reported to credit reporting companies, determine how the medical identity theft affects the provider's responsibilities under FCRA. If patients provide identity theft reports detailing thefts, FCRA states that debt associated with thefts cannot be reported to credit reporting companies. An *identity theft report* is a police report that contains enough detail for credit reporting companies and businesses involved to verify that the consumer is a victim, and it also states which accounts and inaccurate information resulted from the theft.
- *Reviewing data security practices.* Even if information used to commit the fraud was not generated by the provider, it is important to periodically review data security practices and compliance with information safeguard provisions associated with HIPAA privacy and security rules.
- *Providing any necessary breach notifications.* If an investigation reveals that the provider improperly used or shared protected health information (PHI) (e.g., health information was improperly shared with an identity thief), determine whether a breach occurred under the HIPAA Breach Notification Rule (45 CFR part 164 subpart D) or any applicable state breach notification law.

Some practical tips for assisting patients with correcting medical, billing, and financial records include the following:

- *Provide patients with a copy of the provider's notice of privacy practices.* The notice should include contact information for someone who can respond to questions or concerns from patients about the privacy of their health information. Hospitals may also put the person in touch with a patient representative or ombudsman.
- *Provide patients with copies of their records in accordance with the HIPAA privacy rule.* Patients may ask for copies of their medical and billing records to help identify the impact of the theft and to review their records for inaccuracies before seeking additional medical care. There is no central source for medical records, so patients need to contact each provider they do business with, including doctors, clinics, hospitals, pharmacies, laboratories, and health plans. For example, if a thief obtained a prescription in your patient's name, the victim may want a copy of the record from the pharmacy that filled the prescription and the health care provider who wrote the prescription. Explain to the patient that there may be fees and mailing costs to obtain copies of medical or billing files.
- *Educate patients about their right to have their medical and billing records amended or corrected.* Encourage patients to write to their health plan or provider to dispute the inaccurate information. Tell them to include copies (because they should keep the originals) of any documents that support their position. Their letter should identify each disputed item, the reasons for disputing it, and a request that each error be corrected or deleted. Patients may want to include a copy of medical or billing records with items in question circled.
- *Send an accounting of disclosures to patients.* An accounting of disclosures about medical information provided to third parties (e.g., attorneys, third-party payers, and Social Security disability offices) may help indicate to patients whether there has been an inappropriate release of their medical information. HIPAA allows patients to order one free copy of the accounting from each of their providers and

health plans every 12 months. The accounting includes a record of the date of the disclosure, the name of the person or entity who received the information, a brief description of the information disclosed, and a brief statement about the purpose of the disclosure or a copy of the request for disclosure.

- *Inform patients that they have the right to file a complaint if they believe their privacy rights have been violated*. For example, it would be a violation if a medical provider refused to provide someone with a copy of his or her own medical record. Patients can file a complaint with the U.S. Department of Health and Human Services' Office for Civil Rights (www.hhs.gov/ocr).
- *Encourage your patients to notify their health plan if they suspect medical identity theft*. Obtaining a list of benefits paid in their name can help patients determine whether there are any fraudulent charges. Patients also should carefully review EOB statements that third-party payers send after treatment is provided, and patients should verify that the claims paid match care received, ensuring that the name of the provider, dates of service, and services provided are correct. Patients should report discrepancies to their third-party payer.
- *Tell your patients to file a complaint with the FTC*. Patients can file a complaint with the FTC. They also should file a report with local police and send copies of the report to their health plan's fraud department, health care provider(s), and the three nationwide credit reporting companies.
- *Encourage patients to look for signs of other misuses of their personal information*. Someone who engages in medical identity theft also may use their victim's personal information to commit more traditional forms of identity theft, such as opening a credit card account in the victim's name. Tell patients to order copies of credit reports and to review them carefully. Once victims have their reports, they should look for inquiries from companies they did not contact, accounts they did not open, and debts that they cannot explain. They also should verify that their Social Security number, address(es), name and/or initials, and employers' names are listed correctly.

Release of Information

Release of information (ROI) by a covered entity (e.g., provider's office) about protected health information (PHI) requires the patient (or representative) to sign an authorization to release information, which is reviewed for authenticity (e.g., comparing the signature on the authorization form to documents signed in the patient record) and processed within a HIPAA-mandated 60-day time limit. Requests for ROI include those from patients, physicians and other health care providers, third-party payers, Social Security disability, attorneys, and so on. A **release of information log** is used to document patient information released to authorized requestors, and data are entered manually (e.g., three-ring binder) or using ROI tracking software.

The HIPAA privacy rule requires covered entities to track the release of protected health information (PHI) so that individuals can obtain an accounting of disclosures for the 6 years prior to the date of their request, retroactive to April 16, 2003. To respond to this requirement, each covered entity must establish a tracking mechanism and reporting process that includes the date of disclosure, name and address of the entity or person who received the PHI, description of the PHI disclosed, and statement of reason for disclosure (or a copy of the written request for disclosure). If an entity releases PHI to the same entity for the same reason, the first disclosure is documented along with the number of disclosures made during the accounting period and the date of the last disclosure in the accounting period. An individual has the right to receive an accounting of all PHI disclosures made by a covered entity during the 6 years prior to the date an accounting is requested, *except* for disclosures to:

- **Carry out treatment, payment, and health care operations (TPO)**
- **Comply with requests that occurred prior to the compliance date for the covered entity**
- **Create entries in the facility's directory**
- **Fulfill requests from correctional institutions or law enforcement officials**
- **Individuals (e.g., patients), themselves**
- **Persons involved in the individual's care**
- **Send notifications to national security for intelligence purposes**

Telephone Inquiries One area of concern regarding breach of confidentiality involves the clarification of insurance data by telephone. A signed release statement from the patient may be on file, but the office has no assurance of the identity or credentials of a telephone inquirer. It is very simple for a curious individual to place a call to a physician's office and claim to be an insurance company benefits clerk. The rule to follow is, *always require written requests for patient information.* (The only circumstance that would allow the release of information over the telephone is an emergency situation that involves patient care. In this situation, be sure to authenticate the requesting party by using the "call-back method," which involves calling the facility's switchboard and asking to be connected to the requesting party.)

Facsimile Transmission Great care must be taken to ensure that sensitive information sent by fax reaches the intended receiver and is handled properly. It is recommended that health information be faxed only when there is:

1. An urgent need for the health record and mailing the record will cause unnecessary delays in treatment, or
2. Immediate authorization for treatment is required from a primary care physician or other third-party case manager.

In such cases, information transmitted should be limited only to the information required to satisfy the immediate needs of the requesting party. Each transmission of sensitive material should have a cover sheet including the following information:

- **Name of the facility to receive the facsimile**
- **Name and telephone number of the person authorized to receive the transmission**
- **Name and telephone number of the sender**
- **Number of pages being transmitted**
- **A confidentiality notice or disclaimer (Figure 5-11)**
- **Instructions to authorized recipient to send verification of receipt of transmittal to the sender**

If you have received this transmittal in error, please notify the sender immediately.

The material in this transmission contains confidential information that is legally privileged. This information is intended only for the use of the individual or entity named above.

If you are not the intended recipient, you are hereby notified that any disclosure, copying, distribution, or action taken based on the contents of this transmission is strictly prohibited.

FIGURE 5-11 Sample fax confidentiality notice.

The practice should keep a dated log of the transmission of all medically sensitive facsimiles and copies of all "receipt of transmittal" verifications signed and returned by the authorized recipient. Special care must be taken to ensure that proper facsimile destination numbers are keyed into the fax machine prior to transmission.

NOTE: Carefully review all e-mails before sending to ensure receipt by intended recipients only. Sending an e-mail to an unintended recipient can result in a breach of confidentiality (e.g., patient, facility). For example, when an investigator selected "reply all" to an e-mail that included claims abuse information about several providers, state and CMS officials had to be notified and an investigation was conducted.

Confidentiality and the Internet At present, there is no guarantee of confidentiality when patient records are transmitted via the Internet. If time constraints prevent sending sensitive information through a more secure delivery system, special arrangements may be made with the requesting party to transmit the document after deleting specific patient identification information. It is best to call the party requesting the documents to arrange for an identifier code to be added to the document so that the receiving party is assured that the information received is that which was requested. This transmission should be followed by an official unedited copy of the record, sent by overnight delivery, that includes specific patient material that was deleted from the previous transmission. In 1998, the *HCFA Internet Security Policy* issued guidelines for the security and appropriate use of the Internet for accessing and transmitting sensitive information (e.g., Medicare beneficiary information). The information must be encrypted so that information is converted to a secure language format for transmission, and authentication or identification procedures must be implemented to ensure that the sender and receiver of data are known to each other and are authorized to send and/or receive such information.

Breach of Confidentiality Health care providers are required to notify patients when the security of their protected health information has been breached. (A breach occurs when protected health information (PHI) is acquired, accessed, used, or disclosed in a way that poses "significant risk of financial, reputational, or other harm to the individual.") The following rules apply:

- **Providers must notify individuals to whom the PHI pertains within 60 days after discovery of the breach.**
- **Providers also have a duty to notify the media of any breach that affects more than 500 individuals residing in one state or jurisdiction.**

Some situations of unauthorized disclosure, access, or use of unsecured PHI do not constitute a breach requiring notification. Examples include:

- **Employees who unintentionally access PHI within the scope of their authority**
- **PHI that is inadvertently disclosed to an employee who normally has access to certain types of PHI**
- **Individuals to whom PHI was disclosed but who cannot readily retain the information**

HIPAA ALERT!

Privacy violations are subject to a penalty of no more than $100 per person per violation, not to exceed $25,000 per person per year per violation of a single standard. More serious violations are subject to more severe penalties, including the following:

- $50,000 and/or up to 1 year in prison for persons who knowingly obtain and disclose protected health information
- $100,000 and/or up to 5 years in prison for persons who under "false pretense" obtain and disclose protected health information
- $250,000 and up to 10 years in prison for persons with intent to sell, transfer, or use PHI for malicious reasons or personal gain

Title II (continued)—Medical Liability Reform

NOTE: The *Patient Safety and Quality Improvement Act* allows providers to report health care errors on a voluntary and confidential basis. Patient safety organizations (PSOs) analyze the problems, identify solutions, and provide feedback to avoid future errors. A database tracks national trends and recurring problems.

The threat of excessive awards in medical liability cases has increased providers' liability insurance premiums and resulted in increased health care costs. As a result, some providers stop practicing medicine in areas of the country where liability insurance costs are highest, and the direct result for individuals and communities across the country is reduced access to quality medical care. Although medical liability reform was included in HIPAA legislation, no final rule was published. Individual states, such as Ohio, have passed medical liability reform, and the U.S. Congress is also formulating separate federal medical liability reform legislation.

Title III—Tax-Related Health Provisions

HIPAA's *Title III—Tax-Related Health Provisions* provides for certain deductions for medical insurance, and makes other changes to health insurance law. The HIPAA *Title III* subtitles include:

- ***Subtitle A:*** **Medical Savings Accounts**
  - ***Section 302:*** **Medical Savings Accounts**
- ***Subtitle B:*** **Increase in Deduction for Health Insurance Costs of Self-Employed Individuals**
  - ***Section 311:*** **Increase in deduction for health insurance costs of self-employed individuals**

- *Subtitle C:* Long-Term Care Services and Contracts, such as Long-Term Care Insurance
  - *Part I:* General Provisions
    - *Section 321:* Treatment of long-term care insurance
    - *Section 322:* Qualified long-term care services treated as medical care
    - *Section 323:* Reporting requirements
  - *Part II:* Consumer Protection Provisions
    - *Section 325:* Policy requirements
    - *Section 326:* Requirements for issuers of qualified long-term care insurance contracts
    - *Section 327:* Effective dates
- *Subtitle D:* Treatment of Accelerated Death Benefits
  - *Section 331:* Treatment of accelerated death benefits by recipient
  - *Section 332:* Tax treatment of companies issuing qualified accelerated death benefit riders
- *Subtitle E:* State Insurance Pools
  - *Section 341:* Exemption from income tax for state-sponsored organizations providing health coverage for high-risk individuals
  - *Section 342:* Exemption from income tax for state-sponsored worker's compensation reinsurance organizations
- *Subtitle F:* Organizations Subject to Section 833 (Section 833 of the United States Code covers treatment of BlueCross BlueShield organizations, etc.)
  - *Section 351:* Organizations subject to Section 833
- *Subtitle G:* IRA Distributions to the Unemployed
  - *Section 361:* Distributions from certain plans may be used without additional tax to pay financially devastating medical expenses
- *Subtitle H:* Organ and Tissue Donation Information Included with Income Tax Refund Payments
  - *Section 371:* Organ and tissue donation information included with income tax refund payments

(Go to **http://hippo.findlaw.com** to learn more about HIPAA's *Title III—Tax-Related Health Provisions.*)

Title IV—Application and Enforcement of Group Health Plan Requirements

HIPAA's *Title IV—Application and Enforcement of Group Health Plan Requirements* specifies conditions for group health plans regarding coverage of persons with pre-existing conditions and modifies continuation of coverage requirements. The HIPAA *Title IV* subtitles and sections include:

- *Subtitle A:* Application and Enforcement of Group Health Plan Requirements
  - *Section 401:* Group health plan portability, access, and renewability requirements
  - *Section 402:* Penalty on failure to meet certain group health plan requirements

- *Subtitle B:* Clarification of Certain Continuation Coverage Requirements
  - *Section 421:* COBRA clarifications

(Go to **http://hippo.findlaw.com** to learn more about HIPAA's *Title IV—Application and Enforcement of Group Health Plan Requirements.*)

Title V–Revenue Offsets

HIPAA's *Title V—Revenue Offsets* includes provisions related to company-owned life insurance and treatment of individuals who lose U.S. citizenship for income tax purposes. It also repeals the financial institution transition rule to interest allocation rules. For example, regulations were established regarding how employers can deduct company-owned life insurance premiums for income tax purposes. The HIPAA *Title V* subtitles and sections include:

- *Subtitle A:* Company-Owned Life Insurance
  - *Section 501:* Denial of deduction for interest on loans with respect to company-owned life insurance
- *Subtitle B:* Treatment of Individuals Who Lose U.S. Citizenship
  - *Section 511:* Revision of income, estate, and gift taxes on individuals who lose U.S. citizenship
  - *Section 512:* Information on individuals losing U.S. citizenship
  - *Section 513:* Report on tax compliance by U.S. citizens and residents living abroad
- *Subtitle C:* Repeal of Financial Institution Transition Rule to Interest Allocation Rules
  - *Section 521:* Repeal of financial institution transition rule to interest allocation rules

(Go to **http://hippo.findlaw.com** to learn more about HIPAA's *Title V—Revenue Offsets.*)

SUMMARY

Federal and state statutes are laws passed by legislative bodies and implemented as regulations (guidelines written by administrative agencies). The *Federal Register* is a legal newspaper published every business day by the federal government. Medicare program transmittals are legal notices about Medicare policies and procedures, and they are incorporated into the appropriate CMS program manual (e.g., *Medicare Claims Processing Manual*). Federal and state legislation have regulated the health care industry since 1863, when the False Claims Act (FCA) was enacted.

Record retention is the storage of documentation for an established period of time, usually mandated by federal and/or state law. HIPAA mandates the retention of health insurance claims for a minimum of 6 years, unless state law specifies a longer period. HIPAA also mandates that patient records and health insurance claims be retained for a minimum of 2 years after a patient's death.

The Health Insurance Portability and Accountability Act (HIPAA) includes the following provisions: health care access, portability, and renewability; prevention of health care fraud and abuse, administrative simplification, and medical liability reform; tax-related health provisions; application and enforcement of group health plan requirements; and revenue offsets.

HIPAA's administrative simplification regulations established the HIPAA security and privacy rules. Do not confuse the purpose of each rule. The *HIPAA security rule* defines administrative, physical, and technical safeguards to protect the availability, confidentiality, and integrity of electronic protected health information (PHI). The *HIPAA privacy rule* establishes standards for how PHI should be controlled by indicating authorized uses (e.g., continuity of care) and disclosures (e.g., third-party reimbursement) and patients' rights with respect to their health information (e.g., patient access).

INTERNET LINKS

- Administrative Simplification in the Health Care Industry (HIPAA)
  Go to **http://aspe.hhs.gov**, enter HIPAA in the Search box, click Search, and click on the Health Care Administrative Simplification link.
- ANSI ASC X12N 837 implementation guides
  www.wpc-edi.com
- Centers for Medicare and Medicaid Services
  www.cms.gov
- Comprehensive Error Rate Testing (CERT)
  www.cms.gov/cert
- DHHS OIG Prevention and Detection program
  http://oig.hhs.gov
- *Federal Register*
  www.federalregister.gov
- Health care policy and regulatory resources, such as HIPAA
  http://hippo.findlaw.com
- HIPAA Privacy
  Go to **www.hhs.gov**, click on the A-Z Index link, and then click on the H link to locate HIPAA privacy and security documents.
- Medical Identify Theft brochure
  Go to **www.consumer.ftc.gov**, click on the Privacy & Identity link, click on the Repairing Identity Theft link, and then scroll down and click on the Medical Identity Theft link.
- Medical liability reform
  Go to **http://thomas.loc.gov**, and enter "medical liability reform" in the search box to review federal legislation under consideration by the House and/or Senate.
- Payment Error Rate Measurement (PERM)
  www.cms.gov/PERM
- Recovery Audit Program
  www.cms.gov/RAC
- Retail pharmacy standards implementation guide
  www.ncpdp.org
- State and local government information
  Go to **http://thomas.loc.gov**, click on the Government Resources link, scroll down to the General Government Resources heading, and click on the Local Government Resources or the State Government Resources link.

STUDY CHECKLIST

- ☐ Read this textbook chapter and highlight key concepts.
- ☐ Create an index card for each key term.
- ☐ Access the chapter Internet links to learn more about concepts.
- ☐ Answer the chapter review questions, verifying answers with your instructor.
- ☐ Complete the Workbook chapter, verifying answers with your instructor.
- ☐ Form a study group with classmates to discuss chapter concepts in preparation for an exam.

REVIEW

MULTIPLE CHOICE **Select the most appropriate response.**

1. A commercial insurance company sends a letter to the physician requesting a copy of a patient's entire medical record in order to process payment. No other documents accompany the letter. The insurance specialist should

a. contact the patient via telephone to alert him about the request.
b. let the patient's physician handle the situation personally.
c. make a copy of the record and mail it to the insurance company.
d. require a signed patient authorization from the insurance company.

2. An attorney calls the physician's office and requests that a copy of his client's medical record be immediately faxed to the attorney's office. The insurance specialist should

a. call the HIPAA hotline number to report a breach of confidentiality.
b. explain to the attorney that the office does not fax or copy patient records.
c. instruct the attorney to obtain the patient's signed authorization.
d. retrieve the patient's medical record and fax it to the attorney.

3. An insurance company calls the office to request information about a claim. The insurance specialist confirms the patient's dates of service and the patient's negative HIV status. The insurance specialist

a. appropriately released the dates of service, but not the negative HIV status.
b. breached patient confidentiality by confirming the dates of service.
c. did not breach patient confidentiality because the patient's HIV status was negative.
d. was in compliance with HIPAA provisions concerning release of dates of service and HIV status.

4. A patient's spouse comes to the office and requests diagnostic and treatment information about his wife. The spouse is the primary policyholder on a policy for which his wife is named as a dependent. The insurance specialist should

a. allow the patient's spouse to review the actual record in the office, but not release a copy.
b. inform the patient's spouse that he must request the information from his insurance company.
c. obtain a signed patient authorization from the wife before releasing patient information.
d. release a copy of the information to the patient's spouse, because he is the primary policyholder.

5. Which is considered Medicare fraud?

a. billing for services that were not furnished and misrepresenting diagnoses to justify payment
b. charging excessive fees for services, equipment, or supplies provided by the physician
c. submitting claims for services that are not medically necessary to treat a patient's condition
d. violating participating provider agreements with insurance companies and government programs

6. Which is considered Medicare abuse?

a. falsifying certificates of medical necessity, plans of treatment, and medical records to justify payment
b. improper billing practices that result in Medicare payment when the claim is the legal responsibility of another third-party payer
c. soliciting, offering, or receiving a kickback for procedures and/or services provided to patients in the physician's office
d. unbundling codes; that is, reporting multiple CPT codes on a claim to increase reimbursement from a payer

7. The 66-year-old patient was treated in the emergency department (ED) for a fractured arm. The patient said, "I was moving a file cabinet for my boss when it tipped over and fell on my arm." The facility billed Medicare and received reimbursement of $550. The facility later determined that Medicare was not the payer because this was a workers' compensation case. Therefore, the facility

a. is guilty of both fraud and abuse according to HIPAA because of accepting the $550.
b. must give the $550 check to the patient, who should contact workers' compensation.
c. should have billed the employer's workers' compensation payer for the ED visit.
d. was appropriately reimbursed $550 by Medicare for the emergency department visit.

ICD-10-CM Coding

CHAPTER 6

CHAPTER OUTLINE

ICD-9-CM Legacy Coding System

Overview of ICD-10-CM and ICD-10-PCS

ICD-10-CM Coding Conventions

ICD-10-CM Index to Diseases and Injuries

ICD-10-CM Tabular List of Diseases and Injuries

Official Guidelines for Coding and Reporting

OBJECTIVES

Upon successful completion of this chapter, you should be able to:

1. Define key terms.
2. Use ICD-9-CM as a legacy coding system and interpret general equivalence mappings.
3. Describe the purpose and use of the ICD-10-CM and ICD-10-PCS coding systems.
4. Interpret ICD-10-CM coding conventions to accurately assign codes.
5. Interpret diagnostic coding and reporting guidelines for outpatient services.
6. Assign ICD-10-CM codes to outpatient and provider-based office diagnoses.

KEY TERMS

adverse effect
benign
carcinoma (Ca) *in situ*
comorbidity
complication
computer-assisted coding (CAC)
contiguous sites
Cooperating Parties for ICD-10-CM/PCS
encoder
encounter
essential modifier
first-listed diagnosis
general equivalence mapping (GEM)
iatrogenic illness
ICD-10-CM coding conventions
- and
- brackets
- code first underlying disease
- code first underlying disease, such as:
- code, if applicable, any causal condition first

colon
due to
eponym
etiology and manifestation rules
Excludes1 note
Excludes2 note
in
in diseases classified elsewhere
includes note
manifestation

NEC (not elsewhere classifiable)
NOS (not otherwise specified)
other and other specified code
parentheses
see
see also
see category
see condition
Table of Drugs and Chemicals
Table of Neoplasms
unspecified codes
use additional code
with
ICD-10-CM Diagnostic Coding and Reporting Guidelines for Outpatient Services—Hospital-Based Outpatient Services and Provider-Based Office Visits
ICD-10-CM Index to Diseases and Injuries
ICD-10-CM Index to External Causes
ICD-10-CM Official Guidelines for Coding and Reporting
ICD-10-CM Tabular List of Diseases and Injuries
ICD-10-CM/PCS Coordination and Maintenance Committee
ICD-10-PCS Coding Guidelines
legacy classification system
legacy coding system
lesion
main term
malignant
metastasis
morbidity
morphology
mortality
neoplasm
nonessential modifier
outpatient
overlapping sites
physician query process
poisoning: accidental (unintentional)
poisoning: assault
poisoning: intentional self-harm
poisoning: undetermined
preadmission testing (PAT)
primary malignancy
principal diagnosis
qualified diagnosis
qualifiers
re-excision
secondary diagnosis
secondary malignancy
sequela
subterm
trust the index
uncertain behavior
underdosing
unspecified nature

INTRODUCTION

There are four related classifications of diseases with similar titles.

- **The *International Classification of Diseases (ICD)* is published by the World Health Organization (WHO) and is used to classify mortality (death) data from death certificates. In 1994, WHO published the 10th revision of ICD with a new name, *International Statistical Classification of Diseases and Related Health Problems*, and reorganized its three-digit categories. (Although the name of the publication was changed, the familiar abbreviation ICD remains in use.)**
- **The *International Classification of Diseases, 9th Revision, Clinical Modification* (ICD-9-CM) was developed in the United States and implemented in 1979 to code and classify *morbidity* (disease) data from inpatient and outpatient records, including provider-based office records.**
- **The *International Classification of Diseases, 10th Revision, Clinical Modification* (ICD-10-CM) was developed in the United States and is used to classify morbidity (disease) data from inpatient and outpatient records, including provider-based office records.**
- **The *International Classification of Diseases, 10th Revision, Procedure Classification System* (ICD-10-PCS) was developed in the United States and is used to code and classify *procedures* from inpatient records only.**

CODING TIP:

- ICD-10-CM and ICD-10-PCS, also abbreviated as ICD-10-CM/PCS, replaces ICD-9-CM on October 1, 2014.
- All provider offices, outpatient health care settings (e.g., home health care, hospice), and health care facilities (e.g., hospitals, long-term care facilities) report ICD-10-CM diagnosis codes.

(continues)

- All provider-based offices and outpatient health care settings (including hospice and home health care) report CPT and HCPCS level II codes for procedures and services (covered in Chapters 7 and 8 of this textbook). This includes physicians, nurse practitioners, and physician assistants who provide services to inpatients during their hospitalization (e.g., initial hospital care, subsequent hospital care, surgical procedures).
- At the time this textbook was published, CMS had not yet made a decision on whether inpatient long-term care facilities and inpatient hospice programs would report ICD-10-PCS *or* CPT and HCPCS level II procedure and service codes.
- This chapter includes an overview of ICD-10-PCS only because its codes are reported for hospital inpatient services/procedures only. Students should be familiar with the existence of ICD-10-PCS, the effective date of implementation, and the *build-a-code* nature of assigning codes to inpatient procedures. Refer to Cengage Learning's *3-2-1 Code It!* by Michelle A. Green, which extensively covers ICD-10-PCS coding in multiple chapters.

The health insurance specialist employed in a provider's office assigns ICD-10-CM codes to diagnoses, conditions, signs, and symptoms documented by the health care provider. Reporting ICD-10-CM codes on insurance claims results in uniform reporting of medical reasons for health care services provided. (CPT and HCPCS level II codes are reported to the provider's office and outpatient health care setting procedures and services; Chapters 7 and 8 of this textbook cover those coding systems.)

ICD-9-CM LEGACY CODING SYSTEM

Upon implementation of the ICD-10-CM (and ICD-10-PCS) coding systems, the *International Classification of Diseases, 9th Revision, Clinical Modification* (ICD-9-CM) became a **legacy coding system** (or **legacy classification system**), which means it will be used to archive data but will no longer be supported or updated by the ICD-9-CM Coordination and Maintenance Committee. Because ICD-9-CM was used since 1979 in the United States to classify inpatient and outpatient/provider-based office diagnoses (Volumes 1 and 2) and inpatient procedures (Volume 3), *general equivalence mappings (GEMs)* will be annually published by the National Center for Health Statistics (NCHS) and Centers for Medicare and Medicaid Services (CMS).

ICD-9-CM was over 30 years old, had contained outdated and obsolete terminology, used outdated codes that produce inaccurate and limited data, and was inconsistent with current medical practice. It could not accurately describe diagnoses or inpatient procedures for care delivered in the twenty-first century. ICD-9-CM did not provide the necessary detail about patients' medical conditions or procedures performed on hospitalized inpatients; thus, effective October 1, 2014, provider-based offices and health care facilities (e.g., hospitals) implemented ICD-10-CM to code diagnoses. (Hospitals also began using ICD-10-PCS to code inpatient procedures. Provider-based offices and outpatient health

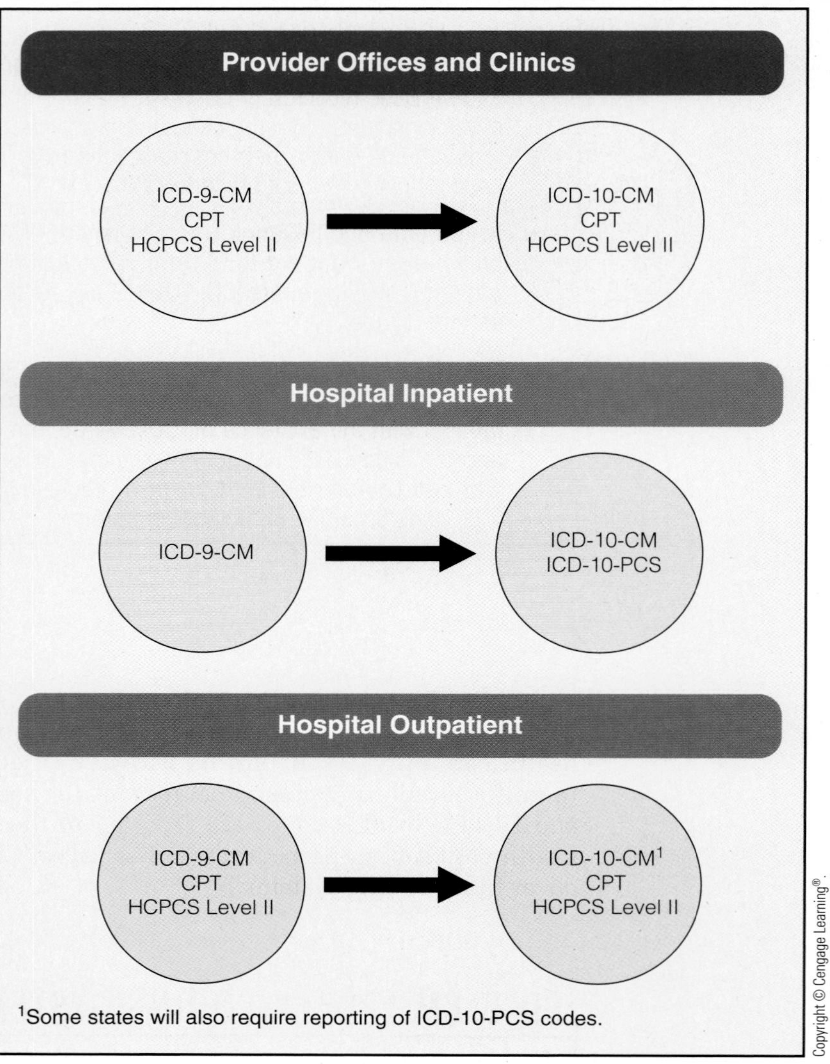

care settings continue to use CPT and HCPCS level II to code procedures and services.)

General Equivalence Mappings (GEMs)

The National Center for Health Statistics (NCHS) and Centers for Medicare and Medicaid Services (CMS) annually publish **general equivalence mappings (GEMs)**, which are translation dictionaries or crosswalks of codes that can be used to roughly identify ICD-10-CM codes for their ICD-9-CM equivalent codes (and vice versa). (GEMs published by the NCHS and CMS do not contain code descriptions; however, other publishers include code descriptions to facilitate code translation.) GEMs facilitate the location of corresponding diagnosis codes between two code sets. In some areas of the classification, the correlation between codes is close; since the two code sets share the conventions of organization and formatting common to both revisions of ICD, translating between them is straightforward.

EXAMPLE: There is straightforward correspondence between the two code sets for infectious diseases, neoplasms, eye diseases, and ear diseases.

GENERAL EQUIVALENCE MAPPING	
ICD-9-CM Diagnosis Code and Description	**ICD-10-CM Diagnosis Code and Description**
003.21 Salmonella meningitis	A02.21 Salmonella meningitis
205.01 Acute myeloid leukemia in remission	C92.01 Acute myeloblastic leukemia, in remission

EXAMPLE: In other areas of the two code sets, such as obstetrics, entire chapters are organized according to a different axis of classification. Translating between them offers a series of possible codes that must be verified in the appropriate tabular list (ICD-9-CM or ICD-10-CM) or table of codes (ICD-10-PCS) to identify the correct code. (Think about translating the English language into Chinese or any other foreign language, and you will see the problems inherent in such translation.)

GENERAL EQUIVALENCE MAPPING	
ICD-9-CM Diagnosis Code and Description	**ICD-10-CM Diagnosis Code and Description**
649.51 Spotting complicating pregnancy, delivered, with or without mention of antepartum condition	O26.851 Spotting complicating pregnancy, first trimester
	O26.852 Spotting complicating pregnancy, second trimester
	O26.853 Spotting complicating pregnancy, third trimester
	O26.859 Spotting complicating pregnancy, unspecified trimester

NOTE: ICD-9-CM was designed to facilitate statistical data groupings and health care trend analysis, and it was implemented in the United States in 1979. Although ICD-9-CM was never intended for reimbursement purposes, the first prospective payment system (called diagnosis-related groups, or DRGs) was implemented in 1983 and relied on ICD-9-CM codes to generate DRG payment amounts. The ICD-10-CM and ICD-10-PCS classifications considered payment systems and processing claims for reimbursement as one of many intents; thus, the huge number of ICD-10-CM/PCS codes is an advantage of its adoption.

OVERVIEW OF ICD-10-CM AND ICD-10-PCS

The *International Classification of Diseases, 10th Revision, Clinical Modification* (ICD-10-CM) is a clinical modification of WHO's *International Classification of Diseases, 10th Revision* (ICD-10) that is used to code and classify disease data from inpatient and outpatient records. The *International Classification of Diseases, 10th Revision, Procedure Classification System* (ICD-10-PCS) is used to code and classify procedure data from inpatient records only. The Centers for Medicare and Medicaid Services (CMS) abbreviates ICD-10-CM and ICD-10-PCS as ICD-10-CM/PCS.

ICD-10-CM includes many more codes and applies to more users than ICD-9-CM because it is designed to collect data on every type of health care encounter (e.g., inpatient, outpatient, hospice, home health care, and long-term care). ICD-10-CM also enhances accurate payment for services rendered and facilitates

EXERCISE 6-1

ICD-9-CM Legacy Coding System

Instructions: Complete each statement.

1. Implementation of ICD-10-CM and ICD-10-PCS resulted in the *International Classification of Diseases, 9th Revision, Clinical Modification* (ICD-9-CM) becoming a ________.
2. The NCHS and CMS publish ________ to facilitate the location of corresponding diagnosis codes between ICD-9-CM and ICD-10-CM.
3. ICD-9-CM was the classification (or coding) system used since ________ in the United States to classify inpatient and outpatient/provider-based office diagnoses (Volumes 1 and 2) and inpatient procedures (Volume 3).
4. Because ICD-9-CM was over 30 years old, it contained ________, used outdated codes that produced inaccurate and limited data, and was inconsistent with current medical practice.
5. When an ICD-9-CM code maps to a single ICD-10-CM code, reviewing the tabular list to validate the code is optional. (TRUE or FALSE)

Instructions: Use the diagnosis GEM depicted in the following table to complete each statement.

ICD-9-CM to ICD-10-CM General Equivalence Mapping

ICD-9-CM Diagnosis Code and Description	ICD-10-CM Diagnosis Code and Description
078.81 Epidemic vertigo	A88.1 Epidemic vertigo
078.82 Epidemic vomiting syndrome	R11.11 Vomiting without nausea
078.88 Other specified diseases due to *Chlamydiae*	A74.89 Other *chlamydial* diseases
078.89 Other specified diseases due to viruses	B33.8 Other specified viral diseases

6. ICD-10-CM code A88.1 maps to ICD-9-CM code(s) ________.
7. ICD-9-CM code 078.81 maps to ICD-10-CM code(s) ________.
8. ICD-9-CM code 078.89 maps to ICD-10-CM code(s) ________.
9. ICD-10-CM code A74.89 maps to ICD-9-CM code(s) ________.
10. ICD-10-CM code B33.8 maps to ICD-9-CM code(s) ________.

evaluation of medical processes and outcomes. The term *clinical* emphasizes the modification's intent, which is to:

- **Describe the clinical picture of the patient, which means codes are more precise (when compared with classification systems designed for statistical data groupings and health care trend analysis)**

- **Serve as a useful tool in the area of classification of morbidity data for indexing patient records, reviewing quality of care, and compiling basic health statistics**

ICD-10-CM was developed by the Centers for Disease Control and Prevention (CDC) for use in *all* U.S. health care treatment settings. ICD-10-CM codes require up to seven characters, are entirely alphanumeric, and have unique *coding conventions*, rules that apply to the assignment of codes, such as Excludes1 and Excludes2 notes.

CODING TIP:

The format of ICD-10-CM is similar to ICD-9-CM Volumes 1 and 2 in that both coding systems use a disease index to initially locate codes for conditions and a tabular list to verify codes.

ICD-10-CM and ICD-10-PCS (Figure 6-1) incorporate much greater specificity and clinical information, which results in:

- **Decreased need to include supporting documentation with claims**
- **Enhanced ability to conduct public health surveillance**
- **Improved ability to measure health care services**
- **Increased sensitivity when refining grouping and reimbursement methodologies**

ICD-10-CM and ICD-10-PCS also include updated medical terminology and classification of diseases, provide codes to allow for the comparison of mortality and morbidity data, and provide better data for:

- **Conducting research**
- **Designing payment systems**

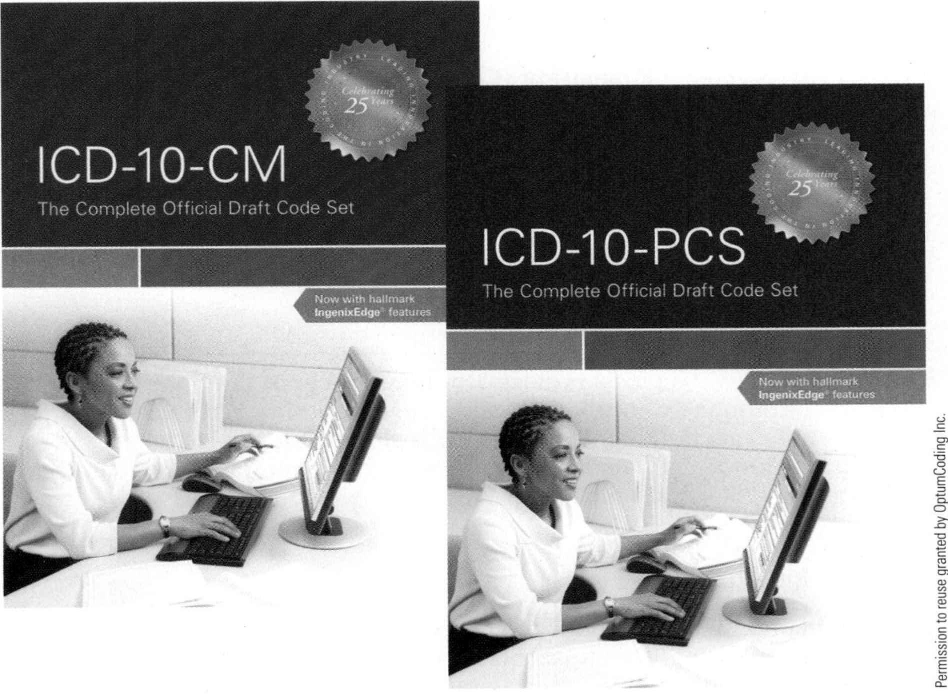

FIGURE 6-1 ICD-10-CM and ICD-10-PCS coding manuals.

- **Identifying fraud and abuse**
- **Making clinical decisions**
- **Measuring care furnished to patients**
- **Processing claims**
- **Tracking public health**

To prepare for implementation of ICD-10-CM/PCS, health care professionals should assess their coding staff to determine their needs and offer appropriate education and training to:

- **Apply advanced knowledge of anatomy and physiology, medical terminology, and pathophysiology**
- **Effectively communicate with members of the medical staff** (e.g., physician queries)
- **Interpret patient record documentation** (e.g., operative reports)
- **Interpret and apply coding guidelines that apply to the assignment of ICD-10-CM/PCS codes**

CODING TIP:

When coders have questions about documented diagnoses or procedures/services, they should use a **physician query process** to contact the responsible physician to request clarification about documentation and the code(s) to be assigned. The process is activated when the coder notices a problem with documentation quality (e.g., an incomplete diagnostic statement when clinical documentation indicates that a more specific ICD-10-CM code should be assigned). (Chapter 1 of Cengage Learning's *3-2-1 Code It!* by Michelle A. Green contains detailed content about the physician query process.)

Comparing ICD-10-CM to ICD-9-CM

ICD-10-CM far exceeds ICD-9-CM in the number of codes provided, having been expanded to (1) include health-related conditions, (2) provide much greater specificity at the sixth digit level, and (3) add a seventh digit extension (for some codes). Assigning the sixth and seventh characters when available for ICD-10-CM codes is mandatory because they report information documented in the patient record.

EXAMPLE 1: The diagnosis is stage 3 pressure ulcer of the right lower back. Refer to the ICD-9-CM codes in column one of the following table, and notice that two separate codes are reported for location and stage, but laterality (e.g., right sidedness) cannot be classified. Refer to the ICD-10-CM codes in column two of the table, and notice that a combination code is reported and the right side (laterality) is classified.

ICD-9-CM: 707.03, 707.23
ICD-10-CM: L89.133

ICD-9-CM contains just 15 codes to classify pressure ulcers according to location and depth. ICD-10-CM contains greater specificity because 125 codes are available to classify pressure ulcers according to location, depth, and laterality.

(continues)

EXAMPLE 1 (continued)

ICD-9-CM TABULAR LIST OF DISEASES	ICD-10-CM TABULAR LIST OF DISEASES AND INJURIES
707.0 Pressure ulcer Bed sore Decubitus ulcer Plaster ulcer Use additional code to identify pressure ulcer stage (707.20–707.25)	**L89.13 Pressure ulcer of right lower back** **L89.130 Pressure ulcer of right lower back, unstageable** **L89.131 Pressure ulcer of right lower back, stage 1** Healing pressure ulcer of right lower back, stage 1 Pressure pre-ulcer skin changes limited to persistent focal edema, right lower back
707.03 Lower back **707.23 Pressure ulcer stages** Code first site of pressure ulcer (707.00–707.09)	**L89.132 Pressure ulcer of right lower back, stage 2** Healing pressure ulcer of right lower back, stage 2 Pressure ulcer with abrasion, blister, partial thickness skin loss involving epidermis and/or dermis, right lower back
707.23 Pressure ulcer stage III Healing pressure ulcer, stage III Pressure ulcer with full thickness skin loss involving damage or necrosis of subcutaneous tissue	**L89.133 Pressure ulcer of right lower back, stage 3** Healing pressure ulcer of right lower back, stage 3 Pressure ulcer with full thickness skin loss involving damage or necrosis of subcutaneous tissue, right lower back
	L89.134 Pressure ulcer of right lower back, stage 4 Healing pressure ulcer of right lower back, stage 4 Pressure ulcer with necrosis of soft tissues through to underlying muscle, tendon, or bone, right lower back
	L89.139 Pressure ulcer of right lower back, unspecified stage Healing pressure ulcer of right lower back NOS Healing pressure ulcer of right lower back, unspecified stage

EXAMPLE 2: The diagnosis is "mechanical breakdown of femoral arterial graft, initial encounter." In ICD-9-CM, just one code is available for any mechanical complication of a vascular graft.

ICD-9-CM: 996.1
ICD-10-CM: T82.312A

In ICD-10-CM, a more specific code is reported, and the right side is classified. ICD-10-CM contains a greatly expanded number of codes because over 150 codes are available to classify mechanical complications of vascular grafts according to type of complication and/or type of graft (which also indicates the location of the graft).

(continues)

EXAMPLE 2 (continued)

ICD-9-CM TABULAR LIST OF DISEASES	ICD-10-CM TABULAR LIST OF DISEASES AND INJURIES
996.1 Mechanical complication of other vascular device, implant, or graft Mechanical complications involving: aortic (bifurcation) graft (replacement) arteriovenous: dialysis catheter, fistula, shunt } Surgically created balloon (counterpulsation) device, intra-aortic carotid artery bypass graft femoral-popliteal bypass graft umbrella device, vena cava **EXCLUDES** *atherosclerosis of biological graft (440.30–440.32)* *embolism [occlusion NOS] [thrombus] of (biological) (synthetic) graft (996.74)* *peritoneal dialysis catheter (996.56)*	**T82 Complications of cardiac and vascular prosthetic devices, implants and grafts** **EXCLUDES2:** *failure and rejection of transplanted organs and tissue (T86-)* The appropriate 7th character is to be added to each code from category T82. A initial encounter D subsequent encounter S sequela **T82.3 Mechanical complication of other vascular grafts** **T82.31 Breakdown (mechanical) of other vascular grafts** **T82.310 Breakdown (mechanical) of aortic (bifurcation) graft (replacement)** **T82.311 Breakdown (mechanical) of carotid arterial graft (bypass)** **T82.312 Breakdown (mechanical) of femoral arterial graft (bypass)** **T82.318 Breakdown (mechanical) of other vascular grafts** **T82.319 Breakdown (mechanical) of unspecified vascular grafts**

ICD-10-PCS

ICD-10-PCS is an entirely new procedure classification system that was developed by CMS for use in inpatient hospital settings *only*. ICD-10-PCS uses a *multiaxial* seven-character alphanumeric code structure (e.g., 047K04Z) that provides a unique code for all substantially different procedures. It also allows new procedures to be easily incorporated as new codes. ICD-10-PCS has more than 87,000 seven-character alphanumeric procedure codes. (ICD-9-CM has about 4,000 three- or four-digit numeric procedure codes.)

CODING TIP:

In ICD-10-PCS, *multiaxial* means the codes contain independent characters, with each axis retaining its meaning across broad ranges of codes to the extent possible. (There is no decimal used in ICD-10-PCS codes.)

Coding Manuals

Many publishers produce their own versions of ICD-10-CM and ICD-10-PCS:

- **ICD-10-CM is published as a single-volume coding manual, with the Index to Diseases and Injuries, Neoplasm, Table of Drugs and Chemicals, and Index to External Causes located in front of the Tabular List of Diseases and Injuries.**
- **ICD-10-PCS is published as a separate single-volume coding manual, with the Index to Procedures located in front of the Tables.**

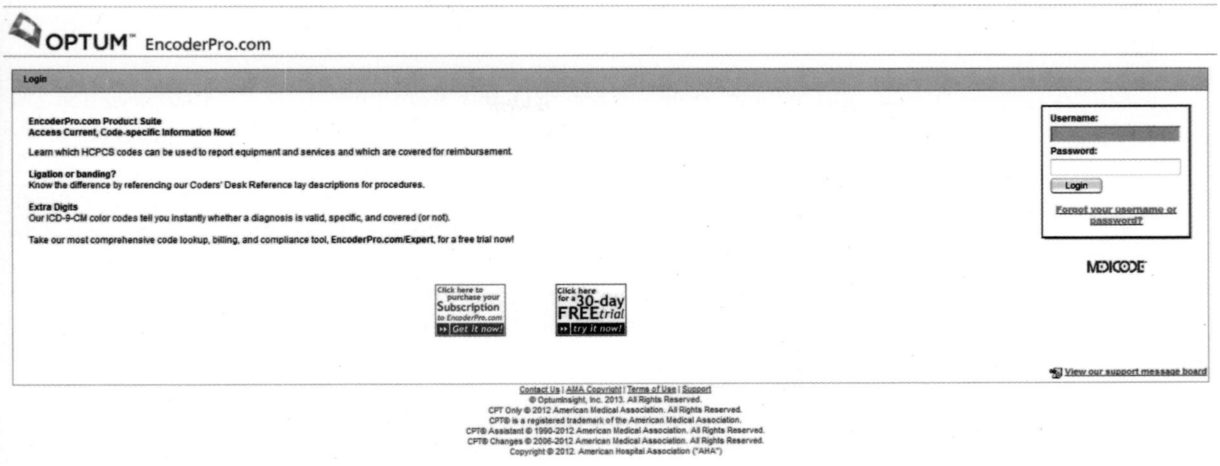

FIGURE 6-2 Encoder software.

Some companies also publish **encoders**, which automate the coding process. This means that computerized or web-based software (Figure 6-2) is used instead of coding manuals. (Coders use the software's Search feature to locate and verify codes.)

Updating ICD-10-CM and ICD-10-PCS

The National Center for Health Statistics (NCHS) and the Centers for Medicare and Medicaid Services (CMS) are the U.S. Department of Health and Human Services (DHHS) agencies that comprise the **ICD-10-CM/PCS Coordination and Maintenance Committee**. That committee is responsible for overseeing all changes and modifications to ICD-10-CM (diagnosis) and ICD-10-PCS (procedure) codes. It also discusses issues such as the creation and update of general equivalence mappings (GEMs).

- **NCHS works with the World Health Organization (WHO) to coordinate official disease classification activities for ICD-10-CM, including the use, interpretation, and periodic revision of the classification system.**
- **CMS is responsible for annually revising and updating the ICD-10-PCS procedure classification.**
- **Updates to ICD-10-CM and ICD-10-PCS are available at the official CMS (www.cms.gov) and NCHS (www.cdc.gov/nchs) websites.**
- **A CD-ROM version of the code sets that contain official coding guidelines are available for purchase from the U.S. Government Bookstore (bookstore.gpo.gov).**

The *Medicare Prescription Drug, Improvement, and Modernization Act (MMA)* requires all code sets (e.g., ICD-10-CM, ICD-10-PCS) to be valid at the time services are provided. This means that midyear (April 1) and end-of-year (October 1) coding updates must be implemented immediately so accurate codes are reported on claims.

It is crucial that updated coding manuals be purchased and/or billing systems be updated with coding changes so that billing delays (e.g., due to waiting for new coding manuals to arrive) and claims rejections are avoided. If outdated codes are submitted on claims, providers and health care facilities will incur administrative costs associated with resubmitting corrected claims and delayed reimbursement for services provided.

- **Updateable coding manuals are available from publishers as a subscription service, and they are usually stored in a three-ring binder so outdated pages can be removed and new pages can be added.**
- **Encoder software is also available as a subscription service. Coders routinely download the most up-to-date encoder software, which contains edits for new, revised, and discontinued codes. An *encoder* automates the coding process using computerized or web-based software; instead of manually looking up conditions (or procedures) in the coding manual index, the coder uses the software's search feature to locate and verify diagnosis and procedure codes.**
- **Automating the medical coding process is the goal of computer-assisted coding (CAC) (Figure 6-3), which uses a natural language processing engine to "read" patient records and generate ICD-10-CM and HCPCS/CPT codes. Because of this process, coders become coding auditors, responsible for ensuring the accuracy of codes reported to payers. (CAC can be compared to speech recognition technology that has transitioned the role of medical transcriptionists in certain fields, such as radiology, to that of medical editors.)**

Mandatory Reporting of ICD-10-CM and ICD-10-PCS Codes

The *Medicare Catastrophic Coverage Act of 1988* mandated the reporting of ICD-9-CM diagnosis codes on Medicare claims; in subsequent years, private third-party payers adopted similar requirements for claims submission. The Administrative Simplification subtitle of the Health Insurance Portability and Accountability Act of 1996 (HIPAA) mandated the adoption of code set standards in the Transactions and Code Sets final rule published in the *Federal Register*. The final rule modifies the standard medical data code sets for coding diagnoses and inpatient hospital procedures by concurrently adopting ICD-10-CM for all diagnosis coding and ICD-10-PCS for inpatient hospital procedure coding. *Effective October 1, 2014, ICD-10-CM and ICD-10-PCS replaced ICD-9-CM.*

Medical Necessity

Today's concept of medical necessity determines the extent to which individuals with health conditions receive health care services. (The concept was introduced in the 1970s when health insurance contracts intended to exclude care, such as voluntary hospitalizations prescribed primarily for the convenience of the provider or patient.) Reporting diagnosis codes (ICD-10-CM) ensures the medical necessity of procedures and services (CPT and/or HCPCS level II) provided to patients during an encounter. Medicare defines *medical necessity* as "the determination that a service or procedure rendered is reasonable and necessary for the diagnosis or treatment of an illness or injury." If it is possible that scheduled tests, services, or procedures may be found "medically unnecessary" by Medicare, the patient must sign an advance beneficiary notice (ABN), which acknowledges patient responsibility for payment if Medicare denies the claim. (Chapter 14 contains a complete explanation about the ABN, including a sample form.)

CODING TIP:

Be sure to clarify the definition of medical necessity by insurance companies (other than Medicare), because the definition can vary.

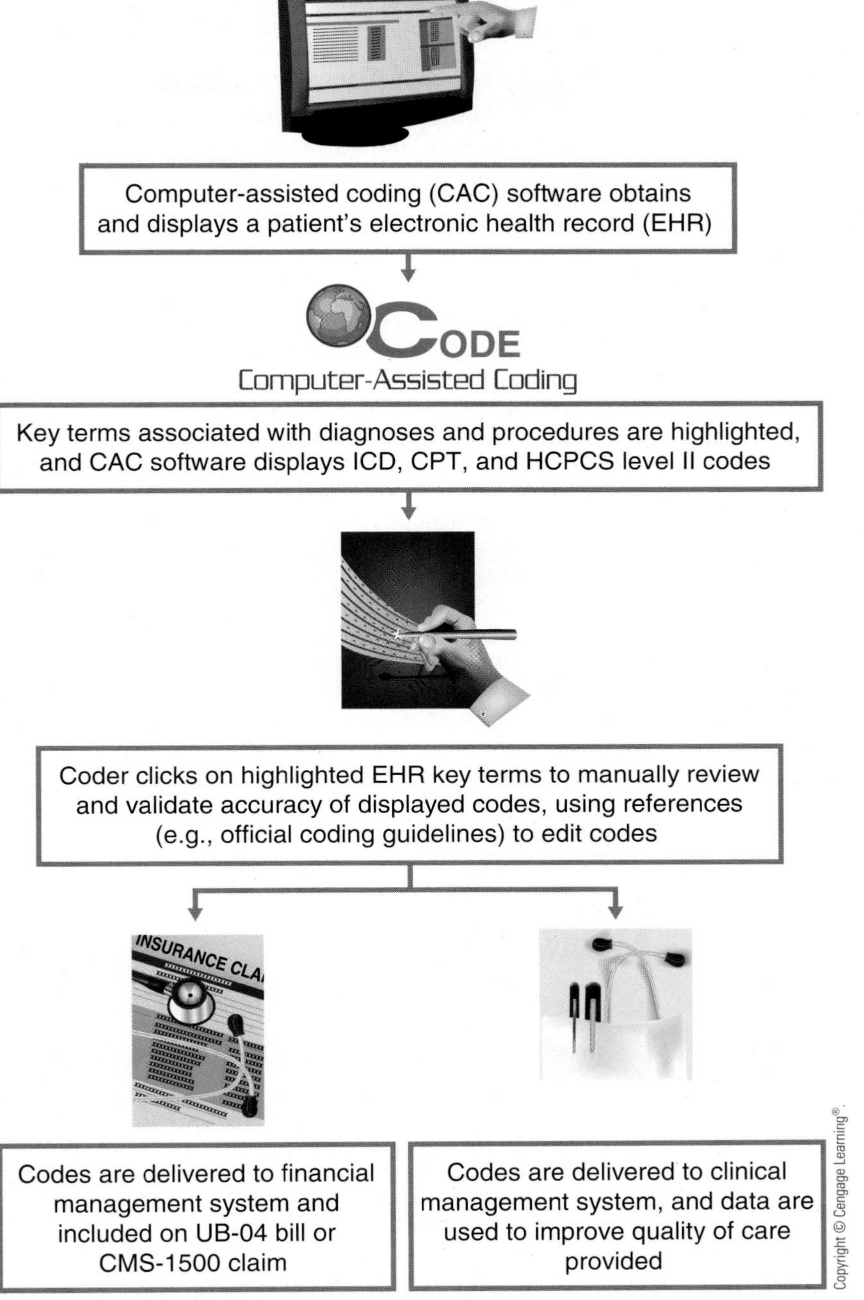
Computer-assisted coding (CAC) software obtains and displays a patient's electronic health record (EHR)
CODE
Computer-Assisted Coding
Key terms associated with diagnoses and procedures are highlighted, and CAC software displays ICD, CPT, and HCPCS level II codes
Coder clicks on highlighted EHR key terms to manually review and validate accuracy of displayed codes, using references (e.g., official coding guidelines) to edit codes
INSURANCE CLA
Codes are delivered to financial management system and included on UB-04 bill or CMS-1500 claim
Codes are delivered to clinical management system, and data are used to improve quality of care provided
Copyright © Cengage Learning®.

FIGURE 6-3 Computer-assisted coding (CAC).

An **encounter** is a face-to-face contact between a patient and a health care provider (e.g., physician, nurse practitioner) who assesses and treats the patient's condition. Thus, medical necessity is the measure of whether a health care procedure or service is appropriate for the diagnosis and/or treatment of a condition. This decision-making process is based on the third-party payer contractual language and treating provider documentation. Generally, the following criteria are used to determine medical necessity:

> **NOTE:** Cost-effective does not necessarily mean least expensive.

- ***Purpose*. The procedure or service is performed to treat a medical condition.**
- ***Scope*. The most appropriate level of service is provided, taking into consideration potential benefit and harm to the patient.**
- ***Evidence*. The treatment is known to be effective in improving health outcomes.**
- ***Value*. The treatment is cost-effective for this condition when compared to alternative treatments, including no treatment.**

EXAMPLE: A 70-year-old male patient with type 1 diabetes mellitus is treated at the physician's office for severe wrist pain resulting from a fall. When the physician asks the patient whether he has been regularly taking his insulin and checking his blood glucose levels, the patient says that most of the time he takes his insulin and sometimes he forgets to check his blood glucose levels. The physician orders a blood glucose test to be done in the office, which reveals elevated blood glucose levels. The physician provides counseling and education to the patient about the importance of taking his daily insulin and checking his blood glucose levels. The physician also orders an x-ray of the wrist, which proves to be negative for a fracture. The physician provides the patient with a wrist brace and instructs the patient to follow up in the office within four weeks.

The insurance specialist reports ICD-10-CM codes for type 1 diabetes mellitus and sprained wrist along with CPT and HCPCS level II codes for an office visit, blood glucose lab test, and the wrist brace. If the only diagnosis reported on the claim was a sprained wrist, the blood glucose lab test would be rejected for payment by the insurance company as an unnecessary medical procedure.

EXERCISE 6-2

Overview of ICD-10-CM and ICD-10-PCS

Instructions: Complete each statement.

1. The *International Classification of Diseases, 10th Revision, Clinical Modification* (ICD-10-CM) codes and classifies __________.
2. The *International Classification of Diseases, 10th Revision, Procedure Classification System* (ICD-10-PCS) codes and classifies __________.
3. The Centers for Medicare and Medicaid Services (CMS) abbreviates ICD-10-CM and ICD-10-PCS as __________.
4. ICD-10-CM includes many more codes and applies to more users than ICD-9-CM because it is designed to collect data on every type of health care encounter, which includes __________.
5. ICD-10-CM also enhances accurate payment for services rendered and facilitates __________.
6. The intent of ICD-10-CM is to describe the clinical picture of the patient, which means codes are more precise than those needed for __________.

(continues)

7. ICD-10-CM codes require up to ________ characters, are entirely alphanumeric, and have unique coding conventions.
8. ICD-10-CM uses a disease index to initially locate codes for conditions and a ________ to verify codes.
9. ICD-10-CM and ICD-10-PCS incorporate much greater ________ (when compared with previous classification systems, such as ICD-9-CM).
10. ICD-10-CM and ICD-10-PCS provide codes to allow for the comparison of ________.
11. The reporting of ICD-9-CM diagnosis codes on Medicare claims was originally mandated by the ________.
12. The reporting of ICD-10-CM/PCS codes was mandated by ________.
13. Reporting ICD-10-CM codes on submitted claims ensures the ________ of procedures and services provided to patients during an encounter, which is defined as "the determination that a service or procedure rendered is reasonable and necessary for the diagnosis or treatment of an illness or injury."
14. The face-to-face contact between a patient and a health care provider who assesses and treats the patient's condition is a(n) ________.
15. The criteria used to determine medical necessity include ________, ________, ________, and ________.

ICD-10-CM CODING CONVENTIONS

ICD-10-CM coding conventions are general rules used in the classification, and they are independent of coding guidelines (located at the Premium Website). The conventions are incorporated into ICD-10-CM as instructional notes, and they include the following:

- **Format and typeface**
- **Eponyms**
- **Abbreviations**
- **Punctuation**
- **Tables**
- **Includes notes, excludes notes, and inclusion terms**
- **Other, other specified, and unspecified codes**
- **Etiology and manifestation rules**
- **And**
- **Due to**
- **With**
- **Cross-references, including, *see, see also, see* category, and *see* condition**

Format and Typeface

The ICD-10-CM index uses an indented format for ease in reference. Index subterms associated with an index entry's main term are indented two spaces, with second and third qualifiers associated with the main term further indented by two and four spaces, respectively. If an index entry requires more than one line, the additional text is printed on the next line and indented five spaces.

> **EXAMPLE:** Locate the main term "Ulcer" in the ICD-10-CM index, and notice that the subterm "aphthous (oral) (recurrent) K12.0" is indented two spaces below the "U" of the main term "Ulcer." Then, notice that the second qualifier "genital organ(s)" is further indented two spaces.

In the tabular list, additional terms are indented below the term to which they are linked. If a definition or disease requires more than one line, the additional text is printed on the next line and indented five spaces.

> **EXAMPLE:** Locate code "P07.3 Preterm [premature] newborn [other]" in Figure 6-9, and notice that the code and description are boldfaced and its definition and synonym (e.g., Prematurity NOS) are indented.

Boldface type is used for main term entries in the alphabetic index and all codes and descriptions of codes in the tabular list. Italicized type is used for all tabular list exclusion notes and to identify manifestation codes, which are never reported as the first-listed diagnoses.

Eponyms

Eponyms are diseases or syndromes that are named for people. They are listed in appropriate alphabetical sequence as main terms in the index. They are also listed as subterms below main terms such as "Disease" or "Syndrome." A description of the disease, syndrome, or procedure is usually included in parentheses following the eponym. (The tabular list usually includes the eponym in the code description.)

> **EXAMPLE:** The index entry for "Barlow's disease" can be located in alphabetic order. (Although the tabular list entry for code E54 does not include the eponym, Barlow's disease, other eponyms are routinely included in the tabular list.)

Abbreviations

The index and tabular list contains abbreviations to save space. The abbreviation **NEC (not elsewhere classifiable)** means "other" or "other specified" and identifies codes that are assigned when information needed to assign a more specific code cannot be located. When a specific code is not available in the index for a condition, the coder is directed to the "other specified" code in the tabular list.

EXAMPLE 1: The index entry for "aberrant, artery, basilar" contains the NEC abbreviation in front of code Q28.1, which means a more specific code cannot be assigned. When verifying code Q28.1 in the tabular list, notice that the code description is "Other malformations of precerebral vessels" and that the NEC abbreviation does not appear in the code description. Code Q28.1 is assigned to "aberrant basilar artery" because the index's NEC abbreviation provides direction to that code.

EXAMPLE 2: Locate code Q28.8 in the tabular list, and notice that the NEC abbreviation is included next to "Congenital aneurysm, specified site NEC" below the code description.

The index and tabular list also contain the abbreviation **NOS (not otherwise specified)**, which is the equivalent of "unspecified." It identifies codes that are to be assigned when information needed to assign a more specific code cannot be obtained from the provider. Because selecting a code from the index based on limited documentation results in the coder being directed to an "unspecified" code in the tabular list, the coder should contact the physician to request that additional documentation be provided so that a more specific diagnosis and/or procedure code can be assigned. A review of the patient record to assign a more specific code is also an important part of the coding process (e.g., laboratory data, radiology reports, operative report, pathology report).

EXAMPLE 1: The index entry for "Bronchomycosis NOS B49 [J99]" provides direction to category B49, which is an unspecified code.

EXAMPLE 2: Locate code A03.9 in the tabular list, and notice that the NOS abbreviation appears after "Bacillary dysentery."

Punctuation

The index includes the following punctuation:

- **Colons**
- **Parentheses**
- **Brackets**

A **colon** is used after an incomplete term or phrase in the index and tabular list when one or more modifiers (additional terms) is needed to assign a code.

EXAMPLE 1: The second qualifier "with retinal:" (located after the index main term "Detachment" and subterm "retina (without retinal break) (serous) H33.2-") requires the type of retinal detachment to be documented in the patient record so that a specific code can be selected.

EXAMPLE 2: The *Excludes2* note below code C32.1 in the tabular list contains the phrase "*malignant neoplasm of aryepiglottic fold or interarytenoid fold:*" that ends with a colon. The three terms indented below the phrase are to be referenced to complete the phrase and assign an additional code (if the condition is documented in the patient record).

Parentheses are used in the index and tabular list to enclose *nonessential modifiers*, which are supplementary words that may be present in or absent from the physician's statement of a disease or procedure without affecting the code number to which it is assigned.

> **EXAMPLE 1:** The index entry "Abasia (-astasia) (hysterical) F44.4" contains two nonessential modifiers in parentheses, which means that the terms may be present or absent from the provider's diagnostic statement.

> **EXAMPLE 2:** In the tabular list, code I47.9 contains nonessential modifier (-Hoffman) in parentheses for *Bouveret (-Hoffman) syndrome*, which means that the term may be present or absent from the provider's diagnostic statement.

Brackets are used in the index to identify manifestation codes and in the index and tabular list to enclose abbreviations, synonyms, alternative wording, or explanatory phrases. A **manifestation** is a condition that occurs as the result of another condition, and manifestation codes are always reported as secondary codes. The code and description may or may not appear in italics in the tabular list. When code descriptions are not italicized in the tabular list, make sure you sequence the codes according to the sequence in the index entry.

> **EXAMPLE 1:** The index entry for "Amyloid heart (disease) E85.4 [I43]" indicates that two codes should be reported: E85.4 and I43. Because code I43 appears in brackets, it is reported as a secondary code. When verifying code I43 in the tabular list, notice that its description is italicized and a *Code first underlying disease, such as:* instruction is provided, prompting you to report code I43 as the second code.

> **EXAMPLE 2:** The index entry for "Abnormal, electrocardiogram [ECG] [EKG] R94.31" encloses abbreviations in square brackets.

> **EXAMPLE 3:** Code I45.89 in the tabular list uses square brackets to enclose the abbreviation for atrioventricular as [AV].

Tables

> **NOTE:** ICD-10-PCS also uses tables, but not in its index; instead of a tabular list of codes, ICD-10-PCS uses tables to assign procedure codes.

The index includes tables which organize subterms, second qualifiers, and third qualifiers and their codes in columns and rows to make it easier to select the proper code. ICD-10-CM organizes the following main terms in tables, which are located at the end of the Index to Diseases and Injuries (before the Index to External Causes):

- **Table of Neoplasms**
- **Table of Drugs and Chemicals**

The **Table of Neoplasms** is an alphabetic index of anatomic sites for which there are six possible code numbers according to whether the neoplasm in question is malignant primary, malignant secondary, malignant *in situ, benign*, of uncertain behavior, or of unspecified nature. The description of the neoplasm will often indicate which of the six columns is appropriate (e.g., malignant melanoma of skin, benign fibroadenoma of breast, carcinoma *in situ* of cervix uteri).

The **Table of Drugs and Chemicals** is an alphabetic index of medicinal, chemical, and biological substances that result in poisonings and adverse effects. The first column of the table lists generic names of drugs and chemicals (although some publishers have added brand names) with six columns for:

- **Poisoning: Accidental (Unintentional)**
- **Poisoning: Intentional Self-harm**
- **Poisoning: Assault**
- **Poisoning: Undetermined**
- **Adverse Effect**
- **Underdosing**

Includes Notes, Excludes Notes, and Inclusion Terms

An **includes note** appears in the ICD-10-CM tabular lists below certain categories to further define, clarify, or give examples of the content of a code category.

> **EXAMPLE:** The *includes note* located below category code "H80 Otosclerosis" in the tabular list indicates that "otospongiosis" is classified to that same category. This means that the provider could document "otosclerosis" or "otospongiosis," and a code from category H80 would be assigned.

Two types of excludes notes are used in the tabular list, and each note has a different definition for use. However, they are similar in that they both indicate that codes excluded from each other are independent of each other. An **Excludes1 note** is a "pure" excludes. It means "not coded here" and indicates mutually exclusive codes; in other words, two conditions that cannot be reported together.

> **EXAMPLE 1:** ICD-10-CM code "Q03 Congenital hydrocephalus" contains an Excludes1 note for *acquired hydrocephalus (G91.-)*. For hydrocephalus that develops later in life, which is an acquired form of the disease, a code from G91.- is assigned. The congenital form of the disease is not reported with an acquired form of the same condition. Thus, code G91.- is *never* reported with a code from category Q03.

> **EXAMPLE 2:** ICD-10-CM code "E10 Type 1 diabetes mellitus" contains an Excludes1 note for *type 2 diabetes mellitus (E11.-)*. Type 1 diabetes mellitus is classified to a code from E10.1x–E10.9. Thus, a code for type 2 diabetes mellitus (E11.0–E11.9) is *never* reported with a code for type 1 diabetes mellitus.

An **Excludes2 note** means "not included here" and indicates that, although the excluded condition is not classified as part of the condition it is excluded from, a patient may be diagnosed with all conditions at the same time. Therefore, when an Excludes2 note appears under a code, it may be acceptable to assign both the code and the excluded code(s) together if supported by the medical documentation.

EXAMPLE: ICD-10-CM code "M19.14 Post-traumatic osteoarthritis, hand" contains an Excludes2 note for *post-traumatic osteoarthritis of first carpometacarpal joint (M18.2-, M18.3-)*. The Excludes2 note means that because a patient can be diagnosed with both "post-traumatic osteoarthritis of the hand" and "post-traumatic osteoarthritis of the first carpometacarpal joint," it is acceptable to assign codes to *both* conditions if supported by medical documentation.

NOTE: Inclusion terms listed below codes in the tabular list are not meant to be exhaustive, and additional terms found only in the index may also be associated with a code. This concept is called **trust the index**.

Lists of inclusion terms are located below certain codes in the ICD-10-CM tabular list. The inclusion terms indicate some of the conditions for which that code number may be assigned. They may be synonyms of the code title, or, in the case of "other specified" codes, the terms may also provide a list of various conditions included within a classification code. The list of inclusion terms in the tabular lists is not exhaustive. Each index may provide additional terms that may also be assigned to a given code.

EXAMPLE 1: The following inclusion terms are located in the Tabular List of Diseases and Injuries for diagnosis code "M54.5, Low back pain:"

- Loin pain
- Lumbago NOS

EXAMPLE 2: If the provider documents "polyalgia" as the patient's condition, assign code M79.89 even though the code description indicates it is an "other specified" code.

EXAMPLE 3: Locate the index entry for "Infection, fish tapeworm, larval B70.1." Then, go to the tabular list to verify code B70.1 where you will notice that "infection due to fish tapeworm, larval" is not listed as an inclusion term. The coder has to *trust the index* and assign code B70.1 for the documented condition.

Other, Other Specified, and Unspecified Codes

Other and other specified codes are assigned when patient record documentation provides detail for which a specific code does not exist in ICD-10-CM. Index entries that contain the abbreviation NEC are classified to "other" codes in the tabular list. These index entries represent specific disease entities for which no specific code exists in the tabular list, so the term is included within an "other" code.

Unspecified codes are assigned when patient record documentation is insufficient to assign a more specific code. (Before assigning an unspecified code, ask the provider to document additional information so that a more specific code can be reported.) When an ICD-10-CM tabular list category does not contain an unspecified code, the "other specified" code may represent both "other and unspecified." In ICD-10-CM, "other and unspecified" category and subcategory codes require assignment of extra character(s) to classify the condition.

When the index directs the coder to an "other, other specified, or unspecified code" in the tabular list, it is important to review the record carefully (or ask the physician for clarification of documentation) to determine if a more specific code can be assigned. This is referred to as "moving up the ladder" of codes in the tabular list.

EXAMPLE:
- D64.89 is an "other specified" code.
- D64.9 is an "unspecified" code.
- I70.9 is an "other and unspecified" code (that contains subcategories).

Etiology and Manifestation Rules

Etiology and manifestation rules include the following notes in the ICD-10-CM Tabular List of Diseases and Injuries:

- **Code first underlying disease**
- **Code first underlying disease, such as:**
- **Code, if applicable, any causal condition first**
- **Use additional code**
- **In diseases classified elsewhere**

To classify certain conditions completely, codes must be assigned to the underlying *etiology* (cause or origin of disease) and multiple body system *manifestations* (resulting symptoms or conditions) due to the underlying etiology. For such conditions, the underlying condition is sequenced first, followed by the manifestation. Wherever an etiology and manifestation combination of codes exists, the tabular list etiology code contains a **use additional code** note and the manifestation code contains a **code first underlying disease** or **code first underlying disease, such as:** note. These instructional notes assist coders in the proper sequencing of the codes: etiology code followed by manifestation code. In most cases, the manifestation code will have in its title **in diseases classified elsewhere**, which indicates that the manifestation code is a component of the etiology/manifestation coding convention. A manifestation code that does not contain "in diseases classified elsewhere" in its title will contain a "use additional code" note. (Sequence the manifestation code *after* the etiology code.)

The instruction to **code, if applicable, any causal condition first** requires the causal condition to be sequenced first if present. A causal condition is a disease (e.g., diabetes mellitus) that manifests (or results in) another condition (e.g., diabetic cataracts). If no causal condition is documented, the code that contains the instruction (code, if applicable, any causal condition first) may be reported without the causal condition code. (This differs from the instruction to code first underlying condition, which does not allow for the code that contains the instruction to be reported without first sequencing the underlying condition.)

EXAMPLE 1: Diagnostic statement "idiopathic pulmonary hemosiderosis" includes two codes in the ICD-10-CM index: E83.19 [J84.03]. Code J84.03 is listed in brackets in the index, which indicates it is the manifestation code and is reported second. The ICD-10-CM tabular list entry for J84.03 is also in italics, and it contains a "code first underlying disease, such as:" note.

EXAMPLE 2: The patient is diagnosed with "benign hypertrophy of the prostate with urge and stress incontinence." Locate subcategory code N40.1 in the ICD-10-CM tabular list, and notice that the "use additional code for . . . urinary incontinence (N39.4-)" note instructs you to report an additional code. Therefore, assign codes N40.1 and N39.46.

Next, notice that category code N39.4 in the tabular list includes a "code also any associated overactive bladder (N32.81)" note. Because the diagnostic statement (above) does not include "overactive bladder," do not assign code N32.81.

EXAMPLE 3: A patient with an alcohol addiction (F10.20) was seen in the office, complaining of urinary incontinence. The physician determined that the condition was nonorganic in origin and most likely the result of the patient being too inebriated to realize he had urinated while unconscious. Thus, code F98.0 is assigned to urinary incontinence that is of nonorganic origin.

And

When the word **and** appears in category titles and code descriptions in the ICD-10-CM Tabular List of Diseases and Injuries, it is interpreted as meaning and/or.

EXAMPLE: Subcategory code "H61.0 Chondritis and perichondritis of external ear" is interpreted as "Chondritis of external ear" *and/or* "Perichondritis of external ear." This means that code H61.0 can be assigned for both conditions or either condition, depending upon documentation.

Due to

The subterm **due to** is located in the index in alphabetical order below a main term to indicate the presence of a cause-and-effect (or causal) relationship between two conditions. When the index includes *due to* as a subterm, the code is assigned *only if* the physician documented the causal relationship between two conditions, such as meningitis due to adenovirus. It is possible that a patient could have meningitis along with an unrelated adenovirus at the same time. (The due to phrase is included in tabular list code descriptions, but it is not a coding instruction.)

ICD-10-CM occasionally presumes a causal relationship between two conditions. This means that the physician is not required to document "due to" in the diagnostic statement, such as when the patient has hypertension and renal failure. This condition is coded as hypertensive renal failure, which is interpreted as hypertension due to renal failure.

EXAMPLE: When the physician documents "pneumonitis due to inhalation of regurgitated food," a causal relationship exists, and code J69.0 is assigned.

In

When the word **in** appears in the ICD-10-CM index, it is located in alphabetical order below the main term. To assign a code from the list of qualifiers below the word *in*, the physician must document both conditions in the patient's record. ICD-10-CM classifies certain conditions as if there were a cause-and-effect relationship present because they occur together much of the time (e.g., pneumonia in Q fever).

EXAMPLE: Locate the main term "pneumonia" in the index, and notice that the word *in (due to)* appears in alphabetical order above a list of second qualifiers. To assign a code from the list, the physician must document a relationship between both conditions, such as "pneumonia in measles" (or "postpneumonia measles") for which combination code B05.2 is assigned. (Other conditions that occur together may require the assignment of multiple codes, one for the etiology and another for the manifestation.)

NOTE: The word *with* is interpreted to mean "associated with" or "due to" when it appears in a code title, the index, or an instructional note in the tabular list. When the word *with* is included in disease and procedure code descriptions in the ICD-10-CM tabular list, the physician must document both conditions (or procedures) for the code to be assigned.

With

When the word **with** appears in the ICD-10-CM index, it is located immediately below the main term, not in alphabetical order. To assign a code from the list of qualifiers below the word *with*, the physician must document the presence of both conditions in the patient's record.

EXAMPLE: Locate the main term "measles" in the index, and notice that the word *with* appears above a list of second qualifiers. To assign a code from the list, the physician must document both conditions, such as measles with keratitis (B05.81). The physician could also document:

- Measles keratitis
- Measles associated with keratitis
- Measles and keratitis
- Measles with keratoconjunctivitis

Cross-References, Including See, See Also, See Category, and See Condition

The ICD-10-CM index includes cross-references, which instruct the coder to refer to another entry in the index (e.g., see, see also, see condition) or to the tabular list (e.g., see category) to assign the correct code.

- **The see instruction after a main term directs the coder to refer to another term in the ICD-10-CM index to locate the code. The coder must go to the referenced main term to locate the correct code.**
- **The see also instruction is located after a main term or subterm in the ICD-10-CM index and directs the coder to another main term (or subterm) that may provide additional useful index entries. The *see also* instruction does *not* have to be followed if the original main term (or subterm) provides the correct code.**
- **The see category instruction directs the coder to the ICD-10-CM tabular list, where a code can be selected from the options provided there.**
- **The see condition instruction directs the coder to the main term for a condition, found in the ICD-10-CM disease index.**

EXAMPLE 1: Locate the main term "Laceration" and subterm "blood vessel" in the ICD-10-CM index. Notice that a cross-reference directs you to "*See* Injury, blood vessel," which is at a different location in the index where the code can be found.

EXAMPLE 2: The *see also* instruction is optional if the correct code can be located below the main term (e.g., ICD-10-CM index entry "Laceration, lower back —*see* Laceration, back, lower"). If the correct code cannot be located, the *see also* cross-reference directs the coder to a different location in the index where the code can be found.

EXAMPLE 3: Locate the main term "Pyelitis," subterm "with," and second qualifier "calculus" in the ICD-10-CM index. Notice that a cross-reference directs you to *see category* N20. To assign the correct code, review category N20 in the tabular list to select the appropriate fourth digit.

EXAMPLE 4: Locate the main term "Accidental" in the ICD-10-CM index, and notice that a cross-reference directs you to *see* condition, which means the patient record needs to be reviewed to determine the condition (e.g., fracture).

EXERCISE 6-3

ICD-10-CM Coding Conventions

Instructions: Assign ICD-10-CM codes to each diagnostic statement, interpreting coding conventions.

1. Acariasis infestation ______
2. Costen's complex ______
3. ST elevation myocardial infarction, anterior wall, involving left main coronary artery ______
4. Malaria with hepatitis ______
5. Acute lymphangitis ______
6. Absence of menstruation ______
7. Arterial atheroembolism ______
8. Cataract in hypoparathyroidism ______
9. Acromegaly ______
10. Cirrhosis due to Wilson's disease ______
11. Keratoconjunctivitis in exanthema ______
12. Appendicitis with perforation ______
13. Abnormal acid–base balance ______
14. Parietoalveolar pneumopathy ______
15. GM2 gangliosidosis, juvenile ______

ICD-10-CM INDEX TO DISEASES AND INJURIES

The **ICD-10-CM Index to Diseases and Injuries** (Figure 6-4) is an alphabetical listing of terms and their corresponding codes, which include:

- **Specific illnesses (e.g., hypertension)**
- **Injuries (e.g., fracture)**
- **Eponyms (e.g., Barlow's disease)**
- **Abbreviations (e.g., BMI)**
- **Other descriptive diagnostic terms (e.g., acute)**

ICD-10-CM Index to Diseases and Injuries

A

Aarskog's syndrome Q87.1
Abandonment — *see* Maltreatment
Abasia (-astasia) (hysterical) F44.4
Abderhalden-Kaufmann-Lignac syndrome (cystinosis) E72.04
Abdomen, abdominal (*see also* condition)
  acute R10.0
  angina K55.1
  muscle deficiency syndrome Q79.4
Abdominalgia — *see* Pain, abdominal
Abduction contracture, hip or other joint — *see* Contraction, joint
Aberrant (congenital) (*see also* Malposition, congenital)
  adrenal gland Q89.1
  artery (peripheral) Q27.8
    basilar NEC Q28.1
    cerebral Q28.3
    coronary Q24.5
    digestive system Q27.8
    eye Q15.8
    lower limb Q27.8
    precerebral Q28.1
    pulmonary Q25.79
    renal Q27.2
    retina Q14.1
    specified site NEC Q27.8
    subclavian Q27.8
    upper limb Q27.8
    vertebral Q28.1
  breast Q83.8
  endocrine gland NEC Q89.2
  hepatic duct Q44.5
  pancreas Q45.3
  parathyroid gland Q89.2
  pituitary gland Q89.2
  sebaceous glands, mucous membrane, mouth, congenital Q38.6
  spleen Q89.09
  subclavian artery Q27.8
  thymus (gland) Q89.2
  thyroid gland Q89.2
  vein (peripheral) NEC Q27.8
    cerebral Q28.3

FIGURE 6-4 ICD-10-CM Index to Diseases and Injuries (partial).

The index is subdivided as follows:

- **Index to Diseases and Injuries**
  - **Table of Neoplasms**
  - **Table of Drugs and Chemicals**
- **Index to External Causes**

Main Terms, Subterms, and Qualifiers

Main terms in the index are boldfaced and listed in alphabetical order, which means hyphens within main terms are ignored, but a single space within a main term is not ignored. A code listed next to a main term in the ICD-10-CM index is referred to as a *default code*. The default code represents the code for the condition most commonly associated with the main term, or it may represent an unspecified code for the condition. (The ICD-10-CM Tabular List of Diseases and Injuries must always be referenced so that the most accurate and complete code is assigned.) When a condition is documented without any additional information (e.g., appendicitis), such as acute or chronic, the *default code* is assigned (after verifying the code in the ICD-10-CM Tabular List of Diseases and Injuries).

EXAMPLE: The hyphen in "Cat-scratch" is ignored, resulting in sequencing that main term after "Catatonic."

Catatonic

Cat-scratch

EXAMPLE: The space between "bee" and "sting" is considered, resulting in that main term being sequenced above "Beer-drinkers' heart (disease)"

Bee sting (with allergic or anaphylactic shock) —see Toxicity, venom, arthropod, bee

Beer drinkers' heart (disease) I42.6

Main terms may or may not be followed by a listing of parenthetical terms that serve as nonessential modifiers of the main term. **Nonessential modifiers** are supplementary words located in parentheses after a main term that do not have to be included in the diagnostic statement for the code to be assigned. **Qualifiers** are supplementary terms that further modify subterms and other qualifiers. **Subterms** (or **essential modifiers**) qualify the main term by listing alternative sites, etiology, or clinical status. A subterm is indented two spaces under the main term. Second qualifiers are indented two spaces under a subterm, and third qualifiers are indented two spaces under a second qualifier (Figure 6-5). Care must be taken when moving from the bottom of one column to the top of the next column or when turning to the next page of the index. The main term will be repeated and followed by *—continued*. When moving from one column to another, watch carefully to determine whether the subterm has changed *or* new second or third qualifiers appear.

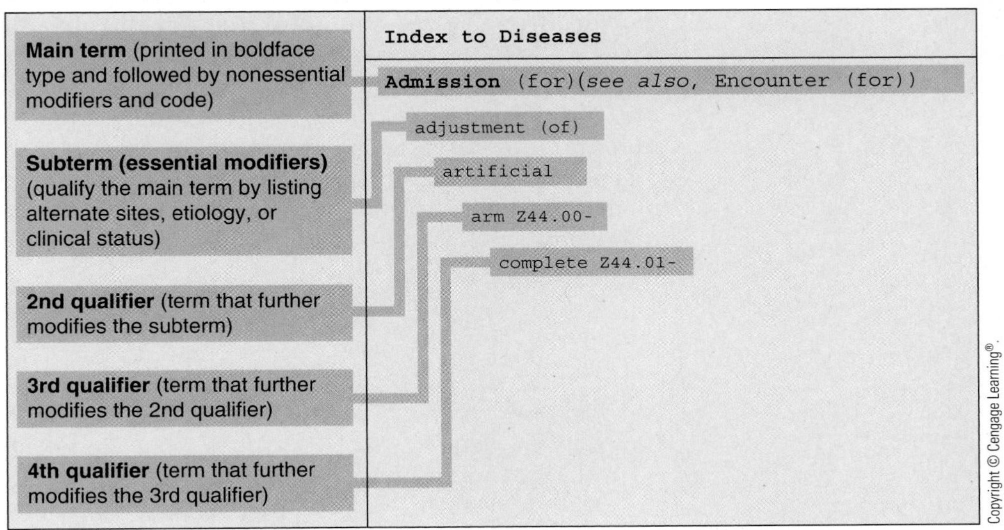

FIGURE 6-5 Display of main terms, subterms (nonessential modifiers), and qualifiers in the ICD-10-CM index.

EXAMPLE: Index to Diseases and Injuries entries are organized according to main terms, subterms, second qualifiers, and third qualifiers. Refer to the index entry for "stricture, aqueduct of Sylvius, with spina bifida, acquired (G91.1)," and note the indented subterm and qualifiers. Notice that when the main term continues at the top of a column (or on the next page of the Index to Diseases and Injuries), the word *—continued* appears after the main term. Subterms and qualifiers are then indented below the main term.

Start of Main Term in Index to Diseases and Injuries		Continuation of Main Term (next column)	
Main term:	Stricture (*see also* Stenosis)	**Main term:**	Stricture – *continued*
Subterm:	aqueduct of Sylvius (congenital) Q03.0	**Subterm:**	bronchus J98.09
Second qualifier:	with spina bifida – *see* spina bifida,	**Second qualifier:**	congenital Q32.3
Continuation line:	by site, with hydrocephalus	**Second qualifier:**	syphilitic A52.72
Third qualifier:	acquired G91.1	**Subterm:**	cardia (stomach) K22.2

Table of Neoplasms

Neoplasms are new growths, or tumors, in which cell reproduction is out of control. For coding purposes, the provider should specify whether the tumor is *benign* (noncancerous, nonmalignant, noninvasive) or **malignant** (cancerous, invasive, capable of spreading to other parts of the body). It is highly advisable that neoplasms be coded directly from the pathology report (generated by a hospital's or stand-alone laboratory's pathology department and mailed to the provider's office); however, until the diagnostic statement specifies whether the neoplasm is benign or malignant, coders should code the patient's sign (e.g., breast lump) or report a subcategory code from the "unspecified nature" column of the documented site using the Index to Diseases Table of Neoplasms.

Another term associated with neoplasms is **lesion**, defined as any discontinuity of tissue (e.g., skin or organ) that may or may not be malignant. Disease index entries for "lesion" contain subterms according to anatomic site (e.g., organs or tissue), and that term should be referenced if the diagnostic statement does not confirm a malignancy. In addition, the following conditions are examples of benign lesions and are listed as separate Index to Diseases entries:

- **Adenosis**
- **Cyst**
- **Dysplasia**
- **Mass (unless the word *neoplasm* is included in the diagnostic statement)**
- **Polyp**

The *Table of Neoplasms* (Figure 6-6) is indexed by anatomic site and contains four cellular classifications: malignant, benign, uncertain behavior, and unspecified nature. The malignant classification is subdivided into three divisions: primary, secondary, and carcinoma *in situ*. The six neoplasm classifications are defined as follows:

- **Primary malignancy—The original tumor site. All malignant tumors are considered primary unless otherwise documented as metastatic or secondary.**

	Malignant Primary	Malignant Secondary	Ca *in situ*	Benign	Uncertain Behavior	Unspecified Nature
Neoplasm, neoplastic	C80.1	C79.9	D09.9	D36.9	D48.9	D49.9

Notes—

The list below gives the code numbers for neoplasms by anatomical site. For each site there are six possible code numbers according to whether the neoplasm in question is malignant, benign, *in situ,* of uncertain behavior, or of unspecified nature. The description of the neoplasm will often indicate which of the six columns is appropriate; e.g., malignant melanoma of skin, benign fibroadenoma of breast, carcinoma *in situ* of cervix uteri.

Where such descriptors are not present, the remainder of the Index should be consulted where guidance is given to the appropriate column for each morphologic (histological) variety listed; e.g., Mesonephroma —*see* Neoplasm, malignant; Embryoma —*see also* Neoplasm, uncertain behavior; Disease, Bowen's —*see* Neoplasm, skin, *in situ.* However, the guidance in the Index can be overridden if one of the descriptors mentioned above is present; e.g., malignant adenoma of colon is coded to C18.9 and not to D12.6 as the adjective "malignant" overrides the Index entry "Adenoma —*see also* Neoplasm, benign."

Codes listed with a dash -, following the code have a required additional character for laterality. The tabular must be reviewed for the complete code.

	Malignant Primary	Malignant Secondary	Ca *in situ*	Benign	Uncertain Behavior	Unspecified Nature
abdomen, abdominal	C76.2	C79.9	D09.7	D36.7	D48.9	D49.9
cavity	C76.2	C79.89	D09.7	D36.7	D48.7	D49.89
organ	C76.2	C79.89	D09.7	D36.7	D48.7	D49.89
viscera	C76.2	C79.89	D09.7	D36.7	D48.7	D49.89
wall —*see also* Neoplasm, abdomen, wall, skin	C44.509	C79.2	D04.5	D23.5	D48.5	D49.2
connective tissue	C49.4	C79.89	—	D21.4	D48.1	D49.2
skin	C44.509	—	—	—	—	—
basal cell carcinoma	C44.519	—	—	—	—	—
specified type NEC	C44.599	—	—	—	—	—
squamous cell carcinoma	C44.529	—	—	—	—	—

FIGURE 6-6 ICD-10-CM Table of Neoplasms (partial).

- **Secondary malignancy**—The tumor has metastasized (spread) to a secondary site, either adjacent to the primary site or to a remote region of the body.
- **Carcinoma (Ca) *in situ***—A malignant tumor that is localized, circumscribed, encapsulated, and noninvasive (has not spread to deeper or adjacent tissues or organs).
- **Benign**—A noninvasive, nonspreading, nonmalignant tumor.
- **Uncertain behavior**—It is not possible to predict subsequent morphology or behavior from the submitted specimen. In order to assign a code from this column, the pathology report must specifically indicate the "uncertain behavior" of the neoplasm.
- **Unspecified nature**—A neoplasm is identified, but no further indication of the histology or nature of the tumor is reflected in the documented diagnosis. Assign a code from this column when the neoplasm was destroyed or removed and a tissue biopsy was performed and results are pending.

To go directly to the Table of Neoplasms, you must know the classification and the site of the neoplasm. Some diagnostic statements specifically document the "neoplasm" classification; others will not provide a clue. If the diagnostic statement classifies the neoplasm, the coder can refer directly to the Table of Neoplasms to assign the proper code (after verifying the code in the tabular list, of course).

EXAMPLE:

Diagnostic Statement	Table of Neoplasms Reference
Tracheal carcinoma *in situ*	trachea (cartilage) (mucosa), Malignant, Ca *in situ* (D02.1)
Cowper's gland tumor, uncertain behavior	Cowper's gland, Uncertain Behavior (D41.3)
Metastatic carcinoma	unknown site or unspecified, Malignant Secondary (C79.9)
Cancer of the breast, primary	breast, Malignant Primary (C50.9-)

If the diagnostic statement *does not* classify the neoplasm, the coder must refer to the disease index entry for the condition documented (instead of the Table of Neoplasms). That entry will either contain a code number that can be verified in the tabular list or will refer the coder to the proper Table of Neoplasms entry under which to locate the code.

EXAMPLE:

Diagnostic Statement	Index to Diseases Entry
non-Hodgkin's lymphoma	**Lymphoma (of) (malignant)** C85.90 non-Hodgkin (*see also* Lymphoma, by type) C85.9- specified NEC C85.8-
Adrenal adenolymphoma	**Adenolymphoma** specified site —*see* Neoplasm, benign, by site unspecified site D11.9

CODING TIP:

1. Assigning codes from the Table of Neoplasms is a two-step process. First, classify the neoplasm by its behavior (e.g., malignant, secondary) and then by its anatomic site (e.g., acoustic nerve).
2. To classify the neoplasm's behavior, review the provider's diagnostic statement (e.g., carcinoma of the throat), and look up "carcinoma" in the index. The entry will classify the behavior for you, directing you to the proper column in the Table of Neoplasms. (If malignant, you will still need to determine whether it is primary, secondary, or *in situ* based on documentation in the patient's record.)

Primary Malignancy

A malignancy is coded as the primary site if the diagnostic statement documents:

- **Metastatic *from* a site**
- **Spread *from* a site**
- ***Primary neoplasm of* a site**
- **A malignancy for which *no specific classification is documented***
- **A *recurrent* tumor**

EXAMPLE: For carcinoma of cervical lymph nodes, metastatic from the breast, assign two codes:

- Primary malignancy of left breast (male) (C50.922)
- Secondary malignancy of cervical lymph nodes (C77.0)

Secondary Malignancy

Secondary malignancies are *metastatic* and indicate that a primary cancer has spread (*metastasized*) to another part of the body. Sequencing of neoplasm codes depends on whether the primary or secondary cancer is being managed and/or treated. To properly code secondary malignancies, consider the following: Cancer described as *metastatic* from a site is *primary* of that site. Assign one code to the primary neoplasm and a second code to the secondary neoplasm of the specified site (if the secondary site is known) or unspecified site (if the secondary site is unknown).

EXAMPLE: For metastatic carcinoma from the right breast (female) to lung, assign two codes:

- Primary malignant neoplasm of right breast (C50.911)
- Secondary malignant neoplasm of right lung (C78.01)

Cancer described as *metastatic* to a site is considered *secondary* of that site. Assign one code to the secondary site and a second code to the specified primary site (if the primary site is known) or unspecified site (if the primary site is unknown).

> **EXAMPLE:** For metastatic carcinoma from the liver to left lung, assign two codes:
>
> - Primary malignant neoplasm of liver (C22.9)
> - Secondary malignant neoplasm of left lung (C78.02)

When anatomic sites are documented as *metastatic*, assign *secondary* neoplasm code(s) to those sites, and assign an *unspecified* site code to the primary malignant neoplasm.

> **EXAMPLE:** For metastatic renal cell carcinoma of the left lung, assign two codes:
>
> - Primary malignant neoplasm of right kidney (C64.1)
> - Secondary malignant neoplasm of left lung (C78.02)

If the diagnostic statement does not specify whether the neoplasm site is primary or secondary, code the site as primary *unless the documented site is bone, brain, diaphragm, heart, liver, lymph nodes, mediastinum, meninges, peritoneum, pleura, retroperitoneum, or spinal cord*. These sites are considered *secondary sites* unless the physician specifies that they are primary.

> **EXAMPLE 1:** For left lung cancer, assign one code (because *lung* does not appear in the above list of secondary sites):
>
> - Primary malignant neoplasm of left lung (C34.92)

> **EXAMPLE 2:** For spinal cord cancer, assign two codes:
>
> - Primary malignant neoplasm of unspecified site (C80.1)
> - Secondary malignant neoplasm of spinal cord (C79.49)

Anatomic Site Is Not Documented

If the cancer diagnosis does not contain documentation of the anatomic site, but the term *metastatic* is documented, assign codes for *unspecified site* for both the primary and secondary sites.

> **EXAMPLE:** For metastatic chromophobe pituitary gland adenocarcinoma, assign two codes as follows:
>
> - Primary malignant neoplasm of pituitary gland (C75.1)
> - Secondary malignant neoplasm of unknown site (C79.9)

Primary Malignant Site Is No Longer Present

If the primary site of malignancy is no longer present, do not assign the code for "primary of unspecified site." Instead, classify the previous primary site by assigning the appropriate code from category Z85, "Personal history of malignant neoplasm."

> **EXAMPLE:** For metastatic carcinoma to right lung from left breast (left radical mastectomy performed last year), assign two codes as follows:
>
> - Secondary malignant neoplasm of right lung (C78.01)
> - Personal history of malignant neoplasm of breast (Z85.3)

Contiguous or Overlapping Sites

Contiguous sites (or **overlapping sites**) occur when the origin of the tumor (primary site) involves two adjacent sites. Neoplasms with overlapping site boundaries are classified to the fourth-digit subcategory .8, "Other."

> **EXAMPLE:** For cancer of the jejunum and ileum, go to the index entry for "intestine, small, overlapping lesion" in the Table of Neoplasms. Locate code C17.8 in the *Malignant Primary* column, and verify the code in the tabular list.

Re-excision of Tumors

A **re-excision** of a tumor occurs when the pathology report recommends that the surgeon perform a second excision to widen the margins of the original tumor site. The re-excision is performed to ensure that all tumor cells have been removed and that a clear border (margin) of normal tissue surrounds the excised specimen. Use the diagnostic statement found in the report of the original excision to code the reason for the re-excision. The pathology report for the re-excision may not specify a malignancy at this time, but the patient is still under treatment for the original neoplasm.

CODING TIP:

1. Read all notes in the Table of Neoplasms that apply to the malignancy that you are coding.
2. Never assign a code directly from the Table of Neoplasms or Index to Diseases and Injuries.
3. Be certain you are submitting codes that represent the current status of the neoplasm.
4. Assign a code from the Table of Neoplasms if the tumor has been excised *and the patient is still undergoing radiation or chemotherapy treatment.*
5. Assign a Z code if the tumor is no longer present *or* if the patient is not receiving treatment, but is returning for follow-up care.
6. Classification stated on a pathology report overrides the morphology classification stated in the Index to Diseases and Injuries.

EXERCISE 6-4

Table of Neoplasms

Instructions: Complete each statement.

1. For *oat cell carcinoma of the right lung with spread to the brain*, the primary site is ________, and the secondary site is ________.
2. For *metastatic carcinoma from right breast (female)*, the primary site is ________, and the secondary site is ________.
3. For *metastatic carcinoma from right kidney to bone*, the primary site is ________, and the secondary site is ________.
4. For *metastatic malignant melanoma of bone*, the primary site is ________, and the secondary site is ________.
5. For *frontal lobe brain cancer*, the primary site is ________, and the secondary site is ________.

Instructions: Assign codes to each diagnostic statement, sequencing the primary site code first.

6. Oat cell carcinoma of the right lung with spread to the brain ________
7. Metastatic carcinoma from right breast (female) ________
8. Metastatic carcinoma from right kidney to bone ________
9. Metastatic malignant melanoma of bone ________
10. Brain cancer ________

Table of Drugs and Chemicals

The Table of Drugs and Chemicals (Figure 6-7) is an alphabetic index of medicinal, chemical, and biological substances that result in poisonings and adverse effects. The first column of the table lists generic names of drugs and chemicals (although some publishers have added brand names) with six columns for:

- **Poisoning: Accidental (Unintentional)** (poisoning that results from an inadvertent overdose, wrong substance administered/taken, or intoxication that includes combining prescription drugs with nonprescription drugs or alcohol)
- **Poisoning: Intentional Self-harm** (poisoning that results from a deliberate overdose, such as a suicide attempt, of substance(s) administered/taken or intoxication that includes purposely combining prescription drugs with nonprescription drugs or alcohol)
- **Poisoning: Assault** (poisoning inflicted by another person who intended to kill or injure the patient)
- **Poisoning: Undetermined** (subcategory used if the patient record does not document whether the poisoning was intentional or accidental)
- **Adverse Effect** (development of a pathologic condition that results from a drug or chemical substance that was properly administered or taken)
- **Underdosing** (taking less of a medication than is prescribed by a provider or a manufacturer's instruction)

NOTE: An **iatrogenic illness** can result from a medical intervention, such as an adverse reaction to contrast material injected prior to a scan, and is classified within individual ICD-10-CM chapters. For example, code E71.43 (iatrogenic carnitine deficiency) is classified in ICD-10-CM Chapter 4, Endocrine, nutritional and metabolic diseases (E00–E90).

Substance	Poisoning, Accidental (unintentional)	Poisoning, Intentional Self-harm	Poisoning, Assault	Poisoning, Undetermined	Adverse Effect	Underdosing
1-Propanol	T51.3x1	T51.3x2	T51.3x3	T51.3x4	—	—
2-Propanol	T51.2x1	T51.2x2	T51.2x3	T51.2x4	—	—
2, 4-D (dichlorophen-oxyacetic acid)	T60.3x1	T60.3x2	T60.3x3	T60.3x4	—	—
2, 4-toluene diisocyanate	T65.0x1	T65.0x2	T65.0x3	T65.0x4	—	—
2, 4, 5-T (trichloro-phenoxyacetic acid)	T60.1x1	T60.1x2	T60.1x3	T60.1x4	—	—
14-hydroxydihydro-morphinone	T40.2x1	T40.2x2	T40.2x3	T40.2x4	T40.2x5	T40.2x6
ABOB	T37.5x1	T37.5x2	T37.5x3	T37.5x4	T37.5x5	T37.5x6
Abrine	T62.2x1	T62.2x2	T62.2x3	T62.2x4	—	—
Abrus (seed)	T62.2x1	T62.2x2	T62.2x3	T62.2x4	—	—
Absinthe	T51.0x1	T51.0x2	T51.0x3	T51.0x4	—	—
beverage	T51.0x1	T51.0x2	T51.0x3	T51.0x4	—	—
Acaricide	T60.8x1	T60.8x2	T60.8x3	T60.8x4	—	—
Acebutolol	T44.7x1	T44.7x2	T44.7x3	T44.7x4	T44.7x5	T44.7x6
Acecarbromal	T42.6x1	T42.6x2	T42.6x3	T42.6x4	T42.6x5	T42.6x6
Aceclidine	T44.1x1	T44.1x2	T44.1x3	T44.1x4	T44.1x5	T44.1x6
Acedapsone	T37.0x1	T37.0x2	T37.0x3	T37.0x4	T37.0x5	T37.0x6
Acefylline piperazine	T48.6x1	T48.6x2	T48.6x3	T48.6x4	T48.6x5	T48.6x6

FIGURE 6-7 ICD-10-CM Table of Drugs and Chemicals (partial).

CODING TIP:

The term *intoxication* indicates that either alcohol was involved (e.g., alcohol intoxication) or that an accumulation effect of a medication in the patient's bloodstream occurred (e.g., Coumadin intoxication). When *alcohol intoxication* occurs, assign an appropriate poisoning code. When an accumulation effect of a medication occurs (because the patient was taking the drug as prescribed), assign the adverse effect code (e.g., daily Coumadin use).

EXAMPLE 1: For *hives due to penicillin taken as prescribed* (initial encounter), report codes T36.0x5A (adverse effect, penicillin, initial encounter) and L50.0 (hives).

EXAMPLE 2: For *coma due to overdose of barbiturates, which was the result of an attempted suicide* (initial encounter), report codes T42.3x2A (poisoning intentional self-harm, barbiturates, initial encounter) and R40.20 (coma).

NOTE: The Table of Drugs and Chemicals lists drugs and chemicals along with codes that identify the drug/chemical intent. *No additional external cause of injury and poisoning codes are assigned in ICD-10-CM.*

Codes in categories T36–T65 are combination codes that include the substances related to adverse effects, poisonings, toxic effects, and underdosing, as well as the external cause. (No additional external cause code is required for poisonings, toxic effects, adverse effects, and underdosing codes.) A code from categories T36–T65 is sequenced first, followed by the code(s) that specify the nature of the adverse effect, poisoning, or toxic effect. *The exception to this rule is the sequencing of underdosing codes (e.g., T36.0x6-) when the condition treated is sequenced first followed by the underdosing code.*

OFFICIAL GUIDELINES FOR CODING AND REPORTING ADVERSE EFFECTS, POISONING, UNDERDOSING, AND TOXIC EFFECTS

According to official coding guidelines, the occurrence of drug toxicity is classified in ICD-10-CM as follows:

1. *Adverse Effect*
   When coding an adverse effect of a drug that has been correctly prescribed and properly administered, assign the appropriate code for the nature of the adverse effect followed by the appropriate code for the adverse effect of the drug (T36–T50). The code for the drug should have a fifth or sixth character "5" (for example, T36.0X5-). Examples of the nature of an adverse effect are tachycardia, delirium, gastrointestinal hemorrhaging, vomiting, hypokalemia, hepatitis, renal failure, or respiratory failure.
2. *Poisoning*
   When coding a poisoning or reaction to the improper use of a medication (e.g., overdose, wrong substance given or taken in error, wrong route of administration), assign the appropriate code from categories T36–T50. The poisoning codes have an associated intent as their fifth or sixth character (accidental, intentional self-harm, assault, and undetermined). Use additional code(s) for all manifestations of poisonings. If there is also a diagnosis of abuse or dependence of the substance, the abuse or dependence is coded as an additional code. Examples of poisoning include:
   - (i) *Error was made in drug prescription*
     Errors made in drug prescription or in the administration of the drug by provider, nurse, patient, or other person.
   - (ii) *Overdose of a drug intentionally taken*
     If an overdose of a drug was intentionally taken or administered and resulted in drug toxicity, it would be coded as a poisoning.
   - (iii) *Nonprescribed drug taken with correctly prescribed and properly administered drug*
     If a nonprescribed drug or medicinal agent was taken in combination with a correctly prescribed and properly administered drug, any drug toxicity or other reaction resulting from the interaction of the two drugs would be classified as a poisoning.
   - (iv) *Interaction of drug(s) and alcohol*
     When a reaction results from the interaction of a drug(s) and alcohol, this would be classified as poisoning.
3. Underdosing
   Underdosing refers to taking less of a medication than is prescribed by a provider or a manufacturer's instruction. For underdosing, assign the code from categories T36–T50 (fifth or sixth character "6"). *Codes for underdosing are never assigned as principal or first-listed codes.* If a patient has a relapse or exacerbation of the medical condition for which the drug is prescribed because of the reduction in dose, then the medical condition itself should be coded.
   Noncompliance (Z91.12-, Z91.13-) or complication of care (Y63.61, Y63.8–Y63.9) codes are to be used with an underdosing code to indicate intent, if known.
4. Toxic Effects
   When a harmful substance is ingested or comes in contact with a person, this is classified as a toxic effect. The toxic effect codes are in categories T51–T65. Toxic effect codes have an associated intent: accidental, intentional self-harm, assault, and undetermined.

CODING TIP:

Complications due to insulin pump malfunction include:

(a) *Underdose of insulin due to insulin pump failure*
An underdose of insulin due to an insulin pump failure should be assigned to a code from subcategory T85.6, Mechanical complication of other specified internal and external prosthetic devices, implants and grafts, that specifies the type of pump malfunction as the principal or first-listed code, followed by code T38.3x6-, Underdosing of insulin and oral hypoglycemic [antidiabetic] drugs. Additional codes for the type of diabetes mellitus and any associated complications due to the underdosing should also be assigned.

(b) *Overdose of insulin due to insulin pump failure*
The principal or first-listed code for an encounter due to an insulin pump malfunction resulting in an overdose of insulin should also be T85.6-, Mechanical complication of other specified internal and external prosthetic devices, implants and grafts, followed by code T38.3x1-, Poisoning by insulin and oral hypoglycemic [antidiabetic] drugs, accidental (unintentional).

EXERCISE 6-5

Table of Drugs and Chemicals

Instructions: Assign ICD-10-CM code(s) to each diagnostic statement.

1. Adverse reaction to pertussis vaccine, initial encounter ________
2. Cardiac arrhythmia caused by interaction between prescribed ephedrine and wine (accident), initial encounter ________
3. Stupor, due to overdose of Nytol (suicide attempt), initial encounter ________
4. High blood pressure due to prescribed albuterol, initial encounter ________
5. Rash due to combining prescribed amoxicillin with prescribed Benadryl, initial encounter ________

Index to External Causes

The **ICD-10-CM Index to External Causes** (Figure 6-8) is arranged in alphabetical order by main term indicating the event. These codes are secondary codes for use in any health care setting. External cause codes are intended to provide data for injury research and evaluation of injury prevention strategies.

These codes are assigned to capture the following:

- ***Cause of injury*** **("how" the injury occurred, such as abuse, accident, assault, burn, collision, and so on)**
- ***Activity being performed*** **("what" the patient was doing at the time of injury, such as playing a sport, gardening, sleeping, using a cell phone, and so on)**
- ***Place of occurrence*** **("where" the patient was when the injury occurred, such as at home or work, in a post office, on a highway, and so on)**
- ***Status at the time of injury*** **(indicates if injury is related to leisure, military, student, volunteer, and so on, as applicable)**

ICD-10-CM EXTERNAL CAUSE INDEX

Abandonment (causing exposure to weather conditions) (with intent to injure or kill) NEC X58
Abuse (adult) (child) (mental) (physical) (sexual) X58
Accident (to) X58
  aircraft (in transit) (powered) – (*see also* Accident, transport, aircraft)
    due to, caused by cataclysm – *see* Forces of nature, by type
  animal-rider – *see* Accident, transport, animal-rider
  animal-drawn vehicle – *see* Accident, transport, animal-drawn vehicle occupant
  automobile – *see* Accident, transport, car occupant
  bare foot water skiier V94.4
  boat, boating (*see also* Accident, watercraft)
    striking swimmer
      powered V94.11
      unpowered V94.12

ICD-10-CM TABULAR LIST OF DISEASES AND INJURIES

CHAPTER 20: External causes of morbidity (V00-Y99)

V94 Other and unspecified water transport accidents

EXCLUDES1: military watercraft accidents in military or war operations (Y36, Y37)

The appropriate 7th character is to be added to each code from category V94
A Initial encounter
D Subsequent encounter
S Sequela

V94.0 Hitting object or bottom of body of water due to fall from watercraft

EXCLUDES2: drowning and submersion due to fall from watercraft (V92.0-)

V94.1 Bather struck by watercraft
Swimmer hit by watercraft

V94.11 Bather struck by powered watercraft

V94.12 Bather struck by nonpowered watercraft

FIGURE 6-8 ICD-10-CM External Causes (partial).

CODING TIP:

Refer to ICD-10-CM Index to External Causes main terms to begin the process of assigning an external cause code. Common main terms include:

- Accident
- Injury, injured
- Misadventure(s) to patient(s) during surgical or medical care

Before assigning an ICD-10-CM external cause code, review the notes located at the beginning of Chapter 21 in the ICD-10-CM tabular list.

EXAMPLE: A patient fell off the toilet in the downstairs bathroom of her single-family house during an attempt to coax her cat to come down from the top of a cabinet. It apparently worked because the cat jumped off the cabinet and landed on the patient. However, the patient was so surprised that she screamed and fell off the toilet onto the floor. The patient landed on her left arm due to the fall and experienced extremely sharp pain. She was evaluated in the emergency department where she was diagnosed with a *closed nondisplaced comminuted fracture of the humerus, left*. She received treatment and was discharged home to follow-up with her primary care physician in the office.

For ICD-10-CM, report the injury (fracture) (S42.355A), cause of injury (fall) (W18.11xA), place of injury (bathroom of patient's home) (Y92.012), activity (other activity involving animal care) (Y93.K9), external cause status (other external cause status) (Y99.8).

ICD-10-CM's level of specificity results in different codes for other locations in the patient's home (e.g., bathroom). For ICD-10-CM code W18.11xA (fall from toilet), the seventh character (A) indicates she received initial treatment. ICD-10-CM place of injury codes for this case indicate that the patient's health insurance policy should be billed (not a homeowner's, liability, or workers' compensation policy). If a guest of a homeowner had been injured in this manner, the homeowner's insurance would be billed. If the place of injury had been at a grocery store or another place of business, that business's liability insurance would be billed instead of the patient's health insurance.

Basic Steps for Using the Index to Diseases and Injuries

It is important to remember that you should never code directly from the Index to Diseases and Injuries. After locating a code in the index, go to that code in the Tabular List of Diseases and Injuries to find important instructions (e.g., includes notes and excludes notes) and to verify the code selected. Instructions may require the assignment of additional codes or indicate conditions that are classified elsewhere.

STEP 1 Locate the main term in the Index to Diseases and Injuries.

Begin the coding process in the ICD-10-CM Index to Diseases and Injuries by locating the condition's boldfaced main term and then reviewing the subterms listed below the main term to locate the proper disorder.

EXAMPLE: The underlined terms in the following conditions are main terms:

Allergens investigation

Auditory agnosia secondary to organic lesion

Intussusception, ileocolic

Status (post) angioplasty

STEP 2 If the instructional phrase – *see condition* is found after the main term, a descriptive term (an adjective) or the anatomic site has been mistakenly referenced instead of the disorder or the disease (the condition) documented in the diagnostic statement.

EXAMPLE: The provider's diagnostic statement is *upper respiratory infection*. In the ICD-10-CM Index to Diseases and Injuries, look up the phrase *upper respiratory*. Notice that the instructional phrase — *see condition* appears next to the phrase *upper respiratory*. This instruction directs you to the condition, which is *infection*.

STEP 3 When the condition in the diagnostic statement is not easily found in the index, use the main terms below to locate the code.

NOTE: To locate a code that classifies an external cause of injury, refer to the separate Index to External Causes, which is located after the Table of Drugs and Chemicals (after the Index to Diseases and Injuries).

Abnormal	Findings	Neoplasm
Anomaly	Foreign body	Obstruction
Complication	Infection	Pregnancy
Delivery	Injury	Puerperal
Disease	Late effects	Syndrome
Disorder	Lesion	Wound

STEP 4 Sometimes terms found in the Index to Diseases and Injuries are not found in the Tabular List of Diseases and Injuries when the code number is reviewed for verification. When this occurs, the coder should *trust the index* because, to save space in the tabular list, more terms are listed in the index than in the tabular list.

EXAMPLE: For the condition "gum attrition," the main term "attrition" and subterm "gum" are found in the ICD-10-CM Index to Diseases and Injuries. When code K06.0 is verified in the tabular list, the term "attrition" is not found; however, code K06.0 is still the correct code. (This is an example of *trust the index*.)

EXERCISE 6-6

ICD-10-CM Index to Diseases and Injuries

Instructions: Complete each statement.

1. The ICD-10-CM alphabetical listing of main terms or conditions printed in boldfaced type that may be expressed as nouns, adjectives, or eponyms is called the ________.
2. The ________ contains adverse effects and poisonings associated with medicinal, chemical, and biological substances.
3. Main terms in the ICD-10-CM index are listed in alphabetical order, which means a single hyphen between words in a main term (is / is not) ________ ignored when locating main terms in the ICD-10-CM indexes, and a single space within a main term (is / is not) ________ ignored.
4. For the following list of main terms found in the ICD-10-CM Index to Diseases and Injuries, the main term ________ is *not* in alphabetical order.

   Lathyrism
   Launois-Cleret syndrome
   Launois' syndrome

(continues)

5. When numerical characters and words appear under a main term, they are listed in ________ order.
6. Main terms are printed in boldfaced type and followed by the ________ code.
7. Qualifying words contained in parentheses after a main term, which do not have to be included in the diagnostic statement for the code number listed after the parentheses to be assigned, are called ________ modifiers.
8. Subterms that qualify the main term by listing alternative sites, etiology, or clinical status are called ________ modifiers.
9. The provider documents "acute angina pectoris." The main term in the ICD-10-CM index is ________.
10. The provider documents "history of nutritional deficiency." The main term in the ICD-10-CM index is ________.

ICD-10-CM TABULAR LIST OF DISEASES AND INJURIES

The **ICD-10-CM Tabular List of Diseases and Injuries** (Table 6-1) is a chronological list of codes contained within 21 chapters, which are based on body system or condition. ICD-10-CM codes are organized within:

- ***Major topic headings*, also called a *code block*, are printed in bold uppercase letters and followed by groups of three-character disease categories within a chapter (e.g., Intestinal Infectious Diseases, A00–A09).**
- ***Categories, subcategories, and codes*, which contain a combination of letters and numbers.**
  - **All categories contain three characters (e.g., A09).**
  - **A three-character category that has no further subdivision is a valid code.**
  - **Subcategories contain either four or five characters.**
  - **Codes may contain three, four, five, six, or seven characters.**
    - **The final level of subdivision is a code.**
    - **All codes in the ICD-10-CM tabular list are boldfaced.**
- **Codes that have an applicable seventh character are referred to as codes (not subcategories).**
- **Codes that have an applicable seventh character are considered invalid without the seventh character.**

Structure

The ICD-10-CM tabular list contains three-character categories, four-, five-, or six-character subcategories, and four-, five-, six-, or seven-character codes (Figure 6-9), which contain letters and numbers. Each level of subdivision within a category is called a subcategory, and the final level of subdivision is a code. Codes that have applicable seventh characters are referred to as codes (not subcategories or subclassifications), and a code that has an applicable seventh character is considered invalid without the seventh character.

- ***Use of codes for reporting purposes.* For reporting purposes, only codes are permissible (not categories or subcategories), and any applicable seventh character is required.**

TABLE 6-1 ICD-10-CM Tabular List of Diseases and Injuries

CHAPTER NUMBER	RANGE OF CODES	CHAPTER TITLE
Chapter 1	A00-B99	Certain Infectious and Parasitic Diseases
Chapter 2	C00-D49	Neoplasms
Chapter 3	D50-D89	Diseases of the Blood and Blood-forming Organs and Certain Disorders Involving the Immune Mechanism
Chapter 4	E00-E89	Endocrine, Nutritional, and Metabolic Disorders
Chapter 5	F01-F99	Mental, Behavioral and Neurodevelopment Disorders
Chapter 6	G00-G99	Diseases of the Nervous System
Chapter 7	H00-H59	Diseases of the Eye and Adnexa
Chapter 8	H60-H95	Diseases of the Ear and Mastoid Process
Chapter 9	I00-I99	Diseases of the Circulatory System
Chapter 10	J00-J99	Diseases of the Respiratory System
Chapter 11	K00-K95	Diseases of the Digestive System
Chapter 12	L00-L99	Diseases of the Skin and Subcutaneous Tissue
Chapter 13	M00-M99	Diseases of the Musculoskeletal System and Connective Tissue
Chapter 14	N00-N99	Diseases of the Genitourinary System
Chapter 15	O00-O9A	Pregnancy, Childbirth, and the Puerperium
Chapter 16	P00-P96	Certain Conditions Originating in the Perinatal Period
Chapter 17	Q00-Q99	Congenital Malformations, Deformations, and Chromosomal Abnormalities
Chapter 18	R00-R99	Symptoms, Signs, and Abnormal Clinical and Laboratory Findings, Not Elsewhere Classified
Chapter 19	S00-T88	Injury, Poisoning, and Certain Other Consequences of External Causes
Chapter 20	V00-Y99	External Causes of Morbidity
Chapter 21	Z00-Z99	Factors Influencing Health Status and Contact with Health Services

- *Placeholder character*. ICD-10-CM utilizes the character "x" as a fifth-character placeholder for certain six-character codes to allow for future expansion without disturbing the six-character structure (e.g., H62.8x1, other disorders of right external ear in diseases classified elsewhere). When a placeholder exists, the x must be entered in order for the code to be considered a valid code.
- *Seventh characters*. Certain ICD-10-CM categories contain applicable seventh characters, which are required for all codes within the category (or as instructed by notes in the tabular list). The seventh character must always be located in the seventh-character data field. If a code that requires a seventh character is not six characters in length, the placeholder x is entered to fill in the empty character(s) (e.g., M48.46xS, reporting sequelae of fracture for previous fatigue fracture of lumbar vertebrae; an additional code is assigned to the sequelae, such as pain).

EXAMPLE 1: ICD-10-CM CATEGORY AND SUBCATEGORY CODES: Go to Figure 6-9, refer to the "Disorders of newborn related to length of gestation and fetal growth (P05–P08)" section, and locate the four-character subcategory code (P07.3) and the five-character subcategory codes (P07.30, P07.31, P07.32, and so on).

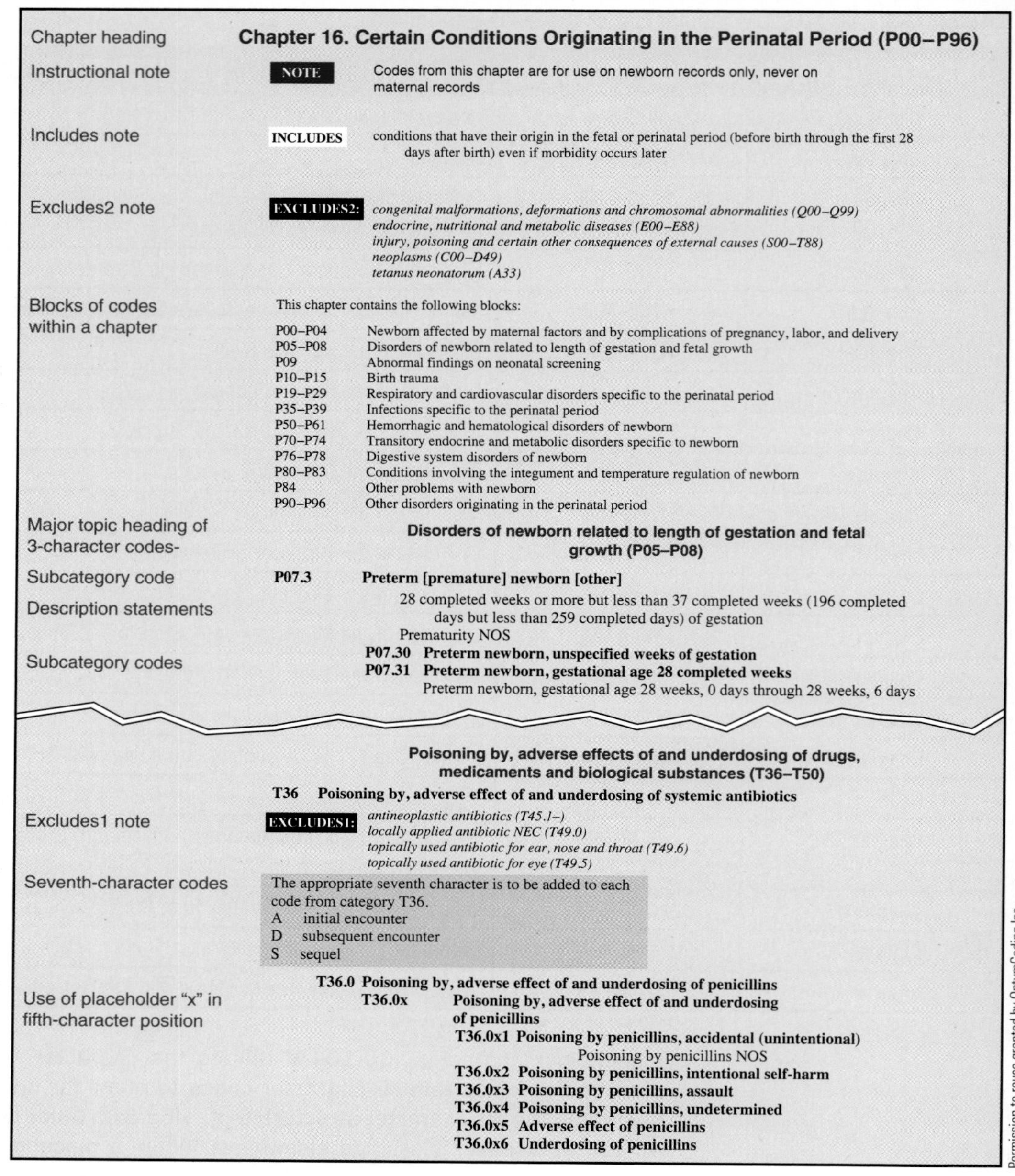

Chapter heading — **Chapter 16. Certain Conditions Originating in the Perinatal Period (P00–P96)**

Instructional note — NOTE Codes from this chapter are for use on newborn records only, never on maternal records

Includes note — INCLUDES conditions that have their origin in the fetal or perinatal period (before birth through the first 28 days after birth) even if morbidity occurs later

Excludes2 note — EXCLUDES2: *congenital malformations, deformations and chromosomal abnormalities (Q00–Q99)*
endocrine, nutritional and metabolic diseases (E00–E88)
injury, poisoning and certain other consequences of external causes (S00–T88)
neoplasms (C00–D49)
tetanus neonatorum (A33)

Blocks of codes within a chapter — This chapter contains the following blocks:

P00–P04	Newborn affected by maternal factors and by complications of pregnancy, labor, and delivery
P05–P08	Disorders of newborn related to length of gestation and fetal growth
P09	Abnormal findings on neonatal screening
P10–P15	Birth trauma
P19–P29	Respiratory and cardiovascular disorders specific to the perinatal period
P35–P39	Infections specific to the perinatal period
P50–P61	Hemorrhagic and hematological disorders of newborn
P70–P74	Transitory endocrine and metabolic disorders specific to newborn
P76–P78	Digestive system disorders of newborn
P80–P83	Conditions involving the integument and temperature regulation of newborn
P84	Other problems with newborn
P90–P96	Other disorders originating in the perinatal period

Major topic heading of 3-character codes- — **Disorders of newborn related to length of gestation and fetal growth (P05–P08)**

Subcategory code — **P07.3 Preterm [premature] newborn [other]**

Description statements — 28 completed weeks or more but less than 37 completed weeks (196 completed days but less than 259 completed days) of gestation
Prematurity NOS

Subcategory codes — **P07.30 Preterm newborn, unspecified weeks of gestation**
P07.31 Preterm newborn, gestational age 28 completed weeks
Preterm newborn, gestational age 28 weeks, 0 days through 28 weeks, 6 days

Poisoning by, adverse effects of and underdosing of drugs, medicaments and biological substances (T36–T50)

T36 Poisoning by, adverse effect of and underdosing of systemic antibiotics

Excludes1 note — EXCLUDES1: *antineoplastic antibiotics (T45.1-)*
locally applied antibiotic NEC (T49.0)
topically used antibiotic for ear, nose and throat (T49.6)
topically used antibiotic for eye (T49.5)

Seventh-character codes — The appropriate seventh character is to be added to each code from category T36.
A initial encounter
D subsequent encounter
S sequel

T36.0 Poisoning by, adverse effect of and underdosing of penicillins

Use of placeholder "x" in fifth-character position — **T36.0x Poisoning by, adverse effect of and underdosing of penicillins**
T36.0x1 Poisoning by penicillins, accidental (unintentional)
Poisoning by penicillins NOS
T36.0x2 Poisoning by penicillins, intentional self-harm
T36.0x3 Poisoning by penicillins, assault
T36.0x4 Poisoning by penicillins, undetermined
T36.0x5 Adverse effect of penicillins
T36.0x6 Underdosing of penicillins

FIGURE 6-9 Sample page from ICD-10-CM Tabular List of Diseases and Injuries.

EXAMPLE 2: ICD-10-CM SIX-CHARACTER AND SEVEN-CHARACTER CODES: Go to Figure 6-9, refer to the "Poisoning by, adverse effects of and underdosing of drugs, medicaments and biological substances (T36–T50)" section, and locate the six-character subcategory codes (T36.0x1, T36.0x2, T36.0x3, T36.0x4, T36.0x5, and T36.0x6), which also contain "x" as a placeholder to allow for future expansion. Then, locate the seventh characters (A, D, and S), one of which is to be added to each code from category T36 (depending on the status of encounter or whether the condition is a sequela). (**Sequela** is defined as the residual late effects of an injury or illness.)

EXAMPLE 3: THE LETTER X AS A PLACEHOLDER: Go to Figure 6-9, refer to code T36.0x1A, and notice that it requires "x" as a placeholder in the fifth-character position. The letter A is added to code T36.0x1 to indicate an initial encounter. (Letters A, D, and S are located in the pink shaded area of Figure 6-9; one of these characters is added to code T36.0x1 to indicate the type of encounter.). If the code is reported as T36.01A (without the "x" placeholder in the fifth-character position), it is an invalid code that results in a denied claim for third-party payer reimbursement.

ICD-10-CM External Cause Codes

Injury, Poisoning, and Certain Other Consequences of External Causes and *External Causes of Morbidity* are incorporated into ICD-10-CM's Tabular List of Diseases and Injuries as Chapter 19 (S and T codes) and Chapter 20 (V through Y codes), respectively. External cause codes are also reported for environmental events, industrial accidents, injuries inflicted by criminal activity, and so on. While assigning the codes does not directly impact reimbursement to the provider, reporting them can expedite insurance claims processing because the circumstances related to an injury are indicated.

CODING TIP:

In ICD-10-CM, codes for external causes are incorporated into ICD-10-CM's tabular list as Chapter 19 (S00-T88) and Chapter 20 (V00-Y99). (The codes are no longer located in a supplementary classification as they were in ICD-9-CM.)

ICD-10-CM Health Status and Contact with Health Services Codes

Factors Influencing Health Status and Contact with Health Services are incorporated into ICD-10-CM's Tabular List of Diseases and Injuries as Chapter 21 (Z codes) (Z00-Z99) (Figure 6-10). The Z codes are located in the last chapter of the ICD-10-CM tabular list, and they are reported for patient encounters when a circumstance other than disease or injury is documented (e.g., well-child visit).

CODING TIP:

- ICD-10-CM Z codes are always reported as diagnosis codes. They are not reported as procedure codes even though some ICD-10-CM Z codes classify situations associated with procedures (e.g., canceled procedure Z53 category code).
- Although indexed in the ICD-10-CM Index to Diseases and Injuries, it can be challenging to locate main terms. Consider using terms from the following list to locate the codes:
  - Admission
  - Aftercare
  - Attention to
  - Contact
  - Counseling
  - Donor
  - Encounter
  - Examination
  - Exposure to
  - Fitting
  - Follow-up
  - History
  - Newborn
  - Observation
  - Outcome of delivery
  - Problem
  - Screening
  - Status
  - Test
  - Therapy
  - Vaccination

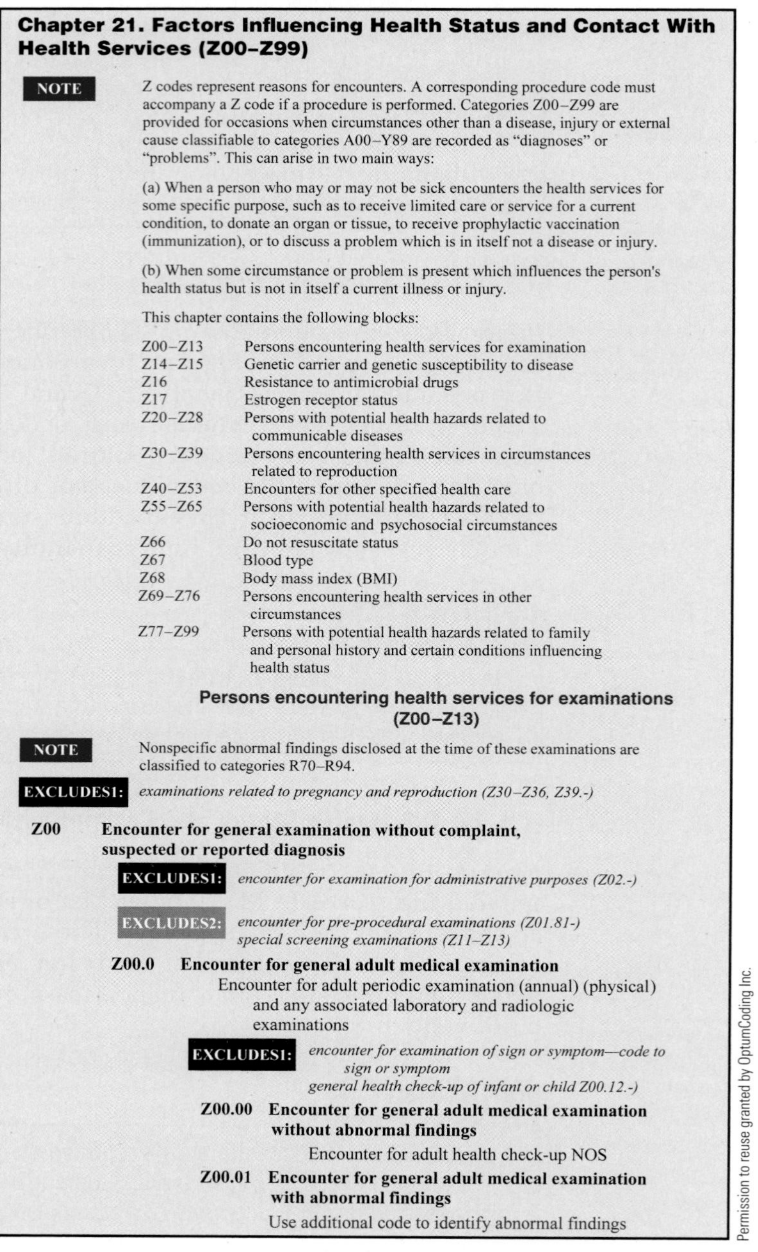

Z Codes

Chapter 21. Factors Influencing Health Status and Contact With Health Services (Z00–Z99)

NOTE Z codes represent reasons for encounters. A corresponding procedure code must accompany a Z code if a procedure is performed. Categories Z00–Z99 are provided for occasions when circumstances other than a disease, injury or external cause classifiable to categories A00–Y89 are recorded as "diagnoses" or "problems". This can arise in two main ways:

(a) When a person who may or may not be sick encounters the health services for some specific purpose, such as to receive limited care or service for a current condition, to donate an organ or tissue, to receive prophylactic vaccination (immunization), or to discuss a problem which is in itself not a disease or injury.

(b) When some circumstance or problem is present which influences the person's health status but is not in itself a current illness or injury.

This chapter contains the following blocks:

Z00–Z13	Persons encountering health services for examination
Z14–Z15	Genetic carrier and genetic susceptibility to disease
Z16	Resistance to antimicrobial drugs
Z17	Estrogen receptor status
Z20–Z28	Persons with potential health hazards related to communicable diseases
Z30–Z39	Persons encountering health services in circumstances related to reproduction
Z40–Z53	Encounters for other specified health care
Z55–Z65	Persons with potential health hazards related to socioeconomic and psychosocial circumstances
Z66	Do not resuscitate status
Z67	Blood type
Z68	Body mass index (BMI)
Z69–Z76	Persons encountering health services in other circumstances
Z77–Z99	Persons with potential health hazards related to family and personal history and certain conditions influencing health status

Persons encountering health services for examinations (Z00–Z13)

NOTE Nonspecific abnormal findings disclosed at the time of these examinations are classified to categories R70–R94.

EXCLUDES1: *examinations related to pregnancy and reproduction (Z30–Z36, Z39.-)*

Z00 Encounter for general examination without complaint, suspected or reported diagnosis

EXCLUDES1: *encounter for examination for administrative purposes (Z02.-)*

EXCLUDES2: *encounter for pre-procedural examinations (Z01.81-)*
special screening examinations (Z11–Z13)

Z00.0 Encounter for general adult medical examination

Encounter for adult periodic examination (annual) (physical) and any associated laboratory and radiologic examinations

EXCLUDES1: *encounter for examination of sign or symptom—code to sign or symptom*
general health check-up of infant or child Z00.12.-)

Z00.00 Encounter for general adult medical examination without abnormal findings

Encounter for adult health check-up NOS

Z00.01 Encounter for general adult medical examination with abnormal findings

Use additional code to identify abnormal findings

FIGURE 6-10 Sample page of Z codes from ICD-10-CM Tabular List of Diseases and Injuries.

Morphology of Neoplasm Codes

Morphology indicates the tissue type of a neoplasm (e.g., adenocarcinoma and sarcoma); and while they are not reported on insurance claims, they are reported to state cancer registries. Neoplasms are new growths, or tumors, in which cell reproduction is out of control. A basic knowledge of morphology coding can be helpful to a coder because the name of the neoplasm documented in the patient's record does not always indicate whether the neoplasm is benign (not cancerous) or malignant (cancerous).

ICD-10-CM Chapter 2 classifies neoplasms primarily by site (topography), with broad groupings for behavior, malignant, *in situ*, benign, and so on. The ICD-10-CM Table of Neoplasms in its Index to Diseases and Injuries is used to identify the correct topography code. Morphology codes for most of ICD-10-CM's Chapter 2 (Neoplasms) codes do not include histologic type. Thus, a comprehensive separate set of morphology codes is used from the *International Classification of Diseases for Oncology, 3rd Revision* (ICD-O-3). (In a few cases, such as for malignant melanoma and certain neuroendocrine tumors, the morphology or histologic type is included in the ICD-10-CM category and code.)

NOTE: Do not confuse morphology codes with ICD-10-CM's Chapter 13, Diseases of the Musculoskeletal System and Connective Tissue (M00–M99) codes.

Morphology codes contain five digits preceded by the letter M and range from M8000/0 to M9989/3. The first four digits (e.g., M8000) indicate the specific histologic term. The fifth digit, after the slash, is a behavior code, which indicates whether a tumor is malignant, benign, *in situ*, or uncertain whether malignant or benign. In addition, a separate one-digit code is assigned for histologic grading to indicate differentiation.

CODING TIP:

Use the *International Classification of Diseases for Oncology, 3rd Revision* (ICD-O-3) to locate morphology codes when assigning topography codes from ICD-10-CM.

EXERCISE 6-7

ICD-10-CM Tabular List of Diseases and Injuries

Instructions: Complete each statement.

1. The *ICD-10-CM Tabular List of Diseases and Injuries* is a chronological list of codes contained within ________, which are based on body system or condition.
2. Intestinal Infectious Diseases (A00–A09) is an example of a(n) ________, which is printed in bold uppercase letters and followed by groups of three-character disease categories within a chapter.
3. ICD-10-CM categories, subcategories, and codes contain a combination of ________.
4. All of ICD-10-CM's categories contain ________ characters.
5. A three-character ICD-10-CM category that has no further subdivision is a ________.
6. ICD-10-CM subcategories contain either ________ or ________ characters.
7. ICD-10-CM codes may contain ________ characters.
8. The final level of an ICD-10-CM tabular list subdivision is a(n) ________.
9. All codes in the ICD-10-CM tabular list are ________.
10. Codes that have an applicable seventh character are referred to as ________.
11. Codes that have an applicable seventh character are considered ________ without the seventh character.

(continues)

12. The seventh character must always be located in the seventh-character data field, and if a code that requires a seventh character is not six characters in length, the placeholder ________ is entered to fill in the empty character(s).
13. *Factors Influencing Health Status and Contact with Health Services* are incorporated into ICD-10-CM's Tabular List of Diseases and Injuries as ________.
14. Morphology codes are abbreviated as ________.
15. ICD-10-CM Chapter 2 classifies neoplasms primarily by site (topography), and morphology codes are classified using the ________.

OFFICIAL GUIDELINES FOR CODING AND REPORTING

NOTE: Official coding advice (e.g., interpretation of ICD-10-CM/PCS coding principles) will be published in the AHA's *Coding Clinic for ICD-10-CM and ICD-10-PCS*.

The **ICD-10-CM Official Guidelines for Coding and Reporting** and the **ICD-10-PCS Coding Guidelines** are prepared by the Centers for Medicare and Medicaid Services (CMS) and the National Center for Health Statistics (NCHS). The guidelines are approved by the **Cooperating Parties for ICD-10-CM/PCS**, which include CMS, NCHS, American Hospital Association (AHA), and American Health Information Management Association (AHIMA). The official guidelines contain rules that accompany and complement ICD-10-CM and ICD-10-PCS coding conventions and instructions. HIPAA regulations require adherence to the guidelines when assigning diagnosis and procedure codes.

- **ICD-10-CM diagnosis codes were adopted under HIPAA for all health care settings.**
- **ICD-10-PCS procedure codes were adopted for inpatient procedures reported by hospitals.**

A joint effort between the health care provider and the coder is essential for complete and accurate (1) documentation, (2) code assignment, and (3) reporting of diagnoses and procedures. The importance of consistent, complete documentation in the medical record cannot be overemphasized because without such documentation, accurate coding cannot be achieved. Review all documentation in the patient record to determine the specific reason for the encounter as well as conditions treated. Official guidelines use the term:

- ***Encounter* to indicate all health care settings, including inpatient hospital admissions**
- ***Provider* to refer to physicians or any qualified health care practitioners who are legally accountable for establishing the patient's diagnosis**

ICD-10-CM official guidelines are organized as:

- **Section I: Conventions, general coding guidelines, and chapter-specific guidelines**
- **Section II: Selection of principal diagnosis**
- **Section III: Reporting additional diagnoses**
- **Section IV: Diagnostic coding and reporting guidelines for outpatient services**
- **Appendix I: Present on admission reporting guidelines**

ICD-10-PCS official guidelines are organized according to:

- **Conventions**
- **Medical and surgical section guidelines**
- **Obstetrics section guidelines**

Diagnostic Coding and Reporting Guidelines Outpatient Services—Hospital-Based Outpatient Services and Provider-Based Office Visits

NOTE: Go to www.cengagebrain.com and log in to locate the *ICD-10-CM Official Guidelines for Coding and Reporting.*

The **ICD-10-CM Diagnostic Coding and Reporting Guidelines for Outpatient Services—Hospital-Based Outpatient Services and Provider-Based Office Visits** were developed by the federal government and approved for use by hospitals and providers for coding and reporting hospital-based outpatient services and provider-based office visits. Although the guidelines were originally developed for use in submitting government claims, insurance companies have also adopted them (sometimes with variation).

The terms *encounter* and *visit* are often used interchangeably when describing outpatient service contacts and, therefore, appear together in the official guidelines without distinguishing one from the other. Though the coding conventions and general coding guidelines apply to all health care settings, coding guidelines for outpatient hospital-based and provider-based office reporting of diagnoses differ from reporting of inpatient diagnoses.

- **The *Uniform Hospital Discharge Data Set (UHDDS)* definition of principal diagnosis applies *only* to inpatients in acute, short-term, long-term care, and psychiatric hospitals. The inpatient principal diagnosis is defined as "the condition determined after study which resulted in the patient's admission to the hospital," and it is reported in Form Locator 67 of the UB-04 (CMS-1450) claim.**
- **Coding guidelines for inconclusive diagnoses (or qualified diagnoses) (e.g., possible, probable, suspected, rule out) were developed for inpatient reporting *only* and do not apply to outpatients.**

A. Selection of First-Listed Condition

NOTE: You may see *principal diagnosis* referred to as *first-listed diagnosis* in medical literature. Remember! An outpatient setting reports the first-listed diagnosis, *not* the principal diagnosis.

In the outpatient setting, the **first-listed diagnosis** is reported (instead of the inpatient hospital *principal diagnosis*) in Block 21 of the CMS-1500 claim; it reflects the reason for the encounter, which often is a sign or symptom. (First-listed diagnosis replaced the outdated primary diagnosis term some years ago.) Physicians do not usually have time during a single encounter to establish a definitive diagnosis. Thus, the first-listed diagnosis code indicates to third-party payers why the physician provided the services. It is determined in accordance with ICD-10-CM *coding conventions* (or rules) as well as general and disease-specific coding guidelines. Because diagnoses are often not established at the time of the patient's initial encounter or visit, two or more visits may be required before a diagnosis is confirmed. An **outpatient** is a person treated in one of four settings:

- ***Ambulatory Surgery Center:*** **Patient is released prior to a 24-hour stay and length of stay must be 23 hours, 59 minutes, and 59 seconds or less.**
- ***Health Care Provider's Office*** **(e.g., physician)**
- ***Hospital Clinic, ED, Outpatient Department, Same-day Surgery Unit:*** **Length of stay must be 23 hours, 59 minutes, and 59 seconds or less.**
- ***Hospital Observation Status or Hospital Observation Unit:*** **Patient's length of stay is 23 hours, 59 minutes, and 59 seconds or less unless documentation for additional observation is medically justified.**

Outpatient Surgery

When a patient presents for outpatient surgery (same-day surgery), code the reason for the surgery as the first-listed diagnosis (reason for the encounter), even if the surgery is not performed due to a contraindication.

Observation Stay

When a patient is admitted for observation for a medical condition, assign a code for the medical condition as the first-listed diagnosis. When a patient presents for outpatient surgery and develops complications requiring admission to observation, code the reason for the surgery as the first-listed diagnosis (reason for the encounter), followed by codes for the complications as secondary diagnoses.

EXAMPLE: A patient received emergency department care for an injury to the right arm, which upon x-ray revealed a closed displaced oblique fracture of the shaft of the right humerus. The first-listed diagnosis code is S42.331A, and it justifies the medical necessity of the x-ray.

B. ICD-10-CM Tabular List of Diseases and Injuries (A00–T88.9, Z00–Z99)

The appropriate code or codes from the ICD-10-CM Tabular List of Diseases and Injuries (A00–T88, Z00–Z99) must be used to identify diagnoses, symptoms, conditions, problems, complaints, or other reason(s) for the encounter/visit.

C. Accurate Reporting of ICD-10-CM Diagnosis Codes

For accurate reporting of ICD-10-CM diagnosis codes, the documentation should describe the patient's condition, using terminology that includes specific diagnoses as well as symptoms, problems, or reasons for the encounter. There are ICD-10-CM codes to describe all of these.

NOTE:

- *Outpatient Surgery:* When a patient presents for outpatient surgery, the first-listed diagnosis is the reason for the surgery even if the surgery is cancelled due to a contraindication (e.g., patient's blood pressure increases unexpectedly upon administration of anesthesia).
- *Observation Stay:* When a patient is admitted for observation of a medical condition, the first-listed diagnosis is the medical condition being observed.

When a patient presents for outpatient surgery and then develops complications requiring admission for observation, the first-listed diagnosis is the reason for the surgery. The secondary diagnosis is the complication(s) (e.g., respiratory distress).

D. Codes That Describe Signs and Symptoms

Codes that describe symptoms and signs, as opposed to definitive diagnoses, are acceptable for reporting purposes when the physician has not documented an established diagnosis or confirmed diagnosis. ICD-10-CM Chapter 18 (Symptoms, Signs, and Abnormal Clinical and Laboratory Findings Not Elsewhere Classified) (R00–R99) contain many, but not all, codes for symptoms. Some symptom codes are located in other ICD-10-CM chapters, which can be found by properly using the ICD-10-CM Index to Diseases and Injuries.

E. Encounters for Circumstances Other than a Disease or Injury (Z Codes)

ICD-10-CM provides codes to deal with encounters for circumstances other than a disease or an injury. In ICD-10-CM, Factors Influencing Health Status and Contact with Health Services (Z00–Z99) classifies occasions when circumstances other than a disease or injury are recorded as diagnosis or problems.

F. Level of Detail in Coding

ICD-10-CM diagnosis codes contain three, four, five, six, or seven characters.

- ***ICD-10-CM codes with three, four, five, six, or seven characters:*** **Disease codes with three characters are included in ICD-10-CM as the heading of a category of codes that may be further subdivided by the use of fourth, fifth, sixth, or seventh characters to provide greater specificity.**

- ***Use of full number of characters required for a code:*** **A three-character code is to be assigned only if it cannot be further subdivided. A code is invalid if it has not been coded to the full number of characters required for that code, including the seventh-character extension, if applicable.**

G. ICD-10-CM Code for the Diagnosis, Condition, Problem, or Other Reason for Encounter/Visit

Report first the ICD-10-CM code for the diagnosis, condition, problem, or other reason for encounter/visit shown in the medical record to be chiefly responsible for the services provided. Then report additional codes that describe any coexisting conditions that were treated or medically managed or that influenced the treatment of the patient during the encounter. In some cases, the first-listed diagnosis may be a symptom when a diagnosis has not been established (confirmed) by the physician.

H. Uncertain Diagnoses

NOTE: Coding guidelines for inpatient stays allow codes for qualified diagnoses to be reported on the UB-04.

Do not code diagnoses documented as probable, suspected, questionable, rule out, or working diagnosis, or other similar terms indicating uncertainty, all of which are considered **qualified diagnoses**. Instead, code condition(s) to the highest degree of certainty for that encounter/visit, such as symptoms, signs, abnormal test results, or other reasons for the visit.

FOR QUALIFIED DIAGNOSIS	CODE THE FOLLOWING SIGNS OR SYMPTOMS
Suspected pneumonia	Shortness of breath
Questionable Raynaud's	Numbness of hands
Possible wrist fracture, right	Wrist pain, right
Rule out pneumonia	Influenza

NOTE: When assigning codes to physician services provided to inpatients, adhere to the outpatient "Uncertain Diagnosis" guideline (so that codes for signs and symptoms are reported instead of qualified diagnoses).

Qualified or uncertain diagnoses are a necessary part of the hospital and office chart until a specific diagnosis can be determined. Although qualified diagnoses are routinely coded for hospital inpatient admissions and reported on the UB-04 claim, CMS *specifically prohibits the reporting of qualified diagnoses on the CMS-1500 claim submitted for outpatient care.* CMS regulations permit the reporting of patients' signs and/or symptoms instead of the qualified diagnoses.

An additional incentive for not coding qualified diagnoses resulted from the Missouri case of *Stafford v. Neurological Medicine Inc., 811 F. 2d 470 (8th Cir., 1987).* In this case, the diagnosis stated in the physician's office chart was *rule out brain tumor.* The claim submitted by the office listed the diagnosis code for *rule out brain tumor* although test results were available that proved a brain tumor did not exist. The physician assured the patient that although she had lung cancer, there was no **metastasis** (spread of cancer from primary to secondary sites) to the brain. Sometime after the insurance company received the provider's claim, it was inadvertently sent to the patient. When the patient received the claim, she was so devastated by the diagnosis that she committed suicide. Her husband sued and was awarded $200,000 on the basis of *negligent paperwork* because the physician's office had reported a *qualified or uncertain diagnosis.*

I. Chronic Diseases

Chronic diseases treated on an ongoing basis may be coded and reported as many times as the patient receives treatment and care for the condition(s).

J. Code All Documented Conditions That Coexist

NOTE: Third-party payers review claims for *family history of* codes to determine reimbursement eligibility. Some plans reimburse for conditions that may not normally be eligible for payment when family history of a related condition is documented in the patient's record and reported on the claim.

Secondary diagnoses include comorbidities and complications. A **comorbidity** is a concurrent condition that coexists with the first-listed diagnosis (outpatient care) (or principal diagnosis, for inpatient care), has the potential to affect treatment of the first-listed diagnosis (outpatient care) (or principal diagnosis for inpatient care), and is an active condition for which the patient is treated and/or monitored. (Insulin-dependent diabetes mellitus is an example of a comorbidity.) A **complication** is a condition that develops after outpatient care has been provided (e.g., ruptured sutures after office surgery) (or during an inpatient admission, such as development of a postoperative wound infection). Secondary diagnoses are reported in Block 21 of the CMS-1500 claim for outpatient care (and Form Locators 67A–67Q of the UB-04 for inpatient care).

Code all documented conditions that coexist at the time of the encounter/visit and that require or affect patient care, treatment, or management. Do not code conditions that were previously treated and no longer exist. However, history codes (ICD-10-CM categories Z80–Z87) may be reported as secondary codes if the historical condition or family history has an impact on current care or influences treatment.

EXAMPLE 1: A patient seeks care at the health care provider's office for an injury to the right leg that, upon x-ray in the office, is diagnosed as a fractured tibia. While in the office, the physician also reviews the current status and treatment of the patient's type 2 diabetes.

- What is the first-listed diagnosis?
- What is the secondary diagnosis?
- Which diagnosis justifies medical necessity of the right leg x-ray?
- Which diagnosis justifies medical necessity of the office visit?

Answer: The first-listed diagnosis is *fracture, shaft, right tibia*, and it justifies medical necessity for the *right leg x-ray*. The secondary diagnosis is *type 2 diabetes mellitus*, and it justifies medical necessity for the *office visit*.

K. Patients Receiving Diagnostic Services Only

NOTE: Do not report codes for qualified diagnoses on outpatient cases; instead, report codes for documented signs and symptoms. This differs from coding practices in hospital inpatient settings regarding abnormal findings on test results, for which the physician may document a qualified diagnosis that is coded and reported.

For patients receiving diagnostic services *only* during an encounter/visit, report first the diagnosis, condition, problem, or other reason for encounter/visit that is documented in the medical record as being chiefly responsible for the outpatient services provided during the encounter/visit. (This is the *first-listed diagnosis*.) Codes for other diagnoses (e.g., chronic conditions) may be reported as additional diagnoses.

For encounters for routine laboratory/radiology testing in the absence of any signs, symptoms, or associated diagnosis, assign Z01.89, Encounter for other specified special examinations. If routine testing is performed during the same encounter as a test to evaluate a sign, symptom, or diagnosis, it is appropriate to assign both the Z code and the code describing the reason for the nonroutine test.

For outpatient encounters for diagnostic tests that have been interpreted by a physician and for which the final report is available at the time of coding, code any confirmed or definitive diagnoses documented in the interpretation. *Do not code related signs and symptoms as additional diagnoses.*

L. Patients Receiving Therapeutic Services Only

For patients receiving *therapeutic services only* during an encounter/visit, sequence first the diagnosis, condition, problem, or other reason for encounter/visit shown in the medical record to be chiefly responsible for the outpatient services provided during the encounter/visit.

Assign codes to other diagnoses (e.g., chronic conditions) that are treated or medically managed or that would affect the patient's receipt of therapeutic services during this encounter/visit.

The only exception to this rule is when the reason for admission/encounter is for chemotherapy or radiation therapy. For these services, the appropriate Z code for the service is listed first and the diagnosis or problem for which the service is being performed is reported second.

NOTE: Preadmission testing (PAT) is routinely completed prior to an inpatient admission or outpatient surgery to facilitate the patient's treatment and reduce the length of stay. As an incentive to facilities that perform PAT, some payers provide higher reimbursement for PAT, making it important to assign codes properly.

M. Patients Receiving Preoperative Evaluations Only

For patients receiving *preoperative evaluations only*, assign and report first the appropriate code from ICD-10-CM subcategory Z01.81 (encounter for preprocedural examinations) to describe the pre-op consultations.

Assign an additional code for the condition that describes the reason for the surgery. Also assign additional code(s) to any findings discovered during the preoperative evaluation.

N. Ambulatory Surgery (or Outpatient Surgery)

For *ambulatory surgery* (or *outpatient surgery*), assign a code to the diagnosis for which the surgery was performed. If the postoperative diagnosis is different from the preoperative diagnosis when the diagnosis is confirmed, assign a code to the postoperative diagnosis instead (because it is more definitive).

O. Routine Outpatient Prenatal Visits

For routine outpatient prenatal visits when no complications are present:

- **Report a code from ICD-10-CM category Z34 (encounter for supervision of normal pregnancy) as the first-listed diagnosis.**
- **Do not report a code from category Z34 in combination with ICD-10-CM Chapter 15 codes.**

For routine prenatal outpatient visits for patients with high-risk pregnancies, report an ICD-10-CM code from category O09 (supervision of high-risk pregnancy) as the first-listed diagnosis. A code from ICD-10-CM Chapter 15 may also be reported as a secondary diagnosis, if appropriate.

P. Encounters for General Medical Examinations with Abnormal Findings

ICD-10-CM category Z00 (encounter for general examination without complaint, suspected, or reported diagnosis) provides codes for encounters with and without abnormal findings. When a general medical examination results in an abnormal finding, report the code for general medical examination with abnormal finding as the first-listed diagnosis. Then, report a secondary code for the abnormal finding.

NOTE: ICD-10-CM Z codes are not procedure codes. A corresponding CPT or HCPCS level II procedure code is reported on the CMS-1500 to justify medical necessity of ICD-10-CM Z code.

Q. Encounters for Routine Health Screenings

ICD-10-CM Z codes are assigned for any health care setting, and they may be reported as either a first-listed or secondary code, depending on the circumstances of the encounter. (Certain Z codes may only be reported as first-listed diagnosis.) *Screening* is the testing for disease or disease precursors in seemingly well individuals so that early detection and treatment can be provided for those who test positive for the disease (e.g., screening mammogram).

The testing of a person to rule out or confirm a suspected diagnosis because the patient has some sign or symptom is a *diagnostic examination*, not a screening. In these cases, the sign or symptom is used to explain the reason for the test.

A screening code may be reported as a *first-listed code* if the reason for the visit is specifically the screening exam. It may also be used as an additional code if the screening is done during an office visit for other health problems. A screening code is not necessary if the screening is inherent to a routine examination, such as a pap smear done during a routine pelvic examination.

Should a condition be discovered during the screening, then the code for the condition may be assigned as an additional diagnosis.

The Z code indicates that a screening exam is planned. A procedure code is required to confirm that the screening was performed. The screening Z codes/categories are:

Z11 Encounter for screening for infectious and parasitic diseases

Z12 Encounter for screening for malignant neoplasms

Z13 Encounter for screening for other diseases and disorders

Except: Z13.9, Encounter for screening, unspecified

Z36 Encounter for antenatal screening of mother

ICD-10-CM Z codes describe encounters for routine examinations (e.g., general check-up) or examinations for administrative purposes (e.g., pre-employment physical). Z codes are not to be reported *if the examination is for diagnosis of a suspected condition or for treatment purposes.* In such cases, report an ICD-10-CM diagnosis code.

- **During a routine exam, if a diagnosis or condition is discovered, report it as an additional ICD-10-CM code.**
- **Pre-existing conditions, chronic conditions, and history codes may also be reported as additional ICD-10-CM codes if the examination performed is for administrative purposes and does not focus on any particular condition.**
- **Some ICD-10-CM codes for routine health examinations distinguish between "with" and "without" abnormal findings. Code assignment depends on the information that is known at the time the encounter is being coded.**
  - **If no abnormal findings were found during examination, but the encounter is being coded before test results are back, it is acceptable to assign the code for "without abnormal findings."**
  - **When assigning a code for "with abnormal findings," additional code(s) should be assigned to identify the specific abnormal finding(s).**
- **Preoperative examination and preprocedural laboratory examination Z codes are reported only for those situations when a patient is being cleared for a procedure or surgery *and no treatment is provided.***

EXERCISE 6-8

Official Guidelines for Coding and Reporting

Instructions: Complete each statement.

1. The guidelines for coding and reporting using ICD-10-CM and ICD-10-PCS have been approved by the four organizations that comprise the ________.
2. The abbreviations for the four organizations that develop and approve the coding guidelines are ________, ________, ________, and ________.
3. Adherence to the coding guidelines when assigning ICD-10-CM and ICD-10-PCS diagnosis and procedure codes is required by ________ legislation.
4. The guidelines use the term ________ to indicate all health care settings, including inpatient hospital admissions.
5. The term ________ is used throughout the guidelines to refer to physicians or any qualified health care practitioners who are legally accountable for establishing the patient's diagnosis.

Instructions: Select the first-listed diagnosis in each statement.

6. The physician treated the patient's chronic asthma during an office visit, and she also received a renewed prescription for hypertension.
7. The physician ordered an ultrasound to rule out cholecystitis; the patient presented to the office with severe abdominal pain.
8. The patient slipped on ice and fell as she was walking down the steps of her porch. She was treated in the emergency department for severe swelling of the left leg, and x-ray of the left leg was negative for fracture.
9. The patient was treated in the office for nausea and vomiting. The physician diagnosed gastroenteritis.
10. The patient was treated in the outpatient department for a sore throat, which was cultured. The physician documented possible strep throat in the record.
11. The patient was treated on an outpatient basis for both acute and chronic bronchitis, for which each was assigned an ICD-10-CM diagnosis code.
12. The patient was treated for acne in the physician's office during this visit. The physician also documented that his previously diagnosed hives had totally resolved.
13. The patient was seen for complaints of fainting accompanied by nausea and vomiting. Her blood was drawn and sent to the lab to have a blood glucose level performed. Lab results were normal. The patient was scheduled for outpatient testing to rule out seizure disorder.
14. The patient underwent outpatient radiation therapy for treatment of prostate cancer during today's encounter; the patient had previously complained of painful urination.
15. The patient's preoperative diagnosis was possible appendicitis and right lower quadrant pain; he underwent a laparoscopic appendectomy. The postoperative diagnosis was acute appendicitis.

SUMMARY

ICD-10-CM is used to classify *morbidity* (disease) data from inpatient and outpatient records, including provider-based office records. (ICD-10-PCS is used to code and classify *procedures* from inpatient records only.) ICD-10-CM and ICD-10-PCS, also abbreviated as ICD-10-CM/PCS, replaced ICD-9-CM on October 1, 2014. All provider offices, outpatient health care settings, and health care facilities will report ICD-10-CM diagnosis codes.

Implementation of the ICD-10-CM (and ICD-10-PCS) coding systems resulted in ICD-9-CM becoming a *legacy coding system* (or *legacy classification system*), which means it will be used as archive data but it will no longer be supported or updated. *General equivalence mappings (GEMs)*, which are translation dictionaries or crosswalks of codes that can be used to roughly identify ICD-10-CM codes for their ICD-9-CM equivalent codes (and vice versa), will be annually published by NCHS and CMS.

The ICD-10-CM Index to Diseases and Injuries is organized according to alphabetical main terms (boldfaced conditions), nonessential modifiers (in parentheses), and subterms (essential modifiers that are indented below main terms). The index also contains a Table of Neoplasms, a Table of Drugs and Chemicals, and an index to external causes and injuries. To properly assign an ICD-10-CM code, locate the main term in the index, apply coding conventions (and guidelines), and verify the code in the ICD-10-CM Tabular List of Diseases and Injuries. Medical necessity is the measure of whether a health care procedure or service is appropriate for the diagnosis and/or treatment of a condition. Third-party payers use medical necessity measurements to make a decision about whether or not to pay a claim. ICD-10-CM coding conventions are incorporated into the coding system as instructional notes.

Outpatient care includes any health care service provided to a patient who is not admitted to a facility. Such care may be provided in a physician's office, a stand-alone health care facility, a hospital outpatient or emergency department, or the patient's home. The CMS *Diagnostic Coding and Reporting Guidelines for Outpatient Services: Hospital-Based and Provider-Based Office* were developed by the federal government and have been approved for use by hospitals and providers for coding and reporting hospital-based outpatient services and provider-based office visits. Although the guidelines were originally developed for use in submitting government claims, insurance companies have also adopted them (sometimes with variation).

INTERNET LINKS

- CDC Topics A–Z
  Go to **www.cdc.gov** and click on a letter from the A–Z Index link (e.g., letter I to locate ICD-10-CM content).
- Coding Pro Listserv (free)
  www.decisionhealth.com/codingpro-l-enroll
- Encoder Pro
  www.encoderpro.com
- HCPro, Inc.
  Go to **www.hcmarketplace.com**, and click on the Sign up for our FREE e-Newsletters link. Click on the box located in front of *JustCoding News: Outpatient* (along with other e-Newsletters of interest) to subscribe.
- ICD-9-CM to ICD-10-CM GEMs
  Go to **www.findacode.com**, click on the FREE TRIAL & DEMOS demos link (to register for a free trial), and click on the Cross-a-Code™ link (located below the *Search* heading) to subscribe to use the general equivalence mapping (GEM).

- ICD-10 Training (free)
  Go to **www.who.int**, click on the Health Topics link, click on the Classifications of Disease link, click on the International Classification of Diseases (ICD) link, and click on the ICD-10 Training link. Content at ICD-10 Training is based on the WHO's ICD-10 classification system (not ICD-10-CM). According to the website, "the course provides an overview of coding, focuses on the different chapters, gives a minimum of medical background, and provides short summaries."
- ICD-10-CM MS-DRG Definitions (Draft) (free)
  Go to **www.cms.gov**, click on the Medicare link, click on the ICD-10 link under Coding, click on the ICD-10 MS-DRG Conversion Project link, and click on a definitions manual link.
- ICD-10-CM search engines (free)
  www.findacode.com
- Web-based training courses (free)
  Go to **http://cms.meridianksi.com** and register to complete Web-Based Training Courses.

STUDY CHECKLIST

- ☐ Read this textbook chapter and highlight key concepts.
- ☐ Create an index card for each key term.
- ☐ Access chapter Internet links to learn more about concepts.
- ☐ Answer the chapter review questions, verifying answers with your instructor.
- ☐ Complete the Workbook chapter, verifying answers with your instructor.
- ☐ Form a study group with classmates to discuss chapter concepts in preparation for an exam.

REVIEW

NOTE: Although the review is organized by chapter, codes from outside a particular chapter or supplemental classification may be required to completely classify a case.

Instructions: The ICD-10-CM coding review is organized according to the ICD-10-CM chapters. To properly code, refer first to the Index to Diseases and Injuries (to locate the main term and subterm entries) and then to the Tabular List of Diseases and Injuries (to review notes and verify the code selected). Underline the main term in each item; then, use coding conventions and guidelines to assign the code(s). Enter the code(s) on the line next to each diagnostic statement. Be sure to list the first-listed code first.

CERTAIN INFECTIOUS AND PARASITIC DISEASES

1. Aseptic meningitis due to AIDS ____________
2. Asymptomatic HIV infection ____________
3. Septicemia due to streptococcus ____________
4. Dermatophytosis of the foot ____________
5. Measles; no complications noted ____________
6. Nodular pulmonary tuberculosis ____________
7. Acute cystitis due to *E. coli* ____________
8. Tuberculous osteomyelitis of left lower leg ____________
9. Gas gangrene ____________
10. Rotaviral enteritis ____________

NEOPLASMS

11. Primary malignant melanoma of skin of scalp ______
12. Lipoma of face ______
13. Glioma of the parietal lobe of the brain ______
14. Primary adenocarcinoma of prostate ______
15. Carcinoma *in situ* of vocal cord ______
16. Hodgkin's granuloma of intra-abdominal lymph nodes and spleen ______
17. Paget's disease with primary infiltrating duct carcinoma of nipple and areola of right breast (female) ______
18. Secondary liver cancer ______
19. Metastatic adenocarcinoma from breast to brain (right mastectomy performed 5 years ago; breast cancer is no longer present) ______
20. Cancer of the pleura (primary site) ______

DISEASES OF THE BLOOD AND BLOOD-FORMING ORGANS AND CERTAIN DISORDERS INVOLVING THE IMMUNE MECHANISM

21. Sickle cell disease with crisis ______
22. Iron deficiency anemia secondary to chronic blood loss ______
23. Von Willebrand's disease ______
24. Chronic congestive splenomegaly ______
25. Congenital nonspherocytic hemolytic anemia ______
26. Essential thrombocytopenia ______
27. Malignant neutropenia ______
28. Fanconi's anemia ______
29. Microangiopathic hemolytic anemia ______
30. Aplastic anemia secondary to antineoplastic medication for breast cancer ______

ENDOCRINE, NUTRITIONAL, AND METABOLIC DISEASES

31. Cushing's syndrome ______
32. Hypokalemia ______
33. Type 2 diabetes mellitus with malnutrition ______
34. Hypogammaglobulinemia ______
35. Hypercholesterolemia ______
36. Nephrosis due to type 2 diabetes ______
37. Toxic diffuse goiter with thyrotoxic crisis ______
38. Cystic fibrosis ______
39. Panhypopituitarism ______
40. Rickets ______

MENTAL AND BEHAVIORAL DISORDERS

41. Acute exacerbation of chronic undifferentiated schizophrenia ________

42. Reactive depressive psychosis due to the death of a child ________

43. Hysterical neurosis ________

44. Anxiety reaction manifested by fainting ________

45. Alcoholic gastritis due to chronic alcoholism (episodic) ________

46. Juvenile delinquency; patient was caught shoplifting ________

47. Depression ________

48. Hypochondria; patient also has continuous laxative habit ________

49. Acute senile dementia with Alzheimer's disease ________

50. Epileptic psychosis with generalized grand mal epilepsy ________

DISEASES OF THE NERVOUS SYSTEM

51. *Neisseria* meningitis ________

52. Intracranial abscess ________

53. Postvaricella encephalitis ________

54. Hemiplegia due to old CVA ________

55. Encephalitis ________

56. Congenital diplegic cerebral palsy ________

57. Tonic-clonic epilepsy ________

58. Bell's palsy ________

59. Spastic quadriplegia ________

60. Intraspinal abscess ________

DISEASES OF THE EYE AND ADNEXA

61. Retinal detachment with single retinal break, right eye ________

62. Infantile glaucoma ________

63. Senile cataract, right eye ________

64. Blepharochalasis of right upper eyelid ________

65. Xanthelasma of right lower eyelid ________

66. Lacrimal gland dislocation, bilateral lacrimal glands ________

67. Stenosis of bilateral lacrimal sacs ________

68. Cyst of left orbit ________

69. Acute toxic conjunctivitis, left eye ________

70. Ocular pain, right eye ________

DISEASES OF THE EAR AND MASTOID PROCESS

71. Acute contact otitis externa, right ear ________

72. Chronic perichondritis, left external ear ________

73. Chronic serous otitis media, bilateral ________

74. Acute eustachian salpingitis, right ear ________

75. Postauricular fistula, left ear ________

76. Attic perforation of tympanic membrane, left ear ________

77. Cochlear otosclerosis, right ear ________

78. Labyrinthitis, right ear ________

79. Tinnitus, left ear ________

80. Postprocedural stenosis of right external ear canal ________

DISEASES OF THE CIRCULATORY SYSTEM

81. Congestive rheumatic heart failure ________

82. Mitral valve stenosis with aortic valve disease ________

83. Acute rheumatic heart disease ________

84. Hypertensive cardiovascular disease ________

85. Congestive heart failure; hypertension ________

86. Secondary hypertension; stenosis of renal artery ________

87. Hypertensive nephropathy with chronic uremia ________

88. Hypertensive chronic end-stage renal disease ________

89. Acute STEMI myocardial infarction of inferolateral wall, initial episode of care ________

90. Arteriosclerotic heart disease (native coronary artery) with angina pectoris ________

DISEASES OF THE RESPIRATORY SYSTEM

91. Aspiration pneumonia due to regurgitated food ________

92. Streptococcal Group B pneumonia ________

93. Respiratory failure due to myasthenia gravis ________

94. Mild intrinsic asthma with status asthmaticus ________

95. COPD with emphysema ________

96. Acute tracheitis with obstruction ________

97. Chlamydial pneumonia ________

98. Chronic tonsillitis and adenoiditis ________

99. Simple chronic bronchitis ________

100. Moderate persistent asthma with (acute) exacerbation ________

DISEASES OF THE DIGESTIVE SYSTEM

101. Supernumerary tooth __________

102. Unilateral femoral hernia with gangrene __________

103. Cholesterolosis of gallbladder __________

104. Diarrhea __________

105. Acute perforated peptic ulcer __________

106. Acute hemorrhagic gastritis with acute blood loss anemia __________

107. Acute appendicitis peritoneal abscess __________

108. Acute cholecystitis with cholelithiasis __________

109. Aphthous stomatitis __________

110. Diverticulosis and diverticulitis of large intestine __________

DISEASES OF THE SKIN AND SUBCUTANEOUS TISSUE

111. Diaper rash __________

112. Acne vulgaris __________

113. Postinfective skin cicatrix __________

114. Cellulitis of left foot; culture reveals staphylococcus __________

115. Infected ingrowing nail, thumb, left hand __________

116. Carbuncle of face __________

117. Pemphigus foliaceous __________

118. Pressure ulcer of right elbow, stage 2 __________

119. Factitial dermatitis __________

120. Seborrhea __________

DISEASES OF THE MUSCULOSKELETAL SYSTEM AND CONNECTIVE TISSUE

121. Displacement of thoracic intervertebral disc __________

122. Primary localized osteoarthrosis of the left hip __________

123. Acute juvenile rheumatoid arthritis __________

124. Chondromalacia of the right patella __________

125. Pathologic fracture, cervical vertebra (initial encounter) __________

126. Staphylococcal arthritis, left knee __________

127. Postimmunization arthropathy, right ankle and foot __________

128. Idiopathic chronic gout, right shoulder __________

129. Kaschin-Beck disease, left shoulder __________

130. Fibromyalgia __________

DISEASES OF THE GENITOURINARY SYSTEM

131. Vesicoureteral reflux with bilateral reflux nephropathy ______

132. Acute glomerulonephritis with necrotizing glomerulitis ______

133. Actinomycotic cystitis ______

134. Subserosal uterine leiomyoma, cervical polyp, and endometriosis of uterus ______

135. Dysplasia of the cervix ______

136. Recurrent and persistent hematuria with dense deposit disease ______

137. Chronic obstructive pyelonephritis ______

138. Acute kidney failure with medullary necrosis ______

139. Stage 3 chronic kidney disease ______

140. Urethral stricture due to childbirth ______

DISEASES OF PREGNANCY, CHILDBIRTH, AND THE PUERPERIUM

141. Defibrination syndrome following termination of pregnancy procedure 2 weeks ago ______

142. Miscarriage at 19 weeks gestation ______

143. Incompetent cervix resulting in miscarriage and fetal death ______

144. Postpartum varicose veins of legs ______

145. Spontaneous breech delivery ______

146. Triplet pregnancy, delivered spontaneously ______

147. Retained placenta without hemorrhage, delivery this admission ______

148. Postpartum pyrexia of unknown origin (delivery during previous admission) ______

149. Late vomiting of pregnancy, undelivered ______

150. Pre-eclampsia complicating pregnancy, delivered this admission ______

CERTAIN CONDITIONS ORIGINATING IN THE PERINATAL PERIOD

151. Erythroblastosis fetalis ______

152. Hyperbilirubinemia of prematurity, prematurity (birthweight 2,000 grams) ______

153. Erb's palsy ______

154. Hypoglycemia in infant with diabetic mother ______

155. Premature "crack" baby born in hospital to cocaine-dependent mother (birthweight 1,247 grams); neonatal withdrawal; cocaine dependence ______

156. Neonatal hematemesis ______

157. Sclerema neonatorum ______

158. Failure to thrive in newborn ______

159. Grey baby syndrome ______

160. Congenital renal failure ______

CONGENITAL MALFORMATIONS, DEFORMATIONS, AND CHROMOSOMAL ABNORMALITIES

161. Congenital diaphragmatic hernia __________

162. Single liveborn male (born in the hospital, vaginally) with polydactyly of fingers __________

163. Unilateral cleft lip and palate, incomplete __________

164. Patent ductus arteriosus __________

165. Congenital talipes equinovarus __________

166. Cervical spina bifida __________

167. Coloboma of left iris __________

168. Tetralogy of Fallot __________

169. Atresia of vas deferens __________

170. Klinefelter syndrome, karyotype 47, XXY __________

SYMPTOMS, SIGNS, AND ABNORMAL CLINICAL AND LABORATORY FINDINGS

171. Abnormal cervical Pap smear __________

172. Sudden infant death syndrome __________

173. Sleep apnea __________

174. Fluid retention and edema __________

175. Elevated blood pressure reading __________

176. Epistaxis __________

177. Acute abdomen __________

178. Dysphagia, pharyngeal phase __________

179. Retrograde amnesia __________

180. Irritable infant __________

INJURY, POISONING, AND CERTAIN OTHER CONSEQUENCES OF EXTERNAL CAUSES

181. Open frontal fracture with traumatic subarachnoid hemorrhage and no loss of consciousness (initial encounter) __________

182. Traumatic anterior dislocation, left elbow (initial encounter) __________

183. Sprain of lateral collateral ligament, right knee (subsequent encounter) __________

184. Chronic headaches due to old traumatic avulsion, left eye __________

185. Traumatic below-the-knee amputation, right (initial encounter) __________

BURNS

Instructions: Burns require two codes:

- One code for *each* site and highest degree (which means more than one code can be assigned)
- One code for the percentage of body surface (not body part) affected

Refer to the following chart to calculate the percentage of burns for an extent of body surface. The percentage of total body area or surface affected follows the "rule of nines," as depicted in the following chart:

BODY SURFACE	PERCENTAGE
Head and neck	9%
Back (trunk)	18%
Chest (trunk)	18%
Leg (each)	18%
	18%
Arm (each)	9%
	9%
Genitalia	1%
TOTAL BODY SURFACE	**100%**

186. Third-degree burn of left lower leg and second-degree burn of left thigh (initial encounter) __________

187. Third-degree burn of right forearm (initial encounter) __________

188. Third-degree burn of upper back (subsequent encounter) __________

189. Thirty percent body burns with 10 percent third-degree burns (initial encounter) __________

190. Painful scarring due to old first- and second-degree burns of right palm __________

FOREIGN BODIES

NOTE: Refer to the main term "Foreign body" in the ICD-10-CM Index to Diseases and Injuries to begin the process of locating each code.

191. Coin in the bronchus causing asphyxiation (initial encounter) __________

192. Foreign body in right eye (initial encounter) __________

193. Marble in colon (initial encounter) __________

194. Bean in nose (initial encounter) __________

195. Q-tip stuck in left ear (initial encounter) __________

COMPLICATIONS

NOTE: Refer to the main term "Complication" in the ICD-10-CM Index to Diseases and Injuries to begin the process of locating each code.

196. Infected ventriculoperitoneal shunt (initial encounter) ____________

197. Displaced left breast prosthesis (initial encounter) ____________

198. Leakage of mitral valve prosthesis (initial encounter) ____________

199. Postoperative superficial thrombophlebitis of right leg (initial encounter) ____________

200. Dislocated left hip internal prosthesis (initial encounter) ____________

POISONINGS, ADVERSE EFFECTS, AND UNDERDOSING

NOTE: Use the ICD-10-CM Table of Drugs and Chemicals to begin the process of locating each code.

201. Accidental lead poisoning (child discovered eating paint chips) (initial encounter) ____________

202. Anaphylactic shock due to allergic reaction to penicillin (initial encounter) ____________

203. Theophylline toxicity (initial encounter) ____________

204. Carbon monoxide poisoning from car exhaust (suicide attempt) (initial encounter) ____________

205. Hypertension due to underdosing of Aldomet (initial encounter) ____________

EXTERNAL CAUSES OF MORBIDITY

NOTE: Use the ICD-10-CM Index to External Causes to begin the process of locating each code.

206. Bicyclist fell off bicycle in parking lot, lacerating chin (initial encounter) ____________

207. Boy wearing heelies-type sneakers used the wheels (in the sneaker's heels) to glide and collided with tree in yard of single-family home; the boy started crying and became emotionally upset (initial encounter) ____________

208. Pedestrian was walking through deep snow at local college and fell, spraining right wrist (initial encounter) ____________

209. Patient walked into lamppost while walking on sidewalk, striking her head causing dizziness (initial encounter) ____________

210. Patient lacerated right hand while slicing tomatoes in college dormitory kitchen (initial encounter) ____________

FACTORS INFLUENCING HEALTH STATUS AND CONTACT WITH HEALTH SERVICES

211. Exposure to tuberculosis __________

212. Family history of colon carcinoma __________

213. Postoperative follow-up examination, human kidney donor __________

214. Encounter for removal of cast from healed pathologic fracture of right ankle __________

215. Admitted as bone marrow donor __________

216. Encounter for chemotherapy for patient with Hodgkin lymphoma __________

217. Encounter for reprogramming (adjustment) of cardiac pacemaker __________

218. Encounter for replacement of tracheostomy tube __________

219. Encounter for renal dialysis in patient with end-stage renal failure __________

220. Encounter for speech therapy for patient with dysphasia secondary to an old CVA __________

CPT Coding

CHAPTER 7

CHAPTER OUTLINE

Overview of CPT

CPT Sections, Subsections, Categories, and Subcategories

CPT Index

CPT Modifiers

Coding Procedures and Services

Evaluation and Management Section

Anesthesia Section

Surgery Section

Radiology Section

Pathology and Laboratory Section

Medicine Section

National Correct Coding Initiative

OBJECTIVES

Upon successful completion of this chapter, you should be able to:

1. Define key terms.
2. Explain the format used in CPT.
3. Locate main terms and subterms in the CPT index.
4. Select appropriate modifiers to add to CPT codes.
5. Assign CPT codes to procedures and services.

KEY TERMS

care plan oversight services
case management services
Category I codes
Category II codes
Category III codes
comprehensive assessment
concurrent care
consultation
contributory components
coordination of care
counseling
CPT Coding Conventions
- boldface type
- cross-reference *(See)*
- descriptive qualifier
- guidelines
- inferred words
- instructional notes
- italicized type

CPT Symbols
- 
- ▲
- 
- ;

+
⊘
⊙
ϟ
○
#
critical care services
direct patient contact
emergency department services
established patient
Evaluation and Management Documentation Guidelines
Evaluation and Management (E/M) section
extent of examination (CPT)
- comprehensive examination
- detailed examination
- expanded problem focused examination
- problem focused examination

extent of history (CPT)
- comprehensive history
- detailed history
- expanded problem focused history
- problem focused history

face-to-face time
global period
global surgery
history
home services
hospital discharge services
indented code
initial hospital care
key components
level of service
medical decision making
medically unlikely edit (MUE)
moderate (conscious) sedation
modifier
monitored anesthesia care (MAC)
multiple surgical procedures
nature of the presenting problem
NCCI code pairs
NCCI edit pairs
new patient
newborn care
nursing facility services
observation or inpatient care services
observation services
organ- or disease-oriented panel
partial hospitalization
physical examination
physical status modifier
place of service (POS)
preoperative clearance
preventive medicine services
professional component
prolonged services
qualifying circumstances
radiologic views
referral
resequenced code
separate procedure
special report
stand-alone code
standby services
subsequent hospital care
surgical package
technical component
transfer of care
type of service (TOS)
unit/floor time
unlisted procedure
unlisted service
without direct patient contact

INTRODUCTION

This chapter introduces the assignment of *Current Procedural Terminology* (CPT) service and procedure codes reported on insurance claims. CPT is published by the American Medical Association and includes codes for procedures performed and services provided to patients. It is level I of the Healthcare Common Procedure Coding System (HCPCS), which also contains level II (national codes). Because of the introductory nature of this chapter, you are encouraged to obtain a comprehensive textbook that covers CPT principles and practice (e.g., Cengage Learning's *3-2-1 Code It!* by Michelle A. Green).

OVERVIEW OF CPT

Current Procedural Terminology (CPT) is a listing of descriptive terms and identifying codes for reporting medical services and procedures. It provides a uniform language that describes medical, surgical, and diagnostic services to facilitate communication among providers, patients, and insurers. The American Medical Association (AMA) first published CPT in 1966, and subsequent editions expanded its descriptive terms and codes for diagnostic and therapeutic procedures. Five-digit codes were introduced in 1970, replacing the four-digit classification. In 1983, CPT was adopted as part of the Healthcare Common Procedure Coding System (HCPCS), and its use was mandated for reporting Medicare Part B services. In 1986, HCPCS was required for reporting to Medicaid agencies, and in July 1987, as part of the Omnibus Budget Reconciliation

Act (OBRA), CMS mandated that CPT codes be reported for outpatient hospital surgical procedures.

HIPAA ALERT!

HIPAA named CPT and HCPCS level II as the procedure code set for physician or other qualified health care professional services, physical and occupational therapy services, radiological procedures, clinical laboratory tests, other medical diagnostic procedures, hearing and vision services, and transportation services, including ambulance. HIPAA also named ICD-9-CM (now ICD-10-CM) as the code set for diagnosis codes and (ICD-10-PCS) inpatient hospital procedures and services, CDT for dental services, and NDC for drugs. It eliminated the use of HCPCS level III local codes effective December 2003.

NOTE: The MMA requires that new, revised, and deleted ICD-10-CM and ICD-10-PCS codes be implemented each October 1 and updated each April, and changes to CPT and HCPCS level II national codes be implemented each January 1.

CMS enforced regulations resulting from the Medicare Prescription Drug, Improvement, and Modernization Act (MMA) on October 1, 2004, which required that new, revised, and deleted CPT codes be implemented each January 1. In the past, a 90-day grace period (from January 1 through March 31) had been allowed so providers and health care facilities had time to update billing systems and coders had an opportunity to undergo training regarding new, revised, and deleted codes. Be sure to purchase updated coding manuals to avoid billing delays and claims rejections. If outdated codes are submitted on claims, providers and health care facilities will incur administrative costs associated with resubmitting corrected claims and delayed reimbursement for services provided.

CPT codes are used to report services and procedures performed on patients:

- **By providers in offices, clinics, and private homes**
- **By providers in institutional settings such as hospitals, nursing facilities, and hospices**
- **When the provider is employed by the health care facility (e.g., many of the physicians or other qualified health care professionals associated with Veterans Administration Medical Centers are employees of that organization)**
- **By a hospital outpatient department (e.g., ambulatory surgery, emergency department, and outpatient laboratory or radiographic procedures)**

Procedures and services submitted on a claim must be linked to the ICD-10-CM code that justifies the need for the service or procedure. That ICD-10-CM code must demonstrate medical necessity for the service or procedure to receive reimbursement consideration by insurance payers.

The assignment of CPT codes simplifies reporting and assists in the accurate identification of procedures and services for third-party payer consideration. CPT codes and descriptions are based on consistency with contemporary medical practice as performed by clinical providers throughout the country.

In response to the electronic data interchange requirements of the Health Insurance Portability and Accountability Act of 1996 (HIPAA), the American Medical Association reviewed and revised the *Current Procedural Coding* system. Among HIPAA's requirements is that code sets and classification systems be implemented in a cost-effective manner that includes low-cost, efficient distribution, as well as application to all users. Although CPT was identified as the procedure coding standard for the reporting of physician services in 2000, the May 7, 1998, *Federal Register* reported that "CPT is not always precise or unambiguous. . . ."

CPT codes are five digits in length, and code descriptions reflect health care services and procedures performed in modern medical practice. In addition, the AMA reviews and updates CPT codes and descriptions on an annual basis.

Changes to CPT

CPT supports electronic data interchange (EDI), the computer-based patient record (CPR) or electronic medical record (EMR), and reference/research databases. CPT can also be used to track new technology and performance measures. Code descriptors were improved to eliminate ambiguous terms, and guidelines and notes underwent revision to make them more comprehensive, easier to interpret, and more specific. A CPT glossary was created to standardize definitions and differentiate the use of synonymous terms; and a searchable, electronic CPT index is under development, along with a computerized database to delineate relationships among CPT code descriptions.

Improvements to CPT address the needs of hospitals, managed care organizations, and long-term care facilities. In 2000, the AMA established three categories of CPT codes:

- **Category I codes: procedures/services identified by a five-digit CPT code and descriptor nomenclature; these are codes traditionally associated with CPT and organized within six sections**
- **Category II codes: contain "performance measurements" tracking codes that are assigned an alphanumeric identifier with a letter in the last field (e.g., 1234A); these codes will be located after the Medicine section, and *their use is optional***
- **Category III codes: contain "emerging technology" temporary codes assigned for data collection purposes that are assigned an alphanumeric identifier with a letter in the last field (e.g., 0001T); these codes are located after the Medicine section, and they will be archived after five years unless accepted for placement within Category I sections of CPT**

CPT Sections

CPT organizes Category I procedures and services within six sections:

- **Evaluation and Management (E/M) (99201–99499)**
- **Anesthesia (00100–01999, 99100–99140)**
- **Surgery (10021–69990)**
- **Radiology (70010–79999)**
- **Pathology and Laboratory (80047–89398)**
- **Medicine (90281–99199, 99500–99607)**

NOTE:

- The E/M section is located at the beginning of CPT because these codes are reported by all specialties.
- Medicine section codes (99100–99140) that classify *Qualifying Circumstances for Anesthesia Services* are explained in the Anesthesia section guidelines; they are to be reported with Anesthesia section codes.

CPT Code Number Format

A five-digit code number and a narrative description identify each procedure and service listed in CPT. Most procedures and services are classified as **stand-alone codes**, which include a complete description of the procedure or service. To save space, some descriptions are not printed in their entirety next to a code number. Instead, an **indented code** appears below a stand-alone code, requiring the coder to refer back to the common portion of the code description that is located before the semicolon.

EXAMPLE 1: Stand-alone code description

27870 Arthrodesis, ankle, open

EXAMPLE 2: Indented code description

27780 Closed treatment of proximal fibula or shaft fracture; without manipulation

27781 with manipulation

The code description for 27781 is *closed treatment of proximal fibula or shaft fracture with manipulation*.

CPT Category II Codes

CPT category II codes are supplemental tracking codes used for performance measurement in compliance with the Physician Quality Reporting System (PQRS). They (as well as certain HCPCS level II G codes defined by CMS) are assigned for certain services or test results, which support nationally established performance measures that have proven to contribute to quality patient care. CPT category II codes are alphanumeric and consist of four digits followed by the alpha character F. (HCPCS level II G codes are alphanumeric and consist of the alpha character G followed by four digits.)

The reporting of category II codes (and CMS-defined HCPCS level II G codes) is optional and is *not* a substitute for the assignment of CPT category I codes. When reported on the CMS-1500 claim, the submitted charge is zero ($0.00). CPT category II codes are arranged according to the following categories:

- Modifiers (1P–8P), reported with CPT category II codes only
- Composite Measures (0001F–0015F)
- Patient Management (0500F–0575F)
- Patient History (1000F–1494F)
- Physical Examination (2000F–2060F)
- Diagnostic/Screening Processes or Results (3000F–3750F)
- Therapeutic, Preventive or Other Interventions (4000F–4526F)
- Follow-up or Other Outcomes (5000F–5250F)
- Patient Safety (6000F–6150F)
- Structural Measures (7010F–7025F)

The purpose of reporting category II codes is to facilitate the collection of information about the quality of services provided to patients. The use of category II is expected to decrease the time required for patient record abstracting and review, thus minimizing the administrative burden on health care providers (e.g., physicians, hospitals).

EXAMPLE: Dr. Ryan is a dermatologist who is participating in a nationwide quality management study about malignant melanoma. CPT category II code 0015F is reported for each patient who receives melanoma follow-up services, which include obtaining a history about new or changing moles (code 1050F), performing a complete physical skin examination (code 2029F), and providing patient counseling to perform a monthly skin self-examination (code 5005F). Thus, codes 0015F, 1050F, 2029F, and 5005F are reported on the CMS-1500 claim, and the charge for each is zero ($0.00). In addition, ICD-10-CM reason for encounter code(s) and CPT category I service/procedure code(s) are reported on the same CMS-1500 claim with appropriate charges entered for each CPT category I code.

CPT Category III Codes

CPT category III codes are temporary codes that allow for utilization tracking of emerging technology, procedures, and services. They facilitate data collection on and assessment of new services and procedures during the Food and Drug Administration (FDA) approval process or to confirm that a procedure/service is generally provided. According to the CPT coding manual, "the inclusion of a service or procedure in this section neither implies nor endorses clinical efficacy, safety, or the applicability to clinical practice." CPT category III codes are alphanumeric and consist of four digits followed by the alpha character T, and they range from 0019T–0317T. In 2002, CMS began designating certain CPT category III codes as covered by Medicare, which means charges are entered when reporting the codes on a CMS-1500 claim.

In the past, researchers were hindered by the length and requirements of the CPT approval process. Thus, CPT category III (temporary) codes facilitate the reporting of emerging technology, procedures, and services. They are generally retired if the emerging technology, procedure, or service is not assigned a CPT category I code within five years. When a category III code is available, it must be reported instead of an unlisted CPT category I code (because reporting an unlisted code does not offer the opportunity for collection of specific data). Category III codes were initially released in July 2001 and are included as a separate section in CPT (following the category II codes). (HCPCS level II codes also describe emerging technology, procedures, and services; when an HCPCS level II code exists, it must be reported for Medicare claims.)

EXAMPLE: The patient's physician administered low-energy extracorporeal shock wave therapy of the musculoskeletal system. Report category III code 0019T and its charge on the CMS-1500 claim.

CPT Appendices

CPT contains appendices that are located between the Medicine section and the index. Insurance specialists should carefully review these appendices to become familiar with coding changes that affect the practice annually:

CPT APPENDIX	DESCRIPTION
Appendix A	Detailed descriptions of each CPT modifier. **CODING TIP:** Place a marker at the beginning of Appendix A because you will refer to this appendix often.
Appendix B	Annual CPT coding changes (added, deleted, and revised CPT codes). **CODING TIP:** Carefully review Appendix B because it will serve as the basis for updating encounter forms and chargemasters.
Appendix C	Clinical examples for Evaluation and Management (E/M) section codes. **NOTE:** The AMA halted the project to revise E/M code descriptions using clinical examples (or vignettes) in 2004. However, previously developed clinical examples are still included in Appendix C.

(continues)

(continued)

CPT APPENDIX	DESCRIPTION
Appendix D	Summary list of CPT add-on codes. **CODING TIP:** Add-on codes are identified in CPT with the + symbol.
Appendix E	Summary list of CPT codes exempt from modifier -51 reporting rules. **CODING TIP:** Exempt codes are identified in CPT with the ⃠ symbol.
Appendix F	Summary list of CPT codes exempt from modifier -63 reporting rules. **CODING TIP:** Below the codes that are exempt from modifier -63 is the parenthetical instruction "(Do not report modifier -63 in conjunction with . . . .)"
Appendix G	Summary list of CPT codes that include moderate (conscious) sedation. **CODING TIP:** Codes that include moderate (conscious) sedation are identified in CPT with the ⊙ symbol.
Appendix H	Alphabetic clinical topics listing located at www.ama-assn.org by clicking on links for Resources, *CPT*, Category II Codes, and *CPT Category II Codes Alphabetical Clinical Topics Listing,* which is a document that includes performance measures.
Appendix I	Molecular laboratory procedure codes for genetic testing were deleted from CPT 2013. This resulted in removal of Appendix I because its genetic testing modifiers were applied to those codes.
Appendix J	Summary electrodiagnostic medicine listing of sensory, motor, and mixed nerves (reported for motor and nerve studies codes).
Appendix K	Products pending Food and Drug Administration (FDA) approval but that have been assigned a CPT code. In the CPT manual, these codes are preceded by the flash symbol (⚡).
Appendix L	List of vascular families to assist in selecting first-, second-, third-, and beyond third-order branch arteries.
Appendix M	Crosswalk of deleted and renumbered CPT codes.
Appendix N	Summary list of resequenced CPT codes.
Appendix O	List of administrative codes for multianalyte assays with algorithmic analyses (MAAA) procedures, which are procedures that use multiple results generated from assays of various types, including molecular pathology assays, and so on.

NOTE: Examples of CPT symbols are included for illustrative purposes only and may not match the current CPT manual. Refer to your CPT coding manual to locate current uses of the bullet, triangle, and horizontal triangles.

CPT Symbols

Symbols located throughout the CPT coding book include the following:

- A bullet located to the left of a code number identifies new procedures and services added to CPT.

EXAMPLE: CPT code 81479 was added to a new edition of the coding manual.

• **81479** Unlisted molecular pathology procedure

▲ A triangle located to the left of a code number identifies a code description that has been revised.

EXAMPLE: CPT code 72040 was revised to change "2 or 3 views" to "3 views or less."

▲ 72040 Radiologic examination, spine, cervical; 2 or 3 views

►◄ Horizontal triangles surround revised guidelines and notes. *This symbol is not used for revised code descriptions.*

EXAMPLE: The parenthetical instruction below code 83887

► (83890–83914 have been deleted. To report, see 81200–81479) ◄

CODING TIP:

A complete list of code additions, deletions, and revisions is found in Appendix B of CPT. Revisions marked with horizontal triangles (►◄) are *not* included in Appendix B, and coders need to carefully review all CPT guidelines and notes in the new edition of CPT.

; A semicolon is used to save space in CPT, and some code descriptions are not printed in their entirety next to a code number. Instead, the entry is indented and the coder must refer back to the common portion of the code description that is located before the semicolon. The common portion begins with a capital letter, and the abbreviated (or subordinate) descriptions are indented and begin with lowercase letters.

EXAMPLE: The code description for 67255 is *scleral reinforcement with graft.*

67250 Scleral reinforcement (separate procedure); without graft
67255 with graft

CODING TIP:

CPT is printed using proportional spacing, and careful review of code descriptions to locate the semicolon may be necessary.

+ The plus symbol identifies add-on codes (Appendix D of CPT) for procedures that are commonly, but not always, performed at the same time and by the same surgeon as the primary procedure. Parenthetical notes, located below add-on codes, often identify the primary procedure to which add-on codes apply.

EXAMPLE:

22210	Osteotomy of spine, posterior or posterolateral approach, one vertebral segment; cervical
+ 22216	each additional vertebral segment (List separately in addition to primary procedure) (Use 22216 in conjunction with codes 22210, 22212, 22214)

CODING TIP:

Codes identified with **+** are *never* reported as stand-alone codes; they are reported with primary codes. Also, *do not* append add-on codes with modifier -51.

⃠ The forbidden symbol identifies codes that are *not* to be used with modifier -51. These codes are reported in addition to other codes, but they are *not* classified as add-on codes.

NOTE: A complete list of codes that are exempt from modifier -51 is found in Appendix E of CPT.

EXAMPLE:

⃠ 20974	Electrical stimulation to aid bone healing; noninvasive (nonoperative)

⊙ The bull's-eye symbol indicates a procedure that includes moderate (conscious) sedation.

Moderate (conscious) sedation is the administration of moderate sedation or analgesia, which results in a drug-induced depression of consciousness. CPT established a package concept for moderate (conscious) sedation, and the bull's-eye (⊙) symbol located next to the code number identifies moderate (conscious) sedation as an inherent part of providing specific procedures. Because these codes include moderate (conscious) sedation, it is inappropriate for a physician to report a separate moderate (conscious) sedation code from the CPT Medicine section (99143–99150).

If, however, the patient undergoes a procedure for which the CPT code has a bull's-eye symbol and the patient does *not* receive moderate (conscious) sedation, report the CPT procedure code only (e.g., 33208). Do *not* assign modifier -52 (reduced services) to the procedure code. If the patient receives general anesthesia, the anesthesiologist reports an Anesthesia section code.

NOTE: A complete list of codes that include moderate (conscious) sedation is located in Appendix G of CPT.

EXAMPLE:

⊙ 33206	Insertion or replacement of permanent pacemaker with transvenous electrode(s); atrial

⚡ The flash symbol indicates codes that classify products that are pending FDA approval but have been assigned a CPT code (e.g., code 90673).

○ The hollow circle symbol indicates a reinstated or recycled CPT code.

The number symbol precedes CPT **resequenced codes**, which appear out of numerical order (e.g., code 99224).

➲ The **green reference symbol** located below a code description in some CPT coding manuals indicates that the coder should refer to the *CPT Assistant* monthly newsletter and/or the *CPT Changes: An Insider's View* annual publication that contains all coding changes for the current year.

EXAMPLE: 43882 Revision or removal of gastric neurostimulator electrodes, antrum, open

➲ *CPT Assistant* Mar 07:4; *CPT Changes: An Insider's View* 2007

➲ The **red reference symbol** located below a code description in some CPT coding manuals indicates that the coder should refer to the *Clinical Examples in Radiology* quarterly newsletter.

EXAMPLE:

➲ 73500 Radiologic examination, hip, unilateral; 1 view
Clinical Examples in Radiology Spring 05:12

CPT SECTIONS, SUBSECTIONS, CATEGORIES, AND SUBCATEGORIES

CPT Category I codes are organized according to six sections that are subdivided into subsections, categories, and subcategories (Figure 7-1).

Guidelines

Guidelines are located at the beginning of each CPT section, and *should be carefully reviewed before attempting to code.* **Guidelines** define terms and explain the assignment of codes for procedures and services located in a particular section (Figure 7-2). This means that guidelines in one section do not apply to another section in CPT.

Unlisted Procedures/Services

NOTE: Medicare and other third-party payers often require providers to report HCPCS level II (national) codes instead of unlisted procedure or service CPT codes.

An **unlisted procedure** or **unlisted service** code is assigned when the provider performs a procedure or service for which there is no CPT code. When an unlisted procedure or service code is reported, a **special report** (e.g., copy of procedure report) must accompany the claim to describe the nature, extent, and need for the procedure or service along with the time, effort, and equipment necessary to provide the service.

Notes

NOTE:

- Terminology in the CPT code example need not appear in the procedural statement documented by the provider.
- Parenthetical notes within a code series provide information about deleted codes.

Instructional notes appear throughout CPT sections to clarify the assignment of codes. They are typeset in two patterns (Figure 7-3):

1. A *blocked unindented note* is located below a subsection title and contains instructions that apply to all codes in the subsection.
2. An *indented parenthetical note* is located below a subsection title, code description, or code description that contains an example.

Parenthetical notes that contain the abbreviation "eg" are examples.

> **NOTE:** CPT is inconsistent in its use of subsection, category, and subcategory terminology. For example, Table 1 in the CPT Evaluation and Management section guidelines lists categories and subcategories (instead of the more logical subsections and categories).
>
> Remaining CPT section guidelines include lists of subsections except for the Radiology section, which includes some subcategories in the list of subsections.
>
> To make matters even more complicated, CPT refers to headings and subheadings in some section guidelines and categories and subcategories in other section guidelines.
>
> In addition, the Surgery section guidelines include "Subsection Information" that refers to "subheadings or subsections." It would be more logical if the latter phrase had been written as "subheadings or *subcategories*."

SYMBOL / CONVENTION	CPT ENTRY:	
Section	**Surgery**	
Subsection	**Integumentary System**	
Category / Heading	**Skin, Subcutaneous and Accessory Structures**	
Subcategory / Subheading	**Incision and Drainage**	
Note		(For excision, see 11400, et seq)
Code number / Description	**10040**	Acne surgery (eg, marsupialization, opening or removal of multiple milia, comedones, cysts, pustules)
Use of semicolon	**11000**	Debridement of extensive eczematous or infected skin; up to 10% of body surface
Use of plus symbol	**+11001**	each additional 10% of the body surface, or part thereof (List separately in addition to code for primary procedure)
Use of -51 modifier exemption symbol	⊘ **93503**	Insertion and placement of flow-directed catheter (eg, Swan-Ganz) for monitoring purposes

FIGURE 7-1 Selection from CPT that illustrates symbols and conventions.

Surgery Guidelines

Guidelines to direct general reporting of services are presented in the **Introduction**. Some of the commonalities are repeated here for the convenience of those referring to this section on **Surgery**. Other definitions and items unique to Surgery are also listed.

Physicians' Services

Services rendered in the office, home, or hospital, consultations, and other medical services are listed in **Evaluation and Management Services** section (99201-99499), beginning on page 11. "Special Services and Reports" (99000-99091) are listed in the **Medicine** section.

Supplied Materials

Supplies and materials (eg, sterile trays/drugs) over and above those usually included with the procedure(s) rendered are reported separately. List drugs, trays, supplies, and materials provided. Identify as 99070 or specific supply code.

FIGURE 7-2 Portion of CPT Surgery Guidelines.

	Cardiovascular System
Blocked unindented note	Selective vascular catheterizations should be coded to include introduction and all lesser order selective catheterizations used in the approach (eg, the description for a selective right middle cerebral artery catheterization includes the introduction and placement catheterization of the right common and internal carotid arteries). Additional second and/or third order arterial catheterizations within the same family of arteries supplied by a single first order artery should be expressed by 36218 or 36248. Additional first order or higher catheterizations in vascular families supplied by a first order vessel different from a previously selected and coded family should be separately coded using the conventions described above.
Indented parenthetical note located below subsection title	(For monitoring, operation of pump, and other nonsurgical services, see 99190-99192, 99291, 99292, 99354-99360) (For other medical or laboratory related services, see appropriate section) (For radiological supervision and interpretation, see 75600-75978)
	Heart and Pericardium
	Pericardium
	⊙ **33010** Pericardiocentesis; initial
Parenthetical note located below code description	(For radiological supervision and interpretation, use 76930)

FIGURE 7-3 Selection from CPT that illustrates types of instructional notes.

Descriptive Qualifiers

Descriptive qualifiers are terms that clarify the assignment of a CPT code. They can occur in the middle of a main clause or after the semicolon and may or may not be enclosed in parentheses. Be sure to read all code descriptions very carefully to properly assign CPT codes that require descriptive qualifiers.

EXAMPLE: **17000** Destruction (eg, laser surgery, electrosurgery, cryosurgery, chemosurgery, surgical curettement), premalignant lesions (eg, actinic keratoses); first lesion

+ 17003 <u>second through 14 lesions, each</u> (List separately in addition to code for first lesion)

The underlining identifies descriptive qualifiers in the code description for 17003.

CODING TIP:

Coders working in a provider's office should highlight descriptive qualifiers in CPT that pertain to the office's specialty. This will help ensure that qualifiers are not overlooked when assigning codes.

EXERCISE 7-1

Working with CPT Symbols and Conventions

Instructions: If the statement is true, place a T in front of the number. If the statement is false, enter an F and correct the statement.

_____ **1.** The major sections of CPT are Surgery, Pathology and Laboratory, Radiology, and Medicine.

_____ **2.** The triangle indicates a new procedure code number.

_____ **3.** CPT requires a two- or five-digit modifier to be attached to the five-digit CPT code.

_____ **4.** "Notes" should be applied to all codes located under a heading.

_____ **5.** Semicolons save space in CPT where a series of related codes are found.

_____ **6.** Qualifiers for a particular code are always found in an indented code description.

_____ **7.** Parenthetical statements beginning with "eg" provide examples of terms that must be included in the health care provider's documentation of services/procedures performed.

_____ **8.** Horizontal triangles (▶◀) surround revised guidelines, notes, and procedure descriptions.

_____ **9.** The bullet (●) located to the left of a CPT code indicates a code new to that edition of CPT.

_____ **10.** Upon review of the CPT tabular listing below, code 50620 would be reported for a *ureterolithotomy performed on the upper or middle one-third of the ureter.*

50610 Ureterolithotomy; upper one-third of ureter

50620 middle one-third of ureter

50630 lower one-third of ureter

CPT INDEX

The CPT index (Figure 7-4) is organized by alphabetical main terms printed in boldface.

Main Terms

The CPT index is organized according to main terms, which can stand alone or be followed by modifying terms. Main terms can represent:

- **Procedure or service (e.g., endoscopy)**
- **Organ or anatomic site (e.g., colon)**
- **Condition (e.g., abscess)**
- **Synonyms, eponyms, and abbreviations (e.g., Bricker Operation, Fibrinase, EEG)**

Modifying Terms

A main term may be followed by subterms that modify the main term and/or terms they follow. The subterms may also be followed by additional subterms that are indented.

Code Ranges

Index code numbers for specific procedures may be represented as a single code number, a range of codes separated by a dash, a series of codes separated by commas, or a combination of single codes and ranges of codes. All listed numbers should be investigated before assigning a code for the procedure or service.

	N
Cross-referenced term	**N. Meningitidis** *See* Neisseria Meningitidis
Main term (boldface type) Subterm (not indented)	**Nails** Avulsion 11730-11732
	Biopsy 11755
Range of codes to investigate	Debridement 11720-11721
	Drainage 10060-10061
	Evacuation
Subterm (indented)	Hematoma, Subungual 11740

FIGURE 7-4 Selection from CPT index.

Conventions

Main terms in the CPT index are printed in **boldface type**, along with CPT categories, subcategories, headings, and code numbers. ***See*** is a **cross-reference** that directs coders to an index entry under which codes are listed. No codes are listed under the original entry. **Italicized type** is used for the cross-reference term, *See*, in the CPT index.

> **EXAMPLE: AV Shunt**
> *See* Arteriovenous Shunt
>
> In this example, the coder is directed to the index entry for Arteriovenous Shunt because no codes are listed for AV Shunt.

To save space in the CPT index when referencing subterms, **inferred words** are used.

> **EXAMPLE: Abdomen**
> Exploration (of) 49000,49002
>
> In this example, the word (of) is inferred and does not actually appear in the CPT index.

EXERCISE 7-2

Working with the CPT Index

Instructions: Answer each item below.

1. Turn to code number 47300 and review all procedural descriptions through code 47362. What does the term *marsupialization* mean? If you don't know the meaning, look it up in your medical dictionary.

   ____

   ____

2. How do codes 47350, 47360–47362 differ?

   47350 ______________________________

   ____

(continues)

47360 ____________________

47361 ____________________

47362 ____________________

3. The cross-reference that directs coders to refer to a different index entry because no codes are found under the original entry is called *See*. TRUE or FALSE.
4. Main terms appear in *italics* in the CPT index. TRUE or FALSE.
5. Inferred words appear in the CPT index to assist coders in assigning appropriate codes. TRUE or FALSE.

CODING TIP:

The descriptions of *all* codes listed for a specific procedure must be carefully investigated before selecting a final code. As with ICD-10-CM, CPT coding must *never* be performed solely from the index.

CPT MODIFIERS

NOTE: CPT modifiers are included at the beginning of this chapter because as students assign CPT codes, they must remember to add appropriate modifier(s).

CPT **modifiers** clarify services and procedures performed by providers. Although the CPT code and description remain unchanged, modifiers indicate that the description of the service or procedure performed has been altered. CPT modifiers are reported as two-digit numeric codes added to the five-digit CPT code.

EXAMPLE: 30630-77.

A patient undergoes repair of a deviated nasal septum (code 30630), which was unsuccessful. The patient undergoes repeat repair of the deviated nasal septum by a different surgeon (modifier -77). The same CPT code is assigned, and a modifier is added to indicate the repeat repair.

CPT modifiers have always been reported on claims submitted for provider office services and procedures. In April 2000, hospitals also began reporting CPT and HCPCS level II (national) modifiers for outpatient services.

NOTE: HCPCS level II national modifiers are detailed in Chapter 8.

CODING TIP:

A list of all CPT modifiers with brief descriptions is located inside the front cover of the coding manual. CPT and HCPCS level II national modifiers approved for hospital outpatient reporting purposes are also identified. Appendix A of the CPT coding manual contains a list of modifiers with descriptions.

NOTE: In an attempt to simplify the explanation of modifiers, the wording in this textbook does not correspond word-for-word with descriptions found in CPT.

Not all CPT modifiers apply to each section of CPT. Software (e.g., Optum's *EncoderPro.com Expert*) can be used to select modifiers associated with a CPT (or HCPCS level II) code.

The AMA develops new modifiers on a continuous basis, and next available numbers are assigned. This means there is no relationship among groups of modifier numbers. Reviewing modifiers in strict numerical order does not allow for comparison of those that are related to one another in terms of content; therefore, Table 7-1 organizes modifiers according to reporting similarity.

TABLE 7-1 Organization of CPT modifiers according to reporting similarity

SPECIAL EVALUATION AND MANAGEMENT (E/M) SERVICES		
MODIFIER	**DESCRIPTION**	**INTERPRETATION**
-24	Unrelated Evaluation and Management Service by the Same Physician or Other Qualified Health Care Professional During a Postoperative Period	Assign to indicate that an E/M service was performed during the standard postoperative period for a condition unrelated to the surgery. The procedure to which the modifier is attached *must be* linked to a diagnosis that is *unrelated* to the surgical diagnosis previously submitted. Be sure to submit a copy of documentation with the claim to explain the circumstances.
	EXAMPLE: One week after surgical release of a frozen shoulder, patient received level 3 evaluation and management services for treatment of the flu. Report code 99213-24.	
-25	Significant, Separately Identifiable Evaluation and Management Service by the Same Physician or Other Qualified Health Care Professional on the Same Day of the Procedure or Other Services	Assign when a documented E/M service was performed on the same day as another procedure because the patient's condition required the assignment of significant, separately identifiable, additional E/M services that are normally not a part of the other procedure. **NOTE:** The documented history, examination, and medical decision making must "stand on its own" to justify reporting modifier -25 with the E/M code. The E/M service provided must be "above and beyond" what is normally performed during a procedure. Many payers restrict the reporting of modifier -25. Be sure to obtain payer reporting guidelines.
	EXAMPLE: During routine annual examination, it was discovered that a 65-year-old established patient had an enlarged liver, necessitating expansion of the scope of level 4 E/M services. Report 99397 and 99214-25. (Be sure to submit supporting documentation to the payer.)	
-57	Decision for Surgery	Assign when the reported E/M service resulted in the *initial* decision to perform surgery on the day before *or* the day of surgery, to exempt it from the global surgery package.
	EXAMPLE: The patient received level 4 E/M services for chest pain in the emergency department, and a decision was made to insert a coronary arterial stent. Report 99284-57.	
GREATER, REDUCED, OR DISCONTINUED PROCEDURES OR SERVICES		
MODIFIER	**DESCRIPTION**	**INTERPRETATION**
-22	Increased Procedural Services	Assign when a procedure *requires greater than usual service(s).* Documentation that would support using this modifier includes difficult, complicated, extensive, unusual, or rare procedure(s). **NOTE:** This modifier has been overused. Be sure special circumstances are documented, and send a copy of documentation with the claim.
	EXAMPLE: Procedure report documents blood loss of 600 cc or greater. Operative report documents prolonged operative time due to …	

(continues)

TABLE 7-1 (continued)

GREATER, REDUCED, OR DISCONTINUED PROCEDURES OR SERVICES (continued)		
MODIFIER	**DESCRIPTION**	**INTERPRETATION**
-52	Reduced Services	Report when a service has been partially reduced at the physician's discretion and does not completely match the CPT code description. **NOTE:** Attach a copy of documentation to the claim.
	EXAMPLE: A surgeon removed a coccygeal pressure ulcer and performed a coccygectomy. However, the surgeon did not use a primary suture or perform a skin flap closure because the wound had to be cleansed for a continued period of time postoperatively. Report code 15920-52. (When the surgeon eventually performs the wound closure procedure, an appropriate code would be reported.)	
-53	Discontinued Procedure	Report when a provider elects to terminate a procedure because of extenuating circumstances that threaten the well-being of the patient. **NOTE:** This modifier applies only to provider office settings *and only if* surgical prep has begun or induction of anesthesia has been initiated. Do *not* report for procedures electively canceled prior to induction of anesthesia and/or surgical prep.
	EXAMPLE: Record documented that the procedure was started and terminated due to equipment failure.	
-73	Discontinued Outpatient Procedure Prior to Anesthesia Administration	Report to describe procedures discontinued *prior to the administration of any anesthesia* because of extenuating circumstances threatening the well-being of the patient. Do not report for elective cancellations. **NOTE:** Report a code from ICD-10-CM category Z53 to document the reason the procedure was halted.
	EXAMPLE: Patient developed heart arrhythmia prior to anesthesia administration for left breast simple complete mastectomy, and surgery was halted. Report 19303-73-LT.	
-74	Discontinued Outpatient Procedure After Anesthesia Administration	Report to describe procedures discontinued *after the administration of anesthesia* due to extenuating circumstances. **NOTE:** Report a code from ICD-10-CM category Z53 to document the reason the procedure was halted.
	EXAMPLE: Patient was prepped and draped, and general anesthesia administered prior to performance of a laparoscopic cholecystectomy. Anesthesiologist noted a sudden increase in blood pressure, and the procedure was terminated. Report 47562-74.	
GLOBAL SURGERY		
NOTE: • These modifiers apply to the four areas related to the CPT surgical package (Figure 7-5), which includes the procedure; local infiltration, metacarpal/digital block or topical anesthesia when used; and normal, uncomplicated follow-up care. • These modifiers do not apply to obstetric coding where the CPT description of specific codes clearly describes separate antepartum, postpartum, and delivery services for both vaginal and cesarean deliveries.		

(continues)

TABLE 7-1 (continued)

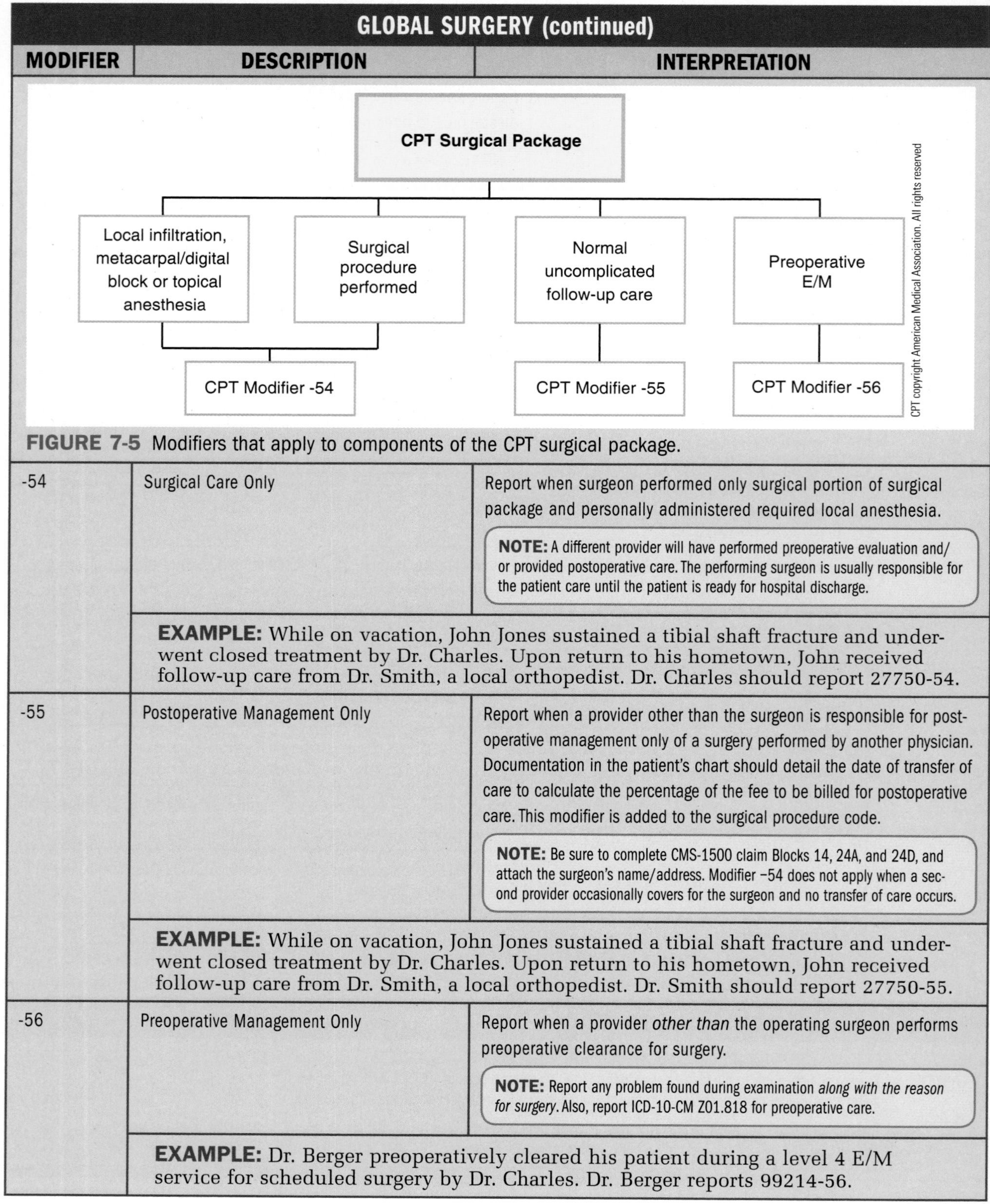

GLOBAL SURGERY (continued)

FIGURE 7-5 Modifiers that apply to components of the CPT surgical package.

MODIFIER	DESCRIPTION	INTERPRETATION
-54	Surgical Care Only	Report when surgeon performed only surgical portion of surgical package and personally administered required local anesthesia. **NOTE:** A different provider will have performed preoperative evaluation and/or provided postoperative care. The performing surgeon is usually responsible for the patient care until the patient is ready for hospital discharge.
	EXAMPLE: While on vacation, John Jones sustained a tibial shaft fracture and underwent closed treatment by Dr. Charles. Upon return to his hometown, John received follow-up care from Dr. Smith, a local orthopedist. Dr. Charles should report 27750-54.	
-55	Postoperative Management Only	Report when a provider other than the surgeon is responsible for postoperative management only of a surgery performed by another physician. Documentation in the patient's chart should detail the date of transfer of care to calculate the percentage of the fee to be billed for postoperative care. This modifier is added to the surgical procedure code. **NOTE:** Be sure to complete CMS-1500 claim Blocks 14, 24A, and 24D, and attach the surgeon's name/address. Modifier −54 does not apply when a second provider occasionally covers for the surgeon and no transfer of care occurs.
	EXAMPLE: While on vacation, John Jones sustained a tibial shaft fracture and underwent closed treatment by Dr. Charles. Upon return to his hometown, John received follow-up care from Dr. Smith, a local orthopedist. Dr. Smith should report 27750-55.	
-56	Preoperative Management Only	Report when a provider *other than* the operating surgeon performs preoperative clearance for surgery. **NOTE:** Report any problem found during examination *along with the reason for surgery*. Also, report ICD-10-CM Z01.818 for preoperative care.
	EXAMPLE: Dr. Berger preoperatively cleared his patient during a level 4 E/M service for scheduled surgery by Dr. Charles. Dr. Berger reports 99214-56.	

(continues)

TABLE 7-1 (continued)

<table>
<tr><th colspan="3">SPECIAL SURGICAL AND PROCEDURAL SERVICES (continued)</th></tr>
<tr><th>MODIFIER</th><th>DESCRIPTION</th><th>INTERPRETATION</th></tr>
<tr><td rowspan="3">-58</td><td>Staged or Related Procedure or Service by the Same Physician or Other Qualified Health Care Professional During the Postoperative Period</td><td>Report to indicate that additional related surgery was required during the postoperative period of a previously completed surgery and was performed by the same physician. Documentation should include one of the following:
• Original plan for surgery included additional stages to be performed within the postoperative period of the first stage of the procedure.
• Underlying disease required performance of a second related, but unplanned, procedure.
• Additional related therapy is required after the performance of a diagnostic surgical procedure.</td></tr>
<tr><td colspan="2">EXAMPLE: A surgical wound is not healing properly because of the patient's underlying diabetes. Patient was told prior to the original surgery that if this happened, additional surgery would be required for subcutaneous tissue debridement of the wound. Report code 11042-58 for debridement surgery.</td></tr>
<tr><td colspan="2">CODING TIP:
Do not report modifier -58 if the CPT code description describes multiple sessions of an event.</td></tr>
<tr><td rowspan="2">-59</td><td>Distinct Procedural Service</td><td>Report when the same physician performs one or more distinctly independent procedures on the same day as other procedures or services, according to the following criteria:
• Procedures are performed at different sessions or during different patient encounters.
• Procedures are performed on different sites or organs and require a different surgical prep.
• Procedures are performed for multiple or extensive injuries, using separate incisions/excisions; for separate lesions; or for procedures not ordinarily encountered/performed on the same day.
NOTE: Modifier -51, multiple procedures, may also be added to reported secondary procedures codes.</td></tr>
<tr><td colspan="2">EXAMPLE: Patient has two basal cell carcinomas removed, one from the forehead with a simple closure (11640) and the other from the nose requiring adjacent tissue transfer (14060). Report as 14060, 11640-51 (forehead), 11640-59-51 (nose).</td></tr>
<tr><td rowspan="2">-63</td><td>Procedure Performed on Infants Less Than 4 kg</td><td>Report when infant weighs less than 4 kilograms (kg) because procedures performed may require increased complexity and provider work.</td></tr>
<tr><td colspan="2">EXAMPLE: Baby Girl Markel's weight was 3.5 kg at the time she underwent diagnostic thoracoscopy. Report 32601-63.</td></tr>
</table>

(continues)

TABLE 7-1 (continued)

SPECIAL SURGICAL AND PROCEDURAL SERVICES (continued)		
MODIFIER	**DESCRIPTION**	**INTERPRETATION**
-78	Unplanned Return to the Operating/Procedure Room by the Same Physician or Other Qualified Health Care Professional Following Initial Procedure for a Related Procedure During the Postoperative Period	Report for unplanned circumstances that require a return to the operating room for complications of the initial operation.
	EXAMPLE: Surgical sutures of the axilla did not hold, and a 12 cm layer closure of the axillary wound was performed. Report 12034-78.	
	CODING TIP: To ensure payment, medical necessity for the return to the operating room must reflect the surgical complication.	
-79	Unrelated Procedure or Service by the Same Physician or Other Qualified Health Care Professional During the Postoperative Period	Report when a new procedure or service is performed by a surgeon during the normal postoperative period of a previously performed but unrelated surgery.
	EXAMPLE: Six weeks following cataract surgery performed on the left eye, the patient underwent diathermic repair of retinal detachment, right eye. Report 67101-79.	

BILATERAL AND MULTIPLE PROCEDURES OR ENCOUNTERS		
MODIFIER	**DESCRIPTION**	**INTERPRETATION**
-27	Multiple Outpatient Hospital E/M Encounters on the Same Date	Report for patients who receive multiple E/M services performed by *different providers* on the same day. **NOTE:** Do *not* report for multiple E/M services performed by the same provider on the same day.
	EXAMPLE: A patient was seen in the hospital's emergency department and received level 4 evaluation and management services due to a fractured ankle. The patient was seen later the same day in the urgent care center and received level 3 evaluation and management services due to a migraine that did not respond to prescribed medication taken at home. Report codes 99284-27 and 99213-27.	
-50	Bilateral Procedure	Report when a procedure was performed bilaterally *during the same session and when the code description does not specify that the procedure is bilateral.*
	EXAMPLE: Patient underwent bilateral athrodesis, knees. Report 27580-50 (or report HCPCS level II national modifiers as codes 27580-LT and 27580-RT).	
	CODING TIP: • Although CPT modifier −50 refers to *operative session*, both diagnostic and therapeutic procedures can be reported with the bilateral modifier *if the anatomic structures are found bilaterally and the identical procedure is performed on both sides.* • Reporting HCPCS modifiers -LT (left side) and -RT (right side) with procedure codes will remove any doubt that a bilateral procedure was performed. Documentation should accompany the submitted claim. *Do not report modifier −50 with HCPCS modifiers -LT and -RT.*	

(continues)

TABLE 7-1 (continued)

BILATERAL AND MULTIPLE PROCEDURES OR ENCOUNTERS (continued)		
MODIFIER	**DESCRIPTION**	**INTERPRETATION**
-51	Multiple Procedures	Report when multiple procedures *other than E/M services* are performed at the same session by the same provider. The procedures performed are characterized as: • Multiple, related surgical procedures performed at the same session • Surgical procedures performed in combination, whether through the same or another incision, or involving the same or different anatomy • Combination medical and surgical procedures performed at the same session **NOTE:** This modifier is reported with the secondary or lesser procedure(s).
	EXAMPLE: Patient underwent right tibial shaft fracture repair and arthrodesis of left knee. Report codes 27750 and 27580-51.	

CODING TIP:

Do not report modifier -51 if:

- Notes at the beginning of a category instruct the coder to *report additional codes in addition to . . .* (see note before code 22305).
- The code description states *List separately in addition to the code for primary procedure* (see code 22116).
- The code description includes the words *each or each additional segment* (e.g., code 22103).
- The symbol **+** precedes a code; this designates an add-on code.
- Codes are reported from the Laboratory and Pathology 80000 series.

REPEAT PROCEDURES		
MODIFIER	**DESCRIPTION**	**INTERPRETATION**
-76	Repeat Procedure or Service by Same Physician or Other Qualified Health Care Professional	Report when a procedure was repeated because of special circumstances involving the original service, and the same physician performed the repeat procedure.
	EXAMPLE: A repeat EKG is performed because of changes in the patient's condition or the need to assess the effect of therapeutic procedures. Report 93041-76.	
-77	Repeat Procedure or Service by Another Physician or Other Qualified Health Care Professional	Report when a physician *other than the original physician* performs a repeat procedure because of special circumstances involving the original study or procedure.
	EXAMPLE: Patient underwent sterilization procedure (e.g., tubal ligation), but became pregnant. After C-section delivery, she underwent a second sterilization procedure. Report 58611-77 for the second sterilization procedure.	

(continues)

TABLE 7-1 (continued)

MULTIPLE SURGEONS		
MODIFIER	**DESCRIPTION**	**INTERPRETATION**
-62	Two Surgeons	Report when two primary surgeons are required during an operative session, each performing distinct parts of a reportable procedure. Ideally, the surgeons represent different specialties.
	EXAMPLE: A spinal surgeon and a general surgeon work together as primary surgeons to perform an anterior spinal fusion of L5–S1; the spinal surgeon also inserts an intervertebral synthetic cage and performs iliac bone grafting. *Each surgeon reports code 22558-62.* The spinal surgeon also reports codes 22851 and 20937. **NOTE:** Surgeons should document the procedure(s) they performed in individual operative reports.	
CODING TIP: Report modifiers -62 and -50 (bilateral procedure) when co-surgery is done by surgeons of the same specialty (e.g., bilateral knee replacement that required two surgeons to operate on both knees at the same time due to the patient's condition or risk).		
CODING TIP: If either surgeon acts as the assistant surgeon for additional unrelated procedure(s) performed during the same operative session, report modifier -80 or -81 with the additional procedures code(s).		
-66	Surgical Team	Report when surgery performed is highly complex and requires the services of a skilled team of three or more physicians. The procedure reported on the claim for each participating physician must include this modifier. The operative reports must document the complexity of the surgery and refer to the actions of each team member.
	EXAMPLE: A surgical team of three physicians performed the reattachment of a severed arm. Each surgeon reports 20805-66.	
-80	Assistant Surgeon	Report when one physician assists another during an operative session. The assistant surgeon reports the same CPT code as the operating physician.
	EXAMPLE: Dr. Landry assisted Dr. Bartron during single CABG surgery. Dr. Landry reports code 33510-80.	
-81	Minimum Assistant Surgeon	Report when primary operating physician planned to perform a surgical procedure alone, but circumstances arise that require the services of an assistant surgeon for a short time. The second surgeon reports the same CPT code as the operating physician.
	EXAMPLE: Dr. Kelly begins an invasive cholecystectomy procedure on a patient and discovers that the gallbladder is the size of a hot dog bun, which necessitates calling Dr. Pietro to assist for a short time. Dr. Pietro reports 47600-81. (A gallbladder is supposed to be the size of your little finger.)	

(continues)

TABLE 7-1 (continued)

MODIFIER	DESCRIPTION	INTERPRETATION
MULTIPLE SURGEONS (continued)		
-82	Assistant Surgeon (when qualified resident surgeon not available)	Report when a qualified resident surgeon is unavailable to assist with a procedure. In teaching hospitals, the physician acting as the assistant surgeon is usually a qualified resident surgeon. If circumstances arise (e.g., rotational changes) and a qualified resident surgeon is not available, another surgeon may assist with a procedure. The nonresident-assistant surgeon reports the same CPT code as the operating physician.
	EXAMPLE: Resident surgeon Dr. Smith was to assist surgeon Dr. Manlin with a routine laparoscopic appendectomy. Dr. Smith was temporarily reassigned to the emergency department due to a staffing problem. Therefore, Dr. Manlin's partner, Dr. Lando, assisted with the procedure. Dr. Lando reports 44970-82.	
CODING TIP: Do not report modifiers -80, -81, and -82 for nonphysician surgical assistant services (e.g., physician assistant, nurse practitioner) *unless the payer authorizes this reporting.*		
PREVENTIVE SERVICES		
-33	Preventive Service	Alerts third-party payers that the procedure or service was preventive under applicable laws and that patient cost sharing (e.g., coinsurance, copayment, deductible) does not apply when furnished by in-network providers.
	EXAMPLE: The patient's primary care provider provided 20 minutes of smoking and tobacco use cessation counseling. Report code 99407-33.	
CODING TIP: • When multiple *preventive* procedures or services are provided on the same day, add modifier -33 to each code. • When procedure or service code descriptions contain the word *screening* (e.g., screening mammography), do not add modifier -33 to the code.		
PROFESSIONAL COMPONENTS		
MODIFIER	**DESCRIPTION**	**INTERPRETATION**
-26	Professional Component	Report when the physician either interprets test results or operates equipment for a procedure. *Do not report this modifier when a specific separately identifiable code describes the professional component of a procedure (e.g., 93010).*
	EXAMPLE: Independent radiologist Dr. Minion interprets a stereo frontal chest x-ray that was performed on Mary Sue Patient by another provider. Dr. Minion reports code 71021-26.	

(continues)

TABLE 7-1 (continued)

MANDATED SERVICES		
MODIFIER	**DESCRIPTION**	**INTERPRETATION**
-32	Mandated Services	Report when services (e.g., second or third opinion for a surgical procedure) provided were mandated by a third party (e.g., attorney, payer).
	EXAMPLE: Mary Sue Patient is seen by her primary care provider who recommends respiratory therapy. Before the payer will approve reimbursement for respiratory therapy, Mary Sue Patient receives a level 3 E/M service by respiratory specialist Dr. Powell. Dr. Powell reports code 99213-32.	
UNUSUAL ANESTHESIA OR ANESTHESIA BY SURGEON		
MODIFIER	**DESCRIPTION**	**INTERPRETATION**
-23	Unusual Anesthesia	Report when circumstances (e.g., extent of service, patient's physical condition) require anesthesia for procedures that usually require either no anesthesia or local anesthesia.
	EXAMPLE: The 30-year-old patient is mentally handicapped, extremely apprehensive, and requires general anesthesia for sliding hernia repair. Report 00832-23.	
-47	Anesthesia by Surgeon	Report when the surgeon provides regional or general anesthesia in addition to performing the surgical procedure.
	EXAMPLE: Instead of calling in an anesthesiologist to assist with a surgical case, Dr. Borja administers regional anesthesia and performs the spigelian hernia repair. Dr. Borja reports code 49590-47.	
CODING TIP: Modifier -47 is added to the CPT surgery code. It is not reported with Anesthesia section codes 00100–01999.		
LABORATORY SERVICES		
MODIFIER	**DESCRIPTION**	**INTERPRETATION**
-90	Reference (Outside) Laboratory	Report when a laboratory test is performed by an outside or reference laboratory.
	EXAMPLE: The provider orders a complete blood count (CBC). Because the office does not perform lab testing, arrangements are made with an outside laboratory to perform the CBC and bill the physician. The physician reports the CBC as code 85025-90. Code 36415 is also reported for routine venipuncture.	
-91	Repeat Clinical Diagnostic Laboratory Test	Report when a clinical diagnostic laboratory test is repeated on the same day to obtain subsequent (multiple) test results. *This modifier is not reported when lab tests are repeated to confirm initial results* (e.g., due to equipment problems).
	EXAMPLE: The patient was in the emergency department for 18 hours for observation of chest pain. He underwent serial (repeated) lab tests for cardiac enzyme testing every six hours. Report codes 82657, 82657-91, and 82657-91.	

(continues)

TABLE 7-1 (continued)

LABORATORY SERVICES (continued)		
MODIFIER	**DESCRIPTION**	**INTERPRETATION**
-92	Alternative Laboratory Platform Testing	When a single-use disposable kit or transportable instrument is used to perform HIV laboratory testing (CPT codes 86701-86703), add modifier −92 to the reported code.
	EXAMPLE: The hospital laboratory technician brought all of the HIV-1 testing materials to emergency department examination room #1 and performed an HIV-1 test on Mary Jones. Report code 86701-92.	
MULTIPLE MODIFIERS		
MODIFIER	**DESCRIPTION**	**INTERPRETATION**
-99	Multiple Modifiers	Report to alert third-party payers that more than three modifiers are being added to a procedure/service code.
	NOTE: The CMS-1500 claim allows up to four modifiers to be listed after a CPT or HCPCS level II code. (If more than four modifiers are required to report a procedure or service, enter the first three modifiers and modifier 99 on line 1 of Block 24D. On line 2, report the same CPT or HCPCS level II code and enter the remaining modifiers.) Line 1: 49540 22 47 50 99 NPI Line 2: 49540 80 NPI Courtesy of the Centers for Medicare & Medicaid Services, www.cms.gov	
	NOTE: The UB-04 claim allows up to two modifiers to be listed after a CPT or HCPCS level II code in Form Locator 44. If more than two modifiers are required to report a procedure or service, enter the first modifier and modifier 99 on the first line. On the subsequent line(s), enter the same CPT or HCPCS level II code and enter the remaining modifiers. 42 REV. CO. | 43 DESCRIPTION | 44 HCPCS/RATES | 45 SERV. DATE | 46 SERV. UNITS | 47 TOTAL CHARGES | 48 NON-COVERED CHARGES | 49 44 HCPCS/RATES: 49540 22 47 99 44 HCPCS/RATES: 49540 50 80 Courtesy of the Centers for Medicare & Medicaid Services, www.cms.gov	

EXAMPLE: Mrs. T has a history of gallbladder disease. After several hours of acute pain, she was referred to Dr. S for an evaluation of her condition. Dr. S performed a complete history and physical examination and decided to admit the patient to the hospital for an immediate work-up for cholecystitis. When the results of the laboratory tests and sonogram were received, the patient was scheduled for an emergency laparoscopic cholecystectomy.

The surgeon was Dr. S and the assistant surgeon was Dr. A. The surgery was successful, and the patient was discharged the next day and told to return to the office in seven days. Four days later, Mrs. T returned to Dr. S's office complaining of chest pains. Dr. S performed another examination and ordered the necessary tests. After reviewing the test results and confirming with the patient's primary care physician, it was determined that the patient was suffering from mild angina.

Dr. S submitted a claim (Figure 7-6) for the following services:

- Initial hospital visit, comprehensive, with medical decision making of high complexity (99223-57) (Modifier -57 indicates that the decision to perform surgery was made during the hospital evaluation.)
- Laparoscopic cholecystectomy (47562)
- Office visit, established patient, expanded problem focused, with medical decision making of low complexity (99213-24) (Modifier -24 indicates that the reexamination of the patient revealed the problem to be unrelated to the normal postoperative care provided to a cholecystectomy patient. The diagnosis linked to this visit is angina.)

(continues)

Dr. A submits a claim (Figure 7-7) for the following service: Laparoscopic cholecystectomy 47562-80. (Modifier -80 indicates that Dr. A is the assistant surgeon.)

	24. A. DATE(S) OF SERVICE From MM DD YY	To MM DD YY	B. PLACE OF SERVICE	C. EMG	D. PROCEDURES, SERVICES, OR SUPPLIES (Explain Unusual Circumstances) CPT/HCPCS	MODIFIER	E. DIAGNOSIS POINTER	F. $ CHARGES	G. DAYS OR UNITS	H. EPSDT Family Plan	I. ID. QUAL.	J. RENDERING PROVIDER ID. #
1					99223	57					NPI	
2					47562						NPI	
3					99213	24					NPI	

Courtesy of the Centers for Medicare & Medicaid Services, www.cms.gov; Copyright © Cengage Learning®.

FIGURE 7-6 Completed Block 24D on CMS-1500 claim.

	24. A. DATE(S) OF SERVICE From MM DD YY	To MM DD YY	B. PLACE OF SERVICE	C. EMG	D. PROCEDURES, SERVICES, OR SUPPLIES (Explain Unusual Circumstances) CPT/HCPCS	MODIFIER	E. DIAGNOSIS POINTER	F. $ CHARGES	G. DAYS OR UNITS	H. EPSDT Family Plan	I. ID. QUAL.	J. RENDERING PROVIDER ID. #
1					47562	80					NPI	

Courtesy of the Centers for Medicare & Medicaid Services, www.cms.gov; Copyright © Cengage Learning®.

FIGURE 7-7 Completed Block 24D on CMS-1500 claim.

EXERCISE 7-3

Assigning CPT Modifiers

Instructions: Assign the appropriate modifier(s) to each statement below.

_____ 1. Assistant surgeon reporting patient's cesarean section, delivery only.

_____ 2. Cholecystectomy reported during postoperative period for treatment of leg fracture.

_____ 3. Treatment for chronic conditions at same time preventive medicine is provided.

_____ 4. Inpatient visit performed by surgeon, with decision to perform surgery tomorrow.

_____ 5. Office consultation as preoperative clearance for surgery.

_____ 6. Postoperative management of vaginal hysterectomy.

_____ 7. Repeat gallbladder x-ray series, same physician.

_____ 8. Arthroscopy of right elbow and closed fracture reduction of left wrist.

_____ 9. Needle core biopsy of right and left breast.

_____ 10. Consultation required by payer.

CODING PROCEDURES AND SERVICES

STEP 1 Read the introduction in the CPT coding manual.

STEP 2 Review guidelines at the beginning of each section.

STEP 3 Review the procedure or service listed in the source document (e.g., charge slip, progress note, operative report, laboratory report, or pathology report). Code only what is documented in the source document; do not make assumptions about conditions, procedures, or services not stated. If necessary, obtain clarification from the provider.

STEP 4 **Refer to the CPT index, and locate the main term for the procedure or service documented. Main terms can be located by referring to the:**

a. *Procedure or service* documented.
EXAMPLE: Arthroscopy
Consultation

b. *Organ or anatomic site.*
EXAMPLE: Arm

c. *Condition documented in the record.*
EXAMPLE: Hernia

d. *Substance being tested.*
EXAMPLE: Blood

e. *Synonym* (terms with similar meanings).
EXAMPLE: Pyothorax is abscess, thorax; both are found in the index.

f. *Eponym* (procedures and diagnoses named for an individual).
EXAMPLE: Babcock Operation is ligation, saphenous vein. Both are found in the index.

g. *Abbreviation*
EXAMPLE: CBC

STEP 5 **Locate subterms and follow cross-references.**

STEP 6 **Review descriptions of service/procedure codes, and compare all qualifiers to descriptive statements.**

HINT:

If the main term is located at the bottom of a CPT index page, turn the page and check to see if the main term and subterm(s) continue.

STEP 7 **Assign the applicable code number and any add-on (+) or additional codes needed to accurately classify the statement being coded.**

CODING TIP:

You may have to refer to synonyms, translate medical terms to ordinary English, or substitute medical words for English terms documented in the provider's statement to find the main term in the index. Some examples are:

Procedure Statement	Word Substitution
Placement of a shunt	Insertion of shunt
Pacemaker implantation	Pacemaker insertion
Resection of tumor	Excision or removal of tumor
Radiograph of the chest	X-ray of chest
Suture laceration	Repair open wound
Placement of nerve block	Injection of nerve anesthesia

EXERCISE 7-4

Finding Procedures in the Index

Instructions: Using only the CPT index, find the code or range of codes to be investigated. Note the code or range of codes and any word substitution you made that led to selected code numbers.

1. Closed treatment of wrist dislocation ________
2. Dilation of cervix ________
3. Placement of upper GI feeding tube ________
4. Radiograph and fluoroscopy of chest, four views ________
5. Magnetic resonance imaging (MRI), lower spine ________
6. Arthrodesis of glenohumeral joint ________
7. Automated CBC ________
8. Electrosurgical removal, skin tags ________
9. Molar pregnancy excision ________
10. Muscle denervation, hip joint ________

EVALUATION AND MANAGEMENT SECTION

The **Evaluation and Management (E/M) section** (codes 99201–99499) is located at the beginning of CPT because these codes describe services most frequently provided by physicians. Accurate assignment of *E/M codes* is essential to the success of a physician's practice because most of the revenue generated by the office is based on provision of these services. Before assigning E/M codes, make sure you review the guidelines (located at the beginning of the E/M section) and apply any notes (located below the category and subcategory titles).

Most E/M services are cognitive services—this means that the provider must acquire information from the patient, use reasoning skills to process the information, interact with the patient to provide feedback, and respond by creating an appropriate plan of care. E/M services do not include significant procedural services (e.g., diagnostic tests or surgical procedures), which are coded separately. However, some services that arise directly from the E/M service provided are included (e.g., cleansing traumatic lesions, closing lacerations with adhesive strips, applying dressings, and providing counseling and educational services).

Overview of Evaluation and Management Section

CPT 1992 introduced the E/M level of service codes, replacing the brief, limited office visit codes included in the Medicine section of past CPT revisions. The E/M section is organized according to place of service (POS) (e.g., office, hospital, home, nursing facility [NF], emergency department [ED], or critical care), type of service (TOS) (e.g., new or initial encounter, follow-up or subsequent encounter, or consultation), and miscellaneous services (e.g., prolonged physician service or care plan oversight service). The E/M **level of service** reflects the amount of work involved in providing health care to a patient, and correct coding requires determining the extent of history and examination performed as well as the complexity of medical decision making.

Between three and five levels of service are included in E/M categories, and documentation in the patient's chart must support the level of service reported. CMS often refers to E/M codes by level numbers, and the level often corresponds to the last digit of the CPT code (e.g., 99204 is a level 4 E/M service).

EXAMPLE: Refer to the Office or Other Outpatient Services category in the E/M section, and notice that it contains two subcategories:

- New patient (contains five codes)
- Established patient (contains five codes)

Each code represents a level of E/M service, ranked from lowest to highest level. CMS would consider E/M code 99201 a level 1 code.

Accurate assignment of E/M codes depends on (1) identifying the place of service (POS) and/or type of service (TOS) provided to the patient, (2) determining whether the patient is new or established to the practice, (3) reviewing the patient's record for documentation of level of service components, (4) applying CMS's *Documentation Guidelines for Evaluation and Management Services*, and (5) determining whether E/M guidelines (e.g., unlisted service) apply.

Place of Service (POS)

Place of service (POS) refers to the physical location where health care is provided to patients (e.g., office or other outpatient settings, hospitals, NFs, home health care, or EDs).

EXAMPLE 1: The provider treated the patient in her office.

Place of Service: Office

E/M Category: Office or Other Outpatient Services

EXAMPLE 2: The patient received care in the hospital's ED.

Place of Service: Hospital ED

E/M Category: Emergency Department Services

Type of Service (TOS)

Type of service (TOS) refers to the kind of health care services provided to patients. It includes critical care, consultation, initial hospital care, subsequent hospital care, and confirmatory consultation.

EXAMPLE 1: The patient underwent an annual physical examination in the provider's office.

Type of Service: Preventive care

E/M Category: Preventive Medicine Services

EXAMPLE 2: The hospital inpatient was transferred to the regular medical-surgical unit where he was recovering from surgery. He suddenly stopped breathing and required respirator management by his physician.

Type of Service: Critical care

E/M Category: Critical Care Services

Sometimes *both the TOS and POS* must be identified before the proper code can be assigned.

EXAMPLE 1: Dr. Smith completed Josie Black's history and physical examination on the first day of her inpatient admission.

Place of Service: Hospital

Type of Service: Initial inpatient care

E/M Category: Hospital Inpatient Services

E/M Subcategory: Initial Hospital Care

EXAMPLE 2: Dr. Charles saw Josie Black in her office to render a second opinion.

Place of Service: Office

Type of Service: Consultation

E/M Category: Consultations

E/M Subcategory: Office or Other Outpatient Consultations

CODING TIP:

Refer to the CPT Medicine section for codes that describe specialty services (e.g., ophthalmologic services, psychiatric services) that require evaluation and management. When codes for specialty services are reported from the Medicine section, a code from the CPT E/M section is *not* reported on the same date *unless a significant, separately identifiable E/M service was provided (and modifier -25 is attached).*

New and Established Patients

A **new patient** is one who has *not* received any professional services from the physician, or from another physician of the same specialty who belongs to the same group practice, within the past three years. An **established patient** is one who *has* received professional services from the physician, or from another physician of the same specialty who belongs to the same group practice, within the past three years.

CODING TIP:

- Professional services may not require a face-to-face encounter with a provider.
- Definitions of new and established patients include professional services rendered by other physicians of the same specialty in the same group practice.

EXAMPLE 1: Sally Dunlop had a prescription renewed by Dr. Smith's office on January 1, 2005, but she did not see the physician. She has been Dr. Smith's patient since her initial office visit on March 15, 2002. On December 1, 2005, Dr. Smith treated Sally during an office visit.

New Patient: March 15, 2002.

Established Patient: January 1, 2005, and December 1, 2005.

Sally is considered a new patient on January 1, 2005, because that date is more than three years past March 15, 2002. Then, because she received professional services (the prescription renewal) on January 1, 2005, Sally is considered an established patient for the December 1, 2005, visit.

EXAMPLE 2: Dr. Charles and Dr. Black share a general practice. Dr. Charles treated Mary Smith in the office on July 1, 2005. Mary was first seen by the practice on February 15, 2002, when Dr. Black provided preventive care services to her. Mary returned to the practice on November 1, 2005, for her annual physical examination conducted by Dr. Black.

New Patient: February 15, 2002, and July 1, 2005.

Established Patient: November 1, 2005.

EXAMPLE 3: Dr. Corey left Alfred Medical Group to join Buffalo Physician Group as a family practitioner. At Buffalo Physician Group, when Dr. Corey provides professional services to patients, are those patients considered new or established?

Answer: Patients who have not received professional services from Dr. Corey or another physician of the same specialty at Buffalo Physician Group are considered new. Patients who have been treated by another family practitioner at Buffalo Physician Group within the past three years are considered established. If any of Dr. Corey's patients from the Alfred Medical Group choose to seek care from him at the Buffalo Physician Group, they will be considered established patients.

Concurrent Care and Transfer of Care

Concurrent care is the provision of similar services, such as hospital inpatient visits, to the same patient by more than one provider on the same day. Effective October 1995, CMS published new regulations that permit concurrent care by two or more providers on the same day even if the providers are of the same specialty. To avoid reimbursement denials by third-party payers and Medicare administrative contracts, the provider should report different ICD-10-CM diagnosis codes from those reported by other providers who see the patient on the same day. **Transfer of care** occurs when a physician who is managing some or all of a patient's problems releases the patient to the care of another physician who is not providing consultative services.

EXAMPLE: Laurie Birch was admitted to the hospital on October 5 for an acute myocardial infarction. On October 7, her attending physician (a cardiologist) wrote a physician's order requesting a psychiatrist to consult with the patient regarding her anxiety and depression. The cardiologist's insurance specialist should report the ICD code for "acute myocardial infarction" to justify inpatient E/M services provided to the patient. The psychiatrist's insurance specialist should report the ICD codes for "anxiety and depression" to justify inpatient consultation E/M services provided to the patient. If each provider reported the ICD code for "acute myocardial infarction," the provider who submitted the claim first would be reimbursed (and the other provider's claim would be denied).

Evaluation and Management Guidelines

Evaluation and management guidelines clarify that an *unlisted service* code is assigned when the provider furnishes an E/M service for which there is no CPT code. When an unlisted procedure or service code is reported, a special report (e.g., copy of documented encounter note record) must accompany the claim to describe the nature of, extent of, and need for the procedure or service.

CODING TIP:

Medicare and third-party payers often require providers to report HCPCS level II national codes instead of unlisted procedure or service CPT codes. (HCPCS level II national codes are discussed in Chapter 8 of this textbook.)

When an unlisted service code is reported, a *special report* must be submitted with the insurance claim to demonstrate medical appropriateness. The provider should document the following elements in the special report:

- **Complexity of patient's symptoms**
- **Description of, nature of, extent of, and need for service**
- **Diagnostic and therapeutic procedures performed**
- **Follow-up care**
- **Patient's final diagnosis and concurrent problems**
- **Pertinent physical findings**
- **Time, effort, and equipment required to provide the service**

Appendix C of the CPT coding manual contains clinical examples of E/M service codes. Along with a careful review of the E/M code descriptions, they assist providers in selecting the appropriate code for documented E/M services. The AMA cautions providers that the clinical examples "do not encompass the entire scope of medical practice." They can be used in addition to document key components (history, examination, and/or medical decision making) that are required to determine a particular level of service.

Levels of Evaluation and Management Services

Evaluation and Management (E/M) categories and subcategories contain codes that are classified according to level of services for reporting to third-party payers. Although the last number of some E/M codes represents the level of service (e.g., code 99213 is a level 3 E/M service), the levels within categories and subcategories are not interchangeable. Levels of E/M services include conferences with or about patients, evaluations, examinations, preventive adult and pediatric health supervision, treatments, and other medical services (e.g., determining the need for and/or location of appropriate care, such as hospice care for a terminally ill patient).

EXAMPLE: CPT code 99201 classifies a level 1 office or other outpatient service reported for new patients, and it includes a problem focused history and examination and straightforward medical decision making. CPT code 99211 classifies a level 1 office or other outpatient service reported for established patients, but it is reported when the physician's presence may not be required (e.g., office nurse takes patient's blood pressure and records it in the record).

Typically, just one E/M code is reported each day by a provider for a patient. When a separately identifiable E/M service is provided in addition to a surgical procedure, the E/M code is reported with modifier -25.

EXAMPLE 1: A physician sutured a patient's 2.5 centimeter scalp wound in the ED and performed a comprehensive neurological history and exam of the patient. The patient had sustained head trauma as the result of a car accident, and EMT personnel documented that he had been unconscious at the scene. Medical decision making was of high complexity. Report code 12001 for the simple repair of the scalp wound, and report code 99285-25 for the E/M service provided.

EXAMPLE 2: A physician sutured a 5 centimeter laceration of a patient's left hand and confirmed that the patient was up-to-date regarding her tetanus toxoids immunization status. Report code 12002 for the simple repair of the skin laceration, hand. Do not report an E/M code because the patient was not evaluated other than confirmation of her tetanus immunization status.

NOTE: Because they were believed to be insufficient to guarantee consistent coding by providers and reliable medical review by payers, CMS developed **Evaluation and Management Documentation Guidelines**, which explain how E/M codes are assigned according to elements associated with comprehensive multisystem and single-system examinations. The first set of guidelines created by CMS in 1995 was criticized by providers as containing unclear criteria for single-system specialty examinations. Therefore, CMS created an alternate set of guidelines in 1997, which was also criticized as being confusing and requiring extensive counting of services and other elements. In response, CMS instructed Medicare administrative contractors to use both sets of guidelines when reviewing records. Providers use whichever set of guidelines is most advantageous to their practice reimbursement.

The levels of E/M services code descriptions include seven components, six of which determine the level of E/M service code to be assigned:

- **History**
- **Examination**
- **Medical decision making**
- **Counseling**
- **Coordination of care**
- **Nature of presenting problem**
- **Time**

The **key components** of history, examination, and medical decision making are required when selecting an E/M level of service code. **Contributory components** include counseling, coordination of care, nature of presenting problem, and time; and they are used to select the appropriate E/M service code when patient record documentation indicates that they were the focus of the visit.

Key Components

E/M code selection is based on three key components:

- **Extent of history**
- **Extent of examination**
- **Complexity of medical decision making**

> **NOTE:**
> - When assigning codes for new patients, all three key components must be considered.
> - For established patients, two of three key components must be considered.

All three key components must be considered when assigning codes for new patients. For established patients, two of the three key components must be considered. This means that documentation in the patient's chart must support the key components used to determine the E/M code selected. The E/M code reported to a payer must be supported by documentation in the patient's record (e.g., office progress note, diagnostic test results, operative findings). Although providers are responsible for selecting the E/M code at the time patient care is rendered, insurance specialists audit records to make sure that the appropriate level of E/M code was reported to the third-party payer.

Extent of History

A **history** is an interview of the patient that includes the following elements: history of present illness (HPI) (including the patient's chief complaint, CC), a review of systems (ROS), and a past/family/social history (PFSH). The **extent of history (CPT)** (Figure 7-8A) is categorized according to four levels:

- **Problem focused history**: chief complaint, brief history of present illness or problem
- **Expanded problem focused history**: chief complaint, brief history of present illness, problem pertinent system review
- **Detailed history**: chief complaint, extended history of present illness, problem pertinent system review extended to include a limited number of additional systems, pertinent past/family/social history directly related to patient's problem
- **Comprehensive history**: chief complaint, extended history of present illness, review of systems directly related to the problem(s) identified in the history of the present illness in addition to a review of all additional body systems, complete past/family/social history

> **NOTE:** Physicians and providers can use either the 1995 or 1997 documentation guidelines for Evaluation and Management services, which were jointly developed by CMS and the American Medical Association. Each set of guidelines defines documentation elements that determine the level of examination.
> - The 1995 guidelines are typically used by general practitioners and others who do not perform single-system examinations.
> - The 1997 guidelines are often used by specialists who perform organ- or body area specific examinations.
>
> Regardless of guidelines used, documentation in the patient record must support the level of examination selected.

Extent of Examination

A **physical examination** is an assessment of the patient's body areas (e.g., extremities) and organ systems (e.g., cardiovascular). The **extent of examination (CPT)** (Figure 7-8B) is categorized according to four levels:

- **Problem focused examination**: limited examination of the affected body area or organ system
- **Expanded problem focused examination**: limited examination of the affected body area or organ system and other symptomatic or related organ system(s)
- **Detailed examination**: extended examination of the affected body area(s) and other symptomatic or related organ system(s)
- **Comprehensive examination**: general multisystem examination or a complete examination of a single organ system

SELECTING EXTENT OF HISTORY: To select extent of history, review the following elements documented in the patient record. If an element is not documented, it cannot be considered when selecting the level of E/M service code.

- History of Present Illness (HPI)
- Review of Systems (ROS)
- Past, Family, and Social History (PFSH)

HISTORY OF PRESENT ILLNESS (HPI): Review the patient's record, and for each documented HPI element listed below place an **x** in the box located in front of the element on this form. Then, count the number of **x**'s, and enter that number in the box located in front of the Total Score (below). Select the level of history based on the total number of elements documented, and place an **x** in the appropriate box.

☐ **Duration:** of pain/discomfort: length of time the condition has persisted (e.g., pain began three days ago)
☐ **Location:** of pain/discomfort (e.g., is pain diffuse/localized, unilateral/bilateral, does it radiate or refer?)
☐ **Quality:** a description of the quality of the symptom (e.g., is pain described as sharp, dull, throbbing, stabbing, constant, intermittent, acute or chronic, stable, improving or worsening?)
☐ **Severity:** use of self-assessment scale to measure subjective levels (e.g.,"on a scale of 1–10, how severe is the pain?"), or comparison of pain quantitatively with previously experienced pain
☐ **Timing:** establishing onset of pain and chronology of pain development (e.g., migraine in the morning)
☐ **Context:** where was the patient and what was he doing when pain begins (e.g., was patient at rest or involved in an activity; was pain aggravated or relieved, or does it recur, with a specific activity; did situational stress or some other factor precede or accompany the pain?)
☐ **Modifying factors:** what has patient attempted to do to relieve pain (e.g., heat vs. cold; does it relieve or exacerbate pain; what makes the pain worse; have over-the-counter drugs been attempted—with what results?)
☐ **Associated signs/symptoms:** clinician's impressions formulated during the interview may lead to questioning about additional sensations or feelings (e.g., diaphoresis associated with indigestion or chest pain, blurred vision accompanying a headache, etc.)

______ **Total Score:** Enter the number of **x**'s entered above. Place an **x** in front of the HPI type below.

☐ BRIEF HPI (1-3 elements)
☐ EXTENDED HPI (4 or more elements)

REVIEW OF SYSTEMS (ROS): Review the clinic or SOAP note in the patient's record, and for each documented ROS element listed below, place an **x** in the box located in front of the element on this form. Then, total the **x**'s and enter that number in the box located in front of the Total Score (below). Finally, select the level of ROS based on the total number of elements documented, and place an **x** in the appropriate box.

☐ Allergic / Immunologic
☐ Constitutional symptoms
☐ Cardiovascular
☐ Ears, nose, mouth, throat
☐ Endocrine
☐ Eyes
☐ Gastrointestinal
☐ Genitourinary
☐ Hematologic/Lymphatic
☐ Integumentary (including skin and breast)
☐ Musculoskeletal
☐ Neurologic
☐ Psychiatric
☐ Respiratory

______ **Total Score:** Enter the number of **x**'s entered above. Place an **x** in front of the ROS type below.

☐ NONE
☐ PROBLEM PERTINENT ROS (1 body system documented)
☐ EXTENDED ROS (2–9 body systems documented)
☐ COMPLETE ROS (all body systems documented)

PAST, FAMILY, AND/OR SOCIAL HISTORY (PFSH): Review the clinic or SOAP note in the patient's record, and for each documented PFSH element (below), place an **x** in the box located in front of the element on this form. Then, total the **x**'s entered and enter that number in the box located in front of the Total Score (below). Finally, select the level of PFSH based on the total number of elements documented, and place an **x** in the appropriate box.

☐ Past history (current medications, drug allergies, immunizations, and prior illnesses/ injuries, hospitalizations, surgeries)
☐ Family history (health status/cause of death of relatives, specific disease related to CC, HPI, ROS, hereditary diseases for which patient is at risk)
☐ Social history (alcohol use, current employment, illicit drug use, level of education, nutritional status, occupational history, sexual history, tobacco use)

______ **Total Score:** Enter the number of **x**'s selected. Place an **x** in front of the PFSH type below.

☐ NONE
☐ PERTINENT PFSH (1 history area documented)
☐ COMPLETE PFSH (2 or 3 history areas documented)

Circle the type of HPI, ROS, and PFSH. Select the Extent of History. (3 of 3 elements must be met or exceeded.)

HPI	Brief	Brief	Extended	Extended
ROS	None	Problem Pertinent	Extended	Complete
PFSH	None	None	Pertinent	Complete
EXTENT OF HISTORY	PROBLEM FOCUSED	EXPANDED PROBLEM FOCUSED	DETAILED	COMPREHENSIVE

FIGURE 7-8A Extent of history.

SELECTING EXTENT OF EXAMINATION: To select the level of examination, first determine whether a *single organ examination* (e.g., specialist exam, such as ophthalmologist) or a *general multisystem examination* (e.g., family practitioner) was completed.

SINGLE ORGAN SYSTEM EXAMINATION: Refer to single organ system examination requirements in CMS's *Documentation Guidelines for Evaluation and Management Services.* Place an **x** in front of the appropriate exam type below.

- ☐ PROBLEM FOCUSED EXAMINATION (1–5 elements identified by a bullet)
- ☐ EXPANDED PROBLEM FOCUSED EXAMINATION (at least 6 elements identified by a bullet)
- ☐ DETAILED EXAMINATION (at least 12 elements identified by a bullet)
- ☐ COMPREHENSIVE EXAMINATION (all elements identified by a bullet; document every element in each box with a shaded border and at least 1 element in each box with an unshaded border)

  NOTE: For eye and psychiatric examinations, at least 9 elements in each box with a shaded border and at least 1 element in each box with a shaded or unshaded border is documented.

GENERAL MULTISYSTEM EXAM: Refer to the general multisystem examination requirements in CMS's *Documentation Guidelines for Evaluation and Management Services.* Place an **x** in front of the organ system or body area for up to the total number of allowed elements (e.g., up to 2 marks can be made for the Neck exam).

- ☐ Constitutional (2)
- ☐ Cardiovascular (7)
- ☐ Chest (Breasts) (2)
- ☐ Eyes (3)
- ☐ Ears, nose, mouth, throat (6)
- ☐ Gastrointestinal (5)
- ☐ Genitourinary (M–3; F–6)
- ☐ Musculoskeletal (6)
- ☐ Neck (2)
- ☐ Neurologic (3)a
- ☐ Psychiatric (4)
- ☐ Respiratory (4)
- ☐ Skin (2)

______ **Total Score:** Enter the number of **x**'s entered above. Place an **x** in front of the Examination type below.

- ☐ PROBLEM FOCUSED EXAMINATION (1–5 elements identified by a bullet on CMS's *E/M Documentation Guidelines*)
- ☐ EXPANDED PROBLEM FOCUSED EXAMINATION (at least 6 elements identified by a bullet on CMS's *E/M Documentation Guidelines*)
- ☐ DETAILED EXAMINATION (at least 2 elements identified by a bullet from each of 6 organ systems or body areas or at least 12 elements identified by a bullet in 2 or more systems or areas, on CMS's *E/M Documentation Guidelines*)
- ☐ COMPREHENSIVE EXAMINATION (documentation of all elements identified by a bullet in at least 9 organ systems or body areas, and documentation of at least 2 elements identified by a bullet from each of 9 organ systems or body areas, on CMS's *E/M Documentation Guidelines*)

FIGURE 7-8B Extent of examination.

CRITERIA TO DETERMINE COMPLEXITY OF MEDICAL DECISION MAKING

Number of Diagnoses or Management Options	Amount/Complexity of Data to Be Reviewed	Risk of Complications and/or Morbidity/Mortality	Complexity of Medical Decision Making
Minimal	Minimal or none	Minimal	Straightforward
Limited	Limited	Low	Low complexity
Multiple	Moderate	Moderate	Moderate complexity
Extensive	Extensive	High	High complexity

FIGURE 7-8C Criteria to determine complexity of medical decision making.

Complexity of Medical Decision Making

Medical decision making (Figure 7-8C) refers to the complexity of establishing a diagnosis and/or selecting a management option as measured by the:

- **Number of diagnoses or management options**
- **Amount and/or complexity of data to be reviewed**
- **Risk of complications and/or morbidity or mortality**

Complexity of medical decision-making criteria reflects the provider's level of uncertainty, volume of data to review, and risk to the patient. Documentation in the patient's record includes:

- **Laboratory, imaging, and other test results that are significant to the management of the patient's care**
- **List of known diagnoses as well as those that are suspected**
- **Opinions of other physicians who have been consulted**
- **Planned course of action for the patient's treatment (plan of treatment)**
- **Review of patient records obtained from other facilities**

The physician is responsible for determining the complexity of medical decision making, and that decision must be supported by documentation in the patient's chart. CPT includes a table in the E/M guidelines that can assist in determining the complexity of medical decision making. Once the key components for extent of history and examination are determined, the type of medical decision making can be selected as follows:

- **Straightforward**
- **Low complexity**
- **Moderate complexity**
- **High complexity**

HOW TO SELECT COMPLEXITY OF MEDICAL DECISION MAKING

When assigning codes from the Evaluation and Management section of CPT, use the E/M CodeBuilder located in Appendix III of this textbook. It contains the *criteria to determine the complexity of medical decision-making* table (Figure 7-8C). To select the complexity of medical decision making:

STEP 1. Review the entire patient record to locate documented diagnoses and/or management options. Then, decide whether the documentation represents a minimal, limited, multiple, or extensive *number of diagnoses or management options*.

STEP 2. Review the entire patient record to locate documented data (e.g., lab reports, x-ray reports, consultation reports, and so on). Then, decide if the documentation represents a minimal (or none), limited, moderate, or extensive *amount/complexity of data to be reviewed*.

STEP 3. Review the entire patient record to determine the risk of complications and/or morbidity or mortality. This review requires knowledge of pathophysiology and pharmacology to select among minimal, low, moderate, or high *risk of complications and/or morbidity/mortality*.

STEP 4. Finally, select straightforward, low, moderate, or *high complexity of medical decision making* based on the criteria selected in steps 1 to 3.

Select the E/M code based on extent of history, extent of examination, and complexity of medical decision making:					
History	Problem focused	Expanded problem focused	Expanded problem focused	Detailed	Comprehensive
Examination	Problem focused	Expanded problem focused	Expanded problem focused	Detailed	Comprehensive
Medical Decision Making	Straightforward	Low complexity	Moderate complexity	Moderate complexity	High complexity
Go to the appropriate E/M category/subcategory, and select the code based upon the information above.					

FIGURE 7-8D E/M code selection based on extent of history and examination and complexity of medical decision making.

Assigning the E/M Code

Once the extent of history, extent of examination, and complexity of medical decision making are determined, select the appropriate E/M code (Figure 7-8D).

CODING TIP:

Use the E/M CodeBuilder located in Appendix III to select the correct E/M code.

EXAMPLE: Review the progress note below (documented using the SOAP format), and use Figures 7-8A, 7-8B, 7-8C, and 7-8D to determine the extent of history and examination and complexity of medical decision making for a patient who is seen by his general practitioner.

SUBJECTIVE: The patient is a 35-year-old established male patient seen today with a chief complaint of severe snoring. He says that this has gone on for years and that he's finally ready to do something about it because it causes him to awaken during the night, and his wife to lose sleep as well. He says that he wakes up in the morning feeling very tired and notices that he gets very tired during the day. Review of systems reveals allergies. He denies smoking or alcohol use. He is on no medications.

OBJECTIVE: Blood pressure is 126/86. Pulse is 82. Weight is 185. EYES: Pupils equal, round, and reactive to light and accommodation; extraocular muscles intact. EARS & NOSE: Tympanic membranes normal; oropharynx benign. NECK: Supple without jugular venous distention, bruits, or thyromegaly. RESPIRATORY: Breath sounds are clear to percussion and auscultation. EXTREMITIES: Without edema; pulses intact.

ASSESSMENT: Possible sleep apnea.

PLAN: Patient to undergo sleep study in two weeks. Results to be evaluated by Dr. Jones, ENT specialist, to determine whether patient is candidate for laser-assisted uvuloplasty (LAUP) surgery.

(continues)

To assign the E/M code, the following is determined:

NEW OR ESTABLISHED PATIENT: This is an established patient.

EXTENT OF HISTORY: HPI elements include quality, severity, timing, and context; in the above case, an extended HPI (four elements) is documented. ROS elements *include allergic*; in the above case, a problem pertinent ROS (one body system) is documented. PFSH elements include documentation of social history; in the above case, a pertinent PFSH (one history area) is documented *for a score of* 1. Because three out of three HPI/ROS/PFHS types must be selected to determine the higher-level extent of history, an expanded problem focused history is assigned.

EXTENT OF EXAMINATION: Constitutional (1), Eyes (1), ENT (2), Neck (1), Respiratory (1), Cardiovascular (1); thus, an expanded problem focused examination (six elements) is documented.

COMPLEXITY OF MEDICAL DECISION MAKING: Undiagnosed new problem with uncertain prognosis is documented (possible sleep apnea). Although "physiologic test not under stress" (sleep study) is documented as being ordered, results are not reviewed by this provider. In addition, this provider will not follow through on management options because the patient is referred to an ENT specialist. Therefore, complexity of medical decision making is straightforward because two of three elements are required and just one element is documented.

E/M CODE ASSIGNED: 99213 (Two of three key components are required.)

Contributory Components

The contributory components of counseling, coordination of care, nature of presenting illness, and time play an important role in selecting the E/M code when documentation in the patient record indicates that they were the focus of the visit. Counseling and/or coordination of care components drive CPT code selection only when they dominate the encounter (e.g., office visit), requiring that more than 50 percent of the provider's time be spent on such components. In such circumstances, the provider must be sure to carefully document these elements so as to support the higher-level code selected. (Some E/M code descriptions include notes about time and nature of the presenting problem to assist in determining the appropriate code number to report.)

Counseling

CPT defines **counseling** as it relates to E/M coding as a discussion with a patient and/or family concerning one or more of the following areas: diagnostic results, impressions, and/or recommended diagnostic studies; prognosis; risks and benefits of management (treatment) options; instructions for management (treatment) and/or follow-up; importance of compliance with chosen management (treatment) options; risk factor reduction; patient and family education.

Providers typically select the level of E/M code based on extent of history and examination and complexity of medical decision making. However, some patients require counseling services (e.g., nutrition instruction, smoking cessation, and weight management) during an E/M visit. If provided, such counseling should be properly documented and the appropriate level of E/M code selected.

Coordination of Care

When the physician makes arrangements with other providers or agencies for services to be provided to a patient, this is called **coordination of care**.

Nature of the Presenting Problem

CPT defines **nature of the presenting problem** as "a disease, condition, illness, injury, symptom, sign, finding, complaint, or other reason for the encounter, with or without a diagnosis being established at the time of the encounter." The *nature of the presenting problem* is considered when determining the number of diagnoses or management options for medical decision-making complexity.

Five types of presenting problems are recognized:

- **Minimal (problem may not require the presence of the physician, but service is provided under the physician's supervision, such as a patient who comes to the office once a week to have blood pressure taken and recorded)**
- **Self-limited or minor (problem that runs a definite and prescribed course, is transient in nature, and is not likely to permanently alter health status or that has a good prognosis with management/compliance, such as a patient diagnosed with adult-onset diabetes mellitus controlled by diet and exercise)**
- **Low severity (problem where the risk of morbidity without treatment is low; there is little to no risk of mortality without treatment; full recovery without functional impairment is expected, such as a patient who is diagnosed with eczema and who does not respond to over-the-counter medications)**
- **Moderate severity (problem where the risk of morbidity without treatment is moderate; there is moderate risk of mortality without treatment; uncertain prognosis; increased probability of prolonged functional impairment, such as a 35-year-old male patient diagnosed with chest pain on exertion)**
- **High severity (problem where the risk of morbidity without treatment is high to extreme; there is a moderate to high risk of mortality without treatment; high probability of severe, prolonged functional impairment, such as an infant hospitalized with a diagnosis of respiratory syncytial virus)**

Time (Face-to-Face versus Unit/Floor)

Face-to-face time is the amount of time the office or outpatient care provider spends with the patient and/or family. **Unit/floor time** is the amount of time the provider spends at the patient's bedside and managing the patient's care on the unit or floor (e.g., documenting orders for diagnostic tests or reviewing test results). Unit/floor time applies to inpatient hospital care, hospital observation care, initial and follow-up inpatient hospital consultations, and nursing facility services.

As mentioned previously, although the key components of history, examination, and medical decision making usually determine the E/M code, visits consisting predominantly of counseling and/or coordination of care are the exception. When the physician spends more than 50 percent of the encounter providing counseling and/or coordination of care, it is considered dominant and can be considered a key factor in selecting a particular E/M code. The extent of counseling must be documented in the patient's chart to support the E/M code selected.

EXAMPLE: Anne Sider is seen by Dr. Cyrix in the office for her three-month check-up. (She has chronic hypertension controlled by diet and exercise.) During the visit, Dr. Cyrix notes that the patient seems distracted and stressed, and he asks her about these symptoms. Anne starts to cry and spends 10 minutes telling Dr. Cyrix that her "life is falling apart" and that she wakes up in the middle of the night with a pounding heart, feeling as though she's going to die. Dr. Cyrix spends the next 45 minutes (of the 70-minute visit) counseling Anne about these symptoms. He determines that Anne is suffering from panic attacks, so he prescribes a medication and contacts ABC Counseling Associates to arrange an appointment for mental health counseling. In this example, a routine three-month check-up (for which code 99212 or 99213 would be selected) evolves into a higher-level service (for which code 99215 can be reported). The provider must carefully document all aspects of this visit, which includes the recheck for hypertension, provision of counseling, coordination of care provided, and length of time spent face-to-face with the patient. The coder should report an ICD-10-CM disease code from category Z71, in addition to the hypertension disease code, when counseling and/or coordination of care dominates the patient encounter *and is documented by the provider.*

To properly bill an E/M level of service for an encounter based on time, the provider must provide counseling and/or coordination of care *in the presence of the patient* and document the following:

- **Total length of time of the encounter**
- **Length of time spent coordinating care and/or counseling patient**
- **Issues discussed**
- **Relevant history, exam, and medical decision making (if performed)**

Evaluation and Management Subsections

The E/M section (99201–99499) contains notes unique to each category and subcategory (Table 7-2). *Remember to review notes before assigning an E/M code.* (For a complete list of categories and subcategories, refer to Table 1, Categories and Subcategories of Service, in the E/M Services Guidelines of your CPT coding manual.) (CPT refers to E/M subsections and categories as categories and subcategories, respectively.)

EXAMPLE: Lucy Moreno is a 45-year-old established female patient who was seen in the office on April 22 for a problem focused history and examination as follow-up for her diagnosis of lower back pain. Patient states that she is having great difficulty managing her pain, and she says that she realizes part of the problem is that she needs to lose 50 pounds. A variety of weight-loss management options were discussed with the patient, including an appropriate exercise program; and she is scheduled to return in one month for recheck. Today's visit was 30 minutes in length, more than half of which was spent discussing weight-loss management. Report code 99214.

TABLE 7-2 Evaluation and Management subsections (categories)

SUBSECTION (CATEGORY)	DESCRIPTION
Office or Other Outpatient Services	E/M services provided in a physician's office, a hospital outpatient department, or another ambulatory care facility (e.g., stand-alone ambulatory care center). Before assigning an E/M level of service code from this category, make sure you apply the definition of *new* and *established* patient. **NOTE:** Code 99211 is commonly thought of as a "nurse visit" because it is typically reported when ancillary personnel provide E/M services. However, the code can be reported when the E/M service is rendered by any other provider (e.g., nurse practitioner, physician assistant, or physician). • CMS "incident to" guidelines apply when the 99211 level of service is provided by ancillary personnel (e.g., nurse). Guidelines state that the physician must be physically present in the office suite when the service is provided. • Documentation of a 99211 level of service includes a chief complaint and a description of the service provided. Because the presenting problem is of minimal severity, documentation of a history and examination is not required. • When prescription drug management services are provided during an office visit, report a minimum level 3 E/M code. Reporting a level 1 or 2 E/M code is considered undercoding.
Hospital Observation Services	**Observation services** are furnished in a hospital outpatient setting, and the patient is considered an outpatient. Services include use of a bed and at least periodic monitoring by a hospital's nursing or other staff that is reasonable and necessary to evaluate an outpatient's condition or determine the need for possible admission to the hospital as an inpatient. Observation services are reimbursed only when ordered by a physician (or another individual authorized by state licensure law and hospital staff bylaws to admit patients to the hospital or to order outpatient tests). Medicare requires the physician to order an inpatient admission if the duration of observation care is expected to be 48 hours or more. (Other payers require an inpatient admission order if the duration of observation care is expected to be 24 hours or more.) Subcategories include: • Observation care discharge services • Initial observation care • Subsequent observation care
Hospital Inpatient Services	E/M services provided to hospital inpatients, including partial hospitalization services; they are indicated when the patient's condition requires services and/or procedures that cannot be performed in any other POS without putting the patient at risk. Subcategories include: • **Initial hospital care** (covers first inpatient encounter) • **Subsequent hospital care** (includes review of chart for changes in patient's condition, results of diagnostic studies, and/or reassessment of patient's condition since performance of last assessment) • **Observation or inpatient care services** (assigned only if the patient is admitted to and discharged from observation/inpatient status on the same day) • **Hospital discharge services** (include final examination of the patient, discussion of hospital stay with patient/caregiver, instructions for continued care, and preparation of discharge records, prescriptions, and referral forms) **NOTE:** A *hospital inpatient* is someone who is admitted and discharged and has a length of stay (LOS) of one or more days. **Partial hospitalization** is a short-term, intensive treatment program where individuals who are experiencing an acute episode of an illness (e.g., geriatric, psychiatric, or rehabilitative) can receive medically supervised treatment during a significant number of daytime or nighttime hours. This type of program is an alternative to 24-hour inpatient hospitalization and allows the patients to maintain their everyday life without the disruption associated with an inpatient hospital stay.

(continues)

TABLE 7-2 (continued)

<table>
<tr><th>SUBSECTION (CATEGORY)</th><th>DESCRIPTION</th></tr>
<tr><td>Consultations</td><td>A consultation is an examination of a patient by a health care provider, usually a specialist, for the purpose of advising the referring or attending physician in the evaluation and/or management of a specific problem with a known diagnosis. Consultants may initiate diagnostic and/or therapeutic services as necessary during the consultation.

CODING TIP:
Do not confuse a consultation with a referral, which occurs when a patient reports that another provider “referred” the patient to the provider. Because the referring provider did not schedule the appointment or document a request for the referral, the referral is not a consultation.

Preoperative clearance occurs when a surgeon requests a specialist or other physician (e.g., general practitioner) to examine a patient and provide an opinion about whether the patient can withstand the expected risks of a specific surgery. If the referring surgeon documents a written request for preoperative clearance, this service is considered a consultation, even when provided by the patient’s primary care physician.

NOTE: In 2010, CMS and the federal Office of Workers’ Compensation Board eliminated reporting of CPT consultation codes. Providers are required to report codes from the “Office or Other Outpatient Services” or “Inpatient Hospital Services” subsections of CPT. For the hospital inpatient setting, the admitting or attending physician will attach modifier -A1 (Principal Physician of Record) to the initial visit code. This will distinguish the admitting or attending physician’s service from those who provide consultation services.

The OIG reported that most consultation services reported to Medicare in 2001 were inappropriate, and subsequent education efforts to improve reporting failed to produce desired results. Other third-party payers will likely adopt the elimination of CPT’s consultation codes. It is unknown whether the AMA will eliminate the “Consultations” subsection from a future revision of CPT.

EXAMPLE: On May 1, Mary Smith is seen in the hospital’s emergency department (ED) and receives level 4 E/M services from Dr. Axel (ED physician) for complaints of severe shortness of breath, chest pain radiating down the left arm, back pain, and extreme anxiety. The patient is admitted to the hospital, and Dr. Rodney (attending physician) provides level 3 initial hospital care. Dr. Axel reports code 99284, and Dr. Rodney reports code 99222-A1.</td></tr>
<tr><td>Emergency Department Services</td><td>Emergency department services are provided in a hospital, which is open 24 hours for the purpose of providing unscheduled episodic services to patients who require immediate medical attention.<ul><li>While ED physicians employed by the facility usually provide ED services, any physician who provides services to a patient registered in the ED may report the ED services codes. The physician does not have to be assigned to the hospital’s ED.</li><li>When services provided in the ED are determined not to be an actual emergency, ED services codes (99281-99288) are still reportable if ED services were provided. Typically, the hospital reports a lower-level ED services code for nonemergency conditions.</li><li>If a physician provides emergency services to a patient in the office, it is not appropriate to assign codes from the Emergency Department Services category of E/M. If the patient’s primary care provider asks the patient to meet him in the hospital’s ED as an alternative to the physician’s office and the patient is not registered as a patient in the ED, the physician should report a code from the Office or Other Outpatient Services category of E/M. ED services codes are reported only if the patient receives services in the hospital’s ED.</li></ul></td></tr>
</table>

(continues)

TABLE 7-2 (continued)

<table>
<tr><th>SUBSECTION (CATEGORY)</th><th>DESCRIPTION</th></tr>
<tr><td>Emergency Department Services (continued)</td><td>

NOTE: Instead of developing national emergency department coding guidelines, CMS instructed hospitals to develop internal guidelines for reporting emergency department E/M visits. The guidelines must reflect hospital resources (not physician resources) used in providing the service. CMS reviews hospital claims to evaluate patterns associated with reporting different levels of emergency department E/M codes to:

- Verify appropriate billing of Medicare services
- Ensure that hospitals follow their own internally developed guidelines

NOTE:

- A medical emergency is the sudden and unexpected onset of a medical condition, or the acute exacerbation of a chronic condition that is threatening to life, limb, or sight. It requires immediate medical treatment or manifests painful symptomatology requiring immediate palliative effort to relieve suffering.
- A maternity emergency is a sudden unexpected medical complication that puts the mother or fetus at risk.
- A psychiatric inpatient admission is an emergency situation in which, based on a psychiatric evaluation performed by a physician (or another qualified mental health care professional with hospital admission authority), the patient is at immediate risk of serious harm to self or others as a result of a mental disorder, and requires immediate continuous skilled observation at the acute level of care.

CODING TIP:

Code 99288 (Other Emergency Services) is reported when the physician is in two-way communication contact with ambulance or rescue crew personnel located outside the hospital.

</td></tr>
<tr><td>Critical Care Services</td><td>

Critical care is the direct delivery of medical care by a physician to a patient who is critically ill or injured. **Critical care services** are reported when a physician directly delivers medical care for a critically ill or critically injured patient. Critical care services can be provided on multiple days even if no changes are made to the treatment rendered to the patient, as long as the patient's condition requires the direct delivery of critical care services by the provider. *The provider should document the total time spent delivering critical care services.*

NOTE: It is not necessary for a patient to be admitted to a critical care unit or an intensive care unit to receive critical care services. Patients can receive critical care services in the hospital emergency department, medical/surgical unit, and so on.

EXAMPLE: Dr. Smith delivers critical care services to his patient on June 15th from 8:00 to 9:00 a.m., 10:30 to 10:45 a.m., and 3:00 to 3:45 p.m. To assign codes to this case, total the minutes of critical care services directly delivered by the provider. (Refer to the table located in the CPT coding manual's Critical Care Services category to select the codes.) Report codes 99291 and 99292 × 2.

CODING TIP:

When critical care service codes are reported in addition to another E/M service code (e.g., ED care and initial hospital care), add modifier -25 to the E/M service code to report it as a separately identified service provided to the patient. Remember! Critical care services are reported based on the total time the physician spends in constant attendance, and the time need not be continuous.

</td></tr>
</table>

(continues)

TABLE 7-2 (continued)

SUBSECTION (CATEGORY)	DESCRIPTION
Nursing Facility Services	**Nursing facility services** are provided at a nursing facility (NF), skilled nursing facility (SNF), intermediate care facility/mentally handicapped (ICF), long-term care facility (LTCF), or psychiatric residential treatment facility. NFs provide convalescent, rehabilitative, or long-term care for patients. A comprehensive assessment must be completed on each patient upon admission, and then annually (unless the patient's condition requires more frequent assessments). Subcategories include: • Initial nursing facility care • Subsequent nursing facility care • Nursing facility discharge services • Other nursing facility services **NOTE:** The **comprehensive assessment** documents the patient's functional capacity, identification of potential problems, and nursing plan to enhance (or at least maintain) the patient's physical and psychosocial functions. The assessments are written when the patient is admitted or readmitted to the facility or when a reassessment is necessary because of a substantial change in the patient's status. The nursing facility assessment code (99318) is reported when the nursing facility patient's attending physician conducts an annual assessment.
Domiciliary, Rest Home (e.g., Boarding Home), or Custodial Care Services	These services are provided to residents of a facility that offers room, board, and other personal assistance services, usually on a long-term basis. Medical services (e.g., 24-hour nursing care) are *not* provided to residents.
Domiciliary, Rest Home (e.g., Assisted Living Facility), or Home Care Plan Oversight Services	**Care plan oversight services** cover the physician's time supervising a complex and multidisciplinary care treatment program for a specific patient who is under the care of a domiciliary or rest home, or who resides at home.
Home Services	**Home services** are provided to individuals in their place of residence to promote, maintain, or restore health and/or to minimize the effects of disability and illness, including terminal illness.
Prolonged Services	Physicians' services involving patient contact that are considered beyond the usual service in either an inpatient or outpatient setting may be reported as **prolonged services**. Subcategories include: • Prolonged service with direct patient contact (**Direct patient contact** refers to face-to-face patient contact on an inpatient or outpatient basis, and these codes are reported in addition to other E/M services provided.) • Prolonged service without direct patient contact (**Without direct patient contact** refers to *non*-face-to-face time spent by the provider on an inpatient or outpatient basis *and occurring before and/or after direct patient care*.) • **Standby services** cover providers who spend prolonged periods of time without direct patient contact, until physician's services are required
Case Management Services	**Case management services** include "processes in which a physician is responsible for direct care of a patient, and for coordinating and controlling access to or initiating and/or supervising other health care services needed by the patient." Subcategories include: • Anticoagulant management • Medical team conferences

(continues)

TABLE 7-2 (continued)

SUBSECTION (CATEGORY)	DESCRIPTION
Care Plan Oversight Services	These services cover the physician's time spent supervising a complex and multidisciplinary care treatment program for a specific patient who is under the care of a home health agency, hospice, or nursing facility. These codes are classified separately from other E/M codes when the physician is involved in direct patient examinations. The billing covers a 30-day period, and only one physician in a group practice may bill for this service in any given 30-day period.

Preventive Medicine Services	**Preventive medicine services** include routine examinations or risk management counseling for children and adults who exhibit no overt signs or symptoms of a disorder while presenting to the medical office for a preventive medical physical. Such services are also called *wellness visits*. Discussion of risk factors such as diet and exercise counseling, family problems, substance abuse counseling, and injury prevention are an integral part of preventive medicine.
	Care must be taken to select the proper code according to the age of the patient and the patient's status (new or established). Subcategories include:
	● New patient
	● Established patient
	● Counseling risk factor reduction and behavior change intervention
	  • Preventive medicine, individual counseling
	  • Behavior change interventions, individual
	  • Preventive medicine, group counseling
	● Other preventive medicine services

Non-Face-to-Face Physician Services	Non-face-to-face physician services include telephone services and online medical evaluation.
Special Evaluation and Management Services	Provided for establishment of baseline information prior to basic life or disability insurance certificates being issued and for examination of a patient with a work-related or medical disability problem. During special evaluation and management services, the examining provider does *not* assume active management of the patient's health problems.
Newborn Care Services	**Newborn care** includes services provided to newborns in a variety of health care settings (e.g., hospital, birthing center, and home birth). Also included is delivery/birthing room attendance and resuscitation services.
Inpatient Neonatal Intensive Care Services and Pediatric and Neonatal Critical Care Services	These services are provided to critically ill neonates and infants by a physician. A neonate is a newborn, up to 28 days old. An infant is a very young child, up to one year old. (The same definitions for critical care services codes apply to adult, child, and neonate.) Subcategories include: ● Pediatric critical care patient transport ● Inpatient neonatal and pediatric critical care ● Initial and continuing intensive care services Pediatric patient transport includes the physical attendance and direct face-to-face care provided by a physician during the interfacility transport of a critically ill or critically injured patient, aged 24 months or less.
Complex Chronic Care Coordination Services	Patient-centered management and support services provided to patients who reside at home or in a domiciliary, rest home, or assisted living facility.

(continues)

TABLE 7-2 (continued)

SUBSECTION (CATEGORY)	DESCRIPTION
Transitional Care Management Services	Services provided to established patients whose medical and/or psychosocial problems require moderate or high complexity medical decision making during transitions in care from one setting (e.g., acute care hospital) to the patient's community setting (e.g., home).
Other Evaluation and Management Services	Code 99499 is assigned when the E/M service provided is not described in any other listed E/M codes. The use of modifiers with this code is not appropriate. In addition, a special report must be submitted with the CMS-1500 claim.

EXERCISE 7-5

Evaluation and Management Section

Instructions: Review each statement, and use your CPT coding manual to assign the appropriate level-of-service E/M section code.

1. Home visit, problem focused, established patient ________
2. ED service, new patient, low complexity ________
3. Hospital care, new patient, initial, high complexity ________
4. Hospital care, subsequent, detailed ________
5. ED care, problem focused, counseling 15 minutes ________
6. Patient requested consultation, new patient, moderate complexity ________
7. Office consultation, high complexity, established patient ________
8. Follow-up consultation, office, problem focused counseling 15 minutes, encounter was 25 minutes ________
9. Follow-up consultation, inpatient, detailed, 35 minutes ________
10. Blood pressure check by nurse (established patient) ________
11. New patient, routine preventive medicine, age 11. Risk factor discussion, 20 minutes. ________
12. Critical care, 1.5 hours ________
13. Nursing facility visit, subsequent visit, expanded problem focused H&PE ________
14. Medical team conference, 50 minutes, nurse practitioner and discharge planner ________
15. Follow-up visit, ICU patient, stable, expanded problem focused H&PE ________
16. Resuscitation of newborn in delivery room ________
17. Telephone E/M service by physician to established patient, 10 minutes ________
18. Custodial care, established patient, detailed H&PE, high complexity ________
19. Pediatrician on standby, high-risk birth, 65 minutes ________
20. Heart risk factor education, group counseling, asymptomatic attendees, 65 minutes ________

ANESTHESIA SECTION

Anesthesia services are associated with the administration of analgesia and/or anesthesia as provided by an anesthesiologist (physician) or certified registered nurse anesthetist (CRNA). Services include the administration of local, regional, epidural, general anesthesia, monitored anesthesia care (MAC), and/or the administration of anxiolytics (drug that relieves anxiety) or amnesia-inducing medications. The patient's physiological parameters are also monitored during the administration of local or peripheral block anesthesia with sedation (when medically necessary), and other supportive services are provided when the anesthesiologist deems them necessary during any procedure.

NOTE: Monitored anesthesia care (MAC) is the provision of local or regional anesthetic services with certain conscious-altering drugs when provided by a physician, anesthesiologist, or medically directed CRNA. MAC requires sufficiently monitoring the patient to anticipate the potential need for administration of general anesthesia, and it requires continuous evaluation of vital physiologic functions as well as recognition and treatment of adverse changes.

Anesthesia care requires the preoperative evaluation of a patient, which includes documenting the history and physical examination to minimize the risk of adverse reactions, planning alternative approaches to administering anesthesia, and answering all questions asked by the patient about the anesthesia procedure. The anesthesiologist or CRNA is responsible for the patient's post-anesthesia recovery period until patient care is assumed by the surgeon or another physician; this occurs when the patient is discharged from the post-anesthesia recovery area.

Assigning Anesthesia Codes

Anesthesia codes describe a general anatomic area or service that is associated with a number of surgical procedures, often from multiple CPT sections.

- **Codes 00100–01860 are reported for anesthesia services during surgical procedures.**
- **Codes 01916–01936 are reported for anesthesia services during radiology procedures.**
- **CPT codes 01951–01953 are reported for anesthesia services during burn excisions or debridement.**
- **CPT codes 01958–01969 are reported for anethesia services during obstetric procedures.**
- **CPT codes 01990–01999 are reported for anesthesia services during other procedures.**

NOTE: Interventional radiology uses image guidance to perform minimally invasive procedures (e.g., angiography, angioplasty).

A one-to-one correspondence for Anesthesia to Surgery section codes does not exist, and one Anesthesia section code is often reported for many different surgical procedures that share similar anesthesia requirements. Anesthesia section guidelines also include four codes (99100–99140) that are located in the Medicine section, which are used to report qualifying circumstances for anesthesia.

Separate or Multiple Procedures

When multiple surgical procedures are performed during the single administration of anesthesia, report the anesthesia code that represents the most complex procedure performed. The time reported is the combined total for all procedures performed. (Content about anesthesia time reporting begins on page 267.)

Qualifying Circumstances for Anesthesia

When anesthesia services are provided during situations or circumstances that make anesthesia administration more difficult, report a **qualifying circumstances** code from the CPT Medicine section (in addition to the Anesthesia section code). Difficult circumstances depend on factors such as extraordinary condition of patient, notable operative conditions, or unusual risk factors. These code(s) are reported in addition to the Anesthesia section code(s). Qualifying circumstances codes include:

- **99100 (Anesthesia for patient of extreme age, younger than one year and older than 70)**
- **99116 (Anesthesia complicated by utilization of total body hypothermia)**
- **99135 (Anesthesia complicated by utilization of controlled hypotension)**
- **99140 (Anesthesia complicated by emergency conditions [specify]) (An *emergency condition* results when a delay in treatment of the patient would lead to a significant increase in threat to life or body part.)**

> **EXAMPLE:** A 92-year-old female patient with hypertension received general anesthesia services from a CRNA, who was monitored by an anesthesiologist, during total left hip arthroplasty. Report codes 01214-P2-QY and 99100.

Anesthesia Modifiers

All anesthesia services require the following types of modifiers to be reviewed for assignment with reported Anesthesia section codes:

- **Physical status modifiers**
- **HCPCS level II modifiers**
- **CPT modifiers**

Physical Status Modifiers

A **physical status modifier** is added to each reported Anesthesia section code to indicate the patient's condition at the time anesthesia was administered. The modifier also serves to identify the complexity of services provided. (The physical status modifier is determined by the anesthesiologist or CRNA and is documented as such in the patient record.) Physical status modifiers are represented by the letter "P" followed by a single digit, from 1 to 6, as indicated below:

- **-P1 (normal healthy patient; e.g., no biochemical, organic, physiologic, psychiatric disturbance)**
- **-P2 (patient with mild systemic disease; e.g., anemia, chronic asthma, chronic bronchitis, diabetes mellitus, essential hypertension, heart disease that only slightly limits physical activity, obesity)**
- **-P3 (patient with moderate systemic disease; e.g., angina pectoris, chronic pulmonary disease that limits activity, history of prior myocardial infarction, heart disease that limits activity, poorly controlled essential hypertension, morbid obesity, diabetes mellitus, type I and/or with vascular complications)**
- **-P4 (patient with severe systemic disease that is a constant threat to life; e.g., advanced pulmonary/renal/hepatic dysfunction, congestive heart failure, persistent angina pectoris, unstable/rest angina)**
- **-P5 (moribund patient who is not expected to survive without the operation; e.g., abdominal aortic aneurysm)**
- **-P6 (declared brain-dead patient whose organs are being removed for donor purposes)**

EXAMPLE: An anesthesiologist provided general anesthesia services to a 65-year-old male with mild systemic disease who underwent total knee replacement. Report code 01402-P2.

HCPCS Level II Anesthesia Modifiers

When applicable, the following HCPCS level II modifiers are added to reported Anesthesia section codes:

- **-AA (anesthesia services performed personally by anesthesiologist)**
- **-AD (medically supervised by a physician for more than four concurrent procedures)**
- **-G8 (monitored anesthesia care [MAC] for deep complex, complicated, or markedly invasive surgical procedure)**
- **-G9 (monitored anesthesia care [MAC] for patient who has a history of severe cardiopulmonary condition)**
- **-QK (medical direction of two, three, or four concurrent anesthetic procedures involving qualified individuals)**
- **-QS (monitored anesthesia care service)**
- **-QX (CRNA service, with medical direction by physician)**
- **-QY (medical direction of one Certified Registered Nurse Anesthetist [CRNA] by an anesthesiologist)**
- **-QZ (CRNA service, without medical direction by physician)**

NOTE: Report modifier -G8 with CPT codes 00100, 00400, 00160, 00300, 00532, 00920 only. Do not report modifier -G8 with modifier -QS.

EXAMPLE: A CRNA provided general anesthesia services to an otherwise healthy patient who underwent a vaginal hysterectomy due to uterine fibroids. The CRNA received medical direction from an anesthesiologist. Report code 00944-P1-QY.

CPT Modifiers

The following CPT modifiers should be reviewed to determine whether they should be added to the reported Anesthesia section codes:

- **-23 (unusual anesthesia) (When a patient's circumstances warrant the administration of general or regional anesthesia instead of the usual local anesthesia, add modifier -23 to the Anesthesia section code [e.g., extremely apprehensive patients, mentally handicapped individuals, patients who have a physical condition, such as spasticity or tremors])**
- **-53 (discontinued procedure)**
- **-59 (distinct procedural service)**
- **-74 (discontinued outpatient hospital/ambulatory surgery center procedure after anesthesia administration)**
- **-99 (multiple modifiers)**

EXAMPLE: An anesthesiologist provided general anesthesia services to a 49-year-old male patient with chronic obstructive pulmonary disease who underwent extracorporeal shock wave lithotripsy, with water bath. The patient was extremely anxious about the procedure, which normally does not require general anesthesia. Report code 00872-P2-23-AA.

Anesthesia Time Reporting

NOTE: Anesthesia time is calculated as the continuous actual presence of the anesthesiologist or CRNA during the administration of anesthesia. Anesthesia time begins when the anesthesiologist or CRNA begins to prepare the patient for anesthesia care in the operating room or equivalent area and ends when the anesthesiologist or CRNA is no longer in personal attendance.

When reporting Anesthesia section codes, be sure to report the time units in Block 24G of the CMS-1500. (*Anesthesia time units* are based on the total anesthesia time, and they are reported as one unit for each 15 minutes [or fraction thereof] of anesthesia time. For example, 45 minutes of anesthesia time equals three anesthesia time units. The number 3 is entered in Block 24G of the CMS-1500 claim.) Reimbursement for anesthesia services is based on the reported time units, which represents the continuous actual presence of the anesthesiologist or CRNA during the administration of anesthesia. Anesthesia time starts when the anesthesiologist or CRNA begins to prepare the patient for anesthesia care in the operating room or equivalent area (e.g., patient's room) and ends when the anesthesiologist or CRNA is no longer in personal attendance (e.g., patient is released for postoperative supervision by the surgeon).

When calculating anesthesia time units, do *not* include:

- Examination and evaluation of the patient by the anesthesiologist or CRNA prior to administration of anesthesia (e.g., reviewing patient records prior to the administration of anesthesia). (If surgery is canceled, report an appropriate code from the CPT E/M section. Usually, a consultation code is reported.)
- Nonmonitored interval time (e.g., period of time when patient does not require monitored anesthesia care, period of time during which anesthesiologist or CRNA leaves operating room to assist with another procedure)
- Recovery room time. (The anesthesiologist or CRNA is responsible for monitoring the patient in the recovery room as part of the anesthesia service provided.)
- Routine postoperative evaluation by the anesthesiologist or CRNA. (When postoperative evaluation and management services are significant, separately identifiable services, such as postoperative pain management services or extensive unrelated ventilator management, report an appropriate code from the CPT E/M section. In addition, the management of epidural or subarachnoid medication administration is reported with CPT code 01996 because it is separately payable on dates of service subsequent to surgery *but not on the date of surgery*.)

EXAMPLE: A patient undergoes cataract extraction surgery, which requires monitored anesthesia care by the CRNA. At 9:45 a.m., the CRNA administered a sedative and then performed a retrobulbar injection to administer regional block anesthesia. From 10:00 a.m. until 10:30 a.m., the patient did not require monitored anesthesia care. The CRNA began monitored anesthesia care again at 10:30 a.m. during the cataract extraction procedure, and monitored anesthesia care ended at 10:45 a.m. The patient was admitted to the recovery room at 10:45 a.m. for monitoring by the recovery room nurse; the patient was released from the recovery room to the surgeon for postoperative care at 11:30 a.m.

Carefully read the procedure outlined in the operative report. Sometimes the discriminating factor between one code and another will be the surgical approach or type of procedure documented.

The total time calculated for monitored anesthesia care is 30 minutes, or 2 time units. (Total time calculated does not include the 30 minutes of nonmonitored interval time [9:00–9:30 a.m.] or the 45 minutes of recovery room time [10:45–11:30 a.m.].)

EXERCISE 7-6

Anesthesia Section

Instructions: Review each statement, and use your CPT coding manual to assign the appropriate Anesthesia section code, including CPT and HCPCS level II modifiers.

1. Anesthesiologist provided anesthesia services to a 77-year-old female patient with hypertension who received a corneal transplant. The patient has a history of prior stroke.
   ____
2. Anesthesiologist provided anesthesia services to a 50-year-old diabetic patient with coronary arteriosclerosis who underwent direct coronary artery bypass grafting.
   ____
3. Anesthesiologist provided anesthesia services for hernia repair in the lower abdomen of an otherwise healthy 9-month-old infant.
   ____
4. CRNA provided anesthesia services under physician direction during an extensive procedure on the cervical spine of an otherwise healthy patient.
   ____
5. CRNA provided anesthesia services to a morbidly obese female patient who underwent repair of malunion, humerus.
   ____

SURGERY SECTION

The Surgery section contains subsections that are organized by body system. Each subsection is subdivided into categories by specific organ or anatomic site. Some categories are further subdivided by procedure subcategories in the following order:

- **Incision**
- **Excision**
- **Introduction or Removal**
- **Repair, Endoscopy**
- **Revision or Reconstruction**
- **Destruction**
- **Grafts**
- **Suture**
- **Other Procedures**

To code surgeries properly, three questions must be asked:

1. What body system was involved?
2. What anatomic site was involved?
3. What type of procedure was performed?

Carefully read the procedure outlined in the operative report. Sometimes the discriminating factor between one code and another will be the surgical approach or type of procedure documented.

EXAMPLE 1: Surgical approach

57540	Excision of cervical stump, abdominal approach;
57545	with pelvic floor repair
57550	Excision of cervical stump, vaginal approach;
57556	with repair of enterocele

When reporting the code number for the excision of cervical stump, code 57540 would be reported for an abdominal approach, and code 57550 would be reported for a vaginal approach.

EXAMPLE 2: Type of procedure

11600	Excision, malignant lesion including margins, trunk, arms, or legs; excised diameter 0.5 cm or less
17260	Destruction, malignant lesion (e.g, laser surgery, electrosurgery, cryosurgery, chemosurgery, surgical curettement), trunk, arms, or legs; lesion diameter 0.5 cm or less

When reporting the code for removal of a 0.5 cm malignant lesion of the arm, code 11600 would be reported for a surgical excision, and code 17260 would be reported for a destruction procedure (e.g., laser ablation).

Surgical Package

The **surgical package** (or **global surgery**) includes a variety of services provided by a surgeon (Figure 7-9), including:

- **Surgical procedure performed**
- **Local infiltration, metacarpal/metatarsal/digital block, or topical anesthesia**
- **One related Evaluation and Management (E/M) encounter on the date immediately prior to *or* on the date of the procedure (including history and physical)**
- **Immediate postoperative care, including dictating operative notes, talking with family and other physicians, documenting postoperative orders, and evaluating the patient in the postanesthesia recovery area**
- **Typical postoperative follow-up care, including pain management, suture removal, dressing changes, local incisional care, removal of operative packs/cutaneous sutures/staples/lines/wires/tubes/drains/casts/splints (however, casting supplies can usually be billed separately)**

The **global period** is the number of days associated with the surgical package (or global surgery) and is designated by the payer as 0, 10, or 90 days. During

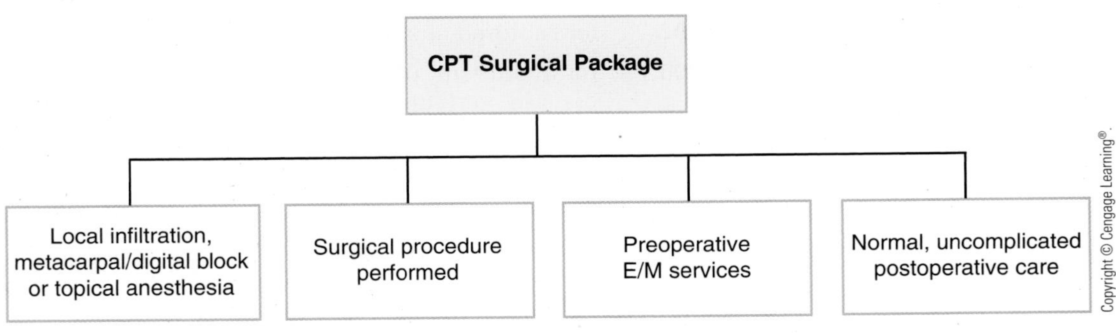

FIGURE 7-9 Components of the surgical package.

the global period, all postoperative services are included in the procedure code; postoperative services (except services provided to treat complications) cannot be separately reported and billed. (Obtain global period information from each payer.) The following designations are also associated with the surgical package:

NOTE: The surgical package does *not* apply to treatment of patients for surgical complications. Procedures and/or services provided to treat complications are reported in addition to the surgical package CPT code.

- **MMM (global period policy does not apply)**
- **XXX (global period policy does not apply)**
- **YYY (payer-determined global period)**
- **ZZZ (procedure/service is related to another service; falls within the global period of another service)**

When different physicians in a same-specialty group practice participate in the pre- and postoperative care of a patient, the physician who performs the surgery reports the CPT code, patient care is shared by the physicians, and reimbursement is distributed within the group. Do *not* bill separately for services included in the global package, even though a different physician in a same-specialty group practice provides the service.

Coders must be aware that *unbundling* is not allowed; unbundling means assigning multiple codes to procedures/services when just one comprehensive code *should be* reported. Examples of procedures that are bundled (included) with the surgical package code include:

- **Local infiltration of medication**
- **Closure of surgically created wounds**
- **Minor debridement**
- **Exploration of operative area**
- **Fulguration of bleeding points**
- **Application of dressings**
- **Application of splints with musculoskeletal procedures**

NOTE: Another indication that a code might not be reportable with another code is the presence of the parenthetical note (separate procedure) that indicates the procedure is included as part of a more comprehensive code.

Read the descriptions of surgical procedures carefully, and remember that the main clause—the narrative to the left of the semicolon (;)—of an indented surgical description is stated only once in a series of related intraoperative procedures. The complexity of the related intraoperative procedures increases as you proceed through the listings of indented code descriptions. *Always report the comprehensive code rather than codes for individual components of a surgery.*

EXAMPLE:

35001 Direct repair of aneurysm, pseudoaneurysm, or excision (partial or total) and graft insertion, with or without patch graft; for aneurysm and associated occlusive disease, carotid, subclavian artery, by neck incision

35002 for ruptured aneurysm, carotid, subclavian artery, by neck incision

35005 for aneurysm, pseudoaneurysm, and associated occlusive disease, vertebral artery

35011 for aneurysm and associated occlusive disease, axillary-brachial artery, by arm incision

35013 for ruptured aneurysm, axillary-brachial artery, by arm incision

Only one code from this series of five codes is assigned *if the procedures performed and reported were rendered during the same operative session.* Note the increasing complexity of procedures as code numbers increase within a series.

Exceptions to reporting one combination code occur either when the code number is marked by a + symbol (add-on code) or when a parenthetical note indicates that a code should be reported in addition to the primary code. The following statements appear in CPT code descriptions or as parenthetical notes when it is appropriate to report additional codes:

- **List separately in addition to code for primary procedure.**
- **Use . . . in conjunction with . . .**
- **Each additional . . .**
- **Each separate/additional . . .**

EXERCISE 7-7

Working with the Surgical Package

Instructions: Review each statement, and use your CPT coding manual to assign the appropriate Surgery section code.

1. Incision and drainage (I&D), finger abscess ________
2. Percutaneous I&D, abscess, appendix ________
3. Therapeutic agent injection, L-5 paravertebral nerve, with image guidance ________
4. Laparoscopic cholecystectomy with cholangiography ________
5. Flexible esophagoscopy with removal of foreign body and radiologic supervision and interpretation (S&I) ________

Separate Procedure

The parenthetical note, **separate procedure**, follows a code description identifying procedures that are an integral part of another procedure or service. In addition, a *separate procedure* code is reported if the procedure or service is performed independently of the comprehensive procedure or service or is unrelated to or distinct from another procedure or service performed at the same time. The *separate procedure* code is *not* reported if the procedure or service performed is included in the description of another reported code.

EXAMPLE: The patient undergoes only a cystourethroscopy (passage of an endoscope through the urethra to visualize the urinary bladder). CPT codes for cystourethroscopy include:

52000 Cystourethroscopy (separate procedure)

52001 Cystourethroscopy, with irrigation and evacuation of multiple obstructing clots

52005 Cystourethroscopy, with ureteral catheterization, with or without irrigation, instillation, or ureteropyelography, exclusive of radiologic service;

52007 with brush biopsy of ureter and/or renal pelvis

52010 Cystourethroscopy, with ejaculatory duct catheterization, with or without irrigation, instillation, or duct radiography, exclusive of radiologic service

Report code 52000, because only the cystourethroscopy was performed. A code from 52001–52010 would be reported *only* if the operative report documented additional procedures that were included in the code description.

The placement of the phrase "separate procedure" is critical to correct coding. When it appears after the semicolon, it applies to that specific code.

EXAMPLE:

38100 Splenectomy; total (separate procedure)

The phrase that appears to the left of the semicolon applies to all indented code descriptions.

EXAMPLE:

10080 Incision and drainage of pilonidal cyst; simple
10081 complicated

Multiple Surgical Procedures

Great care must be taken when billing **multiple surgical procedures** (two or more surgeries performed during the same operative session). The major surgical procedure (the procedure reimbursed at the highest level) should be reported first on the claim, and the lesser surgeries listed on the claim in descending order of expense. Modifier -51 is added to the CPT number for each lesser surgical procedure that does not have the symbol ⊘ or **+** in front of the code. (Appendix E in the CPT coding manual provides a complete list of modifier -51 exemptions.)

The ranking into major and minor procedures is done to accommodate the fact that most insurance companies will reduce the fee for the second surgery by 50 percent of the regular fee and for the third, fourth, and so on, by 50 to 75 percent. If a lesser procedure is listed first, it may be paid at 100 percent and the major or most expensive surgery reduced by 50 to 75 percent, resulting in a lower payment for the combined surgeries. Insurance companies reason that when multiple surgical procedures are performed during the same operative session, they share the same pre- and postoperative session; therefore, the fee is reduced because the pre- and postoperative portions are covered in the full payment for the major procedure.

BILLING TIP:

Computerized practices must be sure that *multiple surgeries performed during the same operative session are entered into the computer in the proper order* to ensure that they will print correctly on the computer-generated claim.

RADIOLOGY SECTION

The Radiology section includes subsections (Table 7-3) for diagnostic radiology (imaging), diagnostic ultrasound, radiation oncology, and nuclear medicine. These subsections are further subdivided into anatomic categories.

The number of **radiologic views** (studies taken from different angles) described in the report or on the encounter form determines the code selection for many diagnostic radiologic procedures. The term *complete* in the discussion of views

EXERCISE 7-8

Coding Separate and Multiple Procedures

Instructions: Review each statement, and use your CPT coding manual to assign the appropriate Surgery section code.

1. Diagnostic arthroscopy, right wrist, with synovial biopsy ________
2. Simple vaginal mucosal biopsy ________
3. Diagnostic nasal endoscopy, bilateral, and facial chemical peel ________
4. Diagnostic thoracoscopy, lungs and pleural space, with right lung biopsy ________
5. Needle biopsy of testis ________
6. Total abdominal hysterectomy with removal of ovaries and anterior colporrhaphy ________
7. Laparoscopic appendectomy and lumbar hernia repair ________
8. Biopsy of larynx (indirect) via laryngoscopy and laryngoplasty ________
9. Excision of chest wall lesion with removal of ribs and plastic reconstruction ________
10. Debridement of extensive eczematous skin involving 5 percent of body surface ________

is a reference to the number of views required for a full study of a designated body part. Carefully review code descriptions to understand how many views constitute a "complete study" for a specific type of radiologic procedure.

EXAMPLE:

70120 Radiologic examination, mastoids; less than three views per side

70130 complete, minimum of three views per side

TABLE 7-3 Radiology subsections

SUBSECTION (CATEGORY)	DESCRIPTION
Diagnostic Radiology (Diagnostic Imaging)	Codes for noninvasive (noninterventional) and invasive (interventional) diagnostic and therapeutic procedures, in addition to CT, MRI, and magnetic resonance angiography (MRA). These diagnostic procedures can be as simple as a routine chest x-ray or as complex as a carotid angiography, which requires selective vascular catheterization. To code diagnostic radiology procedures accurately, identify the following: • Anatomic site • Type of procedure • Number of views • Laterality of the procedure (e.g., unilateral or bilateral) • Use of contrast media **EXAMPLE 1:** Patient underwent complete x-ray of facial bones. Report code 70150. **EXAMPLE 2:** Patient underwent CT of the cervical spine. Report code 72125. (There is no mention of "contrast material" in this example.)

(continues)

TABLE 7-3 (continued)

SUBSECTION (CATEGORY)	DESCRIPTION
Diagnostic Ultrasound	Use of high-frequency sound waves (e.g., mechanical oscillations) to produce an image. Codes are organized according to anatomic site; procedures are often performed as follow-up studies for inconclusive diagnostic radiology procedures, intraoperatively (e.g., during endoscopic procedures), and as guidance for biopsies, cyst localization, invasive procedures, paracentesis, pericardiocentesis, placement of radiation therapy fields, and thoracentesis. **EXAMPLE:** Patient underwent ultrasound of the spinal canal and contents. Report code 76800.
Radiologic Guidance	Performed during a procedure to visualize access to an anatomic site; contains four headings: fluoroscopic guidance, computed tomography guidance, magnetic resonance guidance, and other radiologic guidance. **EXAMPLE:** Patient underwent fluoroscopic guidance for needle placement prior to biopsy procedure. Report code 77002.
Breast, Mammography	Radiological examination of the soft tissue and internal structures of the breast. Screening mammography is performed when a patient presents *without* signs and symptoms of breast disease (e.g., routine annual screening for early detection of unsuspected breast cancer). Diagnostic mammography includes an assessment of suspected disease (e.g., suspicious mass is palpated on physical examination) and is reported when an abnormality is found or suspected. **EXAMPLE:** Patient underwent bilateral screening mammography, which was reviewed and interpreted by the radiologist. Report code 77057.
Bone/Joint Studies	CPT codes 77071–77084 classify bone and joint studies. **EXAMPLE:** Female patient, age 51, underwent complete osseous survey. Report code 77075.
Radiation Oncology	Uses high-energy ionizing radiation to treat malignant neoplasms and certain nonmalignant conditions. Therapeutic modalities (methods) directed at malignant and benign lesions include brachytherapy, hyperthermia, stereotactic radiation, and teletherapy. **EXAMPLE:** Radiation oncologist provided intermediate therapeutic radiology treatment planning services to a 49-year-old male patient. Report code 77262.
Nuclear Medicine	Use of radioactive elements (e.g., radionuclides and radioisotopes) for diagnostic imaging (e.g., scan) and radiopharmaceutical therapy (destroys diseased tissue, such as a malignant neoplasm). The isotope emits gamma rays as it deteriorates, which enables the radiologist to visualize internal abnormalities (e.g., tumors). The images created by the contrast media (radioactive element) are detected by a gamma camera. Nuclear medicine codes do not include the provision of radium, which means that the nuclear medicine report must be reviewed to identify the diagnostic or therapeutic radiopharmaceutical provided. Then an appropriate HCPCS level II code is reported for the radiopharmaceutical administered. (The injection of the radionuclide is included as part of the procedure, and a separate injection code is not reported.) Common diagnostic nuclear medicine procedures include bone scans, cardiac scans (e.g., thallium scan and MUGA), renal scans, thyroid scans, and hepatobiliary scans (e.g., HIDA scans). Therapeutic nuclear medicine procedures are used to treat diseases such as chronic leukemia, hyperthyroidism, and thyroid cancer. **EXAMPLE:** Patient underwent particulate pulmonary perfusion imaging, which required venous injection of 10 mc of radioactive Technetium Tc-99m macroaggregated albumin. Report codes 78580, 36000, and A9540.

Complete Procedure

Do not confuse use of the term *complete* in the code description with its use in a parenthetical note. When the word *complete* is found in the code description, one code is reported to "completely" describe the procedure performed.

> **EXAMPLE:** For a clavicle x-ray, one code is reported (by the radiologist).
>
> **73000** Radiologic examination; clavicle, complete

When the word *complete* is found in a parenthetical note below a code, it may be necessary to report more than one code to "completely" describe the procedure performed. In this case, when each component is performed by the same physician (e.g., radiologist), that physician reports all codes. However, when multiple physicians (e.g., radiologist and surgeon or other physician) perform each component of the procedure, each physician reports an appropriate code.

> **EXAMPLE:** For a cervical/thoracic myelography via cervical contrast injection procedure, two codes are reported to completely describe the procedure performed.
>
> - Code 72270 is reported for the myelography procedure with radiological supervision and interpretation.
> - The parenthetical note located below code 72270 indicates that codes 61055, 62284, and 72270 should be reviewed to determine whether additional code(s) need to be reported. Thus, code 61055 is reported for the cervical contrast injection procedure.
>
> **72270** Myelography, two or more regions (e.g, lumbar/thoracic, cervical/thoracic, lumbar/cervical, lumbar/thoracic/cervical), radiological supervision and interpretation
>
> (For complete myelography of entire spinal canal, see 61055, 62284, 72270.)
>
> **61055** Cisternal or lateral cervical (C1-C2) puncture; with injection of medication or other substance for diagnosis or treatment (e.g., C1-C2)
>
> (For radiological supervision and interpretation, see Radiology.)
>
> **62284** Injection procedure for myelography and/or computed tomography, spinal (other than C1-C2 and posterior fossa)
>
> (For injection procedure at C1-C2, see 61055.)
>
> (For radiological supervision and interpretation, see Radiology.)

Professional versus Technical Component

Another consideration in Radiology section coding involves determining which physician is responsible for the professional and technical components of an examination.

- **The professional component of a radiologic examination covers the supervision of the procedure and the interpretation and documentation of a report describing the examination and its findings.**
- **The technical component of an examination covers the use of the equipment, supplies provided, and employment of the radiologic technicians.**

When the examination takes place in a clinic or private office that owns the equipment, and professional services are performed by a physician employed by the clinic or private office, both professional and technical components are billed on the same claim. If, however, the equipment and supplies are owned by a hospital or other corporation and the radiologist performs only the professional component of the examination, two separate billings are generated: one by the physician for the professional component and one by the hospital for the technical component.

When two separate billings are required, the professional component is billed by adding the modifier -26 to the CPT code number. (HCPCS level II modifier -TC, Technical Component, is added to the Radiology section code reported by the provider who performs the radiologic procedure.)

An exception to this rule is when the code description restricts the use of the code to "supervision and interpretation."

CODING TIP:

Report code 76140 when physician consultation is requested to review x-rays produced in another facility and the consultant generates a written report.

Special care must be taken when coding interventional diagnostic procedures that involve injection of contrast media, local anesthesia, or needle localization of a mass. CPT assigns two separate codes to these interventional procedures: a 70000 series Supervision and Interpretation section code, and a Surgery section code. This is done because these procedures may be performed by two physicians, each billing separately. If only one physician is involved, the claim should still include both codes.

EXAMPLE:

75710 Angiography, extremity, unilateral, radiologic supervision and interpretation

EXERCISE 7-9

Radiology Coding

Instructions: Review each statement, and use your CPT coding manual to assign the appropriate Radiology section code.

1. GI series (x-ray), with small bowel and air studies, without KUB ________
2. Chest x-ray, frontal & left lateral ________
3. Cervical spine x-ray, complete, with flexion and extension (spine) ________
4. X-ray pelvis, AP ________
5. Abdomen, flat plate, AP (x-ray) ________
6. BE, colon, with air (x-ray colon) ________
7. Postoperative radiologic supervision and interpretation of cholangiography by radiologist ________
8. Bilateral screening mammography ________
9. Retrograde pyelography with KUB (Urography) via cystourethroscopy ________
10. SPECT liver imaging ________

PATHOLOGY AND LABORATORY SECTION

This section is organized according to the type of pathology or laboratory procedure performed (Table 7-4). Within each subsection, procedures are listed alphabetically.

NOTE: The Clinical Laboratory Improvement Act (CLIA) established quality standards for all laboratory testing to ensure the accuracy, reliability, and timeliness of patient test results regardless of where the test was performed.

TABLE 7-4 Pathology and Laboratory subsections

SUBSECTION(S)	DESCRIPTION
Organ or Disease-Oriented Panels	Single code numbers are assigned to **organ- or disease-oriented panels**, which consist of a series of blood chemistry studies routinely ordered by providers at the same time for the purpose of investigating a specific organ or disorder. The composition of the panel is very specific, and no substitutions are allowed. **EXAMPLE:** Report code 80061 when the physician orders a "lipid panel." The following tests are performed on the blood sample: cholesterol, serum, total (82465); lipoprotein, direct measurement, high-density cholesterol (HDL cholesterol) (83718); and triglycerides (84478). **NOTE:** Refer to "Blood Tests, Panels" in the CPT index to locate organ- or disease-oriented panel codes.
Drug Testing	Codes for laboratory tests that determine whether a drug or a specific classification of drugs is present in blood or urine. **EXAMPLE:** Report code 80102 to confirm the presence of a single drug class (e.g., cocaine and metabolites).
Therapeutic Drug Assays	Codes for laboratory tests performed to determine how much of a specific prescribed drug is in the patient's blood. **EXAMPLE:** Report code 80162 when the physician orders a therapeutic drug assay to determine the patient's digoxin level. (Patient digoxin levels are routinely monitored for therapeutic purposes.)
Evocative/Suppression Testing	Codes for laboratory tests when substances are injected for the purpose of confirming or ruling out specific disorders. **EXAMPLE:** Report 80400 when the physician orders an adrenocorticotropic hormone (ACTH) stimulation panel to determine whether the patient has adrenal insufficiency.
Consultations (Clinical Pathology)	Codes reported by pathologists who perform clinical pathology consultations requested by attending physicians when a test result requires additional medical interpretive judgment: • For face-to-face patient contact, assign codes 99241-99255. • For consultative review of tissue specimen slides, report codes 88321-88325. • For pathologic consultation during surgery, report codes 88329-88332. **EXAMPLE:** Report code 80500 when a pathologist reviews the patient's lab tests for a limited diagnosis problem and prepares a report.

(continues)

TABLE 7-4 (continued)

SUBSECTION(S)	DESCRIPTION
• Urinalysis • Molecular Pathology • Multianalyte Assays with Algorithmic Analyses • Chemistry • Hematology and Coagulation • Immunology	Codes for laboratory tests performed on body fluids (e.g., urine, blood). Tests are ordered by physicians and performed by technologists under the supervision of a physician (usually a pathologist). **EXAMPLE:** Report code 81025 for a urine pregnancy test.
Transfusion Medicine	Codes reported for procedures and products (e.g., fresh frozen plasma) associated with blood transfusions. **EXAMPLE:** Report code 86900 for ABO blood typing. (ABO refers to the four blood groups: A, B, AB, and O.) **NOTE:** Codes for transfusion of blood and blood components (e.g., packed cells) are located in the CPT Surgery section (36430-36460, except for "leukocyte transfusion," which is assigned code 86950).
Microbiology	Codes reported for bacteriology, mycology, parasitology, and virology procedures. **EXAMPLE:** Report code 87086 for a urine culture that tests for bacteria.
Anatomic Pathology	Codes reported for postmortem examination (also called *autopsy* or *necropsy*). **EXAMPLE:** Report code 88027 for a gross and microscopic autopsy performed on an adult, which includes the central nervous system (CNS, brain, and spinal cord).
• Cytopathology • Cytogenetic Studies	Codes reported for pathology screening tests (cytopathology) and for tissue cultures and chromosome analysis studies (cytogenetic studies). **EXAMPLE:** Report code 88125 for forensic cytopathology of a sperm specimen.
Surgical Pathology	Codes reported when specimen(s) removed during surgery require pathologic diagnosis. Codes are organized according to level. (Refer to codes 88300-88309 for descriptions of levels and associated procedures.) **EXAMPLE 1:** Report code 88304 for a gallbladder specimen removed during cholecystectomy. This subsection also includes additional codes reported for histochemistry, consultation and report on referred material, and so on. **EXAMPLE 2:** Report code 88321 when a pathologist reviews tissue slides prepared elsewhere to render a second opinion regarding pathologic diagnosis.
In Vivo (e.g., Transcutaneous) Laboratory Procedures	Reported for *noninvasive* laboratory procedures that are performed transcutaneously, which means the measurement is obtained by pressing a laboratory instrument against the patient's skin or using visible and near-infrared optical bands to obtain a laboratory value. **EXAMPLE:** Report code 88720 for transcutaneous total bilirubin testing.
Other Procedures	Codes reported for miscellaneous laboratory procedures, not elsewhere classified in the CPT Pathology and Laboratory section. **EXAMPLE:** Report code 89230 for sweat collection by iontophoresis.

(continues)

TABLE 7-4 (continued)

SUBSECTION(S)	DESCRIPTION
Reproductive Medicine Procedures	Codes reported for oocyte or embryo procedures are coded for the female partner, and codes involving sperm alone are coded for the male partner. They address the coding needs in the evolving reproductive medicine area. (The AMA states that, alternatively, *all* "reproductive medicine procedures" codes may also be applied to the female.) **EXAMPLE:** Report code 89259 for cryopreservation of sperm. (Patient can be male or female because a male could have donated the sperm for purchase by a female who will arrange to have it stored.)

EXERCISE 7-10

Pathology and Laboratory Coding

Instructions: Review each statement, and use your CPT coding manual to assign the appropriate Pathology and Laboratory section code.

1. Hepatic function panel ________
2. Acute hepatitis panel ________
3. TB skin test, PPD ________
4. UA (Urinalysis) by dip stick with micro, automated ________
5. WBC count with Diff, automated ________
6. Stool for occult blood ________
7. Wet mount, vaginal smear ________
8. Glucose/blood sugar, quantitative ________
9. Sedimentation rate, automated ________
10. Throat culture, bacterial ________
11. Urine sensitivity, disk ________
12. Microhematocrit blood count, spun ________
13. Monospot test ________
14. Strep test, group A, rapid ________
15. One-year storage of sperm ________

MEDICINE SECTION

The CPT Medicine section classifies *noninvasive* or *minimally invasive* diagnostic and therapeutic procedures and services.

- ***Noninvasive*** **procedures require no surgical incision or excision, and they are not open procedures.**
- ***Minimally invasive*** **procedures include percutaneous access.**

Medicine is the last section of CPT, and its codes are reported with those from all other sections. The Medicine section includes subsections (Table 7-5) that:

- **Classify procedures and procedure-oriented services (e.g., immunizations)**
- **Apply to various medical specialties (e.g., gastroenterology, ophthalmology, otorhinolaryngology, and psychiatry)**
- **Apply to different types of health care providers (e.g., physical therapists and occupational therapists)**

TABLE 7-5 Medicine subsections

MEDICINE SUBSECTION	DESCRIPTION
Immune Globulins, Serum or Recombinant Products	Reported for the *supply of the immune globulin product,* including broad-spectrum and anti-infective immune globulins, antitoxins, and other isoantibodies. (The *administration* of an immune globulin is reported separately with a code from the Therapeutic, Prophylactic, and Diagnostic Injections and Infusions subsection.)
Immunization Administration for Vaccines/Toxoids	Reported for intradermal, intramuscular, percutaneous, and subcutaneous injections and intranasal/oral administration.
Vaccines, Toxoids	Reported to identify the vaccine/toxoid product only, in addition to immunization administration for vaccines/toxoids codes.
Psychiatry	Reported by psychiatrists, psychologists, and licensed clinical social workers for provision of psychiatric diagnostic services, psychotherapy, and other services to an individual, family, or group.
Biofeedback	Reported for biofeedback services, including review of the patient's history; preparation of biofeedback equipment; placement of electrodes on patient; reading and interpreting responses; monitoring the patient; and control of muscle responses. (*Biofeedback* is a technique that trains the patient to gain some control over autonomic body functions.)
Dialysis	Reported for hemodialysis, miscellaneous dialysis procedures, end-stage renal disease services, and other dialysis procedures.
Gastroenterology	Reported for gastric physiology services and other procedures.
Ophthalmology	Reported for general ophthalmological services, special ophthalmological services, contact lens services, and spectacle services (including prosthesis for aphakia).
Special Otorhinolaryngologic Services	Reported for vestibular function tests without electrical recording, vestibular function tests with recording (e.g., ENG, PENG), audiologic function tests, evaluative and therapeutic services, special diagnostic procedures, and other procedures. When otorhinolaryngologic services are performed during provision of an Evaluation and Management (E/M) service, do *not* code and report the component procedures separately (e.g., otoscopy, tuning fork test, whispered voice test). However, any special otorhinolaryngologic services (92502–92700) that are *not* typically included in a comprehensive otorhinolaryngologic evaluation *are* reported separately.
Cardiovascular	Reported for therapeutic services and procedures, cardiography, cardiovascular monitoring services, implantable and wearable cardiac device evaluations, echocardiography, cardiac catheterization, intracardiac electrophysiological procedures/studies, peripheral arterial disease rehabilitation, noninvasive physiologic studies and procedures, and other vascular studies.

(continues)

TABLE 7-5 (continued)

MEDICINE SUBSECTION	DESCRIPTION
Noninvasive Vascular Diagnostic Studies	Reported for cerebrovascular arterial studies, extremity arterial and venous studies, visceral and penile vascular studies, extremity arterial-venous studies, and noninvasive vascular diagnostic studies (e.g., a duplex scan). (A *duplex scan* is a noninvasive test that is performed to evaluate a vessel's blood flow.)
Pulmonary	Reported for ventilator management and pulmonary diagnostic testing and therapies.
Allergy and Clinical Immunology	Reported for allergy testing, ingestion challenge testing, and allergen immunotherapy.
Endocrinology	Reported for subcutaneous placement of a sensor for continual glucose (blood sugar) monitoring (up to 72 hours) and physician interpretation/report of results of monitoring.
Neurology and Neuromuscular Procedures	Reported for neurology and neuromuscular diagnostic and therapeutic services that do *not* require surgical procedures (e.g., sleep testing, EEG, EMG, motion analysis).
Medical Genetics and Genetic Counseling Services	Reported for counseling of an individual, couple, or family to investigate family genetic history and assess risks associated with genetic defects in offspring.
Central Nervous System Assessments/Tests	Reported for tests performed to measure cognitive function of the central nervous system (e.g., cognitive processes, visual motor responses, and abstractive abilities).
Health and Behavior Assessment/Intervention	Reported for tests that identify the psychological, behavioral, emotional, cognitive, and social elements involved in the prevention, treatment, or management of physical health problems.
Hydration, Therapeutic, Prophylactic, Diagnostic Injections and Infusions, and Chemotherapy and Other Highly Complex Drug or Highly Complex Biologic Agent Administration	Reported for hydration IV infusion that consists of prepackaged fluid and electrolytes (but no drugs or other substances). Codes include the administration of local anesthesia; intravenous (IV) insertion; access to catheter, IV, or port; routine syringe, tubing, and other supplies; and flushing performed upon completion of infusion. Reported for the administration of chemotherapeutic agents by multiple routes (e.g., intravenously). These codes can be separately billed when an E/M service is rendered on the same day as the chemotherapy administration. *Chemotherapy* is the treatment of cancer with drugs that serve to destroy cancer cells or slow the growth of cancer cells, keep cancer from spreading to other parts of the body, and prevent recurrence of the cancer. Chemotherapy administered in addition to other cancer treatments, such as surgery and/or radiation therapy, is called *adjuvant chemotherapy*.
Photodynamic Therapy	Reported for the administration of light therapy to destroy premalignant/malignant lesions or ablate abnormal tissue using photosensitive drugs.
Special Dermatological Procedures	Reported for dermatology procedures that are typically performed in addition to an appropriate E/M service code.
Physical Medicine and Rehabilitation	Reported for services that focus on the prevention, diagnosis, and treatment of disorders of the musculoskeletal, cardiovascular, and pulmonary systems that may produce temporary or permanent impairment.
Medical Nutrition Therapy	Reported for medical nutrition therapy, which is classified according to type of assessment, individual or group therapy, and length of time.
Acupuncture	Reported for acupuncture treatment, which is classified as face-to-face patient contact for 15-minute increments of time and according to whether electrical stimulation was provided.
Osteopathic Manipulative Treatment	Reported for manual treatment applied by a physician to eliminate or alleviate somatic dysfunction and related disorders.

(continues)

TABLE 7-5 (continued)

MEDICINE SUBSECTION	DESCRIPTION
Chiropractic Manipulative Treatment	Reported for manual treatments that influence joint and neurophysiological function.
Education and Training for Patient Self-Management	Reported for education and training services provided for patient self-management by a qualified, nonphysician health care professional using a standard curriculum. The codes are classified according to the length of time spent face-to-face with one or more patients.
Non-Face-to-Face Nonphysician Services	Reported for telephone services provided to an established patient, parent, or guardian; and online medical evaluation.
Special Services, Procedures, and Reports	Reported for special services, procedures, and reports (e.g., handling/conveyance of specimen for transfer from physician's office to laboratory).
Qualifying Circumstances for Anesthesia	Reported for situations that complicate the administration of anesthesia services (e.g., emergencies, extreme age, hypotension, and hypothermia). Codes 99100–99140 are add-on codes, which means they are reported in addition to a code from the Anesthesia section.
Moderate (Conscious) Sedation	Reported for a drug-induced depression of consciousness that requires no interventions to maintain airway patency or ventilation. • CPT specifies that moderate (conscious) sedation does not include minimal sedation (e.g., anxiolysis), deep sedation, or monitored anesthesia care (MAC). • Subsection notes specify services that are included in moderate (conscious) sedation codes (e.g., IV access, administration of agent, and monitoring oxygen saturation). • The surgeon who performs a surgical procedure usually provides moderate (conscious) sedation services. When another physician (e.g., an anesthesiologist) provides general anesthesia, regional anesthesia, or monitored anesthesia care, that other physician reports an appropriate Anesthesia section code and its modifiers. • CPT's Appendix G lists procedures that include moderate (conscious) sedation as an inherent part of the procedure, identified with the bull's-eye symbol (⊙).
Other Services and Procedures	Reported for services and procedures that cannot be classified in another subsection of the Medicine section (e.g., anogenital examination, vision screening by nonoptical professionals, hypothermia treatment).
Home Health Procedures/ Services	Reported by nonphysician health care professionals who perform procedures and provide services to the patient in the patient's residence (the patient's home, assisted living facility, or group home).
Medication Therapy Management Services	Reported when a pharmacist provides individual management of medication therapy with assessment and intervention.

EXERCISE 7-11

Medicine Section

Instructions: Review each statement, and use your CPT coding manual to assign the appropriate Medicine section code, including modifiers.

1. Cardiac catheterization, right side only, with moderate (conscious) sedation, IV, and measurements of oxygen saturation and cardiac output ________

(continues)

2. Routine ECG, tracing only ________
3. Spirometry ________
4. CPR, in office ________
5. Diagnostic psychiatric examination ________
6. Influenza vaccine, age 18 months ________
7. Whirlpool and paraffin bath therapy ________
8. WAIS-R and MMPI psychological tests and report, 1 hour ________
9. Office services on emergency basis ________
10. Physical therapy evaluation (and management) ________

NATIONAL CORRECT CODING INITIATIVE

The Centers for Medicare and Medicaid Services (CMS) implemented the National Correct Coding Initiative (NCCI) to promote national correct coding methodologies and to control the improper assignment of codes that result in inappropriate reimbursement of Medicare Part B claims. (Table 7-6 contains a list of NCCI terms, definitions, and examples.)

There are more than 140,000 **NCCI code pairs** (or **NCCI edit pairs**) that cannot be reported on the same claim for the same date of service. CMS contracts with Correct Coding Solutions, LLC, to develop, maintain, and refine the NCCI and

TABLE 7-6 NCCI terms and definitions

TERM	DEFINITION
CCI edits	Pairs of CPT and/or HCPCS level II codes that are not separately payable except under certain circumstances (e.g., reporting an appropriate modifier). CCI edits apply to services billed by the same provider for the same beneficiary on the same date of service. **EXAMPLE:** The surgeon intends to perform a laparoscopic cholecystectomy, but upon visualization of an inflamed and huge gallbladder, the procedure is changed to an open cholecystectomy. If CPT codes for open cholecystectomy and laparoscopic cholecystectomy are reported, NCCI edits result in a claims denial. (When a laparoscopic procedure becomes an open procedure, report only the open procedure code.)
Column 1 code	The major procedure or service when reported with another code. The column 1 code represents greater work, effort, and time than to the other code reported. Thus, higher payments are associated with column 1 codes (previously called *comprehensive codes*). **EXAMPLE:** The patient undergoes a superficial biopsy and a deep biopsy of the same site (during the same operative episode). If CPT codes for both deep and superficial biopsies are reported, NCCI edits result in claims denial. (When both deep and superficial biopsies are performed on the same site, report only the deep biopsy code.)
Column 2 code (continues)	The lesser procedure or service when reported with another code. The *column 2 code* is part of another major procedure or service, and it is often represented by a lower work relative value unit (RVU) under the Medicare Physician Fee Schedule. Thus, lower payments are associated with column 2 codes (previously called *component codes*).

(continues)

TABLE 7-6 (continued)

TERM	DEFINITION
Column 2 code (continued)	**EXAMPLE:** The patient undergoes a superficial biopsy and a deep superficial biopsy of the same site (during the same operative episode). Documentation supports the significant work, effort, and time associated with each biopsy, which means codes for both the superficial biopsy and deep biopsy are reported. An NCCI-associated modifier (e.g., -59, Distinct Procedural Service) is added to the superficial biopsy code so that NCCI edits do not result in claims denial. (Reduced payment for the superficial biopsy might be processed by the payer after review of documentation.)
NCCI column 1/ column 2 edits (Figure 7-10A)	Code pairs (or edit pairs), where one code is a component (column 1) of the more comprehensive code (column 2), and only the comprehensive code is paid. (When clinical circumstances justify reporting both codes, add an NCCI-associated modifier to either code of the code pair so that payment of both codes might be allowed.)
	Refer to Figure 7-10A, which contains a sample listing of column 1/column 2 codes. Column 1 code 10021 is reported on the CMS-1500 claim, and none of the codes from column 2 are reported on the same claim (unless an NCCI-associated modifier is attached to one of the codes and supporting documentation justifies reporting multiple codes).
Mutually exclusive codes	Procedures or services that could not reasonably be performed during the same operative episode, by the same provider, on the same beneficiary. **EXAMPLE:** A claim contains CPT codes for cystourethroscopy, with internal urethrotomy of a female *and that of a male*. NCCI edits will result in claims denial.
NCCI mutually exclusive codes (Figure 7-10B)	Code pairs (or edit pairs), where one of the procedures/services could not reasonably be performed with the other. (When clinical circumstances justify reporting both codes, add an NCCI-associated modifier to either code of the code pair so that payment of both codes might be allowed.) **EXAMPLE:** A claim contains CPT codes for initial inpatient E/M services and critical care E/M *services (with NCCI-associated modifier -59) for the same date of service*. Documentation supports initial inpatient E/M services provided at 3 a.m. on the day of admission (when the patient did not require critical care) and critical care services later that same day (when the patient did require critical care).

medically unlikely edits (MUEs) (discussed below), which are published by the National Technical Information Service (NTIS).

In 2007, CMS incorporated **medically unlikely edits (MUEs)** into the NCCI program, which are used to compare units of service (UOS) with CPT and HCPCS level II codes reported on claims and indicate the maximum number of UOS allowable by the same provider for the same beneficiary on the same date of service under most circumstances.

> **EXAMPLE:** Mary Jones underwent a cataract extraction in her left eye. The claim submitted by the provider contained a 3 in the units column of Block 24, which means the patient underwent cataract extraction surgery on three left eyes. The *medically unlikely edit* process rejected the claim (because the patient has just one left eye). If 1 had been entered in the units column of Block 24, the claim would have passed the *medically unlikely edit* and payment would have been processed.

NATIONAL CORRECT CODING INITIATIVE COLUMN 1 / COLUMN 2 EDITS					
Column 1	**Column 2**	* = In existence prior to 1996	**Effective Date**	**Deletion Date** * = no data	**Modifier** 0 = not allowed 1 = allowed 9 = not applicable
10021	J2001		20040701	*	1
10021	19303		20020101	*	1
10021	36000		20021001	*	1
10021	36410		20021001	*	1
10021	37202		20021001	*	1
10021	62318		20021001	*	1
10021	62319		20021001	*	1
10021	64415		20021001	*	1
10021	64416		20030101	*	1
10021	64417		20021001	*	1

FIGURE 7-10A Sample NCCI column 1/column 2 code edits.

NATIONAL CORRECT CODING INITIATIVE MUTUALLY EXCLUSIVE EDITS					
Column 1	**Column 2**	* = In existence prior to 1996	**Effective Date**	**Deletion Date** * = no data	**Modifier** 0 = not allowed 1 = allowed 9 = not applicable
10060	11401		19960101	*	1
10060	11402		19960101	*	1
10060	11403		19960101	*	1
10060	11404		19960101	*	1
10060	11406		19960101	*	1

FIGURE 7-10B Sample NCCI mutually exclusive edits.

NCCI code edits (*or NCCI edit pairs*) (Table 7-7) are used to process Medicare Part B claims, and NCCI coding policies are based on the:

- **Analysis of standard medical and surgical practice**
- **Coding conventions included in CPT**
- **Coding guidelines developed by national medical specialty societies (e.g., CPT Advisory Committee, which contains representatives of major medical societies)**
- **Local and national coverage determinations**
- **Review of current coding practices**

The NCCI was initially developed for use by Medicare administrative contractors (MACs) that process Medicare Part B claims for physician office services. NCCI edits (Table 7-7) were added to the outpatient code editor (OCE) in August 2000, and they are used by MACs to process Medicare Part B claims for

TABLE 7-7 Partial listing of National Correct Coding Initiative (NCCI) edits

NCCI EDIT	DESCRIPTION	DISPOSITION OF CLAIM
1	Invalid diagnosis code	Return to Provider
2	Diagnosis and age conflict	Return to Provider
3	Diagnosis and sex conflict	Return to Provider
4	Medicare secondary payer alert	Suspend
19	Mutually exclusive procedure that is not allowed by NCCI even if appropriate modifier is present	Line Item Rejection
20	Component of a comprehensive procedure that is not allowed by NCCI even if appropriate modifier is present	Line Item Rejection
39	Mutually exclusive procedure that would be allowed by NCCI if appropriate modifier were present	Line Item Rejection
40	Component of a comprehensive procedure that would be allowed by NCCI if appropriate modifier were present	Line Item Rejection

NOTE: OCE edits are packaged with commercial software, such as Optum's *EncoderPro.com Expert.*

outpatient hospital services. (Some OCE edits that apply to outpatient hospital services claims differ from comparable edits in the NCCI used to process physician office services claims.)

Carefully review parenthetical notes below CPT code descriptions to locate procedures that are separately reported (in addition to the major procedure performed). When reporting codes for outpatient hospital services and physician office services, be sure to use outpatient code editor (OCE) software or NCCI software, respectively, to identify bundled codes for procedures and services considered necessary to accomplish the major procedure. Bundled procedure codes are *not* separately coded or reported with the major procedure code. Reporting bundled procedure codes in addition to the major procedure code is characterized as unbundling (fraud). The OCE edits are packaged with commercial software, such as Optum's *EncoderPro.com Expert.* The NCCI edits are available at **www.cms.gov**. (The OCE and NCCI edits are available for purchase from the National Technical Information Service [NTIS] at **www.ntis.gov**.)

EXAMPLE: Code 67911 describes the "Correction of lid retraction." A parenthetical note below the code description advises that, if autogenous graft materials are used during the same operative session, tissue graft codes 20920, 20922, or 20926 are reported in addition to code 67911.

According to the Medicare Code Editor (MCE), *other procedures necessary to accomplish* the "correction of lid retraction" are included in code 67911, such as full-thickness graft placement (15260). Other such procedures are not separately coded and reported when performed during the same operative session as the "correction of lid retraction."

NOTE: Locate Medlearn articles that contain OCE updates by going to **www.cms.gov**, clicking on the Outreach and Education link, and clicking on the MLN Matters Articles link.

CMS POSTS CORRECT CODING INITIATIVE (CCI) EDITS ON INTERNET

(Permission to reuse in accordance with www.cms.gov Web site Content Reuse Policy.)

The Centers for Medicare & Medicaid Services (CMS) today make it easier for physicians and other providers to bill properly and be paid promptly for their services to people with Medicare coverage. CMS has posted on its website (**www.cms.gov**) the automated edits used to identify questionable claims and adjust payments to reflect what would have been paid if the claim had been filed correctly. The edits, known as the National Correct Coding Initiative (NCCI), identify pairs of services that normally should not be billed by the same physician for the same patient on the same day. The NCCI also promotes uniformity among the contractors that process Medicare claims in interpreting Medicare payment policies.

The posting of NCCI edits is the most recent in a series of steps CMS has taken to use the Internet creatively to reduce the regulatory burden on physicians and make it easier for them to work with Medicare to improve services to beneficiaries. CMS has also added a feature to its website that makes it possible for physicians to determine in advance what they will be paid for a particular service or range of services. The Medicare Physician Fee Schedule look-up provides both the unadjusted payment rates, as well as the payment rates by geographic location. While the NCCI is a cornerstone of efforts to ensure that Medicare and beneficiaries do not pay twice for the same service or for duplicative services, CMS believes physicians should have easy access to the edits used to identify incorrect claims. The NCCI includes two types of edits:

- Comprehensive/component edits (code pairs that should not be billed together because one service inherently includes the other)
- Mutually exclusive edits (code pairs that, for clinical reasons, are unlikely to be performed on the same patient on the same day; for example, two different types of testing that yield equivalent results)

CPT codes representing services denied based on NCCI edits may not be billed to Medicare beneficiaries. Since these denials are based on incorrect coding rather than medical necessity, the provider cannot submit an Advance Beneficiary Notice (ABN) to seek payment from a Medicare beneficiary. An Advance Beneficiary Notice (ABN) is a form completed and signed by a Medicare beneficiary each time a provider believes a normally covered service will not be covered *and* the provider wants to bill the beneficiary directly for the service. In addition, because the denials are based on incorrect coding (rather than a legislated Medicare benefit exclusion) the provider *cannot* seek payment from the beneficiary even if a Notice of Exclusions from Medicare Benefits (NEMB) was obtained.

A *Notice of Exclusions from Medicare Benefits (NEMB)* is a form completed and signed by a Medicare beneficiary before items, procedures, and services excluded from Medicare benefits are provided; alerts Medicare beneficiaries in advance that Medicare does not cover certain items and services because they do not meet the definition of a Medicare benefit or because they are specifically excluded by law; NEMB is completed when an ABN is not appropriate.

(continues)

(continued)

The NCCI edits, which are updated quarterly, were previously available to physicians and other providers on a paid subscription basis, but they are now available to anyone with a personal computer. The NCCI edits are posted as a spreadsheet that will allow users to sort by procedural code and effective date. A "find" feature will allow users to look for a specific code. The NCCI edit files are also indexed by procedural code ranges for easy navigation.

The new web page also includes links to documents that explain the edits, including the:

- Medicare Claims Processing Manual
- NCCI Edits Program Transmittals
- NCCI FAQs (frequently asked questions)
- NCCI Policy Manual for Part B MACs

Unbundling CPT Codes

Providers are responsible for reporting the CPT (and HCPCS level II) code that most comprehensively describes the services provided. NCCI edits determine the appropriateness of CPT code combinations for claims submitted to Medicare administrative contractors. NCCI edits are designed to detect unbundling, which involves reporting multiple codes for a service when a single comprehensive code should be assigned. The practice of unbundling occurs because:

- **Provider's coding staff unintentionally reports multiple codes based on misinterpreted coding guidelines.**
- **Reporting multiple codes is intentional and is done to maximize reimbursement.**

Unbundling occurs when one service is divided into its component parts, and a code for each component part is reported as if they were performed as separate services.

EXAMPLE: A 64-year-old female patient undergoes total abdominal hysterectomy with bilateral salpingectomy and oophorectomy. Review CPT Surgery section code descriptions for 58150, 58700, and 58720. Reporting codes 58700 and 58720 in addition to 58150 is considered unbundling. If all three codes are submitted on a claim, reimbursement for codes 58700 and 58720 would be disallowed (and the provider might be subject to allegations of fraud and abuse).

Unbundling occurs when a code for the separate surgical approach (e.g., laparotomy) is reported in addition to a code for the surgical procedure. Procedures performed to gain access to an area or organ system are not separately reported.

EXAMPLE: A 54-year-old female patient underwent excision of ileoanal reservoir with ileostomy, which required lysis of adhesions to gain access to the site of surgery. Review CPT Surgery section code descriptions for 45136 and 44005. Report CPT code 45136 only because code 44005 is considered a component part of the total procedure (45136). Reporting both codes would be considered unbundling.

SUMMARY

CPT codes are reported for services and procedures provided by home health care and hospice agencies, outpatient hospital departments, physicians who are employees of a health care facility, and physicians who see patients in their offices or clinics and in patients' homes. CPT organizes Category I procedures and services into six sections:

- Evaluation and Management (E/M) (99201–99499)
- Anesthesia (00100–01999, 99100–99140)
- Surgery (10021–69990)
- Radiology (70010–79999)
- Pathology and Laboratory (80048–89398)
- Medicine (90281–99199, 99500–99607)

CPT also contains Category II codes (supplemental tracking codes used for performance measurement in compliance with the PQRS) and Category III codes (temporary codes that allow for utilization tracking of emerging technology, procedures, and services).

The CPT index is organized by alphabetical main terms printed in boldface; appendices are located between the Medicine section and the index. CPT Category I codes are organized according to six sections that are subdivided into subsections, categories, and subcategories. Guidelines, notes, and descriptive qualifiers are also organized according to sections, subsections, categories, and subcategories. Two-digit modifiers are added to five-digit CPT codes to clarify services and procedures performed by providers.

The Centers for Medicare and Medicaid Services (CMS) implemented the *National Correct Coding Initiative (NCCI)* to promote national correct coding methodologies and to control the improper assignment of codes that result in inappropriate reimbursement of Medicare Part B claims. CMS has posted on its website **(www.cms.gov)** the automated edits used to identify questionable claims and adjust payments to reflect what would have been paid if the claim had been filed correctly.

INTERNET LINKS

- American Medical Association
  www.ama-assn.org
- E/M Documentation Guidelines
  Go to **www.cms.gov**, click on the Outreach and Education link, click on the MLN Educational Web Guides link, and click on the Documentation Guidelines for Evaluation and Management (E/M) Services link.
- Decision Health billing and reimbursement newsletters (free)
  http://ezines.decisionhealth.com
- Family Practice Management
  Go to **www.aafp.org**, click on Journals, and click on the Family Practice Management (FPM) link to view past and current issues in this helpful journal.
- Novitas Solutions
  www.novitas-solutions.com

STUDY CHECKLIST

- ☐ Read this textbook chapter and highlight key concepts.
- ☐ Create an index card for each key term.
- ☐ Access the chapter Internet links to learn more about concepts.

- ☐ Answer the chapter review questions, verifying answers with your instructor.
- ☐ Complete the Workbook chapter, verifying answers with your instructor.
- ☐ Form a study group with classmates to discuss chapter concepts in preparation for an exam.

REVIEW

EVALUATION AND MANAGEMENT SECTION

Refer to the CPT coding manual to answer each of the following items.

1. Which category is used to report services for patients seen in stand-alone ambulatory care centers? ________
2. Office or Other Outpatient Services is used to report services rendered by a physician to a patient in a hospital observation area. TRUE or FALSE. ________
3. Which category is used to report services provided to patients in a partial hospital setting? ________
4. What is the name of the service provided by a physician whose opinion is requested? ________
5. The service identified in question 4 must be requested by another physician (e.g., attending physician). TRUE or FALSE. ________
6. Consultations provided in a physician's office are reported using office or other outpatient services codes. TRUE or FALSE. ________
7. Only one initial consultation is to be reported by a consultant per hospital inpatient admission. TRUE or FALSE. ________
8. A consultant who participates in management of an inpatient after conducting an initial consultation will report services using codes from which subcategory? ________
9. Which modifier is reported for mandated services? ________
10. A distinction is made between new and established patients when reporting E/M emergency department services. TRUE or FALSE. ________
11. Which code would you assign to report for a physician who provides directed emergency care? ________
12. What is meant by the phrase *directed emergency care?* ________
13. Critical care services must be provided in a critical care unit area (e.g., ICU). TRUE or FALSE. ________
14. Which code(s) would be assigned to report 2 1/2 hours of critical care provided by the attending physician? ________
15. SNFs, ICFs, and LTCFs are classified in CPT as ________. ________
16. Which category would be used when reporting a physician's visit to a patient residing in a boarding home? ________
17. Services provided by a physician to patients in a private residence are reported using codes from which category? ________
18. Which code would be reported when a physician calls a patient about recent lab test results? ________
19. A physical examination was performed on an 18-year-old who is scheduled to attend college in the fall. Which code(s) would you assign? ________

20. Assign code(s) to well-baby care of a 9-month-old established patient that includes the administration of DTaP and oral polio vaccines. ____________

HINT:

You'll also need to refer to the Medicine section of CPT.

21. Assign a code for preventive medicine service to a 56-year-old established patient. ____________

22. Assign code(s) to a patient who was admitted to observation services on June 30 and also discharged from observation services on that date. ____________

23. Assign code(s) to a patient who received critical care services for a total of 210 minutes on July 15. On this date, the patient also underwent an inpatient comprehensive history and examination with medical decision making of high complexity. ____________

24. Identify the code to assign to a patient who underwent a medical disability evaluation by his own physician. ____________

In questions 25–29, identify the E/M category and subcategory you would use to code each of the following cases. The key components of history, examination, and medical decision making are identified in each case, and you are required to assign the correct code based on that information.

25. Dr. Jones is an internist who performed a hospital admission, examination, and initiation of treatment program for a 67-year-old male with uncomplicated pneumonia who requires IV antibiotic therapy. Dr. Jones completed a comprehensive history and examination; the medical decision making is of low complexity. Minimal patient counseling was provided. The patient's problem was of low severity.

    Identify the CPT category and subcategory ____________.

    Identify the appropriate CPT code ____________.

26. Dr. Smith completed an office consultation for management of systolic hypertension in a 70-year-old male scheduled for elective prostate resection. Dr. Smith conducted an expanded problem focused history and examination; medical decision making was straightforward. The patient's problem is of low severity. Dr. Smith spent 20 minutes counseling the patient.

    Identify the CPT category and subcategory ____________.

    Identify the appropriate CPT code ____________.

27. Dr. Choi conducted subsequent hospital care for the evaluation and management of a healthy newborn on the second day of inpatient stay.

    Identify the CPT category ____________.

    Identify the appropriate CPT code ____________.

28. Dr. Lange saw an established patient in the office for recent syncopal attacks. Comprehensive history and examination were performed. Medical decision making is of high complexity.

    Identify the CPT category and subcategory ____________.

    Identify the appropriate CPT code ____________.

29. Dr. Doolittle conducted a follow-up hospital visit for a 54-year-old patient, post myocardial infarction, who is out of the CCU but is now having frequent premature ventricular contractions on telemetry. Expanded problem focused interval history and examination were completed. Medical

decision making is of moderate complexity. Dr. Doolittle coordinated care with the patient's providers and discussed the case with the patient's immediate family.

Identify the CPT category and subcategory ______________________.

Identify the appropriate CPT code ______________________.

SURGERY SECTION

Use your CPT manual to assign procedure codes, adding appropriate modifier(s).

30. Percutaneous needle biopsy, mediastinum; assistant surgeon reporting ____________

31. Electrodesiccation, basal cell carcinoma (1 cm), face ____________

32. Complicated bilateral repair of recurrent inguinal hernia ____________

33. Biopsy of anorectal wall via proctosigmoidoscopy ____________

34. Mastectomy for gynecomastia, bilateral ____________

35. Open reduction, right tibia/fibula shaft fracture, with insertion of screws ____________

36. Excision, condylomata, penis ____________

37. Replacement of breast tissue expander with breast prosthesis (permanent) ____________

38. Closed reduction of closed fracture, clavicle ____________

39. Incision and drainage of infected bursa, wrist ____________

40. Cystourethroscopy with biopsy of urinary bladder ____________

41. Endoscopic right maxillary sinusotomy with partial polypectomy ____________

42. Insertion of nontunneled Hickman catheter (short-term) (age 70) ____________

43. Avulsion of four nail plates ____________

RADIOLOGY, PATHOLOGY AND LABORATORY, AND MEDICINE SECTIONS

Use your CPT manual to assign procedure and service codes, adding appropriate modifier(s).

44. Arthrography of the shoulder, supervision and interpretation ____________

45. Chest x-ray, frontal, single view (professional component only) ____________

46. Transabdominal ultrasound of pregnant uterus, first pregnancy (real time with image documentation), fetal and maternal evaluation, second trimester ____________

47. Application of radioactive needles (radioelement), intracavitary of uterus, intermediate ____________

48. Lipid panel blood test ____________

49. Drug screen for opiates (outside laboratory performed drug screen) ____________

50. Hemogram (manual) (complete CBC) ____________

51. Cervical cytopathology slides, manual screening under physician supervision ____________

52. Gross and microscopic examination of gallbladder ____________

53. Complete echocardiography, transthoracic (real-time with image documentation [2D] with M-mode recording) ____________

54. Mumps vaccine immunization ________

55. Intermittent positive pressure breathing of a newborn ________

56. Gait training, first 30 minutes ________

57. Medical psychoanalysis ________

58. Ultraviolet light is used to treat a skin disorder ________

59. Chemotherapy, IV infusion technique, 10 hours, requiring use of portable pump (including refill) ________

60. Combined right cardiac catheterization and retrograde left heart catheterization for congenital anomalies ________

CATEGORY II CODES

Use your CPT manual to assign procedure and service codes, adding appropriate modifier(s).

61. Initial prenatal care visit ________

62. Assessment of tobacco use ________

63. Recording of vital signs ________

64. Documentation and review of spirometry results ________

65. Inhaled bronchodilator prescribed for COPD patient ________

CATEGORY III CODES

Use your CPT manual to assign procedure and service codes, adding appropriate modifier(s).

66. Ligation, hemorrhoidal vascular bundle, including ultrasound guidance ________

67. Antiprothrombin antibody IgA test ________

68. Remote real-time interactive videoconferenced critical care, evaluation and management of critically ill patient, 45 minutes ________

69. Insertion of posterior spinous process distraction device, lumbar, single level ________

70. High dose rate electronic brachytherapy, two fractions ________

HCPCS Level II Coding

CHAPTER 8

CHAPTER OUTLINE

OBJECTIVES

Upon successful completion of this chapter, you should be able to:

1. Define key terms.
2. Describe the HCPCS levels.
3. Assign HCPCS level II codes and modifiers.
4. Identify claims to be submitted to Medicare administrative contractors according to HCPCS level II code number.
5. List situations in which both HCPCS levels I and II codes are assigned.

KEY TERMS

certificate of medical necessity (CMN)
durable medical equipment (DME)
durable medical equipment, prosthetics, orthotics, and supplies (DMEPOS)
durable medical equipment, prosthetics, orthotics, and supplies (DMEPOS) dealers
Medicare Pricing, Data Analysis and Coding (PDAC) Contractor
orthotics
prosthetics
transitional pass-through payments
Types of HCPCS level II codes:
- miscellaneous codes
- modifier
- permanent national codes
- temporary codes

INTRODUCTION

NOTE: HCPCS used to be called the HCFA Common Procedure Coding System when the Centers for Medicare and Medicaid Services (CMS) was titled the Health Care Financing Administration (HCFA). The change to Healthcare Common Procedure Coding System occurred in 2002 when CMS became the new name for HCFA.

This chapter presents the procedure/service coding reference developed by CMS, the *Healthcare Common Procedure Coding System* (HCPCS, pronounced "hick-picks"). HCPCS level II was introduced in 1983 after Medicare found that its payers used more than 100 different coding systems, making it difficult to analyze claims data. HCPCS furnishes health care providers and suppliers with a standardized language for reporting professional services, procedures, supplies, and equipment. Most state Medicaid programs and many commercial payers also use the HCPCS level II coding system.

OVERVIEW OF HCPCS

Two levels of codes are associated with HCPCS, commonly referred to as HCPCS level I and II codes:

- **HCPCS level I: *Current Procedural Terminology* (CPT)**
- **HCPCS level II: national codes**

NOTE: Effective December 31, 2003, HCPCS level III codes were no longer required. They had the same structure as level II codes, but were assigned by the local Medicare carriers (LMCs) who process Medicare claims. HCPCS level III codes began with the letters W, X, Y, or Z.

The majority of procedures and services are reported using CPT (HCPCS level I) codes. However, CPT does not describe durable medical equipment, prosthetics, orthotics, and supplies (DMEPOS), as well as certain other services reported on claims submitted for Medicare and some Medicaid patients. Therefore, the CMS developed HCPCS level II national codes to report DMEPOS and other services. (Medicare carriers previously developed HCPCS level III local codes, which were discontinued December 31, 2003. Medicare administrative contractors (MACs) replaced carriers, DMERCs, and fiscal intermediaries.

HCPCS Level I

HCPCS level I includes the five-digit CPT codes developed and published by the American Medical Association (AMA). The AMA is responsible for the annual update of this coding system and its two-digit modifiers. (CPT coding is covered in Chapter 7 of this textbook.)

HCPCS Level II

HCPCS level II (or HCPCS national codes) were created in 1983 to describe common medical services and supplies not classified in CPT. HCPCS level II national codes are five characters in length, and they begin with letters A–V, followed by four numbers. HCPCS level II codes identify services performed by physician and nonphysician providers (e.g., nurse practitioners and speech therapists), ambulance companies, and durable medical equipment (DME) companies (called durable medical equipment, prosthetics, orthotics, and supplies [DMEPOS] dealers). **Orthotics** is a branch of medicine that deals with the design and fitting of orthopedic devices. **Prosthetics** is a branch of medicine that deals with the design, production, and use of artificial body parts.

- **Durable medical equipment (DME) is defined by Medicare as equipment that can withstand repeated use, is primarily used to serve a medical purpose, is used in the patient's home, and would not be used in the absence of illness or injury.**
- **Durable medical equipment, prosthetics, orthotics, and supplies (DMEPOS) include artificial limbs, braces, medications, surgical dressings, and wheelchairs.**
- **Durable medical equipment, prosthetics, orthotics, and supplies (DMEPOS) dealers supply patients with DME (e.g., canes, crutches, walkers, commode chairs, and blood-glucose monitors). DMEPOS claims are submitted to DME Medicare administrative contractors (DME MACs) that replaced durable medical equipment regional carriers (DMERCs) that were awarded contracts by CMS. Each DME MAC covers a specific geographic region of the country and is responsible for processing DMEPOS claims for its specific region.**

NOTE: Originally, HCPCS level II codes were simply listed on a health care facility's *chargemaster* (or *charge description master*) for selection by the health care professional who provided patient services. However, implementation of the outpatient prospective payment system (OPPS) resulted in more invasive procedures being assigned HCPCS level II codes for outpatient encounters. Coders must review patient records to assign the codes.

When an appropriate HCPCS level II code exists, it is often assigned instead of a CPT code (with the same or similar code description) for Medicare accounts and for some state Medicaid systems. (Other payers may not require the reporting of HCPCS level II codes instead of CPT codes, so coders should check with individual payers to determine their policies.) CMS creates HCPCS level II codes:

- **For services and procedures that will probably never be assigned a CPT code (e.g., medications, equipment, supplies)**
- **To determine the volumes and costs of newly implemented technologies**

New HCPCS level II codes are reported for several years until CMS initiates a process to create corresponding CPT codes. When the CPT codes are published, they are reported instead of the original HCPCS level II codes. (HCPCS level II codes that are replaced by CPT codes are often deleted. If not deleted, they are probably continuing to be reported by another payer or government demonstration program.)

EXAMPLE: HCPCS level II device code C1725 is reported for the surgical supply of a "catheter, transluminal angioplasty, nonlaser method (may include guidance, infusion/perfusion capability)" during vascular surgery. Thus, when a CPT code from range 35450–35476 is reported for a transluminal balloon angioplasty procedure, HCPCS level II device code C1725 is also reported as the surgical supply of the catheter.

CODING TIP:

When people refer to HCPCS codes, they are most likely referring to HCPCS level II national codes. CMS is responsible for the annual updates to HCPCS level II codes and two-character alphanumeric modifiers.

HCPCS LEVEL II NATIONAL CODES

The HCPCS level II national coding system classifies similar medical products and services for the purpose of efficient claims processing. Each HCPCS level II code contains a description, and the codes are used primarily for billing purposes.

EXAMPLE: DMEPOS dealers report HCPCS level II codes to identify items on claims billed to private or public health insurers.

HCPCS is *not* a reimbursement methodology or system, and it is important to understand that just because codes exist for certain products or services, coverage (e.g., payment) is not guaranteed. The HCPCS level II coding system has the following characteristics:

- **It ensures uniform reporting of medical products or services on claims.**
- **Code descriptors identify similar products or services (rather than specific products or brand/trade names).**
- **HCPCS is not a reimbursement methodology for making coverage or payment determinations. (Each payer makes determinations on coverage and payment outside this coding process.)**

REMEMBER!

Effective January 1, 2005, CMS no longer allows a 90-day grace period (traditionally, January 1 through March 31) for reporting discontinued, revised, and new HCPCS level II national codes on claims. There is also no 90-day grace period for implementing mid-year HCPCS level II national coding updates.

Responsibility for HCPCS Level II Codes

HCPCS level II codes are developed and maintained by the CMS HCPCS Workgroup and do not carry the copyright of a private organization. They are in the public domain, and many publishers print annual coding manuals.

Some HCPCS level II references contain general instructions or guidelines for each section; an Appendix summarizing additions, deletions, and terminology revisions for codes (similar to Appendix B in CPT); or separate tables of drugs or deleted codes. Others use symbols to identify codes excluded from Medicare coverage, codes where payment is left to the discretion of the payer, or codes with special coverage instructions. In addition, most references provide a complete Appendix of current HCPCS level II national modifiers. CMS has stated that it is not responsible for any errors that might occur in or from the use of these private printings of HCPCS level II codes.

Types of HCPCS Level II Codes

HCPCS level II codes are organized by type, depending on the purpose of the codes and the entity responsible for establishing and maintaining them. The four types are:

- **Permanent national codes**
- **Miscellaneous codes**
- **Temporary codes**
- **Modifiers**

Permanent National Codes

HCPCS level II **permanent national codes** are maintained by the CMS HCPCS Workgroup, which is composed of representatives of the major components of CMS, Medicaid State agencies, and the Pricing, Data Analysis and Coding (PDAC). The CMS HCPCS Workgroup is responsible for making decisions about additions, revisions, and deletions to the permanent national alphanumeric codes. Decisions regarding changes to the permanent national codes are made only by unanimous consent of all three parties. As HCPCS level II is a national coding system, none of the parties, including CMS, can make unilateral decisions regarding permanent national codes. These codes are for the use of all private and public health insurers.

NOTE: When claims are to be submitted to one of the four regional MACs, DMEPOS dealers that have coding questions should check with the **Medicare Pricing, Data Analysis and Coding (PDAC) Contractor**, which is responsible for providing suppliers and manufacturers with assistance in determining HCPCS codes to be used. The PDAC has a toll-free helpline for this purpose at (877) 735-1326. PDACs have replaced SADMERCs (statistical analysis durable medical equipment regional carriers).

Miscellaneous Codes

HCPCS level II **miscellaneous codes** include *miscellaneous/not otherwise classified* codes that are reported when a DMEPOS dealer submits a claim for a product or service for which there is no existing HCPCS level II code. Miscellaneous codes allow DMEPOS dealers to submit a claim for a product or service as soon as it is approved by the Food and Drug Administration (FDA), even though there is no code that describes the product or service. The use of miscellaneous codes also helps avoid the inefficiency of assigning codes for items or services that are rarely furnished or for which payers expect to receive few claims.

Claims that contain miscellaneous codes are manually reviewed by the payer, and the following must be provided for use in the review process:

- **Complete description of product or service**
- **Pricing information for product or service**
- **Documentation to explain why the item or service is needed by the beneficiary**

Before reporting a miscellaneous code on a claim, a DMEPOS dealer should check with the payer to determine if a specific code has been identified for use (instead of a miscellaneous code).

NOTE: Decisions regarding MAC temporary codes are made by an internal CMS HCPCS workgroup, and other payers may also use these codes.

NOTE: Whenever a permanent code is established by the HCPCS National Panel to replace a temporary code, the temporary code is deleted and cross-referenced to the new permanent code.

Temporary Codes

HCPCS level II **temporary codes** are maintained by the CMS and other members of the HCPCS National Panel, independent of permanent national codes. Permanent codes are updated once a year on January 1, but temporary codes allow payers the flexibility to establish codes that are needed before the next January 1 annual update. Approximately 35 percent of the HCPCS level II codes are temporary codes. Certain sections of the HCPCS level II codes were set aside to allow HCPCS National Panel members to develop temporary codes, and decisions regarding the number and type of temporary codes and how they are used are made independently by each HCPCS National Panel member. Temporary codes serve the purpose of meeting the short-time-frame operational needs of a particular payer.

Although the HCPCS National Panel may decide to replace temporary codes with permanent codes, if permanent codes are not established, the temporary codes remain "temporary" indefinitely.

Categories of Temporary Codes

C codes permit implementation of section 201 of the Balanced Budget Refinement Act of 1999, and they identify items that may qualify for **transitional pass-through payments** under the hospital outpatient prospective payment system (OPPS). These are temporary additional payments (over and above the OPPS payment) made for certain innovative medical devices, drugs, and biologicals provided to Medicare beneficiaries. These codes are used exclusively for OPPS purposes and are only valid for Medicare claims submitted by hospital outpatient departments.

G codes identify professional health care procedures and services that do not have codes identified in CPT. G codes are reported to all payers.

H codes are reported to state Medicaid agencies that are mandated by state law to establish separate codes for identifying mental health services (e.g., alcohol and drug treatment services).

K codes are reported to MACs when existing permanent codes do not include codes needed to implement a MAC medical review coverage policy.

Q codes identify services that would not ordinarily be assigned a CPT code (e.g., drugs, biologicals, and other types of medical equipment or services).

S codes are used by the BCBSA and the HIAA when no HCPCS level II codes exist to report drugs, services, and supplies, but codes are needed to implement private payer policies and programs for claims processing.

T codes are reported to state Medicaid agencies when no permanent national codes exist, but codes are needed to administer the Medicaid program. (T codes are not reported to Medicare, but can be reported to private payers.)

Modifiers

HCPCS level II **modifiers** are attached to any HCPCS level I (CPT) or II (national) code to clarify services and procedures performed by providers. Although the HCPCS level II code and description remain unchanged, modifiers indicate that the description of the service or procedure performed has been altered. HCPCS modifiers are reported as two-character alphabetic or alphanumeric codes added to the five-character CPT or HCPCS level II code.

EXAMPLE: Modifier -UE indicates the product is "used equipment."
Modifier -NU indicates the product is "new equipment."

CODING TIP:

Depending on the publisher, the HCPCS level II coding manual includes a list of modifiers inside the front and back covers *or* as a separate appendix. (Figure 8-1 contains a brief sample listing of HCPCS level II modifiers, regardless of location in the coding manual.)

The CPT coding manual includes an abbreviated list of all CPT modifiers inside the front cover; also included are some HCPCS level II modifiers. Appendix A of the CPT coding manual includes a detailed list of all CPT modifiers.

Coders assign CPT and HCPCS level II modifiers to CPT and HCPCS level II codes. Thus, familiarity with all modifiers is crucial to reporting accurate CPT and HCPCS level II codes for reimbursement purposes. A careful review of the patient record will help determine which modifier(s), if any, should be added to CPT and HCPCS level II codes.

HCPCS level II modifiers are either alphabetic (two letters) or alphanumeric (one letter followed by one number) (Figure 8-1).

EXAMPLE 1: A patient sees a clinical psychologist for 30 minutes of individual psychotherapy (CPT code 90832). Report:

90832-AH

	24. A. DATE(S) OF SERVICE From MM DD YY	To MM DD YY	B. PLACE OF SERVICE	C. EMG	D. PROCEDURES, SERVICES, OR SUPPLIES (Explain Unusual Circumstances) CPT/HCPCS	MODIFIER	E. DIAGNOSIS POINTER	F. $ CHARGES	G. DAYS OR UNITS	H. EPSDT Family Plan	I. ID. QUAL.	J. RENDERING PROVIDER ID. #
1					90832	AH					NPI	

Courtesy of the Centers for Medicare & Medicaid Services, www.cms.gov; Copyright © 2015 Cengage Learning®.

EXAMPLE 2: A Medicare patient undergoes tendon excision, right palm (CPT code 26170) and left middle finger (CPT code 26180). Report:

26170-RT

26180-59-F2

	24. A. DATE(S) OF SERVICE From MM DD YY	To MM DD YY	B. PLACE OF SERVICE	C. EMG	D. PROCEDURES, SERVICES, OR SUPPLIES (Explain Unusual Circumstances) CPT/HCPCS	MODIFIER	E. DIAGNOSIS POINTER	F. $ CHARGES	G. DAYS OR UNITS	H. EPSDT Family Plan	I. ID. QUAL.	J. RENDERING PROVIDER ID. #
1					26170	RT					NPI	
2					26180	59 F2					NPI	

Courtesy of the Centers for Medicare & Medicaid Services, www.cms.gov; Copyright © 2015 Cengage Learning®.

HCPCS Level II Modifiers

NOTE: When CPT modifier -50 is reported, do not report modifiers -RT and -LT.

AA	Anesthesia services performed personally by anesthesiologist
AD	Medical supervision by a physician: more than four concurrent anesthesia procedures
AH	Clinical psychologist
AM	Physician, team member service
AP	Ophthalmological examination
AS	Physician assistant, nurse practitioner, or clinical nurse specialist services for assistant at surgery
AT	Acute treatment (this modifier should be used when reporting service 98940, 98941, 98942)
E1	Upper left, eyelid
E2	Lower left, eyelid
E3	Upper right, eyelid
E4	Lower right, eyelid
LT	Left side (used to identify procedures performed on the left side of the body)
RT	Right side (used to identify procedures performed on the right side of the body)

FIGURE 8-1 Sample HCPCS level II modifiers.

NOTE: C codes are reported for new drugs, biologicals, and devices that are eligible for transitional pass-through payments under the ambulatory payment classifications (APCs) under the outpatient prospective payment system.

The alphabetic first character identifies the code sections of HCPCS level II. Some are logical, such as R for radiology, whereas others, such as J for drugs, appear to be arbitrarily assigned. The HCPCS level II code ranges are as follows:

A0021–A0999	Transportation Services Including Ambulance
A4206–A9999	Medical and Surgical Supplies
B4034–B9999	Enteral and Parenteral Therapy
C1300–C9899	Outpatient PPS
E0100–E8002	Durable Medical Equipment
G0008-G9186	Procedures/Professional Services (Temporary)
H0001–H2037	Alcohol and/or Drug Abuse Treatment Services
J0120–J8499	Drugs Administered Other Than Oral Method
J8501–J9999	Chemotherapy Drugs
K0001–K0899	Temporary Codes (durable medical equipment)
L0112–L4631	Orthotic Procedures and Devices
L5000–L9999	Prosthetic Procedures
M0064–M0301	Medical Services
P2028–P9615	Pathology and Laboratory Services
Q0035–Q9969	Q Codes (Temporary)
R0070–R0076	Diagnostic Radiology Services
S0012–S9999	Temporary National Codes (non-Medicare)
T1000–T5999	National T Codes
V2020–V2799	Vision Services
V5008–V5364	Hearing Services

> **NOTE:** The Food and Drug Administration (FDA) publishes the *National Drug Code (NDC) directory*, which includes drug products that are identified and reported using a unique, three-segment number. Go to **www.cengagebrain.com** and log in to UHI's Student Resources to locate information about the NDC directory at Student Resources.

Organization of Coding Manual

Because of the wide variety of services and procedures described in HCPCS level II, the alphabetical index (Figure 8-2) is very helpful in finding the correct code. The various publishers of the reference may include an expanded index that lists "alcohol wipes" and "wipes" as well as "Ancef" and "cefazolin sodium," making the search for codes easier and faster. Some references also include a Table of Drugs (Figure 8-3) that lists J codes assigned to medications. Some publishers print brand names beneath the generic description, and others provide a special expanded index of the drug codes. It is important never to code directly from the index and always to verify the code in the tabular section of the coding manual. You may wish to review the HCPCS level II references from several publishers and select the one that best meets your needs and is the easiest for you to use.

If you have difficulty locating the service or procedure in the HCPCS level II index, review the list of codes and descriptions of the appropriate section of the tabular list of codes to locate the code. Read the code descriptions very carefully. You may need to ask the provider to help select the correct code.

Index

A

Abatacept, J0129
Abciximab, J0130
Abdomen
 dressing holder/binder, A4462
 pad, low profile, L1270
Abduction
 control, each, L2624
 rotation bar, foot L3140-L3170
Abortion, S2260-S2267
AbobotulinumtoxintypeA, J0586
Absorption dressing, A6251-A6256
Accessories
 ambulation devices, E0153-E0159
 artificial kidney and machine (*see also* ESRD), E1510-E1699
 beds, E0271-E0280, E0305-E0326
 wheelchairs E0950-E1030, E1050-E1298, E2300-E2399, K0001-K0109

2014 HCPCS

FIGURE 8-2 HCPCS level II index entries (portion).

Drug Name	Unit Per	Route	Code
5% DEXTROSE AND .45% NORMAL SALINE	1000 ML	IV	S5010
5% DEXTROSE IN LACTATED RINGERS	1000 ML	IV	S5011
5% DEXTROSE WITH POTASSIUM CHLORIDE	1000 ML	IV	S5013
5% DEXTROSE/.45% NS WITH KCL AND MAG SULFATE	1500 ML	IV	S5014
5% DEXTROSE/NORMAL SALINE	5%	VAR	J7042
5% DEXTROSE/WATER	500 ML	IV	J7060
10% LMD	500 ML	IV	J7100
ABATACEPT	10 MG	IV	J0129
ABCIXIMAB	10 MG	IV	J0130
ABELCET	10 MG	IV	J0287
ABILIFY	0.25 MG	IM	J0400
ABLAVAR	1 ML	IV	A9583
ABOBOTULINUMTOXINA	5 UNITS	IM	J0586
ABRAXANE	1 MG	IV	J9264

Figure 8-3 HCPCS level II table of drugs (portion).

EXERCISE 8-1

HCPCS Level II National Codes

Instructions: Using the HCPCS level II index, identify the key word(s) used to search the index and enter the code in front of the description after reviewing the tabular list of codes.

1. ______ Unclassified drug
   Key word(s): ______
2. ______ Fern test
   Key word(s): ______
3. ______ Benesch boot, pair, junior
   Key word(s): ______
4. ______ Safety belt for wheelchair
   Key word(s): ______
5. ______ Miscellaneous dialysis supplies
   Key word(s): ______

NOTE: At one time, the local Medicare carriers (LMCs) (replaced by Medicare administrative contractors) processed all claims for DME. The emphasis on keeping seniors in their own homes led to a rapid expansion in DME services and dealers. Also, many of the larger companies operated in several states and sent their claims to multiple Medicare carriers. Unfortunately, a few dealers formed for the sole purpose of collecting as much money as possible from the Medicare program and then closed down. When CMS began to investigate and pursue fraudulent claims, it became apparent that DME billings were out of control, so CMS decided to have all DME claims processed by only four regional MACs. This allowed the local MACs to concentrate on the familiar, traditional claims of providers billing for services, not equipment.

DETERMINING PAYER RESPONSIBILITY

The specific HCPCS level II code determines whether the claim is sent to the:

- **Primary MAC that processes provider claims**
- **DME MAC that processes DMEPOS dealer claims**

Annual lists of valid HCPCS level II codes give providers complete billing instructions for those services.

When the doctor treats a Medicare patient for a broken ankle and supplies the patient with crutches, two claims are generated. The one for the fracture care, or professional service, is sent to the primary Medicare administrative contractor (MAC); the claim for the crutches is sent to the DME MAC. The physician must register with both, review billing rules, comply with claims instructions, and forward claims correctly to secure payment for both services. If the doctor is not registered with the DME MAC to provide medical equipment and supplies, the patient is given a prescription for crutches to take to a local DMEPOS dealer.

Some services, such as most cosmetic procedures, are excluded as Medicare benefits by law and will not be covered by either MAC. Splints and casts for traumatic injuries have CPT numbers that would be used to report these supplies or services to the local MAC. Because the review procedure for adding new codes to level II is a much shorter process, new medical and surgical services may first be assigned a level II code and then incorporated into CPT at a later date.

Patient Record Documentation

The patient record includes documentation that justifies the medical necessity of procedures, services, and supplies coded and reported on an insurance claim. This means that the diagnoses reported on the claim must justify diagnostic and/or therapeutic procedures or services provided. The patient's record should include documentation of the following:

- **Patient history, including review of systems**
- **Physical examination, including impression**
- **Diagnostic test results, including analysis of findings**
- **Diagnoses, including duration (e.g., acute or chronic) and comorbidities that impact care**
- **Patient's prognosis, including potential for rehabilitation**

When DMEPOS items are reported on a claim, the DMEPOS dealer must keep the following documents on file:

- **Provider order for DMEPOS item, signed and dated**
- **Signed advance beneficiary notice (ABN) if medical necessity for an item cannot be established**

An *advance beneficiary notice (ABN)* (discussed further in Chapter 14 of this textbook) is a waiver signed by the patient acknowledging that because medical necessity for a procedure, service, or supply cannot be established (e.g., due to the nature of the patient's condition, injury, or illness), the patient accepts responsibility for reimbursing the provider or DMEPOS dealer for costs associated with the procedure, service, or supply. When the provider reports DMEPOS items on a claim, the provider must keep the following documents on file:

- **Diagnosis establishing medical necessity for the item**
- **Clinical notes that justify the DMEPOS item ordered**
- **Provider order for DMEPOS item, signed and dated**
- **Signed advance beneficiary notice if medical necessity for an item cannot be established**

DMEPOS Claims

For certain items or services reported on a claim submitted to the DME MAC, the DMEPOS dealer must receive a signed **certificate of medical necessity (CMN)** (Figure 8-4) from the treating physician before submitting a claim to Medicare. A copied, electronic, faxed, or original certificate of medical necessity (CMN) must be maintained by the DMEPOS dealer and must be available to the DME MAC on request. The certificate of medical necessity (CMN) is a prescription for DME, services, and supplies. DME MAC medical review policies include local coverage determinations (LCDs) (formerly called local medical review policies, or LMRPs) and national coverage determinations (NCDs), both of which define coverage criteria, payment rules, and documentation required as applied to DMEPOS claims processed by DME MACs for frequently ordered DMEPOS equipment, services, and supplies. (National policies are included in the *Medicare Benefit Policy Manual, Medicare Program Integrity Manual, and Medicare National Coverage Determinations Manual.*) If DMEPOS equipment, services, or supplies do not have medical review policies established for coverage, the general coverage criteria applies. The DMEPOS equipment, services, or supplies must:

- **Fall within a benefit category**
- **Not be excluded by statute or by national CMS policy**
- **Be reasonable and necessary to diagnose and/or treat an illness or injury or to improve the functioning of a malformed body**

DME MACs are required to follow national policy when it exists; when there is no national policy on a subject, DME MACs have the authority and responsibility to establish local policies. Because many DMEPOS dealers operate nationally, the CMS requires that the medical review policies published by the DME MACs be identical in all four regions.

EXERCISE 8-2

Recognizing Payer Responsibility

Instructions: Complete each statement below.

1. The specific ______ code determines whether the claim is sent to the primary MAC that processes provider claims or the DME MAC that processes DMEPOS dealer claims.
2. Providers and DMEPOS dealers obtain annual lists of valid HCPCS level II codes, which include ______ instructions for services.
3. CMS decided to have all DME claims processed by only four DME MACs to reduce ______ claims.
4. When a physician treats a Medicare patient for a fractured femur and supplies the patient with crutches, two claims are generated. The physician's claim for the fracture care is sent to the ______, and the claim for the crutches is sent to the ______.
5. For certain items or services reported on a claim submitted to the DME MAC, the DMEPOS dealer must receive a signed ______.

U.S. DEPARTMENT OF HEALTH & HUMAN SERVICES
CENTERS FOR MEDICARE & MEDICAID SERVICES

FORM APPROVED
OMB NO. 0938-0679

CERTIFICATE OF MEDICAL NECESSITY **DMERC 01.02A**

HOSPITAL BEDS

SECTION A **Certification Type/Date:** **INITIAL __/__/__** **REVISED __/__/__**

PATIENT NAME, ADDRESS, TELEPHONE and HIC NUMBER		SUPPLIER NAME, ADDRESS, TELEPHONE and NSC NUMBER
(___) ___-____ HICN ________		(___) ___-____ NSC # ________
PLACE OF SERVICE _____ NAME and ADDRESS of FACILITY if applicable (See reverse)	HCPCS CODE ____ ____ ____ ____	**PT DOB __/__/__; Sex ___ (M/F); HT.___(in.); WT.___(lbs.)** **PHYSICIAN NAME, ADDRESS (Printed or Typed)** **PHYSICIAN'S UPIN:** ______ **PHYSICIAN'S TELEPHONE #: (___) ___-____**

SECTION B **Information in this Section May Not Be Completed by the Supplier of the Items/Supplies.**

EST. LENGTH OF NEED (# OF MONTHS): ____ 1-99 (99=LIFETIME) | **DIAGNOSIS CODES (ICD-9):** ____ ____ ____ ____

ANSWERS	ANSWER QUESTIONS 1, AND 3-7 FOR HOSPITAL BEDS (Circle **Y** for Yes, **N** for No, or **D** for Does Not Apply)
	QUESTION 2 RESERVED FOR OTHER OR FUTURE USE.
Y N D	1. Does the patient require positioning of the body in ways not feasible with an ordinary bed due to a medical condition which is expected to last at least one month?
Y N D	3. Does the patient require, for the alleviation of pain, positioning of the body in ways not feasible with an ordinary bed?
Y N D	4. Does the patient require the head of the bed to be elevated more than 30 degrees most of the time due to congestive heart failure, chronic pulmonary disease, or aspiration?
Y N D	5. Does the patient require traction which can only be attached to a hospital bed?
Y N D	6. Does the patient require a bed height different than a fixed height hospital bed to permit transfers to chair, wheelchair, or standing position?
Y N D	7. Does the patient require frequent changes in body position and/or have an immediate need for a change in body position?

NAME OF PERSON ANSWERING SECTION B QUESTIONS, IF OTHER THAN PHYSICIAN (Please Print):
NAME: ________ TITLE: ________ EMPLOYER: ________

SECTION C **Narrative Description Of Equipment And Cost**

(1) Narrative description of all items, accessories and options ordered; **(2)** Supplier's charge; and **(3)** Medicare Fee Schedule Allowance for each item, accessory, and option. *(See Instructions On Back)*

SECTION D **Physician Attestation and Signature/Date**

I certify that I am the physician identified in Section A of this form. I have received Sections A, B and C of the Certificate of Medical Necessity (including charges for items ordered). Any statement on my letterhead attached hereto, has been reviewed and signed by me. I certify that the medical necessity information in Section B is true, accurate and complete, to the best of my knowledge, and I understand that any falsification, omission, or concealment of material fact in that section may subject me to civil or criminal liability.

PHYSICIAN'S SIGNATURE ________ DATE __/__/__ (SIGNATURE AND DATE STAMPS ARE NOT ACCEPTABLE)

CMS-841 (04/96)

FIGURE 8-4 Sample certificate of medical necessity required of DMEPOS dealer.

ASSIGNING HCPCS LEVEL II CODES

Some services must be reported by assigning both a CPT and a HCPCS code. The most common scenario uses the CPT code for administration of an injection and the HCPCS level II code to identify the medication administered. Most drugs have qualifying terms such as dosage limits that could alter the quantity reported (see Figure 8-3). If a drug stating "per 50 mg" is administered in a 70-mg dose, the quantity billed would be "2." If you administered only 15 mg of a drug stating "up to 20 mg," the quantity is "1." Imagine how much money providers lose by reporting only the CPT code for injections. Unless the payer or insurance plan advises the provider that it does not pay separately for the medication injected, always report this combination of codes.

It is possible that a particular service would be assigned a CPT code and a HCPCS level II code. Which one should you report? The answer is found in the instructions from the payer. Most commercial payers require the CPT code. Medicare gives HCPCS level II codes the highest priority if the CPT code is general and the HCPCS level II code is more specific.

Most supplies are included in the charge for the office visit or the procedure. CPT provides code 99070 for all supplies and materials exceeding those usually included in the primary service or procedure performed. However, this CPT code may be too general to ensure correct payment. If the office provides additional supplies when performing a service, the HCPCS level II codes may identify the supplies in sufficient detail to secure proper reimbursement.

Although CMS developed this system, some HCPCS levels I and II services are not payable by Medicare. Medicare may also place qualifications or conditions on payment for some services. As an example, an ECG is a covered service for a cardiac problem but is not covered when performed as part of a routine examination. Also, the payment for some services may be left to the payer's discretion. Two CMS publications assist payers in correctly processing claims. The *Medicare National Coverage Determinations Manual* advises the MAC whether a service is covered or excluded under Medicare regulations. The *Medicare Benefit Policy Manual* directs the MAC to pay a service or reject it using a specific "remark" or explanation code.

There are more than 4,000 HCPCS level II codes, but you may find that no code exists for the procedure or service you need to report. Unlike CPT, HCPCS level II does not have a consistent method of establishing codes for reporting "unlisted procedure" services. If the MAC does not provide special instructions for reporting these services in HCPCS, report them with the proper "unlisted procedure" code from CPT. Remember to submit documentation explaining the procedure or service when using the "unlisted procedure" codes.

NOTE: CMS developed the HCPCS level II codes for Medicare, but commercial payers also adopt them.

SUMMARY

Two levels of codes are associated with HCPCS, commonly referred to as HCPCS level I and II codes. (HCPCS level III codes were discontinued effective December 31, 2003.) HCPCS level I includes the five-digit *Current Procedural Terminology* (CPT) codes developed and published by the American Medical Association (AMA). HCPCS level II (or HCPCS national codes) were created in the 1980s to describe common medical services and supplies not classified in CPT.

The HCPCS level II national coding system classifies similar medical products and services for the purpose of efficient claims processing. Each code contains a description, and the codes are used primarily for billing purposes. The codes describe DME devices, accessories, supplies, and repairs; prosthetics; medical and surgical supplies; medications; provider services; temporary Medicare codes (e.g., Q codes);

and other items and services (e.g., ambulance services). Some services must be reported by assigning both a CPT and a HCPCS level II national code. The most common scenario uses the CPT code for the administration of an injection and the HCPCS code to identify the medication.

The specific HCPCS level II code determines whether the claim is sent to the primary Medicare administrative contractor (MAC) that processes provider claims or the DME MAC that processes DMEPOS dealer claims. Providers and DMEPOS dealers obtain annual lists of valid HCPCS level II national codes, which include billing instructions for services.

INTERNET LINKS

- HCPCS level II coding files
  Go to **www.cms.gov**, click on the Medicare link, scroll down to the Coding heading, and click on the HCPCS Release & Code Sets link.
- HCPCS/CPT drug and product reimbursement coding and pricing information
  www.reimbursementcodes.com

STUDY CHECKLIST

- ☐ Read this textbook chapter and highlight key concepts.
- ☐ Create an index card for each key term.
- ☐ Access chapter Internet links to learn more about concepts.
- ☐ Answer the chapter review questions, verifying answers with your instructor.
- ☐ Complete the Workbook chapter, verifying answers with your instructor.
- ☐ Form a study group with classmates to discuss chapter concepts in preparation for an exam.

REVIEW

MULTIPLE CHOICE **Select the most appropriate response.**

1. HCPCS level II was introduced in 1983 after Medicare found that its payers used more than 100 different coding systems, making it _______________.

a. difficult to analyze claims data
b. expensive to reimburse services
c. proficient to assign codes
d. unmanageable to publish manuals

2. HCPCS furnishes health care providers and suppliers with a _______________ language for reporting professional services, procedures, supplies, and equipment.

a. medical
b. proficient
c. standardized
d. therapeutic

3. Although the majority of procedures and services are reported using CPT (HCPCS level I), that coding system does not describe _______________ (services) and certain other services reported on claims submitted for Medicare and some Medicaid patients.

a. DMEPOS
b. LCD/NCD
c. PDAC
d. SADMERC

4. HCPCS level II national codes are five characters in length, and they begin with letters ________________, followed by four numbers.

a. A-B, E-V
b. A-V
c. A-Z
d. W-Z

5. Because HCPCS level II is not a reimbursement methodology or system, its procedure, product, and service codes ________________ coverage (e.g., payment).

a. are assured
b. bear out
c. correspond with
d. do not guarantee

6. HCPCS level II codes are developed and maintained by ________________ and do not carry the copyright of a private organization, which means they are in the public domain and many publishers print annual coding manuals.

a. BCBS
b. CMS
c. NCCI
d. OIG

7. The four types of HCPCS level II codes are ________________.

a. miscellaneous, modifier, permanent, and temporary codes
b. miscellaneous, investigational, permanent, and temporary codes
c. miscellaneous, investigational, medical/surgical supply, and transportation service codes
d. orthotic, prosthetic, radiology, and temporary codes

8. HCPCS level II codes that begin with ________________ are reported to the local MAC.

a. A, J, Q, or V
b. B, E, K, or L
c. G, M, P, or F
d. W, X, Y, or Z

9. HCPCS level II codes that begin with ________________ are reported to the regional DME MAC.

a. A, J, Q, or V
b. B, E, K, or L
c. G, M, P, or F
d. W, X, Y, or Z

10. HCPCS level II codes that begin with ________________ are reported to either the local MAC or regional DME MAC.

a. A, J, Q, or V
b. B, E, K, or L
c. G, M, P, or F
d. W, X, Y, or Z

ASSIGNING HCPCS LEVEL II CODES

11. Patient received ALS 1 emergency transport ambulance service from home to hospital emergency department. ________________

12. Patient received supplies for self-administered injections. ________________

13. Patient was administered artificial saliva, 60 milliliters, orally. ____________

14. Stroke patient was administered four ounces of food thickener, orally. ____________

15. Patient underwent insertion of catheter for intravascular ultrasound (prior to scheduled ultrasound procedure). ____________

16. Patient purchased a used heavy-duty wheeled walker (after being informed about purchase and rental options). ____________

17. Patient underwent left tibia bone marrow aspiration and left tibia bone marrow biopsy (through the same incision on the same date of service). ____________

18. Patient underwent 60 minutes of behavioral health counseling and therapy. ____________

19. Patient received intramuscular administration of a 250-milligram injection of tetracycline. ____________

20. Patient supplied with lightweight wheelchair. ____________

21. Patient supplied with brand new protective body sock for use under her new cervical-thoracic-lumbar-sacral-orthotic (CTLSO) (Milwaukee) spinal orthotic. ____________

22. Schizophrenic patient underwent brief office visit for purpose of monitoring prescription medications. The psychiatrist provided this service in an unlisted health professional shortage area (HPSA). ____________

23. Patient underwent office screening Pap smear, cervix, which was interpreted by pathologist. ____________

24. Medicare patient underwent the Fern test, which was administered by a substitute physician under a reciprocal billing arrangement. ____________

25. Provider transported portable EKG equipment to a nursing facility for the purpose of testing five patients. ____________

26. Commercial insurance patient received 100 milligrams of oral Zidovudine. ____________

27. Patient received 15 minutes of sign language services. ____________

28. Patient purchased frames (to replace broken frames). ____________

FILL-IN-THE-BLANK

29. **Using the current edition of the HCPCS level II coding manual, assign the correct codes, HCPCS modifier(s), and quantity to each of the following services.**

    a. B-12 injection not covered by Medicare, but patient agrees to pay.

    Code ____________ Modifier(s) ____________ Quantity ____________

    b. Purchase of new rolling chair with six-inch wheels. Rental declined.

    Code ____________ Modifier(s) ____________ Quantity ____________

    c. 100 reagent strips for home glucose monitor. Patient not on insulin.

    Code ____________ Modifier(s) ____________ Quantity ____________

d. Cervical cancer screening, including pelvic and clinical breast exam, at clinic in rural underserved area.

Code ________________ Modifier(s) ________________ Quantity ________________

e. Rental of immersion external heater for nebulizer.

Code ________________ Modifier(s) ________________ Quantity ________________

30. Using the current editions of CPT and HCPCS level II coding manuals, assign the correct code and the HCPCS modifier(s) and quantity to each of the following scenarios.

a. Metatarsophalangeal synovectomy, third digit, left foot.

Code ________________ Modifier(s) ________________ Quantity ________________

b. HemoCue 3 sample GTT performed at a CLIA-waived site.

Code ________________ Modifier(s) ________________ Quantity ________________

c. Closed manipulation, left Potts fracture, by physician who has opted out of Medicare.

Code ________________ Modifier(s) ________________ Quantity ________________

d. Anesthesiologist provides medical direction of one CRNA during radical nasal surgery.

Code ________________ Modifier(s) ________________ Quantity ________________

e. Neuropsychological testing, two hours, by clinical psychologist.

Code ________________ Modifier(s) ________________ Quantity ________________

CHAPTER 9

CMS Reimbursement Methodologies

CHAPTER OUTLINE

Historical Perspective of CMS Reimbursement Systems
CMS Payment Systems
Ambulance Fee Schedule
Ambulatory Surgical Center Payment Rates
Clinical Laboratory Fee Schedule
Durable Medical Equipment, Prosthetics/Orthotics, and Supplies Fee Schedule
End-Stage Renal Disease (ESRD) Composite Rate Payment System
Home Health Prospective Payment System
Hospital Inpatient Prospective Payment System
Hospital Outpatient Prospective Payment System
Inpatient Psychiatric Facility Prospective Payment System
Inpatient Rehabilitation Facility Prospective Payment System
Long-Term (Acute) Care Hospital Prospective Payment System
Skilled Nursing Facility Prospective Payment System
Medicare Physician Fee Schedule
Chargemaster
Revenue Cycle Management
UB-04 Claim

OBJECTIVES

Upon successful completion of this chapter, you should be able to:

1. Define key terms.
2. Explain the historical development of CMS reimbursement systems.
3. List and define each CMS payment system.
4. Apply special rules for the Medicare physician fee schedule payment system.
5. Interpret a chargemaster.
6. Explain hospital revenue cycle management.
7. Complete a UB-04 claim.

KEY TERMS

allowable charge
All-Patient diagnosis-related group (AP-DRG)
All-Patient Refined diagnosis-related group (APR-DRG)
ambulance fee schedule
ambulatory surgical center (ASC)
ambulatory surgical center payment rate
balance billing
case mix
chargemaster (charge description master [CDM])
chargemaster maintenance
chargemaster team
clinical laboratory fee schedule
clinical nurse specialist (CNS)
CMS program transmittal
CMS Quarterly Provider Update (QPU)
conversion factor
data analytics
Diagnostic and Statistical Manual (DSM)
disproportionate share hospital (DSH) adjustment
durable medical equipment, prosthetics/orthotics, and supplies (DMEPOS) fee schedule
employer group health plan (EGHP)
End-Stage Renal Disease (ESRD) composite payment rate system
grouper software
health insurance prospective payment system (HIPPS) code set
Home Assessment Validation and Entry (HAVEN)
home health resource groups (HHRGs)
incident to
indirect medical education (IME) adjustment
inpatient prospective payment system (IPPS)
Inpatient Rehabilitation Validation and Entry (IRVEN)
intensity of resources
IPPS 3-day payment window
IPPS 72-hour rule
IPPS transfer rule
large group health plan (LGHP)
limiting charge
long-term (acute) care hospital prospective payment system (LTCH PPS)
major diagnostic category (MDC)
Medicare physician fee schedule (MPFS)
Medicare Secondary Payer (MSP)
Medicare severity diagnosis-related groups (MS-DRGs)
Medicare Summary Notice (MSN)
metrics
nurse practitioner (NP)
Outcomes and Assessment Information Set (OASIS)
outlier
outpatient encounter (outpatient visit)
payment system
physician assistant (PA)
prospective cost-based rates
prospective price-based rates
relative value units (RVUs)
Resident Assessment Validation and Entry (RAVEN)
resource allocation
resource allocation monitoring
retrospective reasonable cost system
revenue code
revenue cycle auditing
revenue cycle management
revenue cycle monitoring
risk of mortality (ROM)
severity of illness (SOI)
site of service differential
wage index

INTRODUCTION

NOTE:

- Content about the Medicare physician fee schedule (MPFS) begins later in this chapter. (Medical assistant academic programs often cover just the MPFS in this chapter.)
- Coding and health information management academic programs cover all content in this chapter.

Since the Medicare program was implemented in 1966, expenditures have increased at an unanticipated rate, and the news media frequently report that the program will be bankrupt in a few years. In 1983 the Health Care Financing Administration (HCFA, now called CMS) implemented the first prospective payment system (PPS) to control the cost of hospital inpatient care.

In subsequent years, similar reimbursement systems were implemented for alternate care (e.g., physician office, long-term care). This chapter details CMS's reimbursement systems and related issues, including the Medicare physician fee schedule (MPFS), UB-04 claim, and chargemaster.

HISTORICAL PERSPECTIVE OF CMS REIMBURSEMENT SYSTEMS

NOTE: According to the American Enterprise Institute for Public Policy Research, in 1966, Medicare cost $3 billion. At that time, Congress's House Ways and Means Committee estimated that by 1990 Medicare would cost $12 billion (adjusting for inflation). However, in 1990, Medicare actually cost $107 billion.

In 1964 the Johnson administration avoided opposition from hospitals for passage of the Medicare and Medicaid programs by adopting retrospective reasonable cost-basis payment arrangements originally established by BlueCross. Reimbursement according to a **retrospective reasonable cost system** meant that hospitals reported actual charges for inpatient care to payers after discharge of the patient from the hospital. Payers then reimbursed hospitals 80 percent of allowed charges. Although this policy helped secure passage of Medicare and Medicaid (by enticing hospital participation), subsequent spiraling reimbursement costs ensued.

Shortly after the passage of Medicare and Medicaid, Congress began investigating prospective payment systems (PPS) (Table 9-1), which established predetermined rates based on patient category or the type of facility (with annual increases based on an inflation index and a geographic wage index):

- **Prospective cost-based rates are also established in advance, but they are based on reported health care costs (charges) from which a predetermined *per diem* (Latin meaning "for each day") rate is determined. Annual rates are usually adjusted using actual costs from the prior year. This method may be based on the facility's case mix (patient acuity) (e.g., resource utilization groups [RUGs] for skilled nursing care facilities).**
- **Prospective price-based rates are associated with a particular category of patient (e.g., inpatients), and rates are established by the payer (e.g., Medicare) prior to the provision of health care services (e.g., diagnosis-related groups [DRGs] for inpatient care).**

TABLE 9-1 Prospective payment systems, year implemented, and type

PROSPECTIVE PAYMENT SYSTEM	YEAR	TYPE
Ambulance Fee Schedule	2002	Cost-based
Ambulatory Surgical Center (ASC) Payment Rates	1994	Cost-based
Clinical Laboratory Fee Schedule	1985	Cost-based
Durable Medical Equipment, Prosthetics/Orthotics, and Supplies (DMEPOS) Fee Schedule	1989	Cost-based
End-Stage Renal Disease (ESRD) Composite Payment Rate System	2005	Price-based
Home Health Prospective Payment System (HH PPS) (Home Health Resource Groups [HHRG])	2000	Price-based
Hospital Inpatient Prospective Patient System (IPPS)	1983	Price-based
Hospital Outpatient Prospective Payment System (HOPPS)	2001	Price-based
Inpatient Psychiatric Facility Prospective Payment System (IPF PPS)	2004	Cost-based
Inpatient Rehabilitation Facility Prospective Payment System (IRF PPS)	2002	Price-based
Long-Term (Acute) Care Hospital Prospective Payment System (LTCH PPS)	2001	Price-based
Resource-Based Relative Value Scale (RBRVS) System (or Medicare Physician Fee Schedule [MPFS])	1992	Cost-based
Skilled Nursing Facility Prospective Payment System (SNF PPS)	1998	Cost-based

EXAMPLE: Prior to 1983, acute care hospitals generated invoices based on total charges for an inpatient stay. In 1982 an eight-day inpatient hospitalization at $225 per day (including ancillary service charges) would be billed $1,800. This *per diem* reimbursement rate actually discouraged hospitals from limiting inpatient lengths of stay. In 1983 the hospital would have been reimbursed a PPS rate of $950 for the same inpatient hospitalization, regardless of length of stay (unless the case qualified for additional reimbursement as an outlier). The PPS rate encourages hospitals to limit inpatient lengths of stay because any reimbursement received in excess of the actual cost of providing care is retained by the facility. (In this example, if the $950 PPS rate had been paid in 1980, the hospital would have absorbed the $850 loss.)

CMS PAYMENT SYSTEMS

The federal government administers several health care programs, some of which require services to be reimbursed according to a predetermined reimbursement methodology (**payment system**). Federal health care programs (an overview of each is located in Chapter 2) include:

- **CHAMPVA**
- **Indian Health Service (IHS)**
- **Medicaid (including the State Children's Health Insurance Program, or SCHIP)**
- **Medicare**
- **TRICARE (formerly CHAMPUS)**
- **Workers' Compensation (also a state health care program)**

NOTE: The Medicare physician fee schedule (MPFS) is discussed last in the series within this chapter because additional content is included to explain the intricacies of this payment system.

Depending on the type of health care services provided to beneficiaries, the federal government requires that one of the payment systems listed in Table 9-1 be used for the CHAMPVA, Medicaid, Medicare, and TRICARE programs.

AMBULANCE FEE SCHEDULE

The Balanced Budget Act of 1997 required establishment of an **ambulance fee schedule** payment system for ambulance services provided to Medicare beneficiaries. Starting in April 2002, the ambulance fee schedule was phased in over a five-year period replacing a retrospective reasonable cost payment system for providers and suppliers of ambulance services (because such a wide variation of payment rates resulted for the same service). This schedule requires:

- **Ambulance suppliers to accept Medicare assignment**
- **Reporting of HCPCS codes on claims for ambulance services**
- **Establishment of increased payment under the fee schedule for ambulance services furnished in rural areas based on the location of the beneficiary at the time the beneficiary is placed onboard the ambulance**
- **Revision of the certification requirements for coverage of nonemergency ambulance services**
- **Medicare to pay for beneficiary transportation services when other means of transportation are contraindicated. Ambulance services are divided into different levels of ground (land and water transportation) and air ambulance services based on the medically necessary treatment provided during transport**

NOTE: For the purpose of this example, the charges and rates remain the same for each year. Medicare actually adjusts ambulance fee schedule rates according to an inflationary formula.

EXAMPLE: A patient was transported by ambulance from her home to the local hospital for care. Under the retrospective reasonable cost payment system, the ambulance company charged $600, and Medicare paid 80 percent of that amount, or $480. The ambulance fee schedule requires Medicare to reimburse the ambulance company $425, which is an amount equal to the predetermined rate or *fee schedule*.

AMBULATORY SURGICAL CENTER PAYMENT RATES

An **ambulatory surgical center (ASC)** is a state-licensed, Medicare-certified supplier (not provider) of surgical health care services that must *accept assignment* on Medicare claims. An ASC must be a separate entity distinguishable from any other entity or facility, and it must have its own employer identifier number (EIN) as well as processes for:

NOTE: An ASC can be physically located within a health care organization and still be considered separate for Medicare reimbursement purposes if all the preceding criteria are met.

- **Accreditation**
- **Administrative functions**
- **Clinical services**
- **Financial and accounting systems**
- **Governance (of medical staff)**
- **Professional supervision**
- **Recordkeeping**
- **State licensure**

NOTE: Hospital outpatient departments that perform surgery are reimbursed under the outpatient prospective payment system (OPPS), which uses ambulatory payment classifications (APCs) as its reimbursement methodology, as discussed later in this chapter.

In 1980 Medicare authorized implementation of **ambulatory surgical center payment rates** as a fee to ambulatory surgery centers (ASCs) for facility services furnished in connection with performing certain surgical procedures. (Physician's professional services are separately reimbursed by the Medicare physician fee schedule, discussed later in this chapter.)

Effective January 1, 2008, the MMA of 2003 mandated implementation of the outpatient prospective payment system (OPPS) payment amount as a substitute for the ASC standard overhead amount for surgical procedures performed at an ASC. Medicare allows payment of an ASC facility fee for any surgical procedure performed at an ASC, *except those surgical procedures that Medicare has determined are not eligible for the ASC facility fee*. This means that instead of maintaining and updating an "inclusive list of procedures," Medicare maintains and updates an "exclusionary list of procedures" for which an ASC facility fee would *not* be paid (e.g., any procedure included on the OPPS inpatient list).

Under the payment system (Table 9-2), Medicare uses the ambulatory payment classification (APC) groups and relative payment weights for surgical procedures established under the OPPS as the basis of the payment groups and the relative payment weights for surgical procedures performed at ASCs. These payment weights would be multiplied by an ASC conversion factor to calculate the ASC payment rates.

The ASC relative payment weights are updated each year using the national OPPS relative payment weights for that calendar year and, for office-based procedures, the practice expense payments under the physician fee schedule for that calendar year. Medicare makes the relative payment weights budget neutral to ensure that changes in the relative payment weights from year to year do not cause the estimated amount of expenditures to ASCs to increase or decrease as a function of those changes.

TABLE 9-2 Sample list of Medicare-approved ASC procedures under ASC payment system

HCPCS CODE	HCPCS CODE DESCRIPTION	ASC RELATIVE PAYMENT WEIGHT	ASC FACILITY FEE PAYMENT	PATIENT COPAYMENT
G0104	Colorectal cancer screening; flexible sigmoidoscopy	1.7292	$68.63	$13.73
G0105	Colorectal cancer screening; colonoscopy on individual at high risk	7.8134	$310.10	$62.02
G0121	Colorectal cancer screening; colonoscopy on individual not meeting criteria for high risk	7.8134	$310.10	$62.02
G0127	Trimming of dystrophic nails, any number	0.2665	$10.58	$2.12
G0186	Destruction of localized lesion of choroid (for example, choroidal neovascularization); photocoagulation, feeder vessel technique (one or more sessions)	4.0750	$161.73	$32.35
G0260	Injection procedure for sacroiliac joint; provision of anesthetic, steroid and/or other therapeutic agent, with or without arthrography	5.5439	$220.03	$44.01
G0268	Removal of impacted cerumen (one or both ears) by physician on same date of service as audiologic function testing	0.5409	$21.47	$4.29
G0364	Bone marrow aspiration performed with bone marrow biopsy through the same incision on the same date of service	0.1293	$5.13	$1.03

CLINICAL LABORATORY FEE SCHEDULE

The Deficit Reduction Act of 1984 established the Medicare **clinical laboratory fee schedule** (Figure 9-1), which is a data set based on local fee schedules (for outpatient clinical diagnostic laboratory services). Medicare reimburses laboratory services according to the (1) submitted charge, (2) national limitation amount, or (3) local fee schedule amount, whichever is lowest. The local fee schedules are developed by Medicare administrative contractors who are:

NOTE: The clinical laboratory fee schedule contains approximately 1,000 separate clinical laboratory codes currently listed in the 80048–89399 CPT code series, along with a small number (less than 50) of HCPCS level II national codes.

- **Local contractors that process Medicare Part B claims, including claims submitted by independent laboratories and physician office laboratories**
- **Local contractors that process Medicare Part A claims, including outpatient laboratory tests performed by hospitals, nursing homes, and end-stage renal disease centers**

DURABLE MEDICAL EQUIPMENT, PROSTHETICS/ ORTHOTICS, AND SUPPLIES FEE SCHEDULE

NOTE: A valid ICD-10-CM diagnosis code must be reported for each line item on electronically submitted claims. If an electronic claim that is submitted to a regional DME MAC does not contain a valid ICD-10-CM diagnosis code, it will be rejected.

The Deficit Reduction Act of 1984 also established the Medicare **durable medical equipment, prosthetics/orthotics, and supplies (DMEPOS) fee schedule** (Figure 9-2). Medicare reimburses DMEPOS either 80 percent of the actual charge for the item *or* the fee schedule amount, whichever is lower. (Fee schedule amounts are annually updated and legislated by Congress.)

Clinical Diagnostic Laboratory Fee Schedule
12/10/YYYY

CPT code	Modifier	National Limit	Mid Point	N.Y.S. rate	Short Description of HCPCS code
78267		$10.98	$14.84	$10.98	Breath test attain/anal c-14
78268		$94.11	$127.18	$94.11	Breath test analysis, c-14
80048		$11.83	$15.98	$11.83	Basic metabolic panel
80051		$9.80	$13.24	$8.93	Electrolyte panel
80053		$14.77	$19.96	$14.77	Comprehensive metabolic panel
80061		$0.00	$0.00	$15.88	Lipid panel
80061	-QW	$0.00	$0.00	$15.88	Lipid panel
80069		$12.13	$16.39	$12.13	Renal function panel
80074		$0.00	$0.00	$64.46	Acute hepatitis panel
80076		$11.42	$15.43	$11.42	Hepatic function panel
80100		$20.32	$27.46	$20.32	Drug screen, qualitative/multi

FIGURE 9-1 Sample clinical lab fee schedule data (modifier -QW is reported for a CLIA-waived laboratory test).

Durable Medical Equipment, Prosthetics, Orthotics, and Supplies (DMEPOS)
8/16/YYYY

HCPCS code	Modifier	Jurisdiction[1]	Category[2]	Ceiling[3]	Floor[4]	N.Y.S. rate	Short Description of HCPCS code
A4217		D	SU	$3.13	$2.66	$2.66	Sterile water/saline, 500 mL
A4217	-AU	D	OS	$3.13	$2.66	$2.66	Sterile water/saline, 500 mL
A4221		D	SU	$22.64	$19.24	$22.64	Supplies for maint drug infus cath, per wk.
A4222		D	SU	$46.73	$39.72	$46.73	External drug infusion pump supplies, per cassette or bag
A4253		D	IN	$38.52	$32.74	$38.52	Blood glucose/reagent strips, per 50
A4255		D	SU	$4.11	$3.49	$4.11	Glucose monitor platforms, 50 per box

[1]**Jursidiction**
D (Regional DME MAC jurisdiction)
L (Local Part B administrative contractor jurisdiction)
J (Joint regional DME MAC/local MAC jurisdiction)

[2]**Category**
IN (inexpensive and other routinely purchased items)
FS (frequently serviced items)
CR (capped rental items)
OX (oxygen and oxygen equipment)
OS (ostomy, tracheostomy, & urological items)
SD (surgical dressings)
PO (prosthetics & orthotics)
SU (supplies)
TE (transcutaneous electrical nerve stimulators)

[3]**Ceiling** (maximum fee schedule amount)

[4]**Floor** (minimum fee schedule amount)

FIGURE 9-2 Sample DMEPOS fee schedule data.

The Medicare Prescription Drug, Improvement, and Modernization Act of 2003 (MMA) authorized Medicare to replace the current durable medical equipment (DME) payment methodology for *certain items* with a competitive acquisition process to improve the effectiveness of its methodology for establishing DME payment amounts. The new bidding process established payment amounts for certain durable medical equipment, enteral nutrition, and off-the-shelf orthotics. Competitive bidding provides a way to create incentives for suppliers to provide quality items and services in an efficient manner and at reasonable cost.

END-STAGE RENAL DISEASE (ESRD) COMPOSITE RATE PAYMENT SYSTEM

Medicare's ESRD benefit allows patients to receive dialysis treatments, which remove excess fluids and toxins from the bloodstream. Patients also receive items and services related to their dialysis treatments, including drugs to treat conditions resulting from the loss of kidney function, such as anemia and low blood calcium. CMS traditionally divided ESRD items and services into two groups for payment purposes:

- **Dialysis and associated routine services (e.g., nursing, supplies, equipment, certain drugs, and certain laboratory tests) are reimbursed according to a composite rate (one rate for a defined set of services). Paying according to a composite rate (or fixed) is a common form of Medicare payment, also known as *bundling*.**
- **End-Stage Renal Disease (ESRD) composite payment rate system bundles ESRD drugs and related laboratory tests with the composite rate payments, resulting in one reimbursement amount paid for ESRD services provided to patients. The rate is case-mix adjusted to provide a mechanism to account for differences in patients' utilization of health care resources (e.g., patient's age, documentation and reporting of comorbidities) (Table 9-3).**

NOTE: A facility's case mix is a measure of the types of patients treated, and it reflects patient utilization of varying levels of health care resources. Patients are classified according to age, gender, health status, and so on.

For example, elderly patients usually require more complex care than teenage patients, which means a greater amount of money is spent on patient care provided to the elderly.

The Medicare Prescription Drug, Improvement and Modernization Act (MMA) of 2003 required Medicare to change the way it pays facilities for dialysis treatments and separately billable drugs. A key purpose of the MMA was to eliminate the cross-subsidization of composite rate payments by drug payments. These revisions also resulted in more accurate reimbursement for drugs and the composite rate. Medicare spends the same amount of money as would have been spent under the prior system, but the cross-subsidy was eliminated.

TABLE 9-3 Case-mix adjustments to composite rates based on patient age

AGE RANGE	CASE-MIX INDEX MULTIPLIER
18-44	1.023
45-59	1.055
60-69	1.000
70-79	1.094
80+	1.174

EXAMPLE: A health care facility's composite rate is $128.35, which means that Medicare reimburses the facility $128.35 for an ESRD service. According to Table 9-3, that rate applies only to patients whose ages range from 60 to 69. When a 58-year-old patient receives ESRD services, the facility's reimbursement increases to $135.41 because the composite rate ($128.35) is multiplied by the case-mix index (1.055).

HOME HEALTH PROSPECTIVE PAYMENT SYSTEM

The BBA of 1997 called for implementation of a Medicare *home health prospective payment system* (HH PPS), which uses a classification system called *home health resource groups* (HHRGs) to establish prospective reimbursement rates for each 60-day episode of home health care. **Home health resource groups (HHRGs)** classify patients into one of 80 groups, which range in severity level. Each HHRG has an associated weight value that increases or decreases Medicare's payment for an episode of home health care. HHRGs are reported to Medicare on HH PPS claims (UB-04, discussed later in this chapter) using the **health insurance prospective payment system (HIPPS) code set**. Codes in this set are five-character alphanumeric codes that represent case-mix groups about which payment determinations are made for the HH PPS. CMS originally created the HIPPS code set for the skilled nursing facility prospective payment system (SNF PPS) in 1998, and reporting requirements for the HH PPS (and inpatient rehabilitation facility PPS) were added later. HIPPS codes are determined after patient assessments using the **Outcomes and Assessment Information Set (OASIS)** are completed.

NOTE: ICD-10-CM codes are used to determine the appropriate HH PPS payment level.

Grouper software is used to determine the appropriate HHRG after Outcomes and Assessment Information Set (OASIS) data (Figure 9-3) are input on each patient (to measure the outcome of all adult patients receiving home health services). **Home Assessment Validation and Entry (HAVEN)** data entry software is then used to collect OASIS assessment data for transmission to state databases.

HOSPITAL INPATIENT PROSPECTIVE PAYMENT SYSTEM

NOTE: ICD-10-CM and ICD-10-PCS codes directly affect DRG assignment. CPT codes play no role in DRG assignments.

NOTE: Cancer hospitals are excluded from the IPPS and continue to be paid on a reasonable cost basis subject to per-discharge limits.

Before 1983, Medicare payments for hospital inpatient care were based on a *retrospective reasonable cost system*, which meant hospitals received 80 percent of reasonable charges. Since 1983, when the **inpatient prospective payment system (IPPS)** was implemented, Medicare has reimbursed hospitals for inpatient hospital services according to a predetermined rate for each discharge. Each discharge is categorized into a *diagnosis-related group (DRG)*, which is based on the patient's principal and secondary diagnoses (including comorbidities and complications) as well as surgical and other procedures (if performed) (Figure 9-4). The DRG determines how much payment the hospital receives. Diagnosis-related groups are organized into mutually exclusive categories called **major diagnostic categories (MDCs)**, which are loosely based on body systems (e.g., nervous system).

Because the IPPS payment is based on an adjusted average payment rate, some cases receive Medicare reimbursement in excess of costs (rather than billed charges), whereas other cases receive payment that is less than costs incurred. The system is designed to provide hospitals with an incentive to manage their operations more efficiently by finding areas in which increased efficiencies can be instituted without affecting the quality of care and by treating a mix of patients to balance cost and payments. Note that a hospital's payment is not affected by the length of stay prior to discharge (unless the patient

Home Health Patient Tracking Sheet

(M0010) CMS Certification Number: __ __ __ __ __ __

(M0014) Branch State: __ __

(M0016) Branch ID Number: __ __ __ __ __ __ __ __ __ __

(M0018) National Provider Identifier (NPI) for the attending physician who has signed the plan of care:

__ __ __ __ __ __ __ __ __ __ ☐ UK - Unknown or Not Available

(M0020) Patient ID Number: __

(M0030) Start of Care Date: __ __/__ __/__ __ __ __
month / day / year

(M0032) Resumption of Care Date: __ __/__ __/__ __ __ __ ☐ NA - Not Applicable
month / day / year

(M0040) Patient Name: __
(First) (MI) (Last) (Suffix)

(M0050) Patient State of Residence: __ __

(M0060) Patient Zip Code: __ __ __ __ __ __ __ __ __

(M0063) Medicare Number: __ __ __ __ __ __ __ __ __ __ __ __ ☐ NA - No Medicare
(including suffix)

(M0064) Social Security Number: __ __ __-__ __-__ __ __ __ ☐ UK - Unknown or Not Available

☐ NA - No Medicaid

(M0065) Medicaid Number: __ __ __ __ __ __ __ __ __ __ __ __ __ __

(M0066) Birth Date: __ __/__ __/__ __ __ __
month / day / year

(M0069) Gender:

☐ 1 - Male

☐ 2 - Female

(M0140) Race/Ethnicity: (Mark all that apply.)

☐ 1 - American Indian or Alaska Native

☐ 2 - Asian

☐ 3 - Black or African-American

☐ 4 - Hispanic or Latino

☐ 5 - Native Hawaiian or Pacific Islander

☐ 6 - White

OMB #0938-0760

FIGURE 9-3 Page 1 of the *Home Health Patient Tracking Sheet* completed by home health agencies to capture Outcome and Assessment Information Set (OASIS) data.

is transferred). It is expected that some patients will stay longer than others and that hospitals will offset the higher costs of a longer stay with the lower costs of a reduced stay.

Each DRG has a payment weight assigned to it, based on the average resources used to treat Medicare patients in that DRG, and the reimbursement rate can be adjusted according to the following guidelines:

> **NOTE:** Decision trees are not used by coders or billers to calculate reimbursement, but they do serve as the basis for the development of grouper software that is used to enter patient data (e.g., ICD-10-CM and ICD-10-PCS codes) for DRG assignment to calculate payment.

- **Disproportionate share hospital (DSH) adjustment. Hospitals that treat a high-percentage of low-income patients receive increased Medicare payments.**
- **Indirect medical education (IME) adjustment. Approved teaching hospitals receive increased Medicare payments. The adjustment varies depending on the ratio of residents-to-beds (to calculate operating costs) and residents-to-average-daily-census (to calculate capital costs).**

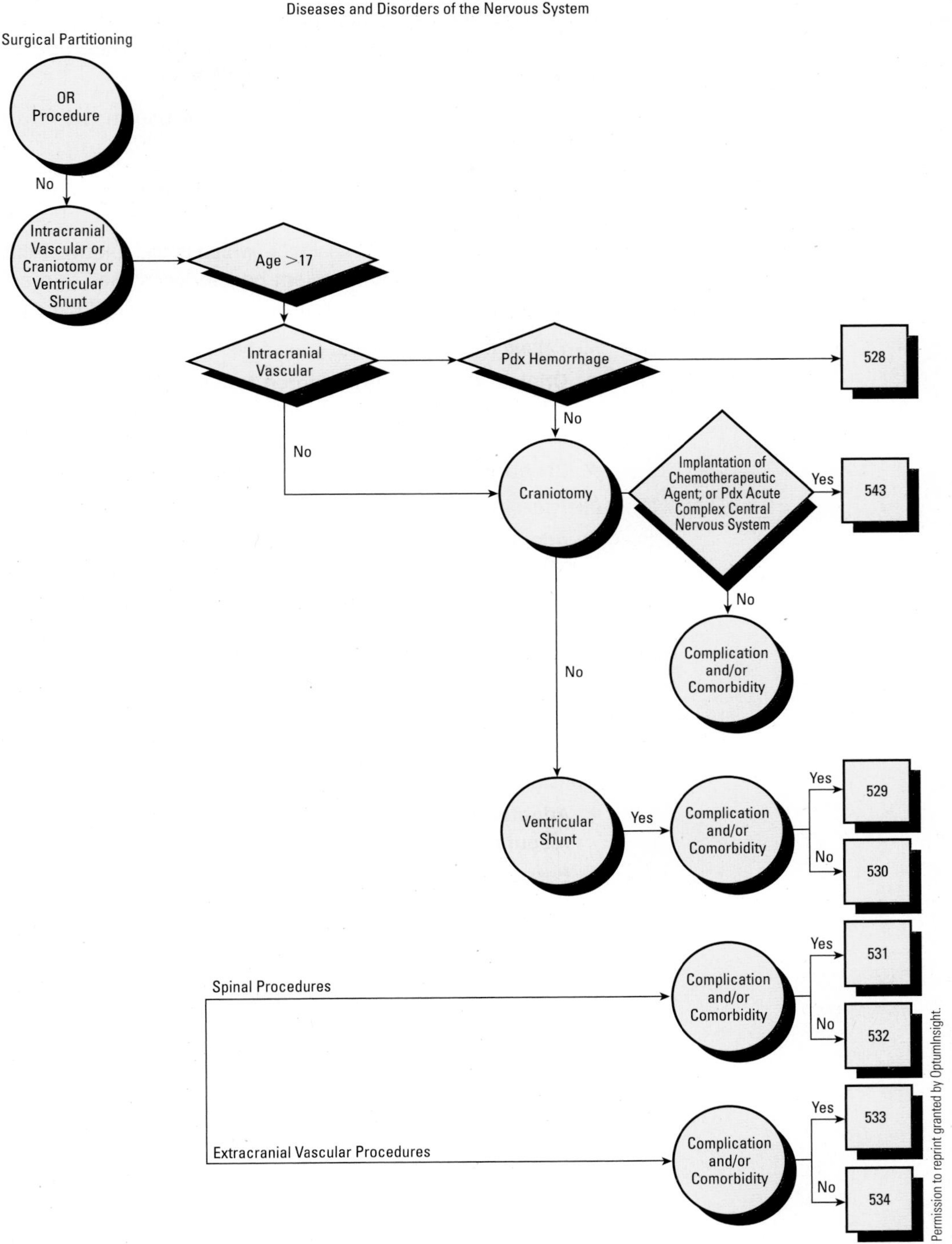

FIGURE 9-4 Sample DRG decision tree.

- Outlier. Hospitals that treat unusually costly cases receive increased medical payments. The additional payment is designed to protect hospitals from large financial losses due to unusually expensive cases. Outlier payments are added to DSH or IME adjustments, when applicable.

Several DRG systems were developed for use in the United States, including:

- *Diagnosis-related groups (DRGs)*
  - Original system used by CMS to reimburse hospitals for inpatient care provided to Medicare beneficiaries
  - Based on intensity of resources, which is the relative volume and types of diagnostic, therapeutic, and inpatient bed services used to manage an inpatient disease
  - Replaced in 2008 by Medicare severity DRGs (MS-DRGs) (discussed below)
- All-Patient diagnosis-related groups (AP-DRGs)
  - Original DRG system adapted for use by third-party payers to reimburse hospitals for inpatient care provided to *non*-Medicare beneficiaries (e.g., BlueCross BlueShield, commercial health plans, TRICARE)
  - Based on intensity of resources
- All-Patient Refined diagnosis-related groups (APR-DRGs)
  - Adopted by Medicare in 2007 to reimburse hospitals for inpatient care provided to Medicare beneficiaries (but discontinued when MS-DRGs were adopted in 2008)
  - Expanded original DRG system (based on intensity of resources) to add two subclasses to each DRG that adjusts Medicare inpatient hospital reimbursement rates for severity of illness (SOI) (extent of physiological decompensation or organ system loss of function) and risk of mortality (ROM) (likelihood of dying)
  - Each subclass, in turn, is subdivided into four areas: (1) minor, (2) moderate, (3) major, and (4) extreme.
- Medicare severity diagnosis-related groups (MS-DRGs)
  - Adopted by Medicare in 2008 to improve recognition of severity of illness and resource consumption and reduce cost variation among DRGs
  - Bases DRG relative weights on hospital *costs* (instead of hospital charges that are associated with pre-2008 DRGs), and expanded number from 538 DRGs to over 750 MS-DRGs, but retained improvements and refinements made to DRGs since 1983
  - Recognized approximately 335 "base" DRGs, which are further refined by *complications* (undesirable effect of disease or treatment that can change the patient's outcome and may require additional treatment), conditions that arise during hospitalization, and/or *comorbidities* (coexisting conditions treated during hospitalization) (CC)
  - Re-evaluated CC list to assign *all* ICD-10-CM codes as non-CC status (conditions that should not be treated as CCs for specific clinical conditions), CC status, *or* major CC status, which prevents Medicare from paying additional costs of treating patients who acquire conditions (e.g., infections) during hospitalization
  - Assigned diagnoses closely associated with patient mortality (cardiogenic shock, cardiac arrest, other shock without mention of trauma, respiratory arrest, and ventricular fibrillation) to different CC subclasses, depending on whether the patient lived or expired
  - Emphasized the importance of proper documentation of patient care, relating it to reimbursement optimization (e.g., increased diagnosis specificity to justify more severe illnesses, resulting in increased reimbursement)—facilities implemented clinical documentation improvement (CDI) programs to ensure thorough and accurate documentation in patient records

CODING FOR DIAGNOSIS-RELATED GROUPS (DRGs)

Diagnoses and procedures are assigned ICD-10-CM and ICD-10-PCS codes, and they are sequenced according to CMS official coding guidelines and the Uniform Hospital Discharge Data Set (UHDDS). This means that hospitals are not required to assign codes to every diagnosis and procedure documented in the patient record. However, hospitals must evaluate their institutional data needs to develop coding policies, which will determine the assignment of ICD-10-CM and ICD-10-PCS codes to diagnoses and procedures.

When assigning codes to comorbidities (coexisting conditions) and complications (conditions that develop during inpatient admission), be sure to carefully review patient record documentation to assign the most specific code possible. Revisions to the MS-DRGs comorbidities and complications (CC) list eliminated many diagnoses that were considered CCs in the past. As a result, physicians must be educated about the importance of proper documentation practices.

EXAMPLE: Under MS-DRGs:

- Chronic obstructive pulmonary disease (COPD) (J44.9) is not a CC. However, acute exacerbation of COPD (J44.1) is a CC.
- Congestive heart failure (CHF) (I50.9) is not a CC. However, chronic systolic heart failure (I50.22) is a CC and acute systolic heart failure (I50.21) is a major CC (MCC).

ICD-10-PCS codes are assigned for documented OR (operating room) and non-OR procedures. (Non-OR procedures are performed in the patient's room, emergency department, radiology department, and so on.) Whether ICD-10-PCS codes are assigned to other procedures, such as ancillary tests (e.g., EKG, laboratory tests, and so on), is dependent on the hospital's coding policy.

The *present on admission (POA) indicator* differentiates between patient conditions present upon inpatient admission and those that develop during the inpatient admission. Claims that do not report the POA indicator are returned to the facility for correction. Hospital-acquired conditions that are reported as not present at the time of admission are not considered when calculating the MS-DRG payment. This means that such conditions, even if included on the CC and MCC lists, are not considered a CC or MCC if diagnosed during the inpatient stay and the facility will not receive additional payment for such conditions.

To determine an IPPS payment, hospitals submit a UB-04 claim for each patient to a Medicare administrative contractor (MAC), which is a third-party payer that contracts with Medicare to carry out the operational functions of the Medicare program. Based on the information provided on the UB-04, the case is categorized into a DRG, which determines the reimbursement provided to the hospital. (DRG payments are adjusted as discussed previously.)

The **IPPS 3-day payment window** (or **IPPS 72-hour rule**) requires outpatient preadmission services provided by a hospital on the day of or during the three days prior to a patient's inpatient admission to be covered by the IPPS DRG payment and reported on the UB-04 with ICD-10-PCS procedure codes (*not* CPT codes) for:

- **Diagnostic services (e.g., lab testing)**
- **Therapeutic (or nondiagnostic) services for which the inpatient principal diagnosis code (ICD-10-CM) exactly matches that for preadmission services**

NOTE: Services that are distinct from and unrelated to the inpatient admission are separately billed by the hospital *if documentation supports that the service is unrelated to the inpatient admission.*

In addition, an **IPPS transfer rule** states that certain patients discharged to a post-acute provider are treated as transfer cases, which means hospitals are paid a graduated *per diem* rate for each day of the patient's stay, not to exceed the prospective payment DRG rate. (Outliers are also recognized for extraordinarily high-cost cases.)

MEDICARE AND MEDICAID NO LONGER PAY FOR HOSPITAL MISTAKES

Payment under the Medicare program for inpatient hospital services is generally based on the *inpatient prospective payment system* (IPPS), and hospitals receive reimbursement for each inpatient discharge based in part on diagnosis codes that identify a *Medicare severity diagnosis-related group (MS-DRG)*. Assignment of an MS-DRG can take into account the presence of secondary diagnoses, and payment levels are adjusted to account for a number of hospital-specific factors. The Deficit Reduction Act of 2005 (DRA) expanded hospital quality measures collected by Medicare and allowed for the adjustment of payments to hospitals for certain preventable hospital-acquired conditions (HACs) that (1) have high cost, high volume, or both; (2) result in the assignment of a case to a MS-DRG that has a higher payment when present as a secondary diagnosis; and (3) could reasonably have been prevented through the application of evidence-based guidelines.

In 2002, the National Quality Forum (NQF) published *Serious Reportable Events in Healthcare: A Consensus Report*, which listed the previously noted adverse events, which were *serious, largely preventable, and of concern to both the public and health care providers*. These events were originally known as *never events* (now called *adverse events*). The Medicare program addressed certain *adverse events* through national coverage determinations (NCDs). Similar to any other patient population, Medicare (and Medicaid) beneficiaries may experience serious injury and/or death if they undergo erroneous surgical or other invasive procedures and may require additional health care to correct adverse outcomes that may result from such errors. To address and reduce the occurrence of these surgeries, CMS issued three national coverage determinations (NCDs). Under these NCDs, CMS does not cover a particular surgical or other invasive procedure performed to treat a particular medical condition when the practitioner erroneously performs (1) a different procedure altogether; (2) the correct procedure but on the wrong body part; or (3) the correct procedure but on the wrong patient. Medicare and Medicaid also do not cover hospitalizations and other services related to these noncovered procedures.

Since October 1, 2007, hospitals subject to the IPPS have been required to submit information on Medicare claims specifying whether diagnoses were present on admission (POA). The POA-indicator reporting requirement and the HAC payment provision apply to IPPS hospitals only, and the following is a list of the Medicare HACs for which CMS does not reimburse hospitals. (Effective July 2012, Medicaid also does not reimburse hospitals for these HACs.)

- Foreign object retained after surgery
- Air embolism
- Blood incompatibility
- Stage III and IV pressure ulcers

(continues)

(continued)

- Falls and trauma
    - Fractures
    - Dislocations
    - Intracranial injuries
    - Crushing injuries
    - Burns
    - Electric shock
- Catheter-associated urinary tract infection (UTI)
- Vascular catheter-associated infection
- Manifestations of poor glycemic control
    - Diabetic ketoacidosis
    - Nonketotic hyperosmolar coma
    - Hypoglycemic coma
    - Secondary diabetes with ketoacidosis
    - Secondary diabetes with hyperosmolarity
- Surgical site infection following:
    - Coronary artery bypass graft (CABG)—mediastinitis
    - Bariatric surgery
        - Laparoscopic gastric bypass
        - Gastroenterostomy
        - Laparoscopic gastric restrictive surgery
    - Orthopedic procedures
        - Spine
        - Neck
        - Shoulder
        - Elbow
- Deep vein thrombosis (DVT)/pulmonary embolism (PE) following:
    - Total knee replacement
    - Hip replacement
- Surgery on the wrong patient, wrong surgery on a patient, and wrong site surgery

Source: Federal Register. 42 CFR Parts 434, 438, and 447. May 25, 2011 (www.ofr.gov)

HOSPITAL OUTPATIENT PROSPECTIVE PAYMENT SYSTEM

The BBA of 1997 authorized CMS to implement an *outpatient prospective payment system (OPPS)* for hospital outpatient services provided to Medicare patients. (The OPPS was implemented in 2000.) Also reimbursed under the

NOTE: The OPPS does not cover payments for professional services, which are reported on the CMS-1500 claim and reimbursed according to a fee schedule, such as the Medicare physician fee schedule (MPFS) discussed later in this chapter. Hospitals report outpatient encounters on the UB-04 (or CMS-1450) claim using ICD-10-CM for diagnoses and HCPCS/CPT for procedures and services.

NOTE: A Medicare patient's coinsurance amount is initially calculated for each APC based on 20 percent of the national median charge for services in the APC. The coinsurance amount for an APC does not change until the amount becomes 20 percent of the total APC payment, and no coinsurance amount can be greater than the hospital inpatient deductible in a given year.

OPPS are certain Medicare Part B services furnished to hospital inpatients who have no Part A coverage, as well as partial hospitalization services furnished by community mental health centers. All services are paid according to *ambulatory payment classifications* (APCs), which group services according to similar clinical characteristics and in terms of resources required. A payment rate is established for each APC and, depending on services provided, hospitals may be paid for more than one APC for a patient encounter (Figure 9-5). The Medicare beneficiary coinsurance was also recalculated under the OPPS and was based on 20 percent of the national median charge for services in the APC. (Both the total APC payment and the portion paid as coinsurance amounts are adjusted to reflect geographic wage variations.)

Each CPT and HCPCS level II code is assigned a *status indicator (SI)* as a payment indicator to identify how each code is paid (or not paid) under the OPPS. For example, status indicator "S" refers to "significant procedures for which the multiple procedure reduction does not apply." This means that the CPT and/or HCPCS level II code is paid the full APC reimbursement rate. OPPS status indicator "T" refers to "services to which the multiple procedure payment reduction applies." (CPT modifier, -51 is not added to codes reported for OPPS payment consideration.) This means that the reported CPT and/or HCPCS level II code will be paid a discounted APC reimbursement rate when reported with other procedures on the same claim.

APC grouper software is used to assign an APC to each CPT and/or HCPCS level II code reported on an outpatient claim, as well as to appropriate ICD-10-CM diagnosis codes. Outpatient code editor (OCE) software is used in conjunction

Outpatient Prospective Payment System (OPPS) Formula

(APC Weight x Conversion Factor x Wage Index) + Add-On Payments = Payment

NOTE: When a patient undergoes multiple procedures and services on the same day, multiple APCs are generated and payments are added together. APC software automatically discounts multiple APC payments when appropriate (e.g., bilateral procedure).

EXAMPLE: Using the sample data below, the OPPS payment for a patient who underwent a cataract procedure with intraocular lens implant, chest X-ray, and ureteral reflux study in Buffalo, New York, is calculated as $1,253.73. (NOTE: Add-on payments do not apply to this example and APC payments were not discounted.)

(22.98 x $54.561 x 0.8192) + (0.78 x $54.561 x 0.8192) + (4.29 x $54.561 x 0.8192)

$1,027.12 + $34.86 + $191.75 = $1,253.73

Conversion Factor = $54.561
Wage Index = 0.8192

HCPCS Code	Description	APC	APC Weight
66984	Cataract procedure with intraocular lens implant	246	22.98
71020	Chest x-ray, 2 views	260	0.78
78740	Ureteral reflux study	292	4.29

FIGURE 9-5 Formula for determining OPPS payments.

NOTE: Health care personnel routinely discuss "pass-through payments" due to new technology, such as innovative medical devices (e.g., using surgical glue instead of stitches) and new drugs and vaccines (e.g., human papillomavirus [HPV] vaccine).

with the APC grouper to identify Medicare claims edits and assign APC groups to reported codes.

EXAMPLE: OCE software reviews "to/from" dates of service to identify and reject claims that are submitted for reimbursement as hospital-based outpatient care when, in fact, the claim should be processed as inpatient care.

The unit of payment for the OPPS is an outpatient visit or encounter. (The unit of payment for the IPPS discussed earlier is an inpatient hospital admission.) An **outpatient encounter** (or **outpatient visit**) includes all outpatient procedures and services (e.g., same-day surgery, x-rays, laboratory tests, and so on) provided during one day to the same patient. Thus, a patient who undergoes multiple outpatient procedures and receives multiple services on the same day will be assigned to one or more outpatient groups (called *APCs*). Each APC is weighted and has a prospective payment amount associated with it; if a patient is assigned multiple APCs, the payments are totaled to provide reimbursement to the hospital for the encounter. (APC payments may be discounted when certain procedures or services are provided, such as bilateral procedures.) A **wage index** adjusts payments to account for geographic variations in hospitals' labor costs. In addition, *add-ons* such as *pass-through payments* provide additional reimbursement to hospitals that use innovative (new and improved) biologicals, drugs, and technical devices. *Outlier payments* for high-cost services, *hold harmless payments* for certain hospitals, and *transitional payments* to limit losses under the OPPS can also increase payments. (The hospital profits if the payment rate is higher than the cost of care provided; the hospital loses money if the payment rate is lower than the cost of care provided.)

INPATIENT PSYCHIATRIC FACILITY PROSPECTIVE PAYMENT SYSTEM

The *inpatient psychiatric facility prospective payment system (IPF PPS)* was implemented as a result of Medicare, Medicaid, and SCHIP Balanced Budget Refinement Act of 1999 (BBRA) provisions that required implementation of a *per diem* patient classification system that reflects differences in patient resource use and costs. The IPF PPS replaced a reasonable cost-based payment system, affecting approximately 2,000 facilities, to promote long-term cost control and utilization management. Licensed psychiatric facilities and hospital-based psychiatric units were reimbursed according to the new PPS, which was phased in over a three-year period beginning in 2004. (General health care facilities that are not licensed for specialty care but that occasionally treat patients with behavioral health or chemical dependency diagnoses are exempt from the IPF PPS.)

NOTE: New York State will phase in *ambulatory patient groups* (APGs) as a new payment methodology for most Medicaid outpatient services (e.g., outpatient clinic, ambulatory surgery, and emergency department services). Implementation of APGs will result in:

- Higher payments for higher intensity services and lower payments for lower intensity services.
- The transition of funds from inpatient to outpatient services to support quality outpatient care and to address the problem of avoidable hospitalizations.

Health information department coders will use ICD-10-CM and ICD-10-PCS to assign codes to inpatient behavioral health diagnoses and procedures and will enter data into DRG software to calculate the IPF PPS rates. Inpatient psychiatric facilities are reimbursed according to a *per diem* payment that is calculated using DRG data, wage-adjusted rates, and facility-level adjusters (Figure 9-6). (IPPS MS-DRGs reimburse acute care hospitals a flat payment based on ICD-10-CM and ICD-10-PCS codes and other data.) Providers will use the ***Diagnostic and Statistical Manual* (DSM)** published by the American Psychiatric Association. Although DSM codes do not affect IPF PPS rates, the manual contains diagnostic assessment criteria that are used as tools to identify psychiatric disorders. The DSM includes psychiatric disorders and codes, provides a mechanism for communicating and recording diagnostic information, and is used in the areas of research and statistics.

Inpatient Psychiatric Hospital PPS Calculator

		Adjustment Factors
Patient Age	Patient is under age 65	1
Principal Diagnosis	DRG 12: Degenerative Nervous System Disorders (select as many comorbidities that apply below)	1.07
Comorbidity	Renal Failure, Chronic	1.14
Comorbidity	Arteriosclerosis of the Extremity with Gangrene	1.17
Comorbidity	Infectious Diseases	1.08
LOS (Days)	18	
Geographic Location	Rural	1.16
Teaching Adj.	0.6	1.28
Wage Area	Utah	0.9312

After making selections (above), scroll down for payment calculation information.

Budget Neutral Base Rate	$530

Calculate Wage Adjusted Rate	
The labor portion of the base rate	$386
Apply wage index factor of 0.9312 to the labor portion of $386	$359
The non-labor portion of the Federal base rate	$144
The total wage-adjusted rate	$503

Apply Facility Level Adjusters	
Teaching Adjustment	1.28
Rural Adjustment (if applicable)	1.16

Apply Patient Level Adjusters	
DRG 12: Degenerative Nervous System Disorders	1.07
Apply age adjustment	1
Apply comorbidity adjusters:	
Renal Failure, Chronic	1.14
Arteriosclerosis of the Extremity with Gangrene	1.17
Infectious Diseases	1.08

Total PPS Adjustment Factor	2.2846

The wage-adjusted and PPS-adjusted per diem amount is $1,150 (2.2846 * $503)

Apply variable per diem adjustment for 18 days:	Per Diem Amount	Unit	Extended
Day 1 (adjustment factor=1.26):	$1,150 * 1.26 = $1,449	1	$1,449
Days 2–4 (adjustment factor=1.12):	$1,150 * 1.12 = $1,288	3	$3,865
Days 5–8 (adjustment factor=1.05):	$1,150 * 1.05 = $1,208	4	$4,831
Days over 8 (adjustment factor=1.00):	$1,150 * 1.00 = $1,150	10	$11,502

Total Inpatient Psychiatric Hospital PPS Payment:	**$21,646**

FIGURE 9-6 Psychiatric hospital IPF PPS calculator worksheet.

INPATIENT REHABILITATION FACILITY PROSPECTIVE PAYMENT SYSTEM

The BBA of 1997 authorized the implementation of a per-discharge prospective payment system (PPS) for inpatient rehabilitation hospitals and rehabilitation units, also called inpatient rehabilitation facilities (IRFs). Implemented in 2002, the IRF PPS utilizes information from a patient assessment instrument to classify patients into distinct groups based on clinical characteristics and expected resource needs. Separate payments are calculated for each group, including the application of case- and facility-level adjustments.

A *patient assessment instrument* classifies patients into IRF PPS groups based on clinical characteristics and expected resource needs. Separate IRF PPS payments are calculated for each group and include case- and facility-level adjustments. Elements of the IRF PPS include:

- ***Minimum Data Set for Post Acute Care (MDS-PAC)*** **(patient-centered assessment instrument completed by each Medicare patient that emphasizes the patient's care needs instead of the provider's characteristics; it classifies patients for Medicare payment and contains an appropriate quality-of-care monitoring system, including the use of quality indicators)**
- ***Case-mix groups (CMGs)*** **(classification of patients into 97 function-related groups, which predict resources needed to furnish patient care to different types of patients; data elements from the MDS-PAC are used to classify a patient into a CMG)**
- ***CMG relative weights*** **(weights that account for the variance in cost per discharge and resource utilization among CMGs; reimbursement is based on a national formula that adjusts for case mix)**
- ***CMG payment rates*** **(predetermined, per-discharge reimbursement amount that includes all operating and capital costs associated with providing covered inpatient rehabilitation services)**

Inpatient Rehabilitation Validation and Entry (IRVEN) software (Figure 9-7) is the computerized data entry system used by inpatient rehabilitation facilities to create a file in a standard format that can be electronically transmitted to a national database. The data collected are used to assess the clinical characteristics of patients in rehabilitation hospitals and rehabilitation units in acute care hospitals. It provides agencies and facilities with a means to objectively measure and compare facility performance and quality. It will also provide researchers with information to support the development of improved standards.

LONG-TERM (ACUTE) CARE HOSPITAL PROSPECTIVE PAYMENT SYSTEM

The BBRA of 1999 authorized the implementation of a per-discharge DRG **long-term (acute) care hospital prospective payment system (LTCH PPS)** for cost reporting periods beginning on or after October 1, 2002. This new prospective payment system replaced the reasonable cost-based payment system under which long-term (acute) care hospitals (LTCHs) were previously paid. (In 2008, Medicare severity long-term care diagnosis-related groups [MS-LTC-DRGs] were adopted for the LTCH PPS.) Long-term (acute) care hospitals are defined by Medicare as having an average inpatient length of stay of greater than 25 days.

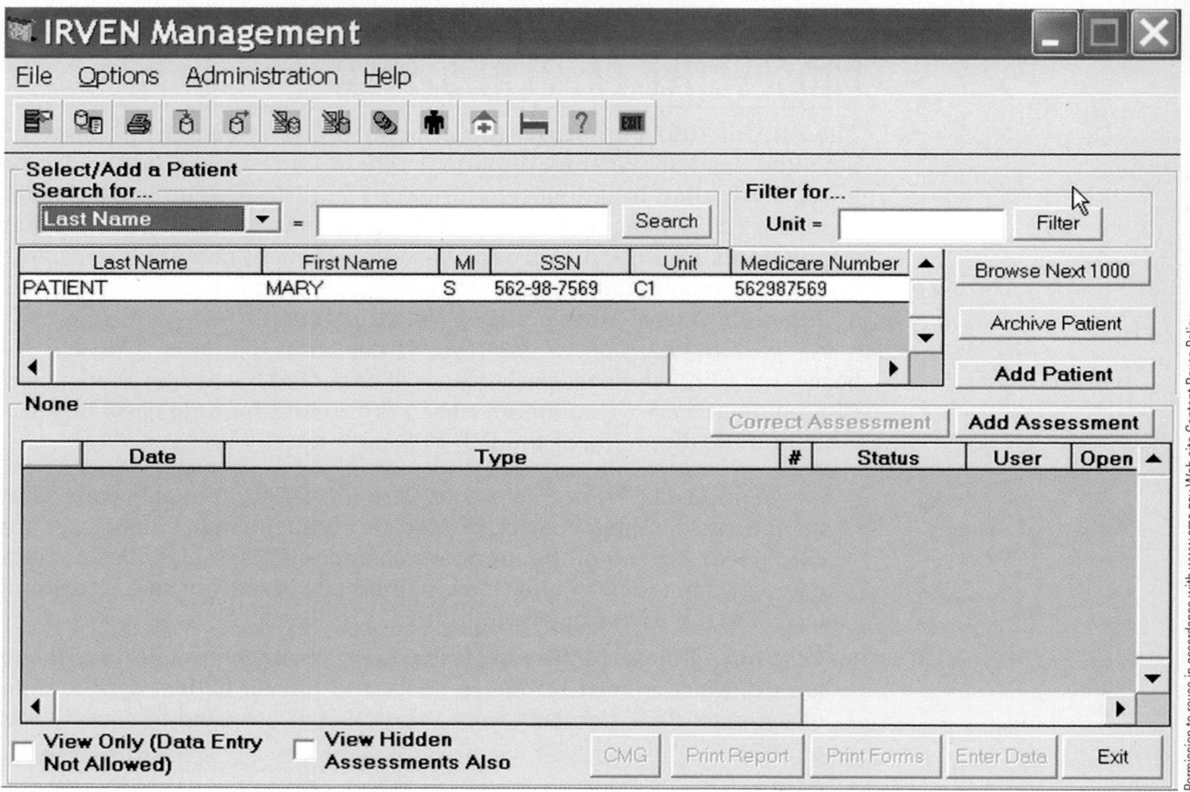

FIGURE 9-7 Opening screen from IRVEN software.

Major elements of the LTCH PPS include:

- ***Patient classification system*** **(patients are classified according to long-term [acute] care diagnosis-related groups [LTC DRGs] based on clinical characteristics and average resource needs; the LTC DRGs are based on existing IPPS DRGs, which have been weighted to reflect the resources required to treat medically complex patients in long-term care hospitals)**
- ***Relative weights*** **(the MS-LTC-DRGs primary element that accounts for variations in cost per discharge, because the weights reflect severity of illness and resource consumption for each diagnosis)**
- ***Payment rate*** **(LTCH PPS payments for Medicare patients will be predetermined, per-discharge amounts for each MS-LTC-DRG)**
- ***Adjustments*** **(LTCH PPS payments are adjusted for short stay cases, interrupted stay cases, cases discharged and readmitted to co-located providers, and high-cost outlier cases. In addition, adjustments are made for differences in area wages and a cost-of-living adjustment [COLA] for LTCHs in Alaska and Hawaii.)**

SKILLED NURSING FACILITY PROSPECTIVE PAYMENT SYSTEM

The BBA of 1997 modified reimbursement for Medicare Part A (inpatient) skilled nursing facility (SNF) services. Beginning in 1998, SNFs were no longer paid on a reasonable cost basis but rather on the basis of a prospective payment system.

```
RAVEN - Clinical Data Collection Design System Report

Assessment Data Entry

Date:     June 04, YYYY
Requested by:     MDS
------------------------------------------------------------------
ASSESSMENT DATA ENTRY REPORT FOR ASSESSMENT ID = 1-00001
Last entry Date:  05/23/YYYY    Dictionary Version:    MDS700
Data entry Time:  00:08:41      Data Entry Version:    MDS700
Data entry user:  MDS
MDS Module, Screen Set:
Full Assessment
------------------------------------------------------------------
Header Records
------------------------------------------------------------------
(Assessment Date)                       : 05/23/YYYY
Assessment Form Type                    : RAVEN Assessment
Facility Option AB and AC               : 5
Quarter type                            :
Include section t and u                 :
```


FIGURE 9-8 Sample report generated from RAVEN software.

Major elements of the SNF PPS include:

- ***Payment rate*** **(Federal rates are determined using allowable costs from facility cost reports, and data are aggregated nationally by urban and rural area to determine standardized federal *Per diem* rates to which case-mix and wage adjustments apply.)**
- ***Case-mix adjustment*** **(*Per diem* payments for each admission are case-mix adjusted using a resident classification system called Resource Utilization Groups, based on data from resident assessments and relative weights developed from staff time data.)**
- ***Geographic adjustment*** **(Labor portions of federal rates are adjusted for geographic variation in wages using the hospital wage index.)**

Computerized data entry software entitled **Resident Assessment Validation and Entry (RAVEN)** is used to enter MDS data about SNF patients and transmit those assessments in CMS-standard format to individual state databases. RAVEN also allows facilities to generate system reports (Figure 9-8).

MEDICARE PHYSICIAN FEE SCHEDULE

As of 1992, physician services and procedures are reimbursed according to a payment system known as the *Resource-Based Relative Value Scale (RBRVS).* The RBRVS replaced the Medicare physician payment system of "customary, prevailing, and reasonable" (CPR) charges under which physicians were reimbursed according to the historical record of the charge for the provision of each service. This system, now called the **Medicare physician fee schedule (MPFS)**, reimburses providers according to predetermined rates assigned to services and is revised by CMS each year. All services are standardized to measure the value of a service as compared with other services provided. These standards, called **relative value units (RVUs)**, are payment components consisting of:

NOTE: Most third-party payers, including state Medicaid programs, have adopted aspects of the MPFS.

- ***Physician work*****, which reflects the physician's time and intensity in providing the service (e.g., judgment, technical skill, and physical effort)**

- *Practice expense*, which reflects overhead costs involved in providing a service (e.g., rent, utilities, equipment, and staff salaries)
- *Malpractice expense*, which reflects malpractice expenses (e.g., costs of liability insurance)

Payment limits were also established by adjusting the RVUs for each locality by geographic adjustment factors (GAF), called *geographic cost practice indices (GCPIs)*, so that Medicare providers are paid differently in each state and also within each state (e.g., New York state has five separate payment localities). An annual **conversion factor** (dollar multiplier) converts RVUs into payments using a formula (Figure 9-9).

Although the Medicare physician fee schedule is used to determine payment for Medicare Part B (physician) services, other services, such as anesthesia, pathology/laboratory, and radiology, require special consideration.

NOTE: The Medicare physician fee schedule may list fees for services not commonly provided to Medicare patients (e.g., obstetrical services) because private payers also adopt the schedule.

- Anesthesia services payments are based on the actual time an anesthesiologist spends with a patient and the American Society of Anesthesiologists' relative value system.
- Radiology services payments vary according to place of service (e.g., hospital radiology department vs. freestanding radiology center).
- Pathology services payments vary according to the number of patients served:
  - Pathology services that include clinical laboratory management and supervision of technologists are covered and paid as hospital services.
  - Pathology services that are directed to an individual patient in a hospital setting (e.g., pathology consultation) are paid under the physician fee schedule.

Nonparticipating Physicians

NOTE: NonPARs can accept assignment on a case-by-case basis, as discussed in Chapter 14.

When the nonparticipating provider (nonPAR) does not accept assignment from Medicare, the amount Medicare reimburses for services provided is subject to a 5 percent reduction of the Medicare physician fee schedule (MPFS) amount. In addition, Medicare requires the nonPAR to charge the patient no more than the difference between what Medicare reimburses and the **limiting charge**, which is calculated by multiplying the reduced MPFS (or allowable charge) by 115 percent.

Use the following formula to calculate the limiting charge:

[MPFS – (MPFS × 5 percent)] × 115 percent = limiting charge

For example, [$80 – ($80 × 5 percent)] × 115 percent = $76 × 115 percent = $87.40 (limiting charge). (Medicare reimburses the nonPAR based on the $76 reduced MPFS amount, such as 80 percent of that reduced MPFS. The patient is responsible for reimbursing the nonPAR for the difference between what Medicare reimburses the nonPAR and the limiting charge, or $26.60, which includes any copayment.)

Limiting charge information appears on the **Medicare Summary Notice (MSN)** (Figure 9-10) (previously called an *Explanation of Medicare Benefits*, or *EOMB*), which notifies Medicare beneficiaries of actions taken on claims. The limiting charge policy is intended to reduce the amount patients enrolled in Medicare are expected to pay when they receive health care services. If a participating (PAR) and a nonparticipating (nonPAR) physician charge the same fee for an office visit, amounts billed and reimbursement received are different for each physician.

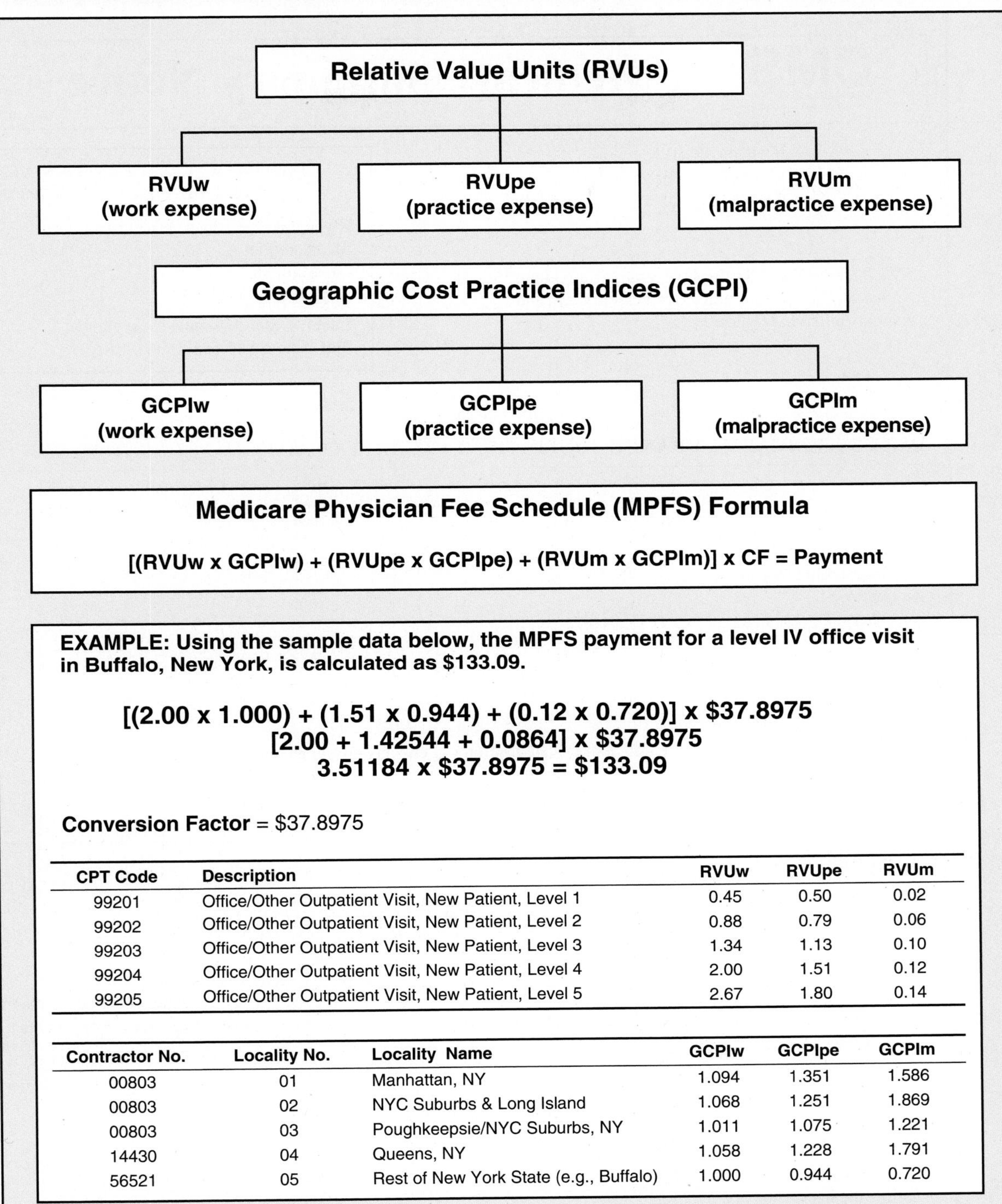

CPT Code	Description	RVUw	RVUpe	RVUm
99201	Office/Other Outpatient Visit, New Patient, Level 1	0.45	0.50	0.02
99202	Office/Other Outpatient Visit, New Patient, Level 2	0.88	0.79	0.06
99203	Office/Other Outpatient Visit, New Patient, Level 3	1.34	1.13	0.10
99204	Office/Other Outpatient Visit, New Patient, Level 4	2.00	1.51	0.12
99205	Office/Other Outpatient Visit, New Patient, Level 5	2.67	1.80	0.14

Contractor No.	Locality No.	Locality Name	GCPIw	GCPIpe	GCPIm
00803	01	Manhattan, NY	1.094	1.351	1.586
00803	02	NYC Suburbs & Long Island	1.068	1.251	1.869
00803	03	Poughkeepsie/NYC Suburbs, NY	1.011	1.075	1.221
14430	04	Queens, NY	1.058	1.228	1.791
56521	05	Rest of New York State (e.g., Buffalo)	1.000	0.944	0.720

FIGURE 9-9 Formula for determining physician fee schedule payments.

Medicare Summary Notice

July 10, YYYY

JOHN Q. PUBLIC
10A SENATE ST.
ANYWHERE, NY 12345

CUSTOMER SERVICE INFORMATION
Your Medicare Number: 112-34-9801A

If you have questions, write or call:
Medicare Part A
101 Main St
Anywhere, NY 12345

Local: 1-800-555-4606 (Maryland)
Toll-free: 1-800-555-1636 (Others)

HELP STOP FRAUD: Read your Medicare Summary Notice carefully for accuracy of dates, services, and amounts billed to Medicare.

This is a summary of claims processed on 06/26/YYYY.

PART B MEDICAL INSURANCE - OUTPATIENT FACILITY CLAIMS

Dates of Service	Services Provided	Amount Charged	Non-Covered Charged	Deductible and Coinsurance	You May Be Billed	See Notes Section
Claim number 12345678901245 **Goodmedicine Hospital** **Anywhere St.** **Anywhere, US 12345** Referred by: E Helper						a, b
05/25/YY	CAT scan for therapy guide (76370)	$212.00	$0.00	$122.40	$0.00	c

Notes Section:

a. This information is being sent to your private insurer(s). Send any questions regarding your benefits to them.
b. $100.00 of the money approved by your primary insurer has been credited to your Medicare Part B deductible. You do not have to pay this amount.
c. $100.00 of this approved amount has been applied toward your deductible.

Your Medicare Number: 112-34-9801A

Deductible Information:

You have met the Part B deductible for YYYY.

General Information:

Who pays? You pay. Report Medicare fraud by calling 1-800-447-8477. An example of fraud would be claims for Medicare items or services you did not receive. If you have any other questions about your claim, please contact the Medicare contractor telephone number shown on this notice.

You can protect yourself from some pneumococcal infections by getting a pneumococcal vaccination. Medicare Part B will pay for your vaccination. One pneumococcal vaccination may be all you ever need.

Appeals Information - Part B (Outpatient)

If you disagree with any claims decision on this notice, you can request an appeal by **January 10, YYYY.** Follow the instructions below:

1. Circle the item(s) you disagree with and explain why you disagree.
2. Send this notice, or a copy, to the address in the "Customer Service Information" box on Page 1.
3. Sign here ______________________________ Phone number (______) ____________________

THIS IS NOT A BILL - Keep this notice for your records.

FIGURE 9-10 Sample Medicare Summary Notice (MSN).

NOTE: Medicare discounts its physician fee schedule 5 percent for nonPAR providers, which is called the **allowable charge** or allowed charge.

EXAMPLE: A PAR and nonPAR physician each charge $50 for an office visit (CPT code 99213). The Medicare physician fee schedule for CPT code 99213 is $40. The nonPAR is reimbursed a maximum of $38 by Medicare (because of the 5 percent reduction of the MPFS rate) and the limiting charge is $43.70 ($38 × 115 percent).

The PAR physician is reimbursed:

Medicare payment (80 percent of $40)	$32.00
Beneficiary coinsurance (20 percent of $40)	+ $8.00
TOTAL REIMBURSEMENT TO PAR	$40.00

The nonPAR physician is reimbursed:

Medicare payment (80 percent of $38)	$30.40
Beneficiary is billed the balance of the $43.70 limiting charge	+ $13.30
TOTAL REIMBURSEMENT TO NONPAR	$43.70

Generally, participating physicians report their actual fees to Medicare but adjust, or write off, the uncollectible portion of the charge when they receive payment. NonPAR doctors usually report only the *limiting charge* as their fee. Billing write-off or adjustment amounts to beneficiaries is called **balance billing** and is prohibited by Medicare regulations. In the preceding example, using CPT code 99213, the write-off amounts are:

Participating physician	$10.00 (because $50 – $40 = $10)
NonPAR physician	$6.30 (because $50 – $43.70 = $6.30)

The patient pays $5.30 more ($13.30 – $8 = $5.30) to the nonPAR, which can be significant for people living on a fixed income. Beneficiaries frequently ask, "Does the doctor participate in Medicare?" when calling for an appointment. With very few exceptions, people who qualify for Medicare are not allowed to purchase other primary health insurance. CMS must be certain that Medicare beneficiaries are not required to pay excessive out-of-pocket amounts for health care services. To protect Medicare enrollees financially, providers must comply with extensive rules and regulations.

Medicare Secondary Payer

Medicare Secondary Payer (MSP) refers to situations in which the Medicare program does not have primary responsibility for paying a beneficiary's medical expenses. The Medicare beneficiary may be entitled to other coverage that should pay before Medicare. From the time the Medicare program began in 1966, providers of health care grew accustomed to billing Medicare first for services to Medicare beneficiaries. Thus, the MSP program was initiated in 1980, and when a Medicare beneficiary also has coverage from one of the following groups, Medicare is a secondary payer:

- Automobile medical or no-fault insurance
- Disabled individual covered by a large group health plan (LGHP) or who has coverage under the LGHP of a family member who is currently employed. A **large group health plan (LGHP)** is provided by an employer who has 100 or more

employees *or* a multi-employer plan in which at least one employer has 100 or more full- or part-time employees.

- End-stage renal disease program. *Exception:* For a Medicare patient who has ESRD and who is covered by both Medicare and an employer or union group health plan, the group health plan is primary and Medicare is secondary. After the first 30 months, Medicare is primary and the group health plan is secondary.
- Federal black-lung program
- Other liability insurance (e.g., general casualty insurance, homeowner's liability insurance, malpractice insurance, or product liability insurance)
- Veterans Administration benefits
- Workers' compensation
- Working aged coverage by an employer group health plan (EGHP), or an individual age 65 or older who is covered by a working spouse's EGHP. (The working spouse can be any age.) An **employer group health plan (EGHP)** is contributed to by an employer or employee pay-all plan and provides coverage to employees and dependents without regard to the enrollee's employment status (i.e., full-time, part-time, or retired). These provisions are applicable regardless of the size of the employer.

Upon claims submission, the amount of secondary benefits payable is the lowest of the:

- Actual charge by the physician or supplier minus the amount paid by the primary payer
- Amount Medicare would pay if services were not covered by the primary payer
- Higher of the Medicare physician fee schedule (or other amount payable under Medicare or the third-party payer's allowable charge) minus the amount actually paid by the primary payer

To calculate the amount of Medicare secondary benefits payable on a given claim, the following information is required:

- Amount paid by the primary payer
- Primary payer's allowable charge

This information can be obtained from the primary payer's remittance advice or the patient's explanation of benefits (EOB).

EXAMPLE: An individual received treatment from a physician who charged $250. The individual's Medicare Part B deductible had previously been met. As primary payer, the employer group health plan's (EGHP) allowed charge was $200, and the EGHP paid 80 percent of this amount (or $160). The Medicare physician fee schedule amount is $150. The Medicare secondary payment is calculated as follows:

1. Physician charge minus EGHP payment ($250 – $160 = $90)
2. Medicare payment (determined in usual manner) (80 percent of $150 = $120)
3. EGHP allowable charge minus EGHP payment ($200 – $160 = $40)
4. Medicare pays $40 (lowest of amounts in steps 1, 2, or 3)

Some Medicare beneficiaries are covered by an employer plan if they are still working or if the spouse is employed and the health plan covers family members. Medicare has very specific rules about payment when another insurance is primary. This billing order is discussed in Chapter 14 of this text.

Nonphysician Practitioners

Medicare reimburses professional services provided by nonphysician practitioners, including nurse practitioners, clinical nurse specialists, and physician assistants. A **nurse practitioner (NP)** is a registered nurse licensed to practice as an NP in the state in which services are furnished, is certified by a national association (e.g., American Academy of Nurse Practitioners), and has a master's degree in nursing. NPs often work as primary care providers along with physicians, and they must *accept assignment* to receive reimbursement from Medicare. A **clinical nurse specialist (CNS)** is an advanced practice registered nurse licensed by the state in which services are provided, has a graduate degree in a defined clinical area of nursing from an accredited educational institution, and is certified as a CNS. A **physician assistant (PA)** must be legally authorized and licensed by the state to furnish services, have graduated from a physician assistant educational program that is accredited by the Accreditation Review Commission on Education for the Physician Assistant, and have passed the national certification examination of the National Commission on Certification of Physician Assistants (NCCPA). Some states (e.g., Texas) require PAs to work under a supervising physician who is approved by the state to direct and manage professional activities and who ensures that services provided are medically appropriate for the patient.

Nonphysician practitioner reimbursement rules include the following:

> **NOTE:** Nonphysician practitioners that bill Medicare under an incident-to provision report the physician's provider number on the CMS-1500 claim (instead of their own provider number). This provision is based on the Medicare regulation that permits billing of ancillary personnel services under the physician's provider number (e.g., office EKG performed by a medical assistant).

- Reimbursement for services provided by nonphysician practitioners is allowed *only* if no facility or other provider is paid in connection with such services.
- Payment is based on 80 percent of the actual charge or 85 percent of the Medicare physician fee schedule, whichever is less. Medicare reimburses 80 percent of the resultant payment, and the patient pays 20 percent.
- Direct payment can be made to the nonphysician practitioner, the employer, or the contractor (except for services provided by PAs, for which payment *must* be made to the employer).
- If nonphysician practitioners provide services outside of the office setting, they must obtain their own Medicare provider numbers.
- Services provided by nonphysician practitioners may also be reported to Medicare as **incident to** the supervising physician's service. (Nonphysician practitioners *do not* have to have their own Medicare provider numbers when billing incident-to services.) *Incident-to* services are reimbursed at 100 percent of the Medicare physician fee schedule, and Medicare pays 80 percent of that amount directly to the physician.
- Reimbursement is available for services provided by nonphysician practitioners who work *in collaboration with* a physician (e.g., DO or MD), which means that a written agreement is in place specifying the services to be provided by the nonphysician practitioner, who must work with one or more physicians to deliver health care services. These providers receive medical direction and appropriate supervision as required by state law.

> **NOTE:** The collaborating physician need *not* be present when the nonphysician practitioner provides services to patients, and the physician does *not* have to independently evaluate each patient seen by the nonphysician practitioner. The written agreement must be made available to Medicare upon request, and any services provided by the nonphysician practitioner that are not included in the agreement cannot be billed to Medicare.

The types of services nonphysician practitioners provide include those traditionally reserved to physicians, such as physical examination, minor surgery, setting casts for simple fractures, interpreting x-rays, and other activities that involve independent evaluation or treatment of the patient's condition. Also, if authorized under the scope of their state licenses, nonphysician practitioners may furnish services billed under all levels of evaluation and management codes and diagnostic tests *if furnished in collaboration with a physician.*

Location of Service Adjustment

Physicians are usually reimbursed on a fee-for-service basis with payments established by the Medicare physician fee schedule (MPFS) based on RBRVS. When office-based services are performed in a facility, such as a hospital or outpatient setting, payments are reduced because the doctor did not provide supplies, utilities, or the costs of running the facility. This is known as the **site of service differential**. Other rules govern the services performed by hospital-based providers and teaching physicians. This chapter discusses rules that affect private practice physicians billing under the MPFS.

CMS Manual System

The Centers for Medicare and Medicaid Services (CMS) publish Internet-only manuals (IOMs) (e.g., Medicare Claims Processing Manual) on their website. The manuals include CMS program issuances (e.g., transmittal notices, national coverage determinations, and so on), day-to-day operating instructions, policies, and procedures that are based on statutes, regulations, guidelines, models, and directives. The CMS program components, providers, contractors, Medicare Advantage organizations, and state survey agencies use the IOMs to administer CMS programs. They are also a good source of Medicare and Medicaid information for the general public.

CMS program transmittals communicate new or changed policies and/or procedures that are being incorporated into a specific CMS Internet-only program manual. The ***CMS Quarterly Provider Update*** **(QPU)** is an online CMS publication that contains information about regulations and major policies currently under development, regulations and major policies completed or canceled, and new or revised manual instructions.

CHARGEMASTER

The **chargemaster** (or **charge description master [CDM]**) is a document that contains a computer-generated list of procedures, services, and supplies with charges for each. Chargemaster data are entered in the facility's patient accounting system, and charges are automatically posted to the patient's bill (UB-04). The bill is then submitted to the payer to generate payment for inpatient, ancillary, and other services (e.g., emergency department, laboratory, radiology, and so on). The chargemaster allows the facility to accurately and efficiently bill the payer for services rendered, and it usually contains the following:

- Department code (refers to the specific ancillary department where the service is performed)
- Service code (internal identification of specific service rendered)
- Service description (narrative description of the service, procedure, or supply)
- Revenue code (UB-04 revenue code that is assigned to each procedure, service, or product)
- Charge amount (dollar amount facility charges for each procedure, service, or supply)
- Relative value units (RVUs) (numeric value assigned to a procedure; based on difficulty and time consumed)

Chargemaster maintenance is the process of updating and revising key elements of the chargemaster (or charge description master [CDM]) to ensure accurate reimbursement. Because a chargemaster allows a health care facility to capture charges as procedures are performed and services are provided, inaccurate and outdated chargemasters can result in claims rejection, fines and penalties (for submitting false information on a claim), and overpayment or underpayment. A **chargemaster team** jointly shares the responsibility of updating and revising the chargemaster to ensure its accuracy, and it consists of representatives of a variety of departments, such as coding compliance financial services (e.g., billing department), health information management, information services, other departments (e.g., laboratory, pharmacy, radiology, and so on), and physicians. Chargemaster maintenance requires expertise in billing regulations, clinical procedures, coding guidelines, and patient record documentation. While the entire chargemaster is reviewed periodically (e.g., annually to incorporate coding updates), the chargemaster team could be gathered any time a new procedure or service is offered by the facility so that appropriate data can be added to the chargemaster.

EXAMPLE: CHARGEMASTER

GOODMEDICINE HOSPITAL
ANYWHERE, US 12345

Printed on:
04/15/YYYY

DEPARTMENT CODE: 01-855
DEPARTMENT: Radiology

SERVICE CODE	SERVICE DESCRIPTION	REVENUE CODE	CPT CODE	CHARGE	RVU
8550001	Chest x-ray, single view	0324	71010	74.50	0.70
8550002	Chest x-ray, two views	0324	71020	82.50	0.95
8550025	Computed tomography, lumbar spine; with contrast material	0350	72132	899.50	8.73
8550026	Computed tomography, lumbar spine; without contrast material followed by contrast material(s) and further sections	0350	72133	999.50	11.10

Personnel who render services to institutional patients (e.g., nursing, laboratory, radiology) enter data into the commercial software product. The data reside in the patient's computerized account; upon discharge from the institution, the data are verified by billing office personnel and transmitted electronically (Figure 9-11) as a UB-04 claim to a third-party payer or a clearinghouse. When submitted directly to the payer, the claim is processed to authorize reimbursement to the facility. When submitted to a clearinghouse, electronic claims are edited and validated to ensure that they are error-free, reformatted to the specifications of the payer, and submitted electronically to the appropriate payer for further processing to generate reimbursement to the facility.

UB-04 data elements in ASC X12N format	Description of data elements
ST*837*123456~ BHT*0019*00*A98765*YYYY0504*0830~	Header
NM1*41*2*GOODMEDICINE HOSPITAL*****54*888229999~	Submitter name
NM1*40*2*CAPITAL BLUE CROSS*****54*16000~	Receiver name
HL*1**20*1~	Service provider hierarchical level for submitter
NM1*85*2*GOODMEDICINE HOSPITAL*****54*888229999~ REF*1J*898989~	Service provider name
HL*2*1*22*1~ SBR*P********BL~	Subscriber (patient) hierarchical level
NM1*IL*1*PUBLIC*JOHN*Q**MI*GRNESSC1234~ N3*1247 HILL STREET~ N4*ANYWHERE*US*12345~ DMG*D8*19820805*M**::RET:3::RET:2~ REF*SY*150259874~	Subscriber (patient) name
NM1*PR*2*CAPITAL BLUE CROSS*****PI*00303~	Payer name
CLM*ABH123456*5015***11:A:1~ DTP*096*TM*1200~ DTP*434*RD8*YYYY0504-YYYY0510~ DTP*435*DT*YYYY05101100~ CL1*2*1*01~ HI*BK:66411*BJ:66411~ HI*BF:66331:::::::Y*BF:66111:::::::N*BF:V270:::::::N~ HI*BR:7569:D8:YYYY0510~	Claim information
SE*91*123456~	Trailer

FIGURE 9-11 Portion of UB-04 data submitted in ASC X12N electronic protocol format.

EXAMPLE: During an inpatient admission, the attending physician documents an order in the patient's record for a blood glucose level to be performed by the laboratory. The patient's nurse processes the order by contacting the laboratory (e.g., telephone or computer message), which sends a technician to the patient's room to perform a venipuncture (blood draw, or withdrawing blood from the patient's arm using a syringe). The blood specimen is transported to the laboratory by the technician where the blood glucose test is completed. The technician enters the results into the patient record information technology (IT) system using a computer terminal, and UB-04 data elements are input into the patient's account. This data resides in the patient's computerized account until it is verified by the billing office (at patient discharge) and is then transmitted to a clearinghouse that processes the claim and submits it to the third-party payer. The clearinghouse also uses the network to send an acknowledgment to the institution upon receipt of the submitted claim.

A **revenue code** is a four-digit code preprinted on a facility's chargemaster to indicate the location or type of service provided to an institutional patient. (They are reported in FL42 of the UB-04.)

NOTE: Prior to 2002, revenue codes contained just three digits.

EXAMPLE: REVENUE CODES

CODE	COMPLETE DESCRIPTION	ABBREVIATED DESCRIPTION
0270	Medical/surgical supplies	MED SURG SUPPLIES
0450	Emergency department services	EMER/FACILITY CHARGE
0981	Emergency department physician fee	EMER/PHYSICIAN FEE

REVENUE CYCLE MANAGEMENT

Revenue cycle management (Figure 9-12) is the process by which health care facilities and providers ensure their financial viability by increasing revenue, improving cash flow, and enhancing the patient's experience. Revenue cycle management includes the following features, typically in this order:

- ***Physician ordering*** **(Physician order for inpatient admission or outpatient services is documented by the responsible physician.)**

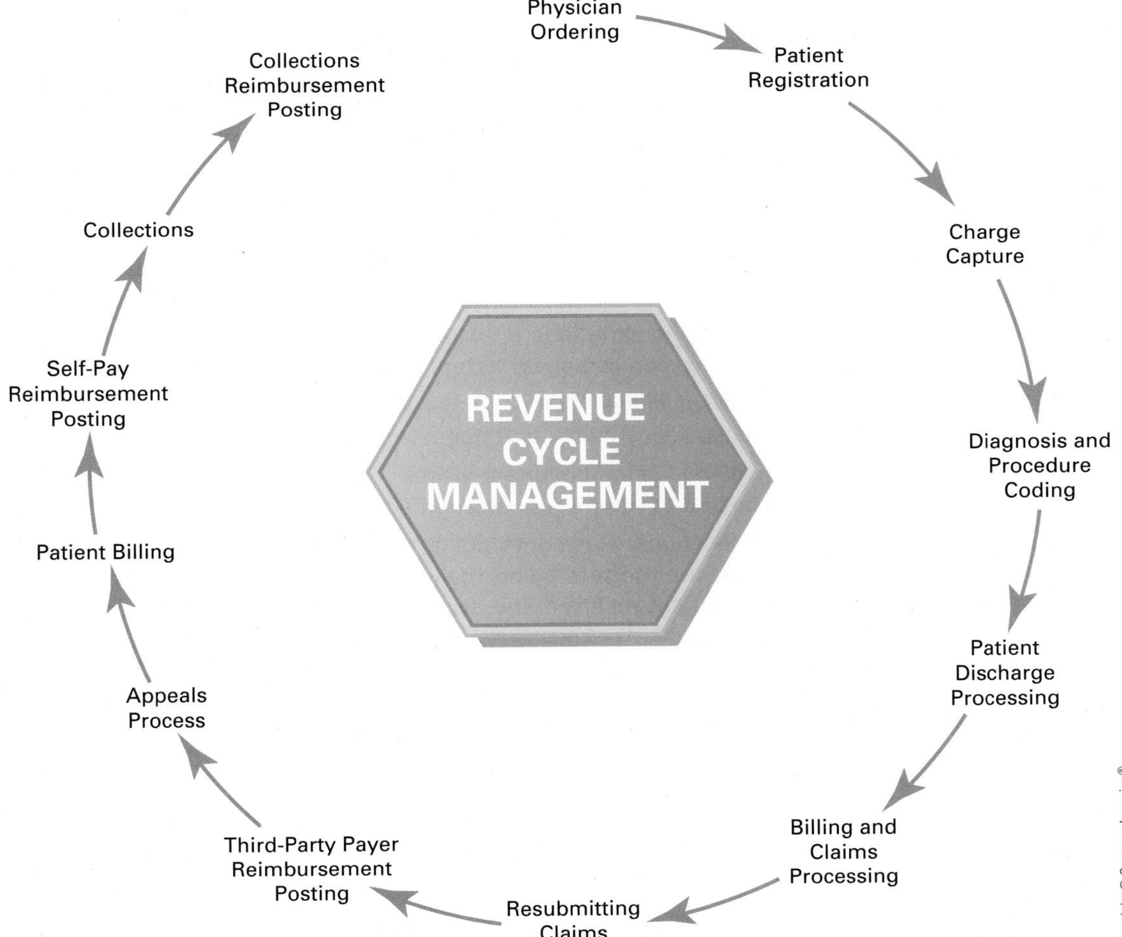

FIGURE 9-12 The revenue cycle.

> **NOTE:** When registering for outpatient services, patients provide the facility with requisition forms (physician orders) for procedures/services. Occasionally, patients forget to provide the paper-based requisition form, and providers and facilities who have implemented the electronic health record (EHR) can retrieve the electronic requisition from the EHR so that patients do not have to delay the registration process.

- *Patient registration* (Patient is admitted as an inpatient or scheduled for outpatient services.)
  - Appropriate consents for treatment and release of information are obtained.
  - Patient demographic and insurance information is collected.
  - Patient's insurance coverage is validated and utilization management is performed (e.g., clinical reviews) to determine medical necessity.
  - Preadmission clearance (e.g., precertification, preauthorization, screening for medical necessity) is given.
- *Charge capture* (or *data capture*) (Providers use chargemasters or encounter forms to select procedures or services provided. Ancillary departments, such as the laboratory, use automated systems that link to the chargemaster.)
- *Diagnosis and procedure coding* (Assignment of appropriate ICD-10-CM and ICD-10-PCS or CPT/HCPCS level II codes is typically performed by health information management personnel, to assign APCs, DRGs, and so on.)
- *Patient discharge processing* (Patient information is verified, discharge instructions are provided, patient follow-up visit is scheduled, consent forms are reviewed for signatures, and patient policies are explained to the patient.)
- *Billing and claims processing* (All patient information and codes are input into the billing system, and CMS-1500 or UB-04 claims are generated and submitted to third-party payers.)
- *Resubmitting claims* (Before reimbursement is received from third-party payers, late charges, lost charges, or corrections to previously processed CMS-1500 or UB-04 claims are entered, and claims are resubmitted to payers—this may result in payment delays and claims denials.)
- *Third-party payer reimbursement posting* (Payment from third-party payers is posted to appropriate accounts, and rejected claims are resubmitted with appropriate documentation; this process includes *electronic remittance*, which involves receiving reimbursement from third-party payers electronically.)
- *Appeals process* (Analysis of reimbursement received from third-party payers identifies variations in expected payments or contracted rates and may result in submission of appeal letters to payers.)
- *Patient billing* (Self-pay balances are billed to the patient; these include deductibles, copayments, and noncovered charges.)
- *Self-pay reimbursement posting* (Self-pay balances received from patients are posted to appropriate accounts.)
- *Collections* (Payments not received from patients in a timely manner result in collection letters being mailed to patients until payment is received; if payment is still not received, the account is turned over to an outside collections agency.)
- *Collections reimbursement posting* (Payments received from patients are posted to appropriate accounts.)

> **NOTE:** In a physician practice, revenue cycle management is also called *accounts receivable management*.

Revenue Cycle Monitoring

Revenue cycle monitoring involves assessing the revenue cycle to ensure financial viability and stability using the following **metrics**, which are standards of measurement:

- *Cash flow* (total amount of money transferred into and out of a business; measure of *liquidity*, which is the amount of capital available for investment and expenditures)

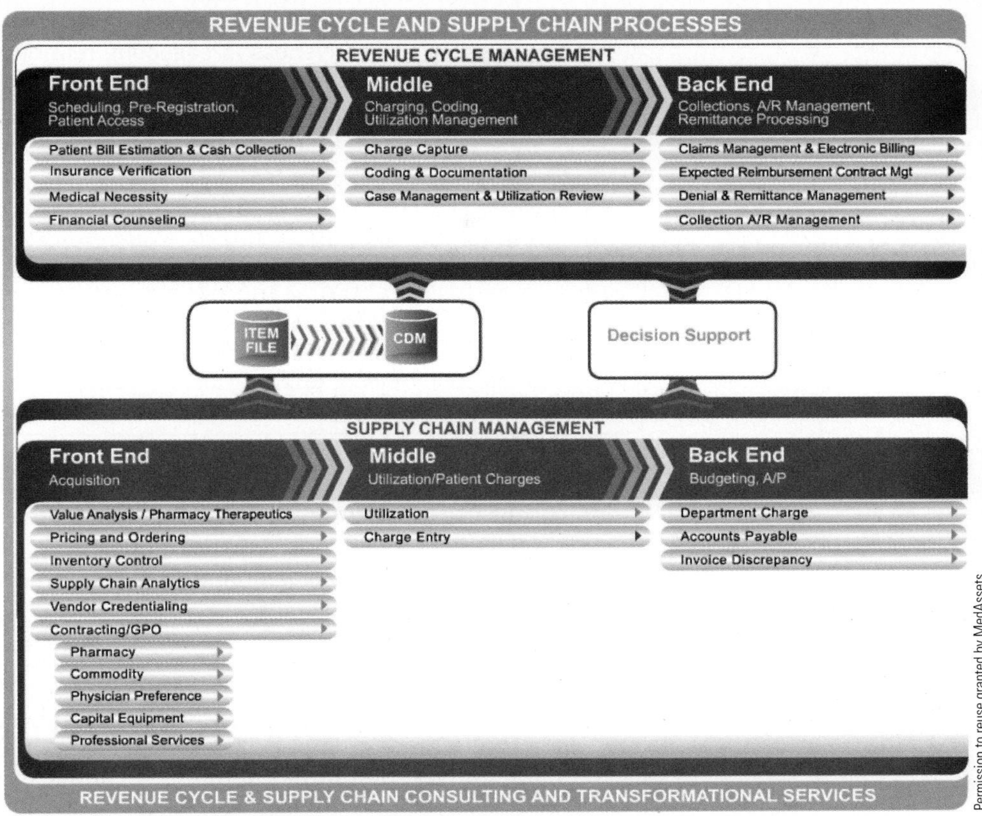

- ***Days in accounts receivable*** **(number of days outstanding money is owed the organization; measure of how long it usually takes for a service/procedure to be paid by all financially responsible parties, such as third-party payers, government health programs, and patients)**

> **EXAMPLE:** Last year, the medical practice's gross charges for procedures/services totaled $750,000. The current accounts receivables (A/R) are $95,000, and the credit balance (from the previous year) is $9,500. The formula for calculating *Days in A/R* = [Receivables – (Credit Balance)] ÷ [Gross Charges ÷ 365 days]. Thus, [$95,000 – ($9,500)] ÷ [$750,000 ÷ 365] = $104,500 ÷ $2,054 = 51 days. According to national standards, A/R should average 35 days or less; therefore, this medical practice needs to audit its revenue cycle to identify and improve areas of poor performance so that the number of *days in A/R* decreases.

- ***Percentage of accounts receivable older than 30, 60, 90, and 120 days*** **(measure of the organization's ability to get procedures/services paid in a timely manner)**

Anywhere Medical Center
Report of Percentage of Accounts Receivable Older Than 30, 60, 90, and 120 Days

0-30	31-60	61-90	91-120	> 121	TOTAL A/R
$66,500	$55,000	$9,000	$7,500	$5,000	$143,000
46.5%	38.5%	6.3%	5.2%	3.5%	100%

According to national standards, A/R > 120 should be less than 12 percent. This organization's A/R > 120 is 3.5 percent, which is excellent.

- ***Net collection rate*** **(percentage received of allowed reimbursement; measure of the organization's effectiveness in collecting reimbursement)**

> **EXAMPLE:** The hospital's payments received is $945,000. Refunds paid to payers and patients (for charges not supported by documentation in the patient record) total $30,000. The total charge for inpatient and outpatient services is $1,500,000. Total write-offs are $525,000. The formula for calculating the *Net Collection Rate* = [(Payments – Refunds) ÷ (Charges – Write-offs)] × 100. Thus, [($945,000 – $30,000) ÷ ($1,500,000 – $525,000)] × 100 = [$915,000 ÷ $975,000] × 100 = 0.938 × 100 = 93.8 percent. The calculated net collection rate of 93.8 percent is very poor, which means the hospital needs to audit its revenue cycle to identify and correct areas of poor performance such as chargemaster accuracy, filing claims in a timely manner, obtaining preauthorization, and so on.

- ***Denial rate*** **(percentage of claims denied by payers; measure of the organization's effectiveness in submitting *clean claims*, which are claims paid in full upon initial submission; the formula for calculating the *denial rate* = [total dollar amount of denied claims ÷ total dollar amount of claims submitted] × 100; denial rates should be less than 5 percent)**

> **EXAMPLE:** The hospital's total dollar amount of denied claims is $250,000, and the total dollar amount of claims submitted is $2,500,000. The formula for calculating the *Denial Rate* = [total dollar amount of denied claims ÷ total dollar amount of claims submitted] × 100. Thus, [$250,000 ÷ $2,500,000] × 100 = 10 percent. The calculated denial rate of 10 percent is unacceptable, which means the hospital needs to audit its revenue cycle to identify and correct areas of filing claims in a timely manner, following up on rejected and unpaid claims, and so on.

Revenue Cycle Auditing

Revenue cycle auditing is an assessment process that is conducted as a follow-up to revenue cycle monitoring so that areas of poor performance can be identified and corrected. Auditing processes include:

- ***Compliance monitoring*** **(level of compliance with established managed care contracts is monitored; provider performance per managed care contractual requirement is monitored; compliance risk is monitored)**
- ***Denials management*** **(claims denials are analyzed to prevent future denials; rejected claims are resubmitted with appropriate documentation)**
- ***Tracking resubmitted claims and appeals for denied claims*** **(resubmitted claims and appealed claims are tracked to ensure payment by payers)**
- ***Posting late charges and lost charges*** **(performed after reimbursement for late claims is received and appeals for denied claims have been exhausted)**

Resource Allocation and Data Analytics

Resource allocation is the distribution of financial resources among competing groups (e.g., hospital departments, state health care organizations). **Resource allocation monitoring** uses data analytics to measure whether a health care provider or organization achieves operational goals and objectives within the confines of the distribution of financial resources, such as appropriately expending budgeted amounts as well as conserving resources and protecting assets while providing quality patient care. **Data analytics** are tools and systems that are used to analyze clinical and financial data, conduct research, and evaluate the effectiveness of disease treatments:

- **Data warehouses** (databases that use *reporting interfaces* to consolidate multiple databases, allowing reports to be generated from a single request)
- **Data mining** (extracting and analyzing data to identify patterns, whether predictable or unpredictable)

EXAMPLE 1: The quality manager at a medical center has been charged with performing a study to determine the quality of care and costs of providing procedures and services to the practice's patient population. The manager will access and study clinical and financial data that is located in reports generated by the facility's electronic health record, and preestablished criteria will be used when conducting the study. The manager submits a report request to the information technology department, which then uses a data warehouse to generate the results. The request submitted by the manager is specific as to patient demographics, conditions, procedures and services, and so on. The manager uses the generated reports to conduct data mining, which results in the identification of quality-of-care issues associated with providing patient care as well as procedures/services that are profitable and nonprofitable. The manager then prepares a report of findings for discussion with the quality management committee (consisting of facility staff and physicians). The result is an action plan to:

- Eliminate deficiencies in quality of care to its patient population (e.g., in-service education to facility staff, purchase of technologically advanced equipment)
- Increase the number of profitable procedures/services (e.g., increase human and other resources)
- Decrease or eliminate nonprofitable procedures/services (e.g., partner with another health care organization that offers such procedures/services)

EXAMPLE 2: The Department of Veterans Affairs (VA) provides health care services to almost three million veterans annually, but veterans nationwide have traditionally not had equitable access to these services. Congress enacted legislation in 1996 requiring the VA to develop a plan for equitably allocating resources to "ensure that veterans who have similar economic status and eligibility priority and who are eligible for medical care have similar access to such care regardless of the region of the United States in which such veterans reside." In response, the VA implemented the *Veterans Equitable Resource Allocation (VERA)* resource allocation monitoring system to improve equity of access to veterans' health care services. VERA allocated resources to regional VA health care networks, known as *Veterans Integrated Services Networks (VISN)*, which allocate resources to their hospitals and clinics. The VA continuously assesses the effectiveness of VERA by monitoring changes in health care delivery and overseeing the network allocation process used to provide veterans with equitable access to services.

> **NOTE:** UB-04 claims are not manually completed (unlike CMS-1500 claims that continue to be manually completed by many physician practices). Instead, the UB-04 claim is automatically generated when data is transmitted to the facility's billing department by providers who:
>
> - Circle procedure/service CPT/HCPCS codes on a paper-based chargemaster (after which keyboarding specialists enter the codes into the facility's computer)
> - Select codes using a hand-held computer, such as a personal digital assistant (PDA) (and click to transmit the codes)

UB-04 CLAIM

The UB-04 claim (Figure 9-13) (previously called the UB-92) contains data entry blocks called form locators (FLs) that are similar to the CMS-1500 claim blocks used to input information about procedures or services provided to a patient. Although some institutions manually complete the UB-04 claim and submit it to third-party payers for reimbursement, others perform data entry of UB-04 information using commercial software (Figure 9-14). However, most institutions do not complete the UB-04 because it is automatically generated from chargemaster data entered by providers (e.g., nurses, therapists, laboratory, and so on).

UB-04 Claim Development and Implementation

Institutional and other selected providers submit UB-04 (CMS-1450) claim data to payers for reimbursement of patient services. The National Uniform Billing Committee (NUBC) is responsible for developing data elements reported on the UB-04 in cooperation with State Uniform Billing Committees (SUBCs).

National Uniform Billing Committee (NUBC)

Like the role of the National Uniform Claims Committee (NUCC) in the development of the CMS-1500 claim, the National Uniform Billing Committee (NUBC) is responsible for identifying and revising data elements (information entered into UB-04 form locators or submitted by institutions using electronic data interchange). (The claim was originally designed as the first uniform bill and called the UB-82 because of its 1982 implementation date. Then, the UB-92 was implemented in 1992.) The current claim is called the UB-04 because it was developed in 2004 (although it was implemented in 2007).

> **NOTE:** UB-04 claims data for Medicare Part A reimbursement is submitted to Medicare administrative contractors (MACs, replacing carriers, DMERCs, and fiscal intermediaries) and other third-party payers. Payments are processed for hospitals, skilled nursing facilities, home health and hospice agencies, dialysis facilities, rehabilitation facilities, and rural health clinics.

The NUBC was created by the American Hospital Association (AHA) in 1975 and is represented by major national provider (e.g., AHA state hospital association representatives) and payer (e.g., BlueCross BlueShield Association) organizations. The intent was to develop a single billing form and standard data set that could be used by all institutional providers and payers for health care claims processing. In 1982 the NUBC voted to accept the UB-82 and its data set (a compilation of data elements that are reported on the uniform bill) for implementation as a national uniform bill. Once the UB-82 was adopted, the focus of the NUBC shifted to the state level, and a State Uniform Billing Committee (SUBC) was created in each state to handle implementation and distribution of state-specific UB-82 manuals (that contained national guidelines along with unique state billing requirements).

When the NUBC established the UB-82 data set design and specifications, it also implemented an evaluation process through 1990 to determine whether the UB-82 data set was appropriate for third-party payer claims processing. The NUBC surveyed SUBCs to obtain suggestions for improving the design of the UB-82, and the UB-92 was implemented in 1992 to incorporate the best of the UB-82 with data set design improvements (e.g., providers no longer had to include as many attachments to UB-92 claims submitted). UB-04 revisions emphasize clarification of definitions for data elements and codes to eliminate ambiguity and to create consistency. The UB-04 also addresses emergency department (ED) coding and data collection issues to respond to concerns of state public health reporting systems. The NUBC continues to emphasize the need for data sources to continue to support public health data reporting needs.

Data Specifications for the UB-04

When reviewing data specifications for the UB-04, the NUBC balanced the payers' need to collect information against the burden of providers to report

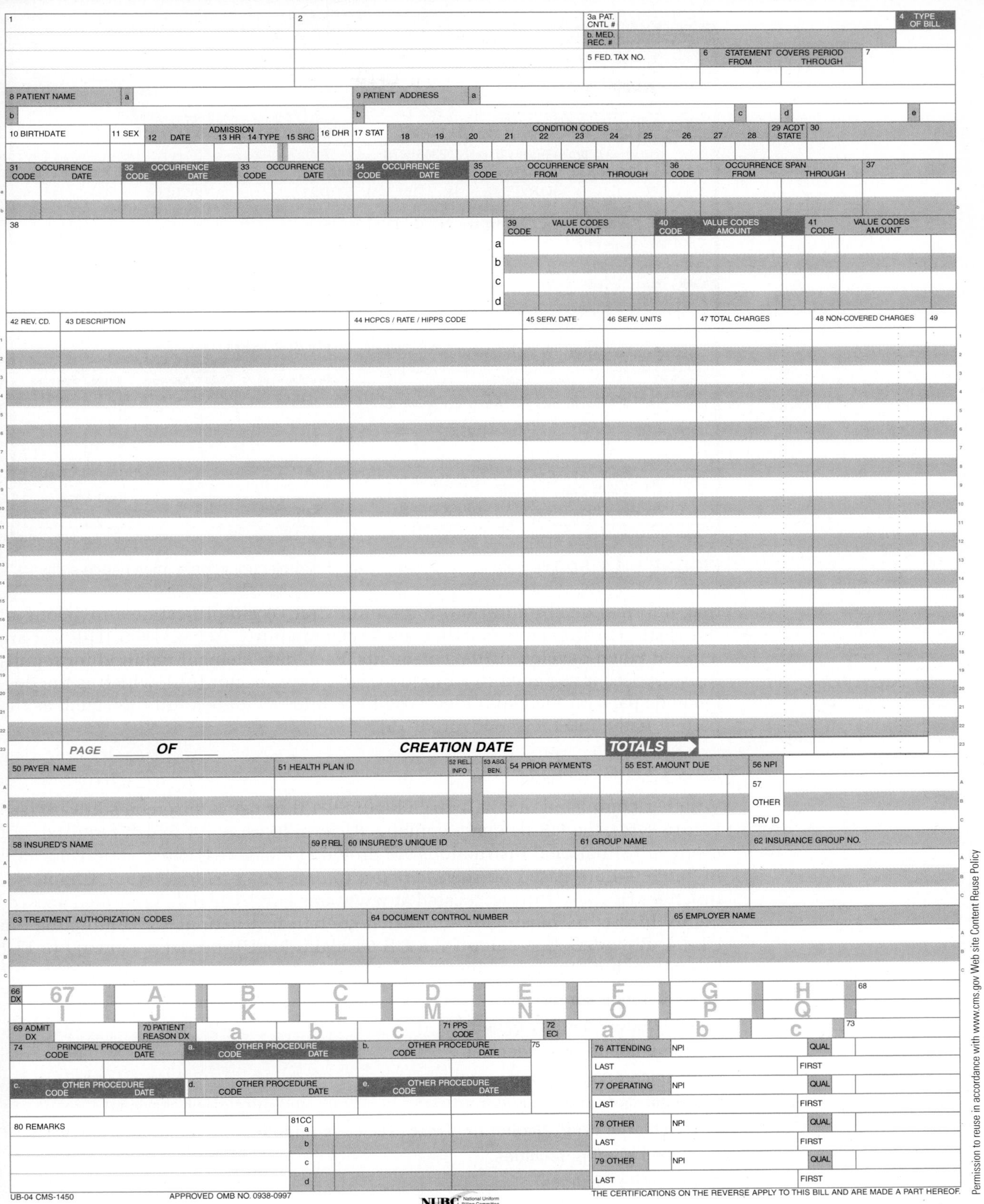

1
2
3a PAT. CNTL #
b. MED. REC. #
4 TYPE OF BILL
5 FED. TAX NO.
6 STATEMENT COVERS PERIOD FROM THROUGH
7
8 PATIENT NAME a
b
9 PATIENT ADDRESS a
b c d e
10 BIRTHDATE
11 SEX
ADMISSION 12 DATE 13 HR 14 TYPE 15 SRC
16 DHR
17 STAT
CONDITION CODES 18 19 20 21 22 23 24 25 26 27 28
29 ACDT STATE
30
31 OCCURRENCE CODE DATE
32 OCCURRENCE CODE DATE
33 OCCURRENCE CODE DATE
34 OCCURRENCE CODE DATE
35 OCCURRENCE SPAN CODE FROM THROUGH
36 OCCURRENCE SPAN CODE FROM THROUGH
37
38
39 VALUE CODES CODE AMOUNT
40 VALUE CODES CODE AMOUNT
41 VALUE CODES CODE AMOUNT
a b c d
42 REV. CD.
43 DESCRIPTION
44 HCPCS / RATE / HIPPS CODE
45 SERV. DATE
46 SERV. UNITS
47 TOTAL CHARGES
48 NON-COVERED CHARGES
49
1 2 3 4 5 6 7 8 9 10 11 12 13 14 15 16 17 18 19 20 21 22 23
PAGE ____ OF ____
CREATION DATE
TOTALS
50 PAYER NAME
51 HEALTH PLAN ID
52 REL. INFO
53 ASG. BEN.
54 PRIOR PAYMENTS
55 EST. AMOUNT DUE
56 NPI
57 OTHER PRV ID
A B C
58 INSURED'S NAME
59 P. REL
60 INSURED'S UNIQUE ID
61 GROUP NAME
62 INSURANCE GROUP NO.
A B C
63 TREATMENT AUTHORIZATION CODES
64 DOCUMENT CONTROL NUMBER
65 EMPLOYER NAME
A B C
66 DX
67 A B C D E F G H
I J K L M N O P Q
68
69 ADMIT DX
70 PATIENT REASON DX a b c
71 PPS CODE
72 ECI a b c
73
74 PRINCIPAL PROCEDURE CODE DATE
a. OTHER PROCEDURE CODE DATE
b. OTHER PROCEDURE CODE DATE
75
c. OTHER PROCEDURE CODE DATE
d. OTHER PROCEDURE CODE DATE
e. OTHER PROCEDURE CODE DATE
76 ATTENDING NPI QUAL
LAST FIRST
77 OPERATING NPI QUAL
LAST FIRST
80 REMARKS
81CC a b c d
78 OTHER NPI QUAL
LAST FIRST
79 OTHER NPI QUAL
LAST FIRST
UB-04 CMS-1450
APPROVED OMB NO. 0938-0997
NUBC National Uniform Billing Committee
THE CERTIFICATIONS ON THE REVERSE APPLY TO THIS BILL AND ARE MADE A PART HEREOF.

FIGURE 9-13 Blank UB-04 claim.

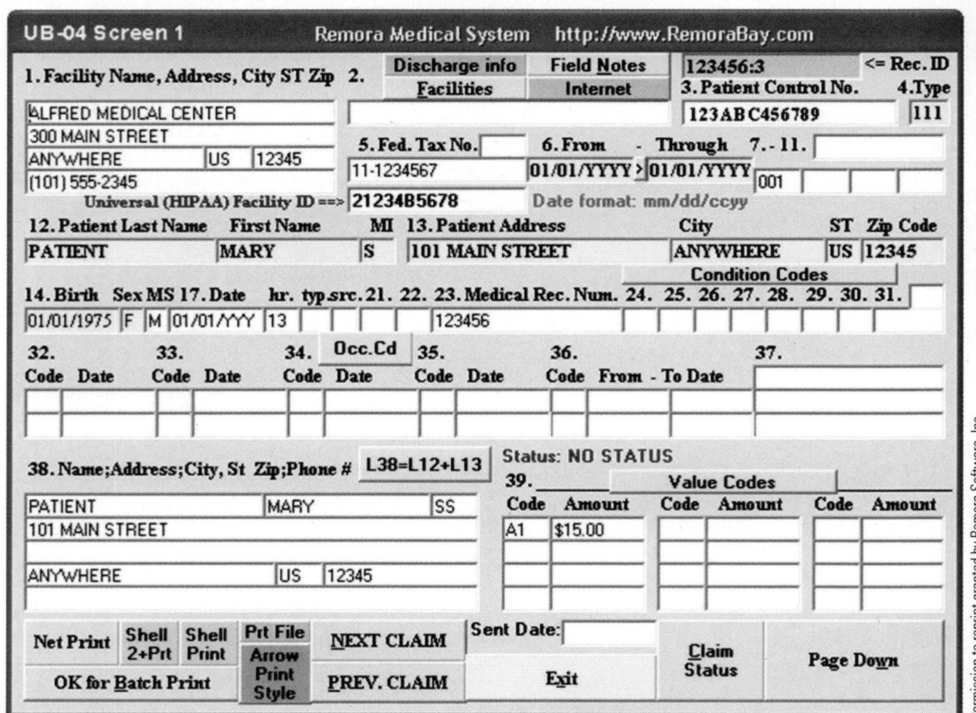

FIGURE 9-14 Sample data entry screen using UB-04 electronic data interchange software.

that information. In addition, the administrative simplification provisions of the Health Insurance Portability and Accountability Act of 1996 (HIPAA) are applied when developing data elements. Each data element required for reporting purposes is assigned to a unique UB-04 form locator (FL), which is the designated space on the claim identified by a unique number and title, such as the patient name in FL8 (see Figure 9-13).

UB-04 Claims Submission

Whether completed manually (see Figure 9-13) or using onscreen software (see Figure 9-14), the UB-04 claim contains 81 form locators for which required, not used, and situational instructions are provided (Table 9-4). (Instructions located in Table 9-4 are based on the *Medicare Claims Processing Manual*, Chapter 3, Inpatient Hospital Billing, located at **www.cms.gov**.) The data is entered according to third-party payer guidelines that contain instructions for completing the UB-04. Providers that submit the UB-04 claim (or UB-04 data elements in EDI format) include the following:

- **Ambulance companies**
- **Ambulatory surgery centers**
- **Home health care agencies**
- **Hospice organizations**
- **Hospitals (emergency department, inpatient, and outpatient services)**
- **Psychiatric drug/alcohol treatment facilities (inpatient and outpatient services)**
- **Skilled nursing facilities**
- **Subacute facilities**
- **Stand-alone clinical/laboratory facilities**
- **Walk-in clinics**

TABLE 9-4 UB-04 (CMS-1450) form locator (FL) descriptions and Medicare claims completion instructions

FL	DESCRIPTION	INSTRUCTIONS
NOTE: Form locator (FL) descriptions indicate whether data entry for Medicare claims is required (mandatory), not required (optional), not used (leave FL blank), or situational (dependent on circumstances clarified in the FL instructions). Payer-specific instructions can be located by conducting Internet searches.		
1	Provider name, street address, city, state, zip code, telephone number, country code, and fax number (REQUIRED)	Enter the provider name, city, state, zip code, telephone number, fax number, and country code. Either the provider's post office box number or street name and number may be included. The state can be abbreviated using standard post office abbreviations, and five- or nine-digit zip codes are acceptable. **NOTE:** Payer compares FL1 information to data on file for provider number reported in FL51 (to verify provider identity).
2	Pay-to name, address, and secondary ID fields (SITUATIONAL)	Enter provider name, address, city, state, zip code, and identification number *if the pay-to name and address information is different from the Billing Provider information in FL1*. Otherwise, leave blank.
3a	Patient control number (unique claim number) (REQUIRED)	Enter the alphanumeric control number *if assigned by the provider and needed to facilitate retrieval of patient financial records and for posting payments.*
3b	Medical record number (or health record number) (SITUATIONAL)	Enter the medical record number *if assigned by the provider and needed to facilitate retrieval of patient records*. Otherwise, leave blank.
4	Type of bill (TOB) (REQUIRED)	**NOTE:** The four-digit alphanumeric TOB code provides three specific pieces of information after a leading zero. Digit 1 (the leading 0) is ignored by CMS. Digit 2 identifies the type of facility. Digit 3 classifies the type of care provided. Digit 4 indicates the sequence of this bill for this particular episode of care, and it is called a *frequency code.* Enter a valid four-digit TOB classification number. • Digit 1: Leading Zero • Digit 2: Type of Facility 1 Hospital 2 Skilled nursing 3 Home health (includes HH PPS claims, for which CMS determines whether services are paid from the Medicare Part A or Part B) 4 Religious nonmedical (hospital) 5 Reserved for national assignment (discontinued 10/1/05) 6 Intermediate care 7 Clinic or hospital-based renal dialysis facility (requires assignment of special information as Digit 3 below) 8 Special facility or hospital ASC surgery (requires assignment of special information as Digit 3 below) 9 Reserved for national assignment • Digit 3: Bill Classification, Except Clinics and Special Facilities 1 Inpatient (Medicare Part A) 2 Inpatient (Medicare Part B) 3 Outpatient 4 Other (Medicare Part B) 5 Intermediate Care - Level I 6 Intermediate Care - Level II 7 Reserved for national assignment (discontinued 10/1/05) 8 Swing bed 9 Reserved for national assignment

(continues)

TABLE 9-4 (continued)

FL	DESCRIPTION	INSTRUCTIONS
4	Type of bill (TOB) (REQUIRED)—continued	• Digit 3 (Clinics Only) 1 Rural health clinic (RHC) 2 Hospital-based or independent renal dialysis facility 3 Freestanding provider-based federally qualified health center (FQHC) 4 Other rehabilitation facility (ORF) 5 Comprehensive outpatient rehabilitation facility (CORF) 6 Community mental health center (CMHC) 7–8 Reserved for national assignment 9 Other • Digit 3 (Special Facilities Only) 1 Hospice (non-hospital-based) 2 Hospice (hospital-based) 3 Ambulatory surgical center services to hospital outpatients 4 Freestanding birthing center 5 Critical access hospital 6–8 Reserved for national assignment 9 Other • Digit 4 (Frequency - Definition) A Admission/election notice (hospice or religious nonmedical health care institution) B Termination/revocation notice (hospice/Medicare coordinated care demonstration or religious nonmedical health care institution) C Change of provider notice (hospice) D Health care institution void/cancel notice (hospice) E Change of ownership (hospice) F Beneficiary initiated adjustment claim G Common working file (CWF) initiated adjustment claim H CMS initiated adjustment claim I Internal adjustment claim (other than QIO or provider) J Initiated adjustment claim (other entities) K OIG initiated adjustment claim M Medicare as secondary payer (MSP) initiated adjustment claim P Quality improvement organization (QIO) adjustment claim 0 Nonpayment/zero claims provider 1 Admit through discharge claim 2 Interim - first claim 3 Interim - continuing claim(s) 4 Interim - last claim 5 Late charge only (There is no code 6) 7 Replacement of prior claim 8 Void/cancel of a prior claim 9 Final claim for HH PPS episode • Sample Bill Type Codes 011X Hospital inpatient (Medicare Part A) 012X Hospital inpatient (Medicare Part B) 013X Hospital outpatient 014X Hospital other (Medicare Part B)

(continues)

TABLE 9-4 (continued)

FL	DESCRIPTION	INSTRUCTIONS
4	Type of bill (TOB) (REQUIRED)—continued	• Sample Bill Type Codes (continued) 018X Hospital swing bed 021X SNF inpatient 022X SNF inpatient (Medicare Part B) 023X SNF outpatient 028X SNF swing bed 032X Home health 033X Home health 034X Home health (Medicare Part B only) 041X Religious nonmedical health care institutions 071X Clinical rural health 072X Clinic ESRD 073X Federally qualified health centers 074X Clinic outpatient physical therapy (OPT) 075X Clinic CORF 076X Community mental health centers 081X Non-hospital-based hospice 082X Hospital-based hospice 083X Hospital outpatient (ASC) 085X Critical access hospital
5	Federal tax number (REQUIRED)	Enter the facility's federal tax identification number in 00-0000000 format.
6	Statement covers period (from-through) (REQUIRED)	Enter beginning and ending dates of the period included on this bill as MMDDYY.
7	Unlabeled (NOT USED)	Leave blank.
8a	Patient identifier (SITUATIONAL)	Enter the patient's payer identification (ID) number, *which is the subscriber/insured ID number entered in FL60.*
8b	Patient name (REQUIRED)	Enter patient's last name, first name, and middle initial (if any). Use a comma to separate the last name, first name, and middle initial. **NOTE:** When the patient's last name contains a prefix, do not enter a space after the prefix (e.g., VonSchmidt). When the patient's name contains a suffix, enter as LastName Suffix, FirstName (e.g., Smith III, James).
9a–e	Patient address (REQUIRED)	• Enter the patient's street address in 9a. • Enter the patient's city in 9b. • Enter the patient's state in 9c. • Enter the patient's five- or nine-digit zip code in 9d. • Enter the patient's country code *if the patient resides outside of the United States* in 9e.
10	Patient birth date (REQUIRED)	Enter the patient's date of birth as MMDDCCYY. **NOTE:** If birth date is unknown, enter zeros for all eight digits.
11	Patient sex (REQUIRED)	Enter the patient's gender as a one-character letter: M Male F Female
12	Admission date (REQUIRED for inpatient and home health)	Enter the inpatient date of admission (or home health start-of-care date) as MMDDYY.

(continues)

TABLE 9-4 (continued)

FL	DESCRIPTION	INSTRUCTIONS
13	Admission hour (SITUATIONAL)	Enter the admission hour using military time (e.g., 03 for admission hour of 3:00 through 3:59 a.m.), *if required by the payer.*
14	Type of admission/visit (REQUIRED FOR INPATIENT CLAIMS)	Enter one-digit type of admission/visit code: 1 Emergency 2 Urgent 3 Elective 4 Newborn 5 Trauma center 6–8 Reserved for national assignment 9 Information not available
15	Source of referral for admission or visit (REQUIRED)	Enter one-digit source of admission or visit code: 1 Physician referral 2 Clinic referral 3 Managed care plan referral 4 Transfer from a hospital 5 Transfer from a skilled nursing facility 6 Transfer from another health care facility 7 Emergency room 8 Court/law enforcement 9 Information not available A Transfer from a critical access hospital B Transfer from another home health agency C Readmission to same home health agency D Transfer from hospital inpatient in the same facility resulting in a separate claim to the payer E–Z Reserved for national assignment
16	Discharge hour (SITUATIONAL)	Enter the discharge hour using military time (e.g., 03 for admission hour of 3:00 through 3:59 a.m.), *if required by the payer.*
17	Patient discharge status (REQUIRED)	Enter two-digit patient discharge status code: 01 Discharged to home or self-care (routine discharge) 02 Discharged/transferred to a short-term general hospital for inpatient care 03 Discharged/transferred to SNF with Medicare certification in anticipation of covered skilled care (effective 2/23/05) 04 Discharged/transferred to an intermediate care facility (ICF) 05 Discharged/transferred to another type of institution not defined elsewhere in this code list (effective 2/23/05) (e.g., cancer hospitals excluded from Medicare PPS and children's hospitals) 06 Discharged/transferred to home under care of organized home health service organization in anticipation of covered skills care (effective 2/23/05) 07 Left against medical advice or discontinued care 08 Reserved for national assignment 09 Admitted as an inpatient to this hospital **NOTE:** For patient status code 09, in situations where a patient is admitted before midnight of the third day following the day of an outpatient diagnostic service or a service related to the reason for the admission, the outpatient services are considered inpatient. Therefore, code 09 would apply only to services that began longer than three days earlier or were unrelated to the reason for admission, such as observation following outpatient surgery, which results in admission.

(continues)

TABLE 9-4 (continued)

FL	DESCRIPTION	INSTRUCTIONS
17	Patient discharge status (REQUIRED)—continued	Enter two-digit patient discharge status code: (continued) 10-19 Reserved for national assignment 21 Expired (or did not recover - religious nonmedical health care patient) Discharged/transferred to court/law enforcement 22-29 Reserved for national assignment 30 Still patient or expected to return for outpatient services 31-39 Reserved for national assignment 40 Expired at home (Hospice claims only) 41 Expired in a medical facility (e.g., hospital, SNF, ICF, or freestanding hospice) (Hospice claims only) 42 Expired - place unknown (Hospice claims only) 43 Discharged/transferred to a federal health care facility (effective 10/1/03) (e.g., Department of Defense hospital, Veteran's Administration hospital) 44-49 Reserved for national assignment 50 Discharged/transferred to Hospice (home) 51 Discharged/transferred to Hospice (medical facility) 52-60 Reserved for national assignment 61 Discharged/transferred within this institution to a hospital-based Medicare-approved swing bed 62 Discharged/transferred to an inpatient rehabilitation facility including distinct parts/units of a hospital 63 Discharged/transferred to long-term care hospital 64 Discharged/transferred to a nursing facility certified under Medicaid *but not certified under Medicare* 65 Discharged/transferred to a psychiatric hospital or psychiatric distinct part/unit of a hospital 66 Discharged/transferred to a critical access hospital (effective 1/1/06) 67-99 Reserved for national assignment
18-28	Condition codes (SITUATIONAL)	Enter the two-digit code (in numerical order) that describes any of the following conditions or events that apply to this billing period, *if required by the payer*. Otherwise, leave blank. (*Sample of condition codes listed below.*) 02 Condition is employment-related 03 Patient covered by insurance not reflected here 04 Information only bill 05 Lien has been filed **NOTE:** For a comprehensive list of condition codes, refer to Chapter 25 of the *Medicare Claims Processing Manual* (**www.cms.gov**).
29	Accident State (SITUATIONAL)	Enter the state (e.g., NY) in which an accident occurred, *if required by the payer.*
30	Unlabeled (NOT USED)	Leave blank.

(continues)

TABLE 9-4 (continued)

FL	DESCRIPTION	INSTRUCTIONS
31-34	Occurrence code(s) and date(s) (SITUATIONAL)	Enter occurrence code(s) and associated date(s) (MMDDYY) to report specific event(s) related to this billing period *if condition code(s) were entered in FL18–28.* Otherwise, leave blank. (*Sample of occurrence codes listed below.*) 01 = Accident/medical coverage 02 = No Fault Insurance Involved 03 = Accident/Tort Liability 04 = Accident Employment Related 05 = Accident No Medical/Liability Coverage 06 = Crime Victim **NOTE:** For a comprehensive list of occurrence codes, refer to Chapter 25 of the *Medicare Claims Processing Manual* (**www.cms.gov**).
35-36	Occurrence span code and dates (SITUATIONAL FOR INPATIENT CLAIMS)	Enter occurrence span code(s) and beginning/ending dates defining a specific event relating to this billing period as MMDDYY *for inpatient claims.* (*Sample of occurrence span codes listed below.*) 70 Qualifying stay dates (Medicare Part A SNF level of care only) or non-utilization dates (for payer use on hospital bills only) 71 Hospital prior stay dates 72 First/last visit (occurring in this billing period where these dates are different from those in FL6) 74 Noncovered level of care 75 SNF level of care **NOTE:** For a comprehensive list of occurrence span codes, refer to Chapter 25 of the *Medicare Claims Processing Manual* (**www.cms.gov**).
37	Untitled (NOT USED)	Leave blank.
38	Responsible party name and address (SITUATIONAL)	Enter the responsible party name and address, *if required by the payer.* Enter the responsible party last name, first name, and middle initial (if any). Use a comma to separate the last name, first name, and middle initial. Enter responsible party street address, city, state, and zip code.
39-41	Value codes and amounts (REQUIRED)	Enter two-character value code(s) and dollar/unit amount(s). Codes and related dollar or unit amounts identify data of a monetary nature necessary for processing the claim. Negative amounts are not allowed, except in FL41. If more than one value code is entered for the same billing period, enter in ascending numeric sequence. Lines "a" through "d" allow for entry of up to four lines of data. Enter data in FL39a through 41a before FL39b through 41b, and so on. Codes 80-83 are only available for use on the UB-04. (*Sample of value codes listed below.*) 01 = Most Common Semi-Private Rooms 02 = Provider Has No Semi-Private Rooms 08 = Lifetime Reserve Amount in the First Calendar Year 45 = Accident Hour 50 = Physical Therapy Visit A1 = Inpatient Deductible Part A A2 = Inpatient Coinsurance Part A A3 = Estimated Responsibility Part A B1 = Outpatient Deductible B2 = Outpatient Coinsurance **NOTE:** For a comprehensive list of value codes, refer to Chapter 25 of the *Medicare Claims Processing Manual* (**www.cms.gov**).

(continues)

TABLE 9-4 (continued)

FL	DESCRIPTION	INSTRUCTIONS
42	Revenue code(s) (REQUIRED)	Enter four-character revenue code(s) to identify accommodation and/or ancillary charges. **NOTE:** When completing UB-04 claims in this chapter, revenue codes are provided in case studies (Figure 9-15). *Revenue codes* entered in FL42 explain charges entered in FL47. They are entered in ascending numeric sequence, and do not repeat on the same bill. (*Sample revenue codes listed below.*) 010X All-inclusive rate (e.g., 0100, 0101) 0 All-inclusive room and board plus ancillary 1 All-inclusive room and board **NOTE:** For a comprehensive list of revenue codes, refer to Chapter 25 of the *Medicare Claims Processing Manual* (**www.cms.gov**).
43	Revenue description (NOT REQUIRED)	Enter the narrative description (or standard abbreviation) for each revenue code, reported in FL42, on the adjacent line in FL43. (This information assists clerical bill review by the facility/provider and payer.)
44	HCPCS/Rates/HIPPS Rate Codes (REQUIRED if applicable)	• *For outpatient claims,* enter the HCPCS (CPT and/or HCPCS level II) code that describes outpatient services or procedures. • *For inpatient claims,* enter the accommodation rate. • *For SNF claims,* enter the Health Insurance Prospective Payment System (HIPPS) rate code (obtained from resource utilization groups, RUGs, grouper software) and the two-character assessment indicator (AI) to specify the type of assessment associated with the RUG code obtained from the grouper.
45	Service date (REQUIRED FOR OUTPATIENT CLAIMS)	Enter line item dates of service, including claims where "from" and "through" dates are the same *for outpatient claims.*
46	Units of service (SITUATIONAL)	Enter the number of units that quantify services reported as revenue codes (FL42) (e.g., number of days for type of accommodation, number of pints of blood), *if required by the payer.* When HCPCS codes are reported for procedures/services, units equal the number of times the procedure/service reported was performed.
47	Total charges (REQUIRED)	• Enter charges for procedures/services reported as revenue codes (FL42) *on each line.* Be sure to consider the units of service (FL46) in your calculations. • Enter the sum of all charges reported on the last line (same line as revenue code 0001).
48	Noncovered charges (SITUATIONAL)	Enter noncovered charge(s) (e.g., copayment, day after active care ended) *if related revenue codes were entered in FL42.* (Do not enter negative charges.)
49	Untitled (NOT USED)	Leave blank.
50A–C	Payer name (REQUIRED)	Enter the name of the health insurance payer as follows: • Line A (Primary Payer) • Line B (Secondary Payer) • Line C (Tertiary Payer)
51A–C	Health plan ID (REQUIRED)	Report the payer's 10-character national health plan identifier (health plan ID).

(continues)

TABLE 9-4 (continued)

FL	DESCRIPTION	INSTRUCTIONS
52A–C	Release of information certification indicator (REQUIRED)	Enter the appropriate identifier for release of information certification for each payer, which is needed to permit the release of data to other organizations to adjudicate (process) the claim. I Informed consent to release medical information for conditions or diagnoses regulated by federal statutes Y Provider has on file a signed statement permitting the release of medical/billing date related to a claim
53A–C	Assignment of benefits certification indicator (SITUATIONAL)	Enter the assignment of benefits certification indicator, *if required by the payer.*
54A–C	Prior payment(s) (SITUATIONAL)	Enter the sum of payments collected from the patient toward payer deductibles/coinsurance or blood deductibles, *if required by the payer.* **EXAMPLE:** The first three pints of blood are treated as noncovered by Medicare. If total inpatient hospital charges were $350, including $50 for a deductible pint of blood, the hospital would enter $300 (toward the Part A deductible) and $50 (toward the blood deductible) in 54A and 54B, respectively.
55A–C	Estimated amount due from patient (SITUATIONAL)	Enter the estimated amount due from the patient, *if required by the payer.*
56	National provider identifier (NPI) (REQUIRED)	Enter the billing provider's NPI.
57A–C	Other provider ID (SITUATIONAL)	Enter other provider identification number(s), *if required by the payer.*
58A–C	Insured's name (REQUIRED)	Enter the insured's name (last, first, middle initial), as verified on the patient's health insurance card, *on the same lettered line (A, B, or C) that corresponds to the line on which payer information was entered in FL50A–C.*
59A–C	Patient's relationship to insured (REQUIRED)	Enter the "patient's relationship to subscriber/insured" code to indicate the relationship of the patient to the insured. 01 Spouse 18 Self 19 Child 20 Employee 21 Unknown 39 Organ Donor 40 Cadaver Donor 53 Life Partner G8 Other Relationship
60A–C	Insured's unique identification number (REQUIRED)	Enter the patient's health insurance identification number *on the same lettered line (A, B, or C) that corresponds to the line on which payer information was entered in FL50A–C.*

(continues)

TABLE 9-4 (continued)

FL	DESCRIPTION	INSTRUCTIONS
61A-C	Insured's group name (SITUATIONAL)	Enter the name of the health insurance group *on the same lettered line (A, B, or C) if workers' compensation or an employer group health plan (EGHP) was entered in FL50A–C.*
62A-C	Insured's group number (SITUATIONAL)	Enter the group number (or other identification number) of the health insurance group *on the same lettered line (A, B, or C) if workers' compensation or an employer group health plan (EGHP) was entered in FL50A–C.*
63A-C	Treatment authorization code (SITUATIONAL)	Enter the treatment authorization code or referral number assigned by the payer *if procedures/services reported on this claim were preauthorized or a referral was required.* **NOTE:** When quality improvement organization (QIO) review is performed for Medicare outpatient preadmission, preprocedure, or home IV therapy services, enter the treatment authorization number for all approved admissions or services.
64A-C	Document control number (SITUATIONAL)	Enter the control number assigned to the original bill by the health plan or the health plan's fiscal agent as part of their internal control *if this is not the original UB-04 submitted for procedures/services provided* (e.g., this UB-04 is a corrected claim).
65A-C	Employer name (SITUATIONAL)	Enter the name of the employer that provides health care coverage for the insured (identified on the same line in FL58) *if workers' compensation or an employer group health plan (EGHP) was entered in FL50A–C.*
66	Diagnosis version qualifier (REQUIRED)	Enter the indicator to designate which version of ICD was used to report diagnosis codes. 9 Ninth revision (ICD-9-CM) 0 Tenth revision (ICD-10-CM)
67	Principal diagnosis code (REQUIRED)	Enter the ICD code for the principal diagnosis (hospital inpatient) and the present on admission (POA) indicator *or* the first-listed diagnosis (hospital outpatient). **NOTE:** • Do *not* enter the decimal in the reported ICD-10-CM code because it is implied (e.g., E119 instead of E11.9). • Do *not* report ICD-10-CM diagnosis codes on *nonpatient claims for laboratory services*, where the hospital functions as an independent laboratory.
67A–Q	Other diagnosis code(s) (SITUATIONAL)	Enter ICD-10-CM codes for up to eight additional diagnoses *if they coexisted (in addition to the principal diagnosis) at the time of admission or developed subsequently, and which had an effect upon the treatment or the length of stay* (hospital inpatient) or *if they coexisted in addition to the first-listed diagnosis* (hospital outpatient). **NOTE:** • Do *not* enter the decimal in the reported ICD-10-CM code because it is implied (e.g., E119 instead of E11.9). • Do *not* report ICD-10-CM diagnosis codes on *nonpatient claims for laboratory services* when the hospital functions as an independent laboratory. • Effective January 1, 2011, CMS expanded the number of other (secondary) significant diagnosis codes reported from 8 to 24. CMS is conducting an analysis of the entire claims processing system to determine the changes needed to process the additional ICD codes (e.g., increasing the number of procedure code fields required for electronic submission of UB-04 data). It is unknown whether the paper-based UB-04 claim will be similarly revised to expand the number of procedure code (and date) fields.
68	Untitled (NOT USED)	Leave blank.

(continues)

TABLE 9-4 (continued)

FL	DESCRIPTION	INSTRUCTIONS
69	Admitting diagnosis code (REQUIRED FOR HOSPITAL INPATIENT CLAIMS)	Enter the ICD-10-CM code for the admitting diagnosis, which is the condition identified by the physician at the time of the patient's admission to the hospital, *if completing an inpatient claim.*
70a–c	Patient's reason for visit diagnosis code (SITUATIONAL)	Enter the ICD-10-CM code for the patient's reason for visit (e.g., sign, symptom, diagnosis) *if the patient received care for an unscheduled outpatient visit* (e.g., emergency department).
71	Prospective payment system (PPS) code (SITUATIONAL)	Enter the PPS code, *if required by the payer.*
72a–c	ECI (external cause of injury) (E-codes) (SITUATIONAL)	Enter ICD-10-CM external cause of injury code(s) and POA indicator(s), *if required by the payer.* **NOTE:** Check to determine if your state (e.g., New York) requires entry of E-codes for data capture purposes (e.g., statistical analysis).
73	Untitled (NOT USED)	Leave blank.
74	Principal procedure code and date (SITUATIONAL FOR INPATIENT CLAIMS)	Enter the ICD-10-PCS code for the principal procedure *if an inpatient procedure was performed.* Enter the date as MMDDYY. (Leave blank for outpatient claims.) **NOTE:** Do *not* enter the decimal in the reported ICD code because it is implied (e.g., 1471 instead of 14.71).
74a–e	Other procedure code(s) and date(s) (SITUATIONAL)	Enter the ICD-10-PCS code *if additional inpatient procedure(s) were performed.* Enter the date as MMDDYY. (Leave blank for outpatient claims.) **NOTE:** Effective January 1, 2011, CMS expanded the number of other (secondary) significant procedure codes reported from 5 to 24. CMS is conducting an analysis of the entire claims processing system to determine the changes needed to process the additional ICD-10-PCS codes (e.g., increasing the number of procedure code fields required for electronic submission of UB-04 data). It is unknown whether the paper-based UB-04 claim will be similarly revised to expand the number of procedure code (and date) fields.
75	Untitled (NOT USED)	Leave blank.
76	Attending provider name and identifiers (SITUATIONAL)	• Enter the name and NPI of the attending provider for all claims *except those submitted for nonscheduled transportation services.* • Leave the QUAL field blank. **NOTE:** The *attending provider* is the individual who has overall responsibility for the patient's medical care and treatment reported on this claim.
77	Operating physician name and NPI (SITUATIONAL)	Enter the name and NPI of the operating physician *if a surgical procedure ICD-10-PCS code is reported on this claim.* (Leave the QUAL field blank.)

(continues)

TABLE 9-4 (continued)

FL	DESCRIPTION	INSTRUCTIONS
78-79	Other provider name and NPI (SITUATIONAL)	Enter the name and NPI number of the provider *that corresponds to the following qualifier codes*: DN Referring Provider (The provider who sends the patient to another provider for services. Required on outpatient claims when the referring provider is different from the attending provider.) ZZ Other Operating Physician (The individual who performs a secondary surgical procedure or assists the operating physician. Required when another operating physician is involved.) 82 Rendering Provider (The health care professional who delivers or completes a particular medical service or nonsurgical procedure. Required when state or federal regulations call for a combined claim, such as a claim that includes both facility and professional fee components.)
80	Remarks (SITUATIONAL)	Enter remarks *for the following situations*: • DME billings (provider enters rental rate, cost, and anticipated months of usage so that payer may determine whether to approve the rental or purchase of the equipment) • Medicare is not primary payer (because workers' compensation, EGHP, automobile medical, no-fault, or liability insurer is primary) • Renal dialysis facilities (provider enters first month of the 30-month period during which Medicare benefits are secondary to benefits payable under an EGHP) • Other information not entered elsewhere on the UB-04, which is necessary for proper payment
81a-d	Code-Code (SITUATIONAL)	Enter the code qualifier (from the list below) and additional codes (e.g., occurrence codes) as related to a form locator or to report from the external code list approved by the NUBC for inclusion in the institutional data set, *if required by the payer.* 01-A0 Reserved for national assignment A1 National Uniform Billing Committee condition codes – not used for Medicare A2 National Uniform Billing Committee occurrence codes – not used for Medicare A3 National Uniform Billing Committee occurrence span codes – not used for Medicare A4 National Uniform Billing Committee value codes – not used for Medicare A5-B0 Reserved for national assignment B3 Health care provider taxonomy code B4-ZZ Reserved for national assignment CODE SOURCE: ASC X12 External Code Source 682 (National Uniform Claim Committee)

The UB-04 (CMS-1450) and its data elements serve the needs of many third-party payers. Although some payers do not collect certain data elements, it is important to capture all NUBC-approved data elements for audit trail purposes. In addition, NUBC-approved data elements are reported by facilities that have established coordination of benefits agreements with the payers.

UB-04 Case Study

NOTE: Many form locators will remain blank on the completed UB-04 claim.

Use the blank UB-04 claim (Figure 9-13) to enter data from the outpatient case study (Figure 9-15). Codes (e.g., ICD, CPT/HCPCS, revenue) required for completion of the UB-04 claim are included in the case study. Refer to Table 9-4 for instructions on completing the UB-04 claim. Then, compare your completed claim to the answer key in Figure 9-16.

Alfred Medical Center • 548 N Main St • Alfred, NY 14802
(607) 555-1234 **EIN:** 87-1349061 **NPI:** 9876543211 **TOB:** 0131

OUTPATIENT CASE

PATIENT NAME	DATE & START/END TIME OF VISIT		SOURCE OF ADMISSION	
John Q Public	0505YY 0900 1300		Physician referral	
PATIENT ADDRESS		**PATIENT TELEPHONE NUMBER**	**BIRTH DATE**	**GENDER**
15 Hill St Alfred NY 14802		(607)555-1234	08-05-70	M (Male)
MARITAL STATUS	**MEDICAL RECORD #**	**PATIENT CONTROL #**	**PATIENT DISCHARGE STATUS**	
Widowed	987654	859ABC451562	01 (Discharged home)	
PAYER	**HEALTH INSURANCE ID NUMBER (HICN)**			
Aetna	524856254			
PRIMARY PAYER MAILING ADDRESS			**Health Plan ID**	
Aetna, P.O. Box 650, Canandaigua, NY 14424			3429872450	
PATIENT RELATIONSHIP TO INSURED		**EMPLOYMENT STATUS**	**NAME OF EMPLOYER**	
18 (Self)		Employed full time	Alstom, Hornell NY	
RESPONSIBLE PHYSICIAN		**RESPONSIBLE PHYSICIAN N.P.I.**	**TYPE OF ADMISSION**	
John Smith, M.D.		1265891895	Elective	
RELEASE OF INFORMATION FORM		**ASSIGNMENTS OF BENEFITS FORM**		
Signed by patient		Signed by patient		

CASE SUMMARY	DIAGNOSES	ICD CODES
Patient was registered in the outpatient clinic and underwent single view chest x-ray for chronic obstructive pulmonary disease (COPD). Patient discharged home, to be followed by primary care physician.	COPD	J44.9

CHARGE DESCRIPTION MASTER (PARTIAL)

ALFRED MEDICAL CENTER
548 N MAIN ST
ALFRED, NY 14802

Printed on 05/05/YY

DEPARTMENT CODE: 01.855 DEPARTMENT: Radiology

	SERVICE CODE	SERVICE DESCRIPTION	REVENUE CODE	CPT CODE	CHARGE	RVU
X	8550001	Chest x-ray, single view	0324	71010	74.50	0.70
	8550002	Chest x-ray, two views	0324	71020	82.50	0.95

FIGURE 9-15 Outpatient case.

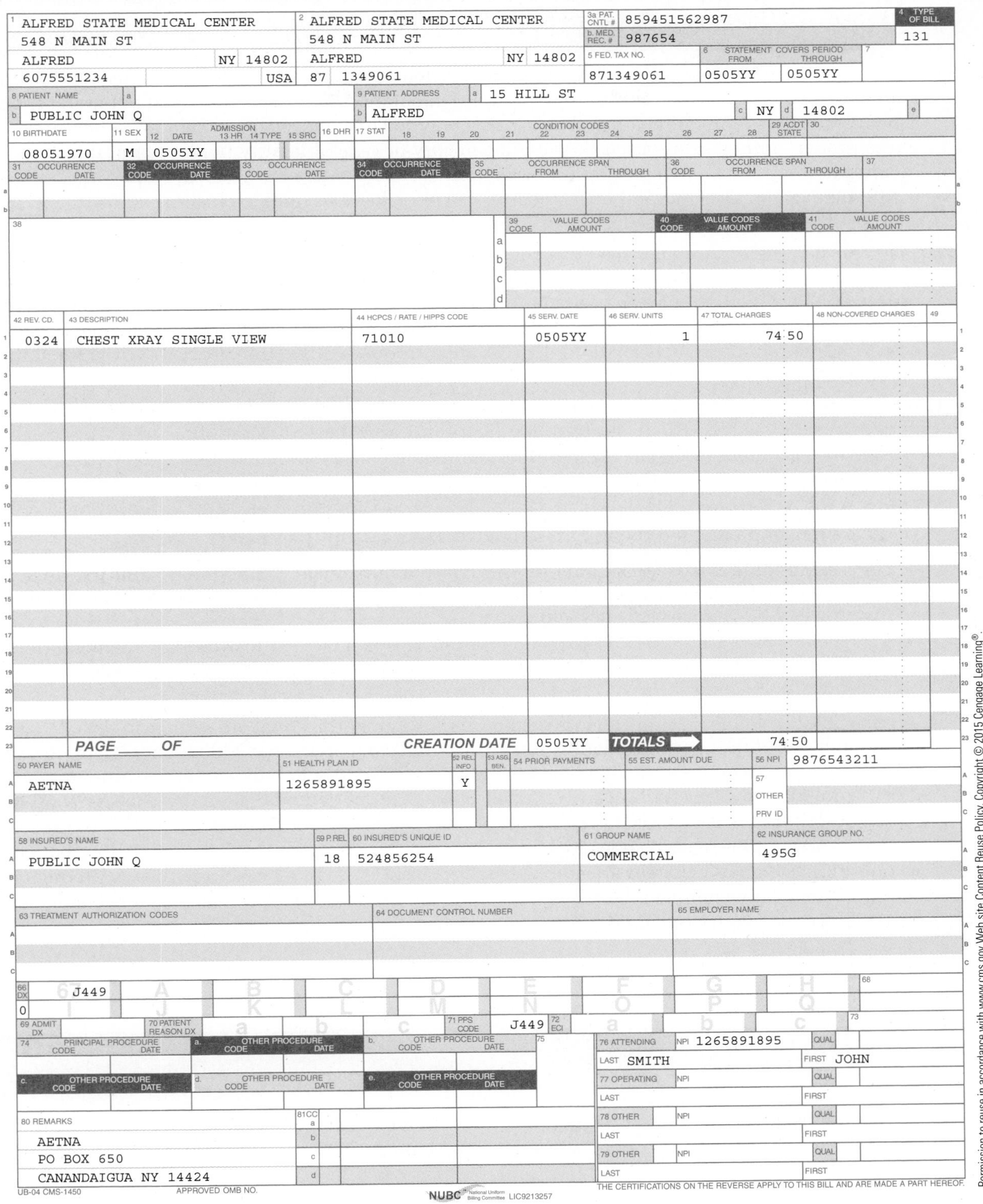

1	ALFRED STATE MEDICAL CENTER, 548 N MAIN ST, ALFRED NY 14802, 6075551234 USA
2	ALFRED STATE MEDICAL CENTER, 548 N MAIN ST, ALFRED NY 14802, 87 1349061
3a PAT. CNTL #	859451562987
b. MED. REC. #	987654
4 TYPE OF BILL	131
5 FED. TAX NO.	871349061
6 STATEMENT COVERS PERIOD FROM / THROUGH	0505YY / 0505YY
8 PATIENT NAME	b PUBLIC JOHN Q
9 PATIENT ADDRESS	a 15 HILL ST; b ALFRED; c NY; d 14802
10 BIRTHDATE	08051970
11 SEX	M
12 ADMISSION DATE	0505YY

42 REV. CD.	43 DESCRIPTION	44 HCPCS / RATE / HIPPS CODE	45 SERV. DATE	46 SERV. UNITS	47 TOTAL CHARGES	48 NON-COVERED CHARGES
0324	CHEST XRAY SINGLE VIEW	71010	0505YY	1	74 50	
	PAGE ____ OF ____	CREATION DATE	0505YY	TOTALS	74 50	

50 PAYER NAME	AETNA
51 HEALTH PLAN ID	1265891895
52 REL. INFO	Y
56 NPI	9876543211
58 INSURED'S NAME	PUBLIC JOHN Q
59 P.REL	18
60 INSURED'S UNIQUE ID	524856254
61 GROUP NAME	COMMERCIAL
62 INSURANCE GROUP NO.	495G
66 DX	0
67	J449
71 PPS CODE / 72 ECI	J449
76 ATTENDING NPI	1265891895
LAST / FIRST	SMITH / JOHN
80 REMARKS	AETNA, PO BOX 650, CANANDAIGUA NY 14424

UB-04 CMS-1450 APPROVED OMB NO. NUBC National Uniform Billing Committee LIC9213257

THE CERTIFICATIONS ON THE REVERSE APPLY TO THIS BILL AND ARE MADE A PART HEREOF.

FIGURE 9-16 UB-04 claim answer key.

SUMMARY

Health care costs increased dramatically with the implementation of government-sponsored health programs in 1965. This led to the creation and implementation of prospective payment systems and fee schedules for government health programs as a way to control costs by reimbursing facilities according to predetermined rates based on patient category or type of facility (with annual increases based on an inflation index and a geographic wage index). The Centers for Medicare and Medicaid Services (CMS) manage implementation of Medicare PPS, fee schedules, and exclusions according to prospective cost-based rates and prospective price-based rates.

Prospective cost-based rates are based on reported health care costs (e.g., charges) from which a prospective *per diem* rate is determined. Annual rates are usually adjusted using actual costs from the prior year. This method may be based on the facility's *case mix* (types and categories of patients that reflect the need for different levels of service based on acuity). Prospective payment systems based on this reimbursement methodology include resource utilization groups (RUGs) for skilled nursing care.

Prospective price-based rates are associated with a particular category of patient (e.g., inpatients), and rates are established by the payer (e.g., Medicare) prior to the provision of health care services. Prospective payment systems based on this reimbursement methodology include Medicare severity diagnosis-related groups (MS-DRGs) for inpatient care.

Typically, third-party payers adopt prospective payment systems, fee schedules, and exclusions after Medicare has implemented them; payers modify them to suit their needs.

- A fee schedule is cost-based, fee-for-service reimbursement methodology that includes a list of maximum fees and corresponding procedures/services, which payers use to compensate providers for health care services delivered to patients.
- Exclusions are "Medicare PPS Excluded Cancer Hospitals" (e.g., Roswell Park Memorial Institute in Buffalo, New York) that applied for and were granted waivers from mandatory participation in the hospital inpatient PPS.

The UB-04 claim contains data entry blocks called form locators (FLs) that are similar to the CMS-1500 claim blocks used to input information about procedures or services provided to a patient. Revenue codes are four-digit codes preprinted on a facility's chargemaster to indicate the location or type of service provided to an institutional patient, and they are reported on the UB-04. The chargemaster (or charge description master, CDM) is a document that contains a computer-generated list of procedures, services, and supplies with charges for each. Chargemaster data is entered in the facility's patient accounting system, and charges are automatically posted to the patient's bill (UB-04). Although some institutions actually complete the UB-04 claim and submit it to third-party payers for reimbursement, most perform data entry of UB-04 information using commercial software.

INTERNET LINKS

- CMS manuals
  Go to **www.cms.gov**, click on the Regulations and Guidance link, click on the Manuals link (below the Guidance heading), and click on the Internet-Only Manuals (IOMs) or Paper-Based Manuals link to access CMS manuals.
- *Diagnostic Statistical Manual*
  www.appi.org
- HIPPS rate codes
  Go to **www.cms.gov**, click on Medicare, click on the Prospective Payment Systems - General Information link under the Medicare Fee-for-Service Payment section, and click on the HIPPS Codes link.

- *Medicare Claims Processing Manual*, Chapter 25
  Go to **www.cms.gov**, click on the Regulations and Guidance link, click on the Manuals link (below the Guidance heading), click on the Internet-Only Manuals (IOMs) link, click on the 100-04 (Medicare Claims Processing Manual) link, and click on the Chapter 25 - Completing and Processing the Form CMS-1450 Data Set link.
- Medicare payment systems
  Go to **www.cms.gov**, click on the Medicare link, scroll to the Medicare Fee-for-Service Payment heading, and click on any payment system link.
- NUBC
  Go to **www.nubc.org** to learn more about the implementation of the UB-04.
- Quarterly Medicare provider updates
  Go to **www.cms.gov**, click on the Regulations and Guidance link, scroll down to the Regulations & Policies heading, and click on the Quarterly Provider Updates link.
  (Click on the CMS Quarterly Provider Updates Email Updates link to join and receive e-mail updates.)

STUDY CHECKLIST

- ☐ Read this textbook chapter and highlight key concepts.
- ☐ Create an index card for each key term.
- ☐ Access the chapter Internet links to learn more about concepts.
- ☐ Answer the chapter review questions, verifying answers with your instructor.
- ☐ Complete the Workbook chapter, verifying answers with your instructor.
- ☐ Form a study group with classmates to discuss chapter concepts in preparation for an exam.

REVIEW

SHORT ANSWER Complete the following.

1. Calculate the following amounts for a participating provider who bills Medicare:

Submitted charge (based on provider's regular fee for office visit)	$ 75
Medicare physician fee schedule (PFS)	$ 60
Coinsurance amount (paid by patient or supplemental insurance)	$ 12
Medicare payment (80 percent of the allowed amount)	______
Medicare write-off (not to be paid by Medicare or the beneficiary)	______

2. Calculate the following amounts for a nonPAR who bills Medicare:

Submitted charge (based on provider's regular fee)	$ 650
NonPAR Medicare physician fee schedule allowed amount	$ 450
Limiting charge [MPFS – (MPFS × 5 percent)] × 115 percent	______
Medicare payment (80 percent of the MPFS allowed amount, less 5 percent)	______
Beneficiary is billed the balance of the limiting charge	$ 149.63
Medicare write-off (*not* to be paid by Medicare or the beneficiary)	______

3. Calculate the following amounts for a nurse practitioner who bills Medicare:

Submitted charge (based on provider's regular fee for office visit)	$ 75
Medicare allowed amount (according to the Medicare physician fee schedule)	$ 60
Nurse practitioner allowed amount (100 percent of MPFS)	________
Medicare payment (80 percent of the allowed amount)	________

MATCHING Match the type of rate with the prospective payment system.

a. cost-based

b. price-based

_____ **4. Ambulance fee schedule**

_____ **5. Ambulatory surgical center payment rates**

_____ **6. IPPS**

_____ **7. Inpatient psychiatric facility PPS**

_____ **8. SNF PPS**

MULTIPLE CHOICE Select the most appropriate response.

9. Which PPS provides a predetermined payment that depends on the patient's principal diagnosis, comorbidities, complications, and principal and secondary procedures?

a. OPPS

b. IPPS

c. MPFS

d. SNF PPS

10. Which abbreviation indicates where services were provided to beneficiaries?

a. ABN

b. MSP

c. POS

d. TOS

11. The chargemaster is a(n)

a. computer-generated list used by facilities, which contains procedures, services, supplies, revenue codes, and charges.

b. data entry screen used by coders to assign diagnosis and procedure codes to generate a diagnosis-related group.

c. document used by third-party payers and government plans to generate national provider identification numbers.

d. encounter form used by physicians and other providers to collect data about office procedures provided to patients.

12. Resource utilization groups (RUGs) use a _____ reimbursement methodology used by skilled nursing facilities.

a. fee-for-service-based

b. cost-based

c. managed care

d. price-based

13. Which of the following legislated implementation of the long-term (acute) care hospital inpatient prospective payment system?

a. BBA
b. BBRA
c. OBRA
d. TEFRA

14. The Resource-Based Relative Value Scale (RBRVS) system is more commonly called the

a. clinical laboratory fee schedule.
b. long-term care prospective payment system.
c. Medicare physician fee schedule.
d. outpatient prospective payment system.

15. Reimbursement rates based on the anticipated care needs of patients result in reduced risks to facilities and to payers. The process by which health care facilities and payers determine anticipated care needs by reviewing types and/or categories of patients treated by a facility is called its

a. capitation.
b. case mix.
c. chargemaster.
d. claims.

16. Diagnosis-related groups are organized into mutually exclusive categories called _____, which are loosely based on body systems.

a. ambulatory payment classifications
b. major diagnostic categories
c. Outcomes and Assessment Information Sets
d. resource utilization groups

17. Physician work, practice expense, and malpractice expense are components in computing _____ for the Resource-Based Relative Value Scale system.

a. conversion factors
b. limiting charges
c. relative-value units
d. site of service differentials

18. Four-digit _____ codes are preprinted on a facility's chargemaster to indicate the location or type of service provided to an institutional patient.

a. disease and procedure
b. place-of-service
c. revenue
d. type-of-service

19. The type of bill (TOB) is a required element that is entered in FL4 on the UB-04, and it contains _____ digits.

a. 3
b. 4
c. 5
d. 10

20. Which is responsible for developing data elements reported on the UB-04?

a. AHA
b. CMS
c. NUBC
d. NUCC

21. A 50-year-old female patient reports to the hospital's registration department to begin the patient registration process. The patient tells the patient registration clerk that her physician wants her to undergo a screening mammogram. The clerk asks the patient for the requisition form (physician order for screening mammogram) and is told that the patient left it at home. The registration clerk is aware that the patient's physician office has implemented use of the electronic health record, and so the patient registration process is

a. continued after the patient returns from having obtained a new paper-based requisition form from the physician's nearby office.
b. continued because an electronic version of the requisition form is available from the physician office in the hospital's EHR system.
c. halted until the the radiology department approves performing the screening mammogram procedure without the requisition form.
d. halted so the switchboard operator can page the physician to ask that a telephone order for the mammogram be called in.

22. An 18-year-old male patient arrives at the hospital's registration department to begin the patient registration process for scheduled wisdom teeth extraction under anesthesia. In addition to obtaining appropriate consents for treatment and release of information along with collecting patient demographic and insurance information, the patient registration clerk

a. authorizes preadmission clearance for the patient.
b. conducts utilization management for medical necessity.
c. posts charges associated with the surgical procedure.
d. validates the patient's health insurance coverage.

23. A female patient is properly registered for scheduled blood work and arrives at the hospital's laboratory department. The laboratory technician who performs venipuncture

a. assigns diagnosis and laboratory procedure codes using ICD-10-CM and CPT/HCPCS level II.
b. captures charge data by using an automated system that links to the hospital's chargemaster.
c. determines ambulatory payment classification (APC) revenue the hospital can expect to receive.
d. forwards the record generated to the billing department so an encounter form can be completed.

24. Diagnosis and procedure coding required for the assignment of APCs, DRGs, and so on, is typically performed by _____ personnel.

a. health information management
b. medical staff
c. patient registration
d. third-party payer

25. During the patient discharge processing stage of revenue cycle management

a. all patient information and codes are input into the billing system, and CMS-1500 or UB-04 claims are generated and submitted to third-party payers.
b. late charges, lost charges, or corrections to previously processed CMS-1500 or UB-04 claims are entered, and claims are resubmitted to payers.
c. patient information is verified, discharge instructions are provided, patient follow-up visit is scheduled, consent forms are reviewed for signatures, and patient policies are explained to the patient.
d. reimbursement from third-party payers is posted to appropriate accounts, and rejected claims are resubmitted with appropriate documentation.

CHAPTER 10

Coding for Medical Necessity

CHAPTER OUTLINE

Applying Coding Guidelines
Coding and Billing Considerations
Coding from Case Scenarios
Coding from Patient Reports

OBJECTIVES

Upon successful completion of this chapter, you should be able to:

1. Define key terms.
2. Select and code diagnoses and procedures from case studies and sample reports.
3. Research local coverage determinations.

KEY TERMS

assessment
auditing process
local coverage determination (LCD)
medically managed
Medicare coverage database (MCD)
narrative clinic note
national coverage determination (NCD)
objective
operative report
outpatient code editor (OCE)
plan
SOAP note
subjective

INTRODUCTION

In Chapters 7 through 9, coding practice exercises consisted of statements for which diagnosis or procedure/service codes were assigned. The next step in learning to code properly is to select diagnoses and procedures/services from a case and link each procedure/service with the diagnosis code that justifies the medical necessity for performing it. (Medical necessity of procedures/services is required by payers for reimbursement consideration.) This chapter requires you to review case scenarios and patient reports to determine diagnoses and procedures/services to be coded, as well as medical necessity issues.

Coding for medical necessity requires a background in patient record documentation practices and the ability to interpret provider documentation. Cengage Learning's *Essentials of Health Information Management*, by Mary Jo Bowie and Michelle A. Green, contains detailed content about patient record documentation practices.

This chapter includes case studies that will allow you to practice interpreting provider documentation to select appropriate diagnoses and procedures/services for coding purposes and medical necessity determination.

APPLYING CODING GUIDELINES

In Chapters 6 through 8, diagnosis and procedure statements were coded according to ICD-10-CM, CPT, or HCPCS level II. In preparation for entering codes in the diagnosis blocks on the CMS-1500 claim, it is necessary to apply the CMS-established *Official Coding Guidelines for Physician and Outpatient Hospital Services* and to understand the limitations of the CMS-1500 claim when billing payers.

Coding may not be a problem when you are reviewing short, one-line diagnosis or procedure/service statements such as those that appeared in most of the earlier exercises. When working with case scenarios, sample reports, or patient records, however, you must select the diagnosis and procedure/service to code based on provider documentation.

Be sure to code and report only those diagnoses, conditions, procedures, and/or services that are documented in the patient record as having been *treated* or *medically managed*. **Medically managed** means that even though a diagnosis (e.g., hypertension) may not receive direct treatment during an encounter, the provider has to consider that diagnosis when determining treatment for other conditions. It is appropriate to code and report medically managed diagnoses and conditions. Questions that should be considered before coding and reporting a diagnosis or condition include:

1. Does the diagnosis or condition support a procedure or service provided during this encounter?
2. Did the provider prescribe a new medication or change a prescription for a new or existing diagnosis or condition?
3. Are positive diagnostic test results documented in the patient record to support a diagnosis or condition?
4. Did the provider have to consider the impact of treatment for chronic conditions when treating a newly diagnosed condition?

> **NOTE:** A diagnosis or condition code is linked with each procedure or service code reported on the CMS-1500 claim. Up to 12 ICD-10-CM codes are entered next to letters A–L in Block 21 of the CMS-1500 claim. The appropriate diagnosis pointer (letter) from Block 21 is reported in Block 24E to justify medical necessity of the procedure or service code reported in Block 24D.

Up to 12 ICD-10-CM diagnosis codes can be reported on one CMS-1500. When reporting procedure/service codes on the CMS-1500, it is important to carefully match the appropriate diagnosis code with the procedure or service provided. Providers often document past conditions that are not active problems for the patient, and these conditions are not coded or reported on the claim. (However, for data capture purposes, an ICD-10-CM Z code can be assigned to past conditions.)

Report ICD-10-CM codes on the claim, beginning with the *first-listed diagnosis* and followed by any secondary diagnoses (e.g., coexisting conditions) that were treated or medically managed. Then, link the code for each procedure or service provided with the diagnosis or condition that proves the *medical necessity* for performing the procedure or service.

EXAMPLE: Tim Johnson's primary care provider performed a level 3 E/M service (99213) in the office on June 1 to evaluate Tim's symptoms of upset stomach (K30) and vomiting without nausea (R11.11). Tim's type 2 diabetes mellitus (E11.9) was medically managed during the encounter when venipuncture (36415) and a blood glucose test (82947) were performed; test results were within normal limits. Table 10-1 demonstrates how diagnoses and conditions are linked with procedures or services performed during the encounter. Figure 10-1 illustrates completion of Blocks 21 and 24A–E on the CMS-1500 claim. Note that Block 24E, line 1, contains two diagnosis code indicators from Block 21 whereas Block 24E, lines 2 and 3, each contain just one diagnosis code indicator from Block 21. If a payer allows multiple diagnosis codes to be linked to procedures/services in Block 24, enter A B *or* A B C in Block 24E, line 1.

TABLE 10-1 Linking diagnosis and procedure/service codes from Block 21 with Block 24E of the CMS-1500 claim

DIAGNOSES DOCUMENTED ON PATIENT'S CHART	ICD-10-CM CODE (ENTER IN BLOCK 21 OF CMS-1500)	PROCEDURE OR SERVICE RENDERED TO PATIENT	CPT CODE (ENTER IN BLOCK 24D OF CMS-1500)	DIAGNOSIS POINTER (ENTER IN BLOCK 24E OF CMS-1500)
Upset stomach	K30	Office visit	99213	A
Vomiting	R11.11	Office visit	99213	B
Diabetes mellitus	E11.9	Venipuncture	36415	C
		Blood-sugar test	82947	C

21. DIAGNOSIS OR NATURE OF ILLNESS OR INJURY Relate A-L to service line below (24E) ICD Ind. 0

A. K30 B. R11.11 C. E11.9 D.
E. F. G. H.
I. J. K. L.

22. RESUBMISSION CODE ORIGINAL REF. NO.

23. PRIOR AUTHORIZATION NUMBER

	24. A. DATE(S) OF SERVICE From MM	DD	YY	To MM	DD	YY	B. PLACE OF SERVICE	C. EMG	D. PROCEDURES, SERVICES, OR SUPPLIES (Explain Unusual Circumstances) CPT/HCPCS	MODIFIER	E. DIAGNOSIS POINTER	F. $ CHARGES	G. DAYS OR UNITS	H. EPSDT Family Plan	I. ID. QUAL.	J. RENDERING PROVIDER ID. #
1	06	01	YY				11		99213		A B	75 00	1		NPI	
2	06	01	YY				11		36415		C	15 00	1		NPI	
3	06	01	YY				11		82947		C	35 00	1		NPI	

Courtesy of the Centers for Medicare & Medicaid Services, www.cms.gov; Copyright © 2015 Cengage Learning®.

FIGURE 10-1 Completed Blocks 21 and 24 of the CMS-1500 claim with ICD-10-CM codes.

EXERCISE 10-1

Choosing the First-Listed Diagnosis

Review the list of symptoms, complaints, and disorders in each case and underline the first-listed diagnosis, which is reported in Block 21 of the CMS-1500 claim.

1. Occasional bouts of urinary frequency, but symptom-free today
Sore throat with swollen glands and enlarged tonsils
Acute pharyngitis with negative rapid strep test
Urinalysis test negative

2. Edema, left lateral malleolus
Limited range of motion due to pain
Musculoligamentous sprain, left ankle
X-ray negative for fracture

3. Distended urinary bladder
Benign prostatic hypertrophy (BPH) with urinary retention
Enlarged prostate

4. Pale, diaphoretic, and in acute distress
Bacterial endocarditis
Limited chest expansion, scattered bilateral wheezes
Pulse 112 and regular, respirations 22 with some shortness of breath

5. Right leg still weak
Partial drop foot gait, right
Tightness in lower back

EXERCISE 10-2

Linking Diagnoses with Procedures/Services

Link the diagnosis with the procedure/service by entering just one letter in the DIAGNOSIS POINTER column.

REMEMBER!

To link the diagnosis with the procedure/service means to match up the appropriate diagnosis with the procedure/service that was rendered to treat or manage the diagnosis.

(continues)

EXAMPLE: The patient was treated by the doctor in the office for a fractured thumb, and x-rays were taken. The following diagnoses and procedures were documented in the patient's chart:

A. diabetes mellitus, non-insulin-dependent, controlled

B. benign essential hypertension

C. simple fracture, right thumb

DIAGNOSIS POINTER	PROCEDURE/SERVICE
C	Office visit
C	X-ray, right thumb

Based on the procedure performed and service delivered, the patient was seen for the thumb fracture. Because the diabetes and hypertension are under control, they require no treatment or management during this visit. Therefore, only the fracture is linked to the procedure and service.

CASE 1

The patient was treated in the office for abdominal cramping and bloody stools. A hemoccult test was positive for blood in the stool. The patient was scheduled for proctoscopy with biopsy two days later, and Duke C carcinoma of the colon was diagnosed. The patient was scheduled for proctectomy to be performed in seven days. The following diagnoses were documented on the patient's chart:

A. abdominal cramping

B. blood in the stool

C. Duke C carcinoma, colon

DIAGNOSIS POINTER	PROCEDURE/SERVICE
	Hemoccult lab test
	Proctoscopy with biopsy
	Proctectomy

CASE 2

The patient was treated in the office for urinary frequency with dysuria, sore throat with cough, and headaches. The urinalysis was negative, and the rapid strep test was positive for streptococcus infection. The patient was placed on antibiotics and was scheduled to be seen in 10 days. The following diagnoses were documented on the patient's chart:

A. urinary frequency with dysuria

B. sore throat with cough

C. headaches

D. strep throat

(continues)

DIAGNOSIS POINTER	PROCEDURE/SERVICE
	Office visit
	Urinalysis
	Rapid strep test

CASE 3

The patient was treated in the office to rule out pneumonia. She had been experiencing wheezing and congestion, and her respirations were labored. The chest x-ray done in the office was positive for pneumonia. The following diagnoses were documented on the patient's chart:

A. pneumonia

B. wheezing

C. congestion

D. labored respirations

DIAGNOSIS POINTER	PROCEDURE/SERVICE
	Office visit
	Chest x-ray

CASE 4

The doctor treated the patient in the nursing facility for the second time since she was admitted. The patient complained of malaise. It was noted that the patient had a cough as well as a fever of 103°F and that her pharynx was erythematous (abnormally red in appearance, which is a sign of infection). The following diagnoses were documented on the patient's chart:

A. malaise

B. cough

C. fever of 103°F

D. erythematous pharynx

DIAGNOSIS POINTER	PROCEDURE/SERVICE
	Nursing facility visit

CASE 5

The patient was treated in the emergency department for chills and fever. The physician noted left lower abdominal quadrant pain and tenderness. The physician diagnosed *acute diverticulitis*. The following diagnoses were documented on the patient's chart:

A. chills

B. fever

C. acute diverticulitis

DIAGNOSIS POINTER	PROCEDURE/SERVICE
	Emergency department visit

CODING AND BILLING CONSIDERATIONS

In addition to applying coding guidelines and rules to accurately assign and report codes on insurance claims, you should also incorporate the following as part of practice management:

- **Completion of an advance beneficiary notice of noncoverage (ABN) when appropriate**
- **Implementation of an auditing process**
- **Review of local coverage determinations (LCDs) and national coverage determinations (NCDs)**
- **Complete and timely patient record documentation**
- **Use of outpatient code editor (OCE) software (for outpatient hospital claims)**

Patient Record Documentation

Patient record documentation must justify and support the medical necessity of procedures and services reported to payers. The following characteristics are associated with patient record documentation in all health care settings:

- **Documentation should be generated at the time of service or shortly thereafter.**
- **Delayed entries within a reasonable time frame (24 to 48 hours) are acceptable for purposes of clarification, correction of errors, addition of information not initially available, and when certain unusual circumstances prevent documentation at the time of service. Delayed entries cannot be used to authenticate services or substantiate medical necessity for the purpose of reimbursement.**
- **The patient record cannot be altered. Doing so is considered tampering with documentation. This means that errors must be legibly corrected so that a reviewer can determine the origin of the corrections, and the use of correction fluid (e.g., Wite-Out™) is prohibited.**
- **Corrections or additions to the patient record must be dated, timed, and legibly signed or initialed.**
- **Patient record entries must be legible.**
- **Entries should be dated, timed, and authenticated by the author.**

NOTE: It is recommended that an *authentication legend* be generated that contains the word-processed provider's name and, next to it, the provider's signature.

Advance Beneficiary Notice of Noncoverage (ABN)

An *advance beneficiary notice of noncoverage (ABN)* (located in Chapter 14 of this textbook, Figure 14-1) is a waiver required by Medicare for all outpatient and physician office procedures/services that are not covered by the Medicare program. Before providing a procedure or service that is not medically necessary and/or that Medicare will not cover, the patient must be informed and required to sign the waiver. (Even though a provider considers a procedure or service medically necessary, Medicare may not cover that procedure or service.) Patients sign the waiver to indicate that they understand the procedure or service is not covered by Medicare and that they will be financially responsible for reimbursing the provider for the procedure or service performed. If the waiver is not signed before the procedure/service is provided *and* Medicare denies coverage, the perception is that the provider is providing free services to Medicare patients—this is considered *fraud* by the Office of the Inspector General for CMS!

EXAMPLE: A Medicare patient is seen by her health care provider for severe left shoulder pain. There is no history of trauma, and in the office the patient has full range of motion with moderate pain. The patient insists that she wants the shoulder scanned to make sure she does not have cancer. Her physician explains that Medicare will reimburse for a scanning procedure *only if medically necessary* and that her symptoms and past history do not justify his ordering the scan. The patient insists again that she wants the scan even if she has to pay for it herself. The physician explains that this is an option for her and that she can sign the facility's ABN so that if Medicare denies the claim, the facility can bill her for the scan. The patient signs the ABN, which the physician keeps on file in the office, and the scan is ordered. The claim is submitted to Medicare, but it is denied due to lack of medical necessity to justify the scan. The patient is billed for the scan and is responsible for reimbursing the facility.

Auditing Process

Medical practices and health care facilities should routinely participate in an **auditing process**, which involves reviewing patient records and CMS-1500 or UB-04 claims to assess coding accuracy and completeness of documentation. Medical practices should also review encounter forms to ensure the accuracy of ICD-10-CM, CPT, and HCPCS level II codes. In addition, health care facilities should audit chargemasters to ensure the accuracy of HCPCS/CPT and UB-04 revenue codes. Physicians use an *encounter form* (or *superbill*) to select diagnoses treated or medically managed and procedures, services, and supplies provided to patients during an office visit. Physicians and other personnel use *chargemasters* to select procedures, services, and supplies provided to hospital emergency department patients and outpatients. (No diagnosis codes are included on chargemasters because diagnoses are documented in the patient record, coded by health information personnel, entered using an automated abstracting system, and reported on the UB-04 by billing office personnel. Nursing and other personnel typically use automated order-entry software to capture procedures, services, and supplies provided to health care facility inpatients.)

NOTE: Appendix III contains an E/M CodeBuilder that can be used to audit patient record documentation to ensure that codes submitted to payers are accurate.

EXAMPLE: Upon routine audit of outpatient records and UB-04 claims submitted to payers, a claim for $4,890 submitted to a commercial payer was paid based on 80 percent of total billed charges, or $3,912. Review of the patient record revealed that the patient was actually treated in the hospital for 36 hours—this case should have been billed as an inpatient at a DRG rate of $1,500 (based on the patient's diagnosis). The result of the audit was an overpayment of $2,412, which the facility has an obligation to refund to the payer.

Medicare Coverage Database (MCD)

The **Medicare coverage database (MCD)** is used by Medicare administrative contractors, providers, and other health care industry professionals to determine whether a procedure or service is reasonable and necessary for the diagnosis or treatment of an illness or injury. The MCD contains:

- **National coverage determinations (NCDs), including draft policies and proposed decisions**
- **Local coverage determinations (LCDs), including policy articles**

The MCD also includes other types of national coverage analyses (NCAs), coding analyses for labs (CALs), Medicare Evidence Development & Coverage Advisory Committee (MedCAC) proceedings, and Medicare coverage guidance documents.

CMS develops **national coverage determinations (NCDs)** on an ongoing basis, and Medicare administrative contractors create edits for NCD rules, called local coverage determinations (LCDs) (discussed below). NCDs (and LCDs) link ICD-10-CM diagnosis codes with procedures or services that are considered reasonable and necessary for the diagnosis or treatment of an illness or injury. When review of NCDs (or LCDs) indicates that a procedure or service is not medically necessary, the provider is permitted to bill the patient only if an advance beneficiary notice of noncoverage (ABN) is signed by the patient prior to providing the procedure or service.

- **Claims submitted with diagnosis and procedure/service codes that fail NCD or LCD edits may be denied.**
- **When an LCD and an NCD exist for the same procedure or service, the NCD takes precedence.**

EXAMPLE: The Centers for Medicare and Medicaid Services (CMS) published national coverage determinations (NCDs) that will prevent Medicare from paying for the following surgical errors:

- Wrong surgical or other invasive procedures performed on a patient
- Surgical or other invasive procedures performed on the wrong body part
- Surgical or other invasive procedures performed on the wrong patient

Local coverage determinations (LCDs) (formerly called *local medical review policies*, LMRPs) specify under what clinical circumstances a service is covered (including under what clinical circumstances it is considered to be reasonable and necessary) and coded correctly. They list covered and noncovered codes, but they do not include coding guidelines. LCDs assist Medicare administrative contractors (MACs) (previously called carriers and fiscal intermediaries) and providers (e.g., hospitals, physicians, and suppliers) by outlining how contractors will review claims to ensure that they meet Medicare coverage requirements. MACs publish LCDs to provide guidance to the public and medical community within a specified geographic area. CMS requires that LCDs be consistent with national guidance (although they can be more detailed or specific), developed with scientific evidence and clinical practice, and created using specified federal guidelines. If a MAC develops an LCD, it applies only within the area serviced by that contractor. Although another MAC may come to a similar decision, CMS does not require it to do so.

EXAMPLE: A Medicare administrative contractor (MAC) established an LCD for *MRI and CT Scans of Thorax and Chest* (LCD ID # L26732), which defines indications and limitations of coverage and/or medical necessity, reasons for denials, documentation requirements, and a list of ICD-10-CM codes that support medical necessity. Before submitting a claim for payment of an MRI or CT scan of thorax and chest to the MAC, the insurance specialist should review this LCD to make sure the procedure is covered, that the ICD-10-CM codes reported are accurate, and that the patient record documentation supports medical necessity of the procedure.

Outpatient Code Editor (OCE)

The **outpatient code editor (OCE)** is software that edits outpatient claims submitted by hospitals, community mental health centers, comprehensive out-patient rehabilitation facilities, and home health agencies. The software is used during the assignment of ambulatory payment classifications (APCs) and to review submissions for coding validity (e.g., missing characters from codes) and coverage (e.g., medical necessity). OCE edits result in one of the following dispositions: rejection, denial, return to provider (RTP), or suspension.

EXAMPLE: The OCE reviews data elements submitted on the UB-04 claim such as from/through dates, ICD-10-CM diagnosis codes, type of bill, age, gender, HCPCS/CPT codes, revenue codes, service units, and so on.

EXERCISE 10-3

National Coverage Determinations

Go to **www.cms.gov**, scroll to the Top 5 Resources, click on the Medicare Coverage Database link, click the **INDEXES** link, click on the **National Coverage** link, and click on the **NCDs Listed Alphabetically** link to locate the procedure/service and carefully review its contents to determine whether Medicare covers that procedure/service.

EXAMPLE: A 67-year-old black female, status post menopause, underwent a bone (mineral) density study for osteoporosis screening.

Answer: Upon review of the NCD entitled *Bone (Mineral) Density Studies*, it is noted that conditions for coverage of "bone mass measurements" are located in the *Medicare Benefit Policy Manual*, which indicates that "bone mass measurement" (BMM) is covered under certain conditions (e.g., BMM is ordered by the treating physician, is reasonable and necessary for treating the patient's condition, and so on).

1. A 72-year-old male undergoes left heart *cardiac* catheterization by cutdown for coronary artery disease and angina pectoris, which was performed in an ambulatory surgery center. The patient is status post myocardial infarction four weeks ago.
2. A 66-year-old female undergoes cardiac rehabilitation with continuous ECG monitoring for status post coronary angioplasty, status post coronary bypass, and unstable angina.
3. An 81-year-old female undergoes diagnostic colonoscopy (endoscopy) through a stoma for history of colon cancer (treatment complete), Crohn's disease, blood in stool, and abdominal pain.
4. A 94-year-old male undergoes a CT (computed tomography) scan of the head for a laceration of the scalp, closed head trauma, contusion of the scalp, suspected brain lesion, and suspected brain metastasis.

CODING FROM CASE SCENARIOS

Case scenarios summarize medical data from patient records; in this text, they introduce the student to the process of selecting (or abstracting) diagnoses and procedures. Once this technique is learned, it will be easier to move on to selecting diagnoses and procedures from patient records.

STEP 1 Read the entire case scenario to obtain an overview of the problems presented and procedures/services performed. Research any word or abbreviation not understood.

NOTE: Do *not* use a highlighter or other marker on an original document because copies of the document will be illegible. Highlighting marks photocopy as a thick, black or gray line. Instead, make a copy of the original document for mark-up purposes, and then destroy the copy after the coding process has been completed.

STEP 2 Reread the problem and highlight the diagnoses, symptoms, or health status that supports, justifies, and/or proves the medical necessity of any procedure or service performed.

STEP 3 Assign codes to documented diagnoses, symptoms, procedure(s), signs, health status, and/or service(s).

STEP 4 Assign modifiers to CPT and HCPCS level II codes, if applicable.

STEP 5 Identify the first-listed condition.

STEP 6 Link each procedure or service to a diagnosis, symptom, or health status for medical necessity.

Case 1

The patient returned to the surgeon's office during the postoperative period because of symptoms of shortness of breath, dizzy spells, and pain in the left arm. A level 3 re-examination (detailed history and examination was documented) of the patient was performed. The wound is healing nicely. There is no abnormal redness or abnormal pain from the incision. A 3-lead ECG rhythm strip was performed, which revealed an inversion of the T wave. The abnormal ECG was discussed with the patient and he agreed to an immediate referral to Dr. Cardiac for a cardiac work-up.

Answer

Procedure(s) performed	Code	Diagnosis(es)
1. Office visit, established patient, level 3	99213-24	A. Postoperative status (Z98.89)
2. 3-lead ECG rhythm strip	93040	B. Shortness of breath (R06.02) and dizziness (R42)
		C. Pain, left arm (M79.602)
		D. Abnormal ECG-inverted T wave (R94.31)

Rationale

- **The service provided is a level 3 office visit, established patient.**
- **The words "re-examination" and "during postoperative period, by same surgeon" justify the use of the -24 modifier because this examination was conducted during the postoperative period.**

- **Abnormal ECG illustrates an inversion of the T wave, the documented problem.**
- **"Shortness of breath, dizzy spells, and pain in the left arm" are symptoms of a possible cardiac condition that is causing the abnormal ECG.**

Case 2

This 72-year-old man with multiple chronic conditions registered for hospital outpatient surgery and was scheduled for repair of an initial, uncomplicated left inguinal hernia. The patient was cleared for surgery by his primary care physician. General anesthesia was administered by the anesthesiologist, after which the incision was made. At this point, the patient went into shock, the surgery was halted, and the wound was closed. The patient was sent to Recovery.

Answer

Procedure(s) performed	Code	Diagnosis(es)
1. Hernia repair, initial	49505-74	A. Inguinal hernia (K40.90)
		B. Shock due to surgery (T81.11xA)
		C. Surgery cancelled (Z53.09)

Rationale

- **Procedure was initiated for the repair of an uncomplicated, inguinal hernia.**
- **Modifier -74 indicates surgery was stopped after anesthesia had been administered because of the threat to the patient's well-being from the shock.**
- **The first-listed diagnosis is inguinal hernia, which is the reason the patient sought health care.**
- **Secondary diagnoses include shock resulting from surgery (explains the discontinuation of the surgery) and cancelled surgery.**

EXERCISE 10-4

Coding Case Scenarios

A. List and code the procedures, services, and diagnosis(es) for each of the following case scenarios.

B. Be sure to include all necessary CPT and/or HCPCS modifiers.

C. Underline the first-listed condition.

1. A 66-year-old Medicare patient came to the office for his annual physical. He has a past history of hypertension, controlled by medication, and new complaints of dizziness and tiredness (which the physician determined was related to today's increased blood pressure). During the course of the examination, the physician found blood pressure of 160/130. A detailed history and exam of this established patient was performed in addition to the preventive medicine encounter.

   Procedures/Services **Diagnoses**

   ____

   ____

   ____

(continues)

2. A 67-year-old woman came to the surgery center for a scheduled diagnostic arthroscopy of her right shoulder because of constant pain on rotation of the shoulder. Prior to entering the operating room she told the nurse, "I have been feeling weak, depressed, and tired ever since my last visit." The surgeon performs a re-examination with a detailed history, expanded problem-focused physical, and moderate-complexity decision making prior to the surgery. The findings were negative and the procedure was performed uneventfully.

Procedures/Services **Diagnoses**

____

____

____

3. The patient was seen in the emergency department (ED) at 10:00 a.m. for right lower quadrant pain; the ED physician performed an expanded problem-focused history and exam. Ultrasound revealed an inflamed appendix. A surgeon was called in, who evaluated the patient (conducting a level 3 new patient E/M office or other outpatient service) and performed an outpatient laparoscopic appendectomy at 1:00 p.m. for the ruptured appendix with abscess. The patient was discharged at 9:00 a.m. the next morning.

Procedures/Services **Diagnoses**

____

____

____

4. An emergency department (ED) physician performed a level 3 evaluation on a patient who was seen for complaints of severe abdominal pain, nausea, and vomiting. An ultrasound revealed an enlarged gallbladder. A surgeon was called in, evaluated the patient (conducting a level 3 new patient E/M office or other outpatient service), and performed a laparoscopic cholecystectomy, which revealed acute cholecystitis. The patient's stay was less than 24 hours.

Procedures/Services **Diagnoses**

____

____

____

5. Dr. B performed an expanded problem-focused, postoperative examination on an established patient. He also removed the sutures from an open appendectomy that the patient underwent while on vacation in another part of the country.

Procedures/Services **Diagnoses**

____

____

____

Additional scenarios are found at the end of this chapter and in the Workbook that accompanies this text.

CODING FROM PATIENT REPORTS

A patient record serves as the business record for a patient encounter, and is maintained in a manual record or automated format (e.g., electronic medical record). The patient record contains documentation of all health care services provided to a patient to support diagnoses, justify treatment, and record treatment results. The primary purpose of the patient record is to provide *continuity of care* (documentation of patient care services so that others who treat the patient have a source of information from which to base additional care and treatment). Secondary purposes of the patient record do not relate directly to patient care, and they include:

NOTE: Health insurance specialists review the patient record when assigning codes to diagnoses, procedures, and services. In addition, copies of reports from the patient record may be requested from third-party payers to process insurance claims.

- **Evaluating the quality of patient care**
- **Providing information to third-party payers for reimbursement**
- **Serving the medico-legal interests of the patient, facility, and providers of care**
- **Providing data for use in clinical research, epidemiology studies, education, public policy making, facilities planning, and health care statistics**

VETERANS HEALTH INFORMATION SYSTEMS AND TECHNOLOGY ARCHITECTURE (VISTA®)

The Veterans Health Information Systems and Technology Architecture (VistA®) electronic health record was developed by the U.S. Department of Veterans Affairs (VA) and is used by VA medical centers and outpatient clinics to document health care provided to military veterans. (An electronic health record allows for immediate access to information such as laboratory data, office notes, radiology reports, and so on.) Originally called the Decentralized Hospital Computer Program (DHCP), which was introduced in 1985 when all VA computers were operational, the software was renamed "VistA" in 1994. (VistA's origins predate its programming to that of its conception and design, when President Lyndon Johnson signed the Social Security Amendments Act [or Medicare Act] into law on July 30, 1965.)

The CMS (Centers for Medicare and Medicaid Services) has made VistA-Office EHR (VOE) software available to physician offices, and it includes the following features:

- Patient registration
- Progress note templates (including customization)
- Graphing (e.g., lab test results can be viewed as a graph)
- Clinical reminders (e.g., assist in clinical decision making)
- Report generation (e.g., patient treatment profile)
- HIPAA compliance (e.g., role-based access security controls, electronic signature, audit capabilities)
- Codified data (e.g., allows assignment of ICD-10 codes)
- Risk, social, and medical factors (e.g., alcohol and drug use, marital status)

(continues)

- Hospitalization functionality (e.g., document inpatient hospital discharge summary)
- Immunization history
- Laboratory functionality (e.g., order lab tests and view results)
- Pharmacy functionality (e.g., order medications, print prescriptions for signature, fax prescriptions to a local pharmacy with electronic signature)
- Laboratory interface
- Billing/practice management interface

NOTE: Abbreviations are commonly used by providers when documenting patient care. The Joint Commission has implemented a patient safety goal to help reduce the numbers of medical errors related to incorrect use of terminology. To facilitate compliance with the goal, the Joint Commission issued a list of abbreviations, acronyms, and symbols that should no longer be used by providers.

To locate the list, go to **www.jointcommission.org**, click on the Standards link, click on the National Patient Safety Goals link, and click on the Official "Do Not Use" Abbreviations List link.

Diagnoses, procedures, and services are selected and coded from clinic notes, consultation reports, and diagnostic reports. This process is the same as that used for case scenarios. The major difference is that clinic notes, consultations, and diagnostic reports contain more detail.

Clinic Notes

Health care providers use two major formats for documenting clinic notes:

- **Narrative clinic notes**
- **SOAP notes**

Diagnoses, procedures, and services can be selected and coded from either format. Both require documentation to support the level of Evaluation and Management (E/M) service coded and reported on the CMS-1500 claim, even if the provider selects the E/M code from a preprinted encounter form (e.g., superbill).

EXAMPLE: Portion of an encounter form containing E/M service, date, code, and charge

New Patient E/M Service	01-01-YYYY	☑99203	$70.00

Narrative Clinic Note

A **narrative clinic note** is written in paragraph format.

EXAMPLE: Narrative clinic note

A 21-year-old female patient comes to the office today, having been referred by Dr. Bandaid for pain in the RLQ of the abdomen, 2 days' duration. Temp: 102°F. Detailed history and physical examination revealed rebound tenderness over McBurney's point with radiation to the RUQ and RLQ. The remainder of the physical examination is normal. For additional information, see the complete history and physical in this chart. Laboratory data ordered by Dr. Bandaid (oral report given by Goodtechnique Lab) is as follows: WBC 19.1; RBC 4.61; platelets 234,000; hematocrit 42; hemoglobin 13.5; bands 15 percent, and PMNs 88 percent. UA and all other blood work were within normal limits. Patient is to be admitted to Goodmedicine Hospital for further work-up and possible appendectomy.

T.J. Stitcher, M.D.

SOAP Notes

A **SOAP note** is written in outline format ("SOAP" is an acronym derived from the first letter of the topic headings used in the note: Subjective, Objective, Assessment, and Plan).

The **subjective** part of the note contains the chief complaint and the patient's description of the presenting problem. It can also include the response to treatment prescribed earlier, past history, review of symptoms, and relevant family and social history. The documentation may appear in quotes because it represents the patient's statement verbatim.

The **objective** part of the note contains documentation of measurable or objective observations made during physical examination and diagnostic testing. Some health care providers may also include historical information obtained from previous encounters in this section.

The **assessment** contains the diagnostic statement and may include the physician's rationale for the diagnosis. If this section is missing from the report, look for positive diagnostic test results documented in the objective data or code the symptoms presented in either the subjective or objective data.

The **plan** is the statement of the physician's future plans for the work-up and medical management of the case. This includes plans for medications, diet, and therapy; future diagnostic tests to be performed; suggested lifestyle changes; items covered in the informed consent discussions; items covered in patient education sessions; and suggested follow-up care.

EXAMPLE: SOAP note

3/29/YYYY

S: Pt states "no complaints, no new symptoms since last visit, which was seven days ago."

O: Patient seen today, on 10th day postop. T 98.6°F; P 80; R 20; BP 120/86, right arm, sitting, WT 120 lb.

Incision, inner aspect of left breast, healing well. No sign of inflammation or infection.

A: Papilloma with fibrocystic changes, no malignancy.

Size 3.0 × 1.5 × 0.2 cm.

P: 1. Suture removal today.

2. Return visit, 3 months for follow-up.

Janet B. Surgeon, M.D.

In this example, the chief complaint (S:) and the vital signs (O:) were documented by the medical assistant (or nurse). The provider then performed an examination (O:), documented her findings (A:), and established a plan for the patient (P:). Because this note documents a postoperative follow-up office visit within the global period, no diagnoses or procedures/services are selected or coded. Neither the third-party payer nor the patient is billed for this postoperative visit. However, when the patient returns in three months for follow-up, that visit is billed to the payer (because it is not within the postoperative global period).

Diagnostic Test Results

Diagnostic test results are documented in two locations:

- **Clinic notes**
- **Laboratory reports**

Laboratory reports quantify data, and diagnostic implications are summarized in *clinic notes* documented by the provider. Other diagnostic tests (e.g., x-ray and pathology reports) include an interpretation by the responsible physician (e.g., radiologist or pathologist).

The laboratory report in Figure 10-2 documents a high glucose level (denoted by the **H** on the report). Upon review of the clinic note, if the insurance specialist finds documentation of signs and symptoms like a high glucose level, the provider should be asked whether a definitive diagnosis is to be coded instead.

The x-ray in Figure 10-3 was justified by the diagnosis of mild fibrocystic changes of the breast. (If the diagnosis is not documented in the patient's record, be sure to check with the provider before coding this as the diagnosis.)

MILLION, IMA **Patient No.** 12345 **PROVIDER:** Erin Helper, M.D.

Specimen: Blood (collected 03/03/YYYY). Test completed: 03/03/YYYY at 04:50 P.M. Technician: 099

Test	Result		Normal Values
Sodium	142 mEq/L		(135–148)
Potassium	4.4 mEq/L		(3.5–5.1)
Chloride	105 mEq/L		(97–107)
Glucose	176 mg/dL	**H**	(70–110)
BUN	14 mg/dL		(5–20)
Creatinine	1.0 mg/dL		(0.8–1.5)

FIGURE 10-2 Sample laboratory report with abnormal glucose level.

MILLION, IMA **Patient No.** 12345 **PROVIDER:** Erin Helper, M.D.

Baseline Mammogram

There are mild fibrocystic changes in both breasts but without evidence of a dominant mass, grouped microcalcifications, or retractions. Density on the left side is slightly greater and thought to be simply asymmetric breast tissue. There are some small axillary nodes bilaterally.

IMPRESSION: Class 1 (normal or clinically insignificant findings).

Follow-up in 1 year is suggested to assess stability in view of the fibrocystic asymmetric findings. Thereafter, biannual follow-up if stable. No dominant mass is present particularly in the upper inner quadrant of the left breast.

Maryanne Iona, M.D.

FIGURE 10-3 Sample radiology report.

EXERCISE 10-5

Coding SOAP Notes

Review the following SOAP notes, then select and code the diagnoses.

1. S: Patient complains of stomach pain, 3 days' duration. She also stated that her legs still get painful from the knees down.
O: Ht 5'6"; Wt 164 lb; BP 122/86; pulse 92 and regular; temp 97.0°F, oral; chest normal; heart normal. The Doppler arteriogram of lower extremities taken last week at the hospital is reported as within normal limits bilaterally.
A: Another episode of chronic atrophic gastritis. Leg pain, left.
P: Carafate 1 g. Take 1 tablet qid before meals and at bedtime, #120 tabs.

DIAGNOSES	ICD-10-CM CODES

2. S: Patient seems to be doing quite well, postop cholecystectomy; however, the pain that he had prior to his surgery is not gone.
O: Incision is well healed. Abdomen is soft and nontender.
A: Surgical aftercare. Pathology report revealed chronic cholecystitis and cholelithiasis.
P: 1. Lengthy discussion with patient and his wife about treatment in the future. Asked that they call any time they have questions.
2. Return visit here on a prn basis.

DIAGNOSES	ICD-10-CM CODES

3. S: Patient complains of generalized stiffness and being tired. She also notes that her left knee was swollen and felt hot to the touch last week. She was last seen 18 months ago on Penicillamine and 2 mg prednisone bid. Her other meds are loperamide for loose stool and Tagamet 300 mg bid.
O: Examination reveals some swelling of the left knee with active synovitis of the left knee and minimal fluid. Her present weight is 134 lb, BP 116/72. The hematocrit performed today is 37.5 and her sed rate is 65.
A: This patient has active rheumatoid arthritis, left knee.
P: 1. Increase prednisone to 5 mg bid, and Penicillamine to 500 mg bid.
2. X-ray of left knee tomorrow.

(continues)

3. Recheck CBC, sed rate, and urinalysis in 4 weeks.
4. Discussed with her the possibility of injecting steroids into the left knee if she shows no improvement.

DIAGNOSES	ICD-10-CM CODES

4. S: Patient returns today for follow-up of chronic angina and dyspnea. She says the angina still appears mainly when she is resting, and particularly just as she is waking up in the morning. This is accompanied by some dyspnea and pain occasionally radiating into the left jaw, but no palpitations. The angina is relieved by nitroglycerin. She continues to take Inderal 40 mg qid.

O: BP, left arm, sitting, 128/72; weight is 150 lb. Chest is clear. No wheezing or rales.

A: Unstable angina. Patient again refused to consider a heart catheterization.

P: New RX: Isordil Tembids 40 mg.
Refill nitroglycerin.

DIAGNOSES	ICD-10-CM CODES

5. S: This 17-year-old, single, white female presents to the office with a sore throat, fever, and swollen glands, 2 days' duration.

O: Oral temp 102.4°F; pulse 84; respirations 18; BP 118/78; wt 138 lb. The throat is markedly erythematous with evidence of exudative tonsillitis. Ears show normal TMs bilaterally. Few tender, submandibular nodes, bilaterally.

A: Acute tonsillitis.

P:
1. Obtained throat culture that was sent to the lab. Waiting for results.
2. Patient started on an empiric course of Pen Vee K 250 mg #40 to be taken qid × 10 days
3. Encouraged patient to increase oral fluid intake.
4. Patient to call office in 48 hours to obtain culture results and report her progress.

DIAGNOSES	ICD-10-CM CODES

(continues)

6. S: This is a 50-year-old widow who comes to the office following a possible seizure. Her friend reports she was seated at her desk, and after a crash was heard, they found her lying on the floor. She had urinary incontinence, and now complains of confusion and headache. Patient says this was her first episode and denies ever having chest pain, palpitations, or paresthesias. She cannot recall any recent head trauma or auras. She reports no allergies to medication and currently denies taking a medication.

She does have a history of well-differentiated nodular lymphoma, which was treated successfully by a course of radiation at the Goodmedicine Hospital in Anywhere, US. She has had no clinical evidence of recurrence. She reports no hospitalizations except for normal delivery of her son 25 years ago. She does admit to mild COPD. Her family history is negative for seizures.

O: Review of systems is noncontributory. Wt 155 lb; BP 116/72, both arms; pulse 72 and regular; respirations 18 and unlabored. Head is normocephalic and atraumatic. PERRLA. EOMs are intact. The sclerae are white. Conjunctivae are pink. Funduscopic examination is benign. The ears are normal bilaterally. No evidence of Battle sign. Mouth and throat are normal; tongue is midline and normal. The neck is supple and negative. Chest is clear. Heart rate and rhythm are regular with a grade II/IV systolic ejection murmur along the left sternal border without gallop, rub, click, or other adventitious sounds. Abdomen is soft, nontender, and otherwise negative. Bowel sounds are normal. Pelvic was deferred. There is good rectal sphincter tone. No masses are felt. Hemoccult test was negative. Extremities and lymphatics are noncontributory.

Neurologic exam shows normal mental status. Cranial nerves II–XII are intact. Motor, sensory, cerebellar function, and Romberg are normal. Babinski is absent. Reflexes are 2+ and symmetric in both upper and lower extremities.

A: New-onset seizure disorder. Rule out metabolic versus vascular etiologies.

P: The patient will be scheduled for MRI of the brain and EEG at Goodmedicine Hospital. Obtain electrolytes, calcium, albumin, liver function tests, and CBC with platelet and sed rate at the same visit.

DIAGNOSES	ICD-10-CM CODES

Operative Reports

Operative reports will vary from a short narrative description of a minor procedure that is performed in the physician's office (Figure 10-4) to more formal reports dictated by the surgeon in a format required by hospitals and ambulatory surgical centers (ASCs) (Figure 10-5).

MILLION, IMA **Patient No.** 12345 **PROVIDER:** Erin Helper, M.D.

12/5/YYYY

Reason for Visit: Postpartum exam and colposcopy.

Vital Signs: Temperature 97.2F. Blood pressure 88/52. Weight 107.

Labs: Glucose negative; Albumin, trace.

Patient seems to be doing fine, thinks the bleeding has just about stopped at this point. Her daughter is apparently doing fine; she is to get back chromosomal analysis in a couple of days. No other system defects have been found yet.

Examination: *Breasts:* Negative bilaterally. Patient is breastfeeding. *Abdomen:* Soft, flat, no masses, nontender. *Pelvic:* Cervix appeared clear, no bleeding noted. Uterus anteverted, small, nontender. Adnexa negative. Vagina appeared atrophic. Episiotomy healing well.

Procedure: Colposcopy of cervix performed with staining of acetic acid. Entire squamocolumnar junction could not be visualized even with aid of endocervical speculum. Exam was made more difficult because of very thick cervical mucus, which could not be completely removed, and because the vagina and cervix were somewhat atrophic appearing. Whitening of epithelium around entire circumference of cervix noted, but no abnormal vasculature noted. Numerous biopsies were taken from posterior and anterior lip of cervix. Endocervical curettage done. Repeat Pap smear of cervix also done.

Plan: Patient to call at the end of this week for biopsy results. Patient told she could have intercourse after five days, to use condoms, or to come back to office first to have size of diaphragm checked.

Erin Helper, M.D.

FIGURE 10-4 Sample physician's office operative report.

MILLION, IMA **Patient No.** 12345 **PROVIDER:** Gail R. Bones, M.D.
Room #: 101B **DATE OF SURGERY:** 01/01/YYYY

Preoperative Diagnosis: Displaced supracondylar fracture, left humerus

Postoperative Diagnosis: Same

Procedure: Closed reduction and casting, left humeral fracture

Surgeon: Gail R. Bones, M.D.

Assistant Surgeon: T.J. Stitcher, M.D.

Findings and Procedure:
After adequate general anesthesia, the patient's left elbow was gently manipulated and held at 110 degrees of flexion, at which point the patient continued to maintain a good radial pulse. X-rays revealed a good reduction; therefore, a plaster splint was applied, care being taken not to put any constriction in the antecubital fossa. X-rays were taken again, and showed excellent reduction has been maintained. Patient maintained good radial pulse, was awake, and was taken to Recovery in good condition.

Gail R. Bones, M.D.

FIGURE 10-5 Sample hospital outpatient surgery or ambulatory surgery center operative report.

Hospital and ASC formats may vary slightly, but all contain the following information in outline form:

- **Date of the surgery**
- **Patient identification**
- **Pre- and postoperative diagnosis(es)**
- **List of the procedure(s) performed**
- **Name(s) of primary and secondary surgeons who performed surgery**

The body of the report contains a detailed narrative of:

- **Positioning and draping of the patient for surgery**
- **Achievement of anesthesia**
- **Detailed description of how the procedure(s) was performed; identification of the incision made; and instruments, drains, dressings, special packs, and so on, used during surgery**
- **Identification of abnormalities found during the surgery**
- **Description of how hemostasis was obtained and the closure of the surgical site(s)**
- **Condition of the patient when (s)he left the operating room**
- **Signature of surgeon**

Procedure for Coding Operative Reports

STEP 1 Make a copy of the operative report.

This will allow you to freely make notations in the margin and highlight special details without marking up the original (which must remain in the patient's record).

STEP 2 Carefully review the list of procedures performed.

STEP 3 Read the narrative of the report and make a note of procedures to be coded.

Key words to look for include:

Simple versus complicated
Partial, complete, total, or incomplete
Unilateral versus bilateral
Initial versus subsequent
Incision versus excision
Open versus closed treatment, surgery, or fracture
Reconstructive surgery
Repair
Endoscopy
Biopsy
Ligation
Debridement
Complex, simple, intermediate, repair
Micronerve repair
Reconstruction
Graft (bone, nerve, or tendon requires additional code)
Diagnostic versus surgical procedure

Be alert to the following:

1. Additional procedures documented in the narrative of the report that are not listed in the heading of the report (e.g., Procedures Performed) should be coded.

> **EXAMPLE:**
>
> *Postoperative Diagnosis*: Chronic cholecystitis and cholelithiasis without obstruction
>
> *Procedures Performed*: Laparoscopic cholecystectomy with cholangiography
>
> In the body of the operative report, the surgeon describes the laparoscopic cholecystectomy and a cholangiogram. The surgeon also documents the operative findings and a biopsy of a suspicious liver nodule. The insurance specialist should contact the surgeon so that the liver biopsy is added to the *Procedures Performed* statement and then assign a CPT code to it (in addition to the laparoscopic cholecystectomy and cholangiogram).

2. When the *Procedures Performed* heading lists procedures performed that are not described in the body of the operative report, the surgeon will have to add a written addendum to the operative report documenting the performance of any listed procedure that should be coded.

> **EXAMPLE:**
>
> *Procedures Performed*: Arthroscopy, right knee. Open repair, right knee, collateral and cruciate ligaments
>
> Upon review of the body of the report, the insurance specialist notes that the surgeon did not document removal of the scope. Even though the removal of a scope is not coded, the insurance specialist should instruct the surgeon to document this as an addendum to the operative report.

STEP 4 **Identify main term(s) and subterms for the procedure(s) to be coded.**

STEP 5 **Underline and research any terms in the report that you cannot define.**

Many coding errors are made when the coder does not understand critical medical terms in the report.

STEP 6 **Locate the main term(s) in the CPT index.**

Check for the proper anatomic site or organ.

STEP 7 **Research all suggested codes.**

Read all notes and guidelines pertaining to the codes you are investigating. Watch for add-on procedures described in any notes/guidelines.

STEP 8 **Return to the CPT index and research additional codes if you cannot find a particular code(s) that matches the description of the procedure(s) performed in the operative report.**

Because a monetary value is associated with each CPT code, and to avoid bundling, never assign multiple, separate codes to describe a procedure if CPT has a single code that classifies all the individual components of the procedure described by the physician.

REMEMBER!

Global surgery includes the preoperative assessment (e.g., H&PE); the procedure; local infiltration, metacarpal/digital block or topical anesthesia when used; and normal, uncomplicated follow-up care.

Never assign a code number described in CPT as a "separate procedure" when it is performed within the same incision as the primary procedure and is an integral part of a larger procedure.

STEP 9 **Investigate the possibility of adding modifiers to a specific code description to fully explain the procedure(s) performed.**

EXAMPLE: Key word indicators for use of modifier -22

Extensive debridement/lysis or adhesions

Excessive bleeding (>500 mL)

Friable tissue

Prolonged procedure due to _____

Unusual anatomy, findings, or circumstances

Very difficult

STEP 10 **Code the postoperative diagnosis. This should explain the medical necessity for performing the procedure(s). If the postoperative diagnosis does not support the procedure performed, be sure the patient's chart contains documentation to justify the procedure.**

EXAMPLE: The patient is seen in the emergency department (ED) with right lower quadrant pain, and evaluation reveals elevated temperature and increased white blood count. Preoperative diagnosis is *appendicitis*, and the patient undergoes *appendectomy;* however, the postoperative diagnosis is *normal appendix*. In this situation, the documentation of the patient's signs and symptoms in the ED chart justifies the surgery performed even though the postoperative diagnosis does not support the surgery performed.

Look for additional findings in the body of the report if the postoperative diagnosis listed on the operative report does not completely justify the medical necessity for the procedure.

Compare the postoperative diagnosis with the biopsy report on all excised neoplasms to determine whether the tissue is benign or malignant.

When doing the exercises in this text and the Workbook, use any stated pathology report to determine whether excised tissue is benign or malignant if it is not covered in the postoperative diagnosis(es).

When working in a medical practice, do not code an excision until the pathology report is received.

STEP 11 **Review code options with the physician who performed the procedure if the case is unusual.**

Before assigning an "unlisted CPT procedure" code, review HCPCS level II codes. Remember that a description of the procedure performed must accompany the claim if an unlisted CPT code is reported.

STEP 12 **Assign final code numbers for procedures verified in steps 3 and 4 and any addendum the physician added to the original report.**

STEP 13 **Properly sequence the codes, listing first the most significant procedure performed during the episode.**

STEP 14 **Be sure to destroy the copy of the operative report (e.g., shred it) after the abstracting and coding process is completed.**

EXERCISE 10-6

Coding Operative Reports

When working with the case studies in this text, code procedures as listed in the case. When working in a medical practice, refer to the Medicare physician fee schedule or the payer's fee schedule to determine which surgical procedure receives the highest reimbursement.

CASE 1

Preoperative Diagnosis:	Questionable recurrent basal cell carcinoma, frontal scalp
Postoperative Diagnosis:	Benign lesion, frontal scalp, 0.3 cm in diameter
Operation:	Biopsy of granulating area with electrodessication of possible recurrent basal cell carcinoma of frontal scalp

History: About 1 year ago, the patient had an excision and grafting of a very extensive basal cell carcinoma of the forehead at the edge of the scalp. The patient now has a large granular area at 12 o'clock on the grafted area. This may be a recurrence of the basal cell carcinoma.

Procedure: The patient was placed in the dorsal recumbent position and draped in the usual fashion. The skin and subcutaneous tissues at the junction of the skin grafts of the previous excision and the normal scalp were infiltrated with 1/2 percent xylocaine containing epinephrine. An elliptical excision of the normal skin and the granulating area was made. After hemostasis was obtained, the entire area of granulating tissue was thoroughly electrodesiccated.

Pathology Report: The entire specimen measures 0.7 × 0.4 × 0.3 cm depth. Part of the specimen is a slightly nodular hemorrhagic lesion measuring 0.3 cm in diameter.

(continues)

Resected piece of skin shows partial loss of epithelium accompanied by acute and chronic inflammation of granulation tissue from a previous excision of basal cell carcinoma.

Diagnosis: This specimen is benign; there is no evidence of tumor.

DIAGNOSES/PROCEDURES	ICD-10-CM/CPT CODES

CASE 2

Preoperative Diagnosis: Tumor of the skin of the back with atypical melanocyte cells

Postoperative Diagnosis: Same

Operation Performed: Wide excision

Anesthesia: General

Indications: The patient had a previous biopsy of a nevus located on the back. The pathology report indicated atypical melanocyte cells in the area close to the margin of the excision. The pathologist recommended that a wide re-excision be performed. The patient was informed of the situation during an office visit last week, and he agreed to be readmitted for a wider excision of the tumor area.

Procedure: The patient was placed on his left side, and general anesthesia was administered. The skin was prepped and draped in a usual fashion. A wide excision, 5.0 cm in length and 4.0 cm wide, was made. The pathologist was alerted, and the specimen was sent to the lab. The frozen section was reported as negative for melanocytes on the excisional margin at this time. After the report was received, the wound was closed in layers and a dressing was applied. The patient tolerated the procedure well and was sent to Recovery in good condition.

DIAGNOSES/PROCEDURES	ICD-10-CM/CPT CODES

CASE 3

Preoperative Diagnosis: Colonic polyps

Postoperative Diagnosis: Benign colonic polyps; Melanosis coli

Operation Performed: Colonoscopy

Anesthesia: An additional 25 mg of Demerol and 2.5 mg of Valium were administered for sedation.

(continues)

Procedure: The Olympus video colonoscope was passed into the rectum and slowly advanced. The cecum was identified by the ileocecal valve. The prep was suboptimal.

The colonic mucosa had diffuse dark pigmentation suggestive of melanosis coli. The ascending colon, transverse colon, and proximal descending colon appeared unremarkable. There were two polyps which were about 8 mm in size adjacent to each other in the sigmoid colon. They were fulgurated with hot wire biopsy forceps. After this, the colonoscope was gradually withdrawn. The patient tolerated the procedure well and was sent to Recovery.

Because of the suboptimal prep, small polyps or arteriovenous malformations could have been missed.

DIAGNOSES/PROCEDURES	ICD-10-CM/CPT CODES

CASE 4

Preoperative Diagnosis: Serous otitis media, bilateral

Postoperative Diagnosis: Same

Operation Performed: Bilateral myringotomy with insertion of ventilating tubes

Anesthesia: General

Procedure: The patient was placed in a supine position and induction of general anesthesia was achieved by face mask. The ears were examined bilaterally using an operating microscope. An incision was made in the anteroinferior quadrants. A large amount of thick fluid was aspirated from both ears, more so from the left side. Ventilating tubes were introduced with no difficulties. Patient tolerated the procedure well and was sent to Recovery in satisfactory condition.

DIAGNOSES/PROCEDURES	ICD-10-CM/CPT CODES

CASE 5

Preoperative Diagnosis: Lesion, buccal mucosa, left upper lip

Postoperative Diagnosis: Ca in situ, buccal mucosa, left upper lip

Operation Performed: Excisional biopsy of lesion, left buccal mucosa

Anesthesia: Local

(continues)

Procedure: The patient was placed in the supine position, and a 3 × 4 mm hard lesion could be felt under the mucosa of the left upper lip. After application of 1 percent xylocaine with 1:1000 epinephrine, the lesion was completely excised. The surgical wound was closed using #4-00 chromic catgut.

The patient tolerated the procedure well and returned to the Outpatient Surgery Unit in satisfactory condition.

DIAGNOSES/PROCEDURES	ICD-10-CM/CPT CODES

CASE 6

Preoperative Diagnosis: Pilonidal cyst

Postoperative Diagnosis: Same

Operation Performed: Pilonidal cystectomy

Anesthesia: Local with 4 mL of 1/2 percent xylocaine

Estimated Blood Loss: Minimal

Fluids: 550 mL intraoperatively

Procedure: The patient was brought to the operating room and placed in a jackknife position. After sterile prepping and draping, 40 mL of 1/2 percent xylocaine was infiltrated into the surrounding tissue of the pilonidal cyst that had a surface opening on the median raphe over the sacrum. After adequate anesthesia was obtained and 1 gram of IV Ancef administered intraoperatively, the surface opening was probed. There were no apparent tracks demonstrated upon probing. Next, a scalpel was used to make an approximately 8 × 8 cm elliptical incision around the pilonidal cyst. The incision was carried down through subcutaneous tissue to the fascia and the tissue was then excised. Attention was turned to achieving hemostasis with Bovie electrocautery. The pilonidal cyst was then opened and found to contain fibrous tissue. The wound was closed with 0 Prolene interrupted vertical mattress. Estimated blood loss was minimal, and the patient received 550 mL of crystalloid intraoperatively. The patient tolerated the procedure well and was sent to Recovery in stable condition.

DIAGNOSES/PROCEDURES	ICD-10-CM/CPT CODES

(continues)

CASE 7

Preoperative Diagnosis:	Incarcerated right femoral hernia
Postoperative Diagnosis:	Same
Operation Performed:	Right femoral herniorrhaphy
Anesthesia:	General

Procedure: Patient is a 37-year-old male. Initially, the patient was placed in the supine position, and the abdomen was prepped and draped with Betadine in the appropriate manner. Xylocaine (1 percent) was infiltrated into the skin and subcutaneous tissue. Because of the patient's reaction to pain, general anesthesia was also administered. An oblique skin incision was performed from the anterior superior iliac spine to the pubic tubercle. The skin and subcutaneous tissues were sharply incised. Dissection was carried down until the external oblique was divided in the line of its fibers with care taken to identify the ilioinguinal nerve to avoid injury. Sharp and blunt dissection were used to free the inguinal cord. The cremasteric muscle was transected. Attempts at reduction of the incarcerated femoral hernia from below were unsuccessful.

The femoral canal was opened in an inferior to superior manner, and finally this large incarcerated hernia was reduced. The conjoint tendon was then sutured to Cooper's ligament with 0 Prolene interrupted suture. The conjoint tendon was somewhat attenuated and of poor quality. A transition suture was placed from the conjoint tendon to Cooper's ligament and then to the inguinal ligament with care taken to obliterate the femoral space without stenosis of the femoral vein. The conjoint tendon was then sutured laterally to the shelving border or Poupart's ligament. The external oblique was closed over the cord with 0 chromic running suture. 3-0 plain was placed in the subcutaneous tissue and the skin was closed with staples. Sterile dressings were applied. The patient tolerated the operative procedure well and was gently taken to Recovery in satisfactory condition.

DIAGNOSES/PROCEDURES	ICD-10-CM/CPT CODES

SUMMARY

Medically managed means that even though a diagnosis may not receive direct treatment during an encounter, the provider has to consider that diagnosis when determining treatment for other conditions. Up to 12 diagnosis codes can be reported on one CMS-1500, and the appropriate diagnosis code must be linked to the procedure or service provided. Patient record documentation must justify and support the medical necessity of procedures and services reported to payers for reimbursement. Medical practices and health care facilities should routinely participate in an auditing process, which involves reviewing patient records and CMS-1500 or UB-04 claims to assess coding accuracy and completeness of documentation. Medical practices should also review encounter forms to ensure the accuracy of ICD-10-CM and HCPCS/CPT codes. In addition, health care facilities should audit chargemasters to ensure the accuracy of HCPCS/CPT and UB-04 revenue codes.

National coverage determinations (NCDs) and local coverage determinations (LCDs) specify under what clinical circumstances a service is covered, and they list covered and noncovered codes (but they do not include coding guidelines). The outpatient code editor (OCE) is software that edits outpatient claims, assigns ambulatory payment classifications (APCs), and reviews submissions for coding validity and coverage. NCDs and LCDs comprise the Medicare coverage database (MCD).

Health care providers document narrative clinic notes and SOAP notes, and diagnostic test results are documented in clinic notes and laboratory reports. Operative reports can include a short narrative description of a minor procedure or dictated reports as typically required by hospitals and ambulatory surgical centers (ASCs).

INTERNET LINKS

- MedicalNecessityPro.com
  Go to **www.MedicalReferenceEngine.com** to register for a 30-day online trial of Optum's web-based subscription service that serves as a comprehensive regulatory, coding, billing, and reimbursement search and research tool. LCDs/LMRPs for Medicare Part A and Part B items, services, and procedures (as well as national coverage decisions [NCDs] and detailed code crosswalk information) help hospitals, physicians, and payers accurately determine medical necessity criteria for coverage.
- Medicare Coverage Database (MCD)
  Go to **www.cms.gov**, click on the Regulations and Guidance link, click on the Medicare Coverage link under the Special Topics heading and click on the Medicare Coverage Database link.
- My Family Health Portrait
  Go to **https:// familyhistory.hhs.gov** and click on Create a Family Health History.
- The FPM Toolbox
  Go to **www.aafp.org**, click on the Journals link, click on the View FPM link, and then click on Toolbox to view practice management tools (e.g., medical decision-making reference) that can be used for physician practices.
- WorldVistA EHR (open source software)
  Go to **www.worldvista.org** and click on the About VistA and About WorldVistA links.

STUDY CHECKLIST

- ☐ Read this textbook chapter and highlight key concepts.
- ☐ Create an index card for each key term.
- ☐ Access the chapter Internet links to learn more about concepts.
- ☐ Answer the chapter review questions, verifying answers with your instructor.
- ☐ Complete the Workbook chapter, verifying answers with your instructor.
- ☐ Form a study group with classmates to discuss chapter concepts in preparation for an exam.

REVIEW

COMPREHENSIVE CODING PRACTICE

Instructions: Code all diagnoses, procedures, and services in the following case scenarios, and link the diagnoses to the appropriate procedure/service. Review each case, and underline the condition(s) to which ICD-10-CM codes are assigned and procedures/services to which CPT/HCPCS level II codes and modifiers are assigned. (ICD-10-CM diagnosis codes and CPT/HCPCS level II procedure/services codes are included in the Instructor's Manual.)

1. A 42-year-old white male was referred to a gastroenterologist by his primary care physician because of a two-month history of gross rectal bleeding. The new patient was seen on Wednesday, and the doctor performed a comprehensive history and exam. Medical decision making was of moderate complexity. The patient was scheduled for a complete diagnostic colonoscopy four days later. The patient was given detailed instructions for the bowel prep that was to be started at home on Friday at 1:00 p.m.

   On Friday, the patient was registered for outpatient surgery at the hospital, conscious sedation was administered, and the flexible colonoscopy was started. The examination had to be halted at the splenic flexure because of inadequate bowel preparation. The patient was rescheduled for Monday and given additional instructions for bowel prep to be performed starting at 3:00 p.m. on Sunday.

   On Monday, the patient was again registered for outpatient surgery at the hospital, conscious sedation was again administered, and a successful total colonoscopy was performed. Diverticulosis was noted in the ascending colon and two polyps were excised from the descending colon using the snare technique. The pathology report indicated the polyps were benign.

   ____

2. The patient underwent an upper GI series on Tuesday, which included both a KUB and delayed films. The request form noted severe esophageal burning daily for the past six weeks. The radiology impression was Barrett's esophagus.

   ____

3. The patient was referred to a cardiologist for transesophageal echocardiography for cardiac arrhythmia. The patient underwent transesophageal echocardiography on Thursday, and the cardiologist supervised and interpreted the echocardiography, which included probe placement and image acquisition. The report stated the "transesophageal echocardiogram showed cardiac arrhythmia but normal valvular function with no intra-atrial or intraventricular thrombus, and no significant aortic atherosclerosis."

   ____

4. The patient had been seen in the office for a level 2 E/M service on Monday morning, and a diagnosis of sinusitis was made.

   Her husband called at 8:00 p.m. that same evening to report his wife had become very lethargic and her speech was slightly slurred. The patient was admitted to the hospital at 8:30 p.m. by the primary care physician. The doctor performed a comprehensive history and examination, and medical decision making was of high complexity.

   At 9:00 a.m. the next day, the patient was comatose and was transferred to the critical care unit. The doctor was in constant attendance from 8:10 a.m. until the patient expired at 9:35 a.m. The attending physician listed CVA (stroke) as the diagnosis.

   ____

EVALUATION AND MANAGEMENT CODING PRACTICE

Review each case, and select the appropriate level of history, examination, and medical decision making (key components) before referring to the CPT E/M section to assign the code. To assist in the process of assigning E/M codes, use the E/M CodeBuilder that is located in Appendix III. The first E/M coding practice (below) indicates how answers were determined.

HPI documents duration, symptoms, and timing, which is a "brief HPI."

ROS documents HEENT, neurological, cardiovacular, respiratory, GI, and GU, which is an "extended ROS."

PE documents seven elements, which is an "expanded problem-focused examination."

5. *History of Present Illness (HPI):* Mary Adams was initially seen by her physician, Dr. Thompson, as an inpatient on May 1 with the chief complaint of having taken an overdose of Ornade. She had been suffering from flu-like symptoms for one week and had been taking the prescribed drug, Ornade, for several days. She states that she apparently took too many pills this morning and started exhibiting symptoms of dizziness and nausea. She called the office complaining of these symptoms and was told to meet Dr. Thompson at the hospital emergency department. From the emergency department, she was admitted to the hospital.

Past History revealed no history of hypertension, diabetes, or rheumatic fever. The patient denies any chest pain or past history of previously having taken an overdose of Ornade as mentioned above. Social history reveals she does not smoke or drink. She has two healthy children. Family history is unremarkable.

Systemic Review revealed HEENT within normal limits. Review of the CNS revealed headache and dizziness. She had a fainting spell this morning. No paresthesias. Cardiorespiratory revealed cough but no chest pain or hemoptysis. GI revealed nausea; she had one episode of vomiting early this morning. No other abdominal distress noted. GU revealed no frequency, dysuria, or hematuria.

Physical Examination revealed the patient to be stable without any major symptoms upon arrival to the telemetry area. Head & Neck Exam revealed pupil reaction normal to light and accommodation. Fundoscopic examination is normal. Thyroid is not palpable. ENT normal. No lymphadenopathy noted. Cardiovascular Exam revealed the point of maximum impulse is felt in the left fifth intercostal space in the midclavicular line. No S_3 or S_4 gallop. Ejection click was heard and grade 2/6 systolic murmur in the left third and fourth intercostal space was heard. No diastolic murmur. Chest is clear to auscultation. Abdomen reveals no organomegaly. Neurologic Exam is normal. Peripheral Vascular System is intact.

ECG reveals a sinus tachycardia, and there was no evidence of myocardial ischemia. A pattern of early repolarization syndrome was noted.

Assessment: Will be briefly observed in the telemetry area to rule out any specific evidence of cardiac arrhythmia. She will also have a routine biochemical and hematologic profile, chest x-ray, and cardiogram. Estimated length of stay will be fairly short.

Impression: Rule out dizziness. Rule out cardiac arrhythmias.

Identify the E/M category/subcategory **Hospital Inpatient Services, Initial and Subsequent**

Determine the extent of history obtained **Expanded problem focused**

Determine the extent of examination performed **Expanded problem focused**

Determine the complexity of medical decision making **Straightforward**

CPT E/M code number: **99221**

6. Sandy White is a 52-year-old white female established patient who was seen in the office by Dr. Kramer on January 15 with the chief complaint of low back pain. The patient has complained of lumbosacral pain off and on for many months, but it has been getting worse for the last two to three weeks. The pain is constant and gets worse with sneezing and coughing. There is no radiation of the pain to the legs.

Past History reveals no history of trauma, no history of urinary symptoms, and no history of weakness or numbness in the legs. She had measles during childhood. She's had high blood pressure for a few years. Sandy also has a previous history of rectal bleeding from hemorrhoids. She had an appendectomy and cholecystectomy in 1975. She also has diabetes mellitus, controlled by diet alone.

Family History: Sandy's mother died postoperatively at age 62 of an abdominal operation, the exact nature of which is not known. She had massive bleeding. Her father died at the age of 75 of a myocardial infarction. He also had carcinoma of the bladder and diabetes mellitus. One sister has high blood pressure.

Social History: She is widowed. She smokes and drinks, but just socially. Her job at the *Evening Tribune* involves heavy lifting.

Systemic Review reveals no history of cough, expectoration, or hemoptysis. No history of weight loss or loss of appetite. No history of thyroid or kidney disease. The patient has been overweight for many years. HEENT is unremarkable; hearing and vision are normal. Cardiorespiratory reveals *no known murmurs.* GI reveals no food allergies or chronic constipation. GU reveals no nocturia, enuresis, or GI infection. Neuromuscular reveals no history of paralysis or numbness in the past.

Physical Examination in the office reveals a slightly obese, middle-aged female in acute distress with lower back pain. Pulse is 80, blood pressure is 140/85, respirations 16, temperature 98.4°F. HEENT: PERRLA. Conjunctivae are not pale. Sclerae are not icteric. Fundi show arteriolar narrowing. Neck: No thyroid or lymph node palpable. No venous engorgement. No bruit heard in the neck. Chest: PMI is not palpable. S_1, S_2 normal. No gallop or murmur heard. Chest moves equally on both sides with respirations. Breath sounds are diminished. No adventitious sounds heard. Abdomen: She has scars from her previous surgery. There is no tenderness. Liver, spleen, and kidneys are not palpable. Bowel sounds normal. Extremities: Leg-raising sign is negative on both sides. Both femorals and dorsalis pedis are palpable and equal bilaterally. There is no ankle edema. Central Nervous System: Speech is normal. Cranial nerves are intact. Motor system is normal. Sensory system is normal. Reflexes are equal bilaterally.

Impression: The impression is lumbosacral pain. The patient is being referred for physical therapy treatment twice per week. Darvocet-N will be prescribed for the pain.

Identify the E/M category/subcategory ______________________________

Determine the extent of history obtained ______________________________

Determine the extent of examination performed ______________________________

Determine the complexity of medical decision making ______________________________

CPT E/M code number: ______________________________

7. S: Monica Sullivan was seen in the office by Dr. White on 12/13 for the second time. She presented with a chief complaint of dizziness and weakness; she stated that she wanted to have her blood pressure checked.

O: Patient has been on Vasotec 5 mg and Hydrodiuril 25 mg. BP has been going up at home. Patient has felt ill, weak, and dizzy, with headache for three days. Cardiovascular exam reveals a BP of 130/110 and pulse rate of 84. Her temperature is 98.6°F and normal.

A: Accelerated hypertension. Bell's palsy.

P: Increase Vasotec to 5 mg a.m. and 2.5 mg p.m. SMA & CBC.

Identify the E/M category/subcategory __________

Determine the extent of history obtained __________

Determine the extent of examination performed __________

Determine the complexity of medical decision making __________

CPT E/M code number: __________

8. Ginny Tallman is a 73-year-old female who is followed in the Alfred State Medical Clinic for COPD. Her medications include Theo-Dur 300 mg p.o. q a.m. History of present illness reveals that she seems to have adequate control of her bronchospasm using this medication. She also uses an albuterol inhaler two puffs p.o. q6h. She has no recent complaints of acute shortness of breath and no chest tightness. She has a chronic, dry cough, productive of scanty sputum. At this time, she is complaining of shortness of breath.

PE reveals an elderly female in no real distress. BP in the left arm, sitting, is 110/84, pulse 74 per minute and regular, respiratory rate 12 per minute and somewhat labored. Lungs reveal scattered wheezes in both lung fields. There is also noted an increased expiratory phase. CV exam reveals no S_3, S_4, or murmurs.

The impression is COPD with asthmatic bronchitis. The patient will have present medications increased to Theo-Dur 300 mg p.o. q a.m. and 400 mg p.o. q p.m. She should receive follow-up care in the clinic in approximately two months time.

Identify the E/M category/subcategory __________

Determine the extent of history obtained __________

Determine the extent of examination performed __________

Determine the complexity of medical decision making __________

CPT E/M code number: __________

9. Dr. Linde telephoned an established patient, Mark Jones, at 8:00 a.m. to discuss the results of his blood-glucose level test. The doctor concluded the call at 9:00 a.m. after discussing the test results and proposed therapy regimen. Mr. Jones had numerous questions that Dr. Linde took the time to answer completely.

Identify the E/M category/subcategory __________

Identify the appropriate code(s) __________

CORRECTING CLAIMS SUBMISSION ERRORS

Review each case scenario, identify the coding error(s), and enter the corresponding letter to describe the error.

- **a.** Code is inappropriate for patient's age.
- **b.** Code is incomplete (e.g., missing digits).
- **c.** Code reported is incorrect (e.g., wrong code).
- **d.** Medical necessity not met.
- **e.** Procedure codes are unbundled.

EXAMPLE: A patient was treated for excision of a 1-cm skin lesion on her right arm. The pathology diagnosis was benign nevus. The physician documented benign nevus as the final diagnosis.

Coding Error	Procedure Code	Diagnosis Code
b	11401	D22.6

Select "b" because the coder referred to Nevus, Skin, Arm in the ICD-10-CM Index to Diseases and Injuries to assign D22.6. That code requires assignment of a fifth digit to report D22.61 as the correct code.

10. The physician performed an automated urinalysis without microscopy in the office on a patient who complained of dysuria. The urinalysis revealed more than 100,000 white cells and was positive for bacteria.

Coding Error	Procedure Code	Diagnosis Code
	81003	N39.0
		B96.20

11. An office single-view frontal chest x-ray was performed on a patient referred for shortness of breath. The radiologist reported no acute findings, but an incidental note was made of a small hiatal hernia.

Coding Error	Procedure Code	Diagnosis Code
	71010	K44.9

12. A healthy 20-year-old male underwent a physical examination performed by his family physician, prior to starting soccer training.

Coding Error	Procedure Code	Diagnosis Code
	99394	Z02.5

13. The patient was diagnosed with incipient cataract, and on March 5 underwent extracapsular cataract removal that required phacoemulsification, with insertion of intraocular lens prosthesis.

Coding Error	Procedure Code	Diagnosis Code
	66984	H26.9
	66985-51	

14. Patient underwent physical therapy evaluation for right dominant side hemiplegia due to CVA (stroke).

Coding Error	Procedure Code	Diagnosis Code
	97001	I69.35

CHAPTER 11

Essential CMS-1500 Claim Instructions

CHAPTER OUTLINE

OBJECTIVES

Upon successful completion of this chapter, you should be able to:

1. Define key terms.
2. List and define general insurance billing guidelines.
3. Apply optical scanning guidelines when completing claims.
4. Enter patient and policyholder names, provider names, mailing addresses, and telephone numbers according to claims completion guidelines.
5. Describe how funds are recovered from responsible payers.
6. Explain the use of the national provider identifier (NPI).
7. Differentiate between assignment of benefits and accept assignment.
8. Report ICD-10-CM, HCPCS level II, and CPT codes according to claims completion guidelines. (ICD-10-PCS codes are reported on inpatient UB-04 claims.)

9. Explain the use of the national standard employer identifier.
10. Explain when the signature of a physician or supplier is required on a claim.
11. Enter the billing entity according to claims completion guidelines.
12. Explain how secondary claims are processed.
13. List and describe common errors that delay claims processing.
14. State the final steps required in claims processing.
15. Establish insurance claim files for a physician's practice.

KEY TERMS

billing entity
diagnosis pointer letters
National Plan and Provider Enumeration System (NPPES)
optical character reader (OCR)
optical scanning
supervising physician
supplemental plan

INTRODUCTION

This chapter presents universal instructions that must be considered before entering data on the CMS-1500 claim. In addition, there is a discussion of common errors made on claims, guidelines for maintaining the practice's insurance claim files, processing assigned claims, and the Federal Privacy Act of 1974.

REMEMBER!

To prevent breach of patient confidentiality, all health care professionals involved in processing insurance claims should check to be sure the patient has signed an "Authorization for Release of Medical Information" statement before completing the claim. The release can be obtained in one of two ways:

- Ask the patient to sign Block 12, Patient's or Authorized Person's Signature, of the CMS-1500 claim.
- Ask the patient to sign a special release form that is customized by each practice and specifically names the patient's health plan and to enter SIGNATURE ON FILE (or SOF) in Block 12 of the CMS-1500 claim.

Don't forget! HIPAA privacy standards require providers to notify patients about their right to privacy, and providers should obtain their patients' written acknowledgment of receipt of this notice. Patients will also be required to authorize in advance the nonroutine use or disclosure of information. In addition, state or other applicable laws govern the control of health information about minor children and provide parents with new rights to control that information.

EXAMPLE: Before Aetna will pay the claim submitted for Mary Sue Patient's office visit, the provider is required to submit a copy of the patient's entire medical record. HIPAA regulations specify that providers can disclose protected health information for payment activities. Typically, this information includes just the patient's diagnosis and procedures/services rendered. Therefore, the provider should require Mary Sue Patient to sign an authorization to release medical information before sending a copy of her record to Aetna.

Distinguishing between a patient's primary and secondary insurance policies as determined during the preclinical interview and check-in procedures is discussed in Chapter 4.

NOTE: Federal and state regulations also determine primary and secondary insurance coverage.

REMEMBER!

The development of an insurance claim begins when the patient contacts a health care provider's office and schedules an appointment. At this time, it is important to determine whether the patient is requesting an initial appointment or is returning to the practice for additional services. (The preclinical interview and check-in of a new patient are more extensive than that of an established patient.)

EXAMPLE: Section 1862 of Title XVIII—Health Insurance for the Aged and Disabled of the Social Security Act specifies that for an individual covered by both workers' compensation (WC) and Medicare, WC is primary. For an individual covered by both Medicare and Medicaid, Medicare is primary.

INSURANCE BILLING GUIDELINES

General billing guidelines common to most payers include:

1. Provider services for *inpatient care* are billed on a fee-for-service basis. Each physician service results in a unique and separate charge designated by a CPT/HCPCS service/procedure code. (Hospital inpatient charges are reported on the UB-04, discussed in Chapter 9.)

NOTE: Members of the same practice *cannot* bill for inpatient services on the same day unless circumstances are documented that justify medical necessity and modifiers are assigned to reported code number(s). Otherwise, this is considered duplication of services.

EXAMPLE: The patient was admitted on June 1 with a diagnosis of bronchopneumonia. The doctor sees the patient each morning until the patient is discharged on June 5. Billing for this inpatient includes:

6/1	Initial hospital visit (99xxx)
6/2–6/4	Three subsequent hospital visits (99xxx × 3)
6/5	Discharge visit (99xxx)

EXAMPLE: Dr. Adams and Dr. Lowry are partners in an internal medicine group practice. Dr. Adams' patient, Irene Ahearn, was admitted on May 1 with a chief complaint of severe chest pain, and Dr. Adams provided E/M services at 11:00 a.m. at which time the patient was stable. (Dr. Lowry is on call as of 5:00 p.m. on May 1.) At 7:00 p.m., Dr. Lowry was summoned to provide critical care because the patient's condition became unstable. Dr. Adams reports an initial hospital care CPT code, and Dr. Lowry reports appropriate E/M critical care code(s) with modifier -25 attached.

2. Appropriately report observation services. The Medicare Benefit Policy manual (PUB 100-02), Section 20.5—Outpatient Observation Services, defines *observation care* as "a well-defined set of specific, clinically appropriate services, which include ongoing short-term treatment, assessment, and reassessment before a decision can be made regarding whether patients will require further treatment as hospital inpatients or if they are able to be discharged from the hospital. Observation status is commonly assigned to patients who present to the emergency department and who then require a significant period of treatment or monitoring before a

> **NOTE:** Observation services are reimbursed as an alternative to inpatient admission under the Outpatient Prospective Payment System (OPPS) using the UB-04 (CMS-1450). Medicare coverage is limited to not more than 48 hours unless the Medicare administrative contractor grants an exception. Although outpatient observation care can progress to inpatient admission, an inpatient admission *cannot* be converted to outpatient observation. If an inpatient admission is warranted, *observation services are not billed separately and are reported on the inpatient claim!*

decision is made concerning their admission or discharge. Observation services are covered only when provided by the order of a physician or another individual authorized by state licensure law and hospital staff bylaws (policies) to admit patients to the hospital or to order outpatient tests. In the majority of cases, the decision whether to discharge a patient from the hospital following resolution of the reason for the observation care or to admit the patient as an inpatient can be made in less than 48 hours, usually in less than 24 hours. In only rare and exceptional cases do reasonable and necessary outpatient observation services span more than 48 hours. Hospitals may bill for patients who are direct admissions to observation. A *direct admission* occurs when a physician in the community refers a patient to the hospital for observation, bypassing the clinic or emergency department (ED)."

> **EXAMPLE:** A 66-year-old male experiences three or four annual episodes of mild lower substernal chest pressure after meals. The condition is unresponsive to nitroglycerin and usually subsides after 15 to 30 minutes. The patient's physician has diagnosed stable angina versus gastrointestinal pain. On one occasion, while in recovery following outpatient bunion repair, the patient experiences an episode of lower substernal chest pressure. The patient's physician is contacted and seven hours of observation services are provided, after which the patient is released.

3. The surgeon's charges for inpatient and outpatient surgery are billed according to a global fee (or global surgery package), which means that one charge covers presurgical evaluation and management, initial and subsequent hospital visits, surgical procedure, the discharge visit, and uncomplicated postoperative follow-up care in the surgeon's office.
4. Postoperative complications requiring a return to the operating room for surgery related to the original procedure are billed as an additional procedure. (Be sure to use the correct modifier, and link the additional procedure to a new diagnosis that describes the complication.)
5. *Combined medical/surgical cases* in which the patient is admitted to the hospital as a medical case but, after testing, requires surgery are billed according to the instructions in items 3–4.

> **EXAMPLE:** Patient is admitted on June 1 for suspected pancreatic cancer. Tests are performed on June 2 and 3. On June 4 the decision is made to perform surgery. Surgery is performed on June 5. The patient is discharged on June 10.
>
> This case begins as a medical admission.
>
> The billing will show:

6/1	Initial hospital visit (99xxx)
6/2 and 6/3	Two subsequent hospital visits (99xxx × 2)
6/4	One subsequent hospital visit with modifier -57 (99xxx-57) (indicating the decision for surgery was made on this day)

> At this point this becomes a surgery case.
>
> The billing continues with:

6/5	Pancreatic surgery (48xxx)

> **NOTE:** No subsequent hospital visits or discharge day codes are reported because the global surgery package concept applies.

6. Some claims require attachments, such as operative reports, discharge summaries, clinic notes, or letters, to aid in determination of the fee to be paid by the third-party payer. Attachments are also required when CPT unlisted codes are reported. Each claims attachment (medical report substantiating the medical condition) should include patient and policy identification information. Instructions for submitting *electronic media claims (EMC)* and paper-generated claims are discussed in Chapter 4.

   Any *letter* written by the provider should contain clear and simple English rather than "medicalese." The letter can describe an unusual procedure, special operation, or a patient's medical condition that warranted performing surgery in a setting different from the CMS-stipulated site for that surgery. A letter should be used in any of the following circumstances:

   - **Surgery defined as an inpatient procedure that is performed at an *ambulatory surgical center (ASC)* or physician's office.**
   - **Surgery typically categorized as an office or outpatient procedure that is performed in an ASC or on a hospital inpatient.**
   - **A patient's stay in the hospital is prolonged because of medical or psychological complications.**
   - **An outpatient or office procedure is performed as an inpatient procedure because the patient is a high-risk case.**
   - **Explanation of why a fee submitted to an insurance company is higher than the health care provider's normal fee for the coded procedure. (Modifier -22 should be added to the procedure code number.)**
   - **A procedure is submitted with an "unlisted procedure" CPT code number, or an explanation or report of a procedure is required before reimbursement can be determined.**

NOTE: HIPAA regulations require all payers to accept electronic attachments (e.g., notes, reports, referrals).

NOTE: Most computer programs have a claim form test pattern to assist with the alignment of paper in printers. Print this test pattern before printing claims. If claims must be completed on a typewriter, each must be meticulously aligned in both the horizontal and vertical planes.

7. For paper-generated claims, great care must be taken to ensure that the data prints well within the boundaries of the properly designated blocks on the form. Data that run over into the adjacent blocks or appear in the wrong block will cause rejection of claims.

8. Policies located on the back of the CMS-1500 claim provide additional guidance to providers (Figure 11-1). (Electronic versions of the CMS-1500 embed the policies in block instructions.)

9. The provider's return address can be entered in the upper right-hand corner of the CMS-1500 claims, as permitted by third-party payers.

NOTE: If entering patient claim data directly into practice management software, such as Medical Manager®, the software may require that all data be entered using upper- and lowercase and other data to be entered without regard to OCR guidelines. In these cases, the computer program converts the data to the OCR format when claims are printed or electronically transmitted to a payer.

OPTICAL SCANNING GUIDELINES

The CMS-1500 paper claim was designed to accommodate **optical scanning** of paper claims (Figure 11-2). This process uses a device (e.g., scanner) to convert printed or handwritten characters into text that can be viewed by an **optical character reader (OCR)** (a device used for optical character recognition). Entering data into the computer using this technology greatly increases productivity associated with claims processing because the need to manually enter data from the claim into a computer is eliminated. OCR guidelines were established when the HCFA-1500 (now called CMS-1500) claim was developed and are now used by all payers that process claims using the official CMS-1500 claim.

BECAUSE THIS FORM IS USED BY VARIOUS GOVERNMENT AND PRIVATE HEALTH PROGRAMS, SEE SEPARATE INSTRUCTIONS ISSUED BY APPLICABLE PROGRAMS.

NOTICE: Any person who knowingly files a statement of claim containing any misrepresentation or any false, incomplete or misleading information may be guilty of a criminal act punishable under law and may be subject to civil penalties.

MEDICARE AND TRICARE PAYMENTS

A patient's signature requests that payment be made and authorizes release of any information necessary to process the claim and certifies that the information provided in Blocks 1 through 12 is true, accurate and complete. In the case of a Medicare claim, the patient's signature authorizes any entity to release to Medicare medical and nonmedical information and whether the person has employer group health insurance, liability, no-fault, worker's compensation or other insurance which is responsible to pay for the services for which the Medicare claim is made. See 42 CFR 411.24(a). If item 9 is completed, the patient's signature authorizes release of the information to the health plan or agency shown. In Medicare assigned or TRICARE participation cases, the physician agrees to accept the charge determination of the Medicare carrier or TRICARE fiscal intermediary as the full charge and the patient is responsible only for the deductible, coinsurance and non-covered services. Coinsurance and the deductible are based upon the charge determination of the Medicare carrier or TRICARE fiscal intermediary if this is less than the charge submitted. TRICARE is not a health insurance program but makes payment for health benefits provided through certain affiliations with the Uniformed Services. Information on the patient's sponsor should be provided in those items captioned in "Insured"; i.e., items 1a, 4, 6, 7, 9, and 11.

BLACK LUNG AND FECA CLAIMS

The provider agrees to accept the amount paid by the Government as payment in full. See Black Lung and FECA instructions regarding required procedure and diagnosis coding systems.

SIGNATURE OF PHYSICIAN OR SUPPLIER (MEDICARE, TRICARE, FECA AND BLACK LUNG)

In submitting this claim for payment from federal funds, I certify that: 1) the information on this form is true, accurate and complete; 2) I have familiarized myself with all applicable laws, regulations, and program instructions, which are available from the Medicare contractor; 3) I have provided or will provide sufficient information required to allow the government to make an informed eligibility and payment decision; 4) this claim, whether submitted by me or on my behalf by my designated billing company, complies with all applicable Medicare and/or Medicaid laws, regulations, and program instructions for payment including but not limited to the Federal anti-kickback statute and Physician Self-Referral law (commonly known as Stark law); 5) the services on this form were medically necessary and personally furnished by me or were furnished incident to my professional service by my employee under my direct supervision, except as otherwise expressly permitted by Medicare or TRICARE; 6) for each service rendered incident to my professional service, the identity (legal name and NPI, license #, or SSN) of the primary individual rendering each service is reported in the designated section.

For services to be considered "incident to" a physician's professional services, 1) they must be rendered under the physician's direct supervision by his/her employee, 2) they must be an integral, although incidental part of a covered physician service, 3) they must be of kinds commonly furnished in physician's offices, and 4) the services of non-physicians must be included on the physician's bills.

For TRICARE claims, I further certify that I (or any employee) who rendered services am not an active duty member of the Uniformed Services or a civilian employee of the United States Government or a contract employee of the United States Government, either civilian or military (refer to 5 USC 5536).

For Black-Lung claims, I further certify that the services performed were for a Black Lung-related disorder.

No Part B Medicare benefits may be paid unless this form is received as required by existing law and regulations (42 CFR 424.32).

NOTICE: Anyone who misrepresents or falsifies essential information to receive payment from Federal funds requested by this form may upon conviction be subject to fine and imprisonment under applicable Federal laws.

NOTICE TO PATIENT ABOUT THE COLLECTION AND USE OF MEDICARE, TRICARE, FECA, AND BLACK LUNG INFORMATION

(PRIVACY ACT STATEMENT)

We are authorized by CMS, TRICARE and OWCP to ask you for information needed in the administration of the Medicare, TRICARE, FECA, and Black Lung programs. Authority to collect information is in section 205(a), 1862, 1872 and 1874 of the Social Security Act as amended, 42 CFR 411.24(a) and 424.5(a) (6), and 44 USC 3101;41 CFR 101 et seq and 10 USC 1079 and 1086; 5 USC 8101 et seq; and 30 USC 901 et seq; 38 USC 613; E.O. 9397.

The information we obtain to complete claims under these programs is used to identify you and to determine your eligibility. It is also used to decide if the services and supplies you received are covered by these programs and to insure that proper payment is made.

The information may also be given to other providers of services, carriers, intermediaries, medical review boards, health plans, and other organizations or Federal agencies, for the effective administration of Federal provisions that require other third parties payers to pay primary to Federal program, and as otherwise necessary to administer these programs. For example, it may be necessary to disclose information about the benefits you have used to a hospital or doctor. Additional disclosures are made through routine uses for information contained in systems of records.

FOR MEDICARE CLAIMS: See the notice modifying system No. 09-70-0501, titled, 'Carrier Medicare Claims Record,' published in the Federal Register, Vol. 55 No. 177, page 37549, Wed. Sept. 12, 1990, or as updated and republished.

FOR OWCP CLAIMS: Department of Labor, Privacy Act of 1974, "Republication of Notice of Systems of Records," Federal Register Vol. 55 No. 40, Wed Feb. 28, 1990, See ESA-5, ESA-6, ESA-12, ESA-13, ESA-30, or as updated and republished.

FOR TRICARE CLAIMS: PRINCIPLE PURPOSE(S): To evaluate eligibility for medical care provided by civilian sources and to issue payment upon establishment of eligibility and determination that the services/supplies received are authorized by law.

ROUTINE USE(S): Information from claims and related documents may be given to the Dept. of Veterans Affairs, the Dept. of Health and Human Services and/or the Dept. of Transportation consistent with their statutory administrative responsibilities under TRICARE/CHAMPVA; to the Dept. of Justice for representation of the Secretary of Defense in civil actions; to the Internal Revenue Service, private collection agencies, and consumer reporting agencies in connection with recoupment claims; and to Congressional Offices in response to inquiries made at the request of the person to whom a record pertains. Appropriate disclosures may be made to other federal, state, local, foreign government agencies, private business entities, and individual providers of care, on matters relating to entitlement, claims adjudication, fraud, program abuse, utilization review, quality assurance, peer review, program integrity, third-party liability, coordination of benefits, and civil and criminal litigation related to the operation of TRICARE.

DISCLOSURES: Voluntary; however, failure to provide information will result in delay in payment or may result in denial of claim. With the one exception discussed below, there are no penalties under these programs for refusing to supply information. However, failure to furnish information regarding the medical services rendered or the amount charged would prevent payment of claims under these programs. Failure to furnish any other information, such as name or claim number, would delay payment of the claim. Failure to provide medical information under FECA could be deemed an obstruction.

It is mandatory that you tell us if you know that another party is responsible for paying for your treatment. Section 1128B of the Social Security Act and 31 USC 3801-3812 provide penalties for withholding this information.

You should be aware that P.L. 100-503, the "Computer Matching and Privacy Protection Act of 1988", permits the government to verify information by way of computer matches.

MEDICAID PAYMENTS (PROVIDER CERTIFICATION)

I hereby agree to keep such records as are necessary to disclose fully the extent of services provided to individuals under the State's Title XIX plan and to furnish information regarding any payments claimed for providing such services as the State Agency or Dept. of Health and Human Services may request.

I further agree to accept, as payment in full, the amount paid by the Medicaid program for those claims submitted for payment under that program, with the exception of authorized deductible, coinsurance, co-payment or similar cost-sharing charge.

SIGNATURE OF PHYSICIAN (OR SUPPLIER): I certify that the services listed above were medically indicated and necessary to the health of this patient and were personally furnished by me or my employee under my personal direction.

NOTICE: This is to certify that the foregoing information is true, accurate and complete. I understand that payment and satisfaction of this claim will be from Federal and State funds, and that any false claims, statements, or documents, or concealment of a material fact, may be prosecuted under applicable Federal or State laws.

According to the Paperwork Reduction Act of 1995, no persons are required to respond to a collection of information unless it displays a valid OMB control number. The valid OMB control number for this information collection is 0938-XXXX. The time required to complete this information collection is estimated to average 10 minutes per response, including the time to review instructions, search existing data resources, gather the data needed, and complete and review the information collection. If you have any comments concerning the accuracy of the time estimate(s) or suggestions for improving this form, please write to: CMS, 7500 Security Boulevard, Attn: PRA Reports Clearance Officer, Baltimore, Maryland 21244-1850. This address is for comments and/or suggestions only. DO NOT MAIL COMPLETED CLAIM FORMS TO THIS ADDRESS.

FIGURE 11-1 Reverse of CMS-1500, which contains special instructions for government programs.

HEALTH INSURANCE CLAIM FORM

APPROVED BY NATIONAL UNIFORM CLAIM COMMITTEE (NUCC) 02/12

PICA | PICA

CARRIER

1. MEDICARE (Medicare#) | MEDICAID (Medicaid#) | TRICARE (ID#/DoD#) | CHAMPVA (Member ID#) | GROUP HEALTH PLAN (ID#) | FECA BLK LUNG (ID#) | OTHER (ID#)

1a. INSURED'S I.D. NUMBER (For Program in Item 1)

2. PATIENT'S NAME (Last Name, First Name, Middle Initial)

3. PATIENT'S BIRTH DATE MM DD YY SEX M F

4. INSURED'S NAME (Last Name, First Name, Middle Initial)

5. PATIENT'S ADDRESS (No., Street)

6. PATIENT RELATIONSHIP TO INSURED Self Spouse Child Other

7. INSURED'S ADDRESS (No., Street)

CITY STATE

8. RESERVED FOR NUCC USE

CITY STATE

ZIP CODE TELEPHONE (Include Area Code) ( )

ZIP CODE TELEPHONE (Include Area Code) ( )

9. OTHER INSURED'S NAME (Last Name, First Name, Middle Initial)

10. IS PATIENT'S CONDITION RELATED TO:

11. INSURED'S POLICY GROUP OR FECA NUMBER

a. OTHER INSURED'S POLICY OR GROUP NUMBER

a. EMPLOYMENT? (Current or Previous) YES NO

a. INSURED'S DATE OF BIRTH MM DD YY SEX M F

b. RESERVED FOR NUCC USE

b. AUTO ACCIDENT? YES NO PLACE (State)

b. OTHER CLAIM ID (Designated by NUCC)

c. RESERVED FOR NUCC USE

c. OTHER ACCIDENT? YES NO

c. INSURANCE PLAN NAME OR PROGRAM NAME

d. INSURANCE PLAN NAME OR PROGRAM NAME

10d. CLAIM CODES (Designated by NUCC)

d. IS THERE ANOTHER HEALTH BENEFIT PLAN? YES NO *If yes*, complete items 9, 9a, and 9d.

READ BACK OF FORM BEFORE COMPLETING & SIGNING THIS FORM.

12. PATIENT'S OR AUTHORIZED PERSON'S SIGNATURE I authorize the release of any medical or other information necessary to process this claim. I also request payment of government benefits either to myself or to the party who accepts assignment below.

SIGNED DATE

13. INSURED'S OR AUTHORIZED PERSON'S SIGNATURE I authorize payment of medical benefits to the undersigned physician or supplier for services described below.

SIGNED

PATIENT AND INSURED INFORMATION

14. DATE OF CURRENT ILLNESS, INJURY, or PREGNANCY (LMP) MM DD YY QUAL.

15. OTHER DATE QUAL. MM DD YY

16. DATES PATIENT UNABLE TO WORK IN CURRENT OCCUPATION FROM MM DD YY TO MM DD YY

17. NAME OF REFERRING PROVIDER OR OTHER SOURCE

17a.

17b. NPI

18. HOSPITALIZATION DATES RELATED TO CURRENT SERVICES FROM MM DD YY TO MM DD YY

19. ADDITIONAL CLAIM INFORMATION (Designated by NUCC)

20. OUTSIDE LAB? YES NO $ CHARGES

21. DIAGNOSIS OR NATURE OF ILLNESS OR INJURY Relate A-L to service line below (24E) ICD Ind.

A. B. C. D.
E. F. G. H.
I. J. K. L.

22. RESUBMISSION CODE ORIGINAL REF. NO.

23. PRIOR AUTHORIZATION NUMBER

24. A. DATE(S) OF SERVICE From MM DD YY	To MM DD YY	B. PLACE OF SERVICE	C. EMG	D. PROCEDURES, SERVICES, OR SUPPLIES (Explain Unusual Circumstances) CPT/HCPCS	MODIFIER	E. DIAGNOSIS POINTER	F. $ CHARGES	G. DAYS OR UNITS	H. EPSDT Family Plan	I. ID. QUAL.	J. RENDERING PROVIDER ID. #
1										NPI	
2										NPI	
3										NPI	
4										NPI	
5										NPI	
6										NPI	

PHYSICIAN OR SUPPLIER INFORMATION

25. FEDERAL TAX I.D. NUMBER SSN EIN

26. PATIENT'S ACCOUNT NO.

27. ACCEPT ASSIGNMENT? (For govt. claims, see back) YES NO

28. TOTAL CHARGE $

29. AMOUNT PAID $

30. Rsvd for NUCC Use

31. SIGNATURE OF PHYSICIAN OR SUPPLIER INCLUDING DEGREES OR CREDENTIALS (I certify that the statements on the reverse apply to this bill and are made a part thereof.)

SIGNED DATE

32. SERVICE FACILITY LOCATION INFORMATION

a. NPI b.

33. BILLING PROVIDER INFO & PH # ( )

a. NPI b.

NUCC Instruction Manual available at: www.nucc.org

PLEASE PRINT OR TYPE

Courtesy of the Centers for Medicare & Medicaid Services, www.cms.gov

FIGURE 11-2 CMS-1500 claim.

6. PATIENT RELATIONSHIP TO INSURED			
Self [X]	Spouse [ ]	Child [ ]	Other [ ]

FIGURE 11-3 Examples of correct placement of the X within a box on the CMS-1500 claim.

All claims for case studies in this text are prepared according to OCR standards.

- **All data must be entered on the claim within the borders of the data field. "X"s must be contained completely within the boxes, and no letters or numbers should be printed on vertical solid or dotted lines (Figure 11-3).**

Computer-generated paper claims: Software programs should have a test pattern program that fills the claim with "X"s so that you can test the alignment of forms. This is a critical operation with a pin-fed printer. Check the alignment and make any necessary adjustments each time a new batch of claims is inserted into the printer.

- **Enter all alpha characters in uppercase (capital letters).**
- **Do not enter the alpha character "O" for a zero (0).**
- ***Enter a space* for the following, which are preprinted on the claim:**
  - **Dollar sign or decimal in all charges or totals**
  - **Parentheses surrounding the area code in a telephone number**
- **Do *not* enter a hyphen between the CPT or HCPCS code and modifier. Enter a space between the code and modifier. If multiple modifiers are reported for one CPT or HCPCS level II code, enter one space between each modifier.**
- **Do *not* enter hyphens or spaces in the social security number, in the employer identification number (EIN), or in the Health Plan Identifier (HPID) number.**
- **Enter commas between the patient or policyholder's last name, first name, and middle initial.**
- ***Do not* use any other punctuation in a patient's or policyholder's name, except for a hyphen in a compound name.**

EXAMPLE: GARDNER-BEY

- ***Do not* enter a person's title or other designations, such as Sr., Jr., II, or III, unless printed on the patient's insurance ID card.**

EXAMPLE: The name on the ID card states:

Wm F. Goodpatient, IV

Name on claim is entered as:

GOODPATIENT IV, WILLIAM, F

- **Enter two zeroes in the cents column when a fee or a monetary total is expressed in whole dollars. *Do not* enter any leading zeroes in front of the dollar amount.**

EXAMPLES:

Six dollars is entered as 6 00

Six thousand dollars is entered as 6000 00

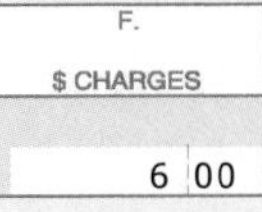

3. PATIENT'S BIRTH DATE MM DD YY 03 08 YYYY SEX M [ ] F [X]

Copyright © Cengage Learning®.

FIGURE 11-4 Proper entry for birth date.

- Birth dates are entered as eight digits with spaces between the digits representing the month, day, and the *four-digit year (MM DD YYYY)* except for Blocks 24A (MM DD YY) and 31 (MMDDYYYY). Care should be taken to ensure that none of the digits fall on the vertical separations within the block (Figure 11-4). Two-digit code numbers for the months are:

Jan—01	Apr—04	July—07	Oct—10
Feb—02	May—05	Aug—08	Nov—11
Mar—03	June—06	Sept—09	Dec—12

- For an electronic media claim, all corrections must be made within the computer data set. On a computer-generated paper claim, for errors caught before mailing, correct the data in the computer and reprint the claim. Errors should then be corrected in the computer database.
- *Handwritten claims:* Claims that contain handwritten data, with the exception of the blocks that require signatures, must be manually processed because they cannot be processed by scanners. This will cause a delay in payment of the claim.
- Extraneous data, such as handwritten notes, printed material, or special stamps, should be placed on an attachment to the claim.
- The third-party payer (carrier) block is located from the upper center to the right margin of the CMS-1500 claim form. Enter the name and address of the payer to which the claim is being sent, in the following format. Do not use punctuation (e.g., commas, periods) or other symbols in the address (e.g., enter 123 N Main Street 101, not 123 N. Main Street, #101). When entering a nine-digit zip code, include the hyphen (e.g., 12345-6789).

  Line 1 - Name of third-party payer

  Line 2 - First line of address

  Line 3 - Second line of address, if necessary; otherwise, leave blank

  Line 4 - City, state (2 characters), and zip code

NOTE: Typewritten and handwritten claims have higher error rates, resulting in payment delays.

HEALTH INSURANCE CLAIM FORM

APPROVED BY NATIONAL UNIFORM CLAIM COMMITTEE (NUCC) 02/12

PICA

ABC INSURANCE COMPANY
SUITE 500 567 INSURANCE LANE
BIG CITY IL 60605

CARRIER

PICA

Courtesy of the Centers for Medicare & Medicaid Services, www.cms.gov

- **List only one procedure per line, starting with line one of Block 24. (To report more than six procedures or services for the same date of service, generate a new claim.)**
- **Photocopies of claims are not allowed because they cannot be optically scanned. All resubmissions must also be prepared on an original (red-print) CMS-1500 claim. (In addition, information located on the reverse of the claim must be present.)**

EXERCISE 11-1

Applying Optical Scanning Guidelines

On a blank sheet of paper, enter the following items according to optical scanning guidelines.

1. Patient name: Jeffrey L. Green, D.D.S.
2. Total charge of three hundred dollars.
3. Procedure code 12345 with modifiers -22 and -51.
4. ID number 123-45-6789.
5. Illustrate improper marking of boxes.
6. Enter the birth date for a person who was born on March 8, 2000.

Answer the following questions.

7. Your medical office management software automatically enters the name of the payer and its mailing address on the claim. Where should this be placed?
8. Your computer uses pin-fed paper. You just ran a batch of 50 claims that will be mailed to one insurance company. All claims are properly processed. What must be done to the claims before they are placed in the envelope for mailing?
9. What is the rule for placing handwritten material on the claim?
10. Name the computer/typewriter font style and print size requirements acceptable for optical scanning of claims.

ENTERING PATIENT AND POLICYHOLDER NAMES

When entering the patient's name in Block 2, separate the last name, first name, and middle initial with commas (e.g., DOE, JOHN, S). When entering the policyholder's name in Block 4, separate the last name, first name, and middle initial with commas (e.g., DOE, JOHN, S). If the patient is the policyholder, enter the patient's name as last name, first name, and middle initial (separated by commas).

When entering the name of the patient and/or policyholder on the CMS-1500 claim, it is:

- **Acceptable to enter a last name suffix (e.g., JR, SR) after the last name (e.g., DOE JR, JOHN, S) and/or a hyphen for hyphenated names (e.g., BLUM-CONDON, MARY, T)**
- **Unacceptable to enter periods, titles (e.g., Sister, Capt, Dr), or professional suffixes (e.g., PhD, MD, Esq.) within a name**

ENTERING PROVIDER NAMES

When entering the name of a provider on the CMS-1500 claim, enter the first name, middle initial (if known), last name, and credentials (e.g., MARY SMITH MD). *Do not enter any punctuation.*

In Block 31, some third-party payers allow providers to:

- **Use a signature stamp and handwrite the date.**
- **Sign and date a printed CMS-1500 claim.**
- **Enter SIGNATURE ON FILE or SOF for electronic claims transmissions if a certification letter is filed with the payer; the date is entered as MMDDYYYY (without spaces).**

NOTE:

- Do not enter commas, periods, or other punctuation in the address.
- When entering a nine-digit zip code, enter the hyphen.
- Do not enter parentheses for the area code because they are preprinted on the claim.
- Do not enter spaces in the telephone number.

ENTERING MAILING ADDRESSES AND TELEPHONE NUMBERS

When entering a patient's and/or policyholder's (Blocks 5 and 7) mailing address and telephone number, enter the street address on line 1. Enter the city and state on line 2. Enter the five- or nine-digit zip code and telephone number on line 3.

The patient's address refers to the patient's permanent residence. Do not enter a temporary address or a school address.

When entering a provider's name, mailing address, and telephone number (Block 33), enter the provider's name on line 1, enter the provider's billing address on line 2, and enter the provider's city, state, and five- or nine-digit zip code on line 3. Enter the telephone number in the area next to the Block title.

NOTE: In ICD-10-CM, the majority of codes assigned to external causes of morbidity are located in Chapter 20. Other conditions stated as due to external causes are also classified elsewhere in ICD-10-CM's Chapters 1–25. For these other conditions, ICD-10-CM codes from Chapter 20 are also reported to provide additional information regarding external causes of the condition (e.g., place of occurrence).

RECOVERY OF FUNDS FROM RESPONSIBLE PAYERS

Payers flag claims for investigation when an X is entered in one or more of the YES boxes in Block 10 of the CMS-1500 claim, or an ICD-10-CM code that begins with the letter V, W, X, or Y is reported in Block 21. Such an entry indicates that payment might be the responsibility of a workers' compensation payer (Block 10a); automobile insurance company (Block 10b); or homeowners, business, or other liability policy insurance company (Block 10c). Some payers reimburse the claim and outsource (to a vendor that specializes in "backend recovery") the pursuit of funds from the appropriate payer. Other payers deny payment until the provider submits documentation to support reimbursement processing by the payer (e.g., remittance advice from workers' compensation or other liability payer denying the claim).

Entering an X in any of the YES boxes in Block 10 of the CMS-1500 alerts the commercial payer that another insurance company might be liable for payment. The commercial payer will not consider the claim unless the provider submits a remittance advice from the liable party (e.g., automobile policy) indicating that the claim was denied. For employment-related conditions, another option is to attach a letter from the workers' compensation payer that documents rejection of payment for an on-the-job injury.

10. IS PATIENT'S CONDITION RELATED TO:

a. EMPLOYMENT? (Current or Previous)

☐ YES ☐ NO

b. AUTO ACCIDENT? PLACE (State)

☐ YES ☐ NO

c. OTHER ACCIDENT?

☐ YES ☐ NO

Third-party payers also screen submitted claims when codes for accidents and injuries are reported. When an external cause of injury code is reported on Block 21, the claims examiner "pends" the claim and submits a letter to the insured to request details about a possible accident or injury. Depending on the insured's responses, the payer might deny the claim and instruct the insured to resubmit the claim to another payer (e.g., automobile insurance company, liability insurance company) for processing.

NATIONAL PROVIDER IDENTIFIER (NPI)

The *national provider identifier* (NPI) is a unique 10-digit number issued to individual providers (e.g., physicians, dentists, pharmacists) and health care organizations (e.g., group physician practices, hospitals, nursing facilities). The NPI replaced health care provider identifiers (e.g., PIN, UPIN) previously generated by health plans and government programs. Submission of the NPI has been required on the CMS-1500 claim for:

- **Large health plans (e.g., private payers, Medicare, Medicaid) and all health care clearinghouses, effective May 23, 2007**
- **Small health plans, effective May 23, 2008**

NOTE: If an NPI is used fraudulently by another, a new NPI will be issued to the individual provider or health care organization affected.

Even if an individual provider moves, changes specialty, or changes practices, the provider will keep the same NPI (but must notify CMS to supply the new information). *The NPI will identify the provider throughout his or her career.*

The NPI issued to a health care organization is also permanent *except in rare situations when a health care provider does not wish to continue an association with a previously used NPI.*

HIPAA mandated the adoption of standard unique identifiers to improve the efficiency and effectiveness of the electronic transmission of health information for:

- Employers—national standard employer identifier number (EIN)
- Health care providers—national provider identifier (NPI)
- Health plans—health plan identifier (HPID)
- Individuals—national individual identifier (has been placed on hold)

(continues)

HIPAA *covered entities* include health plans, health care clearinghouses, and health care providers that conduct electronic transactions. HIPAA mandated use of the NPI to identify health care providers in standard transactions, which include claims processing, patient eligibility inquiries and responses, claims status inquiries and responses, patient referrals, and generation of remittance advices. Health care providers (and organizations) that transmit health information electronically to submit claims data are required by HIPAA to obtain an NPI even if the provider (or organization) uses business associates (e.g., billing agencies) to prepare the transactions.

NPI Application Process

The **National Plan and Provider Enumeration System (NPPES)** was developed by CMS to assign the unique health care provider and health plan identifiers and to serve as a database from which to extract data (e.g., health plan verification of provider NPI). Each health plan will develop a process by which NPI data will be accessed to verify the identity of providers who submit HIPAA transactions.

Providers apply for an NPI by submitting the following:

- **Web-based application**
- **Paper-based application**
- **Electronic file (e.g., hospital submits an electronic file that contains information about all physician employees, such as emergency department physicians, pathologists, and radiologists)**

Practices That Bill "Incident To"

When a nonphysician practitioner (NPP) (e.g., nurse practitioner, physician assistant) in a group practice bills incident-to a physician, but that physician is out of the office on the day the NPP provides services to the patient, another physician in the same group can provide direct supervision to meet the incident-to requirements. A **supervising physician** is a licensed physician in good standing who, according to state regulations, engages in the direct supervision of nurse practitioners and/or physician assistants whose duties are encompassed by the supervising physician's scope of practice. A supervising physician is not required to be physically present in the patient's treatment room when services are provided; however, the supervising physician must be present in the office suite or facility to render assistance, if necessary.

NOTE: A *rendering physician* provides (or renders) care to patients. A supervising physician engages in the direct supervision of nonphysician practitioners who provide care to patients.

When incident-to services are billed, the following entries are made on the CMS-1500:

- **Enter the ordering physician's name in Block 17 (*not* the supervising physician's name).**
- **Enter the applicable qualifier (in the space preceding the name) to identify which provider is being reported.**
  - **DN (referring provider)**
  - **DK (ordering provider)**
  - **DQ (supervising provider)**
- **Enter the ordering physician's NPI in Block 17b.**

- **Enter the supervising physician's NPI in Block 24I.**
- **Enter the supervising physician's name (or signature) in Block 31.**

17. NAME OF REFERRING PHYSICIAN OR OTHER SOURCE	17a.		
	17b.	NPI	

ASSIGNMENT OF BENEFITS VERSUS ACCEPT ASSIGNMENT

An area of confusion for health insurance specialists is differentiating between *assignment of benefits* and *accept assignment*. Patients sign Block 13 of the CMS-1500 claim to instruct the payer to directly reimburse the provider. This is called *assignment of benefits*. If the patient does not sign Block 13, the payer sends reimbursement to the patient. The patient is then responsible for reimbursing the provider.

When the YES box in Block 27 contains an X, the provider agrees to accept as payment in full whatever the payer reimburses. This is called *accept assignment*. The provider can still collect deductible, copayment, and coinsurance amounts from the patient. If the NO box in Block 27 contains an X, the provider does not accept assignment. The provider can bill the patient for the amount not paid by the payer.

13. INSURED'S OR AUTHORIZED PERSON'S SIGNATURE I authorize payment of medical benefits to the undersigned physician or supplier for services described below.

SIGNED ______

27. ACCEPT ASSIGNMENT? (for govt. claims, see back)
☐ YES ☐ NO

REPORTING DIAGNOSES: ICD-10-CM CODES

Block 21

Diagnosis codes (with decimal points) are entered in Block 21 of the claim. A maximum of *12* ICD-10-CM codes may be entered on a single claim. In the ICD Ind (ICD indicator) box, enter 0 for ICD-10-CM.

If more than 12 diagnoses are required to justify the procedures and/or services on a claim, generate additional claims. In such cases, be sure that the diagnoses justify the medical necessity for performing the procedures/services reported on each claim. Diagnoses must be documented in the patient's record to validate medical necessity of procedures or services billed.

NOTE:

- When entering ICD-10-CM codes in Block 21, enter the decimal.
- When a payer allows more than one diagnosis pointer letter to be entered in Block 24E of the CMS-1500 claim, enter a space between each letter (e.g., A B C D). *Do not enter commas between pointer letters.*

21. DIAGNOSIS OR NATURE OF ILLNESS OR INJURY Relate A-L to service line below (24E) ICD Ind. **0**

A. **E11.8**	B. **I10**	C. **Z00.00**	D. **Y92.099**
E.	F.	G.	H.
I.	J.	K.	L.

Courtesy of the Centers for Medicare & Medicaid Services, **www.cms.gov**

Sequencing Multiple Diagnoses

The first-listed code reported is the major reason the patient was treated by the health care provider. *Secondary diagnoses codes are entered in letters B through L of Block 21 and should be included on the claim only if they are necessary to justify procedures/services reported in Block 24D.* Do not enter any diagnoses stated in the patient record that were not treated or medically managed (e.g., existing diagnosis that impacts treatment of a new diagnosis) during the encounter.

Be sure code numbers are placed within the designated field on the claim. Enter the decimal point, if appropriate for the reported code.

Accurate Coding

For physician office and outpatient claims processing, *never* report a code for diagnoses that includes such terms as "rule out," "suspicious for," "probable," "ruled out," "possible," or "questionable." Code either the patient's symptoms or complaints, or do not complete this block until a definitive diagnosis is determined.

NOTE: Coders should be aware that some chronic conditions always affect patient care because they require medical management and should, therefore, be coded and reported on the CMS-1500 claim. Examples include diabetes mellitus and hypertension.

Be sure all diagnosis codes are reported to the highest degree of specificity known at the time of the treatment.

If the computerized billing system displays a default diagnosis code (e.g., condition last treated) when entering a patient's claim information, determine if the code validates the current procedure/service reported. It may frequently be necessary to edit this code because, although the diagnosis may still be present, it may not have been treated or medically managed during the current encounter.

REPORTING PROCEDURES AND SERVICES: HCPCS LEVEL II AND CPT CODES

Instructions in this section are for those blocks that are universally required. All other blocks are discussed individually in Chapters 12 through 17.

Block 24A—Dates of Service

When the claim form was designed, space was allotted for a six-digit date pattern with spaces between the month, day, and two-digit year (MM DD YY). No allowance was made for the year 2000 or beyond and the need for a four-digit year. Therefore, a six-digit date is entered *with* spaces (e.g., MM DD YY).

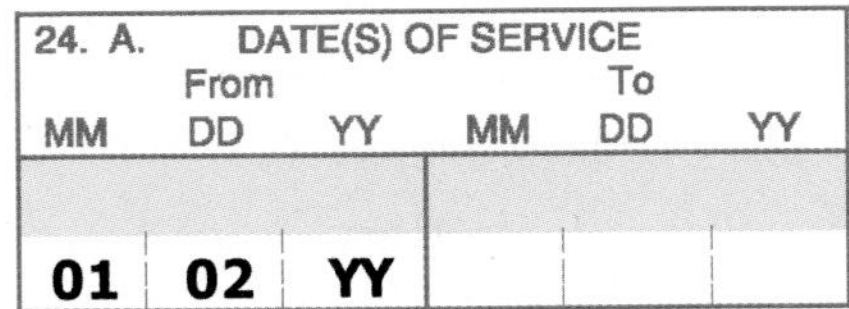

24. A. DATE(S) OF SERVICE From MM	DD	YY	To MM	DD	YY
01	02	YY			

Block 24B—Place of Service

All payers require entry of a place of service (POS) code on the claim. The POS code reported must be consistent with the CPT procedure/service code description, and it will be one or two digits, depending on the payer. (Refer to Appendix II for POS codes.)

When third-party payers and government programs (e.g., Medicaid) audit submitted claims, they require evidence of documentation in the patient's record about encounters and inpatient hospital visits. It is recommended that when a provider submits a claim for inpatient visits, a copy of hospital documentation (e.g., progress notes) supporting the visits be filed in the office patient record. Without such documentation, payers and government programs deny reimbursement for the visits.

BLUESHIELD POS CODES	MEDICARE POS CODES	DESCRIPTION
1	21	Inpatient Hospital
2	22	Outpatient Hospital
3	11	Office
4	12	Home

Block 24C–EMG

Check with the payer for their definition of emergency (EMG) treatment. If the payer requires completion of Block 24C, and EMG treatment was provided, enter a Y (for YES). Otherwise, leave blank.

Block 24D–Procedures and Services

NOTE: Do not report procedure and/or service codes if no fee was charged.

Procedure codes and modifiers are reported in Block 24D. A maximum of six procedures and/or services may be reported on one claim. If the reporting of additional procedure and/or service codes is necessary, generate additional CMS-1500 claim(s).

Below the heading in Block 24D is a parenthetical instruction that says *(Explain Unusual Circumstances)*, which means to enter official CPT or HCPCS level II modifiers, attach documentation from the patient's record, or include a letter written by the provider.

NOTE: Shaded rows were added to Block 24 because:

- Blocks 24I and 24J were split to accommodate reporting of the NPI (effective May 2007) and other identification numbers (prior to May 2007).
- Input from the health insurance industry indicated a need to report supplemental information about services reported.

The completely shaded area across rows 1-6 in Block 24 will be used to report supplemental information for each reported service (e.g., anesthesia, National Drug Codes, product numbers).

When reporting more than one CPT Surgery code on a CMS-1500 claim, enter the code with the highest fee in line 1 of Block 24, and then enter additional codes (and modifiers) in descending order of charges. Be sure to completely enter data on each horizontal line before beginning to enter data on another line.

Identical procedures or services can be reported on the same line *if* the following circumstances apply:

- **Procedures were performed on consecutive days in the same month.**
- **The same code is assigned to the procedures/services reported.**
- **Identical charges apply to the assigned code.**
- **Block 24G (Days or Units) is completed.**

Modifiers

To accurately report a procedure or service, up to four CPT/HCPCS modifiers can be entered to the right of the solid vertical line in Block 24D on the claim. The first modifier is entered between the solid vertical line and the dotted line.

EXAMPLE: Patient is admitted to the hospital on June 1. The doctor reports detailed subsequent hospital visits on June 2, 3, and 4.

Date of service 0601YY (no spaces) is entered on a separate line in Block 24 because the CPT code assigned for initial inpatient care (on the day of admission) is different from subsequent hospital visits (reported for June 2, 3, and 4 as 0602YY through 0604YY).

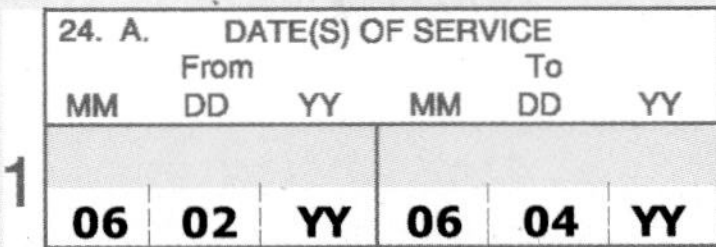

	24. A. DATE(S) OF SERVICE From MM	DD	YY	To MM	DD	YY
1	06	02	YY	06	04	YY

If identical consecutive procedures fall within a two-month span, use two lines, one for the first month and one for the second.

EXAMPLE: Patient is admitted to the hospital on May 29. The doctor reports an initial E/M service on May 29 and subsequent E/M services on May 30, May 31, June 1, June 2, and June 3.

	24. A. DATE(S) OF SERVICE From MM	DD	YY	To MM	DD	YY
1	05	29	YY			
2	05	30	YY	05	31	YY
3	06	01	YY	06	03	YY

When reporting consecutive days on one line, the first date is reported in 24A in the *From* column and the last day in the *To* column. The *DAYS OR UNITS* column (24G) should reflect the number of days reported in 24A.

If additional modifier(s) are added, enter one blank space between modifiers. *Do not* enter a hyphen in front of the modifier.

D. PROCEDURES, SERVICES, OR SUPPLIES (Explain Unusual Circumstances) CPT/HCPCS	MODIFIER			
99221	57			
44960	22	47	60	

Block 24E–Diagnosis Pointer

Diagnosis pointer letters A through L are preprinted in Block 21 of the CMS-1500 claim, and they are reported in Block 24E. Although reporting of diagnosis pointer letters rather than ICD-10-CM code numbers is required, some payers require just one pointer letter to be entered in Block 24E; others allow multiple pointer letters (separated by one blank space) to be entered in Block 24E. Be sure to consult individual payers for specific instructions on how many pointer letters can be reported in Block 24E.

REMEMBER!

If more than one pointer letter is reported, the first-listed code is the reason the patient sought care from the provider.

21. DIAGNOSIS OR NATURE OF ILLNESS OR INJURY Relate A-L to service line below (24E) ICD Ind. **0**

A. **R94.01**	B. **I20.1**	C. **S06.0X0A**	D. **W06.XXXA**
E.	F.	G.	H.
I.	J.	K.	L.

Courtesy of the Centers for Medicare & Medicaid Services, **www.cms.gov**

Block 24F—Charges

Careful alignment of the charges in Block 24F, as well as the totals in Blocks 28 and 29, is critical. Precise entry of dollars and cents is also critical. The block has room for five characters in the dollar column and three in the cents column. Dollar amounts and cents must be entered in their own blocks with only one blank space between them (Figure 11-5).

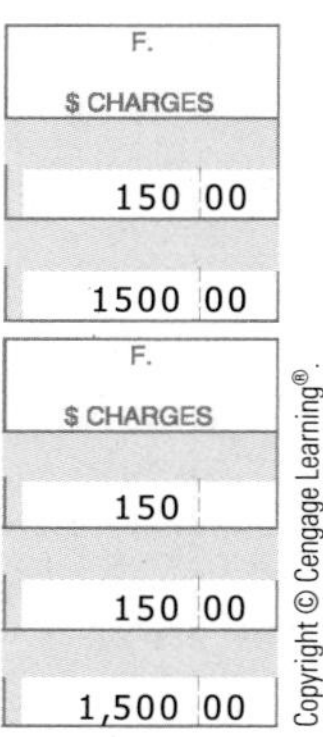

FIGURE 11-5 Correct and incorrect entry of charges in Block 24F.

Block 24G—Days or Units

Block 24G requires reporting of the number of encounters, units of service or supplies, amount of drug injected, and so on, for the procedure reported on the same line in Block 24D. This block has room for only three digits.

The most common number entered in Block 24G is "1" to represent the delivery of a single procedure/service.

The entry of a number greater than "1" is required if identical procedures are reported on the same line. Do not confuse the number of units assigned on one line with the number of days the patient is in the hospital.

EXAMPLE: The patient is in the hospital for three days following an open cholecystectomy. The number of units assigned to the line reporting the surgery is "1" (only one cholecystectomy was performed).

REMEMBER!

When a procedure is performed more than once a day, enter the appropriate modifier(s) in Block 24D and attach a copy of supporting documentation to the claim.

Rules to follow when reporting multiple days/units include:

- *Anesthesia time:* Report elapsed time as one unit for each 15 minutes (or fraction thereof) of anesthesia time. Convert hours to minutes, first.

> **EXAMPLE:** Elapsed time 3 hours and 15 minutes, reported as 13 units (195 minutes divided by 15 minutes equals 13).

- *Multiple procedures:* Enter the procedure code that will be reimbursed highest first, and then enter secondary procedure codes in descending order of charges. Enter a "1" in the units column for each procedure entered. Then enter any required modifiers to the secondary procedures in Block 24D (e.g., modifier 51 for multiple procedures).
- *Inclusive dates of similar services:* Report the number of days indicated in the *From* and *To* blocks (Block 24A); the number of days is reported in Block 24G.

> **EXAMPLE:** The physician treated Mr. Greenstalk on 01/02 through 01/04 and performed a detailed inpatient subsequent exam each day. The same E/M code is reported on one line in Block 24 and a 3 is entered as the units in Block 24G.

- *Radiology services*: Enter a number greater than "1" when the same radiology study is performed more than once on the same day. *Do not report the number of x-ray views taken for a specific study*.

> **EXAMPLE:** 71030 Chest, four views
>
> Enter 1 in Block 24G.

MEDICALLY UNLIKELY EDITS (MUE) PROJECT

In 2007 CMS implemented the medically unlikely edits *(MUE) project* as part of the NCCI to improve the accuracy of Medicare payments by detecting and denying unlikely Medicare claims on a prepayment basis. The project is CMS's response to the May 2006 Office of Inspector General (OIG) report, entitled *Excessive Payments for Outpatient Services Processed by Mutual of Omaha*, which reported errors due to inappropriate units of service, accounting for $2.8 million in outpatient service overpayments (2003) from one third-party payer. The OIG determined that the payer made these overpayments because sufficient edits were not in place during the year 2003 to detect billing errors related to units of service.

The following examples illustrate ways providers overstated the units of service on individual claims:

- A provider billed 10,001 units of service for 1 CT scan as the result of a typing error. The payer was overpaid approximately $958,000.

(continues)

- A provider billed 141 units of service (the number of minutes in the operating room) for 1 shoulder arthroscopy procedure. The payer was overpaid approximately $97,000.
- A provider billed 8 units of service (the number of 15-minute time increments in the operating room) for 1 cochlear implant procedure. The payer was overpaid approximately $67,000.

MUEs are used to compare units of service with code numbers as reported on submitted claims:

- **CMS-1500:** Block 24G (units of service) is compared with Block 24D (code number) on the same line.
- **UB-04:** Form Locator 46 (service units) is compared with Form Locator 44 (HCPCS/RATE/HIPPS CODE).

NOTE: If the EIN is unavailable, enter the provider's SSN.

NATIONAL STANDARD EMPLOYER IDENTIFIER

NOTE: Reporting correct EIN and/or SSN information is crucial because payers report reimbursement to the Internal Revenue Service (IRS) according to EIN or SSN.

Block 25 requires entry of either the provider's social security number (SSN) or the employer tax identification number (EIN). If completing claims for a group practice, enter the practice's EIN in this block. Do not enter the hyphen (e.g., 111234567). The SSN is also entered without hyphens or spaces.

25. FEDERAL TAX I.D. NUMBER	SSN	EIN
111233412	☐	X

EXERCISE 11-2

Entering Procedures in Block 24

Review the following unrelated scenarios and enter the data into columns A, D, F, and G of Block 24. If a procedure is performed on consecutive dates, enter them on one line.

1.	10/10	OV, est pt, detailed history and physical exam	99214	$65.00
2.	10/10	Subsequent hosp visit, expanded problem focused	99232	$45.00

NOTE: The physician visited the patient twice in the hospital on 10/10.

	10/12	Subsequent hosp visit, problem focused	99231	$35.00
3.	10/15	X-ray, pelvis, 4 views	72190	$150.00
4.	11/09	Cholecystectomy, open	47600	$900.00
	11/09	Diagnostic arthroscopy, knee	29870-51	$500.00

	24. A. DATE(S) OF SERVICE From MM DD YY	To MM DD YY	B. PLACE OF SERVICE	C. EMG	D. PROCEDURES, SERVICES, OR SUPPLIES (Explain Unusual Circumstances) CPT/HCPCS | MODIFIER	E. DIAGNOSIS POINTER	F. $ CHARGES	G. DAYS OR UNITS	H. EPSDT Family Plan	I. ID. QUAL.	J. RENDERING PROVIDER ID. #
1										NPI	
2										NPI	
3										NPI	
4										NPI	
5										NPI	
6										NPI	

NOTE: When a nonphysician practitioner bills incident to a physician in the same group, but that physician is out of the office on a day the nonphysician practitioner treats the physician's patient, another physician in the same group can provide direct supervision to meet the incident-to requirements. The ordering physician's name is entered in Block 17 of the CMS-1500 claim. The supervising physician's NPI is entered in Block 24J, and the supervising physician authenticates the claim in Block 31.

SIGNATURE OF PHYSICIAN OR SUPPLIER

The provider signature in Block 31 of the CMS-1500 provides attestation (confirmation) that the procedures and services were billed properly. This means that the provider is responsible for claims submitted in their name, even if they did not have actual knowledge of a billing impropriety.

31. SIGNATURE OF PHYSICIAN OR SUPPLIER INCLUDING DEGREES OR CREDENTIALS
(I certify that the statements on the reverse apply to this bill and are made a part thereof.)

SIGNED DATE

REPORTING THE BILLING ENTITY

Block 33 requires entry of the name, address, and telephone number of the billing entity. The **billing entity** is the legal business name of the practice (e.g., Goodmedicine Clinic). In the case of a solo practitioner, the name of the practice may be entered as the name of the physician followed by initials that designate how the practice is incorporated (e.g., Irvin M. Gooddoc, M.D., PA). The phone number, including area code, should be entered on the same line as the printed words "& PH #." Below this line is a blank space for a three-line billing entity mailing address.

The last line of Block 33 is for entering the provider and/or group practice national provider number (NPI).

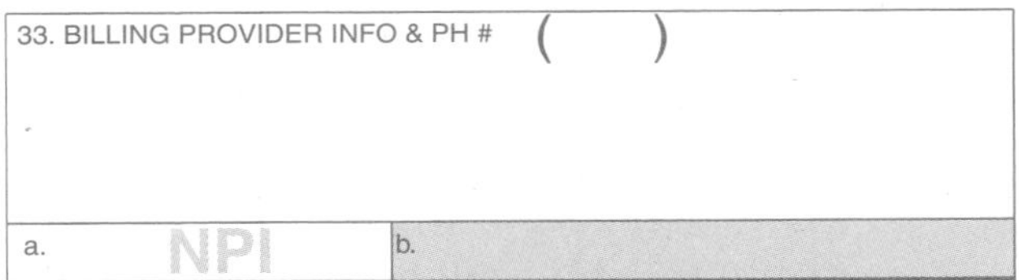
33. BILLING PROVIDER INFO & PH # ( )

a. NPI b.

EXERCISE 11-3

Completing Block 33

What is the name of the billing entity in these cases?

1. Dr. Cardiac is employed by Goodmedicine Clinic.
2. Dr. Blank is a solo practitioner. The official name of his practice is Timbuktu Orthopedics.
3. Dr. Jones shares office space with Dr. Blank at Timbuktu Orthopedics; Dr. Jones, PA, and Timbuktu Orthopedics have separate EIN numbers.

PROCESSING SECONDARY CLAIMS

The secondary insurance claim is filed only after the remittance advice generated as a result of processing the primary claim has been received by the medical practice. When submitting the secondary claim, attach the remittance advice to the claim sent to the secondary payer.

HEALTH INSURANCE CLAIM FORM

APPROVED BY NATIONAL UNIFORM CLAIM COMMITTEE (NUCC) 02/12

PICA | PICA

1. MEDICARE (Medicare#) / MEDICAID (Medicaid#) / TRICARE (ID#/DoD#) / CHAMPVA (Member ID#) / GROUP HEALTH PLAN (ID#) / FECA BLK LUNG (ID#) / OTHER (ID#) — **Primary Insurance Payer is Marked**		1a. INSURED'S I.D. NUMBER (For Program in Item 1) — **Primary Insurance Number**
2. PATIENT'S NAME (Last Name, First Name, Middle Initial)	3. PATIENT'S BIRTH DATE MM DD YY; SEX M ☐ F ☐	4. INSURED'S NAME (Last Name, First Name, Middle Initial)
5. PATIENT'S ADDRESS (No., Street)	6. PATIENT RELATIONSHIP TO INSURED: Self ☐ Spouse ☐ Child ☐ Other ☐	7. INSURED'S ADDRESS (No., Street)
CITY / STATE	8. RESERVED FOR NUCC USE	CITY / STATE
ZIP CODE / TELEPHONE (Include Area Code) ( )		ZIP CODE / TELEPHONE (Include Area Code) ( )
9. OTHER INSURED'S NAME (Last Name, First Name, Middle Initial)	10. IS PATIENT'S CONDITION RELATED TO:	11. INSURED'S POLICY GROUP OR FECA NUMBER
a. OTHER INSURED'S POLICY OR GROUP NUMBER	a. EMPLOYMENT? (Current or Previous) ☐ YES ☐ NO	a. INSURED'S DATE OF BIRTH MM DD YY; SEX M ☐ F ☐
b. RESERVED FOR NUCC USE — **Secondary Insurance Information**	b. AUTO ACCIDENT? ☐ YES ☐ NO; PLACE (State)	b. OTHER CLAIM ID (Designated by NUCC) — **Primary Insurance Information**
c. RESERVED FOR NUCC USE	c. OTHER ACCIDENT? ☐ YES ☐ NO	c. INSURANCE PLAN NAME OR PROGRAM NAME
d. INSURANCE PLAN NAME OR PROGRAM NAME	10d. CLAIM CODES (Designated by NUCC)	d. IS THERE ANOTHER HEALTH BENEFIT PLAN? ☐ YES ☐ NO *If yes*, complete items 9, 9a, and 9d.

FIGURE 11-6 Entry of secondary policy information in Block 9 of primary CMS-1500 claim (primary policy information is entered in Blocks 1, 1a, and 11).

When primary and secondary information is entered on the same CMS-1500 claim, primary insurance policy information is entered in Block 11 through 11c, and an X is entered in the YES box in Block 11d. The secondary insurance policy information is entered in Blocks 9–9d of the same claim (Figure 11-6).

When generating claims from this text and the Workbook, a single CMS-1500 claim is generated when the patient's primary and secondary insurance policies are with the same payer (e.g., BlueCross BlueShield). Multiple claims are generated when the patient is covered by multiple insurance policies with different companies (e.g., Aetna and United Healthcare). For example, if the patient has both primary and secondary insurance with different payers, two claims are generated. The primary claim is completed according to step-by-step instructions, and the secondary claim is completed by following special instructions included in each chapter.

Supplemental Plans

Supplemental plans usually cover the deductible and copay or coinsurance of a primary health insurance policy. Some plans may also cover additional benefits not included in the primary policy. The best known supplemental plans are the *Medigap* plans, which are supplemental plans designed by the federal government but sold by private commercial insurance companies to "cover the gaps in Medicare." Supplemental plan information is entered in Blocks 9–9d on the primary insurance claim (Figure 11-7).

9. OTHER INSURED'S NAME (Last Name, First Name, Middle Initial)
a. OTHER INSURED'S POLICY OR GROUP NUMBER
b. RESERVED FOR NUCC USE
c. RESERVED FOR NUCC USE
d. INSURANCE PLAN NAME OR PROGRAM NAME

FIGURE 11-7 Supplemental plan information is entered in Block 9.

COMMON ERRORS THAT DELAY PROCESSING

> **NOTE:** Because the first character of each ICD-10-CM code is alphabetic *and the letters I and O are used*, carefully enter ICD-10-CM I and O codes (so that the numbers 1 and 0 are not mistakenly entered as the first characters).

After the claim has been completed, check for these common errors:

1. Keyboarding errors or incorrectly entered information, as follows:
   - **Procedure code number**
   - **Diagnosis code number**
   - **Policy identification numbers**
   - **Dates of service**
   - **Federal employer tax ID number (EIN)**
   - **Total amount due on a claim**
   - **Incomplete or incorrect name of the patient or policyholder (name must match the name on the policy; no nicknames)**
2. Omission of the following:
   - **Current diagnosis (because of failure to change the patient's default diagnosis in the computer program)**
   - **Required fourth-, fifth-, sixth-, and/or seventh-characters for ICD-10-CM**
   - **Procedure service dates**
   - **Hospital admission and/or discharge dates**
   - **Name and NPI of the referring provider**
   - **Required prior treatment authorization numbers**
   - **Units of service**
3. Attachments without patient and policy identification information on each page.
4. Failure to properly align the claim form in the printer to ensure that each item fits within the proper field on the claim.
5. Handwritten items or messages on the claim other than required signatures.
6. Failure to properly link each procedure with the correct diagnosis (Block 24E).

FINAL STEPS IN PROCESSING CLAIMS

STEP 1 Double-check each claim for errors and omissions.

STEP 2 Add any necessary attachments.

STEP 3 If required by the payer, obtain the provider's signature on claims.

STEP 4 Post submission of the claim on the patient's account/ledger.

STEP 5 Place a copy of the claim in the practice's claims files.

STEP 6 Submit the claim to the payer.

MAINTAINING INSURANCE CLAIM FILES FOR THE PRACTICE

Medicare *Conditions of Participation (CoP)* require providers to keep copies of any government insurance claims and copies of all attachments filed by the provider for a period of five years, unless state law specifies a longer period. "Providers and billing services filing claims electronically can comply with the federal regulation by retaining the source documents (routing slip, charge slip, encounter form, superbill) from which they generated the claim and the daily summary of claims transmitted and received for" these years.

Although there are no specific laws covering retention of commercial or BlueCross BlueShield claims, health care provider contracts with specific insurance carriers may stipulate a specific time frame for all participating providers. It is good business practice to keep these claims until you are sure all transactions have been completed.

Insurance File Set-Up

Files should be organized in the following manner:

1. File *open assigned cases* by month and payer. (These claims have been sent to the payer, but processing is not complete.)
2. File *closed assigned cases* by year and payer.
3. File *batched remittance advice notices.*
4. File *unassigned or nonparticipating claims* by year and payer.

Processing Assigned Paid Claims

When the remittance advice arrives from the payer, pull the claim(s) and review the payment(s). Make a notation of the amount of payment, remittance advice notice processing date, and applicable batch number on the claim. Claims with no processing errors and payment in full are marked "closed." They are moved to the closed assigned claims file. Single-payment remittance advice notices may be stapled to the claim before filing in the closed assigned claims file. Batched remittance advice notices are refiled and if, after comparing the remittance advice notices and the claim, an error in processing is found, the following steps should be taken:

STEP 1 Write an immediate appeal for reconsideration of the payment.

STEP 2 Make a copy of the original claim, the remittance advice notices, and the written appeal.

STEP 3 Generate a new CMS-1500 claim, and attach it to the remittance advice notices and the appeal. (Black-and-white copies cannot be read by the payer's optical scanner.) Make sure the date in Block 31 matches the date on the original claim.

STEP 4 Mail the appeal and claim to the payer.

STEP 5 Make a notation of the payment (including the check number) on the office copy of the claim.

STEP 6 Refile the claim and attachments in the assigned open claims file.

Federal Privacy Act

The Federal Privacy Act of 1974 prohibits a payer from notifying the provider about payment or rejection of unassigned claims or payments sent directly to the patient/policyholder. If the provider is to assist the patient with the appeal of a claim, the patient must provide a copy of the explanation of benefits (EOB) received from the payer and a letter that explains the error. The letter is to be signed by the patient and policyholder, to give the payer permission to allow the provider to appeal the unassigned claim. The EOB and letter must accompany the provider's request for reconsideration of the claim. If the policyholder writes the appeal, the provider must supply the policyholder with the supporting documentation required to have the claim reconsidered.

SUMMARY

The CMS-1500 paper claim was designed to accommodate optical scanning of paper claims, which requires use of a scanner to convert printed or handwritten characters into text that can be viewed by an optical character reader (OCR). Entering data into the computer using this technology greatly increases productivity associated with claims processing because the need to manually enter data from the claim into a computer is eliminated. The 10-digit *national provider identifier (NPI)* is issued to individual providers and health care organizations and replaces health care provider identifiers (e.g., PIN, UPIN) previously generated by health plans and government programs.

INTERNET LINKS

- Consumer guides for getting and keeping health insurance
  www.healthinsuranceinfo.net
- Insure Kids Now!
  www.insurekidsnow.gov
- National Plan and Provider Enumeration System (NPPES)
  https://nppes.cms.hhs.gov

STUDY CHECKLIST

- ☐ Read this textbook chapter and highlight key concepts.
- ☐ Create an index card for each key term.
- ☐ Access the chapter Internet links to learn more about concepts.
- ☐ Answer the chapter review questions, verifying answers with your instructor.
- ☐ Complete the Workbook chapter, verifying answers with your instructor.
- ☐ Form a study group with classmates to discuss chapter concepts in preparation for an exam.

REVIEW

MULTIPLE CHOICE **Select the most appropriate response.**

1. Physician services for inpatient care are billed on a fee-for-service basis, and physicians submit ______ service/procedure codes to payers.

a. CPT/HCPCS level II
b. DSM-5
c. HCPCS level III
d. ICD-10-CM

2. A patient develops surgical complications and returns to the operating room to undergo surgery related to the original procedure. The return surgery is

a. billed as an additional surgical procedure.
b. coded for office data capture purposes only.
c. included as part of the original procedure.
d. not reported on the CMS-1500 or UB-04.

3. Outpatient surgery and surgeon charges for inpatient surgery are billed according to a global fee, which means that the presurgical evaluation and management, initial and subsequent hospital visits, surgical procedure, discharge visit, and uncomplicated postoperative follow-up care in the surgeon's office are billed as

a. DRG payments.
b. multiple charges.
c. one charge.
d. separate charges.

4. **When one charge covers presurgical evaluation and management, initial and subsequent hospital visits, surgical procedure, the discharge visit, and uncomplicated postoperative follow-up care in the surgeon's office, this is called a(n)**
   a. combined medical/surgical case.
   b. fee-for-service charge.
   c. global fee.
   d. itemized list of separate charges.

5. **Which situation requires the provider to write a letter explaining special circumstances?**
   a. A patient's inpatient stay was prolonged because of medical or psychological complications.
   b. Charges submitted to the payer are lower than the provider's normal fee (e.g., -22 added to code).
   c. Surgery defined as an inpatient procedure was performed while the patient was in the hospital.
   d. Surgery typically categorized as an ASC procedure was performed in a hospital outpatient setting.

6. **The optical character reader (OCR) is a device that is used to**
   a. convert CMS-1500 claims.
   b. enter CMS-1500 claims.
   c. scan CMS-1500 claims.
   d. view CMS-1500 text.

7. **When entering patient claims data onto the CMS-1500 claim, enter alpha characters using**
   a. lower case.
   b. sentence case.
   c. title case.
   d. upper case.

8. **Which statement is an accurate interpretation of the phrase "assignment of benefits"? If signed by the patient on the CMS-1500 claim**
   a. the payer is instructed to reimburse the provider directly.
   b. the payer sends reimbursement for services to the patient.
   c. the provider accepts as payment what the payer reimburses.
   d. the provider cannot collect copayments from the patient.

9. **When an X is entered in one or more of the YES boxes in Block 10 of the CMS-1500 claim, payment might be the responsibility of a ______ insurance company.**
   a. disability
   b. homeowner's
   c. life
   d. managed care

10. **The billing entity, as reported in Block 33 of the CMS-1500 claim, includes the legal business name of the**
   a. acute care hospital.
   b. insurance company.
   c. medical practice.
   d. patient (or spouse).

CHAPTER 12

Commercial Insurance

CHAPTER OUTLINE

Commercial Health Insurance

Automobile, Disability, and Liability Insurance

Commercial Claims

Claims Instructions

Commercial Secondary Coverage

Commercial Group Health Plan Coverage

OBJECTIVES

Upon successful completion of this chapter, you should be able to:

1. Define key terms.
2. Explain the characteristics of commercial insurance plans.
3. Differentiate among automobile, disability, and liability insurance.
4. Differentiate between primary and secondary commercial claims.
5. Complete commercial primary and secondary fee-for-service claims.

KEY TERMS

automobile insurance policy
base period
commercial health insurance
disability insurance
indemnity insurance
liability insurance
lien
subrogation

INTRODUCTION

This chapter contains instructions for completing fee-for-service claims that are generally accepted nationwide by most commercial health insurance companies, including Aetna, United Healthcare, Prudential, Cigna, and others. (Instructions for filing BlueCross BlueShield, Medicare, Medicaid, TRICARE, CHAMPVA, and workers' compensation claims are found in later chapters.)

NOTE: Information presented in this chapter builds on the claims completion instructions presented in Chapter 11.

These instructions apply to *all primary commercial and HMO fee-for-service (noncapitated) claims.* Separate instructions are provided when the patient has secondary and/or supplemental health insurance coverage.

To assist you in learning how to process commercial claims, this chapter includes:

- Separate instructions for primary, secondary, and supplemental commercial insurance plans
- Instructions in a table format for completing claims
- A case study and completed claim to illustrate the instructions
- A case-study exercise, a blank claim, and the completed claim that allows the student to practice completing a claim. The completed claim allows the student to receive immediate feedback. (Additional case-study claims-completion exercises are located in Appendices I and II.)

COMMERCIAL HEALTH INSURANCE

Commercial health insurance covers the medical expenses of individuals (e.g., private health insurance) and groups (e.g., employer group health insurance). Premiums and benefits vary according to the type of plan offered, but group health insurance usually costs less than individual private health insurance.

Individual Health Insurance

Individual health insurance policies are regulated by individual states and include the following:

- *Fee-for-service* (or *indemnity*) *insurance* (traditional health insurance that covers a portion of services, such as inpatient hospitalizations or physician office visits, with the patient paying the remaining costs)
- *High-risk pools* ("last resort" health insurance for individuals who cannot obtain coverage due to a serious medical condition; certain eligibility requirements apply, such as refusal by at least one or two insurance companies)
- *Managed care* (e.g., health maintenance organization, preferred provider organization) (Review Chapter 3 of this textbook for comprehensive information about managed care.)
- *Association health insurance* (offered to members of a professional association and marketed to small business owners as a way to provide coverage to employees; however, these plans are not subject to the same regulations as group health insurance plans and, therefore, are more risky)

Group Health Insurance

Group health insurance is available through employers and other organizations (e.g., labor unions, rural and consumer health cooperatives), and all or part of the premium costs are paid by employers. Employer-based group health insurance:

- Covers all employees, regardless of health status, and cannot be cancelled if an employee becomes ill

- **Is portable, which means if an employee had insurance before enrolling in employer group health insurance**
- **Offers COBRA continuation coverage, which means when an employee resigns (or has another qualifying event) the employee must be offered COBRA continuation coverage that lasts for 18 to 36 months, depending on the employee's situation**
- **Has employer-limited plan options (e.g., prescription drug plan that covers a certain list of medications, called a *formulary*)**

AUTOMOBILE, DISABILITY, AND LIABILITY INSURANCE

Automobile, disability, and liability insurance plans are included in this chapter for informational purposes. (They are not commercial health insurance plans.) It is recommended that financial records for such plans be maintained separately.

Automobile Insurance

Indemnity insurance compensates policyholders for actual economic losses, up to limiting amounts on the insurance policy, and it usually requires the insured to prove losses before payment is made. Automobile insurance is an example of indemnity insurance. An **automobile insurance policy** is a contract between an individual and an insurance company whereby the individual pays a premium and, in exchange, the insurance company agrees to pay for specific car-related financial losses during the term of the policy. Available coverage typically includes the following:

- **Collision (pays for damage to a covered vehicle caused by collision with another object or by an automobile accident; a deductible is required)**
- **Comprehensive (pays for loss of or damage to a covered vehicle, such as that caused by fire, flood, hail, impact with an animal, theft, vandalism, or wind; a deductible may apply)**
- **Emergency road service (pays expenses incurred for having an automobile towed as a result of a breakdown)**
- **Liability (pays for accidental bodily injury and property damage to others, including medical expenses, pain and suffering, lost wages, and other special damages; property damage includes damaged property and may include loss of use)**
- **Medical payments (reimburses medical and funeral expenses for covered individuals, regardless of fault, when those expenses are related to an automobile accident)**
- **Personal injury protection (PIP) (reimburses medical expenses for covered individuals, regardless of fault, for treatment due to an automobile accident; also pays for funeral expenses, lost earnings, rehabilitation, and replacement of services such as child care if a parent is disabled)**
- **Rental reimbursement (pays expenses incurred for renting a car when an automobile is disabled because of an automobile accident)**
- **Underinsured motorist (pays damages when a covered individual is injured in an automobile accident caused by another driver who has insufficient liability insurance—not available in every state)**

NOTE: Not all states require PIP insurance, and reimbursement from the PIP payer is based on individual state laws.

Medical payments and PIP coverage usually reimburse, up to certain limits, the medical expenses of an injured driver and any passengers in a vehicle that was involved in an automobile accident. (Coverage might also be available for pedestrians injured by a vehicle.) The automobile insurance company's *medical adjuster* reviews health care bills submitted to the insurance company for treatment of injuries sustained as the result of a motor vehicle accident to determine coverage. Medical expenses that may be reimbursed include ambulance services; emergency department care; laboratory services; medical supplies (e.g., crutches); physical therapy; prescription drugs; services provided by chiropractors, dentists, physicians, and specialists; x-rays; and so on. (In addition, nonautomobile health insurance policies may include coverage that pays medical bills regardless of who was at fault during an automobile accident.)

Disability Insurance

Disability insurance is defined as reimbursement for income lost as a result of a temporary or permanent illness or injury. When patients are treated for disability diagnoses and other medical problems, separate patient records must be maintained. Offices that generate one patient record for the treatment of disability diagnoses as well as other medical problems often confuse the submission of diagnostic and procedural data for insurance processing. This can result in payment delays and claims denials. For example, under certain circumstances, other insurance coverage (e.g., workers' compensation) is primary to basic medical coverage.

NOTE: Disability insurance generally does not pay for health care services, but provides the disabled person with financial assistance.

Disability benefits are usually paid if an individual:

- Has been unable to do regular or customary work for a certain number of days (number of days depends on the policy)
- Was employed when disabled (e.g., individuals must have lost wages because of a disability)
- Has disability insurance coverage
- Was under the care and treatment of a licensed provider during initial disability; to continue receiving benefits, the individual must remain under care and treatment
- Processes a claim within a certain number of days after the date the individual was disabled (number of days depends on the policy)
- Has the licensed provider complete the disability medical certification document(s)

Individuals may be found ineligible for disability benefits if they:

- Are claiming or receiving unemployment insurance benefits
- Became disabled while committing a crime that resulted in a felony conviction
- Are receiving workers' compensation benefits at a weekly rate equal to or greater than the disability rate
- Are in jail, prison, or a recovery home (e.g., halfway house) because of being convicted of a crime
- Fail to have an independent medical examination when requested to do so

NOTE: The federal Social Security Disability Insurance (SSDI) and Supplemental Security Income (SSI) disability programs provide assistance to people with disabilities. Both programs are administered by the federal Social Security Administration, and only individuals who have a disability and meet medical criteria qualify for benefits under either program. Social Security Disability Insurance pays benefits to you and certain members of your family if you are "insured," meaning that you worked long enough and paid social security taxes. Supplemental Security Income pays benefits based on financial need.

A disability claim begins on the date of disability, and the disability payer calculates an individual's weekly benefit amount using a base period. The **base period** usually covers 12 months and is divided into four consecutive quarters. It includes taxed wages paid approximately 6 to 18 months before the disability claim begins. The base period does not include wages being paid at the time the disability began.

A final payment notice is sent when records show that an individual has been paid through the doctor's estimated date of recovery. If the individual is still disabled, the doctor must submit appropriate documentation so that the case can be reviewed. When an individual has recovered or returned to work and becomes disabled again, a new claim should be submitted along with a report of the dates worked.

Liability Insurance

Although processing of liability insurance claims is not covered in this text, it is important to understand how it influences the processing of health insurance claims. **Liability insurance** is a policy that covers losses to a third party caused by the insured, by an object owned by the insured, or on premises owned by the insured. Liability insurance claims are made to cover the cost of medical care for traumatic injuries and lost wages, and, in many cases, remuneration (compensation) for the "pain and suffering" of the injured party. Most health insurance contracts state that health insurance benefits are secondary to liability insurance. In this situation, the patient is *not* the insured. This means that the insured (e.g., employer) is responsible for payment, and the patient's health insurance plan is billed as secondary (and reimburses only the remaining costs of health care *not* covered by the insured). When negligence by another party is suspected in an injury claim, the health insurance company will not reimburse the patient for medical treatment of the injury until one of two factors is established: (1) it is determined that there was no third-party negligence, or (2) in cases in which third-party negligence did occur, the liability payer determines that the incident is not covered by the negligent party's liability contract.

EXAMPLE: Dr. Small treats Jim Keene in the office for scalp lacerations (cuts) from a work-related injury. Mr. Keene is covered by an employer-sponsored group health plan called HealthCareUSA, and his employer provides workers' compensation insurance coverage for on-the-job injuries.

The insurance claim for treatment of Mr. Keene's lacerations should be submitted to the employer's workers' compensation insurance payer.

If the claim were submitted to HealthCareUSA, it would be subject to review because the diagnosis code submitted would indicate trauma (injury), which activates the review of patient records by an insurance company. Upon reviewing requested copies of patient records, HealthCareUSA would determine that another insurance plan should have been billed for this treatment. HealthCareUSA would deny payment of the claim, and Dr. Small's office would then submit the claim to the workers' compensation carrier payer. In this scenario, a delay in payment for treatment results.

To file a claim with a liability payer, a regular patient billing statement is often used rather than an insurance claim. Be sure to include the name of the policyholder and the liability policy identification numbers. If the liability payer denies payment, a claim is then filed with the patient's health insurance plan. *A photocopy of the written denial of responsibility from the liability payer must accompany the health insurance claim.*

EXAMPLE: California's Medical Care Services operates Medi-Cal, which is California's Medicaid program. Its Third Party Liability Branch is responsible for ensuring that Medi-Cal complies with state and federal laws relating to the legal liability of third parties to reimburse health care services to beneficiaries. The Branch ensures that all reasonable measures are taken to ensure that the Medi-Cal program is the *payer of last resort*. As a result, within one year, the Branch recovered more than $202 million, which was recycled back into the Medi-Cal program.

PURSUING REIMBURSEMENT FROM LIABILITY PAYERS

Third-party payers implement a "pay and chase" method to aggressively pursue the recovery and coordination of payment for health care expenses from liability payers (e.g., malpractice cases, public property injuries, and automobile accidents). Third-party payers review diagnosis codes reported on claims (e.g., trauma) to determine whether a liability payer should be considered primary. Once this initial determination has been made, third-party payers often outsource the recovery and coordination of payment for health care expenses from liability payers to subrogation vendors, which further screen data to identify potential liability claims and recover reimbursement paid on claims by third-party payers.

Subrogation refers to the contractual right of a third-party payer to recover health care expenses from a liable party. (For example, if a patient is injured on the job, the workers' compensation payer is responsible for reimbursing the patient's health care expenses.) Third-party recovery standards for investigation of liability coverage and the process for filing a **lien** (securing a debtor's property as security or payment for a debt) in a potential liability case vary on federal and state bases.

COMMERCIAL CLAIMS

NOTE: As you review the CMS-1500 claims instructions in Table 12-1, refer to the John Q. Public case study (Figure 12-1) and completed CMS-1500 claim (Figure 12-2). The completed claim will also assist you when you begin work on Exercise 12-1.

The commercial claims completion instructions in this chapter are generally recognized nationwide. Some payers may require variations in a few of the blocks, and their requirements should be followed accordingly. Throughout the year, commercial payers implement changes to claims completion requirements that are discovered by providers when claims are denied—commercial payers do not typically make available their billing manual or updates.

Primary claims submission is covered in this chapter's claims completion instructions (Table 12-1), as determined by *one* of the following criteria:

- **The patient is covered by just one commercial plan.**
- **The patient is covered by a large employer group health plan (EGHP), *and* the patient is also a Medicare beneficiary. (EGHP is primary.)**
- **The patient is covered by a small *or* large employer group health plan on which the patient is designated as policyholder (or insured), *and* the patient is also listed as a dependent on another EGHP.**
- **The patient is a child covered by two or more plans. The primary policyholder is the parent whose birthday occurs first in the year.**

REMEMBER!

The birthday rule for a child covered by two or more plans states that the policyholder whose birth month and day occur earlier in the calendar year holds the primary policy when each parent subscribes to a different health insurance plan.

Before working with commercial claims, complete the Review at the end of this chapter.

TABLE 12-1 CMS-1500 claims completion instructions for commercial payers

NOTE: Refer to Chapter 11 for clarification of claims completion (e.g., entering names, mailing addresses, ICD-10-CM codes, diagnosis pointer letters, NPI, and so on).

BLOCK	INSTRUCTIONS
1	Enter an X in the *Other* box if the patient is covered by an individual or family health plan. Or, enter an X in the *Group Health Plan* box if the patient is covered by a group health plan. **NOTE:** The patient is covered by a group health plan if a group number is printed on the patient's insurance identification card (or a group number is included on case studies located in this textbook, workbook, and SimClaim™ software).
1a	Enter the health insurance identification number as it appears on the patient's insurance card. *Do not enter hyphens or spaces in the number.*
2	Enter the patient's last name, first name, and middle initial (separated by commas) (e.g., DOE, JANE, M).
3	Enter the patient's birth date as MM DD YYYY (with spaces). Enter an X in the appropriate box to indicate the patient's gender. If the patient's gender is unknown, leave blank.
4	Enter the policyholder's last name, first name, and middle initial (separated by commas) (e.g., DOE, JANE, M).
5	Enter the patient's mailing address and telephone number. Enter the street address on line 1, enter the city and state on line 2, and enter the five- or nine-digit zip code and phone number on line 3.
6	Enter an X in the appropriate box to indicate the patient's relationship to the policyholder. If the patient is an unmarried domestic partner, enter an X in the *Other* box.
7	Enter the policyholder's mailing address and telephone number. Enter the street address on line 1, enter the city and state on line 2, and enter the five- or nine-digit zip code and phone number on line 3.
8	Leave blank.
9, 9a, 9d	Leave blank. *Blocks 9, 9a, and 9d are completed if the patient has secondary insurance coverage (discussed later in this chapter).* **NOTE:** When the patient is covered by a primary commercial health insurance plan and another health insurance plan (e.g., another commercial health insurance plan, Medicaid, Medicare, and so on), complete Blocks 9, 9a, and 9d.
9b–9c	Leave blank.
10a–c	Enter an X in the appropriate boxes to indicate whether the patient's condition is related to employment, an automobile accident, and/or another type of accident. If an X is entered in the YES box for auto accident, enter the two-character state abbreviation of the patient's residence.
10d	Leave blank.
11	Enter the policyholder's commercial group number if the patient is covered by a group health plan. *Do not enter hyphens or spaces in the group number.* Otherwise, leave blank. **NOTE:** The policyholder's group number refers to the alphanumeric or numeric identifier for group health plan coverage. (The FECA number is the nine-digit alphanumeric identifier assigned to a patient claiming work-related condition(s) under the Federal Employees Compensation Act. The FECA number is discussed in Chapter 17 of this textbook.) (Entering the group number is discussed later in this chapter.)

(continues)

TABLE 12-1 (continued)

BLOCK	INSTRUCTIONS
11a	Enter the policyholder's birth date as MM DD YYYY (with spaces). Enter an X in the appropriate box to indicate the policyholder's gender. If the policyholder's gender is unknown, leave blank.
11b	Leave blank. This is reserved for property and casualty or worker's compensation claims.
11c	Enter the name of the policyholder's commercial health insurance plan.
11d	Enter an X in the NO box (if the patient does not have secondary insurance coverage). **NOTE:** When the patient is covered by a primary commercial health insurance plan and another health insurance plan (e.g., another commercial health insurance plan, Medicaid, Medicare, and so on), enter an X in the YES box (discussed later in this chapter).
12	Enter SIGNATURE ON FILE. Leave the date field blank. (The abbreviation SOF is also acceptable.) **NOTE:** Entering SIGNATURE ON FILE means that the patient has previously signed an authorization to release medical information to the payer, and it is maintained "on file" by the provider. If the patient has not signed an authorization, the patient must sign and date the block.
13	Enter SIGNATURE ON FILE to authorize direct payment to the provider for benefits due the patient. (The abbreviation SOF is also acceptable.)
14	Enter the date as MM DD YYYY (with spaces) to indicate when the patient first experienced signs *or* symptoms of the present illness, actual date of injury, *or* the date of the last menstrual period (LMP) for obstetric visits. *If the date is not documented in the patient's record, but the history indicates an appropriate date (e.g., three weeks ago), simply count back to the approximate date and enter it on the claim.* Enter the applicable qualifier to identify which date is being reported: 431 (onset of current symptoms/illness or injury) *or* 484 (last menstrual period). **EXAMPLE:** For encounter date 06/08/YYYY, when the record documents that the patient was "injured three months ago," enter 03 08 YYYY and 431 in Block 14.
15	Enter the date as MM DD YYYY (with spaces) to indicate that a prior episode of the same or similar illness began, *if documented in the patient's record. Previous pregnancies are not a similar illness.* If a date is entered in Block 15, also enter the applicable qualifier to identify which date is being reported (e.g., 454 for initial treatment). Otherwise, leave blank.
16	Enter dates as MM DD YYYY (with spaces) to indicate the period of time the patient was unable to work in his current occupation, *if documented in the patient's record. An entry in this block might indicate employment-related insurance coverage.* Otherwise, leave blank.
17	If applicable, enter the first name, middle initial (if known), last name, and credentials of the professional who referred, ordered, or supervised health care service(s) or supply(ies) reported on the claim. *Do not enter any punctuation.* In front of the name, enter the applicable qualifier to identify which provider is being reported, as follows: DN (referring provider), DK (ordering provider), or DQ (supervising provider). Otherwise, leave blank.
17a	Leave blank.
17b	Enter the 10-digit national provider identifier (NPI) of the provider entered in Block 17. Otherwise, leave blank.
18	Enter the admission date and discharge date as MM DD YYYY (with spaces) if the patient received inpatient services (e.g., hospital, skilled nursing facility). Otherwise, leave blank. *If the patient has not been discharged at the time the claim is completed, leave the discharge date blank.*

(continues)

TABLE 12-1 (continued)

BLOCK	INSTRUCTIONS
19	Leave blank. **NOTE:** Refer to third-party payer instructions regarding use of this block because some require certain identifiers and appropriate qualifiers that describe the identifier, such as photographs available upon request of the provider (e.g., XP AA).
20	Enter an X in the NO box if all laboratory procedures reported on the claim were performed in the provider's office. Enter an X in the YES box if laboratory procedures reported on the claim were performed by an outside laboratory and billed to the provider. Enter the total amount charged by the outside laboratory in $ CHARGES, and enter the outside laboratory's name, mailing address, and NPI in Block 32. (Charges are entered *without* punctuation. For example, $1,100.00 is entered as 110000 below $ CHARGES.)
21	Enter the ICD-10-CM code for up to 12 diagnoses or conditions treated or medically managed during the encounter. Lines A through L in Block 21 will relate to CPT/HCPCS service/procedure codes reported in Block 24E. In the *ICD Ind* (ICD indicator) box, enter 0 for ICD-10-CM (or 9 for ICD-9-CM).
22	Leave blank. This is reserved for resubmitted claims.
23	Enter prior authorization number, referral number, mammography precertification number, or Clinical Laboratory Improvement Amendments (CLIA) number, as assigned by the payer for the current service. *Do not enter hyphens or spaces in the number.* Otherwise, leave blank.
24A	Enter the date the procedure or service was performed in the FROM column as MM DD YY (with spaces). Enter a date in the TO column *if the procedure or service was performed on consecutive days during a range of dates. Then, enter the number of consecutive days in Block 24G.* **NOTE:** The shaded area in each line is used to enter supplemental information to support reported services *if instructed by the payer to enter such information.* Data entry in Block 24 is limited to reporting six services. *Do not use the shaded lines to report additional services.* If additional services were provided, generate new CMS-1500 claim(s) to report the additional services.
24B	Enter the appropriate two-digit place-of-service (POS) code to identify the location where the reported procedure or service was performed. (Refer to Appendix II for POS codes.)
24C	Leave blank.
24D	Enter the CPT or HCPCS level II code and applicable required modifier(s) for procedures or services performed. *Separate the CPT/HCPCS code and first modifier with one space. Separate additional modifiers with one space each. Up to four modifiers can be entered.*
24E	Enter the diagnosis pointer letter from Block 21 that relates to the procedure/service performed on the date of service.
24F	Enter the fee charged for each reported procedure or service (e.g., 55 00). When multiple procedures or services are reported on the same line, enter the total fee charged. *Do not enter commas, periods, or dollar signs. Do not enter negative amounts. Enter 00 in the cents area if the amount is a whole number.*
24G	Enter the number of days or units for procedures or services reported in Block 24D. *If just one procedure or service was reported in Block 24D, enter a 1 in Block 24G.*
24H	Leave blank. This is reserved for Medicaid claims.
24I	Leave blank. (The NPI abbreviation is preprinted on the CMS-1500 claim.)

(continues)

TABLE 12-1 (continued)

BLOCK	INSTRUCTIONS
24J	Enter the 10-digit NPI for the: • Provider who performed the service *if the provider is a member of a group practice* (Leave blank if the provider is a solo practitioner.) • Supervising provider *if the service was provided incident-to the service of a physician or nonphysician practitioner* **and** *the physician or practitioner who ordered the service did not supervise the provider* (Leave blank if the incident-to service was performed under the supervision of the physician or nonphysician practitioner.) • DMEPOS supplier or outside laboratory *if the physician submits the claim for services provided by the DMEPOS supplier or outside laboratory* (Leave blank if the DMEPOS supplier or outside laboratory submits the claim.) Otherwise, leave blank. **EXAMPLE:** Dr. Sanderlee evaluates Mary Smith during a three-month recheck of her chronic anemia. He performs venipuncture and sends the patient's blood sample to an outside laboratory where a complete blood count test will be performed. Dr. Sanderlee's insurance specialist enters the outside laboratory's NPI in Block 24J because the complete blood count test is reported in Block 24D on that line.
25	Enter the provider's social security number (SSN) or employer identification number (EIN). *Do not enter hyphens or spaces in the number.* Enter an X in the appropriate box to indicate which number is reported. **EXAMPLE:** • Dr. Brilliant is a solo practitioner. Enter Dr. Brilliant's EIN in Block 25. • Dr. Healer practices at the Goodmedicine Clinic. Enter Dr. Healer's EIN in Block 25.
26	Enter the patient's account number as assigned by the provider.
27	Enter an X in the YES box to indicate that the provider agrees to accept assignment. Otherwise, enter an X in the NO box.
28	Enter the total charges for services and/or procedures reported in Block 24. **NOTE:** If multiple claims are submitted for one patient because more than six procedures or services were reported, be sure the total charge reported on each claim accurately represents the total of the items on each submitted claim.
29	Enter the total amount the patient (or another payer) paid *toward covered services only.* If no payment was made, leave blank.
30	Leave blank.
31	Enter the provider's name and credential (e.g., MARY SMITH MD) and the date the claim was completed as MMDDYYYY (without spaces). *Do not enter any punctuation.*
32	Enter the name and address where procedures or services were provided *if at a location other than the provider's office or the patient's home, such as a hospital, outside laboratory facility, skilled nursing facility, or DMEPOS supplier.* Otherwise, leave blank. Enter the name on line 1, the address on line 2, and the city, state, and five- or nine-digit zip code on line 3. *For a nine-digit zip code, enter the hyphen.* **NOTE:** If Block 18 contains dates of service for inpatient care and/or Block 20 contains an X in the YES box, enter the name and address of the facility that provided services.
32a	Enter the 10-digit NPI of the facility or supplier entered in Block 32.
32b	Leave blank.

(continues)

TABLE 12-1 (continued)

BLOCK	INSTRUCTIONS
33	Enter the provider's *billing* name, address, and telephone number. Enter the phone number in the area next to the block title. *Do not enter parentheses for the area code.* Enter the name on line 1, enter the address on line 2, and enter the city, state, and five- or nine-digit zip code on line 3. *For a nine-digit zip code, enter the hyphen.* **EXAMPLE:** • Dr. Brilliant is a solo practitioner. Enter Dr. Brilliant's name, credential, and address in Block 33. • Dr. Healer practices at the Goodmedicine Clinic. Enter Goodmedicine Clinic as the billing provider along with its address and telephone number in Block 33.
33a	Enter the 10-digit NPI of the *billing* provider (e.g., solo practitioner) or group practice (e.g., clinic). **EXAMPLE:** Dr. Healer (NPI: 6789012345) practices at Goodmedicine Clinic (NPI: 3345678901). Enter 3345678901 in Block 33a.
33b	Leave blank.

ERIN A. HELPER, M.D.
101 Medic Drive, Anywhere, NY 12345
(101) 111-1234 (Office) • (101) 111-9292 (Fax)
EIN: 11-1234523
NPI: 1234567890

Case Study

PATIENT INFORMATION:		**INSURANCE INFORMATION:**	
Name:	Public, John Q.	**Patient Number:**	12-1
Address:	10A Senate Avenue	**Place of Service:**	Office
City:	Anywhere	**Primary Insurance Plan:**	Metropolitan
State:	NY	**Primary Insurance Plan ID #:**	225120661W
Zip Code:	12345-1234	**Primary Policyholder:**	Public, John Q.
Telephone:	(101) 201-7891	**Policyholder Date of Birth:**	03-09-1945
Gender:	Male	**Relationship to Patient:**	Self
Date of Birth:	03-09-1945	**Secondary Insurance Plan:**	
Occupation:	Supervisor	**Secondary Insurance Plan ID #:**	
Employer:	Legal Research, Inc.	**Secondary Policyholder:**	

Patient Status ☐ Married ☐ Divorced ☒ Single ☐ Student

DIAGNOSIS INFORMATION

Diagnosis	Code	Diagnosis	Code
1. Bronchopneumonia	J18.0	5.	
2. Urinary frequency	R35.0	6.	
3.		7.	
4.		8.	

PROCEDURE INFORMATION

Description of Procedure or Service	Date	Code	Charge
1. Established patient office visit, level III	01-09-YYYY	99213	75.00
2. Urinalysis, dipstick, automatic microscopy	01-09-YYYY	81001	10.00
3. Chest x-ray, 2 views	01-09-YYYY	71020	50.00
4.			
5.			

SPECIAL NOTES:
• Date symptoms started: 01-05-YYYY
• Recheck: 01/19/YYYY
• Referring physician: Ivan Goodoc, MD (NPI: 3456789012)
• Amount patient paid: $10 copayment

FIGURE 12-1 John Q. Public case study.

CARRIER

HEALTH INSURANCE CLAIM FORM

APPROVED BY NATIONAL UNIFORM CLAIM COMMITTEE (NUCC) 02/12

PICA PICA

1. MEDICARE (Medicare#) MEDICAID (Medicaid#) TRICARE (ID#/DoD#) CHAMPVA (Member ID#) GROUP HEALTH PLAN (ID#) FECA BLK LUNG (ID#) OTHER [X] (ID#)

1a. INSURED'S I.D. NUMBER (For Program in Item 1): 225120661W

2. PATIENT'S NAME (Last Name, First Name, Middle Initial): PUBLIC, JOHN, Q

3. PATIENT'S BIRTH DATE MM DD YY: 03 09 1945 SEX M [X] F

4. INSURED'S NAME (Last Name, First Name, Middle Initial): PUBLIC, JOHN, Q

5. PATIENT'S ADDRESS (No., Street): 10A SENATE AVENUE

6. PATIENT RELATIONSHIP TO INSURED: Self [X] Spouse Child Other

7. INSURED'S ADDRESS (No., Street): 10A SENATE AVENUE

CITY: ANYWHERE STATE: NY

8. RESERVED FOR NUCC USE

CITY: ANYWHERE STATE: NY

ZIP CODE: 12345-1234 TELEPHONE (Include Area Code): (101) 2017891

ZIP CODE: 12345-1234 TELEPHONE (Include Area Code): (101) 2017891

9. OTHER INSURED'S NAME (Last Name, First Name, Middle Initial)

10. IS PATIENT'S CONDITION RELATED TO:

11. INSURED'S POLICY GROUP OR FECA NUMBER

a. OTHER INSURED'S POLICY OR GROUP NUMBER

a. EMPLOYMENT? (Current or Previous) YES [X] NO

a. INSURED'S DATE OF BIRTH MM DD YY: 03 09 1945 SEX M [X] F

b. RESERVED FOR NUCC USE

b. AUTO ACCIDENT? YES [X] NO PLACE (State)

b. OTHER CLAIM ID (Designated by NUCC)

c. RESERVED FOR NUCC USE

c. OTHER ACCIDENT? YES [X] NO

c. INSURANCE PLAN NAME OR PROGRAM NAME: METROPOLITAN

d. INSURANCE PLAN NAME OR PROGRAM NAME

10d. CLAIM CODES (Designated by NUCC)

d. IS THERE ANOTHER HEALTH BENEFIT PLAN? YES [X] NO *If yes, complete items 9, 9a, and 9d.*

READ BACK OF FORM BEFORE COMPLETING & SIGNING THIS FORM.

12. PATIENT'S OR AUTHORIZED PERSON'S SIGNATURE I authorize the release of any medical or other information necessary to process this claim. I also request payment of government benefits either to myself or to the party who accepts assignment below.

SIGNED SIGNATURE ON FILE DATE

13. INSURED'S OR AUTHORIZED PERSON'S SIGNATURE I authorize payment of medical benefits to the undersigned physician or supplier for services described below.

SIGNED SIGNATURE ON FILE

PATIENT AND INSURED INFORMATION

14. DATE OF CURRENT ILLNESS, INJURY, or PREGNANCY (LMP) MM DD YY: 01 05 YYYY QUAL. 431

15. OTHER DATE QUAL. MM DD YY

16. DATES PATIENT UNABLE TO WORK IN CURRENT OCCUPATION MM DD YY FROM TO

17. NAME OF REFERRING PROVIDER OR OTHER SOURCE: DN IVAN GOODOC MD

17a.

17b. NPI 3456789012

18. HOSPITALIZATION DATES RELATED TO CURRENT SERVICES MM DD YY FROM TO

19. ADDITIONAL CLAIM INFORMATION (Designated by NUCC)

20. OUTSIDE LAB? YES [X] NO $ CHARGES

21. DIAGNOSIS OR NATURE OF ILLNESS OR INJURY Relate A-L to service line below (24E) ICD Ind. 0

A. J18.0 B. R35.0 C. D.
E. F. G. H.
I. J. K. L.

22. RESUBMISSION CODE ORIGINAL REF. NO.

23. PRIOR AUTHORIZATION NUMBER

	24. A. DATE(S) OF SERVICE From MM DD YY	To MM DD YY	B. PLACE OF SERVICE	C. EMG	D. PROCEDURES, SERVICES, OR SUPPLIES (Explain Unusual Circumstances) CPT/HCPCS	MODIFIER	E. DIAGNOSIS POINTER	F. $ CHARGES	G. DAYS OR UNITS	H. EPSDT Family Plan	I. ID. QUAL.	J. RENDERING PROVIDER ID. #
1	01 09 YY		11		99213		A	75 00	1		NPI	
2	01 09 YY		11		81001		B	10 00	1		NPI	
3	01 09 YY		11		71020		A	50 00	1		NPI	
4											NPI	
5											NPI	
6											NPI	

25. FEDERAL TAX I.D. NUMBER SSN EIN [X]: 111234523

26. PATIENT'S ACCOUNT NO.: 12-1

27. ACCEPT ASSIGNMENT? (For govt. claims, see back) [X] YES NO

28. TOTAL CHARGE $ 135 00

29. AMOUNT PAID $ 10 00

30. Rsvd for NUCC Use

31. SIGNATURE OF PHYSICIAN OR SUPPLIER INCLUDING DEGREES OR CREDENTIALS (I certify that the statements on the reverse apply to this bill and are made a part thereof.)

ERIN A HELPER MD MMDDYYYY
SIGNED DATE

32. SERVICE FACILITY LOCATION INFORMATION

a. NPI b.

33. BILLING PROVIDER INFO & PH # (101) 1111234
ERIN A HELPER MD
101 MEDIC DRIVE
ANYWHERE NY 12345

a. 1234567890 b.

PHYSICIAN OR SUPPLIER INFORMATION

NUCC Instruction Manual available at: www.nucc.org *PLEASE PRINT OR TYPE*

FIGURE 12-2 Completed John Q. Public primary claim.

EXERCISE 12-1

Completing the Mary S. Patient CMS-1500 Claim

1. Obtain a blank claim by making a copy of the CMS-1500 claim form in Appendix III.
2. Review the Mary S. Patient case study (Figure 12-3).
3. Select the information needed for Blocks 1 through 33, and enter the required information on the blank CMS-1500 claim using optical scanning guidelines.
4. Review the completed claim to be sure that all required blocks are completed accurately.
5. Compare your claim with the completed Mary S. Patient claim (Figure 12-4).

ERIN A. HELPER, M.D.
101 Medic Drive, Anywhere, NY 12345
(101) 111-1234 (Office) • (101) 111-9292 (Fax)
EIN: 11-1234523
NPI: 1234567890

Case Study

PATIENT INFORMATION:		**INSURANCE INFORMATION:**	
Name:	Patient, Mary S.	**Patient Number:**	12-2
Address:	91 Home Street	**Place of Service:**	Hospital Inpatient
City:	Nowhere	**Primary Insurance Plan:**	Conn General
State:	NY	**Primary Insurance Plan ID #:**	222017681
Zip Code:	12367-1234	**Primary Policyholder:**	James W. Patient
Telephone:	(101) 201-8989	**Policyholder Date of Birth:**	03-01-1948
Gender:	Female	**Employer:**	Alstom
Date of Birth:	10-10-1959	**Relationship to Patient:**	Spouse
Occupation:	Homemaker	**Secondary Insurance Plan:**	
Employer:	Alstom	**Secondary Insurance Plan ID #:**	
		Secondary Policyholder:	

Patient Status ☒ Married ☐ Divorced ☐ Single ☐ Student

DIAGNOSIS INFORMATION

Diagnosis	**Code**	**Diagnosis**	**Code**
1. Abnormal ECG	R94.30	5.	
2. Prinzmetal angina	I20.1	6.	
3. Familial combined hyperlipidemia	E78.4	7.	

PROCEDURE INFORMATION

Description of Procedure or Service	**Date**	**Code**	**Charge**
1. Initial hospital visit, level III	01-07-YYYY	99223	150.00
2. Subsequent hospital visit, level I	01-08-YYYY	99231	75.00
3. Discharge visit, 30 minutes	01-09-YYYY	99238	75.00
4.			
5.			

SPECIAL NOTES:
- Date symptoms started: 01-07-YYYY
- Referred to: Dr. Cardiac for Thallium Stress test on 01-10-YYYY
- Recheck: 01/17/YYYY
- Hospital Information: Goodmedicine Hospital, Anywhere Street, Anywhere, NY 12345-1234 (NPI: 2345678901)

FIGURE 12-3 Mary S. Patient case study.

HEALTH INSURANCE CLAIM FORM

APPROVED BY NATIONAL UNIFORM CLAIM COMMITTEE (NUCC) 02/12

PICA | PICA

CARRIER

1. MEDICARE (Medicare#) | MEDICAID (Medicaid#) | TRICARE (ID#/DoD#) | CHAMPVA (Member ID#) | GROUP HEALTH PLAN (ID#) | FECA BLK LUNG (ID#) | OTHER [X] (ID#)

1a. INSURED'S I.D. NUMBER (For Program in Item 1): 222017681

2. PATIENT'S NAME (Last Name, First Name, Middle Initial): PATIENT, MARY, S

3. PATIENT'S BIRTH DATE MM DD YY: 10 10 1959 — SEX M [ ] F [X]

4. INSURED'S NAME (Last Name, First Name, Middle Initial): PATIENT, MARY, S

5. PATIENT'S ADDRESS (No., Street): 91 HOME STREET

6. PATIENT RELATIONSHIP TO INSURED: Self [ ] Spouse [X] Child [ ] Other [ ]

7. INSURED'S ADDRESS (No., Street): 91 HOME STREET

CITY: NOWHERE — STATE: NY

8. RESERVED FOR NUCC USE

CITY: NOWHERE — STATE: NY

ZIP CODE: 12367-1234 — TELEPHONE (Include Area Code): (101) 2018989

ZIP CODE: 12367-1234 — TELEPHONE (Include Area Code): (101) 2018989

9. OTHER INSURED'S NAME (Last Name, First Name, Middle Initial)

10. IS PATIENT'S CONDITION RELATED TO:

11. INSURED'S POLICY GROUP OR FECA NUMBER

a. OTHER INSURED'S POLICY OR GROUP NUMBER

a. EMPLOYMENT? (Current or Previous) [ ] YES [X] NO

a. INSURED'S DATE OF BIRTH MM DD YY: 03 01 1948 — SEX M [X] F [ ]

b. RESERVED FOR NUCC USE

b. AUTO ACCIDENT? [ ] YES [X] NO — PLACE (State)

b. OTHER CLAIM ID (Designated by NUCC)

c. RESERVED FOR NUCC USE

c. OTHER ACCIDENT? [ ] YES [X] NO

c. INSURANCE PLAN NAME OR PROGRAM NAME: CONN GENERAL

d. INSURANCE PLAN NAME OR PROGRAM NAME

10d. CLAIM CODES (Designated by NUCC)

d. IS THERE ANOTHER HEALTH BENEFIT PLAN? [ ] YES [X] NO *If yes, complete items 9, 9a, and 9d.*

READ BACK OF FORM BEFORE COMPLETING & SIGNING THIS FORM.

12. PATIENT'S OR AUTHORIZED PERSON'S SIGNATURE I authorize the release of any medical or other information necessary to process this claim. I also request payment of government benefits either to myself or to the party who accepts assignment below.

SIGNED SIGNATURE ON FILE — DATE

13. INSURED'S OR AUTHORIZED PERSON'S SIGNATURE I authorize payment of medical benefits to the undersigned physician or supplier for services described below.

SIGNED SIGNATURE ON FILE

PATIENT AND INSURED INFORMATION

14. DATE OF CURRENT ILLNESS, INJURY, or PREGNANCY (LMP) MM DD YY: 01 07 YYYY — QUAL. 431

15. OTHER DATE QUAL. MM DD YY

16. DATES PATIENT UNABLE TO WORK IN CURRENT OCCUPATION MM DD YY FROM — TO

17. NAME OF REFERRING PROVIDER OR OTHER SOURCE — 17a. — 17b. NPI

18. HOSPITALIZATION DATES RELATED TO CURRENT SERVICES MM DD YY FROM 01 07 YYYY TO 01 09 YYYY

19. ADDITIONAL CLAIM INFORMATION (Designated by NUCC)

20. OUTSIDE LAB? [ ] YES [X] NO — $ CHARGES

21. DIAGNOSIS OR NATURE OF ILLNESS OR INJURY Relate A-L to service line below (24E) — ICD Ind. 0

A. R94.30 B. I20.1 C. E78.4 D.

E. F. G. H.

I. J. K. L.

22. RESUBMISSION CODE — ORIGINAL REF. NO.

23. PRIOR AUTHORIZATION NUMBER

	24. A. DATE(S) OF SERVICE From MM	DD	YY	To MM	DD	YY	B. PLACE OF SERVICE	C. EMG	D. PROCEDURES, SERVICES, OR SUPPLIES (Explain Unusual Circumstances) CPT/HCPCS	MODIFIER	E. DIAGNOSIS POINTER	F. $ CHARGES	G. DAYS OR UNITS	H. EPSDT Family Plan	I. ID. QUAL.	J. RENDERING PROVIDER ID. #
1	01	07	YY				21		99223		A	150 00	1		NPI	
2	01	08	YY				21		99231		A	75 00	1		NPI	
3	01	09	YY				21		99238		A	75 00	1		NPI	
4															NPI	
5															NPI	
6															NPI	

25. FEDERAL TAX I.D. NUMBER: 111234523 — SSN [ ] EIN [X]

26. PATIENT'S ACCOUNT NO.: 12-2

27. ACCEPT ASSIGNMENT? (For govt. claims, see back) [X] YES [ ] NO

28. TOTAL CHARGE: $ 300 00

29. AMOUNT PAID: $

30. Rsvd for NUCC Use

31. SIGNATURE OF PHYSICIAN OR SUPPLIER INCLUDING DEGREES OR CREDENTIALS (I certify that the statements on the reverse apply to this bill and are made a part thereof.)

SIGNED ERIN A HELPER MD — DATE MMDDYYYY

32. SERVICE FACILITY LOCATION INFORMATION
GOODMEDICINE HOSPITAL
ANYWHERE STREET
ANYWHERE NY 12345-1234
a. 2345678901 b.

33. BILLING PROVIDER INFO & PH # (101) 1111234
ERIN A HELPER MD
101 MEDIC DRIVE
ANYWHERE NY 12345
a. 1234567890 b.

PHYSICIAN OR SUPPLIER INFORMATION

NUCC Instruction Manual available at: www.nucc.org — *PLEASE PRINT OR TYPE*

FIGURE 12-4 Completed Mary S. Patient primary claim.

CLAIMS INSTRUCTIONS

Additional commercial claim case studies are found in Appendices I and II of this text.

COMMERCIAL SECONDARY COVERAGE

Modifications are made to the primary CMS-1500 claim instructions when patients are covered by primary and secondary or supplemental health insurance plans. Secondary health insurance plans provide coverage similar to that of primary plans; supplemental plans usually cover only deductible, copayment, and coinsurance expenses.

When the same payer issues the primary and secondary or supplemental policies (Table 12-2), submit just one CMS-1500 claim (Figure 12-5). If the payers for the primary and secondary or supplemental policies are different (Table 12-3), submit a CMS-1500 claim to the primary payer. When the primary payer has processed the claim (e.g., provider is reimbursed), generate a second CMS-1500 claim (Figure 12-6) to send to the secondary payer, and include a copy of the primary payer's remittance advice.

TABLE 12-2 Modifications to commercial primary CMS-1500 claims completion instructions when the same commercial health insurance company provides a secondary or supplemental policy (Refer to Table 12-1 for primary CMS-1500 claims completion instructions.)

BLOCK	INSTRUCTIONS
9	Enter the secondary or supplemental policyholder's last name, first name, and middle initial (if known) (separated by commas).
9a	Enter the secondary or supplemental policyholder's policy or group number.
9d	Enter the name of the secondary or supplemental policyholder's commercial health insurance plan.
11d	Enter an X in the YES box.

Courtesy of the Centers for Medicare & Medicaid Services, www.cms.gov

EXERCISE 12-2

Filing Commercial Secondary Claims When the Same Commercial Payer Provides Primary and Secondary Coverage

1. Obtain a blank claim by making a copy of the CMS-1500 claim form in Appendix III.
2. Underline Blocks 9, 9a, 9d, and 11d on the claim.
3. Refer to the Mary S. Patient case study (Figure 12-3). Enter the following additional information in the appropriate blocks for the secondary policy (Table 12-2):
   Conn General ID # 22335544
   Policyholder: James W. Patient
   Birth date: 03/01/48
   Relationship: Spouse
4. Review the completed claim to be sure all required blocks are properly completed.
5. Compare your claim with the completed Mary S. Patient claim in Figure 12-5.

HEALTH INSURANCE CLAIM FORM

APPROVED BY NATIONAL UNIFORM CLAIM COMMITTEE (NUCC) 02/12

PICA | PICA

CARRIER

PATIENT AND INSURED INFORMATION

1. MEDICARE (Medicare#) MEDICAID (Medicaid#) TRICARE (ID#/DoD#) CHAMPVA (Member ID#) GROUP HEALTH PLAN (ID#) FECA BLK LUNG (ID#) OTHER [X] (ID#)

1a. INSURED'S I.D. NUMBER (For Program in Item 1): 222017681

2. PATIENT'S NAME (Last Name, First Name, Middle Initial): PATIENT, MARY, S

3. PATIENT'S BIRTH DATE MM DD YY: 10 10 1959 SEX M [ ] F [X]

4. INSURED'S NAME (Last Name, First Name, Middle Initial): PATIENT, JAMES, W

5. PATIENT'S ADDRESS (No., Street): 91 HOME STREET

6. PATIENT RELATIONSHIP TO INSURED: Self [ ] Spouse [X] Child [ ] Other [ ]

7. INSURED'S ADDRESS (No., Street): 91 HOME STREET

CITY: NOWHERE STATE: NY

8. RESERVED FOR NUCC USE

CITY: NOWHERE STATE: NY

ZIP CODE: 12367-1234 TELEPHONE (Include Area Code): (101) 2018989

ZIP CODE: 12367-1234 TELEPHONE (Include Area Code): (101) 2018989

9. OTHER INSURED'S NAME (Last Name, First Name, Middle Initial): PATIENT, JAMES, W

10. IS PATIENT'S CONDITION RELATED TO:

11. INSURED'S POLICY GROUP OR FECA NUMBER

a. OTHER INSURED'S POLICY OR GROUP NUMBER: 22335544

a. EMPLOYMENT? (Current or Previous) [ ] YES [X] NO

a. INSURED'S DATE OF BIRTH MM DD YY: 03 01 1948 SEX M [X] F [ ]

b. RESERVED FOR NUCC USE

b. AUTO ACCIDENT? [ ] YES [X] NO PLACE (State)

b. OTHER CLAIM ID (Designated by NUCC)

c. RESERVED FOR NUCC USE

c. OTHER ACCIDENT? [ ] YES [X] NO

c. INSURANCE PLAN NAME OR PROGRAM NAME: CONN GENERAL

d. INSURANCE PLAN NAME OR PROGRAM NAME: CONN GENERAL

10d. CLAIM CODES (Designated by NUCC)

d. IS THERE ANOTHER HEALTH BENEFIT PLAN? [X] YES [ ] NO *If yes, complete items 9, 9a, and 9d.*

READ BACK OF FORM BEFORE COMPLETING & SIGNING THIS FORM.

12. PATIENT'S OR AUTHORIZED PERSON'S SIGNATURE I authorize the release of any medical or other information necessary to process this claim. I also request payment of government benefits either to myself or to the party who accepts assignment below.

SIGNED SIGNATURE ON FILE DATE

13. INSURED'S OR AUTHORIZED PERSON'S SIGNATURE I authorize payment of medical benefits to the undersigned physician or supplier for services described below.

SIGNED SIGNATURE ON FILE

PHYSICIAN OR SUPPLIER INFORMATION

14. DATE OF CURRENT ILLNESS, INJURY, or PREGNANCY (LMP) MM DD YY: 01 07 YYYY QUAL. 431

15. OTHER DATE QUAL. MM DD YY

16. DATES PATIENT UNABLE TO WORK IN CURRENT OCCUPATION FROM TO

17. NAME OF REFERRING PROVIDER OR OTHER SOURCE 17a. 17b. NPI

18. HOSPITALIZATION DATES RELATED TO CURRENT SERVICES FROM 01 07 YYYY TO 01 09 YYYY

19. ADDITIONAL CLAIM INFORMATION (Designated by NUCC)

20. OUTSIDE LAB? [ ] YES [X] NO $ CHARGES

21. DIAGNOSIS OR NATURE OF ILLNESS OR INJURY Relate A-L to service line below (24E) ICD Ind. 0

A. R94.30 B. I20.1 C. E78.4 D.
E. F. G. H.
I. J. K. L.

22. RESUBMISSION CODE ORIGINAL REF. NO.

23. PRIOR AUTHORIZATION NUMBER

	24. A. DATE(S) OF SERVICE From MM DD YY	To MM DD YY	B. PLACE OF SERVICE	C. EMG	D. PROCEDURES, SERVICES, OR SUPPLIES CPT/HCPCS	MODIFIER	E. DIAGNOSIS POINTER	F. $ CHARGES	G. DAYS OR UNITS	H. EPSDT Family Plan	I. ID. QUAL.	J. RENDERING PROVIDER ID. #
1	01 07 YY		21		99223		A	150 00	1		NPI	
2	01 08 YY		21		99231		A	75 00	1		NPI	
3	01 09 YY		21		99238		A	75 00	1		NPI	
4											NPI	
5											NPI	
6											NPI	

25. FEDERAL TAX I.D. NUMBER: 111234523 SSN [ ] EIN [X]

26. PATIENT'S ACCOUNT NO.: 12-2

27. ACCEPT ASSIGNMENT? (For govt. claims, see back) [X] YES [ ] NO

28. TOTAL CHARGE: $ 300 00

29. AMOUNT PAID: $

30. Rsvd for NUCC Use

31. SIGNATURE OF PHYSICIAN OR SUPPLIER INCLUDING DEGREES OR CREDENTIALS (I certify that the statements on the reverse apply to this bill and are made a part thereof.)

SIGNED ERIN A HELPER MD DATE MMDDYYYY

32. SERVICE FACILITY LOCATION INFORMATION
GOODMEDICINE HOSPITAL
ANYWHERE STREET
ANYWHERE NY 12345-1234

a. 2345678901 b.

33. BILLING PROVIDER INFO & PH # (101) 1111234
ERIN A HELPER MD
101 MEDIC DRIVE
ANYWHERE NY 12345

a. 1234567890 b.

NUCC Instruction Manual available at: www.nucc.org PLEASE PRINT OR TYPE

FIGURE 12-5 Completed Mary S. Patient claim when primary and secondary payers are the same.

TABLE 12-3 Modifications to commercial primary CMS-1500 claims completion instructions when a different commercial health insurance company provides a secondary or supplemental policy

BLOCK	INSTRUCTIONS
	NOTE: If the primary and secondary/supplemental payers are the same, do not generate a second CMS-1500 claim. Instead, modify the primary CMS-1500 claim using the instructions in Table 12-2.
1a	Enter the secondary or supplemental policyholder's health insurance identification number (HICN) as it appears on the insurance card. *Do not enter hyphens or spaces in the number.*
4	Enter the secondary or supplemental policyholder's last name, first name, and middle initial (separated by commas).
7	Enter the secondary or supplemental policyholder's mailing address and telephone number.
9	Enter the primary policyholder's last name, first name, and middle initial (if known) (separated by commas).
9a	Enter the primary policyholder's policy or group number.
9d	Enter the name of the primary policyholder's commercial health insurance plan.
11	Enter the secondary or supplemental policyholder's policy or group number. *Do not enter hyphens or spaces in the policy or group number.*
11a	Enter the secondary or supplemental policyholder's birth date as MM DD YYYY (with spaces). Enter an X in the appropriate box to indicate the policyholder's gender. If the policyholder's gender is unknown, leave blank.
11c	Enter the name of the secondary or supplemental policyholder's commercial health insurance plan.
11d	Enter an X in the YES box.
26	Add an S to the patient's account number to indicate the secondary policy.

Courtesy of the Centers for Medicare & Medicaid Services, www.cms.gov

EXERCISE 12-3

Filing Commercial Secondary Claims When Different Commercial Payers Provide Primary and Secondary Coverage

1. Obtain a blank claim by making a copy of the CMS-1500 claim form in Appendix III.
2. Underline Blocks 1a, 4, 7, 9, 9a, 9d, 11, 11a, 11c, 11d, and 26 on the claim.
3. Refer to the Mary S. Patient case study (Figure 12-3). Enter the following information in the appropriate blocks for the secondary policy:
   Aetna ID # 987654321
   Policyholder: James W. Patient
   Birth date: 03/01/48
   Relationship: Spouse
   Add an "S" to the patient's account number in Block 26 (e.g., 12-2S)
4. Review the completed claim to be sure all required blocks are properly completed.
5. Compare your claim with the completed Mary S. Patient claim in Figure 12-6.

HEALTH INSURANCE CLAIM FORM

APPROVED BY NATIONAL UNIFORM CLAIM COMMITTEE (NUCC) 02/12

PICA — PICA — CARRIER

1. MEDICARE (Medicare#) / MEDICAID (Medicaid#) / TRICARE (ID#/DoD#) / CHAMPVA (Member ID#) / GROUP HEALTH PLAN (ID#) / FECA BLK LUNG (ID#) / OTHER (ID#): [X] OTHER

1a. INSURED'S I.D. NUMBER (For Program in Item 1): 987654321

2. PATIENT'S NAME (Last Name, First Name, Middle Initial): PATIENT, MARY, S

3. PATIENT'S BIRTH DATE (MM DD YY): 10 10 1959 — SEX: M [ ] F [X]

4. INSURED'S NAME (Last Name, First Name, Middle Initial): PATIENT, JAMES, W

5. PATIENT'S ADDRESS (No., Street): 91 HOME STREET — CITY: NOWHERE — STATE: NY — ZIP CODE: 12367-1234 — TELEPHONE (Include Area Code): (101) 2018989

6. PATIENT RELATIONSHIP TO INSURED: Self [ ] Spouse [X] Child [ ] Other [ ]

7. INSURED'S ADDRESS (No., Street): 91 HOME STREET — CITY: NOWHERE — STATE: NY — ZIP CODE: 12367-1234 — TELEPHONE (Include Area Code): (101) 2018989

8. RESERVED FOR NUCC USE

9. OTHER INSURED'S NAME (Last Name, First Name, Middle Initial): PATIENT, JAMES, W

a. OTHER INSURED'S POLICY OR GROUP NUMBER: 222017681

b. RESERVED FOR NUCC USE

c. RESERVED FOR NUCC USE

d. INSURANCE PLAN NAME OR PROGRAM NAME: CONN GENERAL

10. IS PATIENT'S CONDITION RELATED TO:
a. EMPLOYMENT? (Current or Previous) YES [ ] NO [X]
b. AUTO ACCIDENT? YES [ ] NO [X] PLACE (State)
c. OTHER ACCIDENT? YES [ ] NO [X]
10d. CLAIM CODES (Designated by NUCC)

11. INSURED'S POLICY GROUP OR FECA NUMBER
a. INSURED'S DATE OF BIRTH (MM DD YY): 03 01 1948 — SEX: M [X] F [ ]
b. OTHER CLAIM ID (Designated by NUCC)
c. INSURANCE PLAN NAME OR PROGRAM NAME: AETNA
d. IS THERE ANOTHER HEALTH BENEFIT PLAN? [X] YES [ ] NO *If yes, complete items 9, 9a, and 9d.*

READ BACK OF FORM BEFORE COMPLETING & SIGNING THIS FORM.

12. PATIENT'S OR AUTHORIZED PERSON'S SIGNATURE I authorize the release of any medical or other information necessary to process this claim. I also request payment of government benefits either to myself or to the party who accepts assignment below.
SIGNED SIGNATURE ON FILE DATE

13. INSURED'S OR AUTHORIZED PERSON'S SIGNATURE I authorize payment of medical benefits to the undersigned physician or supplier for services described below.
SIGNED SIGNATURE ON FILE

PATIENT AND INSURED INFORMATION

14. DATE OF CURRENT ILLNESS, INJURY, or PREGNANCY (LMP) (MM DD YY): 01 07 YYYY QUAL. 431

15. OTHER DATE QUAL. MM DD YY

16. DATES PATIENT UNABLE TO WORK IN CURRENT OCCUPATION FROM TO

17. NAME OF REFERRING PROVIDER OR OTHER SOURCE — 17a. — 17b. NPI

18. HOSPITALIZATION DATES RELATED TO CURRENT SERVICES FROM 01 07 YYYY TO 01 09 YYYY

19. ADDITIONAL CLAIM INFORMATION (Designated by NUCC)

20. OUTSIDE LAB? [ ] YES [X] NO — $ CHARGES

21. DIAGNOSIS OR NATURE OF ILLNESS OR INJURY Relate A-L to service line below (24E) ICD Ind. 0
A. R94.30 B. I20.1 C. E78.4 D.
E. F. G. H.
I. J. K. L.

22. RESUBMISSION CODE — ORIGINAL REF. NO.

23. PRIOR AUTHORIZATION NUMBER

	24. A. DATE(S) OF SERVICE From MM DD YY	To MM DD YY	B. PLACE OF SERVICE	C. EMG	D. PROCEDURES, SERVICES, OR SUPPLIES (Explain Unusual Circumstances) CPT/HCPCS	MODIFIER	E. DIAGNOSIS POINTER	F. $ CHARGES	G. DAYS OR UNITS	H. EPSDT Family Plan	I. ID. QUAL.	J. RENDERING PROVIDER ID. #
1	01 07 YY		21		99223		A	150 00	1		NPI	
2	01 08 YY		21		99231		A	75 00	1		NPI	
3	01 09 YY		21		99238		A	75 00	1		NPI	
4											NPI	
5											NPI	
6											NPI	

25. FEDERAL TAX I.D. NUMBER: 111234523 — SSN [ ] EIN [X]

26. PATIENT'S ACCOUNT NO.: 12-2S

27. ACCEPT ASSIGNMENT? (For govt. claims, see back) [X] YES [ ] NO

28. TOTAL CHARGE: $ 300 00

29. AMOUNT PAID: $

30. Rsvd for NUCC Use

31. SIGNATURE OF PHYSICIAN OR SUPPLIER INCLUDING DEGREES OR CREDENTIALS (I certify that the statements on the reverse apply to this bill and are made a part thereof.)
ERIN A HELPER MD MMDDYYYY
SIGNED DATE

32. SERVICE FACILITY LOCATION INFORMATION
GOODMEDICINE HOSPITAL
ANYWHERE STREET
ANYWHERE NY 12345-1234
a. 2345678901 b.

33. BILLING PROVIDER INFO & PH # (101) 1111234
ERIN A HELPER MD
101 MEDIC DRIVE
ANYWHERE NY 12345
a. 1234567890 b.

PHYSICIAN OR SUPPLIER INFORMATION

NUCC Instruction Manual available at: www.nucc.org — PLEASE PRINT OR TYPE

FIGURE 12-6 Completed Mary S. Patient claim when primary and secondary payers are different.

COMMERCIAL GROUP HEALTH PLAN COVERAGE

NOTE: Individual and family health plans cover individuals and their families, and each person covered must qualify individually. Group health plans are required to accept employees and their family members, and may be less expensive than individual/family health plans.

Employers include group health plan coverage (Table 12-4) in fringe benefit programs to retain high-quality employees and ensure productivity by providing preventive medical care to create a healthy workforce. There are many group health plan options available to employers, including various payment options from paying 100 percent of annual premium costs for each employee to sharing a percentage (e.g., 80 percent) of the annual insurance costs with employees.

EXAMPLE: Linda Ryan is employed by a public school, which provides individual and family group health plan coverage. Her employer pays 80 percent of her annual premium. Linda selected family coverage for her group health plan, which means her employer pays $9,600 per year (of the $12,000 annual premium). Linda is responsible for 20 percent of the annual premium (or $2,400), which means $92.31 is deducted from each of her 26 biweekly paychecks. (Copayments and deductibles also apply to her group health plan, such as a $20 copayment for office visits, a $50 copayment for hospital emergency department visits, and a $35 copayment for hospital outpatient ancillary tests.)

TABLE 12-4 Modifications to commercial primary CMS-1500 claims completion instructions when the policy is a group health plan (Refer to Table 12-1 for primary CMS-1500 claims completion instructions.)

BLOCK	INSTRUCTIONS
1	Enter an X in the Group Health Plans box.
11	Enter the policyholder's group number. **NOTE:** Locate the group number on the policyholder's insurance identification card (or in case studies located in this textbook, workbook, and SimClaim software).

Courtesy of the Centers for Medicare & Medicaid Services, www.cms.gov

EXERCISE 12-4

Filing Group Health Plan Claims

1. Obtain a blank claim by making a copy of the CMS-1500 claim form in Appendix III.
2. Underline Blocks 1 and 11 on the claim.
3. Refer to the Mary S. Patient case study (see Figure 12-3), and complete the group health plan claim. Enter the following information in the appropriate blocks for the group health plan policy:

   Group number: 123A
4. Review the completed claim to be sure all required blocks are properly completed.
5. Compare your claim with the completed Mary S. Patient claim in Figure 12-7.

HEALTH INSURANCE CLAIM FORM

APPROVED BY NATIONAL UNIFORM CLAIM COMMITTEE (NUCC) 02/12

PICA | PICA

CARRIER

1. MEDICARE (Medicare#) ☐ MEDICAID (Medicaid#) ☐ TRICARE (ID#/DoD#) ☐ CHAMPVA (Member ID#) ☐ GROUP HEALTH PLAN (ID#) ☒ FECA BLK LUNG (ID#) ☐ OTHER (ID#) ☐

1a. INSURED'S I.D. NUMBER (For Program in Item 1): 987654321

2. PATIENT'S NAME (Last Name, First Name, Middle Initial): PATIENT, MARY, S

3. PATIENT'S BIRTH DATE MM DD YY: 10 10 1959 SEX M ☐ F ☒

4. INSURED'S NAME (Last Name, First Name, Middle Initial): PATIENT, MARY, S

5. PATIENT'S ADDRESS (No., Street): 91 HOME STREET

6. PATIENT RELATIONSHIP TO INSURED: Self ☐ Spouse ☒ Child ☐ Other ☐

7. INSURED'S ADDRESS (No., Street): 91 HOME STREET

CITY: NOWHERE STATE: NY

8. RESERVED FOR NUCC USE

CITY: NOWHERE STATE: NY

ZIP CODE: 12367-1234 TELEPHONE (Include Area Code): (101) 2018989

ZIP CODE: 12367-1234 TELEPHONE (Include Area Code): (101) 2018989

9. OTHER INSURED'S NAME (Last Name, First Name, Middle Initial): PATIENT, JAMES, W

10. IS PATIENT'S CONDITION RELATED TO:

11. INSURED'S POLICY GROUP OR FECA NUMBER: 123A

a. OTHER INSURED'S POLICY OR GROUP NUMBER: 222017681

a. EMPLOYMENT? (Current or Previous) ☐ YES ☒ NO

a. INSURED'S DATE OF BIRTH MM DD YY: 03 01 1948 SEX M ☒ F ☐

b. RESERVED FOR NUCC USE

b. AUTO ACCIDENT? ☐ YES ☒ NO PLACE (State)

b. OTHER CLAIM ID (Designated by NUCC)

c. RESERVED FOR NUCC USE

c. OTHER ACCIDENT? ☐ YES ☒ NO

c. INSURANCE PLAN NAME OR PROGRAM NAME: AETNA

d. INSURANCE PLAN NAME OR PROGRAM NAME: CONN GENERAL

10d. CLAIM CODES (Designated by NUCC)

d. IS THERE ANOTHER HEALTH BENEFIT PLAN? ☒ YES ☐ NO *If yes*, complete items 9, 9a, and 9d.

READ BACK OF FORM BEFORE COMPLETING & SIGNING THIS FORM.

12. PATIENT'S OR AUTHORIZED PERSON'S SIGNATURE I authorize the release of any medical or other information necessary to process this claim. I also request payment of government benefits either to myself or to the party who accepts assignment below.

SIGNED SIGNATURE ON FILE DATE

13. INSURED'S OR AUTHORIZED PERSON'S SIGNATURE I authorize payment of medical benefits to the undersigned physician or supplier for services described below.

SIGNED SIGNATURE ON FILE

PATIENT AND INSURED INFORMATION

14. DATE OF CURRENT ILLNESS, INJURY, or PREGNANCY (LMP) MM DD YY: 01 07 YYYY QUAL. 431

15. OTHER DATE QUAL. MM DD YY

16. DATES PATIENT UNABLE TO WORK IN CURRENT OCCUPATION FROM MM DD YY TO MM DD YY

17. NAME OF REFERRING PROVIDER OR OTHER SOURCE 17a. 17b. NPI

18. HOSPITALIZATION DATES RELATED TO CURRENT SERVICES FROM 01 07 YYYY TO 01 09 YYYY

19. ADDITIONAL CLAIM INFORMATION (Designated by NUCC)

20. OUTSIDE LAB? ☐ YES ☒ NO $ CHARGES

21. DIAGNOSIS OR NATURE OF ILLNESS OR INJURY Relate A-L to service line below (24E) ICD Ind. 0

A. R94.30 B. I20.1 C. E78.4 D.
E. F. G. H.
I. J. K. L.

22. RESUBMISSION CODE ORIGINAL REF. NO.

23. PRIOR AUTHORIZATION NUMBER

	24. A. DATE(S) OF SERVICE From MM DD YY	To MM DD YY	B. PLACE OF SERVICE	C. EMG	D. PROCEDURES, SERVICES, OR SUPPLIES (Explain Unusual Circumstances) CPT/HCPCS	MODIFIER	E. DIAGNOSIS POINTER	F. $ CHARGES	G. DAYS OR UNITS	H. EPSDT Family Plan	I. ID. QUAL.	J. RENDERING PROVIDER ID. #
1	01 07 YY		21		99223		A	150 00	1		NPI	
2	01 08 YY		21		99231		A	75 00	1		NPI	
3	01 09 YY		21		99238		A	75 00	1		NPI	
4											NPI	
5											NPI	
6											NPI	

25. FEDERAL TAX I.D. NUMBER: 111234523 SSN ☐ EIN ☒

26. PATIENT'S ACCOUNT NO.: 12-2

27. ACCEPT ASSIGNMENT? (For govt. claims, see back) ☒ YES ☐ NO

28. TOTAL CHARGE: $ 300 00

29. AMOUNT PAID: $

30. Rsvd for NUCC Use

31. SIGNATURE OF PHYSICIAN OR SUPPLIER INCLUDING DEGREES OR CREDENTIALS (I certify that the statements on the reverse apply to this bill and are made a part thereof.)

SIGNED ERIN A HELPER MD DATE MMDDYYYY

32. SERVICE FACILITY LOCATION INFORMATION
GOODMEDICINE HOSPITAL
ANYWHERE STREET
ANYWHERE NY 12345-1234
a. 2345678901 b.

33. BILLING PROVIDER INFO & PH # (101) 1111234
ERIN A HELPER MD
101 MEDIC DRIVE
ANYWHERE NY 12345
a. 1234567890 b.

PHYSICIAN OR SUPPLIER INFORMATION

NUCC Instruction Manual available at: www.nucc.org PLEASE PRINT OR TYPE

FIGURE 12-7 Completed Mary S. Patient claim for commercial payer group health plan.

SUMMARY

Automobile insurance coverage includes medical payments and PIP; disability insurance provides an individual with reimbursement for lost wages; liability insurance covers losses to a third party caused by the insured or on premises owned by the insured.

Although commercial claims completion instructions are generally recognized nationwide, it is important to check with each payer to determine if they require alternate information to be entered on the claim. Commercial payers also implement changes to claims completion requirements throughout the year, and most providers discover these changes when claims are denied. Commercial payers do not typically make available their billing manuals or updates, which is another reason it is important to routinely contact payers to request their specific CMS-1500 claims completion instructions.

When patients are covered by primary *and* secondary/supplemental health insurance plans, modifications are made to the CMS-1500 claim instructions:

- If the same payer provides both primary and secondary/supplemental coverage, just one claim is submitted, and information is entered in Blocks 9, 9a, 9d, 11, 11a, 11c, and 11d.
- If the secondary/supplemental payer is different from the primary payer, a primary claim is submitted to the primary payer, and a new claim is generated and submitted to the secondary payer, with information entered in Blocks 1a, 4, 7, 9, 9a, 9d, 11, 11a, 11c, and 11d. A copy of the primary payer's remittance advice is attached to the secondary claim.

When completing commercial CMS-1500 claims for case studies in the Workbook, the following special instructions apply:

- Block 12—Enter SIGNATURE ON FILE.
- Block 13—Enter SIGNATURE ON FILE.
- Block 20—Enter an X in the NO box.
- Block 26—Enter the case study number (e.g., 12-2). If the patient has both primary and secondary coverage, enter a P (for primary) (e.g., 12-2P) next to the number (on the primary claim) and an S (for secondary) (e.g., 12-2S) next to the number (on the secondary claim).
- Block 27—Enter an X in the YES box.
- Block 31—Enter the provider's complete name with credentials and the date as MMDDYYYY.

INTERNET LINKS

- Aetna
  www.aetna.com
- *Commercial Insurance*
  www.medhealthinsurance.com
- eHealthInsurance Services, Inc.
  www.ehealthinsurance.org
- Insurance Information Institute
  www.iii.org
- *International Insurance Fact Book*
  www.internationalinsurance.org
- State of Wisconsin Office of the Commissioner of Insurance
  www.oci.wi.gov
- Washington State Office of the Insurance Commissioner
  www.insurance.wa.gov
- Wolters Kluwer Financial Services, Insurance Compliance Solutions
  https://insurance.wolterskluwerfs.com

STUDY CHECKLIST

- ☐ Read this textbook chapter and highlight key concepts.
- ☐ Access SimClaim software at the online companion, and complete commercial claims using the software's case studies.
- ☐ Complete CMS-1500 claims for each chapter case study.
- ☐ Answer the chapter review questions, verifying answers with your instructor.
- ☐ Complete the Workbook chapter, verifying answers with your instructor.
- ☐ Form a study group with classmates to discuss chapter concepts in preparation for an exam.

REVIEW

MULTIPLE CHOICE Select the most appropriate response.

1. **When a patient is covered by a large employer group health plan (EGHP) and Medicare, which is primary?**
   a. EGHP
   b. Medicare
   c. no distinction is made between the plans
   d. the plan that has been in place longest
2. **When a child who is covered by two or more plans lives with his married parents, the primary policyholder is the parent**
   a. who is older.
   b. who is younger.
   c. whose birthday occurs first in the year.
   d. whose birthday occurs later in the year.
3. **When an insurance company uses the patient's social security number as the patient's insurance identification number, Block 1a of the CMS-1500 claim**
   a. contains the dashes associated with social security numbers.
   b. contains the identification number without hyphens or spaces.
   c. is left blank, because social security numbers are private.
   d. can contain spaces or dashes when the number is entered.
4. **When the CMS-1500 claim requires spaces in the data entry of a date, the entry looks like which of the following?**
   a. MM DD YYYY or MM DD YY
   b. MM-DD-YYYY or MM-DD-YY
   c. MM/DD/YYYY or MM/DD/YY
   d. MMDDYYYY or MMDDYY
5. **When completing a CMS-1500 claim using computer software, text should be entered in _____ case.**
   a. lower
   b. small caps
   c. title
   d. upper

6. When the CMS-1500 claim requires a response to *YES* or *NO* entries, enter

a. a checkmark.

b. an X.

c. either an X or a checkmark.

d. nothing.

7. When SIGNATURE ON FILE is the appropriate entry for a CMS-1500 claim block, which is also acceptable as an entry?

a. FILED

b. S/F

c. SIGNED

d. SOF

8. Block 14 of the CMS-1500 claim requires entry of the date the patient first experienced signs or symptoms of an illness or injury (or the date of last menstrual period for obstetric visits). Upon completion of Jean Mandel's claim, you notice that there is no documentation of that date in the record. The provider does document that her pain began five days ago. Today is May 10, YYYY. What do you enter in Block 14?

a. 05 05 YYYY

b. 05 10 YYYY

c. the word NONE

d. nothing (leave the block blank)

9. Blocks 24A–24J of the CMS-1500 contain shaded rows, which can contain

a. additional dates of service and code numbers.

b. attachments to the CMS-1500 claim.

c. modifiers that didn't fit in the unshaded block.

d. supplemental information, per payer instructions.

10. Block 24A of the CMS-1500 claim contains dates of service (*FROM* and *TO*). If a procedure was performed on May 10, YYYY, in the office, what is entered in the *TO* block?

a. 0510YYYY

b. 05 10 YY

c. 05-10-YY

d. 05-10-YYYY

11. Nancy White's employer provides individual and family group health plan coverage, and it pays 80 percent of her annual premium. Nancy selected family coverage for her group health plan, which means her employer pays $12,000 per year (of the $15,000 annual premium). Nancy is responsible for the remaining $3,000 of the annual premium, which means approximately _____ is deducted from each of her 26 biweekly paychecks.

a. $90

b. $100

c. $115

d. $125

12. When Block 25 of the CMS-1500 contains the provider's EIN, enter _____ after the first two digits of the EIN.

a. a hyphen

b. a space

c. no punctuation or space

d. the provider's SSN

13. When a patient is covered by the same primary and secondary commercial health insurance plan,

a. complete and submit two CMS-1500 claims.
b. mail the remittance advice to the payer.
c. send the secondary CMS-1500, but not the primary claim.
d. submit just one CMS-1500 to the payer.

14. When entering the patient's name in Block 2 of the CMS-1500 claim, separate the last name, first name, and middle initial (if known) with

a. commas.
b. hyphens.
c. parentheses.
d. slashes.

15. Block 33a of the CMS-1500 claim contains the provider's

a. EIN.
b. NPI.
c. PIN.
d. SSN.

CHAPTER 13

BlueCross BlueShield

CHAPTER OUTLINE

History of BlueCross and BlueShield

BlueCross BlueShield Plans

Billing Notes

Claims Instructions

BlueCross BlueShield Secondary Coverage

OBJECTIVES

Upon successful completion of this chapter, you should be able to:

1. Define key terms.
2. Explain the history of BlueCross and BlueShield.
3. Differentiate among BlueCross BlueShield plans.
4. Apply BlueCross BlueShield billing notes when completing CMS-1500 claims.
5. Complete BlueCross BlueShield primary and secondary claims.

KEY TERMS

Away From Home Care® Program
BCBS basic coverage
BCBS major medical (MM) coverage
BlueCard® Program
BlueCross
BlueCross BlueShield (BCBS)
BlueShield
BlueWorldwide *Expat*
coordinated home health and hospice care
Federal Employee Health Benefits Program (FEHBP)
Federal Employee Program (FEP)
for-profit corporation
Government-Wide Service Benefit Plan
Healthcare Anywhere
indemnity coverage
medical emergency care rider
Medicare supplemental plans
member
member hospital
nonprofit corporation
outpatient pretreatment authorization plan (OPAP)
PPN provider
precertification
preferred provider network (PPN)
prepaid health plan
prospective authorization
rider
second surgical opinion (SSO)
service location
special accidental injury rider
usual, customary, and reasonable (UCR)

INTRODUCTION

NOTE: Instructions for completing CMS-1500 claims in this chapter are for BCBS fee-for-service claims only.

BlueCross and BlueShield plans are perhaps the best known medical insurance programs in the United States. They began as two separate *prepaid health plans* selling contracts to individuals or groups for coverage of specified medical expenses as long as the premiums were paid.

HISTORY OF BLUECROSS AND BLUESHIELD

Origin of BlueCross

The forerunner of what is known today as the **BlueCross** plan began in 1929 when Baylor University Hospital in Dallas, Texas, approached teachers in the Dallas school district with a plan that would guarantee up to 21 days of hospitalization per year for subscribers and each of their dependents, in exchange for a $6 annual premium. This **prepaid health plan** was accepted by the teachers and worked so well that the concept soon spread across the country. Early plans specified which hospital subscribers and their dependents could use for care. By 1932 some plans modified this concept and organized community-wide programs that allowed the subscriber to be hospitalized in one of several **member hospitals**, which had signed contracts to provide services for special rates.

The blue cross symbol was first used in 1933 by the St. Paul, Minnesota, plan and was adopted in 1939 by the *American Hospital Association (AHA)* when it became the approving agency for accreditation of new prepaid hospitalization plans. In 1948 the need for additional national coordination among plans arose, and the Blue Cross Association was created. In 1973 the AHA deeded the right to both the name and the use of the blue cross symbol to the Blue Cross Association. At that time the symbol was updated to the trademark in use today.

Origin of BlueShield

The **BlueShield** plans began as a resolution passed by the House of Delegates at an American Medical Association meeting in 1938. This resolution supported the concept of voluntary health insurance that would encourage physicians to cooperate with prepaid health care plans. The first known plan was formed in Palo Alto, California, in 1939 and was called the California Physicians' Service. This plan stipulated that physicians' fees for covered medical services would be paid in full by the plan if the subscriber earned less than $3,000 a year. When the subscriber earned more than $3,000 a year, a small percentage of the physician's fee would be paid by the patient. This patient responsibility for a small percentage of the health care fee is the forerunner of today's industry-wide required patient coinsurance and copayment requirements.

The blue shield design was first used as a trademark by the Buffalo, New York, plan in 1939. The name and symbol were formally adopted by the Associated Medical Care Plans, formed in 1948, as the approving agency for accreditation of new BlueShield plans adopting programs created in the spirit of the California Physicians' Service program. In 1951 this accrediting organization changed its name to the National Association of BlueShield Plans. Like the BlueCross plans, each BlueShield plan in the association was established as a separate, nonprofit corporate entity that issued its own contracts and plans within a specific geographic area.

BlueCross BlueShield Joint Ventures

BlueCross plans originally covered only hospital bills, and BlueShield plans covered fees for physician services. Over the years, both programs increased their coverage to include almost all health care services. In many areas of the country, there was close cooperation between BlueCross and BlueShield plans that resulted in the formation of joint ventures in some states where the two corporations were housed in one building. In these joint ventures, **BlueCross BlueShield (BCBS)** shared one building and computer services but maintained separate corporate identities.

BlueCross BlueShield Association

In 1977 the membership of the separate BlueCross and BlueShield national associations voted to combine personnel under the leadership of a single president, responsible to both boards of directors. Further consolidation occurred in 1986 when the boards of directors of the separate national BlueCross and BlueShield associations merged into a single corporation named the BlueCross BlueShield Association (BCBSA).

Today, BCBSA consists of more than 450 independent, locally operated BlueCross BlueShield plans that collectively provide health care coverage to more than 80 million Americans and serve more than 1 million enrolled in the Medicare+Choice program (discussed in Chapter 14). The BCBSA is located in Chicago, Illinois, and performs the following functions:

- Establishes standards for new plans and programs
- Assists local plans with enrollment activities, national advertising, public education, professional relations, and statistical and research activities
- Serves as a contractor for processing Medicare hospital, hospice, and home health care claims
- Coordinates nationwide BCBS plans

The association is also the registered owner of the BlueCross and BlueShield trademarks.

The Changing Business Structure

Strong competition among all health insurance companies in the United States emerged during the 1990s and resulted in the following:

- **Mergers occurred among BCBS regional corporations (within a state or with neighboring states) and names no longer had regional designations.**

> **EXAMPLE:** Care First BCBS is the name of the corporation that resulted from a merger between BCBS of Maryland and Washington, DC, BCBS.

- **The BlueCross BlueShield Association no longer required plans to be nonprofit (as of 1994).**

Nonprofit and Profit Corporations

Regional corporations that needed additional capital to compete with commercial for-profit health insurance plans petitioned their respective state legislatures to allow conversion from their nonprofit status to for-profit corporations. **Nonprofit corporations** are charitable, educational, civic, or humanitarian organizations whose profits are returned to the corporation rather than distributed to shareholders and officers of the corporation. Because no profits of the organization are distributed to shareholders, the government does not tax the organization's income. **For-profit corporations** pay taxes on profits generated by the corporation's enterprises and pay dividends to shareholders on after-tax profits.

Although some BCBS plans have converted to for-profit companies, state regulators and courts are scrutinizing these transactions, some on a retroactive basis, to ensure that charitable assets are preserved. For example, Empire BCBS in New York State publicly acknowledges its nonprofit obligations and agrees to preserve 100 percent of its assets for nonprofit charitable purposes as part of proposed conversions to for-profit corporations.

BCBS Distinctive Features

The "Blues" were pioneers in nonprofit, prepaid health care, and they possess features that distinguish them from other commercial health insurance groups.

> **NOTE:** For-profit commercial plans have the right to cancel a policy at renewal time if the patient moves into a region of the country in which the company is not licensed to sell insurance *or* if the person is a high user of benefits and has purchased a plan that does not include a non-cancellation clause.

1. They maintain negotiated contracts with providers of care. In exchange for such contracts, BCBS agrees to perform the following services:
   - **Make prompt, direct payment of claims**
   - **Maintain regional professional representatives to assist participating providers with claim problems**
   - **Provide educational seminars, workshops, billing manuals, and newsletters to keep participating providers up to date on BCBS insurance procedures**
2. BCBS plans, in exchange for tax relief for their nonprofit status, are forbidden by state law from cancelling coverage for an individual because he or she is in poor health or BCBS payments to providers have far exceeded the average. Policies issued by the nonprofit entity can be canceled, or an individual unenrolled, only:
   - **When premiums are not paid**
   - **If the plan can prove that fraudulent statements were made on the application for coverage**

3. BCBS plans must obtain approval from their respective state insurance commissioners for any rate increases and/or benefit changes that affect BCBS members within the state. For-profit commercial plans have more freedom to increase rates and modify general benefits without state approval when the premium is due for annual renewal *if there is no clause restricting such action in the policy.*

4. BCBS plans must allow conversion from group to individual coverage and guarantee the transferability of membership from one local plan to another when a change in residency moves a policyholder into an area served by a different BCBS corporation.

NOTE: The insurance claim is submitted to the BCBS plan in the state where services were rendered. That *local plan* forwards the claim to the *home plan* for adjudication.

Participating Providers

As mentioned earlier, the "Blues" were pioneers in negotiating contracts with providers of care. A *participating provider (PAR)* is a health care provider who enters into a contract with a BCBS corporation and agrees to:

- **Submit insurance claims for all BCBS subscribers**
- **Provide access to the Provider Relations Department, which assists the PAR provider in resolving claims or payment problems**
- **Write off (make a fee adjustment for) the difference or balance between the amount charged by the provider for covered procedures/services and the approved fee established by the insurer (For noncovered procedures/services, the patient is billed by the provider.)**
- **Bill patients for only the deductible and copay/coinsurance amounts that are based on BCBS-allowed fees and the full charged fee for any uncovered service**

In return, BCBS corporations agree to:

- **Make direct payments to PARs**
- **Conduct regular training sessions for PAR billing staff**
- **Provide free billing manuals and PAR newsletters**
- **Maintain a provider representative department to assist with billing/payment problems**
- **Publish the name, address, and specialty of all PARs in a directory distributed to BCBS subscribers and PARs**

Preferred Provider Network (PPN)

PARs can also contract to participate in the plan's **preferred provider network (PPN)**, a program that requires providers to adhere to managed care provisions. In this contractual agreement, the **PPN provider** (a provider who has signed a PPN contract) agrees to accept the PPN allowed rate, which is generally 10 percent lower than the PAR allowed rate. The provider further agrees to abide by all cost-containment, utilization, and quality assurance provisions of the PPN program. In return for a PPN agreement, the "Blues" agree to notify PPN providers in writing of new employer groups and hospitals that have entered into PPN contracts and to maintain a PPN directory.

Nonparticipating Providers

Nonparticipating providers (nonPARs) have not signed participating provider contracts, and they expect to be paid the full fee charged for services rendered. In these cases, the patient may be asked to pay the provider in full and then be reimbursed by BCBS for the allowed fee for each service, minus the patient's deductible and copayment obligations. Even when the provider agrees to file the claim for the patient, the insurance company sends the payment for the claim directly to the patient and not to the provider.

BLUECROSS BLUESHIELD PLANS

BlueCross BlueShield coverage includes the following programs:

- Fee-for-service (traditional coverage)
- Indemnity
  - Managed care plans
  - Coordinated home health and hospice care
  - Exclusive provider organization (EPO)
  - Health maintenance organization (HMO)
  - Outpatient pretreatment authorization plan (OPAP)
  - Point-of-service (POS) plan
  - Preferred provider organization (PPO)
  - Second surgical opinion (SSO)
- Federal Employee Program (FEP)
- Medicare supplemental plans
- Healthcare Anywhere

Fee-for-Service (Traditional Coverage)

BCBS *fee-for-service* or *traditional coverage* is selected by (1) individuals who do not have access to a group plan and (2) many small business employers. These contracts are divided into two types of coverage within one policy:

- Basic coverage
- Major medical (MM) benefits

Minimum benefits under **BCBS basic coverage** routinely include the following services:

- Hospitalizations
- Diagnostic laboratory services
- X-rays
- Surgical fees
- Assistant surgeon fees
- Obstetric care
- Intensive care
- Newborn care
- Chemotherapy for cancer

BCBS major medical (MM) coverage includes the following services in addition to basic coverage:

- Office visits
- Outpatient nonsurgical treatment
- Physical and occupational therapy
- Purchase of durable medical equipment (DME)
- Mental health encounters
- Allergy testing and injections

- **Prescription drugs**
- **Private duty nursing (when medically necessary)**
- **Dental care required as a result of a covered accidental injury**

Major medical services are usually subject to patient deductible and copayment requirements, and in a few cases the patient may be responsible for filing claims for these benefits.

Some of the contracts also include one or more **riders**, which are special clauses that stipulate additional coverage over and above the standard contract. Common riders include special accidental injury and medical emergency care coverage.

The **special accidental injury rider** covers 100 percent of nonsurgical care sought and rendered within 24 to 72 hours (varies according to the policy) of the accidental injury. Surgical care is subject to any established contract basic plan deductible and copayment requirements. Outpatient follow-up care for these accidental injuries is not included in the accidental injury rider, but will be covered if the patient has supplemental coverage.

The **medical emergency care rider** covers *immediate treatment sought and received for sudden, severe, and unexpected conditions* that if not treated would place the patient's health in permanent jeopardy or cause permanent impairment or dysfunction of an organ or body part. Chronic or subacute conditions do not qualify for treatment under the medical emergency rider unless the symptoms suddenly become acute and require immediate medical attention. Special attention must be paid to the ICD-10-CM coding (Blocks 21 and 24D) on the CMS-1500 claim to ensure that services rendered under the medical emergency rider are linked to diagnoses or reported symptoms generally accepted as conditions that require immediate care. Nonspecific conditions such as "acute upper respiratory infection" or "bladder infection" would not be included on the medical emergency diagnosis list.

Indemnity Coverage

BCBS **indemnity coverage** offers choice and flexibility to subscribers who want to receive a full range of benefits along with the freedom to use any licensed health care provider. Coverage includes hospital-only or comprehensive hospital and medical coverage. Subscribers share the cost of benefits through coinsurance options, do not have to select a primary care provider, and do not need a referral to see a provider.

Managed Care Plans

Managed care is a health care delivery system that provides health care and controls costs through a network of physicians, hospitals, and other health care providers. BCBS managed care plans include the coordinated home health and hospice care program, exclusive provider organizations, health maintenance organizations, outpatient pretreatment authorization plans, point-of-service plans, preferred provider organizations, and second surgical opinions.

The **coordinated home health and hospice care** program allows patients with this option to elect an alternative to the acute care setting. The patient's physician must file a treatment plan with the case manager assigned to review and coordinate the case. All authorized services must be rendered by personnel from a licensed home health agency or approved hospice facility.

An *exclusive provider organization (EPO)* is similar to a health maintenance organization that provides health care services through a network of doctors, hospitals, and other health care providers, except that members are not required to select a primary care provider (PCP), and they do not need a referral to see a specialist. However, they must obtain services from EPO providers only or the patient is responsible for the charges. A *primary care provider (PCP)* is a physician or other medical professional who serves as a subscriber's first contact with a plan's health care system. The PCP is also known as a *personal care physician* or *personal care provider*.

All BCBS corporations now offer at least one *health maintenance organization (HMO)* plan that assumes or shares the financial and health care delivery risks associated with providing comprehensive medical services to subscribers in return for a fixed, prepaid fee. Some plans were for-profit acquisitions; others were developed as separate nonprofit plans. Examples of plan names are *Capital Care* and *Columbia Medical Plan*. Because familiar BCBS names are not always used in the plan name, some HMOs may not be easily recognized as BCBS plans. The BCBS trademarks, however, usually appear on the plan's ID cards and advertisements.

The **outpatient pretreatment authorization plan (OPAP)** requires preauthorization of outpatient physical, occupational, and speech therapy services. In addition, OPAP requires periodic treatment/progress plans to be filed. OPAP is a requirement for the delivery of certain health care services and is issued prior to the provision of services. OPAP is also known as **prospective authorization** or **precertification**.

A *point-of-service (POS) plan* allows subscribers to choose, at the time medical services are needed, whether they will go to a provider within the plan's network or outside the network. When subscribers go outside the network to seek care, out-of-pocket expenses and copayments generally increase. POS plans provide a full range of inpatient and outpatient services, and subscribers choose a primary care provider (PCP) from the payer's PCP list. The PCP assumes responsibility for coordinating subscriber and dependent medical care, and the PCP is often referred to as the *gatekeeper* of the patient's medical care. The name and telephone number of the PCP appear on POS plan ID cards, and written referral notices issued by the PCP are usually mailed to the appropriate local processing address following the transmission of an electronic claim. Because the PCP is responsible for authorizing all inpatient hospitalizations, a specialist's office should contact the PCP when hospitalization is necessary and follow up that call with one to the utilization control office at the local BCBS plan office.

NOTE: When subscribers go outside the network for health care, the approval of the PCP is not required, and costs are usually higher. When subscribers undergo procedures/services that are not covered by their policy, they are responsible for reimbursing the provider for such care.

A *preferred provider organization (PPO)* offers discounted health care services to subscribers who use designated health care providers (who contract with the PPO) but also provides coverage for services rendered by health care providers who are not part of the PPO network. The BCBS PPO plan is sometimes described as a subscriber-driven program, and BCBS substitutes the terms *subscriber* (or **member**) for *policyholder* (used by other commercial carriers). In this type of plan, the subscriber (member) is responsible for remaining within the network of PPO providers and must request referrals to PPO specialists whenever possible. The subscriber must also adhere to the managed care requirements of the PPO policy, such as obtaining required second surgical opinions and/or hospital admission review. Failure to adhere to these requirements will result in denial of the surgical claim or reduced payment to the provider. In such cases, the patient is responsible for the difference or balance between the reduced payment and the normal PPO allowed rate.

The mandatory **second surgical opinion (SSO)** requirement is necessary when a patient is considering elective, nonemergency surgical care. The initial surgical recommendation must be made by a physician qualified to perform the anticipated surgery. If a second surgical opinion is not obtained prior to surgery, the patient's out-of-pocket expenses may be greatly increased. The patient or surgeon should contact the subscriber's BCBS local plan for instructions. In some cases, the second opinion must be obtained from a member of a select surgical panel. In other cases, the concurrence of the need for surgery from the patient's PCP may suffice.

Federal Employee Program

The **Federal Employee Health Benefits Program (FEHBP)** (or **Federal Employee Program [FEP]**) is an employer-sponsored health benefits program established by an Act of Congress in 1959. The FEP began covering federal employees on July 1, 1960, and now provides benefits to more than 9 million federal enrollees and dependents through contracts with about 300 insurance carriers. FEP is underwritten and administered by participating insurance plans (e.g., BlueCross BlueShield plans) that are called *local plans.* Claims are submitted to local plans that serve the location where the patient was seen (called a **service location**), regardless of the member's FEP plan affiliation.

FEP cards contain the phrase **Government-Wide Service Benefit Plan** under your insurance company's trademark. FEP enrollees have identification numbers that begin with the letter "R" followed by eight numeric digits (Figure 13-1). All ID cards contain the name of the government employee. Dependents' names do *not* appear on the card. A three-digit enrollment code is located on the front of the card to specify the option(s) selected when the government employee enrolled in the program. This code should be entered as the group ID number on insurance claims.

The four enrollment options are:

- **101—Individual, High Option Plan**
- **102—Family, High Option Plan**
- **104—Individual Standard (Low) Option Plan**
- **105—Family Standard (Low) Option Plan**

> **NOTE:** The federal government's Office of Personnel Management (OPM) oversees administration of the FEHBP, and BCBS is just one of several payers who reimburse health care services. Others include the Alliance Health Plan (AHP), American Postal Workers Union (APWU) Health Plan, Government Employee Hospital Association (GEHA), Mail Handlers Benefit Plan (MHBP), National Association of Letter Carriers (NALC), and People Before Profit (PBP) Health Plan sponsored by the National League of Postmasters.

The FEP is considered a managed fee-for-service program and has generally operated as a PPO plan. The patient is responsible for ensuring that precertification is obtained for all hospitalizations except routine maternity care, home health and hospice care, and emergency hospitalization within 48 hours of admission. In 1997, a POS product was introduced in specific geographic sections of the country, and gradual expansion to a nationwide POS program was

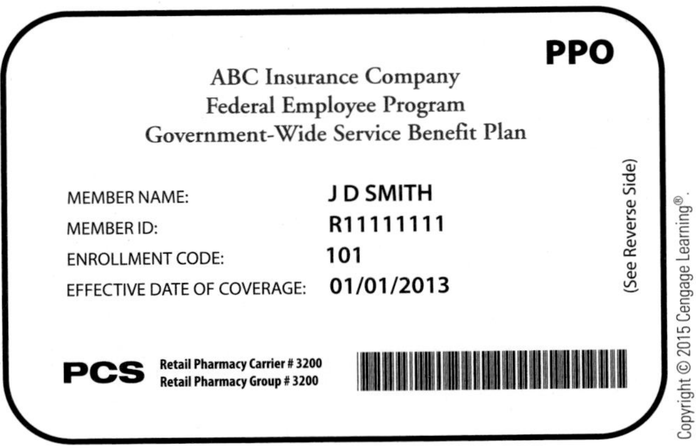

FIGURE 13-1 Mock-up of an insurance FEP PPO plan ID card.

implemented. The federal POS program requires that the subscriber select a PCP. This plan offers enhanced benefits and reduced out-of-pocket expenses when PCP referrals are obtained for specialty care.

Medicare Supplemental Plans

BCBS corporations offer several federally designed and regulated **Medicare supplemental plans** (described in Chapter 14), which augment the Medicare program by paying for Medicare deductibles and copayments. These plans are better known throughout the industry as *Medigap Plans* and are usually identified by the word *Medigap* on the patient's plan ID card.

Healthcare Anywhere

Healthcare Anywhere coverage allows "members of the independently owned and operated BCBS plans [to] have access to health care benefits throughout the United States and around the world, depending on their home plan benefits. Generally, the **BlueCard® Program** enables such members obtaining health care services while traveling or living in another BCBS plan's service area to receive the benefits of their home plan contract and to access local provider networks. As instructed by their home BCBS plan, members call the phone number on their Plan ID card to arrange for pre-certification or prior authorization number, if necessary. Member identification cards (Figure 13-2) displaying a (suitcase) logo indicate that the BlueCard® Program is available to the member. The **Away From Home Care® Program** allows the participating BCBS plan members who are temporarily residing outside of their home HMO service area for at least 90 days to temporarily enroll with a local HMO. Such members usually include dependent students attending school out-of-state, family members who reside in different HMO service areas, long-term travelers whose work assignment is in another state, and retirees with a dual residence." (BlueCard, Away From Home Care, and the PPO suitcase are registered trademarks of the BlueCross BlueShield Association and are used with permission.) **BlueWorldwide *Expat*** provides global medical coverage for active employees and their dependents who spend more than six months outside the United States. Any U.S. corporation, with new or existing Blue coverage, that sends members to work and reside outside the United States for six months or more is eligible for BlueWorldwide *Expat*.

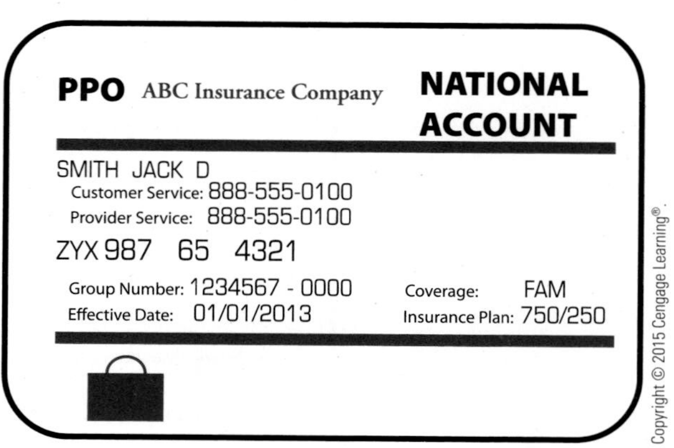

PPO ABC Insurance Company
NATIONAL ACCOUNT
SMITH JACK D
Customer Service: 888-555-0100
Provider Service: 888-555-0100
ZYX 987 65 4321
Group Number: 1234567 - 0000
Effective Date: 01/01/2013
Coverage: FAM
Insurance Plan: 750/250
Copyright © 2015 Cengage Learning®.

FIGURE 13-2 Mock-up of a national account PPO ID insurance card.

BILLING NOTES

A summary follows of nationwide billing issues for traditional BCBS fee-for-service claims. PAR providers are required to submit claims for subscribers.

Claims Processing

Claims for BCBS patients are submitted to the local BCBS payer for processing (and not to the patient's "home" BCBS plan).

> **EXAMPLE:** Mary Smith's "home" health insurance coverage is an employer group health plan (EGHP) through Western New York (WNY) BCBS, which is located in Buffalo, New York. She receives health care services from her local physician in Syracuse, New York, because that is the city in which Mary works and resides. Her physician's office submits claims to Central BCBS in Syracuse, which contacts WNY BCBS to determine contractual coverage and reimbursement rates for treatment provided to Mary.

Deadline for Filing Claims

The general deadline is customarily one year from the date of service, unless otherwise specified in the subscriber's or provider's contracts. (Some BCBS payers require claims to be submitted as soon as 120 days from the date of service, while others allow as long as 18 months from the date of service.)

Form Used

BCBS payers currently accept the CMS-1500 claim.

Inpatient and Outpatient Coverage

Inpatient and outpatient coverage may vary according to the plan. Many plans require second surgical opinions and prior authorization for elective hospitalizations. Information on the individual program requirements can be obtained from your BCBS payer(s).

Deductible

The deductible will vary according to the BCBS plan. Consult the BCBS billing manual or eligibility status computerized phone bank for specific patient requirements. Patients enrolled in PPO plans may have no applicable deductibles for certain preventive medicine services.

Copayment/Coinsurance

Patient copayment/coinsurance requirements vary according to the patient plan. The most common coinsurance amounts are 20 percent or 25 percent, although they may be as high as 50 percent for mental health services on some policies. (The subscriber is allowed a pre-established number of mental health visits.)

Allowable Fee Determination

The allowable fee varies according to the plan. Many corporations use the physician fee schedule to determine the allowed fees for each procedure. Other plans use a **usual, customary, and reasonable (UCR)** basis, which is the amount commonly charged for a particular medical service by providers within a particular geographic region for establishing their allowable rates. Participating providers must accept the allowable rate on all covered services and write off or adjust the difference or balance between the plan-determined allowed amount and the amount billed. Patients are responsible for any deductible and copay/coinsurance described in the policy, as well as full charges for uncovered services.

The remittance advice sent to PAR and PPN providers clearly states the patient's total deductible and copayment/coinsurance responsibility for each claim submission.

NonPARs may collect the full fee from the patient. BCBS payments are then sent directly to the patient.

Assignment of Benefits

All claims filed by participating providers qualify for an *assignment of benefits* to the provider. This means that payment is made directly to the provider by BCBS.

Special Handling

The following special handling guidelines should be followed:

1. Make it a habit and priority to retain a current photocopy of the front and back of all patient insurance plan ID cards in the patient's file.
2. Resubmit claims not paid within 30 days.
3. Some mental health claims are forwarded to a *third-party administrator (TPA)* that provides administrative services to health care plans and specializes in mental health case management. Check the back of the ID card and billing manual for special instructions.

Before working with BCBS claims, complete the Review located at the end of this chapter.

NOTE: As you review the CMS-1500 claims instructions in Table 13-1, refer to the John Q. Public case study (Figure 13-3) and completed CMS-1500 claim (Figure 13-4). The completed claim will also assist you when you begin work on Exercise 13-1.

CLAIMS INSTRUCTIONS

The claims instructions (Table 13-1) in this section are used for completing primary BCBS claims. (At the end of the chapter, you will find instructions for completing secondary and supplemental claims.)

BCBS primary claim status is determined when the patient is:

- **Covered by only one BCBS policy**
- **Covered by both a government-sponsored plan and an employer-sponsored BCBS plan**
- **Covered by a non-BCBS plan that is not employer-sponsored**
- **Designated as the policyholder of one employer-sponsored plan and is also listed as a dependent on another employer-sponsored plan**

NOTE: Insurance companies frequently change billing rules and instructions. Obtain updates from a variety of sources (e.g., professional publications, Internet-based listservs, and payer websites).

Your instructor may substitute local requirements for specific CMS-1500 blocks. *Enter these local instructions in the margins of this text for quick reference when working with case study assignments that are to be graded by the instructor.*

TABLE 13-1 CMS-1500 claims completion instructions for BCBS fee-for-service plans

NOTE: Refer to Chapter 11 for clarification of claims completion (e.g., entering names, mailing addresses, ICD-10-CM codes, diagnosis pointer letters, NPI, and so on).

BLOCK	INSTRUCTIONS
1	Enter an X in the *Other* box if the patient is covered by an individual or family health plan. Or, enter an X in the *Group Health Plan* box if the patient is covered by a group health plan. **NOTE:** The patient is covered by a group health plan if a group number is printed on the patient's insurance identification card (or a group number is included on case studies located in this textbook, workbook, and SimClaim™ software).
1a	Enter the BCBS plan identification number as it appears on the patient's insurance card. *Do not enter hyphens or spaces in the number.*
2	Enter the patient's last name, first name, and middle initial (separated by commas) (e.g., DOE, JANE, M).
3	Enter the patient's birth date as MM DD YYYY (with spaces). Enter an X in the appropriate box to indicate the patient's gender. If the patient's gender is unknown, leave blank.
4	Enter the policyholder's last name, first name, and middle initial (separated by commas).
5	Enter the patient's mailing address and telephone number. Enter the street address on line 1, enter the city and state on line 2, and enter the five- or nine-digit zip code and phone number on line 3.
6	Enter an X in the appropriate box to indicate the patient's relationship to the policyholder. If the patient is an unmarried domestic partner, enter an X in the *Other* box.
7	Enter the policyholder's mailing address and telephone number. Enter the street address on line 1, enter the city and state on line 2, and enter the five- or nine-digit zip code and phone number on line 3.
8	Leave blank.
9, 9a, 9d	Leave blank. *Blocks 9, 9a, and 9d are completed if the patient has secondary insurance coverage (discussed later in this chapter).*
9b–9c	Leave blank.
10a–c	Enter an X in the appropriate boxes to indicate whether the patient's condition is related to employment, an automobile accident, and/or another accident. If an X is entered in the YES box for auto accident, enter the two-character state abbreviation of the patient's residence.
10d	Leave blank.
11	Enter the policyholder's BCBS group number if the patient is covered by a group health plan. *Do not enter hyphens or spaces in the policy or group number.* Otherwise, leave blank.
11a	Enter the policyholder's birth date as MM DD YYYY (with spaces). Enter an X in the appropriate box to indicate the policyholder's gender. If the policyholder's gender is unknown, leave blank.
11b	Leave blank. This is reserved for property and casualty or worker's compensation claims.
11c	Enter the name of the policyholder's BCBS health insurance plan.
11d	Enter an X in the NO box. *Block 11d is completed by entering an X in the YES box if the patient has secondary insurance coverage (discussed later in this chapter).*
12	Enter SIGNATURE ON FILE. Leave the date field blank. (The abbreviation SOF is also acceptable.)
13	Leave blank. *Assignment of benefits is a provision of BCBS contracts signed by policyholders, which authorizes BCBS to reimburse providers directly for plan benefits.*

(continues)

TABLE 13-1 (continued)

BLOCK	INSTRUCTIONS
14	Enter the date as MM DD YYYY (with spaces) to indicate when the patient first experienced signs or symptoms of the present illness, actual date of injury, *or* the date of the last menstrual period (LMP) for obstetric visits. Enter the applicable qualifier to identify which date is being reported: 431 (onset of current symptoms/illness or injury) *or* 484 (last menstrual period). *If the date is not documented in the patient's record, but the history indicates an appropriate date (e.g., three weeks ago), simply count back to the approximate date and enter it on the claim.*
15–16	Leave blank.
17	If applicable, enter the first name, middle initial (if known), last name, and credentials of the professional who referred, ordered, or supervised health care service(s) or supply(ies) reported on the claim. *Do not enter any punctuation.* In front of the name, enter the applicable qualifier to identify which provider is being reported, as follows: DN (referring provider), DK (ordering provider), or DQ (supervising provider). Otherwise, leave blank.
17a	Leave blank.
17b	Enter the 10-digit national provider identifier (NPI) of the provider entered in Block 17. Otherwise, leave blank.
18	Enter the admission date and discharge date as MM DD YYYY (with spaces) if the patient received inpatient services (e.g., hospital, skilled nursing facility). Otherwise, leave blank. *If the patient has not been discharged at the time the claim is completed, leave the discharge date blank.*
19	Leave blank.
20	Enter an X in the NO box if all laboratory procedures reported on the claim were performed in the provider's office. Otherwise, enter an X in the YES box and enter the total amount charged by the outside laboratory in $ CHARGES. Also enter the outside laboratory's name, mailing address, and NPI in Block 32. (Charges are entered *without* punctuation. For example, $1,100.00 is entered as 110000 below $ CHARGES.)
21	Enter the ICD-10-CM code for up to 12 diagnoses or conditions treated or medically managed during the encounter. Lines A through L in Block 21 will relate to CPT/HCPCS service/procedure codes reported in Block 24E. In the *ICD Ind* (ICD indicator) box, enter 0 for ICD-10-CM (or 9 for ICD-9-CM).
22	Leave blank. Reserved for resubmitted claims.
23	Enter prior authorization number, referral number, mammography precertification number, or Clinical Laboratory Improvement Amendments (CLIA) number, as assigned by the payer for the current service. *Do not enter hyphens or spaces in the number.* Otherwise, leave blank.
24A	Enter the date the procedure or service was performed in the FROM column as MM DD YY (with spaces). Enter a date in the TO column *if the procedure or service was performed on consecutive days during a range of dates. Then, enter the number of consecutive days in Block 24G.* **NOTE:** The shaded area in each line is used to enter supplemental information to support reported services *if instructed by the payer to enter such information.* Data entry in Block 24 is limited to reporting six services. *Do not use the shaded lines to report additional services.* If additional services were provided, generate new CMS-1500 claim(s) to report the additional services.
24B	Enter the appropriate two-digit place-of-service (POS) code to identify the location where the reported procedure or service was performed. (Refer to Appendix II for POS codes.)
24C	Leave blank.
24D	Enter the CPT or HCPCS level II code and applicable required modifier(s) for procedures or services performed. *Separate the CPT/HCPCS code and first modifier with one space. Separate additional modifiers with one space each. Up to four modifiers can be entered.*

(continues)

TABLE 13-1 (continued)

BLOCK	INSTRUCTIONS
24E	Enter the diagnosis pointer letter from Block 21 that relates to the procedure/service performed on the date of service. **NOTE:** When completing CMS-1500 claims for case studies in this textbook, its workbook, and SimClaim software, enter just one diagnosis pointer letter on each line of Block 24E.
24F	Enter the fee charged for each reported procedure or service. When multiple procedures or services are reported on the same line, enter the total fee charged. *Do not enter commas, periods, or dollar signs. Do not enter negative amounts. Enter 00 in the cents area if the amount is a whole number.*
24G	Enter the number of days or units for procedures or services reported in Block 24D. *If just one procedure or service was reported in Block 24D, enter a 1 in Block 24G.*
24H	Leave blank. This is reserved for Medicaid claims.
24I	Leave blank. The NPI abbreviation is preprinted on the CMS-1500 claim.
24J	Enter the 10-digit NPI for the: • Provider who performed the service *if the provider is a member of a group practice.* (Leave blank if the provider is a solo practitioner.) • Supervising provider *if the service was provided incident-to the service of a physician or nonphysician practitioner* **and** *the physician or practitioner who ordered the service did not supervise the provider.* (Leave blank if the incident-to service was performed under the supervision of the physician or nonphysician practitioner.) • DMEPOS supplier or outside laboratory *if the physician submits the claim for services provided by the DMEPOS supplier or outside laboratory.* (Leave blank if the DMEPOS supplier or outside laboratory submits the claim.) Otherwise, leave blank.
25	Enter the provider's social security number (SSN) or employer identification number (EIN). *Do not enter hyphens or spaces in the number.* Enter an X in the appropriate box to indicate which number is reported.
26	Enter the patient's account number as assigned by the provider.
27	Enter an X in the YES box to indicate that the provider agrees to accept assignment. Otherwise, enter an X in the NO box.
28	Enter the total charges for services and/or procedures reported in Block 24. **NOTE:** If multiple claims are submitted for one patient because more than six procedures or services were reported, be sure the total charge reported on each claim accurately represents the total of the items on each submitted claim.
29-30	Leave blank.
31	Enter the provider's name and credential (e.g., MARY SMITH MD) and the date the claim was completed as MMDDYYYY (without spaces). *Do not enter any punctuation.*
32	Enter the name and address where procedures or services were provided *if at a location other than the provider's office or the patient's home, such as a hospital, outside laboratory facility, skilled nursing facility, or DMEPOS supplier.* Otherwise, leave blank. Enter the name on line 1, the address on line 2, and the city, state, and five- or nine-digit zip code on line 3. *For a nine-digit zip code, enter the hyphen.* **NOTE:** If Block 18 contains dates of service for inpatient care and/or Block 20 contains an X in the YES box, enter the name and address of the facility that provided services.
32a	Enter the 10-digit NPI of the facility entered in Block 32.
32b	Leave blank.

(continues)

TABLE 13-1 (continued)

BLOCK	INSTRUCTIONS
33	Enter the provider's *billing* name, address, and telephone number. Enter the phone number in the area next to the block title. *Do not enter parentheses for the area code.* Enter the provider's name on line 1, enter the address on line 2, and enter the city, state, and five- or nine-digit zip code on line 3. *For a nine-digit zip code, enter the hyphen.*
33a	Enter the 10-digit NPI of the *billing* provider (e.g., solo practitioner) or group practice (e.g., clinic).
33b	Leave blank.

ERIN A. HELPER, M.D.
101 Medic Drive, Anywhere, NY 12345
(101) 111-1234 (Office) • (101) 111-9292 (Fax)
EIN: 11-1234523
NPI: 1234567890

Case Study

PATIENT INFORMATION:		**INSURANCE INFORMATION:**	
Name:	Public, John Q.	**Patient Number:**	13-1
Address:	10A Senate Avenue	**Place of Service:**	Office
City:	Anywhere	**Primary Insurance Plan:**	BlueCross BlueShield
State:	NY	**Primary Insurance Plan ID #:**	WW123456
Zip Code:	12345-1234	**Group #:**	50698
Telephone:	(101) 201-7891	**Primary Policyholder:**	Public, John Q.
Gender:	Male	**Policyholder Date of Birth:**	03-09-1945
Date of Birth:	03-09-1945	**Relationship to Patient:**	Self
Occupation:	Supervisor	**Secondary Insurance Plan:**	
Employer:	Legal Research Inc	**Secondary Insurance Plan ID #:**	
		Secondary Policyholder:	

Patient Status ☒ Married ☐ Divorced ☐ Single ☐ Student

DIAGNOSIS INFORMATION

Diagnosis	Code	Diagnosis	Code
1. Bronchopneumonia	J18.0	5.	
2. Urinary frequency	R35.0	6.	
3.		7.	
4.		8.	

PROCEDURE INFORMATION

Description of Procedure or Service	Date	Code	Charge
1. Established patient office visit, level III	01-12-YYYY	99213	75.00
2. Urinalysis, dipstick, automatic microscopy	01-12-YYYY	81001	10.00
3. Chest x-ray, 2 views	01-12-YYYY	71020	50.00
4.			
5.			

SPECIAL NOTES: Recheck 01-19-YYYY. Referring Physician: Ivan Gooddoc, M.D. (NPI 3456789012).

FIGURE 13-3 John Q. Public case study.

HEALTH INSURANCE CLAIM FORM

APPROVED BY NATIONAL UNIFORM CLAIM COMMITTEE (NUCC) 02/12

PICA | PICA

CARRIER

1. MEDICARE (Medicare#) | MEDICAID (Medicaid#) | TRICARE (ID#/DoD#) | CHAMPVA (Member ID#) | [X] GROUP HEALTH PLAN (ID#) | FECA BLK LUNG (ID#) | OTHER (ID#)

1a. INSURED'S I.D. NUMBER (For Program in Item 1): WW123456

2. PATIENT'S NAME (Last Name, First Name, Middle Initial): PUBLIC, JOHN, Q

3. PATIENT'S BIRTH DATE MM DD YY: 03 09 1945 SEX M [X] F

4. INSURED'S NAME (Last Name, First Name, Middle Initial): PUBLIC, JOHN, Q

5. PATIENT'S ADDRESS (No., Street): 10A SENATE AVENUE

6. PATIENT RELATIONSHIP TO INSURED: Self [X] Spouse Child Other

7. INSURED'S ADDRESS (No., Street): 10A SENATE AVENUE

CITY: ANYWHERE STATE: NY

8. RESERVED FOR NUCC USE

CITY: ANYWHERE STATE: NY

ZIP CODE: 12345-1234 TELEPHONE (Include Area Code): (101) 2017891

ZIP CODE: 12345-1234 TELEPHONE (Include Area Code): (101) 2017891

9. OTHER INSURED'S NAME (Last Name, First Name, Middle Initial)

10. IS PATIENT'S CONDITION RELATED TO:

11. INSURED'S POLICY GROUP OR FECA NUMBER: 50698

a. OTHER INSURED'S POLICY OR GROUP NUMBER

a. EMPLOYMENT? (Current or Previous) YES [X] NO

a. INSURED'S DATE OF BIRTH MM DD YY: 03 09 1945 SEX M [X] F

b. RESERVED FOR NUCC USE

b. AUTO ACCIDENT? YES [X] NO PLACE (State)

b. OTHER CLAIM ID (Designated by NUCC)

c. RESERVED FOR NUCC USE

c. OTHER ACCIDENT? YES [X] NO

c. INSURANCE PLAN NAME OR PROGRAM NAME: BLUECROSS BLUESHIELD

d. INSURANCE PLAN NAME OR PROGRAM NAME

10d. CLAIM CODES (Designated by NUCC)

d. IS THERE ANOTHER HEALTH BENEFIT PLAN? YES [X] NO *If yes, complete items 9, 9a, and 9d.*

PATIENT AND INSURED INFORMATION

READ BACK OF FORM BEFORE COMPLETING & SIGNING THIS FORM.

12. PATIENT'S OR AUTHORIZED PERSON'S SIGNATURE I authorize the release of any medical or other information necessary to process this claim. I also request payment of government benefits either to myself or to the party who accepts assignment below.

SIGNED SIGNATURE ON FILE DATE

13. INSURED'S OR AUTHORIZED PERSON'S SIGNATURE I authorize payment of medical benefits to the undersigned physician or supplier for services described below.

SIGNED

14. DATE OF CURRENT ILLNESS, INJURY, or PREGNANCY (LMP) MM DD YY: 01 12 YYYY QUAL. 431

15. OTHER DATE QUAL. MM DD YY

16. DATES PATIENT UNABLE TO WORK IN CURRENT OCCUPATION FROM TO

17. NAME OF REFERRING PROVIDER OR OTHER SOURCE: DN IVAN GOODDOC MD

17a.

17b. NPI 3456789012

18. HOSPITALIZATION DATES RELATED TO CURRENT SERVICES FROM TO

19. ADDITIONAL CLAIM INFORMATION (Designated by NUCC)

20. OUTSIDE LAB? YES [X] NO $ CHARGES

21. DIAGNOSIS OR NATURE OF ILLNESS OR INJURY Relate A-L to service line below (24E) ICD Ind. 0

A. J18.0 B. R35.0 C. D.
E. F. G. H.
I. J. K. L.

22. RESUBMISSION CODE ORIGINAL REF. NO.

23. PRIOR AUTHORIZATION NUMBER

	24. A. DATE(S) OF SERVICE From MM	DD	YY	To MM	DD	YY	B. PLACE OF SERVICE	C. EMG	D. PROCEDURES, SERVICES, OR SUPPLIES (Explain Unusual Circumstances) CPT/HCPCS	MODIFIER	E. DIAGNOSIS POINTER	F. $ CHARGES	G. DAYS OR UNITS	H. EPSDT Family Plan	I. ID. QUAL.	J. RENDERING PROVIDER ID. #
1	01	12	YY				11		99213		A	75 00	1		NPI	
2	01	12	YY				11		81001		B	10 00	1		NPI	
3	01	12	YY				11		71020		A	50 00	1		NPI	
4															NPI	
5															NPI	
6															NPI	

25. FEDERAL TAX I.D. NUMBER: 111234523 SSN EIN [X]

26. PATIENT'S ACCOUNT NO.: 13-1

27. ACCEPT ASSIGNMENT? (For govt. claims, see back) [X] YES NO

28. TOTAL CHARGE: $ 135 00

29. AMOUNT PAID: $

30. Rsvd for NUCC Use

31. SIGNATURE OF PHYSICIAN OR SUPPLIER INCLUDING DEGREES OR CREDENTIALS (I certify that the statements on the reverse apply to this bill and are made a part thereof.)

ERIN A HELPER MD MMDDYYYY
SIGNED DATE

32. SERVICE FACILITY LOCATION INFORMATION

a. NPI b.

33. BILLING PROVIDER INFO & PH # (101) 1111234

ERIN A HELPER MD
101 MEDIC DRIVE
ANYWHERE NY 12345

a. 1234567890 b.

PHYSICIAN OR SUPPLIER INFORMATION

NUCC Instruction Manual available at: www.nucc.org PLEASE PRINT OR TYPE

FIGURE 13-4 Completed John Q. Public claim.

EXERCISE 13-1

Completing the Mary S. Patient BCBS CMS-1500 Claim

1. Obtain a blank claim by making a copy of the CMS-1500 claim form in Appendix III.
2. Review the Mary S. Patient case study (Figure 13-5).
3. Select the information needed from the case study, and enter the required information on the claim using optical scanning guidelines.
4. Review the completed claim to be sure all required blocks are completed accurately.
5. Compare your claim with the completed Mary S. Patient claim (Figure 13-6).

ERIN A. HELPER, M.D.
101 Medic Drive, Anywhere, NY 12345
(101) 111-1234 (Office) • (101) 111-9292 (Fax)
EIN: 11-1234523
NPI: 1234567890

Case Study

PATIENT INFORMATION:		**INSURANCE INFORMATION:**	
Name:	Patient, Mary S.	**Patient Number:**	13-2
Address:	91 Home Street	**Place of Service:**	Office
City:	Nowhere	**Primary Insurance Plan:**	BlueCross BlueShield
State:	NY	**Primary Insurance Plan ID #:**	WWW1023456
Zip Code:	12367-1234	**Primary Policyholder:**	Mary S. Patient
Telephone:	(101) 201-8989	**Policyholder Date of Birth:**	10-10-1959
Gender:	Female	**Relationship to Patient:**	Self
Date of Birth:	10-10-1959	**Secondary Insurance Plan:**	
Occupation:	Manager	**Secondary Insurance Plan ID #:**	
Employer:	Happy Farm Day Care	**Secondary Policyholder:**	

Patient Status ☒ Married ☐ Divorced ☐ Single ☐ Student

DIAGNOSIS INFORMATION

Diagnosis	Code	Diagnosis	Code
1. Strep throat	J02.0	5.	
2. Type 1 diabetes mellitus	E10.9	6.	
3.		7.	
4.		8.	

PROCEDURE INFORMATION

Description of Procedure or Service	Date	Code	Charge
1. Office visit, level II	01-12-YYYY	99212	65.00
2. Strep test	01-12-YYYY	87880	12.00
3.			
4.			
5.			

SPECIAL NOTES:

FIGURE 13-5 Mary S. Patient case study.

HEALTH INSURANCE CLAIM FORM

APPROVED BY NATIONAL UNIFORM CLAIM COMMITTEE (NUCC) 02/12

PICA | PICA | CARRIER

1. MEDICARE (Medicare#) MEDICAID (Medicaid#) TRICARE (ID#/DoD#) CHAMPVA (Member ID#) GROUP HEALTH PLAN (ID#) FECA BLK LUNG (ID#) OTHER (ID#) [X]

1a. INSURED'S I.D. NUMBER (For Program in Item 1): WWW1023456

2. PATIENT'S NAME (Last Name, First Name, Middle Initial): PATIENT, MARY, S

3. PATIENT'S BIRTH DATE MM DD YY: 10 10 1959 SEX M [ ] F [X]

4. INSURED'S NAME (Last Name, First Name, Middle Initial): PATIENT, MARY, S

5. PATIENT'S ADDRESS (No., Street): 91 HOME STREET

6. PATIENT RELATIONSHIP TO INSURED: Self [X] Spouse [ ] Child [ ] Other [ ]

7. INSURED'S ADDRESS (No., Street): 91 HOME STREET

CITY: NOWHERE STATE: NY

8. RESERVED FOR NUCC USE

CITY: NOWHERE STATE: NY

ZIP CODE: 12367-1234 TELEPHONE (Include Area Code): (101) 2018989

ZIP CODE: 12367-1234 TELEPHONE (Include Area Code): (101) 2018989

9. OTHER INSURED'S NAME (Last Name, First Name, Middle Initial)

10. IS PATIENT'S CONDITION RELATED TO:

11. INSURED'S POLICY GROUP OR FECA NUMBER

a. OTHER INSURED'S POLICY OR GROUP NUMBER

a. EMPLOYMENT? (Current or Previous) [ ] YES [X] NO

a. INSURED'S DATE OF BIRTH MM DD YY: 10 10 1959 SEX M [ ] F [X]

b. RESERVED FOR NUCC USE

b. AUTO ACCIDENT? [ ] YES [X] NO PLACE (State)

b. OTHER CLAIM ID (Designated by NUCC)

c. RESERVED FOR NUCC USE

c. OTHER ACCIDENT? [ ] YES [X] NO

c. INSURANCE PLAN NAME OR PROGRAM NAME: BLUECROSS BLUESHIELD

d. INSURANCE PLAN NAME OR PROGRAM NAME

10d. CLAIM CODES (Designated by NUCC)

d. IS THERE ANOTHER HEALTH BENEFIT PLAN? [ ] YES [X] NO *If yes, complete items 9, 9a, and 9d.*

READ BACK OF FORM BEFORE COMPLETING & SIGNING THIS FORM.

12. PATIENT'S OR AUTHORIZED PERSON'S SIGNATURE I authorize the release of any medical or other information necessary to process this claim. I also request payment of government benefits either to myself or to the party who accepts assignment below.

SIGNED SIGNATURE ON FILE DATE

13. INSURED'S OR AUTHORIZED PERSON'S SIGNATURE I authorize payment of medical benefits to the undersigned physician or supplier for services described below.

SIGNED

PATIENT AND INSURED INFORMATION

14. DATE OF CURRENT ILLNESS, INJURY, or PREGNANCY (LMP) MM DD YY: 01 12 YYYY QUAL. 431

15. OTHER DATE QUAL. MM DD YY

16. DATES PATIENT UNABLE TO WORK IN CURRENT OCCUPATION FROM TO

17. NAME OF REFERRING PROVIDER OR OTHER SOURCE 17a. 17b. NPI

18. HOSPITALIZATION DATES RELATED TO CURRENT SERVICES FROM TO

19. ADDITIONAL CLAIM INFORMATION (Designated by NUCC)

20. OUTSIDE LAB? [ ] YES [X] NO $ CHARGES

21. DIAGNOSIS OR NATURE OF ILLNESS OR INJURY Relate A-L to service line below (24E) ICD Ind. 0

A. J02.0 B. E10.9 C. D. E. F. G. H. I. J. K. L.

22. RESUBMISSION CODE ORIGINAL REF. NO.

23. PRIOR AUTHORIZATION NUMBER

	24. A. DATE(S) OF SERVICE From MM DD YY	To MM DD YY	B. PLACE OF SERVICE	C. EMG	D. PROCEDURES, SERVICES, OR SUPPLIES (Explain Unusual Circumstances) CPT/HCPCS	MODIFIER	E. DIAGNOSIS POINTER	F. $ CHARGES	G. DAYS OR UNITS	H. EPSDT Family Plan	I. ID. QUAL.	J. RENDERING PROVIDER ID. #
1	01 12 YY		11		99212		A	65 00	1		NPI	
2	01 12 YY		11		87880		A	12 00	1		NPI	
3											NPI	
4											NPI	
5											NPI	
6											NPI	

25. FEDERAL TAX I.D. NUMBER: 111234523 SSN [ ] EIN [X]

26. PATIENT'S ACCOUNT NO.: 13-2

27. ACCEPT ASSIGNMENT? (For govt. claims, see back) [X] YES [ ] NO

28. TOTAL CHARGE: $ 77 00

29. AMOUNT PAID: $

30. Rsvd for NUCC Use

31. SIGNATURE OF PHYSICIAN OR SUPPLIER INCLUDING DEGREES OR CREDENTIALS (I certify that the statements on the reverse apply to this bill and are made a part thereof.)

SIGNED ERIN A HELPER MD DATE MMDDYYYY

32. SERVICE FACILITY LOCATION INFORMATION

a. NPI b.

33. BILLING PROVIDER INFO & PH # (101) 1111234

ERIN A HELPER MD
101 MEDIC DRIVE
ANYWHERE NY 12345

a. 1234567890 b.

PHYSICIAN OR SUPPLIER INFORMATION

NUCC Instruction Manual available at: www.nucc.org *PLEASE PRINT OR TYPE*

FIGURE 13-6 Completed Mary S. Patient claim.

BLUECROSS BLUESHIELD SECONDARY COVERAGE

Modifications are made to the CMS-1500 claim when patients are covered by primary and secondary or supplemental health insurance plans. Secondary health insurance plans provide coverage similar to that of primary plans, whereas supplemental health plans usually cover only deductible, copayment, and coinsurance expenses.

When the same BCBS payer issues the primary and secondary or supplemental policies (Table 13-2), submit only one CMS-1500 claim (Figure 13-7). If BCBS payers for the primary and secondary or supplemental policies are different (Table 13-3), submit a CMS-1500 claim to the primary payer. After the primary payer processes the claim, generate a second CMS-1500 claim (Figure 13-8) to send to the secondary or supplemental payer and include a copy of the primary payer's remittance advice.

TABLE 13-2 Modifications to BCBS primary CMS-1500 claims completion instructions when patient is covered by same BCBS payer for primary *and* secondary or supplemental plans (Refer to Table 13-1 for primary CMS-1500 claims completion instructions.)

BLOCK	INSTRUCTIONS
9	Enter the secondary or supplemental policyholder's last name, first name, and middle initial (if known) (separated by commas).
9a	Enter the secondary or supplemental policyholder's policy or group number.
9d	Enter the name of the secondary or supplemental policyholder's commercial health insurance plan.
11d	Enter an X in the YES box.

Courtesy of the Centers for Medicare

EXERCISE 13-2

Filing a Claim When a Patient Is Covered by the Same BCBS Payer for Primary and Secondary Policies

1. Obtain a blank claim by making a copy of the CMS-1500 claim form in Appendix III.
2. Underline Blocks 9, 9a, 9d, 11d, and 26 on the claim.
3. Refer to the case study for Mary S. Patient (Figure 13-5). Enter the following information in the appropriate blocks for the secondary policy (Table 13-2):
   BlueCross BlueShield POLICY NO. R152748
   Policyholder: James W. Patient
   Birth date: 03/01/48
   Relationship: Spouse
   Employer: NAVAL STATION
   Add BB to the patient account number in Block 26, entering 13-2BB (to indicate two BCBS policies).
4. Complete the secondary claim on Mary S. Patient using the data from the case study (Figure 13-5), entering claims information in the blocks indicated in step 2.
5. Review the completed claim to be sure all required blocks are properly completed. Compare your claim with Figure 13-7.

HEALTH INSURANCE CLAIM FORM

APPROVED BY NATIONAL UNIFORM CLAIM COMMITTEE (NUCC) 02/12

PICA | PICA

CARRIER

1. MEDICARE (Medicare#) [ ] MEDICAID (Medicaid#) [ ] TRICARE (ID#/DoD#) [ ] CHAMPVA (Member ID#) [ ] GROUP HEALTH PLAN (ID#) [ ] FECA BLK LUNG (ID#) [ ] OTHER (ID#) [X]

1a. INSURED'S I.D. NUMBER (For Program in Item 1): WWW1023456

2. PATIENT'S NAME (Last Name, First Name, Middle Initial): PATIENT, MARY, S

3. PATIENT'S BIRTH DATE MM DD YY: 10 10 1959 SEX M [ ] F [X]

4. INSURED'S NAME (Last Name, First Name, Middle Initial): PATIENT, MARY, S

5. PATIENT'S ADDRESS (No., Street): 91 HOME STREET

CITY: NOWHERE STATE: NY

ZIP CODE: 12367-1234 TELEPHONE (Include Area Code): (101) 2018989

6. PATIENT RELATIONSHIP TO INSURED: Self [X] Spouse [ ] Child [ ] Other [ ]

8. RESERVED FOR NUCC USE

7. INSURED'S ADDRESS (No., Street): 91 HOME STREET

CITY: NOWHERE STATE: NY

ZIP CODE: 12367-1234 TELEPHONE (Include Area Code): (101) 2018989

9. OTHER INSURED'S NAME (Last Name, First Name, Middle Initial): PATIENT, JAMES, W

a. OTHER INSURED'S POLICY OR GROUP NUMBER: R152748

b. RESERVED FOR NUCC USE

c. RESERVED FOR NUCC USE

d. INSURANCE PLAN NAME OR PROGRAM NAME: BLUECROSS BLUESHIELD

10. IS PATIENT'S CONDITION RELATED TO:

a. EMPLOYMENT? (Current or Previous) [ ] YES [X] NO

b. AUTO ACCIDENT? [ ] YES [X] NO PLACE (State)

c. OTHER ACCIDENT? [ ] YES [X] NO

10d. CLAIM CODES (Designated by NUCC)

11. INSURED'S POLICY GROUP OR FECA NUMBER

a. INSURED'S DATE OF BIRTH MM DD YY: 10 10 1959 SEX M [ ] F [X]

b. OTHER CLAIM ID (Designated by NUCC)

c. INSURANCE PLAN NAME OR PROGRAM NAME: BLUECROSS BLUESHIELD

d. IS THERE ANOTHER HEALTH BENEFIT PLAN? [X] YES [ ] NO *If yes, complete items 9, 9a, and 9d.*

PATIENT AND INSURED INFORMATION

READ BACK OF FORM BEFORE COMPLETING & SIGNING THIS FORM.

12. PATIENT'S OR AUTHORIZED PERSON'S SIGNATURE I authorize the release of any medical or other information necessary to process this claim. I also request payment of government benefits either to myself or to the party who accepts assignment below.

SIGNED SIGNATURE ON FILE DATE

13. INSURED'S OR AUTHORIZED PERSON'S SIGNATURE I authorize payment of medical benefits to the undersigned physician or supplier for services described below.

SIGNED

14. DATE OF CURRENT ILLNESS, INJURY, or PREGNANCY (LMP) MM DD YY: 01 12 YYYY QUAL. 431

15. OTHER DATE QUAL. MM DD YY

16. DATES PATIENT UNABLE TO WORK IN CURRENT OCCUPATION FROM MM DD YY TO MM DD YY

17. NAME OF REFERRING PROVIDER OR OTHER SOURCE 17a. 17b. NPI

18. HOSPITALIZATION DATES RELATED TO CURRENT SERVICES FROM MM DD YY TO MM DD YY

19. ADDITIONAL CLAIM INFORMATION (Designated by NUCC)

20. OUTSIDE LAB? [ ] YES [X] NO $ CHARGES

21. DIAGNOSIS OR NATURE OF ILLNESS OR INJURY Relate A-L to service line below (24E) ICD Ind. 0

A. J02.0 B. E10.9 C. D.
E. F. G. H.
I. J. K. L.

22. RESUBMISSION CODE ORIGINAL REF. NO.

23. PRIOR AUTHORIZATION NUMBER

	24. A. DATE(S) OF SERVICE From MM DD YY	To MM DD YY	B. PLACE OF SERVICE	C. EMG	D. PROCEDURES, SERVICES, OR SUPPLIES (Explain Unusual Circumstances) CPT/HCPCS	MODIFIER	E. DIAGNOSIS POINTER	F. $ CHARGES	G. DAYS OR UNITS	H. EPSDT Family Plan	I. ID. QUAL.	J. RENDERING PROVIDER ID. #
1	01 12 YY		11		99212		A	65 00	1		NPI	
2	01 12 YY		11		87880		A	12 00	1		NPI	
3											NPI	
4											NPI	
5											NPI	
6											NPI	

PHYSICIAN OR SUPPLIER INFORMATION

25. FEDERAL TAX I.D. NUMBER: 111234523 SSN [ ] EIN [X]

26. PATIENT'S ACCOUNT NO.: 13-2BB

27. ACCEPT ASSIGNMENT? (For govt. claims, see back) [X] YES [ ] NO

28. TOTAL CHARGE: $ 77 00

29. AMOUNT PAID: $

30. Rsvd for NUCC Use

31. SIGNATURE OF PHYSICIAN OR SUPPLIER INCLUDING DEGREES OR CREDENTIALS (I certify that the statements on the reverse apply to this bill and are made a part thereof.)

SIGNED ERIN A HELPER MD DATE MMDDYYYY

32. SERVICE FACILITY LOCATION INFORMATION

a. NPI b.

33. BILLING PROVIDER INFO & PH #: (101) 1111234
ERIN A HELPER MD
101 MEDIC DRIVE
ANYWHERE NY 12345

a. 1234567890 b.

NUCC Instruction Manual available at: www.nucc.org *PLEASE PRINT OR TYPE*

Courtesy of the Centers for Medicare & Medicaid Services, www.cms.gov; Copyright © 2015 Cengage Learning®.

FIGURE 13-7 Completed Mary S. Patient claim (same BCBS payer for primary and secondary policies).

TABLE 13-3 Modifications to BCBS secondary CMS-1500 claims completion instructions when patient is covered by BCBS secondary or supplemental plan (and primary payer is *not* BCBS)

BLOCK	INSTRUCTIONS
	NOTE: If the primary and secondary/supplemental payers are the same, do not generate a second CMS-1500 claim. Refer to Table 13-2 instructions.
1a	Enter the secondary or supplemental policyholder's BCBS identification number as it appears on the insurance card. *Do not enter hyphens or spaces in the number.*
4	Enter the secondary or supplemental policyholder's last name, first name, and middle initial (if known) (separated by commas).
7	Enter the secondary or supplemental policyholder's mailing address and telephone number. Enter the street address on line 1, enter the city and state on line 2, and enter the five- or nine-digit zip code and phone number on line 3.
9	Enter the primary policyholder's last name, first name, and middle initial (if known) (separated by commas).
9a	Enter the primary policyholder's policy or group number. *Do not enter hyphens or spaces in the number.*
9d	Enter the name of the primary policyholder's health insurance plan (e.g., commercial health insurance plan name or government program).
11	Enter the secondary or supplemental policyholder's policy or group number. *Do not enter hyphens or spaces in the policy or group number.*
11a	Enter the secondary or supplemental policyholder's birth date as MM DD YYYY (with spaces). Enter an X in the appropriate box to indicate the policyholder's gender. If the policyholder's gender is unknown, leave blank.
11c	Enter the name of the secondary or supplemental policyholder's BCBS health insurance plan.
11d	Enter an X in the YES box.
29	Enter the reimbursement amount received from the primary payer.

Courtesy of the Centers for Medicare & Medicaid Services, www.cms.gov

EXERCISE 13-3

Filing BCBS Secondary Claims When Patient Is Covered by BCBS Secondary or Supplemental Plan, and Primary Payer Is *Not* BCBS

1. Obtain a blank claim by making a copy of the CMS-1500 claim form in Appendix III.
2. Underline Blocks 1a, 4, 7, 9, 9d, 11, 11a, 11c, 11d, and 29, and note the entries discussed in Table 13-3. Add an "S" to the patient's account number in Block 26 (e.g., 13-3S).
3. Review Figure 13-8. Complete the BCBS secondary claim for this case using data from the case study.
4. Review the completed claim to be sure all required blocks are properly completed.
5. Compare your claim with Figure 13-9.

Additional BCBS claim case studies are found in Appendices I and II.

Case studies in Appendix II require reading the case study chart entries and selecting and coding diagnostic/procedural information. Necessary clinic, hospital, and physician data are included in the case studies patient records in Appendix II.

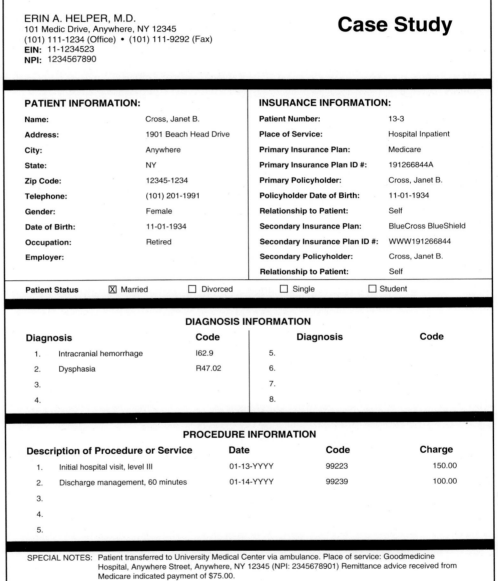

ERIN A. HELPER, M.D.
101 Medic Drive, Anywhere, NY 12345
(101) 111-1234 (Office) • (101) 111-9292 (Fax)
EIN: 11-1234523
NPI: 1234567890

Case Study

PATIENT INFORMATION:		**INSURANCE INFORMATION:**	
Name:	Cross, Janet B.	**Patient Number:**	13-3
Address:	1901 Beach Head Drive	**Place of Service:**	Hospital Inpatient
City:	Anywhere	**Primary Insurance Plan:**	Medicare
State:	NY	**Primary Insurance Plan ID #:**	191266844A
Zip Code:	12345-1234	**Primary Policyholder:**	Cross, Janet B.
Telephone:	(101) 201-1991	**Policyholder Date of Birth:**	11-01-1934
Gender:	Female	**Relationship to Patient:**	Self
Date of Birth:	11-01-1934	**Secondary Insurance Plan:**	BlueCross BlueShield
Occupation:	Retired	**Secondary Insurance Plan ID #:**	WWW191266844
Employer:		**Secondary Policyholder:**	Cross, Janet B.
		Relationship to Patient:	Self

Patient Status ☒ Married ☐ Divorced ☐ Single ☐ Student

DIAGNOSIS INFORMATION

Diagnosis	**Code**	**Diagnosis**	**Code**
1. Intracranial hemorrhage	I62.9	5.	
2. Dysphasia	R47.02	6.	
3.		7.	
4.		8.	

PROCEDURE INFORMATION

Description of Procedure or Service	**Date**	**Code**	**Charge**
1. Initial hospital visit, level III	01-13-YYYY	99223	150.00
2. Discharge management, 60 minutes	01-14-YYYY	99239	100.00
3.			
4.			
5.			

SPECIAL NOTES: Patient transferred to University Medical Center via ambulance. Place of service: Goodmedicine Hospital, Anywhere Street, Anywhere, NY 12345 (NPI: 2345678901) Remittance advice received from Medicare indicated payment of $75.00.

FIGURE 13-8 Janet B. Cross case study.

HEALTH INSURANCE CLAIM FORM

APPROVED BY NATIONAL UNIFORM CLAIM COMMITTEE (NUCC) 02/12

PICA | PICA — CARRIER

1. MEDICARE (Medicare#) | MEDICAID (Medicaid#) | TRICARE (ID#/DoD#) | CHAMPVA (Member ID#) | GROUP HEALTH PLAN (ID#) | FECA BLK LUNG (ID#) | OTHER (ID#) [X]

1a. INSURED'S I.D. NUMBER (For Program in Item 1): WWW191266844

2. PATIENT'S NAME (Last Name, First Name, Middle Initial): CROSS, JANET, B

3. PATIENT'S BIRTH DATE MM DD YY: 11 01 1934 SEX M [ ] F [X]

4. INSURED'S NAME (Last Name, First Name, Middle Initial): CROSS, JANET, B

5. PATIENT'S ADDRESS (No., Street): 1901 BEACH HEAD DRIVE

6. PATIENT RELATIONSHIP TO INSURED: Self [X] Spouse [ ] Child [ ] Other [ ]

7. INSURED'S ADDRESS (No., Street): 1901 BEACH HEAD DRIVE

CITY: ANYWHERE STATE: NY

8. RESERVED FOR NUCC USE

CITY: ANYWHERE STATE: NY

ZIP CODE: 12345-1234 TELEPHONE (Include Area Code): (101) 2011991

ZIP CODE: 12345-1234 TELEPHONE (Include Area Code): (101) 2011991

9. OTHER INSURED'S NAME (Last Name, First Name, Middle Initial): CROSS, JANET, B

10. IS PATIENT'S CONDITION RELATED TO:

11. INSURED'S POLICY GROUP OR FECA NUMBER

a. OTHER INSURED'S POLICY OR GROUP NUMBER: 191266844A

a. EMPLOYMENT? (Current or Previous) [ ] YES [X] NO

a. INSURED'S DATE OF BIRTH MM DD YY: 11 01 1934 SEX M [ ] F [X]

b. RESERVED FOR NUCC USE

b. AUTO ACCIDENT? [ ] YES [X] NO PLACE (State)

b. OTHER CLAIM ID (Designated by NUCC)

c. RESERVED FOR NUCC USE

c. OTHER ACCIDENT? [ ] YES [X] NO

c. INSURANCE PLAN NAME OR PROGRAM NAME: BLUECROSS BLUESHIELD

d. INSURANCE PLAN NAME OR PROGRAM NAME: MEDICARE

10d. CLAIM CODES (Designated by NUCC)

d. IS THERE ANOTHER HEALTH BENEFIT PLAN? [X] YES [ ] NO *If yes,* complete items 9, 9a, and 9d.

READ BACK OF FORM BEFORE COMPLETING & SIGNING THIS FORM.

12. PATIENT'S OR AUTHORIZED PERSON'S SIGNATURE I authorize the release of any medical or other information necessary to process this claim. I also request payment of government benefits either to myself or to the party who accepts assignment below.

SIGNED SIGNATURE ON FILE DATE

13. INSURED'S OR AUTHORIZED PERSON'S SIGNATURE I authorize payment of medical benefits to the undersigned physician or supplier for services described below.

SIGNED

PATIENT AND INSURED INFORMATION

14. DATE OF CURRENT ILLNESS, INJURY, or PREGNANCY (LMP) MM DD YY: 01 13 YYYY QUAL. 431

15. OTHER DATE QUAL. MM DD YY

16. DATES PATIENT UNABLE TO WORK IN CURRENT OCCUPATION FROM MM DD YY TO MM DD YY

17. NAME OF REFERRING PROVIDER OR OTHER SOURCE 17a. 17b. NPI

18. HOSPITALIZATION DATES RELATED TO CURRENT SERVICES FROM 01 13 YYYY TO 01 14 YYYY

19. ADDITIONAL CLAIM INFORMATION (Designated by NUCC)

20. OUTSIDE LAB? [ ] YES [X] NO $ CHARGES

21. DIAGNOSIS OR NATURE OF ILLNESS OR INJURY Relate A-L to service line below (24E) ICD Ind. 0

A. I62.9 B. R47.02 C. D. E. F. G. H. I. J. K. L.

22. RESUBMISSION CODE ORIGINAL REF. NO.

23. PRIOR AUTHORIZATION NUMBER

	24. A. DATE(S) OF SERVICE From MM DD YY	To MM DD YY	B. PLACE OF SERVICE	C. EMG	D. PROCEDURES, SERVICES, OR SUPPLIES (Explain Unusual Circumstances) CPT/HCPCS	MODIFIER	E. DIAGNOSIS POINTER	F. $ CHARGES	G. DAYS OR UNITS	H. EPSDT Family Plan	I. ID. QUAL.	J. RENDERING PROVIDER ID. #
1	01 13 YY		21		99223		B	150 00	1		NPI	
2	01 14 YY		21		99239		A	100 00	1		NPI	
3											NPI	
4											NPI	
5											NPI	
6											NPI	

25. FEDERAL TAX I.D. NUMBER: 111234523 SSN [ ] EIN [X]

26. PATIENT'S ACCOUNT NO.: 13-3S

27. ACCEPT ASSIGNMENT? (For govt. claims, see back) [X] YES [ ] NO

28. TOTAL CHARGE: $ 250 00

29. AMOUNT PAID: $ 75 00

30. Rsvd for NUCC Use

31. SIGNATURE OF PHYSICIAN OR SUPPLIER INCLUDING DEGREES OR CREDENTIALS (I certify that the statements on the reverse apply to this bill and are made a part thereof.)

ERIN A HELPER MD MMDDYYYY
SIGNED DATE

32. SERVICE FACILITY LOCATION INFORMATION
GOODMEDICINE HOSPITAL
ANYWHERE STREET
ANYWHERE NY 12345
a. 2345678901 b.

33. BILLING PROVIDER INFO & PH # (101) 1111234
ERIN A HELPER MD
101 MEDIC DRIVE
ANYWHERE NY 12345
a. 1234567890 b.

PHYSICIAN OR SUPPLIER INFORMATION

NUCC Instruction Manual available at: www.nucc.org PLEASE PRINT OR TYPE

FIGURE 13-9 Completed Janet B. Cross secondary payer claim.

SUMMARY

BlueCross plans were initiated in 1929 and originally provided coverage for hospital bills, whereas BlueShield was created in 1938 and originally covered fees for physician services. BlueCross and BlueShield (BCBS) plans entered into joint ventures that increased coverage of almost all health care services, and the BlueCross BlueShield Association (BCBSA) was created in 1986 when the separate BlueCross association merged with the BlueShield association. The BCBS plans were pioneers in nonprofit, prepaid health care; and competition among all health insurance payers in the United States resulted in further mergers. BCBS negotiates contracts with providers who are designated *participating providers (PARs)*. PARs are eligible to contract with preferred provider networks, and they qualify for assignment of benefits.

Nonparticipating providers do not sign such contracts, and they expect to be reimbursed the complete fee. They collect payment from the patient, and the patient receives reimbursement from BCBS. BCBS plans include fee-for-service, indemnity, managed care, Federal Employee Program, Medicare supplemental, and Healthcare Anywhere plans.

When completing BCBS CMS-1500 claims for case studies in this text (including *SimClaim* software) and the Workbook, the following special instructions apply:

- Block 12—Enter SIGNATURE ON FILE, and leave date blank.
- Block 20—Enter an X in the *NO* box.
- Block 23—Leave blank.
- Block 24E—Enter just one diagnosis pointer on each line.
- Block 26—Enter the case study number (e.g., 13-4). If the patient has both primary and secondary coverage, enter a P (for primary) next to the case study number (on the primary claim) and an S (for secondary) next to the number (on the secondary claim); if the same BCBS plan provides both primary and secondary coverage, enter a BB next to the case study number.
- Block 27—Enter an X in the *YES* box.
- When completing secondary claims, enter REMITTANCE ADVICE ATTACHED in the top margin of the CMS-1500 claim (to simulate the attachment of a primary payer's remittance advice with a claim submitted to a secondary payer).

INTERNET LINKS

- BCBS Federal Employee Program
  www.fepblue.org
- BlueCross BlueShield Association
  www.bcbsa.com

STUDY CHECKLIST

- ☐ Read this textbook chapter and highlight key concepts.
- ☐ Access SimClaim software at the online companion, and complete BlueCross BlueShield claims using the software's case studies.
- ☐ Complete CMS-1500 claims for each chapter case study.
- ☐ Answer the chapter review questions, verifying answers with your instructor.
- ☐ Complete the Workbook chapter, verifying answers with your instructor.
- ☐ Form a study group with classmates to discuss chapter concepts in preparation for an exam.

REVIEW

MULTIPLE CHOICE Select the most appropriate response.

1. **One of the requirements that a participating provider must comply with is to**
   a. maintain a provider representative department to assist with billing and payment problems for submitted claims.
   b. make fee adjustments for the difference between amounts charged to patients for services provided and payer-approved fees.
   c. purchase billing manuals and newsletters published by the payer and pay registration fees to attend payer training sessions.
   d. write off deductible and copay/coinsurance amounts and accept as payment in full the BCBS-allowed fees.

2. **Which is a program that requires providers to adhere to managed care provisions?**
   a. fee-for-service
   b. indemnity
   c. preferred provider network
   d. traditional coverage

3. **One of the expectations that a nonparticipating provider has is to _____ for services rendered.**
   a. file the CMS-1500 claim on behalf of the patient
   b. obtain payment for the full fee charged
   c. receive reimbursement directly from the payer
   d. waive patient deductibles and copay/coinsurance

4. **Which is considered a minimum benefit under BCBS basic coverage?**
   a. hospitalizations
   b. office visits
   c. physical therapy
   d. prescription drugs

5. **Which is considered a service reimbursed by BCBS major medical coverage?**
   a. assistant surgeon fees
   b. chemotherapy for cancer
   c. diagnostic laboratory services
   d. mental health visits

6. **Which is a special clause in an insurance contract that stipulates additional coverage over and above the standard contract?**
   a. coinsurance
   b. copayment
   c. deductible
   d. rider

7. **BCBS indemnity coverage is characterized by certain limitations, including**
   a. hospital-only or comprehensive hospital and medical coverage.
   b. the requirement that patients identify and select a primary care provider.
   c. provision of care by participating licensed health care providers.
   d. the requirement that patients obtain a referral before seeing a provider.

8. Prospective authorization or precertification is a requirement of the _____ BCBS managed care plan.

a. coordinated home health and hospice care
b. outpatient pretreatment authorization
c. second surgical opinion
d. point-of-service

9. Which phrase is located on a Federal Employee Program plan ID card?

a. *Family, High Option Plan*
b. *Government-Wide Service Benefit Plan*
c. *Office of Personnel Management*
d. *Preferred Provider Organization*

10. The plan ID card for a subscriber who opts for BCBS's Healthcare Anywhere PPO coverage uniquely contains the _____ logo.

a. dental
b. eyeglass
c. prescription drug
d. suitcase

Medicare

CHAPTER 14

CHAPTER OUTLINE

Medicare Eligibility
Medicare Enrollment
Medicare Part A
Medicare Part B
Medicare Part C
Medicare Part D
Other Medicare Health Plans
Employer and Union Health Plans
Medigap
Participating Providers
Nonparticipating Providers
Mandatory Claims Submission
Private Contracting
Advance Beneficiary Notice of Noncoverage
Experimental and Investigational Procedures
Medicare as Primary Payer
Medicare as Secondary Payer
Medicare Summary Notice
Billing Notes
Claims Instructions
Medicare and Medigap Claims
Medicare-Medicaid (Medi-Medi) Crossover Claims
Medicare as Secondary Payer Claims
Roster Billing for Mass Vaccination Programs

OBJECTIVES

Upon successful completion of this chapter, you should be able to:

1. Define key terms.
2. Explain Medicare eligibility guidelines.
3. Describe the Medicare enrollment process.
4. Differentiate among Medicare Part A, Part B, Part C, and Part D coverage.

5. Define other Medicare health plans, employer and union health plans, Medigap, and private contracting.
6. Calculate Medicare reimbursement amounts for participating and nonparticipating providers.
7. Determine when a Medicare advance beneficiary notice of noncoverage is required.
8. Explain the Medicare mandatory claims submission process.
9. List and explain Medicare's experimental and investigational procedures.
10. Differentiate between Medicare as primary payer and Medicare as secondary payer.
11. Interpret a Medicare Summary Notice.
12. Apply Medicare billing notes when completing CMS-1500 claims.
13. Complete Medicare primary, Medigap, Medicare-Medicaid (Medi-Medi) crossover, secondary, and roster billing claims.

KEY TERMS

advance beneficiary notice of noncoverage (ABN)
benefit period
conditional primary payer status
coordinated care plan
demonstration/pilot program
general enrollment period (GEP)
hospice
initial enrollment period (IEP)
lifetime reserve days
medical necessity denial
Medicare Advantage (Medicare Part C)
Medicare Cost Plan
Medicare fee-for-service plan
Medicare Hospital Insurance (Medicare Part A)
Medicare Medical Insurance (Medicare Part B)
Medicare Part A
Medicare Part B
Medicare Part C
Medicare Part D coverage gap
Medicare Part D "donut hole"
Medicare Prescription Drug Plans (Medicare Part D)
Medicare private contract
Medicare SELECT
Medicare special needs plans
Medicare Supplementary Insurance (MSI)
Medicare-Medicaid (Medi-Medi) crossover
Medigap
original Medicare plan
private fee-for-service (PFFS)
Programs of All-Inclusive Care for the Elderly (PACE)
qualified disabled working individual (QDWI)
qualified Medicare beneficiary program (QMBP)
qualifying individual (QI)
respite care
roster billing
special enrollment period (SEP)
specified low-income Medicare beneficiary (SLMB)
spell of illness

INTRODUCTION

Medicare, the largest single health care program in the United States, is a federal program authorized by Congress and administered by the Centers for Medicare and Medicaid Services (CMS, formerly HCFA). CMS is responsible for the operation of the Medicare program and for selecting Medicare administrative contractors (MACs) to process Medicare fee-for-service Part A, Part B, and durable medicine equipment (DME) claims. The Medicare Prescription Drug, Improvement, and Modernization Act of 2003 (MMA) created *Medicare administrative contractors (MACs)*, which replaced carriers and fiscal intermediaries and process both Medicare Part A and Part B claims. Medicare is a two-part program:

- **Medicare Part A reimburses institutional providers for inpatient, hospice, and some home health services.**
- **Medicare Part B reimburses institutional providers for outpatient services and physicians for inpatient and office services.**

The Medicare program includes the following:

- **Medicare Hospital Insurance (Medicare Part A)** pays for inpatient hospital critical care access; skilled nursing facility stays, hospice care, and some home health care. (Submit UB-04 [CMS-1450] claim for services.)
- **Medicare Medical Insurance (Medicare Part B)** pays for physician services, outpatient hospital care, durable medical equipment, and some medical services that are not covered by Part A. (Submit CMS-1500 claim for services.)
- **Medicare Advantage (Medicare Part C)**, formerly called Medicare+Choice, includes managed care and private fee-for-service plans that provide contracted care to Medicare patients. Medicare Advantage is an alternative to the original Medicare plan reimbursed under Medicare Part A. (Submit CMS-1500 or UB-04, depending on type of services provided.)
- **Medicare Prescription Drug Plans (Medicare Part D)** add prescription drug coverage to the Original Medicare Plan, some Medicare Cost Plans, some Medicare Private Fee-for-Service Plans, and Medicare Medical Savings Account Plans. (Medicare beneficiaries present a Medicare prescription drug discount card to pharmacies.)

Medicare beneficiaries can also obtain supplemental insurance, called *Medigap*, which helps cover costs not reimbursed by the original Medicare plan. Depending on the region of the country, more than one Medicare health plan may be available to enrollees.

The billing instructions in this chapter cover Medicare Part B services only. Medicare Part A claims are not filed by insurance specialists working in health care provider offices; the UB-04 is filed by hospitals, hospices, and home health care providers.

MEDICARE ELIGIBILITY

General Medicare eligibility requires:

1. Individuals or their spouses to have worked at least 10 years in Medicare-covered employment.
2. Individuals to be the minimum of 65 years old.
3. Individuals to be citizens or permanent residents of the United States.

Individuals can also qualify for coverage if they are younger than 65 *and* have a disability or End-Stage Renal Disease. The *Social Security Administration (SSA)* (an agency of the federal government) bases its definition of *disability* on an individual's ability to work; an individual can be considered disabled if unable to do work as before and if it is determined that adjustments cannot be made to do other work because of a medical condition(s). In addition, the disability must last or be expected to last a year or to result in death. There is no premium for Part A if individuals meet one of these conditions; however, they do pay for Part B coverage. The Part B monthly premium changes annually and is deducted from Social Security, Railroad Retirement, or Civil Service Retirement checks.

Medicare Part A coverage is available to individuals *age 65 and over* who:

- Are already receiving retirement benefits from Social Security or the Railroad Retirement Board (RRB)
- Are eligible to receive Social Security or Railroad benefits but have not yet filed for them
- Had Medicare-covered government employment

Medicare Part A coverage is available to individuals *under age 65* who have:

- **Received Social Security or RRB disability benefits for 24 months**
- **End-Stage Renal Disease and meet certain requirements**

Provider Telephone Inquiries for Medicare Eligibility Information

The standard method for providers to obtain Medicare eligibility information is through electronic data interchange (EDI). EDI is the most efficient and cost-effective way to make eligibility information available because provider agreements ensure privacy safeguards. Instructions regarding provider EDI access to limited eligibility information can be found in Chapter 3 (Provider Inquiries) of the *Medicare Contractor Beneficiary and Provider Communications Manual*.

Eligibility information is also available over the telephone, subject to conditions intended to ensure the protection of the beneficiary's privacy rights. The eligibility information that can be released by telephone is limited to *that information available via EDI*.

The provider's name and identification number must be verified and the following information obtained about each beneficiary:

NOTE: The Privacy Act of 1974 prohibits release of information unless all the listed required information is accurately provided.

- **Last name and first initial**
- **Date of birth**
- **HICN (health insurance claim number)**
- **Gender**

MEDICARE ENROLLMENT

Medicare enrollment is handled in two ways: either individuals are enrolled automatically, or they apply for coverage. Individuals age 65 and over do not pay a monthly premium for Medicare Part A *if they or a spouse paid Medicare taxes while they were working*. Individuals who are age 65 and over and who have not paid Medicare taxes (e.g., overseas workers who were exempt from paying Medicare taxes) can "buy in" to Medicare Part A by paying monthly premiums. The Medicare Part A buy-in premiums for 2013 are:

- **$441/month (less than 40 quarters of Medicare-covered employment)**
- **$248/month (between 30 and 39 quarters of Medicare-covered employment)**

Medicare Part B premiums are based on the modified adjusted gross income reported on an individual or joint tax return (Table 14-1).

TABLE 14-1 Medicare Part B monthly premiums based on annual income (2014)

INDIVIDUAL TAX RETURN (SINGLE)	JOINT TAX RETURN (MARRIED)	MONTHLY PREMIUM
$85,000 or less	$170,000 or less	$123.10
$85,001-$107,000	$170,001-$214,000	$156.90
$107,001-$160,000	$214,001-$320,000	$224.20
$160,001-$213,000	$320,001-$426,000	$291.50
Over $213,000	Over $426,000	$358.70

Courtesy of the Centers for Medicare & Medicaid Services

Automatic Enrollment

Individuals not yet age 65 who already receive Social Security, Railroad Retirement Board, or disability benefits are automatically enrolled in Part A and Part B effective the month of their 65th birthday. About three months before the 65th birthday, or the 24th month of disability, individuals are sent an initial enrollment package that contains information about Medicare, a questionnaire, and a Medicare card. If the individual wants both Medicare Part A (hospital insurance) and Part B (supplemental medical insurance), he or she just signs the Medicare card and keeps it in a safe place.

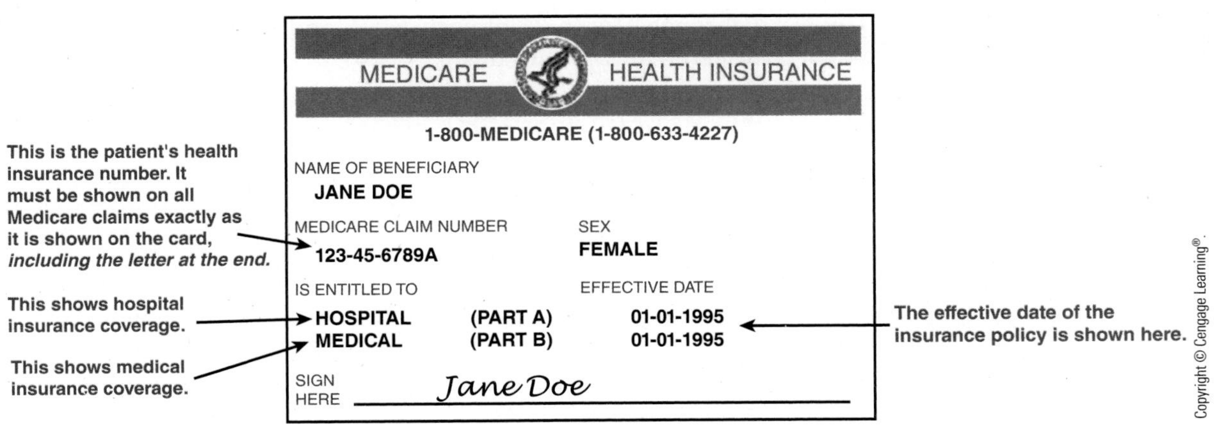

MEDICARE
HEALTH INSURANCE
1-800-MEDICARE (1-800-633-4227)
NAME OF BENEFICIARY
JANE DOE
MEDICARE CLAIM NUMBER
123-45-6789A
SEX
FEMALE
IS ENTITLED TO
EFFECTIVE DATE
HOSPITAL (PART A) 01-01-1995
MEDICAL (PART B) 01-01-1995
SIGN HERE
Jane Doe
This is the patient's health insurance number. It must be shown on all Medicare claims exactly as it is shown on the card, *including the letter at the end.*
This shows hospital insurance coverage.
This shows medical insurance coverage.
The effective date of the insurance policy is shown here.

Individuals who do not want Part B coverage (because there is a monthly premium associated with it) must follow the instructions that accompany the Medicare card; these instructions direct the individual to mark an "X" in the refusal box on the back of the Medicare card form, sign the form, and return it *with* the Medicare card to the address indicated. The individual is then sent a new Medicare card showing coverage for Part A only.

Applying for Medicare

Individuals who do not receive Social Security, Railroad Retirement Board, or disability benefits must apply for Medicare Part A and Part B by contacting the Social Security Administration (or Railroad Retirement Board) approximately three months before the month in which they turn 65 or the 24th month of disability. A seven-month **initial enrollment period (IEP)** for applying provides an opportunity for the individual to enroll in Medicare Part A and/or Part B. Those who wait until they actually turn 65 to apply for Medicare will cause a delay in the start of Part B coverage, because they will have to wait until the next **general enrollment period (GEP)**, which is held January 1 through March 31 of each year; Part B coverage starts on July 1 of that year. The Part B premium is also increased by 10 percent for each 12-month period during which an individual was eligible for Part B coverage but did not participate.

Under certain circumstances, individuals can delay Part B enrollment without having to pay higher premiums:

- **Individuals age 65 or older who are working, or whose spouse is working, and who have group health insurance through the employer or union**
- **Disabled individuals who are working and who have group health insurance or who have group health insurance coverage from a working family member**

If Part B enrollment is delayed for one of these reasons, individuals can enroll anytime during the **special enrollment period (SEP)**, a set time when they can sign up for Medicare Part B, if they did not enroll in Part B during the initial enrollment period. For individuals who enroll in Medicare Part B while covered by a group health plan or during the first full month after group health plan coverage ends, coverage starts on the first day of the month of enrollment. Individuals can also delay the start date for Medicare Part B coverage until the first day of any of the subsequent three months. If the individual enrolls during any of the seven remaining months of the special enrollment period, coverage begins the month after enrollment. If an individual does not enroll during the special enrollment period, he or she must wait until the next general enrollment period (January 1 through March 31 of each year), and then may be required to pay a higher Medicare Part B premium.

Dual Eligible Medicare Beneficiary Groups

Medicare Savings Programs help people with low income and asset levels pay for health care coverage, and certain income and asset limits must be met to qualify for the following programs:

- **Qualified Medicare beneficiary program (QMBP)** (helps individuals whose assets are not low enough to qualify them for Medicaid by requiring states to pay their Medicare Part A and B premiums, deductibles, and coinsurance amounts)
- **Specified low-income Medicare beneficiary (SLMB)** (helps low-income individuals by requiring states to pay their Medicare Part B premiums)
- **Qualifying individual (QI)** (helps low-income individuals by requiring states to pay their Medicare Part B premiums)
- **Qualified disabled working individual (QDWI)** (helps individuals who received Social Security and Medicare because of disability, but who lost their Social Security benefits and free Medicare Part A because they returned to work and their earnings exceed the limit allowed, by requiring states to pay their Medicare Part A premiums)

The asset limits are the same for all programs. Personal assets (e.g., cash, money in the bank, stocks, bonds, and so on) cannot exceed $4,000 for an individual or $6,000 for married couples. Exclusions include a home, household goods and personal belongings, one car, a life insurance policy up to a cash value of $1,500 per person, a prepaid burial plan (unlimited if irrevocable; up to $1,500 if revocable), a burial plot, and retroactive Social Security or SSI benefits (for six months after qualification in a Medicare savings program).

MEDICARE PART A

NOTE: The **original Medicare plan** (or **Medicare fee-for-service plan**) includes Medicare Part A and Medicare Part B and is available nationwide to anyone who is eligible for Medicare coverage. Original Medicare plan subscribers also subscribe to *Medigap* supplemental insurance coverage, which helps pay for health care costs not covered by the original Medicare plan (e.g., deductible and coinsurance amounts).

Medicare Part A (Medicare Hospital Insurance) helps cover inpatient care in acute care hospitals, critical access hospitals, and skilled nursing facilities. (Physician services provided to patients during an inpatient stay are covered by Medicare Part B.) It also covers hospice care and some home health care services.

Hospitalizations

Medicare pays only a portion of a patient's acute care and critical access hospital (CAH) inpatient hospitalization expenses, and the patient's out-of-pocket expenses are calculated on a benefit-period basis. A **benefit period** begins with the first day of hospitalization and ends when the patient has been out of the hospital for 60 consecutive days. (Some Medicare literature uses the term

spell of illness instead of *benefit period*.) After 90 continuous days of hospitalization, the patient may elect to use some or all of the allotted lifetime reserve days, or pay the full daily charges for hospitalization. **Lifetime reserve days** (60 days) may be used only once during a patient's lifetime and are usually reserved for use during the patient's final, terminal hospital stay. The 2013 Part A deductibles per benefit period are:

Days 1–60	$1,184 total
Days 61–90	$296/day
Days 91–150	Patient pays total charges, or elects to use lifetime reserve days at $592/day
150+ continuous days	Patient pays total charges

A person who has been out of the hospital for a period of 60 consecutive days will enter a new benefit period if rehospitalized, and a new benefit period is started. Persons confined to a psychiatric hospital are allowed 190 lifetime reserve days instead of the 60 days allotted for a stay in an acute care hospital.

Skilled Nursing Facility Stays

Individuals who become inpatients at a skilled nursing facility after a three-day-minimum acute hospital stay, and who meet Medicare's qualified diagnosis and comprehensive treatment plan requirements, pay 2013 rates of:

Days 1–20	Nothing
Days 21–100	$148 per day
Days 101+	Full daily rate

NOTE: Medicare Part B also covers some home health services if the patient is *not* covered by Medicare Part A.

Home Health Services

Individuals receiving physician-prescribed, Medicare-covered home health services have no deductible or coinsurance responsibilities for services provided. Patients must be confined to the home, but they do not have to be hospitalized in an acute care hospital before qualifying for home health benefits. The patient is responsible for a 20 percent deductible of the approved amount for durable medical equipment.

Hospice Care

All terminally ill patients qualify for hospice care. **Hospice** is an autonomous, centrally administered program of coordinated inpatient and outpatient palliative (relief of symptoms) services for terminally ill patients and their families. This program is for patients for whom the provider can do nothing further to stop the progression of disease; the patient is treated only to relieve pain or other discomfort. In addition to medical care, a physician-directed interdisciplinary team provides psychological, sociological, and spiritual care. Medicare coverage includes:

- $0 for hospice care, and there is no deductible
- Copayment of up to $5 per prescription for outpatient prescription drugs for pain and symptom management
- 5 percent of the Medicare-approved amount for inpatient **respite care** (short-term care given by another caregiver, so the usual caregiver can rest)

Respite care can also include the temporary hospitalization of a terminally ill, dependent hospice patient for the purpose of providing relief for the nonpaid person who has the major day-to-day responsibility for care of that patient.

When a patient's health improves or his illness goes into remission, he no longer needs hospice care. Also, the patient always has the right to stop hospice care at any time for any reason. If the patient stops hospice care, he will receive the type of Medicare coverage he had prior to choosing a hospice program (e.g., treatment to cure a terminal illness). If eligible, the patient can return to hospice care at any time.

EXAMPLE: A patient has terminal cancer and received hospice care. Her cancer went into remission, and she and her physician decided that, due to remission, she could stop receiving hospice care. The patient's physician explained that if she becomes eligible for hospice services in the future, she can be recertified and return to hospice care.

MEDICARE PART B

Medicare Part B (Medicare Medical Insurance) helps cover physician services, outpatient hospital care, and other services not covered by Medicare Part A, including physical and occupational therapy and some home health care for patients who do not have Medicare Part A.

NOTE: The Affordable Care Act eliminated coinsurance and the Medicare Part B deductible for recommended preventive services (e.g., annual depression screenings, annual wellness visit, cancer screenings). Such services complement the *Welcome to Medicare Visit*, which allows people joining Medicare to evaluate current health conditions, prescriptions, medical and family history, and risk factors and make a plan for appropriate preventive care with their primary health care professional.

Deductible and Coinsurance Expenses

Medicare Part B costs (2013) to the patient include:

- **$104.90 standard monthly premium for aged enrollees (and higher, based on modified adjusted gross income)**
- **$147 annual deductible**
- **20 percent coinsurance of Medicare-approved amount after deductible is met**
- **20 percent of all occupational, physical, and speech-language therapy services**
- **20 percent of the Medicare-approved amount for durable medical equipment**
- **50 percent of most outpatient mental health care**
- **Blood from a blood bank at no charge, or if the hospital has to buy blood, hospital costs are paid for the first three units of blood in a calendar year (or have the blood donated)**

Providers who do not routinely collect the patient's deductible and coinsurance are in violation of Medicare regulations and are subject to large fines and exclusion from the Medicare program.

In hospital outpatient settings, the coinsurance amount is based on a national median amount per ambulatory payment classification (APC), which could be higher than 20 percent. Hospitals have the option of charging patients either the 20 percent or the higher national median coinsurance amount. Regardless, Medicare will reimburse hospitals the difference between the Medicare-approved amount and the national coinsurance of 20 percent. However, if the hospital collects the higher median coinsurance amount from the patient, Medicare will reduce its reimbursement accordingly.

NOTE: Medicare enrollees whose incomes are more than $85,000 (individual) or $170,000 (couple) pay higher Part B premiums than people with lower incomes.

Physician Fee Schedule

Since 1992, Medicare has reimbursed provider services according to a *physician fee schedule* (also called the *Resource-Based Relative Value Scale, RBRVS*), which also limits the amounts nonparticipating providers (nonPARs) can charge beneficiaries. Reimbursement under the fee schedule is based on relative value units (RVUs) that consider resources used in providing a service (physician work, practice expense, and malpractice expense). The schedule is revised annually and is organized in a table format that includes HCPCS/CPT code numbers and the Medicare-allowed fee for each.

EXAMPLE: CPT E/M codes are listed in the physician fee schedule as indicated below. (This represents a sample listing, not based on any particular year.)

99201	$ 35.68	99211	$ 21.47
99202	$ 64.48	99212	$ 38.02
99203	$ 96.32	99213	$ 52.76
99204	$136.57	99214	$ 82.57
99205	$173.30	99215	$120.93

NOTE: Medicare Part C includes managed care plans, such as Medicare health maintenance organizations (HMOs).

MEDICARE PART C

Medicare Advantage Plans (**Medicare Part C**, formerly called *Medicare+Choice* as established by the Balanced Budget Act of 1997) are health plan options that are approved by Medicare but managed by private companies. These plans provide all Medicare Part A (hospital) and Medicare Part B (medical) coverage and must cover medically necessary services. There is no need to purchase a Medigap policy. Medicare Advantage Plans may:

- Require referrals to see specialists
- Offer lower premiums or copayments and deductibles than the Original Medicare Plan
- Have networks, which means patients may have to see doctors who belong to the plan or go to certain hospitals to get covered services
- Offer extra benefits, such as prescription drug coverage
- Coordinate patient care, using networks and referrals, which can help with overall care management and result in cost savings

Medicare enrollees have the option of enrolling in one of the following plans:

NOTE: Refer to Chapter 3 for discussion of HMO and PPO plans, which Medicare categorizes as **coordinated care plans**.

- Medicare health maintenance organization (HMO)
- Medicare medical savings account (MSA) plan
- Medicare special needs plan
- Preferred provider organization (PPO)
- Private fee-for-service (PFFS) plan

A *Medicare medical savings account (MSA)* is used by an enrollee to pay health care bills, whereas Medicare pays the cost of a special health care policy that has a high deductible. Medicare also annually deposits into an account the difference between the policy costs and what Medicare pays for an average enrollee in the patient's region. The money deposited annually by Medicare into an MSA is managed by a Medicare-approved insurance company or other qualified company. It is not taxed if the enrollee uses it to pay qualified health care expenses. It may earn interest or dividends, and any funds left in the account at the end of a calendar year are carried over to the next year. The enrollee pays health care expenses using money from the MSA account until the high deductible has been met. (If the MSA is exhausted before the high deductible has been met, the enrollee pays out of pocket until the deductible has been met.) Once the deductible has been met, the insurance policy pays health care expenses.

NOTE: MSA enrollees are required to pay the monthly Medicare Part B premium.

EXAMPLE: Jill selects the Medicare MSA plan option, establishes an account, and selects an MSA insurance policy with a $5,000 deductible. Medicare deposits $1,200 into Jill's MSA account on January 1. During the first year of the MSA plan, Jill receives health care services for which she pays $300, leaving $900 remaining in her MSA account. On January 1, Medicare deposits another $1,200 into her account; Jill now has $2,100 that she can use for health care expenses. During that next year, Jill undergoes surgery that costs $8,000. She uses the $2,100 in her account plus $2,900 of her own money to meet the policy's high deductible of $5,000; the remaining $3,000 is reimbursed by the MSA insurance policy.

NOTE: Do not confuse Medicare savings accounts with health savings accounts. The Medicare Prescription Drug, Improvement, and Modernization Act of 2003 (the Medicare Modernization Act or MMA) created health savings accounts (and gave employers a tax break for providing retiree prescription drug coverage). Health savings accounts (HSAs) provide tax-favored treatment for current medical expenses as well as the ability to save, on a tax-favored basis, for future medical expenses. Eligible individuals are those covered by a high-deductible health plan. Medicare enrollees are not eligible to make contributions to an HSA (because they are eligible to make contributions to an MSA). A high-deductible health plan has a deductible of at least $1,000 for self-only coverage, or $2,000 for family coverage, and has an out-of-pocket expense limit that is no more than $5,000 for self-only coverage ($10,000 for family coverage).

Private fee-for-service (PFFS) plans are offered by private insurance companies and are available in some regions of the country. Medicare pays a pre-established amount of money each month to the insurance company, which decides how much it will pay for services. Such plans reimburse providers on a fee-for-service basis and are authorized to charge enrollees up to 115 percent of the plan's payment schedule.

Medicare special needs plans cover all Medicare Part A and Part B health care services for individuals who can benefit the most from special care for chronic illnesses, care management of multiple diseases, and focused care management. Such plans may limit membership to individuals who:

- **Are eligible for both Medicare and Medicaid (Medi-Medi coverage)**
- **Have certain chronic or disabling conditions**
- **Reside in certain institutions (e.g., nursing facility)**

MEDICARE PART D

Medicare Prescription Drug Plans (*Medicare Part D*) offer prescription drug coverage to all Medicare beneficiaries that may help lower prescription drug costs and help protect against higher costs in the future. Medicare Part D is optional, and individuals who join a Medicare drug plan pay a monthly premium. (Individuals who decide not to enroll in a Medicare prescription drug plan when first eligible may be required to pay a penalty if they choose to join later.)

Medicare prescription drug plans are administered by insurance companies and other private companies approved by Medicare. There are two ways to obtain Medicare prescription drug coverage:

1. Join a Medicare Prescription Drug Plan that adds coverage to the original Medicare plan, some Medicare private fee-for-service plans, some Medicare cost plans, and Medicare medical savings account plans. This plan requires subscribers to pay a monthly premium and an annual deductible.

2. Join a Medicare Advantage Plan (e.g., HMO) that includes prescription drug coverage as part of the plan. Monthly premiums and annual deductibles will vary, depending on the plan. In addition, all Medicare health care (including prescription drug coverage) is provided by such plans.

TABLE 14-2 Medicare Part D monthly premiums based on annual income (2013)

INDIVIDUAL TAX RETURN	JOINT TAX RETURN	MONTHLY PREMIUM
Less than or equal to $85,000	Less than or equal to $170,000	$0.00 + plan premium
Greater than $85,000 and less than or equal to $107,000	Greater than $170,000 and less than or equal to $214,000	$11.60 + plan premium
Greater than $107,000 and less than or equal to $160,000	Greater than $214,000 and less than or equal to $320,000	$29.90 + plan premium
Greater than $160,000 and less than or equal to $214,000	Greater than $320,000 and less than or equal to $428,000	$48.30 + plan premium
Greater than $214,000	Greater than $428,000	$66.60 + plan premium

Courtesy of the Centers for Medicare & Medicaid Services, www.cms.gov

The Patient Protection and Affordable Care Act (PPACA) requires Medicare Part D enrollees *whose incomes exceed the same thresholds that apply to higher income Medicare Part B enrollees* to also pay a monthly adjustment amount (Table 14-2). Federal subsidies are available to states that implement programs to pay some or all of Parts A, B, and D premiums and coinsurance *for Medicare beneficiaries with limited incomes and assets.*

The **Medicare Part D coverage gap** (or **Medicare Part D "donut hole"**) is the difference between the initial coverage limit and the catastrophic coverage threshold for the Medicare Part D prescription drug program. Medicare beneficiaries who surpass the prescription drug-coverage limit are financially responsible for the entire cost of prescription drugs until expenses reach the catastrophic coverage threshold. Starting in 2011, the PPACA (abbreviated as the Affordable Care Act) provided for a 50 percent discount on brand-name drugs when Medicare beneficiaries reach the prescription drug "donut hole." Then, each year thereafter, Medicare beneficiaries pay less for prescription drugs in the "donut hole" until complete coverage of the donut hole is implemented in 2020.

OTHER MEDICARE HEALTH PLANS

Other Medicare health plans generally provide all of an individual's Medicare-covered health care, and some cover prescription drugs. Other Medicare health plans include:

- **Medicare Cost Plans**
- **Demonstration/pilot program**
- **Programs of All-inclusive Care for the Elderly (PACE)**

A **Medicare Cost Plan** is a type of HMO that works in much the same way and has some of the same rules as a Medicare Advantage Plan. In a Medicare Cost Plan, if the individual receives health care services from a non-network provider, the Original Medicare Plan provides coverage. The individual pays Medicare Part A and Part B coinsurance and deductibles.

A **demonstration/pilot program** is a special project that tests improvements in Medicare coverage, payment, and quality of care. Some follow Medicare Advantage Plan rules, but others do not. Demonstrations usually apply to a specific group of people and/or are offered only in specific areas. They also include

NOTE: The Medicare Prescription Drug, Improvement, and Modernization Act of 2003 (MMA) required implementation of *Medicare Prescription Drug Plans (Medicare Part D)* in 2006 to assist Medicare beneficiaries with outpatient prescription drug costs. The MMA also requires coordination of Medicare Part D with state pharmaceutical assistance programs (SPAP), Medicaid plans, group health plans, Federal Employee Health Benefit plans (FEHBP), and military plans such as TRICARE. Enrollment in Medicare Part D is voluntary, and beneficiaries must apply for the benefit.

pilot programs for individuals with multiple chronic illnesses that are designed to reduce health risks, improve quality of life, and provide health care savings.

Programs of All-Inclusive Care for the Elderly (PACE) combine medical, social, and long-term care services for frail people who live and receive health care in the community. PACE is a joint Medicare and Medicaid option in some states. To be eligible, an individual must be:

- **55 years old, or older**
- **A resident of the service area covered by the PACE program**
- **Able to live safely in the community**
- **Certified as eligible for nursing facility care by the appropriate state agency**

The goal of PACE is to help people stay independent and live in their community as long as possible, while receiving the high quality care they need.

EMPLOYER AND UNION HEALTH PLANS

Some employer and union health insurance policies provide coverage for individuals who reach age 65 and who retire. Medicare has special rules that apply to beneficiaries who have group health plan coverage through their own or their spouse's current employment. Group health plans of employers with 20 or more employees must offer the same health insurance benefits under the same conditions that younger workers and spouses receive. When the individual or the individual's spouse stops working and the individual is already enrolled in Part B, individuals are responsible for:

- **Notifying Medicare that their or their spouse's employment situation has changed**
- **Providing Medicare with the name and address of the employer plan, policy number of the plan, date the coverage stopped, and reason coverage stopped**
- **Telling their provider that Medicare is their primary payer and should be billed first (The individual should also provide the date their group health coverage stopped.)**

MEDIGAP

Medigap (or **Medicare Supplementary Insurance, MSI**), which is offered by commercial health insurance companies and some BCBS companies, is designed to supplement Medicare benefits by paying for services that Medicare does not cover. Although Medicare covers many health care costs, enrollees must still pay Medicare's deductibles and coinsurance amounts. In addition, there are many health care services that Medicare does not cover. A Medigap policy provides reimbursement for out-of-pocket costs not covered by Medicare, in addition to those that are the beneficiary's share of health care costs. There are 12 Medigap policies (Table 14-3), each offering a different combination of benefits. (Premium amounts are determined by payers.)

Medicare SELECT is a type of Medigap insurance that requires enrollees to use a network of providers (doctors and hospitals) in order to receive full benefits. Because of this requirement, Medicare SELECT policies may have lower premiums. However, if an out-of-network provider is used, Medicare SELECT generally will not pay benefits for nonemergency services. Medicare, however, will still pay its share of approved charges. Currently, Medicare SELECT is available only in limited geographic areas of the country.

TABLE 14-3 Medigap plans

MEDIGAP BENEFITS	A	B	C	D	F[1]	G	K	L	M	N
Yes = Plan covers 100% of benefit. No = Policy doesn't cover benefit. % = Plan covers that percentage of benefit. N/A = Not applicable to plan.										
Part A coinsurance and hospital costs up to an additional 365 days after Medicare benefits are used up	Yes	Yes	Yes	Yes	Yes	Yes	Yes	Yes	Yes	Yes
Part B coinsurance or copayment	Yes	Yes	Yes	Yes	Yes	Yes	50%	75%	Yes	Yes[3]
Blood (first 3 pints)	Yes	Yes	Yes	Yes	Yes	Yes	50%	75%	Yes	Yes
Part A hospice care coinsurance or copayment	Yes	Yes	Yes	Yes	Yes	Yes	50%	75%	Yes	Yes
Skilled nursing facility care coinsurance	No	No	Yes	Yes	Yes	Yes	50%	75%	Yes	Yes
Part A deductible	No	Yes	Yes	Yes	Yes	Yes	50%	75%	50%	Yes
Part B deductible	No	No	Yes	No	Yes	No	No	No	No	No
Part B excess charges	No	No	No	No	Yes	Yes	No	No	No	No
Foreign travel exchange (up to plan limits)	No	No	Yes	Yes	Yes	Yes	No	No	Yes	Yes
Out-of-pocket limit[2]	N/A	N/A	N/A	N/A	N/A	N/A	$4,800	$2,400	N/A	N/A

Courtesy of the Centers for Medicare & Medicaid Services, www.cms.gov

[1]Plan F also offers a high-deductible plan. If you choose this option, this means you must pay for Medicare-covered costs up to the deductible amount of $2,110 (in 2013) before your Medigap plan pays anything.

[2]After you meet your out-of-pocket yearly limit and your yearly Part B deductible, the Medigap plan pays 100% of covered services for the rest of the calendar year.

[3]Plan N pays 100% of the Part B coinsurance, except for a copayment of up to $20 for some office visits and up to a $50 copayment for emergency room visits that don't result in inpatient admission.

PARTICIPATING PROVIDERS

Medicare has established a *participating provider (PAR)*, an agreement in which the provider contracts to *accept assignment* on all claims submitted to Medicare. By 2000, more than 85 percent of all physicians, practitioners, and suppliers in the United States were PARs. Congress mandated special incentives to increase the number of health care providers signing PAR agreements with Medicare, including:

- **Direct payment of all claims**
- **Bonuses provided to Medicare administrative contractors (MACs) for recruitment and enrollment of PARs**
- **Publication of an annual, regional PAR directory (MedPARD) made available to all Medicare patients**
- **A special message printed on all unassigned Medicare Summary Notice (MSN) forms mailed to patients, reminding them of the reduction in out-of-pocket expenses if they use PARs and stating how much they would save with PARs**
- **Hospital referrals for outpatient care that provide the patient with the name and full address of at least one PAR provider each time the hospital provides a referral for care**
- **Faster processing of assigned claims**

Regardless of the type of Medicare Part B services billed, PARs have "one-stop" billing for beneficiaries who have Medigap coverage and who assign both Medicare and Medigap payments to PARs. After Medicare has made payment, the claim will automatically be sent to the Medigap insurer for payment of all coinsurance and deductible amounts due under the Medigap policy. The Medigap insurer must pay the PAR directly.

NONPARTICIPATING PROVIDERS

Medicare *nonparticipating providers (nonPARs)* may elect to accept assignment on a claim-by-claim basis, but several restrictions must be adhered to:

- **NonPARs must file all Medicare claims.**
- **Fees are restricted to not more than the "limiting charge" on nonassigned claims.**
- **Balance billing of the patient by a nonPAR is forbidden.**
- **Collections are restricted to only the deductible and coinsurance due at the time of service on an assigned claim.**
- **Patients must sign an advance beneficiary notice of noncoverage for all non-assigned surgical fees over $500.**
- **NonPARs must accept assignment on clinical laboratory charges.**

Limiting Charge

Nonparticipating (nonPAR) providers who do not accept assignment on Medicare claims are subject to a limit regarding what can be charged to beneficiaries for covered services. The Medicare-allowed fee for nonPARs is 5 percent below the PAR Medicare fee schedule, but the nonPAR physician may charge a maximum of 15 percent above the nonPAR approved rate (or 10 percent above the PAR Medicare fee schedule). The 15 percent allowance is based on the 95 percent reduced Medicare fee schedule, which means nonPAR providers receive somewhat less than 110 percent of the allowed PAR amount. The *limiting charge* is the maximum fee a nonPAR may charge for a covered service. It applies regardless of who is responsible for payment and whether Medicare is primary or secondary.

EXAMPLE: Compare the PAR and nonPAR Medicare reimbursement rates.

Participating (PAR) Provider Medicare Reimbursement		Nonparticipating (nonPAR) Provider Medicare Reimbursement	
PAR usual charge for office visit	$110	nonPAR limiting charge[1]	$110
PAR Medicare-allowed fee schedule	$100	nonPAR Medicare-allowed fee schedule[2]	$95
Medicare pays 80% of fee schedule	$80	Medicare pays 80% of fee schedule	$76
PAR writes off amount[3]	$10	nonPAR bills patient[4]	$15
Patient coinsurance[5] (20% of PAR Medicare-allowed fee schedule)	$20	Patient coinsurance[6]	$19
Total payment to PAR	$100	Total payment to nonPAR	$110

Although it appears that the nonPAR is paid more than the PAR ($110 versus $100), the nonPAR has to collect $34 ($15 + $19) from the patient, whereas the PAR has to collect just $20 from the patient. (It is also more cost-effective for patients to seek treatment from PARs.)

[1]Even if the nonPAR's usual charge for an office visit is greater than $110, the limiting charge in this example remains $110.

[2]The nonPAR Medicare-allowed fee schedule is 5% below the PAR Medicare-allowed fee schedule. (In the nonPAR example above, the $95 nonPAR Medicare-allowed fee schedule is calculated as: (1) $100 × 5% = $5 and (2) $100 – $5 = $95.)

[3]PAR writes off the difference between the usual charge and the Medicare-allowed fee schedule.

[4]nonPAR can bill the patient for the difference between the limiting charge and the Medicare-allowed fee schedule.

[5]This is 20% of the PAR Medicare-allowed fee schedule.

[6]This is 20% of the nonPAR Medicare-allowed fee schedule.

HIPAA ALERT!

With the passage of the Health Insurance Portability and Accountability Act (HIPAA) of 1996, Congress increased the potential fine from $2,000 to $10,000 if a nonPAR does not heed Medicare administrative contractor (MAC) warnings to desist from flagrant abuse of the limiting charge rules.

Accepting Assignment on a Claim

A nonparticipating provider who agrees to accept assignment on a claim will be reimbursed the Medicare-allowed fee. The nonPAR may also collect any previously unpaid deductible and the 20 percent coinsurance determined from the Medicare Physician Fee Schedule (MPFS). If the nonPAR collects the entire charge at the time of the patient's encounter, the assigned status of the claim is voided and the nonPAR limiting fee is then in effect. The nonPAR may also be subject to a fine or may be in violation of MPFS requirements.

The nonPAR cannot revoke the agreement for an assigned claim *unless* it is by mutual written consent of the provider and the beneficiary. Even then, such an agreement must be communicated to the MAC *before* the MAC has determined the allowed amount. Providers who repeatedly violate the assignment agreement could be charged and found guilty of a misdemeanor, which is punishable by a fine, imprisonment, or both. In addition, a criminal violation may result in suspension from Medicare participation.

The following practitioners who submit claims for services must accept assignment:

- **Anesthesiologist assistants**
- **Certified nurse midwives**
- **Certified registered nurse anesthetists**
- **Clinical nurse specialists**
- **Clinical psychologists**
- **Clinical social workers**
- **Mass immunization roster billers**
- **Nurse practitioners**
- **Physician assistants**
- **Registered dietitians**

Providers who submit claims for the following services must accept assignment:

- **Ambulance services**
- **Ambulatory surgical center services**
- **Clinical diagnostic laboratory services**
- **Home dialysis supplies and equipment**
- **Medications**
- **Physician lab services**
- **Physician services to Medicare-Medicaid (Medi-Medi) crossover patients**

EXAMPLE: A patient undergoes laboratory procedures and sees the nonPAR physician during an office visit (E/M service). If the nonPAR accepts assignment for just the laboratory procedures, two claims must be submitted: one for the laboratory services and another for the office visit.

Waiver of Medicare Billing Contracts

Medicare law specifically states that nonPARs are subject to sanctions, including fines and exclusions from the Medicare program, if they (1) require patients to sign agreements stating that the patient waives the right to have the nonPAR provider file the patient's Medicare claims or (2) require that the patient agrees to pay charges for services that are in excess of the nonPAR charge limits.

Privacy Act of 1974

In addition to the other restrictions, the *Privacy Act of 1974* forbids the Medicare administrative contractor (MAC) from disclosing the status of any unassigned claim beyond the following:

- **Date the claim was received by the MAC**
- **Date the claim was paid, denied, or suspended**
- **General reason the claim was suspended**

The nonPAR provider will *not* be told payment amounts or approved charge information.

MANDATORY CLAIMS SUBMISSION

Federal law requires that all providers and suppliers submit claims to Medicare if they provide a Medicare-covered service to a patient enrolled in Medicare Part B. This regulation does not apply if the:

- **Patient is not enrolled in Part B.**
- **Patient disenrolled before the service was furnished.**
- **Patient or the patient's legal representative refuses to sign an authorization for release of medical information.**
- **Provider opts out of the Medicare program, and those patients enter into private contracts with the provider (see section on Private Contracting).**

An exception may occur if a patient refuses to sign an authorization for the release of medical information to Medicare. However, if the patient later opts to sign a Medicare authorization and requests that claims for all prior services be filed with Medicare, the request must be honored.

PRIVATE CONTRACTING

Under the Balanced Budget Act of 1997, physicians were provided the option of withdrawing from Medicare and entering into private contracts with their Medicare patients. As of 2003, dentists, optometrists, and podiatrists were added to the list of providers who may opt out of Medicare. This **Medicare private contract** is an agreement between the Medicare beneficiary and a physician or other practitioner who has "opted out" of Medicare for two years for *all* covered items and services furnished to Medicare beneficiaries. This means that the physician or other health care practitioner will not bill for any service or supplies provided to any Medicare beneficiary for at least two years.

Under a private contract:

- **No Medicare payment will be made for services or procedures provided to a patient.**

- **The patient is required to pay whatever the physician/practitioner charges, and there is no limit on what the physician/practitioner can charge for Medicare-approved services (the limiting charge will not apply).**
- **Medicare managed care plans will not pay for services rendered under a private contract.**
- **No claim is to be submitted to Medicare, and Medicare will not pay if a claim is submitted.**
- **Supplemental insurance (Medigap) will not pay for services or procedures rendered.**
- **Other insurance plans may not pay for services or procedures rendered.**

The private contract applies only to services and procedures rendered by the physician or practitioner with whom the patient signed an agreement. Patients cannot be asked to sign a private contract when facing an emergency or urgent health situation. If patients want to pay for services that the original Medicare plan does not cover, the physician does not have to leave Medicare or ask the patient to sign a private contract. The patient is welcome to obtain noncovered services and to pay for those services.

A physician who enters into a Medicare private contract with one patient will be unable to bill Medicare for any patient for a period of two years with the exception of emergency or urgent care provided to a patient who has not signed an agreement with the provider to forgo Medicare benefits. In these cases, the claim for urgent or emergency care must be accompanied by an attachment explaining the following: (1) the nature of the emergency or urgent problem, and (2) a statement affirming that this patient has not signed an agreement with the provider to forgo Medicare. If a provider submits a nonemergency or urgent care claim for any patient before the opt-out agreement becomes effective, the provider must submit claims for all Medicare patients thereafter and abide by the limiting-fee rules. If, however, the patient files the claim, the provider will not be penalized.

ADVANCE BENEFICIARY NOTICE OF NONCOVERAGE

An **advance beneficiary notice of noncoverage (ABN)** is a written document provided to a Medicare beneficiary by a supplier, physician, or provider prior to service being rendered (Figure 14-1) to inform beneficiaries in the traditional fee-for-service Medicare program about possible noncovered charges when *limitation of liability (LOL)* applies. The ABN indicates that the service is unlikely to be reimbursed by Medicare, specifies why Medicare denial is anticipated, and requests the beneficiary to sign an agreement that guarantees personal payment for services. A beneficiary who signs an ABN agreement will be held responsible for payment of the bill if Medicare denies payment. ABNs should be generated whenever the supplier or provider believes that a claim for the services is likely to receive a Medicare **medical necessity denial** (a denial of otherwise covered services that were found to be not "reasonable and necessary") or when the service would be considered custodial care. The provider is held liable for the service and cannot bill the Medicare administrative contractor (MAC) or the Medicare beneficiary *unless the beneficiary signs an ABN*, which makes the beneficiary liable for payment if they opt to receive the service after notice was provided. Providers must also have patients sign an ABN prior to providing preventative services that are usually covered by Medicare but will not be covered because the frequency of providing such services has been exceeded.

***(A)* Notifier:**
***(B)* Patient Name:** ***(C)* Identification Number:**

ADVANCE BENEFICIARY NOTICE OF NONCOVERAGE (ABN)

NOTE: If Medicare doesn't pay for ***(D)***____________ below, you may have to pay.

Medicare does not pay for everything, even some care that you or your health care provider have good reason to think you need. We expect Medicare may not pay for the ***(D)***____________below.

(D)	***(E)* Reason Medicare May Not Pay:**	***(F)* Estimated Cost:**

WHAT YOU NEED TO DO NOW:

- Read this notice, so you can make an informed decision about your care.
- Ask us any questions that you may have after you finish reading.
- Choose an option below about whether to receive the ***(D)***____________ listed above.

  Note: If you choose Option 1 or 2, we may help you to use any other insurance that you might have, but Medicare cannot require us to do this.

***(G)* OPTIONS:** **Check only one box. We cannot choose a box for you.**

☐ **OPTION 1.** I want the ***(D)***__________ listed above. You may ask to be paid now, but I also want Medicare billed for an official decision on payment, which is sent to me on a Medicare Summary Notice (MSN). I understand that if Medicare doesn't pay, I am responsible for payment, but **I can appeal to Medicare** by following the directions on the MSN. If Medicare does pay, you will refund any payments I made to you, less copays or deductibles.

☐ **OPTION 2.** I want the ***(D)***__________ listed above, but do not bill Medicare. You may ask to be paid now as I am responsible for payment. **I cannot appeal if Medicare is not billed**.

☐ **OPTION 3.** I don't want the ***(D)***__________listed above. I understand with this choice I am **not** responsible for payment,and **I cannot appeal to see if Medicare would pay.**

***(H)* Additional Information:**

This notice gives our opinion, not an official Medicare decision. If you have other questions on this notice or Medicare billing, call **1-800-MEDICARE** (1-800-633-4227/**TTY**: 1-877-486-2048). Signing below means that you have received and understand this notice. You also receive a copy.

***(I)* Signature:**	***(J)* Date:**

According to the Paperwork Reduction Act of 1995, no persons are required to respond to a collection of information unless it displays a valid OMB control number. The valid OMB control number for this information collection is 0938-0566. The time required to complete this information collection is estimated to average 7 minutes per response, including the time to review instructions, search existing data resources, gather the data needed, and complete and review the information collection. If you have comments concerning the accuracy of the time estimate or suggestions for improving this form, please write to: CMS, 7500 Security Boulevard, Attn: PRA Reports Clearance Officer, Baltimore, Maryland 21244-1850.

Form CMS-R-131 (03/11) Form Approved OMB No. 0938-0566

FIGURE 14-1 Advance beneficiary notice of noncoverage form approved for use by CMS.

BILLING TIP:

The purpose of obtaining the ABN is to ensure payment for a procedure or service that might not be reimbursed under Medicare.

CAUTION:

Do not obtain ABNs on every procedure or service to be rendered to a patient "just in case" Medicare denies the claim. To do so is considered fraudulent.

NOTE: Electronic ABNs allow beneficiaries to view the notice on a computer screen prior to signing, and the beneficiary is provided with a printout of the signed document.

- Providers must retain copies of ABNs for five years from the date of service, and electronic retention of the signed paper document is acceptable (e.g., scanned ABN).
- An ABN is in effect for one year from date of signature unless there are changes to what is described on the form.

Cost estimates are unnecessary when an ABN is generated, because the purpose of the ABN is to document that the beneficiary has received notice that a service is unlikely to be reimbursed by Medicare. Hospital ABNs are called Hospital-Issued Notices of Noncoverage (HINN) or Notices of Noncoverage (NONC).

Do not have a patient sign an ABN when a service is *never* covered by Medicare. Instead, have those patients sign a different form, called the Notice of Exclusion of Medicare Benefits (NEMB). The ABN is used when the service is sometimes covered by Medicare, but the provider does not think it will be covered for that patient. It communicates that the patient will be responsible for provider charges if Medicare denies the service. The NEMB clearly states that the service is never covered by Medicare, and that the patient is responsible for paying provider charges. Unlike the ABN, providers are not required to have patients sign an NEMB for a never-covered Medicare service in order to bill the patient; however, use of the form makes it clear to the patient *before* a service is provided that the patient will have to pay for it.

There are four modifiers that can be added to codes assigned to procedures and services that may be denied. Depending on the procedure performed or the service provided and specific circumstances, the modifier may be required by Medicare or voluntarily added to the code. The following modifiers are added to codes when Medicare is expected to deny the service or item as not reasonable and necessary.

- **-GA: Waiver of liability statement (ABN) issued as required by payer policy, individual case, which is used to report that a required ABN was issued for a service and is on file. Medicare will automatically deny these services and assign liability to the beneficiary. Because the provider obtained an ABN, the patient can be billed for this service.**
- **-GZ: Item or service expected to be denied as not reasonable and necessary, which indicates an ABN was not issued for this service. Medicare will automatically deny these services and indicate the beneficiary is not responsible for payment. Because the provider did not obtain an ABN prior to performing the service, the patient cannot be billed.**

The following modifiers are added to codes when procedures and services do not meet medical necessity as determined by a Medicare Local Coverage Determination (LCD) or National Coverage Determination (NCD). These modifiers may also be added to codes for procedures and services that are statutorily (by law) excluded from the Medicare program. The use of an ABN is optional for such situations, but it is proof that the beneficiary understands (s)he will be liable for payment for these services.

- **-GX: Notice of liability issued, voluntary under payer policy, which is used to report that a voluntary ABN was issued for a procedure or service that is statutorily excluded from Medicare reimbursement. Medicare will reject noncovered procedures and services appended with -GX and assign liability to the beneficiary.**
- **-GY: Item or service statutorily excluded or does not meet the definition of any Medicare benefit, which is used when a procedure or service is excluded by Medicare and an ABN was not issued to the beneficiary. Medicare will deny these claims, and the beneficiary will be liable.**

Modifiers -GX and -GY are informational only, and when used, they allow the provider to bill the beneficiary.

EXAMPLE: Mary Jones is a 70-year-old female Medicare beneficiary who is evaluated for possible cosmetic surgery on her face. Because cosmetic surgery is excluded from the Medicare program, the provider's office has the patient sign an *advance beneficiary notice of noncoverage (ABN)* so that the Medicare beneficiary (Mary Jones) can be billed for all procedures performed and services provided. Modifier -GY is added to codes submitted for all procedures and services.

EXPERIMENTAL AND INVESTIGATIONAL PROCEDURES

Medicare law allows payment only for services or supplies that are considered reasonable and necessary for the stated diagnosis. Medicare will not cover procedures deemed to be experimental in nature. There are cases in which the provider determines that treatments or services are fully justified and such treatment options are then explained to the patient, who must pay the full cost of the noncovered procedure.

Medicare regulations specify that the provider must refund any payment received from a patient for a service denied by Medicare as investigational, unnecessary, unproved, or experimental, unless the patient agreed in writing prior to receiving the services to personally pay for such services. Figure 14-2

Goodmedicine Clinic ■ 1 Provider St ■ Anywhere, US 12345 ■ (101) 111-2222

To My Medicare Patients:

My primary concern as your physician is to provide you with the best possible care. Medicare does not pay for all services and will only allow those which it determines, under the guidelines spelled out in the Omnibus Budget Reconciliation Act of 1986 Section 1862(a)(1), to be reasonable and necessary. Under this law, a procedure or service deemed to be medically unreasonable or unnecessary will be denied. Since I believe each scheduled visit or planned procedure is both reasonable and necessary, I am required to notify you in advance that the following procedures or services listed below, which we have mutually agreed on, may be denied by Medicare.

Date of Service ____________________

Description of Service	Charge
____________________	__________
____________________	__________
____________________	__________

Denial may be for the following reasons:

1. Medicare does not usually pay for this many visits or treatments,
2. Medicare does not usually pay for this many services within this period of time, and/or
3. Medicare does not usually pay for this type of service for your condition.

I, however, believe these procedures/services to be both reasonable and necessary for your condition, and will assist you in collecting payment from Medicare. In order for me to assist you in this matter, the law requires that you read the following agreement and sign it.

I have been informed by (fill in the name and title of the provider) that he/she believes, in my case, Medicare is likely to deny payment for the services and reasons stated above. If Medicare denies payment, I agree to be personally and fully responsible for payment.

Beneficiary's Name: ____________________ Medicare ID# ____________________ or

Beneficiary's Signature: ____________________

or

Authorized Representative's Signature ____________________

FIGURE 14-2 Sample letter of medical necessity.

shows a CMS-approved medical necessity statement. An appeal of the denial of payment must be made in writing, and if the appeal is not granted, a refund must be paid to the patient within 30 days. A refund is not required if the provider "could not have known a specific treatment would be ruled unnecessary."

MEDICARE AS PRIMARY PAYER

Medicare is considered the primary payer under the following circumstances:

- **The employee is eligible for a group health plan but has declined to enroll, or has recently dropped coverage.**
- **The individual is currently employed, but is not yet eligible for group plan coverage or has exhausted benefits under the plan.**
- **The health insurance plan is only for self-employed individuals.**
- **The health insurance plan was purchased as an individual plan and not obtained through a group.**
- **The patient is also covered by TRICARE, which provides health benefits to retired members of the uniformed services and spouses/children of active duty, retired, and deceased service members.**
- **The patient is under age 65, has Medicare because of a disability or ESRD, and is not covered by an employer-sponsored plan.**
- **The patient is under age 65, has ESRD, and has an employer-sponsored plan but has been eligible for Medicare for more than 30 months.**
- **The patient has left a company and has elected to continue coverage in the group health plan under federal COBRA rules.**
- **The patient has both Medicare and Medicaid (Medi-Medi crossover patient).**

The Consolidated Omnibus Budget Reconciliation Act of 1985 (COBRA) requires employers with 20 or more employees to allow employees and their dependents to keep their employer-sponsored group health insurance coverage for up to 18 months for any of the following occurrences:

- **Death of the employed spouse**
- **Loss of employment or reduction in work hours**
- **Divorce**

The employee or dependents may have to pay their share as well as the employer's share of the premium.

Medicare Conditional Primary Payer Status

Medicare will award an assigned claim **conditional primary payer status** and process the claim under the following circumstances:

- **A plan that is normally considered primary to Medicare issues a denial of payment that is under appeal.**
- **A patient who is physically or mentally impaired fails to file a claim with the primary payer.**

- **A workers' compensation claim has been denied, and the case is slowly moving through the appeal process.**
- **There is no response from a liability payer within 120 days of filing the claim.**

Medicare is to be reimbursed immediately if payment is received from the primary payer at a later date.

MEDICARE AS SECONDARY PAYER

The *Medicare Secondary Payer* (MSP) rules state that Medicare is secondary when the patient is eligible for Medicare and is also covered by one or more of the following plans:

- **An employer-sponsored group health plan (EGHP) that has more than 20 covered employees**
- **Disability coverage through an employer-sponsored group health plan that has more than 100 covered employees**
- **An End-Stage Renal Disease case covered by an employer-sponsored group plan of any size during the first 18 months of the patient's eligibility for Medicare**
- **A third-party liability policy, if the Medicare-eligible person is seeking treatment for an injury covered by such a policy (this category includes automobile insurance, no-fault insurance, and self-insured liability plans)**
- **A workers' compensation program; if the claim is contested, the provider should file a Medicare primary claim and include a copy of the workers' compensation notice declaring that the case is "pending a Compensation Board decision"**
- **Veterans Administration (VA) preauthorized services for a beneficiary who is eligible for both VA benefits and Medicare**
- **Federal Black Lung Program that covers currently or formerly employed coal miners**

NOTE: Providers are required to collect or verify Medicare Secondary Payer (MSP) information during the initial beneficiary encounter instead of each time the patient is seen. Providers are also encouraged to retain MSP questionnaires for at least 10 years, even though five years is the required retention period.

All primary plans, which are collectively described in the Medicare literature as *MSP plans*, must be billed first. Medicare is billed only after the remittance advice from the primary plan or plans has been received. (The remittance advice must be attached to the Medicare claim when the claim is submitted.)

Independent and hospital labs are to enter NONE in Block 11 of the CMS-1500 claim when they bill Medicare for reference lab services when there is no face-to-face encounter with a Medicare patient. CMS does not require labs to collect Medicare secondary payer information to bill Medicare if they have had no face-to-face encounter with the patient. Entering NONE in Block 11 will prevent claims from being denied as unprocessable. When independent or hospital labs have face-to-face encounters with Medicare patients, they must collect MSP information.

Federal law requires that Medicare recover any money spent for care as a secondary payer before a settlement is dispersed, and standardized options for beneficiaries to manage any settlements relating to auto, liability, and workers' compensation insurance include the following:

NOTE: Be sure to submit a claim to Medicare for services paid by a primary payer, even if the primary payer reimbursed the entire amount charged. Failure to submit claims to Medicare could result in patients being denied credit toward their Medicare deductible.

- **The individual or beneficiary pays for all related future medical care until his or her settlement is exhausted and documents it accordingly.**
- **Medicare would not pursue *future medicals* if the individual or beneficiary's case fits a number of conditions in the proposal.**
- **The individual or beneficiary acquires and provides an attestation regarding the date of care completion from the treating physician.**

- **The individual or beneficiary submits proposed Medicare Set-Aside Arrangement (MSA) amounts for CMS review and obtains approval.**
- **The beneficiary participates in one of Medicare's recover options.**
- **The beneficiary makes an up-front payment.**
- **The beneficiary obtains a compromise or waiver of recovery.**

To avoid fines and penalties for routinely billing Medicare as primary when it is the secondary payer, a more detailed Medicare secondary payer questionnaire (Figure 14-3) should be provided to all Medicare patients when they register/reregister (update demographic and/or insurance information) with the practice. This form is used to clarify primary and secondary insurance payers.

Goodmedicine Clinic ■ 1 Provider St ■ Anywhere, US 12345 ■ (101) 111-2222

To: All Medicare Patients
In order for us to comply with the Medicare as Secondary Payer laws, you must complete this form before we can properly process your insurance claim.

Please complete this questionnaire and return it to the front desk. We will also need to make photocopies of all your insurance identification cards. Do not hesitate to ask for clarification of any item on this form.

CHECK ALL ITEMS THAT DESCRIBE YOUR HEALTH INSURANCE COVERAGE

1. I am working full time _____ part time ______ . I retired on ___/___/___.
2. _____ I am enrolled in a Medicare HMO plan.
   _____ I am entitled to Black Lung Benefits.
   _____ I had a job-related injury on ___/___/___.
   _____ I have a fee service card from the VA.
   _____ I had an organ transplant on ___/___/___.
   _____ I have been on kidney dialysis since ___/___/___.
   _____ I am being treated for an injury received in a car accident ________.
   _____ Other vehicle (please identify)
   _____ Other type of accident (please identify) ______________________________
   ____.
3. _____ I am employed/My spouse is employed and I am covered by an employer-sponsored health care program covering more than 20 employees. Name of policy:
   ____
4. _____ I/My spouse has purchased a private insurance policy to supplement Medicare.
   Name of policy:
   ____
5. _____ I have health insurance through my/my spouse's previous employer or union. Name of previous employer or union:
   ____
6. _____ I am covered by Medicaid and my ID number is: ______________________
7. _____ I am retired and covered by an employer-sponsored retiree health care plan.
   Name of plan:
   ____
8. _____ I am retired, but have been called back temporarily and have employee health benefits while I am working. Name of plan:
   ____

Patient Signature ______________________________ Date ____/____/____

FIGURE 14-3 Sample Medicare secondary payer questionnaire.

EXERCISE 14-1

Medicare as Secondary Payer

Review the following cases and determine the CMS-prescribed billing order for each.

EXAMPLE: Patient is retired and covered by Medicare, an employer-sponsored retirement plan, and his spouse's employer-sponsored large group plan.

Billing order: Employer-sponsored large group plan, Medicare, employer-sponsored retirement plan.

1. The patient is the policyholder in an employer-sponsored large group plan and has Medicare, a Medigap policy, and a $100-per-day extra coverage hospital plan.
   Billing order: ______________________________
2. The patient has Medicare and an employer-sponsored retirement plan, and the patient is a dependent on the spouse's employer-sponsored large group plan. The claim is for an injury received in a car accident.
   Billing order: ______________________________
3. The patient has a retirement plan through his former employer, Medicare, and a cancer policy. The patient is diagnosed with cancer. The spouse is deceased.
   Billing order: ______________________________
4. The patient is 67, working full time, and covered by Medicare, an employer-sponsored large group plan, and a Medigap plan. The spouse is retired, 62, and covered by an employer-sponsored plan for 18 employees.
   Billing order: ______________________________
5. The patient is 50 and disabled and has Medicare and an employer-sponsored group health plan that covers 50 employees.
   Billing order: ______________________________

MEDICARE SUMMARY NOTICE

The *Medicare Summary Notice* (MSN) (Figure 14-4) is an easy-to-read, monthly statement that clearly lists health insurance claims information. It replaced the Explanation of Medicare Benefits (EOMB), the Medicare Benefits Notice (Part A), and benefit denial letters.

BILLING NOTES

Following is a summary of nationwide billing information for original Medicare plan claims submission.

Medicare Administrative Contractor (MAC)

The regional MAC for traditional Medicare claims is selected by CMS through a competitive bidding process. Obtain the name and mailing address of the MAC for your region.

Medicare Summary Notice
for Part B (Medical Insurance)

The Official Summary of Your Medicare Claims from the Centers for Medicare & Medicaid Services

Page 1 of 5

THIS IS NOT A BILL

Facility Name
Your Name Here
Street Address
City, State 12345-6789

Notice for Your Name

Medicare Number	**XXX-XX-1234A**
Date of This Notice	**September 16, 2011**
Claims Processed Between	**June 15 – September 15, 2011**

Your Deductible Status

Your deductible is what you must pay for most health services before Medicare begins to pay.

Part B Deductible: You have now met **$85** of your **$162** deductible for 2011.

Be Informed!

Register at www.MyMedicare.gov for direct access to your Original Medicare claims, track your preventive services and print an "On the Go" report to share with your provider. Visit the Web site to sign up and access your personal Medicare information.

Your Claims & Costs This Period

Did Medicare Approve All Services?	**NO**
Number of Services Medicare Denied See claims starting on page 3. Look for **NO** in the "Service Approved?" column. See the last page for how to handle a denied claim.	**2**
Total You May Be Billed	**$150.86**

Providers with Claims This Period

June 18, 2011
Jane Doe, M.D.

June 28, 2011
John Doe, M.D.

June 29 – June 30, 2011
Any Doctor, M.D.

¿Sabía que puede recibir este aviso y otro tipo de ayuda de Medicare en español? Llame y hable con un agente en española.
如果需要国语帮助，请致电联邦医疗保险，请先说"agent"，然后说"Mandarin"。 **1-800-MEDICARE (1-800-633-4227)**

FIGURE 14-4 Sample Medicare Summary Notice (Page 1 of 5).

Medicare Split/Shared Visit Payment Policy

The *Medicare split/shared visit payment policy* applies when the physician and a qualified nonphysician provider (NPP) (e.g., nurse practitioner, physician assistant) each personally perform a substantive portion of a medically necessary evaluation and management (E/M) service for the same patient on the same date of service. A *substantive portion of an E/M visit* involves performing all or some portion of the history, examination, or medical decision making (the key components of an E/M service). The physician and qualified NPP must be in the same group practice or be employed by the same employer.

Durable Medical Equipment Claims

Durable medical equipment (DME) claims must be sent to one of four regional Medicare administrative contractors in the country. Check the Medicare manual for the one responsible for processing DME claims for your region.

Deadline for Filing Claims

The claim filing deadline for both regular Medicare and Railroad Retirement claims is one calendar year from the date of service. Any claims received after that date will be denied due to being past the timely filing statute.

EXAMPLE 1: A claim for services performed on January 28 this year must be received by the Medicare administrative contractor (MAC) by January 28 of next year.

EXAMPLE 2: A claim for services performed on November 5 this year must be received by the MAC by November 5 of next year.

Form Used

All claims must be submitted on the CMS-1500 claim. A minimum of 45 days should pass before an unpaid paper claim is resubmitted. An advance beneficiary notice of noncoverage is required for all nonassigned surgeries totaling $500 or more. A letter of medical necessity is required if the provider is to collect fees from the patient for procedures deemed by Medicare to be unreasonable, experimental, unproved, or investigational.

Medicare does not differentiate between basic and major medical benefits. Medicare is *not* the primary payer for accidental injuries covered by any third-party liability program.

Special Handling

All providers are required to file Medicare claims for their patients. Noncompliance with MSP rules and regulations may result in a substantial penalty or fine. For each filing, when Medicare is the secondary payer, a copy of the primary payer's remittance advice must be attached to the Medicare claim.

Two claims may be needed to describe one encounter in the following circumstances:

- **When multiple referring, ordering, or supervising names and provider identifier numbers are required in Blocks 17 through 17a**
- **When multiple facility names and addresses are required in Block 32**

- **When DME is charged to the patient at the same time the patient had a reimbursable medical or surgical encounter**
- **When the patient has received covered lab services and other medical or surgical services during an encounter with a nonPAR provider**

When more than one claim is needed to describe an encounter, be sure that the diagnoses on each claim prove the medical necessity for performing the service, and that the proper names and numbers required in Blocks 17, 17a, and 32 appear on the correct claims.

Before continuing with this chapter, complete the Review questions located at the end of this chapter.

CLAIMS INSTRUCTIONS

The law requires that all Medicare claims be filed using optical scanning guidelines. Practices must make certain that forms generated by computer software follow Medicare claims processing guidelines. Extraneous data on the claims or data appearing in blocks not consistent with Medicare guidelines will cause the claim to be rejected.

You should review Chapter 11, Essential CMS-1500 Claim Instructions, before working with Medicare claims instructions.

Read the following instructions carefully. Medicare requires many details that are not required for other payers discussed in this text.

These instructions (Table 14-4) are for filing primary original Medicare plan claims when the patient is not covered by additional insurance. (Instructions for filing Medicare-HMO fee-for-service claims are found in Chapter 12.)

During review of the instructions, refer to the John Q. Public case study in Figure 14-5 and the completed CMS-1500 claim (Figure 14-6).

TABLE 14-4 CMS-1500 claims completion instructions for Medicare primary claims

NOTE: Refer to Chapter 11 for clarification of claims completion (e.g., entering names, mailing addresses, ICD-10-CM codes, diagnosis pointer letters, NPI, and so on).

BLOCK	INSTRUCTIONS
1	Enter an X in the Medicare box.
1a	Enter the Medicare identification number as it appears on the patient's insurance card. *Do not enter hyphens or spaces in the number.*
2	Enter the patient's last name, first name, and middle initial (separated by commas) (e.g., DOE, JOHN, J).
3	Enter the patient's birth date as MM DD YYYY (with spaces). Enter an X in the appropriate box to indicate the patient's gender. If the patient's gender is unknown, leave blank.
4	Leave blank. *Block 4 is completed if the patient has other insurance primary to Medicare (e.g., employer group health plan) (discussed later in this chapter).*
5	Enter the patient's mailing address and telephone number. Enter the street address on line 1, enter the city and state on line 2, and enter the five- or nine-digit zip code and phone number on line 3.
6	Leave blank.

(continues)

TABLE 14-4 (continued)

BLOCK	INSTRUCTIONS
7	Leave blank. *Block 7 is completed if the patient has other insurance primary to Medicare (e.g., employer group health plan) (discussed later in this chapter).*
8	Leave blank.
9, 9a, 9d	Leave blank. *Blocks 9, 9a, and 9d are completed if the patient has secondary insurance coverage, such as Medigap (discussed later in this chapter).*
9b–9c	Leave blank.
10a–c	Enter an X in the NO boxes. (If an X is entered in the YES box for auto accident, enter the two-character state abbreviation of the patient's residence.)
10d	Leave blank.
11	Enter NONE, which indicates the provider has made a good-faith effort to determine whether Medicare is the primary or secondary payer.
11a	Leave blank.
11b	Leave blank. This is reserved for property and casualty or workers' compensation claims.
11c–d	Leave blank.
12	Enter SIGNATURE ON FILE. Leave the date field blank. (The abbreviation SOF is also acceptable.)
13	Leave blank. *Block 13 is completed if the patient has Medigap coverage.*
14	Enter the date as MM DD YYYY (with spaces) to indicate when the patient first experienced signs or symptoms of the present illness, actual date of injury, *or* the date of the last menstrual period (LMP) for obstetric visits. Enter the applicable qualifier to identify which date is being reported: 431 (onset of current symptoms/illness or injury) *or* 484 (last menstrual period). *If the date is not documented in the patient's record, but the history indicates an appropriate date (e.g., three weeks ago), simply count back to the approximate date and enter it on the claim.*
15	Leave blank.
16	Enter dates as MM DD YYYY (with spaces) to indicate the period of time the patient was unable to work in his current occupation, *if documented in the patient's record. An entry in this block might indicate employment-related insurance coverage.* Otherwise, leave blank.
17	If applicable, enter the first name, middle initial (if known), last name, and credentials of the professional who referred, ordered, or supervised health care service(s) or supply(ies) reported on the claim. *Do not enter any punctuation.* In front of the name, enter the applicable qualifier to identify which provider is being reported, as follows: DN (referring provider), DK (ordering provider), or DQ (supervising provider). Otherwise, leave blank.
17a	Leave blank.
17b	Enter the 10-digit national provider identifier (NPI) of the professional in Block 17. Otherwise, leave blank.
18	Enter the admission date and discharge date as MM DD YYYY (with spaces) if the patient received inpatient services (e.g., hospital, skilled nursing facility). Otherwise, leave blank. *If the patient has not been discharged at the time the claim is completed, leave the discharge date blank.*
19	Leave blank.

(continues)

TABLE 14-4 (continued)

BLOCK	INSTRUCTIONS
20	Enter an X in the NO box if all laboratory procedures reported on the claim were performed in the provider's office. Otherwise, enter an X in the YES box, enter the total amount charged by the outside laboratory in $ CHARGES, and enter the outside laboratory's name, mailing address, and NPI in Block 32. (Charges are entered *without* punctuation. For example, $1,100.00 is entered as 110000 below $ CHARGES.)
21	Enter the ICD-10-CM code for up to 12 diagnoses or conditions treated or medically managed during the encounter. Lines A through L in Block 21 will relate to CPT/HCPCS service/procedure codes reported in Block 24E. In the *ICD Ind* (ICD indicator) box, enter 0 for ICD-10-CM (or 9 for ICD-9-CM).
22	Leave blank. This is reserved for resubmitted claims.
23	Enter the applicable quality improvement organization (QIO) prior authorization number, investigational device exemption (IDE) number, NPI for a physician performing care plan oversight services of a home health agency or hospice, referral number, mammography precertification number, 10-digit Clinical Laboratory Improvement Amendments (CLIA) certification number, or skilled nursing facility NPI. *Do not enter hyphens or spaces in the number.* Otherwise, leave blank.
24A	Enter the date the procedure or service was performed in the FROM column as MM DD YY (with spaces). Enter a date in the TO column *if the procedure or service was performed on consecutive days during a range of dates. Then, enter the number of consecutive days in Block 24G.* **NOTE:** The shaded area in each line is used to enter supplemental information to support reported services *if instructed by the payer to enter such information.* Data entry in Block 24 is limited to reporting six services. *Do not use the shaded lines to report additional services.* If additional services were provided, generate new CMS-1500 claim(s) to report the additional services.
24B	Enter the appropriate two-digit place-of-service (POS) code to identify the location where the reported procedure or service was performed. (Refer to Appendix II for POS codes.)
24C	Leave blank.
24D	Enter the CPT or HCPCS level II code and applicable required modifier(s) for procedures or services performed. *Separate the CPT/HCPCS code and first modifier with one space. Separate additional modifiers with one space each. Up to four modifiers can be entered.*
24E	Enter the diagnosis pointer letter from Block 21 that relates to the procedure/service performed on the date of service. **NOTE:** When completing CMS-1500 claims for case studies in this textbook, its Workbook, and SimClaim™ software, enter just one diagnosis pointer letter on each line of Block 24E.
24F	Enter the fee charged for each reported procedure or service. When multiple procedures or services are reported on the same line, enter the total fee charged. *Do not enter commas, periods, or dollar signs. Do not enter negative amounts. Enter 00 in the cents area if the amount is a whole number.*
24G	Enter the number of days or units for procedures or services reported in Block 24D. *If just one procedure or service was reported in Block 24D, enter a 1 in Block 24G.*
24H	Leave blank. Reserved for Medicaid claims.
24I	Leave blank. The NPI abbreviation is preprinted on the CMS-1500 claim.
24J	Enter the 10-digit NPI for the: ● Provider who performed the service *if the provider is a member of a group practice* (Leave blank if the provider is a solo practitioner.)

(continues)

TABLE 14-4 (continued)

BLOCK	INSTRUCTIONS
	• Supervising provider *if the service was provided incident-to the service of a physician or nonphysician practitioner* **and** *the physician or practitioner who ordered the service did not supervise the provider* (Leave blank if the incident-to service was performed under the supervision of the physician or nonphysician practitioner.) • DMEPOS supplier or outside laboratory *if the physician submits the claim for services provided by the DMEPOS supplier or outside laboratory* (Leave blank if the DMEPOS supplier or outside laboratory submits the claim.) Otherwise, leave blank.
25	Enter the provider's social security number (SSN) or employer identification number (EIN*). Do not enter hyphens or spaces in the number.* Enter an X in the appropriate box to indicate which number is reported.
26	Enter the patient's account number as assigned by the provider.
27	Enter an X in the YES box to indicate that the provider agrees to accept assignment. Otherwise, enter an X in the NO box.
28	Enter the total charges for services and/or procedures reported in Block 24. **NOTE:** If multiple claims are submitted for one patient because more than six procedures or services were reported, be sure the total charge reported on each claim accurately represents the total of the items on each submitted claim.
29	Enter the total amount the patient (or another payer) paid *toward covered services only.* If no payment was made, leave blank.
30	Leave blank.
31	Enter the provider's name and credential (e.g., MARY SMITH MD) and the date the claim was completed as MMDDYYYY (without spaces). *Do not enter any punctuation.*
32	Enter the name and address where procedures or services were provided, *such as the patient's home, a hospital, an outside laboratory facility, a physician's office, a skilled nursing facility, or a DMEPOS supplier.* Enter the name on line 1, the address on line 2, and the city, state, and five- or nine-digit zip code on line 3. *For a nine-digit zip code, enter the hyphen.* **EXAMPLE:** • Dr. Brilliant is a solo practitioner. Enter Dr. Brilliant's name, credential, and address in Block 32. • Dr. Healer practices at the Goodmedicine Clinic. Enter Goodmedicine Clinic and its address in Block 32. **NOTE:** If Block 18 contains dates of service for inpatient care and/or Block 20 contains an X in the YES box, enter the name and address of the facility that provided services.
32a	Enter the 10-digit NPI of the provider entered in Block 32.
32b	Leave blank.
33	Enter the provider's *billing* name, address, and telephone number. Enter the phone number in the area next to the block title. *Do not enter parentheses for the area code.* Enter the name on line 1, enter the address on line 2, and enter the city, state, and five- or nine-digit zip code on line 3. *For a nine-digit zip code, enter the hyphen.*
33a	Enter the 10-digit NPI of the *billing* provider (e.g., solo practitioner) or group practice (e.g., clinic).
33b	Leave blank.

Courtesy of the Centers for Medicare & Medicaid Services, www.cms.gov

ERIN A. HELPER, M.D.
101 Medic Drive, Anywhere, NY 12345
(101) 111-1234 (Office) • (101) 111-9292 (Fax)
EIN: 11-1234523
NPI: 1234567890

Case Study

PATIENT INFORMATION:

Name:	Public, John Q.
Address:	10A Senate Avenue
City:	Anywhere
State:	NY
Zip Code:	12345-1234
Telephone:	(101) 201-7891
Gender:	Male
Date of Birth:	09-25-1930
Occupation:	
Employer:	
Spouse's Employer:	

INSURANCE INFORMATION:

Patient Number:	14-1
Place of Service:	Office
Primary Insurance Plan:	Medicare
Primary Insurance Plan ID #:	112349801A
Policy #:	
Primary Policyholder:	Public, John Q.
Policyholder Date of Birth:	09-25-1930
Relationship to Patient:	Self
Secondary Insurance Plan:	
Secondary Insurance Plan ID #:	
Secondary Policyholder:	

Patient Status ☐ Married ☐ Divorced ☒ Single ☐ Student

DIAGNOSIS INFORMATION

Diagnosis	Code	Diagnosis	Code
1. Abdominal pain	R10.9	5.	
2.		6.	
3.		7.	
4.		8.	

PROCEDURE INFORMATION

Description of Procedure or Service	Date	Code	Charge
1. New patient office visit, level III	01-20-YYYY	99203	75.00
2.			
3.			
4.			
5.			

SPECIAL NOTES: Referring physician: Ivan Gooddoc, M.D. (NPI 3456789012).

FIGURE 14-5 John Q. Public case study.

HEALTH INSURANCE CLAIM FORM

APPROVED BY NATIONAL UNIFORM CLAIM COMMITTEE (NUCC) 02/12

PICA | PICA

CARRIER

1. MEDICARE (Medicare#) / MEDICAID (Medicaid#) / TRICARE (ID#/DoD#) / CHAMPVA (Member ID#) / GROUP HEALTH PLAN (ID#) / FECA BLK LUNG (ID#) / OTHER (ID#)	X MEDICARE
1a. INSURED'S I.D. NUMBER (For Program in Item 1)	112349801A
2. PATIENT'S NAME (Last Name, First Name, Middle Initial)	PUBLIC, JOHN, Q
3. PATIENT'S BIRTH DATE MM DD YY / SEX M F	09 25 1930 / M X
4. INSURED'S NAME (Last Name, First Name, Middle Initial)	
5. PATIENT'S ADDRESS (No., Street)	10A SENATE AVENUE
6. PATIENT RELATIONSHIP TO INSURED: Self / Spouse / Child / Other	
7. INSURED'S ADDRESS (No., Street)	
CITY / STATE	ANYWHERE / NY
8. RESERVED FOR NUCC USE	
CITY / STATE	
ZIP CODE / TELEPHONE (Include Area Code)	12345-1234 / (101) 2017891
ZIP CODE / TELEPHONE (Include Area Code)	( )
9. OTHER INSURED'S NAME (Last Name, First Name, Middle Initial)	
10. IS PATIENT'S CONDITION RELATED TO:	
11. INSURED'S POLICY GROUP OR FECA NUMBER	NONE
a. OTHER INSURED'S POLICY OR GROUP NUMBER	
a. EMPLOYMENT? (Current or Previous) YES NO	X NO
a. INSURED'S DATE OF BIRTH MM DD YY / SEX M F	
b. RESERVED FOR NUCC USE	
b. AUTO ACCIDENT? YES NO PLACE (State)	X NO
b. OTHER CLAIM ID (Designated by NUCC)	
c. RESERVED FOR NUCC USE	
c. OTHER ACCIDENT? YES NO	X NO
c. INSURANCE PLAN NAME OR PROGRAM NAME	
d. INSURANCE PLAN NAME OR PROGRAM NAME	
10d. CLAIM CODES (Designated by NUCC)	
d. IS THERE ANOTHER HEALTH BENEFIT PLAN? YES NO *If yes,* complete items 9, 9a, and 9d.	

READ BACK OF FORM BEFORE COMPLETING & SIGNING THIS FORM.

12. PATIENT'S OR AUTHORIZED PERSON'S SIGNATURE I authorize the release of any medical or other information necessary to process this claim. I also request payment of government benefits either to myself or to the party who accepts assignment below.

SIGNED SIGNATURE ON FILE DATE

13. INSURED'S OR AUTHORIZED PERSON'S SIGNATURE I authorize payment of medical benefits to the undersigned physician or supplier for services described below.

SIGNED

PATIENT AND INSURED INFORMATION

14. DATE OF CURRENT ILLNESS, INJURY, or PREGNANCY (LMP) MM DD YY	01 20 YYYY QUAL. 431
15. OTHER DATE QUAL. MM DD YY	
16. DATES PATIENT UNABLE TO WORK IN CURRENT OCCUPATION FROM TO	
17. NAME OF REFERRING PROVIDER OR OTHER SOURCE	DN IVAN GOODDOC MD
17a.	
17b. NPI	3456789012
18. HOSPITALIZATION DATES RELATED TO CURRENT SERVICES FROM TO	
19. ADDITIONAL CLAIM INFORMATION (Designated by NUCC)	
20. OUTSIDE LAB? YES NO / $ CHARGES	X NO
21. DIAGNOSIS OR NATURE OF ILLNESS OR INJURY Relate A-L to service line below (24E) ICD Ind.	0
A.	R10.9
B. C. D. E. F. G. H. I. J. K. L.	
22. RESUBMISSION CODE / ORIGINAL REF. NO.	
23. PRIOR AUTHORIZATION NUMBER	

	24. A. DATE(S) OF SERVICE From MM DD YY	To MM DD YY	B. PLACE OF SERVICE	C. EMG	D. PROCEDURES, SERVICES, OR SUPPLIES (Explain Unusual Circumstances) CPT/HCPCS	MODIFIER	E. DIAGNOSIS POINTER	F. $ CHARGES	G. DAYS OR UNITS	H. EPSDT Family Plan	I. ID. QUAL.	J. RENDERING PROVIDER ID. #
1	01 20 YY		11		99203		A	75 00	1		NPI	
2											NPI	
3											NPI	
4											NPI	
5											NPI	
6											NPI	

25. FEDERAL TAX I.D. NUMBER SSN EIN	111234523 / X EIN
26. PATIENT'S ACCOUNT NO.	14-1
27. ACCEPT ASSIGNMENT? (For govt. claims, see back) YES NO	X YES
28. TOTAL CHARGE	$ 75 00
29. AMOUNT PAID	$
30. Rsvd for NUCC Use	
31. SIGNATURE OF PHYSICIAN OR SUPPLIER INCLUDING DEGREES OR CREDENTIALS (I certify that the statements on the reverse apply to this bill and are made a part thereof.)	ERIN A HELPER MD SIGNED / MMDDYYYY DATE
32. SERVICE FACILITY LOCATION INFORMATION	ERIN A HELPER MD 101 MEDIC DRIVE ANYWHERE NY 12345
32a. / b.	1234567890
33. BILLING PROVIDER INFO & PH #	(101) 1111234 ERIN A HELPER MD 101 MEDIC DRIVE ANYWHERE NY 12345
33a. / b.	1234567890

PHYSICIAN OR SUPPLIER INFORMATION

NUCC Instruction Manual available at: www.nucc.org PLEASE PRINT OR TYPE

FIGURE 14-6 Completed CMS-1500 claim for John Q. Public case study.

EXERCISE 14-2

Completing the Mary S. Patient Medicare Primary CMS-1500 Claim

1. Obtain a blank claim by making a copy of the CMS-1500 claim form in Appendix III.
2. Refer to the claims completion instructions in Table 14-4.
3. Review the Mary S. Patient case study (Figure 14-7).
4. Select the information needed from the case study, and enter the required information on the claim using optical scanning guidelines.
5. Review the claim to be sure all required blocks are properly completed.
6. Compare your claim with the completed Mary S. Patient claim in Figure 14-8.

ERIN A. HELPER, M.D.
101 Medic Drive, Anywhere, NY 12345
(101) 111-1234 (Office) • (101) 111-9292 (Fax)
EIN: 11-1234523
NPI: 1234567890

Case Study

PATIENT INFORMATION:		**INSURANCE INFORMATION:**	
Name:	Patient, Mary S.	**Patient Number:**	14-2
Address:	91 Home Street	**Place of Service:**	Office
City:	Nowhere	**Primary Insurance Plan:**	Medicare
State:	NY	**Primary Insurance Plan ID #:**	001287431D
Zip Code:	12367-1234	**Policy #:**	
Telephone:	(101) 201-8989	**Primary Policyholder:**	Mary S. Patient
Gender:	Female	**Policyholder Date of Birth:**	03-08-1933
Date of Birth:	03-08-1933	**Relationship to Patient:**	Self
Occupation:		**Secondary Insurance Plan:**	
Employer:		**Secondary Insurance Plan ID #:**	
		Secondary Policyholder:	

Patient Status ☐ Married ☐ Divorced ☒ Single ☐ Student

DIAGNOSIS INFORMATION

Diagnosis	**Code**	**Diagnosis**	**Code**
1. Pleurisy	R09.1	5.	
2. Atrial tachycardia	I47.1	6.	
3. History of pulmonary embolism	Z86.711	7.	
4.		8.	

PROCEDURE INFORMATION

Description of Procedure or Service	**Date**	**Code**	**Charge**
1. Office consultation, Level III, new patient	01-30-YYYY	99203	150.00
2. Chest x-ray, two views (frontal and lateral)	01-30-YYYY	71020	50.00
3. 12-lead ECG with interpretation and report	01-30-YYYY	93000	50.00
4.			
5.			

SPECIAL NOTES: Date of onset 01-28-YYYY. Referred by Ivan M. Gooddoc M.D. (NPI 3456789012). CPT office or other outpatient E/M code 99203 is reported (instead of CPT consultation E/M code 99243) because effective January 1, 2010, Medicare no longer recognizes CPT consultation codes for Medicare Part B payment.

FIGURE 14-7 Mary S. Patient case study.

HEALTH INSURANCE CLAIM FORM

APPROVED BY NATIONAL UNIFORM CLAIM COMMITTEE (NUCC) 02/12

PICA | PICA | CARRIER

1. MEDICARE [X] (Medicare#) | MEDICAID [ ] (Medicaid#) | TRICARE [ ] (ID#/DoD#) | CHAMPVA [ ] (Member ID#) | GROUP HEALTH PLAN [ ] (ID#) | FECA BLK LUNG [ ] (ID#) | OTHER [ ] (ID#)

1a. INSURED'S I.D. NUMBER (For Program in Item 1): 001287431D

2. PATIENT'S NAME (Last Name, First Name, Middle Initial): PATIENT, MARY, S

3. PATIENT'S BIRTH DATE MM DD YY: 03 08 1933 SEX M [ ] F [X]

4. INSURED'S NAME (Last Name, First Name, Middle Initial):

5. PATIENT'S ADDRESS (No., Street): 91 HOME STREET

6. PATIENT RELATIONSHIP TO INSURED: Self [ ] Spouse [ ] Child [ ] Other [ ]

7. INSURED'S ADDRESS (No., Street):

CITY: NOWHERE STATE: NY

8. RESERVED FOR NUCC USE

CITY STATE

ZIP CODE: 12367-1234 TELEPHONE (Include Area Code): (101) 2018989

ZIP CODE TELEPHONE (Include Area Code) ( )

9. OTHER INSURED'S NAME (Last Name, First Name, Middle Initial)

10. IS PATIENT'S CONDITION RELATED TO:

11. INSURED'S POLICY GROUP OR FECA NUMBER: NONE

a. OTHER INSURED'S POLICY OR GROUP NUMBER

a. EMPLOYMENT? (Current or Previous) [ ] YES [X] NO

a. INSURED'S DATE OF BIRTH MM DD YY SEX M [ ] F [ ]

b. RESERVED FOR NUCC USE

b. AUTO ACCIDENT? [ ] YES [X] NO PLACE (State)

b. OTHER CLAIM ID (Designated by NUCC)

c. RESERVED FOR NUCC USE

c. OTHER ACCIDENT? [ ] YES [X] NO

c. INSURANCE PLAN NAME OR PROGRAM NAME

d. INSURANCE PLAN NAME OR PROGRAM NAME

10d. CLAIM CODES (Designated by NUCC)

d. IS THERE ANOTHER HEALTH BENEFIT PLAN? [ ] YES [ ] NO *If yes, complete items 9, 9a, and 9d.*

READ BACK OF FORM BEFORE COMPLETING & SIGNING THIS FORM.

12. PATIENT'S OR AUTHORIZED PERSON'S SIGNATURE I authorize the release of any medical or other information necessary to process this claim. I also request payment of government benefits either to myself or to the party who accepts assignment below.

SIGNED SIGNATURE ON FILE DATE

13. INSURED'S OR AUTHORIZED PERSON'S SIGNATURE I authorize payment of medical benefits to the undersigned physician or supplier for services described below.

SIGNED

PATIENT AND INSURED INFORMATION

14. DATE OF CURRENT ILLNESS, INJURY, or PREGNANCY (LMP) MM DD YY: 01 28 YYYY QUAL. 431

15. OTHER DATE QUAL. MM DD YY

16. DATES PATIENT UNABLE TO WORK IN CURRENT OCCUPATION FROM TO

17. NAME OF REFERRING PROVIDER OR OTHER SOURCE: DN IVAN M GOODDOC MD

17a. | 17b. NPI 3456789012

18. HOSPITALIZATION DATES RELATED TO CURRENT SERVICES FROM TO

19. ADDITIONAL CLAIM INFORMATION (Designated by NUCC)

20. OUTSIDE LAB? [ ] YES [X] NO $ CHARGES

21. DIAGNOSIS OR NATURE OF ILLNESS OR INJURY Relate A-L to service line below (24E) ICD Ind. 0

A. R09.1 B. I47.1 C. Z86.711 D.
E. F. G. H.
I. J. K. L.

22. RESUBMISSION CODE ORIGINAL REF. NO.

23. PRIOR AUTHORIZATION NUMBER

	24. A. DATE(S) OF SERVICE From MM DD YY	To MM DD YY	B. PLACE OF SERVICE	C. EMG	D. PROCEDURES, SERVICES, OR SUPPLIES (Explain Unusual Circumstances) CPT/HCPCS	MODIFIER	E. DIAGNOSIS POINTER	F. $ CHARGES	G. DAYS OR UNITS	H. EPSDT Family Plan	I. ID. QUAL.	J. RENDERING PROVIDER ID. #
1	01 30 YY		11		99203		A	150 00	1		NPI	
2	01 30 YY		11		71020		A	50 00	1		NPI	
3	01 30 YY		11		93000		B	50 00	1		NPI	
4											NPI	
5											NPI	
6											NPI	

25. FEDERAL TAX I.D. NUMBER: 111234523 SSN [ ] EIN [X]

26. PATIENT'S ACCOUNT NO.: 14-2

27. ACCEPT ASSIGNMENT? (For govt. claims, see back) [X] YES [ ] NO

28. TOTAL CHARGE: $ 250 00

29. AMOUNT PAID: $

30. Rsvd for NUCC Use

31. SIGNATURE OF PHYSICIAN OR SUPPLIER INCLUDING DEGREES OR CREDENTIALS (I certify that the statements on the reverse apply to this bill and are made a part thereof.)

SIGNED ERIN A HELPER MD DATE MMDDYYYY

32. SERVICE FACILITY LOCATION INFORMATION
ERIN A HELPER MD
101 MEDIC DRIVE
ANYWHERE NY 12345
a. 1234567890 b.

33. BILLING PROVIDER INFO & PH # (101) 1111234
ERIN A HELPER MD
101 MEDIC DRIVE
ANYWHERE NY 12345
a. 1234567890 b.

PHYSICIAN OR SUPPLIER INFORMATION

NUCC Instruction Manual available at: www.nucc.org *PLEASE PRINT OR TYPE*

FIGURE 14-8 Completed Medicare primary CMS-1500 claim for Mary S. Patient case study.

MEDICARE AND MEDIGAP CLAIMS

Modifications must be made to the Medicare primary claim (Table 14-5 and Figure 14-9) when the health care provider is a Medicare PAR, the patient has a Medigap policy in addition to Medicare, and the patient has signed an Authorization for Release of Medigap Benefits. If a separate Medigap release is on file, the words SIGNATURE ON FILE must appear in Block 13. No benefits will be paid to the PAR if Block 27, Accept Assignment, contains an X in the NO box.

TABLE 14-5 CMS-1500 claims completion instructions for Medicare and Medigap claims

BLOCK	INSTRUCTIONS
1	Enter an X in the *Medicare* and the *Other* boxes.
9	Enter SAME if the patient is the Medigap policyholder. If the patient is *not* the Medigap policyholder, enter the policyholder's last name, first name, and middle initial (if known) (separated by commas).
9a	Enter MEDIGAP followed by the policy number and group number, separated by spaces (e.g., MEDIGAP 123456789 123). (The abbreviations MG or MGAP are also acceptable.)
9d	Enter the Medigap Plan ID number.
13	Enter SIGNATURE ON FILE. (The abbreviation SOF is also acceptable.) Leave the date field blank.

Courtesy of the Centers for Medicare & Medicaid Services, www.cms.gov

EXERCISE 14-3

Medicare and Medigap Claims Processing

Additional information needed for this case:

Dr. Helper is a Medicare PAR. The billing entity is Erin Helper, M.D.

1. Obtain a blank claim by making a copy of the CMS-1500 claim form in Appendix III.
2. Underline the block identifiers on the new claim for the blocks listed in the Medicare and Medigap claim form instructions (Table 14-5).
3. Refer to the case study for John Q. Public (see Figure 14-5). Enter the following information in the blocks for the secondary policy:

   Aetna Medigap ID # 22233544

   Plan ID: 11543299

   Policyholder: John Q. Public

   Employer: Retired
4. Complete the Medicare-Medigap claim using the data from the case study.
5. Compare the completed claim to the claim in Figure 14-9 to be sure all required blocks are properly completed.

HEALTH INSURANCE CLAIM FORM

APPROVED BY NATIONAL UNIFORM CLAIM COMMITTEE (NUCC) 02/12

PICA

1. MEDICARE [X] (Medicare#) MEDICAID (Medicaid#) TRICARE (ID#/DoD#) CHAMPVA (Member ID#) GROUP HEALTH PLAN (ID#) FECA BLK LUNG (ID#) OTHER [X] (ID#)

1a. INSURED'S I.D. NUMBER (For Program in Item 1): 112349801A

2. PATIENT'S NAME (Last Name, First Name, Middle Initial): PUBLIC, JOHN, Q

3. PATIENT'S BIRTH DATE MM DD YY: 09 25 1930 SEX M [X] F

4. INSURED'S NAME (Last Name, First Name, Middle Initial):

5. PATIENT'S ADDRESS (No., Street): 10A SENATE AVENUE

CITY: ANYWHERE STATE: NY

ZIP CODE: 12345-1234 TELEPHONE (Include Area Code): (101) 2017891

6. PATIENT RELATIONSHIP TO INSURED: Self Spouse Child Other

7. INSURED'S ADDRESS (No., Street): CITY STATE ZIP CODE TELEPHONE (Include Area Code) ( )

8. RESERVED FOR NUCC USE

9. OTHER INSURED'S NAME (Last Name, First Name, Middle Initial): SAME

a. OTHER INSURED'S POLICY OR GROUP NUMBER: MEDIGAP 22233544

b. RESERVED FOR NUCC USE

c. RESERVED FOR NUCC USE

d. INSURANCE PLAN NAME OR PROGRAM NAME: 11543299

10. IS PATIENT'S CONDITION RELATED TO:

a. EMPLOYMENT? (Current or Previous) YES [X] NO

b. AUTO ACCIDENT? YES [X] NO PLACE (State)

c. OTHER ACCIDENT? YES [X] NO

10d. CLAIM CODES (Designated by NUCC)

11. INSURED'S POLICY GROUP OR FECA NUMBER: NONE

a. INSURED'S DATE OF BIRTH MM DD YY SEX M F

b. OTHER CLAIM ID (Designated by NUCC)

c. INSURANCE PLAN NAME OR PROGRAM NAME

d. IS THERE ANOTHER HEALTH BENEFIT PLAN? YES NO *If yes*, complete items 9, 9a, and 9d.

READ BACK OF FORM BEFORE COMPLETING & SIGNING THIS FORM.

12. PATIENT'S OR AUTHORIZED PERSON'S SIGNATURE I authorize the release of any medical or other information necessary to process this claim. I also request payment of government benefits either to myself or to the party who accepts assignment below.

SIGNED SIGNATURE ON FILE DATE

13. INSURED'S OR AUTHORIZED PERSON'S SIGNATURE I authorize payment of medical benefits to the undersigned physician or supplier for services described below.

SIGNED SIGNATURE ON FILE

14. DATE OF CURRENT ILLNESS, INJURY, or PREGNANCY (LMP) MM DD YY: 01 09 YYYY QUAL. 431

15. OTHER DATE QUAL. MM DD YY

16. DATES PATIENT UNABLE TO WORK IN CURRENT OCCUPATION FROM TO

17. NAME OF REFERRING PROVIDER OR OTHER SOURCE: DN IVAN GOODDOC MD

17a. 17b. NPI 3456789012

18. HOSPITALIZATION DATES RELATED TO CURRENT SERVICES FROM TO

19. ADDITIONAL CLAIM INFORMATION (Designated by NUCC)

20. OUTSIDE LAB? YES [X] NO $ CHARGES

21. DIAGNOSIS OR NATURE OF ILLNESS OR INJURY Relate A-L to service line below (24E) ICD Ind. 0

A. R10.9 B. C. D. E. F. G. H. I. J. K. L.

22. RESUBMISSION CODE ORIGINAL REF. NO.

23. PRIOR AUTHORIZATION NUMBER

24. A. DATE(S) OF SERVICE From MM DD YY	To MM DD YY	B. PLACE OF SERVICE	C. EMG	D. PROCEDURES, SERVICES, OR SUPPLIES (Explain Unusual Circumstances) CPT/HCPCS	MODIFIER	E. DIAGNOSIS POINTER	F. $ CHARGES	G. DAYS OR UNITS	H. EPSDT Family Plan	I. ID. QUAL.	J. RENDERING PROVIDER ID. #
1 01 20 YY		11		99203		A	75 00	1		NPI	
2										NPI	
3										NPI	
4										NPI	
5										NPI	
6										NPI	

25. FEDERAL TAX I.D. NUMBER SSN EIN [X]: 111234523

26. PATIENT'S ACCOUNT NO.: 14-1

27. ACCEPT ASSIGNMENT? (For govt. claims, see back) [X] YES NO

28. TOTAL CHARGE: $ 75 00

29. AMOUNT PAID $

30. Rsvd for NUCC Use

31. SIGNATURE OF PHYSICIAN OR SUPPLIER INCLUDING DEGREES OR CREDENTIALS (I certify that the statements on the reverse apply to this bill and are made a part thereof.)

SIGNED ERIN A HELPER MD DATE MMDDYYYY

32. SERVICE FACILITY LOCATION INFORMATION
ERIN A HELPER MD
101 MEDIC DRIVE
ANYWHERE NY 12345
a. 1234567890 b.

33. BILLING PROVIDER INFO & PH # (101) 1111234
ERIN A HELPER MD
101 MEDIC DRIVE
ANYWHERE NY 12345
a. 1234567890 b.

NUCC Instruction Manual available at: www.nucc.org *PLEASE PRINT OR TYPE*

CARRIER — PATIENT AND INSURED INFORMATION — PHYSICIAN OR SUPPLIER INFORMATION

FIGURE 14-9 Completed Medicare-Medigap CMS-1500 claim for John Q. Public case study.

MEDICARE-MEDICAID (MEDI-MEDI) CROSSOVER CLAIMS

A **Medicare-Medicaid (Medi-Medi) crossover** plan provides both Medicare and Medicaid coverage to certain eligible beneficiaries (Medicare beneficiaries with low incomes).

The following modifications must be added to the Medicare primary claim when the patient is covered by Medicare and also has Medicaid coverage for services rendered on a fee-for-service basis (Table 14-6 and Figure 14-10).

TABLE 14-6 CMS-1500 claims completion instructions for Medicare-Medicaid (Medi-Medi) crossover claims

BLOCK	INSTRUCTIONS
1	Enter an X in both the Medicare *and* Medicaid boxes. **NOTE:** According to NUCC claims instructions, an X is to be entered in just one box in Block 1. However, at the time this textbook was printed, Medicare-Medicaid crossover claims instructions require an X to be entered in both the Medicare and Medicaid boxes.
10d	Enter the abbreviation MCD followed by the patient's Medicaid ID number.
27	Enter an X in the YES box. (NonPAR providers must accept assignment on Medicare-Medicaid crossover claims.)

Courtesy of the Centers for Medicare & Medicaid Services, www.cms.gov

EXERCISE 14-4

Medicare-Medicaid Crossover Claims Processing

Additional information needed for this case:

Dr. Helper is a Medicare PAR. The billing entity is Erin Helper, M.D.

1. Obtain a blank claim by making a copy of the CMS-1500 claim form in Appendix III.
2. Underline the blocks discussed in the Medicare-Medicaid crossover claims instructions (Table 14-6).
3. Refer to the Mary S. Patient case study in Figure 14-7, and enter additional Medicaid information in the secondary policy blocks:

   Insurance policy: Medicaid

   ID #: 101234591XT

   Relationship: Self
4. Complete the Medicare-Medicaid (Medi-Medi) claim.
5. Compare the completed claim with the claim in Figure 14-10.

MEDICARE AS SECONDARY PAYER CLAIMS

CMS-1500 claims instructions are modified when Medicare is secondary to another insurance plan (Table 14-7 and Figure 14-7). The Medicare Secondary Payer (MSP) program coordinates benefits between Medicare and other payers to determine if another insurance plan is primary. CMS awards a coordination-of-benefits (COB) contract to consolidate activities that support the collection, management, and reporting of other insurance coverage primary to

HEALTH INSURANCE CLAIM FORM

APPROVED BY NATIONAL UNIFORM CLAIM COMMITTEE (NUCC) 02/12

PICA

1. MEDICARE (Medicare#) X | MEDICAID (Medicaid#) X | TRICARE (ID#/DoD#) | CHAMPVA (Member ID#) | GROUP HEALTH PLAN (ID#) | FECA BLK LUNG (ID#) | OTHER (ID#)

1a. INSURED'S I.D. NUMBER (For Program in Item 1): 001287431D

2. PATIENT'S NAME (Last Name, First Name, Middle Initial): PATIENT, MARY, S

3. PATIENT'S BIRTH DATE MM DD YY: 03 08 1933 SEX M ☐ F X

4. INSURED'S NAME (Last Name, First Name, Middle Initial):

5. PATIENT'S ADDRESS (No., Street): 91 HOME STREET

6. PATIENT RELATIONSHIP TO INSURED: Self ☐ Spouse ☐ Child ☐ Other ☐

7. INSURED'S ADDRESS (No., Street):

CITY: NOWHERE STATE: NY

8. RESERVED FOR NUCC USE

CITY STATE

ZIP CODE: 12367-1234 TELEPHONE (Include Area Code): (101) 2018989

ZIP CODE TELEPHONE (Include Area Code) ( )

9. OTHER INSURED'S NAME (Last Name, First Name, Middle Initial)

10. IS PATIENT'S CONDITION RELATED TO:

11. INSURED'S POLICY GROUP OR FECA NUMBER: NONE

a. OTHER INSURED'S POLICY OR GROUP NUMBER

a. EMPLOYMENT? (Current or Previous) ☐ YES X NO

a. INSURED'S DATE OF BIRTH MM DD YY SEX M ☐ F ☐

b. RESERVED FOR NUCC USE

b. AUTO ACCIDENT? ☐ YES X NO PLACE (State)

b. OTHER CLAIM ID (Designated by NUCC)

c. RESERVED FOR NUCC USE

c. OTHER ACCIDENT? ☐ YES X NO

c. INSURANCE PLAN NAME OR PROGRAM NAME

d. INSURANCE PLAN NAME OR PROGRAM NAME

10d. CLAIM CODES (Designated by NUCC): MCD 101234591XT

d. IS THERE ANOTHER HEALTH BENEFIT PLAN? ☐ YES ☐ NO *If yes, complete items 9, 9a, and 9d.*

READ BACK OF FORM BEFORE COMPLETING & SIGNING THIS FORM.

12. PATIENT'S OR AUTHORIZED PERSON'S SIGNATURE I authorize the release of any medical or other information necessary to process this claim. I also request payment of government benefits either to myself or to the party who accepts assignment below.

SIGNED SIGNATURE ON FILE DATE

13. INSURED'S OR AUTHORIZED PERSON'S SIGNATURE I authorize payment of medical benefits to the undersigned physician or supplier for services described below.

SIGNED

14. DATE OF CURRENT ILLNESS, INJURY, or PREGNANCY (LMP) MM DD YY: 01 28 YYYY QUAL. 431

15. OTHER DATE QUAL. MM DD YY

16. DATES PATIENT UNABLE TO WORK IN CURRENT OCCUPATION FROM TO

17. NAME OF REFERRING PROVIDER OR OTHER SOURCE: DN IVAN M GOODDOC MD

17a. 17b. NPI 3456789012

18. HOSPITALIZATION DATES RELATED TO CURRENT SERVICES FROM TO

19. ADDITIONAL CLAIM INFORMATION (Designated by NUCC)

20. OUTSIDE LAB? ☐ YES X NO $ CHARGES

21. DIAGNOSIS OR NATURE OF ILLNESS OR INJURY Relate A-L to service line below (24E) ICD Ind. 0

A. R09.1 B. I47.1 C. Z86.711 D.
E. F. G. H.
I. J. K. L.

22. RESUBMISSION CODE ORIGINAL REF. NO.

23. PRIOR AUTHORIZATION NUMBER

	24. A. DATE(S) OF SERVICE From MM DD YY	To MM DD YY	B. PLACE OF SERVICE	C. EMG	D. PROCEDURES, SERVICES, OR SUPPLIES (Explain Unusual Circumstances) CPT/HCPCS	MODIFIER	E. DIAGNOSIS POINTER	F. $ CHARGES	G. DAYS OR UNITS	H. EPSDT Family Plan	I. ID. QUAL.	J. RENDERING PROVIDER ID. #
1	01 30 YY		11		99203		A	150 00	1		NPI	
2	01 30 YY		11		71020		A	50 00	1		NPI	
3	01 30 YY		11		93000		B	50 00	1		NPI	
4											NPI	
5											NPI	
6											NPI	

25. FEDERAL TAX I.D. NUMBER: 111234523 SSN ☐ EIN X

26. PATIENT'S ACCOUNT NO.: 14-2

27. ACCEPT ASSIGNMENT? (For govt. claims, see back) X YES ☐ NO

28. TOTAL CHARGE: $ 250 00

29. AMOUNT PAID: $

30. Rsvd for NUCC Use

31. SIGNATURE OF PHYSICIAN OR SUPPLIER INCLUDING DEGREES OR CREDENTIALS (I certify that the statements on the reverse apply to this bill and are made a part thereof.)

SIGNED ERIN A HELPER MD DATE MMDDYYYY

32. SERVICE FACILITY LOCATION INFORMATION
ERIN A HELPER MD
101 MEDIC DRIVE
ANYWHERE NY 12345

a. 1234567890 b.

33. BILLING PROVIDER INFO & PH # (101) 1111234
ERIN A HELPER MD
101 MEDIC DRIVE
ANYWHERE NY 12345

a. 1234567890 b.

NUCC Instruction Manual available at: www.nucc.org *PLEASE PRINT OR TYPE*

CARRIER — PATIENT AND INSURED INFORMATION — PHYSICIAN OR SUPPLIER INFORMATION

FIGURE 14-10 Completed Medicare-Medicaid (Medi-Medi) CMS-1500 claim for Mary S. Patient case study.

Medicare. The COB contractor uses the following to identify insurance primary to Medicare:

- ***Initial Enrollment Questionnaire (IEQ)***—Medicare beneficiaries complete a questionnaire about other insurance coverage about three months before they are entitled to Medicare
- ***IRS/SSA/CMS Data Match***—Employers complete a questionnaire that provides group health plan (GHP) information about identified workers who are either entitled to Medicare or married to a Medicare beneficiary
- ***MSP Claims Investigation***—Collects data about other health insurance that may be primary to Medicare; is based on information submitted on a CMS-1500 claim or from other sources
- ***Voluntary MSP Data Match Agreements***—Voluntary agreements between CMS and employers and payers that allow the electronic data exchange of group health plan eligibility and Medicare information

NOTE: Effective 2007, HCPCS level II modifier -M2 (Medicare secondary payer) was added to reported codes to communicate to private payers that Medicare is the secondary payer. Reporting modifier -M2 prevents claims denial based on the patient's age or another edit specific to a private payer.

TABLE 14-7 CMS-1500 claims completion instructions for Medicare as secondary payer claims

BLOCK	INSTRUCTIONS
1	Enter an X in the *Medicare* and *Other* boxes. **NOTE:** According to NUCC claims instructions, an X is to be entered in just one box in Block 1. However, at the time this textbook was printed, Medicare as secondary payer claims instructions require an X to be entered in both the Medicare and Other boxes.
4	If the policyholder is the patient, enter SAME. If the patient is not the policyholder, enter the primary insurance policyholder's name.
6	Enter an X in the appropriate box to indicate the patient's relationship to the primary insurance policyholder.
7	Enter SAME.
10a-10c	Enter an X in the appropriate boxes to indicate whether the patient's condition is related to employment or an auto or other accident. **NOTE:** Entering an X in any of the YES boxes alerts the Medicare administrative contractor that another insurance plan might be liable for payment. Medicare will not process the claim until the provider submits a remittance advice from the liable party (e.g., auto insurance, workers' compensation).
11	Enter the primary policyholder's group number if the patient is covered by a group health plan. *Do not enter hyphens or spaces in the policy or group number.* Otherwise, leave blank.
11a	Enter the primary insurance policyholder's date of birth as MM DD YYYY (with spaces). Enter an X in the appropriate box to indicate the policyholder's gender.
11c	Enter the name of the primary policyholder's insurance plan. **NOTE:** Be sure to attach a copy of the remittance advice to the claim, which must contain the payer's name and address.
11d	Enter an X in the NO box. **NOTE:** Medicare is secondary, which is indicated by entering an X in the Medicare box in Block 1. However, an X is entered in the YES box if the patient is covered by a secondary or supplemental health plan (e.g., commercial health plan) in addition to a primary health plan (e.g., employer-based group health plan) and Medicare as secondary coverage.
16	If the patient is employed full time, enter the dates the patient is or was unable to work (if applicable).

Courtesy of the Centers for Medicare & Medicaid Services, www.cms.gov

EXERCISE 14-5

Medicare as Secondary Payer Claims Processing

Additional information needed for this case:

Dr. Helper is a Medicare PAR. The billing entity is Erin Helper, M.D. The ambulatory surgical center NPI is 5678901234.

1. Obtain a blank claim by making a copy of the CMS-1500 claim form in Appendix III.
2. Underline the blocks discussed in the Medicare Secondary Payer claims instructions in Table 14-7. Add an "S" to the patient's account number in Block 26 (e.g., 14-3S).
3. Refer to the Jack L. Neely case study (Figure 14-11) and complete the Medicare Secondary Payer claim for this case.
4. Review the completed claim to be sure all required blocks are filled in.
5. Compare your claim with Figure 14-12.

ERIN A. HELPER, M.D.
101 Medic Drive, Anywhere, NY 12345
(101) 111-1234 (Office) • (101) 111-9292 (Fax)
EIN: 11-1234523
NPI: 1234567890

Case Study

PATIENT INFORMATION:		**INSURANCE INFORMATION:**	
Name:	Jack L. Neely	**Patient Number:**	14-3
Address:	329 Water Street	**Place of Service:**	Anywhere Surgical Center
City:	Nowhere	**Primary Insurance Plan:**	BCBS Federal
State:	NY	**Primary Insurance Plan ID #:**	R1234567
Zip Code:	12367-1234	**Primary Group #:**	103
Telephone:	(101) 201-1278	**Primary Policyholder:**	Mary Neely
Gender:	Male	**Primary Policyholder Birth Date:**	03-19-1935
Date of Birth:	09-09-1929	**Relationship to Patient:**	Spouse
Occupation:	Retired	**Secondary Policy:**	Medicare
Spouse's Employer:	Federal Investigative Service	**Secondary Insurance Plan ID #:**	111223344A
		Secondary Policyholder:	Jack L. Neely

Patient Status ☒ Married ☐ Divorced ☐ Single ☐ Student

DIAGNOSIS INFORMATION

Diagnosis	**Code**	**Diagnosis**	**Code**
1. Rectal bleeding (3 days)	K62.5	5.	
2. History of polyps, ascending colon	Z85.038	6.	
3.		7.	
4.		8.	

PROCEDURE INFORMATION

Description of Procedure or Service	**Date**	**Code**	**Charge**
1. Colonoscopy, flexible to ileum	01-08-YYYY	45378	700.00
2.			
3.			
4.			
5.			

SPECIAL NOTES: Referring physician: Arnold Younglove M.D. (NPI 4567890123)
Anywhere Surgical Center, 101 Park St, Anywhere, NY 12345 (NPI 5678901234)

FIGURE 14-11 Jack L. Neely case study.

HEALTH INSURANCE CLAIM FORM

APPROVED BY NATIONAL UNIFORM CLAIM COMMITTEE (NUCC) 02/12

PICA — PICA — CARRIER

PATIENT AND INSURED INFORMATION

1. MEDICARE (Medicare#) / MEDICAID (Medicaid#) / TRICARE (ID#/DoD#) / CHAMPVA (Member ID#) / GROUP HEALTH PLAN (ID#) / FECA BLK LUNG (ID#) / OTHER (ID#)	X MEDICARE; X OTHER
1a. INSURED'S I.D. NUMBER (For Program in Item 1)	111223344A
2. PATIENT'S NAME (Last Name, First Name, Middle Initial)	NEELY, JACK, L
3. PATIENT'S BIRTH DATE MM DD YY / SEX	09 09 1929 / M X
4. INSURED'S NAME (Last Name, First Name, Middle Initial)	NEELY, MARY
5. PATIENT'S ADDRESS (No., Street)	329 WATER STREET
CITY / STATE	NOWHERE / NY
ZIP CODE / TELEPHONE (Include Area Code)	12367-1234 / (101) 2011278
6. PATIENT RELATIONSHIP TO INSURED: Self / Spouse / Child / Other	Spouse X
7. INSURED'S ADDRESS (No., Street)	SAME
CITY / STATE	
ZIP CODE / TELEPHONE (Include Area Code)	( )
8. RESERVED FOR NUCC USE	
9. OTHER INSURED'S NAME (Last Name, First Name, Middle Initial)	
a. OTHER INSURED'S POLICY OR GROUP NUMBER	
b. RESERVED FOR NUCC USE	
c. RESERVED FOR NUCC USE	
d. INSURANCE PLAN NAME OR PROGRAM NAME	
10. IS PATIENT'S CONDITION RELATED TO: a. EMPLOYMENT? (Current or Previous) YES / NO	X NO
b. AUTO ACCIDENT? YES / NO PLACE (State)	X NO
c. OTHER ACCIDENT? YES / NO	X NO
10d. CLAIM CODES (Designated by NUCC)	
11. INSURED'S POLICY GROUP OR FECA NUMBER	103
a. INSURED'S DATE OF BIRTH MM DD YY / SEX	03 19 1935 / F X
b. OTHER CLAIM ID (Designated by NUCC)	
c. INSURANCE PLAN NAME OR PROGRAM NAME	BCBS FEDERAL
d. IS THERE ANOTHER HEALTH BENEFIT PLAN? YES / NO *If yes, complete items 9, 9a, and 9d.*	X NO

READ BACK OF FORM BEFORE COMPLETING & SIGNING THIS FORM.

12. PATIENT'S OR AUTHORIZED PERSON'S SIGNATURE I authorize the release of any medical or other information necessary to process this claim. I also request payment of government benefits either to myself or to the party who accepts assignment below.

SIGNED SIGNATURE ON FILE DATE

13. INSURED'S OR AUTHORIZED PERSON'S SIGNATURE I authorize payment of medical benefits to the undersigned physician or supplier for services described below.

SIGNED

PHYSICIAN OR SUPPLIER INFORMATION

14. DATE OF CURRENT ILLNESS, INJURY, or PREGNANCY (LMP) MM DD YY / QUAL.	01 08 YYYY / QUAL. 431
15. OTHER DATE QUAL. MM DD YY	
16. DATES PATIENT UNABLE TO WORK IN CURRENT OCCUPATION FROM / TO	
17. NAME OF REFERRING PROVIDER OR OTHER SOURCE	DN ARNOLD YOUNGLOVE MD
17a.	
17b. NPI	4567890123
18. HOSPITALIZATION DATES RELATED TO CURRENT SERVICES FROM / TO	
19. ADDITIONAL CLAIM INFORMATION (Designated by NUCC)	
20. OUTSIDE LAB? YES / NO $ CHARGES	X NO
21. DIAGNOSIS OR NATURE OF ILLNESS OR INJURY Relate A-L to service line below (24E) ICD Ind.	A. K62.5 B. Z85.038 C. D. E. F. G. H. I. J. K. L.
22. RESUBMISSION CODE / ORIGINAL REF. NO.	
23. PRIOR AUTHORIZATION NUMBER	

	24. A. DATE(S) OF SERVICE From MM DD YY	To MM DD YY	B. PLACE OF SERVICE	C. EMG	D. PROCEDURES, SERVICES, OR SUPPLIES (Explain Unusual Circumstances) CPT/HCPCS	MODIFIER	E. DIAGNOSIS POINTER	F. $ CHARGES	G. DAYS OR UNITS	H. EPSDT Family Plan	I. ID. QUAL.	J. RENDERING PROVIDER ID. #
1	01 08 YY		24		45378		A	700 00	1		NPI	
2											NPI	
3											NPI	
4											NPI	
5											NPI	
6											NPI	

25. FEDERAL TAX I.D. NUMBER SSN EIN	111234523 / EIN X
26. PATIENT'S ACCOUNT NO.	14-3S
27. ACCEPT ASSIGNMENT? (For govt. claims, see back) YES / NO	X YES
28. TOTAL CHARGE	$ 700 00
29. AMOUNT PAID	$
30. Rsvd for NUCC Use	
31. SIGNATURE OF PHYSICIAN OR SUPPLIER INCLUDING DEGREES OR CREDENTIALS (I certify that the statements on the reverse apply to this bill and are made a part thereof.)	SIGNED ERIN A HELPER MD DATE MMDDYYYY
32. SERVICE FACILITY LOCATION INFORMATION	ANYWHERE SURGICAL CENTER 101 PARK ST ANYWHERE NY 12345 a. 5678901234 b.
33. BILLING PROVIDER INFO & PH #	(101) 1111234 ERIN A HELPER MD 101 MEDIC DRIVE ANYWHERE NY 12345 a. 1234567890 b.

NUCC Instruction Manual available at: www.nucc.org PLEASE PRINT OR TYPE

FIGURE 14-12 Completed Medicare Secondary Payer CMS-1500 claim for Jack L. Neely case study.

Additional Medicare case studies are found in Appendices I and II.

Completing case studies requires you to read the case study chart entries, then select and code the diagnostic information. Necessary hospital and physician data are included in the case studies in Appendix II.

ROSTER BILLING FOR MASS VACCINATION PROGRAMS

NOTE: There is no minimum requirement as to the number of beneficiaries to be reported on the same date (the rule used to be a minimum of five beneficiaries reported on the same date to qualify for roster billing). *However, the date of service for each vaccination administered must be entered.*

NOTE: Roster billing is not used to submit single patient bills.

The simplified **roster billing** process was developed to enable Medicare beneficiaries to participate in mass pneumococcal polysaccharide vaccine (PPV) and influenza virus vaccination programs offered by public health clinics (PHCs) and other entities that bill Medicare payers. (Medicare has not yet developed roster billing for hepatitis B vaccinations.) Properly licensed individuals and entities conducting mass immunization programs may submit claims using a simplified claims filing procedure to bill for the PPV and influenza virus vaccine benefit for multiple beneficiaries if they agree to accept assignment for these claims. Entities that submit claims on roster bills (and therefore must accept assignment) may not collect any donations or other cost-sharing of any kind from Medicare beneficiaries for PPV or influenza vaccinations. However, the entity may bill Medicare for the amount not subsidized from its own budget.

NOTE: Providers should establish a computer edit to identify individuals and entities that plan to participate in the Medicare program only for the purpose of mass immunizing beneficiaries.

EXAMPLE: A public health clinic (PHC) sponsors an influenza virus vaccination clinic for Medicare beneficiaries. The cost is $12.50 per vaccination, and the PHC pays $2.50 of the cost from its budget.

The PHC is therefore eligible to roster-bill Medicare the $10 cost difference for each beneficiary. The PHC submits both the roster billing form (Figure 14-13) and CMS-1500 claim (Figure 14-14).

NOTE: During a mass immunization clinic, beneficiaries receive either the PPV *or* the influenza virus vaccination, not both. (This note applies to Blocks 21 and 24D.)

Provider Enrollment Criteria

All individuals and entities that submit PPV and influenza virus vaccination benefit claims to Medicare on roster bills must complete Form CMS-855, the Provider/Supplier Enrollment Application. Specialized instructions must be followed to simplify the enrollment process, and providers may not bill Medicare for any services other than PPV and influenza virus vaccinations.

NOTE: If the provider is not charging for the vaccine or its administration, enter 0 00 or NC (for "no charge") on the appropriate line for that item. This information is required for both paper claims and electronic submissions.

Completing the CMS-1500 Claim for Roster Billing Purposes

Providers that qualify for roster billing may use a preprinted CMS-1500 claim that contains standardized information about the entity and the benefit (Table 14-8). Providers that submit roster bills to carriers must complete certain blocks on a single modified CMS-1500 claim, which serves as the cover sheet for the roster bill.

Provider	Allegany Health Clinic 100 Main St, Anywhere, NY 12345 (101) 555-1111
EIN	98-7654321
NPI	1123456789
Date of Service	November 15, YYYY
Diagnosis	Encounter for immunization (ICD code Z23)
Type of Service	Flu vaccine (Afluria) (HCPCS level II codes Q2035-33 and G0008-33) $10.00 ($50.00 to be billed to Medicare) (Q2035-33)
Cost	$1.00 ($5.00 to be billed to Medicare) (G0008-33)

Patient Information

HICN	Name	DOB	Sex	Address	Signature
215659849	Doe, John A	02/05/34	M	1 Hill, Anywhere, NY 12345	John A. Doe
236595428	Doe, Jane M	12/24/30	F	5 Main, Anywhere, NY 12345	Jane M. Doe
236595214	Smith, May J	02/18/32	F	8 Roe, Anywhere, NY 12345	May J Smith
956325954	Brown, Lou	05/15/20	F	2 Sims, Anywhere, NY 12345	Lou Brown
596524854	Green, Julie	09/30/25	F	6 Pine, Anywhere, NY 12345	Julie Green

FIGURE 14-13 Sample roster billing form (attach to CMS-1500 claim).

TABLE 14-8 CMS-1500 claims completion instructions for Medicare roster billing

BLOCK	INSTRUCTIONS
1	Enter an X in the Medicare box.
2	Enter SEE ATTACHED ROSTER.
11	Enter NONE.
20	Enter an X in the NO box.
21	On line 1, enter V03.82 for PPV *or* V04.81 for influenza virus.
24B	Enter 60 (place of service, POS, code for "mass immunization center").
24D	On line 1, enter 90732 for PPV *or* Q2305 for influenza virus (Afluria). On line 2, enter G0009 (administration code for PPV) *or* G0008 (administration code for influenza). Then, enter 33 as the modifier.
24E	On lines 1 and 2, enter the diagnosis pointer letter from Block 21.
24F	On lines 1 and 2, enter the total charges for each service.
25	Enter the provider's EIN (without the hyphen). Enter an X in the EIN box.
27	Enter an X in the YES box.
29	Enter the total amount paid by Medicare beneficiaries (e.g., coinsurance amounts). If no amount was paid, leave blank.
31	Have the provider sign the claim or use a signature stamp. Enter the date as MMDDYYYY (without spaces).
32	Enter the provider's name and address.
32a	Enter the provider's NPI.
33	Enter the provider's name, address, and telephone number.
33a	Enter the provider's NPI.

Courtesy of the Centers for Medicare & Medicaid Services, www.cms.gov

HEALTH INSURANCE CLAIM FORM

APPROVED BY NATIONAL UNIFORM CLAIM COMMITTEE (NUCC) 02/12

PICA | PICA

CARRIER

1. MEDICARE [X] (Medicare#) MEDICAID (Medicaid#) TRICARE (ID#/DoD#) CHAMPVA (Member ID#) GROUP HEALTH PLAN (ID#) FECA BLK LUNG (ID#) OTHER (ID#)

1a. INSURED'S I.D. NUMBER (For Program in Item 1)

2. PATIENT'S NAME (Last Name, First Name, Middle Initial): SEE ATTACHED ROSTER

3. PATIENT'S BIRTH DATE MM DD YY SEX M F

4. INSURED'S NAME (Last Name, First Name, Middle Initial)

5. PATIENT'S ADDRESS (No., Street)

6. PATIENT RELATIONSHIP TO INSURED Self Spouse Child Other

7. INSURED'S ADDRESS (No., Street)

CITY STATE

8. RESERVED FOR NUCC USE

CITY STATE

ZIP CODE TELEPHONE (Include Area Code) ( )

ZIP CODE TELEPHONE (Include Area Code) ( )

9. OTHER INSURED'S NAME (Last Name, First Name, Middle Initial)

10. IS PATIENT'S CONDITION RELATED TO:

11. INSURED'S POLICY GROUP OR FECA NUMBER: NONE

a. OTHER INSURED'S POLICY OR GROUP NUMBER

a. EMPLOYMENT? (Current or Previous) YES NO

a. INSURED'S DATE OF BIRTH MM DD YY SEX M F

b. RESERVED FOR NUCC USE

b. AUTO ACCIDENT? YES NO PLACE (State)

b. OTHER CLAIM ID (Designated by NUCC)

c. RESERVED FOR NUCC USE

c. OTHER ACCIDENT? YES NO

c. INSURANCE PLAN NAME OR PROGRAM NAME

d. INSURANCE PLAN NAME OR PROGRAM NAME

10d. CLAIM CODES (Designated by NUCC)

d. IS THERE ANOTHER HEALTH BENEFIT PLAN? YES NO *If yes,* complete items 9, 9a, and 9d.

READ BACK OF FORM BEFORE COMPLETING & SIGNING THIS FORM.

12. PATIENT'S OR AUTHORIZED PERSON'S SIGNATURE I authorize the release of any medical or other information necessary to process this claim. I also request payment of government benefits either to myself or to the party who accepts assignment below.

SIGNED DATE

13. INSURED'S OR AUTHORIZED PERSON'S SIGNATURE I authorize payment of medical benefits to the undersigned physician or supplier for services described below.

SIGNED

PATIENT AND INSURED INFORMATION

14. DATE OF CURRENT ILLNESS, INJURY, or PREGNANCY (LMP) MM DD YY QUAL.

15. OTHER DATE QUAL. MM DD YY

16. DATES PATIENT UNABLE TO WORK IN CURRENT OCCUPATION MM DD YY FROM TO

17. NAME OF REFERRING PROVIDER OR OTHER SOURCE 17a. 17b. NPI

18. HOSPITALIZATION DATES RELATED TO CURRENT SERVICES MM DD YY FROM TO

19. ADDITIONAL CLAIM INFORMATION (Designated by NUCC)

20. OUTSIDE LAB? YES NO $ CHARGES

21. DIAGNOSIS OR NATURE OF ILLNESS OR INJURY Relate A-L to service line below (24E) ICD Ind. 0

A. Z23 B. C. D. E. F. G. H. I. J. K. L.

22. RESUBMISSION CODE ORIGINAL REF. NO.

23. PRIOR AUTHORIZATION NUMBER

	24. A. DATE(S) OF SERVICE From MM	DD	YY	To MM	DD	YY	B. PLACE OF SERVICE	C. EMG	D. CPT/HCPCS	MODIFIER	E. DIAGNOSIS POINTER	F. $ CHARGES	G. DAYS OR UNITS	H. EPSDT Family Plan	I. ID. QUAL.	J. RENDERING PROVIDER ID. #
1	11	15	YY				60		Q2035	33	A	50 00	1		NPI	
2	11	15	YY				60		G0008	33	A	5 00	1		NPI	
3															NPI	
4															NPI	
5															NPI	
6															NPI	

25. FEDERAL TAX I.D. NUMBER SSN EIN [X]: 987654321

26. PATIENT'S ACCOUNT NO.

27. ACCEPT ASSIGNMENT? (For govt. claims, see back) [X] YES NO

28. TOTAL CHARGE $

29. AMOUNT PAID $ 0 00

30. Rsvd for NUCC Use

31. SIGNATURE OF PHYSICIAN OR SUPPLIER INCLUDING DEGREES OR CREDENTIALS (I certify that the statements on the reverse apply to this bill and are made a part thereof.)

SIGNATURE STAMP SIGNED MMDDYYYY DATE

32. SERVICE FACILITY LOCATION INFORMATION
ALLEGANY HEALTH CLINIC
100 MAIN ST
ANYWHERE NY 12345
a. 1123456789 b.

33. BILLING PROVIDER INFO & PH # (101) 5551111
ALLEGANY HEALTH CLINIC
100 MAIN ST
ANYWHERE NY 12345
a. 1123456789 b.

PHYSICIAN OR SUPPLIER INFORMATION

NUCC Instruction Manual available at: www.nucc.org PLEASE PRINT OR TYPE

FIGURE 14-14 Completed CMS-1500 claim as cover sheet for Medicare roster billing form.

SUMMARY

Medicare Part A reimburses institutional providers for inpatient hospital and skilled nursing facility stays; home health and hospice services; ESRD and kidney donor coverage; and heart/heart-lung, liver, and bone marrow transplants. Medicare Part B reimburses noninstitutional health care providers for all outpatient services, including physician services, diagnostic testing, ambulance services, DME, supplies used in the home and certified by a physician, and so on.

Medicare Advantage plans (Medicare Part C) include managed care plans and private fee-for-service plans that provide care under contract to Medicare and may include such benefits as coordination of care, reductions in out-of-pocket expenses, and prescription drugs. The Medicare outpatient prescription drug program consists of private prescription drug plans (PDPs) and Medicare Advantage prescription drug plans (MA–PDs), collectively referred to as Medicare Part D.

Participating providers (PARs) agree to accept assignment on all Medicare claims submitted, and PARs receive special incentives as part of the agreement. Nonparticipating providers (nonPARs) may elect to accept assignment on a claim-by-claim basis, and restrictions apply (e.g., limiting charge).

When completing Medicare CMS-1500 claims for case studies in this text and the Workbook, the following special instructions apply:

- Block 9a—Enter MEDIGAP followed by the policy and/or group number (this instruction applies to Medigap claims only); otherwise, leave blank.
- Block 12—Enter SIGNATURE ON FILE (patients have signed a customized authorization that is filed in the patient's record), and leave date blank.
- Block 20—Enter an X in the *NO* box.
- Block 23—Leave blank.
- Block 24E—Enter just one diagnosis pointer letter on each line.
- Block 26—Enter the case study number (e.g., 14-7). If the patient has both primary and secondary coverage, enter a P (for primary) next to the case study number (on the primary claim) and an S (for secondary) next to the number (on the secondary claim); if the patient is eligible for the Medicare-Medicaid crossover plan, enter MM next to the case study number.
- Block 27—Enter an X in the *YES* box.
- When completing secondary claims, enter REMITTANCE ADVICE ATTACHED in the top left margin of the CMS-1500 claim (to simulate the attachment of a primary payer's remittance advice with a claim submitted to a secondary payer).

INTERNET LINKS

- *Medicare Contractor Beneficiary and Provider Communications Manual*
  Go to **www.cms.gov**, scroll down to the Top 5 Resources heading, click on the Manuals link, click on the Internet-Only Manuals (IOMs) link, click on the Publication 100-09 link, and click on the Chapter 3 - Provider Inquiries link.
- Medicare coverage information
  Go to **www.cms.gov**, click on the Medicare link, scroll down to the Coverage heading, and click on the Medicare Coverage - General Information link.
- Medicare Learning Network® (MLN)
  Go to **https://cms.meridianski.com** to register (free) for web-based training and to browse available MLN products (e.g., electronic data interchange standards).
- Medicare physician fee schedules
  Go to **www.cms.gov**, click on the Medicare link, scroll down to the Medicare Fee-for-Service Payment heading, and click on the Fee Schedules - General Information link.

- Medicare program manuals
  Go to **www.cms.gov**, scroll down to the Top 5 Resources heading, click on the Manuals link, click on the Internet-Only Manuals (IOMs) link, and click on the Publication #100-04 (*Medicare Claims Processing Manual*) and #100-05 (*Medicare Secondary Payer Manual*) links.
- Medicare Summary Notice (MSN)
  Go to **www.medicare.gov**, scroll over the Forms, Help, & Resources link, click on the Publications link, and click on the Download link. The Medicare & You publication contains information about the MSN.
- QualityNet health care quality data exchange
  www.qualitynet.org
- RBRVS EZ-Fees software
  www.rbrvs.net
- U.S. government site for people with Medicare
  www.medicare.gov

STUDY CHECKLIST

- ☐ Read this textbook chapter and highlight key concepts.
- ☐ Access SimClaim software at the online companion, and complete Medicare claims using the software's case studies.
- ☐ Complete CMS-1500 claims for each chapter case study.
- ☐ Answer the chapter review questions, verifying answers with your instructor.
- ☐ Complete the Workbook chapter, verifying answers with your instructor.
- ☐ Form a study group with classmates to discuss chapter concepts in preparation for an exam.

REVIEW

MULTIPLE CHOICE Select the most appropriate response.

1. CMS is responsible for administering the _____ program.

a. Medicaid
b. Medicare
c. TRICARE
d. workers' compensation

2. Medicare Part _____ reimburses institutional providers for inpatient, hospice, and some home health services.

a. A
b. B
c. C
d. D

3. Which is a characteristic of Medicare enrollment?

a. Eligible individuals are automatically enrolled, or they apply for coverage.
b. Individuals who qualify for SSA benefits must "buy in" to Medicare Part A.
c. The general enrollment period is between January 1 and December 31.
d. Those who enroll in Medicare Part A must also enroll in Medicare Part B.

4. A Medicare benefit period is defined as beginning the first day of hospitalization and ending when

a. the patient has been admitted to a skilled nursing facility.
b. the patient has been officially discharged from the hospital.
c. the patient has been out of the hospital for 60 consecutive days.
d. the spell of illness has ended for the patient.

5. Skilled nursing facility (SNF) inpatients who meet Medicare's qualified diagnosis and comprehensive treatment plan requirements when they are admitted after a three-day-minimum acute hospital stay are required to pay the Medicare rate for SNF inpatient care during which period?

a. days 1–20
b. days 21–100
c. days 101+
d. days 1–101

6. Which is the total number of Medicare *lifetime reserve days* (defined as the number of days that can be used just once during a patient's lifetime)?

a. 30
b. 60
c. 90
d. 120

7. The original Medicare plan is also called Medicare

a. Advantage.
b. fee-for-service.
c. SELECT.
d. supplemental insurance.

8. Medigap coverage is offered to Medicare beneficiaries by

a. commercial payers.
b. Medicaid.
c. employers.
d. federal health plans.

9. Which is forbidden as the result of legislation passed by some states?

a. assignment of benefits
b. balance billing
c. limiting charges
d. private contracting

10. Which is a written document provided to a Medicare beneficiary by a provider prior to rendering a service that is unlikely to be reimbursed by Medicare?

a. advance beneficiary notice of noncoverage
b. medical necessity denial
c. MSP questionnaire
d. waiver of Medicare billing contract

CHAPTER 15

Medicaid

CHAPTER OUTLINE

Medicaid Eligibility
Medicaid-Covered Services
Payment for Medicaid Services
Billing Notes
Claims Instructions
Medicaid as Secondary Payer Claims
Mother/Baby Claims
SCHIP Claims

OBJECTIVES

Upon successful completion of this chapter, you should be able to:

1. Define key terms.
2. Explain Medicaid eligibility guidelines.
3. List Medicaid-covered services required by the federal government.
4. Describe how payments for Medicaid services are processed.
5. Apply Medicaid billing notes when completing CMS-1500 claims.
6. Complete Medicaid primary, secondary, mother/baby, and SCHIP claims.

KEY TERMS

adjusted claim
dual eligibles
Early and Periodic Screening, Diagnostic, and Treatment (EPSDT) services
Federal Medical Assistance Percentage (FMAP)
federal poverty level (FPL)
Medicaid
Medicaid eligibility verification system (MEVS)
Medicaid remittance advice
medical assistance program
mother/baby claim
recipient eligibility verification system (REVS)
surveillance and utilization review subsystem (SURS)
Temporary Assistance for Needy Families (TANF)
voided claim

INTRODUCTION

In 1965 Congress passed Title 19 of the Social Security Act, establishing a federally mandated, state-administered medical assistance program for individuals with incomes below the federal poverty level. The federal name for this program is Medicaid; several states assign local designations (e.g., California uses *MediCal;* Massachusetts uses *MassHealth*; Tennessee uses *TennCare*). Unlike Medicare, which is a nationwide entitlement program, the federal government mandated national requirements for Medicaid and gave states the flexibility to develop eligibility rules and additional benefits if they assumed responsibility for the program's support.

***Medicaid* provides medical and health-related services to certain individuals and families with low incomes and limited resources (the "medically indigent"). It is jointly funded by the federal and state governments to assist states in providing adequate medical care to qualified individuals. Within broad federal guidelines, each state:**

- Establishes its own eligibility standards
- Determines the type, amount, duration, and scope of services
- Sets rates of payment for services
- Administers its own program

Thus, Medicaid varies considerably from state to state, and each state has modified its program over time.

MEDICAID ELIGIBILITY

Medicaid policies for eligibility are complex and vary considerably, even among states of similar size and geographic proximity. Thus, a person who is eligible for Medicaid in one state may not be eligible in another state, and the services provided by one state may differ considerably in amount, duration, or scope as compared with services provided in a similar or neighboring state. In addition, state legislatures may change Medicaid eligibility requirements during the year.

Medicaid Eligibility

Medicaid does not provide medical assistance for all poor persons, and it is important to realize that low income is only one test for Medicaid eligibility; an individual's resources are also compared to limits established by each state in accordance with federal guidelines. To be eligible for federal funds, states are required to provide Medicaid coverage for certain individuals who receive federally assisted income-maintenance payments and for related groups that do not receive cash payments. In addition to their Medicaid programs, most states implement "state-only" programs to provide medical assistance for specified poor persons who do not qualify for Medicaid. (Federal funds are *not* provided for state-only programs.) The federal government provides matching funds to state Medicaid programs when certain health care services are provided to eligible individuals (e.g., children, disabled, seniors). Each state administers its own Medicaid program, and CMS monitors the programs and establishes requirements for the delivery, funding, and quality of services as well as eligibility criteria.

Medicaid eligibility is limited to individuals who can be classified into three eligibility groups:

- **Categorically needy**
- **Medically needy**
- **Special groups**

Categorically Needy Groups

State Medicaid programs must be available to the following *mandatory Medicaid eligibility groups* (or *mandatory populations*) because the federal government provides matching funds:

- **Families who meet states' Temporary Assistance for Needy Families (TANF) eligibility requirements in effect on July 16, 1996**
- **Pregnant women and children under age 6 whose family income is at or below 133 percent of the federal poverty level (FPL) (annual income guidelines established by the federal government)**
- **Caretakers (relatives or legal guardians who take care of children under age 18, or age 19 if still in high school)**
- **Supplemental Security Income (SSI) recipients (or, in certain states, aged, blind, and disabled people who meet more restrictive requirements than those of the SSI program)**
- **Individuals and couples living in medical institutions who have a monthly income up to 300 percent of the SSI income**

NOTE: Go to **www.coverageforall.org**, click on the Resources link, and click on the Federal Poverty Level (FPL) Chart link to view benefit levels; calculations are based on family size (e.g., a pregnant woman counts as two in the chart) and state of residence (e.g., calculations for the states of Alaska and Hawaii are higher than the 48 contiguous states).

Medically Needy Program

States that establish a *medically needy Medicaid program* expand eligibility to additional qualified persons who may have too much income to qualify under the categorically needy group. (Federal matching funds are available.) This option allows:

- **Individuals to "spend down" to Medicaid eligibility by incurring medical and/or remedial care expenses to offset their excess income. Thus, their income is reduced to a level below the maximum allowed by their state's Medicaid plan.**
- **Families to establish eligibility as medically needy by paying monthly premiums in an amount equal to the difference between family income (reduced by unpaid expenses, if any, incurred for medical care in previous months) and the income eligibility standard.**

States that implement a medically needy Medicaid program are required to include pregnant women through a 60-day postpartum period, children under age 18, certain newborns for one year, and certain protected blind persons. States may also choose to provide coverage to other medically needy persons, including aged, blind, and/or disabled persons, as well as caretaker relatives or legal guardians who live with and take care of children and other eligible children up to age 21 who are full-time students.

NOTE: Temporary Assistance for Needy Families (TANF) makes cash assistance available, for a limited time, for children deprived of support because of a parent's absence, death, incapacity, or unemployment. TANF was previously called the Aid to Families with Dependent Children (AFDC) program.

NOTE: States are required to extend Medicaid eligibility to all children born after September 30, 1983, who reside in families with incomes at or below the federal poverty level, until they reach age 19. (States may choose to establish an earlier date.)

Special Groups

States are required to assist the following special groups:

- ***Qualified Medicare beneficiaries (QMB)* (states pay Medicare premiums, deductibles, and coinsurance amounts for individuals whose income is at or below 100 percent of the federal poverty level and whose resources are at or below twice the standard allowed under SSI)**

- *Qualified working disabled individuals (QWDI)* (states pay Medicare Part A premiums for certain disabled individuals who lose Medicare coverage because of work; these individuals have incomes below 200 percent of the federal poverty level and resources that are no more than twice the standard allowed under SSI)
- *Qualifying individual (QI)* (states pay Medicare Part B premiums for individuals with incomes between 120 percent and 175 percent of the federal poverty level)
- *Specified low-income Medicare beneficiary (SLMB)* (states pay Medicare Part B premiums for individuals with incomes between 100 percent and 120 percent of the federal poverty level)

States may also improve access to employment, training, and placement of people with disabilities who want to work by providing expanded Medicaid eligibility to:

- Working disabled people between ages 16 and 65 who have income and resources greater than that allowed under the SSI program
- Working individuals who become ineligible for the group described above because their medical conditions improve (States may require these individuals to share in the cost of their medical care.)

Two additional eligibility groups are related to specific medical conditions, and states may provide coverage under their Medicaid plans:

- Time-limited eligibility for women who have breast or cervical cancer
- Individuals diagnosed with tuberculosis (TB) who are uninsured

Women with breast or cervical cancer receive all Medicaid plan services. TB patients receive only services related to the treatment of TB.

State Children's Health Insurance Program

The *State Children's Health Insurance Program (SCHIP)* was implemented in accordance with the Balanced Budget Act (BBA), which allows states to create or expand existing insurance programs, providing more federal funds to states for the purpose of expanding Medicaid eligibility to include a greater number of currently uninsured children. With certain exceptions, these include low-income children who would not otherwise qualify for Medicaid. SCHIP may also be used to provide medical assistance to children during a presumptive eligibility period for Medicaid. Medicaid coverage can begin as early as the third month *prior to* application *if* the person would have been eligible for Medicaid had he or she applied during that time. Medicaid coverage is usually discontinued at the end of the month in which a person no longer meets the criteria for any Medicaid eligibility group. The BBA allows states to provide 12 months of continuous Medicaid coverage (without reevaluation) for eligible children under the age of 19.

The *Affordable Care Act* provides uninsured Americans with access to affordable coverage through affordable insurance exchanges (or health insurance exchanges), resulting in improvements to Medicaid and the State Children's Health Insurance Program (SCHIP). The purpose of these programs is to use consistent standards and systems to seamlessly and efficiently meet consumers' health care needs, improve quality, and lower costs. Coverage eligibility was expanded to low-income adults who are not offered health insurance by their employers or who are not eligible for Medicaid, including adults who are childless and who do not have disabilities. Beginning in 2014, the Affordable Care Act extended Medicaid coverage to all individuals between ages 19 and 64 with incomes up to 133 percent of the federal poverty level, or $15,282 for an individual and $31,322 for a family of four (based on the 2013 federal poverty level).

EXAMPLE: An uninsured 45-year-old woman (who has no children) who is employed as a restaurant hostess, where health insurance is not offered, could qualify for Medicaid if she earns less than $14,000 in a year.

Coordination among affordable insurance exchanges (or health insurance exchanges), Medicaid, and SCHIP will help ensure the success of the Affordable Care Act by providing all Americans access to quality, affordable health insurance. An affordable insurance exchange (or health insurance exchange) can determine Medicaid eligibility based on state Medicaid eligibility rules and can also determine eligibility for advance payment of premium tax credits. An affordable insurance exchange (or health insurance exchange) can make a preliminary Medicaid eligibility assessment and rely on state Medicaid and SCHIP agencies for a final eligibility determination. Either approach helps ensure that timely and coordinated eligibility determinations are maintained.

Programs of All-inclusive Care for the Elderly (PACE)

Programs of All-inclusive Care for the Elderly (PACE) use a capitated payment system to provide a comprehensive package of community-based services as an alternative to institutional care for persons age 55 or older who require a *nursing facility level of care*. PACE is part of the Medicare program, but is an optional service for state Medicaid plans. Thus, PACE programs operate only in states that have selected to include this option. PACE programs enter into contracts with various types of providers, physicians, and other entities to furnish care to participants. This PACE team offers and manages *all* health, medical, and social services and mobilizes other services as needed to provide preventive, rehabilitative, curative, and supportive care. The care is provided in day health centers, homes, hospitals, and nursing facilities, and its purpose is to help the person maintain independence, dignity, and quality of life. PACE providers receive payment only through the PACE agreement and must make available all items and services covered under both Medicaid and Medicare, without amount, duration, or scope limitations and without application of any deductibles, copayments, or other cost-sharing requirements. The individuals enrolled in PACE receive benefits solely through the PACE program.

NOTE: When a PACE participant needs to use a noncontract provider, physician, or other entity, there is a limit on the amount that these noncontract entities can charge the PACE program.

Spousal Impoverishment Protection

The *Medicare Catastrophic Coverage Act of 1988 (MCCA)* implemented Spousal Impoverishment Protection Legislation in 1989 to prevent married couples from being required to *spend down* income and other *liquid assets* (cash and property) before one of the partners could be declared eligible for Medicaid coverage for nursing facility care. The spouse residing at home is called the *community spouse* (which has nothing to do with community property). Before monthly income is used to pay nursing facility costs, a minimum monthly maintenance needs allowance (MMMNA) is deducted.

To determine whether the spouse residing in a facility meets the state's resource standard for Medicaid, a *protected resource amount (PRA)* is subtracted from the couple's combined countable resources. The PRA is the greatest of the:

- **Spousal share, up to a maximum of $115,920 in 2013**
- **State spousal resource standard, which a state could set at any amount between $23,184 and $115,920 in 2013**

NOTE: The couple's home, household goods, automobile, and burial funds are *not* included in the couple's combined countable resources.

NOTE: The community spouse's income is *not* available to the spouse who resides in the facility, and the two individuals are not considered a couple for income eligibility purposes. The state uses the income eligibility standard for one person rather than two, and the standard income eligibility process for Medicaid is used.

- **Amount transferred to the community spouse for her or his support as directed by a court order**
- **Amount designated by a state officer to raise the community spouse's protected resources up to the minimum monthly maintenance needs standard**

After the PRA is subtracted from the couple's combined countable resources, the remainder is considered available as resources to the spouse residing in the facility. If the amount of resources is below the state's resource standard, the individual is eligible for Medicaid. Once resource eligibility is determined, any resources belonging to the community spouse are no longer considered available to the spouse in the facility.

EXAMPLE: John Q. Public is required to reside in a nursing facility. His wife, Nancy Public, resides in the family home. At the time of Mr. Public's Medicaid application, they have $160,000 in resources (not including the family home, which is not included in resources as long as the spouse is in residence). John Q. Public's monthly Social Security income (SSI) is $1,000, and Nancy Public's monthly SSI is $600, totaling $1,600.

- Under the *income-first approach*, the state attributes one-half of the resources (or $80,000) to Mrs. Public as her community spouse resource allowance (CSRA). This allows Mr. Public to retain $80,000, which must be reduced to $1,500 before he becomes eligible for Medicaid. This means the Publics are expected to convert the $78,500 in resources (e.g., stocks, bonds, summer home) to cash and spend it on nursing facility care for Mr. Public. Because the state's minimum monthly maintenance needs allowance (MMMNA) is $1,751 (in 2009), Mrs. Public keeps all her monthly SSI, in addition to all $1,000 of her husband's monthly SSI. None of the monthly income is expended on nursing facility care for Mr. Public.
- Under the *resources-first approach*, Mr. Public is expected to expend his $1,000 monthly SSI on nursing facility care. This means that Mrs. Public has a monthly income of only $600, and because the state's MMMNA is $1,751, Mr. Public can transfer his $80,000 in resources to Mrs. Public. This increases her CSRA to an amount that generates an additional $1,000 per month. As a result, Mr. Public becomes immediately eligible for Medicaid, and Mrs. Public is allowed to retain all $160,000 in resources.

Confirming Medicaid Eligibility

Any time patients state that they receive Medicaid, they must present a valid Medicaid identification card.

pacifica
BENEFITS IDENTIFICATION CARD
Issue Date 02/01/YYYY
ID Number
TW965
Card Number
5621 9865 569 86 0
Gender
Male
Date of Birth
05/25/1978
First Name/M.I.
John Q.
Last Name
Patient

Sample Medicaid identification card

Eligibility, in many cases, will depend on the patient's monthly income. As eligibility may fluctuate from one month to the next, most states have a dedicated telephone line for verification of eligibility. Confirmation of eligibility should be obtained for each visit; failure to do so may result in a denial of payment. If residing in one of these states, be sure to access the Medicaid verification line. Some states have a point-of-service device similar to those used by credit card companies. Beneficiaries carry plastic cards containing encoded data strips. When the card is swiped, the printout indicates eligibility or noneligibility data.

Retroactive eligibility is sometimes granted to patients whose income has fallen below the state-set eligibility level and who had high medical expenses prior to filing for Medicaid. When patients notify the practice that they have become retroactively eligible for Medicaid benefits, confirm this information before proceeding. A refund of any payments made by the patient during the retroactive period must be made and Medicaid billed for these services.

MEDICAID-COVERED SERVICES

Medicaid allows considerable flexibility within state plans, but some federal requirements are mandatory if federal matching funds are to be received. A state's Medicaid program *must* offer medical assistance for certain *basic* services to eligible groups.

NOTE: **Early and Periodic Screening, Diagnostic, and Treatment (EPSDT) services** consist of routine pediatric checkups provided to all children enrolled in Medicaid, including dental, hearing, vision, and other screening services to detect potential problems. Other necessary diagnostic services to detect potential problems, treatment, and other measures must also be performed to correct or ameliorate defects and physical and mental illnesses and conditions discovered by the screening services, whether or not such services are covered by the state Medicaid plan.

Mandatory Services

To receive federal matching funds, states must offer the following services:

Services for Categorically Needy Eligibility Groups

Medicaid eligibility groups classified as categorically needy are entitled to the following services unless waived under the Medicaid law. (These service entitlements do not apply to the SCHIP programs.)

- Inpatient hospital (excluding inpatient services in institutions for mental disease)
- Outpatient hospital including Federally Qualified Health Centers (FQHCs) and, if permitted under state law, rural health clinic (RHC) and other ambulatory services provided by a rural health clinic that are otherwise included under states' plans
- Other laboratory and x-ray
- Certified pediatric and family nurse practitioners (when licensed to practice under state law)
- Nursing facility services for beneficiaries age 21 and older
- Early and Periodic Screening, Diagnosis, and Treatment (EPSDT) for children under age 21
- Family planning services and supplies
- Physicians' services
- Medical and surgical services of a dentist
- Home health services for beneficiaries entitled to nursing facility services under the state's Medicaid plan
- Intermittent or part-time nursing services provided by a home health agency or by a registered nurse when there is no home health agency in the area
- Home health aides
- Medical supplies and appliances for use in the home

- **Nurse midwife services**
- **Pregnancy-related services and service for other conditions that might complicate pregnancy**
- **Sixty (60) days postpartum pregnancy-related services**

Services for Medically Needy Eligibility Groups

States must provide at least the following services when the medically needy are included under the Medicaid plans:

- **Prenatal and delivery services**
- **Postpartum pregnancy-related services for beneficiaries who are under age 18 and are entitled to institutional and ambulatory services defined in a state's plan**
- **Home health services to beneficiaries entitled to receive nursing facility services under the state's Medicaid plan**

States may provide different services to different groups of medically needy individuals, such as specified services for beneficiaries under age 21 and/or over age 65 in institutions for mental disease (IMDs); and/or intermediate care facilities for the mentally retarded (ICF/MRs), if included as medically needy. The services provided to a particular group must also be available to everyone within that group (unless the state has obtained a waiver).

Preauthorized Services

Most states that have not placed all Medicaid beneficiaries into a prepaid HMO have some form of prior approval or preauthorization for recipients. Preauthorization guidelines include:

- **Elective inpatient admission (document medical necessity justification of inpatient treatment and admission diagnosis and treatment plan)**
- **Emergency inpatient admission (document medical necessity justification for inpatient treatment and admission diagnosis and treatment plan)**
- **More than one preoperative day (document reason[s] surgery cannot be performed within 24 hours of indication for surgery and specify number of additional preoperative day[s] requested)**
- **Outpatient procedure(s) to be performed in an inpatient setting (submit CPT code and description of surgical procedure along with medical necessity justification for performing surgery on an inpatient basis)**
- **Days exceeding state hospital stay limitation due to complication(s) (submit diagnosis stated on original preauthorization request, beginning and ending dates originally preauthorized, statement describing the complication[s], date complication[s] presented, principal diagnosis, and complication[s] diagnosis)**
- **Extension of inpatient days (document medical necessity justification for the extension and specify number of additional days requested)**

NOTE: Preauthorization is required for certain procedures and services (e.g., inpatient hospitalizations) as mandated by state and federal law. To be eligible for reimbursement, the provider must submit the appropriate preauthorization form, such as California's Department of Health Care Services (DHCS) *treatment authorization request* (TAR) and/or *service authorization request* (SAR), to the appropriate state Medicaid field office. Once approved, the procedure or service is provided to the patient and the provider is reimbursed by Medicaid.

- Go to **https://learn.medi-cal.ca.gov**, and register as a student to complete Medi-Cal (California's Medicaid) eLearning Tutorials.
- Go to **www.westernhighlands.org**, click on Provider, click on the Activation, Registration & Authorization link, and click on the Enrollee Registration Form (ERF) link to view it.

PAYMENT FOR MEDICAID SERVICES

Medicaid operates as a vendor-payment program, which means that states pay health care providers on a fee-for-service basis *or* states pay for Medicaid services using prepayment arrangements (e.g., an HMO). When Medicaid makes payment directly to providers, those participating in Medicaid must accept the reimbursement as payment in full. States determine their own reimbursement methodology and payment rates for services, with three exceptions: (1) for institutional services, payment may not exceed amounts that would be paid under Medicare payment rates; (2) for *disproportionate share hospitals (DSHs)*, hospitals that treat a disproportionate number of Medicaid patients, different limits apply; and (3) for hospice care services, rates cannot be lower than Medicare rates.

States can require nominal deductibles, coinsurance, or copayments for certain services performed for some Medicaid recipients. Emergency services and family planning services are exempt from copayments. Certain Medicaid recipients are also excluded from this cost-sharing requirement, including pregnant women, children under age 18, and hospital or nursing home patients who are expected to contribute most of their income to institutional care.

The portion of the Medicaid program paid by the federal government is known as the **Federal Medical Assistance Percentage (FMAP)** and is determined annually for each state using a formula that compares the state's average per capita income level with the national average. Wealthier states receive a smaller share of reimbursed costs, and the federal government shares in administration expenses (minimum 50 percent match).

The federal government also reimburses states for 100 percent of the cost of services provided through facilities of the Indian Health Service, provides financial help to the 12 states that furnish the highest number of emergency services to undocumented aliens, and shares in each state's expenditures for the administration of the Medicaid program. Most administrative costs are matched at 50 percent, although higher percentages are paid for certain activities and functions, such as development of mechanized claims processing systems.

Medicare-Medicaid Relationship

Medicare beneficiaries with low incomes and limited resources may also receive help from the Medicaid program. For those eligible for *full* Medicaid coverage, Medicare coverage is supplemented by services available under a state's Medicaid program. These additional services may include, for example, nursing facility care beyond the 100-day limit covered by Medicare, prescription drugs, eyeglasses, and hearing aids.

NOTE: When an individual has both Medicare and Medicaid coverage, covered services are paid by Medicare first before any payments are made by the Medicaid program. The reason for this is because Medicaid is always the *payer of last resort*.

Dual Eligibles

Medicare beneficiaries with low incomes and limited resources may receive help with out-of-pocket medical expenses from state Medicaid programs. Various benefits are available to **dual eligibles**, individuals entitled to Medicare *and* eligible for some type of Medicaid benefit (abbreviated as Medi-Medi). Individuals eligible for full Medicaid coverage receive program supplements to their Medicare coverage via services and supplies available from the state's Medicaid program. Services covered by both programs are paid first by Medicare and the difference by Medicaid, up to the state's payment limit. Medicaid also covers the following additional services:

- **Nursing facility care beyond the 100-day limit covered by Medicare**
- **Prescription drugs**
- **Eyeglasses**
- **Hearing aids**

Medicaid as a Secondary Payer

Medicaid is always the *payer of last resort*. If the patient is covered by another medical or liability policy, including Medicare, TRICARE (formerly CHAMPUS), CHAMPVA, or Indian Health Services (IHS), this coverage must be billed first. Medicaid is billed only if the other coverage denies responsibility for payment, pays less than the Medicaid fee schedule, or if Medicaid covers procedures not covered by the other policy.

Participating Providers

Any provider who accepts a Medicaid patient must accept the Medicaid-determined payment as payment in full. Providers are forbidden by law to bill *(balance billing)* patients for Medicaid-covered benefits. A patient may be billed for any service that is not a covered benefit; however, some states have historically required providers to sign formal participating Medicaid contracts. Other states do not require contracts.

Medicaid and Managed Care

Medicaid managed care grew rapidly in the 1990s. In 1991, 2.7 million beneficiaries were enrolled in some form of managed care. By 2004 that number had grown to 27 million, an increase of 900 percent. That represents 60 percent of the Medicaid population who receive benefits through managed care. States can make managed care enrollment voluntary, or they can seek a waiver of the Social Security Act from CMS to require certain populations to enroll in an MCO.

Medicaid *managed care* does not always mean a comprehensive health care plan that requires a monthly premium and is at financial risk for the cost of care provided to all enrollees. Medicaid beneficiaries are also enrolled in *primary care case management (PCCM)* plans, which are similar to fee-for-service plans except that each PCCM enrollee has a primary care provider who authorizes access to specialty care. (Primary care providers are not at risk for the cost of specialty care provided to managed care patients, which means the providers do not pay for care out of their managed care contract funds. Specialty care is paid by the patient's managed care contract.)

Most states that have not placed all Medicaid beneficiaries into a prepaid HMO have some form of prior approval or preauthorization for recipients. Preauthorization guidelines include:

- **Elective inpatient admission (document medical necessity justification of inpatient treatment and admission diagnosis and treatment plan)**
- **Emergency inpatient admission (document medical necessity justification for inpatient treatment and admission diagnosis and treatment plan)**
- **More than one preoperative day (document reason[s] surgery cannot be performed within 24 hours of indication for surgery and specify number of additional preoperative day[s] requested)**
- **Outpatient procedure(s) to be performed in an inpatient setting (submit CPT code and description of surgical procedure along with medical necessity justification for performing surgery on an inpatient basis)**
- **Days exceeding state hospital stay limitation due to complication(s) (submit diagnosis stated on original preauthorization request, beginning and ending dates originally preauthorized, statement describing the complication[s], date complication[s] presented, principal diagnosis, and complication[s] diagnosis)**
- **Extension of inpatient days (document medical necessity justification for the extension and specify number of additional days requested)**

NOTE: Go to **www.eMedNY.org** to view a web-based electronic Medicaid system.

Medicaid Eligibility Verification System

The **Medicaid eligibility verification system (MEVS)** (sometimes called **recipient eligibility verification system**, or **REVS**) allows providers to electronically access the state's eligibility file using the following methods. Then, a "receipt ticket" (Figure 15-1) is generated upon eligibility verification by MEVS.

NOTE: The provider should compare content on the remittance advice to claims submitted to determine whether proper payment was received. If improper payment was issued, the provider has the option to appeal the claim.

- *Point-of-service device:* The patient's medical identification card contains a magnetic strip, and when the provider "swipes" the card through a reader, accurate eligibility information is displayed. (The provider purchases magnetic card reader equipment.)
- *Computer software:* When the provider enters a Medicaid recipient's identification number into special computer software, accurate eligibility information is displayed.
- *Automated voice response:* Providers can call the state's Medicaid office to receive eligibility verification information through an automated voice response system.

US MEDICAID

Eligibility

05/15/YYYY 14:44:58
Date of Service 05/15/YYYY
Provider NPI 1234567890

Individual Status

Verification Number 23659856236541
Name .... John Q. Public
RID # 562365951
Card Generation # 001
DOB/(age) 03/09/1945
Gender .... M
Restriction .... None
Copay .... N

Managed Care

Managed Care .... N
PCP Name .... Dr. Erin Helper
PCP Telephone # 101-111-1234

Third-Party Liability

Coverage Code LDO–4
Policy # DD1234
Payer Name .... Any Insurance
Address .... 111 Main St
City/State/Zip .... Anywhere, NY 12345
Phone # .... (101) 555-1234

Legend
LDO-4 = large dialysis organization #4

FIGURE 15-1 Sample Medicaid eligibility verification system (MEVS) receipt ticket.

Medicaid Remittance Advice

> **NOTE:** Remittance advice documents should be maintained according to the statute of limitations of the state in which the provider practices.

Providers receive reimbursement from Medicaid on a lump-sum basis, which means they will receive payment for several claims at once. A **Medicaid remittance advice** (Figure 15-2) is sent to the provider which contains the current status of all claims (including adjusted and voided claims). The provider should compare content on the remittance advice to claims submitted to determine whether proper payment was received. If improper payment was issued, the provider has the option to appeal the claim. An **adjusted claim** has a payment correction, resulting in additional payment(s) to the provider. A **voided claim** is one that Medicaid should not have originally paid and results in a deduction from the lump-sum payment made to the provider. If a year-to-date negative balance appears on the Medicaid remittance advice as a result of voided claims, the provider receives no payment until the amount of paid claims exceeds the negative balance amount.

Utilization Review

The federal government requires states to verify the receipt of Medicaid services. Thus, a sample of Medicaid recipients is sent a monthly survey letter requesting verification of services paid the previous month on their behalf. (Such services are identified in nontechnical terms, and confidential services are omitted.) Federal regulations also require Medicaid to establish and maintain a **surveillance and utilization review subsystem (SURS)**, which safeguards against unnecessary or inappropriate use of Medicaid services or excess payments and assesses the quality of those services. A postpayment review process monitors both the use of health services by recipients and the delivery of health services by providers. Overpayments to providers may be recovered by the SURS unit, regardless of whether the payment error was caused by the provider or by the Medicaid program.

The SURS unit is also responsible for identifying possible fraud or abuse, and most states organize the unit under the state's Office of Attorney General, which is certified by the federal government to detect, investigate, and prosecute fraudulent practices or abuse against the Medicaid program.

State of New York Medicaid

Provider Number: 999   Remittance Advice as of 01-06-YY   RA#: 256295987

RECIPIENT NAME	MEDICAID ID	INTERNAL CONTROL NO.	SERVICE DATES FROM	TO	POS	CPT CODE	QUANTITY	BILLED AMOUNT	ALLOWED AMOUNT	CUT/ BACK	PAYMENT AMOUNT	ADJUSTMENT REASON CODE
DOE, JOHN	123654	4400367890	0105YY	0105YY	11	99213	1	45.00	24.00	21.00	24.00	A2
REMARK CODES: N59			*** CLAIMS TOTALS ***				1		24.00	21.00	24.00	
JONES, MARY	569562	5626594589	0106YY	0106YY	11	99213	1	54.00	24.00	30.00	24.00	A2
			0106YY	0106YY	11	82948	1	18.00	1.00	17.00	1.00	A2
REMARK CODES: N59 MA66			0106YY	0106YY	11	36415	1	4.00	0.00	4.00	0.00	125
			*** CLAIMS TOTALS ***				3		25.00	51.00	25.00	
*** CATEGORY TOTALS:			NUMBER OF CLAIMS:			2	4	121.00	49.00	72.00	49.00	

RA# 256295987 CHECK AMOUNT: $ 49.00

****

*** EARNINGS DATA ***

NO. OF CLAIMS PROCESSED YEAR TO DATE: 75

DOLLAR AMOUNT PROCESSED YEAR TO DATE: $1459.82

CHECK AMOUNT YEAR TO DATE: $1459.82

*** CODE LEGEND ***

11 = Office

125 = Submission/billing error(s)

A2 = Contractual adjustment

N59 = Refer to provider manual for program/provider information

FIGURE 15-2 Sample Medicaid remittance advice (RA).

Medical Necessity

Medicaid-covered services are payable only when the service is determined by the provider to be medically necessary. Covered services must be:

- **Consistent with the patient's symptoms, diagnosis, condition, or injury**
- **Recognized as the prevailing standard and consistent with generally accepted professional medical standards of the provider's peer group**
- **Provided in response to a life-threatening condition; to treat pain, injury, illness, or infection; to treat a condition that could result in physical or mental disability; or to achieve a level of physical or mental function consistent with prevailing community standards for diagnosis or condition**

In addition, medically necessary services are:

- **Not furnished primarily for the convenience of the recipient or the provider**
- **Furnished when there is no other equally effective course of treatment available or suitable for the recipient requesting the service that is more conservative or substantially less costly**

BILLING NOTES

Following is information on nationwide fee-for-service billing. Consult your state's Medicaid MCO billing manual to bill for noncapitated MCO services.

Fiscal Agent

The name of the state's Medicaid fiscal agent will vary from state to state. Contact the local county government for information about the Medicaid program in your area. (In some states, third-party payers contract with Medicaid to process claims.)

Timely Filing Deadline

Deadlines vary from state to state. Check with your state's Medicaid office. It is important to file a Medicaid fee-for-service claim as soon as possible. The only time a claim should be delayed is when the patient does not identify Medicaid eligibility or if the patient has applied for retroactive Medicaid coverage.

Medicare-Medicaid crossover claims follow the Medicare, not Medicaid, deadlines for claims.

Accept Assignment

NOTE: Medicaid patients must assign benefits to providers.

Accept assignment must be selected on the CMS-1500 claim, or reimbursement (depending on state policy) may be denied. It is illegal to attempt collection of the difference between the Medicaid payment and the fee the provider charged, even if the patient did not reveal his or her Medicaid status at the time services were rendered.

Deductibles

A deductible may be required. In such cases, eligibility cards usually are not issued until after the stated deductible has been met.

Copayments

Copayments are required for some Medicaid recipients.

Inpatient Benefits

All nonemergency hospitalizations must be preauthorized. If the patient's condition warrants an extension of the authorized inpatient days, the hospital must seek an authorization for additional inpatient days.

Major Medical/Accidental Injury Coverage

There is no special treatment for major medical or accidental injury categories. Medicaid will conditionally subrogate claims when there is liability insurance to cover a person's injuries. *Subrogation* is the assumption of an obligation for which another party is primarily liable.

Medicaid Eligibility

Because Medicaid eligibility is determined by income, patients can be eligible one month and not the next. Check eligibility status on each visit. New work requirements may change this, as beneficiaries may continue coverage for a specific time even if their income exceeds the state eligibility levels. Prior authorization is required for many procedures and most nonemergency hospitalizations. Consult the current Medicaid handbook for a listing of the procedures that must have prior authorization. When in doubt, contact the state agency for clarification.

Medicaid Cards

Cards may be issued for the "Unborn child of . . ." (the name of the pregnant woman is inserted in the blank space). These cards are good only for services that promote the life and good health of the unborn child.

Remittance Advice

Because other health and liability programs are primary to Medicaid, the remittance advice from the primary coverage must be attached to the Medicaid claim.

A combined Medicare-Medicaid (Medi-Medi) claim should be filed by the Medicare deadline on the CMS-1500 claim.

Before working with Medicaid claims, complete the Review located at the end of this chapter.

CLAIMS INSTRUCTIONS

The instructions in Table 15-1 are for filing primary Medicaid fee-for-service claims when the patient is not covered by additional insurance. If the patient is covered by Medicare and Medicaid, follow the instructions for Medicare-Medicaid (Medi-Medi) crossover claims in Chapter 14.

Refer to the John Q. Public case study in Figure 15-3 and the completed claim in Figure 15-4 as you study Table 15-1.

TABLE 15-1 CMS-1500 claims completion instructions for Medicaid primary claims

NOTE: Refer to Chapter 11 for clarification of claims completion (e.g., entering names, mailing addresses, ICD-10-CM codes, diagnosis pointer letters, NPI, and so on).

BLOCK	INSTRUCTIONS
1	Enter an X in the *Medicaid* box.
1a	Enter the Medicaid identification number as it appears on the patient's Medicaid card. *Do not enter hyphens or spaces in the number.*
2	Enter the patient's last name, first name, and middle initial (separated by commas) (DOE, JANE, M).
3	Enter the patient's birth date as MM DD YYYY (with spaces). Enter an X in the appropriate box to indicate the patient's gender. If the patient's gender is unknown, leave blank.
4	Leave blank.
5	Enter the patient's mailing address and telephone number. Enter the street address on line 1, enter the city and state on line 2, and enter the five- or nine-digit zip code and phone number on line 3.
6-8	Leave blank.
9, 9a, 9d	Leave blank. *Blocks 9, 9a, and 9d are completed if the patient has additional insurance coverage, such as commercial insurance.*
9b-9c	Leave blank.
10a-c	Enter an X in the NO boxes. (If an X is entered in the YES box for auto accident, enter the two-character state abbreviation of the patient's residence.)
10d	Leave blank. For Medicaid managed care programs, enter an E for emergency care or U for urgency care (if instructed to do so by the administrative contractor).
11-16	Leave blank.
17	If applicable, enter the first name, middle initial (if known), last name, and credentials of the professional who referred, ordered, or supervised health care service(s) or supply(ies) reported on the claim. *Do not enter any punctuation.* In front of the name, enter the applicable qualifier to identify which provider is being reported, as follows: DN (referring provider), DK (ordering provider), or DQ (supervising provider). Otherwise, leave blank.
17a	Leave blank.
17b	Enter the 10-digit national provider identifier (NPI) of the professional in Block 17. Otherwise, leave blank.
18	Enter the admission date and discharge date as MM DD YYYY (with spaces) if the patient received inpatient services (e.g., hospital, skilled nursing facility). Otherwise, leave blank. *If the patient has not been discharged at the time the claim is completed, leave the discharge date blank.*
19	Leave blank.
20	Enter an X in the NO box if all laboratory procedures reported on the claim were performed in the provider's office. Otherwise, enter an X in the YES box, enter the total amount charged by the outside laboratory in $ CHARGES, and enter the outside laboratory's name, mailing address, and NPI in Block 32. (Charges are entered *without* punctuation. For example, $1,100.00 is entered as 110000 below $ CHARGES.)

(continues)

TABLE 15-1 (continued)

BLOCK	INSTRUCTIONS
21	Enter the ICD-10-CM code for up to 12 diagnoses or conditions treated or medically managed during the encounter. Lines A through L in Block 21 will relate to CPT/HCPCS service/procedure codes reported in Block 24E. In the *ICD Ind* (ICD indicator) box, enter 0 for ICD-10-CM (or 9 for ICD-9-CM).
22	Leave blank. This is reserved for submitted claims.
23	Enter the Medicaid preauthorization number, which was assigned by the payer, if applicable. If written preauthorization was obtained, attach a copy to the claim. Otherwise, leave blank.
24A	Enter the date the procedure or service was performed in the FROM column as MM DD YY (with spaces). Enter a date in the TO column *if the procedure or service was performed on consecutive days during a range of dates. Then, enter the number of consecutive days in Block 24G.* **NOTE:** The shaded area in each line is used to enter supplemental information to support reported services *if instructed by the payer to enter such information.* Data entry in Block 24 is limited to reporting six services. *Do not use the shaded lines to report additional services.* If additional services were provided, generate new CMS-1500 claim(s) to report the additional services.
24B	Enter the appropriate two-digit place-of-service (POS) code to identify the location where the reported procedure or service was performed. (Refer to Appendix II for POS codes.)
24C	Enter an E *if the service was provided for a medical emergency,* regardless of where it was provided. Otherwise, leave blank.
24D	Enter the CPT or HCPCS level II code and applicable required modifier(s) for procedures or services performed. *Separate the CPT/HCPCS code and first modifier with one space. Separate additional modifiers with one space each. Up to four modifiers can be entered.*
24E	Enter the diagnosis pointer letter from Block 21 that relates to the procedure/service performed on the date of service. **NOTE:** When completing CMS-1500 claims for case studies in this textbook, its Workbook, and SimClaim™ software, enter just one diagnosis pointer letter on each line of Block 24E.
24F	Enter the fee charged for each reported procedure or service. When multiple procedures or services are reported on the same line, enter the total fee charged. *Do not enter commas, periods, or dollar signs. Do not enter negative amounts. Enter 00 in the cents area if the amount is a whole number.*
24G	Enter the number of days or units for procedures or services reported in Block 24D. *If just one procedure or service was reported in Block 24D, enter a 1 in Block 24G.*
24H	Enter an E if the service was provided under the EPSDT program, or enter an F if the service was provided for family planning. Enter a B if the service can be categorized as both EPSDT and family planning. Otherwise, leave blank.
24I	Leave blank. The NPI abbreviation is preprinted on the CMS-1500 claim.

(continues)

TABLE 15-1 (continued)

BLOCK	INSTRUCTIONS
24J	Enter the 10-digit NPI for the: • Provider who performed the service *if the provider is a member of a group practice* (Leave blank if the provider is a solo practitioner.) • Supervising provider *if the service was provided incident-to the service of a physician or nonphysician practitioner* **and** *the physician or practitioner who ordered the service did not supervise the provider* (Leave blank if the incident-to service was performed under the supervision of the physician or nonphysician practitioner.) • DMEPOS supplier or outside laboratory *if the physician submits the claim for services provided by the DMEPOS supplier or outside laboratory* (Leave blank if the DMEPOS supplier or outside laboratory submits the claim.) Otherwise, leave blank.
25	Enter the provider's social security number (SSN) or employer identification number (EIN). *Do not enter hyphens or spaces in the number.* Enter an X in the appropriate box to indicate which number is reported.
26	Enter the patient's account number as assigned by the provider.
27	Enter an X in the YES box to indicate that the provider agrees to accept assignment. Otherwise, enter an X in the NO box.
28	Enter the total charges for services and/or procedures reported in Block 24. **NOTE:** If multiple claims are submitted for one patient because more than six procedures or services were reported, be sure the total charge reported on each claim accurately represents the total of the items on each submitted claim.
29-30	Leave blank.
31	Enter the provider's name and credential (e.g., MARY SMITH MD) and the date the claim was completed as MMDDYYYY (without spaces). *Do not enter any punctuation.*
32	Enter the name and address where procedures or services were provided *if at a location other than the patient's home, such as a hospital, outside laboratory facility, skilled nursing facility, or DMEPOS supplier.* Otherwise, leave blank. Enter the name on line 1, the address on line 2, and the city, state, and five- or nine-digit zip code on line 3. *For a nine-digit zip code, enter the hyphen.* **NOTE:** If Block 18 contains dates of service for inpatient care and/or Block 20 contains an X in the YES box, enter the name and address of the facility that provided services.
32a	Enter the 10-digit NPI of the provider entered in Block 32.
32b	Leave blank.
33	Enter the provider's *billing* name, address, and telephone number. Enter the phone number in the area next to the Block title. *Do not enter parentheses for the area code.* Enter the name on line 1, enter the address on line 2, and enter the city, state, and five- or nine-digit zip code on line 3. *For a nine-digit zip code, enter the hyphen.*
33a	Enter the 10-digit NPI of the *billing* provider (e.g., solo practitioner) or group practice (e.g., clinic).
33b	Leave blank.

Courtesy of the Centers for Medicare & Medicaid Services, www.cms.gov

ERIN A. HELPER, M.D.
101 Medic Drive, Anywhere, NY 12345
(101) 111-1234 (Office) • (101) 111-9292 (Fax)
EIN: 11-1234523
NPI: 1234567890

Case Study

PATIENT INFORMATION:		**INSURANCE INFORMATION:**	
Name:	Public, John Q.	**Patient Number:**	15-1
Address:	10A Senate Avenue	**Place of Service:**	Office
City:	Anywhere	**Primary Insurance Plan:**	Medicaid
State:	NY	**Primary Insurance Plan ID #:**	99811948
Zip Code:	12345-1234	**Policy #:**	
Telephone:	(101) 201-7891	**Primary Policyholder:**	Public, John Q.
Gender:	Male	**Policyholder Date of Birth:**	10-10-1959
Date of Birth:	10-10-1959	**Relationship to Patient:**	Self
Occupation:		**Secondary Insurance Plan:**	
Employer:		**Secondary Insurance Plan ID #:**	
		Secondary Policyholder:	

Patient Status ☒ Married ☐ Divorced ☐ Single ☐ Student

DIAGNOSIS INFORMATION

	Diagnosis	Code		Diagnosis	Code
1.	Benign sebaceous cyst	L72.3	5.		
2.	Malignant lesion, skin of trunk	C44.509	6.		
3.			7.		
4.			8.		

PROCEDURE INFORMATION

	Description of Procedure or Service	Date	Code	Charge
1.	Excision, 1.4 cm malignant lesion, skin of trunk, with intermediate repair	01-21-YYYY	11602 12031-51	75.00 75.00
2.	Excision, 2.1 cm benign cyst, skin of back	01-21-YYYY	11403-51	50.00
3.				
4.				
5.				

SPECIAL NOTES: Medicaid Preauthorization No. YY8301

FIGURE 15-3 John Q. Public case study.

HEALTH INSURANCE CLAIM FORM

APPROVED BY NATIONAL UNIFORM CLAIM COMMITTEE (NUCC) 02/12

PICA — PICA — CARRIER

1. MEDICARE (Medicare#) [ ] MEDICAID (Medicaid#) [X] TRICARE (ID#/DoD#) [ ] CHAMPVA (Member ID#) [ ] GROUP HEALTH PLAN (ID#) [ ] FECA BLK LUNG (ID#) [ ] OTHER (ID#) [ ]

1a. INSURED'S I.D. NUMBER (For Program in Item 1): **99811948**

2. PATIENT'S NAME (Last Name, First Name, Middle Initial): **PUBLIC, JOHN, Q**

3. PATIENT'S BIRTH DATE MM DD YY: **10 10 1959** SEX M [X] F [ ]

4. INSURED'S NAME (Last Name, First Name, Middle Initial)

5. PATIENT'S ADDRESS (No., Street): **10A SENATE AVENUE**

6. PATIENT RELATIONSHIP TO INSURED: Self [ ] Spouse [ ] Child [ ] Other [ ]

7. INSURED'S ADDRESS (No., Street)

CITY: **ANYWHERE** STATE: **NY**

8. RESERVED FOR NUCC USE

CITY STATE

ZIP CODE: **12345-1234** TELEPHONE (Include Area Code): **(101) 2017891**

ZIP CODE TELEPHONE (Include Area Code) ( )

9. OTHER INSURED'S NAME (Last Name, First Name, Middle Initial)

10. IS PATIENT'S CONDITION RELATED TO:

11. INSURED'S POLICY GROUP OR FECA NUMBER

a. OTHER INSURED'S POLICY OR GROUP NUMBER

a. EMPLOYMENT? (Current or Previous) [ ] YES [X] NO

a. INSURED'S DATE OF BIRTH MM DD YY SEX M [ ] F [ ]

b. RESERVED FOR NUCC USE

b. AUTO ACCIDENT? [ ] YES [X] NO PLACE (State)

b. OTHER CLAIM ID (Designated by NUCC)

c. RESERVED FOR NUCC USE

c. OTHER ACCIDENT? [ ] YES [X] NO

c. INSURANCE PLAN NAME OR PROGRAM NAME

d. INSURANCE PLAN NAME OR PROGRAM NAME

10d. CLAIM CODES (Designated by NUCC)

d. IS THERE ANOTHER HEALTH BENEFIT PLAN? [ ] YES [ ] NO *If yes, complete items 9, 9a, and 9d.*

READ BACK OF FORM BEFORE COMPLETING & SIGNING THIS FORM.

12. PATIENT'S OR AUTHORIZED PERSON'S SIGNATURE I authorize the release of any medical or other information necessary to process this claim. I also request payment of government benefits either to myself or to the party who accepts assignment below.

SIGNED ______ DATE ______

13. INSURED'S OR AUTHORIZED PERSON'S SIGNATURE I authorize payment of medical benefits to the undersigned physician or supplier for services described below.

SIGNED ______

PATIENT AND INSURED INFORMATION

14. DATE OF CURRENT ILLNESS, INJURY, or PREGNANCY (LMP) MM DD YY QUAL.

15. OTHER DATE QUAL. MM DD YY

16. DATES PATIENT UNABLE TO WORK IN CURRENT OCCUPATION FROM MM DD YY TO MM DD YY

17. NAME OF REFERRING PROVIDER OR OTHER SOURCE 17a. 17b. NPI

18. HOSPITALIZATION DATES RELATED TO CURRENT SERVICES FROM MM DD YY TO MM DD YY

19. ADDITIONAL CLAIM INFORMATION (Designated by NUCC)

20. OUTSIDE LAB? [ ] YES [X] NO $ CHARGES

21. DIAGNOSIS OR NATURE OF ILLNESS OR INJURY Relate A-L to service line below (24E) ICD Ind. **0**

A. **L72.3** B. **C44.509** C. D. E. F. G. H. I. J. K. L.

22. RESUBMISSION CODE ORIGINAL REF. NO.

23. PRIOR AUTHORIZATION NUMBER: **YY8301**

	24. A. DATE(S) OF SERVICE From MM DD YY	To MM DD YY	B. PLACE OF SERVICE	C. EMG	D. PROCEDURES, SERVICES, OR SUPPLIES (Explain Unusual Circumstances) CPT/HCPCS	MODIFIER	E. DIAGNOSIS POINTER	F. $ CHARGES	G. DAYS OR UNITS	H. EPSDT Family Plan	I. ID. QUAL.	J. RENDERING PROVIDER ID. #
1	01 21 YY		11		11602		B	75 00	1		NPI	
2	01 21 YY		11		12031	51	B	75 00	1		NPI	
3	01 21 YY		11		11403	51	A	50 00	1		NPI	
4											NPI	
5											NPI	
6											NPI	

25. FEDERAL TAX I.D. NUMBER: **111234523** SSN [ ] EIN [X]

26. PATIENT'S ACCOUNT NO.: **15-1**

27. ACCEPT ASSIGNMENT? (For govt. claims, see back) [X] YES [ ] NO

28. TOTAL CHARGE: $ **200 00**

29. AMOUNT PAID: $

30. Rsvd for NUCC Use

31. SIGNATURE OF PHYSICIAN OR SUPPLIER INCLUDING DEGREES OR CREDENTIALS (I certify that the statements on the reverse apply to this bill and are made a part thereof.)

SIGNED: **ERIN A HELPER MD** DATE: **MMDDYYYY**

32. SERVICE FACILITY LOCATION INFORMATION a. NPI b.

33. BILLING PROVIDER INFO & PH #: **(101) 1111234**

ERIN A HELPER MD
101 MEDIC DRIVE
ANYWHERE NY 12345

a. **1234567890** b.

PHYSICIAN OR SUPPLIER INFORMATION

NUCC Instruction Manual available at: www.nucc.org *PLEASE PRINT OR TYPE*

FIGURE 15-4 Completed primary Medicaid CMS-1500 claim for John Q. Public case study.

EXERCISE 15-1

Completion of Medicaid as Primary CMS-1500 Claim

1. Obtain a blank claim by making a copy of the CMS-1500 claim form in Appendix III.
2. Review the claims instructions in Table 15-1.
3. Review Figure 15-5, Mary S. Patient case study.
4. Select the information needed from the case study, and enter the required information on the claim using optical scanning guidelines.
5. Review the claim to be sure all required blocks are properly completed.
6. Compare your claim with the completed claim in Figure 15-6.

ERIN A. HELPER, M.D.
101 Medic Drive, Anywhere, NY 12345
(101) 111-1234 (Office) • (101) 111-9292 (Fax)
EIN: 11-1234523
NPI: 1234567890

Case Study

PATIENT INFORMATION:		**INSURANCE INFORMATION:**	
Name:	Patient, Mary S.	**Patient Number:**	15-2
Address:	91 Home Street	**Place of Service:**	Office
City:	Nowhere	**Primary Insurance Plan:**	Medicaid
State:	NY	**Primary Insurance Plan ID #:**	99811765
Zip Code:	12367-1234	**Policy #:**	
Telephone:	(101) 201-8989	**Primary Policyholder:**	Patient, Mary S.
Gender:	Female	**Policyholder Date of Birth:**	03-08-1980
Date of Birth:	03-08-1980	**Relationship to Patient:**	Self
Occupation:		**Secondary Insurance Plan:**	
Employer:		**Secondary Insurance Plan ID #:**	
		Secondary Policyholder:	

Patient Status ☒ Married ☐ Divorced ☐ Single ☐ Student

DIAGNOSIS INFORMATION

Diagnosis	**Code**	**Diagnosis**	**Code**
1. Annual physical exam	Z00.00	5.	
2. Hypertension	I10	6.	
3.		7.	
4.		8.	

PROCEDURE INFORMATION

Description of Procedure or Service	**Date**	**Code**	**Charge**
1. Preventive Medicine Office Visit	01-05-YYYY	99386	150.00
2. Established Patient Office Visit, Level III	01-05-YYYY	99213-25	75.00
3. Urinalysis, with microscopy	01-05-YYYY	81001	10.00
4. Venipuncture, routine	01-05-YYYY	36415	8.00
5.			

SPECIAL NOTES: Patient scheduled for outpatient chest x-ray and mammogram at RadioDiagnostics.

FIGURE 15-5 Mary S. Patient case study.

CARRIER

HEALTH INSURANCE CLAIM FORM

APPROVED BY NATIONAL UNIFORM CLAIM COMMITTEE (NUCC) 02/12

PICA | PICA

1. MEDICARE (Medicare#) ☐ MEDICAID (Medicaid#) ☒ TRICARE (ID#/DoD#) ☐ CHAMPVA (Member ID#) ☐ GROUP HEALTH PLAN (ID#) ☐ FECA BLK LUNG (ID#) ☐ OTHER (ID#) ☐

1a. INSURED'S I.D. NUMBER (For Program in Item 1): 99811765

2. PATIENT'S NAME (Last Name, First Name, Middle Initial): PATIENT, MARY, S

3. PATIENT'S BIRTH DATE MM DD YY: 03 08 1980 SEX M ☐ F ☒

4. INSURED'S NAME (Last Name, First Name, Middle Initial)

5. PATIENT'S ADDRESS (No., Street): 91 HOME STREET

6. PATIENT RELATIONSHIP TO INSURED: Self ☐ Spouse ☐ Child ☐ Other ☐

7. INSURED'S ADDRESS (No., Street)

CITY: NOWHERE STATE: NY

8. RESERVED FOR NUCC USE

CITY STATE

ZIP CODE: 12367-1234 TELEPHONE (Include Area Code): (101) 2018989

ZIP CODE TELEPHONE (Include Area Code) ( )

9. OTHER INSURED'S NAME (Last Name, First Name, Middle Initial)

10. IS PATIENT'S CONDITION RELATED TO:

11. INSURED'S POLICY GROUP OR FECA NUMBER

a. OTHER INSURED'S POLICY OR GROUP NUMBER

a. EMPLOYMENT? (Current or Previous) ☐ YES ☒ NO

a. INSURED'S DATE OF BIRTH MM DD YY SEX M ☐ F ☐

b. RESERVED FOR NUCC USE

b. AUTO ACCIDENT? ☐ YES ☒ NO PLACE (State)

b. OTHER CLAIM ID (Designated by NUCC)

c. RESERVED FOR NUCC USE

c. OTHER ACCIDENT? ☐ YES ☒ NO

c. INSURANCE PLAN NAME OR PROGRAM NAME

d. INSURANCE PLAN NAME OR PROGRAM NAME

10d. CLAIM CODES (Designated by NUCC)

d. IS THERE ANOTHER HEALTH BENEFIT PLAN? ☐ YES ☐ NO *If yes*, complete items 9, 9a, and 9d.

READ BACK OF FORM BEFORE COMPLETING & SIGNING THIS FORM.

12. PATIENT'S OR AUTHORIZED PERSON'S SIGNATURE I authorize the release of any medical or other information necessary to process this claim. I also request payment of government benefits either to myself or to the party who accepts assignment below.

SIGNED DATE

13. INSURED'S OR AUTHORIZED PERSON'S SIGNATURE I authorize payment of medical benefits to the undersigned physician or supplier for services described below.

SIGNED

PATIENT AND INSURED INFORMATION

14. DATE OF CURRENT ILLNESS, INJURY, or PREGNANCY (LMP) MM DD YY QUAL.

15. OTHER DATE QUAL. MM DD YY

16. DATES PATIENT UNABLE TO WORK IN CURRENT OCCUPATION FROM MM DD YY TO MM DD YY

17. NAME OF REFERRING PROVIDER OR OTHER SOURCE 17a. 17b. NPI

18. HOSPITALIZATION DATES RELATED TO CURRENT SERVICES FROM MM DD YY TO MM DD YY

19. ADDITIONAL CLAIM INFORMATION (Designated by NUCC)

20. OUTSIDE LAB? ☐ YES ☒ NO $ CHARGES

21. DIAGNOSIS OR NATURE OF ILLNESS OR INJURY Relate A-L to service line below (24E) ICD Ind. 0

A. Z00.00 B. I10 C. D.
E. F. G. H.
I. J. K. L.

22. RESUBMISSION CODE ORIGINAL REF. NO.

23. PRIOR AUTHORIZATION NUMBER

	24. A. DATE(S) OF SERVICE From MM DD YY	To MM DD YY	B. PLACE OF SERVICE	C. EMG	D. PROCEDURES, SERVICES, OR SUPPLIES (Explain Unusual Circumstances) CPT/HCPCS	MODIFIER	E. DIAGNOSIS POINTER	F. $ CHARGES	G. DAYS OR UNITS	H. EPSDT Family Plan	I. ID. QUAL.	J. RENDERING PROVIDER ID. #
1	01 05 YY		11		99386		A	150 00	1		NPI	
2	01 05 YY		11		99213	25	B	75 00	1		NPI	
3	01 05 YY		11		81001		A	10 00	1		NPI	
4	01 05 YY		11		36415		A	8 00	1		NPI	
5											NPI	
6											NPI	

25. FEDERAL TAX I.D. NUMBER: 111234523 SSN ☐ EIN ☒

26. PATIENT'S ACCOUNT NO.: 15-2

27. ACCEPT ASSIGNMENT? (For govt. claims, see back) ☒ YES ☐ NO

28. TOTAL CHARGE: $ 243 00

29. AMOUNT PAID: $

30. Rsvd for NUCC Use

31. SIGNATURE OF PHYSICIAN OR SUPPLIER INCLUDING DEGREES OR CREDENTIALS (I certify that the statements on the reverse apply to this bill and are made a part thereof.)

ERIN A HELPER MD MMDDYYYY
SIGNED DATE

32. SERVICE FACILITY LOCATION INFORMATION

a. NPI b.

33. BILLING PROVIDER INFO & PH # (101) 1111234

ERIN A HELPER MD
101 MEDIC DRIVE
ANYWHERE NY 12345

a. 1234567890 b.

PHYSICIAN OR SUPPLIER INFORMATION

NUCC Instruction Manual available at: www.nucc.org *PLEASE PRINT OR TYPE*

FIGURE 15-6 Completed primary Medicaid CMS-1500 claim for Mary S. Patient case study.

> **NOTE:** The instructions *do not* apply to Medicare-Medicaid (Medi-Medi) crossover cases, which are discussed in Chapter 14.

MEDICAID AS SECONDARY PAYER CLAIMS

Modifications are made to the CMS-1500 claim when patients are covered by Medicaid and a secondary or supplemental health insurance plan (Table 15-2), which means just one CMS-1500 claim is submitted (Figures 15-7 and 15-8).

TABLE 15-2 CMS-1500 claims completion instructions for Medicaid as secondary payer (Refer to Table 15-1 for primary CMS-1500 claims completion instructions.)

BLOCK	INSTRUCTIONS
4	Enter the primary policyholder's last name, first name, and middle initial (separated by commas).
6	Enter an X in the appropriate box to indicate the patient's relationship to the primary policyholder. If the patient is an unmarried domestic partner, enter an X in the *Other* box.
7	Enter the primary policyholder's mailing address and telephone number. Enter the street address on line 1, enter the city and state on line 2, and enter the five- or nine-digit zip code and phone number on line 3.
9	Enter the primary policyholder's last name, first name, and middle initial (if known) (separated by commas). If the primary policyholder is the patient, enter SAME.
9a	Enter the primary policyholder's policy or group number. *Do not enter hyphens or spaces in the number.*
9d	Enter the name of the primary policyholder's health insurance plan (e.g., commercial health insurance plan name or government program).
10a-c	Enter an X in the appropriate box.
10d	Leave blank.
11	Enter the rejection code provided by the payer *if the patient has other third-party payer coverage and the submitted claim was rejected by that payer.* Otherwise, leave blank. **NOTE:** When a third-party payer has rejected the submitted claim, and a CMS-1500 claim is sent to Medicaid, enter the code that describes the reason for rejection by the payer (e.g., service not covered). The rejection code reported in Block 11 alerts Medicaid that another payer is not responsible for reimbursement of procedures/services provided. (The other payer's remittance advice or explanation of benefits may need to be submitted to Medicaid as proof.)
11d	Enter an X in the YES box.
28	Enter the total charges for services and/or procedures reported in Block 24.
29	Enter the amount paid by the other payer. If the other payer denied the claim, enter 0 00.

Courtesy of the Centers for Medicare & Medicaid Services, www.cms.gov

ERIN A. HELPER, M.D.
101 Medic Drive, Anywhere, NY 12345
(101) 111-1234 (Office) • (101) 111-9292 (Fax)
EIN: 11-1234523
NPI: 1234567890

Case Study

PATIENT INFORMATION:

Name:	Connelly, Jennifer
Address:	45 Main Street
City:	Nowhere
State:	NY
Zip Code:	12367-1234
Telephone:	(101) 555-5624
Gender:	Female
Date of Birth:	05-05-1955
Occupation:	
Employer:	

INSURANCE INFORMATION:

Patient Number:	15-3
Place of Service:	Office
Primary Insurance Plan:	Aetna
Primary Insurance Plan ID #:	56265897
Policy #:	
Primary Policyholder:	Thomas Connelly
Policyholder Date of Birth:	05-25-1956
Employer:	Turbodyne
Relationship to Patient:	Spouse
Secondary Insurance Plan:	Medicaid
Secondary Insurance Plan ID #:	56215689
Secondary Policyholder:	Jennifer Connelly

Patient Status ☒ Married ☐ Divorced ☐ Single ☐ Student

DIAGNOSIS INFORMATION

Diagnosis	Code	Diagnosis	Code
1. Hypertension	I10	5.	
2.		6.	
3.		7.	
4.		8.	

PROCEDURE INFORMATION

Description of Procedure or Service	Date	Code	Charge
1. New patient, office visit, level III	01-07-YYYY	99203	150.00
2.			
3.			
4.			
5.			

SPECIAL NOTES: Aetna paid $105.00 as primary payer.

FIGURE 15-7 Jennifer Connelly case study.

HEALTH INSURANCE CLAIM FORM

APPROVED BY NATIONAL UNIFORM CLAIM COMMITTEE (NUCC) 02/12

PICA PICA

CARRIER

PATIENT AND INSURED INFORMATION

1. MEDICARE (Medicare#) [ ] MEDICAID (Medicaid#) [X] TRICARE (ID#/DoD#) [ ] CHAMPVA (Member ID#) [ ] GROUP HEALTH PLAN (ID#) [ ] FECA BLK LUNG (ID#) [ ] OTHER (ID#) [ ]

1a. INSURED'S I.D. NUMBER (For Program in Item 1): 56215689

2. PATIENT'S NAME (Last Name, First Name, Middle Initial): CONNELLY, JENNIFER

3. PATIENT'S BIRTH DATE MM DD YY: 05 05 1955 SEX M [ ] F [X]

4. INSURED'S NAME (Last Name, First Name, Middle Initial): CONNELLY, THOMAS

5. PATIENT'S ADDRESS (No., Street): 45 MAIN STREET

CITY: NOWHERE STATE: NY

ZIP CODE: 12367-1234 TELEPHONE (Include Area Code): (101) 5555624

6. PATIENT RELATIONSHIP TO INSURED: Self [ ] Spouse [X] Child [ ] Other [ ]

7. INSURED'S ADDRESS (No., Street): 45 MAIN STREET

CITY: NOWHERE STATE: NY

ZIP CODE: 12367-1234 TELEPHONE (Include Area Code): (101) 5555624

8. RESERVED FOR NUCC USE

9. OTHER INSURED'S NAME (Last Name, First Name, Middle Initial): CONNELLY, THOMAS

a. OTHER INSURED'S POLICY OR GROUP NUMBER: 56265897

b. RESERVED FOR NUCC USE

c. RESERVED FOR NUCC USE

d. INSURANCE PLAN NAME OR PROGRAM NAME: AETNA

10. IS PATIENT'S CONDITION RELATED TO:

a. EMPLOYMENT? (Current or Previous) [ ] YES [X] NO

b. AUTO ACCIDENT? [ ] YES [X] NO PLACE (State)

c. OTHER ACCIDENT? [ ] YES [X] NO

10d. CLAIM CODES (Designated by NUCC)

11. INSURED'S POLICY GROUP OR FECA NUMBER

a. INSURED'S DATE OF BIRTH MM DD YY SEX M [ ] F [ ]

b. OTHER CLAIM ID (Designated by NUCC)

c. INSURANCE PLAN NAME OR PROGRAM NAME

d. IS THERE ANOTHER HEALTH BENEFIT PLAN? [X] YES [ ] NO *If yes*, complete items 9, 9a, and 9d.

READ BACK OF FORM BEFORE COMPLETING & SIGNING THIS FORM.

12. PATIENT'S OR AUTHORIZED PERSON'S SIGNATURE I authorize the release of any medical or other information necessary to process this claim. I also request payment of government benefits either to myself or to the party who accepts assignment below.

SIGNED ____ DATE ____

13. INSURED'S OR AUTHORIZED PERSON'S SIGNATURE I authorize payment of medical benefits to the undersigned physician or supplier for services described below.

SIGNED ____

PHYSICIAN OR SUPPLIER INFORMATION

14. DATE OF CURRENT ILLNESS, INJURY, or PREGNANCY (LMP) MM DD YY QUAL.

15. OTHER DATE QUAL. MM DD YY

16. DATES PATIENT UNABLE TO WORK IN CURRENT OCCUPATION FROM MM DD YY TO MM DD YY

17. NAME OF REFERRING PROVIDER OR OTHER SOURCE 17a. 17b. NPI

18. HOSPITALIZATION DATES RELATED TO CURRENT SERVICES FROM MM DD YY TO MM DD YY

19. ADDITIONAL CLAIM INFORMATION (Designated by NUCC)

20. OUTSIDE LAB? [ ] YES [X] NO $ CHARGES

21. DIAGNOSIS OR NATURE OF ILLNESS OR INJURY Relate A-L to service line below (24E) ICD Ind. 0

A. I10 B. C. D. E. F. G. H. I. J. K. L.

22. RESUBMISSION CODE ORIGINAL REF. NO.

23. PRIOR AUTHORIZATION NUMBER

	24. A. DATE(S) OF SERVICE From MM DD YY	To MM DD YY	B. PLACE OF SERVICE	C. EMG	D. PROCEDURES, SERVICES, OR SUPPLIES (Explain Unusual Circumstances) CPT/HCPCS	MODIFIER	E. DIAGNOSIS POINTER	F. $ CHARGES	G. DAYS OR UNITS	H. EPSDT Family Plan	I. ID. QUAL.	J. RENDERING PROVIDER ID. #
1	01 07 YY		11		99203		A	150 00	1		NPI	
2											NPI	
3											NPI	
4											NPI	
5											NPI	
6											NPI	

25. FEDERAL TAX I.D. NUMBER: 111234523 SSN [ ] EIN [X]

26. PATIENT'S ACCOUNT NO.: 15-3S

27. ACCEPT ASSIGNMENT? (For govt. claims, see back) [X] YES [ ] NO

28. TOTAL CHARGE: $ 150 00

29. AMOUNT PAID: $ 105 00

30. Rsvd for NUCC Use

31. SIGNATURE OF PHYSICIAN OR SUPPLIER INCLUDING DEGREES OR CREDENTIALS (I certify that the statements on the reverse apply to this bill and are made a part thereof.)

ERIN A HELPER MD MMDDYYYY
SIGNED DATE

32. SERVICE FACILITY LOCATION INFORMATION
a. NPI b.

33. BILLING PROVIDER INFO & PH #: (101) 1111234
ERIN A HELPER MD
101 MEDIC DRIVE
ANYWHERE NY 12345
a. 1234567890 b.

NUCC Instruction Manual available at: www.nucc.org *PLEASE PRINT OR TYPE*

Courtesy of the Centers for Medicare & Medicaid Services, www.cms.gov; Copyright © 2015 Cengage Learning®.

FIGURE 15-8 Completed Medicaid secondary payer CMS-1500 claim for Jennifer Connelly case study.

MOTHER/BABY CLAIMS

The instructions in Table 15-3 are for mother/baby claims. They modify the primary Medicaid instructions. Refer to Figures 15-9 and 15-10 for a completed claim based on a case study.

The infant of a Medicaid recipient is automatically eligible for Medicaid for the entire first year of life. Individual state Medicaid programs determine reimbursement procedures for services provided to newborns. When claims are submitted under the *mother's Medicaid identification number*, coverage is usually limited to the baby's first 10 days of life (during which time an application is made so the baby is assigned its own identification number). Medicaid usually covers babies through the end of the month of their first birthday (e.g., baby born on January 5 this year is covered until January 31 next year). The baby must continuously live with its mother to be eligible for the full year, and the baby remains eligible for Medicaid even if changes in family size or income occur and the mother is no longer eligible for Medicaid.

NOTE: Medicaid *Baby Your Baby* programs cover the mother's prenatal care only.

A **mother/baby claim** is submitted for services provided to a baby under the mother's Medicaid identification number. (The mother's services are *not* reimbursed on the mother/baby claim; they are submitted on a separate CMS-1500 claim according to the instructions in Table 15-1.)

TABLE 15-3 CMS-1500 claims completion instructions for Medicaid mother/baby claims

BLOCK	INSTRUCTIONS
1a	Enter the mother's Medicaid ID number as it appears on the patient's Medicaid card. *Do not enter hyphens or spaces in the number.*
2	Enter the mother's last name followed by the word NEWBORN (separated by a comma). **EXAMPLE:** VANDERMARK, NEWBORN **NOTE:** A Medicaid payer may require BABYBOY or BABYGIRL to be entered instead of NEWBORN (e.g., VANDERMARK, BABYGIRL).
3	Enter the infant's birth date as MM DD YYYY (with spaces). Enter an X to indicate the infant's gender.
4	Enter the mother's name (separated by a comma), followed by (MOM), as the responsible party. **EXAMPLE:** VANDERMARK, JOYCE (MOM) **NOTE:** A Medicaid payer may require just the mother's last name and first name, separated by a comma (e.g., VANDERMARK, JOYCE).
21	Enter ICD-10-CM secondary diagnosis codes in fields B through L, if applicable.

Courtesy of the Centers for Medicare & Medicaid Services, www.cms.gov

KIM A. CARRINGTON, M.D.
900 Medic Drive, Anywhere, NY 12345
(101) 111-2365 (Office) • (101) 111-5625 (Fax)
EIN: 11-5623567
NPI: 7890123456

Case Study

PATIENT INFORMATION:		**INSURANCE INFORMATION:**	
Name:	Muracek, Newborn	**Patient Number:**	15-4
Address:	515 Hill Street	**Place of Service:**	Inpatient Hospital
City:	Anywhere	**Primary Insurance Plan:**	Medicaid
State:	NY	**Primary Insurance Plan ID #:**	56265987
Zip Code:	12367-1234	**Policy #:**	
Telephone:	(101) 555-5598	**Primary Policyholder:**	Yvonne Muracek
Gender:	Female	**Policyholder Date of Birth:**	12-24-1980
Date of Birth:	01-10-2010	**Employer:**	
Occupation:		**Relationship to Patient:**	Mother
Employer:		**Secondary Insurance Plan:**	
		Secondary Insurance Plan ID #:	
		Secondary Policyholder:	

Patient Status ☐ Married ☐ Divorced ☒ Single ☐ Student

DIAGNOSIS INFORMATION

	Diagnosis	Code		Diagnosis	Code
1.	Healthy single liveborn infant, delivered vaginally	Z38.00	5.		
2.			6.		
3.			7.		
4.			8.		

PROCEDURE INFORMATION

	Description of Procedure or Service	Date	Code	Charge
1.	History and examination of normal newborn	01-10-2010	99460	150.00
2.	Attendance at delivery	01-10-2010	99464	400.00
3.	Subsequent care for normal newborn	01-11-2010	99462	100.00
4.				
5.				

SPECIAL NOTES: Inpatient care provided at Goodmedicine Hospital, Anywhere St, Anywhere, NY 12345. (NPI: 2345678901) Application for infant's Medicaid ID number has been submitted.

FIGURE 15-9 Newborn Muracek case study.

HEALTH INSURANCE CLAIM FORM

APPROVED BY NATIONAL UNIFORM CLAIM COMMITTEE (NUCC) 02/12

PICA

1. MEDICARE (Medicare#) | MEDICAID (Medicaid#) [X] | TRICARE (ID#/DoD#) | CHAMPVA (Member ID#) | GROUP HEALTH PLAN (ID#) | FECA BLK LUNG (ID#) | OTHER (ID#)

1a. INSURED'S I.D. NUMBER (For Program in Item 1): 56265987

2. PATIENT'S NAME (Last Name, First Name, Middle Initial): MURACEK, NEWBORN

3. PATIENT'S BIRTH DATE MM DD YY: 01 10 2010 SEX: M [ ] F [X]

4. INSURED'S NAME (Last Name, First Name, Middle Initial): MURACEK, YVONNE (MOM)

5. PATIENT'S ADDRESS (No., Street): 515 HILL STREET

6. PATIENT RELATIONSHIP TO INSURED: Self [ ] Spouse [ ] Child [ ] Other [ ]

7. INSURED'S ADDRESS (No., Street):

CITY: ANYWHERE STATE: NY

8. RESERVED FOR NUCC USE

ZIP CODE: 12367-1234 TELEPHONE (Include Area Code): (101) 5555598

9. OTHER INSURED'S NAME (Last Name, First Name, Middle Initial)

10. IS PATIENT'S CONDITION RELATED TO:

11. INSURED'S POLICY GROUP OR FECA NUMBER

a. OTHER INSURED'S POLICY OR GROUP NUMBER

a. EMPLOYMENT? (Current or Previous) YES [ ] NO [X]

a. INSURED'S DATE OF BIRTH MM DD YY SEX M [ ] F [ ]

b. RESERVED FOR NUCC USE

b. AUTO ACCIDENT? YES [ ] NO [X] PLACE (State)

b. OTHER CLAIM ID (Designated by NUCC)

c. RESERVED FOR NUCC USE

c. OTHER ACCIDENT? YES [ ] NO [X]

c. INSURANCE PLAN NAME OR PROGRAM NAME

d. INSURANCE PLAN NAME OR PROGRAM NAME

10d. CLAIM CODES (Designated by NUCC)

d. IS THERE ANOTHER HEALTH BENEFIT PLAN? YES [ ] NO [ ] *If yes*, complete items 9, 9a, and 9d.

READ BACK OF FORM BEFORE COMPLETING & SIGNING THIS FORM.

12. PATIENT'S OR AUTHORIZED PERSON'S SIGNATURE I authorize the release of any medical or other information necessary to process this claim. I also request payment of government benefits either to myself or to the party who accepts assignment below.

SIGNED DATE

13. INSURED'S OR AUTHORIZED PERSON'S SIGNATURE I authorize payment of medical benefits to the undersigned physician or supplier for services described below.

SIGNED

14. DATE OF CURRENT ILLNESS, INJURY, or PREGNANCY (LMP) MM DD YY QUAL.

15. OTHER DATE QUAL. MM DD YY

16. DATES PATIENT UNABLE TO WORK IN CURRENT OCCUPATION FROM TO

17. NAME OF REFERRING PROVIDER OR OTHER SOURCE 17a. 17b. NPI

18. HOSPITALIZATION DATES RELATED TO CURRENT SERVICES FROM 01 10 YYYY TO 01 11 YYYY

19. ADDITIONAL CLAIM INFORMATION (Designated by NUCC)

20. OUTSIDE LAB? YES [ ] NO [X] $ CHARGES

21. DIAGNOSIS OR NATURE OF ILLNESS OR INJURY Relate A-L to service line below (24E) ICD Ind. 0

A. Z38.00 B. C. D. E. F. G. H. I. J. K. L.

22. RESUBMISSION CODE ORIGINAL REF. NO.

23. PRIOR AUTHORIZATION NUMBER

24. A. DATE(S) OF SERVICE From MM DD YY	To MM DD YY	B. PLACE OF SERVICE	C. EMG	D. CPT/HCPCS	MODIFIER	E. DIAGNOSIS POINTER	F. $ CHARGES	G. DAYS OR UNITS	H. EPSDT Family Plan	I. ID. QUAL.	J. RENDERING PROVIDER ID. #
1 01 10 YY		21		99460		A	150 00	1		NPI	
2 01 10 YY		21		99464		A	400 00	1		NPI	
3 01 10 YY		21		99462		A	100 00	1		NPI	
4										NPI	
5										NPI	
6										NPI	

25. FEDERAL TAX I.D. NUMBER SSN [ ] EIN [X]: 115623567

26. PATIENT'S ACCOUNT NO.: 15-4

27. ACCEPT ASSIGNMENT? (For govt. claims, see back) YES [X] NO [ ]

28. TOTAL CHARGE $ 650 00

29. AMOUNT PAID $

30. Rsvd for NUCC Use

31. SIGNATURE OF PHYSICIAN OR SUPPLIER INCLUDING DEGREES OR CREDENTIALS (I certify that the statements on the reverse apply to this bill and are made a part thereof.)

KIM A CARRINGTON MD MMDDYYYY
SIGNED DATE

32. SERVICE FACILITY LOCATION INFORMATION
GOODMEDICINE HOSPITAL
ANYWHERE ST
ANYWHERE NY 12345
a. 2345678901 b.

33. BILLING PROVIDER INFO & PH # (101) 11112365
KIM A CARRINGTON MD
900 MEDIC DRIVE
ANYWHERE NY 12345
a. 7890123456 b.

NUCC Instruction Manual available at: www.nucc.org PLEASE PRINT OR TYPE

CARRIER — PATIENT AND INSURED INFORMATION — PHYSICIAN OR SUPPLIER INFORMATION

FIGURE 15-10 Completed Medicaid mother/baby CMS-1500 claim for Newborn Muracek case study.

SCHIP CLAIMS

Each state selects a payer that administers its State Children's Health Insurance Program (SCHIP), and the payer develops its own CMS-1500 claims instructions. General instructions included in Table 15-4 are used to complete SCHIP CMS-1500 claims for case studies in this textbook and its Workbook. (Refer to Figures 15-11 and 15-12 for a completed claim based on the case study.) It is important to obtain official CMS-1500 claims completion instructions from the SCHIP payer in your state.

> **EXAMPLE 1:** California's Healthy Kids program is administered by the Partnership HealthPlan of California (**www.PartnershipHP.org**), which requires entry of an X in the *Group Health Plan* box.

> **EXAMPLE 2:** New York State's Child Health Plus program is administered by Excellus BlueCross BlueShield (**www.ExcellusBCBS.com**), which requires entry of an X in the *Other* box.

TABLE 15-4 CMS-1500 claims completion instructions for SCHIP claims

BLOCK	INSTRUCTIONS
1	Enter an X in the *Other* box. **NOTE:** Some SCHIP payers, such as California's Healthy Kids program (administered by the Partnership HealthPlan of California), require an X to be entered in the *Group Health Plan box.*
1a	Enter the SCHIP identification number (assigned by the Health Plan) of the subscriber (person who holds the policy).
29	Enter the total amount the patient (or another payer) paid toward covered services only. If no payment was made, leave blank.

ANGELA DILALIO, M.D.
99 Provider Street • Injury, NY 12347 • (101) 201-4321
EIN: 11-1982342
NPI: 4567890123

Case Study

PATIENT INFORMATION:

Name:	Edgar Vasquez
Address:	1018 Bonita Ave
City:	Anywhere
State:	US
Zipcode:	12345
Telephone:	(101) 690-5244
Gender:	Male
Date of Birth:	10-18-2008
Occupation:	
Employer:	
Spouse's Employer	

INSURANCE INFORMATION:

Patient Number:	15-5
Place of Service:	Office
Primary Insurance Plan:	SCHIP
Primary Insurance Plan ID#:	CAM101919690
Group #:	987654Y
Primary Policyholder:	Edgar Vasquez
Policyholder Date of Birth:	10-18-2008
Relationship to Patient:	Self
Secondary Insurance Plan:	
Secondary Insurance Plan ID #:	
Secondary Policyholder:	

Patient status: ☐ Married ☐ Divorced ☒ Single ☐ Employed ☐ Student ☐ Other

DIAGNOSIS INFORMATION

	Diagnosis	Code		Diagnosis	Code
1.	Asthma	J45.909	5.		
2.			6.		
3.			7.		
4.			8.		

PROCEDURE INFORMATION

	Description of Procedure or Service	Date	Code	Charge
1.	Office visit, established visit, level II	12-18-YYYY	99212	$40.00
2.				
3.				
4.				
5.				

SPECIAL NOTES:

FIGURE 15-11 Edgar Vasquez case study.

HEALTH INSURANCE CLAIM FORM

APPROVED BY NATIONAL UNIFORM CLAIM COMMITTEE (NUCC) 02/12

PICA | PICA

CARRIER

1. MEDICARE (Medicare#) | MEDICAID (Medicaid#) | TRICARE (ID#/DoD#) | CHAMPVA (Member ID#) | GROUP HEALTH PLAN (ID#) | FECA BLK LUNG (ID#) | OTHER (ID#) [X]

1a. INSURED'S I.D. NUMBER (For Program in Item 1): CAM101919690

2. PATIENT'S NAME (Last Name, First Name, Middle Initial): VASQUEZ, EDGAR

3. PATIENT'S BIRTH DATE MM DD YY: 10 18 2008 SEX M [X] F [ ]

4. INSURED'S NAME (Last Name, First Name, Middle Initial)

5. PATIENT'S ADDRESS (No., Street): 1018 BONITA AVE

6. PATIENT RELATIONSHIP TO INSURED: Self [ ] Spouse [ ] Child [ ] Other [ ]

7. INSURED'S ADDRESS (No., Street)

CITY: ANYWHERE STATE: US

8. RESERVED FOR NUCC USE

CITY STATE

ZIP CODE: 12345 TELEPHONE (Include Area Code): (101) 6905244

ZIP CODE TELEPHONE (Include Area Code) ( )

9. OTHER INSURED'S NAME (Last Name, First Name, Middle Initial)

10. IS PATIENT'S CONDITION RELATED TO:

11. INSURED'S POLICY GROUP OR FECA NUMBER

a. OTHER INSURED'S POLICY OR GROUP NUMBER

a. EMPLOYMENT? (Current or Previous) [ ] YES [X] NO

a. INSURED'S DATE OF BIRTH MM DD YY SEX M [ ] F [ ]

b. RESERVED FOR NUCC USE

b. AUTO ACCIDENT? [ ] YES [X] NO PLACE (State)

b. OTHER CLAIM ID (Designated by NUCC)

c. RESERVED FOR NUCC USE

c. OTHER ACCIDENT? [ ] YES [X] NO

c. INSURANCE PLAN NAME OR PROGRAM NAME

d. INSURANCE PLAN NAME OR PROGRAM NAME

10d. CLAIM CODES (Designated by NUCC)

d. IS THERE ANOTHER HEALTH BENEFIT PLAN? [ ] YES [ ] NO *If yes,* complete items 9, 9a, and 9d.

READ BACK OF FORM BEFORE COMPLETING & SIGNING THIS FORM.

12. PATIENT'S OR AUTHORIZED PERSON'S SIGNATURE I authorize the release of any medical or other information necessary to process this claim. I also request payment of government benefits either to myself or to the party who accepts assignment below.

SIGNED DATE

13. INSURED'S OR AUTHORIZED PERSON'S SIGNATURE I authorize payment of medical benefits to the undersigned physician or supplier for services described below.

SIGNED

PATIENT AND INSURED INFORMATION

14. DATE OF CURRENT ILLNESS, INJURY, or PREGNANCY (LMP) MM DD YY QUAL.

15. OTHER DATE QUAL. MM DD YY

16. DATES PATIENT UNABLE TO WORK IN CURRENT OCCUPATION MM DD YY FROM TO

17. NAME OF REFERRING PROVIDER OR OTHER SOURCE 17a. 17b. NPI

18. HOSPITALIZATION DATES RELATED TO CURRENT SERVICES MM DD YY FROM TO

19. ADDITIONAL CLAIM INFORMATION (Designated by NUCC)

20. OUTSIDE LAB? [ ] YES [X] NO $ CHARGES

21. DIAGNOSIS OR NATURE OF ILLNESS OR INJURY Relate A-L to service line below (24E) ICD Ind. 0

A. J45.909 B. C. D.
E. F. G. H.
I. J. K. L.

22. RESUBMISSION CODE ORIGINAL REF. NO.

23. PRIOR AUTHORIZATION NUMBER

	24. A. DATE(S) OF SERVICE From MM	DD	YY	To MM	DD	YY	B. PLACE OF SERVICE	C. EMG	D. PROCEDURES, SERVICES, OR SUPPLIES (Explain Unusual Circumstances) CPT/HCPCS	MODIFIER	E. DIAGNOSIS POINTER	F. $ CHARGES	G. DAYS OR UNITS	H. EPSDT Family Plan	I. ID. QUAL.	J. RENDERING PROVIDER ID. #
1	12	18	YY				11		99212		A	40 00	1		NPI	
2															NPI	
3															NPI	
4															NPI	
5															NPI	
6															NPI	

25. FEDERAL TAX I.D. NUMBER: 111982342 SSN [ ] EIN [X]

26. PATIENT'S ACCOUNT NO.: 15-5

27. ACCEPT ASSIGNMENT? (For govt. claims, see back) [X] YES [ ] NO

28. TOTAL CHARGE $ 40 00

29. AMOUNT PAID $

30. Rsvd for NUCC Use

31. SIGNATURE OF PHYSICIAN OR SUPPLIER INCLUDING DEGREES OR CREDENTIALS (I certify that the statements on the reverse apply to this bill and are made a part thereof.)

ANGELA DILALIO MD MMDDYYYY
SIGNED DATE

32. SERVICE FACILITY LOCATION INFORMATION

a. NPI b.

33. BILLING PROVIDER INFO & PH # (101) 2014321
ANGELA DILALIO
99 PROVIDER STREET
INJURY NY 12347

a. 4567890123 b.

PHYSICIAN OR SUPPLIER INFORMATION

NUCC Instruction Manual available at: www.nucc.org PLEASE PRINT OR TYPE

FIGURE 15-12 Completed SCHIP CMS-1500 claim for Edgar Vasquez case study.

SUMMARY

Title 19 of the SSA created Medicaid, a medical assistance program for individuals with incomes below the FPL. The federal government establishes Medicaid eligibility requirements, and individual states have discretion in determining coverage policies as well as establishing financial criteria for eligibility. Medicaid eligibility criteria depend on which of the following categories a recipient is placed in: mandatory eligibility groups, optional eligibility groups, SCHIP, and disabled Medicaid beneficiaries who work.

Preauthorization for services is often required by Medicaid programs that have not implemented managed care (e.g., HMOs). A *dual eligible* is an individual who is covered by both Medicare and Medicaid—Medicare is billed as the primary payer. Medicaid is always the *payer of last resort* when a recipient is covered by other insurance (e.g., Medicare, TRICARE, IHS, or commercial health insurance). Participating providers accept Medicaid payments as payment in full, and balance billing is illegal.

MEVS (or REVS) allow providers to electronically verify a recipient's eligibility for Medicaid coverage via a point-of-service device, computer software, or an automated voice response system. The Medicaid remittance advice sent to providers contains the status of claims submitted, including paid, adjusted, and voided claims. Medicaid's surveillance utilization review system assesses unnecessary or inappropriate use of Medicaid services or excess payments, as well as the quality of services rendered.

When completing Medicaid CMS-1500 claims for case studies in this text (including SimClaim software) and the Workbook, the following special instructions apply:

- Block 20—Enter an X in the NO box.
- Block 24C—Leave blank.
- Block 24E—Enter just one diagnosis pointer letter on each line.
- Block 24H—Leave blank.
- Block 26—Enter the case study number (e.g., 15-5). If the patient has Medicaid as secondary coverage, enter an S (for secondary) next to the number (on the secondary claim).
- Block 27—Enter an X in the YES box.
- Block 32—If Block 18 contains dates and/or Block 20 contains an X in the YES box, enter the name, address, and Medicaid NPI of the responsible provider (e.g., hospital, outside laboratory).
- When completing secondary claims, enter REMITTANCE ADVICE ATTACHED in the top margin of the CMS-1500 claim (to indicate that a primary payer's remittance advice would be attached to the claim submitted to the secondary payer).

INTERNET LINKS

- BenefitsCheckUp®
  Go to **www.benefitscheckup.org** to locate information useful to seniors with limited income and resources.
- Medicaid
  Go to **www.medicaid.gov**
- Programs of All-inclusive Care for the Elderly (PACE)
  Go to **www.medicaid.gov**, scroll over Medicaid, click on By-Topic, click on Long-Term Services and Support, and click on PACE.
- State Children's Health Insurance Program (SCHIP)
  Go to **www.medicaid.gov**, and click on the CHIP link.

- Ticket to Work and Work Incentives Improvement Act (TWWIA)
  Go to **www.medicaid.gov**, scroll over Medicaid, click on By-Topic, click on Delivery Systems, click on Grant Programs, and click on the Ticket to Work & Work Incentives Improvement Act (TWWIIA) link. (Scroll down to view information about TWWIIA.)
- Your Path to Government Benefits
  Go to **www.govbenefits.gov** (official benefits website of the U.S. government) for improved, personalized access to government assistance programs.

STUDY CHECKLIST

☐ Read this textbook chapter and highlight key concepts.
☐ Access SimClaim software at the online companion, and complete Medicaid claims using the software's case studies.
☐ Complete CMS-1500 claims for each chapter case study.
☐ Answer the chapter review questions, verifying answers with your instructor.
☐ Complete the Workbook chapter, verifying answers with your instructor.
☐ Form a study group with classmates to discuss chapter concepts in preparation for an exam.

REVIEW

MULTIPLE CHOICE Select the most appropriate response.

1. **Medicaid is jointly funded by federal and state governments, and each state**
   a. administers its own Medicaid program.
   b. adopts the federal scope of services.
   c. establishes uniform eligibility standards.
   d. implements managed care for payment.
2. **State legislatures may change Medicaid eligibility requirements**
   a. as directed by the federal government.
   b. during the year, sometimes more than once.
   c. no more than once during each year.
   d. to clarify services and payments only.
3. **Which requirements are used to determine Medicaid eligibility for mandatory categorically needy eligibility groups?**
   a. AFDC
   b. EPSDT
   c. PACE
   d. TANF
4. **States that opt to include a medically needy eligibility group in their Medicaid program are required to include certain children who are under the age of ____ and who are full-time students.**
   a. 18
   b. 19
   c. 21
   d. 25

5. **Which allows states to create or expand existing insurance programs to include a greater number of children who are currently uninsured?**
   a. FMAP
   b. SCHIP
   c. SSDI
   d. TWWIA
6. **Which is considered a mandatory Medicaid service that states must offer to receive federal matching funds?**
   a. family planning services and supplies
   b. nursing facility services for those under age 21
   c. rehabilitation and physical therapy services
   d. transportation services
7. **Individuals who are eligible for both Medicare and Medicaid coverage are called**
   a. dual eligibles.
   b. Medicaid allowables.
   c. PACE participants.
   d. participating providers.
8. **When a patient has Medicaid coverage in addition to other, third-party payer coverage, Medicaid is always considered the**
   a. adjusted claim.
   b. medically necessary service.
   c. payer of last resort.
   d. remittance advice.
9. **Which is considered a voided claim?**
   a. a claim that has a negative balance for which the provider receives no payment until amounts exceed the negative balance amount
   b. a claim that has a payment correction submitted on it, which results in additional reimbursement being made to the provider
   c. a claim that Medicaid should not have originally paid and results in a deduction from the lump-sum payment made to the provider
   d. a claim that underwent review to safeguard against unnecessary or inappropriate use of Medicaid services or excess payments
10. **Medicaid-covered services are paid only when the service is determined by the provider to be medically necessary, which means the services are**
   a. consistent with the patient's symptoms, diagnosis, condition, or injury.
   b. furnished primarily for the convenience of the recipient or the provider.
   c. provided when other equally effective treatments are available or suitable.
   d. recognized as being inconsistent with generally accepted standards.

TRICARE

CHAPTER 16

CHAPTER OUTLINE

TRICARE Background
TRICARE Administration
CHAMPVA
TRICARE Options
TRICARE Special Programs
TRICARE Supplemental Plans
Billing Notes
Claims Instructions
TRICARE as Secondary Payer
TRICARE and Supplemental Coverage

OBJECTIVES

Upon successful completion of this chapter, you should be able to:

1. Define key terms.
2. Explain the historical background of TRICARE.
3. Describe how TRICARE is administered.
4. Define CHAMPVA.
5. List and explain the TRICARE options, programs and demonstration projects, and supplemental plans.
6. Apply TRICARE billing notes when completing CMS-1500 claims.
7. Complete TRICARE claims properly.

KEY TERMS

beneficiary counseling and assistance coordinator (BCAC)
beneficiary services representative (BSR)
catastrophic cap benefit
catchment area
CHAMPUS Reform Initiative (CRI)
common access card (CAC)
critical pathway
debt collection assistance officer (DCAO)
Defense Enrollment Eligibility Reporting System (DEERS)
demonstration project or pilot
emergency care
fiscal year
Health Affairs (HA)
health care finder (HCF)
lead agent (LA)
Military Health Services System (MHSS)
military treatment facility (MTF)
nonavailability statement (NAS)
nurse advisor
practice guidelines
primary care manager (PCM)
Program Integrity (PI) Office

TRICARE
TRICARE beneficiary
TRICARE Extra
TRICARE Management Activity (TMA)
TRICARE Prime
TRICARE Service Centers (TSCs)
TRICARE sponsors
TRICARE Standard
uniformed services

INTRODUCTION

TRICARE is a health care program for (1) active-duty members of the military and their qualified family members, (2) CHAMPUS-eligible retirees and their qualified family members, and (3) eligible survivors of members of the uniformed services. CHAMPUS (now called TRICARE Standard) is an abbreviation for the Civilian Health and Medical Program of the Uniformed Services, a federal program created in 1966 (and implemented in 1967) as a benefit for dependents of personnel serving in the uniformed services (U.S. military branches that include the Army, Navy, Air Force, Marines, and Coast Guard), Public Health Service Commissioned Corps, and the National Oceanic and Atmospheric Administration (NOAA) Commissioned Corps. TRICARE was created to expand health care access, ensure quality of care, control health care costs, and improve medical readiness.

TRICARE BACKGROUND

CHAMPUS (now called TRICARE) was implemented in 1967 as the result of an initiative to provide military medical care for families of active-duty members. The original budget was $106 million; the current budget is more than $24 billion (*2002 Tricare Stakeholders' Report*, volume IV). In the 1980s the Department of Defense (DoD) began researching ways to improve access to quality care while controlling costs and authorizing demonstration projects. One demonstration project, the CHAMPUS Reform Initiative (CRI) carried out in California and Hawaii, offered military families a choice of how their health care benefits could be used. The DoD noted the successful operation and high levels of patient satisfaction associated with the CRI, and determined that its concepts should be expanded to a nationwide uniform program.

TRICARE

This new program became known as TRICARE, a regionally managed health care program that joins the health care resources of the uniformed services (e.g., Army) and supplements them with networks of civilian health care professionals to provide access and high-quality service while maintaining the capability to support military operations. TRICARE is a health care program for active-duty members of the uniformed services and their families, retirees and their families, and survivors of all uniformed services who are not eligible for Medicare.

NOTE: The original 12 TRICARE regions were consolidated as part of restructuring initiatives in 2004.

There are four TRICARE regions: three in the United States and TRICARE overseas (Figure 16-1). Each is managed by a lead agent staff that is responsible for the military health system in that region. Commanders of selected military treatment facilities (MTFs) are selected as lead agents (LA) for the TRICARE regions. The lead agent staff serves as a federal health care team created to work with regional military treatment facility commanders, uniformed service headquarters' staffs, and Health Affairs (HA) to support the mission of the Military Health Services System (MHSS). The Military Health Services System (MHSS) is the entire health care system of the U.S. uniformed services and includes MTFs as well as various programs in the civilian health care market, such as TRICARE. Health Affairs (HA) refers to the Office of the Assistant Secretary of Defense for Health Affairs, which is responsible for both military readiness and peacetime health care.

Eligibility for TRICARE is specified in Table 16-1.

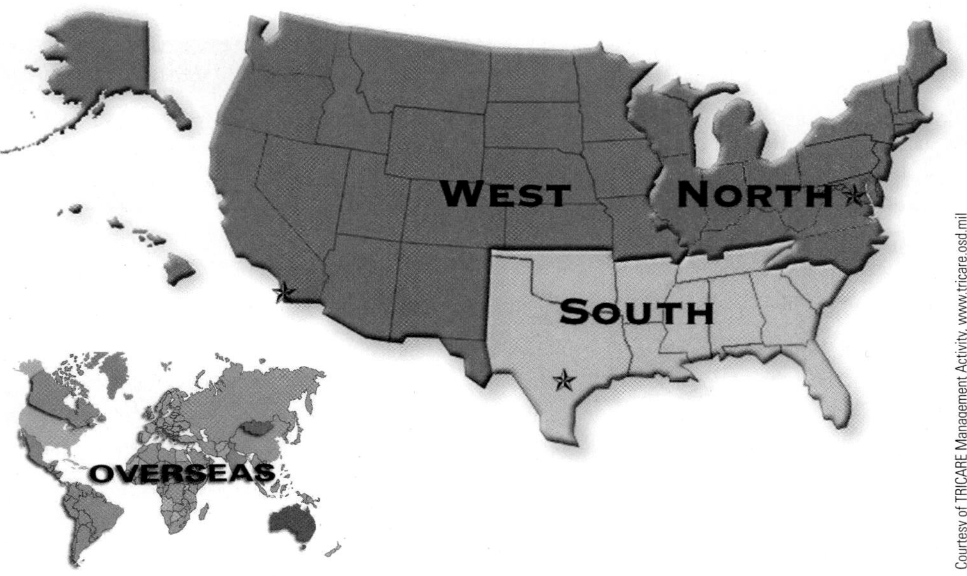

FIGURE 16-1 Map of TRICARE regions.

TABLE 16-1 TRICARE eligibility

BENEFICIARY CATEGORY	DESCRIPTION
Active-duty and retired service members	Includes any of the seven uniformed services: • Air Force • Army • Coast Guard • Marine Corps • National Oceanic and Atmospheric Administration • Navy • Public Health Service
Spouses and unmarried children (including stepchildren) of active-duty or retired service members	• Remain eligible even if parents divorce or remarry • Eligibility ends at age 21 unless child is a full-time student (validation of student status is required), in which case eligibility ends at age 23 or when the full-time student status ends • Eligibility may extend past age 21 if the child is incapable of self-support because of a mental or physical incapacity and the condition existed prior to age 21, or if the condition occurred between ages 21 and 23 while the child was a full-time student • Illegitimate children of current or former service members or their spouses may be eligible under certain conditions • Children placed in the custody of a service member or former service member, either by a court or by a recognized adoption agency, in anticipation of legal adoption by the member **NOTE:** Stepchildren lose eligibility after a divorce unless they are adopted by the sponsor.
National Guard and Reserve Component members on active duty for more than 30 days—under federal orders	Includes National Guard and any of the following Reserve Component services: • Air Force • Army • Coast Guard • Marine Corps • National Oceanic and Atmospheric Administration • Navy • Public Health Service

(continues)

TABLE 16-1 (continued)

BENEFICIARY CATEGORY	DESCRIPTION
Spouses and unmarried children of National Guard and Reserve Component service members	• Covered while sponsor is on active duty for more than 30 consecutive days • Covered if sponsor was injured or died during, or on the way to or from, active-duty training for a period of 30 days or less
Retired National Guard and Reserve Component service members and their family members	• When retired service member is eligible for retirement pay (usually at age 60), member and his or her eligible family members become eligible for TRICARE
Widows or widowers and unmarried children of deceased active-duty or retired service members	• Are eligible as family members of deceased member *if* sponsor was serving or was ordered to active duty for more than 30 days at time of death • Claims will be cost-shared at the active-duty family member rate for three years after death of active-duty sponsor, and thereafter at the retiree rate. • Widows or widowers remain eligible until they remarry (loss of benefits remains applicable even if remarriage ends in death or divorce). • Children remain eligible until age 21, unless they meet the exceptions listed earlier.
Medal of Honor recipients and their family members	• Any service member who was awarded the Medal of Honor • Awardee's eligible family members and widow or widower are eligible for medical and dental benefits under TRICARE.

Certain eligible former spouses of active-duty or retired service members	• Must not have remarried (if remarried, loss of benefits remains applicable even if remarriage ends in death or divorce)
	• Starting October 1, 2003, eligibility and medical records are listed under former spouse's own social security number, not that of the sponsor.
	• Must not be covered by an employer-sponsored health plan
	• Must not be former spouse of a North Atlantic Treaty Organization (NATO) or Partners for Peace (PFP) nation member
	• Must meet the requirements of one of the following three situations:
	  • SITUATION 1: Must have been married to the *same* member or former member for at least 20 years, and at least 20 of those years must have been creditable in determining the member's eligibility for retirement pay. If the date of the final decree of divorce or annulment was on or after February 1, 1983, the former spouse is eligible for TRICARE coverage of health care that is received after that date. If the date of the final decree is before February 1, 1983, the former spouse is eligible for TRICARE coverage of health care received on or after January 1, 1985.
	  • SITUATION 2: Must have been married to the *same* military member or former member for at least 20 years, and at least 15—but less than 20—of those married years must have been creditable in determining the member's eligibility for retirement pay. If the date of the final decree of divorce or annulment is before April 1, 1985, the former spouse is eligible only for care received on or after January 1, 1985, or the date of the decree, whichever is later.
	  • SITUATION 3: Must have been married to the *same* military member or former member for at least 20 years, and at least 15—but less than 20—of those married years must have been creditable in determining the member's eligibility for retirement pay. If the date of the final decree of divorce or annulment is on or after September 29, 1988, the former spouse is eligible for care received for only one year from the date of the decree. Upon completion of the period of eligibility for TRICARE, explained in Situation 3, a former spouse is eligible for the Continued Health Care Benefit Program (CHCBP).

Courtesy of TRICARE Management Activity, www.tricare.osd.mil

TRICARE ADMINISTRATION

The **TRICARE Management Activity (TMA)** (formerly called OCHAMPUS, which meant Office of CHAMPUS) is the office that coordinates and administers the TRICARE program and is accountable for quality health care provided to members of the uniformed services and their families. The TMA also serves as arbitrator for denied claims submitted for consideration by TRICARE sponsors and beneficiaries; its offices are located in Aurora, Colorado. **TRICARE sponsors** are uniformed service personnel who are either active duty, retired, or deceased. (Dependents of deceased sponsors are eligible for TRICARE benefits.) Sponsor information (e.g., SSN, DOB, and last name) can be verified in the **Defense Enrollment Eligibility Reporting System (DEERS)**, a computer system that contains up-to-date Defense Department workforce personnel information. **TRICARE beneficiaries** include sponsors and dependents of sponsors.

> **NOTE:** Do not submit TRICARE claims to the TMA; claims are processed by TRICARE contractors (similar to Medicare administrative contractors) for different regions of the country and overseas.

TRICARE Service Centers

TRICARE regions are served by one or more **TRICARE Service Centers (TSCs)**, business offices staffed by one or more beneficiary services representatives and health care finders who assist TRICARE sponsors with health care needs and answer questions about the program.

Beneficiary Services Representatives

A **beneficiary services representative (BSR)** is employed at a TRICARE Service Center, provides information about using TRICARE, and assists with other matters affecting access to health care (e.g., appointment scheduling).

Health Care Finders

A **health care finder (HCF)** is a registered nurse or physician assistant who assists primary care providers with preauthorizations and referrals to health care services in a military treatment facility or civilian provider network. A *preauthorization* is formal approval obtained from a health care finder before certain specialty procedures and inpatient care services are rendered. A *referral* is a request for a member to receive treatment from another provider.

Nurse Advisors

In most TRICARE regions, **nurse advisors** are also available 24/7 for advice and assistance with treatment alternatives and to discuss whether a sponsor should see a provider based on a discussion of symptoms. Nurse advisors will also discuss preventive care and ways to improve a family's health.

Military Treatment Facilities

A **military treatment facility (MTF)** is a health care facility operated by the military that provides inpatient and/or ambulatory (outpatient and emergency department) care to eligible TRICARE beneficiaries. The capabilities of MTFs vary from limited acute care clinics to teaching and tertiary care medical centers.

Beneficiary counseling and assistance coordinators (BCACs) are located at MTFs, and they are available to answer questions, help solve health care–related problems, and assist beneficiaries in obtaining medical care through TRICARE. BCACs were previously called *Health Benefits Advisors (HBAs)*. **Debt collection assistance officers (DCAOs)** are located at military treatment facilities to assist beneficiaries in resolving health care collection–related issues.

Case Management

TRICARE *case management* is organized under TRICARE utilization management and is a collaborative process that coordinates and monitors a beneficiary's health care options and services by assessing available resources to promote quality and cost-effective outcomes. The use of critical pathways, practice guidelines, and discharge planning can enhance the case management process. A **critical pathway** is the sequence of activities that can normally be expected to result in the most cost-effective clinical course of treatment. **Practice guidelines** are decision-making tools used by providers to determine appropriate health care for specific clinical circumstances. They offer the opportunity to improve health care delivery processes by reducing unwanted variation. The Institute of Medicine specifies that practice guidelines should be valid, reliable and reproducible, clinically applicable and flexible, a multidisciplinary process, reviewed on a scheduled basis, and well documented. *Discharge planning* assesses requirements so that arrangements can be made for the appropriate and timely discharge of patients from acute care or outpatient settings.

> **EXAMPLE:** Inpatient records undergo quarterly review (using predetermined screening criteria) to identify individuals whose frequency of services or cost of services makes them candidates for case management.

Program Integrity Office

The TMA **Program Integrity (PI) Office** is responsible for the surveillance of fraud and abuse activities worldwide involving purchased care for beneficiaries in the Military Health Care System. The PI Office develops policies and procedures for the prevention, detection, investigation, and control of TRICARE fraud, waste, and program abuse. It monitors contractor program integrity activities, coordinates with the Department of Defense and external investigative agencies, and initiates administrative remedies as required. TRICARE-authorized providers can be excluded from program participation if one of the following conditions applies:

- Any criminal conviction or civil judgment involving fraud
- Fraud or abuse under TRICARE
- Exclusion or suspension by another federal, state, or local government agency
- Participation in a conflict-of-interest situation
- When it is in the best interest of the TRICARE program or its beneficiaries

> **EXAMPLE:** A Colorado psychologist pled guilty to two felony counts of health care fraud, one felony count of conspiracy to defraud with respect to claims, and one felony count of criminal forfeiture. This judgment was the culmination of a six-year investigation of a counseling center where a billing-fraud scam involved filing claims for services not provided as well as using an authorized provider's identification number to submit claims for services that were provided by an unauthorized provider. TRICARE will recover almost $500,000 in damages. The psychologist received a sentence of 21 months of imprisonment and three years of released supervision.

CHAMPVA

The *Civilian Health and Medical Program of the Department of Veterans Affairs (CHAMPVA)* is a comprehensive health care program for which the Department of Veterans Affairs (VA) shares costs of covered health care services and supplies with eligible beneficiaries. The Health Administration Center, located in Denver, Colorado, administers the CHAMPVA program by:

- **Processing applications**
- **Determining eligibility**
- **Authorizing benefits**
- **Processing claims**

> **NOTE:** Due to the similarity between CHAMPVA and TRICARE (previously called CHAMPUS), the two are often confused. CHAMPVA is the Department of Veterans Affairs health care program. TRICARE is a regionally managed health care program for active-duty and retired members of the uniformed services, their families, and survivors.

Eligibility for CHAMPVA

The *CHAMPVA sponsor* is a veteran who is permanently and totally disabled from a service-connected condition, died as a result of a service-connected condition, was rated permanently and totally disabled from a service-connected condition at the time of death, or died on active duty and whose dependents are not otherwise entitled to TRICARE benefits. The *CHAMPVA beneficiary* is a CHAMPVA-eligible spouse, widow(er), or child. To be eligible for CHAMPVA, the beneficiary must be:

- **The spouse or child of a veteran who has been rated permanently and totally disabled for a service-connected disability by a VA regional office**
- **The surviving spouse or child of a veteran who died from a VA-rated service connected disability**
- **The surviving spouse or child of a veteran who at the time of death was rated as permanently and totally disabled as the result of a service-connected disability**
- **The surviving spouse or child of a military member who died in the line of duty (not due to misconduct) (However, these individuals may be eligible for TRICARE instead of CHAMPVA.)**

Eligible CHAMPVA sponsors may be entitled to receive medical care through the VA health care system based on their veteran status. If an eligible CHAMPVA sponsor is the spouse of another eligible CHAMPVA sponsor, both may be eligible for CHAMPVA benefits. In each instance where an eligible spouse requires medical attention, the spouse may choose to receive health care from the VA system or through CHAMPVA coverage.

> **NOTE:** For a CHAMPVA beneficiary who also has Medicare coverage, CHAMPVA is always the secondary payer to Medicare. Therefore, submit the beneficiary's claim to Medicare first. (CHAMPVA requires electronic submission of CMS-1500 claims.)

TRICARE OPTIONS

TRICARE offers three health care options:

1. *TRICARE Prime*: Military treatment facilities are the principal source of health care under this option.
2. *TRICARE Extra*: This is a preferred provider organization (PPO) option.
3. *TRICARE Standard* (formerly CHAMPUS): This is a fee-for-service option.

> **NOTE:** The TRICARE Extra option is not offered in all regions because of the limited availability of PPOs in some civilian markets; instead, TRICARE Standard is available.

TRICARE Prime

TRICARE Prime is a managed care option similar to a civilian health maintenance organization (HMO). Enrollment in TRICARE Prime guarantees priority access to care at military treatment facilities.

Features of TRICARE Prime

- **Guaranteed access to timely medical care**
- **Priority for care at military treatment facilities**
- **Assignment of a primary care manager (PCM)**
- **Lowest cost option of the three TRICARE options**
- **Requires enrollment for one year**
- **Retired military pay an annual enrollment fee**
- **Care sought outside of TRICARE Prime network is costly**
- **May be unavailable in some TRICARE regions**

TRICARE Prime provides comprehensive health care benefits at the lowest cost of the three options. *Eligible individuals are required to enroll in TRICARE Prime so that adequate professional staffing and resources are available in military treatment facilities and supporting civilian facilities.* Individuals eligible for TRICARE Prime include (1) active-duty military personnel, (2) family members of active-duty sponsors (no enrollment fee), and (3) retirees and their family members, all of whom are under age 65. See Tables 16-2 and 16-3, which list out-of-pocket costs for TRICARE Prime.

TABLE 16-2 TRICARE deductible, copayment, and coinsurance amounts (sample)

	TRICARE PRIME	TRICARE EXTRA/STANDARD
Annual deductible	$0	$150 individual (E-5 and above) $300 family (E-5 and above) $50 individual (E-4 and below) $100 family (E-4 and below)
Civilian outpatient visit	$0	Extra: 15% of negotiated fee Standard: 20% of allowed charge
Civilian inpatient admission	$0	$15.65/day or $25 minimum, whichever is greater
Civilian inpatient behavioral health	$0	$20/day or $25 minimum, whichever is greater
Civilian inpatient SNF care	$0	$15.65/day or $25 minimum, whichever is greater

Reprinted according to reuse policy at

TABLE 16-3 TRICARE out-of-pocket expenses for retirees and their family members (sample)

	TRICARE PRIME	TRICARE EXTRA	TRICARE STANDARD
Annual deductible	$0	$150 individual $300 family	$150 individual $300 family
Annual enrollment fees	$230 individual $460 family	$0	$0
Civilian Provider Copays Outpatient visit Emergency care Mental health visit	 $12 $30 $25 $17 (group visit)	 20% of negotiated fees 20% of negotiated fees 20% of negotiated fees 20% of negotiated fees	 25% of allowed charges 25% of allowed charges 25% of allowed charges 25% of allowed charges
Civilian inpatient cost share	$11/day ($25 minimum)	Lesser of $250/day or 25% of billed charges; plus 20% of negotiated professional fees	Lesser of $535/day or 25% of billed charges; plus 25% of allowed professional charges
Civilian inpatient behavioral health	$40/day	20% of institutional charges; plus 25% of professional charges	Lesser of $193/day or 25% of institutional charges; plus 25% of professional charges

Reprinted according to reuse policy at www.tricare.osd.mil/main/privacy.html.

A **primary care manager (PCM)** is a doctor assigned to a sponsor and is part of the TRICARE provider network. The PCM guides TRICARE Prime members through the health care system and coordinates all specialty medical needs. Prime members can choose a PCM from the MTF or the TRICARE provider directory. TRICARE Prime beneficiaries also receive care if they reside and work outside an MTF **catchment area**, the region defined by code boundaries within a 40-mile radius of an MTF. Note that certain TRICARE regions only allow a military doctor or medical clinic to serve as a PCM.

The PCM provides nonemergency care to eligible beneficiaries and arranges referrals for specialty care if needed, usually through a military hospital. If military specialty care is unavailable, the PCM authorizes care from a civilian specialist. For beneficiaries to receive coverage for specialty care, the PCM must make these arrangements. TRICARE Prime guarantees enrollees access to care; urgent care is rendered within one day, while less urgent care is provided within one week. In addition, travel is limited to no more than 30 minutes to the PCM. Preventive care is emphasized, and the following services are provided at no additional charge: eye exams, immunizations, hearing screenings, mammograms, Pap smears, prostate exams, and other cancer-prevention and early diagnosis exams.

TRICARE Prime covers nonemergency care if the beneficiary is away from home and receives prior approval from the PCM. Such authorization is required for all routine medical care provided out of the area or at another facility. If the beneficiary seeks medical care without prior approval, the *point-of-service option* is activated, requiring payment of an annual deductible plus 50 percent or more of visit or treatment fees.

Beneficiaries who require emergency care should seek that care at the nearest civilian or military treatment facility.

Catastrophic Cap Benefit

The **catastrophic cap benefit** protects TRICARE beneficiaries from devastating financial loss due to serious illness or long-term treatment by establishing limits over which payment is not required. Under TRICARE Prime, the maximum out-of-pocket cost per year for covered medical services is $1,000 for active-duty military sponsors' family members and $3,000 for retirees and their families per enrollment year.

TRICARE Extra

TRICARE Extra allows TRICARE Standard users to save 5 percent of their TRICARE Standard cost-shares by using health care providers in the TRICARE network. To receive care, enrollees simply go to any network doctor, hospital, or other provider and present their uniformed services **common access card (CAC)** (identification card issued by the Department of Defense, DoD) (Figure 16-2), which is scanned. Care is also available at an MTF on a space-available basis.

NOTE: All active-duty members are enrolled in TRICARE Prime and are not eligible for TRICARE Extra.

Features of TRICARE Extra

- **Choice of any physician in the network**
- **Less costly than TRICARE Standard**
- **May be more expensive than TRICARE Prime**
- **Annual enrollment is not required**
- **Lower priority for care provided at MTFs**

Unlike for TRICARE Prime, individuals eligible for TRICARE Extra do not have to enroll or pay an enrollment fee. They can use the option whenever they choose by selecting any health care provider from within the TRICARE Extra provider network. When a TRICARE Extra network provider renders care, it is

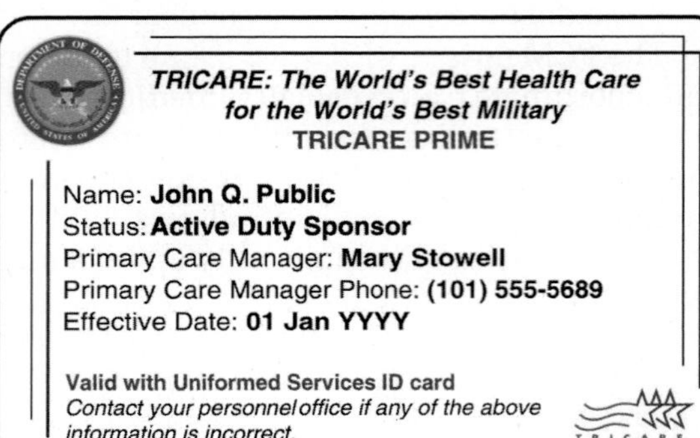

(A)

(B)

FIGURE 16-2 (A) Sample TRICARE enrollment card. (B) Sample uniformed services common access card (CAC) inserted into point-of-service (POS) device.

just like using TRICARE Standard (formerly CHAMPUS), with the bonus of a 5 percent discount on most cost-shares (e.g., copayments).

TRICARE Extra offers enrollees the choice of receiving health care services from participating civilian hospitals, physicians, and other medical providers who have agreed to charge an approved fee for medical treatment and procedures. Two groups that usually prefer TRICARE Extra are (1) individuals and families whose regular physician is a participating member of the TRICARE Extra network, and (2) individuals who do not have convenient access to MTFs and want reduced health care costs as compared with TRICARE Standard.

Those eligible for TRICARE Extra coverage include (1) family members of active-duty sponsors (no enrollment fee) and (2) retirees (except most Medicare-eligible beneficiaries) and their family members under age 65.

TRICARE Extra Coverage

Individuals eligible to enroll in TRICARE Extra are not required to pay an annual fee, can seek care from a network provider, receive a discount on services, and usually pay reduced copayments (5 percent less than TRICARE Standard; participating providers are reimbursed the approved rate plus 5 percent). In addition, network providers file insurance claims for enrollees and are prohibited from balance billing. *Balance billing* refers to the practice of a provider billing a patient for all charges not reimbursed by a health plan.

TRICARE Extra enrollees can also seek health care services from an MTF on a space-available basis, and they can select between TRICARE Extra and TRICARE Standard options on a visit-by-visit basis. Tables 16-2 and 16-3 list out-of-pocket costs for TRICARE Extra.

> **NOTE:** A **nonavailability statement (NAS)** (Figure 16-3) is a certificate issued by an MTF that cannot provide needed care to TRICARE Standard beneficiaries. This means the beneficiary can seek care from a civilian provider and reimbursement will be approved. NAS certificates are not required for **emergency care**, defined by TRICARE as the sudden and unexpected onset of a medical or mental health condition that is threatening to life, limb, or sight.
>
> Individuals who meet TRICARE eligibility criteria are covered by TRICARE Standard, *except* for active-duty service members (who are covered by TRICARE Prime).

Catastrophic Cap Benefit

Under TRICARE Extra, active-duty sponsors' family members are responsible for up to $1,000 and retirees for up to $3,000 per year in out-of-pocket costs for covered services.

TRICARE Standard

TRICARE Standard is the new name for traditional CHAMPUS. To use this option, enrollees either make an appointment at an MTF or seek care from any TRICARE-certified civilian health care provider (fee-for-service option). Enrollees are responsible for annual deductibles and copayments. It provides beneficiaries with the greatest freedom in selecting civilian providers; however,

UNIFORMED SERVICES MEDICAL TREATMENT FACILITY NONAVAILABILITY STATEMENT (NAS)	REPORT CONTROL SYMBOL

Privacy Act Statement

AUTHORITY: 44 USC 3101, 41 CFR 101 et seq., 10 USC 1066 and 1079, and EO 9397, November 1943 (SSN).

PRINCIPAL PURPOSE: To evaluate eligibility for civilian health benefits authorized by 10 USC, Chapter 55, and to issue payment upon establishment of eligibility and determination that the medical care received is authorized by law. The information is subject to verification with the appropriate Uniformed Service.

ROUTINE USE: CHAMPUS and its contractors use the information to control and process medical claims for payment; for control and approval of medical treatments and interface with providers of medical care; to control and accomplish reviews of utilization; for review of claims related to possible third party liability cases and initiation of recovery actions; and for referral to Peer Review Committees or similar professional review organizations to control and review providers' medical care.

DISCLOSURE: Voluntary; however, failure to provide information will result in denial of, or delay in payment of, the claim.

1. NAS NUMBER *(Facility) (Yr-Julian) (Seq. No.)*	2. PRIMARY REASON FOR ISSUANCE *(X one)*
	a. PROPER FACILITIES ARE TEMPORARILY NOT AVAILABLE IN A SAFE OR TIMELY MANNER
3. MAJOR DIAGNOSIC CATEGORY FOR WHICH NAS IS ISSUED *(Use code from reverse)*	b. PROFESSIONAL CAPABILITY IS TEMPORARILY NOT AVAILABLE IN A SAFE OR TIMELY MANNER
	c. PROPER FACILITIES OR PROFESSIONAL CAPABILITY ARE PERMANENTLY NOT AVAILABLE AT THIS FACILITY
	d. IT WOULD BE MEDICALLY INAPPROPRIATE TO REQUIRE THE BENEFICIARY TO USE THE MTF *(Explain in Remarks)*

4. PATIENT DATA		
a. NAME *(Last, First, Middle Initial)*	b. DATE OF BIRTH *(YYMMDD)*	c. SEX
d. ADDRESS *(Street, City, State, and ZIP Code)*	e. PATIENT CATEGORY *(X one)*	f. OTHER NON CHAMPUS HEALTH INSURANCE *(X one)*
	(1) Dependent of Active Duty	
	(2) Dependent of Retiree	(1) Yes, but only CHAMPUS Supplemental
	(3) Retiree	
	(4) Survivor	(2) Yes *(List in Remarks)*
	(5) Former Spouse	(3) No

5. SPONSOR DATA *(if you marked 4e(3) Retiree above, print "Same" in 5a.)*	
a. NAME *(Last, First, Middle Initial)*	b. SPONSOR'S OR RETIREE'S SOCIAL SECURITY NO.

6. ISSUING OFFICIAL DATA		
a. NAME *(Last, First, Middle Initial)*	b. TITLE	
c. SIGNATURE	d. PAY GRADE	e. DATE ISSUED *(YYMMDD)*

7. REMARKS *(Indicate block number to which the answer applies.)*

DD Form 1251

Outside the United States and Puerto Rico, previous editions may be used until exhausted
Inside the United States and Puerto Rico, previous editions are obsolete

FIGURE 16-3 Sample nonavailability statement (NAS).

it has the highest out-of-pocket costs of the three plans. There is no enrollment requirement for TRICARE Standard.

Features of TRICARE Standard

- **Greatest flexibility in selecting health care providers**
- **Most convenient when traveling or away from home**
- **Potentially most expensive of all options**
- **Enrollment not required**
- **TRICARE Extra can be used**
- **Space-available care in MTFs is a provision (low priority is assigned to TRICARE Standard enrollees)**

TRICARE Standard Coverage

NOTE: TRICARE Standard does not enroll participating providers; they participate voluntarily and may do so on a case-by-case basis. When using TRICARE Standard, enrollees should ask the selected providers whether they participate in TRICARE Standard.

Under TRICARE Standard, enrollees can select their health care provider; however, out-of-pocket costs are higher when compared with other TRICARE options.

Also, enrollees who seek care from nonparticipating providers may have to file their own claims and, perhaps, pay more for care (up to 15 percent more than the allowable charge). Participating providers accept the TRICARE Standard allowable charge as payment in full for care rendered and they will file insurance claims for enrollees.

Catastrophic Cap Benefit

Under TRICARE Standard, active-duty sponsors' family members are responsible for up to $1,000 and retirees for up to $3,000 per year in out-of-pocket costs for covered services.

Dual Medicare and TRICARE Eligibility

NOTE: *TRICARE for Life* (TFL) is TRICARE's Medicare-wraparound coverage available to all Medicare-eligible TRICARE beneficiaries, regardless of age or place of residence, provided they have Medicare Parts A and B.

While Medicare is the primary payer, TRICARE acts as the secondary payer minimizing out-of-pocket expenses. TRICARE benefits also cover Medicare's coinsurance and deductible.

Sponsors and dependents who are eligible for Medicare qualify for *dual Medicare/TRICARE eligibility* in the following situations:

- **Beneficiaries who become eligible for Medicare Part A on the basis of age and who also purchase Medicare Part B coverage continue to be eligible for TRICARE, which is secondary to Medicare.**
- **Family members of active-duty service members who are eligible for Medicare for any reason are also eligible for TRICARE Prime, Extra, or Standard, whether or not they purchase Medicare Part B.**
- **Beneficiaries under age 65 who are entitled to Medicare Part A because of disability or end-stage renal disease (ESRD) and who have purchased Medicare Part B are also eligible for TRICARE Prime, Extra, or Standard until they turn 65 (when they become eligible only for TRICARE for Life).**

TRICARE SPECIAL PROGRAMS

TRICARE offers special programs, which include demonstration projects and pilots, that are tailored specifically to beneficiary health concerns or conditions. Some programs have specific eligibility requirements based on beneficiary category, plan, or status; are for specific beneficiary populations while others offer services for specific health conditions; or are limited to a certain number of participants or a certain geographic location. A **demonstration project or pilot** tests and establishes the feasibility of implementing a new program during a trial period, after which the program is evaluated, modified, and/or abandoned. If, upon evaluation, it is determined that program implementation criteria are met (e.g., it is cost-effective and meets the intended needs of a population), the demonstration project is approved as a program, and enrollment is expanded to include all eligible individuals. (TRICARE was originally a demonstration project.)

EXAMPLE 1: The *Chiropractic Health Care Program* emphasizes the recuperative power of the body to heal itself without the use of drugs or surgery. The program is available to active-duty service members (including activated National Guard and Reserve members) at designated military hospitals and clinics.

EXAMPLE 2: The *TRICARE Philippine Demonstration* is designed to ensure high-quality health care for eligible TRICARE Standard beneficiaries who live in the Philippines, and who will receive care in a designated demonstration area.

EXAMPLE 3: The *Applied Behavior Analysis Pilot* is available to non-active-duty family members who have been diagnosed with an autism spectrum disorder.

TRICARE SUPPLEMENTAL PLANS

TRICARE supplemental insurance policies are offered by most military associations and by some private firms. They are designed to reimburse patients for the civilian medical care expenses that must be paid after TRICARE reimburses the government's share of health care costs. Each TRICARE supplemental policy has its own rules concerning pre-existing conditions, eligibility requirements for family members, deductibles, mental health limitations, long-term care illnesses, well-baby care, disability care, claims processed under the diagnosis-related group (DRG) payment system for inpatient hospital charges, and rules concerning allowable charges.

BILLING NOTES

The following is a summary of the nationwide billing information for TRICARE Standard and TRICARE Extra out-of-network services. Providers of services are required to file these claims.

TRICARE Contractors

In recent years, TRICARE contractors were grouped in large regional districts covering many states. Each regional contractor assigned post office box numbers and an associated nine-digit zip code for each state served. Be sure to use and proofread carefully both the post office box number and its associated zip code when submitting claims or correspondence to the contractor. Contact the nearest military facility to obtain the current address of the contractor assigned to your area, or access the TRICARE website of the U.S. Department of Defense Military Health System at **www.tricare.mil**.

Forms Used

NOTE: Inpatient and outpatient hospital (and other institution) claims are submitted on the UB-04 (CMS-1450). If inpatient or outpatient health care was provided at a civilian hospital, a *nonavailability statement (NAS)* must be submitted electronically. (Do not submit an NAS for emergency care provided at a civilian hospital.)

Providers submit the CMS-1500 claim to TRICARE. If the patient has *other health insurance (OHI)*, attach the remittance advice to the TRICARE claim. This includes coverage such as automobile insurance and workers' compensation. If the other health insurance plan does not pay the claim, submit the exclusion section of its policy or a copy of the denial. (A denial from an HMO or PPO stating that the patient did not use available services is not considered an exclusion.) If hospital care was provided (or physician's charges are $500 or higher) for an accidental injury, submit a *DD Form 2527* (Personal Injury Questionnaire) that was completed by the patient.

- **Providers receive a remittance advice from TRICARE third-party payers, which illustrates how claims were processed and the amount for which the enrollee**

is responsible. If a claim is denied, an explanation of the denial is also provided.

- **Enrollees receive a TRICARE explanation of benefits (EOB), which is an itemized statement that includes the action taken by TRICARE submitted CMS-1500 claims.**

Filing Deadline

Claims will be denied if they are filed more than one year after the date of service for outpatient care or more than one year from the date of discharge for inpatient care.

NOTE: Patients who file claims directly with TRICARE submit a *DD Form 2642* (Patient's Request for Medical Payment) and attach a copy of the provider's itemized bill to the claim. (Go to **www.tricare.mil**, click on Forms, click on Claim Forms, click on Medical Claim Forms, and click on the *DD Form 2462*.)

Allowable Fee Determination

TRICARE follows the principles of the RBRVS system, but has made some adjustments to the geographic regions and assigned a slightly higher conversion factor. Fee schedules are available from regional carriers. The TRICARE fee schedule must still be followed when TRICARE is a secondary payer.

Deductibles

All deductibles are applied to the government's **fiscal year**, which runs from October 1 of one year to September 30 of the next. This is different from other insurance programs, for which deductibles are usually calculated on a calendar-year basis.

Confirmation of Eligibility

Confirmation of TRICARE eligibility is obtained by entering the sponsor's social security number in the nationwide computerized Defense Enrollment Eligibility Reporting System (DEERS). The SSN is located on the reverse of the sponsor's uniformed services common access card (CAC). (The CAC is a smart card that replaced the military identification card. Photocopying the CAC is permitted to facilitate eligibility verification and to provide health care services.)

Accepting Assignment

Accepting assignment for nonPARs is determined on a claim-by-claim basis. Be sure to indicate the provider's choice in Block 27 of the claim. All deductibles and cost-shares may be collected at the time service is rendered. When assignment is elected, the local beneficiary services representative can assist if there are problems collecting the deductible and cost-share (copayment) from the patient. The TRICARE contractor's provider representative can assist with claims review or intervene when a claim payment is overdue.

TRICARE has established a "good faith policy" for assigned claims when the copy of the front and back of the patient's uniformed services common access card (CAC) on file turns out to be invalid. If copies of the CAC are on file and TRICARE provides notification that the patient is ineligible for payment, the local BSR can help in investigation of the claim. If the investigation reveals that the CAC is invalid, refile the claim with a note stating: "We treated this patient in good faith. Please note the enclosed copy of the CAC that was presented at the time the treatment was rendered." *Do not send* your file copy of the CAC card. The provider should receive payment of the TRICARE-approved fee for these services.

TRICARE Limiting Charges

All TRICARE nonPAR providers are subject to a limiting charge of 15 percent above the TRICARE fee schedule for PAR providers. Patients cannot be billed for the difference between the provider's normal fee and the TRICARE limiting charge (called *balance billing*). Exceptions to the 15 percent limiting charge are claims from independent laboratory and diagnostic laboratory companies, for durable medical equipment, and from medical supply companies.

Special Handling

1. Always make a copy of the front and back of the patient's uniformed services common access card (CAC).
2. Check to determine whether the patient knows the date of his or her next transfer. If it is within six months, it would be wise to accept assignment on the claim to avoid interstate collection problems.
3. Make sure the patient has obtained the necessary nonavailability statement for all nonemergency civilian inpatient care and specified outpatient surgeries if the sponsor lives within a catchment area.
4. Nonemergency inpatient mental health cases require preauthorization, and a nonavailability statement must be obtained.
5. TRICARE Mental Health Treatment Reports should be submitted for inpatient hospitalizations and outpatient encounters. This report should cover the following points:
   - Date treatment began
   - Age, sex, and marital status of patient
   - Diagnosis and DSM axis information
   - Presenting symptoms
   - Historical data
   - Prior treatment episodes
   - Type and frequency of therapy
   - Explanation of any deviation from standard treatment for the diagnosis
   - Mental status and psychological testing
   - Progress of patient
   - Physical examination and/or pertinent laboratory data
   - Future plans and treatment goals

NOTE: DSM is the *Diagnostic & Statistical Manual* published by the American Psychiatric Association. It classifies mental health disorders and is based on ICD-10-CM.

6. A *Personal Injury–Possible Third-Party Liability Statement* is required for all injuries that have been assigned ICD-10-CM codes in the 800 to 959 range. If there is no third-party liability, call the BSR for information on how to file the claim.
7. When filing a claim for services that fall under the special handicap benefits, enter DEPENDENT DISABILITY PROGRAM at the top of the claim.
8. Contact the regional contractor's representative if there has been no response within 45 days of filing the claim.
9. For hospice claims, enter HOSPICE CLAIMS on the envelope to ensure the claim arrives at the regional carrier's hospice desk.

Before working with TRICARE claims, complete the Review located at the end of this chapter.

Military Time

Time tracking using military time (Table 16-4) for providers is typically performed on a monthly basis, which allows for monitoring the time physicians spend with each patient. Provider office staff use the patient record to prepare the time tracking report, and it is used to manage office procedures (e.g., appointment scheduling, staff scheduling). As such, providers are responsible for documenting the start and stop time each time they provide patient care.

TABLE 16-4 Standard time and military time conversion table

STANDARD TIME		MILITARY TIME	STANDARD TIME		MILITARY TIME
12:00	AM	2400	12:00	PM	1200
12:30	AM	2430	12:30	PM	1230
1:00	AM	0100	1:00	PM	1300
1:30	AM	0130	1:30	PM	1330
2:00	AM	0200	2:00	PM	1400
2:30	AM	0230	2:30	PM	1430
3:00	AM	0300	3:00	PM	1500
3:30	AM	0330	3:30	PM	1530
4:00	AM	0400	4:00	PM	1600
4:30	AM	0430	4:30	PM	1630
5:00	AM	0500	5:00	PM	1700
5:30	AM	0530	5:30	PM	1730
6:00	AM	0600	6:00	PM	1800
6:30	AM	0630	6:30	PM	1830
7:00	AM	0700	7:00	PM	1900
7:30	AM	0730	7:30	PM	1930
8:00	AM	0800	8:00	PM	2000
8:30	AM	0830	8:30	PM	2030
9:00	AM	0900	9:00	PM	2100
9:30	AM	0930	9:30	PM	2130
10:00	AM	1000	10:00	PM	2200
10:30	AM	1030	10:30	PM	2230
11:00	AM	1100	11:00	PM	2300
11:30	AM	1130	11:30	PM	2330

Courtesy of the Centers for Medicare & Medicaid Services, www.cms.gov

CLAIMS INSTRUCTIONS

Table 16-5 contains instructions for completing claims to be submitted to TRICARE Extra and TRICARE Standard contractors. When reviewing the instructions, refer to the John Q. Public case study in Figure 16-4 and the completed CMS-1500 claim in Figure 16-5.

TABLE 16-5 CMS-1500 claims completion instructions for TRICARE fee-for-service claims

NOTE: Refer to Chapter 11 for clarification of claims completion (e.g., entering names, mailing addresses, ICD-10-CM codes, diagnosis pointer letters, NPI, and so on).

BLOCK	INSTRUCTIONS
1	Enter an X in the *TRICARE/CHAMPUS* box.
1a	Enter the sponsor's social security number (SSN) as it appears on the reverse of the uniformed services common access card (CAC). *Do not enter hyphens or spaces in the number.* **NOTE:** The reverse side of the CAC, in the Medical block, states whether the sponsor is eligible for medical care from military or civilian sources.
2	Enter the patient's last name, first name, and middle initial (separated by commas) (e.g., DOE, JANE, M).
3	Enter the patient's birth date as MM DD YYYY (with spaces). Enter an X in the appropriate box to indicate the patient's gender. If the patient's gender is unknown, leave blank.
4	Enter the sponsor's last name, first name, and middle initial (separated by commas).
5	Enter the patient's mailing address and telephone number. Enter the street address on line 1, enter the city and state on line 2, and enter the five- or nine-digit zip code and telephone number on line 3. **NOTE:** Do not enter APO or FPO addresses as the mailing address. The patient's residence is the mailing address.
6	Enter an X in the appropriate box to indicate the patient's relationship to the policyholder. If the patient is an unmarried domestic partner, enter an X in the *Other* box.
7	Enter the sponsor's mailing address and telephone number. Enter the street address on line 1, enter the city and state on line 2, and enter the five- or nine-digit zip code and telephone number on line 3. **NOTE:** For an active-duty sponsor, enter the sponsor's duty station address. For a retiree sponsor, enter the sponsor's home address.
8	Leave blank.
9, 9a, 9d	Leave blank. *Blocks 9, 9a, and 9d are completed if the patient has secondary insurance coverage (discussed later in this chapter).*
10a–c	Enter an X in the appropriate box to indicate whether the patient's condition is related to employment, an automobile accident, and/or another accident. If an X is entered in the YES box for auto accident, enter the two-character state abbreviation of the patient's residence.
10d	If DD Form 2527 is attached to the CMS-1500 claim, enter DD FORM 2527 ATTACHED. Otherwise, leave blank.
11, 11a–11c	Leave blank.
11d	Enter an X in the NO box. *Block 11d is completed by entering an X in the YES box if the patient has secondary insurance coverage (discussed later in this chapter).*
12	Enter SIGNATURE ON FILE. Leave the date field blank. (The abbreviation SOF is also acceptable.) **NOTE:** Entering SIGNATURE ON FILE means that the patient has previously signed an authorization to release medical information to the payer, and it is maintained "on file" by the provider. If the patient has not signed an authorization, the patient must sign and date the block.

(continues)

TABLE 16-5 (continued)

BLOCK	INSTRUCTIONS
13	Enter SIGNATURE ON FILE to authorize direct payment to the provider for benefits due the patient. (The abbreviation SOF is also acceptable.)
14	Enter the date as MM DD YYYY (with spaces) to indicate when the patient first experienced signs or symptoms of the present illness, actual date of injury, *or* the date of the last menstrual period (LMP) for obstetric visits. Enter the applicable qualifier to identify which date is being reported: 431 (onset of current symptoms/illness or injury) *or* 484 (last menstrual period). *If the date is not documented in the patient's record, but the history indicates an appropriate date (e.g., three weeks ago), simply count back to the approximate date and enter it on the claim.*
15	Enter the date as MM DD YYYY (with spaces) to indicate that a prior episode of the same or similar illness began, *if documented in the patient's record. Previous pregnancies are not a similar illness*. Otherwise, leave blank.
16	Leave blank.
17	If applicable, enter the first name, middle initial (if known), last name, and credentials of the professional who referred, ordered, or supervised health care service(s) or supply(ies) reported on the claim. *Do not enter any punctuation*. In front of the name, enter the applicable qualifier to identify which provider is being reported, as follows: DN (referring provider), DK (ordering provider), or DQ (supervising provider). Otherwise, leave blank. **NOTE:** If the patient was referred by a military treatment facility (MTF), enter the name of the MTF and attach DD Form 2161 (Referral for Civilian Medical Care) or SF 513 (Medical Record–Consultation Sheet).
17a	Leave blank.
17b	Enter the 10-digit national provider identifier (NPI) of the professional in Block 17. Otherwise, leave blank.
18	Enter the admission date and discharge date as MM DD YYYY (with spaces) if the patient received inpatient services (e.g., hospital, skilled nursing facility). Otherwise, leave blank. *If the patient has not been discharged at the time the claim is completed, leave the discharge date blank.*
19	Leave blank.
20	Enter an X in the NO box if all laboratory procedures reported on the claim were performed in the provider's office. Enter an X in the YES box if laboratory procedures reported on the claim were performed by an outside laboratory and billed to the provider. Enter the total amount charged by the outside laboratory in $ CHARGES, and enter the outside laboratory's name, mailing address, and NPI in Block 32. (Charges are entered *without* punctuation. For example, $1,100.00 is entered as 110000 below $ CHARGES.)
21	Enter the ICD-10-CM code for up to 12 diagnoses or conditions treated or medically managed during the encounter. Lines A through L in Block 21 will relate to CPT/HCPCS service/procedure codes reported in Block 24E. In the *ICD Ind* (ICD indicator) box, enter 0 for ICD-10-CM (or 9 for ICD-9-CM).
22	Leave blank. This is reserved for resubmitted claims.
23	If applicable, enter the prior authorization number. *Do not enter hyphens or spaces in the number.* Otherwise, leave blank.
24A	Enter the date the procedure or service was performed in the FROM column as MM DD YY (with spaces). Enter a date in the TO column *if the procedure or service was performed on consecutive days during a range of dates. Then, enter the number of consecutive days in Block 24G.* **NOTE:** The shaded area in each line is used to enter supplemental information to support reported services *if instructed by the payer to enter such information.* Data entry in Block 24 is limited to reporting six services. *Do not use the shaded lines to report additional services.* If additional services were provided, generate new CMS-1500 claim(s) to report the additional services.
24B	Enter the appropriate two-digit place-of-service (POS) code to identify the location where the reported procedure or service was performed. (Refer to Appendix II for POS codes.)

(continues)

TABLE 16-5 (continued)

BLOCK	INSTRUCTIONS
24C	Leave blank.
24D	Enter the CPT or HCPCS level II code and applicable required modifier(s) for procedures or services performed. *Separate the CPT/HCPCS code and first modifier with one space. Separate additional modifiers with one space each. Up to four modifiers can be entered.*
24E	Enter the diagnosis pointer letter from Block 21 that relates to the procedure/service performed on the date of service. **NOTE:** When completing CMS-1500 claims for case studies in this textbook, its Workbook, and SimClaim™ software, enter just one diagnosis pointer letter on each line of Block 24E.
24F	Enter the fee charged for each reported procedure or service. When multiple procedures or services are reported on the same line, enter the total fee charged. *Do not enter commas, periods, or dollar signs. Do not enter negative amounts. Enter 00 in the cents area if the amount is a whole number.*
24G	Enter the number of days or units for procedures or services reported in Block 24D. *If just one procedure or service was reported in Block 24D, enter a 1 in Block 24G.*
24H–24I	Leave blank.
24J	Enter the 10-digit NPI for the: ● Provider who performed the service *if the provider is a member of a group practice* (Leave blank if the provider is a solo practitioner.) ● Supervising provider *if the service was provided incident-to the service of a physician or nonphysician practitioner* ***and*** *the physician or practitioner who ordered the service did not supervise the provider* (Leave blank if the incident-to service was performed under the supervision of the physician or nonphysician practitioner.) ● DMEPOS supplier or outside laboratory *if the physician submits the claim for services provided by the DMEPOS supplier or outside laboratory* (Leave blank if the DMEPOS supplier or outside laboratory submits the claim.) Otherwise, leave blank.
25	Enter the provider's social security number (SSN) or employer identification number (EIN). *Do not enter hyphens or spaces in the number.* Enter an X in the appropriate box to indicate which number is reported.
26	Enter the patient's account number as assigned by the provider.
27	Enter an X in the YES box to indicate that the provider agrees to accept assignment. Otherwise, enter an X in the NO box.
28	Enter the total charges for services and/or procedures reported in Block 24. **NOTE:** If multiple claims are submitted for one patient because more than six procedures or services were reported, be sure the total charge reported on each claim accurately represents the total of the items on each submitted claim.
29	Leave blank. *Block 29 is completed if the patient has secondary insurance (discussed later in this chapter).*
30	Leave blank.
31	Enter the provider's name and credential (e.g., MARY SMITH MD) and the date the claim was completed as MMDDYYYY (without spaces). *Do not enter any punctuation.*
32	Enter the name and address where procedures or services were provided *if at a location other than the provider's office or the patient's home, such as a hospital, outside laboratory facility, skilled nursing facility, or DMEPOS supplier.* Otherwise, leave blank. Enter the name on line 1, the address on line 2, and the city, state, and five- or nine-digit zip code on line 3. *For a nine-digit zip code, enter the hyphen.* **NOTE:** If Block 18 contains dates of service for inpatient care and/or Block 20 contains an X in the YES box, enter the name and address of the facility that provided services (e.g., military treatment facility).

(continues)

TABLE 16-5 (continued)

BLOCK	INSTRUCTIONS
32a	Enter the 10-digit NPI of the facility entered in Block 32.
32b	Leave blank.
33	Enter the provider's *billing* name, address, and telephone number. Enter the phone number in the area next to the block title. *Do not enter parentheses for the area code.* Enter the name on line 1, enter the address on line 2, and enter the city, state, and five- or nine-digit zip code on line 3. *For a nine-digit zip code, enter the hyphen.*
33a	Enter the 10-digit NPI of the *billing* provider (e.g., solo practitioner) or group practice (e.g., clinic).
33b	Leave blank.

ERIN A. HELPER, M.D.
101 Medic Drive, Anywhere, NY 12345
(101) 111-1234 (Office) • (101) 111-9292 (Fax)
EIN: 11-1234523
NPI: 1234567890

Case Study

PATIENT INFORMATION:		**INSURANCE INFORMATION:**	
Name:	Public, John Q.	**Patient Number:**	16-1
Address:	10A Senate Avenue	**Place of Service:**	Inpatient Hospital
City:	Anywhere	**Primary Insurance Plan:**	TRICARE Standard
State:	NY	**Primary insurance Plan ID#:**	100 23 9678
Zip Code:	12345-1234	**Policy #:**	
Telephone:	(101) 201-7891	**Primary Policyholder:**	Public, John Q.
Gender:	Male	**Policyholder Date of Birth:**	03-09-1965
Date of Birth:	03-09-1965	**Relationship to Patient:**	Self
Occupation:	Retired	**Secondary Insurance Plan:**	
Employer:		**Secondary Insurance Plan ID #:**	
		Secondary Policyholder:	

Patient Status ☒ Married ☐ Divorced ☐ Single ☐ Student

DIAGNOSIS INFORMATION

Diagnosis	Code	Diagnosis	Code
1. Mycoplasma pneumonia	J15.7	5.	
2. Type 1 diabetes mellitus	E10.9	6.	
3.		7.	
4.		8.	

PROCEDURE INFORMATION

Description of Procedure or Service	Date	Code	Charge
1. Initial hospital visit, level III	01-09-YYYY	99223	150.00
2. Subsequent hospital visit, level II	01-10-YYYY	99232	75.00
3. Subsequent hospital visit, level II	01-11-YYYY	99232	75.00
4. Subsequent hospital visit, level I	01-12-YYYY	99231	50.00
5. Discharge, 30 minutes	01-13-YYYY	99238	50.00

SPECIAL NOTES: Goodmedicine Hospital, Anywhere Street, Anywhere, NY 12345. (NPI: 2345678901) Return visit one week.

FIGURE 16-4 John Q. Public case study.

CARRIER

HEALTH INSURANCE CLAIM FORM

APPROVED BY NATIONAL UNIFORM CLAIM COMMITTEE (NUCC) 02/12

PICA PICA

PATIENT AND INSURED INFORMATION

1. MEDICARE (Medicare#) MEDICAID (Medicaid#) TRICARE (ID#/DoD#) [X] CHAMPVA (Member ID#) GROUP HEALTH PLAN (ID#) FECA BLK LUNG (ID#) OTHER (ID#)

1a. INSURED'S I.D. NUMBER (For Program in Item 1): 100239678

2. PATIENT'S NAME (Last Name, First Name, Middle Initial): PUBLIC, JOHN, Q

3. PATIENT'S BIRTH DATE MM DD YY: 03 09 1965 SEX M [X] F [ ]

4. INSURED'S NAME (Last Name, First Name, Middle Initial): PUBLIC, JOHN, Q

5. PATIENT'S ADDRESS (No., Street): 10A SENATE AVENUE

6. PATIENT RELATIONSHIP TO INSURED: Self [X] Spouse [ ] Child [ ] Other [ ]

7. INSURED'S ADDRESS (No., Street): 10A SENATE AVENUE

CITY: ANYWHERE STATE: NY

8. RESERVED FOR NUCC USE

CITY: ANYWHERE STATE: NY

ZIP CODE: 12345-1234 TELEPHONE (Include Area Code): (101) 2017891

ZIP CODE: 12345-1234 TELEPHONE (Include Area Code): (101) 2017891

9. OTHER INSURED'S NAME (Last Name, First Name, Middle Initial)

10. IS PATIENT'S CONDITION RELATED TO:

11. INSURED'S POLICY GROUP OR FECA NUMBER

a. OTHER INSURED'S POLICY OR GROUP NUMBER

a. EMPLOYMENT? (Current or Previous) YES [ ] NO [X]

a. INSURED'S DATE OF BIRTH MM DD YY SEX M [ ] F [ ]

b. RESERVED FOR NUCC USE

b. AUTO ACCIDENT? YES [ ] NO [X] PLACE (State)

b. OTHER CLAIM ID (Designated by NUCC)

c. RESERVED FOR NUCC USE

c. OTHER ACCIDENT? YES [ ] NO [X]

c. INSURANCE PLAN NAME OR PROGRAM NAME

d. INSURANCE PLAN NAME OR PROGRAM NAME

10d. CLAIM CODES (Designated by NUCC)

d. IS THERE ANOTHER HEALTH BENEFIT PLAN? YES [ ] NO [X] *If yes, complete items 9, 9a, and 9d.*

READ BACK OF FORM BEFORE COMPLETING & SIGNING THIS FORM.

12. PATIENT'S OR AUTHORIZED PERSON'S SIGNATURE I authorize the release of any medical or other information necessary to process this claim. I also request payment of government benefits either to myself or to the party who accepts assignment below.

SIGNED SIGNATURE ON FILE DATE

13. INSURED'S OR AUTHORIZED PERSON'S SIGNATURE I authorize payment of medical benefits to the undersigned physician or supplier for services described below.

SIGNED SIGNATURE ON FILE

PHYSICIAN OR SUPPLIER INFORMATION

14. DATE OF CURRENT ILLNESS, INJURY, or PREGNANCY (LMP) MM DD YY: 01 09 YYYY QUAL. 431

15. OTHER DATE QUAL. MM DD YY

16. DATES PATIENT UNABLE TO WORK IN CURRENT OCCUPATION FROM TO

17. NAME OF REFERRING PROVIDER OR OTHER SOURCE 17a. 17b. NPI

18. HOSPITALIZATION DATES RELATED TO CURRENT SERVICES FROM 01 09 YYYY TO 01 13 YYYY

19. ADDITIONAL CLAIM INFORMATION (Designated by NUCC)

20. OUTSIDE LAB? YES [ ] NO [X] $ CHARGES

21. DIAGNOSIS OR NATURE OF ILLNESS OR INJURY Relate A-L to service line below (24E) ICD Ind. 0

A. J15.7 B. E10.9 C. D.
E. F. G. H.
I. J. K. L.

22. RESUBMISSION CODE ORIGINAL REF. NO.

23. PRIOR AUTHORIZATION NUMBER

	24. A. DATE(S) OF SERVICE From MM	DD	YY	To MM	DD	YY	B. PLACE OF SERVICE	C. EMG	D. PROCEDURES, SERVICES, OR SUPPLIES (Explain Unusual Circumstances) CPT/HCPCS	MODIFIER	E. DIAGNOSIS POINTER	F. $ CHARGES	G. DAYS OR UNITS	H. EPSDT Family Plan	I. ID. QUAL.	J. RENDERING PROVIDER ID. #
1	01	09	YY				21		99223		A	150 00	1		NPI	
2	01	10	YY	01	11	YY	21		99232		A	150 00	2		NPI	
3	01	12	YY				21		99231		A	50 00	1		NPI	
4	01	13	YY				21		99238		A	50 00	1		NPI	
5															NPI	
6															NPI	

25. FEDERAL TAX I.D. NUMBER SSN EIN: 111234523 [X] EIN

26. PATIENT'S ACCOUNT NO.: 16-1

27. ACCEPT ASSIGNMENT? (For govt. claims, see back) YES [X] NO [ ]

28. TOTAL CHARGE $ 400 00

29. AMOUNT PAID $

30. Rsvd for NUCC Use

31. SIGNATURE OF PHYSICIAN OR SUPPLIER INCLUDING DEGREES OR CREDENTIALS (I certify that the statements on the reverse apply to this bill and are made a part thereof.)

SIGNED ERIN A HELPER MD DATE MMDDYYYY

32. SERVICE FACILITY LOCATION INFORMATION
GOODMEDICINE HOSPITAL
ANYWHERE STREET
ANYWHERE NY 12345
a. 2345678901 b.

33. BILLING PROVIDER INFO & PH # (101) 1111234
ERIN A HELPER MD
101 MEDIC DRIVE
ANYWHERE NY 12345
a. 1234567890 b.

NUCC Instruction Manual available at: www.nucc.org *PLEASE PRINT OR TYPE*

FIGURE 16-5 Completed TRICARE as primary CMS-1500 claim for John Q. Public case study.

EXERCISE 16-1

Completion of TRICARE as Primary CMS-1500 Claim

1. Obtain a blank claim by making a copy of the CMS-1500 claim form in Appendix III.
2. Review the claims instructions in Table 16-5.
3. Review Figure 16-6, Mary S. Patient case study.
4. Select the information needed from the case study, and enter the required information on the claim using optical scanning guidelines.
5. Review the claim to be sure all required blocks are properly completed.
6. Compare your claim with the completed claim in Figure 16-7.

ERIN A. HELPER, M.D.
101 Medic Drive, Anywhere, NY 12345
(101) 111-1234 (Office) • (101) 111-9292 (Fax)
EIN: 11-1234523
NPI: 1234567890

Case Study

PATIENT INFORMATION:		INSURANCE INFORMATION:	
Name:	Patient, Mary S.	**Patient Number:**	16-2
Address:	91 Home Street	**Place of Service:**	Office
City:	Nowhere	**Primary Insurance Plan:**	TRICARE Standard
State:	NY	**Primary Insurance Plan ID #:**	101 23 9945
Zip Code:	12367-1234	**Policy #:**	
Telephone:	(101) 201-8989	**Primary Policyholder:**	James L. Patient
Gender:	Female	**Policyholder Date of Birth:**	08-22-1944
Occupation:	Homemaker	**Employer:**	Turbodyne
Date of Birth:	10-10-1959	**Relationship to Patient:**	Spouse
Employer:		**Secondary Insurance Plan:**	US Navy
		Secondary Insurance Plan ID #:	Dept 07 Naval Station Nowhere, NY 12367-1234
		Secondary Policyholder:	

Patient Status ☒ Married ☐ Divorced ☐ Single ☐ Student

DIAGNOSIS INFORMATION

Diagnosis	Code	Diagnosis	Code
1. Fracture, distal radius, left (initial encounter)	S52.509A	5.	
2. Fell at home	Y92.009	6.	
3. Fell down stairs (initial encounter)	W10.8xxA	7.	
4.		8.	

PROCEDURE INFORMATION

Description of Procedure or Service	Date	Code	Charge
1. Closed manipulation, left distal radius	01-10-YYYY	25600-LT	300.00
2. X-ray, left wrist, 3 views	01-10-YYYY	73110-LT	50.00
3. X-ray, left forearm, 1 view	01-10-YYYY	73090-LT	25.00
4.			
5.			

SPECIAL NOTES: Fell down stairs at home today.

FIGURE 16-6 Mary S. Patient case study.

HEALTH INSURANCE CLAIM FORM

APPROVED BY NATIONAL UNIFORM CLAIM COMMITTEE (NUCC) 02/12

PICA | PICA

CARRIER

1. MEDICARE (Medicare#) | MEDICAID (Medicaid#) | TRICARE (ID#/DoD#) [X] | CHAMPVA (Member ID#) | GROUP HEALTH PLAN (ID#) | FECA BLK LUNG (ID#) | OTHER (ID#)

1a. INSURED'S I.D. NUMBER (For Program in Item 1): 101239945

2. PATIENT'S NAME (Last Name, First Name, Middle Initial): PATIENT, MARY, S

3. PATIENT'S BIRTH DATE (MM DD YY): 10 10 1959 — SEX: M [ ] F [X]

4. INSURED'S NAME (Last Name, First Name, Middle Initial): PATIENT, JAMES, L

5. PATIENT'S ADDRESS (No., Street): 91 HOME STREET

6. PATIENT RELATIONSHIP TO INSURED: Self [ ] Spouse [X] Child [ ] Other [ ]

7. INSURED'S ADDRESS (No., Street): DEPT 07 NAVAL STATION

CITY: NOWHERE — STATE: NY

8. RESERVED FOR NUCC USE

CITY: NOWHERE — STATE: NY

ZIP CODE: 12367-1234 — TELEPHONE (Include Area Code): (101) 2018989

ZIP CODE: 12367-1234 — TELEPHONE (Include Area Code): ( )

9. OTHER INSURED'S NAME (Last Name, First Name, Middle Initial)

10. IS PATIENT'S CONDITION RELATED TO:

11. INSURED'S POLICY GROUP OR FECA NUMBER

a. OTHER INSURED'S POLICY OR GROUP NUMBER

a. EMPLOYMENT? (Current or Previous) YES [ ] NO [X]

a. INSURED'S DATE OF BIRTH (MM DD YY) — SEX M [ ] F [ ]

b. RESERVED FOR NUCC USE

b. AUTO ACCIDENT? YES [ ] NO [X] PLACE (State)

b. OTHER CLAIM ID (Designated by NUCC)

c. RESERVED FOR NUCC USE

c. OTHER ACCIDENT? YES [ ] NO [X]

c. INSURANCE PLAN NAME OR PROGRAM NAME

d. INSURANCE PLAN NAME OR PROGRAM NAME

10d. CLAIM CODES (Designated by NUCC)

d. IS THERE ANOTHER HEALTH BENEFIT PLAN? YES [ ] NO [X] *If yes*, complete items 9, 9a, and 9d.

READ BACK OF FORM BEFORE COMPLETING & SIGNING THIS FORM.

12. PATIENT'S OR AUTHORIZED PERSON'S SIGNATURE I authorize the release of any medical or other information necessary to process this claim. I also request payment of government benefits either to myself or to the party who accepts assignment below.

SIGNED SIGNATURE ON FILE DATE

13. INSURED'S OR AUTHORIZED PERSON'S SIGNATURE I authorize payment of medical benefits to the undersigned physician or supplier for services described below.

SIGNED SIGNATURE ON FILE

PATIENT AND INSURED INFORMATION

14. DATE OF CURRENT ILLNESS, INJURY, or PREGNANCY (LMP) (MM DD YY): 01 10 YYYY — QUAL. 431

15. OTHER DATE — QUAL. MM DD YY

16. DATES PATIENT UNABLE TO WORK IN CURRENT OCCUPATION — FROM MM DD YY TO MM DD YY

17. NAME OF REFERRING PROVIDER OR OTHER SOURCE — 17a. — 17b. NPI

18. HOSPITALIZATION DATES RELATED TO CURRENT SERVICES — FROM MM DD YY TO MM DD YY

19. ADDITIONAL CLAIM INFORMATION (Designated by NUCC)

20. OUTSIDE LAB? YES [ ] NO [X] — $ CHARGES

21. DIAGNOSIS OR NATURE OF ILLNESS OR INJURY Relate A-L to service line below (24E) — ICD Ind. 0

A. S52.509A B. Y92.009 C. W10.8XXA D.
E. F. G. H.
I. J. K. L.

22. RESUBMISSION CODE — ORIGINAL REF. NO.

23. PRIOR AUTHORIZATION NUMBER

	24. A. DATE(S) OF SERVICE From MM	DD	YY	To MM	DD	YY	B. PLACE OF SERVICE	C. EMG	D. PROCEDURES, SERVICES, OR SUPPLIES (Explain Unusual Circumstances) CPT/HCPCS	MODIFIER	E. DIAGNOSIS POINTER	F. $ CHARGES	G. DAYS OR UNITS	H. EPSDT Family Plan	I. ID. QUAL.	J. RENDERING PROVIDER ID. #
1	01	10	YY				11		25600	LT	A	300 00	1		NPI	
2	01	10	YY				11		73110	LT	A	50 00	1		NPI	
3	01	10	YY				11		73090	LT	A	25 00	1		NPI	
4															NPI	
5															NPI	
6															NPI	

25. FEDERAL TAX I.D. NUMBER: 111234523 — SSN [ ] EIN [X]

26. PATIENT'S ACCOUNT NO.: 16-2

27. ACCEPT ASSIGNMENT? (For govt. claims, see back) [X] YES [ ] NO

28. TOTAL CHARGE: $ 375 00

29. AMOUNT PAID: $

30. Rsvd for NUCC Use

31. SIGNATURE OF PHYSICIAN OR SUPPLIER INCLUDING DEGREES OR CREDENTIALS (I certify that the statements on the reverse apply to this bill and are made a part thereof.)

SIGNED ERIN A HELPER MD — DATE MMDDYYYY

32. SERVICE FACILITY LOCATION INFORMATION — a. NPI b.

33. BILLING PROVIDER INFO & PH # (101) 1111234

ERIN A HELPER MD
101 MEDIC DRIVE
ANYWHERE NY 12345

a. 1234567890 b.

PHYSICIAN OR SUPPLIER INFORMATION

NUCC Instruction Manual available at: www.nucc.org — *PLEASE PRINT OR TYPE*

FIGURE 16-7 Completed TRICARE as primary CMS-1500 claim for Mary S. Patient case study.

TRICARE AS SECONDARY PAYER

Table 16-6 contains modifications to the CMS-1500 claims instructions when a second CMS-1500 claim is generated with TRICARE as the secondary payer. In this situation, the patient's primary health insurance coverage is another payer, such as Medicare or an employer group health plan (e.g., BCBS).

TABLE 16-6 Modifications to CMS-1500 claims completion instructions when TRICARE is the secondary payer (Refer to Table 16-5 for primary CMS-1500 claims completion instructions.)

BLOCK	INSTRUCTIONS
NOTE: Blocks 11 and 11a–11c remain blank on a TRICARE as Secondary CMS-1500 claim.	
1a	Enter the secondary policyholder's health insurance identification number (HICN) as it appears on the insurance card. *Do not enter hyphens or spaces in the number.*
4	Enter the *TRICARE as secondary* policyholder's last name, first name, and middle initial (separated by commas).
7	Enter the *TRICARE as secondary* policyholder's mailing address and telephone number.
9	Enter the primary policyholder's last name, first name, and middle initial (if known) (separated by commas).
9a	Enter the primary policyholder's policy or group number.
9d	Enter the name of the primary policyholder's health insurance plan.
11, 11a-c	Leave blank.
11d	Enter an X in the YES box.
29	Enter the reimbursement amount received from the primary payer. Attach the remittance advice received from the primary payer to the CMS-1500 claim.

EXERCISE 16-2

Completion of TRICARE as Secondary CMS-1500 Claim

1. Obtain a blank CMS-1500 claim.
2. Refer to Figure 16-8, the John R. Neely case study.
3. Complete the TRICARE secondary claim for this case. Enter the patient account number as 16-3S.
4. Review the completed claim to be sure all required blocks are properly completed. Refer to Figure 16-9.

ERIN A. HELPER, M.D.
101 Medic Drive, Anywhere, NY 12345
(101) 111-1234 (Office) • (101) 111-9292 (Fax)
EIN: 11-1234523
NPI: 1234567890

Case Study

PATIENT INFORMATION:

Name:	John R. Neely
Address:	1 Military Drive
City:	Nowhere
State:	NY
Zip Code:	12345-1234
Telephone:	(101) 111-9941
Gender:	M
Date of Birth:	10-25-1945
Occupation:	Retired Navy Captain
Employer:	
Spouse's Employer:	

INSURANCE INFORMATION:

Patient Number:	16-3
Place of Service:	Office
Primary Insurance Plan:	BlueCross BlueShield
Primary Insurance Plan ID #:	WXY7031
Policy #:	AS101
Primary Policyholder:	Janet B. Neely
Policyholder Date of Birth:	09-09-1945
Employer:	State College
Relationship to Patient:	Spouse
Secondary Insurance Plan:	TRICARE Standard
Secondary Insurance Plan ID #:	001 06 7019
Secondary Policyholder:	John R. Neely

Patient Status ☒ Married ☐ Divorced ☐ Single ☐ Student

DIAGNOSIS INFORMATION

Diagnosis	Code	Diagnosis	Code
1. Abnormal ECG	R94.31	5.	
2. Coronary artery disease, native vessel	I25.10	6.	
3. Family history of heart disease	Z82.49	7.	
4.		8.	

PROCEDURE INFORMATION

Description of Procedure or Service	Date	Code	Charge
1. Established patient office visit, level III	03-10-YYYY	99213	75.00
2. ECG, 12-lead with interpretation and report	03-10-YYYY	93000	60.00
3.			
4.			

SPECIAL NOTES: Schedule stress test for tomorrow. BCBS paid $80 on claim.

FIGURE 16-8 John R. Neely case study.

HEALTH INSURANCE CLAIM FORM

APPROVED BY NATIONAL UNIFORM CLAIM COMMITTEE (NUCC) 02/12

PICA | PICA | CARRIER

1. MEDICARE (Medicare#) | MEDICAID (Medicaid#) | TRICARE (ID#/DoD#) [X] | CHAMPVA (Member ID#) | GROUP HEALTH PLAN (ID#) | FECA BLK LUNG (ID#) | OTHER (ID#)

1a. INSURED'S I.D. NUMBER (For Program in Item 1): 001067019

2. PATIENT'S NAME (Last Name, First Name, Middle Initial): NEELY, JOHN, R

3. PATIENT'S BIRTH DATE MM DD YY: 10 25 1945 SEX M [X] F

4. INSURED'S NAME (Last Name, First Name, Middle Initial): NEELY, JOHN, R

5. PATIENT'S ADDRESS (No., Street): 1 MILITARY DRIVE

6. PATIENT RELATIONSHIP TO INSURED: Self | Spouse [X] | Child | Other

7. INSURED'S ADDRESS (No., Street): 1 MILITARY DRIVE

CITY: NOWHERE STATE: NY

8. RESERVED FOR NUCC USE

CITY: NOWHERE STATE: NY

ZIP CODE: 12345-1234 TELEPHONE (Include Area Code): (101) 1119941

ZIP CODE: 12345-1234 TELEPHONE (Include Area Code): (101) 1119941

9. OTHER INSURED'S NAME (Last Name, First Name, Middle Initial): NEELY, JANET, B

10. IS PATIENT'S CONDITION RELATED TO:

11. INSURED'S POLICY GROUP OR FECA NUMBER

a. OTHER INSURED'S POLICY OR GROUP NUMBER: AS101

a. EMPLOYMENT? (Current or Previous) YES NO [X]

a. INSURED'S DATE OF BIRTH MM DD YY SEX M F

b. RESERVED FOR NUCC USE

b. AUTO ACCIDENT? YES NO [X] PLACE (State)

b. OTHER CLAIM ID (Designated by NUCC)

c. RESERVED FOR NUCC USE

c. OTHER ACCIDENT? YES NO [X]

c. INSURANCE PLAN NAME OR PROGRAM NAME

d. INSURANCE PLAN NAME OR PROGRAM NAME: BLUECROSS BLUESHIELD

10d. CLAIM CODES (Designated by NUCC)

d. IS THERE ANOTHER HEALTH BENEFIT PLAN? YES [X] NO *If yes, complete items 9, 9a, and 9d.*

READ BACK OF FORM BEFORE COMPLETING & SIGNING THIS FORM.

12. PATIENT'S OR AUTHORIZED PERSON'S SIGNATURE I authorize the release of any medical or other information necessary to process this claim. I also request payment of government benefits either to myself or to the party who accepts assignment below.

SIGNED SIGNATURE ON FILE DATE

13. INSURED'S OR AUTHORIZED PERSON'S SIGNATURE I authorize payment of medical benefits to the undersigned physician or supplier for services described below.

SIGNED SIGNATURE ON FILE

PATIENT AND INSURED INFORMATION

14. DATE OF CURRENT ILLNESS, INJURY, or PREGNANCY (LMP) MM DD YY: 03 10 YYYY QUAL. 431

15. OTHER DATE QUAL. MM DD YY

16. DATES PATIENT UNABLE TO WORK IN CURRENT OCCUPATION FROM TO

17. NAME OF REFERRING PROVIDER OR OTHER SOURCE | 17a. | 17b. NPI

18. HOSPITALIZATION DATES RELATED TO CURRENT SERVICES FROM TO

19. ADDITIONAL CLAIM INFORMATION (Designated by NUCC)

20. OUTSIDE LAB? YES NO [X] $ CHARGES

21. DIAGNOSIS OR NATURE OF ILLNESS OR INJURY Relate A-L to service line below (24E) ICD Ind. 0

A. R94.31 B. I25.10 C. Z82.49 D.

E. F. G. H.

I. J. K. L.

22. RESUBMISSION CODE | ORIGINAL REF. NO.

23. PRIOR AUTHORIZATION NUMBER

	24. A. DATE(S) OF SERVICE From MM DD YY	To MM DD YY	B. PLACE OF SERVICE	C. EMG	D. PROCEDURES, SERVICES, OR SUPPLIES (Explain Unusual Circumstances) CPT/HCPCS	MODIFIER	E. DIAGNOSIS POINTER	F. $ CHARGES	G. DAYS OR UNITS	H. EPSDT Family Plan	I. ID. QUAL.	J. RENDERING PROVIDER ID. #
1	03 10 YY		11		99213		A	75 00	1		NPI	
2	03 10 YY		11		93000		A	60 00	1		NPI	
3											NPI	
4											NPI	
5											NPI	
6											NPI	

25. FEDERAL TAX I.D. NUMBER: 111234523 SSN EIN [X]

26. PATIENT'S ACCOUNT NO.: 16-3S

27. ACCEPT ASSIGNMENT? (For govt. claims, see back) YES [X] NO

28. TOTAL CHARGE $ 135 00

29. AMOUNT PAID $ 80 00

30. Rsvd for NUCC Use

31. SIGNATURE OF PHYSICIAN OR SUPPLIER INCLUDING DEGREES OR CREDENTIALS (I certify that the statements on the reverse apply to this bill and are made a part thereof.)

SIGNED ERIN A HELPER MD DATE MMDDYYYY

32. SERVICE FACILITY LOCATION INFORMATION a. NPI b.

33. BILLING PROVIDER INFO & PH # (101) 1111234
ERIN A HELPER MD
10 MEDIC DRIVE
ANYWHERE NY 12345

a. 1234567890 b.

PHYSICIAN OR SUPPLIER INFORMATION

NUCC Instruction Manual available at: www.nucc.org *PLEASE PRINT OR TYPE*

FIGURE 16-9 Completed TRICARE as secondary CMS-1500 claim for John R. Neely case study.

TRICARE AND SUPPLEMENTAL COVERAGE

When the patient has a supplemental health plan (e.g., BCBS) *in addition to TRICARE*, participating providers submit just one claim. Claims completion modifications (Table 16-7) are made to the TRICARE primary claim (Figure 16-10.)

TABLE 16-7 Modifications to TRICARE primary CMS-1500 claims completion instructions when patient has a supplemental health plan (Refer to Table 16-5 for primary CMS-1500 claims completion instructions.)

BLOCK	INSTRUCTIONS
1	Enter an X in the *TRICARE* and *OTHER* boxes.
9	Enter the supplemental policyholder's last name, first name, and middle initial (if known) (separated by commas).
9a	Enter the supplemental policyholder's policy or group number.
9d	Enter the name of the supplemental policyholder's health insurance plan.
11, 11a-c	Leave blank.
11d	Enter an X in the YES box.
29-30	Leave blank.

Courtesy of the Centers for Medicare & Medicaid Services, www.cms.gov

EXERCISE 16-3

Completion of Primary TRICARE with Supplemental Policy CMS-1500 Claim

1. Obtain a blank claim by making a copy of the CMS-1500 claim form in Appendix III.
2. Refer to the Mary S. Patient case study (Figure 16-6), and select the information needed from the case study and the following list to complete the claim:
   - Supplemental policyholder: Mary S. Patient
   - Supplemental policyholder policy number: 123456
   - Supplemental policyholder health insurance plan: Aetna
   - Patient's Account No. 16-2SUPP
3. Review the completed claim to be sure all required blocks are properly completed.
4. Compare your claim with the completed Mary S. Patient claim in Figure 16-10.

HEALTH INSURANCE CLAIM FORM

APPROVED BY NATIONAL UNIFORM CLAIM COMMITTEE (NUCC) 02/12

PICA | PICA

CARRIER

PATIENT AND INSURED INFORMATION

1. MEDICARE (Medicare#) [ ] MEDICAID (Medicaid#) [ ] TRICARE (ID#/DoD#) [X] CHAMPVA (Member ID#) [ ] GROUP HEALTH PLAN (ID#) [ ] FECA BLK LUNG (ID#) [ ] OTHER (ID#) [X]

1a. INSURED'S I.D. NUMBER (For Program in Item 1): 101239945

2. PATIENT'S NAME (Last Name, First Name, Middle Initial): PATIENT, MARY, S

3. PATIENT'S BIRTH DATE MM DD YY: 10 10 1957 SEX M [ ] F [X]

4. INSURED'S NAME (Last Name, First Name, Middle Initial): PATIENT, JAMES, L

5. PATIENT'S ADDRESS (No., Street): 91 HOME STREET

6. PATIENT RELATIONSHIP TO INSURED: Self [ ] Spouse [X] Child [ ] Other [ ]

7. INSURED'S ADDRESS (No., Street): DEPT 07 NAVAL STATION

CITY: NOWHERE STATE: NY

8. RESERVED FOR NUCC USE

CITY: NOWHERE STATE: NY

ZIP CODE: 12367-1234 TELEPHONE (Include Area Code): (101) 2018989

ZIP CODE: 12367-1234 TELEPHONE (Include Area Code): ( )

9. OTHER INSURED'S NAME (Last Name, First Name, Middle Initial): PATIENT, MARY, S

10. IS PATIENT'S CONDITION RELATED TO:

11. INSURED'S POLICY GROUP OR FECA NUMBER

a. OTHER INSURED'S POLICY OR GROUP NUMBER: 123456

a. EMPLOYMENT? (Current or Previous) [ ] YES [X] NO

a. INSURED'S DATE OF BIRTH MM DD YY SEX M [ ] F [ ]

b. RESERVED FOR NUCC USE

b. AUTO ACCIDENT? [ ] YES [X] NO PLACE (State)

b. OTHER CLAIM ID (Designated by NUCC)

c. RESERVED FOR NUCC USE

c. OTHER ACCIDENT? [ ] YES [X] NO

c. INSURANCE PLAN NAME OR PROGRAM NAME

d. INSURANCE PLAN NAME OR PROGRAM NAME: AETNA

10d. CLAIM CODES (Designated by NUCC)

d. IS THERE ANOTHER HEALTH BENEFIT PLAN? [X] YES [ ] NO *If yes,* complete items 9, 9a, and 9d.

READ BACK OF FORM BEFORE COMPLETING & SIGNING THIS FORM.

12. PATIENT'S OR AUTHORIZED PERSON'S SIGNATURE I authorize the release of any medical or other information necessary to process this claim. I also request payment of government benefits either to myself or to the party who accepts assignment below.

SIGNED SIGNATURE ON FILE DATE

13. INSURED'S OR AUTHORIZED PERSON'S SIGNATURE I authorize payment of medical benefits to the undersigned physician or supplier for services described below.

SIGNED SIGNATURE ON FILE

PHYSICIAN OR SUPPLIER INFORMATION

14. DATE OF CURRENT ILLNESS, INJURY, or PREGNANCY (LMP) MM DD YY: 01 10 YYYY QUAL. 431

15. OTHER DATE QUAL. MM DD YY

16. DATES PATIENT UNABLE TO WORK IN CURRENT OCCUPATION FROM MM DD YY TO MM DD YY

17. NAME OF REFERRING PROVIDER OR OTHER SOURCE 17a. 17b. NPI

18. HOSPITALIZATION DATES RELATED TO CURRENT SERVICES FROM MM DD YY TO MM DD YY

19. ADDITIONAL CLAIM INFORMATION (Designated by NUCC)

20. OUTSIDE LAB? [ ] YES [X] NO $ CHARGES

21. DIAGNOSIS OR NATURE OF ILLNESS OR INJURY Relate A-L to service line below (24E) ICD Ind. 0

A. S52.509A B. Y92.009 C. W10.8XXA D.
E. F. G. H.
I. J. K. L.

22. RESUBMISSION CODE ORIGINAL REF. NO.

23. PRIOR AUTHORIZATION NUMBER

	24. A. DATE(S) OF SERVICE From MM DD YY	To MM DD YY	B. PLACE OF SERVICE	C. EMG	D. PROCEDURES, SERVICES, OR SUPPLIES (Explain Unusual Circumstances) CPT/HCPCS	MODIFIER	E. DIAGNOSIS POINTER	F. $ CHARGES	G. DAYS OR UNITS	H. EPSDT Family Plan	I. ID. QUAL.	J. RENDERING PROVIDER ID. #
1	01 10 YY		11		25600	LT	A	300 00	1		NPI	
2	01 10 YY		11		73110	LT	A	50 00	1		NPI	
3	01 10 YY		11		73090	LT	A	25 00	1		NPI	
4											NPI	
5											NPI	
6											NPI	

25. FEDERAL TAX I.D. NUMBER SSN EIN: 111234523 [ ] [X]

26. PATIENT'S ACCOUNT NO.: 16-2SUPP

27. ACCEPT ASSIGNMENT? (For govt. claims, see back) [X] YES [ ] NO

28. TOTAL CHARGE $ 375 00

29. AMOUNT PAID $

30. Rsvd for NUCC Use

31. SIGNATURE OF PHYSICIAN OR SUPPLIER INCLUDING DEGREES OR CREDENTIALS (I certify that the statements on the reverse apply to this bill and are made a part thereof.)

SIGNED ERIN A HELPER MD DATE MMDDYYYY

32. SERVICE FACILITY LOCATION INFORMATION

a. NPI b.

33. BILLING PROVIDER INFO & PH # (101) 1111234

ERIN A HELPER MD
101 MEDIC DRIVE
ANYWHERE NY 12345

a. 1234567890 b.

NUCC Instruction Manual available at: www.nucc.org PLEASE PRINT OR TYPE

FIGURE 16-10 Completed primary TRICARE with supplemental policy CMS-1500 claim for Mary S. Patient case study.

SUMMARY

TRICARE is a regionally managed health care program for active-duty and retired military members and their qualified family members, as well as eligible survivors of deceased uniformed services members. CHAMPUS (now called TRICARE) was created in 1966 as a benefit for dependents of personnel serving in the uniformed services. TRICARE regions are managed by lead agent staff, who are responsible for the military health system in their region. Lead agents serve as a federal health care team to support the mission of the Military Health Services System (MHSS), which is the entire health care system of the U.S. uniformed services. TRICARE Management Activity (TMA) (formerly OCHAMPUS, which meant Office of CHAMPUS) coordinates and administers the TRICARE program. TRICARE options include TRICARE Prime, TRICARE Extra, and TRICARE Standard. All active-duty military personnel are enrolled in TRICARE Prime. TRICARE beneficiaries who have other health insurance (OHI) that is primary to TRICARE must submit documentation (e.g., remittance advice) when submitting TRICARE claims. TRICARE is the secondary payer to civilian insurance plans, workers' compensation, liability insurance plans, and employer-sponsored HMO plans. TRICARE is the primary payer to Medicaid and TRICARE supplemental plans. CHAMPVA is a health care benefits program for dependents of veterans who are rated by Veterans Affairs (VA) as having a total and permanent disability, survivors of veterans who died from VA-rated service-connected conditions, and survivors of veterans who died in the line of duty and not from misconduct.

When completing TRICARE CMS-1500 claims for case studies in this text (including SimClaim software) and the Workbook, the following special instructions apply:

- Blocks 9, 9a, and 9d—Complete if the TRICARE beneficiary has a secondary or supplemental plan; otherwise, leave blank.
- Block 14—Leave blank.
- Block 15—Leave blank.
- Block 16—Leave blank.
- Block 20—Enter an X in the NO box.
- Block 23—Leave blank.
- Block 24E—Enter just one diagnosis pointer letter on each line.
- Block 24H through Block 24I—Leave blank.
- Block 26—Enter the case study number (e.g., 16-5). If the patient has TRICARE as secondary coverage, enter an S (for secondary) next to the number (on the secondary claim).
- Block 27—Enter an X in the YES box.
- Block 32—Enter the name and address of the MTF.
- When completing secondary claims, enter REMITTANCE ADVICE ATTACHED in the top margin of the CMS-1500 (to simulate the attachment of a primary payer's remittance advice with a claim submitted to a secondary payer).

INTERNET LINKS

- CHAMPVA
  Go to **www.va.gov**, click on the Veteran Services link, click on the A-Z Health Topic Finder link under the Health & Well-Being heading, click on "C" in the A-Z index, and click on the CHAMPVA link.
- TRICARE manuals
  http://manuals.tricare.osd.mil
- TRICARE Retiree Dental Program
  www.trdp.org

- TRICARE Supplemental Insurance
  Go to **www.tricare.mil**, click on the Skip to Most Popular Topics link, click on the Getting Care link, click on the Medical Claims link, click on the Other Health Insurance link, and click on the Supplemental Insurance link.
- US Family Health Plan
  www.usfamilyhealthplan.org

STUDY CHECKLIST

- ☐ Read this textbook chapter and highlight key concepts.
- ☐ Access SimClaim software at the online companion, and complete TRICARE claims using the software's case studies.
- ☐ Complete CMS-1500 claims for each chapter case study.
- ☐ Answer the chapter review questions, verifying answers with your instructor.
- ☐ Complete the Workbook chapter, verifying answers with your instructor.
- ☐ Form a study group with classmates to discuss chapter concepts in preparation for an exam.

REVIEW

MULTIPLE CHOICE **Select the most appropriate response.**

1. The health care program for active-duty members of the military and their qualified dependents is called

a. CHAMPUS.
b. CHAMPVA.
c. MHSS.
d. TRICARE.

2. Commanders of selected military treatment facilities for TRICARE regions are called

a. health care finders.
b. lead agents.
c. service centers.
d. sponsors.

3. Which office coordinates and administers the TRICARE program and is accountable for the quality of health care provided to members of the uniformed services and their eligible dependents?

a. Defense Enrollment Eligibility Reporting System (DEERS)
b. Military Health Services System (MHSS)
c. Military Treatment Facility (MTF)
d. TRICARE Management Activity (TMA)

4. Who assists TRICARE sponsors with information about the health program, along with other matters affecting access to health care (e.g., appointment scheduling)?

a. beneficiary services representative
b. health care finder
c. nurse advisor
d. primary care manager

5. **A critical pathway is the**
   a. approval process obtained from a health care finder before certain specialty procedures are provided.
   b. decision-making tool used by providers to determine appropriate health care for specific clinical circumstances.
   c. mechanism for surveillance of fraud and abuse activities worldwide involving purchased care.
   d. sequence of activities that can normally be expected to result in the most cost-effective clinical course of treatment.
6. **The managed care option that is similar to a civilian HMO is called TRICARE**
   a. Extra.
   b. Prime.
   c. Standard.
   d. Worldwide.
7. **The new name for CHAMPUS is TRICARE**
   a. Extra.
   b. Prime.
   c. Standard.
   d. Worldwide.
8. **TRICARE nonparticipating providers are subject to a limiting charge of _____ above the TRICARE fee schedule for participating providers.**
   a. 5 percent
   b. 10 percent
   c. 15 percent
   d. 20 percent
9. **What is the abbreviation for the computer system that contains up-to-date Defense Department workforce personnel information and is used to verify TRICARE eligibility?**
   a. DEERS
   b. HCF
   c. MHSS
   d. TMA
10. **The number of TRICARE regions has _____ since 1999.**
   a. decreased
   b. diminished in scope
   c. increased
   d. remained the same

CHAPTER 17

Workers' Compensation

CHAPTER OUTLINE

OBJECTIVES

Upon successful completion of this chapter, you should be able to:

1. Define key terms.
2. Describe federal and state workers' compensation programs.
3. List eligibility requirements for workers' compensation coverage.
4. Classify workers' compensation cases.
5. Describe special handling practices for workers' compensation cases.
6. Explain how managed care applies to workers' compensation coverage.
7. Submit first report of injury and progress reports.
8. Describe workers' compensation appeals and adjudication processes.
9. State examples of workers' compensation fraud and abuse.
10. Apply workers' compensation billing notes when completing CMS-1500 claims.
11. Complete workers' compensation claims properly.

KEY TERMS

adjudication
arbitration
Energy Employees Occupational Illness Compensation Program (EEOICP)
Federal Black Lung Program
First Report of Injury
Longshore and Harbor Workers' Compensation Program
Material Safety Data Sheet (MSDS)
Merchant Marine Act (Jones Act)
Mine Safety and Health Administration (MSHA)
Occupational Safety and Health Administration (OSHA)
Office of Workers' Compensation Programs (OWCP)
on-the-job injury
permanent disability
State Insurance Fund (State Compensation Fund)
survivor benefits
temporary disability
vocational rehabilitation
Workers' Compensation Board (Workers' Compensation Commission)

INTRODUCTION

Federal and state laws require employers to maintain workers' compensation coverage to meet minimum standards, covering a majority of employees for work-related illnesses and injuries (as long as the employee was not negligent in performing the assigned duties). Employees receive health care and monetary awards (if applicable), and dependents of workers killed on the job receive benefits. Workers' compensation laws also protect employers and fellow workers by limiting the award an injured employee can recover from an employer and by eliminating the liability of coworkers in most accidents. Federal workers' compensation statutes (laws) apply to federal employees or workers employed in a significant aspect of interstate commerce. Individual state workers' compensation laws establish comprehensive programs and are applicable to most employers. For example, California laws (1) limit the liability of the employer and fellow employees for work-related illnesses and injuries, (2) require employers to obtain workers' compensation coverage for potential claims, and (3) establish a state fund to pay claims when employers have illegally failed to obtain coverage.

> **NOTE:** *Workers' compensation* is sometimes mistakenly referred to by its previous name, *workman's compensation*. The name change occurred years ago to reflect an increase in the number of women in the workforce.

FEDERAL WORKERS' COMPENSATION PROGRAMS

The U.S. Department of Labor's (DOL) **Office of Workers' Compensation Programs (OWCP)** administers programs that provide wage-replacement benefits, medical treatment, vocational rehabilitation, and other benefits to federal workers (or eligible dependents) who are injured at work or acquire an occupational disease. The four programs are:

- **Energy Employees Occupational Illness Compensation Program**
- **Federal Black Lung Program**
- **Federal Employees' Compensation Act (FECA) Program**
- **Longshore and Harbor Workers' Compensation Program**

The Department of Labor also manages the following programs designed to prevent work-related injuries and illnesses:

- **Mine Safety and Health Administration (MSHA)**
- **Occupational Safety and Health Administration (OSHA)**

Other federal programs include:

- **Federal Employment Liability Act (FELA)**
- **Merchant Marine Act (Jones Act)**

Energy Employees Occupational Illness Compensation Program

Effective July 31, 2001, the **Energy Employees Occupational Illness Compensation Program (EEOICP)** started providing benefits to eligible employees and former employees of the Department of Energy, its contractors and subcontractors or to certain survivors of such individuals, and to certain beneficiaries of the Radiation Exposure Compensation Act. The Office of Workers' Compensation Programs (OWCP) is responsible for adjudicating and administering claims filed by employees, former employees, or certain qualified survivors.

Federal Black Lung Program

The **Federal Black Lung Program**, enacted in 1969 as part of the *Black Lung Benefits Act*, provides medical treatment and other benefits for respiratory conditions related to former employment in the nation's coal mines. The *Division of Coal Mine Workers' Compensation* administers and processes claims filed by coal miners (and their surviving dependents) who are or were employed in or around U.S. coal mines. Monthly benefit checks are sent to coal miners (or their eligible surviving dependents) who are totally disabled by *pneumoconiosis* (black lung disease) arising from their employment in or around the nation's coal mines.

Federal Employees' Compensation Act Program

NOTE: Federal agencies reimburse FECA for workers' compensation expenses through an annual *budget chargeback process*, which transfers funds from a responsible federal agency's budget (e.g., U.S. Postal Service) to the DFEC.

Enacted in 1908, the *Federal Employees' Compensation Act (FECA)* is administered by the OWCP and provides workers' compensation coverage to all federal and postal workers throughout the world for employment-related injuries and occupational diseases. Benefits include wage replacement, payment for medical care, and, where necessary, medical and vocational rehabilitation assistance in returning to work. The OWCP's *Division of Federal Employees' Compensation (DFEC)* processes new claims for benefits and manages ongoing cases, pays medical expenses and compensation benefits to injured workers and survivors, and helps injured employees return to work when they are medically able to do so.

Longshore and Harbor Workers' Compensation Program

NOTE: The program is also responsible for more than $2 billion in negotiable securities, cash, and bonds maintained for the payment of benefits in the event an employer or insurance payer goes out of business.

The **Longshore and Harbor Workers' Compensation Program**, administered by the U.S. Department of Labor, provides medical benefits, compensation for lost wages, and rehabilitation services to longshoremen, harbor workers, and other maritime workers who are injured during the course of employment or suffer from diseases caused or worsened by conditions of employment. The program also covers private-industry workers who are engaged in the extraction of natural resources from the outer continental shelf, employees on American defense bases, and those working under contract with the U.S. government for defense or public-works projects outside the continental United States.

Mine Safety and Health Administration

The U.S. Labor Department's **Mine Safety and Health Administration (MSHA)** helps to reduce deaths, injuries, and illnesses in U.S. mines through a variety of activities

> **NOTE:** U.S. federal mine safety laws were first enacted in 1911 and have since become increasingly stronger, culminating in the 1977 law.

and programs. MSHA develops and enforces safety and health rules that apply to all U.S. mines, helps mine operators who have special compliance problems, and makes available technical, educational, and other types of assistance. MSHA works cooperatively with industry, labor, and other federal and state agencies toward improving safety and health conditions for all miners. MSHA's responsibilities are delineated in the *Federal Mine Safety and Health Act of 1977.*

Occupational Safety and Health Administration

The *Occupational Safety and Health Act of 1970* created the **Occupational Safety and Health Administration (OSHA)** to protect employees against injuries from occupational hazards in the workplace. OSHA and its state partners (of approximately 2,100 inspectors) establish protective standards, enforce those standards, and reach out to employers and employees by providing technical assistance and consultation programs. OSHA has special significance for those employed in health care because employers are required to obtain and retain manufacturers' **Material Safety Data Sheets (MSDS)**, which contain information about chemical and hazardous substances used on site. Training employees in the safe handling of these substances is also required.

> **NOTE:** Comprehensive records of all vaccinations administered and any accidental exposure incidences (e.g., needle sticks) must be retained for 20 years.

Health care workers who might come into contact with human blood and infectious materials must be provided specific training in their handling (including use of Standard Precautions) to avoid contamination. Health care workers who might be exposed to infectious materials must also be offered hepatitis B vaccinations.

Federal Employment Liability Act

The *Federal Employment Liability Act (FELA)* is not a workers' compensation statute; rather, this legislation, signed into law by President Roosevelt in 1908, provides railroad employees with protection from employer negligence and makes railroads engaged in interstate commerce liable for injuries to employees if the railroad was negligent.

Merchant Marine Act (Jones Act)

The **Merchant Marine Act (Jones Act)** is not a workers' compensation statute; however, it provides seamen with the same protection from employer negligence as FELA provides railroad workers.

STATE WORKERS' COMPENSATION PROGRAMS

> **NOTE:** In New York State (NYS), the maximum weekly benefit was $800 in 2013 (ranking fifth lowest in the country). (**www.wcb.ny.gov**)

Workers' compensation insurance provides weekly cash payments and reimburses health care costs for covered employees who develop a work-related illness or sustain an injury while on the job. It also provides payments to qualified dependents of a worker who dies from a compensable illness or injury. Each state establishes a **Workers' Board (Workers' Compensation Commission)**, a state agency responsible for administering workers' compensation laws and handling appeals for denied claims or cases in which a worker feels compensation was too low.

State workers' compensation legislation resulted in the following types of coverage:

- **State Insurance Fund (State Compensation Fund): a quasi-public agency that provides workers' compensation insurance coverage to private and public employers and acts as an agent in state workers' compensation cases involving state employees.**

- *Self-insurance plans:* employers with sufficient capital to qualify can self-insure, which means they are required to set aside a state-mandated percentage of capital funds to cover medical expenses, wage compensation, and other benefits (e.g., death benefit to an employee's dependents) payable to employees who develop on-the-job illnesses and/or incur injuries.
- *Commercial workers' compensation insurance:* employers are permitted to purchase policies from commercial insurance companies that meet state mandates for workers' compensation coverage.
- *Combination programs:* employers in some states are allowed to choose a combination of any of the above to comply with workers' compensation coverage requirements (e.g., companies with a majority of employees who are at high risk for injury participate in the State Insurance Fund, but may purchase commercial insurance coverage for office workers).

NOTE: The *State Insurance Fund* (or *State Compensation Board*) must offer workers' compensation insurance to any employer requesting it, thereby making the fund an insurer of last resort for employers otherwise unable to obtain coverage.

ELIGIBILITY FOR WORKERS' COMPENSATION COVERAGE

To qualify for workers' compensation benefits, the employee must be injured while working within the scope of the job description, be injured while performing a service required by the employer, or develop a disorder that can be directly linked to employment, such as asbestosis or mercury poisoning. In some states, coverage has been awarded for stress-related disorders to workers in certain high-stress occupations, including emergency services personnel, air traffic controllers, and persons involved in hostage situations at work.

The worker does not have to be physically on company property to qualify for workers' compensation. An **on-the-job injury** would include, for example, a medical assistant who is injured while picking up reports for the office at the local hospital or a worker who is making a trip to the bank to deposit checks. These both qualify as job-related assignments. An employee sent to a workshop in another state who falls during the workshop would also be eligible for compensation, but not if she was injured while sightseeing.

NOTE: In a workers' compensation case, no one party is determined to be at fault, and the amount a claimant receives is not decreased by proof of carelessness (nor increased by proof of employer's fault). A worker will lose the right to workers' compensation coverage if the injury resulted solely from intoxication from drugs or alcohol or from the intent to injure himself or someone else.

CLASSIFICATION OF WORKERS' COMPENSATION CASES

The injured employee's health care provider determines the extent of disability; cash benefits are directly related to established disability classifications. Federal law mandates the following classifications of workers' compensation cases:

- **Medical treatment**
- **Temporary disability**
- **Permanent disability**
- **Vocational rehabilitation**
- **Survivor benefits**

NOTE: The term *disability* associated with the following classifications does not refer to *disability insurance* (or *benefits*), which are temporary cash benefits paid to an eligible wage earner when he or she is disabled by an off-the-job injury or illness. This concept was discussed in Chapter 2.

Medical Treatment

Medical treatment claims are the easiest to process because they are filed for minor illnesses or injuries that are treated by a health care provider. In these cases, the employee continues to work or returns to work within a few days.

Temporary Disability

Temporary disability claims cover health care treatment for illness and injuries, as well as payment for lost wages. *Temporary disability* is subclassified as:

- ***Temporary total disability*, in which the employee's wage-earning capacity is totally lost, but only on a temporary basis.**
- ***Temporary partial disability*, in which the employee's wage-earning capacity is partially lost, but only on a temporary basis.**

Permanent Disability

Permanent disability refers to an ill or injured employee's diminished capacity to return to work. In this case, a provider has determined that although the employee's illness or injury has stabilized, he or she has been permanently impaired. The employee is therefore unable to return to the position held prior to the illness or injury. Subclassifications include:

- ***Permanent total disability*, in which the employee's wage-earning capacity is permanently and totally lost. (There is no limit on the number of weeks payable, and an employee may continue to engage in business or employment if his or her wages, combined with the weekly benefit, do not exceed the maximums established by law.)**
- ***Permanent partial disability*, in which part of the employee's wage-earning capacity has been permanently lost. Benefits are payable as long as the partial disability exists, except in the following circumstances:**
  - ***Schedule loss of use*, in which the employee has a loss of eyesight, hearing, or a part of the body or its use. Compensation is limited to a certain number of weeks, according to a schedule set by law.**
  - ***Disfigurement*, in which serious and permanent disfigurement to the face, head, or neck may entitle the employee to compensation (up to a maximum benefit, depending on the date of the accident).**

NOTE: Providers who treat established patients for work-related disorders should create a compensation file (separate from the established medical record). Caution must be used to ensure that treatment data, progress notes, diagnostic test reports, and other pertinent chart entries pertaining to non-work-related disorders or injuries are not combined with notes and reports covering work-related disorders.

Vocational Rehabilitation

Vocational rehabilitation claims cover expenses for vocational retraining for both temporary and permanent disability cases. Vocational rehabilitation retrains an ill or injured employee so he or she can return to the workforce, although the employee may be incapable of resuming the position held prior to the illness or injury.

Survivor Benefits

Survivor benefits claims provide death benefits to eligible dependents. These benefit amounts are calculated according to the employee's earning capacity at the time of the illness or injury.

SPECIAL HANDLING OF WORKERS' COMPENSATION CASES

Providers are required to accept the workers' compensation-allowable fee as payment in full for covered services rendered on cases involving on-the-job illnesses and injuries. An adjustment to the patient's account must be made if the amount charged for the treatment is greater than the approved reimbursement for the treatment.

State Compensation Boards/Commissions and insurance payers are entitled by law to review only history and treatment data pertaining to a patient's on-the-job injury.

EXAMPLE: Patient A has been treated for diabetes by his doctor for the past two years. The patient was then treated by the same doctor for a broken ankle after falling at his place of employment. The patient was told to return in five days for a recheck. Three days after the original treatment for the broken ankle, the patient was seen in the office for "strep throat." The doctor also checks on the ankle. The treatment for the throat condition should be reported in the patient's medical record; the progress report on the broken ankle will be recorded in the workers' compensation record.

Out-of-State Treatment

Billing regulations vary from state to state. Contact the workers' compensation board (or workers' compensation commission) in the state where the injury occurred for billing instructions if an injured worker presents for treatment of a work-related injury that occurred in another state.

WORKERS' COMPENSATION AND MANAGED CARE

Both employees and employers have benefited from incorporating managed care into workers' compensation programs, thereby improving the quality of medical benefits and services provided. For employers, managed care protects human resources and reduces workers' compensation costs. For employees, the benefits include:

- More comprehensive coverage, because states continue to eliminate exemptions under current law (e.g., small businesses and temporary workers)
- Expanded health care coverage if the injury or illness is work-related and the treatment/service is reasonable and necessary
- Provision of appropriate medical treatment to facilitate healing and promote prompt return to work (lack of treatment can result in increased permanent disability, greater wage replacement benefits, and higher total claim costs)
- Internal grievance and dispute resolution procedures involving the care and treatment provided by the workers' compensation program, along with an appeals process to the state workers' compensation agency
- Coordination of medical treatment and services with other services designed to get workers back to work (research by the Florida Division of Workers' Compensation suggests that managed care may reduce the time it takes an injured worker to return to work)
- No out-of-pocket costs for coverage or provision of medical services and treatment; cost/time limits do not apply when an injury or illness occurs

NOTE: There is no patient signature line on this form. The law says that when a patient requests treatment for a work-related injury or disorder, the patient has given consent for the filing of compensation claims and reports. The required state forms may be obtained from the state board/commission. Necessary forms for filing federal forms may be obtained from the personnel office where the employee works or from the workers' compensation Federal District Office listed under the United States Government listings in the phone book.

FIRST REPORT OF INJURY FORM

First Report of Injury forms are completed by the provider (e.g., physician) when the patient first seeks treatment for a work-related illness or injury (Figure 17-1). This report must be completed in quadruplicate with one copy distributed to each of the following parties:

- State Workers' Compensation Board/Commission
- Employer-designated compensation payer

INSTRUCTIONS

1. Enter answers to ALL questions and submit original to the Workers' Compensation Board within 72 hours after first treatment.
2. BE SURE to forward to the Workers' Compensation Board PROGRESS REPORTS and FINAL REPORT upon discharge of patient.

WORKERS' COMPENSATION BOARD
100 Main St, Anywhere, NY 12345-1234
PHYSICIAN'S REPORT

This is First Report ☐ Progress Report ☐ Final Report ☐

DO NOT WRITE IN THIS SPACE

WCC CLAIM #

EMPLOYER'S REPORT Yes ☐ No ☐

EVERY QUESTION MUST BE ANSWERED AND FORM SIGNED

1. Name of Injured Person: | Soc. Sec. No. | D.O.B. | Gender M ☐ F ☐
2. Address: (No. and Street) | (City or Town) | (State) | (Zip Code)
3. Name and Address of Employer:
4. Date of Accident or Onset of Disease: | Hour: A.M. ☐ P.M. ☐ | 5. Date Disability Began:
6. Patient's Description of Accident or Cause of Disease:
7. Medical Description of Injury or Disease:
8. Will Injury result in:
   (a) Permanent defect? Yes ☐ No ☐ If so, what? (b) Disfigurement? Yes ☐ No ☐
9. Causes, other than injury, contributing to patient's condition:
10. Is patient suffering from any disease of the heart, lungs, brain, kidneys, blood, vascular system or any other disabling condition not due to this accident? Explain.
11. Is there any history or evidence present of previous accident or disease? Explain.
12. Has normal recovery been delayed for any reason? Explain.
13. Date of first treatment: | Who scheduled your services?
14. Describe treatment provided by you:
15. Were X-rays taken? Yes ☐ No ☐ | By whom? — (Name and Address of Facility) | Date:
16. X-ray diagnosis:
17. Was patient treated by anyone else? Yes ☐ No ☐ | By whom? — (Name and Address of Provider) | Date:
18. Was patient hospitalized? Yes ☐ No ☐ | Name and Address of Hospital | Date of Admission: Date of Discharge:
19. Is further treatment needed? Yes ☐ No ☐ | For how long? | 20. Patient was ☐ will be ☐ able to resume regular work on: Patient was ☐ will be ☐ able to resume light work on:
21. If death ensued give date: | 22. Remarks:
23. I am a qualified specialist in: | I am a duly licensed Physician in the State of: | I graduated from Medical School: (Name) | Year:

Date of this report: | (Signed)

(This report must be signed by Physician.)

Address: | Phone:

FIGURE 17-1 Sample First Report of Injury form completed by provider.

- **Ill or injured party's employer**
- **Patient's work-related injury chart**

The time limit for filing this form varies from 24 hours to 14 calendar days, depending on state requirements. It is best to make a habit of completing the form immediately, thus ensuring that the form is filed on time and not overlooked.

The First Report of Injury form requires some information that is not automatically furnished by a patient. When the patient tells you this was a work-related injury, it will be necessary to obtain the following information:

- **Name and address of the present employer**
- **Name of the immediate supervisor**
- **Date and time of the accident or onset of the disease**
- **Site where the injury occurred**
- **Patient's description of the onset of the disorder; if the patient is claiming injury due to exposure to hazardous chemicals or compounds, these should be included in the patient's description of the problem**

In addition, the patient's employer must be contacted to obtain the name and mailing address of the compensation payer. Ask for a faxed confirmation from the employer of the worker with the on-the-job injury. If the employer disputes the legitimacy of the claim, you should still file the First Report of Injury form. The employer must also file an injury report with the compensation commission/board.

Completing the First Report of Injury Form

Item 1

NOTE: The *physician* is responsible for completing this form.

Enter the employee's full name as shown on personnel files (last, first, middle). Enter the employee's social security number and date of birth (MMDDYYYY). Indicate the employee's gender by entering an X in the appropriate box.

Item 2

NOTE: The date of the claimed accident must be specific. For example, if an employee was lifting heavy boxes on Tuesday (11/6) and called in sick on Thursday (11/8) because of a sore back, the date that is entered in Item 4 is 11/6.

Enter the employee's complete home address. This is very important, as workers' compensation disability payments, when due, will be mailed to this address. An incorrect address will delay receipt.

Item 3

Enter the complete name and address of the employer.

Item 4

Enter the date (MMDDYYYY) on which the accident or onset of disease occurred. Enter the time of the day at which the accident or onset of disease occurred, and check the appropriate box to indicate a.m. or p.m.

Item 5

Enter the last date the employee worked after having the accident. If no time was lost from work, enter STILL WORKING.

Item 6

Enter the employee's word-for-word description of the accident. A complete description of the accident is required. Attach an additional page if space provided on the First Report of Injury form is insufficient.

Item 7

Enter the description of the injury or disease. Explain the physical injuries or disease (e.g., laceration, fracture, or contusion). Enter the anatomic part(s) of the body that required medical attention. Be specific, and indicate the location of the injured part when necessary (e.g., left middle finger, right thumb, left shoulder). Enter the location and address where the accident occurred.

Items 8 through 12

Enter as appropriate.

Item 13

Enter the date (MMDDYYYY) the patient initially received services and/or treatment.

Items 14 through 19

Enter as appropriate.

Item 20

Enter an X in the appropriate box.

Item 21

If the employee died as a result of the injury sustained, enter the date of death (MMDDYYYY). Notify the appropriate state agency immediately upon the work-related death of an employee.

Item 22

Enter additional information of value that was not previously documented on the form.

Item 23

Enter the physician's specialty (e.g., internal medicine), the state in which the physician is licensed, and the name of the medical school from which the physician graduated, along with the year of graduation (YYYY).

Be sure the physician dates (MMDDYYYY) and personally signs the report. Enter the physician's office address and telephone number.

PROGRESS REPORTS

A detailed narrative progress/supplemental report (Figure 17-2) should be filed to document any significant change in the worker's medical or disability status. This report should document:

- **Patient's name and compensation file/case number**
- **Treatment and progress report**
- **Work status at the present time**
- **Statement of further treatment needed**
- **Estimate of the future status with regard to work or permanent loss or disability**
- **Copies of substantiating x-ray, laboratory, or consultation reports**

The physician should *personally sign* the original and all photocopies of these reports. No patient signature is required for the release of any report to the

Employee Name (First, Middle, Last)

Workers' Compensation #: ______

Social Security Number: ______

Date of Injury: ______

Disability Date: ______

Name of Employer:

Type of Report ▯ Initial ▯ Supplement ▯ Final ▯ Reopened

Treatment Now Being Administered:

Diagnosis:

Patient is under my care.	▯ Yes	▯ No	**If no, care was transferred to:** ______			
Patient is totally disabled.	▯ Yes	▯ No	**Patient is partially disabled.**		▯ Yes	▯ No
Patient is working.	▯ Yes	▯ No	**Date patient returned to work:** ______			
Patient may be able to return to work.	▯ Yes	▯ No	**Date patient may be able to return to work:** ______			

Work Limitations:

▯ None: ______

▯ Cannot Work: ______

▯ Light Work: ______

▯ Weightlifting Limit: ______

Present Condition:

▯ Improved: ______

▯ Unchanged: ______

▯ Worsening: ______

Anticipated Date of Maximum Medical Improvement or Discharge:

▯ Weeks: ______

▯ Months: ______

▯ Specific Date: ______

▯ Undetermined: ______

Signature of Provider: ______ **EIN:** ______

FIGURE 17-2 Sample workers' compensation narrative progress (supplemental) report.

compensation payer or commission/board. These reports should be generated in duplicate because:

- **One copy is sent to the compensation payer.**
- **One copy is retained in the patient's file.**

The physician is required to answer all requests for further information sent from the compensation payer or the commission/board. Acknowledgment of receipt of a claim will be made by the payer or the commission/board. This acknowledgment will contain the file or case number assigned to the claim. This file/claim number should be written on all further correspondence forwarded to the employer, the payer, the commission/board, and, of course, on all billings sent to the payer.

APPEALS AND ADJUDICATION

When a workers' compensation claim is denied, the employee (or eligible dependents) can appeal the denial to the state Workers' Compensation Board (or Workers' Compensation Commission) and undergo a process called **adjudication**, a judicial dispute resolution process in which an appeals board makes a final determination. All applications for appeal should include supporting medical documentation of the claim when there is a dispute about medical issues. During the appeal process, involved parties will undergo a *deposition*, a legal proceeding during which a party answers questions under oath (but not in open court). If the appeal is successful, the board (commission) will notify the health care provider to submit a claim to the employer's compensation payer and refund payments made by the patient to cover medical expenses for the on-the-job illness or injury.

NOTE: Adjudication is different from **arbitration**, a dispute resolution process in which a final determination is made by an impartial person who may not have judicial powers.

FRAUD AND ABUSE

Workers' compensation fraud occurs when individuals knowingly obtain benefits for which they are not eligible (e.g., provider submits a false claim for workers' compensation coverage of patient treatment). *Workers' compensation abuse* occurs when the workers' compensation system is used in a way contrary to its intended purpose or to the law; fraud is a form of abuse. Penalties include fines and imprisonment, and most states offer a toll-free hotline to report fraud and abuse. Categories of fraud include:

- ***Employer fraud:*** **committed by an employer who misrepresents payroll amounts or employee classification or who attempts to avoid higher insurance risk by transferring employees to a new business entity that is rated in a lower-risk category**
- ***Employee fraud:*** **committed when an employee lies or provides a false statement, intentionally fails to report income from work, or willfully misrepresents a physical condition to obtain benefits from the state compensation fund**
- ***Provider fraud:*** **committed by health care providers and attorneys who inflate their bills for services or bill for treatment of non-work-related illnesses and/or injuries**

BILLING NOTES

The following is a summary of the general nationwide billing information for workers' compensation claims. Local requirements will vary by state. Be sure to follow all the regulations established by your state commission.

Eligibility

For-profit company/corporation or state employees with work-related injuries are eligible for workers' compensation benefits. Coal miners, longshoremen, harbor workers, and all federal employees except those in the uniformed services with a work-related injury are eligible for federal compensation plans.

Identification Card

Some workers' compensation insurance plans issue identification cards, which are provided to employees who are eligible to receive workers' compensation coverage (because they are being treated for a work-related condition or injury).

Brown Sweeney Health Care Plan

The Workers' Compensation Experts

EMPLOYER NAME: Green Consulting, Inc.
EMPLOYER POLICY # 12-3456789

To report a workers' compensation injury, call (800) 555-1234

Payment processed in accordance with state's workers' compensation treatment parameters and reimbursement rules for submitted workers' compensation claims. Call Brown-Sweeney Health Care Plan to obtain prior authorization for all surgeries, medical imaging, durable medical equipment, and/or any treatment that departs from treatment parameter rules.

Submit all treatment authorization requests and completed CMS-1500 claims to: Brown-Sweeney Health Care Plan
P.O. Box 45392, Clay, NY 12041
(800) 555-1234

Fiscal Agent

State Plans

Any one of the following can be designated the fiscal agent by state law and the corporation involved.

1. State insurance or compensation fund (do not confuse this with the state's Workers' Compensation Board or Workers' Compensation Commission)
2. A third-party payer (e.g., commercial insurance company)
3. The employer's special company capital funds set aside for compensation cases

Federal Plans

Information may be obtained from the human resources officer at the agency where the patient is employed.

Underwriter

The federal or state government is the plan's underwriter, depending on the case.

Forms Used

The forms used include:

- **First Report of Injury form**
- **Narrative progress/supplemental reports**
- **CMS-1500 claim**

Filing Deadline

The filing deadline for the first injury report is determined by state law. The deadline for filing of the claim for services performed will vary from payer to payer.

Deductible

There is no deductible for workers' compensation claims.

Copayment

There is no copayment for workers' compensation cases.

Premium

The employer pays all premiums.

Approved Fee Basis

NOTE: For example, if CPT code 99204 is assigned a fee of $26.00 and RVS of 2.4, the reimbursement is $62.40. ($26 × 2.4 = $62.40)

The state compensation board or commission establishes a schedule of approved fees. Many states use a relative value study (RVS) unit-value scale; others have implemented managed care. Contact the state commission/board for information.

Accept Assignment

All providers must accept the compensation payment as payment in full.

Special Handling

Contact the employer immediately when an injured worker presents for the first visit without a written or personal referral from the employer. Contact the workers' compensation board (workers' compensation commission) of the state where the work-related injury occurred if treatment is sought in another state.

No patient signature is needed on the First Report of Injury form, Progress Report, or billing forms. If an established patient seeks treatment of a work-related injury, a separate compensation chart and ledger/account must be established for the patient.

The First Report of Injury form requires a statement from the patient describing the circumstances and events surrounding the injury. Progress reports should be filed when there is any significant change in the patient's condition and when the patient is discharged. Prior authorization may be necessary for nonemergency treatment.

Private Payer Mistakenly Billed

When a patient fails to inform a provider that an illness or injury is work-related, the patient's primary payer is billed for services or procedures rendered. If the patient subsequently requests that the workers' compensation payer be billed instead, the claim will probably be denied. The patient must then initiate the appeal process (and the provider will be responsible for submitting appropriate documentation to support the workers' compensation claim). Any reimbursement paid by the primary payer must be returned.

Before working with workers' compensation claims, complete the Review located at the end of this chapter.

CLAIMS INSTRUCTIONS

Refer to Figures 17-3 and 17-4 as you study the claims instructions in Table 17-1. Additional workers' compensation cases are found in Appendices I and II.

TABLE 17-1 CMS-1500 claims completion instructions for workers' compensation claims

NOTE: Refer to Chapter 11 for clarification of claims completion (e.g., entering names, mailing addresses, ICD-10-CM codes, diagnosis pointer letters, NPI, and so on).

BLOCK	INSTRUCTIONS
1	Enter an X in the *FECA* box if the claim is submitted to the Division of Federal Employees' Compensation (DFEC). Otherwise, enter an X in the OTHER box. **NOTE:** FECA is the abbreviation for the Federal Employee Compensation Act.
1a	Enter the patient's social security number. *Do not enter hyphens or spaces in the number.*
2	Enter the patient's last name, first name, and middle initial (separated by commas) (e.g., DOE, JANE, M).
3	Enter the patient's birth date as MM DD YYYY (with spaces). Enter an X in the appropriate box to indicate the patient's gender. If the patient's gender is unknown, leave blank.
4	Enter the name of the patient's employer.
5	Enter the patient's mailing address and telephone number. Enter the street address on line 1, enter the city and state on line 2, and enter the five- or nine-digit zip code and phone number on line 3.
6	Enter an X in the *Other* box.
7	Enter the employer's mailing address and telephone number. Enter the street address on line 1, enter the city and state on line 2, and enter the five- or nine-digit zip code and phone number on line 3.
8	Leave blank.
9, 9a–9d	Leave blank.

(continues)

TABLE 17-1 (continued)

BLOCK	INSTRUCTIONS
10a	Enter an X in the YES box.
10b–c	Enter an X in the appropriate boxes to indicate whether the patient's condition is related to an automobile accident and/or another accident. If an X is entered in the YES box for auto accident, enter the two-character state abbreviation of the patient's residence.
10d	Leave blank.
11	Enter the nine-digit FECA number. **NOTE:** If a patient claims work-related condition(s) under the Federal Employees Compensation Act (FECA), the nine-digit FECA identifier assigned to the claim is entered.
11a	Leave blank.
11b	Enter the claim number assigned by the workers' compensation third-party payer.
11c	Enter the name of the workers' compensation payer.
11d	Leave blank.
12–13	Leave blank.
14	Enter the date as MM DD YYYY (with spaces) to indicate when the patient first experienced signs or symptoms of the illness or injury. Enter the qualifier 431 (onset of current symptoms/illness or injury) to identify which date is being reported. *If the date is not documented in the patient's record, but the history indicates an appropriate date (e.g., three weeks ago), simply count back to the approximate date and enter it on the claim.* **EXAMPLE:** For encounter date 06/08/YYYY, when the record documents that the patient was "injured on the job three months ago," enter 03 08 YYYY in Block 14.
15	Enter the date as MM DD YYYY (with spaces) to indicate that a prior episode of the same or similar illness began, *if documented in the patient's record*. Otherwise, leave blank.
16	Enter dates as MM DD YYYY (with spaces) to indicate the period of time the patient was unable to work in his current occupation, *if documented in the patient's record.* Otherwise, leave blank.
17	If applicable, enter the first name, middle initial (if known), last name, and credentials of the professional who referred, ordered, or supervised health care service(s) or supply(ies) reported on the claim. *Do not enter any punctuation.* In front of the name, enter the applicable qualifier to identify which provider is being reported, as follows: DN (referring provider), DK (ordering provider), or DQ (supervising provider). Otherwise, leave blank.
17a	Leave blank.
17b	Enter the 10-digit national provider identifier (NPI) of the professional in Block 17. Otherwise, leave blank.
18	Enter the admission date and discharge date as MM DD YYYY (with spaces) if the patient received inpatient services (e.g., hospital, skilled nursing facility). *If the patient has not been discharged at the time the claim is completed, leave the discharge date blank.* Otherwise, leave blank.
19	Leave blank.

(continues)

TABLE 17-1 (continued)

BLOCK	INSTRUCTIONS
20	Enter an X in the NO box if all laboratory procedures reported on the claim were performed in the provider's office. Enter an X in the YES box if laboratory procedures reported on the claim were performed by an outside laboratory and billed to the provider. Enter the total amount charged by the outside laboratory in $ CHARGES, and enter the outside laboratory's name, mailing address, and NPI in Block 32. (Charges are entered *without* punctuation. For example, $1,100.00 is entered as 110000 below $ CHARGES.)
21	Enter the ICD-10-CM code for up to 12 diagnoses or conditions treated or medically managed during the encounter. Lines A through L in Block 21 will relate to CPT/HCPCS service/procedure codes reported in Block 24E. In the *ICD Ind* (ICD indicator) box, enter 0 for ICD-10-CM (or 9 for ICD-9-CM).
22	Leave blank. This is reserved for resubmitted claims.
23	Enter any preauthorization number assigned by the workers' compensation payer. *Do not enter hyphens or spaces in the number.* Otherwise, leave blank.
24A	Enter the date the procedure or service was performed in the FROM column as MM DD YY (with spaces). Enter a date in the TO column *if the procedure or service was performed on consecutive days during a range of dates. Then, enter the number of consecutive days in Block 24G.* **NOTE:** The shaded area in each line is used to enter supplemental information to support reported services *if instructed by the payer to enter such information.* Data entry in Block 24 is limited to reporting six services. *Do not use the shaded lines to report additional services.* If additional services were provided, generate new CMS-1500 claim(s) to report the additional services.
24B	Enter the appropriate two-digit place-of-service (POS) code to identify the location where the reported procedure or service was performed. (Refer to Appendix II for POS codes.)
24C	Leave blank.
24D	Enter the CPT or HCPCS level II code and applicable required modifier(s) for procedures or services performed. *Separate the CPT/HCPCS code and first modifier with one space. Separate additional modifiers with one space each. Up to four modifiers can be entered.*
24E	Enter the diagnosis pointer letter from Block 21 that relates to the procedure/service performed on the date of service. **NOTE:** When completing CMS-1500 claims for case studies in this textbook, its Workbook, and SimClaim™ software, enter just one diagnosis pointer letter on each line of Block 24E.
24F	Enter the fee charged for each reported procedure or service. When multiple procedures or services are reported on the same line, enter the total fee charged. *Do not enter commas, periods, or dollar signs. Do not enter negative amounts. Enter 00 in the cents area if the amount is a whole number.*
24G	Enter the number of days or units for procedures or services reported in Block 24D. *If just one procedure or service was reported in Block 24D, enter a 1 in Block 24G.*
24H–I	Leave blank.

(continues)

TABLE 17-1 (continued)

BLOCK	INSTRUCTIONS
24J	Enter the 10-digit NPI for the: ● Provider who performed the service *if the provider is a member of a group practice* (Leave blank if the provider is a solo practitioner.) ● Supervising provider *if the service was provided incident-to the service of a physician or nonphysician practitioner* **and** *the physician or practitioner who ordered the service did not supervise the provider* (Leave blank if the incident-to service was performed under the supervision of the physician or nonphysician practitioner.) ● DMEPOS supplier or outside laboratory *if the physician submits the claim for services provided by the DMEPOS supplier or outside laboratory* (Leave blank if the DMEPOS supplier or outside laboratory submits the claim.) Otherwise, leave blank.
25	Enter the provider's social security number (SSN) or employer identification number (EIN). *Do not enter hyphens or spaces in the number.* Enter an X in the appropriate box to indicate which number is reported.
26	Enter the patient's account number as assigned by the provider.
27	Enter an X in the YES box to indicate that the provider agrees to accept assignment. Otherwise, enter an X in the NO box.
28	Enter the total charges for services and/or procedures reported in Block 24. **NOTE:** If multiple claims are submitted for one patient because more than six procedures or services were reported, be sure the total charge reported on each claim accurately represents the total of the items on each submitted claim.
29-30	Leave blank.
31	Enter the provider's name and credential (e.g., MARY SMITH MD) and the date the claim was completed as MMDDYYYY (without spaces). *Do not enter any punctuation.*
32	Enter the name and address where procedures or services were provided *if at a location other than the provider's office or the patient's home, such as a hospital, outside laboratory facility, skilled nursing facility, or DMEPOS supplier.* Otherwise, leave blank. Enter the name on line 1, the address on line 2, and the city, state, and five- or nine-digit zip code on line 3. *For a nine-digit zip code, enter the hyphen.* **NOTE:** If Block 18 contains dates of service for inpatient care and/or Block 20 contains an X in the YES box, enter the name and address of the facility that provided services.
32a	Enter the 10-digit NPI of the facility entered in Block 32.
32b	Leave blank.
33	Enter the provider's *billing* name, address, and telephone number. Enter the phone number in the area next to the block title. *Do not enter parentheses for the area code.* Enter the name on line 1, enter the address on line 2, and enter the city, state, and five- or nine-digit zip code on line 3. *For a nine-digit zip code, enter the hyphen.*
33a	Enter the 10-digit NPI of the *billing* provider (e.g., solo practitioner) or group practice (e.g., clinic).
33b	Leave blank.

Courtesy of the Centers for Medicare & Medicaid Services, www.cms.gov

ERIN A. HELPER, M.D.
101 Medic Drive, Anywhere, NY 12345
(101) 111-1234 (Office) • (101) 111-9292 (Fax)
EIN: 11-1234523
NPI: 1234567890

Case Study

PATIENT INFORMATION:

Name:	Public, John Q.
Address:	10A Senate Avenue
City:	Anywhere
State:	NY
Zip Code:	12345-1234
Telephone:	(101) 201-7891
Gender:	Male
Date of Birth:	10-10-1959
Occupation:	Technician
Employer:	BIO Laboratory
Spouse's Employer:	

INSURANCE INFORMATION:

Patient Number:	17-1
Place of Service:	Office
WC Insurance Plan:	Division of Federal Employees' Compensation (DFEC)
WC Claim #:	BL3638B
FECA #:	456123789
WC Policyholder:	BIO Laboratory
Address:	Bio Drive, Anywhere, NY 12345
Relationship to Patient:	Employer

Patient Status ☒ Married ☐ Divorced ☐ Single ☐ Student

DIAGNOSIS INFORMATION

Diagnosis	Code	Diagnosis	Code
1. Whiplash (subsequent encounter)	S13.4xxD	5.	
2. Motor vehicle accident (subsequent encounter)	V89.9xxD	6.	
3. Place of occurrence (public highway)	Y92.410	7.	
4.		8.	

PROCEDURE INFORMATION

Description of Procedure or Service	Date	Code	Charge
1. Established patient office visit, level III	01-03-YYYY	99213	40.00
2.			
3.			
4.			
5.			

SPECIAL NOTES: Originally injured driving delivery car while working 12/29/YYYY. Return to work 01/05/YYYY. NOTE: Submit claim to workers' compensation payer.

FIGURE 17-3 John Q. Public case study.

NOTE: ICD-10-CM categories S13 and V89 in the tabular list contain notes, which state that each code requires assignment of a seventh character. The "x" placeholder characters are included in the code so that the seventh character can be entered.

HEALTH INSURANCE CLAIM FORM

APPROVED BY NATIONAL UNIFORM CLAIM COMMITTEE (NUCC) 02/12

PICA

1. MEDICARE (Medicare#) / MEDICAID (Medicaid#) / TRICARE (ID#/DoD#) / CHAMPVA (Member ID#) / GROUP HEALTH PLAN (ID#) / FECA BLK LUNG (ID#) [X] / OTHER (ID#)

1a. INSURED'S I.D. NUMBER (For Program in Item 1): 252459568

2. PATIENT'S NAME (Last Name, First Name, Middle Initial): PUBLIC, JOHN, Q

3. PATIENT'S BIRTH DATE (MM DD YY): 10 10 1959 SEX: M [X] F [ ]

4. INSURED'S NAME (Last Name, First Name, Middle Initial): BIO LABORATORY

5. PATIENT'S ADDRESS (No., Street): 10A SENATE AVENUE

CITY: ANYWHERE STATE: NY

ZIP CODE: 12345-1234 TELEPHONE (Include Area Code): (101) 2017891

6. PATIENT RELATIONSHIP TO INSURED: Self [ ] Spouse [ ] Child [ ] Other [X]

7. INSURED'S ADDRESS (No., Street): BIO DRIVE

CITY: ANYWHERE STATE: NY

ZIP CODE: 12345 TELEPHONE (Include Area Code): (101) 5559876

8. RESERVED FOR NUCC USE

9. OTHER INSURED'S NAME (Last Name, First Name, Middle Initial)

a. OTHER INSURED'S POLICY OR GROUP NUMBER

b. RESERVED FOR NUCC USE

c. RESERVED FOR NUCC USE

d. INSURANCE PLAN NAME OR PROGRAM NAME

10. IS PATIENT'S CONDITION RELATED TO:

a. EMPLOYMENT? (Current or Previous) [X] YES [ ] NO

b. AUTO ACCIDENT? [X] YES [ ] NO PLACE (State) NY

c. OTHER ACCIDENT? [ ] YES [X] NO

10d. CLAIM CODES (Designated by NUCC)

11. INSURED'S POLICY GROUP OR FECA NUMBER: 456123789

a. INSURED'S DATE OF BIRTH (MM DD YY) SEX M [ ] F [ ]

b. OTHER CLAIM ID (Designated by NUCC): BL3638B

c. INSURANCE PLAN NAME OR PROGRAM NAME: HIGH RISK INC

d. IS THERE ANOTHER HEALTH BENEFIT PLAN? [ ] YES [ ] NO *If yes, complete items 9, 9a, and 9d.*

READ BACK OF FORM BEFORE COMPLETING & SIGNING THIS FORM.

12. PATIENT'S OR AUTHORIZED PERSON'S SIGNATURE I authorize the release of any medical or other information necessary to process this claim. I also request payment of government benefits either to myself or to the party who accepts assignment below.

SIGNED DATE

13. INSURED'S OR AUTHORIZED PERSON'S SIGNATURE I authorize payment of medical benefits to the undersigned physician or supplier for services described below.

SIGNED

14. DATE OF CURRENT ILLNESS, INJURY, or PREGNANCY (LMP) (MM DD YY): 12 29 YYYY QUAL. 431

15. OTHER DATE QUAL. MM DD YY

16. DATES PATIENT UNABLE TO WORK IN CURRENT OCCUPATION FROM 12 29 YYYY TO 01 03 YYYY

17. NAME OF REFERRING PROVIDER OR OTHER SOURCE 17a. 17b. NPI

18. HOSPITALIZATION DATES RELATED TO CURRENT SERVICES FROM TO

19. ADDITIONAL CLAIM INFORMATION (Designated by NUCC)

20. OUTSIDE LAB? [ ] YES [X] NO $ CHARGES

21. DIAGNOSIS OR NATURE OF ILLNESS OR INJURY Relate A-L to service line below (24E) ICD Ind. 0

A. S13.4XXD B. V89.9XXD C. Y92.410 D.
E. F. G. H.
I. J. K. L.

22. RESUBMISSION CODE ORIGINAL REF. NO.

23. PRIOR AUTHORIZATION NUMBER

	24. A. DATE(S) OF SERVICE From MM DD YY	To MM DD YY	B. PLACE OF SERVICE	C. EMG	D. PROCEDURES, SERVICES, OR SUPPLIES CPT/HCPCS	MODIFIER	E. DIAGNOSIS POINTER	F. $ CHARGES	G. DAYS OR UNITS	H. EPSDT Family Plan	I. ID. QUAL.	J. RENDERING PROVIDER ID. #
1	01 03 YY		11		99213		A	40 00	1		NPI	
2											NPI	
3											NPI	
4											NPI	
5											NPI	
6											NPI	

25. FEDERAL TAX I.D. NUMBER: 111234523 SSN [ ] EIN [X]

26. PATIENT'S ACCOUNT NO.: 17-1

27. ACCEPT ASSIGNMENT? (For govt. claims, see back) [X] YES [ ] NO

28. TOTAL CHARGE: $ 40 00

29. AMOUNT PAID: $

30. Rsvd for NUCC Use

31. SIGNATURE OF PHYSICIAN OR SUPPLIER INCLUDING DEGREES OR CREDENTIALS (I certify that the statements on the reverse apply to this bill and are made a part thereof.)

ERIN A HELPER MD MMDDYYYY
SIGNED DATE

32. SERVICE FACILITY LOCATION INFORMATION
a. NPI b.

33. BILLING PROVIDER INFO & PH # (101) 1111234
ERIN A HELPER MD
101 MEDIC DRIVE
ANYWHERE NY 12345
a. 1234567890 b.

NUCC Instruction Manual available at: www.nucc.org *PLEASE PRINT OR TYPE*

CARRIER — PATIENT AND INSURED INFORMATION — PHYSICIAN OR SUPPLIER INFORMATION

FIGURE 17-4 Completed workers' compensation as primary CMS-1500 claim for John Q. Public case study.

EXERCISE 17-1

Completion of Workers' Compensation as Primary CMS-1500 Claim

1. Obtain a blank claim by making a copy of the CMS-1500 claim form in Appendix III.
2. Review the Mary S. Patient case study (Figure 17-5).
3. Select the information needed from the case study, and enter the required information on the claim using optical scanning guidelines.
4. Review the claim to be sure all required blocks are properly completed. Compare it to the completed claim in Figure 17-6.

ERIN A. HELPER, M.D.
101 Medic Drive, Anywhere, NY 12345
(101) 111-1234 (Office) • (101) 111-9292 (Fax)
EIN: 11-1234523
NPI: 1234567890

Case Study

PATIENT INFORMATION:		**INSURANCE INFORMATION:**	
Name:	Patient, Mary S.	**Patient Number:**	17-2
Address:	91 Home Street	**Place of Service:**	Office
City:	Nowhere	**Primary Insurance Plan:**	
State:	NY	**Primary Insurance Plan ID #:**	
Zip Code:	12367-1234	**Policy #:**	
Telephone:	(101) 201-8989	**Primary Policyholder:**	
Gender:	Female	**Policyholder Date of Birth:**	
Date of Birth:	10-10-1959	**Relationship to Patient:**	
Occupation:	Clerk	**Workers' Compensation Plan:**	State Insurance Fund
Employer:	A1 Grocery	**Workers' Compensation Claim #:**	MSP9761
Address:	1 Main St, Nowhere, NY 12367	**Patient's SSN:**	467980123
Telephone:	(101) 555-4561		

Patient Status ☒ Married ☐ Divorced ☐ Single ☐ Student

DIAGNOSIS INFORMATION

Diagnosis	**Code**	**Diagnosis**	**Code**
1. Muscle spasms, trapezius	M62.830	5.	
2. Cervical osteoarthritis	M47.812	6.	
3. Accident at work	Y92.69	7.	
4.		8.	

PROCEDURE INFORMATION

Description of Procedure or Service	**Date**	**Code**	**Charge**
1. Office visit, established patient, level II	01-27-YYYY	99212	45.00
2. Trigger point injections (upper and medial trapezius muscles)	01-27-YYYY	20552	75.00
3.			
4.			
5.			

SPECIAL NOTES: Injured at work 01-20-YYYY. Return to work 01-22-YYYY.

FIGURE 17-5 Mary S. Patient case study.

HEALTH INSURANCE CLAIM FORM

APPROVED BY NATIONAL UNIFORM CLAIM COMMITTEE (NUCC) 02/12

PICA | PICA

CARRIER

1. MEDICARE (Medicare#) | MEDICAID (Medicaid#) | TRICARE (ID#/DoD#) | CHAMPVA (Member ID#) | GROUP HEALTH PLAN (ID#) | FECA BLK LUNG (ID#) | OTHER (ID#) [X]

1a. INSURED'S I.D. NUMBER (For Program in Item 1): 467980123

2. PATIENT'S NAME (Last Name, First Name, Middle Initial): PATIENT, MARY, S

3. PATIENT'S BIRTH DATE MM DD YY: 10 10 1959 SEX M [ ] F [X]

4. INSURED'S NAME (Last Name, First Name, Middle Initial): A1 GROCERY

5. PATIENT'S ADDRESS (No., Street): 91 HOME STREET

6. PATIENT RELATIONSHIP TO INSURED: Self [ ] Spouse [ ] Child [ ] Other [X]

7. INSURED'S ADDRESS (No., Street): 1 MAIN ST

CITY: NOWHERE STATE: NY

8. RESERVED FOR NUCC USE

CITY: NOWHERE STATE: NY

ZIP CODE: 12367-1234 TELEPHONE (Include Area Code): (101) 2018989

ZIP CODE: 12367 TELEPHONE (Include Area Code): (101) 5554561

9. OTHER INSURED'S NAME (Last Name, First Name, Middle Initial)

10. IS PATIENT'S CONDITION RELATED TO:

11. INSURED'S POLICY GROUP OR FECA NUMBER

a. OTHER INSURED'S POLICY OR GROUP NUMBER

a. EMPLOYMENT? (Current or Previous) [X] YES [ ] NO

a. INSURED'S DATE OF BIRTH MM DD YY SEX M [ ] F [ ]

b. RESERVED FOR NUCC USE

b. AUTO ACCIDENT? [ ] YES [X] NO PLACE (State)

b. OTHER CLAIM ID (Designated by NUCC): MSP9761

c. RESERVED FOR NUCC USE

c. OTHER ACCIDENT? [ ] YES [X] NO

c. INSURANCE PLAN NAME OR PROGRAM NAME: STATE INSURANCE FUND

d. INSURANCE PLAN NAME OR PROGRAM NAME

10d. CLAIM CODES (Designated by NUCC)

d. IS THERE ANOTHER HEALTH BENEFIT PLAN? [ ] YES [ ] NO *If yes*, complete items 9, 9a, and 9d.

READ BACK OF FORM BEFORE COMPLETING & SIGNING THIS FORM.

12. PATIENT'S OR AUTHORIZED PERSON'S SIGNATURE I authorize the release of any medical or other information necessary to process this claim. I also request payment of government benefits either to myself or to the party who accepts assignment below.

SIGNED ________ DATE ________

13. INSURED'S OR AUTHORIZED PERSON'S SIGNATURE I authorize payment of medical benefits to the undersigned physician or supplier for services described below.

SIGNED ________

PATIENT AND INSURED INFORMATION

14. DATE OF CURRENT ILLNESS, INJURY, or PREGNANCY (LMP) MM DD YY: 01 20 YYYY QUAL. 431

15. OTHER DATE QUAL. MM DD YY

16. DATES PATIENT UNABLE TO WORK IN CURRENT OCCUPATION FROM 01 20 YYYY TO 01 21 YYYY

17. NAME OF REFERRING PROVIDER OR OTHER SOURCE | 17a. | 17b. NPI

18. HOSPITALIZATION DATES RELATED TO CURRENT SERVICES MM DD YY FROM TO

19. ADDITIONAL CLAIM INFORMATION (Designated by NUCC)

20. OUTSIDE LAB? [ ] YES [X] NO $ CHARGES

21. DIAGNOSIS OR NATURE OF ILLNESS OR INJURY Relate A-L to service line below (24E) ICD Ind. 0

A. M62.830 B. M47.812 C. Y92.69 D.

E. F. G. H.

I. J. K. L.

22. RESUBMISSION CODE | ORIGINAL REF. NO.

23. PRIOR AUTHORIZATION NUMBER

	24. A. DATE(S) OF SERVICE From MM DD YY	To MM DD YY	B. PLACE OF SERVICE	C. EMG	D. PROCEDURES, SERVICES, OR SUPPLIES (Explain Unusual Circumstances) CPT/HCPCS	MODIFIER	E. DIAGNOSIS POINTER	F. $ CHARGES	G. DAYS OR UNITS	H. EPSDT Family Plan	I. ID. QUAL.	J. RENDERING PROVIDER ID. #
1	01 27 YY		11		99212		A	45 00	1		NPI	
2	01 27 YY		11		20552		A	75 00	1		NPI	
3											NPI	
4											NPI	
5											NPI	
6											NPI	

25. FEDERAL TAX I.D. NUMBER: 111234523 SSN [ ] EIN [X]

26. PATIENT'S ACCOUNT NO.: 17-2

27. ACCEPT ASSIGNMENT? (For govt. claims, see back) [X] YES [ ] NO

28. TOTAL CHARGE $ 120 00

29. AMOUNT PAID $

30. Rsvd for NUCC Use

31. SIGNATURE OF PHYSICIAN OR SUPPLIER INCLUDING DEGREES OR CREDENTIALS (I certify that the statements on the reverse apply to this bill and are made a part thereof.)

ERIN A HELPER MD MMDDYYYY
SIGNED DATE

32. SERVICE FACILITY LOCATION INFORMATION

a. NPI b.

33. BILLING PROVIDER INFO & PH # (101) 1111234

ERIN A HELPER MD
101 MEDIC DRIVE
ANYWHERE NY 12345

a. 1234567890 b.

PHYSICIAN OR SUPPLIER INFORMATION

NUCC Instruction Manual available at: www.nucc.org *PLEASE PRINT OR TYPE*

FIGURE 17-6 Completed Mary S. Patient claim.

SUMMARY

The U.S. DOL Office of Workers' Compensation Programs administers programs that provide wage-replacement benefits, medical treatment, vocational rehabilitation, and other benefits to federal workers (or eligible dependents) who are injured at work or who acquire an occupational disease. Federal programs include the Energy Employees Occupational Illness Compensation Program, Federal Black Lung Program, Federal Employees' Compensation Program, Longshore and Harbor Workers' Compensation Program, Mine Safety and Health Administration, and Occupational Safety and Health Administration. State programs include the following types of coverage: State Insurance (or Compensation) Fund; employer self-insured programs; private, commercial workers' compensation programs; and combination programs.

To qualify for workers' compensation, employees must be injured while working within the scope of their job description, be injured while performing a service required by the employer, or contract an illness that can be directly linked to employment. Workers' compensation cases are classified as (1) medical claims with no disability, (2) temporary disability, (3) permanent disability, (4) vocational rehabilitation, and (5) death of the worker.

Providers are required to accept workers' compensation reimbursement as payment in full. Balance billing of patients is prohibited. Many workers' compensation programs incorporate managed care to improve the quality of medical benefits and services provided, as well as to control costs.

The First Report of Injury form is completed when the patient first seeks treatment for a work-related illness or injury. The report is filed in quadruplicate with a copy distributed to the State Workers' Compensation Board (or Workers' Compensation Commission), employer-designated compensation payer, ill or injured party's employer, and patient's work-related injury chart. When employers initially deny workers' compensation claims, the employee has the right to appeal the denial. Detailed narrative progress/supplemental reports document significant changes in the employee's medical or disability status.

When completing workers' compensation CMS-1500 claims for case studies in this text (including SimClaim software) and the Workbook, the following special instructions apply:

- Block 14—Review the case study to locate the date of the on-the-job illness or injury.
- Block 15—Review the case study to locate the date of any prior episode of the same or similar illness or injury.
- Block 16—Review the case study to locate the dates the patient was unable to work.
- Block 20—Enter an X in the NO box.
- Block 23—Leave blank.
- Block 24E—Enter just one diagnosis pointer letter on each line.
- Block 26—Enter the case study number (e.g., 17-4).
- Blocks 29–30—Leave blank.
- Block 32—If Block 18 contains dates, enter the name and address of the responsible provider (e.g., hospital).

INTERNET LINKS

- California Workers' Compensation Institute
  www.cwci.org
- Federal workers' compensation resources
  Go to **www.dol.gov**, and click on the Workers' Compensation link.
- Mine Safety and Health Administration
  www.msha.gov

- National Workers' Compensation website
  www.workerscompensation.com
- Occupational Safety and Health Administration
  www.osha.gov
- State Compensation Fund of Arizona
  www.scfaz.com

STUDY CHECKLIST

- ☐ Read this textbook chapter and highlight key concepts.
- ☐ Access SimClaim software at the online companion, and complete workers' compensation claims using the software's case studies.
- ☐ Complete CMS-1500 claims for each chapter case study.
- ☐ Answer the chapter review questions, verifying answers with your instructor.
- ☐ Complete the Workbook chapter, verifying answers with your instructor.
- ☐ Form a study group with classmates to discuss chapter concepts in preparation for an exam.

REVIEW

MULTIPLE CHOICE **Select the most appropriate response.**

1. The Office of Workers' Compensation Programs (OWCP) administers programs that provide

a. medical treatment.
b. vocational rehabilitation.
c. wage replacement benefits.
d. all of the above.

2. The Energy Employees Occupational Illness Compensation Program began providing benefits to eligible employees and former employees of the Department of Energy in

a. 1999.
b. 2000.
c. 2001.
d. 2002.

3. The Federal Black Lung Program was enacted in 1969 to provide _____ and other benefits for respiratory conditions related to persons formerly employed in the nation's coal mines.

a. medical treatment
b. vocational rehabilitation
c. wage replacement benefits
d. all of the above

4. The Federal Employees' Compensation Act (FECA) program provides workers' compensation to all federal and postal workers throughout the world for employment-related injuries and occupational diseases and includes

a. medical and vocational rehabilitation.
b. payment for medical care.
c. wage replacement.
d. all of the above.

5. **The Longshore and Harbor Workers' Compensation Program covers private-industry workers who are**
   a. employees that work for American companies in foreign countries.
   b. engaged in extracting natural resources from the outer continental shelf.
   c. those associated with industry, labor, and other federal and state agencies.
   d. working under contract for foreign countries outside the continental United States.

6. **Material Safety Data Sheets contain information about**
   a. activities and programs associated with mining.
   b. chemical and hazardous substances used on site.
   c. interstate commerce injuries from railroads.
   d. occupational hazards in the workplace.

7. **Which is responsible for administering state workers' compensation laws?**
   a. Office of State Workers' Compensation Programs
   b. State Compensation Commission
   c. State Insurance Fund
   d. State Workers' Compensation Board

8. **Which situation qualifies a worker for workers' compensation coverage?**
   a. Cindy Frasier administered an injection to a patient and stuck her finger with the needle; this required immediate treatment at the hospital and follow-up treatment by her primary care provider.
   b. Jenny Baker traveled to the local hospital from her place of employment to have lunch with friends; after eating lunch, she suffered food poisoning and underwent emergency care.
   c. Peter Mills attended an out-of-state conference for which his employer had preapproved reimbursement of his expenses; while attending a concert one evening during the trip, he fell and broke his arm.
   d. Sally Jones left the doctor's office where she is employed and stopped at the bank to deposit the day's accounts receivable; thereafter, while on the way to her residence, she was injured in a car accident.

9. **The judicial dispute resolution process in which an appeals board makes a final determination is called**
   a. adjudication.
   b. intercession.
   c. mediation.
   d. negotiation.

10. **Which is completed when the patient initially seeks treatment for a work-related illness or injury?**
   a. billing information notes
   b. First Report of Injury
   c. Material Safety Data Sheet
   d. progress report

APPENDIX I

SimClaim™ Case Studies: Set One

HOW TO ACCESS SIMCLAIM

To access the SimClaim student practice software program online, please refer to the information on the printed access card found in the front of this textbook. The SimClaim case studies are also available for reference in this appendix. Additional information on how to use the SimClaim software program is provided at the online site.

GENERAL INSTRUCTIONS FOR SIMCLAIM

- **Certain abbreviations are allowed** in the program—For example, 'St' for Street, 'Dr' for Drive, 'Rd' for Road, 'Ct' for Court. No other abbreviations will be accepted as correct by the program.
- **Only one diagnosis pointer in Block 24E per line**—Although SimClaim allows for more than one diagnosis pointer to be entered, only one diagnosis pointer is allowed in Block 24E for each line item as per textbook instructions.
- **No amount paid indicated**—If there is no amount paid indicated on the case study, *leave the field blank*.
- **Secondary insurance claims**—If a case study indicates that a patient's primary insurance carrier has paid an amount, fill out a second claim for the secondary insurance that reflects the amount reimbursed by primary insurance when indicated.
- **Fill out Block 32** only when the facility is other than the office setting, as indicated on the case study.
- **Enter all dates** as listed on the case study.

For additional help using SimClaim, refer to the Block Help within SimClaim or to the specific carrier guidelines found in your textbook.

GENERAL INSTRUCTIONS AND HINTS FOR SIMCLAIM CASE STUDIES (1-1 THROUGH 1-20)

The case studies in Appendix I provide additional practice completing CMS-1500 claims for different payers. These case studies are available in the SimClaim software and are reprinted here for your convenience. Be sure to read through the following instructions prior to beginning work.

TABLE OF SIMCLAIM™ CASES 1-1 THROUGH 1-20

CASE	PAYER	CASE	PAYER
1-1	Commercial	1-11	Commercial/Medicare
1-2	Commercial	1-12	Medicare
1-3	Commercial	1-13	Medicaid
1-4	BlueCross BlueShield	1-14	TRICARE
1-5	BlueCross BlueShield	1-15	TRICARE
1-6	BlueCross BlueShield	1-16	TRICARE
1-7	Medicare	1-17	Commercial/TRICARE
1-8	Medicare	1-18	FECA
1-9	Medicare/Medigap	1-19	Commercial
1-10	BlueCross BlueShield	1-20	Commercial

- **The provider name for all cases in Set One is also the practice name.**
- **Primary and secondary insurance information should be entered on the claim even if the secondary insurance is not being filed at this time.**
- **Pay careful attention to the Special Notes section of each case study for those cases requiring two claims, a primary claim as well as a secondary claim when the primary payer has already processed or adjudicated the claim.**
- **Make certain that diagnosis pointer letters are appropriately matched to the diagnosis that corresponds to the specific service for each line item—only one diagnosis pointer is allowed per line as per textbook instructions.**
- **When commercial insurance is provided and the policy is through an employer, an X should be entered in the "group" box in Block 1 and the appropriate group number should be entered in Block 11.**
- **For these case studies, claims completion should be based on the guidelines found in your *Understanding Health Insurance* textbook.**

CASE STUDY 1-1

Mary S. Hightower

IRMINA BRILL MD
25 MEDICAL DRIVE
INJURY NY 12347
101 2013145

Patient Number: 1-1

EIN: 117654312 **NPI:** 2345678901

PATIENT INFORMATION:
Name: HIGHTOWER, MARY, S
Address: 61 WATER TOWER STREET
City: ANYWHERE
State: NY
Zip/4: 12345-1234
Telephone: 101 2016987

Gender: M F X
Status: Single Married X Other
Date of Birth: 08 07 1951
Employer:
Student: FT PT School:

Work Related? Y N X
Auto Accident? Y N X State:
Other Accident: Y N X
Date of Accident:

Referring Physician: DNIM GOODDOC MD
Address:
Telephone:
NPI #: 5678901234

INSURANCE INFORMATION:
Primary Insurance
Primary Insurance Name: AETNA
Address: PO BOX 45
City: STILLWATER
State: PA
Zip/4: 12345-0045

Plan ID#: 272034109
Group #: NPW
Primary Policyholder: HIGHTOWER, WALTER, W
Address: 61 WATER TOWER STREET
City: ANYWHERE
State: NY
Zip/4: 12345-1234
Policyholder Date of Birth: 04 09 1951
Pt Relationship to Insured: Self Spouse X Child Other
Employer/School Name:

Secondary Insurance
Secondary Insurance Name:
Address:
City:
State:
Zip/4:

Plan ID#:
Group #:
Primary Policyholder:
Address:
City:
State:
Zip/4:
Policyholder Date of Birth:
Pt Relationship to Insured: Self Spouse Child Other
Employer/School Name:

ENCOUNTER INFORMATION:
Place of Service: 22

DIAGNOSIS INFORMATION

	Code	Diagnosis		Code	Diagnosis
1.	I25.810	CAD OF GRAFTED ARTERY	5.		
2.			6.		
3.			7.		
4.			8.		

PROCEDURE INFORMATION

Description of Procedure/Service	Dates	Code	Mod	Dx Order	Unit Charge	Days/Units
1. LEFT HEART CATHETERIZATION	01 10 YY -	93458	26	A	2000 00	1
2.	-					
3.	-					
4.	-					
5.	-					
6.	-					

Special Notes: PT DIAGNOSED WITH CAD 5 YEARS AGO (06/15/YYYY)
REFERRING PROVIDER: IM GOODDOC, MD, NPI: 5678901234. CARE RENDERED AT
GOODMEDICINE HOSPITAL, 1 PROVIDER STREET, ANYWHERE NY 12345 NPI 1123456789 ADMIT/DISCHARGE 1/10/YY

CASE STUDY 1-2

Ima Gayle

SEJAL RAJA MD
1 MEDICAL DRIVE
INJURY NY 12347
101 2022923

Patient Number: 1-2

EIN: 111397992 **NPI:** 7890123456

PATIENT INFORMATION:
Name: GAYLE, IMA
Address: 101 HAPPY DRIVE
City: ANYWHERE
State: NY
Zip/4: 12345-1234
Telephone: 101 1119876

Gender: M F X
Status: Single X Married Other
Date of Birth: 09 30 1945
Employer: MAIL BOXES INCORPORATED
Student: FT PT School:

Work Related? Y N X
Auto Accident? Y N X State:
Other Accident: Y N X
Date of Accident:

Referring Physician:
Address:
Telephone:
NPI #:

INSURANCE INFORMATION:
Primary Insurance
Primary Insurance Name: CONNECTICUT GENERAL
Address: PO BOX 1234
City: HEALTH
State: CT
Zip/4: 01234-1234

Plan ID#: 210010121
Group #: 101
Primary Policyholder: GAYLE, IMA
Address: 101 HAPPY DRIVE
City: ANYWHERE
State: NY
Zip/4: 12345-1234
Policyholder Date of Birth: 09 30 1945
Pt Relationship to Insured: Self X Spouse Child Other
Employer/School Name: MAIL BOXES INCORPORATED

Secondary Insurance
Secondary Insurance Name:
Address:
City:
State:
Zip/4:

Plan ID#:
Group #:
Primary Policyholder:
Address:
City:
State:
Zip/4:
Policyholder Date of Birth:
Pt Relationship to Insured: Self Spouse Child Other
Employer/School Name:

ENCOUNTER INFORMATION:
Place of Service: 11

DIAGNOSIS INFORMATION

	Code	Diagnosis		Code	Diagnosis
1.	R20.0	NUMBNESS, LEFT ARM	5.		
2.	M17.9	OSTEOARTHRITIS, LEFT LEG	6.		
3.			7.		
4.			8.		

PROCEDURE INFORMATION

Description of Procedure/Service	Dates	Code	Mod	Dx Order	Unit Charge	Days/Units
1. OFFICE VISIT, EST PATIENT, LEVEL III	03 01 YY -	99213	25	A	60 00	1
2. TRIGGER POINT INJECTION, TRAPEZIUS, LEFT	03 01 YY -	20552		A	75 00	1
3.	-					
4.	-					
5.	-					
6.	-					

Special Notes: PATIENT PAID $50 OF TODAY'S TOTAL.

CASE STUDY 1-3

Sandy Spencer

IRMINA BRILL MD
25 MEDICAL DRIVE
INJURY NY 12347

101 2013145

Patient Number: 1-3

EIN: 117654312 **NPI:** 2345678901

PATIENT INFORMATION:
Name: SPENCER, SANDY
Address: 101 HIGH STREET
City: ANYWHERE
State: NY
Zip/4: 12345-1234
Telephone: 101 5555698

Gender: M F X
Status: Single X Married Other
Date of Birth: 08 05 1985
Employer: GOODMEDICINE MEDICAL CLINIC
Student: FT PT School:

Work Related? Y N X
Auto Accident? Y N X State:
Other Accident: Y N X
Date of Accident:

Referring Physician:
Address:
Telephone:
NPI #:

INSURANCE INFORMATION:
Primary Insurance
Primary Insurance Name: AFLAC
Address: PO BOX 33
City: ASHBURY
State: TN
Zip/4: 23456-0033

Plan ID#: 5623569
Group #:
Primary Policyholder: SPENCER, SANDY
Address: 101 HIGH STREET
City: ANYWHERE
State: NY
Zip/4: 12345-1234
Policyholder Date of Birth: 08 05 1985
Pt Relationship to Insured: Self X Spouse Child Other
Employer/School Name: GOODMEDICINE MEDICAL CLINIC

Secondary Insurance
Secondary Insurance Name:
Address:
City:
State:
Zip/4:

Plan ID#:
Group #:
Primary Policyholder:
Address:
City:
State:
Zip/4:
Policyholder Date of Birth:
Pt Relationship to Insured: Self Spouse Child Other
Employer/School Name:

ENCOUNTER INFORMATION:
Place of Service: 11

DIAGNOSIS INFORMATION

	Code	Diagnosis		Code	Diagnosis
1.	I10	HYPERTENSION	5.		
2.			6.		
3.			7.		
4.			8.		

PROCEDURE INFORMATION

	Description of Procedure/Service	Dates	Code	Mod	Dx Order	Unit Charge	Days/Units
1.	OFFICE VISIT, EST PATIENT, LEVEL IV	10 15 YY -	99214		A	100 00	1
2.		-					
3.		-					
4.		-					
5.		-					
6.		-					

Special Notes:

CASE STUDY 1-4

Katlyn Tiger

ARNOLD YOUNG MD
21 PROVIDER STREET
INJURY NY 12347
101 2027754

Patient Number: 1-4

EIN: 111234632 **NPI:** 0123456789

PATIENT INFORMATION:
Name: TIGER, KATLYN
Address: 2 JUNGLE ROAD
City: NOWHERE
State: NY
Zip/4: 12346-1234
Telephone: 101 1112222

Gender: M F X
Status: Single X Married Other
Date of Birth: 01 03 1954
Employer: JOHN LION CPA
Student: FT PT School:

Work Related? Y N X
Auto Accident? Y N X State:
Other Accident: Y N X
Date of Accident:

Referring Physician:
Address:
Telephone:
NPI #:

INSURANCE INFORMATION:
Primary Insurance
Primary Insurance Name: BLUECROSS BLUESHIELD
Address: PO BOX 1121
City: MEDICAL
State: PA
Zip/4: 12357-1121

Plan ID#: ZJW334444
Group #: W310
Primary Policyholder: TIGER, KATLYN
Address: 2 JUNGLE ROAD
City: NOWHERE
State: NY
Zip/4: 12346-1234
Policyholder Date of Birth: 01 03 1954
Pt Relationship to Insured: Self X Spouse Child Other
Employer/School Name: JOHN LION CPA

Secondary Insurance
Secondary Insurance Name:
Address:
City:
State:
Zip/4:

Plan ID#:
Group #:
Primary Policyholder:
Address:
City:
State:
Zip/4:
Policyholder Date of Birth:
Pt Relationship to Insured: Self Spouse Child Other
Employer/School Name:

ENCOUNTER INFORMATION:
Place of Service: 22

DIAGNOSIS INFORMATION

	Code	Diagnosis		Code	Diagnosis
1.	J18.0	BRONCHOPNEUMONIA	5.		
2.			6.		
3.			7.		
4.			8.		

PROCEDURE INFORMATION

Description of Procedure/Service	Dates	Code	Mod	Dx Order	Unit Charge	Days/ Units
1. INITIAL OBSERVATION, COMPREHENSIVE	02 28 YY -	99220		A	175 00	1
2. DISCHARGE HOME	03 01 YY -	99217		A	65 00	1
3.	-					
4.	-					
5.	-					
6.	-					

Special Notes: CARE RENDERED AT GOODMEDICINE HOSPITAL, 1 PROVIDER STREET, ANYWHERE, NY 12345, NPI: 1123456789.
ADMISSION 2/28/YY DISCHARGE 3/1/YY

CASE STUDY 1-5

Jeffrey A. Green

SEJAL RAJA MD
1 MEDICAL DRIVE
INJURY NY 12347
101 2022923

Patient Number: 1-5

EIN: 111397992 **NPI:** 7890123456

PATIENT INFORMATION:
Name: GREEN, JEFFREY, A
Address: 103 MOUNTAIN VIEW ROAD
City: NOWHERE
State: NY
Zip/4: 12346-1234
Telephone: 101 1178765

Gender: M X F
Status: Single X Married Other
Date of Birth: 02 03 1997
Employer:
Student: FT X PT School:

Work Related? Y N X
Auto Accident? Y N X State:
Other Accident: Y N X
Date of Accident:

Referring Physician:
Address:
Telephone:
NPI #:

INSURANCE INFORMATION:
Primary Insurance
Primary Insurance Name: BLUECROSS BLUESHIELD
Address: PO BOX 1121
City: MEDICAL
State: PA
Zip/4: 12357-1121

Plan ID#: XWV7794483
Group #: 876
Primary Policyholder: GREEN, JEFFREY, G
Address: 103 MOUNTAIN VIEW ROAD
City: NOWHERE
State: NY
Zip/4: 12346-1234
Policyholder Date of Birth: 07 01 1955
Pt Relationship to Insured: Self Spouse Child X Other
Employer/School Name:

Secondary Insurance
Secondary Insurance Name:
Address:
City:
State:
Zip/4:

Plan ID#:
Group #:
Primary Policyholder:
Address:
City:
State:
Zip/4:
Policyholder Date of Birth:
Pt Relationship to Insured: Self Spouse Child Other
Employer/School Name:

ENCOUNTER INFORMATION:
Place of Service: 11

DIAGNOSIS INFORMATION

	Code	Diagnosis		Code	Diagnosis
1.	J20.9	ACUTE BRONCHITIS	5.		
2.	J31.0	PURULENT RHINITIS	6.		
3.			7.		
4.			8.		

PROCEDURE INFORMATION

	Description of Procedure/Service	Dates	Code	Mod	Dx Order	Unit Charge	Days/Units
1.	OFFICE VISIT, EST PATIENT, LEVEL II	03 10 YY -	99212		A	26 00	1
2.		-					
3.		-					
4.		-					
5.		-					
6.		-					

Special Notes: PATIENT'S MOTHER PAID $15 OF TODAY'S TOTAL. RETURN VISIT AS NEEDED.

CASE STUDY 1-6

Christine Noel

ARNOLD YOUNG MD
21 PROVIDER STREET
INJURY NY 12347

101 2027754

Patient Number: 1-6

EIN: 111234632 **NPI:** 0123456789

PATIENT INFORMATION:
Name: NOEL, CHRISTINE
Address: 100 CHRISTMAS TREE LANE
City: ANYWHERE
State: NY
Zip/4: 12345-1234
Telephone: 101 1158123

Gender: M F X
Status: Single Married X Other
Date of Birth: 09 03 1977
Employer: WORLD UNIVERSITY
Student: FT PT School:

Work Related? Y N X
Auto Accident? Y N X State:
Other Accident: Y N X
Date of Accident:

Referring Physician:
Address:
Telephone:
NPI #:

INSURANCE INFORMATION:
Primary Insurance
Primary Insurance Name: BLUECROSS BLUESHIELD
Address: PO BOX 1121
City: MEDICAL
State: PA
Zip/4: 12357-1121

Plan ID#: 123W476
Group #:
Primary Policyholder: NOEL, CHRISTINE
Address: 100 CHRISTMAS TREE LANE
City: ANYWHERE
State: NY
Zip/4: 12345-1234
Policyholder Date of Birth: 09 03 1977
Pt Relationship to Insured: Self X Spouse Child Other
Employer/School Name: WORLD UNIVERSITY

Secondary Insurance
Secondary Insurance Name:
Address:
City:
State:
Zip/4:

Plan ID#:
Group #:
Primary Policyholder:
Address:
City:
State:
Zip/4:
Policyholder Date of Birth:
Pt Relationship to Insured: Self Spouse Child Other
Employer/School Name:

ENCOUNTER INFORMATION:
Place of Service: 11

DIAGNOSIS INFORMATION

	Code	Diagnosis		Code	Diagnosis
1.	J02.9	ACUTE PHARYNGITIS	5.		
2.	R35.0	URINARY FREQUENCY	6.		
3.			7.		
4.			8.		

PROCEDURE INFORMATION

Description of Procedure/Service	Dates	Code	Mod	Dx Order	Unit Charge	Days/ Units
1. OFFICE VISIT, EST PATIENT, LEVEL II	03 01 YY -	99212		A	45 00	1
2. URINALYSIS, DIPSTICK AND MICROSCOPY	03 01 YY -	81000		B	80 00	1
3. STREP TEST (CLIA-APPROVED OFFICE LAB)	03 01 YY -	87880		A	12 00	1
4.	-					
5.	-					
6.	-					

Special Notes: PATIENT PAID $20 TOWARD TODAY'S BILL.

CASE STUDY 1-7

Gladys Phish

ANGELA DILALIO MD
99 PROVIDER DRIVE
INJURY NY 12347

101 2014321

Patient Number: 1-7

EIN: 111982342 **NPI:** 4567890123

PATIENT INFORMATION:
Name: PHISH, GLADYS
Address: 21 WINDWHISPER DRIVE
City: INJURY
State: NY
Zip/4: 12347-1234
Telephone: 101 1112397

Gender: M F X
Status: Single Married X Other
Date of Birth: 11 21 1930
Employer:
Student: FT PT School:

Work Related? Y N X
Auto Accident? Y N X State:
Other Accident: Y N X
Date of Accident:

Referring Physician: DNIM GOODDOC MD
Address:
Telephone:
NPI #: 5678901234

INSURANCE INFORMATION:
Primary Insurance
Primary Insurance Name: MEDICARE
Address: PO BOX 9929
City: BOXBURY
State: MD
Zip/4: 45678-9929

Plan ID#: 101891701A
Group #: NONE
Primary Policyholder:
Address:
City:
State:
Zip/4:
Policyholder Date of Birth:
Pt Relationship to Insured: Self Spouse Child Other
Employer/School Name:

Secondary Insurance
Secondary Insurance Name:
Address:
City:
State:
Zip/4:

Plan ID#:
Group #:
Primary Policyholder:
Address:
City:
State:
Zip/4:
Policyholder Date of Birth:
Pt Relationship to Insured: Self Spouse Child Other
Employer/School Name:

ENCOUNTER INFORMATION:
Place of Service: 22

DIAGNOSIS INFORMATION

	Code	Diagnosis		Code	Diagnosis
1.	L02.511	CUTANEOUS ABSCESS, RIGHT HAND	5.		
2.			6.		
3.			7.		
4.			8.		

PROCEDURE INFORMATION

Description of Procedure/Service	Dates	Code	Mod	Dx Order	Unit Charge	Days/ Units
1. INCISION & DRAINAGE, ABSCESS, SUBCUT	03 10 YY -	10060		A	450 00	1
2.	-					
3.	-					
4.	-					
5.	-					
6.	-					

Special Notes: HOSPITAL INFO: GOODMEDICINE HOSPITAL, 1 PROVIDER ST, ANYWHERE, NY 12345, NPI: 1123456789.
ADMISSION/DISCHARGE DATE: 3/10/YY.

CASE STUDY 1-8

Elaine Blueberry

IRMINA BRILL MD
5 MEDICAL DRIVE
INJURY NY 12347

101 2013145

Patient Number: 1-8

EIN: 117654312 **NPI:** 2345678901

PATIENT INFORMATION:
Name: BLUEBERRY, ELAINE
Address: 101 BUST STREET
City: ANYWHERE
State: NY
Zip/4: 12345-1234
Telephone: 101 5555689

Gender: M F X
Status: Single X Married Other
Date of Birth: 10 02 1925
Employer:
Student: FT PT School:

Work Related? Y N X
Auto Accident? Y N X State:
Other Accident: Y N X
Date of Accident:

Referring Physician: DNIM GOODDOC MD
Address:
Telephone:
NPI #: 5678901234

INSURANCE INFORMATION:
Primary Insurance
Primary Insurance Name: MEDICARE
Address: PO BOX 9929
City: BOXBURY
State: MD
Zip/4: 45678-9929

Plan ID#: 102623434B
Group #: NONE
Primary Policyholder:
Address:
City:
State:
Zip/4:
Policyholder Date of Birth:
Pt Relationship to Insured: Self Spouse Child Other
Employer/School Name:

Secondary Insurance
Secondary Insurance Name:
Address:
City:
State:
Zip/4:

Plan ID#:
Group #:
Primary Policyholder:
Address:
City:
State:
Zip/4:
Policyholder Date of Birth:
Pt Relationship to Insured: Self Spouse Child Other
Employer/School Name:

ENCOUNTER INFORMATION:
Place of Service: 21

DIAGNOSIS INFORMATION

	Code	Diagnosis		Code	Diagnosis
1.	K92.2	GASTROINTESTINAL BLEEDING	5.		
2.	L22	PERIANAL RASH DUE TO ADULT DIAPER	6.		
3.			7.		
4.			8.		

PROCEDURE INFORMATION

Description of Procedure/Service	Dates	Code	Mod	Dx Order	Unit Charge	Days/Units
1. INPATIENT CONSULTATION, LEVEL III	03 01 YY -	99253		A	125 00	1
2.	-					
3.	-					
4.	-					
5.	-					
6.	-					

Special Notes: CARE RENDERED AT GOODMEDICINE HOSPITAL, 1 PROVIDER STREET, ANYWHERE, NY 12345, NPI: 1123456789. ADMISSION DATE: 03/01/YYYY. DISCHARGE DATE: 03/05/YYYY.

CASE STUDY 1-9

Emma Berry

ARNOLD YOUNG MD
21 PROVIDER STREET
INJURY NY 12347

101 2027754

Patient Number: 1-9

EIN: 111234632 **NPI:** 0123456789

PATIENT INFORMATION:
Name: BERRY, EMMA
Address: 15 GOLDEN AGE ROAD
City: ANYWHERE
State: NY
Zip/4: 12345-1234
Telephone: 101 1117700

Gender: M F X
Status: Single X Married Other
Date of Birth: 03 08 1945
Employer:
Student: FT PT School:

Work Related? Y N X
Auto Accident? Y N X State:
Other Accident: Y N X
Date of Accident:

Referring Physician:
Address:
Telephone:
NPI #:

INSURANCE INFORMATION:
Primary Insurance
Primary Insurance Name: MEDICARE
Address: PO BOX 9929
City: BOXBURY
State: MD
Zip/4: 45678-9929

Plan ID#: 888441234A
Group #: NONE
Primary Policyholder:
Address:
City:
State:
Zip/4:
Policyholder Date of Birth:
Pt Relationship to Insured: Self Spouse Child Other
Employer/School Name:

Secondary Insurance
Secondary Insurance Name: MEDIGAP
Address: PO BOX 212
City: BALTIMORE
State: MD
Zip/4: 45678-0212

Plan ID#: MEDIGAP 995432992
Group #:
Primary Policyholder: BERRY, EMMA
Address:
City:
State:
Zip/4:
Policyholder Date of Birth:
Pt Relationship to Insured: Self X Spouse Child Other
Employer/School Name:

ENCOUNTER INFORMATION:
Place of Service: 31

DIAGNOSIS INFORMATION

	Code	Diagnosis		Code	Diagnosis
1.	F03.90	STABLE SENILE DEMENTIA	5.		
2.	R60.9	PERIPHERAL EDEMA	6.		
3.			7.		
4.			8.		

PROCEDURE INFORMATION

	Description of Procedure/Service	Dates	Code	Mod	Dx Order	Unit Charge	Days/ Units
1.	SNF CARE, SUBSEQUENT, LEVEL II	03 01 YY -	99308		B	45 00	1
2.		-					
3.		-					
4.		-					
5.		-					
6.		-					

Special Notes: CARE RENDERED AT GOOD LIFE SNF, 200 GOLDEN AGE ROAD, ANYWHERE, NY 12345, NPI: 2234567890.
ADMISSION DATE: 03/01/YYYY. DISCHARGE DATE: 03/03/YYYY.
DAUGHTER IS ANNE PEACH, 1234 BENEFICIARY ST, FARAWAY WA 9999

CASE STUDY 1-10

Peter Cartright

ANGELA DILALIO MD
99 PROVIDER DRIVE
INJURY NY 12347

101 2014321

Patient Number: 1-10

EIN: 111982342 **NPI:** 4567890123

PATIENT INFORMATION:
Name: CARTRIGHT, PETER
Address: 250 HILL STREET
City: ANYWHERE
State: NY
Zip/4: 12345-1234
Telephone: 101 5557843

Gender: M X F
Status: Single X Married Other
Date of Birth: 12 24 1975
Employer:
Student: FT PT School:

Work Related? Y N X
Auto Accident? Y N X State:
Other Accident: Y N X
Date of Accident:

Referring Physician:
Address:
Telephone:
NPI #:

INSURANCE INFORMATION:
Primary Insurance
Primary Insurance Name: BLUECROSS BLUESHIELD
Address: PO BOX 1121
City: MEDICAL
State: PA
Zip/4: 12357-1121

Plan ID#: 5626598
Group #:
Primary Policyholder: CARTRIGHT, PETER
Address: 250 HILL STREET
City: ANYWHERE
State: NY
Zip/4: 12345-1234
Policyholder Date of Birth: 12 24 1975
Pt Relationship to Insured: Self X Spouse Child Other
Employer/School Name:

Secondary Insurance
Secondary Insurance Name:
Address:
City:
State:
Zip/4:

Plan ID#:
Group #:
Primary Policyholder:
Address:
City:
State:
Zip/4:
Policyholder Date of Birth:
Pt Relationship to Insured: Self Spouse Child Other
Employer/School Name:

ENCOUNTER INFORMATION:
Place of Service: 11

DIAGNOSIS INFORMATION

	Code	Diagnosis		Code	Diagnosis
1.	E11.9	DIABETES MELLITUS, TYPE II	5.		
2.			6.		
3.			7.		
4.			8.		

PROCEDURE INFORMATION

Description of Procedure/Service	Dates	Code	Mod	Dx Order	Unit Charge	Days/ Units
1. OFFICE VISIT, EST PATIENT, LEVEL II	04 15 YY -	99212		A	50 00	1
2.	-					
3.	-					
4.	-					
5.	-					
6.	-					

Special Notes:

CASE STUDY 1-11

Fred Cartwheel

ANGELA DILALIO MD
99 PROVIDER DRIVE
INJURY NY 12347

101 2014321

Patient Number: 1-11

EIN: 111982342 **NPI:** 4567890123

PATIENT INFORMATION:
Name: CARTWHEEL, FRED
Address: RED WAGON ROAD
City: NOWHERE
State: NY
Zip/4: 12346-1234
Telephone: 101 1135567

Gender: M X F
Status: Single Married X Other
Date of Birth: 01 03 1965
Employer: WORLD UNIVERSITY
Student: FT PT School:

Work Related? Y N X
Auto Accident? Y N X State:
Other Accident: Y N X
Date of Accident:

Referring Physician:
Address:
Telephone:
NPI #:

INSURANCE INFORMATION:
Primary Insurance
Primary Insurance Name: METLIFE
Address: PO BOX 67
City: HIGHLAND
State: TX
Zip/4: 76543-0067

Plan ID#: XYZ332999009
Group #:
Primary Policyholder: CARTWHEEL, FRED
Address: RED WAGON ROAD
City: NOWHERE
State: NY
Zip/4: 12346-1234
Policyholder Date of Birth: 01 03 1965
Pt Relationship to Insured: Self X Spouse Child Other
Employer/School Name: WORLD UNIVERSITY

Secondary Insurance
Secondary Insurance Name: MEDICARE
Address: PO BOX 9929
City: BOXBURY
State: MD
Zip/4: 45678-9929

Plan ID#: 332999999D
Group #:
Primary Policyholder: CARTWHEEL, FRED
Address: RED WAGON ROAD
City: NOWHERE
State: NY
Zip/4: 12346-1234
Policyholder Date of Birth:
Pt Relationship to Insured: Self X Spouse Child Other
Employer/School Name:

ENCOUNTER INFORMATION:
Place of Service: 21

DIAGNOSIS INFORMATION

	Code	Diagnosis		Code	Diagnosis
1.	I10	ESSENTIAL HYPERTENSIVE CRISIS, MALIG.	5.		
2.			6.		
3.			7.		
4.			8.		

PROCEDURE INFORMATION

Description of Procedure/Service	Dates	Code	Mod	Dx Order	Unit Charge	Days/ Units
1. INITIAL HOSPITAL VISIT, LEVEL III	03 14 YY –	99223		A	165 00	1
2. SUBSEQUENT HOSPITAL VISIT, LEVEL II	03 15 YY 03 16 YY	99232		A	190 00	2
3. DISCHARGE MANAGEMENT, 30 MINUTES	03 17 YY –	99238		A	55 00	1
4.	–					
5.	–					
6.	–					

Special Notes: ONSET OF ILLNESS 3/12/YY. DISCHARGE HOME.
CARE PROVIDED AT GOODMEDICINE HOSPITAL, 1 PROVIDER STREET, ANYWHERE, NY 12345,
NPI: 1122345789. ADMITTED 03/14/YY DISCHARGED 03/17/YY

CASE STUDY 1-12

Geraldine T. Makebetter

ARNOLD YOUNG MD
21 PROVIDER STREET
INJURY NY 12347

101 2027754

Patient Number: 1-12

EIN: 111234632 **NPI:** 0123456789

PATIENT INFORMATION:
Name: MAKEBETTER, GERALDINE, T
Address: 7866A MEMORY LANE
City: INJURY
State: NY
Zip/4: 12347-1234
Telephone: 101 1119855

Gender: M F X
Status: Single X Married Other
Date of Birth: 06 20 1945
Employer:
Student: FT PT School:

Work Related? Y N X
Auto Accident? Y N X State:
Other Accident: Y N X
Date of Accident:

Referring Physician:
Address:
Telephone:
NPI #:

INSURANCE INFORMATION:
Primary Insurance
Primary Insurance Name: MEDICARE
Address: PO BOX 9929
City: BOXBURY
State: MD
Zip/4: 45678-9929

Plan ID#: 1012788769W
Group #: NONE
Primary Policyholder:
Address:
City:
State:
Zip/4:
Policyholder Date of Birth:
Pt Relationship to Insured: Self Spouse Child Other
Employer/School Name:

Secondary Insurance
Secondary Insurance Name:
Address:
City:
State:
Zip/4:

Plan ID#:
Group #:
Primary Policyholder:
Address:
City:
State:
Zip/4:
Policyholder Date of Birth:
Pt Relationship to Insured: Self Spouse Child Other
Employer/School Name:

ENCOUNTER INFORMATION:
Place of Service: 11

DIAGNOSIS INFORMATION

	Code	Diagnosis		Code	Diagnosis
1.	Z00.00	ANNUAL PHYSICAL EXAM	5.		
2.	N30.90	BLADDER INFECTION	6.		
3.			7.		
4.			8.		

PROCEDURE INFORMATION

Description of Procedure/Service	Dates	Code	Mod	Dx Order	Unit Charge	Days/ Units
1. PREVENTIVE MEDICINE, EST PATIENT	03 03 YY -	99396		A	75 00	1
2. EST OFFICE VISIT, LEVEL II	03 03 YY -	99212	25	B	40 00	1
3. URINALYSIS W/MICROSCOPY	03 03 YY -	81000		B	8 00	1
4. HEMOCCULT	03 03 YY -	82270		A	8 00	1
5. CBC, AUTOMATED	03 03 YY -	85025		A	40 00	1
6. HEALTH RISK ASSESSMENT	03 03 YY -	99420		A	25 00	1

Special Notes:

CASE STUDY 1-13

Fiona J. Filbert

SEJAL RAJA MD
1 MEDICAL DRIVE
INJURY NY 12347
101 2022923

Patient Number: 1-13

EIN: 111397992 **NPI:** 7890123456

PATIENT INFORMATION:
Name: FILBERT, FIONA, J
Address: 1 BUTTERNUT STREET
City: ANYWHERE
State: NY
Zip/4: 12345-1234
Telephone: 101 7918645

Gender: M F X
Status: Single Married Other
Date of Birth: 03 08 1977
Employer:
Student: FT PT School:

Work Related? Y N X
Auto Accident? Y N X State:
Other Accident: Y N X
Date of Accident:

Referring Physician: DNARNOLD YOUNG MD
Address:
Telephone:
NPI #: 0123456789

INSURANCE INFORMATION:
Primary Insurance
Primary Insurance Name: MEDICAID
Address: PO BOX 9900
City: NEW YORK
State: NY
Zip/4: 12300-9900

Plan ID#: 119850B
Group #:
Primary Policyholder:
Address:
City:
State:
Zip/4:
Policyholder Date of Birth:
Pt Relationship to Insured: Self X Spouse Child Other
Employer/School Name:

Secondary Insurance
Secondary Insurance Name:
Address:
City:
State:
Zip/4:

Plan ID#:
Group #:
Primary Policyholder:
Address:
City:
State:
Zip/4:
Policyholder Date of Birth:
Pt Relationship to Insured: Self Spouse Child Other
Employer/School Name:

ENCOUNTER INFORMATION:
Place of Service: 22

DIAGNOSIS INFORMATION

	Code	Diagnosis		Code	Diagnosis
1.	N60.02	CYST, LEFT BREAST	5.		
2.			6.		
3.			7.		
4.			8.		

PROCEDURE INFORMATION

Description of Procedure/Service	Dates	Code	Mod	Dx Order	Unit Charge	Days/ Units
1. EXCISION, MASS, LEFT BREAST	03 10 YY -	19120		A	975 00	1
2.	-					
3.	-					
4.	-					
5.	-					
6.	-					

Special Notes: HOSPITAL INFO: GOODMEDICINE HOSPITAL, 1 PROVIDER ST, ANYWHERE, NY 12345, NPI: 1123456789.
REFERRED BY ARNOLD J. YOUNGLOVE, M.D., NPI: 0123456789.
PATIENT PAID $10 TOWARD TODAY'S CHARGES. ADMISSION/DISCHARGE DATE: 3/10/YYYY.

CASE STUDY 1-14

Gregory Willowtree

ANGELA DILALIO MD
99 PROVIDER DRIVE
INJURY NY 12347

101 2014321

Patient Number: 1-14

EIN: 111982342 **NPI:** 4567890123

PATIENT INFORMATION:
Name: WILLOWTREE, GREGORY
Address: 150 TREE LANE
City: NOWHERE
State: NY
Zip/4: 12346-1234
Telephone: 101 5552356

Gender: M X F
Status: Single X Married Other
Date of Birth: 12 12 1942
Employer: RETIRED ARMY CAPTAIN
Student: FT PT School:

Work Related? Y N X
Auto Accident? Y N X State:
Other Accident: Y N X
Date of Accident:

Referring Physician:
Address:
Telephone:
NPI #:

INSURANCE INFORMATION:
Primary Insurance
Primary Insurance Name: TRICARE
Address: PO BOX 555
City: TRICITY
State: SC
Zip/4: 76654-0555

Plan ID#: 071269845
Group #:
Primary Policyholder: WILLOWTREE, GREGORY
Address: 150 TREE LANE
City: NOWHERE
State: NY
Zip/4: 12346-1234
Policyholder Date of Birth:
Pt Relationship to Insured: Self X Spouse Child Other
Employer/School Name: RETIRED ARMY CAPTAIN

Secondary Insurance
Secondary Insurance Name:
Address:
City:
State:
Zip/4:

Plan ID#:
Group #:
Primary Policyholder:
Address:
City:
State:
Zip/4:
Policyholder Date of Birth:
Pt Relationship to Insured: Self Spouse Child Other
Employer/School Name:

ENCOUNTER INFORMATION:
Place of Service: 22

DIAGNOSIS INFORMATION

	Code	Diagnosis		Code	Diagnosis
1.	S83.241A	MEDIAL MENISCUS TEAR, RT KNEE, INIT ENCOUNTER	5.		
2.	M67.51	PLICA, RIGHT KNEE	6.		
3.			7.		
4.			8.		

PROCEDURE INFORMATION

	Description of Procedure/Service	Dates	Code	Mod	Dx Order	Unit Charge	Days/ Units
1.	ARTHROSCOPY W/ MEDIAL MENISCECTOMY, RIGHT KNEE	03 19 YY -	29881	RT	A	2000 00	1
2.		-					
3.		-					
4.		-					
5.		-					
6.		-					

Special Notes: HOSPITAL INFO: GOODMEDICINE HOSPITAL, 1 PROVIDER ST, ANYWHERE, NY 12345, NPI: 1123456789.
DATE OF INJURY: 03/19/YY. RETURN VISIT IN 3 DAYS.
ADMISSION/DISCHARGE DATE: 03/19/YY.

CASE STUDY 1-15

Agnes Patty

IRMINA BRILL MD
25 MEDICAL DRIVE
INJURY NY 12347
101 2013145

Patient Number: 1-15

EIN: 117654312 **NPI:** 2345678901

PATIENT INFORMATION:
Name: PATTY, AGNES
Address: 1 PATTY CAKE DRIVE
City: NOWHERE
State: NY
Zip/4: 12346-1234
Telephone: 101 1122701

Gender: M F X
Status: Single Married X Other
Date of Birth: 09 03 1947
Employer: RETIRED
Student: FT PT School:

Work Related? Y N X
Auto Accident? Y N X State:
Other Accident: Y N X
Date of Accident:

Referring Physician:
Address:
Telephone:
NPI #:

INSURANCE INFORMATION:
Primary Insurance
Primary Insurance Name: TRICARE
Address: PO BOX 555
City: TRICITY
State: SC
Zip/4: 76654-0555

Plan ID#: 103236666
Group #:
Primary Policyholder: PATTY, GERRY
Address: 1 PATTY CAKE DRIVE
City: NOWHERE
State: NY
Zip/4: 12346-1234
Policyholder Date of Birth:
Pt Relationship to Insured: Self Spouse X Child Other
Employer/School Name: RETIRED

Secondary Insurance
Secondary Insurance Name:
Address:
City:
State:
Zip/4:

Plan ID#:
Group #:
Primary Policyholder:
Address:
City:
State:
Zip/4:
Policyholder Date of Birth:
Pt Relationship to Insured: Self Spouse Child Other
Employer/School Name:

ENCOUNTER INFORMATION:
Place of Service: 11

DIAGNOSIS INFORMATION

	Code	Diagnosis		Code	Diagnosis
1.	I49.9	CARDIAC ARRHYTHMIA	5.		
2.	R04.0	EPISTAXIS	6.		
3.			7.		
4.			8.		

PROCEDURE INFORMATION

Description of Procedure/Service	Dates	Code	Mod	Dx Order	Unit Charge	Days/ Units
1. OFFICE VISIT, NEW PATIENT, LEVEL III	03 01 YY -	99203		A	100 00	1
2. NASAL CAUTERY	03 01 YY -	30901		B	65 00	1
3. ECG WITH INTERPRETATION	03 01 YY -	93000		A	50 00	1
4.	-					
5.	-					
6.	-					

Special Notes: FIRST SYMPTOMS 2/10/YY. PATIENT PAID $35.00 TOWARD TODAY'S CHARGE.

CASE STUDY 1-16

Terry Lewis

ANGELA DILALIO MD
99 PROVIDER DRIVE
INJURY NY 12347

101 2014321

Patient Number: 1-16

EIN: 111982342 **NPI:** 4567890123

PATIENT INFORMATION:
Name: LEWIS, TERRY
Address: 9 RANDOLPH ROAD
City: ANYWHERE
State: NY
Zip/4: 12345-1234
Telephone: 101 5555169

Gender: M X F
Status: Single X Married Other
Date of Birth: 05 05 1986
Employer: US NAVY
Student: FT PT **School:**

Work Related? Y N X
Auto Accident? Y N X **State:**
Other Accident: Y N X
Date of Accident:

Referring Physician:
Address:
Telephone:
NPI #:

INSURANCE INFORMATION:
Primary Insurance
Primary Insurance Name: TRICARE
Address: PO BOX 555
City: TRICITY
State: SC
Zip/4: 76654-0555

Plan ID#: 562356989
Group #:
Primary Policyholder: LEWIS, TERRY
Address: 9 RANDOLPH ROAD
City: ANYWHERE
State: NY
Zip/4: 12345-1234
Policyholder Date of Birth:
Pt Relationship to Insured: Self X Spouse Child Other
Employer/School Name: US NAVY

Secondary Insurance
Secondary Insurance Name:
Address:
City:
State:
Zip/4:

Plan ID#:
Group #:
Primary Policyholder:
Address:
City:
State:
Zip/4:
Policyholder Date of Birth:
Pt Relationship to Insured: Self Spouse Child Other
Employer/School Name:

ENCOUNTER INFORMATION:
Place of Service: 11

DIAGNOSIS INFORMATION

	Code	Diagnosis		Code	Diagnosis
1.	F41.9	ANXIETY	5.		
2.			6.		
3.			7.		
4.			8.		

PROCEDURE INFORMATION

	Description of Procedure/Service	Dates	Code	Mod	Dx Order	Unit Charge	Days/ Units
1.	OFFICE VISIT, EST VISIT, LEVEL II	06 19 YY -	99212		A	35 00	1
2.		-					
3.		-					
4.		-					
5.		-					
6.		-					

Special Notes:

CASE STUDY 1-17

Mary Parker

ANGELA DILALIO MD
99 PROVIDER DRIVE
INJURY NY 12347

101 2014321

Patient Number: 1-17

EIN: 111982342 **NPI:** 4567890123

PATIENT INFORMATION:
Name: PARKER, MARY
Address: 15 MAIN STREET
City: ANYWHERE
State: NY
Zip/4: 12345-1234
Telephone: 101 5555658

Gender: M F X
Status: Single Married X Other
Date of Birth: 06 06 1975
Employer: WORLD UNIVERSITY
Student: FT PT School:

Work Related? Y N X
Auto Accident? Y N X State:
Other Accident: Y N X
Date of Accident:

Referring Physician:
Address:
Telephone:
NPI #:

INSURANCE INFORMATION:
Primary Insurance
Primary Insurance Name: AETNA
Address: PO BOX 45
City: STILLWATER
State: PA
Zip/4: 12345-0045

Plan ID#: 562156
Group #:
Primary Policyholder: PARKER, MARY
Address: 15 MAIN STREET
City: ANYWHERE
State: NY
Zip/4: 12345-1234
Policyholder Date of Birth: 06 06 1975
Pt Relationship to Insured: Self X Spouse Child Other
Employer/School Name:

Secondary Insurance
Secondary Insurance Name: TRICARE
Address: PO BOX 555
City: TRICITY
State: SC
Zip/4: 76654-0555

Plan ID#: 23562598
Group #:
Primary Policyholder: PARKER, MARK
Address: 15 MAIN STREET
City: ANYWHERE
State: NY
Zip/4: 12345-1234
Policyholder Date of Birth:
Pt Relationship to Insured: Self Spouse X Child Other
Employer/School Name:

ENCOUNTER INFORMATION:
Place of Service: 11

DIAGNOSIS INFORMATION

	Code	Diagnosis		Code	Diagnosis
1.	J45.909	ASTHMA	5.		
2.			6.		
3.			7.		
4.			8.		

PROCEDURE INFORMATION

	Description of Procedure/Service	Dates	Code	Mod	Dx Order	Unit Charge	Days/Units
1.	OFFICE VISIT, EST VISIT, LEVEL II	06 19 YY -	99212		A	35 00	1
2.		-					
3.		-					
4.		-					
5.		-					
6.		-					

Special Notes: MARK PARKER IS STATIONED ON THE USS EISENHOWER. FPO AE 11600-3982.
UPDATE: AETNA PAID $10.00.

CASE STUDY 1-18

Iona J. Million

ANGELA DILALIO MD
99 PROVIDER DRIVE
INJURY NY 12347

101 2014321

Patient Number: 1-18

EIN: 111982342 **NPI:** 4567890123

PATIENT INFORMATION:
Name: MILLION, IONA, J
Address: 100A PASTURES COURT
City: ANYWHERE
State: NY
Zip/4: 12345-1234
Telephone: 101 7590839

Gender: M F X
Status: Single Married Other
Date of Birth: 01 01 1970
Employer: ANYWHERE GOLF COURSE
Student: FT PT School:

Work Related? Y X N
Auto Accident? Y N X State:
Other Accident: Y N X
Date of Accident: 09 08 YY

Referring Physician:
Address:
Telephone:
NPI #:

INSURANCE INFORMATION:
Primary Insurance
Primary Insurance Name: DFEC
Address: 21 WASHINGTON AVE
City: FEDERAL
State: MD
Zip/4: 10001

Plan ID#: 235568956
Group #: 10173
Primary Policyholder: ANYWHERE GOLF COURSE
Address: ROUTE 20
City: GOLF
State: NY
Zip/4: 12348-1234
Policyholder Date of Birth:
Pt Relationship to Insured: Self Spouse Child Other X
Employer/School Name: ANYWHERE GOLF COURSE

Secondary Insurance
Secondary Insurance Name:
Address:
City:
State:
Zip/4:

Plan ID#:
Group #:
Primary Policyholder:
Address:
City:
State:
Zip/4:
Policyholder Date of Birth:
Pt Relationship to Insured: Self Spouse Child Other
Employer/School Name:

ENCOUNTER INFORMATION:
Place of Service: 22

DIAGNOSIS INFORMATION

	Code	Diagnosis		Code	Diagnosis
1.	Z47.2	RETAINED HARDWARE	5.		
2.	Z98.89	STATUS POST FRACTURE SURGERY	6.		
3.	M25.571	PAIN, HEALED FRACTURE SITE, LEFT ANKLE	7.		
4.	M84.472S	DUE TO PREVIOUS PATH FRACTURE, LEFT ANKLE	8.		

PROCEDURE INFORMATION

Description of Procedure/Service	Dates	Code	Mod	Dx Order	Unit Charge	Days/Units
1. REMOVAL, INTERNAL FIXATION DEVICE, LT ANKLE, DEEP	03 10 YY -	20680		A	650 00	1
2.	-					
3.	-					
4.	-					
5.	-					
6.	-					

Special Notes: HOSPITAL INFO: GOODMEDICINE HOSPITAL, 1 PROVIDER ST, ANYWHERE, NY 12345, NPI: 1123456789. CLAIM# 10173 DOI: 09/08/YYYY. PT MAY RETURN TO WORK 04/01/YYYY. ADMISSION/DISCHARGE DATE: 03/10/YYYY. PATIENT'S SSN IS 235-56-8956. DIVISION OF FEDERAL EMPLOYEE'S COMPENSATION (DFEC)

CASE STUDY 1-19

Mike R. Scope

ANGELA DILALIO MD
99 PROVIDER DRIVE
INJURY NY 12347
101 2014321

Patient Number: 1-19

EIN: 111982342 **NPI:** 4567890123

PATIENT INFORMATION:
Name: SCOPE, MIKE, R
Address: 5 SPRUCE STREET
City: NOWHERE
State: NY
Zip/4: 12346-1234
Telephone: 101 1135567

Gender: M X F
Status: Single X Married Other
Date of Birth: 06 20 1972
Employer: BIO LABS
Student: FT PT School:

Work Related? Y X N
Auto Accident? Y N X State:
Other Accident: Y N X
Date of Accident: 03 12 YY

Referring Physician:
Address:
Telephone:
NPI #:

INSURANCE INFORMATION:
Primary Insurance
Primary Insurance Name: HIGH RISK INSURANCE
Address: 22 RISKY PROVIDER STREET
City: RISKERTON
State: IN
Zip/4: 90909

Plan ID#: 356898459
Group #:
Primary Policyholder: BIO LABS
Address: 10 LABORATORY COURT
City: NOWHERE
State: NY
Zip/4: 12346-1234
Policyholder Date of Birth:
Pt Relationship to Insured: Self Spouse Child Other X
Employer/School Name:

Secondary Insurance
Secondary Insurance Name:
Address:
City:
State:
Zip/4:

Plan ID#:
Group #:
Primary Policyholder:
Address:
City:
State:
Zip/4:
Policyholder Date of Birth:
Pt Relationship to Insured: Self Spouse Child Other
Employer/School Name:

ENCOUNTER INFORMATION:
Place of Service: 11

DIAGNOSIS INFORMATION

	Code	Diagnosis		Code	Diagnosis
1.	S13.4XXA	CERVICAL STRAIN, INIT ENCOUNTER	5.		
2.	S33.5XXA	SPRAIN,LUMBAR SPINE LIGAMENTS,INIT ENCOUNTER	6.		
3.	Y92.69	ACCIDENT AT INDUSTRIAL AREA	7.		
4.			8.		

PROCEDURE INFORMATION

	Description of Procedure/Service	Dates	Code	Mod	Dx Order	Unit Charge	Days/Units
1.	OFFICE VISIT, EST PT, LEVEL II	03 20 YY -	99212		A	26 00	1
2.		-					
3.		-					
4.		-					
5.		-					
6.		-					

Special Notes: ONSET OF INJURY 03/12/YY. DISCHARGE HOME. PATIENT'S SSN: 356-89-8459.
PATIENT'S INJURY OCCURRED AT INDUSTRIAL PLACE OF EMPLOYMENT
CLAIM#10199

CASE STUDY 1-20

Jim Gallo

ANGELA DILALIO MD
99 PROVIDER DRIVE
INJURY NY 12347

101 2014321

Patient Number: 1-20

EIN: 111982342 **NPI:** 4567890123

PATIENT INFORMATION:
Name: GALLO, JIM
Address: 115 GLENN STREET
City: ANYWHERE
State: NY
Zip/4: 12345-1234
Telephone: 101 5558457

Gender: M X F
Status: Single Married Other
Date of Birth: 05 02 1975
Employer: WORLD UNIVERSITY
Student: FT PT School:

Work Related? Y X N
Auto Accident? Y N X State:
Other Accident: Y N X
Date of Accident: 02 15 YY

Referring Physician:
Address:
Telephone:
NPI #:

INSURANCE INFORMATION:
Primary Insurance
Primary Insurance Name: HIGH RISK INSURANCE
Address: 22 RISKY PROVIDER STREET
City: RISKERTON
State: IN
Zip/4: 90909

Plan ID#: 467909560
Group #:
Primary Policyholder: WORLD UNIVERSITY
Address: COLLEGE DRIVE
City: ANYWHERE
State: NY
Zip/4: 12345
Policyholder Date of Birth:
Pt Relationship to Insured: Self Spouse Child Other X
Employer/School Name:

Secondary Insurance
Secondary Insurance Name:
Address:
City:
State:
Zip/4:

Plan ID#:
Group #:
Primary Policyholder:
Address:
City:
State:
Zip/4:
Policyholder Date of Birth:
Pt Relationship to Insured: Self Spouse Child Other
Employer/School Name:

ENCOUNTER INFORMATION:
Place of Service: 11

DIAGNOSIS INFORMATION

	Code	Diagnosis		Code	Diagnosis
1.	M62.830	MUSCLE SPASMS, BACK	5.		
2.	W19.XXXA	ACCIDENTAL FALL (INITIAL ENCOUNTER)	6.		
3.	Y92.69	PLACE OF OCCURRENCE, INDUSTRIAL	7.		
4.			8.		

PROCEDURE INFORMATION

Description of Procedure/Service	Dates	Code	Mod	Dx Order	Unit Charge	Days/ Units
1. OFFICE VISIT, EST PT, LEVEL II	02 15 YY -	99212		A	35 00	1
2.	-					
3.	-					
4.	-					
5.	-					
6.	-					

Special Notes: ONSET OF INJURY 02/15/YYYY. RETURN TO WORK 02/21/YYYY. PATIENT'S SSN: 467-90-9560 CLAIM#10225
PATIENT'S INJURY OCCURRED AT INDUSTRIAL PLACE OF EMPLOYMENT AS
RESULT OF A FALL.

Case Studies: Set Two

APPENDIX II

GENERAL INSTRUCTIONS FOR CASE STUDIES 2-1 THROUGH 2-20

NOTE: These cases do not appear in the *SimCLAIM*™ product for this edition; however, you may complete claim forms for these cases using the Blank Form Mode option within *SimCLAIM*™ to print to PDF.

The case studies in Appendix II provide practice completing CMS-1500 claims for physicians who practice at the Goodmedicine Clinic, which is a medical group practice. (A *medical group practice* consists of three or more physicians who enter into a formal agreement to provide single-specialty or multispecialty health care services. They jointly share the use of equipment and personnel, and income generated from the practice is distributed according to a predetermined formula.)

Be sure to make special note of the following information prior to completing CMS-1500 claims for Case Studies 2-1 through 2-20:

- Make at least 20 copies of the blank CMS-1500 claim form in Appendix III, or print 20 blank claims using *SimCLAIM*™ software. You also have the option of entering claims data using the Blank Form Mode in *SimCLAIM*™.
- Unlike the claims in Set One, the provider and practice information is NOT always the same for the cases in Set Two. All of the providers in Set Two are members of the practice, "Goodmedicine Clinic." As such, the information in Block 33 reflects the practice name; however, the information entered in Block 31 reflects the actual service provider.
- All EIN and NPI information needed to complete each CMS-1500 claim is provided on each case study.
- When Goodmedicine Hospital is the place of service, the address and NPI are listed in the Special Notes on the case study and are reported in Block 32.
- All providers participate in all of the third-party payer plans; therefore, enter an X in the Yes box in Block 27 of the CMS-1500.
- Table II-1 contains place-of-service (POS) codes reported in Block 24B of the CMS-1500 claim.
- Table II-2 contains the list of Case Studies in Set Two according to third-party payer.
- Please remember that services for just one place of service or one provider are entered on each CMS-1500. In those instances where services are provided at more than one location or by more than one provider, separate CMS-1500 claims are completed for each.
- Note that the provider who performed the service is entered in the following CMS-1500 blocks:

Block 24J:	NPI for providing physician
Block 25:	EIN for providing physician
Block 31:	Providing physician name
Block 33:	Name of billing provider (Goodmedicine Clinic)
Block 33A:	NPI for Goodmedicine Clinic (3345678901)

- Note that the billing provider is reported in CMS-1500 Blocks 33 and 33A.
- Be sure to carefully review the patient record to properly assign ICD-10-CM diagnosis codes and CPT and HCPCS level II (national) procedure and service codes. Each case study contains the name of the procedure or service and charge, but you still need to review the patient record to accurately assign codes.

TABLE II-1 Place-of-service codes for CMS-1500 claim, Block 24B

CODE	DESCRIPTION	CODE	DESCRIPTION
01	Pharmacy	34	Hospice
02	Unassigned	35-40	Unassigned
03	School	41	Ambulance–Land
04	Homeless Shelter	42	Ambulance–Air or Water
05	Indian Health Service Free-standing Facility	43-48	Unassigned
06	Indian Health Service Provider-based Facility	49	Independent Clinic
07	Tribal 638 Free-standing Facility	50	Federally Qualified Health Center
08	Tribal 638 Provider-based Facility	51	Inpatient Psychiatric Facility
09	Prison Correctional Facility	52	Psychiatric Facility–Partial Hospitalization
10	Unassigned	53	Community Mental Health Center
11	Office	54	Intermediate Care Facility/Mentally Retarded
12	Home	55	Residential Substance Abuse Treatment Facility
13	Assisted Living Facility	56	Psychiatric Residential Treatment Facility
14	Group Home	57	Nonresidential Substance Abuse Treatment Facility
15	Mobile Unit	58-59	Unassigned
16-19	Unassigned	60	Mass Immunization Center
20	Urgent Care Facility	61	Comprehensive Inpatient Rehabilitation Facility
21	Inpatient Hospital	62	Comprehensive Outpatient Rehabilitation Facility
22	Outpatient Hospital	63-64	Unassigned
23	Emergency Room–Hospital	65	End-Stage Renal Disease Treatment Facility
24	Ambulatory Surgical Center	66-70	Unassigned
25	Birthing Center	71	Public Health Clinic
26	Military Treatment Facility	72	Rural Health Clinic
27-30	Unassigned	73-80	Unassigned
31	Skilled Nursing Facility	81	Independent Laboratory
32	Nursing Facility	82-98	Unassigned
33	Custodial Care Facility	99	Other Place of Service

TABLE II-2 List of cases according to payer for Case Studies: Set Two

CASE	PAYER	CASE	PAYER
2-1	Commercial	2-11	Medicaid
2-2	Commercial	2-12	Medicaid
2-3	Commercial	2-13	TRICARE
2-4	BlueCross BlueShield	2-14	TRICARE as Secondary
2-5	BlueCross BlueShield	2-15	Workers' Compensation
2-6	Medicare/Medicaid	2-16	Workers' Compensation
2-7	Medicare	2-17	TRICARE
2-8	Medicare/Medigap	2-18	TRICARE
2-9	Medicare	2-19	Medicare/Medicaid
2-10	Medicare/Medigap	2-20	BlueCross BlueShield

CASE STUDY 2-1

GOODMEDICINE CLINIC
1 Provider Street • Anywhere, NY 12345 • (101) 111-2222
NPI: 3345678901

Case Study

PROVIDER(S): HENRY C. CARDIAC, M.D. EIN: 22-1234567 NPI: 3456789012

PATIENT INFORMATION:		INSURANCE INFORMATION:	
Name:	Jose X. Raul	Patient Number:	2-1
Address:	10 Main Street	Place of Service:	Office
City:	Anywhere	Primary Insurance Plan:	Bell Atlantic
State:	NY	Primary Insurance Plan ID #:	222304040
Zip Code:	12345-1234	Group #:	
Telephone:	(101) 111-5454	Primary Policyholder:	Self
Gender:	Male	Policyholder Date of Birth:	01-01-1968
Date of Birth:	01-01-1968	Relationship to Patient:	
Occupation:	Lineman	Secondary Insurance Plan:	
Employer:	Anywhere Telephone Co.	Secondary Insurance Plan ID #:	
Spouse's Employer:		Secondary Policyholder:	

Patient Status ☐ Married ☐ Divorced ☒ Single ☐ Student ☐ Other

DIAGNOSIS INFORMATION

	Diagnosis	Code		Diagnosis	Code
1.			5.		
2.			6.		
3.			7.		
4.			8.		

PROCEDURE INFORMATION

	Description of Procedure or Service	Date	Code	Charge
1.	Office consultation, level III	06-20-YYYY		100.00
2.				
3.				
4.				
5.				
6.				

SPECIAL NOTES:
Referring Physician is I.M. Gooddoc, M.D. (NPI: 5678901234).

GOODMEDICINE CLINIC
1 Provider Street • Anywhere, NY 12345 • (101) 111-2222

Patient Record

PROVIDER: HENRY C. CARDIAC, M.D.

RAUL, JOSE X.

OFFICE CONSULTATION 06/20/YYYY

S: Patient is an adult Mexican-American single male, referred by Dr. I.M. Gooddoc for consultation. He noted umbilical mass roughly five days ago, two days after the onset of pain in this region. There is no known etiology. He had been physically active, but within the past two months he has not engaged in normal physical activity. He has erratic bowel habits with defecation 2-3-4 days and has a history of having some bright red blood in the stool and on the toilet tissue. He has had no melanotic stool or narrowing of the stool. He denies episodic diarrhea. He has had bronchitis and sinus difficulties, particularly in the fall. He is a nonsmoker. He has no GU symptoms of prostatism. Health history reveals chronic nonspecific dermatitis of eyes, ears, hands and groin, and in fact, felt that bleeding in perianal region was secondary to this. He was a full-term delivery. History reveals maternal uncle had hernia similar to this. Medications include use of halogenated steroid for skin condition. HE HAS ALLERGIES IN THE FALL TO POLLEN. HE HAS SENSITIVITY TO PERCODAN OR PERCOCET, CAUSING NAUSEA, although he has taken Tylenol #3 without difficulty. He takes penicillin without difficulty. The rest of the family and social history are noncontributory. Details can be found in patient's history questionnaire.

O: Supraclavicular fossae are free from adenopathy. Chest is clear to percussion and auscultation. No cutaneous icterus is present. Abdomen is soft and nontender, without masses or organomegaly. Penis is circumcised and normal. Testicles are scrotal and normal. No hernia is palpable in the groin. At the base of the umbilicus, there is suggestion of crepitus but no true hernia at this time. Rectal examination reveals normal tone. There is some induration of perianal tissues. The prostate is 3 x 4 cm and normal in architecture. Hemoccult testing of the formed stool is negative for blood.

A: 1. Umbilical mass. Possible umbilical cyst, possible umbilical hernia.
2. Rectal bleeding.

P: 1. Schedule endoscopic evaluation of lower colon.
2. Schedule follow-up visit to evaluate progression of umbilical change.
3. Note dictated to Dr. Gooddoc.

Henry C. Cardiac, M.D.
Henry C. Cardiac, M.D.

CASE STUDY 2-2

GOODMEDICINE CLINIC

1 Provider Street • Anywhere, NY 12345 • (101) 111-2222
NPI: 3345678901

Case Study

PROVIDER(S): HENRY C. CARDIAC, M.D. EIN: 22-1234567 NPI: 3456789012

PATIENT INFORMATION:		INSURANCE INFORMATION:	
Name:	Kay Moutaine	Patient Number:	2-2
Address:	634 Goodview Avenue	Place of Service:	Office
City:	Anywhere	Primary Insurance Plan:	Connecticut General
State:	NY	Primary Insurance Plan ID #:	877345567
Zip Code:	12345-1234	Group #:	
Telephone:	(101) 115-1234	Primary Policyholder:	Charles W. Moutaine
Gender:	Female	Policyholder Date of Birth:	03-04-1952
Date of Birth:	06-01-1955	Relationship to Patient:	Spouse
Occupation:	Pharmacist	Secondary Insurance Plan:	
Employer:	Goodmedicine Pharmacy	Secondary Insurance Plan ID #:	
Spouse's Employer:	General Electric	Secondary Policyholder:	

Patient Status ☒ Married ☐ Divorced ☐ Single ☐ Student ☐ Other

DIAGNOSIS INFORMATION

	Diagnosis	Code		Diagnosis	Code
1.			5.		
2.			6.		
3.			7.		
4.			8.		

PROCEDURE INFORMATION

	Description of Procedure or Service	Date	Code	Charge
1.	Office visit, level III	06-20-YYYY		75.00
2.				
3.				
4.				
5.				
6.				

SPECIAL NOTES:
Schedule return visit as needed.

GOODMEDICINE CLINIC
1 Provider Street • Anywhere, NY 12345 • (101) 111-2222

Patient Record

PROVIDER: HENRY C. CARDIAC, M.D.

MOUTAINE, KAY

OFFICE VISIT 06/20/YYYY

S: This white female, who appears her stated age, is seen for the first time and will undergo routine annual physical examination. She has history of sensory seizure disorder for which she takes Tegretol. This was diagnosed on EEG in California. Tegretol has been quite efficacious in controlling her symptoms. She has sensations of "slipping away," auditory hallucinations, and déjà vu with these attacks, which last for 45 seconds. She also has history of migraines for which she takes Inderal, with no exacerbation in several years. (I discussed with her the advantages and disadvantages of discontinuing prophylaxis in light of no recurrence of migraines.) She has history of allergies and asthma for which she takes Vanceril daily and Ventolin on a p.r.n. basis. She has history of fibrocystic breast disease for which she takes vitamin E and follows a low-caffeine diet. Recently, she was found to have heme positive stools with negative colonoscopy, BE, and sigmoidoscopy. Currently on Colace and Fiberall for hemorrhoids. No complaints today. Had Pap smear and mammogram in October.

O: NAD. HEENT: PERRL, funduscopic benign. Sinuses nontender. NECK: Supple, no nodes or masses. CHEST: Clear. HEART: RRR, without murmur. ABDOMEN: Soft, nontender. NEURO: Cranial nerves II-XII, sensory, motor, cerebellar grossly intact. Gait coordinated. LAB: Peak expiratory flow equals 510 liters/second.

A: 1. Temporal lobe epilepsy, doing well on Tegretol.
2. Migraines, doing well on prophylaxis.
3. Bronchial asthma, doing well.
4. Allergic rhinosinusitis, doing well on Vanceril.
5. Fibrocystic breast disease, no breast exam done today as it was done in October.
6. History of hemorrhoids.

P: Renew medications: Tegretol, 200 mg, 1 P.O., b.i.d. #100, 1 refill.

Henry C. Cardiac, M.D.
Henry C. Cardiac, M.D.

CASE STUDY 2-3

GOODMEDICINE CLINIC
1 Provider Street • Anywhere, NY 12345 • (101) 111-2222
NPI: 3345678901

Case Study

PROVIDER(S): JANET B. SURGEON, M.D. EIN: 33-1234567 NPI: 9012345678

PATIENT INFORMATION:		INSURANCE INFORMATION:	
Name:	Chang Li Ping	Patient Number:	2-3
Address:	100 Christa St	Place of Service:	Office & Inpatient Hospital
City:	Injury	Primary Insurance Plan:	Connecticut General
State:	NY	Primary Insurance Plan ID #:	333669999
Zip Code:	12347-1234	Group #:	
Telephone:	(101) 111-4545	Primary Policyholder:	Song Ping
Gender:	Male	Policyholder Date of Birth:	06-01-1942
Date of Birth:	01-06-1945	Relationship to Patient:	Spouse
Occupation:	Clerk	Secondary Insurance Plan:	
Employer:	Good Growth, Inc.	Secondary Insurance Plan ID #:	
Spouse's Employer:	Hunan Inc.	Secondary Policyholder:	

Patient Status ☒ Married ☐ Divorced ☐ Single ☐ Student ☐ Other

DIAGNOSIS INFORMATION

	Diagnosis	Code		Diagnosis	Code
1.			5.		
2.			6.		
3.			7.		
4.			8.		

PROCEDURE INFORMATION

	Description of Procedure or Service	Date	Code	Charge
1.	Office visit, level III	06-14-YYYY		75.00
2.	Proctectomy with one-stage colostomy	06-16-YYYY		800.00
3.				
4.				
5.				
6.				

SPECIAL NOTES:
Admitted to Goodmedicine Hospital, 1 Provider Street, Anywhere, NY 12345, on 6/16/YYYY, discharged 6/20/YYYY. (NPI: 1123456789).

GOODMEDICINE CLINIC
1 Provider Street • Anywhere, NY 12345 • (101) 111-2222

Patient Record

PROVIDER: Janet B. Surgeon, M.D.

PING, CHANG LI
OFFICE VISIT 06/14/YYYY

S: Mature adult Asian-American male patient, seen for the first time today, was off work due to hypertension when he noted a change in quality of bowel movements in that they became segmented. Two weeks ago occult blood was found in stool on Hemoccult testing x3. Bowel movements occur every 2-3 hours, and stool is flat and hemispheric. He has no weight loss except that following preparation for his barium enema. Appetite is good. In June, he had abdominal cramping. Health problems include hypertension, present for over 20 years, and a recent episode of parotitis. He admits to NO ALLERGIES.

O: No supraclavicular adenopathy. Chest clear to percussion and auscultation. Diminished breath sounds are present. Cardiac exam revealed regular rhythm without extra sound. Abdomen is soft, nontender. Groin is free from adenopathy. Rectal exam revealed normal tone. There is an external hemorrhoid anteriorly. Prostate is 4 x 4 cm, normal in architecture. Hemoccult testing of stool is positive. No masses palpable in rectum. Written report of BE is not yet available, but verbal report from pathology reveals 2 cm apple core type malignant lesion in sigmoid colon, findings compatible with carcinoma.

A: Malignant lesion, sigmoid colon.

P: Admit to Goodmedicine Hospital for complete colonoscopy and evaluation to include CSR, CEA, and liver function. Surgery to follow, if tests prove positive.

Janet B. Surgeon, M.D.
Janet B. Surgeon, M.D.

PING, CHANG LI
INPATIENT HOSPITALIZATION Admission: 06/16/YYYY Discharge: 06/20/YYYY

Patient admitted for surgery due to constricting lesion, lower sigmoid colon. On 6/16/YYYY, complete proctectomy with one-stage colostomy was performed. Pathology report documents malignant lesion, sigmoid colon. Patient was discharged 6/20/YYYY to be seen in the office in 1 week.

Janet B. Surgeon, M.D.
Janet B. Surgeon, M.D.

CASE STUDY 2-4

GOODMEDICINE CLINIC
1 Provider Street • Anywhere, NY 12345 • (101) 111-2222
NPI: 3345678901

Case Study

PROVIDER(S): JANET B. SURGEON, M.D. EIN: 33-1234567 NPI: 90123456789

PATIENT INFORMATION:		INSURANCE INFORMATION:	
Name:	John J. Recall	Patient Number:	2-4
Address:	10 Memory Lane	Place of Service:	Office & Inpatient Hospital
City:	Anywhere	Primary Insurance Plan:	BlueCross BlueShield
State:	NY	Primary Insurance Plan ID #:	ZJW55544
Zip Code:	12345-1234	Group #:	650
Telephone:	(101) 111-4444	Primary Policyholder:	Self
Gender:	Male	Policyholder Date of Birth:	
Date of Birth:	06-03-1942	Relationship to Patient:	
Occupation:	Research Analyst	Secondary Insurance Plan:	
Employer:	Will Solve It, Inc.	Secondary Insurance Plan ID #:	
Spouse's Employer:		Secondary Policyholder:	

Patient Status ☐ Married ☒ Divorced ☐ Single ☐ Student ☐ Other

DIAGNOSIS INFORMATION

	Diagnosis	Code		Diagnosis	Code
1.			5.		
2.			6.		
3.			7.		
4.			8.		

PROCEDURE INFORMATION

	Description of Procedure or Service	Date	Code	Charge
1.	Office visit, level IV	06-18-YYYY		75.00
2.	Open cholecystectomy	06-19-YYYY		1360.00
3.				
4.				
5.				
6.				

SPECIAL NOTES:
New patient referred by Arnold Young, M.D., for surgery (NPI: 0123456789). Surgery performed at Goodmedicine Hospital, 1 Provider Street, Anywhere, NY 12345 (NPI: 1123456789).

GOODMEDICINE CLINIC
1 Provider Street • Anywhere, NY 12345 • (101) 111-2222

Patient Record

PROVIDER: Janet B. Surgeon, M.D.

RECALL, JOHN J.
OFFICE VISIT 06/18/YYYY

S: This new patient is a white adult, divorced male research analyst who was well until approximately early December when he noted nonradiating pain in the right upper quadrant with bloating. He had possible fever with chills several weeks ago, but has had no recurrence of this. He has chronically had increased gas, which was relieved with belching, and he has had some heartburn. He does have fatty food intolerance dating back several years. His pain has been intermittent since the initial episode. He has been slightly constipated. He has no alcoholic stools, jaundice, or liver disease. He drinks two highballs each night and smokes one pack of cigarettes per day. His weight has decreased 55 lbs in the past six months. As a child, he had jaundice. His family history is negative for gallbladder disease. He has NO KNOWN ALLERGIES. His other medical problems include diabetes, diagnosed 5 years ago; arteriosclerotic cardiovascular disease, without CVA or angina, congestive heart failure or arrhythmia. Studies reveal cholelithiasis and a normal upper gastrointestinal series.

O: Supraclavicular fossae are free from adenopathy. Chest is clear to percussion and auscultation. Cardiac examination reveals a regular rhythm, which is slow, without murmur or extra sound. The abdomen is soft and nontender, without masses or organomegaly. There is a suggestion of a left inguinal hernia. Groin is free of adenopathy. Rectal examination reveals normal tone without masses.

A: Cholelithiasis and chronic cholecystitis. Type II diabetes mellitus. Arteriosclerotic cardiovascular disease. Status post five-coronary artery bypass.

P: Admission for cholecystectomy. Obtain films for review.

Janet B. Surgeon, M.D.
Janet B. Surgeon, M.D.

RECALL, JOHN J.
INPATIENT HOSPITALIZATION Admission: 06/19/YYYY Discharge: 06/20/YYYY
Procedure: Cholecystectomy, open, performed yesterday.
Diagnosis: Chronic gallbladder with stones.
Discharge 10:00 AM today. To be seen in 5 days.

Janet B. Surgeon, M.D.
Janet B. Surgeon, M.D.

CASE STUDY 2-5

GOODMEDICINE CLINIC
1 Provider Street • Anywhere, NY 12345 • (101) 111-2222
NPI: 3345678901

Case Study

PROVIDER(S): HENRY C. CARDIAC, M.D. EIN: 22-1234567 NPI: 3456789012

PATIENT INFORMATION:		INSURANCE INFORMATION:	
Name:	Philamena Islander	Patient Number:	2-5
Address:	129 Henry Court	Place of Service:	Office
City:	Anywhere	Primary Insurance Plan:	BlueCross BlueShield
State:	NY	Primary Insurance Plan ID #:	XWJ473655
Zip Code:	12345-1234	Group #:	
Telephone:	(101) 111-7218	Primary Policyholder:	Richard T. Islander
Gender:	Female	Policyholder Date of Birth:	02-11-1952
Date of Birth:	11-21-1953	Relationship to Patient:	Spouse
Occupation:	Secretary	Secondary Insurance Plan:	
Employer:	Nixon Modeling Agency	Secondary Insurance Plan ID #:	
Spouse's Employer:	Wonderful Photos	Secondary Policyholder:	

Patient Status ☒ Married ☐ Divorced ☐ Single ☐ Student ☐ Other

DIAGNOSIS INFORMATION

	Diagnosis	Code		Diagnosis	Code
1.			5.		
2.			6.		
3.			7.		
4.			8.		

PROCEDURE INFORMATION

	Description of Procedure or Service	Date	Code	Charge
1.	Anoscopy with biopsy	06-20-YYYY		100.00
2.				
3.				
4.				
5.				
6.				

SPECIAL NOTES:

GOODMEDICINE CLINIC
1 Provider Street • Anywhere, NY 12345 • (101) 111-2222

Patient Record

PROVIDER: HENRY C. CARDIAC, M.D.

ISLANDER, PHILAMENA
OFFICE SURGERY 06/20/YYYY

S: This patient had no complaints since her last visit until 3 weeks ago when she noted some intermittent soft stool and decrease in the caliber of stools, with some bleeding that discontinued 4 days ago. She had no crampy abdominal pain.

O: External examination of the anus revealed some external skin tags present in the left anterior position. Anal examination revealed an extremely tight anal sphincter. This was dilated manually to allow instrumentation with the anoscope, which was accomplished in a 360 degree orientation. There was some prominence of the crypts and some inflammation of the rectal mucosa, a portion of which was sent for biopsy. This was friable. In the left anterior position, there was a fistula that was healing with some formation of a sentinel pile on the outside, which had been noticed on external examination.

A: Anal fissure, unusual position, nontraumatic.

P: Rule out inflammatory bowel disease with air contrast barium enema examination and reflux into terminal ileum. Patient to return for sigmoidoscopy after BE.

Henry C. Cardiac, M.D.
Henry C. Cardiac, M.D.

CASE STUDY 2-6

GOODMEDICINE CLINIC
1 Provider Street • Anywhere, NY 12345 • (101) 111-2222
NPI: 3345678901

Case Study

PROVIDER(S): NANCY J. HEALER, M.D. EIN: 44-1234567 NPI: 6789012345

PATIENT INFORMATION:		INSURANCE INFORMATION:	
Name:	Imogene Sugar	Patient Number:	2-6
Address:	120 Young Street	Place of Service:	Home
City:	Injury	Primary Insurance Plan:	Medicare
State:	NY	Primary Insurance Plan ID #:	777228888W
Zip Code:	12347-1234	Group #:	
Telephone:	(101) 111-8675	Primary Policyholder:	Self
Gender:	Female	Policyholder Date of Birth:	
Date of Birth:	03-09-1924	Relationship to Patient:	
Occupation:	Retired	Secondary Insurance Plan:	Medicaid
Employer:		Secondary Insurance Plan ID #:	1155773388
Spouse's Employer:		Secondary Policyholder:	Self

Patient Status ☐ Married ☐ Divorced ☒ Single ☐ Student ☐ Other

DIAGNOSIS INFORMATION

	Diagnosis	Code		Diagnosis	Code
1.			5.		
2.			6.		
3.			7.		
4.			8.		

PROCEDURE INFORMATION

	Description of Procedure or Service	Date	Code	Charge
1.	Home visit, level II	06-20-YYYY		45.00
2.				
3.				
4.				
5.				
6.				

SPECIAL NOTES:

GOODMEDICINE CLINIC
1 Provider Street • Anywhere, NY 12345 • (101) 111-2222

Patient Record

PROVIDER: Nancy J. Healer, M.D.

SUGAR, IMOGENE
HOME VISIT 06/20/YYYY

S: Patient was visited at home in follow-up for her type I uncontrolled diabetes with circulatory problems. On 05/10/YYYY, while visiting her daughter in Somewhere, MD, she saw an orthopedic surgeon who admitted her to the hospital and did a transmetatarsal amputation of her left foot. She had not notified Dr. Bones or me that she had received a second opinion or that she had gone through with surgery.

O: Her blood pressure is 130/70; she looks well. Chest is clear and cardiac examination is unremarkable. Examination of the left leg shows no edema, redness, or heat in the lower extremity. The patient had strict instructions not to allow me to unwrap the wound.

This patient underwent left transmetatarsal amputation although neither Dr. Bones nor I felt a BKA was warranted. I encouraged the patient to be compliant with follow-up planned by her orthopedic surgeon. I will inform Dr. Bones that she had gone ahead with the surgery and, if problems develop, she is to contact me.

A: Diabetes mellitus, type I, uncontrolled, with peripheral vascular disease.

P: Schedule office follow-up visit in 2 weeks.

Nancy J. Healer, M.D.
Nancy J. Healer, M.D.

CASE STUDY 2-7

GOODMEDICINE CLINIC
1 Provider Street • Anywhere, NY 12345 • (101) 111-2222
NPI: 3345678901

Case Study

PROVIDER(S): HENRY C. CARDIAC, M.D. EIN: 22-1234567 NPI: 3456789012

PATIENT INFORMATION:		INSURANCE INFORMATION:	
Name:	Esau Gonzales	Patient Number:	2-7
Address:	14 Ridley St	Place of Service:	Office
City:	Nowhere	Primary Insurance Plan:	Medicare
State:	NY	Primary Insurance Plan ID #:	101234591A
Zip Code:	12346-1234	Group #:	
Telephone:	(101) 111-7689	Primary Policyholder:	Self
Gender:	Male	Policyholder Date of Birth:	
Date of Birth:	09-10-1933	Relationship to Patient:	
Occupation:	Retired	Secondary Insurance Plan:	
Employer:		Secondary Insurance Plan ID #:	
Spouse's Employer:		Secondary Policyholder:	

Patient Status ☐ Married ☐ Divorced ☒ Single ☐ Student ☐ Other

DIAGNOSIS INFORMATION

	Diagnosis	Code		Diagnosis	Code
1.			5.		
2.			6.		
3.			7.		
4.			8.		

PROCEDURE INFORMATION

	Description of Procedure or Service	Date	Code	Charge
1.	Office visit, level IV	06-20-YYYY		100.00
2.	EKG, routine with interpretation	06-20-YYYY		65.00
3.				
4.				
5.				
6.				

SPECIAL NOTES:

GOODMEDICINE CLINIC
1 Provider Street • Anywhere, NY 12345 • (101) 111-2222

Patient Record

PROVIDER: HENRY C. CARDIAC, M.D.

GONZALES, ESAU
OFFICE VISIT 06/20/YYYY

S: Elderly African American male returns, after a two-year hiatus, for follow-up of coronary artery disease and associated problems. Since triple coronary bypass surgery four years ago, he has had no chest discomfort. It should be noted that he had no chest discomfort during a markedly abnormal stress test performed just two weeks before the bypass surgery. He now reports intermittent dyspnea that occurs at rest and spontaneously abates. He does not notice any discomfort on exertion, but he does report that his lifestyle is sedentary. He denies orthopnea, paroxysmal nocturnal dyspnea, or edema. He has continued to follow up with his internist, Dr. Gooddoc, for treatment of his dyslipidemia and hypertension. He is on Cholestin and Tenormin.

O: Patient is a mildly obese, African American male appearing his stated age, in no acute distress. Weight is 210. Height is 5'8". Pulse 16. BP 162/82, 172/82, and then 188/82 in the office. HEENT grossly unremarkable. Neck reveals normal jugular venous pressure, without hepatojugular reflux. Normal carotid pulses; no bruits present. Lungs are clear to A&P. Heart reveals regular rhythm, S1 and S2 are normal. There is no murmur, rub, click, or gallop. Cardiac apex is not palpable. No heaves or thrills are detected. Abdomen is soft, nontender, with normal bowel sounds, and no bruits. No organomegaly, including abdominal aorta, or masses noted. Extremities reveal a surgical scar in the right leg, presumably from saphenous venectomy. Femoral pulses are normal, without bruits. Dorsalis pedis and posterior tibial pulses are also normal. There is no cyanosis, clubbing, or edema. Neurological is grossly within normal limits.

A: 1. Dyspnea.
2. Hypertension.
3. Hypercholesterolemia.
4. Status post aortocoronary bypass surgery four years ago.

Per EKG, an inferior myocardial infarction may have occurred sometime in the past. There is independent suggestion of this on stress-thallium test performed six months ago. Additionally, he still has symptoms of dyspnea.

P: 1. Patient was instructed to follow-up with Dr. Gooddoc for hypertension and dyslipidemia.
2. Schedule treadmill stress test for next week.

Henry C. Cardiac, M.D.
Henry C. Cardiac, M.D.

CASE STUDY 2-8

GOODMEDICINE CLINIC
1 Provider Street • Anywhere, NY 12345 • (101) 111-2222
NPI: 3345678901

Case Study

PROVIDER(S): NANCY J. HEALER, M.D. EIN: 44-1234567 NPI: 6789012345

PATIENT INFORMATION:		INSURANCE INFORMATION:	
Name:	Mary Blooming Bush	Patient Number:	2-8
Address:	9910 Williams Rd	Place of Service:	Office
City:	Nowhere	Primary Insurance Plan:	Medicare
State:	NY	Primary Insurance Plan ID #:	071269645B
Zip Code:	12346-1234	Group #:	
Telephone:	(101) 111-9922	Primary Policyholder:	Self
Gender:	Female	Policyholder Date of Birth:	
Date of Birth:	04-01-1930	Secondary Insurance Plan:	Cigna Medigap
Occupation:	Retired	Secondary Insurance Policy #:	ABC9876
Employer:		Secondary Insurance Plan ID #:	9912345678
Spouse's Employer:		Secondary Policyholder:	Self

Patient Status ☐ Married ☐ Divorced ☒ Single ☐ Student ☐ Other

DIAGNOSIS INFORMATION

	Diagnosis	Code		Diagnosis	Code
1.			5.		
2.			6.		
3.			7.		
4.			8.		

PROCEDURE INFORMATION

	Description of Procedure or Service	Date	Code	Charge
1.	Office visit, level IV	06-20-YYYY		100.00
2.				
3.				
4.				
5.				
6.				

SPECIAL NOTES:

GOODMEDICINE CLINIC
1 Provider Street • Anywhere, NY 12345 • (101) 111-2222

Patient Record

PROVIDER: Nancy J. Healer, M.D.

BUSH, MARY BLOOMING
OFFICE VISIT 06/20/YYYY

S: This elderly, widowed Native American woman returns to the office today after having had a possible seizure at dinner last night. She reports that she was sitting at the table and suddenly fell to the floor. She had urine incontinence at that time and awoke in a slightly confused state with a bad headache. She denies any recent trauma, blows to the head, chest pain, palpitation, paresthesias, aura, or other symptoms. Her history is remarkable for a well-differentiated nodular lymphoma on the upper right arm that was diagnosed and treated with radiation by Dr. Raes in Anywhere, NY. She has had no clinical evidence of recurrence. There has been no prior hospitalization other than for childbirth. Para: 1001. She has had mild COPD for the past 10 years. Her husband died of an unexpected myocardial infarction 2 years ago. She now lives with her daughter. The review of systems is noncontributory. She has no current medications and the only known allergy is to penicillin.

O: Physical exam shows a well-nourished, well-developed female in no acute distress at this time. Her clothed weight is 155 lbs. Blood pressure: 120/72, both arms, with no orthostasis. Pulse: 70 and regular. Respirations: Unlabored at 18. HEENT: Head is normocephalic and atraumatic. PERRLA with intact EOMs. Sclerae are white and the conjunctivae are pink. Funduscopic exam is benign. Ears are normal bilaterally. There is no evidence of Battle's sign. The mouth and throat are unremarkable. Tongue is midline without atrophy or fasciculation. Neck is supple without JVD, adenopathy, thyromegaly, or bruits. The lungs are clear to P&A. Breasts are pendulous with no masses, dimpling, or nipple retraction. Heart rate and rhythm are regular with a grade II/VI SEM along the LSB without gallop, rub, clicks, or other adventitious sounds. Abdomen is soft and nontender without organomegaly, masses, or bruits. Bowel sounds are normal. Rectum has good sphincter tone without masses. Stool is hemoccult negative. Extremities have no edema, cyanosis, jaundice, clubbing, or petechiae. The peripheral pulses are full and palpable. There is no significant cervical, supraclavicular, axillary, or inguinal adenopathy noted. The mental status is normal. Cranial nerves II-XII are intact. Motor, sensory, and cerebellar function is normal. Romberg sign is normal. The Babinski is absent. Reflexes are 2+ and symmetrical in both upper and lower extremities.

A: Seizure. Rule out tumor, metabolic, and vascular etiologies.

P: The patient will be scheduled ASAP for MRI of the brain and an EEG at Goodmedicine Hospital. Obtain blood for electrolytes, calcium, albumin, LFTs, and CBC with platelet count and sed rate, and send to the lab. Patient was instructed to call immediately if she has any further difficulty or questions.

Nancy J. Healer, M.D.
Nancy J. Healer, M.D.

CASE STUDY 2-9

GOODMEDICINE CLINIC

1 Provider Street • Anywhere, NY 12345 • (101) 111-2222
NPI: 3345678901

Case Study

PROVIDER(S): T. J. STITCHER, M.D. EIN: 55-1234567 NPI: 8901234567

PATIENT INFORMATION:		INSURANCE INFORMATION:	
Name:	Mary A. Cadillac	Patient Number:	2-9
Address:	500 Carr St	Place of Service:	Outpatient Hospital
City:	Anywhere	Primary Insurance Plan:	Medicare
State:	NY	Primary Insurance Plan ID #:	001266811B
Zip Code:	12345-1234	Group #:	
Telephone:	(101) 222-3333	Primary Policyholder:	Self
Gender:	Female	Policyholder Date of Birth:	
Date of Birth:	04-30-1929	Relationship to Patient:	
Occupation:		Secondary Insurance Plan:	
Employer:		Secondary Insurance Plan ID #:	
Spouse's Employer:	Anywhere Auto Dealer Association	Secondary Policyholder:	

Patient Status ☒ Married ☐ Divorced ☐ Single ☐ Student ☐ Other

DIAGNOSIS INFORMATION

	Diagnosis	Code		Diagnosis	Code
1.			5.		
2.			6.		
3.			7.		
4.			8.		

PROCEDURE INFORMATION

	Description of Procedure or Service	Date	Code	Charge
1.	Laparoscopic cholecystectomy with cholangiogram	06-20-YYYY		1350.00
2.	Liver biopsy	06-20-YYYY		100.00
3.	Lysis of adhesions	06-20-YYYY		0.00
4.				
5.				
6.				

SPECIAL NOTES:
Outpatient surgery performed at Goodmedicine Hospital, 1 Provider St, Anywhere, NY 12345. (NPI: 1123456789).

GOODMEDICINE CLINIC
1 Provider Street • Anywhere, NY 12345 • (101) 111-2222

Patient Record

PROVIDER: T.J. Stitcher, M.D.

CADILLAC, MARY A.

OUTPATIENT HOSPITAL SURGERY 06/20/YYYY

PREOPERATIVE DIAGNOSIS: Chronic cholecystitis and cholelithiasis without obstruction.

POSTOPERATIVE DIAGNOSIS: Same.

SURGEON: T.J. Stitcher, M.D.

PROCEDURE: Laparoscopic cholecystectomy, intraoperative cholangiogram, lysis of adhesions, liver biopsy.

ANESTHESIA: General endotracheal.

OPERATIVE FINDINGS: Numerous adhesions around the gallbladder area. Gallbladder was distended. Cystic duct normal in caliber. Common bile duct normal. No residual stone on cholangiogram. Patient has two nodules on each side of inferior lobe of the liver, close to the gallbladder, proximally and distally.

OPERATIVE PROCEDURE: The patient was placed in the dorsal supine position after adequate anesthesia, and the abdomen was prepped and draped in the usual fashion. A right lateral infraumbilical incision was made and dissected to the fascia. The fascia was entered, and dissection of the pre-peritoneum was done to enter the peritoneal cavity. Adhesions were lysed with blunt dissection. Hasson trocar was inserted and anchored to the fascia after 1-0 Vicryl was preset on each side of the fascia. Insufflation was started with CO2. After adequate insufflation, patient was placed in the Trendelenburg position, and a trocar was placed under direct visualization. Skin was infiltrated with 0.5 percent Marcaine. After adequate placement of trocars, grasping forceps was inserted. Gallbladder was grasped on the lateral port along the subcostal area, anterior axillary line to lift the gallbladder up for dissection and lysis of the adhesions around the gallbladder. After adequate lysis of adhesions, neck of gallbladder was grasped with the midclavicular subcostal grasping forceps to expose the triangle of Calot. Careful dissection of cystic branch going to the gallbladder was identified and skeletonized, small clip was placed distal to the cystic duct toward the gallbladder, and small opening was made. Cholangiocath was introduced, cholangiogram was performed using 50 percent dye and completed with no evidence of retained stone. Cholangiocath was removed. Cystic duct was clamped twice distally and proximally using endoclips and divided. Gallbladder was excised from liver bed using the spatula cautery. Copious irrigation of liver bed was clear with no evidence of bile leak or bleeding. Gallbladder was removed from liver bed and brought out toward subxyphoid opening under visualization. Bile content was removed and some stones had to be crushed prior to removal of the gallbladder through the 1 cm opening. Trocar was reinserted and biopsy of nodule noted on liver was made, using a true cut needle, cutting going through skin under direct visualization. Two specimens were removed (two nodules). Patient was placed in reverse Trendelenburg position, and irrigation fluid was removed. All trocars and grasping forceps were removed under direct visualization. Gas was deflated. Hasson was removed under laparoscope. Fascia layer on umbilical area was closed using preset sutures and figure of eight. Fascia and subxyphoid were closed using 0 Vicryl, figure of eight. Subcuticular reapproximation using 4-0 Vicryl was completed, and skin was Steri-stripped after application of Benzoin Tincture. Patient tolerated procedure well. Estimated blood loss was less than 25 cc. Foley catheter was removed, and nasogastric tube was removed prior to the patient being extubated. The patient left the operating room in satisfactory condition.

T.J. Stitcher, M.D.

T.J. Stitcher, M.D.

CASE STUDY 2-10

GOODMEDICINE CLINIC
1 Provider Street • Anywhere, NY 12345 • (101) 111-2222
NPI: 3345678901

Case Study

PROVIDER(S): T. J. STITCHER, M.D. EIN: 55-1234567 NPI: 8901234567

PATIENT INFORMATION:		INSURANCE INFORMATION:	
Name:	John W. Hammerclaw	Patient Number:	2-10
Address:	111 Lumber St	Place of Service:	Office
City:	Anywhere	Primary Insurance Plan:	Medicare
State:	NY	Primary Insurance Plan ID #:	101101010A
Zip Code:	12345-1234	Group #:	
Telephone:	(101) 111-9191	Primary Policyholder:	Self
Gender:	Male	Policyholder Date of Birth:	
Date of Birth:	05-30-1930	Secondary Insurance Plan:	BlueCross BlueShield Medigap
Occupation:	Retired	Secondary Insurance Policy #:	YXW10110
Employer:		Secondary Insurance Plan ID #:	8812345678
Spouse's Employer:		Secondary Policyholder:	Self

Patient Status ☐ Married ☐ Divorced ☒ Single ☐ Student ☐ Other

DIAGNOSIS INFORMATION

	Diagnosis	Code		Diagnosis	Code
1.			5.		
2.			6.		
3.			7.		
4.			8.		

PROCEDURE INFORMATION

	Description of Procedure or Service	Date	Code	Charge
1.	Excision, 4.1 cm cyst, back	06-20-YYYY		360.00
2.	Excision, 2.5 cm cyst, neck	06-20-YYYY		300.00
3.				
4.				
5.				
6.				

SPECIAL NOTES:
Referring physician is Nancy J. Healer, M.D. (NPI: 6789012345).

GOODMEDICINE CLINIC
1 Provider Street • Anywhere, NY 12345 • (101) 111-2222

Patient Record

PROVIDER: T.J. Stitcher, M.D.

HAMMERCLAW, JOHN W.

OFFICE SURGERY 06/20/YYYY

PREOPERATIVE DIAGNOSIS: 4.1 cm infected sebaceous cyst, back; 2.5 cm infected sebaceous cyst, posterior neck.

POSTOPERATIVE DIAGNOSIS: Same.

OPERATION: Excision, 4.1 cm benign cyst, back. Excision, 2.5 cm benign cyst, neck.

PROCEDURE: The patient was placed in the prone position and the back and posterior neck were prepared with Betadine scrub and solution. Sterile towels were applied in the usual fashion, and 0.25 percent Marcaine was injected subcutaneously in a linear fashion transversely over each of the cysts asynchronously. The lower cyst was excised, and the cavity was irrigated with copious amounts of Marcaine solutions. The skin edges were loosely reapproximated throughout with #3-0 nylon suture. Following this, Marcaine was injected around the superior cyst, an incision was made transversely, and the cyst was completely excised. The wound was irrigated with Marcaine and packed with Iodoform, and sterile dressings were applied. The patient was discharged with verbal and written instructions, as well as Tylenol #3 for pain and a prescription for 30 days. Return visit in 3 days for packing removal.

T.J. Stitcher, M.D.

T.J. Stitcher, M.D.

CASE STUDY 2-11

GOODMEDICINE CLINIC
1 Provider Street • Anywhere, NY 12345 • (101) 111-2222
NPI: 3345678901

Case Study

PROVIDER(S): HENRY C. CARDIAC, M.D. EIN: 22-1234567 NPI: 3456789012

PATIENT INFORMATION:		INSURANCE INFORMATION:	
Name:	Germane Fontaine	Patient Number:	2-11
Address:	132 Canal St	Place of Service:	Office
City:	Injury	Primary Insurance Plan:	Medicaid
State:	NY	Primary Insurance Plan ID #:	11347765
Zip Code:	12347-1234	Group #:	
Telephone:	(101) 111-9685	Primary Policyholder:	Self
Gender:	Female	Policyholder Date of Birth:	
Date of Birth:	05-07-1965	Relationship to Patient:	
Occupation:	Unemployed	Secondary Insurance Plan:	
Employer:		Secondary Insurance Plan ID #:	
Spouse's Employer:		Secondary Policyholder:	

Patient Status ☐ Married ☐ Divorced ☒ Single ☐ Student ☐ Other

DIAGNOSIS INFORMATION

	Diagnosis	Code		Diagnosis	Code
1.			5.		
2.			6.		
3.			7.		
4.			8.		

PROCEDURE INFORMATION

	Description of Procedure or Service	Date	Code	Charge
1.	Office visit, level II	06-20-YYYY		26.00
2.	Strep test (CLIA-approved lab.)	06-20-YYYY		12.00
3.				
4.				
5.				
6.				

SPECIAL NOTES:

GOODMEDICINE CLINIC
1 Provider Street • Anywhere, NY 12345 • (101) 111-2222

Patient Record

PROVIDER: HENRY C. CARDIAC, M.D.

FONTAINE, GERMANE
OFFICE VISIT 06/20/YYYY

S: This patient returns today complaining of a sore throat for the past three days, temperature to 101 degrees Fahrenheit with pleuritic cough. She has had abundant postnasal drip.

O: NAD. Sinuses are tender about the maxillary and frontal areas. TMs, gray bilaterally. Pharynx is injected, and there is obvious purulent material in the left posterior pharynx. Neck: Supple, no nodes. Chest: Clear. COR: RRR without murmur. Lab: Sinus films normal.

A: Clinical chronic sinusitis; her sore throat is probably from this, but will obtain a strep test to rule out that possibility, at her request.

P: Beconase nasal spray, 1 whiff to each nostril q.i.d. for 1 week, then 1 whiff b.i.d. to each nostril. If she has not improved in 3 weeks, refer to ENT specialist.

Henry C. Cardiac, M.D.
Henry C. Cardiac, M.D.

CASE STUDY 2-12

GOODMEDICINE CLINIC
1 Provider Street • Anywhere, NY 12345 • (101) 111-2222
NPI: 3345678901

Case Study

PROVIDER(S): HENRY C. CARDIAC, M.D. EIN: 22-1234567 NPI: 3456789012
T.J. STITCHER, M.D. EIN: 55-1234567 NPI: 8901234567

PATIENT INFORMATION:		INSURANCE INFORMATION:	
Name:	James Apple	Patient Number:	2-12
Address:	1 Appleblossom Court	Place of Service:	Inpatient Hospital
City:	Hometown	Primary Insurance Plan:	Medicaid
State:	NY	Primary Insurance Plan ID #:	1234567
Zip Code:	15123-1234	Group #:	
Telephone:	(201) 111-2011	Primary Policyholder:	Self
Gender:	Male	Policyholder Date of Birth:	
Date of Birth:	11-12-1984	Relationship to Patient:	
Occupation:	Unemployed	Secondary Insurance Plan:	
Employer:		Secondary Insurance Plan ID #:	
Spouse's Employer:		Secondary Policyholder:	

Patient Status ☐ Married ☐ Divorced ☒ Single ☒ Student ☐ Other

DIAGNOSIS INFORMATION

Diagnosis	Code	Diagnosis	Code
1.		5.	
2.		6.	
3.		7.	
4.		8.	

PROCEDURE INFORMATION

Description of Procedure or Service	Date	Code	Charge
1. Inpatient visit, level III (Cardiac)	06-19-YYYY		165.00
2. Laparoscopic appendectomy (Stitcher)	06-19-YYYY		1400.00
3.			
4.			
5.			
6.			

SPECIAL NOTES:
Dr. Cardiac is the attending physician. Dr. Stitcher is the surgeon. Care was provided at Goodmedicine Hospital, 1 Provider St, Anywhere, NY 12345. (NPI: 1123456789).

GOODMEDICINE CLINIC
1 Provider Street • Anywhere, NY 12345 • (101) 111-2222

Patient Record

PROVIDER: HENRY C. CARDIAC, M.D.; T.J. STITCHER, M.D.

INPATIENT HOSPITALIZATION Admitted: 06/19/YYYY Discharged: 06/20/YYYY

APPLE, JAMES
ADMITTING PROGRESS NOTE 06/19/YYYY

Patient admitted with acute appendicitis. Dr. Stitcher called in as surgeon.

Henry C. Cardiac, M.D.
Henry C. Cardiac, M.D.

APPLE, JAMES
OPERATIVE REPORT 06/19/YYYY

PREOPERATIVE DIAGNOSIS: Acute appendicitis.

POSTOPERATIVE DIAGNOSIS: Acute appendicitis.

OPERATION: Laparoscopic exploration with appendectomy.

SURGEON: T.J. Stitcher, M.D.

PROCEDURE: Patient anesthetized with general anesthesia via endotracheal tube. Abdomen prepped and draped in sterile fashion. Because of patient's size (he is quite small) it was not possible to place a catheter in the bladder. Patient was placed in Trendelenburg position. Abdominal wall was palpated, no masses felt. Incision was made below the umbilicus, and Verres needle inserted toward the pelvis. This was tested with normal saline; when it appeared to be in the peritoneal cavity, the abdomen was insufflated with 3 liters of CO2. A 1/2 cm camera was introduced through this opening. There was no evidence of injury from the needle or trocar, and the area of the appendix was visualized and some exudates and free fluid in the area noted. Under direct vision, a 1/2-cm trocar was passed through the right edge of the rectus sheath in the mid-abdomen. Using blunt and sharp dissection, the appendix and cecum were mobilized. The mesoappendix was serially ligated with hemoclips and then divided and the appendix freed to its base. The base was identified by the fact it was supple and it lay at the convergence of the tinea. A single 0 chromic suture was laced approximately 1 cm distally, and then the appendix divided between and through the 11 mm trocar. The abdomen was irrigated with normal saline, and the contents aspirated. Skin closed with 4-0 Vicryl, and Benzoin and SteriStrips applied. Estimated blood loss was 10 cc. Sponge and needle counts were correct. Patient tolerated the procedure well and returned to the recovery room awake and in stable condition.

T.J. Stitcher, M.D.
T.J. Stitcher, M.D.

APPLE, JAMES
DISCHARGE PROGRESS NOTE 06/20/YYYY

Patient was unremarkable postoperatively. Discharged 9 AM today. Mother was given standard, written pediatric appendectomy discharge sheet. Patient to be seen in the office of J.H. Cutdown, M.D., in 5 days for postop follow-up.

T.J. Stitcher, M.D.
T.J. Stitcher, M.D.

CASE STUDY 2-13

GOODMEDICINE CLINIC

Case Study

1 Provider Street • Anywhere, NY 12345 • (101) 111-2222
NPI: 3345678901

PROVIDER(S): JANET B. SURGEON, M.D. EIN: 33-1234567 NPI: 9012345678

PATIENT INFORMATION:		INSURANCE INFORMATION:	
Name:	Stanley N. Banana	Patient Number:	2-13
Address:	1 Barrack St	Place of Service:	Outpatient Hospital
City:	Anywhere	Primary Insurance Plan:	TRICARE
State:	NY	Primary Insurance Plan ID #:	123445555 (Sponsor SSN)
Zip Code:	12345-1234	Group #:	
Telephone:	(101) 111-7676	Primary Policyholder:	Self
Gender:	Male	Policyholder Date of Birth:	
Date of Birth:	11-11-1956	Relationship to Patient:	
Occupation:		Secondary Insurance Plan:	
Employer:	US Army	Secondary Insurance Plan ID #:	
Spouse's Employer:		Secondary Policyholder:	

Patient Status ☐ Married ☒ Divorced ☐ Single ☐ Student ☐ Other

DIAGNOSIS INFORMATION

	Diagnosis	Code		Diagnosis	Code
1.			5.		
2.			6.		
3.			7.		
4.			8.		

PROCEDURE INFORMATION

	Description of Procedure or Service	Date	Code	Charge
1.	Flexible sigmoidoscopy	06-20-YYYY		600.00
2.				
3.				
4.				
5.				
6.				

SPECIAL NOTES:

Nancy J. Healer, M.D., referred patient. (NPI: 6789012345). Care provided at Goodmedicine Hospital, 1 Provider St, Anywhere, NY 12345. (NPI: 1123456789).

GOODMEDICINE CLINIC
1 Provider Street • Anywhere, NY 12345 • (101) 111-2222

Patient Record

PROVIDER: JANET B. SURGEON, M.D.

BANANA, STANLEY N.
OUTPATIENT HOSPITAL SURGERY 06/20/YYYY

PROCEDURE: Flexible left sigmoidoscopy was performed. The lining of the colon to this point was normal throughout. No signs of inflammation, ulceration, or mass formation were noted. Anoscope was introduced into the anal canal, and this was examined in 4 quadrants. To the left of the midline posteriorly a 4-5 mm, very small, fissure was seen, apparently exposing an underlying vein that was slightly darker. There was no sign of heaped up margin or any true ulceration.

DIAGNOSIS: Fissure in ano.

PLAN:
1. Dietary modification to increase fluid and bulk in diet.
2. Avoid straining.
3. Use simple measures such as Sitz baths and Tucks pads when the fissure is symptomatic.
4. Return visit on a prn basis should any additional bleeding be seen.

Janet B. Surgeon, M.D.
Janet B. Surgeon, M.D.

CASE STUDY 2-14

GOODMEDICINE CLINIC
1 Provider Street • Anywhere, NY 12345 • (101) 111-2222
NPI: 3345678901

Case Study

PROVIDER(S): JANET B. SURGEON, M.D. EIN: 33-1234567 NPI: 9012345678

PATIENT INFORMATION:		INSURANCE INFORMATION:	
Name:	Reginald T. Karot	Patient Number:	2-14
Address:	15 Caring St	Place of Service:	Office
City:	Anywhere	Primary Insurance Plan:	Metropolitan
State:	NY	Primary Insurance Policy #:	222 22 222A
Zip Code:	12345-1234	Group #:	
Telephone:	(101) 222-0022	Primary Policyholder:	Louise Karot
Gender:	Male	Policyholder Date of Birth:	10-11-1936
Date of Birth:	10-01-1936	Relationship to Patient:	Spouse
Occupation:	Construction worker	Secondary Insurance Plan:	TRICARE Standard
Employer:	Is A Construction Co.	Secondary Insurance ID #:	012346543
Spouse's Employer:	Anywhere School District	Secondary Policyholder:	Self

Patient Status ☒ Married ☐ Divorced ☐ Single ☐ Student ☐ Other

DIAGNOSIS INFORMATION

	Diagnosis	Code		Diagnosis	Code
1.			5.		
2.			6.		
3.			7.		
4.			8.		

PROCEDURE INFORMATION

	Description of Procedure or Service	Date	Code	Charge
1.	Office visit, level III, new patient	06-20-YYYY		75.00
2.				
3.				
4.				
5.				
6.				

SPECIAL NOTES:
Nancy J. Healer, M.D., referred patient (NPI: 6789012345).

GOODMEDICINE CLINIC
1 Provider Street • Anywhere, NY 12345 • (101) 111-2222

Patient Record

PROVIDER: JANET B. SURGEON, M.D.

KAROT, REGINALD T.
OFFICE VISIT 06/20/YYYY

S: One year ago today, this new patient noticed a bulge in his left side. He has had possible weakness on the right side, noted in Dr. Healer's evaluation today. He does not smoke; he runs frequently and does not do any heavy lifting or straining. He has had some minor changes in his urinary stream and has been noted to have an enlarged prostate in the past. He reports terminal dribbling, but has no difficulty with initiating a stream and has noticed no change in the force of the stream. He reports his bowel movements have been normal. There has been no blood or black stools. He has no other significant medical problems. See the attached Family and Social History Data Sheet elsewhere in this chart.

O: The supraclavicular fossae are free of adenopathy. The chest is clear to percussion and auscultation. The abdomen is soft and nontender, without masses or organomegaly. There is a right lower quadrant appendectomy incision that is well healed. The penis is circumcised without masses. The testicles are scrotal and normal. In the standing position, there is a left inguinal hernia that exits the external right and a right inguinal external hernia that is beginning to do this. Rectal examination revealed normal tone. The prostate is 4.0 x 4.0 cm and normal in architecture. The stool was hemoccult negative.

A: Bilateral inguinal hernias, left greater than right.

P: Schedule for bilateral inguinal herniorrhaphy in early July.

Janet B. Surgeon, M.D.
Janet B. Surgeon, M.D.

CASE STUDY 2-15

GOODMEDICINE CLINIC
1 Provider Street • Anywhere, NY 12345 • (101) 111-2222
NPI: 3345678901

Case Study

PROVIDER(S): T.J. STICHER, M.D. EIN: 55-1234567 NPI: 8901234567

PATIENT INFORMATION:		INSURANCE INFORMATION:	
Name:	James Lawrence Butcher	Patient Number:	2-15
Address:	14 Pigsfeet Rd	Place of Service:	Emergency Department Hospital
City:	Anywhere	WC Insurance Plan:	Workers Comp Fund
State:	NY	Patient's SSN:	321458765
Zip Code:	12345-1234	WC Claim #:	987123
Telephone:	(101) 333-4567	WC Policyholder:	Piglet Meat Packers
Gender:	Male	Address:	100 Reynolds Way
Date of Birth:	02-29-1977	City, State and Zip Code:	Anywhere, NY 12345
Occupation:	Meat cutter		
Employer:	Piglet Meat Packers		
Spouse's Employer:			

Patient Status ☐ Married ☐ Divorced ☒ Single ☐ Student ☐ Other

DIAGNOSIS INFORMATION

	Diagnosis	Code		Diagnosis	Code
1.			5.		
2.			6.		
3.			7.		
4.			8.		

PROCEDURE INFORMATION

	Description of Procedure or Service	Date	Code	Charge
1.	Extensor tendon repair	06-19-YYYY		1400.00
2.				
3.				
4.				
5.				
6.				

SPECIAL NOTES:
Workers Comp Fund, 113 Insurance Ave, Anywhere, NY 12345. Admission date: 06-19-YYYY. Discharge date: 06-19-YYYY. Return to work on 8-19-YYYY (light duty). Care provided at Goodmedicine Hospital, 1 Provider St, Anywhere, NY 12345. (NPI: 1123456789).

GOODMEDICINE CLINIC
1 Provider Street • Anywhere, NY 12345 • (101) 111-2222

Patient Record

PROVIDER: T. J. STITCHER, M.D.

BUTCHER, JAMES LAWRENCE
ED VISIT 06/19/YYYY

DIAGNOSIS: 2 cm laceration, dorsum of left thumb, including laceration of extensor tendon.

PROCEDURE: Repair of extensor tendon laceration, dorsum of left thumb.

HISTORY: 22-year-old male seen with chief complaint of 2 cm laceration of the back of his left thumb. Patient said, "I was cutting some pieces of lumber using a battery-powered Sawzall (electric power tool) when it slipped and cut the back of my thumb." He cannot extend his thumb since the accident, and he had some bleeding, which he stopped with pressure. Patient had tetanus toxoid administered last year when he sustained a wound to the forearm while at work. He has no past history of serious illnesses, operations, or allergies. Social and family history are noncontributory.

PHYSICAL FINDINGS: Examination reveals a well-developed, well-nourished white male appearing his stated age and in no acute distress. He has no abnormal findings other than the left thumb, which shows a laceration of the dorsum of the thumb proximal to the interphalangeal joint with damage to the nail. The patient cannot extend the thumb; he can flex, adduct, and abduct the thumb. Sensation at this time appears to be normal.

PROCEDURE: With the patient in the supine position, the area was prepped and draped. A digital nerve block using 1 percent of Carbocaine was carried out. When the block was totally effective, the wound was explored. The distal severed end of the tendon was located. The proximal end could not be found. A vertical incision was then made down the lateral aspect of the thumb starting at the corner of the original laceration, thus creating a flap. When the flap was retracted back, the proximal portion of the tendon was located. Both tendon ends had a very clean-cut surface; therefore, the tendon was not trimmed. Examination revealed the joint capsule had been lacerated. After thorough irrigation of the wound with normal saline the joint capsule was repaired with two sutures of 5-0 Dexon. The tendon repair was then carried out using 4-0 nylon. When the tendon repair was complete, the patient was allowed to flex the thumb gently and then fully extend it. The thumb was then held in full extension. The wound was again irrigated well and the skin was then closed with 4-0 nylon. Dressings were applied and a splint was applied holding the interphalangeal joint in neutral position, in full extension but not hyperextension. The patient tolerated the procedure well and left the surgical area in good condition.

DISPOSITION OF CASE: Patient was instructed to elevate the hand, keep his fingers moving, keep the dressing clean and dry, and not to remove the splint or dressing at home. He is to take Percocet, one q4h as needed for pain. He will take Augmentin, 250 mg t.i.d. If he has any problems or difficulties, he is to call or return to the emergency department; otherwise, he will be seen in the office for follow-up in three days.

T.J. Stitcher, M.D.
T.J. Stitcher, M.D.

CASE STUDY 2-16

GOODMEDICINE CLINIC

1 Provider Street • Anywhere, NY 12345 • (101) 111-2222
NPI: 3345678901

Case Study

PROVIDER(S): GAIL R. BONES, M.D. EIN: 66-1234567 NPI: 1234567890

PATIENT INFORMATION:		INSURANCE INFORMATION:	
Name:	David J. Hurts	Patient Number:	2-16
Address:	4321 Nowhere St	Place of Service:	Office
City:	Anywhere	WC Insurance Plan:	Industrial Indemnity Co.
State:	NY	Patient's SSN:	112102121
Zip Code:	12345-1234	WC Claim #:	123987
Telephone:	(101) 314-1414	WC Policyholder:	UC Painters
Gender:	Male	Address:	1 Circle Dr
Date of Birth:	02-28-1955	City, State, and Zip Code:	Anywhere, NY 12345
Occupation:	Painter		
Employer:	UC Painters		
Spouse's Employer:			

Patient Status ☐ Married ☐ Divorced ☒ Single ☐ Student ☐ Other

DIAGNOSIS INFORMATION

	Diagnosis	Code		Diagnosis	Code
1.			5.		
2.			6.		
3.			7.		
4.			8.		

PROCEDURE INFORMATION

	Description of Procedure or Service	Date	Code	Charge
1.	X-ray, left forearm, complete	06-20-YYYY		80.00
2.	Closed fracture repair, left radius	06-20-YYYY		300.00
3.	Wound repair, face, 2 cm	06-20-YYYY		80.00
4.				
5.				
6.				

SPECIAL NOTES:
Industrial Indemnity Co., 10 Policy St, Anywhere, NY 12345. Return to work 8/9/YYYY.

GOODMEDICINE CLINIC
1 Provider Street • Anywhere, NY 12345 • (101) 111-2222

Patient Record

PROVIDER: GAIL R. BONES, M.D.

HURTS, DAVID J.
OFFICE VISIT 06/20/YYYY

S: At 10:30 this morning, Mr. Ima Boss presented himself at the front desk and announced that he was the supervisor at UC Painters, Inc., and he had an injured worker in the car. The patient is David J. Hurts, who was injured when he fell from a ladder while painting at 543 House St. in Anywhere. The injury occurred at 10:15 AM. The patient says he fell when a step broke on the ladder.

O: X-rays revealed a Colles' fracture of the left radius with only minor displacement.

A: Colles' fracture, left radius. Multiple abrasions and lacerations.

P: The fracture was reduced and a plaster cast applied. The patient was given a prescription for Tylenol #3, instructed in cast care, and told to return tomorrow for a cast check. A 2.0 cm medial mandible laceration was closed with 3 black silk sutures. The supervisor and patient were told the patient would not be able to return to his regular painting job for approximately 6 weeks. The doctor stated she does not anticipate any permanent disability.

Gail R. Bones, M.D.
Gail R. Bones, M.D.

CASE STUDY 2-17

GOODMEDICINE CLINIC
1 Provider Street • Anywhere, NY 12345 • (101) 111-2222
NPI: 3345678901

Case Study

PROVIDER(S): JANET B. SURGEON, M.D. EIN: 33-1234567 NPI: 9012345678

PATIENT INFORMATION:		INSURANCE INFORMATION:	
Name:	Peter M. Smith	Patient Number:	2-17
Address:	1000 Main St, Apt B	Place of Service:	Office
City:	Anywhere	Primary Insurance Plan:	TRICARE
State:	NY	Primary Insurance Plan ID #:	235 23 6594
Zip Code:	12345-1234	Group #:	
Telephone:	(101) 562-9654	Primary Policyholder:	Peter M. Smith
Gender:	Male	Policyholder Date of Birth:	02-20-1965
Date of Birth:	02-20-1965	Relationship to Patient:	Self
Occupation:	Accountant	Secondary Insurance Plan:	
Employer:	Peebles & Clark	Secondary Insurance Plan ID #:	
Spouse's Employer:	State University	Secondary Policyholder:	

Patient Status ☒ Married ☐ Divorced ☐ Single ☐ Student ☐ Other

DIAGNOSIS INFORMATION

	Diagnosis	Code		Diagnosis	Code
1.			5.		
2.			6.		
3.			7.		
4.			8.		

PROCEDURE INFORMATION

	Description of Procedure or Service	Date	Code	Charge
1.	Office visit, level IV	06-20-YYYY		100.00
2.				
3.				
4.				
5.				
6.				

SPECIAL NOTES:

GOODMEDICINE CLINIC
1 Provider Street • Anywhere, NY 12345 • (101) 111-2222

Patient Record

PROVIDER: JANET B. SURGEON, M.D.

SMITH, PETER M.
OFFICE VISIT 06/20/YYYY

Mr. Smith comes to the office today complaining of severe left hand pain. I performed tendon repair on his left hand in the emergency department two days ago.

The dressing and splint were removed, taking care to keep the finger in extension. It should be noted that when the dressing was removed, there was a slight flexion to the thumb as it was lying in the splint as the patient had replaced it. The wound was inflamed and hot.

The wound was cleaned with aqueous Zephiran; Betadine Ointment was then applied and it was redressed. A new splint was put on, holding the thumb in a fully extended position.

The patient was instructed to keep the dressing clean and dry, and not remove the splint or the dressing. He is to continue his Augmentin. He will continue on Darvocet-N 100 as needed for pain. He was given a prescription for penicillin. If he has any problems or difficulties, he is to call me or return to the emergency department; otherwise, he will be seen in the office in 2 days.

Diagnosis: Postoperative wound infection, left hand.

Janet B. Surgeon, M.D.
Janet B. Surgeon, M.D.

CASE STUDY 2-18

GOODMEDICINE CLINIC
1 Provider Street • Anywhere, NY 12345 • (101) 111-2222
NPI: 3345678901

Case Study

PROVIDER(S): JANET B. SURGEON, M.D. EIN: 33-1234567 NPI: 9012345678

PATIENT INFORMATION:		INSURANCE INFORMATION:	
Name:	Mary A. Martin	Patient Number:	2-18
Address:	5005 South Ave	Place of Service:	Outpatient Hospital
City:	Anywhere	Primary Insurance Plan:	TRICARE
State:	NY	Sponsor's SSN:	232589571
Zip Code:	12345-1234	Group #:	
Telephone:	(101) 111-7676	Primary Policyholder:	Mary A. Martin
Gender:	Female	Policyholder Date of Birth:	10-05-1955
Date of Birth:	10-05-1955	Relationship to Patient:	Self
Occupation:		Secondary Insurance Plan:	
Employer:	US Navy	Secondary Insurance Plan ID #:	
Spouse's Employer:		Secondary Policyholder:	

Patient Status ☐ Married ☐ Divorced ☒ Single ☐ Student ☐ Other

DIAGNOSIS INFORMATION

Diagnosis	Code	Diagnosis	Code
1.		5.	
2.		6.	
3.		7.	
4.		8.	

PROCEDURE INFORMATION

Description of Procedure or Service	Date	Code	Charge
1. Hysteroscopic endometrial ablation	06-20-YYYY		950.00
2.			
3.			
4.			
5.			
6.			

SPECIAL NOTES:
Surgery performed at Goodmedicine Hospital, 1 Provider St, Anywhere, NY 12345. (NPI: 1123456789).

GOODMEDICINE CLINIC

1 Provider Street • Anywhere, NY 12345 • (101) 111-2222

Patient Record

PROVIDER: JANET B. SURGEON, M.D.

MARTIN, MARY A.

OUTPATIENT HOSPITAL SURGERY 06/20/YYYY

PREOPERATIVE DIAGNOSIS: Menorrhagia

POSTOPERATIVE DIAGNOSIS: Same

PROCEDURE PERFORMED: Endometrial ablation

Patient was anesthetized with general anesthesia via endotracheal tube, and prepped and draped in a sterile fashion. Operative hysteroscope was inserted through the vagina and the cervix into the uterus, and the uterus was filled with saline solution. Thermal ablation of the endometrium was successfully performed, and the hysteroscope and saline were removed. The patient was transferred to the recovery room where her output is to be carefully monitored.

Janet B. Surgeon, M.D.

Janet B. Surgeon, M.D.

CASE STUDY 2-19

GOODMEDICINE CLINIC

1 Provider Street • Anywhere, NY 12345 • (101) 111-2222
NPI: 3345678901

Case Study

PROVIDER(S): NANCY J. HEALER, M.D. EIN: 44-1234567 NPI: 6789012345

PATIENT INFORMATION:		INSURANCE INFORMATION:	
Name:	Cindy Santos	Patient Number:	2-19
Address:	3902 Main St	Place of Service:	Office
City:	Anywhere	Primary Insurance Plan:	Medicare
State:	NY	Primary Insurance Plan ID #:	53231589A
Zip Code:	12345-1234	Group #:	
Telephone:	(101) 111-5128	Primary Policyholder:	Self
Gender:	Female	Policyholder Date of Birth:	
Date of Birth:	04-29-1935	Relationship to Patient:	
Occupation:	Retired	Secondary Insurance Plan:	Medicaid
Employer:		Secondary Insurance Plan ID #:	231562584
Spouse's Employer:		Secondary Policyholder:	Self

Patient Status ☐ Married ☐ Divorced ☒ Single ☐ Student ☐ Other

DIAGNOSIS INFORMATION

	Diagnosis	Code		Diagnosis	Code
1.			5.		
2.			6.		
3.			7.		
4.			8.		

PROCEDURE INFORMATION

	Description of Procedure or Service	Date	Code	Charge
1.	Office visit, level II	06-20-YYYY		50.00
2.				
3.				
4.				
5.				
6.				

SPECIAL NOTES:

GOODMEDICINE CLINIC
1 Provider Street • Anywhere, NY 12345 • (101) 111-2222

Patient Record

PROVIDER: NANCY J. HEALER, M.D.

SANTOS, CINDY
OFFICE VISIT 06/20/YYYY

S: Patient was seen in the office today in follow-up for chronic hypertension. She has no complaints today.

O: Her blood pressure is 120/80. Chest is clear to auscultation and percussion. Heart is unremarkable. Extremities reveal no edema or redness.

A: Chronic hypertension, controlled with medication.

P: Renew hypertensive medication. Schedule office follow-up visit in 3 months.

Nancy J. Healer, M.D.
Nancy J. Healer, M.D.

CASE STUDY 2-20

GOODMEDICINE CLINIC
1 Provider Street • Anywhere, NY 12345 • (101) 111-2222
NPI: 3345678901

Case Study

PROVIDER(S): T.J. STITCHER, M.D. EIN: 55-1234567 NPI: 8901234567

PATIENT INFORMATION:		INSURANCE INFORMATION:	
Name:	Lana Tobias	Patient Number:	2-20
Address:	3920 Hill St	Place of Service:	Office
City:	Anywhere	Primary Insurance Plan:	BlueCross BlueShield
State:	NY	Primary Insurance Plan ID #:	ABC123456
Zip Code:	12345-1234	Group #:	
Telephone:	(101) 555-1235	Primary Policyholder:	Casey Tobias
Gender:	Female	Policyholder Date of Birth:	05-05-1965
Date of Birth:	12-15-1967	Relationship to Patient:	Spouse
Occupation:		Secondary Insurance Plan:	
Employer:		Secondary Insurance Plan ID #:	
Spouse's Employer:	State University	Secondary Policyholder:	

Patient Status ☒ Married ☐ Divorced ☐ Single ☐ Student ☐ Other

DIAGNOSIS INFORMATION

Diagnosis	Code	Diagnosis	Code
1.		5.	
2.		6.	
3.		7.	
4.		8.	

PROCEDURE INFORMATION

Description of Procedure or Service	Date	Code	Charge
1. Office visit, level II	06-20-YYYY		50.00
2.			
3.			
4.			
5.			
6.			

SPECIAL NOTES:

GOODMEDICINE CLINIC
1 Provider Street • Anywhere, NY 12345 • (101) 111-2222

Patient Record

PROVIDER: T.J. STITCHER, M.D.

TOBIAS, LANA

OFFICE VISIT 06/20/YYYY

S: Established patient seen in the office today with complaint of left hip pain. She states that she fell down some stairs in her home two days ago while carrying laundry to her basement. She says when she awakes in the morning, her hip 'really hurts her.'

O: Physical examination reveals good range of motion of her left hip, and she can walk without pain. Bruising is noted in the left hip area.

A: Left hip pain.

P: The patient was instructed to take over-the-counter acetaminophen for pain, as directed. If the pain worsens, she is to call the office.

T.J. Stitcher, M.D.
T.J. Stitcher, M.D.

APPENDIX III

Forms

You are welcome to copy the following forms for use when completing exercises in the textbook and Workbook:

NOTE: The CMS-1500 claim and the UB-04 claim can also be printed from the Student Resources online companion at **www.cengagebrain.com**. You'll need to make approximately 120 copies of the CMS-1500 claim and five copies of the UB-04 claim if you plan to complete all the case studies in the textbook and Workbook.

- **CMS-1500 claim (black and white form suitable for photocopying)**
- **UB-04 claim (black and white form suitable for photocopying)**
- **E/M CodeBuilder (to accompany Chapter 7)**

HEALTH INSURANCE CLAIM FORM

APPROVED BY NATIONAL UNIFORM CLAIM COMMITTEE (NUCC) 02/12

PICA PICA

CARRIER

1. MEDICARE (Medicare#) MEDICAID (Medicaid#) TRICARE (ID#/DoD#) CHAMPVA (Member ID#) GROUP HEALTH PLAN (ID#) FECA BLK LUNG (ID#) OTHER (ID#)

1a. INSURED'S I.D. NUMBER (For Program in Item 1)

2. PATIENT'S NAME (Last Name, First Name, Middle Initial)

3. PATIENT'S BIRTH DATE MM DD YY SEX M F

4. INSURED'S NAME (Last Name, First Name, Middle Initial)

5. PATIENT'S ADDRESS (No., Street)

6. PATIENT RELATIONSHIP TO INSURED Self Spouse Child Other

7. INSURED'S ADDRESS (No., Street)

CITY STATE

8. RESERVED FOR NUCC USE

CITY STATE

ZIP CODE TELEPHONE (Include Area Code) ( )

ZIP CODE TELEPHONE (Include Area Code) ( )

9. OTHER INSURED'S NAME (Last Name, First Name, Middle Initial)

10. IS PATIENT'S CONDITION RELATED TO:

11. INSURED'S POLICY GROUP OR FECA NUMBER

a. OTHER INSURED'S POLICY OR GROUP NUMBER

a. EMPLOYMENT? (Current or Previous) YES NO

a. INSURED'S DATE OF BIRTH MM DD YY SEX M F

b. RESERVED FOR NUCC USE

b. AUTO ACCIDENT? YES NO PLACE (State)

b. OTHER CLAIM ID (Designated by NUCC)

c. RESERVED FOR NUCC USE

c. OTHER ACCIDENT? YES NO

c. INSURANCE PLAN NAME OR PROGRAM NAME

d. INSURANCE PLAN NAME OR PROGRAM NAME

10d. CLAIM CODES (Designated by NUCC)

d. IS THERE ANOTHER HEALTH BENEFIT PLAN? YES NO *If yes*, complete items 9, 9a, and 9d.

READ BACK OF FORM BEFORE COMPLETING & SIGNING THIS FORM.

12. PATIENT'S OR AUTHORIZED PERSON'S SIGNATURE I authorize the release of any medical or other information necessary to process this claim. I also request payment of government benefits either to myself or to the party who accepts assignment below.

SIGNED ____ DATE ____

13. INSURED'S OR AUTHORIZED PERSON'S SIGNATURE I authorize payment of medical benefits to the undersigned physician or supplier for services described below.

SIGNED ____

PATIENT AND INSURED INFORMATION

14. DATE OF CURRENT ILLNESS, INJURY, or PREGNANCY (LMP) MM DD YY QUAL.

15. OTHER DATE QUAL. MM DD YY

16. DATES PATIENT UNABLE TO WORK IN CURRENT OCCUPATION FROM MM DD YY TO MM DD YY

17. NAME OF REFERRING PROVIDER OR OTHER SOURCE 17a. 17b. NPI

18. HOSPITALIZATION DATES RELATED TO CURRENT SERVICES FROM MM DD YY TO MM DD YY

19. ADDITIONAL CLAIM INFORMATION (Designated by NUCC)

20. OUTSIDE LAB? YES NO $ CHARGES

21. DIAGNOSIS OR NATURE OF ILLNESS OR INJURY Relate A-L to service line below (24E) ICD Ind.

A. B. C. D.
E. F. G. H.
I. J. K. L.

22. RESUBMISSION CODE ORIGINAL REF. NO.

23. PRIOR AUTHORIZATION NUMBER

	24. A. DATE(S) OF SERVICE From MM DD YY To MM DD YY	B. PLACE OF SERVICE	C. EMG	D. PROCEDURES, SERVICES, OR SUPPLIES (Explain Unusual Circumstances) CPT/HCPCS MODIFIER	E. DIAGNOSIS POINTER	F. $ CHARGES	G. DAYS OR UNITS	H. EPSDT Family Plan	I. ID. QUAL.	J. RENDERING PROVIDER ID. #
1									NPI	
2									NPI	
3									NPI	
4									NPI	
5									NPI	
6									NPI	

25. FEDERAL TAX I.D. NUMBER SSN EIN

26. PATIENT'S ACCOUNT NO.

27. ACCEPT ASSIGNMENT? (For govt. claims, see back) YES NO

28. TOTAL CHARGE $

29. AMOUNT PAID $

30. Rsvd for NUCC Use

31. SIGNATURE OF PHYSICIAN OR SUPPLIER INCLUDING DEGREES OR CREDENTIALS (I certify that the statements on the reverse apply to this bill and are made a part thereof.)

SIGNED DATE

32. SERVICE FACILITY LOCATION INFORMATION

a. NPI b.

33. BILLING PROVIDER INFO & PH # ( )

a. NPI b.

PHYSICIAN OR SUPPLIER INFORMATION

NUCC Instruction Manual available at: www.nucc.org

PLEASE PRINT OR TYPE

Courtesy of the Centers for Medicare and Medicaid Services, www.cms.gov

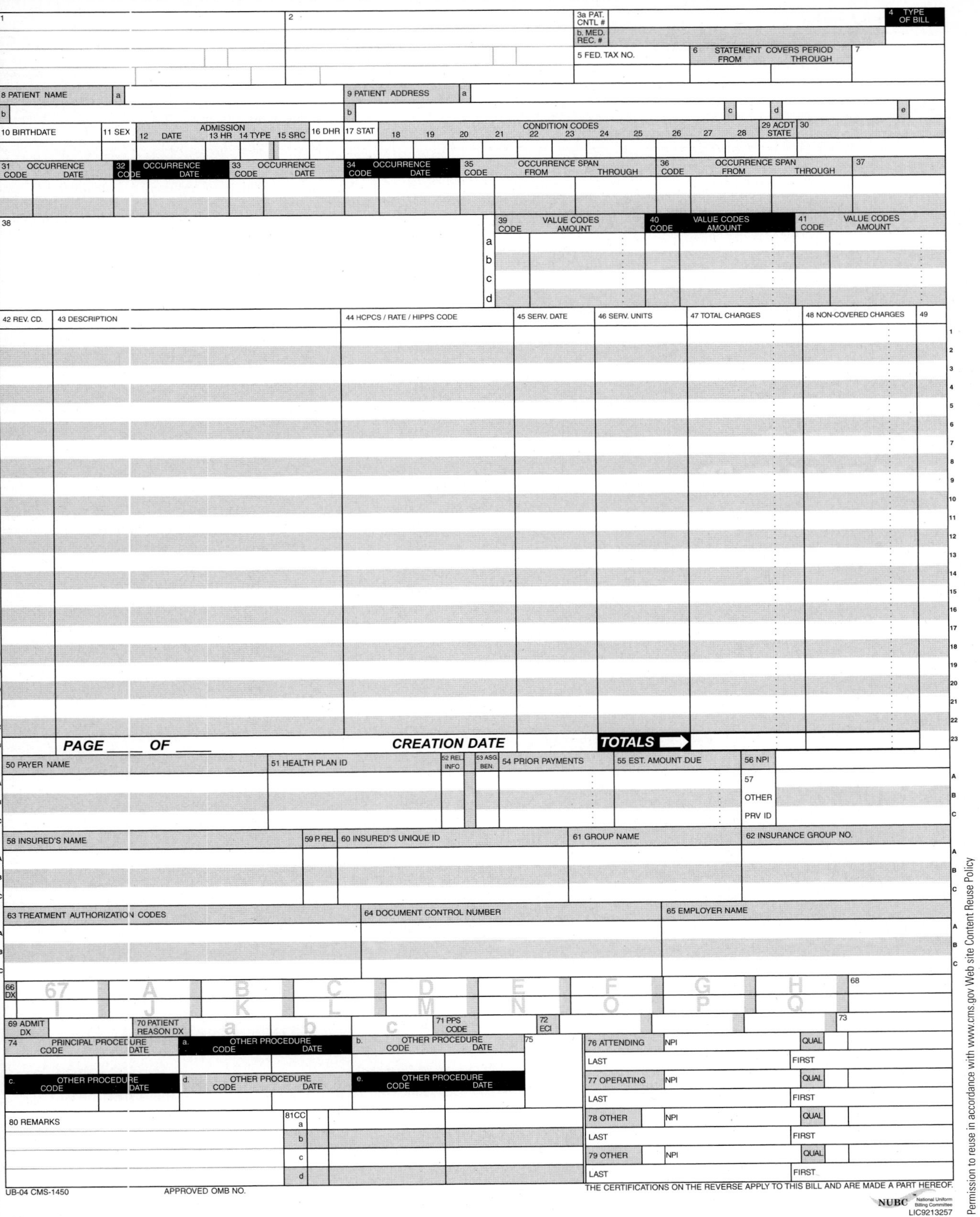

1

2

3a PAT. CNTL #

b. MED. REC. #

4 TYPE OF BILL

5 FED. TAX NO.

6 STATEMENT COVERS PERIOD FROM THROUGH

7

8 PATIENT NAME a

b

9 PATIENT ADDRESS a

b c d e

10 BIRTHDATE | 11 SEX | ADMISSION 12 DATE 13 HR 14 TYPE 15 SRC | 16 DHR | 17 STAT | CONDITION CODES 18 19 20 21 22 23 24 25 26 27 28 | 29 ACDT STATE | 30

31 OCCURRENCE CODE DATE | 32 OCCURRENCE CODE DATE | 33 OCCURRENCE CODE DATE | 34 OCCURRENCE CODE DATE | 35 OCCURRENCE SPAN CODE FROM THROUGH | 36 OCCURRENCE SPAN CODE FROM THROUGH | 37

38

39 VALUE CODES CODE AMOUNT | 40 VALUE CODES CODE AMOUNT | 41 VALUE CODES CODE AMOUNT

a
b
c
d

42 REV. CD. | 43 DESCRIPTION | 44 HCPCS / RATE / HIPPS CODE | 45 SERV. DATE | 46 SERV. UNITS | 47 TOTAL CHARGES | 48 NON-COVERED CHARGES | 49

1
2
3
4
5
6
7
8
9
10
11
12
13
14
15
16
17
18
19
20
21
22
23 PAGE ____ OF ____ CREATION DATE TOTALS

50 PAYER NAME | 51 HEALTH PLAN ID | 52 REL. INFO | 53 ASG. BEN. | 54 PRIOR PAYMENTS | 55 EST. AMOUNT DUE | 56 NPI

A
B
C

57 OTHER PRV ID

58 INSURED'S NAME | 59 P.REL | 60 INSURED'S UNIQUE ID | 61 GROUP NAME | 62 INSURANCE GROUP NO.

A
B
C

63 TREATMENT AUTHORIZATION CODES | 64 DOCUMENT CONTROL NUMBER | 65 EMPLOYER NAME

A
B
C

66 DX 67 A B C D E F G H 68

I J K L M N O P Q

69 ADMIT DX | 70 PATIENT REASON DX a b c | 71 PPS CODE | 72 ECI | 73

74 PRINCIPAL PROCEDURE CODE DATE | a. OTHER PROCEDURE CODE DATE | b. OTHER PROCEDURE CODE DATE | 75

c. OTHER PROCEDURE CODE DATE | d. OTHER PROCEDURE CODE DATE | e. OTHER PROCEDURE CODE DATE

76 ATTENDING NPI QUAL
LAST FIRST

77 OPERATING NPI QUAL
LAST FIRST

80 REMARKS | 81CC a b c d

78 OTHER NPI QUAL
LAST FIRST

79 OTHER NPI QUAL
LAST FIRST

UB-04 CMS-1450 APPROVED OMB NO.

THE CERTIFICATIONS ON THE REVERSE APPLY TO THIS BILL AND ARE MADE A PART HEREOF.

NUBC National Uniform Billing Committee LIC9213257

E/M CODEBUILDER

For use with 1995 and 1997 *CMS Documentation Guidelines for Evaluation & Management Coding.*

Go to **www.cms.gov** and click on Outreach and Education, MLN Educational Web Guides, and Documentation Guidelines for Evaluation and Management (E/M) Services to print the guidelines and use with this *E/M CodeBuilder.*

NOTE: This E/M CodeBuilder can be printed at the Premium Website for use when assigning E/M codes to case studies. Use of this document will reinforce the process required to assign E/M codes, and eventually selecting criteria will make using the form unnecessary.

Introduction

The evaluation and management (E/M) code reported to a third-party payer must be supported by documentation in the patient's record (e.g., SOAP or clinic note, diagnostic test results, operative findings). Although providers are responsible for selecting the E/M code from the encounter form, superbill, or charge-master at the time patient care is rendered, insurance specialists audit records to make sure that the appropriate level of E/M code was reported to the third-party payer.

This *E/M CodeBuilder* form can be used for that purpose, and it can also be used as a tool to teach appropriate assignment of E/M level codes. To assign a code, just review the documentation in the patient's record, record your findings (based on the directions provided), and refer to the CPT coding manual to select the E/M code to be reported.

E/M code selection is based on three key components: *history, examination,* and *medical decision making.* This *E/M CodeBuilder* form emphasizes those components. It is important to be aware that contributory components (*counseling* and *coordination of care*) also play an important role in selecting the E/M code when documentation in the patient record indicates that counseling or coordination of care dominated the visit. In this situation, the contributory component of *time* can be considered a key or controlling factor in selecting a level of E/M service (code).

NOTE: *Time* and *nature of presenting problem* are listed in some E/M code descriptions to assist in determining which code number to report.

Selecting the Level of History

To select the level of history, review the following elements in the patient record. If an element is not documented, it cannot be considered when selecting the level of E/M service code.

- **History of present illness (HPI)**
- **Review of systems (ROS)**
- **Past, family, and/or social history (PFSH)**

History of Present Illness (HPI)

Review the clinic or SOAP note in the patient's record, and for each documented HPI element (below), enter an X in the box in front of the element on this form. Then, total the Xs and enter that number on the line in front of the Total Score (below). Finally, select the level of HPI based on the total number of elements documented, and enter an X in the appropriate box.

☐ Duration: of pain/discomfort; length of time condition has persisted (e.g., pain began three days ago).
☐ Location: of pain/discomfort (e.g., is pain diffused/localized or unilateral/bilateral; does it radiate or refer?).
☐ Quality: a description of the quality of the symptom (e.g., is pain described as sharp, dull, throbbing, stabbing, constant, intermittent, acute or chronic, stable, improving, or worsening?).
☐ Severity: use of self-assessment scale to measure subjective levels (e.g., on a scale of 1–10, how severe is the pain?), or comparison of pain quantitatively with previously experienced pain.
☐ Timing: establishing onset of pain and chronology of pain development (e.g., migraine in the morning).
☐ Context: where was the patient and what was he doing when the pain began (e.g., was patient at rest or involved in an activity; was pain aggravated or relieved, or does it recur, with a specific activity; did situational stress or some other factor precede or accompany the pain?).
☐ Modifying factors: what has the patient attempted to do to relieve the pain (e.g., heat vs. cold; does it relieve or exacerbate the pain; what makes the pain worse; have over-the-counter drugs been attempted—with what results?).
☐ Associated signs/symptoms: clinician's impressions formulated during the interview may lead to questioning about additional sensations or feelings (e.g., diaphoresis associated with indigestion or chest pain, blurred vision accompanying a headache, etc.).

____ **Total Score:** Enter the score for the number of Xs entered above (representing the number of HPI elements), and enter an X in front of the type of HPI below:

☐ Brief HPI (one to three elements) ☐ Extended HPI (four or more elements)

Review of Systems (ROS)

Review the clinic or SOAP note in the patient's record, and for each documented ROS element (below), enter an X in the box in front of the element on this form. Then, total the Xs and enter that number on the line in front of the Total Score (below). Finally, select the level of ROS based on the total number of elements documented, and enter an X in the appropriate box.

NOTE: To properly assess the review of systems documentation, have the *CMS Documentation Guidelines for Evaluation & Management Coding* available as you review the patient's record.

☐ Constitutional symptoms ☐ Ears, nose, mouth, throat ☐ Gastrointestinal ☐ Genitourinary ☐ Neurologic
☐ Eyes ☐ Cardiovascular ☐ Integumentary (including skin & breast) ☐ Allergic/Immunologic ☐ Endocrine
☐ Musculoskeletal ☐ Respiratory ☐ Hematologic/Lymphatic ☐ Psychiatric

____ **Total Score:** Enter the score for the number of Xs entered above (representing the number of ROS elements), and enter an X in front of the type of ROS below:

☐ None ☐ Extended (two to nine body systems documented)
☐ Problem pertinent (one body system documented) ☐ Complete (all body systems documented)

Past, Family, and/or Social History (PFSH)

Review the clinic or SOAP note in the patient's record, and for each documented PFSH element (below), enter an X in the box in front of the element on this form. Then, total the Xs and enter that number on the line in front of the Total Score (below). Finally, select the level of PFSH based on the total number of elements documented, and enter an X in the appropriate box.

☐ Past history (patient's past experience with illnesses, operations, injuries, and treatments)
☐ Family history (review of medical events in the patient's family, including diseases that may be hereditary or place the patient at risk)
☐ Social history (an age-appropriate review of past and current activities)

___ **Total Score:** Enter the score for the number of Xs entered above (representing the number of PFSH elements), and enter an X in front of the type of PFSH below:

☐ None

☐ Pertinent (one history area documented)

☐ Complete (two or three history areas documented)

Level of History

Circle the type of HPI, ROS, and PFSH determined above; then circle the appropriate level of history below.

HPI	Brief	Brief	Extended	Extended
ROS	None	Problem Pertinent	Extended	Complete
PFSH	None	None	Pertinent	Complete
Level of History	Problem Focused	Expanded Problem Focused	Detailed	Comprehensive

Selecting the Level of Examination

To select the level of examination, first determine whether a *single organ examination* (specialist exam; e.g., ophthalmologist) or *a general multisystem examination* (e.g., family practitioner) was completed.

Single Organ System Examination

Refer to the single organ system examination requirements in the *CMS Documentation Guidelines for Evaluation & Management Services*, and enter an X in front of the appropriate level of exam below.

☐ PROBLEM-FOCUSED EXAMINATION (one to five elements identified by a bullet)

☐ EXPANDED PROBLEM-FOCUSED EXAMINATION (at least six elements identified by a bullet)

☐ DETAILED EXAMINATION (at least 12 elements identified by a bullet)

☐ COMPREHENSIVE EXAMINATION (all elements identified by a bullet; document every element in each box with a shaded border and at least one element in each box with an unshaded box)

NOTE: For eye and psychiatric examinations, at least nine elements in each box with a shaded border and at least one element in each box with a shaded or an unshaded border is documented.

General Multisystem Exam

Refer to the general multisystem examination requirements in the *CMS Documentation Guidelines for Evaluation & Management Services.* Enter an X in front of the organ system or body area for up to the total number of allowed elements (e.g., up to two elements can be documented for the Neck exam).

☐ Constitutional (2)
☐ Eyes (3)
☐ Ears, nose, mouth, throat (6)
☐ Neck (2)
☐ Cardiovascular (7)
☐ Respiratory (4)
☐ Gastrointestinal (5)
☐ Chest (breasts) (2)
☐ Skin (2)
☐ Genitourinary (male–3; female–6)
☐ Musculoskeletal (6)
☐ Neurologic (3)
☐ Psychiatric (4)

___ **Total Score:** Enter the score for the number of Xs entered above (representing the number of exam elements), and enter an X in front of the level of exam below:

☐ PROBLEM-FOCUSED EXAMINATION (one to five elements identified by a bullet on *CMS Documentation Guidelines for Evaluation & Management Services*)

☐ EXPANDED PROBLEM-FOCUSED EXAMINATION (at least six elements identified by a bullet on *CMS Documentation Guidelines for Evaluation & Management Services*)

☐ DETAILED EXAMINATION (at least two elements identified by a bullet from each of six organ systems or body areas, or at least 12 elements identified by a bullet in two or more systems or areas, on *CMS Documentation Guidelines for Evaluation & Management Services*)

☐ COMPREHENSIVE EXAMINATION (documentation of all elements identified by a bullet in at least nine organ systems or body areas, and documentation of at least two elements identified by a bullet from each of nine organ systems or body areas, on *CMS Documentation Guidelines for Evaluation & Management Services*)

Medical Decision Making

Circle the appropriate level of medical decision making based upon the following criteria:

CRITERIA TO DETERMINE COMPLEXITY OF MEDICAL DECISION MAKING			
NUMBER OF DIAGNOSIS OR MANAGEMENT OPTIONS	**AMOUNT/COMPLEXITY OF DATA TO BE REVIEWED**	**RISK OF COMPLICATIONS AND/OR MORBIDITY/MORTALITY**	**MEDICAL DECISION MAKING**
Minimal	Minimal or none	Minimal	Straightforward
Limited	Limited	Low	Low complexity
Multiple	Moderate	Moderate	Moderate complexity
Extensive	Extensive	High	High complexity

HOW TO SELECT COMPLEXITY OF MEDICAL DECISION MAKING

To select *criteria to determine complexity of medical decision making,* circle each in the above table.

STEP 1. Review the entire patient record to locate documented diagnoses and/or management options. Then, decide whether the documentation represents a minimal, limited, multiple, or extensive *number of diagnoses or management options.*

STEP 2. Review the entire patient record to locate documented data (e.g., lab reports, x-ray reports, consultation reports, and so on). Then, decide if the documentation represents a minimal (or none), limited, moderate, or extensive *amount/complexity of data to be reviewed.*

STEP 3. Review the entire patient record to determine the risk of complications and/or morbidity or mortality. This review requires knowledge of pathophysiology and pharmacology to select among minimal, low, moderate, or high *risk of complications and/or morbidity/mortality.*

STEP 4. Finally, select straightforward, low, moderate, or *high complexity of medical decision making* based on the criteria selected in steps 1 to 3.

E/M Code Selection

Circle the level of history, examination, and medical decision making. Then, select the code from your CPT coding manual.

History	Problem focused	Expanded problem focused	Expanded problem focused	Detailed	Comprehensive
Examination	Problem focused	Expanded problem focused	Expanded problem focused	Detailed	Comprehensive
Medical Decision Making	Straightforward	Low complexity	Moderate complexity	Moderate complexity	High complexity
Go to the appropriate E/M category/subcategory, of your coding manual and locate the code based upon the information selected above.					

Dental Claims Processing

APPENDIX IV

INTRODUCTION

Dental benefits programs offer a variety of options in the form of either fee-for-service or managed care plans that reimburse a portion of a patient's dental expenses and may exclude certain treatments (e.g., dental sealants). It is, therefore, important for the insurance specialist to become familiar with the specifics of dental plans in which the dental professional participates. It is equally important to become familiar with dental terminology (Table IV-1).

DENTAL CLAIMS PROCESSING

Dental claims (Figures IV-1 and IV-2) are submitted on the American Dental Association (ADA)–approved claim, and instructions (Table IV-2) should be carefully followed. Dental offices also have the option of submitting electronic claims according to HIPAA's electronic transaction standard, *ASC X12N 837 v.4010–Health Care Claim: Dental.*

Dental treatment is reported using codes assigned from the *Current Dental Terminology* (CDT). CDT is published by the American Dental Association (ADA), which ensures that codes are:

- **Created according to a standard format**
- **At an appropriate level of specificity**
- **Uniformly applied to dental treatment**
- **Used to report dental procedures**

The American Dental Association periodically reviews and revises CDT to update codes according to recognized changes in dental procedures. Published revisions are implemented biannually, at the beginning of odd-numbered years. CDT contains the following features:

- **Codes and descriptions**
- **A section on implant-supported prosthetics**
- **Glossaries of dental and dental benefit terminology**
- **Revised ADA claim**
- **An introduction to the Systematized Nomenclature of Dentistry (SNODENT). SNODENT contains standard terms to describe dental disease, captures clinical detail and patient characteristics, and allows for the analysis of patient care services and outcomes**

CURRENT DENTAL TERMINOLOGY (CDT)

The ***Current Dental Terminology* (CDT)** is published by the American Dental Association (ADA) as a biannual revision. It classifies dental procedures and services.

Dental providers and ambulatory care settings use the CDT to report procedures and services. CDT also includes the Code on Dental Procedures and Nomenclature (Code), which contains instructions for use of the Code, questions and answers, ADA dental claim form completion instructions, and tooth numbering systems.

> **EXAMPLE:** Patient underwent incision and drainage of intraoral soft tissue abscess. Report CDT code D7510.

CDT CODING PRACTICE

Instructions: Use the CDT coding manual to assign a code to each item below.

_______________ 1. Frenulectomy

_______________ 2. Sialolithotomy

_______________ 3. Administration of general anesthesia for deep sedation, during dental procedure 45 minutes

_______________ 4. Fixed appliance therapy

_______________ 5. Administration of local anesthesia, during dental procedure

_______________ 6. Enamel microabrasion

_______________ 7. External bleaching, teeth #8 and #9

_______________ 8. Core buildup with pins

_______________ 9. Bone replacement graft, first site in quadrant

_______________ 10. Interim partial denture, mandible

_______________ 11. Repair, cast framework

_______________ 12. Adjust partial denture, maxilla

_______________ 13. Modification of palatal lift prosthesis

_______________ 14. Surgical stent

_______________ 15. Connector bar

_______________ 16. Stress breaker

_______________ 17. Removal of impacted tooth, soft tissue

_______________ 18. Brush biopsy, transepithelial sample collection

_______________ 19. Closure of fistula, salivary

_______________ 20. Surgical removal, residual tooth roots

_______________ 21. Removal of torus mandibularis

_______________ 22. Incision and drainage of abscess, extraoral soft tissue, complicated by drainage of multiple fascial spaces

_______________ 23. Closed reduction of mandible with immobilization of teeth

_______________ 24. Replacement of broken retainer

_______________ 25. Comprehensive orthodontic treatment, adult dentition

ANSWER KEY TO CDT CODING PRACTICE

1. D7960
2. D7980
3. D2220, D2221
4. D8220
5. D9215
6. D9970
7. D9973, D9973
8. D2950
9. D4263
10. D5821
11. D5620
12. D5421
13. D5959
14. D5982
15. D6920
16. D6940
17. D7220
18. D7288
19. D7983
20. D7250
21. D7473
22. D7521
23. D7640
24. D8692
25. D8090

TABLE IV-1 Glossary of common dental terms

DENTAL TERM	DEFINITION
abscess	acute or chronic, localized inflammation associated with tissue destruction
Academy of General Dentistry (AGD)	serves needs and represents interests of general dentists
Alliance for the Best Clinical Practices in Dentistry (ABCPD)	organization that encourages development of evidence-based prevention and treatment protocols through the process of organizing focused seminars
amalgam	alloy used in direct dental restorations; also called a *silver filling*
American Academy of Pediatric Dentistry (AAPD)	dedicated to improving and maintaining the oral health of infants, children, adolescents, and persons with special health care needs
American Academy of Periodontology (AAP)	dedicated to advancing the art and science of periodontics and improving the periodontal health of the public
American Dental Association (ADA)	promotes public health through commitment of member dentists to provide high-quality oral health care and promotes accessible oral health care
attrition	normal wearing away of the surface of a tooth from chewing
baby bottle tooth decay	severe decay in baby teeth due to sleeping with a bottle of milk or juice; natural sugars from drinks combine with bacteria in the mouth to produce acid that decays teeth
bitewing radiograph	x-rays of top and bottom molars and premolars
bruxism	involuntary clenching or grinding of teeth
calculus	hard deposit of mineralized material that adheres to teeth; also called *tartar* or *calcified plaque*
caries	tooth decay
crown	artificial covering of a tooth with metal, porcelain, or porcelain fused to metal
deciduous teeth	baby teeth or primary teeth
endentulous	having no teeth
endodontics	dental specialty concerned with treatment of the root and nerve of a tooth
fluoride	chemical compound that prevents cavities and makes tooth surface stronger
gingivitis	inflammation of gums surrounding teeth, caused by buildup of plaque or food
gum disease	*see* periodontitis
halitosis	bad breath
malocclusion	improper alignment of biting or chewing surfaces of upper and lower teeth
orthodontics	dental specialty concerned with straightening or moving misaligned teeth and/or jaws with braces and/or surgery
panoramic radiograph	single, large x-ray of jaws taken by a machine that rotates around the head
pedodontics	dental specialty concerned with treatment of children; also called *pediatric dentistry*
periodontics	dental specialty concerned with treatment of gums, tissue, and bone that supports the teeth
periodontitis	inflammation and loss of connective tissue of the supporting or surrounding structure of the teeth; also called *gum disease*
plaque	bacteria-containing substance that collects on the surface of teeth, which can cause decay and gum irritation when not removed by daily brushing and flossing
Prevent Abuse and Neglect through Dental Awareness (PANDA)	educational program that educates oral health professionals about child abuse and helps them learn how to diagnose and report potential abuse situations to appropriate authorities
prophylaxis	professional cleaning to remove plaque, calculus, and stains
prosthodontics	dental specialty concerned with restoration and/or replacement of missing teeth with artificial materials
radiograph	x-ray
scaling	removal of plaque, calculus, and stains from teeth
sealant	thin plastic material used to cover biting surface of a child's tooth
supernumerary tooth	extra tooth
tartar	*see* calculus

ADA American Dental Association® Dental Claim Form

HEADER INFORMATION

1. Type of Transaction (Mark all applicable boxes)

☐ Statement of Actual Services ☐ Request for Predetermination/Preauthorization

☐ EPSDT / Title XIX

2. Predetermination/Preauthorization Number

INSURANCE COMPANY/DENTAL BENEFIT PLAN INFORMATION

3. Company/Plan Name, Address, City, State, Zip Code

OTHER COVERAGE (Mark applicable box and complete items 5-11. If none, leave blank.)

4. Dental? ☐ Medical? ☐ (If both, complete 5-11 for dental only.)

5. Name of Policyholder/Subscriber in #4 (Last, First, Middle Initial, Suffix)

6. Date of Birth (MM/DD/CCYY) | 7. Gender ☐ M ☐ F | 8. Policyholder/Subscriber ID (SSN or ID#)

9. Plan/Group Number | 10. Patient's Relationship to Person named in #5 ☐ Self ☐ Spouse ☐ Dependent ☐ Other

11. Other Insurance Company/Dental Benefit Plan Name, Address, City, State, Zip Code

POLICYHOLDER/SUBSCRIBER INFORMATION (For Insurance Company Named in #3)

12. Policyholder/Subscriber Name (Last, First, Middle Initial, Suffix), Address, City, State, Zip Code

13. Date of Birth (MM/DD/CCYY) | 14. Gender ☐ M ☐ F | 15. Policyholder/Subscriber ID (SSN or ID#)

16. Plan/Group Number | 17. Employer Name

PATIENT INFORMATION

18. Relationship to Policyholder/Subscriber in #12 Above ☐ Self ☐ Spouse ☐ Dependent Child ☐ Other | 19. Reserved For Future Use

20. Name (Last, First, Middle Initial, Suffix), Address, City, State, Zip Code

21. Date of Birth (MM/DD/CCYY) | 22. Gender ☐ M ☐ F | 23. Patient ID/Account # (Assigned by Dentist)

RECORD OF SERVICES PROVIDED

	24. Procedure Date (MM/DD/CCYY)	25. Area of Oral Cavity	26. Tooth System	27. Tooth Number(s) or Letter(s)	28. Tooth Surface	29. Procedure Code	29a. Diag. Pointer	29b. Qty.	30. Description	31. Fee
1										
2										
3										
4										
5										
6										
7										
8										
9										
10										

33. Missing Teeth Information (Place an "X" on each missing tooth.)

1	2	3	4	5	6	7	8	9	10	11	12	13	14	15	16
32	31	30	29	28	27	26	25	24	23	22	21	20	19	18	17

34. Diagnosis Code List Qualifier ☐☐ (ICD-9 = B; ICD-10 = AB)

34a. Diagnosis Code(s) A ____ C ____

(Primary diagnosis in "A") B ____ D ____

31a. Other Fee(s)

32. Total Fee

35. Remarks

AUTHORIZATIONS

36. I have been informed of the treatment plan and associated fees. I agree to be responsible for all charges for dental services and materials not paid by my dental benefit plan, unless prohibited by law, or the treating dentist or dental practice has a contractual agreement with my plan prohibiting all or a portion of such charges. To the extent permitted by law, I consent to your use and disclosure of my protected health information to carry out payment activities in connection with this claim.

X ____ Patient/Guardian Signature Date

37. I hereby authorize and direct payment of the dental benefits otherwise payable to me, directly to the below named dentist or dental entity.

X ____ Subscriber Signature Date

ANCILLARY CLAIM/TREATMENT INFORMATION

38. Place of Treatment ☐ (e.g. 11=office; 22=O/P Hospital) (Use "Place of Service Codes for Professional Claims") | 39. Enclosures (Y or N) ☐

40. Is Treatment for Orthodontics? ☐ No (Skip 41-42) ☐ Yes (Complete 41-42) | 41. Date Appliance Placed (MM/DD/CCYY)

42. Months of Treatment | 43. Replacement of Prosthesis ☐ No ☐ Yes (Complete 44) | 44. Date of Prior Placement (MM/DD/CCYY)

45. Treatment Resulting from ☐ Occupational illness/injury ☐ Auto accident ☐ Other accident

46. Date of Accident (MM/DD/CCYY) | 47. Auto Accident State

BILLING DENTIST OR DENTAL ENTITY (Leave blank if dentist or dental entity is not submitting claim on behalf of the patient or insured/subscriber.)

48. Name, Address, City, State, Zip Code

49. NPI | 50. License Number | 51. SSN or TIN

52. Phone Number | 52a. Additional Provider ID

TREATING DENTIST AND TREATMENT LOCATION INFORMATION

53. I hereby certify that the procedures as indicated by date are in progress (for procedures that require multiple visits) or have been completed.

X ____ Signed (Treating Dentist) Date

54. NPI | 55. License Number

56. Address, City, State, Zip Code | 56a. Provider Specialty Code

57. Phone Number | 58. Additional Provider ID

FIGURE IV-1 ADA Dental Claim Form.

ADA American Dental Association®

America's leading advocate for oral health

The following information highlights certain form completion instructions. Comprehensive ADA Dental Claim Form completion instructions are printed in the CDT manual. Any updates to these instructions will be posted on the ADA's web site (ADA.org).

GENERAL INSTRUCTIONS

A. The form is designed so that the name and address (Item 3) of the third-party payer receiving the claim (insurance company/dental benefit plan) is visible in a standard #9 window envelope (window to the left). Please fold the form using the 'tick-marks' printed in the margin.

B. Complete all items unless noted otherwise on the form or in the CDT manual's instructions.

C. Enter the full name of an individual or a full business name, address and zip code when a name and address field is required.

D. All dates must include the four-digit year.

E. If the number of procedures reported exceeds the number of lines available on one claim form, list the remaining procedures on a separate, fully completed claim form.

COORDINATION OF BENEFITS (COB)

When a claim is being submitted to the secondary payer, complete the entire form and attach the primary payer's Explanation of Benefits (EOB) showing the amount paid by the primary payer. You may also note the primary carrier paid amount in the "Remarks" field (Item 35). There are additional detailed completion instructions in the CDT manual.

DIAGNOSIS CODING

The form supports reporting up to four diagnosis codes per dental procedure. This information is required when the diagnosis may affect claim adjudication when specific dental procedures may minimize the risks associated with the connection between the patient's oral and systemic health conditions. Diagnosis codes are linked to procedures using the following fields:

Item 29a – Diagnosis Code Pointer ("A" through "D" as applicable from Item 34a)

Item 34 – Diagnosis Code List Qualifier (B for ICD-9-CM; AB for ICD-10-CM)

Item 34a – Diagnosis Code(s) / A, B, C, D (up to four, with the primary adjacent to the letter "A")

PLACE OF TREATMENT

Enter the 2-digit Place of Service Code for Professional Claims, a HIPAA standard maintained by the Centers for Medicare and Medicaid Services. Frequently used codes are:

11 = Office; 12 = Home; 21 = Inpatient Hospital; 22 = Outpatient Hospital; 31 = Skilled Nursing Facility; 32 = Nursing Facility

The full list is available online at "www.cms.gov/PhysicianFeeSched/Downloads/Website_POS_database.pdf"

PROVIDER SPECIALTY

This code is entered in Item 56a and indicates the type of dental professional who delivered the treatment. The general code listed as "Dentist" may be used instead of any of the other codes.

Category / Description Code	Code
Dentist A dentist is a person qualified by a doctorate in dental surgery (D.D.S.) or dental medicine (D.M.D.) licensed by the state to practice dentistry, and practicing within the scope of that license.	122300000X
General Practice	1223G0001X
Dental Specialty (see following list)	Various
Dental Public Health	1223D0001X
Endodontics	1223E0200X
Orthodontics	1223X0400X
Pediatric Dentistry	1223P0221X
Periodontics	1223P0300X
Prosthodontics	1223P0700X
Oral & Maxillofacial Pathology	1223P0106X
Oral & Maxillofacial Radiology	1223D0008X
Oral & Maxillofacial Surgery	1223S0112X

Provider taxonomy codes listed above are a subset of the full code set that is posted at "www.wpc-edi.com/codes/taxonomy"

Courtesy of the American Dental Association, www.ada.org

FIGURE IV-2 Reverse of ADA Dental Claim Form.

TABLE IV-2 Instructions for completing the ADA claim

BLOCK	INSTRUCTIONS
HEADER INFORMATION	
1	Enter an X in the appropriate box. Select the *Statement of Actual Services* to obtain reimbursement for services provided. Select the *Request for Predetermination/Preauthorization* to obtain preapproval of dental services. Select the *EPSDT/Title XIX* if the patient is covered by Medicaid's Early and Periodic Screening, Diagnosis, and Treatment program for persons under age 21.
2	Enter the predetermination or preauthorization number assigned by the payer, if applicable. Otherwise, leave blank.
PRIMARY PAYER INFORMATION (INSURANCE COMPANY/DENTAL BENEFIT PLAN INFORMATION)	
3	Enter the primary payer's name, address, city, state, and zip code.
OTHER COVERAGE	
NOTE: Always complete Block 4. Complete Blocks 5–11 *only* if the patient has a secondary dental plan.	
4	Enter an X in the NO box if the patient is not covered by another dental insurance plan, and go to Block 12. Enter an X in the YES box if the patient is covered by another dental insurance plan, and complete Blocks 5–11. **REMEMBER!** Complete Blocks 5–11 *only* if the patient has a secondary dental plan. Otherwise, leave Blocks 5–11 blank.
5	*If the patient has secondary dental plan coverage,* enter the complete name (last, first, middle initial, suffix) of the individual named as policyholder on the secondary plan.
6	*If the patient has secondary dental plan coverage,* enter the secondary policyholder's date of birth as MMDDYYYY (without spaces).
7	*If the patient has secondary dental plan coverage,* enter an X in the appropriate box to indicate the secondary policyholder's gender.
8	*If the patient has secondary dental plan coverage,* enter the secondary policyholder's social security number (SSN) or dental plan identification number, as it appears on the dental plan card.
9	*If the patient has secondary dental plan coverage,* enter the secondary policyholder's dental plan number and group number (e.g., 123456 001).
10	*If the patient has secondary dental plan coverage,* enter an X in the appropriate box to indicate the patient's relationship to the policyholder.
11	*If the patient has secondary dental plan coverage,* enter the dental plan's name, address, city, state, and zip code.
PRIMARY SUBSCRIBER INFORMATION (POLICYHOLDER/SUBSCRIBER INFORMATION)	
12	Enter the primary policyholder's complete name, address, city, state, and zip code.
13	Enter the primary policyholder's date of birth as MMDDYYYY (without spaces).
14	Enter an X in the appropriate box to indicate the primary policyholder's gender.
15	Enter the primary policyholder's social security number (SSN) or dental plan identification number and group number, as it appears on the dental plan card.
16	Enter the dental plan number and/or group number.
17	Enter the name of the primary policyholder's employer, if applicable.

(continues)

TABLE IV-2 (continued)

BLOCK	INSTRUCTIONS
	PATIENT INFORMATION
	NOTE: Always complete Block 18. Complete Blocks 19–23 only if the patient is *not* the primary policyholder (e.g., if "Self" does not contain an X in Block 18).
18	Enter an X in the appropriate box to indicate the patient's relationship to the primary subscriber.
19	Leave blank.
20	*If the patient is not the primary policyholder,* enter the patient's complete name, address, city, state, and zip code.
21	*If the patient is not the primary policyholder,* enter the patient's date of birth as MMDDYYYY (without spaces).
22	*If the patient is not the primary policyholder,* enter an X in the appropriate box to indicate the patient's gender.
23	*If the patient is not the primary policyholder,* enter the account number assigned to the patient by the dental practice.
	RECORD OF SERVICES PROVIDED
24	For each procedure performed, enter the date of service (MMDDYYYY) on a different line. **NOTE:** There is no units/days column on the ADA claim.
25	When the CDT procedure code reported in Block 29 refers to a quadrant or arch and the area of the oral cavity is not uniquely defined by the procedure's nomenclature, enter the area of the oral cavity treated using the following two-digit codes: 00 entire oral cavity 01 maxillary arch 02 mandibular arch 10 upper right quadrant 20 upper left quadrant 30 lower left quadrant 40 lower right quadrant
26	Enter the applicable ANSI ASC X12N code list qualifier JP or JO: • JP = ADA's Universal/National Tooth Designation System (numbers teeth 1-32) • JO = International Standards Organization System (numbers teeth 11-18, 21-28, 31-38, 41-48)
27	Identify tooth/teeth number(s) when the procedure directly involves a tooth (e.g., restoration, tooth extraction, root canal, crown, or dentition-related surgical excision), as follows: • Report a range of teeth by entering a hyphen between the first and last tooth (e.g., 1-5) • Report separate individual teeth by entering a comma between teeth numbers (e.g., 1, 3, 5) **NOTE:** Use numerical identification (1–32) for permanent teeth and capital letter identification (A–T) for primary teeth. Leave blank if treatment of a specific tooth (e.g., oral examination) is not performed. For supernumerary tooth numbering, use the ADA's Universal/National Tooth Designation System ("JP") designated by numbers 51 through 82.
28	When procedure(s) directly involve one or more tooth surface(s), enter up to five of the following codes (without spaces): B = Buccal F = Facial (or labial) L = Lingual O = Occlusal D = Distal I = Incisal M = Mesial
29	Enter the CDT procedure code for dental treatment provided.
29a	*Diagnosis Code Pointer:* Enter the letter(s) from Block 34 that identify(ies) the diagnosis code(s) applicable to the dental procedure(s). Report the first-listed diagnosis pointer first.

(continues)

TABLE IV-2 (continued)

BLOCK	INSTRUCTIONS
	RECORD OF SERVICES PROVIDED (continued)
29b	*Quantity:* Enter the number of times (01–99) the procedure identified in Block 29 was delivered to the patient on the date of service reported in Block 24. The default value is "01."
30	Enter terminology to describe the service provided. **NOTE:** If service is for a supernumerary tooth, enter the word "supernumerary" and include information to identify the closest numbered tooth.
31	Enter the fee charged for the procedure.
31a	*Other Fee(s):* Enter the applicable amount when reporting other charges applicable to dental services provided. Such charges may include state tax and other charges imposed by regulatory bodies.
32	Enter other fees (e.g., state taxes where applicable, fees imposed by regulatory agencies).
33	*Missing Teeth Information:* Enter an X on the number of missing tooth (or teeth) (for the identification of missing permanent dentition only).
34	*Diagnosis Code List Qualifier:* Enter the appropriate code to identify the diagnosis code source, as B (ICD-9-CM) or AB (ICD-10-CM).
34a	Enter up to four diagnosis codes after each letter, A–D. The first-listed diagnosis code is entered adjacent to the letter A.
35	Enter additional applicable information (e.g., multiple supernumerary teeth).
	AUTHORIZATIONS
36	Obtain patient/guardian signature and date, which authorizes payment and release of information to dental plan.
37	Obtain policyholder's signature and date, which authorizes the dental plan to make payment directly to the provider (e.g., dentist).
	ANCILLARY CLAIM/TREATMENT INFORMATION
38	Enter the two-digit place of service code for professional claims, such as: 11 (office), 12 (home), 21 (inpatient hospital), 22 (outpatient hospital), 31 (skilled nursing facility), 32 (nursing facility), and so on.
39	Enter a Y or an N in the box to indicate whether or not there are enclosures of any type included with the claim submission (e.g., models, oral images, radiographs).
40	Enter an X in the NO box if treatment is not for orthodontics, and go to Block 43. Enter an X in the YES box if treatment is for orthodontics, and complete Blocks 41 and 42.
41	Enter the date appliances (e.g., braces) were placed as MMDDYYYY (without spaces). Leave blank if an X was entered in the NO box in Block 40.
42	Enter a number that represents the remaining months of treatment (e.g., 26). Leave blank if an X was entered in the NO box in Block 40.
43	Enter an X in the NO box if treatment is not for replacement of a prosthesis, and go to Block 45. Enter an X in the YES box if treatment is for replacement of a prosthesis, and complete Block 44.
44	Enter the date the prior prosthesis was placed as MMDDYYYY (without spaces). Leave blank if an X was entered in the NO box in Block 43.

(continues)

TABLE IV-2 (continued)

BLOCK	INSTRUCTIONS
	ANCILLARY CLAIM/TREATMENT INFORMATION (continued)
45	Enter an X in the appropriate box if dental treatment reported on the claim was provided as a result of an accident or injury and complete Blocks 46 and 47. Otherwise, leave blank.
46	If an X was entered in a box in Block 47, enter the date of the accident as MMDDYYYY (without spaces). Otherwise, leave blank.
47	If an X was entered in the AUTO ACCIDENT box in Block 47, enter the state in which the accident occurred. Otherwise, leave blank.
	BILLING DENTIST OR DENTAL ENTITY
	REMEMBER! Complete Blocks 48–52a *only* if the provider is submitting a claim on behalf of the patient or policyholder.
48	*If the provider is submitting a claim on behalf of the patient or policyholder,* enter the provider's name, address, city, state, and zip code.
49	*If the provider is submitting a claim on behalf of the patient or policyholder,* enter the provider's NPI. **NOTE:** This is *not* the provider's social security number or employer identification number.
50	*If the provider is submitting a claim on behalf of the patient or policyholder,* enter the provider's license number.
51	*If the provider is submitting a claim on behalf of the patient or policyholder,* enter the provider's social security number or tax identification number.
52	*If the provider is submitting a claim on behalf of the patient or policyholder,* enter the provider's telephone number, including area code.
52a	Leave blank.
	TREATING DENTIST AND TREATMENT LOCATION INFORMATION
53	Have the treating dentist provider sign and date the completed claim. **NOTE:** Check with the dental plan to determine if the signature can be typed or stamped, instead of signed by the provider.
54	Enter the treating dentist's NPI.
55	Enter the treating dentist's license number.
56	Enter the treating dentist's address, city, state, and zip code.
56a	Enter the code that indicates the type of dental professional who delivered the treatment, such as 122300000X (dentist), 1223X0400X (orthodontics), and so on.
57	Enter the treating dentist's telephone number.
58	Leave blank.

Courtesy of the American Dental Association, www.ada.org

Abbreviations

APPENDIX V

837 — claims validation tables (as in ANSI ASC X12 837)

A

AAMA — American Association of Medical Assistants
AAPC — American Academy of Professional Coders
ABN — advance beneficiary notice of noncoverage
ADA — Americans with Disabilities Act
AHA — American Hospital Association
AHFS — American Hospital Formulary Service
AHIMA — American Health Information Management Association
AMA — American Medical Association
AMBA — American Medical Billing Association
ANSI — American National Standards Institute
APC — ambulatory payment classification
AP-DRG — All-Patient diagnosis-related group
APR-DRG — All-Patient Refined diagnosis-related group
ARRA — American Recovery and Reinvestment Act
ASC — Accredited Standards Committee
ASC — ambulatory surgical center

B

BBA — Balanced Budget Amendment
BCAC — beneficiary counseling and assistance coordinator
BCBS — BlueCross BlueShield
BCBSA — BlueCross and BlueShield Association
BRAC — base realignment and closure
BSR — beneficiary services representative

C

Ca — cancer or carcinoma
CAC — common access card
CAC — computer-assisted coding
CAT — computerized axial tomography
CCS — Certified Coding Specialist
CDAC — Clinical Data Abstracting Center
CDHP — consumer-directed health plan *or* consumer-driven health plan
CDHS — California Department of Health Services
CDT — *Current Dental Terminology*
CERT — Comprehensive Error Rate Testing
CF — conversion factor
CHAMPUS — Civilian Health and Medical Program of the Uniformed Services
CHAMPVA — Civilian Health and Medical Program of Veterans Affairs
CLIA — Clinical Laboratory Improvement Act
CMP — competitive medical plan
CMS — Centers for Medicare and Medicaid Services
CMS-1450 — UB-04 claim used by institutional and other selected providers to bill payers
CMS-1500 — Insurance claim used by noninstitutional providers and suppliers to bill payers
CNS — clinical nurse specialist
COB — coordination of benefits
COBRA — Consolidated Omnibus Budget Reconciliation Act
copay — copayment
CPC — Certified professional coder
CPT — *Current Procedural Terminology*

CRI	CHAMPUS Reform Initiative
CSCP	customized sub-capitation plan
CT	computed tomography

D

DCAO	debt collection assistance officer
DEERS	Defense Enrollment Eligibility Reporting System
DME	durable medical equipment
DMEPOS	durable medical equipment, prosthetic and orthotic supplies
DoD	Department of Defense
DRG	diagnosis-related groups
DSH	disproportionate share hospital
DSM	*Diagnostic and Statistical Manual*

E

EDI	electronic data interchange
EEOICP	Energy Employees Occupational Illness Compensation Program
EFT	electronic funds transfer
EGHP	employer group health plan
EHNAC	Electronic Healthcare Network Accreditation Commission
EHR	electronic health record
EIN	employer identification number
E/M	evaluation and management
EMC	electronic media claim
EMR	electronic medical record
EOB	explanation of benefits
EPO	exclusive provider organization
EPSDT	early and periodic screening, diagnostic, and treatment
EQRO	external quality review organization
ERA	electronic remittance advice
ERISA	Employee Retirement Income Security Act of 1974
ESRD	End-stage renal disease

F

FATHOM	First-look Analysis for Hospital Outlier Monitoring
FCA	False Claims Act
FCCA	Federal Claims Collection Act
FDCPA	Fair Debt Collection Practices Act
FECA	Federal Employment Compensation Act
FEHBP	Federal Employee Health Benefits Program
FELA	Federal Employment Liability Act
FEP	Federal Employee Program
FMAP	federal medical assistance percentage
FPL	federal poverty level
FR	*Federal Register*
FSA	flexible spending account
FSMA	Federal Services Modernization Act

G

GCPI	geographic cost practice index
GEM	general equivalence mapping
GEP	general enrollment period
GPWW	group practice without walls

H

HA	Health Affairs
HAVEN	Home Assessment Validation and Entry
HCF	health care finder
HCPCS	Healthcare Common Procedure Coding System
HCRA	health care reimbursement account
HEDIS	Health Plan Employer Data and Information Set
HH PPS	home health prospective payment system
HHRG	home health resource group
HICN	health insurance claim number
HIPAA	Health Insurance Portability and Accountability Act of 1996
HIPPS	health insurance prospective payment system (code set)
HITECH	Health Information Technology for Economic and Clinical Health (Act)
HMO	health maintenance organization
HPID	Health Plan Identifier
HPMP	Hospital Payment Monitoring Program
HPSA	health personnel shortage area
HRA	health reimbursement arrangement
HSA	health savings account
HSSA	health savings security account

I

i2 Initiative	Investing in Innovations Initiative
ICD	International Classification of Diseases
ICD-9-CM	*International Classification of Diseases, 9th Revision, Clinical Modification*
ICD-10-CM	*International Classification of Diseases, 10th Revision, Clinical Modification*
ICD-10-PCS	*International Classification of Diseases, 10th Revision, Procedural Coding System*

IDS integrated delivery system
IEP initial enrollment period
IME indirect medical education (adjustment)
IPA independent practice association
IPF PPS inpatient psychiatric facility prospective payment system
IPIA Improper Payments Information Act of 2002
IPO integrated provider organization
IPPS inpatient prospective payment system
IQR inpatient quality reporting
IRF PPP inpatient rehabilitation facility prospective payment system
IRVEN Inpatient Rehabilitation Validation and Entry

L

LA lead agent
LC limiting charge
LCD local coverage determination
LGHP large group health plan
LHWCA Longshore and Harbor Workers' Compensation Act
LLP limited license practitioners
LTC PPS long-term (acute) care hospital prospective payment system

M

MAB Medical Association of Billers
MAC Medicare administrative contractor
MAC monitored anesthesia care
MCD Medicare coverage database
MCO managed care organization
MCR Medicare Contracting Reform (initiative)
MDC major diagnostic category
MDS Minimum Data Set
MEDIC Medicare Drug Integrity Contractors (program)
Medi-Medi Medicare-Medicaid (crossover)
MEVS Medicaid eligibility verification system
MFN most favored nation
MHSS Military Health Services System
MIP Medicaid Integrity Program
MM major medical
MMA Medicare Prescription Drug, Improvement, and Modernization Act
MN medically needy
MPFS Medicare physician fee schedule
MR medical review
MRI magnetic resonance imaging
MSA medical savings account
MS-DRGs Medicare severity diagnosis-related groups
MSDS Material Safety Data Sheet
MSHA Mine Safety and Health Administration
MSI Medicare Supplementary Insurance
MSN Medicare Summary Notice
MSO management service organization
MSP Medicare Secondary Payer
MTF military treatment facility
MUE medically unlikely edit

N

NAS nonavailability statement
NATO North Atlantic Treaty Organization
NCCI National Correct Coding Initiative
NCD national coverage determination
NCHS National Center for Health Statistics
NCQA National Committee for Quality Assurance
NDC *National Drug Code*
NEC not elsewhere classifiable
NMOP National Mail Order Pharmacy
nonPAR nonparticipating provider
NOS not otherwise specified
NP nurse practitioner
NPI national provider identifier
NPPES National Plan and Provider Enumeration System
NSF national standard format
NUCC National Uniform Claims Committee

O

OASIS Outcomes and Assessment Information Set
OBRA Omnibus Budget Reconciliation Act
OCE outpatient code editor
OCR optical character reader
OHI other health insurance
OIG Office of Inspector General
OPAP outpatient pretreatment authorization plan
OPM Office of Personnel Management
OPPS outpatient prospective payment system
OSHA Occupational Safety and Health Administration
OWCP Office of Workers' Compensation Programs

P

PA physician assistant
PAC preadmission certification
PACE Program of All-Inclusive Care for the Elderly
PAR participating provider

PAT	preadmission testing
PATH	Physicians at Teaching Hospitals
PCM	primary care manager
PCP	primary care provider
PDAC	Pricing, Data Analysis and Coding
PEPP	Payment Error Prevention Program
PEPPER	Program for Evaluating Payment Patterns Electronic Report
PERM	Payment Error Rate Measurement
PFFS	private fee-for-service plan
PFPWD	program for persons with disabilities
PHI	protected health information
PHO	physician-hospital organization
PI	program integrity (office)
PIN	provider identification number
PlanID	national health plan identification number
PMO	program management organization (TRICARE)
POR	problem-oriented record
POS	place of service
PPA	preferred provider arrangement
PPN	preferred provider network
PPO	preferred provider organization
PPS	prospective payment system
PQRI	physician quality review initiative
PRN	Provider Remittance Notice
PSC	program safeguard contract
PSO	provider-sponsored organization
PSO	patient safety organization

Q

QAPI	quality assessment and performance improvement
QDWI	qualified disabled and working individual
QI	qualifying individual
QIO	quality improvement organization
QISMC	Quality Improvement System for Managed Care
QMB	qualified Medicare beneficiary
QMBP	qualified Medicare beneficiary program
QPU	Quarterly Provider Update (published by CMS)

R

RAC	recovery audit contractor
RAVEN	Resident Assessment Validation and Entry
RBRVS	resource-based relative value scale
remit	remittance advice
REVS	recipient eligibility verification system
ROI	release of information
ROM	risk of mortality
RUGs	resource utilization groups
RVU	relative value unit

S

SCHIP	State Children's Health Insurance Program
SEP	special enrollment period
SLMB	specified low-income Medicare beneficiary
SNF PPS	skilled nursing facility prospective payment system
SOAP	subjective, objective, assessment, plan
SOI	severity of illness
SSA	Social Security Administration
SSI	Supplemental Security Income
SSN	social security number
SSO	second surgical opinion
SURS	surveillance and utilization review subsystem

T

TANF	Temporary Assistance for Needy Families
TEFRA	Tax Equity and Fiscal Responsibility Act
TMA	TRICARE Management Activity
TOS	type of service
TPA	third-party administrator
TPMS	total practice management system
TRHCA	Tax Relief and Health Care Act
TSC	TRICARE Service Center

U

UB-04	uniform bill implemented in 2004
UCR	usual, customary, and reasonable
UPIN	unique provider identification number
URO	utilization review organization

V

VA	Veterans Administration
VAN	value-added network
VBP	value-based purchasing

W

WHO	World Health Organization

X

X12N	Insurance Subcommittee (as in ANSI ASC X12N 837)

Z

ZPIC	Zone Program Integrity Contractor

APPENDIX VI

Common Medical Terminology

Prefixes, Suffixes, and Combining Forms

a-, an-	no; not
ab-	away from
abdomin-	abdomen
acr-	extremities; top
ad-	toward
-ad	toward
adip-	fat
-al	pertaining to
angi-	vessel
ankyl-	crooked; bent
anti-	against
arthr-	joint
-asis, -esis, -iasis, -isis, -sis	condition
bi-	two
blephar-	eyelid
brachy-	short
brady-	slow
bronch-	bronchial tube
cardi-	heart
cephal-	head
cervic-	neck; cervix
colp-, kolp-	vagina
contra-	against; opposite
crani-	skull
cry-	cold
cyan-	blue
dacry-	tear
dactyl-	fingers; toes
de-	lack of; down
demi-	half
derm-, dermat-	skin
dextr-	right
di-	two
dis-	separation
-dynia	pain
dys-	bad; painful
-ectomy	excision; resection
-emesis	vomiting
-emia	blood condition
en-	in; within
end-, endo-	in; within
epi-	above; upon
erythr-	red
-esis	condition
-esthesia	nervous sensation
eti-	cause
ex-	out; away from
extra-	outside
fibr-	fiber
fore-	before
galact-, lact-	milk
gaster-, gastr-	stomach
genit-	genitals
gloss-	tongue
gluc-, glyc-	sugar; glucose
-gram	record
-graph	instrument for reading
-graphy	process of recording
gyn-, gyne-, gynec-	women; female
hem-, hema-, hemat-	blood
hemi-	half
hepat-	liver
hyp-, hyph-	below; under
hyper-	above; excessive
hyster-	uterus; womb
-ia, -iasis	condition
-ic	pertaining to
ileo-	ileum (small intestine)
ilio-	ilium (hip bone)
in-	in; into; not
infra-	within; into
inter-	between
intra-, intro-	within; into

ipsi-	same
-isis	condition
-itis	inflammation
juxta-	near
laryng-	larynx (voice box)
later-	side
leuk-	white
lingu-	tongue
lip-	fat; lipid
-lith	stone
-lysis	breakdown
mal-	bad
-mania	obsessive preoccupation
med-, medi-	middle
mega-, megal-	large
melan-	black
meta-	change; beyond
metr-, metra-	uterus; measure
mon-	one; single
musculo-, my-	muscle
myel-	spinal cord; bone marrow
nas-	nose
necr-	death
neo-	new
nephr-, nephra-	kidney
non-	not; no
norm-	rule; order
ob-	obstetrics
oculo-, optico-, opto-	eye
-oma	tumor; mass
omphal-	umbilicus (navel)
onych-	nail
oo-, ovi-, ovo-	egg
oophor-, oophoron-	ovary
-osis	condition—usually abnormal
oste-	bone
-ostomosis, -ostomy, -stomosis, -stomy	new opening
ot-	ear
-otomy	incision
-ous	pertaining to
pach-, pachy-	heavy; thick
pan-	all
para-, -para	near; besides
path-, -pathic, -pathy	disease
per-	through
peri-	surrounding
-pexy	fixation
pharyng-	throat (pharynx)
phleb-	vein
-phobia	fear
-plegia	paralysis
pleur-	pleura
pneum-, pneumat-	lung; air
-poiesis, -poietic	formation
poly-	many; much
post-	after; behind
poster-	back; behind
pro-	before; forward
pseud-	false
psych-	mind
pyelo-	renal pelvis
re-	back; again
ren-	kidney
retr-	behind; back
rhe-, -rrhea	flow
rhin-	nose
-rrhage, -rhagia	bursting forth (as of blood)
-rrhaphy	suture
salping-	fallopian tube; auditory tube
scirrh-	hard
-sclerosis	hardening
-scope	instrument for visual examination
-scopy	visual examination
semi-	half
soma-, somat-	body
sphygm-	pulse
splen-	spleen
spondyl-	vertebra
sten-	narrowness
steth-	chest
sub-	below
super-	above, superior
supra-	above, upper
tachy-	fast
tel-, tele-	complete
tend-, ten-	tendon
thorac-, thoraci-	chest; pleural cavity
thromb-	clot
-tomy	process of cutting
trans-	across
trich-, trichi-	hair
tympan-	tympanic membrane
ultra-	beyond; excess
uni-	one
ureter-	ureter
urethr-	urethra
-uria	urination
vas-	vessel; duct
ven-	vein
vesic-	urinary bladder

Bibliography

BOOKS AND MANUALS

Accounts receivable management for the medical practice. (2009). Los Angeles, CA: Practice Management Information Corporation.

American Medical Association. (2013). *CPT 2014.* Chicago, IL.

Blue Cross Association. (1972). *The Blue Cross story.* Chicago, IL.

Blue Cross and Blue Shield Association. (1987). *The history of Blue Cross and Blue Shield plans.* Chicago, IL.

Butler, A., & Dobbins, L. (2010). *Outcomes in coding practice: A roadmap from provider to payer.* Clifton Park, NY: Cengage Learning.

Davis, J. B. (2012). *Medical fees.* Los Angeles, CA: Practice Management Information Corporation.

Davison, J., & Lewis, M. (2007). *Working with insurance and managed care plans: A guide for getting paid.* Los Angeles, CA: Practice Management Information Corporation.

Diamond, M. (2012). *Understanding hospital billing and coding: A worktext.* Clifton Park, NY: Cengage Learning.

Dictionary of coding and billing terminology. (2009). Los Angeles, CA: Practice Management Information Corporation.

E/M coding made easy! (2010). Los Angeles, CA: Practice Management Information Corporation.

Fordney, M. T., French, L. L., & Follis, J. F. (2008). *Administrative medical assisting.* Clifton Park, NY: Cengage Learning.

Frisch, B. (2007). *Correct coding for Medicare, compliance, and reimbursement.* Clifton Park, NY: Cengage Learning.

Garrett, T. M., Baillie, H. W., & Garrett, R. M. (2010). *Health care ethics: Principles and problems.* Upper Saddle River, NJ: Prentice Hall.

Green, M. (2014). *3-2-1 Code It!* Clifton Park, NY: Cengage Learning.

Keir, L., Wise, B., Krebs, C., & Kelley-Arney, C. (2012). *Medical assisting: Administrative and clinical competencies.* Clifton Park, NY: Cengage Learning.

Kelly-Farwell, D., & Favreau, C. (2008). *Coding for medical necessity in the physician's office.* Clifton Park, NY: Cengage Learning.

Krager, D., & Krager, C. (2008). *HIPAA for health care professionals.* Clifton Park, NY: Cengage Learning.

Lindh, W. Q., Pooler, M. S., Tamparo, C. D., & Dahl, B. M. (2010). *Delmar's comprehensive medical assisting: Administrative and clinical competencies.* Clifton Park, NY: Cengage Learning.

Maki, S. E., & Petterson, B. (2008). *Using the electronic health record in the healthcare provider practice.* Clifton Park, NY: Cengage Learning.

Moore, C. D. (2009). *Understanding workers' compensation insurance.* Clifton Park, NY: Cengage Learning.

National Association of Blue Shield Plans. *The Blue Shield story: All of us helping each of us.* Chicago, IL: Blue Cross and Blue Shield Association.

OptumInsight. (2014). *ICD-10-CM: the complete official draft code set.* Salt Lake City, UT: Author.

___ (2014). *ICD-10-CM mapping file.* Salt Lake City, UT: Author.

___ (2014). *ICD-10-PCS: The complete official draft code set.* Salt Lake City, UT: Author.

___ (2014). *ICD-10-PCS mapping files.* Salt Lake City, UT: Author.

___ (2014). *HCPCS level II professional.* Salt Lake City, UT: Author.

___ (2014). *Medicare correct coding guide.* Salt Lake City, UT: Author.

___ (2014). *Medicare desk reference for physicians.* Salt Lake City, UT: Author.

___ (2014). *Uniform billing editor.* Salt Lake City, UT: Author.

Richards, C. (2010). *Coding basics: medical billing and reimbursement fundamentals*. Clifton Park, NY: Cengage Learning.

Rimmer, M. (2008). *Medical Billing 101*. Clifton Park, NY: Cengage Learning.

Rimmer, M. (2009). *Coding basics, understanding medical collections*. Clifton Park, NY: Cengage Learning.

BROCHURES AND BULLETINS

CMS-1500 claim filing instructions. Albuquerque, NM: Blue Cross Blue Shield of New Mexico.

Coverage policy bulletins. Hartford, CT: Aetna US Healthcare, Aetna Life Insurance Company.

Electronic data revolution in the health care industry. Marlborough, MA: 3Com.

The facts about Medicare advantage. Washington, D.C.: Centers for Medicare and Medicaid Services.

The facts about Medicare prescription drug plans. Washington, D.C.: Centers for Medicare and Medicaid Services.

FEP service benefit plan brochure. Chicago, IL: Blue Cross and Blue Shield Federal Employees Program.

Follow that claim: Claims submission, adjudication and payment. Chicago, IL: American Medical Association.

Health Insurance Portability and Accountability Act of 1996—Administrative simplification care fact sheet. Washington, D.C.: Centers for Medicare and Medicaid Services.

Health insurance, the history. Seattle, WA: Health Insurance Association of America.

HIPAA: Health care transformation to electronic communications. Bellevue, WA: Captaris, Inc.

Medicare & you 2013. Washington, D.C.: Centers for Medicare and Medicaid Services.

Medicare and other health benefits: Your guide to who pays first. Washington, D.C.: Centers for Medicare and Medicaid Services.

Medigap policies: The basics. Washington, D.C.: Centers for Medicare and Medicaid Services.

Protecting Medicare and you from fraud. Washington, D.C.: Centers for Medicare and Medicaid Services.

Quick facts about Medicare's new coverage for prescription drugs for people with Medicare and Medicaid. Washington, D.C.: Centers for Medicare and Medicaid Services.

TRICARE grand rounds. Falls Church, VA: TRICARE Management Activity.

Understanding the choice you have in how you get your Medicare health care coverage. Washington, D.C.: Centers for Medicare and Medicaid Services.

Your Medicare benefits. Washington, D.C.: Centers for Medicare and Medicaid Services.

INSURANCE MANUALS

Blue Cross and Blue Shield of Maryland guide to programs & benefits. Owings Mills, MD: Carefirst Blue Cross and Blue Shield.

CHAMPVA handbook. Denver, CO: VA Health Administration Center.

Medicare claims processing manual. Washington, D.C.: Centers for Medicare and Medicaid Services.

Medicare contractor beneficiary and provider communications manual. Washington, D.C.: Centers for Medicare and Medicaid Services.

Medicare financial management manual. Washington, D.C.: Centers for Medicare and Medicaid Services.

Medicare general information, eligibility and entitlement manual. Washington, D.C.: Centers for Medicare and Medicaid Services.

Medicare managed care manual. Washington, D.C.: Centers for Medicare and Medicaid Services.

Medicare prescription drug benefit manual. Washington, D.C.: Centers for Medicare and Medicaid Services.

Medicare program integrity manual. Washington, D.C.: Centers for Medicare and Medicaid Services.

Medicare secondary payer manual. Washington, D.C.: Centers for Medicare and Medicaid Services.

Quality improvement organization manual. Washington, D.C.: Centers for Medicare and Medicaid Services.

State Medicaid manual. Washington, D.C.: Centers for Medicare and Medicaid Services.

TRICARE reimbursement manual. Aurora, CO: TRICARE Management Activity.

JOURNALS, NEWSMAGAZINES, AND NEWSLETTERS

Advance for health information professionals. King of Prussia, PA: Merion Publications.

BlueReview for contracting institutional & professional providers. Chicago, IL: Blue Cross and Blue Shield of Illinois.

Coding edge. Salt Lake City, UT: American Association of Professional Coders.

Compliance (free e-zine). Gaithersburg, MD: DecisionHealth.

Corporate compliance (free e-newsletter). Marblehead, MA: HCPro, Inc.

CPT assistant. Chicago, IL: American Medical Association.

Dental care news. Detroit, MI: Blue Cross and Blue Shield of Michigan.

Family practice management. Leawood, KS: American Academy of Family Physicians.

For the record. Spring City, PA: Great Valley Publishing.

Healthcare Auditing Weekly (free e-newsletter). Marblehead, MA: HCPro, Inc.

InFocus. Owings Mills, MD: CareFirst Blue Cross and Blue Shield.

Journal of Medical Practice Management®. Phoenix, MD: Greenbranch Publishing.

Journal of the American Health Information Management Association. Chicago, IL: American Health Information Management Association.

Managed Care Magazine. Yardley, PA: MultiMedia USA.

Medicare Update for Physician Services (free e-newsletter). Marblehead, MA: HCPro, Inc.

Medicare Weekly Update (free e-newsletter). Marblehead, MA: HCPro, Inc.

Physician billing & reimbursement (free e-zine). Gaithersburg, MD: DecisionHealth.

Physician coding (free e-zine). Gaithersburg, MD: DecisionHealth.

TrailBlazer eBulletin. Denison, TX: TrailBlazer Health Enterprises, LLC.

INTERNET-BASED REFERENCES

www.carefirst.com—BCBS affiliate in Maryland.

https://cms.meridianski.com—self-paced Medicare training by downloading free interactive courses and attending free satellite programs designed to teach Medicare billing guidelines.

www.codecorrect.com—subscription service that provides CPT, ICD-9, CCI, Coding Crosswalk and APC data, and searchable Medicare newsletters and *Federal Register* issues.

www.navicure.com—resource for identifying key metrics in revenue cycle management.

https://www.noridianmedicare.com—Medicare Fees and News (e.g., Fee Schedules, Bulletins).

www.usa.gov—resource for locating government information on the Internet.

www.worldofquotes.com—archive of historic quotes and proverbs.

SOFTWARE

www.EncoderPro.com. Salt Lake City, UT: OptumInsight Publishing.

SimCLAIM™. Clifton Park, NY: Cengage Learning.

Glossary

> **NOTE:** Numbers in parentheses following a glossary term indicate the text chapter(s) in which that term appears as a Key Term.

abuse (5) - actions inconsistent with accepted, sound medical, business, or fiscal practices.

accept assignment (4) - provider accepts as payment in full whatever is paid on the claim by the payer (except for any copayment and/or coinsurance amounts).

accounts receivable (4) - the amount owed to a business for services or goods provided.

accounts receivable aging report (4) - shows the status (by date) of outstanding claims from each payer, as well as payments due from patients.

accounts receivable management (4) - assists providers in the collection of appropriate reimbursement for services rendered; includes functions such as insurance verification/eligibility and preauthorization of services.

accreditation (3) - voluntary process that a health care facility or organization (e.g., hospital or managed care plan) undergoes to demonstrate that it has met standards beyond those required by law.

adjudication (17) - judicial dispute resolution process in which an appeals board makes a final determination.

adjusted claim (15) - payment correction resulting in additional payment(s) to the provider.

advance beneficiary notice of noncoverage (ABN) (14) - document that acknowledges patient responsibility for payment if Medicare denies the claim.

adverse effect (6) - taking less of a medication than is prescribed by a provider or a manufacturer's instruction.

adverse selection (3) - covering members who are sicker than the general population.

allowable charge (9) - *see* limiting charge.

allowed charge (4) - the maximum amount the payer will reimburse for each procedure or service, according to the patient's policy.

All-Patient diagnosis-related group (AP-DRG) (9) - DRG system adapted for use by third-party payers to reimburse hospitals for inpatient care provided to *non*-Medicare beneficiaries (e.g., BlueCross BlueShield, commercial health plans, TRICARE); DRG assignment is based on intensity of resources.

All-Patient Refined diagnosis-related group (APR-DRG) (9) - adopted by Medicare in 2008 to reimburse hospitals for inpatient care provided to Medicare beneficiaries; expanded original DRG system (based on intensity of resources) to add two subclasses to each DRG that adjusts Medicare inpatient hospital reimbursement rates for severity of illness (SOI) (extent of physiological decompensation or organ system loss of function) and risk of mortality (ROM) (likelihood of dying); each subclass, in turn, is subdivided into four areas: (1) minor, (2) moderate, (3) major, and (4) extreme.

ambulance fee schedule (9) - payment system for ambulance services provided to Medicare beneficiaries.

ambulatory payment classifications (APCs) (2) - prospective payment system used to calculate reimbursement for outpatient care according to similar clinical characteristics and in terms of resources required.

ambulatory surgical center (ASC) (9) - state-licensed, Medicare-certified supplier (not provider) of surgical health care services that must *accept assignment* on Medicare claims.

ambulatory surgical center payment rate (9) - predetermined amount for which ASC services are reimbursed, at 80 percent after adjustment for regional wage variations.

Amendment to the HMO Act of 1973 (3) - legislation that allowed federally qualified HMOs to permit members to occasionally use non-HMO physicians and be partially reimbursed.

American Academy of Professional Coders (AAPC) (1) - professional association established to provide a national certification and credentialing process, to support the national and local membership by providing educational products and opportunities to networks, and to increase and promote national recognition and awareness of professional coding.

American Association of Medical Assistants (AAMA) (1) - enables medical assisting professionals to enhance and demonstrate the knowledge, skills, and professionalism required by employers and patients; as well as protect medical assistants' right to practice.

American Health Information Management Association (AHIMA) (1) - founded in 1928 to improve the quality of medical records, and currently advances the health information management (HIM) profession toward an electronic and global environment, including implementation of ICD-10-CM and ICD-10-PCS in 2013.

American Medical Billing Association (AMBA) (1) - offers the Certified Medical Reimbursement Specialist (CMRS) exam, which recognizes competency of members who have met high standards of proficiency.

American Recovery and Reinvestment Act of 2009 (ARRA) (5) - authorized an expenditure of $1.5 billion for grants for construction, renovation, and equipment, and for the acquisition of health information technology systems.

ANSI ASC X12 (4) - an electronic format standard that uses a variable-length file format to process transactions for institutional, professional, dental, and drug claims.

ANSI ASC X12N 837 (5) - variable-length file format used to bill institutional, professional, dental, and drug claims.

appeal (4) - documented as a letter, signed by the provider, explaining why a claim should be reconsidered for payment.

arbitration (17) - dispute-resolution process in which a final determination is made by an impartial person who may not have judicial powers.

assessment (10) - contains the diagnostic statement and may include the provider's rationale for the diagnosis.

assignment of benefits (4) - the provider receives reimbursement directly from the payer.

auditing process (10) - review of patient records and CMS-1500 (or UB-04) claims to assess coding accuracy and whether documentation is complete.

authorization (5) - document that provides official instruction, such as the customized document that gives covered entities permission to use specified protected health information (PHI) for specified purposes or to disclose PHI to a third party specified by the individual.

automobile insurance policy (12) - contract between an individual and an insurance company whereby the individual pays a premium and, in exchange, the insurance company agrees to pay for specific car-related financial losses during the term of the policy; typically includes medical-payments coverage and personal injury protection (PIP) to reimburse health care expenses sustained as the result of injury from an automobile accident.

Away From Home Care® Program (13) - provides continuous BCBS health care coverage for subscribers who will be out of their service area for more than 90 consecutive days.

bad debt (4) - accounts receivable that cannot be collected by the provider or a collection agency.

balance billing (9) - billing beneficiaries for amounts not reimbursed by payers (not including copayments and coinsurance amounts); this practice is prohibited by Medicare regulations.

Balanced Budget Act of 1997 (BBA) (2) - addresses health care fraud and abuse issues, and provides for Department of Health and Human Services (DHHS) Office of the Inspector General (OIG) investigative and audit services in health care fraud cases.

base period (12) - period of time that usually covers 12 months and is divided into four consecutive quarters.

BCBS basic coverage (13) - BlueCross BlueShield (BCBS) coverage for the following services: hospitalization, diagnostic laboratory services, x-rays, surgical fees, assistant surgeon fees, obstetric care, intensive care, newborn care, and chemotherapy for cancer.

BCBS major medical (MM) coverage (13) - BCBS coverage for the following services, in addition to basic coverage: office visits, outpatient nonsurgical treatment, physical and occupational therapy, purchase of durable medical equipment (DME), mental health visits, allergy testing and injections, prescription drugs, private duty nursing (when medically necessary), and dental care required as a result of a covered accidental injury.

beneficiary (4) - the person eligible to receive health care benefits.

beneficiary counseling and assistance coordinator (BCAC) (16) - individual available at a military treatment facility (MTF) to answer questions, help solve health care–related problems, and assist beneficiaries in obtaining medical care through TRICARE; was previously called *health benefits advisor (HBA)*.

beneficiary services representative (BSR) (16) - employed at a TRICARE Service Center; provides information about using TRICARE and assists with other matters affecting access to health care (e.g., appointment scheduling).

benefit period (Medicare) (14) - begins with the first day of hospitalization and ends when the patient has been out of the hospital for 60 consecutive days.

benign (6) - not cancerous.

billing entity (11) - the legal business name of the provider's practice.

birthday rule (4) - determines coverage by primary and secondary policies when each parent subscribes to a different health insurance plan.

black box edits (5) - nonpublished code edits, which were discontinued in 2000.

BlueCard® Program (13) - program that allows BCBS subscribers to receive local Blue Plan health care benefits while traveling or living outside of their plan's area.

BlueCross (13) - insurance plan created in 1929 when Baylor University Hospital, in Dallas, TX, approached teachers in the Dallas school district with a plan that guaranteed up to 21 days of hospitalization per year for subscribers and each dependent for a $6 annual premium.

BlueCross BlueShield (BCBS) (13) - joint venture between BlueCross and BlueShield where the corporations shared one building and computer services but maintained separate corporate identities.

BlueShield (13) - began as a resolution passed by the House of Delegates at an American Medical Association meeting in 1938; incorporates a concept of voluntary health insurance that encourages providers to cooperate with prepaid health plans.

BlueWorldwide *Expat* (13) - provides global medical coverage for active employees and their dependents who spend more than six months outside the United States; any U.S. corporation with new or existing Blue coverage that sends members to work and reside outside the United States for six months or more is eligible for BlueWorldwide *Expat*.

bonding insurance (1) - an insurance agreement that guarantees repayment for financial losses resulting from the act or failure to act of an employee. It protects the financial operations of the employer.

breach of confidentiality (5) - unauthorized release of patient information to a third party.

business liability insurance (1) - protects business assets and covers the cost of lawsuits resulting from bodily injury, personal injury, and false advertising.

cafeteria plan (3) - also called *triple option plan;* provides different health benefit plans and extra coverage options through an insurer or third-party administrator.

capitation (3) - provider accepts preestablished payments for providing health care services to enrollees over a period of time (usually one year).

carcinoma (Ca) *in situ* (6) - a malignant tumor that is localized, circumscribed, encapsulated, and noninvasive (has not spread to deeper or adjacent tissues or organs).

care plan oversight services (7) - cover the provider's time supervising a complex and multidisciplinary care treatment program for a specific patient who is under the care of a home health agency, hospice, or nursing facility.

case law (5) - also called *common law;* based on a court decision that establishes a precedent.

case management (3) - development of patient care plans to coordinate and provide care for complicated cases in a cost-effective manner.

case management services (7) - process by which an attending physician coordinates and supervises care provided to a patient by other providers.

case manager (3) - submits written confirmation, authorizing treatment, to the provider.

case mix (9) - the types and categories of patients treated by a health care facility or provider.

catastrophic cap benefit (16) - protects TRICARE beneficiaries from devastating financial loss due to serious illness or long-term treatment by establishing limits over which payment is not required.

catchment area (16) - the region defined by code boundaries within a 40-mile radius of a military treatment facility.

Category I codes (7) - procedures/services identified by a five-digit CPT code and descriptor nomenclature; these codes are traditionally associated with CPT and organized within six sections.

Category II codes (7) - optional performance measurement tracking codes that are assigned an alphanumeric identifier with a letter in the last field (e.g., 1234A); these codes will be located after the Medicine section; *their use is optional.*

Category III codes (7) - temporary codes for data collection purposes that are assigned an alphanumeric identifier with a letter in the last field (e.g., 0001T); these codes are located after the Medicine section, and will be archived after five years unless accepted for placement within Category I sections of CPT.

Centers for Medicare and Medicaid Services (CMS) (1) - formerly known as the Health Care Financing Administration (HCFA); an administrative agency within the federal Department of Health and Human Services (DHHS).

certificate of medical necessity (CMN) (8) - prescription document for durable medical equipment, services, and supplies that is signed by the treating physician and submitted with the CMS-1500 claim to the DME MAC for reimbursement.

CHAMPUS Reform Initiative (CRI) (2, 16) - conducted in 1988; resulted in a new health program called TRICARE, which includes three options: TRICARE Prime, TRICARE Extra, and TRICARE Standard.

charge description master (CDM) (9) - *see* chargemaster.

chargemaster (4, 9) - document that contains a computer-generated list of procedures, services, and supplies with charges for each; chargemaster data are entered in the facility's patient accounting system, and charges are automatically posted to the patient's bill (UB-04).

chargemaster maintenance (9) - process of updating and revising key elements of the chargemaster (or charge description master [CDM]) to ensure accurate reimbursement.

chargemaster team (9) - jointly shares the responsibility of updating and revising the chargemaster to ensure its accuracy and consists of representatives of a variety of departments, such as coding compliance financial services, health information management, information services, other departments, and physicians.

check digit (5) - one-digit character, alphabetic or numeric, used to verify the validity of a unique identifier.

civil law (5) - area of law not classified as criminal.

Civilian Health and Medical Program of the Department of Veterans Affairs (CHAMPVA) (2) - program that provides health benefits for dependents of veterans rated as 100 percent permanently and totally disabled as a result of service-connected conditions, veterans who died as a result of service-connected conditions, and veterans who died on duty with less than 30 days of active service.

Civilian Health and Medical Program—Uniformed Services (CHAMPUS) (2) - originally designed as a benefit for dependents of personnel serving in the armed forces and uniformed branches of the Public Health Service and the National Oceanic and Atmospheric Administration; now called TRICARE.

claims adjudication (4) - comparing a claim to payer edits and the patient's health plan benefits to verify that the required information is available to process the claim; the claim is not a duplicate; payer rules and procedures have been followed; and procedures performed or services provided are covered benefits.

claims attachment (4) - medical report substantiating a medical condition.

claims examiner (1) - employed by third-party payers to review health-related claims to determine whether the charges are reasonable and medically necessary based on the patient's diagnosis.

claims processing (4) - sorting claims upon submission to collect and verify information about the patient and provider.

claims submission (4) - the transmission of claims data (electronically or manually) to payers or clearinghouses for processing.

clean claim (4) - a correctly completed standardized claim (e.g., CMS-1500 claim).

clearinghouse (4) - performs centralized claims processing for providers and health plans.

Clinical Data Abstracting Center (CDAC) (5) - requests and screens medical records for the Payment Error Prevention Program (PEPP) to survey samples for medical review, DRG validation, and medical necessity.

clinical laboratory fee schedule (9) - data set based on local fee schedules (for outpatient clinical diagnostic laboratory services).

Clinical Laboratory Improvement Act (CLIA) (2) - established quality standards for all laboratory testing to ensure the accuracy, reliability, and timeliness of patient test results regardless of where the test was performed.

clinical nurse specialist (CNS) (9) - a registered nurse licensed by the state in which services are provided, has a master's degree in a defined clinical area of nursing from an accredited educational institution, and is certified as a CNS by the American Nurses Credentialing Center.

closed claim (4) - claims for which all processing, including appeals, has been completed.

closed-panel HMO (3) - health care is provided in an HMO-owned center or satellite clinic or by providers who belong to a specially formed medical group that serves the HMO.

CMS-1500 (2) - form used to submit Medicare claims; previously called the HCFA-1500.

CMS program transmittal (9) - communicate new or changed policies, and/or procedures that are being incorporated into a specific CMS Internet-only program manual.

***CMS Quarterly Provider Update* (QPU) (9)** - an online CMS publication that contains information about regulations and major policies currently under development, regulations and major policies completed or cancelled, and new or revised manual instructions.

coding (1) - process of reporting diagnoses, procedures, and services as numeric and alphanumeric characters on the insurance claim.

coinsurance (2, 4) - also called *coinsurance payment;* the percentage the patient pays for covered services after the deductible has been met and the copayment has been paid.

commercial health insurance (12) - covers the medical expenses of individuals groups; premiums and benefits vary according to the type of plan offered.

common access card (CAC) (16) - identification card issued by the Department of Defense (DoD), which TRICARE enrollees show to receive health care services.

common data file (4) - abstract of all recent claims filed on each patient.

common law (5) - also called *case law;* is based on a court decision that establishes a precedent.

comorbidity (6) - concurrent condition that coexists with the first-listed diagnosis (outpatient care) (or principal diagnosis for inpatient care), has the potential to affect treatment of the first-listed diagnosis (outpatient care) (or principal diagnosis for inpatient care), and is an active condition for which the patient is treated and/or monitored.

competitive medical plan (CMP) (3) - an HMO that meets federal eligibility requirements for a Medicare risk contract, but is not licensed as a federally qualified plan.

complication (6) - condition that develops after outpatient care has been provided or during an inpatient admission.

comprehensive assessment (7) - must include an assessment of the patient's functional capacity, identification of potential problems, and a nursing plan to enhance, or at least maintain, the patient's physical and psychosocial functions.

Comprehensive Error Rate Testing (CERT) program (5) - assesses and measures improper Medicare fee-for-service payments (based on reviewing selected claims and associated medical record documentation).

computer-assisted coding (CAC) (6) - uses a natural language processing engine to "read" patient records and generate ICD-10-CM and HCPCS/CPT codes.

concurrent care (7) - provision of similar services, such as hospital inpatient visits, to the same patient by more than one provider on the same day.

concurrent review (3) - review for medical necessity of tests and procedures ordered during an inpatient hospitalization.

conditional primary payer status (14) - Medicare claim process that includes the following circumstances: a plan that is normally considered to be primary to Medicare issues a denial of payment that is under appeal; a patient who is physically or mentally impaired failed to file a claim to the primary payer; a workers' compensation claim has been denied and the case is slowly moving through the appeal process; or there is no response from a liability payer within 120 days of filing the claim.

confidentiality (5) - restricting patient information access to those with proper authorization and maintaining the security of patient information.

Consolidated Omnibus Budget Reconciliation Act of 1985 (COBRA) (2) - allows employees to continue health care coverage beyond the benefit termination date.

consultation (7) - examination of a patient by a health care provider, usually a specialist, for the purpose of advising the referring or attending physician in the evaluation and/or management of a specific problem with a known diagnosis.

Consumer Credit Protection Act of 1968 (4) - was considered landmark legislation because it launched truth-in-lending disclosures that required creditors to communicate the cost of borrowing money in a common language so that consumers could figure out the charges, compare costs, and shop for the best credit deal.

consumer-directed health plan (CDHP) (3) - *see* consumer-driven health plan.

consumer-driven health plan (CDHP) (2) - health care plan that encourages individuals to locate the best health care at the lowest possible price, with the goal of holding down costs; also called *consumer-directed health plan.*

contiguous sites (6) - also called *overlapping sites;* occurs when the origin of the tumor (primary site) involves two adjacent sites.

continuity of care (2) - documenting patient care services so that others who treat the patient have a source of information on which to base additional care and treatment.

contributory components (7) - include counseling, coordination of care, nature of presenting problem, and time.

conversion factor (9) - dollar multiplier that converts relative value units (RVUs) into payments.

Cooperating Parties for ICD-10-CM/PCS (6) - AHA, AMA, CMS, and NCHS organizations and agencies that approve official guidelines for coding and reporting ICD-10-CM and ICD-10-PCS.

coordinated care plan (14) - also called *managed care plan;* includes health maintenance organizations (HMOs), preferred provider organizations (PPOs), and provider-sponsored organizations (PSOs), through which a Medicare beneficiary may choose to receive health care coverage and services. CCPs often provide a greater array of services and smaller copayment than conventional Medicare.

coordinated home health and hospice care (13) - allows patients with this option to elect an alternative to the acute care setting.

coordination of benefits (COB) (4) - provision in group health insurance policies that prevents multiple insurers from paying benefits covered by other policies; also specifies that coverage will be provided in a specific sequence when more than one policy covers the claim.

coordination of care (7) - provider makes arrangements with other providers or agencies for services to be provided to a patient.

copayment (copay) (2) - provision in an insurance policy that requires the policyholder or patient to pay a specified dollar amount to a health care provider for each visit or medical service received.

counseling (7) - discussion with a patient and/or family concerning one or more of the following areas: diagnostic results, impressions, and/or recommended diagnostic studies; prognosis; risks and benefits of management (treatment) options; instructions for management (treatment) and/or follow-up; importance of compliance with chosen management (treatment) options; risk factor reduction; and patient and family education.

covered entity (4) - private sector health plans (excluding certain small self-administered health plans), managed care organizations, ERISA-covered health benefit plans (Employee Retirement Income Security Act of 1974), and government health plans (including Medicare, Medicaid, Military Health System for active duty and civilian personnel; Veterans Health Administration, and Indian Health Service programs); all health care clearinghouses; and all health care providers that choose to submit or receive transactions electronically.

CPT Coding Conventions (7)

boldface type - highlights main terms in the CPT index and categories, subcategories, headings, and code numbers in the CPT manual.

cross-reference term (See) - directs coders to a different CPT index entry because no codes are found under the original entry.

descriptive qualifiers - terms that clarify assignment of a CPT code.

guidelines - define terms and explain the assignment of codes for procedures and services located in a particular section.

inferred words - used to save space in the CPT index when referencing subterms.

instructional notes - appear throughout CPT sections to clarify the assignment of codes.

italicized type - used for the cross-reference term, *See,* in the CPT index.

separate procedure - follows a code description that identifies procedures that are an integral part of another procedure or service.

CPT Symbols (7)

● bullet located to the left of a code number identifies new CPT procedures and services.

▲ triangle located to the left of a code number identifies a revised code description.

▶◀ horizontal triangles surround revised guidelines and notes. *This symbol is not used for revised code descriptions.*

; semicolon saves space in CPT so that some code descriptions are not printed in their entirety next to a code number; the entry is indented and the coder refers back to the common portion of the code description located before the semicolon.

+ plus symbol identifies add-on codes for procedures that are commonly, but not always, performed at the same time and by the same surgeon as the primary procedure.

⊘ forbidden symbol identifies codes that are not to be appended with modifier -51.

⊙ bull's eye symbol identifies a procedure that includes conscious sedation. (CPT Appendix G includes a list of codes that include conscious sedation.)

↯ flash symbol indicates that a code is pending FDA approval but that it has been assigned a CPT code.

○ hollow circle symbol indicates a reinstated or recycled CPT code (e.g., 1127F).

number symbol precedes CPT codes that appear out of numerical order.

criminal law (5) - public law governed by statute or ordinance that deals with crimes and their prosecution.

critical care services (7) - reported when a provider directly delivers medical care for a critically ill or critically injured patient.

critical pathway (16) - sequence of activities that can normally be expected to result in the most cost-effective clinical course of treatment.

***Current Dental Terminology* (CDT) (5)** - medical code set maintained and copyrighted by the American Dental Association.

***Current Procedural Terminology* (CPT) (1)** - published by the American Medical Association; includes five-digit numeric codes and descriptors for procedures and services performed by providers (e.g., 99203 identifies a detailed office visit for a new patient).

customized sub-capitation plan (CSCP) (3) - managed care plan in which health care expenses are funded by insurance coverage; the individual selects one of each type of provider to create a customized network and pays the resulting customized insurance premium; each provider is paid a fixed amount per month to provide only the care that an individual needs from that provider (called a *sub-capitation payment*).

data analytics (9) - tools and systems that are used to analyze clinical and financial data, conduct research, and evaluate the effectiveness of disease treatments.

day sheet (4) - also called *manual daily accounts receivable journal;* chronological summary of all transactions posted to individual patient ledgers/accounts on a specific day.

debt collection assistance officer (DCAO) (16) - individuals located at military treatment facilities to assist beneficiaries in resolving health care collection-related issues.

decrypt (5) - to decode an encoded computer file so that it can be viewed.

deductible (2, 4) - amount for which the patient is financially responsible before an insurance policy provides coverage.

Defense Enrollment Eligibility Reporting System (DEERS) (16) - computer system that contains up-to-date Defense Department Workforce personnel information.

Deficit Reduction Act of 2005 (5) - Created Medicaid Integrity Program (MIP), which increased resources available to CMS to combat abuse, fraud, and waste in the Medicaid program. Congress requires annual reporting by CMS about the use and effectiveness of funds appropriated for the MIP.

delinquent account (4) - *see* past due account.

delinquent claim (4) - claim usually more than 120 days past due; some practices establish time frames that are less than or more than 120 days past due.

delinquent claim cycle (4) - advances through various aging periods (30 days, 60 days, 90 days, and so on), with practices typically focusing internal recovery efforts on older delinquent accounts (e.g., 120 days or more).

demonstration project or pilot (16) - test and establish the feasibility of implementing a new TRICARE program during a trial period, after which the program is evaluated, modified, and/or abandoned.

demonstration/pilot program (14) - special project that tests improvements in Medicare coverage, payment, and quality of care.

deposition (5) - legal proceeding during which a party answers questions under oath (but not in open court).

diagnosis pointer letters (11) - item letters A through L preprinted in Block 21 of the CMS-1500 claim.

diagnosis-related group (DRG) (2) - prospective payment system that reimburses hospitals for inpatient stays.

***Diagnostic and Statistical Manual* (DSM) (9)** - classifies mental health disorders and is based on ICD; published by the American Psychiatric Association.

digital (5) - application of a mathematical function to an electronic document to create a computer code that can be encrypted (encoded).

direct contract model HMO (3) - contracted health care services delivered to subscribers by individual providers in the community.

direct patient contact (7) - refers to face-to-face patient contact (outpatient or inpatient).

disability insurance (12) - reimbursement for income lost as a result of a temporary or permanent illness or injury.

discharge planning (3) - involves arranging appropriate health care services for the discharged patient (e.g., home health care).

disproportionate share hospital (DSH) adjustment (9) - policy in which hospitals that treat a high percentage of low-income patients receive increased Medicare payments.

downcoding (4) - assigning lower-level codes than documented in the record.

dual eligibles (15) - individuals entitled to Medicare and eligible for some type of Medicaid benefit.

durable medical equipment (DME) (8) - canes, crutches, walkers, commode chairs, blood glucose monitors, and so on.

durable medical equipment, prosthetics, orthotics, and supplies (DMEPOS) (8) - defined by Medicare as equipment that can withstand repeated use, is primarily used to serve a medical purpose, is used in the patient's home, and would not be used in the absence of illness or injury.

durable medical equipment, prosthetics, orthotics, and supplies (DMEPOS) dealers (8) - supply patients with durable medical equipment (DME) (e.g., canes, crutches); DMEPOS claims are submitted to DME Medicare administrative contractors (MACs) who are awarded contracts by CMS; each DME MAC covers a specific geographic region of the country and is responsible for processing DMEPOS claims for its specific region.

durable medical equipment, prosthetics/orthotics, and supplies (DMEPOS) fee schedule (9) - Medicare reimburses DMEPOS dealers according to either the actual charge or the amount calculated according to formulas that use average reasonable charges for items during a base period from 1986 to 1987, whichever is lower.

Early and Periodic Screening, Diagnostic, and Treatment (EPSDT) services (15) - legislation that mandates states to provide routine pediatric checkups to all children enrolled in Medicaid.

electronic data interchange (EDI) (4) - computer-to-computer exchange of data between provider and payer.

electronic flat file format (4) - series of fixed-length records (e.g., 25 spaces for patient's name) submitted to payers to bill for health care services.

electronic funds transfer (EFT) (4) - system by which payers deposit funds to the provider's account electronically.

Electronic Funds Transfer Act (4) - established the rights, liabilities, and responsibilities of participants in electronic funds transfer systems.

electronic health record (EHR) (2) - global concept that includes the collection of patient information documented by a number of providers at different facilities regarding one patient.

Electronic Healthcare Network Accreditation Commission (EHNAC) (4) - organization that accredits clearinghouses.

electronic media claim (4) - *see* electronic flat file format.

electronic medical record (EMR) (2) - considered part of the electronic health record (EHR), the EMR is created on a computer using a keyboard, a mouse, an optical pen device, a voice recognition system, a scanner, or a touch screen; records are created using vendor software, which assists in provider decision making; numerous vendors offer EMR software, mostly to provider office practices that require practice management solutions.

electronic remittance advice (ERA) (4) - remittance advice that is submitted to the provider electronically and contains the same information as a paper-based remittance advice; providers receive the ERA more quickly.

electronic transaction standards (5) - also called *transactions rule;* a uniform language for electronic data interchange.

embezzle (1) - the illegal transfer of money or property as a fraudulent action.

emergency care (16) - care for the sudden and unexpected onset of a medical or mental health condition that is threatening to life, limb, or sight.

emergency department services (7) - services provided in an organized, hospital-based facility, which is open on a 24-hour basis, for the purpose of "providing unscheduled episodic services to patients requiring immediate medical attention."

Employee Retirement Income Security Act of 1974 (ERISA) (2) - mandated reporting and disclosure requirements for group life and health plans (including managed care plans), permitted large employers to self-insure employee health care benefits, and exempted large employers from taxes on health insurance premiums.

employer group health plan (EGHP) (9) - contributed to by an employer or employee pay-all plan; provides coverage to employees and dependents without regard to the enrollee's employment status (i.e., full-time, part-time, or retired).

encoder (6) - automates the coding process using computerized or web-based software; instead of manually looking up conditions (or procedures) in the coding manual's index, the coder uses the software's search feature to locate and verify diagnosis and procedure codes.

encounter (6) - face-to-face contact between a patient and a health care provider (e.g., physician, nurse practitioner) who assesses and treats the patient's condition.

encounter form (4) - financial record source document used by providers and other personnel to record treated diagnoses and services rendered to the patient during the current encounter.

encrypt (5) - to convert information to a secure language format for transmission.

End-Stage Renal Disease (ESRD) composite payment rate system (9) - bundles end-stage renal disease (ESRD) drugs and related laboratory tests with the composite rate payments, resulting in one reimbursement amount paid for ESRD services provided to patients; the rate is case-mix adjusted to provide a mechanism to account for differences in patients' utilization of health care resources (e.g., patient's age).

Energy Employees Occupational Illness Compensation Program (EEOICP) (17) - provides benefits to eligible employees and former employees of the Department of Energy, its contractors and subcontractors, certain survivors of such individuals, and certain beneficiaries of the Radiation Exposure Compensation Act.

enrollees (3) - also called *covered lives;* employees and dependents who join a managed care plan; known as *beneficiaries* in private insurance plans.

Equal Credit Opportunity Act (4) - prohibits discrimination on the basis of race, color, religion, national origin, sex, marital status, age, receipt of public assistance, or good faith exercise of any rights under the Consumer Credit Protection Act.

errors and omissions insurance (1) - *see* professional liability insurance.

essential modifier (6) - *see* subterm.

established patient (7) - one who has received professional services from the provider, or from another provider of the same specialty who belongs to the same group practice, within the past three years.

ethics (1) - principle of right or good conduct; rules that govern the conduct of members of a profession.

etiology and manifestation rules (6) - include the following notes in the ICD-10-CM Tabular List of Diseases and Injuries: code first underlying disease; code, if applicable, any causal condition first; use additional code; and code diseases classified elsewhere.

Evaluation and Management (E/M) (2) - services that describe patient encounters with providers for evaluation and management of general health status.

Evaluation and Management Documentation Guidelines (7) - federal (CMS) guidelines that explain how E/M codes are assigned according to elements associated with comprehensive multisystem and single-system examinations.

Evaluation and Management (E/M) section (7) - located at the beginning of CPT because these codes describe services (e.g., office visits) that are most frequently provided by physicians and other health care practitioners (e.g., nurse practitioner, physician assistant).

exclusive provider organization (EPO) (3) - managed care plan that provides benefits to subscribers if they receive services from network providers.

explanation of benefits (EOB) (1) - report that details the results of processing a claim (e.g., payer reimburses provider $80 on a submitted charge of $100).

extent of examination (CPT) (7) - includes comprehensive, detailed, expanded problem focused, and problem focused levels, based on physician documentation.

comprehensive - general multisystem examination or a complete examination of a single organ system.

detailed - extended examination of the affected body area(s) and other symptomatic or related organ system(s).

expanded problem focused - limited examination of the affected body area or organ system and other symptomatic or related organ system(s).

problem focused - limited examination of the affected body area or organ system.

extent of history (CPT) (7) - includes comprehensive, detailed, expanded problem focused, and problem focused levels, based on physician documentation.

comprehensive - chief complaint, extended history of present illness, review of systems directly related to the problem(s) identified in the history of the present illness, plus a review of all additional body systems and complete past/family/social history.

detailed - chief complaint, extended history of present illness, problem-pertinent system review extended to include a limited number of additional systems, pertinent past/family/social history directly related to patient's problem.

expanded problem focused - chief complaint, brief history of present illness, problem-pertinent system review.

problem focused - chief complaint, brief history of present illness or problem.

external quality review organization (EQRO) (3) - responsible for reviewing health care provided by managed care organizations.

face-to-face time (7) - amount of time the office or outpatient care provider spends with the patient and/or family.

Fair Credit and Charge Card Disclosure Act (4) - amended the Truth in Lending Act, requiring credit and charge card issuers to provide certain disclosures in direct mail, telephone, and other applications and solicitations for open-end credit and charge accounts and under other circumstances; this law applies to providers that accept credit cards.

Fair Credit Billing Act (4) - federal law passed in 1975 that helps consumers resolve billing issues with card issuers; protects important credit rights, including rights to dispute billing errors, unauthorized use of an account, and charges for unsatisfactory goods and services; cardholders cannot be held liable for more than $50 of fraudulent charges made to a credit card.

Fair Credit Reporting Act (4) - protects information collected by consumer reporting agencies such as credit bureaus, medical information companies, and tenant screening services; organizations that provide information to consumer reporting agencies also have specific legal obligations, including the duty to investigate disputed information.

Fair Debt Collection Practices Act (FDCPA) (4) - specifies what a collection source may and may not do when pursuing payment of past due accounts.

False Claims Act (FCA) (5) - passed by the federal government during the Civil War to regulate fraud associated with military contractors selling supplies and equipment to the Union Army.

Federal Black Lung Program (17) - enacted in 1969 as part of the *Black Lung Benefits Act;* provides medical treatment and other benefits for respiratory conditions related to former employment in the nation's coal mines.

Federal Claims Collection Act (FCCA) (5) - requires Medicare administrative contractors (previously called carriers and fiscal intermediaries), as agents of the federal government, to attempt the collection of overpayments.

Federal Employee Health Benefits Program (FEHBP) (13) - also called the *Federal Employee Program (FEP);* an employer-sponsored health benefits program established by an act of Congress in 1959, which now provides benefits to more than 9 million federal enrollees and dependents through contracts with about 300 third-party payers.

Federal Employee Program (FEP) (13) - *see* Federal Employee Health Benefits Program (FEHBP).

Federal Employees' Compensation Act (FECA) (2) - provides civilian employees of the federal government with medical care, survivors' benefits, and compensation for lost wages.

Federal Employers' Liability Act (FELA) (2) - legislation passed in 1908 by President Theodore Roosevelt that protects and compensates railroad workers who are injured on the job.

Federal Medical Assistance Percentage (FMAP) (15) - portion of the Medicaid program paid by the federal government.

federal poverty level (FPL) (15) - income guidelines established annually by the federal government.

***Federal Register* (5)** - legal newspaper published every business day by the National Archives and Records Administration (NARA).

federally qualified HMO (3) - certified to provide health care services to Medicare and Medicaid enrollees.

fee schedule (2) - list of predetermined payments for health care services provided to patients (e.g., a fee is assigned to each CPT code).

fee-for-service (3) - reimbursement methodology that increases payment if the health care service fees increase, if multiple units of service are provided, or if more expensive services are provided instead of less expensive services (e.g., brand-name vs. generic prescription medication).

Financial Services Modernization Act (FSMA) (2) - prohibits sharing of medical information among health insurers and other financial institutions for use in making credit decisions; also allows banks to merge with investment and insurance houses, which allows them to make a profit no matter what the status of the economy, because people usually house their money in one of the options; also called *Gramm-Leach-Bliley Act.*

First Report of Injury (17) - workers' compensation form completed when the patient first seeks treatment for a work-related illness or injury.

first-listed diagnosis (6) - reported on outpatient claims (instead of inpatient *principal diagnosis*); it reflects the reason for the encounter, and it is often a sign or symptom.

First-look Analysis for Hospital Outlier Monitoring (FATHOM) (5) - data analysis tool, which provides administrative hospital and state-specific data for specific CMS target areas.

fiscal year (16) - for the federal government, October 1 of one year to September 30 of the next.

flexible benefit plan (3) - *see* cafeteria plan and triple option plan.

flexible spending account (FSA) (3) - tax-exempt account offered by employers with any number of employees, which individuals use to pay health care bills; participants enroll in a relatively inexpensive, high-deductible insurance plan, and a tax-deductible savings account is opened to cover current and future medical expenses; money deposited (and earnings) is tax-deferred, and money is withdrawn to cover qualified medical expenses tax-free; money can be withdrawn for purposes other than health care expenses after payment of income tax plus a 15 percent penalty; unused balances "roll over" from year to year, and if an employee changes jobs, the FSA can continue to be used to pay for qualified health care expenses; also called *health savings account (HSA)* or *health savings security account (HSSA).*

for-profit corporation (13) - pays taxes on profits generated by the corporation's for-profit enterprises and pays dividends to shareholders on after-tax profits.

fraud (5) - intentional deception or misrepresentation that could result in an unauthorized payment.

gag clause (3) - prevents providers from discussing all treatment options with patients, whether or not the plan would provide reimbursement for services.

gatekeeper (3) - primary care provider for essential health care services at the lowest possible cost, avoiding nonessential care, and referring patients to specialists.

general enrollment period (GEP) (14) - enrollment period for Medicare Part B held January 1 through March 31 of each year.

general equivalence mapping (GEM) (6) - translation dictionaries or crosswalks of codes that can be used to roughly identify ICD-10-CM/PCS codes for their ICD-9-CM equivalent codes (and vice versa). *See also* legacy coding system.

global period (7) - includes all services related to a procedure during a period of time (e.g., 10 days, 30 days, 90 days, depending on payer guidelines).

global surgery (7) - also called *package concept* or *surgical package;* includes the procedure, local infiltration, metacarpal/digital block or topical anesthesia when used, and normal, uncomplicated follow-up care.

Government-Wide Service Benefit Plan (13) - phrase printed below the BCBS trademark on federal employee plan (FEP) insurance cards, which indicates that the enrollee has federal employer-sponsored health benefits.

Gramm-Leach-Bliley Act (2) - *see* Financial Services Modernization Act.

group health insurance (2) - traditional health care coverage subsidized by employers and other organizations (e.g., labor unions, rural and consumer health cooperatives) whereby part or all of premium costs are paid for and/or discounted group rates are offered to eligible individuals.

group model HMO (3) - contracted health care services delivered to subscribers by participating providers who are members of an independent multispecialty group practice.

group practice without walls (GPWW) (3) - contract that allows providers to maintain their own offices and share services (e.g., appointment scheduling and billing).

grouper software (9) - determines appropriate group (e.g., diagnosis-related group, home health resource group, and so on) to classify a patient after data about the patient is input.

guarantor (4) - person responsible for paying health care fees.

HCPCS level II codes (1) - national codes published by CMS, which include five-digit alphanumeric codes for procedures, services, and supplies not classified in CPT.

HCPCS level II code types (8)

miscellaneous codes - reported when a DMEPOS dealer submits a claim for a product or service for which there is no existing permanent national code.

modifiers - provide additional information about a procedure or service (e.g., left-sided procedure).

permanent national codes - maintained by the HCPCS National Panel, composed of representatives from the BlueCross BlueShield Association (BCBSA), the Health Insurance Association of America (HIAA), and CMS.

temporary codes - maintained by the CMS and other members of the HCPCS National Panel; independent of permanent national codes.

Health Affairs (HA) (16) - refers to the Office of the Assistant Secretary of Defense for Health Affairs, which is responsible for both military readiness and peacetime health care.

health care (2) - expands the definition of medical care to include preventive services.

Health Care and Education Reconciliation Act (HCERA) (2) - includes health care reform initiatives that amend the Patient Protection and Affordable Care Act to increase tax credits to buy health care insurance, eliminate special deals provided to senators, close the Medicare "donut hole," delay taxing of "Cadillac-health care plans" until 2018, and so on.

health care finder (HCF) (16) - registered nurse or physician assistant who assists primary care providers with preauthorizations and referrals to health care services in a military treatment facility or civilian provider network.

health care provider (1) - physician or other health care practitioner (e.g., physician's assistant).

health care reimbursement account (HCRA) (3) - tax-exempt account used to pay for health care expenses; individual decides, in advance, how much money to deposit in an HCRA (and unused funds are lost).

health information technician (1) - professionals who manage patient health information and medical records, administer computer information systems, and code diagnoses and procedures for health care services provided to patients.

Health Information Technology for Economic and Clinical Health Act (HITECH Act) (2) - included in the American Recovery and Reinvestment Act of 2009 and amended the Public Health Service Act to establish an Office of National Coordinator for Health Information Technology within HHS to improve health care quality, safety, and efficiency.

health insurance (2) - contract between a policyholder and a third-party payer or government program to reimburse the policyholder for all or a portion of the cost of medically necessary treatment or preventive care by health care professionals.

health insurance claim (1) - documentation submitted to an insurance plan requesting reimbursement for health care services provided (e.g., CMS-1500 and UB-04 claims).

health insurance exchange (2) - *see* health insurance marketplace.

health insurance marketplace (2) - method Americans will use to purchase health coverage that fits their budget and meets their needs effective October 1, 2013.

Health Insurance Portability and Accountability Act of 1996 (HIPAA) (2) - mandates regulations that govern privacy, security, and electronic transactions standards for health care information.

health insurance prospective payment system (HIPPS) code set (9) - Five-digit alphanumeric codes that represent case-mix groups about which payment determinations are made for the HH PPS.

health insurance specialist (1) - person who reviews health-related claims to determine the medical necessity for procedures or services performed before payment (reimbursement) is made to the provider; *see also* reimbursement specialists.

health maintenance organization (HMO) (3) - responsible for providing health care services to subscribers in a given geographical area for a fixed fee.

Health Maintenance Organization (HMO) Assistance Act of 1973 (3) - authorized grants and loans to develop HMOs under private sponsorship; defined a federally qualified HMO as one that has applied for, and met, federal standards established in the HMO Act of 1973; required most employers with more than 25 employees to offer HMO coverage if local plans were available.

Health Plan Identifier (HPID) (5) - unique identifier is assigned to third-party payers (previously called PAYERID and PlanID), which has 10 numeric positions, including a check digit as the tenth position.

health reimbursement arrangement (HRA) (3) - tax-exempt accounts offered by employers with more than 50 employees; individuals use HRAs to pay health care bills; HRAs must be used for qualified health care expenses, require enrollment in a high-deductible insurance policy, and can accumulate unspent money for future years; if an employee changes jobs, the HRA can continue to be used to pay for qualified health care expenses.

health savings account (HSA) (3) - *see* flexible spending account.

health savings security account (HSSA) (3) - *see* flexible spending account.

Healthcare Anywhere (13) - BCBS program that allows members of independently owned and operated plans to have access to health care benefits throughout the United States and around the world.

Healthcare Common Procedure Coding System (HCPCS) (1) - coding system that consists of CPT, national codes (level II), and local codes (level III); local codes were discontinued in 2003; previously known as HCFA Common Procedure Coding System.

Healthcare Effectiveness Data and Information Set (HEDIS) (3) - created standards to assess managed-care systems using data elements that are collected, evaluated, and published to compare the performance of managed health care plans.

Hill-Burton Act (2) - provided federal grants for modernizing hospitals that had become obsolete because of a lack of capital investment during the Great Depression and WWII (1929–1945). In return for federal funds, facilities were required to provide services free, or at reduced rates, to patients unable to pay for care.

history (7) - interview of the patient that includes the following components: history of the present illness (HPI) (including the patient's chief complaint), a review of systems (ROS), and a past/family/social history (PFSH).

hold harmless clause (1) - policy that the patient is not responsible for paying what the insurance plan denies.

Home Assessment Validation and Entry (HAVEN) (9) - data entry software used to collect OASIS assessment data for transmission to state databases.

Home Health Prospective Payment System (HH PPS) (2) - reimbursement methodology for home health agencies that uses a classification system called home health resource groups (HHRGs), which establishes a predetermined rate for health care services provided to patients for each 60-day episode of home health care.

home health resource group (HHRG) (9) - classifies patients into one of 80 groups, which range in severity level according to three domains: clinical, functional, and service utilization.

home services (7) - health care services provided in a private residence.

hospice (14) - autonomous, centrally administered program of coordinated inpatient and outpatient palliative (relief of symptoms) services for terminally ill patients and their families.

hospital discharge service (7) - includes the final examination of the patient; discussion of the hospital stay with the patient and/or caregiver; instructions for continuing care provided to the patient and/or caregiver; and preparation of discharge records, prescriptions, and referral forms.

Hospital Inpatient Quality Reporting (Hospital IQR) program (5) - developed to equip consumers with quality of care information so they can make more informed decisions about health care options; requires hospitals to submit specific quality measures data about health conditions common among Medicare beneficiaries and that typically result in hospitalization; eligible hospitals that do not participate in the Hospital IQR program will receive an annual market basket update with a 2.0 percentage point reduction. (The Hospital IQR program was previously called the *Reporting Hospital Quality Data for Annual Payment Update program.*)

Hospital Payment Monitoring Program (HPMP) (5) - measures, monitors, and reduces the incidence of Medicare fee-for-service payment errors for short-term, acute care, inpatient PPS hospitals.

hospital value-based purchasing (VBP) program (5) - health care reform measure that promotes better clinical outcomes and patient experiences of care; effective October 2012, hospitals receive reimbursement for inpatient acute care services based on care quality (instead of the quantity of the services provided).

iatrogenic illness (6) - illness that results from medical intervention (e.g., adverse reaction to contrast material injected prior to a scan).

ICD-10-CM coding conventions (6) - general coding rules that apply to the assignment of codes, independent of official coding guidelines.

and - when two disorders are separated by the word "and," it is interpreted as "and/or" and indicates that either of the two disorders is associated with the code number.

brackets - used in the index to identify manifestation codes and in the index and tabular list to enclose abbreviations, synonyms, alternative wording, or explanatory phrases.

code first underlying disease - appears when the code referenced is to be sequenced as a secondary code; the code, title, and instructions are italicized.

code first underlying disease, such as: - *see* code first underlying disease.

code, if applicable, any causal condition first - requires causal condition to be sequenced first if present; a causal condition is a disease that manifests (or results in) another condition.

colon - used after an incomplete term and is followed by one or more modifiers (additional terms).

due to - located in the index in alphabetical order to indicate the presence of a cause-and-effect (or causal) relationship between two conditions.

eponym - disease or syndrome named for a person; listed in appropriate alphabetical sequence as main terms in the index.

Excludes1 note - a "pure" excludes, which means "not coded here" and indicates mutually exclusive codes; in other words, two conditions that cannot be reported together.

Excludes2 note - means "not included here" and indicates that although the excluded condition is not classified as part of the condition it is excluded from, a patient may be diagnosed with all conditions at the same time; therefore, it may be acceptable to assign both the code and the excluded code(s) together if supported by medical documentation.

in - located in alphabetical order below the main term; to assign a code from the list of qualifiers below the word "in," the provider must document both conditions in the patient's record; ICD-10-CM classifies certain conditions as if there were a cause-and-effect relationship present because they occur together much of the time, such as *pneumonia in Q fever.*

in diseases classified elsewhere - indicates that the manifestation codes are a component of the etiology/manifestation coding convention.

includes note - appear below certain tabular list categories to further define, clarify, or provide examples.

manifestation - condition that occurs as the result of another condition; manifestation codes are always reported as secondary codes.

NES (not elsewhere classifiable) - means "other" or "other specified" and identifies codes that are assigned when information needed to assign a more specific code cannot be located.

NOS (not otherwise specified) - indicates that the code is unspecified; coders should ask the provider for a more specific diagnosis before assigning the code.

other and other specified code - assigned when patient record documentation provides detail for which a specific code does not exist in ICD-10-CM.

parentheses - enclose supplementary words that may be present or absent in the diagnostic statement, without affecting assignment of the code number.

see - directs the coder to refer to another term in the index to locate the code.

see also - located after a main term or subterm in the index and directs the coder to another main term (or subterm) that may provide additional useful index entries.

see category - instruction directs the coder to the ICD-10-CM tabular list, where a code can be selected from the options provided there.

see condition - directs the coder to the main term for a condition, found in the index.

Table of Drugs and Chemicals - alphabetical index of medicinal, chemical, and biological substances that result in poisonings, adverse effects, and underdosings.

Table of Neoplasms - alphabetical index of anatomic sites for which there are six possible codes according to whether the neoplasm in question is malignant, benign, *in situ*, of uncertain behavior, or of unspecified nature.

unspecified code - assigned because patient record documentation is insufficient to assign a more specific code.

use additional code - indicates that a second code is to be reported to provide more information about the diagnosis.

with - when codes combine one disorder with another (e.g., code that combines primary condition with a complication), the provider's diagnostic statement must clearly indicate that both conditions are present and that a relationship exists between the conditions.

ICD-10-CM Diagnostic Coding and Reporting Guidelines for Outpatient Services Hospital-Based and Provider-Based Office Visits (6) - developed by the federal government, outpatient diagnoses that have been approved for use by hospitals/providers in coding and reporting hospital-based outpatient services and provider-based office visits.

ICD-10-CM Index to Diseases and Injuries (6) - an alphabetical listing of terms and their corresponding codes, which include specific illnesses, injuries, eponyms, abbreviations, and other descriptive diagnostic terms.

ICD-10-CM Index to External Causes - arranged in alphabetical order by main term indicating the event; are secondary codes for use in any health care setting; capture how the injury or health condition happened (cause), the intent (unintentional or accidental; or intentional, such as suicide or assault), the place where the event occurred, the activity of the patient at the time of the event, and the person's status.

ICD-10-CM Official Guidelines for Coding and Reporting (6) - prepared by CMS and NCHS and approved by the cooperating parties for ICD-10-CM/PCS; contain rules that were developed to accompany and complement coding conventions and instructions provided in ICD-10-CM; adherence when assigning diagnosis codes is required under HIPAA.

ICD-10-CM Tabular List of Diseases and Injuries (6) - chronological list of codes contained within 21 chapters, which are based on body system or condition.

ICD-10-CM/PCS Coordination and Maintenance Committee (6) - responsible for overseeing all changes and modifications to ICD-10-CM (diagnosis) and ICD-10-PCS (procedure) codes; discusses issues such as the creation and update of general equivalence mappings (GEMs).

ICD-10-PCS Coding Guidelines (6) - prepared by CMS and NCHS and approved by the cooperating parties for ICD-10-CM/PCS; contain rules that were developed to accompany and complement official conventions and instructions provided in ICD-10-PCS; adherence when assigning procedure codes is required under HIPAA.

Improper Payments Information Act of 2002 (IPIA) (5) - established the *Payment Error Rate Measurement (PERM) program* to measure improper payments in the Medicaid program and the State Children's Health Insurance Program (SCHIP); *Comprehensive Error Rate Testing (CERT) program* to calculate the paid claims error rate for submitted Medicare claims by randomly selecting a statistical sample of claims to determine whether claims were paid properly (based on reviewing selected claims and associated medical record documentation); and the *Hospital Payment Monitoring Program (HPMP)* to measure, monitor, and reduce the incidence of Medicare fee-for-service payment errors for short-term, acute care at inpatient PPS hospitals.

incident to (9) - Medicare regulation which permitted billing Medicare under the physician's billing number for ancillary personnel services when those services were "incident to" a service performed by a physician.

indemnity coverage (13) - offers choice and flexibility to subscribers who want to receive a full range of benefits along with the freedom to use any licensed health care provider.

indemnity insurance (12) - compensates policyholders for actual economic losses, up to limiting amounts on insurance policy, and it usually requires the insured to prove losses before payment is made (e.g., automobile insurance).

indented code (7) - CPT code that is indented below a stand-alone code, requiring the coder to refer back to the common portion of the code description that is located before the semicolon.

independent contractor (1) - defined by the *'Lectric Law Library's Lexicon* as "a person who performs services for another under an express or implied agreement and who is not subject to the other's control, or right to control, of the manner and means of performing the services. The organization that hires an independent contractor is not liable for the acts or omissions of the independent contractor."

independent practice association (IPA) HMO (3) - *see* individual practice association (IPA) HMO.

indirect medical education (IME) adjustment (9) - approved teaching hospitals receive increased Medicare payments, which are adjusted depending on the ratio of residents-to-beds (to calculate operating costs) and residents-to-average daily census (to calculate capital costs).

individual health insurance (2) - private health insurance policy purchased by individuals or families who do not have access to group health insurance coverage; applicants can be denied coverage, and they can also be required to pay higher premiums due to age, gender, and/or pre-existing medical conditions.

individual practice association (IPA) HMO (3) - also called *independent practice association (IPA);* type of HMO where contracted health services are delivered to subscribers by providers who remain in their independent office settings.

initial enrollment period (IEP) (14) - seven-month period that provides an opportunity for the individual to enroll in Medicare Part A and/or Part B.

initial hospital care (7) - covers the first inpatient encounter the *admitting/attending physician* has with the patient for each admission.

inpatient prospective payment system (IPPS) (9) - system in which Medicare reimburses hospitals for inpatient hospital services according to a predetermined rate for each discharge.

Inpatient Psychiatric Facility Prospective Payment System (IPF PPS) (2) - system in which Medicare reimburses inpatient psychiatric facilities according to a patient classification system that reflects differences in patient resource use and costs; it replaces the cost-based payment system with a *per diem* IPF PPS.

Inpatient Rehabilitation Facility Prospective Payment system (IRF PPS) (2) - implemented as a result of the BBA of 1997; utilizes information from a patient assessment instrument to classify patients into distinct groups based on clinical characteristics and expected resource needs.

Inpatient Rehabilitation Validation and Entry (IRVEN) (9) - software used as the computerized data entry system by inpatient rehabilitation facilities to create a file in a standard format that can be electronically transmitted to a national database; data collected is used to assess the clinical characteristics of patients in rehabilitation hospitals and rehabilitation units in acute care hospitals, and provide agencies and facilities with a means to objectively measure and compare facility performance and quality; data also provides researchers with information to support the development of improved standards.

integrated delivery system (IDS) (3) - organization of affiliated provider sites (e.g., hospitals, ambulatory surgical centers, or physician groups) that offer joint health care services to subscribers.

integrated provider organization (IPO) (3) - manages the delivery of health care services offered by hospitals, physicians employed by the IPO, and other health care organizations (e.g., an ambulatory surgery clinic and a nursing facility).

intensity of resources (9) - relative volume and types of diagnostic, therapeutic, and inpatient bed services used to manage an inpatient disease.

International Classification of Diseases (ICD) (2) - classification system used to collect data for statistical purposes.

***International Classification of Diseases, 10th Revision, Clinical Modification* (ICD-10-CM) (1)** - coding system to be implemented on October 1, 2013, and used to report diseases, injuries, and other reasons for inpatient and outpatient encounters.

***International Classification of Diseases, 10th Revision, Procedural Coding System* (ICD-10-PCS) (1)** - coding system to be implemented on October 1, 2013, and used to report procedures and services on inpatient claims.

internship (1) - nonpaid professional practice experience that benefits students and facilities that accept students for placement; students receive on-the-job experience prior to graduation, and the internship assists them in obtaining permanent employment.

interrogatory (5) - document containing a list of questions that must be answered in writing.

Investing in Innovations (i2) Initiative (2) - designed to spur innovations in health information technology (health IT) by promoting research and development to enhance competitiveness in the United States.

IPPS 3-day payment window (9) - requires that outpatient preadmission services provided by a hospital for a period of up to three days prior to a patient's inpatient admission be covered by the IPPS DRG payment for diagnostic services (e.g., lab testing) and therapeutic (or nondiagnostic) services when the inpatient principal diagnosis code (ICD-10-CM) exactly matches that for preadmission services.

IPPS 72-hour rule (9) - *see* IPPS 3-day payment window.

IPPS transfer rule (9) - any patient with a diagnosis from one of ten CMS-determined DRGs, who is discharged to a post acute provider, is treated as a transfer case; this means hospitals are paid a graduated *per diem* rate for each day of the patient's stay, not to exceed the prospective payment DRG rate.

key components (7) - extent of history, extent of examination, and complexity of medical decision making.

large group health plan (LGHP) (9) - provided by an employer that has 100 or more employees *or* a multi-employer plan in which at least one employer has 100 or more full- or part-time employees.

lead agent (LA) (16) - serves as a federal health care team created to work with regional military treatment facility commanders, uniformed service headquarters' staffs, and Health Affairs (HA) to support the mission of the Military Health Services System (MHSS).

legacy classification system (6) - *see* legacy coding system.

legacy coding system (6) - system that is no longer supported or updated, such as ICD-9-CM when ICD-10-CM/PCS replaces it effective October 1, 2013. (*See also* general equivalence mapping.)

legislation (3) - laws.

lesion (6) - any discontinuity of tissue (e.g., skin or organ) that may or may not be malignant.

level of service (7) - reflects the amount of work involved in providing health care to patients.

liability insurance (12) - policy that covers losses to a third party caused by the insured, by an object owned by the insured, or on the premises owned by the insured.

lien (12) - pledges or secures a debtor's property as security or payment for a debt; may be used in a potential liability case, but use varies on a federal and state basis.

lifetime maximum amount (2) - maximum benefit payable to a health plan participant.

lifetime reserve days (14) - may be used only once during a patient's lifetime and are usually reserved for use during the patient's final, terminal hospital stay.

limiting charge (9) - maximum fee a provider may charge.

listserv (5) - subscriber-based question-and-answer forum that is available through e-mail.

litigation (4) - legal action to recover a debt; usually a last resort for a medical practice.

local coverage determination (LCD) (10) - formerly called *local medical review policy (LMRP);* Medicare administrative contractors create edits for national coverage determination rules that are called LCDs.

Longshore and Harbor Workers' Compensation Program (17) - administered by the U.S. Department of Labor; provides medical benefits, compensation for lost wages, and rehabilitation services to longshoremen, harbor workers, and other maritime workers who are injured during the course of employment or suffer from diseases caused or worsened by conditions of employment.

long-term (acute) care hospital prospective payment system (LTCH PPS) (9) - classifies patients according to long-term (acute) care DRGs, which are based on patients' clinical characteristics and expected resource needs; replaced the reasonable cost-based payment system.

main term (6) - bold-faced term located in the ICD-10-CM index; listed in alphabetical order with subterms and qualifiers indented below each main term.

major diagnostic category (MDC) (9) - organizes diagnosis-related groups (DRGs) into mutually exclusive categories, which are loosely based on body systems (e.g., nervous system).

major medical insurance (2) - coverage for catastrophic or prolonged illnesses and injuries.

malignant (6) - cancerous.

managed care organization (MCO) (3) - responsible for the health of a group of enrollees; can be a health plan, hospital, physician group, or health system.

managed health care (managed care) (3) - combines health care delivery with the financing of services provided.

management service organization (MSO) (3) - usually owned by physicians or a hospital and provides practice management (administrative and support) services to individual physician practices.

mandates (3) - laws.

manual daily accounts receivable journal (4) - also called the *day sheet;* a chronological summary of all transactions posted to individual patient ledgers/accounts on a specific day.

Material Safety Data Sheet (MSDS) (17) - contains information about chemical and hazardous substances used on-site.

meaningful EHR user (2) - providers who demonstrate that certified EHR technology is used for electronic prescribing, electronic exchange of health information in accordance with law and HIT standards, and submission of information on clinical quality measures; and hospitals that demonstrate that certified EHR technology is connected in a manner that provides for the electronic exchange of health information to improve quality of care and that the technology is used to submit information on clinical quality measures.

meaningful use (2) - objectives and measures that achieve goals of improved patient care outcomes and delivery through data capture and sharing, advance clinical processes, and improved patient outcomes.

Medicaid (2, 15) - cost-sharing program between the federal and state governments to provide health care services to low-income Americans; originally administered by the Social and Rehabilitation Service (SRS).

Medicaid eligibility verification system (MEVS) (15) - sometimes called *recipient eligibility verification system* or *REVS;* allows providers to electronically access the state's eligibility file through point-of-sale device, computer software, and automated voice response.

Medicaid Integrity Program (MIP) (5) - increased resources available to CMS to combat fraud, waste, and abuse in the Medicaid program; Congress requires annual reporting by CMS about the use and effectiveness of funds appropriated for the MIP.

Medicaid remittance advice (15) - sent to the provider; serves as an explanation of benefits from Medicaid and contains the current status of all claims (including adjusted and voided claims).

medical assistance program (15) - program for individuals with incomes below the federal poverty level.

medical assistant (1) - employed by a provider to perform administrative and clinical tasks that keep the office or clinic running smoothly.

Medical Association of Billers (MAB) (1) - created in 1995 to provide medical billing and coding specialists with a reliable source for diagnosis and procedure coding education and training.

medical care (2) - includes the identification of disease and the provision of care and treatment as provided by members of the health care team to persons who are sick, injured, or concerned about their health status.

medical decision making (7) - refers to the complexity of establishing a diagnosis and/or selecting a management option as measured by the number of diagnoses or management options, amount and/or complexity of data to be reviewed, and risk of complications and/or morbidity or mortality.

medical emergency care rider (13) - covers immediate treatment sought and received for sudden, severe, and unexpected conditions that, if not treated, would place the patient's health in permanent jeopardy or cause permanent impairment or dysfunction of an organ or body part.

medical foundation (3) - nonprofit organization that contracts with and acquires the clinical and business assets of physician practices; the foundation is assigned a provider number and manages the practice's business.

medical identify theft (5) - occurs when someone uses another person's name and/or insurance information to obtain medical and/or surgical treatment, prescription drugs, and medical durable equipment; it can also occur when dishonest people who work in a medical setting use another person's information to submit false bills to health care plans.

medical malpractice insurance (1) - a type of liability insurance that covers physicians and other health care professionals for liability claims arising from patient treatment.

medical necessity (1) - involves linking every procedure or service code reported on an insurance claim to a condition code (e.g., disease, injury, sign, symptom, other reason for encounter) that justifies the need to perform that procedure or service.

medical necessity denial (14) - denial of otherwise covered services that were found to be not "reasonable and necessary."

medical record (2) - *see* patient record.

medical review (MR) (5) - defined by CMS as a review of claims to determine whether services provided are medically reasonable and necessary, as well as to follow up on the effectiveness of previous corrective actions.

medically managed (10) - a particular diagnosis (e.g., hypertension) may not receive direct treatment during an office visit, but the provider had to consider that diagnosis when considering treatment for other conditions.

medically unlikely edit (MUE) (7) - used to compare units of service (UOS) with CPT and HCPCS level II codes reported on claims; indicates the maximum number of UOS allowable by the same provider for the same beneficiary on the same date of service under most circumstances; the MUE project was implemented to improve the accuracy of Medicare payments by detecting and denying unlikely Medicare claims on a prepayment basis. On the CMS-1500, Block 24G (units of service) is compared with Block 24D (code number) on the same line. On the UB-04, Form Locator 46 (service units) is compared with Form Locator 44.

Medicare (2) - reimburses health care services to Americans over the age of 65.

Medicare administrative contractor (MAC) (5) - an organization (e.g., third-party payer) that contracts with CMS to process claims and perform program integrity tasks for Medicare Part A and Part B and DMEPOS; each contractor makes program coverage decisions and publishes a newsletter, which is sent to providers who receive Medicare reimbursement. Medicare is transitioning fiscal intermediaries and carriers to create Medicare administrative contractors (MACs).

Medicare Advantage (Medicare Part C) (14) - includes managed care plans and *private* fee-for-service plans, which provide care under contract to Medicare and may include such benefits as coordination of care, reductions in out-of-pocket expenses, and prescription drugs. Medicare enrollees have the option of enrolling in one of several plans; formerly called Medicare+Choice.

Medicare Catastrophic Coverage Act (2) - mandated the reporting of ICD-9-CM diagnosis codes on Medicare claims; in subsequent years, private third-party payers adopted similar requirements for claims submission. Effective October 1, 2014, ICD-10-CM (diagnosis) codes will be reported.

Medicare contracting reform (MCR) initiative (2) - established to integrate the administration of Medicare Parts A and B fee-for-service benefits with new entities called Medicare administrative contractors (MACs); MACs replaced Medicare carriers, DMERCs, and fiscal intermediaries.

Medicare Cost Plan (14) - type of HMO similar to a medicare Advantage Plan; if an individual receives care from a non-network provider, the original Medicare plan covers the services.

Medicare coverage database (MCD) (10) - used by Medicare administrative contractors, providers, and other health care industry professionals to determine whether a procedure or service is reasonable and necessary for the diagnosis or treatment of an illness or injury; contains national coverage determinations (NCDs), including draft policies and proposed decisions; local coverage determinations (LCDs), including policy articles; and national coverage analyses (NCAs), coding analyses for labs (CALs), Medicare Evidence Development & Coverage Advisory Committee (MedCAC) proceedings, and Medicare coverage guidance documents.

Medicare Drug Integrity Contractors (MEDIC) Program (5) - implemented in 2011 as a presidential action to assist with CMS audit, oversight, anti-fraud, and anti-abuse efforts related to the Medicare Part D benefit.

Medicare fee-for-service plan (14) - *see* original Medicare plan.

Medicare Hospital Insurance (Medicare Part A) (14) - *see* Medicare Part A.

Medicare Integrity Program (MIP) (5) - authorizes CMS to enter into contracts with entities to perform cost report auditing, medical review, anti-fraud activities, and the Medicare Secondary Payer (MSP) program.

Medicare, Medicaid, and SCHIP Benefits Improvement and Protection Act of 2000 (BIPA) (2) - requires implementation of a $400 billion prescription drug benefit, improved Medicare Advantage (formerly called Medicare+Choice) benefits, faster Medicare appeals decisions, and more.

Medicare Medical Insurance (Medicare Part B) (14) - *see* Medicare Part B.

Medicare Part A (14) - reimburses institutional providers for inpatient, hospice, and some home health services.

Medicare Part B (14) - reimburses noninstitutional health care providers for outpatient services.

Medicare Part C (14) - *see* Medicare Advantage.

Medicare Part D coverage gap (14) - the difference between the initial coverage limit and the catastrophic coverage threshold, as described in the Medicare Part D prescription drug program administered; a Medicare beneficiary who surpasses the prescription drug coverage limit is financially responsible for the entire cost of prescription drugs until expenses reach the catastrophic coverage threshold; also called Medicare Part D "donut hole."

Medicare Part D "donut hole" (14) - The *MMA private prescription drug plans (PDPs)* and the *Medicare Advantage prescription drug plans (MA–PDs)* are collectively referred to as *Medicare Part D;* MMA requires coordination of Medicare Part D with State Pharmaceutical Assistance Programs (SPAPs), Medicaid plans, group health plans, Federal Employee Health Benefit Plans (FEHBPs), and military plans such as TRICARE); Medicare Part D enrollment is voluntary, and beneficiaries must apply for the benefit.

Medicare physician fee schedule (MPFS) (9) - payment system that reimburses providers for services and procedures by classifying services according to relative value units (RVUs); also called Resource-Based Relative Value Scale (RBRVS) system.

Medicare Prescription Drug, Improvement, and Modernization Act (MMA) (2) - adds new prescription drug and preventive benefits and provides extra assistance to people with low incomes.

Medicare Prescription Drug Plans (Medicare Part D) (14) - prescription drug coverage added to the original Medicare plan, some Medicare Cost Plans, some Medicare private fee-for-service plans, and Medicare Medical Savings Account Plans; Medicare beneficiaries present a Medicare prescription drug discount card to pharmacies.

Medicare Pricing, Data Analysis, and Coding (PDAC) contractor (8) - responsible for providing suppliers and manufacturers with assistance in determining HCPCS codes to be used; PDACs replaced SADMERCs (statistical analysis durable medical equipment regional carriers).

Medicare private contract (14) - agreement between Medicare beneficiary and physician or other practitioner who has "opted out" of Medicare for two years for *all* covered items and services furnished to Medicare beneficiaries; physician/practitioner will not bill for any service or supplies provided to any Medicare beneficiary for at least two years.

Medicare risk program (3) - federally qualified HMOs and competitive medical plans (CMPs) that meet specified Medicare requirements provide Medicare-covered services under a risk contract.

Medicare Savings Account (MSA) (14) - used by an enrollee to pay health care bills; Medicare pays for a special health care policy that has a high deductible and annually deposits into an account the difference between the policy cost and what it pays for an average Medicare enrollee in the patient's region.

Medicare Secondary Payer (MSP) (9) - situations in which the Medicare program does not have primary responsibility for paying a beneficiary's medical expenses.

Medicare SELECT (14) - type of Medigap policy available in some states where beneficiaries choose from a standardized Medigap plan.

Medicare severity diagnosis-related groups (MS-DRGs) (9) - adopted by Medicare in 2008 to improve recognition of severity of illness and resource consumption and reduce cost variation among DRGs; bases DRG relative weights on hospital costs and greatly expanded the number of DRGs; reevaluated complications/comorbidities (CC) list to assign all ICD-10-CM codes as non-CC status (conditions that should not be treated as CCs for specific clinical conditions), CC status, or major CC status; handles diagnoses closely associated with patient mortality differently depending on whether the patient lived or expired.

Medicare Shared Savings Program (5) - as mandated by the Patient Protection and Portable Care Act (PPACA), CMS established Medicare shared savings programs to facilitate coordination and cooperation among providers to improve quality of care for Medicare fee-for-service beneficiaries and to reduce unnecessary costs; accountable care organizations (ACOs) were created by eligible providers, hospitals, and suppliers to coordinate care, and they are held accountable for the quality, cost, and overall care of traditional fee-for-service Medicare beneficiaries assigned to the ACO.

Medicare special needs plan (14) - covers all Medicare Part A and Part B health care for individuals who can benefit the most from special care for chronic illnesses, care management of multiple diseases, and focused care management; such plans may limit membership to individuals who are eligible for both Medicare and Medicaid, have certain chronic or disabling conditions, and reside in certain institutions (e.g., nursing facility).

Medicare Summary Notice (MSN) (9) - previously called an *Explanation of Medicare Benefits* or *EOMB;* notifies Medicare beneficiaries of actions taken on claims.

Medicare supplemental plans (13) - augment the Medicare program by paying for Medicare deductibles and copayments.

Medicare Supplementary Insurance (MSI) (14) - *see* Medigap.

Medicare-Medicaid (Medi-Medi) crossover (14) - combination of Medicare and Medicaid programs; available to Medicare-eligible persons with incomes below the federal poverty level.

Medigap (14) - supplemental plans designed by the federal government but sold by private commercial insurance companies to cover the costs of Medicare deductibles, copayments, and coinsurance, which are considered "gaps" in Medicare coverage.

member (13) - subscriber.

member hospital (13) - hospital that has signed a contract to provide services for special rates.

Merchant Marine Act (Jones Act) (17) - not a workers' compensation statute, but provides seamen with the same protection from employer negligence as FELA provides railroad workers.

message digest (5) - representation of text as a single string of digits, which was created using a formula; for the purpose of electronic signatures, the message digest is encrypted (encoded) and appended (attached) to an electronic document.

metastasis (6) - spread of cancer from primary to secondary site(s).

metrics (9) - standards of measurement, such as those used to evaluate an organization's revenue cycle to ensure financial viability.

Military Health Services System (MHSS) (16) - entire health care system of the U.S. uniformed services and includes military treatment facilities (MTFs) as well as various programs in the civilian health care market, such as TRICARE.

military treatment facility (MTF) (16) - health care facility operated by the military that provides inpatient and/or ambulatory (outpatient and emergency department) care to eligible TRICARE beneficiaries; capabilities of MTFs vary from limited acute care clinics to teaching and tertiary care medical centers.

Mine Safety and Health Administration (MSHA) (17) - helps reduce deaths, injuries, and illnesses in U.S. mines through a variety of activities and programs.

Minimum Data Set (MDS) (2) - data elements collected by long-term care facilities.

moderate (conscious) sedation (7) - administration of moderate sedation or analgesia, which results in a drug-induced depression of consciousness; CPT established a package concept for moderate (conscious) sedation, and the bull's-eye (⊙) symbol located next to the code number identifies moderate (conscious) sedation as an inherent part of providing specific procedures.

modifier (7, 8) - two-digit or two-character code attached to the main CPT or HCPCS level II code; indicates that a procedure/service has been altered in some manner (e.g., modifier -50 indicates a bilateral procedure).

monitored anesthesia care (MAC) (7) - provision of local or regional anesthetic services with certain consciousness-altering drugs when provided by a physician, anesthesiologist, or medically directed CRNA; monitored anesthesia care involves sufficiently monitoring the patient to anticipate the potential need for administration of general anesthesia, and it requires continuous evaluation of vital physiologic functions as well as recognition and treatment of adverse changes.

morbidity (6) - pertaining to illness or disease.

morphology (6) - indicates the tissue type of a neoplasm; morphology codes are reported to state cancer registries.

mortality (6) - pertaining to death.

mother/baby claim (15) - submitted for services provided to a baby under the mother's Medicaid identification number.

multiple surgical procedures (7) - two or more surgeries performed during the same operative session.

narrative clinic note (10) - using paragraph format to document health care.

national codes (1) - commonly referred to as HCPCS level II codes; include five-digit alphanumeric codes for procedures, services, and supplies that are not classified in CPT (e.g., J-codes are used to assign drugs administered).

National Committee for Quality Assurance (NCQA) (3) - a private, not-for-profit organization that assesses the quality of managed care plans in the United States and releases the data to the public for its consideration when selecting a managed care plan.

National Correct Coding Initiative (NCCI) (2) - developed by CMS to promote national correct coding methodologies and to eliminate improper coding practices.

national coverage determination (NCD) (10) - rules developed by CMS that specify under what clinical circumstances a service or procedure is covered (including clinical circumstances considered reasonable and necessary) and correctly coded; Medicare administrative contractors create edits for NCD rules, called local coverage determinations (LCDs).

***National Drug Code* (NDC) (5)** - maintained by the Food and Drug Administration (FDA); identifies prescription drugs and some over-the-counter products.

National Individual Identifier (5) - unique identifier to be assigned to patients.

National Plan and Provider Enumeration System (NPPES) (5, 11) - developed by CMS to assign unique identifiers to health care providers (NPI) and health plans (HPID).

National Practitioner Data Bank (NPDB) (5) - implemented by Health Care Quality Improvement Act (HCQIA) of 1986 to improve quality of health care by encouraging state licensing boards, hospitals, and other health care entities and professional societies to identify and discipline those who engage in unprofessional behavior; restricts ability of incompetent physicians, dentists, and other health care practitioners to move from state to state without disclosure or discovery of previous medical malpractice payment and adverse action history; impacts licensure, clinical privileges, and professional society memberships as a result of adverse actions; includes Health Integrity and Protection Data Base (HIPDB), originally established by HIPAA, to further combat fraud and abuse in health insurance and health care delivery by serving as a national data collection program for reporting and disclosing certain final adverse actions taken against health care practitioners, providers, and suppliers.

National Provider Identifier (NPI) (5) - unique identifier to be assigned to health care providers as an 8- or possibly 10-character alphanumeric identifier, including a check digit in the last position.

National Standard Employer Identification Number (EIN) (5) - unique identifier assigned to employers who, as sponsors of health insurance for their employees, need to be identified in health care transactions.

National Standard Format (NSF) (5) - flat-file format used to bill provider and noninstitutional services, such as services reported by a general practitioner on a CMS-1500 claim.

nature of the presenting problem (7) - defined by CPT as a disease, condition, illness, injury, symptom, sign, finding, complaint, or other reason for the encounter, with or without a diagnosis being established at the time of the encounter.

NCCI code pairs (7) - pairs of codes included in the National Correct Coding Initiative (NCCI) that cannot be reported on the same claim if each has the same date of service; also called NCCI edit pairs.

NCCI edit pairs (7) - *see* NCCI code pairs.

neoplasm (6) - new growth, or tumor, in which cell reproduction is out of control.

network model HMO (3) - contracted health care services provided to subscribers by two or more physician multispecialty group practices.

network provider (3) - physician, other health care practitioner, or health care facility under contract to the managed care plan.

new patient (7) - one who has *not* received any professional services from the provider, or from another provider of the same specialty who belongs to the same group practice, within the past three years.

newborn care (7) - covers examinations of normal or high-risk neonates in the hospital or other locations, subsequent newborn care in a hospital, and resuscitation of high-risk babies.

nonavailability statement (NAS) (16) - certificate issued by a military treatment facility that cannot provide needed care to TRICARE Standard beneficiaries.

noncovered benefit (4) - any procedure or service reported on a claim that is not included on the payer's master benefit list, resulting in denial of the claim; also called *noncovered procedure* or *uncovered benefit*.

nonessential modifier (6) - supplementary words located in parentheses after an ICD-10-CM main term that do not have to be included in the diagnostic statement for the code number to be assigned.

nonparticipating provider (nonPAR) (4) - does not contract with the insurance plan; patients who elect to receive care from nonPARs will incur higher out-of-pocket expenses.

nonprofit corporation (13) - charitable, educational, civic, or humanitarian organization whose profits are returned to the program of the corporation rather than distributed to shareholders and officers of the corporation.

nurse advisor (16) - available 24/7 for advice and assistance with treatment alternatives and to discuss whether a TRICARE sponsor should see a provider based on a discussion of symptoms.

nurse practitioner (NP) (9) - has two or more years of advanced training, has passed a special exam, and often works as a primary care provider along with a physician.

nursing facility services (7) - performed at the following sites: skilled nursing facilities (SNFs), intermediate care facilities (ICFs), and long-term care facilities (LTCFs).

objective (10) - documentation of measurable or objective observations made during physical examination and diagnostic testing.

observation or inpatient care services (7) - CPT codes used to report observation or inpatient hospital care services provided to patients admitted and discharged on the same date of service.

observation services (7) - furnished in a hospital out-patient setting to determine whether further treatment or inpatient admission is needed; when a patient is placed under observation, the patient is categorized as an outpatient; if the duration of observation care is expected to be 24 hours or more, the physician must order an inpatient admission (and the date the physician orders the inpatient stay is the date of inpatient admission).

Occupational Safety and Health Administration (OSHA) (17) - agency created to protect employees against injuries from occupational hazards in the workplace.

Office of Managed Care (3) - CMS agency that facilitates innovation and competition among Medicare HMOs.

Office of Workers' Compensation Programs (OWCP) (17) - administers programs that provide wage replacement benefits, medical treatment, vocational rehabilitation, and other benefits to federal workers (or eligible dependents) who are injured at work or acquire an occupational disease.

Omnibus Budget Reconciliation Act of 1981 (OBRA) (2) - federal law that requires providers to keep copies of any government insurance claims and copies of all attachments filed by the provider for a period of five years; also expanded Medicare and Medicaid programs.

on-the-job-injury (17) - occurrence when the employee is either injured while working within the scope of the job description, injured while performing a service required by the employer, or succumbs to a disorder that can be directly linked to employment, such as asbestosis or mercury poisoning.

open claim (4) - submitted to the payer, but processing is not complete.

open-panel HMO (3) - health care provided by individuals who are not employees of the HMO or who do not belong to a specially formed medical group that serves the HMO.

operative report (10) - varies from a short narrative description of a minor procedure that is performed in the physician's office to a more formal report dictated by the surgeon in a format required by the hospitals and ambulatory surgical centers (ASCs).

optical character reader (OCR) (11) - device used for optical character recognition.

optical scanning (11) - uses a device (e.g., scanner) to convert printed or handwritten characters into text that can be viewed by an optical character reader.

organ- or disease-oriented panel (7) - series of blood chemistry studies routinely ordered by providers at the same time to investigate a specific organ (e.g., liver panel) or disease (e.g., thyroid panel).

original Medicare plan (14) - fee-for-service or traditional pay-per-visit plans for which beneficiaries are usually charged a fee for each health care service or supply received.

orthotics (8) - branch of medicine that deals with the design and fitting of orthopedic (relating to bone disorders) devices (e.g., braces).

out-of-pocket payment (4) - established by health insurance companies for a health insurance plan; usually has limits of $1,000 or $2,000; when the patient has reached the limit of an out-of-pocket payment (e.g., annual deductible) for the year, appropriate patient reimbursement to the provider is determined; not all health insurance plans include an out-of-pocket payment provision.

Outcomes and Assessment Information Set (OASIS) (2, 9) - group of data elements that represent core items of a comprehensive assessment for an adult home care patient and form the basis for measuring patient outcomes for purposes of outcome-based quality improvement.

outlier (9) - hospitals that treat unusually costly cases receive increased Medicare payments; the additional payment is designed to protect hospitals from large financial losses due to unusually expensive cases.

outpatient (6) - person treated in one of three settings: health care provider's office; hospital clinic, emergency department, hospital same-day surgery unit, or ambulatory surgical center (ASC) where the patient is released within 23 hours; or hospital admission solely for observation where the patient is released after a short stay.

outpatient code editor (OCE) (10) - software that edits outpatient claims submitted by hospitals, community mental health centers, comprehensive outpatient rehabilitation facilities, and home health agencies; the software reviews submissions for coding validity (e.g., missing fifth digits) and coverage (e.g., medical necessity); OCE edits result in one of the following dispositions: rejection, denial, return to provider (RTP), or suspension.

outpatient encounter (9) - includes all outpatient procedures and services (e.g., same-day surgery, x-rays, laboratory tests, and so on) provided during one day to the same patient.

outpatient pretreatment authorization plan (OPAP) (13) - also called *prospective authorization* or *precertification;* requires preauthorization of outpatient physical, occupational, and speech therapy services.

Outpatient Prospective Payment System (OPPS) (2) - uses ambulatory payment classifications (APCs) to calculate reimbursement; was implemented for billing of hospital-based Medicare outpatient claims.

outpatient visit (9) - *see* outpatient encounter.

outsource (4) - contract out.

overlapping sites (6) - *see* contiguous sites.

overpayment (5) - funds that a provider or beneficiary has received in excess of amounts due and payable under Medicare and Medicaid statutes and regulations.

Part A/B Medicare administrative contractor (A/B MAC) (5) - *see* Medicare administrative contractor.

partial hospitalization (7) - short-term, intensive treatment program where individuals who are experiencing an acute episode of an illness (e.g., geriatric, psychiatric, or rehabilitative) can receive medically supervised treatment during a significant number of daytime or nighttime hours; this type of program is an alternative to 24-hour inpatient hospitalization and allows the patients to maintain their everyday lives without the disruption associated with an inpatient hospital stay.

participating provider (PAR) (4) - contracts with a health insurance plan and accepts whatever the plan pays for procedures or services performed.

past-due account (4) - one that has not been paid within a certain time frame (e.g., 120 days); also called *delinquent account.*

patient account record (4) - also called *patient ledger;* a computerized permanent record of all financial transactions between the patient and the practice.

patient ledger (4) - *see* patient account record.

Patient Protection and Affordable Care Act (PPACA) (2) - focuses on private health insurance reform to provide better coverage for individuals with pre-existing conditions, improve prescription drug coverage under Medicare, and extend the life of the Medicare Trust fund by at least 12 years.

patient record (2) - documents health care services provided to a patient.

Patient Safety and Quality Improvement Act (5) - amends Title IX of the Public Health Service Act to provide for improved patient safety by encouraging voluntary and confidential reporting of events that adversely affect patients; creates patient safety organizations (PSOs) to collect, aggregate, and analyze confidential information reported by health care providers; and designates information reported to PSOs as privileged and not subject to disclosure (except when a court determines that the information contains evidence of a criminal act or each provider identified in the information authorizes disclosure).

Payment Error Prevention Program (PEPP) (5) - required facilities to identify and reduce improper Medicare payments and, specifically, the Medicare payment error rate. The hospital payment monitoring program (HPMP) replaced PEPP in 2002.

payment error rate (5) - number of dollars paid in error out of total dollars paid for inpatient prospective payment system services.

Payment Error Rate Measurement (PERM) program (5) - measures improper payments in the Medicaid program and the State Children's Health Insurance Program (SCHIP).

payment system (9) - reimbursement method the federal government uses to compensate providers for patient care.

***per diem* (2)** - Latin term meaning "for each day," which is how retrospective cost-based rates were determined; payments were issued based on daily rates.

permanent disability (17) - refers to an ill or injured employee's diminished capacity to return to work.

personal health record (PHR) (2) - web-based application that allows individuals to maintain and manage their health information (and that of others for whom they are authorized, such as family members) in a private, secure, and confidential environment.

physical examination (7) - assessment of the patient's body areas (e.g., extremities) and organ systems (e.g., cardiovascular).

physical status modifier (7) - indicates the patient's condition at the time anesthesia was administered.

physician assistant (PA) (9) - has two or more years of advanced training, has passed a special exam, works with a physician, and can do some of the same tasks as the doctor.

physician incentive plan (3) - requires managed care plans that contract with Medicare or Medicaid to disclose information about physician incentive plans to CMS or state Medicaid agencies before a new or renewed contract receives final approval.

physician incentives (3) - include payments made directly or indirectly to health care providers to serve as encouragement to reduce or limit services (e.g., discharge an inpatient from the hospital more quickly) to save money for the managed care plan.

Physician Quality Reporting System (5) - the Tax Relief and Health Care Act of 2006 (TRHCA) that established financial incentives for eligible professionals who participate in a *voluntary* quality reporting program; previously called Physician Quality Initiative (PQRI) system.

physician query process (6) - when coders have questions about documented diagnoses or procedures/services, they contact the responsible physician to request clarification about documentation and the code(s) to be assigned.

physician self-referral law (5) - *see* Stark I.

physician-hospital organization (PHO) (3) - owned by hospital(s) and physician groups that obtain managed care plan contracts; physicians maintain their own practices and provide health care services to plan members.

Physicians at Teaching Hospitals (PATH) (5) - HHS implemented audits in 1995 to examine the billing practices of physicians at teaching hospitals; the focus was on two issues: (1) compliance with the Medicare rule affecting payment for physician services provided by residents (e.g., whether a teaching physician was present for Part B services billed to Medicare between 1990 and 1996), and (2) whether the level of the physician service was coded and billed properly.

place of service (POS) (7) - the physical location where health care is provided to patients (e.g., office or other outpatient settings, hospitals, nursing facilities, home health care, or emergency departments); the two-digit location code is required by Medicare.

plan (10) - statement of the physician's future plans for the work-up and medical management of the case.

point-of-service plan (POS) (3) - delivers health care services using both managed care network and traditional indemnity coverage so patients can seek care outside the managed care network.

poisoning: accidental (unintentional) (6) - poisoning that results from an inadvertent overdose, wrong substance administered/taken, or intoxication that includes combining prescription drugs with nonprescription drugs or alcohol.

poisoning: assault (6) - poisoning inflicted by another person who intended to kill or injure the patient.

poisoning: intentional self-harm (6) - poisoning that results from a deliberate overdose, such as a suicide attempt, of substance(s) administered/taken or intoxication that includes purposely combining prescription drugs with nonprescription drugs or alcohol.

poisoning: undetermined (6) - subcategory used if the patient record does not document whether the poisoning was intentional or accidental.

policyholder (2) - a person who signs a contract with a health insurance company and who, thus, owns the health insurance policy; the policyholder is the insured (or enrollee), and the policy might include coverage for dependents.

PPN provider (13) - provider who has signed a preferred provider network (PPN) contract and agrees to accept the PPN allowed rate, which is generally 10 percent lower than the PAR allowed rate.

practice guidelines (16) - decision-making tools used by providers to determine appropriate health care for specific clinical circumstances.

preadmission certification (PAC) (3) - review for medical necessity of inpatient care prior to the patient's admission.

preadmission review (3) - review for medical necessity of inpatient care prior to the patient's admission.

preadmission testing (PAT) (6) - completed prior to an inpatient admission or outpatient surgery to facilitate the patient's treatment and reduce the length of stay.

preauthorization (1) - prior approval.

precedent (5) - standard.

precertification (13) - *see* outpatient pretreatment authorization plan (OPAP).

pre-existing condition (4) - any medical condition that was diagnosed and/or treated within a specified period of time immediately preceding the enrollee's effective date of coverage.

Preferred Provider Health Care Act of 1985 (3) - eased restrictions on preferred provider organizations (PPOs) and allowed subscribers to seek health care from providers outside of the PPO.

preferred provider network (PPN) (13) - program that requires providers to adhere to managed care provision.

preferred provider organization (PPO) (3) - network of physicians, other health care practitioners, and hospitals that have joined together to contract with insurance companies, employers, or other organizations to provide health care to subscribers for a discounted fee.

preoperative clearance (7) - occurs when a surgeon requests that a specialist or other physician (e.g., general practice) examine a patient and give an opinion as to whether that patient can withstand the expected risks of a specific surgery.

prepaid health plan (13) - contract between employer and health care facility (or physician) where specified medical services were performed for a predetermined fee that was paid on either a monthly or yearly basis.

preventive medicine services (7) - routine examinations or risk management counseling for children and adults exhibiting no overt signs or symptoms of a disorder while presenting to the medical office for a preventive medical physical; also called "wellness visits."

preventive services (2) - designed to help individuals avoid problems with health and injuries.

primary care manager (PCM) (16) - provider (e.g., physician) who is assigned to a sponsor and part of the TRICARE provider network.

primary care provider (PCP) (3) - responsible for supervising and coordinating health care services for enrollees and preauthorizing referrals to specialists and inpatient hospital admissions (except in emergencies).

primary insurance (4) - associated with how an insurance plan is billed—the insurance plan responsible for paying health care insurance claims first is considered primary.

primary malignancy (6) - original cancer site.

principal diagnosis (6) - condition determined, after study, that resulted in the patient's admission to the hospital.

privacy (5) - right of individuals to keep their information from being disclosed to others.

Privacy Act of 1974 (5) - forbids the Medicare regional payer from disclosing the status of any unassigned claim beyond the following: date the claim was received by the payer; date the claim was paid, denied, or suspended; or general reason the claim was suspended.

privacy rule (5) - HIPAA provision that creates national standards to protect individuals' medical records and other personal health information.

private fee-for-service (PFFS) (14) - health care plan offered by private insurance companies; not available in all areas of the country.

privileged communication (5) - private information shared between a patient and health care provider; disclosure must be in accordance with HIPAA and/or individual state provisions regarding the privacy and security of protected health information (PHI).

problem-oriented record (POR) (2) - a systematic method of documentation that consists of four components: database, problem list, initial plan, and progress notes.

professional component (7) - supervision of procedure, interpretation, and writing of the report.

professional liability insurance (1) - provides protection from claims resulting from errors and omissions associated with professional services provided to clients as expected of a person in their profession; also called *errors and omissions insurance.*

professionalism (1) - conduct or qualities that characterize a professional person.

Program for Evaluating Payment Patterns Electronic Report (PEPPER) (5) - contains hospital-specific administrative claims data for a number of CMS-identified problem areas (e.g., specific DRGs, types of discharges); a hospital uses PEPPER data to compare its performance with that of other hospitals.

Program Integrity (PI) Office (16) - responsible for the worldwide surveillance of fraud and abuse activities involving purchased care for beneficiaries in the Military Health Services System.

program transmittal (5) - document published by Medicare containing new and changed policies and/or procedures that are to be incorporated into a specific CMS program manual (e.g., *Medicare Claims Processing Manual*); cover page (or transmittal page) summarizes new and changed material, and subsequent pages provide details; transmittals are sent to each Medicare administrative contractor.

Programs of All-Inclusive Care for the Elderly (PACE) (14) - optional Medicaid benefit for eligible enrollees; uses a capitated payment system to provide a comprehensive package of community-based medical and social services as an alternative to institutional care for persons aged 55 or older who require a nursing facility level of care (e.g., adult day health center, home health care, and/or inpatient facilities).

prolonged services (7) - assigned in addition to other E/M services when treatment exceeds by 30 minutes or more the time included in the CPT description of the service.

property insurance (1) - protects business contents (e.g., buildings and equipment) against fire, theft, and other risks.

prospective authorization (13) - *see* outpatient pretreatment authorization plan (OPAP).

prospective cost-based rates (9) - rates established in advance, but based on reported health care costs (charges) from which a prospective *per diem* rate is determined.

prospective payment system (PPS) (2) - issues predetermined payment for services.

prospective price-based rates (9) - rates associated with a particular category of patient (e.g., inpatients) and established by the payer (e.g., Medicare) prior to the provision of health care services.

prospective review (3) - reviewing appropriateness and necessity of care provided to patients prior to administration of care.

prosthetics (8) - branch of medicine that deals with the design, production, and use of artificial body parts (e.g., artificial limbs).

protected health information (PHI) (5) - information that is identifiable to an individual (or individual identifiers) such as name, address, telephone numbers, date of birth, Medicaid ID number, medical record number, social security number (SSN), and name of employer.

Provider Remittance Notice (PRN) (4) - remittance advice submitted by Medicare to providers that includes payment information about a claim.

public health insurance (2) - federal and state government health programs (e.g., Medicare, Medicaid, SCHIP, TRICARE) available to eligible individuals.

qualified diagnosis (6) - working diagnosis that is not yet proven or established; reported for inpatient cases only.

qualified disabled working individual (QDWI) (14) - program that helps individuals who receive Social Security and Medicare because of disability, but who lost their Social Security benefits and free Medicare Part A because they returned to work and their earnings exceeded the limit allowed; states are required to pay their Medicare Part A premiums.

qualified Medicare beneficiary program (QMBP) (14) - program in which the federal government requires state Medicaid programs to pay Medicare premiums, patient deductibles, and coinsurance for individuals who have Medicare Part A, a low monthly income, and limited resources, and who are not otherwise eligible for Medicaid.

qualifiers (6) - supplementary terms in the ICD-10-CM Index to Diseases and Injuries that further modify subterms and other qualifiers.

qualifying circumstances (7) - CPT Medicine Section codes reported in addition to Anesthesia Section codes when situations or circumstances make anesthesia administration more difficult (e.g., patient of extreme age, such as under one year or over 70).

qualifying individual (QI) (14) - program that helps low-income individuals by requiring states to pay their Medicare Part B premiums.

quality assessment and performance improvement (QAPI) (3) - program implemented so that quality assurance activities are performed to improve the functioning of Medicare Advantage organizations.

quality assurance program (3) - activities that assess the quality of care provided in a health care setting.

quality improvement organization (QIO) (2) - performs utilization and quality control review of health care furnished, or to be furnished, to Medicare beneficiaries.

Quality Improvement System for Managed Care (QISMC) (3) - established by Medicare to ensure the accountability of managed care plans in terms of objective, measurable standards.

***qui tam* (5)** - abbreviation for the Latin phrase *qui tam pro domino rege quam pro sic ipso in hoc parte sequitur,* which means "who as well for the king as for himself sues I this matter." It is a provision of the False Claims Act that allows a private citizen to file a lawsuit in the name of the U.S. government, charging fraud by government contractors and other entities.

radiologic views (7) - studies taken from different angles.

recipient eligibility verification system (REVS) (15) - also called *Medicaid eligibility verification system (MEVS);* allows providers to electronically access the state's eligibility file through point-of-sale device, computer software, and automated voice response.

record linkage (2) - allows patient information to be created at different locations according to a unique patient identifier or identification number.

record retention (5) - storage of documentation for an established period of time, usually mandated by federal and/or state law; its purpose is to ensure the availability of records for use by government agencies and other third parties.

Recovery Audit Contractor (RAC) program (5) - mandated by the Medicare Prescription Drug, Improvement, and Modernization Act of 2003 (MMA) to find and correct improper Medicare payments paid to health care providers participating in fee-for-service Medicare.

re-excision (6) - occurs when the pathology report recommends that the surgeon perform a second excision to widen the margins of the original tumor site.

referral (7) - a patient who reports that another provider referred him or her.

regulations (5) - guidelines written by administrative agencies (e.g., CMS).

reimbursement specialist (1) - *see* health insurance specialist.

relative value units (RVUs) (9) - payment components consisting of physician work, practice expense, and malpractice expense.

release of information (ROI) (5) - ROI by a covered entity (e.g., provider's office) about protected health information (PHI) requires the patient (or representative) to sign an authorization to release information, which is reviewed for authenticity (e.g., comparing signature on authorization form to documents signed in the patient record) and processed within a HIPAA-mandated 60-day time limit; requests for ROI include those from patients, physicians, and other health care providers; third-party payers; Social Security Disability attorneys; and so on.

release of information log (5) - used to document patient information released to authorized requestors; data is entered manually (e.g., three-ring binder) or using ROI tracking software.

remittance advice (remit) (1) - electronic or paper-based report of payment sent by the payer to the provider; includes patient name, patient health insurance claim (HIC) number, facility provider number/name, dates of service (from date/thru date), type of bill (TOB), charges, payment information, and reason and/or remark codes.

report card (3) - contains data regarding a managed care plan's quality, utilization, customer satisfaction, administrative effectiveness, financial stability, and cost control.

resequenced code (7) - CPT codes that appear out of numerical order and are preceded by the # symbol (so as to provide direction to the out-of-sequence code).

Resident Assessment Validation and Entry (RAVEN) (9) - data entry system used to enter MDS data about SNF patients and transmit those assessments in CMS-standard format to individual state databases.

resource allocation (9) - distribution of financial resources among competing groups (e.g., hospital departments, state health care organizations).

resource allocation monitoring (9) - uses data analytics to measure whether a health care provider or organization achieves operational goals and objectives within the confines of the distribution of financial resources, such as appropriately expending budgeted amounts as well as conserving resources and protecting assets while providing quality patient care.

Resource Utilization Groups (RUGs) (2) - based on data collected from resident assessments (using data elements called the Minimum Data Set, or MDS) and relative weights developed from staff time data.

Resource-Based Relative Value Scale (RBRVS) system (2) - payment system that reimburses physicians' practice expenses based on relative values for three components of each physician's services: physician work, practice expense, and malpractice insurance expense.

respite care (14) - the temporary hospitalization of a hospice patient for the purpose of providing relief from duty for the nonpaid person who has the major day-to-day responsibility for the care of the terminally ill, dependent patient.

***respondeat superior* (1)** - Latin for "let the master answer"; legal doctrine holding that the employer is liable for the actions and omissions of employees performed and committed within the scope of their employment.

retrospective reasonable cost system (9) - reimbursement system in which hospitals report actual charges for inpatient care to payers after discharge of the patient from the hospital.

retrospective review (3) - reviewing appropriateness and necessity of care provided to patients after the administration of care.

revenue code (9) - a four-digit code that indicates location or type of service provided to an institutional patient; reported in FL 42 of UB-04.

revenue cycle auditing (9) - assessment process that is conducted as a follow-up to revenue cycle monitoring so that areas of poor performance can be identified and corrected.

revenue cycle management (9) - process facilities and providers use to ensure financial viability.

revenue cycle monitoring (9) - involves assessing the revenue cycle to ensure financial viability and stability using metrics (standards of measurement).

rider (13) - special contract clause stipulating additional coverage above the standard contract.

risk contract (3) - an arrangement among providers to provide capitated (fixed, prepaid basis) health care services to Medicare beneficiaries.

risk of mortality (ROM) (9) - likelihood of dying.

risk pool (3) - created when a number of people are grouped for insurance purposes (e.g., employees of an organization); the cost of health care coverage is determined by employees' health status, age, sex, and occupation.

roster billing (14) - enables Medicare beneficiaries to participate in mass PPV (pneumococcal pneumonia virus) and influenza virus vaccination programs offered by Public Health Clinics (PHCs) and other entities that bill Medicare payers.

scope of practice (1) - health care services, determined by the state, that an NP and PA can perform.

second surgical opinion (SSO) (3) - second physician is asked to evaluate the necessity of surgery and recommend the most economical, appropriate facility in which to perform the surgery (e.g., outpatient clinic or doctor's office versus inpatient hospitalization).

secondary diagnosis (6) - coexists with the primary condition, has the potential to affect treatment of the primary condition, and is an active condition for which the patient is treated or monitored.

secondary insurance (4) - billed after primary insurance has paid contracted amount.

secondary malignancy (6) - tumor has metastasized to a secondary site, either adjacent to the primary site or to a remote region of the body.

security (5) - involves the safekeeping of patient information by controlling access to hard copy and computerized records; protecting patient information from alteration, destruction, tampering, or loss; providing employee training in confidentiality of patient information; and requiring employees to sign a confidentiality statement that details the consequences of not maintaining patient confidentiality.

security rule (5) - HIPAA standards and safeguards that protect health information collected, maintained, used, or transmitted electronically; covered entities affected by this rule include health plans, health care clearinghouses, and certain health care providers.

self-insured (or self-funded) employer-sponsored group health plan (2) - allows a large employer to assume the financial risk for providing health care benefits to employees; employer does not pay a fixed premium to a health insurance payer, but establishes a trust fund (of employer and employee contributions) out of which claims are paid.

self-referral (3) - enrollee who sees a non-HMO panel specialist without a referral from the primary care physician.

sequela (6) - residual late effects of injury or illness.

service location (13) - location where the patient was seen.

severity of illness (SOI) (9) - extent of physiological decompensation or organ system loss of function.

single-payer system (2) - centralized health care plan adopted by some Western nations (e.g., Canada, Great Britain) and funded by taxes. The government pays for each resident's health care, which is considered a basic social service.

site of service differential (9) - reduction of payment when office-based services are performed in a facility, such as a hospital or outpatient setting, because the doctor did not provide supplies, utilities, or the costs of running the facility.

Skilled Nursing Facility Prospective Payment System (SNF PPS) (2) - implemented (as a result of the BBA of 1997) to cover all costs (routine, ancillary, and capital) related to services furnished to Medicare Part A beneficiaries.

SOAP note (10) - outline format for documenting health care; "SOAP" is an acronym derived from the first letter of the headings used in the note: Subjective, Objective, Assessment, and Plan.

socialized medicine (2) - type of single-payer system in which the government owns and operates health care facilities and providers (e.g., physicians) receive salaries; the VA health care program is a form of socialized medicine.

source document (4) - the routing slip, charge slip, encounter form, or superbill from which the insurance claim was generated.

special accidental injury rider (13) - covers 100 percent of nonsurgical care sought and rendered within 24 to 72 hours (varies according to policy) of the accidental injury.

special enrollment period (SEP) (14) - a set time when individuals can sign up for Medicare Part B if they did not enroll in Part B during the initial enrollment period.

special report (7) - must accompany the claim when an unlisted procedure or service code is reported to describe the nature, extent, and need for the procedure or service.

specified low-income Medicare beneficiary (SLMB) (14) - federally mandated program that requires states to cover just the Medicare Part B premium for persons whose income is slightly above the poverty level.

spell of illness (14) - formerly called *spell of sickness;* is sometimes used in place of *benefit period.*

staff model HMO (3) - health care services are provided to subscribers by physicians and other health care practitioners employed by the HMO.

stand-alone code (7) - CPT code that includes a complete description of the procedure or service.

standards (3) - requirements.

standby services (7) - cover providers who spend prolonged periods of time without direct patient contact, until provider's services are required.

Stark I (5) - responded to concerns about physicians' conflicts of interest when referring Medicare patients for a variety of services; prohibits physicians from referring Medicare patients to clinical laboratory services in which the physician or a member of the physician's family has a financial ownership/investment interest and/or compensation arrangement; also called *physician self-referral law.*

State Children's Health Insurance Program (SCHIP) (2) - also abbreviated as CHIP; provides health insurance coverage to uninsured children whose family income is up to 200 percent of the federal poverty level (monthly income limits for a family of four also apply).

State Insurance Fund (State Compensation Fund) (17) - a quasi-public agency that provides workers' compensation insurance coverage to private and public employers and acts as an agent in workers' compensation cases involving state employees.

statutes (5) - also called *statutory law;* laws passed by legislative bodies (e.g., federal Congress and state legislatures).

statutory law (5) - *see* statutes.

sub-capitation payment (3) - each provider is paid a fixed amount per month to provide only the care that an individual needs from that provider.

subjective (10) - part of the note that contains the chief complaint and the patient's description of the presenting problem.

subpoena (5) - an order of the court that requires a witness to appear at a particular time and place to testify.

subpoena *duces tecum* (5) - requires documents (e.g., patient record) to be produced.

subrogation (12) - process of the third-party payer recovering health care expenses from the liable party.

subscribers (policyholders) (3) - person in whose name the insurance policy is issued.

subsequent hospital care (7) - includes review of patient's chart for changes in the patient's condition, the results of diagnostic studies, and/or reassessment of the patient's condition since the last assessment performed by the physician.

subterm (6) - qualifies the main term by listing alternative sites, etiology, or clinical status; it is indented two spaces under the main term.

superbill (4) - term used for an encounter form in the physician's office.

supervising physician (11) - a licensed physician in good standing who, according to state regulations, engages in the direct supervision of nurse practitioners and/or physician assistants whose duties are encompassed by the supervising physician's scope of practice.

supplemental plan (11) - covers the deductible and copay or coinsurance of a primary health insurance policy.

surgical package (7) - *see* global surgery.

surveillance and utilization review subsystem (SURS) (15) - safeguards against unnecessary or inappropriate use of Medicaid services or excess payments and assesses the quality of those services.

survey (3) - conducted by accreditation organizations (e.g., The Joint Commission) and/or regulatory agencies (e.g., CMS) to evaluate a facility's compliance with standards and/or regulations.

survivor benefits (17) - claim that provides death benefits to eligible dependents, which are calculated according to the employee's earning capacity at the time of illness or injury.

suspense (4) - pending.

Tax Equity and Fiscal Responsibility Act of 1982 (TEFRA) (2) - created Medicare risk programs, which allowed federally qualified HMOs and competitive medical plans that met specified Medicare requirements to provide Medicare-covered services under a risk contract.

Tax Relief and Health Care Act of 2006 (TRHCA) (5) - created physician quality reporting initiative (PQRI) system that establishes a financial incentive for eligible professionals who participate in a voluntary quality reporting program.

technical component (7) - use of equipment and supplies for services performed.

Temporary Assistance for Needy Families (TANF) (15) - makes cash assistance available on a time-limited basis for children deprived of support because of a parent's death, incapacity, absence, or unemployment.

temporary disability (17) - claim that covers health care treatment for illness and injuries, as well as payment for lost wages.

third-party administrator (TPA) (2) - company that provides health benefits claims administration and other outsourcing services for self-insured companies; provides administrative services to health care plans; specializes in mental health case management; and processes claims, serving as a system of "checks and balances" for labor-management.

third-party payer (2) - a health insurance company that provides coverage, such as BlueCross BlueShield.

total practice management software (TPMS) (2) - used to generate the EMR, automating medical practice functions of registering patients, scheduling appointments, generating insurance claims and patient statements, processing payments from patient and third-party payers, and producing administrative and clinical reports.

transfer of care (7) - occurs when a physician who is managing some or all of a patient's problems releases the patient to the care of another physician who is not providing consultative services.

transitional pass-through payments (8) - temporary additional payments (above the OPPS reimbursement rate) made for certain innovative medical devices, drugs, and biologicals provided to Medicare beneficiaries.

TRICARE (16) - health care program for active duty members of the military and their qualified family members, TRICARE-eligible retirees and their qualified family members, and eligible survivors of members of the uniformed services.

TRICARE beneficiary (16) - includes sponsors and dependents of sponsors.

TRICARE Extra (16) - allows TRICARE Standard users to save 5 percent of their TRICARE Standard cost-shares by using health care providers in the TRICARE network.

TRICARE Management Activity (TMA) (16) - formerly OCHAMPUS; the office that coordinates and administers the TRICARE program and is accountable for quality health care provided to members of the uniformed services and their families.

TRICARE Prime (16) - managed care option similar to a civilian health maintenance organization (HMO).

TRICARE Service Centers (TSCs) (16) - business offices staffed by one or more beneficiary services representatives and health care finders who assist TRICARE sponsors with health care needs and answer questions about the program.

TRICARE sponsors (16) - uniformed service personnel who are either active duty, retired, or deceased.

TRICARE Standard (16) - new name for traditional CHAMPUS; provides fee-for-service health care option.

triple option plan (3) - usually offered by either a single insurance plan or as a joint venture among two or more third-party payers, and provides subscribers or employees with a choice of HMO, PPO, or traditional health insurance plans; also called *cafeteria plan* or *flexible benefit plan*.

trust the index (6) - concept that inclusion terms listed below codes in the tabular list are not meant to be exhaustive, and additional terms found only in the index may also be associated to a code.

Truth in Lending Act (4) - *see* Consumer Credit Protection Act of 1968.

two-party check (4) - check made out to both patient and provider.

type of service (TOS) (7) - refers to the kind of health care services provided to patients; a code required by Medicare to denote anesthesia services.

UB-04 (5) - insurance claim or flat file used to bill institutional services, such as services performed in hospitals.

unassigned claim (4) - generated for providers who do not accept assignment; organized by year.

unauthorized service (4) - services that are provided to a patient without proper authorization or that are not covered by a current authorization.

unbundling (4) - submitting multiple CPT codes when one code should be submitted.

uncertain behavior (6) - it is not possible to predict subsequent morphology or behavior from the submitted specimen.

underdosing (6) - taking less of a medication than is prescribed by a provider or a manufacturer's instruction.

uniformed services (16) - U.S. military branches that include the Army, Navy, Air Force, Marines, Coast Guard, Public Health Service, and the North Atlantic Treaty Organization (NATO).

unique bit string (5) - computer code that creates an electronic signature message digest that is encrypted (encoded) and appended (attached) to an electronic document (e.g., CMS-1500 claim).

unit/floor time (7) - amount of time the provider spends at the patient's bedside and managing the patient's care on the unit or floor (e.g., writing orders for diagnostic tests or reviewing test results).

universal health insurance (2) - goal of providing every individual with access to health coverage, regardless of the system implemented to achieve that goal.

unlisted procedure (7) - also called *unlisted service;* assigned when the provider performs a procedure or service for which there is no CPT code.

unlisted service (7) - *see* unlisted procedure.

unspecified nature (6) - neoplasm is identified, but no further indication of the histology or nature of the tumor is reflected in the documented diagnosis.

upcoding (5) - assignment of an ICD-10-CM diagnosis code that does not match patient record documentation for the purpose of illegally increasing reimbursement (e.g., assigning the ICD-10-CM code for heart attack when angina was actually documented in the record).

usual and reasonable payments (2) - based on fees typically charged by providers in a particular region of the country.

usual, customary, and reasonable (UCR) (13) - description of amount commonly charged for a particular medical service by providers within a particular geographic region; used for establishing allowable rates.

utilization management (utilization review) (3) - method of controlling health care costs and quality of care by reviewing the appropriateness and necessity of care provided to patients prior to the administration of care.

utilization review organization (URO) (3) - entity that establishes a utilization management program and performs external utilization review services.

value-added network (VAN) (4) - clearinghouse that involves value-added vendors, such as banks, in the processing of claims; using a VAN is more efficient and less expensive for providers than managing their own systems to send and receive transactions directly from numerous entities.

vocational rehabilitation (17) - claim that covers expenses for vocational retraining for both temporary and permanent disability cases.

voided claim (15) - claim Medicaid should not have originally paid, resulting in a deduction from the lump-sum payment made to the provider.

wage index (9) - adjusts payments to account for geographic variations in hospitals' labor costs.

whistleblower (5) - individual who makes specified disclosures relating to the use of public funds, such as Medicare payments. ARRA legislation prohibits retaliation (e.g., termination) against such employees who disclose information that they believe is evidence of gross mismanagement of an agency contract or grant relating to covered funds, and so on.

without direct patient contact (7) - includes non-face-to-face time spent by the provider on an outpatient or inpatient basis and occurring before and/or after direct patient care.

Workers' Compensation Board (Workers' Compensation Commission) (17) - state agency responsible for administering workers' compensation laws and handling appeals for denied claims or cases in which a worker feels compensation was too low.

workers' compensation insurance (1) - insurance program, mandated by federal and state governments, that requires employers to cover medical expenses and loss of wages for workers who are injured on the job or who have developed job-related disorders.

World Health Organization (WHO) (2) - developed the International Classification of Diseases (ICD).

Zone Program Integrity Contractor (ZPIC) (5) - program implemented in 2009 by CMS to review billing trends and patterns, focusing on providers whose billings for Medicare services are higher than the majority of providers in the community. ZPICs are assigned to the Medicare administrative contractor (MAC) jurisdictions, replacing Program Safeguard Contracts PSCs).

Index

Page numbers followed by *f* indicate a figure on that page. Page numbers followed by *t* indicate a table on that page.

F

G